COMMON SYMBOLS AND NOTATION

A	market value of assets, premerger total value of acquirer
APR	annual percentage rate
B	risk-free investment in the replicating portfolio
C	cash flow, call option price
$Corr(R_i, R_j)$	correlation between returns of i and j
$Cov(R_i, R_j)$	covariance between returns of i and j
CPN	coupon payment
D	market value of debt
d	debt-to-value ratio
Div_t	dividends paid in year t
dis	discount from face value
E	market value of equity
EAR	effective annual rate
$EBIT$	earnings before interest and taxes
$EBITDA$	earnings before interest, taxes, depreciation, and amortization
EPS_t	earnings per share on date t
$E[R_i]$	expected return of security i
F, F_T	one-year and T-year forward exchange rate
FCF_t	free cash flow at date t
FV	future value, face value of a bond
g	growth rate
I	initial investment or initial capital committed to the project
Int_t	interest expense on date t
IRR	internal rate of return
K	strike price
k	interest coverage ratio, compounding periods per year
L	lease payment, market value of liabilities
$\ln$	natural logarithm
MV_i	total market capitalization of security i
N	number of cash flows, terminal date, notational principal of a swap contract
N_i	number of shares outstanding of security i
$NPER$	annuity spreadsheet notation for the number of periods or dates of the last cash flow
NPV	net present value
P	price, initial principal or deposit, or equivalent present value, put option price

P_i	price of security i
P/E	price-earnings ratio
PMT	annuity spreadsheet notation for cash flow
PV	present value; annuity spreadsheet notation for the initial amount
q	dividend yield
p	risk-neutral probability
r	interest rate, discount rate of cost of capital
R_i	return of security i
R_{mkt}	return of the market portfolio
R_P	return on portfolio P
RATE	annuity spreadsheet notation for interest rate
r_E, r_D	equity and debt costs of capital
r_f	risk-free interest rate
r_i	required return or cost of capital of security i
r_U	unlevered cost of capital
r_{wacc}	weighted average cost of capital
S	stock price, spot exchange rate, value of all synergies
$SD(R_i)$	standard deviation (volatility) of return of security i
T	option expiration date, maturity date, market value of target
U	market value of unlevered equity
V_t	enterprise value on date t
$Var(R)$	variance of return R
x_i	portfolio weight of investment in i
YTC	yield to call on a callable bond
YTM	yield to maturity
α_i	alpha of security i
β_D, β_E	beta of debt or equity
β_i	beta of security i with respect to the market portfolio
β_s^P	beta of security i with respect to portfolio P
β_U	beta of unlevered firm
Δ	shares of stock in the replicating portfolio; sensitivity of option price to stock price
σ	volatility
τ	tax rate
τ_c	marginal corporate tax rate

MyFinanceLab

The Key to Your Success in Three Easy Steps!

1. Take a Sample Test to assess your knowledge.

2. Review your personalized Study Plan to see where you need more work.

3. Use the Study Plan exercises and step-by-step tutorials to get practice—and individualized feedback—where you need it.

If your instructor assigns homework and tests using MyFinanceLab

The MyFinanceLab Course Home page uses graphs to let students know their current progress in the course and it has a detailed calendar that not only displays due dates, but allows instructors to add entries.

CORPORATE FINANCE: THE CORE

THIRD EDITION

GLOBAL EDITION

The Pearson Series in Finance

Bekaert/Hodrick
International Financial Management

Berk/DeMarzo
Corporate Finance*

Berk/DeMarzo
Corporate Finance: The Core*

Berk/DeMarzo/Harford
Fundamentals of Corporate Finance*

Brooks
Financial Management: Core Concepts*

Copeland/Weston/Shastri
Financial Theory and Corporate Policy

Dorfman/Cather
*Introduction to Risk Management
and Insurance*

Eiteman/Stonehill/Moffett
Multinational Business Finance

Fabozzi
Bond Markets: Analysis and Strategies

Fabozzi/Modigliani
Capital Markets: Institutions and Instruments

Fabozzi/Modigliani/Jones
*Foundations of Financial Markets
and Institutions*

Finkler
*Financial Management for Public, Health,
and Not-for-Profit Organizations*

Frasca
Personal Finance

Gitman/Zutter
Principles of Managerial Finance*

Gitman/Zutter
*Principles of Managerial Finance—Brief
Edition**

Goldsmith
Consumer Economics: Issues and Behaviors

Haugen
*The Inefficient Stock Market: What Pays
Off and Why*

Haugen
*The New Finance: Overreaction,
Complexity, and Uniqueness*

Holden
Excel Modeling in Corporate Finance

Holden
Excel Modeling in Investments

Hughes/MacDonald
International Banking: Text and Cases

Hull
Fundamentals of Futures and Options Markets

Hull
Options, Futures, and Other Derivatives

Hull
Risk Management and Financial Institutions

Keown
Personal Finance: Turning Money into Wealth*

Keown/Martin/Petty
*Foundations of Finance: The Logic
and Practice of Financial Management**

Kim/Nofsinger
Corporate Governance

Madura
Personal Finance*

Marthinsen
*Risk Takers: Uses and Abuses of Financial
Derivatives*

McDonald
Derivatives Markets

McDonald
Fundamentals of Derivatives Markets

Mishkin/Eakins
Financial Markets and Institutions

Moffett/Stonehill/Eiteman
Fundamentals of Multinational Finance

Nofsinger
Psychology of Investing

Ormiston/Fraser
Understanding Financial Statements

Pennacchi
Theory of Asset Pricing

Rejda
*Principles of Risk Management
and Insurance*

Seiler
*Performing Financial Studies:
A Methodological Cookbook*

Smart/Gitman/Joehnk
Fundamentals of Investing*

Solnik/McLeavey
Global Investments

Stretcher/Michael
Cases in Financial Management

Titman/Keown/Martin
*Financial Management: Principles
and Applications**

Titman/Martin
*Valuation: The Art and Science
of Corporate Investment Decisions*

Weston/Mitchel/Mulherin
*Takeovers, Restructuring, and Corporate
Governance*

CORPORATE FINANCE:
THE CORE

THIRD EDITION

GLOBAL EDITION

JONATHAN BERK
STANFORD UNIVERSITY

PETER DeMARZO
STANFORD UNIVERSITY

PEARSON

Boston Columbus Indianapolis New York San Francisco Upper Saddle River
Amsterdam Cape Town Dubai London Madrid Milan Munich Paris Montreal Toronto
Delhi Mexico City Sao Paulo Sydney Hong Kong Seoul Singapore Taipei Tokyo

To Rebecca, Natasha, and Hannah, for the love and for being there —J. B.

To Kaui, Pono, Koa, and Kai, for all the love and laughter —P. D.

Editor in Chief: Donna Battista
Acquisitions Editor: Katie Rowland
Executive Development Editor: Rebecca Ferris-Caruso
Editorial Project Manager: Emily Biberger
International Publisher: Laura Dent
International Programme Editor: Leandra Paoli
International Editorial Assistant: Laura Thompson
International Marketing Manager: Dean Erasmus
Managing Editor: Jeff Holcomb
Senior Production Project Manager: Nancy Freihofer

Senior Manufacturing Controller, Production, International Edition: Trudy Kimber
Cover Designer: Jodi Notowitz
Cover Photo: UIG via Getty Images
Media Director: Susan Schoenberg
Content Lead, MyFinanceLab: Miguel Leonarte
Executive Media Producer: Melissa Honig
Project Management and Text Design: Gillian Hall, The Aardvark Group

Pearson Education Limited
Edinburgh Gate
Harlow
Essex CM20 2JE
England

and Associated Companies throughout the world

Visit us on the World Wide Web at: www.pearson.com/uk

© Pearson Education Limited 2014

ISBN-13: 978-0-273-79216-1
ISBN-10: 0-273-79216-4
British Library Cataloguing-in-Publication Data
A catalogue record for this book is available from the British Library

10 9 8 7 6 5 4 3 2
17 16 15 14

Typeset in Adobe Garamond by Laserwords
Printed and bound by Courier/Kendallville in United States of America

The publisher's policy is to use paper manufactured from sustainable forests.

Brief Contents

Detailed Contents

PART 2   TIME, MONEY, AND INTEREST RATES

PART 4 RISK AND RETURN

Chapter 10 Capital Markets and the Pricing of Risk 312

Chapter 11 Optimal Portfolio Choice and the Capital Asset Pricing Model 351

Bridging Theory and Practice

Before the EMU created the euro as a single European currency, the yields of sovereign debt issued by European countries varied widely. These variations primarily reflected differences in inflation expectations and currency risk (see Figure 6.6). However, after the monetary union was put in place at the end of 1998, the yields all essentially converged to the yield on German government bonds. Investors seemed to conclude that there was little distinction between the debt of the European countries in the union—they seemed to feel that all countries in the union were essentially exposed to the same default, inflation and currency risk and thus equally "safe."

Presumably, investors believed that an outright default was unthinkable. They apparently believed that member countries would be fiscally responsible and manage their debt obligations to avoid default at all costs. But as illustrated by Figure 6.6, once the 2008 financial crisis revealed the folly of this assumption, debt yields once again diverged as investors acknowledged the likelihood that some countries (particularly Portugal and Ireland) might be unable to repay their debt and would be forced to default.

In retrospect, rather than bringing fiscal responsibility, the monetary union allowed the weaker member countries to borrow at dramatically lower rates. In response, these countries reacted by increasing their borrowing—and at least in Greece's case, borrowed to the point that default became inevitable.

Focus on the Financial Crisis and Sovereign Debt Crisis

Global Financial Crisis boxes reflect the reality of the recent financial crisis and ongoing sovereign debt crisis, noting lessons learned. 23 boxes across the book illustrate and analyze key details.

The Law of One Price as the Unifying Valuation Framework

The Law of One Price framework reflects the modern idea that the absence of arbitrage is the unifying concept of valuation. This critical insight is introduced in Chapter 3, revisited in each part opener, and integrated throughout the text—motivating all major concepts and connecting theory to practice.

Study Aids with a Practical Focus

To be successful, students need to master the core concepts and learn to identify and solve problems that today's practitioners face.

Common Mistakes boxes alert students to frequently made mistakes stemming from misunderstanding core concepts and calculations—in the classroom and in the field.

The perpetuity formula assumes that the first payment occurs at the end of the first period (at date 1). Sometimes perpetuities have cash flows that start later in the future. In this case, we can adapt the perpetuity formula to compute the present value, but we need to be so carefully to avoid a common mistake.

To illustrate, consider the MBA graduation party described in Example 4.7. Rather than starting immediately, suppose that the first party will be held two years from today (for the current entering class). How would this delay change the amount of the donation required?

Now the timeline looks like this:

We need to determine the present value of these cash flows, as it tells us the amount of money in the bank needed today to finance the future parties. We cannot apply the perpetuity formula directly, however, because these cash flows are not *exactly* a perpetuity as we defined it. Specifically, the cash flow in the first period is "missing." But consider the situation on date 1—at that point, the first party is one period

away and then the cash flows are periodic. From the perspective of date 1, this *is* a perpetuity, and we can apply the formula. From the preceding calculation, we know we need $375,000 on date 1 to have enough to start the parties on date 2. We rewrite the timeline as follows:

Our goal can now be restated more simply: How much do we need to invest today to have $375,000 in one year? This is a simple present value calculation:

$$PV = \$375{,}000/1.08 = \$347{,}222 \text{ today}$$

A common mistake is to discount the $375,000 twice because the first party is in two periods. *Remember—the present value formula for the perpetuity already discounts the cash flows to one period prior to the first cash flow.* Keep in mind that this common mistake may be made with perpetuities, annuities, and all of the other special cases discussed in this section. All of these formulas discount the cash flows to one period prior to the first cash flow.

EXAMPLE 4.14 Evaluating an Annuity with Monthly Cash Flows

Worked Examples accompany every important concept using a step-by-step procedure that guides students through the solution process. Clear labels make them easy to find for help with homework and studying.

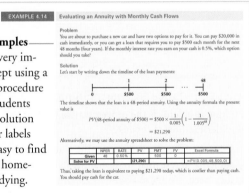

Applications that Reflect Real Practice

Corporate Finance features actual companies and leaders in the field.

Interviews with notable practitioners—seven new for this edition—highlight leaders in the field and address the effects of the financial crisis.

General Interest boxes highlight timely material from financial publications that shed light on business problems and real-company practices.

INTERVIEW WITH
Kevin M. Warsh

Kevin M. Warsh, *a lecturer at Stanford's Graduate School of Business and a distinguished visiting fellow at the Hoover Institution, was a Federal Reserve governor from 2006 to 2011, serving as chief liaison to the financial markets.*

QUESTION: *What are the main policy instruments used by central banks to control the economy?*

ANSWER: The Federal Reserve (Fed) deploys several policy tools to achieve its goals of price stability, maximum sustainable employment, and financial stability. Lowering the federal funds short-term interest rate, the primary policy instrument, stimulates the economy. Raising the federal funds rate generally slows the economy. Buying and selling short-term U.S. Treasury securities through *open market operations* is standard practice. Prior to the 2007–2009 financial crisis, the Fed's balance sheet ranged from $700–$900 billion. But when the Fed was unable to lower interest rates further because rates were so close to zero already, it resorted to large-scale, longer-term open market operations to increase liquidity in the financial system in the hopes of stimulating the economy further, thus growing its balance sheet significantly. With *open mouth operations*, the Fed's announcements of its intent to buy or sell assets indicates its desired degree of future policy accommodation, often prompting markets to react adjusting interest rates immediately. The Fed's Lender-of-

clarity and confidence in the financial wherewithal of each other. One effective, innovative tool, the *Term Auction Facility (TAF)*, stimulated the economy by providing cheap and readily available term funding to banks, large and small, on the front lines of the economy, thus encouraging them to extend credit to businesses and consumers. After reducing the policy rate to near zero to help revive the economy, the Fed instituted two *Quantitative Easing (QE)* programs—special purchases of government and agency securities—to increase money supply, promote lending, and according to some proponents, increase prices of riskier assets.

The Fed also addressed the global financial crisis by establishing temporary *central bank liquidity swap lines* with the European Central Bank and other major central banks. Using this facility, a foreign central bank is able to obtain dollar funding for its customers by swapping Euros for dollars or another currency and agreeing to reverse the swap at a later date. The Fed does not take exchange rate risk, but is subject to the credit risk of its central bank counterparty.

QUESTION: *What tools is the European Central Bank (ECB) using to address the sovereign debt crisis? How does its approach compare to the Fed's approach to the 2007–2009 financial*

Teaching Students to Think Finance

With a consistency in presentation and an innovative set of learning aids, *Corporate Finance* simultaneously meets the needs of both future financial managers and non-financial managers. This textbook truly shows every student how to "think finance."

Simplified Presentation of Mathematics

One of the hardest parts of learning finance is mastering the jargon, math, and non-standardized notation. *Corporate Finance* systematically uses:

Notation Boxes: Each chapter opens by defining the variables and acronyms used in the chapter as a 'legend' for students' reference.

Timelines: Introduced in Chapter 4, timelines are emphasized as the important first step in solving *every* problem that involves cash flows.

Numbered and Labeled Equations: The first time a full equation is given in notation form it is numbered. Key equations are titled and revisited in the summary and in end papers.

Using Excel Boxes: Provide hands-on instruction of Excel techniques and include screenshots to serve as a guide for students.

Spreadsheet Tables: Select tables are available as Excel files, enabling students to change inputs and manipulate the underlying calculations.

TABLE 8.1 SPREADSHEET — HomeNet's Incremental Earnings Forecast

	Year	0	1	2	3	4	5
	Incremental Earnings Forecast ($000s)						
1	Sales	—	26,000	26,000	26,000	26,000	—
2	Cost of Goods Sold	—	(11,000)	(11,000)	(11,000)	(11,000)	—
3	**Gross Profit**	—	15,000	15,000	15,000	15,000	—
4	Selling, General, and Administrative	—	(2,800)	(2,800)	(2,800)	(2,800)	—
5	Research and Development	(15,000)	—	—	—	—	—
6	Depreciation	—	(1,500)	(1,500)	(1,500)	(1,500)	(1,500)
7	**EBIT**	(15,000)	10,700	10,700	10,700	10,700	(1,500)
8	Income Tax at 40%	6,000	(4,280)	(4,280)	(4,280)	(4,280)	600
9	**Unlevered Net Income**	(9,000)	6,420	6,420	6,420	6,420	(900)

Practice Finance to Learn Finance

Working problems is the proven way to cement and demonstrate an understanding of finance.

Concept Check questions at the end of each section enable students to test their understanding and target areas in which they need further review.

End-of-chapter problems written personally by Jonathan Berk and Peter DeMarzo offer instructors the opportunity to assign first-rate materials to students for homework and practice with the confidence that the problems are consistent with chapter content. Both the problems and solutions, which were also written by the authors, have been class-tested and accuracy-checked to ensure quality.

Data Cases present in-depth scenarios in a business setting with questions designed to guide students' analysis. Many questions involve the use of Internet resources and Excel techniques.

MyFinanceLab

Because practice with homework problems is crucial to learning finance, *Corporate Finance* is available with MyFinanceLab, a fully integrated homework and tutorial system. MyFinanceLab revolutionizes homework and practice with material written and developed by Jonathan Berk and Peter DeMarzo.

Online Assessment Using End-of-Chapter Problems

The seamless integration among the textbook, assessment materials, and online resources sets a new standard in corporate finance education.

- **End-of-chapter problems**—every single one —appear online. The values in the problems are algorithmically generated, giving students many opportunities for practice and mastery. Problems can be assigned by professors and completed online by students.

- **Helpful tutorial tools**, along with the same pedagogical aids from the text, support students as they study. Links to the eText direct students right to the material they most need to review.

Additional Resources in MyFinanceLab

- **Video clips** profile high-profile firms such as Boeing, Cisco, Delta, and Intel through interviews and analysis. The videos focus on core topical areas, including capital budgeting, mergers and acquisitions, and risk and return.

- **Interactive animations**, which enable students to manipulate inputs, cover topics such as bonds, stock valuation, NPV, IRR, financial statement modeling, and more.

- **Finance in the News** provides weekly postings of a relevant and current article from a newspaper or journal article with discussion questions that are assignable in MyFinanceLab.

- Live **news and video feeds** from *The Financial Times* and ABC News provide real-term news updates.

To learn more about MyFinanceLab, contact your local Pearson representative or visit www.myfinancelab.com.

Hands-On Practice, Hands-Off Grading

Hands-On, Targeted Practice

Students can take pre-built Practice Tests for each chapter, and their test results will generate an individualized Study Plan. With the Study Plan, students learn to focus their energies on the topics they need to be successful in class, on exams, and, ultimately, in their careers.

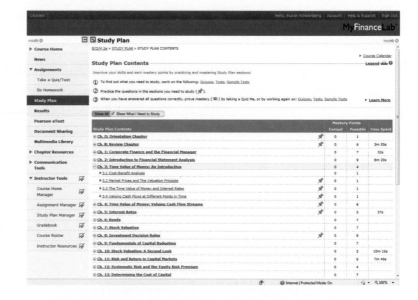

Powerful Instructor Tools

MyFinanceLab provides flexible tools that enable instructors to easily customize the online course materials to suit their needs.

- **Easy-to-Use Homework Manager**. Instructors can easily create and assign tests, quizzes, or graded homework assignments. In addition to pre-built MyFinanceLab questions, the Test Bank is also available so that instructors have ample material with which to create assignments.

- **Flexible Gradebook**. MyFinanceLab saves time by automatically grading students' work and tracking results in an online Gradebook.

- **Downloadable Classroom Resources**. Instructors also have access to online versions of each instructor supplement, including the Instructor's Manual, Solutions Manual, PowerPoint Lecture Notes, and Test Bank.

To learn more about MyFinanceLab, contact your local Pearson representative or visit www.myfinancelab.com.

About the Authors

Jonathan Berk is the A.P. Giannini Professor of Finance at the Graduate School of Business, Stanford University and is a Research Associate at the National Bureau of Economic Research. Before coming to Stanford, he was the Sylvan Coleman Professor of Finance at Haas School of Business at the University of California, Berkeley. Prior to earning his Ph.D., he worked as an Associate at Goldman Sachs (where his education in finance really began).

Professor Berk's research interests in finance include corporate valuation, capital structure, mutual funds, asset pricing, experimental economics, and labor economics. His work has won a number of research awards including the TIAA-CREF Paul A. Samuelson Award, the Smith Breeden Prize, Best Paper of the Year in *The Review of Financial Studies*, and the FAME Research Prize. His paper, "A Critique of Size-Related Anomalies," was selected as one of the two best papers ever published in *The Review of Financial Studies*. In recognition of his influence on the practice of finance he has received the Bernstein-Fabozzi/Jacobs Levy Award, the Graham and Dodd Award of Excellence, and the Roger F. Murray Prize. He

Peter DeMarzo and Jonathan Berk

served as an Associate Editor of the *Journal of Finance* for eight years, is currently a Director of the American Finance Association, an Academic Director of the Financial Management Association, and is a member of the advisory board of the *Journal of Portfolio Management*.

Born in Johannesburg, South Africa, Professor Berk is married, with two daughters, and is an avid skier and biker.

Peter DeMarzo is the Mizuho Financial Group Professor of Finance and Senior Associate Dean for Academic Affairs at the Stanford Graduate School of Business. He is also a Research Associate at the National Bureau of Economic Research. He currently teaches MBA and Ph.D. courses in Corporate Finance and Financial Modeling. In addition to his experience at the Stanford Graduate School of Business, Professor DeMarzo has taught at the Haas School of Business and the Kellogg Graduate School of Management, and he was a National Fellow at the Hoover Institution.

Professor DeMarzo received the Sloan Teaching Excellence Award at Stanford in 2004 and 2006, and the Earl F. Cheit Outstanding Teaching Award at U.C. Berkeley in 1998. Professor DeMarzo has served as an Associate Editor for *The Review of Financial Studies*, *Financial Management*, and the *B.E. Journals in Economic Analysis and Policy*, as well as a Director of the American Finance Association. He has served as Vice President and President of the Western Finance Association. Professor DeMarzo's research is in the area of corporate finance, asset securitization, and contracting, as well as market structure and regulation. His recent work has examined issues of the optimal design of contracts and securities, the regulation of insider trading and broker-dealers, and the influence of information asymmetries on corporate investment. He has received numerous awards including the Western Finance Association Corporate Finance Award and the Barclays Global Investors/Michael Brennan best-paper award from *The Review of Financial Studies*.

Professor DeMarzo was born in Whitestone, New York, and is married with three boys. He and his family enjoy hiking, biking, and skiing.

Preface

WE WERE MOTIVATED TO WRITE THIS TEXTBOOK BY A CENTRAL insight: The core concepts in finance are simple and intuitive. What makes the subject challenging is that it is often difficult for a novice to distinguish between these core ideas and other intuitively appealing approaches that, if used in financial decision making, will lead to incorrect decisions. De-emphasizing the core concepts that underlie finance strips students of the essential intellectual tools they need to differentiate between good and bad decision making.

We present corporate finance as an application of a set of simple, powerful ideas. At the heart is the principal of the absence of arbitrage opportunities, or Law of One Price—*in life, you don't get something for nothing*. This simple concept is a powerful and important tool in financial decision making. By relying on it, and the other core principles in this book, financial decision makers can avoid the bad decisions brought to light by the recent financial crisis. We use the Law of One Price as a compass; it keeps financial decision makers on the right track and is the backbone of the entire book.

New to This Edition

We have updated all text discussions and figures, tables and facts to accurately reflect developments in the field in the last four years. Specific highlights include the following:

- The 2007–2009 financial crisis and European sovereign debt crisis provide a valuable pedagogical illustration of what can go wrong when practitioners ignore the core concepts that underlie financial decision making. We integrate this important lesson into the book in a series of contextual Global Financial Crisis boxes. These boxes—23 in total across the book—bring the relevance of the crises home to students by illustrating and analyzing key details about the financial crisis and sovereign debt dynamics.

- New centralized coverage of financial ratios in Chapter 2 in a specific section provides students with the tools to analyze financial statements.

- The reorganized flow of topics in Chapters 5 and 6—Chapter 6, "Valuing Bonds," now appears after Chapter 5, "Interest Rates"—provides an immediate application of time value of money concepts.

- Seven new practitioner interviews incorporate timely perspectives from leaders in the field related to the recent financial crisis and ongoing European sovereign debt crisis.

- New Using Excel boxes provide hands-on instruction of how to use Excel to solve financial problems and include screenshots to serve as a guide for students.

- We added 45 new problems and refined many others, once again personally writing and solving each one. In addition, every single problem is available in MyFinanceLab, the groundbreaking homework and tutorial system that accompanies the book.

The Law of One Price as the Unifying Principle of Valuation

This book presents corporate finance as an application of a small set of simple core ideas. Modern finance theory and practice is grounded in the idea of the absence of arbitrage—or the Law of One Price—as the unifying concept in valuation. We introduce the Law of One Price concept as the basis for NPV and the time value of money in Chapter 3, *Financial*

Decision Making and the Law of One Price. In the opening of each part and as pertinent throughout the remaining chapters, we relate major concepts to the Law of One Price, creating a framework to ground the student reader and connect theory to practice.

Table of Contents Overview

Corporate Finance offers coverage of the major topical areas for introductory-level MBA students as well as the depth required in a reference textbook for upper-division courses. Most professors customize their classes by selecting a subset of chapters reflecting the subject matter they consider most important. We designed this book from the outset with this need for flexibility in mind. Parts 2 through 6 are the core chapters in the book. We envision that most MBA programs will cover this material—yet even within these core chapters instructors can pick and choose.

Single quarter course: Cover Chapters 3–15; if time allows, or students are previously familiar with the time value of money, add on Chapters 16–19.

Semester-long course: Incorporate options and Part 10, *Special Topics*, chapters as desired.

Single mini-semester: Assign Chapters 3–10, 14, and 15 if time allows.

Chapter	Highlights and Changes
1 The Corporation	Introduces the corporation and its governance; updated to included Dodd-Frank Act
2 Introduction to Financial Statement Analysis: IFRS	Introduces key financial statements; coverage of financial ratios has been centralized to prepare students to analyze financial statements holistically
3 Financial Decision Making and the Law of One Price	Introduces the Law of One Price and net present value as the basis of the book's unifying framework
4 The Time Value of Money	Introduces the mechanics of discounting; new examples with non-annual interest rates provide time value of money applications in a personal loan context; new Using Excel boxes familiarize students with spreadsheet functionality
5 Interest Rates	Discusses key determinants of interest rates and their relation to the cost of capital; new interview with Kevin Warsh, former *Federal Reserve governor*; new Common Mistake box on states' underfunded pensions
6 Valuing Bonds	Analyzes bond prices and yields, addresses the risk level of fixed-debt securities as illustrated by the sovereign debt crisis, overviews European debt problems, and examines whether Treasuries are risk-free securities; new interview with Carmen M. Reinhart, John F. Kennedy School of Government, Harvard University
7 Investment Decision Rules	Introduces the NPV rule as the "golden rule" against which we evaluate other investment decision rules; new appendix on using Excel Data Tables
8 Fundamentals of Capital Budgeting	Provides a clear focus on the distinction between earnings and free cash flow, and shows how to build a financial model to assess the NPV of an investment decision; new Using Excel boxes demonstrate best-practices and sensitivity analysis
9 Valuing Stocks	Provides a unifying treatment of projects within the firm and the valuation of the firm as a whole; new interview with Douglas Kehring, Oracle Corporation
10 Capital Markets and the Pricing of Risk	Establishes the intuition for understanding risk and return, explains the distinction between diversifiable and systematic risk, and introduces beta and the CAPM; new analysis of historical holding period returns for alternative asset classes
11 Optimal Portfolio Choice and the Capital Asset Pricing Model	Presents the CAPM and develops the details of mean-variance portfolio optimization; new interview with John Powers, Stanford Management Company

Chapter	Highlights and Changes
12 Estimating the Cost of Capital	Demonstrates the practical details of estimate the cost of capital for equity, debt, or a project, and introduces asset betas, and the unlevered and weighted-average cost of capital; new interview with Michael Latham, BlackRock Asset Management International Inc.
13 Investor Behavior and Capital Market Efficiency	Examines the role of behavioral finance and ties investor behavior to the topic of market efficiency and alternative models of risk and return; expanded discussion of fund manager performance
14 Capital Structure in a Perfect Market	Presents Modigliani and Miller's results and introduces the market value balance sheet; new Global Financial Crisis box, "Bank Capital Regulation and the ROE Fallacy"
15 Debt and Taxes	Analyzes the tax benefits of leverage, including the debt tax shield and the after-tax WACC
16 Financial Distress, Managerial Incentives, and Information	Examines the role of asymmetric information and introduces the debt overhang and leverage ratchet effect; new interview with John Lipsky, former First Deputy Managing Director of the International Monetary Fund (IMF)
17 Payout Policy	Considers alternative payout policies including dividends and share repurchases; analyzes the role of market imperfections in determining the firm's payout policy
18 Capital Budgeting and Valuation with Leverage	Develops in depth the three main methods for capital budgeting with leverage and market imperfections: the weighted average cost of capital (WACC) method, the adjusted present value (APV) method, and the flow-to-equity (FTE) method
19 Valuation and Financial Modeling: A Case Study	Builds a financial model for a leveraged acquisition; revised discussion of balance sheet and statement of cash flows includes stockholders' equity equation and new Using Excel box, "Auditing Your Financial Model"

A Complete Instructor and Student Support Package

MyFinanceLab

A critical component of the text, MyFinanceLab will give all students the practice and tutorial help they need to succeed. For more details, see pages xix–xx.

Instructor's Resource Center

This password-protected site, accessible at www.pearsonglobaleditions.com/berk, hosts all of the instructor resources that follow. Instructors can find easy-to-follow instructions on getting access or may contact their sales representative for further information.

Solutions Manual

- Prepared by Jonathan Berk and Peter DeMarzo.
- Provides detailed, accuracy-verified, class-tested solutions to every chapter problem.
- See www.pearsonglobaleditions.com/berk for spreadsheet solutions to select chapter problems and Data Cases.

Instructor's Manual

- Written by Janet Payne and William Chittenden of Texas State University.
- Corresponding to each chapter, provides: chapter overview and outline correlated to the PowerPoint Lecture Notes; learning objectives; guide to fresh worked examples in the PowerPoint Lecture Notes; and listing of chapter problems with accompanying Excel spreadsheets.

Test Item File

- Revised by Janet Payne and William Chittenden of Texas State University.
- Provides a wide selection of multiple-choice, short answer, and essay questions qualified by difficulty level and skill type and correlated to chapter topics. Numerical-based problems include step-by-step solutions.
- Available as Computerized Test Bank in TestGen.

PowerPoint Lecture Presentation

- Also authored by Janet Payne and William Chittenden of Texas State University.
- Offers outlines of each chapter with graphs, tables, key terms, and concepts from each chapter.
- Worked examples provide detailed, step-by-step solutions in the same format as the boxes from the text and correlated to parallel specific textbook examples.

Study Guide

- Written by Mark Simonson, Arizona State University.
- Provides the learning tools students need to cement their understanding of key concepts, including chapter synopses, review of select concepts and terms, and 5–10 questions per chapter as a self-test.
- Worked examples with step-by-step solutions guide students through the thought process for arriving at each solution, instilling in them the essential intuition.
- Available for download at MyFinanceLab.

Videos

- Profile well-known firms such as Boeing and Intel through interview and analysis.
- Focus on core topical areas such as capital budgeting and risk and return.
- Available in MyFinanceLab.

Acknowledgments

Looking back, it is hard to believe that this book is in its third edition. We are heartened by its success and impact on the profession through shaping future practitioners. As any textbook writer will tell you, achieving this level of success requires a substantial amount of help. First and foremost we thank Donna Battista, whose leadership, talent, and market savvy are imprinted on all aspects of the project and are central to its success; Denise Clinton, a friend and a leader in fact not just in name, whose experience and knowledge are indispensable; Rebecca Ferris-Caruso, for her unparalleled expertise in managing the complex writing, reviewing, and editing processes and patience in keeping us on track—it is impossible to imagine writing the book without her; Jami Minard, for spearheading marketing efforts;

Katie Rowland, for her energy and fresh perspective as our new editor; and Miguel Leonarte, for his central role on MyFinanceLab. We were blessed to be approached by the best publisher in the business and we are both truly thankful for the indispensable help provided by these and other professionals, including Emily Biberger, Dottie Dennis, Nancy Freihofer, Gillian Hall, Melissa Honig, Carol Melville, and Elissa Senra-Sargent.

Updating a textbook like ours requires a lot of painstaking work, and there are many who have provided insights and input along the way. We would especially like to call out Jared Stanfield for his important contributions and suggestions throughout. We also thank Rebecca Greenberg and Robert James for their tireless efforts to make sure this edition remained as error-free as the past editions have been. We're also appreciative of Marlene Bellamy's work conducting the lively interviews that provide a critically important perspective, and to the interviewees who graciously provided their time and insights.

Of course, this third edition text is built upon the shoulders of the first two, and we have many to thank for helping us make those early versions a reality. We remain forever grateful for Jennifer Koski's critical insights, belief in this project, and tireless effort, all of which were critical to the first edition. Many of the later, non-core chapters required specific detailed knowledge. Nigel Barradale, Reid Click, Jarrad Harford, and Marianne Plunkert ensured that this knowledge was effectively communicated. Joseph Vu and Vance P. Lesseig contributed their talents to the Concept Check questions and Data Cases, respectively.

Creating a truly error-free text is a challenge we could not have lived up to without our team of expert error checkers; we owe particular thanks to Siddharth Bellur, Robert James, Anand Goel, Ian Drummond Gow, Janet Payne, and Jared Stanfield. Thomas Gilbert and Miguel Palacios tirelessly worked examples and problems in the first edition, while providing numerous insights along the way.

A corporate finance textbook is the product of the talents and hard work of many talented colleagues. We are especially gratified with the work of those who updated the impressive array of print supplements to accompany the book: Mark Simonson, for the Study Guide; Janet Payne and William Chittenden, for the Instructor's Manual, Test Item File, and PowerPoint.

As a colleague of both of us, Mark Rubinstein inspired us with his passion to get the history of finance right by correctly attributing the important ideas to the people who first enunciated them. We have used his book, *A History of the Theory of Investments: My Annotated Bibliography*, extensively in this text and we, as well as the profession as a whole, owe him a debt of gratitude for taking the time to write it all down.

We could not have written this text if we were not once ourselves students of finance. As any student knows, the key to success is having a great teacher. In our case we are lucky to have been taught and advised by the people who helped create modern finance: Ken Arrow, Darrell Duffie, Mordecai Kurz, Stephen Ross, and Richard Roll. It was from them that we learned the importance of the core principles of finance, including the Law of One Price, on which this book is based. The learning process does not end at graduation and like most people we have had especially influential colleagues and mentors from which we learned a great deal during our careers and we would like to recognize them explicitly here: Mike Fishman, Richard Green, Vasant Naik, Art Raviv, Mark Rubinstein, Joe Williams, and Jeff Zwiebel. We continue to learn from all of our colleagues and we are grateful to all of them. Finally, we would like to thank those with whom we have taught finance classes over the years: Anat Admati, Ming Huang, Robert Korajczyk, Paul Pfleiderer, Sergio Rebelo, Richard Stanton, and Raman Uppal. Their ideas and teaching strategies have without a doubt influenced our own sense of pedagogy and found their way into this text.

Finally, and most importantly, we owe our biggest debt of gratitude to our spouses, Rebecca Schwartz and Kaui Chun DeMarzo. Little did we (or they) know how much this project would impact our lives, and without their continued love and support—and especially their patience and understanding—this text could not have been completed. We owe a special thanks to Kaui DeMarzo, for her inspiration and support at the start of this project, and for her willingness to be our in-house editor, contributor, advisor, and overall sounding-board throughout each stage of its development.

Jonathan Berk
Peter DeMarzo

Contributors

We are truly thankful to have had so many manuscript reviewers, class testers, and focus group participants. We list all of these contributors below, but Gordon Bodnar, James Conover, Anand Goel, James Linck, Evgeny Lyandres, Marianne Plunkert, Mark Simonson, and Andy Terry went so far beyond the call of duty that we would like to single them out.

We are very grateful for all comments—both informal and in written evaluations—from Second Edition users. We carefully weighed each reviewer suggestion as we sought to streamline the narrative to improve clarity and add relevant new material. The book has benefited enormously for this input.

Reviewers

Ashok B. Abbott, *West Virginia University*
Michael Adams, *Jacksonville University*
Ilan Adler, *University of California, Berkeley*
Ibrahim Affaneh, *Indiana University of Pennsylvania*
Kevin Ahlgrim, *Illinois State University*
Andres Almazan, *University of Texas, Austin*
Confidence Amadi, *Florida A&M University*
Christopher Anderson, *University of Kansas*
Tom Arnold, *University of Richmond*
Nigel Barradale, *Copenhagen Business School*
Peter Basciano, *Augusta State University*
Thomas Bates, *University of Arizona*
Paul Bayes, *East Tennessee State University*
Omar Benkato, *Ball State University*
Gordon Bodnar, *Johns Hopkins University*
Waldo Born, *Eastern Illinois University*
Alex Boulatov, *Higher School of Economics, Moscow*
Tyrone Callahan, *University of Southern California*
Yingpin (George) Chang, *Grand Valley State University*
William G. Christie, *Vanderbilt University*
Ting-Heng Chu, *East Tennessee State University*
Engku Ngah S. Engku Chik, *University Utara Malaysia*
John H. Cochrane, *University of Chicago*
James Conover, *University of North Texas*
James Cordeiro, *SUNY Brockport*
Henrik Cronqvist, *Claremont McKenna College*

Maddur Daggar, *Citigroup*
Hazem Daouk, *Cornell University*
Daniel Deli, *DePaul University*
Andrea DeMaskey, *Villanova University*
B. Espen Eckbo, *Dartmouth College*
Larry Eisenberg, *University of Southern Mississippi*
Riza Emekter, *Robert Morris University*
T. Hanan Eytan, *Baruch College*
Andre Farber, *Universite Libre de Bruxelles*
Eliezer Fich, *Drexel University*
Michael Fishman, *Northwestern University*
Fangjian Fu, *Singapore Management University*
Michael Gallmeyer, *University of Virginia*
Diego Garcia, *University of North Carolina*
Tom Geurts, *Marist College*
Frank Ghannadian, *University of Tampa*
Thomas Gilbert, *University of Washington*
Anand Goel, *DePaul University*
Marc Goergen, *Cardiff Business School*
David Goldenberg, *Rensselaer Polytechnic Institute*
Qing (Grace) Hao, *University of Missouri*
Milton Harris, *University of Chicago*
Christopher Hennessy, *London Business School*
J. Ronald Hoffmeister, *Arizona State University*
Vanessa Holmes, *Xavier University*
Wenli Huang, *Boston University School of Management*

Mark Hutchinson, *University College Cork*
Stuart Hyde, *University of Manchester*
Robert James, *Boston College*
Keith Johnson, *University of Kentucky*
Jouko Karjalainen, *Helsinki University of Technology*
Ayla Kayhan, *Louisiana State University*
Doseong Kim, *University of Akron*
Kenneth Kim, *State University of New York—Buffalo*
Halil Kiymaz, *Rollins College*
Brian Kluger, *University of Cincinnati*
John Knopf, *University of Connecticut*
C.N.V. Krishnan, *Case Western Reserve University*
George Kutner, *Marquette University*
Vance P. Lesseig, *Texas State University*
Martin Lettau, *University of California, Berkeley*
Michel G. Levasseur, *Esa Universite de Lille 2*
Jose Liberti, *DePaul University*
James Linck, *University of Georgia*
David Lins, *University of Illinois at Urbana-Champaign*
Lan Liu, *California State University, Sacramento*
Michelle Lowry, *Pennsylvania State University*
Deborah Lucas, *Massachusetts Institute of Technology*
Peng (Peter) Liu, *Cornell University*
Evgeny Lyandres, *Boston University*
Balasundram Maniam, *Sam Houston State University*
Suren Mansinghka, *University of California, Irvine*
Daniel McConaughy, *California State University, Northridge*
Robert McDonald, *Northwestern University*
Mark McNabb, *University of Cincinnati*
Ilhan Meric, *Rider University*
Timothy Michael, *James Madison University*
Dag Michalsen, *Norwegian School of Management*
Todd Milbourn, *Washington University in St. Louis*
James Miles, *Penn State University*
Darius Miller, *Southern Methodist University*
Emmanuel Morales-Camargo, *University of New Mexico*
Helen Moser, *University of Minnesota*
Arjen Mulder, *Erasmus University*
Michael Muoghalu, *Pittsburg State University*
Jeryl Nelson, *Wayne State College*
Tom Nelson, *University of Colorado*
Chee Ng, *Fairleigh Dickinson University*
Ben Nunnally, *University of North Carolina, Charlotte*
Terrance Odean, *University of California, Berkeley*
Frank Ohara, *University of San Francisco*
Marcus Opp, *University of California, Berkeley*
Henry Oppenheimer, *University of Rhode Island*

Miguel Palacios, *Vanderbilt University*
Mitchell Petersen, *Northwestern University*
Marianne Plunkert, *University of Colorado at Denver*
Paul Povel, *University of Houston*
Eric A. Powers, *University of South Carolina*
Michael Provitera, *Barry University*
Brian Prucyk, *Marquette University*
P. Raghavendra Rau, *University of Cambridge*
Charu Raheja, *TriageLogic Management*
Latha Ramchand, *University of Houston*
Adriano Rampini, *Duke University*
S. Abraham Ravid, *Yeshiva University*
William A. Reese, Jr., *Tulane University*
Ali Reza, *San Jose State University*
Steven P. Rich, *Baylor University*
Antonio Rodriguez, *Texas A&M International University*
Bruce Rubin, *Old Dominion University*
Mark Rubinstein, *University of California, Berkeley*
Doriana Ruffino, *University of Minnesota*
Harley E. Ryan, Jr., *Georgia State University*
Jacob A. Sagi, *Vanderbilt University*
Harikumar Sankaran, *New Mexico State University*
Mukunthan Santhanakrishnan, *Idaho State University*
Frederik Schlingemann, *University of Pittsburgh*
Mark Seasholes, *Hong Kong University of Science and Technology*
Eduardo Schwartz, *University of California, Los Angeles*
Mark Shackleton, *Lancaster University*
Jay Shanken, *Emory University*
Dennis Sheehan, *Penn State University*
Anand Shetty, *Iona College*
Clemens Sialm, *University of Texas at Austin*
Mark Simonson, *Arizona State University*
Rajeev Singhal, *Oakland University*
Erik Stafford, *Harvard Business School*
David Stangeland, *University of Manitoba*
Richard H. Stanton, *University of California, Berkeley*
Mark Hoven Stohs, *California State University, Fullerton*
Ilya A. Strebulaev, *Stanford University*
Ryan Stever, *Bank for International Settlements*
John Strong, *College of William and Mary*
Diane Suhler, *Columbia College*
Lawrence Tai, *Zayed University*
Mark Taranto, *University of Maryland*
Amir Tavakkol, *Kansas State University*
Andy Terry, *University of Arkansas at Little Rock*

John Thornton, *Kent State University*
Alex Triantis, *University of Maryland*
Sorin Tuluca, *Fairleigh Dickinson University*
P. V. Viswanath, *Pace University*
Joe Walker, *University of Alabama at Birmingham*
Edward Waller, *University of Houston, Clear Lake*
Shelly Webb, *Xavier University*
Peihwang Wei, *University of New Orleans*
Peter Went, *Global Association of Risk Professionals (GARP)*
John White, *Georgia Southern University*
Michael E. Williams, *University of Denver*
Annie Wong, *Western Connecticut State University*
K. Matthew Wong, *International School of Management, Paris*
Bob Wood, Jr., *Tennessee Tech University*
Lifan (Frank) Wu, *California State University, Los Angeles*
Tzyy-Jeng Wu, *Pace University*
Jaime Zender, *University of Colorado*
Jeffrey H. Zwiebel, *Stanford University*

Chapter Class Testers

Jack Aber, *Boston University*
John Adams, *University of South Florida*
James Conover, *University of North Texas*
Lou Gingerella, *Rensselaer Polytechnic Institute*
Tom Geurts, *Marist College*
Keith Johnson, *University of Kentucky*
Gautum Kaul, *University of Michigan*
Doseong Kim, *University of Akron*
Jennifer Koski, *University of Washington*
George Kutner, *Marquette University*
Larry Lynch, *Roanoke College*
Vasil Mihov, *Texas Christina University*
Jeryl Nelson, *Wayne State College*
Chee Ng, *Fairleigh Dickinson University*
Ben Nunnally, *University of North Carolina, Charlotte*
Michael Proviteria, *Barry University*
Charu G. Raheja, *Vanderbilt University*
Bruce Rubin, *Old Dominion University*
Mark Seasholes, *University of California, Berkeley*
Dennis Sheehan, *Pennsylvania State University*
Ravi Shukla, *Syracuse University*
Mark Hoven Stohs, *California State University, Fullerton*
Andy Terry, *University of Arkansas*
Sorin Tuluca, *Fairleigh Dickinson University*

Joe Ueng, *University of Saint Thomas*
Bob Wood, *Tennessee Technological University*

End-of-Chapter Problems Class Testers

James Angel, *Georgetown University*
Ting-Heng Chu, *East Tennessee State University*
Robert Kravchuk, *Indiana University*
George Kutner, *Marquette University*
James Nelson, *East Carolina University*
Don Panton, *University of Texas at Arlington*
P. Raghavendra Rau, *Purdue University*
Carolyn Reichert, *University of Texas at Dallas*
Mark Simonson, *Arizona State University*
Diane Suhler, *Columbia College*

Focus Group Participants

Christopher Anderson, *University of Kansas*
Chenchu Bathala, *Cleveland State University*
Matthew T. Billett, *University of Iowa*
Andrea DeMaskey, *Villanova University*
Anand Desai, *Kansas State University*
Ako Doffou, *Sacred Heart University*
Shannon Donovan, *Bridgewater State University*
Ibrahim Elsaify, *Goldey-Beacom College*
Mark Holder, *Kent State University*
Steve Isberg, *University of Baltimore*
Arun Khanna, *Butler University*
Brian Kluger, *University of Cincinnati*
Greg La Blanc, *University of California, Berkeley*
Dima Leshchinskii, *Rensselaer Polytechnic University*
James S. Linck, *University of Georgia*
Larry Lynch, *Roanoke College*
David C. Mauer, *Southern Methodist University*
Alfred Mettler, *Georgia State University*
Stuart Michelson, *Stetson University*
Vassil Mihov, *Texas Christian University*
Jeryl Nelson, *Wayne State College*
Chee Ng, *Fairleigh Dickinson University*
Ben Nunnally, *University of North Carolina at Charlotte*
Sunny Onyiri, *Campbellsville University*
Janet Payne, *Texas State University*
Michael Provitera, *Barry University*
S. Abraham Ravid, *Rutgers University*
William A. Reese, Jr., *Tulane University*
Mario Reyes, *University of Idaho*
Hong Rim, *Shippensburg University*
Robert Ritchey, *Texas Tech University*

Antonio Rodriquez, *Texas A&M International University*

Dan Rogers, *Portland State University*

Harley E. Ryan, Jr., *Georgia State University*

Harikumar Sankaran, *New Mexico State University*

Sorin Sorescu, *Texas A&M University*

David Stangeland, *University of Manitoba*

Jonathan Stewart, *Abilene Christian University*

Mark Hoven Stohs, *California State University, Fullerton*

Tim Sullivan, *Bentley College*

Olie Thorp, *Babson College*

Harry Turtle, *Washington State University*

Joseph Vu, *DePaul University*

Joe Walker, *University of Alabama at Birmingham*

Jill Wetmore, *Saginaw Valley State University*

Jack Wolf, *Clemson University*

Bob Wood, Jr., *Tennessee Tech University*

Donald H. Wort, *California State University, East Bay*

Scott Wright, *Ohio University*

Tong Yao, *University of Arizona*

MyFinanceLab Contributors

Carlos Bazan, *San Diego State University*

Ting-Heng Chu, *East Tennessee State University*

Shannon Donovan, *Bridgewater State College*

Michael Woodworth

Pearson Education wishes to acknowledge and thank the following people for their work on the Global Edition:

Contributors:

Stefan Hirth, *Aarhus University*

Pernille Jessen, *Aarhus University*

Lee Kin Wai, *Nanyang Technological University*

Henrik Nørholm, *Aarhus University*

Jenny Robertson, *University of Brighton*

Håkan Thorsell, *Stockholm School of Economics*

Reviewers:

Wolfgang Bessler, *University of Geissen*

Jaap Bos, *University of Maastricht*

Narjess Boubakri, *American University of Sharjah*

Wajeeh Elali, *Ahlia University*

Nico Dewaelheyns, *Lessius University*

Peter de Goeij, *Tilburg University*

Kenneth Hogholm, *Hanken School of Economics*

Liangliang Jiang, *Lingnan University*

Li Jiang, *Hong Kong Polytechnic*

Jouko Karjalainen, *Helsinki University of Technology*

Timo Korkeamaki, *Hanken School of Economics*

Yue Liu, *University of Edinburgh*

Lynn Pi, *Hong Kong University of Science and Technology*

Alain Praet, *Hogeschool-Universiteit Brussel*

Paulo Rodrigues, *University of Maastricht*

Joel Shapiro, *University of Oxford*

Kenneth Tai, *Singapore Polytechnic*

Introduction

WHY STUDY CORPORATE FINANCE? No matter what your role in a corporation, an understanding of why and how financial decisions are made is essential. The focus of this book is how to make optimal corporate financial decisions. In this part of the book, we lay the foundation for our study of corporate finance. We begin, in Chapter 1, by introducing the corporation and related business forms. We then examine the role of financial managers and outside investors in decision making for the firm. To make optimal decisions, a decision maker needs information. As a result, in Chapter 2, we review an important source of information for corporate decision-making—the firm's financial statements.

We then introduce the most important idea in this book, the concept of *the absence of arbitrage* or *Law of One Price* in Chapter 3. The Law of One Price states that we can use market prices to determine the value of an investment opportunity to the firm. We will demonstrate that the Law of One Price is the one unifying principle that underlies all of financial economics and links all of the ideas throughout this book. We will return to this theme throughout our study of Corporate Finance.

The Corporation

THE MODERN U.S. CORPORATION WAS BORN IN A COURT-room in Washington, D.C., on February 2, 1819. On that day the U.S. Supreme Court established the legal precedent that the property of a corporation, like that of a person, is private and entitled to protection under the U.S. Constitution. Today, it is hard to entertain the possibility that a corporation's private property would not be protected under the Constitution. However, before the 1819 Supreme Court decision, the owners of a corporation were exposed to the possibility that the state could take their business. This concern was real enough to stop most businesses from incorporating and, indeed, in 1816 that concern was realized: The state seized Dartmouth College.

Dartmouth College was incorporated in 1769 as a private educational institution governed by a self-perpetuating board of trustees. Unhappy with the political leanings of the board, the state legislature effectively took control of Dartmouth by passing legislation in 1816 that established a governor-appointed board of overseers to run the school. The legislation had the effect of turning a private university under private control into a state university under state control. If such an act were constitutional, it implied that any state (or the federal government) could, at will, national-ize any corporation.

Dartmouth sued for its independence and the case made it to the Supreme Court under Chief Justice John Marshall in 1818. In a nearly unanimous 5–1 decision, the court struck down the New Hampshire law, ruling that a corporation was a "contract" and that, under Article 1 of the Constitution, "the state legislatures were forbidden to pass any law impairing the obligation of contracts."[1] The precedent was set: Owners of businesses could incorporate and still enjoy the protection of private property, as well as protection from seizure, both guaranteed by the U.S. Constitution. The modern business corporation was born.

---

[1] The full text of John Marshall's decision can be found at http://www.constitution.org/dwebster/dartmouth_decision.htm.

Today, the corporate structure is ubiquitous all over the world, and yet continues to evolve in the face of new forces. In 2008 the financial crisis once again transformed the financial landscape, bringing down giants like Bear Stearns, Lehman Brothers, and AIG and reshaping investment banks like Goldman Sachs into government-guaranteed commercial banks. These changes have as profound an effect on the future of corporate finance as the Dartmouth decision did almost 200 years ago. Government bailouts have provoked challenging questions regarding the role of the federal government in the control and management of private corporations. In the wake of the crisis, significant reforms of the regulation and oversight of financial markets were passed into law. *Understanding the principles of corporate finance has never been more important to the practice of business* than it is now, during this time of great change.

The focus of this book is on how people in corporations make financial decisions. This chapter introduces the corporation and explains alternative business organizational forms. A key factor in the success of corporations is the ability to easily trade ownership shares, and so we will also explain the role of stock markets in facilitating trading among investors in a corporation and the implications that has for the ownership and control of corporations.

1.1 The Types of Firms

We begin our study of corporate finance by introducing the major types of firms: *sole proprietorships, partnerships, limited liability companies,* or *corporations*. We explain each organizational form in turn, but our primary focus is on the most important form—the corporation. In addition to describing what a corporation is, we also provide an overview of why corporations are so successful.

Sole Proprietorships

A **sole proprietorship** is a business owned and run by one person. Sole proprietorships are usually very small with few, if any, employees. Although they do not account for much sales revenue in the economy, they are the most common type of firm in the world, as shown in Figure 1.1. Statistics indicate that 71% of businesses in the United States are sole proprietorships, although they generate only 5% of the revenue.[2] Contrast this with corporations, which make up only 19% of firms but are responsible for 84% of U.S. revenue.

Sole proprietorships share the following key characteristics:

1. Sole proprietorships have the advantage of being straightforward to set up. Consequently, many new businesses use this organizational form.

2. The principal limitation of a sole proprietorship is that there is no separation between the firm and the owner—the firm can have only one owner who runs the business. If there are other investors, they cannot hold an ownership stake in the firm.

3. The owner has unlimited personal liability for the firm's debts. That is, if the firm defaults on any debt payment, the lender can (and will) require the owner to repay

---

[2]This information, as well as other small business statistics, can be found at www.bizstats.com. See their on-site disclosures page for a description of their methodology.

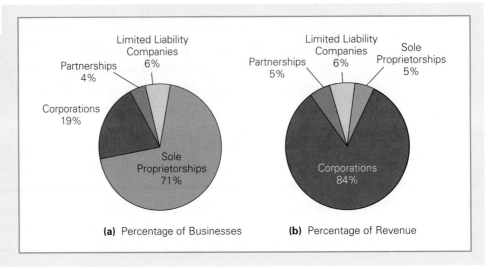

FIGURE 1.1

Types of U.S. Firms

There are four different types of firms in the United States. As (a) and (b) show, although the majority of U.S. firms are sole proprietorships, they generate only a small fraction of total revenue, in contrast to corporations.

Source: www.bizstats.com

the loan from personal assets. An owner who cannot afford to repay the loan must declare personal bankruptcy.

4. The life of a sole proprietorship is limited to the life of the owner. It is also difficult to transfer ownership of a sole proprietorship.

For most businesses, the disadvantages of a sole proprietorship outweigh the advantages. As soon as the firm reaches the point at which it can borrow without the owner agreeing to be personally liable, the owners typically convert the business into a form that limits the owner's liability.

Partnerships

A **partnership** is identical to a sole proprietorship except it has more than one owner. The following are key features of a partnership:

1. *All* partners are liable for the firm's debt. That is, a lender can require *any* partner to repay all the firm's outstanding debts.
2. The partnership ends on the death or withdrawal of any single partner.
3. Partners can avoid liquidation if the partnership agreement provides for alternatives such as a buyout of a deceased or withdrawn partner.

Some old and established businesses remain partnerships or sole proprietorships. Often these firms are the types of businesses in which the owners' personal reputations are the basis for the businesses. For example, law firms, medical practices, and accounting firms are often organized as partnerships. For such enterprises, the partners' personal liability increases the confidence of the firm's clients that the partners will strive to maintain their reputation.

A **limited partnership** is a partnership with two kinds of owners, general partners and limited partners. In this case, the general partners have the same rights and privileges as partners in a (general) partnership—they are personally liable for the firm's debt obligations. Limited partners, however, have **limited liability**—that is, their liability is limited to their investment. Their private property cannot be seized to pay off the firm's outstanding debts. Furthermore, the death or withdrawal of a limited partner does not dissolve the partnership, and a limited partner's interest is transferable. However, a limited partner has no management authority and cannot legally be involved in the managerial decision making for the business.

Private equity funds and venture capital funds are two examples of industries dominated by limited partnerships. In these firms, a few general partners contribute some of their own capital and raise additional capital from outside investors who are limited partners. The general partners control how all the capital is invested. Most often they will actively participate in running the businesses they choose to invest in. The outside investors play no active role in the partnership other than monitoring how their investments are performing.

Limited Liability Companies

A **limited liability company or corporation** limits the owners' liability to their investment, which means the owners cannot be held personally liable for the company's debts. There are two types of limited liability company: *private companies* and *public companies*. The owners of private limited companies are not allowed to trade their shares on an organised exchange.

Private companies are a relatively new phenomenon in the United States. Elsewhere, however, they are more established and known by a variety of names. For example, in Germany they are called *Gesellschaft mit beschränkter Haftnung* (GmbH); in France, *Société a responsabilité limitée (SARL)*; and there are similar names in Italy (SRL) and Spain (SL). Public limited companies are allowed to have their shares traded on an organized exchange. They also have different names in different countries. For example, in the United Kingdom they are called *public limited companies (plc or PLC)*; in Germany, *Aktiengesellschaft (AG)*; in France, *Société Anonyme (SA)*; and in Spain, *Sociedade Anonima (SA)*.

Features of Corporations

The distinguishing feature of a **corporation (or company)** is that it is a legally defined, artificial being (a judicial person or legal entity), separate from its owners. As such, it has many of the legal powers that people have. It can enter into contracts, acquire assets, incur obligations, and, as we have already established, it enjoys protection under most jurisdictions against the seizure of its property. Because a corporation is a legal entity separate and distinct from its owners, it is solely responsible for its own obligations. Consequently, the owners of a corporation (or its employees, customers, etc.) are not liable for any obligations the corporation enters into. Similarly, the corporation is not liable for any personal obligations of its owners.

Formation of a Corporation. Corporations must be legally formed, which means that a legal document (known as a corporate charter in the United States) is created upon the formation of the company. Setting up a corporation is therefore considerably more costly than setting up a sole proprietorship. In the United States, for jurisdictional purposes, a corporation is a citizen of the state in which it is incorporated. Most firms hire lawyers to create a corporate charter that includes formal articles of incorporation and a set of bylaws. The corporate charter specifies the initial rules that govern how the corporation is run.

Ownership of a Corporation. There is no limit on the number of owners a corporation can have. Because most corporations have many owners, each owner owns only a small fraction of the corporation. The entire ownership stake of a corporation is divided into shares known as **stock**. The collection of all the outstanding shares of a corporation is known as the **equity** of the corporation. An owner of a share of stock in the corporation is known as a **shareholder, stockholder,** or **equity holder** and is entitled to **dividend payments**, that is, payments made at the discretion of the corporation to its equity holders.

Shareholders usually receive a share of the dividend payments that is proportional to the amount of stock they own. For example, a shareholder who owns 25% of the firm's shares will be entitled to 25% of the total dividend payment.

A unique feature of a corporation is that there is no limitation on who can own its shares. That is, an owner of a corporation need not have any special expertise or qualification. For publicly owned companies, this feature allows free trade in the shares of the corporation and provides one of the most important advantages of organizing a firm as a corporation rather than as sole proprietorship, partnership, or private limited company. Corporations can raise substantial amounts of capital because they can sell ownership shares to anonymous outside investors.

The availability of outside funding has enabled corporations to dominate the economy, as shown by Panel (b) of Figure 1.1. Let's take one of the world's largest firms, Wal-Mart Stores, as an example. Wal-Mart had over 2 million employees, and reported annual revenue of \$422 billion in 2011. Indeed, the top five companies by sales volume in 2012 (Wal-Mart, Exxon Mobil, Chevron, ConocoPhillips, and General Motors) had combined sales exceeding \$1.5 trillion, an amount comparable to the total sales of the more than 22 million U.S. sole proprietorships.

Tax Implications for Corporate Entities

An important difference between the types of organizational forms is the way they are taxed. Because a corporation is a separate legal entity, a corporation's profits are subject to taxation separate from its owners' tax obligations. In effect, shareholders of a corporation pay taxes twice. First, the corporation pays tax on its profits, and then when the remaining profits are distributed to the shareholders, the shareholders pay their own personal income tax on this income. This system is sometimes referred to as *double taxation*, and is known as the "classical system" of taxation. In addition to the United States, some European countries, such as Austria, Belgium, Denmark, and the Netherlands, have classical systems.

EXAMPLE 1.1	Taxation of Corporate Earnings

Problem

You are a shareholder in a corporation. The corporation earns \$5 per share before taxes. After it has paid taxes, it will distribute the rest of its earnings to you as a dividend. The dividend is income to you, so you will then pay taxes on these earnings. The corporate tax rate is 40% and your tax rate on dividend income is 15%. How much of the earnings remain after all taxes are paid?

Solution

First, the corporation pays taxes. It earned \$5 per share, but must pay $0.40 \times \$5 = \$2$ to the government in corporate taxes. That leaves \$3 to distribute. However, you must pay $0.15 \times \$3 = \$0.45$ in income taxes on this amount, leaving $\$3 - \$0.45 = \$2.55$ per share after all taxes are paid. As a shareholder you only end up with \$2.55 of the original \$5 in earnings; the remaining $\$2 + \$0.45 = \$2.45$ is paid as taxes. Thus, your total effective tax rate is $2.45/5 = 49\%$.

An alternative system is known as the imputation system, whereby the dividend is regarded as a flow of profits direct to the shareholders and is therefore considered to be only one source of income that is not subject to double taxation. For example, in the United States, the U.S. Internal Revenue Code allows an exemption from double taxation for **"S" corporations**, which are corporations that elect subchapter S tax treatment. Under these tax regulations, the firm's profits (and losses) are not subject to corporate taxes, but

Corporate Taxation Around the World

Most countries offer investors in corporations some relief from double taxation. Thirty countries make up the Organization for Economic Co-operation and Development (OECD), and of these countries, only Ireland offers no relief whatsoever. A few countries, including Australia, Mexico, New Zealand, and Norway, offer complete relief by effectively not taxing dividend income. The United States offers partial relief by having a lower tax rate on dividend income than on other sources of income. As of 2012, for most investors qualified dividends are taxed at 15%, a rate significantly below their personal income tax rate.

instead are allocated directly to shareholders based on their ownership share. The shareholders must include these profits as income on their individual tax returns (even if no money is distributed to them). However, after the shareholders have paid income taxes on these profits, no further tax is due.

EXAMPLE 1.2

Taxation of S Corporation Earnings

Problem
Rework Example 1.1 assuming the corporation in that example has elected subchapter S treatment and your tax rate on non-dividend income is 30%.

Solution
In this case, the corporation pays no taxes. It earned $5 per share. Whether or not the corporation chooses to distribute or retain this cash, you must pay $0.30 \times \$5 = \$1.50$ in income taxes, which is substantially lower than the $2.45 paid in Example 1.1.

The U.S. government places strict limitations on the qualifications for subchapter S tax treatment. In particular, the shareholders of such corporations must be individuals who are U.S. citizens or residents, and there can be no more than 100 of them. Because most corporations have no restrictions on who owns their shares or the number of shareholders, they cannot qualify for subchapter S treatment. Thus most corporations are **"C" corporations**, which are corporations subject to corporate taxes.

CONCEPT CHECK

1. What is a limited company? How does it differ from a limited partnership?

2. What are the advantages and disadvantages of organizing a business as a corporation?

1.2 Ownership Versus Control of Corporations

It is often not feasible for the owners of a corporation to have direct control of the firm because there are sometimes many owners, each of whom can freely trade his or her shares. That is, in a corporation, direct control and ownership are often separate. Rather than the owners, the *board of directors* and *chief executive officer* possess direct control of the corporation. In this section, we explain how the responsibilities for the corporation are divided between these two entities and how together they shape and execute the goals of the firm.

The Corporate Management Team

The shareholders of a corporation exercise their control by electing a **board of directors**, a group of people who have the ultimate decision-making authority in the corporation.

David Viniar is Chief Financial Officer and head of the Operations, Technology and Finance Division at Goldman Sachs—the last major investment bank to convert from a partnership to a corporation. As the firm's CFO, he played a leading role in the firm's conversion to a corporation in 1999 and charting the firm's course through the financial crisis of 2008–2009.

QUESTION: *What are the advantages of partnerships and corporations?*

ANSWER: We debated this question at length when we were deciding whether to go public or stay a private partnership in the mid-1990s. There were good arguments on both sides. Those in favor of going public argued we needed greater financial and strategic flexibility to achieve our aggressive growth and market leadership goals. As a public corporation, we would have a more stable equity base to support growth and disperse risk; increased access to large public debt markets; publicly traded securities with which to undertake acquisitions and reward and motivate our employees; and a simpler and more transparent structure with which to increase scale and global reach.

Those against going public argued our private partnership structure worked well and would enable us to achieve our financial and strategic goals. As a private partnership, we could generate enough capital internally and in the private placement markets to fund growth; take a longer-term view of returns on our investments with less focus on earnings volatility, which is not valued in public companies; and retain voting control and alignment of the partners and the firm.

A big perceived advantage of our private partnership was its sense of distinctiveness and mystique, which reinforced our culture of teamwork and excellence and helped differentiate us from our competitors. Many questioned whether the special qualities of our culture would survive if the firm went public.

QUESTION: *What was the driving force behind the conversion?*

ANSWER: We ultimately decided to go public for three main reasons: to secure permanent capital to grow; to be able to use publicly traded securities to finance strategic acquisitions; and to enhance the culture of ownership and gain compensation flexibility.

QUESTION: *Did the conversion achieve its goals?*

ANSWER: Yes. As a public company, we have a simpler, bigger and more permanent capital base, including enhanced long-term borrowing capacity in the public debt markets. We have drawn on substantial capital resources to serve clients, take advantage of new business opportunities, and better control our own destiny through changing economic and business conditions. We have been able to use stock to finance key acquisitions and support large strategic and financial investments. Given how the stakes in our industry changed, how capital demands grew, going public when we did fortunately positioned us to compete effectively through the cycle.

Our distinctive culture of teamwork and excellence has thrived in public form, and our equity compensation programs turned out better than we could have hoped. Making everyone at Goldman Sachs an owner, rather than just 221 partners, energized all our employees. The growing size and scope of our business—not the change to public form—has presented the greatest challenges to the positive aspects of our culture.

QUESTION: *What prompted Goldman's decision to become a bank holding company in Fall 2008?*

ANSWER: The market environment had become extraordinarily unstable following the collapse of Bear Stearns in March 2008. There was an increased focus on the SEC-supervised broker/dealer business model, and in September, market sentiment had become increasingly negative with growing concerns over Lehman Brothers' solvency. Following the bankruptcy of Lehman Brothers and the sale of Merrill Lynch in the middle of September, and notwithstanding the reporting of quite strong earnings by both Goldman Sachs and Morgan Stanley, it became clear to us that the market viewed oversight by the Federal Reserve and the ability to source insured bank deposits as offering a greater degree of safety and soundness. By changing our status, we gained all the benefits available to our commercial banking peers, including access to permanent liquidity and funding, without affecting our ability to operate or own any of our current businesses or investments.

In most corporations, each share of stock gives a shareholder one vote in the election of the board of directors, so investors with the most shares have the most influence. When one or two shareholders own a very large proportion of the outstanding stock, these shareholders may either be on the board of directors themselves, or they may have the right to appoint a number of directors.

The board of directors makes rules on how the corporation should be run (including how the top managers in the corporation are compensated), sets policy, and monitors the performance of the company. The board of directors delegates most decisions that involve day-to-day running of the corporation to its management. The **chief executive officer (CEO)** is charged with running the corporation by instituting the rules and policies set by the board of directors. The size of the rest of the management team varies from corporation to corporation. The separation of powers within corporations between the board of directors and the CEO is not always distinct. In fact, it is not uncommon for the CEO also to be the chairman of the board of directors. The most senior financial manager is the **chief financial officer (CFO)**, who often reports directly to the CEO. Figure 1.2 presents part of a typical organizational chart for a corporation, highlighting the key positions a financial manager may take.

The Financial Manager

Within the corporation, financial managers are responsible for three main tasks: making investment decisions, making financing decisions, and managing the firm's cash flows.

Investment Decisions. The financial manager's most important job is to make the firm's investment decisions. The financial manager must weigh the costs and benefits of all investments and projects and decide which of them qualify as good uses of the money shareholders have invested in the firm. These investment decisions fundamentally shape what the firm does and whether it will add value for its owners. In this book, we will develop the tools necessary to make these investment decisions.

FIGURE 1.2

Organizational Chart of a Typical Corporation

The board of directors, representing the stockholders, controls the corporation and hires the Chief Executive Officer who is then responsible for running the corporation. The Chief Financial Officer oversees the financial operations of the firm, with the Controller managing both tax and accounting functions, and the Treasurer responsible for capital budgeting, risk management, and credit management activities.

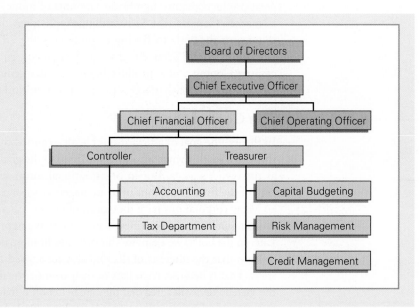

GLOBAL FINANCIAL CRISIS   **The Dodd-Frank Act**

In response to the 2008 financial crisis, the U.S. federal government reevaluated its role in the control and management of financial institutions and private corporations. Signed into law on July 21, 2010, the **Dodd-Frank Wall Street Reform and Consumer Protection Act** brought a sweeping change to financial regulation in response to widespread calls for financial regulatory system reform after the near collapse of the world's financial system in the fall of 2008 and the ensuing global credit crisis. History indeed repeats itself: It was in the wake of the 1929 stock market crash and subsequent Great Depression that Congress passed the Glass-Steagall Act establishing the Federal Deposit Insurance Corporation (FDIC) and instituted significant bank reforms to regulate transactions between commercial banks and securities firms.

The Dodd-Frank Act aims to (i) promote U.S. financial stability by "improving accountability and transparency in the financial system," (ii) put an end to the notion of "too big to fail," (iii) "protect the American taxpayer by ending bailouts," and (iv) "protect consumers from abusive financial services practices." Time will tell whether the Act will actually achieve these important goals.

Implementing the wide-ranging financial reforms in the Dodd-Frank Act requires the work of many federal agencies, either through rulemaking or other regulatory actions. As of mid-2012, two years since Dodd-Frank's passage, 129 of the reforms have been finalized, providing a clear picture of the Dodd-Frank regulatory framework. But another 271 rules or actions, containing many of the core Dodd-Frank reforms, await completion.

Financing Decisions. Once the financial manager has decided which investments to make, he or she also decides how to pay for them. Large investments may require the corporation to raise additional money. The financial manager must decide whether to raise more money from new and existing owners by selling more shares (equity) or to borrow the money (bonds or other debt). In this book, we will discuss the characteristics of each source of funds and how to decide which one to use in the context of the corporation's overall mix of debt and equity.

Cash for Treasury Management. The financial manager must ensure that the firm has enough cash on hand to meet its day-to-day obligations. This job, also commonly known as managing working capital, may seem straightforward, but in a young or growing company, it can mean the difference between success and failure. Even companies with great products require significant amounts of money to develop and bring those products to market. Consider the $150 million Apple spent during its secretive development of the iPhone, or the costs to Boeing of producing the 787—the latter spent billions of dollars before the first 787 left the ground. A company typically spends a significant amount of cash developing a new product before its sales generate income. The financial manager's job is to make sure that access to cash does not hinder the firm's success.

The Goal of the Firm

In theory, the goal of a firm should be determined by the firm's owners. A sole proprietorship has a single owner who runs the firm, so the goals of a sole proprietorship are the same as the owner's goals. But in organizational forms with multiple owners, the appropriate goal of the firm—and thus of its managers—is not as clear.

Many corporations have thousands of owners (shareholders). Each owner is likely to have different interests and priorities. Whose interests and priorities determine the goals of the firm? Later in the book, we examine this question in more detail. However, you might be surprised to learn that the interests of shareholders are aligned for many, if not most, important decisions. That is because, regardless of their own personal financial position and stage in life, all the shareholders will agree that they are better off if management makes decisions that increase the value of their shares. For example, by June 2012, Apple shares were worth over 60 times as much as they were in October 2001, when the first iPod was introduced. Clearly, regardless of their preferences and other differences, all investors who held shares of Apple stock over this period have benefited from the investment decisions Apple's managers have made.

The Firm and Society

Are decisions that increase the value of the firm's equity beneficial for society as a whole? Most often they are. While Apple's shareholders have become much richer since 2001, its customers also are better off with products like the iPod and iPhone that they might otherwise never have had. But even if the corporation only makes its shareholders better off, as long as nobody else is made worse off by its decisions, increasing the value of equity is good for society.

The problem occurs when increasing the value of equity comes at the expense of others. Consider a corporation that, in the course of business, pollutes the environment and does not pay the costs to clean up the pollution. Alternatively, a corporation may not itself pollute, but use of its products may harm the environment. In such cases, decisions that increase shareholder wealth can be costly for society as whole.

The 2008 financial crisis highlighted another example of decisions that can increase shareholder wealth but are costly for society. In the early part of the last decade, banks took on excessive risk. For a while, this strategy benefited the banks' shareholders. But when the bets went bad, the resulting financial crisis harmed the broader economy.

When the actions of the corporation impose harm on others in the economy, appropriate public policy and regulation is required to assure that corporate interests and societal interests remain aligned. Sound public policy should allow firms to continue to pursue the maximization of shareholder value in a way that benefits society overall.

Ethics and Incentives within Corporations

But even when all the owners of a corporation agree on the goals of the corporation, these goals must be implemented. In a simple organizational form like a sole proprietorship, the owner, who runs the firm, can ensure that the firm's goals match his or her own. But a corporation is run by a management team, separate from its owners, giving rise to conflicts of interest. How can the owners of a corporation ensure that the management team will implement their goals?

Agency Problems. Many people claim that because of the separation of ownership and control in a corporation, managers have little incentive to work in the interests of the shareholders when this means working against their own self-interest. Economists call this an **agency problem**—when managers, despite being hired as the agents of shareholders, put their own self-interest ahead of the interests of shareholders. Managers face the ethical dilemma of whether to adhere to their responsibility to put the interests of shareholders first, or to do what is in their own personal best interest.

This agency problem is commonly addressed in practice by minimizing the number of decisions managers must make for which their own self-interest substantially differs from the interests of the shareholders. For example, managers' compensation contracts are designed to ensure that most decisions in the shareholders' interest are also in the managers' interests; shareholders often tie the compensation of top managers to the corporation's profits or perhaps to its share price. There is, however, a limitation to this strategy. By tying compensation too closely to performance, the shareholders might be asking managers to take on more risk than they are comfortable taking. As a result, managers may not make decisions that the shareholders want them to, or it might be hard to find talented managers

> ## GLOBAL FINANCIAL CRISIS The Dodd-Frank Act on Corporate Compensation and Governance
>
> Compensation is one of the most important conflicts of interest between corporate executives and shareholders. To limit senior corporate executives' influence over their own compensation and prevent excessive compensation, the Act directs the SEC to adopt new rules that:
>
> - Mandate the independence of a firm's compensation committee and its advisers.
> - Provide shareholders the opportunity to approve—in a non-binding, advisory vote—the compensation of executive officers at least once every three years (referred to as a "Say-on-Pay" vote).
>
> - Require firm disclosure and shareholder approval of large bonus payments (so-called "golden parachutes") to ousted senior executives as the result of a takeover.
> - Require disclosure of the relationship of executive pay to the company's performance, as well as the ratio between the CEO's total compensation and that of the median employee.
> - Create "clawback" provisions that allow firms to recoup compensation paid based on erroneous financial results.

willing to accept the job. On the other hand, if compensation contracts reduce managers' risk by rewarding good performance but limiting the penalty associated with poor performance, managers may have an incentive to take excessive risk.

Further potential for conflicts of interest and ethical considerations arise when some stakeholders in the corporation benefit and others lose from a decision. Shareholders and managers are two stakeholders in the corporation, but others include the employees and the communities in which the company operates, for example. Managers may decide to take the interests of other stakeholders into account in their decisions, such as keeping a loss-generating factory open because it is the main provider of jobs in a small town, paying above-market wages to factory workers in a developing country, or operating a plant at a higher environmental standard than local law mandates.

In some cases, these actions that benefit other stakeholders also benefit the firm's shareholders by creating a more dedicated workforce, generating positive publicity with customers, or other indirect effects. In other instances, when these decisions benefit other stakeholders at shareholders' expense, they represent a form of corporate charity. Indeed, many if not most corporations explicitly donate (on behalf of their shareholders) to local and global charitable and political causes. For example, in 2010, Wal-Mart Stores gave $320 million in cash to charity (making it the largest corporate donor of cash in that year). These actions are costly and reduce shareholder wealth. Thus, while some shareholders might support such policies because they feel that they reflect their own moral and ethical priorities, it is unlikely that all shareholders will feel this way, leading to potential conflicts of interest amongst shareholders.

Citizens United v. Federal Election Commission

On January 21, 2010, the U.S. Supreme Court ruled on what some scholars have argued is the most important First Amendment case in many years. In *Citizens United v. Federal Election Commission* the Court held, in a controversial 5–4 decision, that the First Amendment allows corporations and unions to make political expenditures in support of a particular candidate. This ruling overturned existing restrictions on political campaigning by corporations. But because it is highly unlikely that all shareholders of a corporation would unanimously support a particular candidate, allowing such activities effectively guarantees a potential conflict of interest.

The CEO's Performance. Another way shareholders can encourage managers to work in the interests of shareholders is to discipline them if they do not. If shareholders are unhappy with a CEO's performance, they could, in principle, pressure the board to oust the CEO. Disney's Michael Eisner, Hewlett Packard's Carly Fiorina, and Yahoo's Scott Thompson were all reportedly forced to resign by their boards. Despite these high-profile examples, directors and top executives are rarely replaced through a grassroots shareholder uprising. Instead, dissatisfied investors often choose to sell their shares. Of course, somebody must be willing to buy the shares from the dissatisfied shareholders. If enough shareholders are dissatisfied, the only way to entice investors to buy (or hold on to) the shares is to offer them a low price. Similarly, investors who see a well-managed corporation will want to purchase shares, which drives the share price up. Thus, the share price of the corporation is a barometer for corporate leaders that continuously gives them feedback on their shareholders' opinion of their performance.

When the share price deteriorates, the board of directors might react by replacing the CEO. In some corporations, however, the senior executives are entrenched because boards of directors do not have the will to replace them. Often the reluctance to fire results because the board members are close friends of the CEO and lack objectivity. In corporations in which the CEO is entrenched and doing a poor job, the expectation of continued poor performance will decrease the share price. Low share prices create a profit opportunity. In a **hostile takeover**, an individual or organization—sometimes known as a corporate raider—can purchase a large fraction of the equity and acquire enough votes to replace the board of directors and the CEO. With a new superior management team, the shares are a much more attractive investment, which would likely result in a price rise and a profit for the corporate raider and the other shareholders. Although the words "hostile" and "raider" have negative connotations, corporate raiders themselves provide an important service to shareholders. The mere threat of being removed as a result of a hostile takeover is often enough to discipline bad managers and motivate boards of directors to make difficult decisions. Consequently, the fact that a corporation's shares can be publicly traded, creates a "market for corporate control" that encourages managers and boards of directors to act in the interests of their shareholders.

Corporate Bankruptcy. Ordinarily, a corporation is run on behalf of its shareholders. But when a corporation borrows money, the holders of the firm's debt also become investors in the corporation. While the debt holders do not normally exercise control over the firm, if the corporation fails to repay its debts, the debt holders are entitled to seize the assets of the corporation in compensation for the default. To prevent such a seizure, the firm may attempt to renegotiate with the debt holders, or file for bankruptcy protection in a court. (We describe the details of the bankruptcy process and its implications for corporate decisions in much more detail in Part 5 of the textbook.) Ultimately, however, if the firm is unable to repay or renegotiate with the debt holders, the control of the corporation's assets will be transferred to them.

Thus, when a firm fails to repay its debts, the end result is a change in ownership of the firm, with control passing from equity holders to debt holders. Importantly, bankruptcy need not result in a **liquidation** of the firm, which involves shutting down the business and selling off its assets. Even if control of the firm passes to the debt holders, it is in the debt holders' interest to run the firm in the most profitable way possible. Doing so often means keeping the business operating. For example, in 1990, Federated Department Stores declared bankruptcy. One of its best-known assets at the time was Bloomingdale's, a nationally recognized department store. Because Bloomingdale's was a profitable business,

Airlines in Bankruptcy

On December 9, 2002, United Airlines filed for bankruptcy protection following an unsuccessful attempt to convince the federal government to bail out the company's investors out by providing loan guarantees. Although United remained in bankruptcy for the next three years, it continued to operate and fly passengers, and even expanded capacity in some markets. One of those expansions was "Ted," an ill-fated attempt by United to start a budget airline to compete directly with Southwest Airlines. In short, although United's original shareholders were wiped out, as far as customers were concerned it was business as usual. People continued to book tickets and United continued to fly and serve them.

It is tempting to think that when a firm files for bankruptcy, things are "over." But often, rather than liquidate the firm, bondholders and other creditors are better off allowing the firm to continue operating as a going concern. United was just one of many airlines to move in and out of bankruptcy since 2002; others include U.S. Airways, Air Canada, Hawaiian Airlines, Northwest Airlines, and Delta Airlines. In November 2011, American Airlines became the latest airline to declare bankruptcy. Like United in 2002, American continues to operate while it cuts costs and reorganizes. These efforts seem to be paying off—excluding the costs associated with the bankruptcy, American reported earnings of $95 million in the second quarter of 2012, the first second-quarter operating profit since 2007.

neither equity holders nor debt holders had any desire to shut it down, and it continued to operate in bankruptcy. In 1992, when Federated Department Stores was reorganized and emerged from bankruptcy, Federated's original equity holders had lost their stake in Bloomingdale's, but this flagship chain continued to perform well for its new owners, and its value as a business was not adversely affected by the bankruptcy.

Thus, a useful way to understand corporations is to think of there being two sets of investors with claims to its cash flows—debt holders and equity holders. As long as the corporation can satisfy the claims of the debt holders, ownership remains in the hands of the equity holders. If the corporation fails to satisfy debt holders' claims, debt holders may take control of the firm. Thus, a corporate bankruptcy is best thought of as a *change in ownership* of the corporation, and not necessarily as a failure of the underlying business.

CONCEPT CHECK
1. What are the three main decisions of a financial manager?

2. What is a principal-agent problem that may exist in a corporation?

3. How may a corporate bankruptcy filing affect the ownership of a corporation?

1.3 The Stock Market

As we have discussed, shareholders would like the firm's managers to maximize the value of their investment in the firm. The value of an investment is determined by the price of a share of the corporation. Because **private companies** have a limited set of shareholders and their shares are not generally traded, the value of their shares can be difficult to determine. But many corporations are **public companies**, whose shares trade on organized markets called a **stock market (or stock exchange or bourse)**. These markets provide *liquidity* and determine a market price for the company's shares. An investment is said to be **liquid** if it can easily be turned into cash by selling it immediately at a competitive market price. This liquidity is attractive to outside investors, as it provides flexibility regarding the timing and duration of their investment in the firm. In this section, we provide an overview of the world's major stock markets. The research and trading of participants in these markets give rise to share prices that provide constant feedback to managers regarding investors' views of their decisions.

Primary and Secondary Stock Markets

When a corporation itself issues new shares and sells them to investors, it does so on the **primary market**. After this initial transaction between the corporation and investors, the shares continue to trade in a **secondary market** between investors without the involvement of the corporation. For example, if you wish to buy 100 shares of Starbucks Coffee, you would place an order on a stock exchange, where Starbucks trades under the ticker symbol SBUX. You would buy your shares from someone who already held shares of Starbucks, not from Starbucks itself.

The Largest Stock Markets

The best-known U.S. stock market and the largest stock market in the world is the New York Stock Exchange (NYSE). Investors exchange billions of dollars of stock every day on the NYSE. Other U.S. stock markets include the American Stock Exchange (AMEX), the National Association of Security Dealers Automated Quotation (NASDAQ), and regional exchanges such as the Midwest Stock Exchange. Most other countries have at least one stock market. Outside the United States, the largest and most active stock markets are the Tokyo Stock Exchange (TSE), the London Stock Exchange (LSE), and NYSE Euronext. Figure 1.3 displays the world's largest stock markets by two of the most common measures—the total annual volume of shares traded on the exchange and the total value of all domestic corporations listed on the exchange.

FIGURE 1.3 **Worldwide Stock Markets Ranked by Two Common Measures**

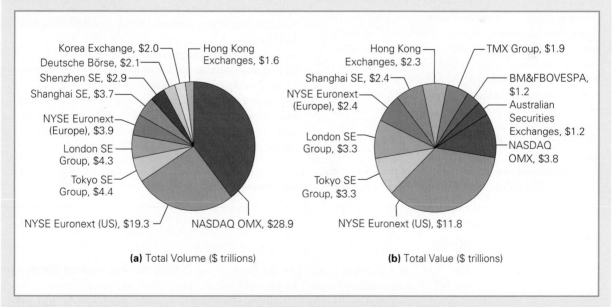

(a) Total Volume ($ trillions)

(b) Total Value ($ trillions)

The 10 biggest stock markets in the world (a) by total volume of shares traded on the exchange in 2011 and (b) by total value of all domestic corporations listed on the exchange at year-end 2011.

Source: www.world-exchanges.org

Jean-François Théodore *

Jean-François Théodore is the Deputy CEO of NYSE Euronext, the largest stock exchange group in the world.

QUESTION: *How have technological innovations shaped financial markets?*

ANSWER: At the end of the 1980s, the electronic execution of market orders transformed the organization and operation of the financial markets, resulting in continuous securities trading. Since then, technology has become a key driver of change in the financial industry, enabling markets to become faster and increasingly more competitive, at a time when client requirements are growing and diversifying, particularly regarding the speed of execution and volumes, notably from algorithmic traders.

QUESTION: *The Paris Stock Exchange has experienced profound upheavals recently. What have the most important changes been?*

ANSWER: The Paris Stock Exchange, like other leading stock markets, has changed significantly in recent years.

With the decompartmentalization and globalization of financial activities, securities markets, which were once national, public, or cooperative institutions, have abandoned their cooperative status or listed for trading on their own market. This change is transforming securities markets into real capitalistic enterprises oriented toward innovation and the optimization of their resources. It also favors mergers among the various market operators, with the objective of creating greater homogeneity in the financial markets, capital fluidity, diversity in the service offering, and reduced costs for publicly traded companies, investors, and intermediaries.

A few months after the introduction of the euro in September 2000, the Paris Stock Exchange played a pioneering role by merging with the Amsterdam and Brussels exchanges to become the first pan-European stock exchange: Euronext. Two years later, after its own initial public offering, Euronext acquired the British derivatives market Liffe and integrated the Lisbon exchange. In April 2007, in an unprecedented event for our business sector, Euronext merged with the New York Stock Exchange, resulting in NYSE Euronext, the largest and most liquid securities market group in the world.

QUESTION: *What benefits do companies and investors receive from the merger of NYSE and Euronext?*

ANSWER: In 2007, over 4000 companies from 55 different countries were listed for trading on NYSE Euronext, representing a total market capitalization of close to 21,000 billion euros, more than the next four exchanges combined.

Present in six countries in the world, NYSE Euronext has an unequaled listing offer, with increased visibility and liquidity and expanded financing opportunities for issuers. Backed by a globally recognized label, NYSE Euronext enables companies to be listed on a market adapted to their size and location, within a stable regulatory environment, in dollars and/or in euros (the world's two leading currencies), and under the accounting standards of their choice (IFRS or US GAAP).

In addition, the integration of the different NYSE Euronext markets, combined with the technological excellence of its digital market information system and the diverse array of financial products and services, encourages cross-border trading and increased liquidity, benefiting all users. In fact, more than one spot trade out of every three trades in the world is made on NYSE Euronext.

*This interview was conducted by Gunther Capelle-Blancard and Nicolas Couderc.

NYSE

The NYSE is a physical place. On the floor of the NYSE, **market makers** (known on the NYSE as **specialists**) match buyers and sellers. They post two prices for every stock they make a market in: the price they stand willing to buy the stock at (the **bid price**) and the price they stand willing to sell the stock for (the **ask price**). If a customer comes to them wanting to make a trade at these prices, they will honor the price (up to a limited number of shares) and make the trade even if they do not have another customer willing to take the other side of the trade. In this way, they ensure that the market is liquid because customers can always be assured they can trade at the posted prices. The exchange has rules that attempt to ensure that bid and ask prices do not get too far apart and that large price changes take place through a series of small changes, rather than one big jump.

Ask prices exceed bid prices. This difference is called the **bid-ask spread**. Customers always buy at the ask (the higher price) and sell at the bid (the lower price). The bid-ask spread is a **transaction cost** investors have to pay in order to trade. Because specialists in a physical market like the NYSE take the other side of the trade from their customers, this cost accrues to them as a profit. It is the compensation they demand for providing a liquid market by standing ready to honor any quoted price. Investors also pay other forms of transactions costs like commissions.

Over-the-Counter Stock Markets

In today's technology-driven economy, a stock market does not need to have a physical location. Investors can make stock transactions (perhaps more efficiently) over the phone or by computer network. Consequently, some stock markets are such as NASDAQ, which are called **over-the-counter (OTC) markets**, are a collection of dealers or market makers connected by computer network and telephone. An important difference between the NYSE and NASDAQ is that on the NYSE, each share has only one market maker. On NASDAQ, shares can and do have multiple market makers who compete with each other. Each market maker must post bid and ask prices in the NASDAQ network where they can be viewed by all participants. Because investors do not directly interact to set the prices, NASDAQ and other over-the-counter markets are **dealer markets**. The NASDAQ system posts the best prices first and fills orders accordingly. This process guarantees investors the best possible price at the moment, whether they are buying or selling.

In this chapter, we provided an overview of corporate finance, described the financial manager's role, and stressed the importance of stock markets. In upcoming chapters, we will develop the tools of financial analysis together with a clear understanding of when to apply them and why they work. These tools will provide the foundation that will allow you to use the financial market information provided by stock markets and other sources to make the best possible financial management decisions.

CONCEPT CHECK
1. What is the New York Stock Exchange (NYSE)?
2. What advantage does a stock market provide to corporate investors?

MyFinanceLab

Here is what you should know after reading this chapter. MyFinanceLab will help you identify what you know and where to go when you need to practice.

1.1 The Types of Firms

- The main types of firms are sole proprietorships, partnerships, and limited liability companies or corporations.
- Firms with unlimited personal liability include sole proprietorships and partnerships.
- Firms with limited liability include limited partnerships and limited liability companies, which include private and public companies (corporations).
- A corporation is a legally defined artificial being (a judicial person or legal entity) that has many of the same legal powers as people have. It can enter into contracts, acquire assets,

incur obligations, and it enjoys the protection under some jurisdictions against seizure of its property.

- Under the classical system, the shareholders in most companies effectively pay tax twice. The corporation pays tax once and then investors must pay personal tax on any funds that are distributed. In the U.S., S corporations are exempt from corporate income tax.

1.2 Ownership Versus Control of Corporations

- The ownership of a corporation is divided into shares collectively known as equity. Investors in these shares are called shareholders, stockholders, or equity holders.
- The ownership and control of a corporation are separate. Shareholders exercise their control indirectly through the board of directors.
- Financial managers within the firm are responsible for three main tasks: making investment decisions, making financing decisions, and managing the firm's cash flows.
- Good public policy should ensure that when firms take actions that benefit their shareholders, they are also benefiting society.
- While the firm's shareholders would like managers to make decisions that maximize the firm's share price, managers often must balance this objective with the desires of other stakeholders (including themselves).
- Corporate bankruptcy can be thought of as a change in ownership and control of the corporation. The equity holders give up their ownership and control to the debt holders.

1.3 The Stock Market

- The shares of public corporations are traded on stock markets. The shares of private corporations do not usually trade on a stock market.

Key Terms

agency problem *p. 11*
ask price *p. 16*
bid price *p. 16*
bid-ask spread *p. 17*
board of directors *p. 7*
"C" corporations *p. 7*
chief executive officer (CEO) *p. 9*
chief financial officer (CFO) *p. 9*
corporation (or company) *p. 5*
dealer markets *p. 17*
dividend payments *p. 5*
Dodd-Frank Act *p. 6*
equity *p. 5*
equity holder *p. 5*
hostile takeover *p. 13*
limited liability *p. 4*
limited liability company or corporation *p. 5*
limited partnership *p. 4*

liquid *p. 14*
liquidation *p. 13*
market makers *p. 16*
over-the-counter (OTC) markets *p. 17*
partnership *p. 4*
primary market *p. 15*
private companies *p. 14*
public companies *p. 14*
"S" corporations *p. 6*
secondary market *p. 15*
shareholder *p. 5*
sole proprietorship *p. 3*
specialists *p. 16*
stock *p. 5*
stock market (or stock exchange or bourse) *p. 14*
stockholder *p. 5*
transaction cost *p. 17*

Further Reading

Readers interested in John Marshall's decision that led to the legal basis for the corporation can find a more detailed description of the decision in J. Smith, *John Marshall: Definer of a Nation* (Henry Holt, 1996): 433–38.

An informative discussion that describes the objective of a corporation can be found in M. Jensen, "Value Maximization, Stakeholder Theory, and the Corporate Objective Function," *Journal of Applied Corporate Finance* (Fall 2001): 8–21.

For background on what determines the goals of corporate managers and how they differ from shareholders' goals, read M. Jensen and W. Meckling, "Theory of the Firm: Managerial Behavior, Agency Costs and Ownership Structure," *Journal of Financial Economics* 3 (1976): 305–60; J. Core, W. Guay, and D. Larker, "Executive Equity Compensation and Incentives: A Survey," *Federal Reserve Bank of New York Economic Policy Review* 9 (April 2003): 27–50.

The following papers explain corporate governance and ownership around the world: F. Barca and M. Becht, *The Control of Corporate Europe* (Oxford University Press, 2001); D. Denis and J. McConnell, "International Corporate Governance," *Journal of Financial Quantitative Analysis* 38 (2003): 1–36; R. La Porta, F. Lopez-de-Silanes, and A. Shleifer, "Corporate Ownership Around the World," *Journal of Finance* 54 (1999): 471–517. Readers interested in a more detailed discussion of how taxes affect incorporation can consult J. Mackie-Mason and R. Gordon, "How Much Do Taxes Discourage Incorporation?" *Journal of Finance* 52 (1997): 477–505.

Problems

All problems are available in MyFinanceLab.

The Types of Firms

1. What is the most important difference between a corporation and *all* other organizational forms?

2. What does the phrase *limited liability* mean in a corporate context?

3. Which organizational forms give their owners limited liability?

4. What are the main advantages and disadvantages of organizing a firm as a corporation?

5. Explain the difference between an S corporation and a C corporation in the United States.

 6. You are a shareholder in a C corporation. The corporation earns $2 per share before taxes. Once it has paid taxes it will distribute the rest of its earnings to you as a dividend. The corporate tax rate is 40% and the personal tax rate on (both dividend and non-dividend) income is 30%. How much is left for you after all taxes are paid?

 7. Repeat Problem 6 assuming the corporation is an S corporation.

Ownership Versus Control of Corporations

8. You have decided to form a new start-up company developing applications for the iPhone. Give examples of the three distinct types of financial decisions you will need to make.

9. When a pharmaceutical company develops a new drug, it often receives patent protection for that medication, allowing it to charge a higher price. Explain how this public policy of providing patent protection might help align the corporation's interests with society's interests.

10. Corporate managers work for the owners of the corporation. Consequently, they should make decisions that are in the interests of the owners, rather than their own interests. What strategies are available to shareholders to help ensure that managers are motivated to act this way?

11. Suppose you are considering renting an apartment. You, the renter, can be viewed as an agent while the company that owns the apartment can be viewed as the principal. What principal-agent conflicts do you anticipate? Suppose, instead, that you work for the apartment company. What features would you put into the lease agreement that would give the renter incentives to take good care of the apartment?

12. You are the CEO of a company and you are considering entering into an agreement to have your company buy another company. You think the price might be too high, but you will be the CEO of the combined, much larger company. You know that when the company gets bigger, your pay and prestige will increase. What is the nature of the agency conflict here and how is it related to ethical considerations?

13. Are hostile takeovers necessarily bad for firms or their investors? Explain.

The Stock Market

14. What is the difference between a public and a private company?

15. Explain why the bid-ask spread is a transaction cost.

16. The following quote on Yahoo! stock appeared on July 9, 2012, on Yahoo! Finance:

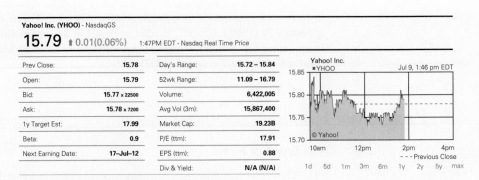

If you wanted to buy Yahoo!, what price per share would you pay? How much would you receive per share if you wanted to sell Yahoo!?

Introduction to Financial Statement Analysis: IFRS

AS WE DISCUSSED IN CHAPTER 1, ONE OF THE GREAT advantages of the corporate organizational form is that it places no restriction on who can own shares in the corporation. Anyone with money to invest is a potential investor. As a result, corporations are often widely held, with investors ranging from individuals who hold 100 shares to mutual funds and institutional investors who own millions of shares. For example, in 2012, International Business Machines Corporation (IBM) had about 1.2 billion shares outstanding held by nearly 600,000 shareholders. Most shareholders were small. Warren Buffett's Berkshire Hathaway was the largest shareholder with about a 6% stake. Less than 1% of the company was owned by insiders (IBM executives).

Although the corporate organizational structure greatly facilitates the firm's access to investment capital, it also means that share ownership is most investors' sole tie to the company. How, then, do investors learn enough about a company to know whether or not they should invest in it? How can financial managers assess the success of their own firm and compare it to the performance of competitors? One way firms evaluate their performance and communicate this information to investors is through their *financial statements*.

Firms issue financial statements regularly to communicate financial information to the investment community. A detailed description of the preparation and analysis of these statements is sufficiently complicated that to do it justice would require an entire book. Here, we briefly review the subject, emphasizing only the material that investors and corporate financial managers need in order to make the corporate-finance decisions we discuss in the text.

We review the four main types of financial statements, present examples of these statements for a firm, and discuss where an investor or manager might find various types of information about the company. We also discuss some of the financial ratios that investors and analysts use to assess a firm's performance and value. We close the chapter with a look at a few highly publicized financial reporting abuses.

2.1 Firms' Disclosure of Financial Information

Financial statements are accounting reports issued by a firm periodically (usually quarterly and annually) that present past information and a shapshot of the firm's financial position. Public companies around the world are required to file their financial statements with the relevant listing authorities. They must also send an **annual report** with their financial statements to their shareholders each year. Private companies often prepare financial statements as well, but they usually do not have to disclose these reports to the public. Financial statements are important tools through which investors, financial analysts, and other interested outside parties (such as creditors) obtain information about a corporation. They are also useful for managers within the firm as a source of information for corporate financial decisions. In this section, we examine the guidelines for preparing financial statements and introduce the types of financial statements.

Preparation of Financial Statements

Reports about a company's performance must be understandable and accurate. **Generally Accepted Accounting Principles (GAAP)** together with the **International Financial Reporting Standards** (issued by the IASB) provide a common set of rules and a standard format for public companies to use when they prepare their reports. This standardization also makes it easier to compare the financial results of different firms.

Investors also need some assurance that the financial statements are prepared accurately. Corporations are required to hire a neutral third party, known as an **auditor**, to check the annual financial statements, to ensure that the annual financial statements are reliable and prepared according to accounting standards and provide evidence to support the reliability of the information.

International Financial Reporting Standards

Because Generally Accepted Accounting Principles (GAAP) differ among countries, companies operating internationally face tremendous accounting complexity. Investors also face difficulty interpreting financial statements of foreign companies, which is often considered a major barrier to international capital mobility. As companies and capital markets become more global, however, interest in harmonizing accounting standards across countries has increased.

The most important harmonization project began in 1973 when representatives of 10 countries (including the United States) established the International Accounting Standards Committee. This effort led to the creation of the International Accounting Standards Board (IASB) in 2001, with headquarters in London. Now the IASB has issued a set of International Financial Reporting Standards (IFRS).

The IFRS are taking root throughout the world. The European Union (EU) approved an accounting regulation in 2002 requiring all publicly traded EU companies to follow IFRS in their consolidated financial statements starting in 2005. As of 2012, over 120 jurisdictions either require or permit the use of IFRS, including the EU, Australia, Brazil, Canada, Russia, Hong Kong, Taiwan, and Singapore. China, India and Japan will soon follow suit. Indeed, currently all major stock exchanges around the world accept IFRS except the United States (for local companies) and Japan, which maintain their local GAAP.

The main difference between U.S. GAAP and IFRS is conceptual—U.S. GAAP are based primarily on accounting rules with specific guidance in applying them, whereas IFRS are based more on principles requiring professional judgment by accountants, and specific guidance in application is limited. Even so, some differences in rules also exist. For example, U.S. GAAP generally prohibit the upward revaluation of non-financial assets, whereas the IFRS allow the revaluation of some such assets to fair value. U.S. GAAP also rely more heavily on historical cost, as opposed to "fair value," to estimate the value of assets and liabilities.

Effort to achieve convergence between U.S. GAAP and IFRS was spurred by the Sarbanes-Oxley Act of 2002 in the United States. It included a provision that U.S. accounting standards move toward international convergence on high-quality accounting standards. Currently SEC regulations still require public U.S. firms to report using U.S. GAAP. That said, modifications to both IFRS and U.S. GAAP have brought the two closer together, with the key remaining differences in the areas of revenue recognition, impairment charges, leasing, insurance, and the treatment of financial instruments. As of mid-2012, the SEC continues to deliberate as to whether and how to incorporate IFRS into U.S. GAAP.

Sue Frieden is Ernst & Young's Global Managing Partner, Quality & Risk Management. A member of the Global Executive board, she is responsible for every aspect of quality and risk management—employees, services, procedures, and clients. She has also served on the SEC Regulations Committee for the American Institute for Certified Public Accountants.

INTERVIEW WITH
Sue Frieden

QUESTION: *Do today's financial statements give the investing public what they need?*

ANSWER: Globally, we are seeing an effort to provide more forward-looking information to investors. But fundamental questions remain, such as how fully do investors understand financial statements and how fully do they read them? Research shows that most individual investors don't rely on financial statements much at all. We need to determine how the financial statement and related reporting models can be improved. To do that we will need a dialogue involving investors, regulators, analysts, auditors, stock exchanges, academics, and others to ensure that financial statements and other reporting models are as relevant as they can be.

QUESTION: *Ernst & Young is a global organization. How do accounting standards in the U.S. compare to those elsewhere?*

ANSWER: In January 2005, 100 countries outside the United States began the process of adopting new accounting standards (International Financial Reporting Standards) that would be in large measure based on principles rather than rules. As global markets become more complex, we all need to be playing by the same set of rules. As a first step, we need consistency from country to country. There are definite challenges to overcome in reconciling principle-based and rules-based systems, but we are optimistic that these challenges will inevitably get resolved. At the same time, there are efforts underway to ensure that auditing standards are globally consistent. Ultimately, financial statements prepared under global standards and audited under consistent global auditing standards will better serve investors.

QUESTION: *What role does the audit firm play in our financial markets, and how has that changed since the collapse of Arthur Andersen?*

ANSWER: The accounting profession has seen unprecedented change in the past few years. The passage of Sarbanes-Oxley and other changes are helping to restore public trust. We're now engaging on a regular basis with a wider range of stakeholders—companies, boards, policymakers, opinion leaders, investors, and academia. And we've had the chance to step back and ask ourselves why we do what we do as accounting professionals, and why it matters. In terms of the services we offer, much of what we do helps companies comply with regulations, guard against undue risks, and implement sound transactions. Part of the value in what we do is providing all stakeholders the basis to understand whether companies are playing by the rules—be they accounting, financial reporting, or tax rules. We help create confidence in financial data. The public may not understand precisely what auditors do or how we do it, but they care that we exist, because it provides them the confidence they so badly need and want.

QUESTION: *Accounting standards seem to be shifting from historical cost-based methods to methods that rely on current market values of assets. During the financial crisis, however, many financial institutions complained that "mark-to-market" rules exacerbated their financial difficulties. Do you believe accounting professionals should rethink the wisdom of moving to market-based accounting methods?*

ANSWER: Fair value accounting can certainly be improved, particularly in light of the difficulty in applying fair value in illiquid markets, which the financial crisis highlighted, and because of some of the anomalies that fair value accounting can produce. But by and large, fair value accounting provided transparency into reality for investors. It is the most transparent way to reflect the economic reality of prevailing market conditions and provide investors and companies with current financial information on which they can base investment and management decisions. Fair value accounting did not cause the economic crisis; it simply kept a fair scorecard.

Types of Financial Statements

Every public company is required to produce four financial statements: the *balance sheet* or *statement of financial position*, the *income statement*, the *statement of cash flows*, and the *statement of changes in shareholders' equity*. These financial statements provide investors and creditors with an overview of the firm's financial performance. In the sections that follow, we take a close look at the content of these financial statements.

CONCEPT CHECK

1. What are the main financial statements that all public companies must produce?
2. What is the role of an auditor?

2.2 The Balance Sheet or Statement of Financial Position

The **balance sheet**, or **statement of financial position**,[1] lists the firm's *assets* and *liabilities*, providing a snapshot of the firm's financial position at a given point in time. Table 2.1 shows the balance sheet for Vodafone Group Plc as at 31 March, 2012 and 2011. Notice that the balance sheet is divided into two parts, with the assets in the top part and the liabilities and shareholders' equity in the bottom part. The **assets** list the firm's cash, inventory, property, plant, and equipment, and other investments the company has made; the **liabilities** show the firm's obligations to creditors. Also shown with liabilities in the bottom part of the balance

TABLE 2.1	Vodafone Group Plc Balance Sheet for 2012 and 2011

VODAFONE GROUP PLC

Statements of Financial Position,
prepared according to IFRS (in £ million)

	2012	2011
Non-current Assets		
Goodwill & other intangible assets	59,514	68,558
Net property plant and equipment	18,655	20,181
Other non-current assets	41,382	45,478
	119,551	134,217
Current Assets		
Inventory	486	537
Accounts receivable	10,744	9,259
Other current assets	1,657	955
Bank and cash	7,138	6,252
	20,025	17,003
Total Assets	**139,576**	**151,220**
Total Shareholders' Equity	78,202	87,561
Non-current liabilities		
Long-term borrowings	37,349	36,584
Current Liabilites		
Short-term financial debt	8,789	12,377
Accounts payable	15,236	14,698
	24,025	27,075
Total Liabilities	61,374	63,659
Total Equity and Liabilities	**139,576**	**151,220**

Source: Data compiled from Vodafone Group Plc's 2012 Annual Report.

[1] In IFRS and recent U.S. GAAP pronouncements, the balance sheet is referred to as the *statement of financial position*.

sheet is the *shareholders' equity*. **Shareholders' equity** (or stockholders' equity), the difference between the firm's assets and liabilities, is an accounting measure of the firm's net worth.

The assets in the top part show how the firm uses its capital (its investments), and the bottom part summarizes the sources of capital, or how a firm raises the money it needs. Because of the way shareholders' equity is calculated, the top and bottom parts must balance:

The Balance Sheet Equation

$$\text{Assets} = \text{Liabilities} + \text{Shareholders' Equity} \qquad (2.1)$$

In Table 2.1, total assets for 2012 (£139,576 million) are equal to total liabilities (£61,374 million) plus shareholders' equity (£78,202 million).

Let's examine Vodafone's assets, liabilities, and shareholders' equity in more detail.

Assets

In Table 2.1, Vodafone's assets are divided into current and non-current assets. We discuss each in turn.

Current Assets. **Current assets** are either cash or assets that could be converted into cash within one year. This category includes the following:

1. **Cash** and other **marketable securities**, which are short-term, low-risk investments that can be easily sold and converted to cash (such as money market investments like government debt that matures within a year);

2. **Accounts receivable**, which are amounts owed to the firm by customers who have purchased goods or services on credit;

3. **Inventories**, which are composed of raw materials as well as work-in-progress and finished goods;

4. Other current assets, which is a catch-all category that includes items such as pre-paid expenses (expenses that have been paid in advance, such as rent or insurance).

Non-current Assets. Assets such as property or machinery that produce tangible benefits for more than one year are called **non-current (or fixed) assets**. If Vodafone spends £2 million on new equipment, this £2 million will be included with property, plant, and equipment under non-current assets on the balance sheet. Because equipment tends to wear out or become obsolete over time, Vodafone will reduce the amount recorded for this equipment each year by deducting a **depreciation expense**. An asset's **accumulated depreciation** is the total amount deducted over its life. The firm reduces the amount of fixed assets (other than land) over time according to a depreciation schedule that depends on the asset's life span. Depreciation is not an actual cash expense that the firm pays; it is a way of recognizing that buildings and equipment wear out and thus it is an allocation of the asset's cost. The **book value (or carrying amount)** of an asset, which is the value shown in the firm's financial statements, is equal to its acquisition cost less accumulated depreciation. The figures for property, plant, and equipment shows the total book value of these assets.

When a firm acquires another company, it will acquire a set of tangible assets (such as inventory or property, plant, and equipment) that will then be included on its balance sheet. In many cases, however, the firm may pay more for the company than the total book value of the assets it acquires. In this case, the difference between the price paid for the company and the book value assigned to its tangible assets is recorded separately as **goodwill** (an **intangible asset**). For example, if Vodafone paid £25 million in 2011 for a firm whose tangible assets has a book value of £5 million, then the difference of £20 million would appear as goodwill in Table 2.1. The total amount shown for goodwill and other intangible assets on the balance sheet captures the value of other "intangibles" that the firm acquired through the acquisition (e.g., brand names and trademarks, patents, customer relationships, and employees). If the firm assesses that the value of these intangible assets declined over time, it will reduce the amount listed on the balance sheet by an **amortization** or **impairment charge** that captures the change in value of the acquired assets. Like depreciation, amortization is not an actual cash expense.

Other non-current assets can include such items as property not used in business operations, start-up costs in connection with a new business, investments in long-term securities, and property held for sale. The sum of all the firms' assets is the total assets shown at the bottom of the top part of the balance sheet in Table 2.1.

Liabilities

We now examine the liabilities shown on the bottom part of the balance sheet, which are divided into *current* and *non-current liabilities*.

Current Liabilities. Liabilities that will be satisfied within one year are known as **current liabilities**. They include the following:

1. **Accounts payable**, the amounts owed to suppliers for products or services purchased with credit;

2. **Short-term debt** (or notes payable) are loans that must be repaid in the next year. Any repayment of non-current debt that will occur within the next year would also be listed here as current maturities of long-term debt

3. **Accrual items**, such as salary or taxes, that are owed but have not yet been paid, and deferred or unearned revenue, which is revenue that has been received for products that have not yet been delivered.

The difference between current assets and current liabilities is the firm's **net working capital**, the capital available in the short term to run the business. For example, in 2012, Vodafone's net working capital totaled – £4000 i.e. negative (£20,025 million in current assets – £24,025 million in current liabilities). Firms with low (or negative) net working capital may face a shortage of funds unless they generate sufficient cash from their ongoing activities. In Vodafone's and other cases, the liabilities due in the short term exceed the company's cash and expected payments due from receivables.

Non-current (Long-Term) Liabilities. Non-current liabilities are liabilities that extend beyond one year. The main types as follows:

1. **Long-term debt** is any loan or debt obligation with a maturity of more than a year. When a firm needs to raise funds to purchase an asset or make an investment, it may borrow those funds through a long-term loan.

2. **Capital leases** are long-term lease contracts that obligate the firm to make regular lease payments in exchange for use of an asset.[2] They allow a firm to gain use of an asset by leasing it from the asset's owner. For example, a firm may lease a building to serve as its corporate headquarters.

3. **Deferred taxes** are taxes that are owed but have not yet been paid. Firms generally keep two sets of financial statements: one for financial reporting and one for tax purposes. Occasionally, the rules for the two types of statements differ. Deferred tax liabilities generally arise when the firm's financial income exceeds its income for tax purposes. Because deferred taxes will eventually be paid, they appear as a liability on the balance sheet.[3]

---

[2]See Chapter 25 for a precise definition of a capital lease.

[3]A firm may also have deferred tax assets related to tax credits it has earned that it will receive in the future.

Shareholders' Equity

The sum of the current liabilities and non-current liabilities is total liabilities. The difference between the firm's assets and liabilities is the shareholders' equity; it is also called the **book value of equity**. As we stated earlier, it represents an accounting measure of the net worth of the firm.

Ideally, the balance sheet would provide us with an accurate assessment of the true value of the firm's equity. Unfortunately, this is unlikely to be the case. First, many of the assets listed on the balance sheet are valued based on their historical cost rather than their true value today. For example, an office building is listed on the balance sheet according to its historical cost net of depreciation. But the actual value of the office building today may be very different (and possibly much *more*) than the amount the firm paid for it years ago. The same is true for other property, plant, and equipment: The true value today of an asset may be very different from, and even exceed, its book value. A second, and probably more important, problem is that *many of the firm's valuable assets are not captured on the balance sheet*. Consider, for example, the expertise of the firm's employees, the firm's reputation in the marketplace, the relationships with customers and suppliers, the value of future research and development innovations, and the quality of the management team. These are all assets that add to the value of the firm that do not appear on the balance sheet.

Market Value Versus Book Value

For the reasons cited above, the book value of equity is an inaccurate assessment of the actual value of the firm's equity. Successful firms are often able to borrow in excess of the book value of their assets because creditors recognize that the market value of the assets is far higher than the book value. Thus, it is not surprising that the book value of equity will often differ substantially from the amount investors are willing to pay for the equity. The total *market* value of a firm's equity equals the number of shares outstanding times the firm's market price per share:

$$\text{Market Value of Equity} = \text{Shares outstanding} \times \text{Market price per share} \qquad (2.2)$$

The market value of equity is often referred to as the company's **market capitalization** (or "market cap"). The market value of a share does not depend on the historical cost of the firm's assets; instead, it depends on what investors expect those assets to produce in the future.

EXAMPLE 2.1 **Market Versus Book Value**

Problem
On March 31, 2012, Vodafone had 50,664 million shares outstanding, and these shares were trading for a price of £1.72 per share. What is Vodafone's market capitalization? How does the market capitalization compare to Vodafone's book value of equity?

Solution
Vodafone's market capitalization is (50,664 million shares) × (£1.72/share) = £87,142 million. This market capitalization is higher than Vodafone's book value of equity of £78,202 million. Thus, investors are willing to pay 87,142/78,202 = 1.1 times the amount Vodafone's shares are "worth" according to their book value.

Market-to-Book Ratio. In Example 2.1, we compared the market and book values of Vodafone's equity. A common way to make this comparison is to compute the **market-to-book ratio** (also called the **price-to-book [P/B] ratio**), which is the ratio of a firm's market capitalization to the book value of shareholders' equity.

$$\text{Market-to-Book Ratio} = \frac{\text{Market Value of Equity}}{\text{Book Value of Equity}} \qquad (2.3)$$

It is one of the many financial ratios used by analysts to evaluate a firm. The market-to-book ratio for most successful firms substantially exceeds 1, indicating that the value of the firm's assets when put to use exceeds their historical cost. Variations in this ratio reflect differences in fundamental firm characteristics as well as the value added by management. Thus, this ratio is one way a company's share price provides feedback to its managers on the market's assessment of their decisions.

In July 2012, Citigroup (C) had a market-to-book ratio of 0.43, a reflection of investors' assessment that many of Citigroup's assets (such as mortgage securities) were worth far less than their book value. At the same time, the average market-to-book ratio for major U.S. banks and financial firms was 1.2, and for all large U.S. firms it was 2.3. In contrast, Pepsico (PEP) had a market-to-book ratio of 4.8, and IBM had a market-to-book ratio of 10.7. Analysts often classify firms with low market-to-book ratios as **value stocks** (shares), and those with high market-to-book ratios as **growth stocks** (shares).

Enterprise Value

A firm's market capitalization measures the market value of the firm's equity, or the value that remains after the firm has paid its debts. But what is the value of the business itself? The **enterprise value** of a firm (also called the **total enterprise value** or **TEV**) assesses the value of the underlying business assets, unencumbered by debt and separate from any cash and marketable securities. We compute it as follows:

$$\text{Enterprise Value} = \text{Market Value of Equity} + \text{Debt} - \text{Cash} \qquad (2.4)$$

From Example 2.1, Vodafone's market capitalization in 2012 is £87,142 million. Its debt is £46,138 million (£8,789 million of short-term financial debt and long-term borrowings of £37,349 million). Therefore, given its cash balance of £7,138 million, Vodafone's enterprise value is $87,142 + 46,138 - 7,138 = £126,142$ million. The enterprise value can be interpreted as the cost to take over the business. That is, it would cost $87,142 + 46,138 = £133,280$ million to buy all of Vodafone's equity and pay off its debts, but because we would acquire Vodafone's £7,138 million in cash, the net cost of the business is only $133,280 - 7138 = £126,142$ million.

CONCEPT CHECK

1. What is the balance sheet equation?

2. The book value of a company's assets usually does not equal the market value of those assets. What are some reasons for this difference?

3. What is a firm's enterprise value, and what does it measure?

2.3   The Income Statement

When you want somebody to get to the point, you might ask him or her for the "bottom line." This expression comes from the *income statement*. The **income statement** or **statement of comprehensive income**[4] lists the firm's revenues and expenses over a period of time. The last or "bottom" line of the income statement shows the firm's **net income (or net profit)**, which is a measure of its profitability during the period. The income statement is sometimes called a profit and loss, or "P&L" account, and the net income is also referred to as the firm's **earnings**. In this section, we examine the components of the income statement in detail and later introduce ratios we can use to analyze this data.

---

[4]In recent IFRS pronouncements, the income statement is referred to as the *statement of comprehensive income*.

Earnings Calculations

Whereas the statement of financial position, or balance sheet shows the firm's assets and liabilities at a given point in time, the income statement shows the flow of revenues and expenses generated by those assets and liabilities between two dates. Table 2.2 shows Vodafone's income statement for 2012. We examine each category on the statement.

Gross Profit. The first two lines of the income statement list the revenues from sales of products and the costs incurred to make and sell the products. Cost of sales shows costs directly related to producing the goods or services being sold, such as manufacturing costs. Other costs such as administrative expenses, research and development, and interest expenses are not included in the cost of sales. The third line is **gross profit**, which is the difference between sales revenues and the cost of sales.

Operating Expenses. The next group of items is operating expenses. These are expenses from the ordinary course of running the business that are not directly related to producing the goods or services being sold. They include administrative expenses and overhead, salaries, marketing costs, and research and development expenses. The third type of operating expense, depreciation and amortization, is not an actual cash expense but represents an estimate of the costs that arise from wear and tear or obsolescence of the firm's assets.[5] The firm's gross profit net of operating expenses is called **operating income (or profit)**.

TABLE 2.2	Vodafone Group Plc Income Statement for 2012 and 2011 in £m

VODAFONE GROUP PLC

Income Statement
Year Ended March 31 (in £ million)

	2012	2011
Revenue	46,417	45,884
Cost of sales	–31,546	–30,814
Gross Profit	14,871	15,070
Selling, distribution and administrative expenses	–8,302	–8,367
Impairment losses/Depreciation	–4,050	–6,150
Share of results in associated companies	4,963	5,059
Other income	3,705	–16
Operating Income	11,187	5,596
Other income	294	4,331
Earnings Before Interest and Taxes (EBIT)	11,481	9,927
Interest income (expense)	–1,932	–429
Profit before taxation	9,549	9,498
Tax	–2,546	–1,628
Net Income	7,003	7,870
Earnings per share	13.74p	15.20p
Diluted earnings per share	13.65p	15.11p

Source: Data compiled from Vodafone Group Plc's 2012 Annual Report.

[5]Only certain types of amortization are deductible as a pretax expense (e.g., amortization of the cost of an acquired patent). Also, firms often do not separately list depreciation and amortization on the income statement, but rather include them with the expenses by function (e.g., depreciation of R&D equipment would be included with R&D expenses). When depreciation and amortization has been separated in this way, practitioners sometimes refer to the expense items as "clean" (e.g., "clean R&D" is R&D expenses excluding any depreciation or amortization).

Earnings before Interest and Taxes. We next include other sources of income or expenses that arise from activities that are not the central part of a company's business. Income from the firm's financial investments is one example of other income that would be listed here. After we have adjusted for other sources of income or expenses, we have the firm's earnings before interest and taxes, or **EBIT**.

Pretax and Net Income. From EBIT, we deduct the interest expense related to outstanding debt to compute Vodafone's pretax income (profit before taxation), and then we deduct corporate taxes to determine the firm's net income (or net profit).

Net income represents the total earnings of the firm's equity holders. It is often reported on a per-share basis as the firm's **earnings per share (EPS)**, which we compute by dividing net income by the total number of shares outstanding:

$$\text{EPS} = \frac{\text{Net Income}}{\text{Shares Outstanding}} = \frac{£6,967 \text{ Million}^6}{50,664 \text{ Shares}} = 13.74\text{p per Share} \qquad (2.5)$$

Although Vodafone has 50,664 million shares outstanding as of the end of 31 March 2012, the number of shares outstanding may grow if Vodafone compensates its employees or executives with **share (stock) options** that give the holder the right to buy a certain number of shares by a specific date at a specific price. If the options are "exercised," the company issues new shares and the number of shares outstanding will grow. The number of shares may also grow if the firm issues **convertible bonds**, a form of debt that can be converted to shares. Because there will be more total shares to divide the same earnings, this growth in the number of shares is referred to as **dilution**. Firms disclose the potential for dilution by reporting **diluted EPS**, which represents earnings per share for the company calculated as though, for example, in-the-money stock options or other stock-based compensation had been exercised or dilutive convertible debt had been converted. For example, in 2012, Vodafone's diluted EPS was £6,967 million/50958 million shares = 13.65p.

CONCEPT CHECK

1. What it is the difference between a firm's gross profit and its net income?
2. What is the diluted earnings per share?

2.4 The Statement of Cash Flows

The income statement provides a measure of the firm's profit over a given time period. However, it does not indicate the amount of *cash* the firm has generated. There are two reasons that net income does not correspond to cash earned. First, there are non-cash entries on the income statement, such as depreciation and amortization. Second, certain uses of cash, such as the purchase of a building or expenditures on inventory, are not reported on the income statement. The firm's **statement of cash flows** utilizes the information from the income statement and statement of financial position or balance sheet to determine how much cash the firm has generated, and how that cash has been allocated, during a set period. As we will see, from the perspective of an investor attempting to value the firm, the statement of cash flows provides what may be the most important information of the four financial statements.

The statement of cash flows is divided into three sections: operating activities, investment activities, and financing activities. The first section, operating activity, starts with

---

[6]Adjusted for non-controlling interests i.e. shareholders outside the Vodafone Group.

net income from the income statement. It then adjusts this number by adding back all non-cash entries related to the firm's operating activities. The next section, investment activity, lists the cash used for investment. The third section, financing activity, shows the flow of cash between the firm and its investors. Vodafone Group's statement of cash flows is shown in Table 2.3. In this section, we take a close look at each component of the statement of cash flows.

Operating Activity

The first section of Vodafone's statement of cash flows adjusts net income by all non-cash items related to operating activity. For instance, depreciation is deducted when computing net income, but it is not an actual cash outflow. Thus, we add it back to net income when determining the amount of cash the firm has generated. Similarly, we add back any other non-cash expenses (for example, deferred taxes).

Next, we adjust for changes to net working capital that arise from changes to accounts receivable, accounts payable, or inventory. When a firm sells a product, it records the revenue as income even though it may not receive the cash from that sale immediately. Instead, it may grant the customer credit and let the customer pay in the future. The customer's

| TABLE 2.3 | Vodafone Group Plc Statement of Cash Flows for 2012 and 2011 |

VODAFONE GROUP PLC

Statement of Cash Flows
Year Ended March 31 (in £ million)

	2012	2011
Operating activities		
Net income	7,003	7,870
Depreciation and amortization	4,050	6,150
Cash effect of changes in:		
Accounts receivable	−689	−387
Accounts payable	871	1,060
Inventory	24	−107
Other adjustments	−1,496	−2,591
Cash from operating activities	**12,755**	**11,995**
Investment activities		
Capital expenditures	−7,852	−8,640
Acquisitions and other investing activity	11,695	6,758
Cash from investing activities	**3,843**	**−1,882**
Financing activities		
Dividends paid	−6,947	−4,788
Interest paid	−1,633	−1,578
Increase/decrease in share capital	−6,117	−2,117
Increase/decrease in borrowings	−672	224
Cash from financing activities	**−15,369**	**−8,259**
Foreign exchange adjustment	**−343**	**−12**
Change in cash and cash equivalents	**886**	**1,842**

Source: Data compiled from Vodafone Group Plc's 2012 Annual Report.

obligation adds to the firm's accounts receivable. We use the following guidelines to adjust for changes in working capital:

1. *Accounts Receivable*: When a sale is recorded as part of net income, but the cash has not yet been received from the customer, we must adjust the cash flows by *deducting* the increases in accounts receivable. This increase represents additional lending by the firm to its customers, and it reduces the cash available to the firm.

2. *Accounts Payable*: Conversely, we *add* increases in accounts payable. Accounts payable represents borrowing by the firm from its suppliers. This borrowing increases the cash available to the firm.

3. *Inventory*: Finally, we *deduct* increases to inventory. Increases to inventory are not recorded as an expense and do not contribute to net income (the cost of the goods are only included in net income when the goods are actually sold). However, the cost of increasing inventory is a cash expense for the firm and must be deducted.

The statement of cash flows in Table 2.3 shows Vodafone's accounts receivable and accounts payable increased by £689 million and £871 million respectively from 2011. We deduct the increase of £689 million and add the increase of £871 million on the statement of cash flows. The net result of accounts receivable and accounts payable is positive on cash flow from operations. For ease of preparation, other adjustments relating to operating activities are included after changes in net working capital.

Investment Activity

The next section of the statement of cash flows shows the cash required for investment activities. Purchases of new property, plant, and equipment are referred to as **capital expenditures**. Recall that capital expenditures do not appear immediately as expenses on the income statement. Instead, the firm depreciates these assets and deducts depreciation expenses over time. To determine the firm's cash flow, we already added back depreciation because it is not an actual cash outflow. Now, we subtract the actual capital expenditure that the firm made. Similarly, we also deduct other assets purchased or long-term investments made by the firm, such as acquisitions or purchases of marketable securities. In Table 2.3, we see that in 2012, Vodafone saved £3,843 million in cash on investing activities.

Financing Activity

The last section of the statement of cash flows shows the cash flows from financing activities. Dividends paid to shareholders are a cash outflow. Vodafone paid £6,947 million to its shareholders as dividends in 2012. The difference between a firm's net income and the amount it spends on dividends is referred to as the firm's **retained earnings** for that year:

$$\text{Retained Earnings} = \text{Net Income} - \text{Dividends} \qquad (2.6)$$

Vodafone retained £7,003 million − £6,947 million = £56 million of its earnings in 2012.

Also listed under financing activity is any cash the company received from the sale of its own stock, or cash spent buying (repurchasing) its own shares. Vodafone issued and repurchased its shares in 2012. The last items to include in this section result from changes to Vodafone's short-term and long-term borrowing. Vodafone spent money by repaying debt, so the decrease in borrowing represents a cash outflow.

The final line of the statement of cash flows combines the cash flows from these three activities to calculate the overall change in the firm's cash balance over the period of the statement. In this case, Vodafone had cash inflows of £886 million, which matches the change in cash from 2011 to 2012 shown earlier on the statement of financial position. By looking at the statement in Table 2.3 as a whole, we can determine that Vodafone has spent cash on financing activities (including the dividend and interest payments) and capital expenditure and has covered the cost by generating cash from investing activity together with a cash inflow from operating activities. This has resulted in an increase in Vodafone's cash balance.

EXAMPLE 2.2

The Impact of Depreciation on Cash Flow

Problem

Suppose Vodafone had an additional £100 million depreciation expense in 2012. If Vodafone's tax rate on pretax income is 26%, what would be the impact of this expense on Vodafone's earnings? How would it impact Vodafone's cash balance at the end of the year?

Solution

Depreciation is an operating expense, so Vodafone's operating income, EBIT, and pretax income would fall by £100 million. This decrease in pretax income would reduce Vodafone's tax bill by $26\% \times £100$ million $= £26$ million. Therefore, net income would fall by $100 - 26 = £74$ million.

On the statement of cash flows, net income would fall by £74 million, but we would add back the additional depreciation of £100 million because it is not a cash expense. Thus, cash from operating activities would rise by $-74 + 100 = £26$ million. Thus, Vodafone's cash balance at the end of the year would increase by £26 million, the amount of the tax savings that resulted from the additional depreciation expense.

CONCEPT CHECK

1. Why does a firm's net income not correspond to cash earned?

2. What are the components of the statement of cash flows?

2.5 Other Financial Statement Information

The most important elements of a firm's financial statements are the statement of financial position or balance sheet, the income statement, and the statement of cash flows, which we have already discussed. Several other pieces of information contained in the financial statements warrant brief mention: the statement of changes in shareholders' equity, the management discussion and analysis, and notes to the financial statements.

Statement of Changes in Shareholders' Equity

The **statement of changes in shareholders' equity** provides a reconciliation of the opening and closing equity position. It provides details of the movements in share capital and reserves; for example, a revaluation reserve and retained earnings derived from the income statement. Its usefulness for financial managers is limited because of the use of book values rather than the market value. The statement breaks down the shareholders' equity computed on the balance sheet into the amount that came from issuing shares (par value plus paid-in capital) versus retained earnings. Because the book value of shareholders' equity is not a useful assessment of value for financial purposes, financial managers use the statement of changes in shareholders' equity infrequently (so we will skip the computational details here). We can, however, determine the change in shareholders' equity using information from the firm's other financial statements as follows:

$$\text{Change in Shareholders' Equity} = \text{Retained Earnings} + \text{Net sales of shares}$$
$$= \text{Net Income} - \text{Dividends} +$$
$$\text{Sales of shares} - \text{Repurchases of shares} \quad (2.7)$$

In this example, during 2012, Vodafone made share sales and repurchases and together with the addition of net income and the payment of dividends, the result was a decrease in its shareholders' equity shown earlier on Vodafone's balance sheet.

Management Discussion and Analysis

The **management discussion and analysis (MD&A)** or business and operating review is a preface to the financial statements in which the company's management discusses the recent year's performance, providing a background on the company and any significant events that may have occurred. Management may also discuss the coming year, and outline goals, new projects, and future plans.

Management should also discuss any important risks that the firm faces or issues that may affect the firm's liquidity or resources. Management is also required to disclose any **off-balance sheet transactions**, which are transactions or arrangements that can have a material impact on the firm's future performance yet do not appear on the balance sheet. For example, if a firm has made guarantees that it will compensate a buyer for losses related to an asset purchased from the firm these guarantees represent a potential future liability for the firm that must be disclosed as part of the review.

Notes to the Financial Statements

In addition to the four financial statements, companies provide extensive notes with additional details on the information provided in the statements. For example, the notes document important accounting assumptions that were used in preparing the statements. They often provide information specific to a firm's subsidiaries or its separate product lines. They show the details of the firm's share-based compensation plans for employees and the different types of debt the firm has outstanding. Details of acquisitions, spin-offs, leases, taxes, debt repayment schedules, and risk management activities are also given. The information provided in the notes is often very important to interpret fully the firm's financial statements.

EXAMPLE 2.3	Sales by Product Category

Problem

In the MD&A section of its financial statements, H. J. Heinz (HNZ) reported the following sales revenues by product category ($ million):

	2012	2011
Ketchup and sauces	$5,233	$4,608
Meals and snacks	4,480	4,282
Infant/Nutritional foods	1,232	1,175
Other	705	641

Which category showed the highest percentage growth? If Heinz has the same percentage growth by category from 2012 to 2013, what will its total revenues be in 2013?

Solution

The percentage growth in the sales of ketchup and sauces was $5233/4608 - 1 = 13.6\%$. Similarly, growth in meals and snacks was 4.6%, infant/nutritional foods was 4.9%, and other categories were 10.0%. Thus, ketchup and sauces showed the highest growth.

If these growth rates continue for another year, sales of ketchup and sauces will be $5233 \times 1.136 = \$5945$ million, and the other categories will be \$4686 million, \$1292 million, and \$776 million, respectively, for total revenues of \$12.7 billion.

CONCEPT CHECK

1. Where do off-balance sheet transactions appear in a firm's financial statements?

2. What information do the notes to financial statements provide?

2.6 Financial Statement Analysis

Investors often use accounting statements to evaluate a firm in one of two ways:

1. Compare the firm with itself by analyzing how the firm has changed over time.
2. Compare the firm to other similar firms using a common set of financial ratios.

In this section we will describe the most commonly used ratios—related to profitability, liquidity, working capital, interest coverage, leverage (or gearing), valuation, and operating returns—and explain how each one is used in practice.

Profitability Ratios

The income statement provides very useful information regarding the profitability of a firm's business and how it relates to the value of the firm's shares. The **gross margin** of a firm is the ratio of gross profit to revenues (sales):

$$\text{Gross Margin} = \frac{\text{Gross Profit}}{\text{Sales}} \tag{2.8}$$

A firm's gross margin reflects its ability to sell a product for more than the cost of producing it. For example, in 2012, Vodafone had gross margin of $14,871/46,417 = 32.04\%$.

Because there are additional expenses of operating a business beyond the direct costs of goods sold, another important profitability ratio is the **operating margin**, the ratio of operating income to revenues:

$$\text{Operating Margin} = \frac{\text{Operating Income}}{\text{Sales}} \tag{2.9}$$

The operating margin reveals how much a company earns before interest and taxes from each dollar of sales. In 2012, Vodafone's operating margin was $11,187/46,417 = 24.10\%$, an increase from its 2011 operating margin of $5,596/45,884 = 12.20\%$. We can similarly compute a firm's **EBIT margin** = (EBIT/Sales).

By comparing operating or EBIT margins across firms within an industry, we can assess the relative efficiency of the firms' operations. For example, Figure 2.1 compares the EBIT margins of four major U.S. airlines from 2007 to 2012. Notice the impact on profitability from the financial crisis during 2008–2009, as well as the consistently low profits of the largest and oldest of the carriers, United-Continental (UAL), relative to its competitors.

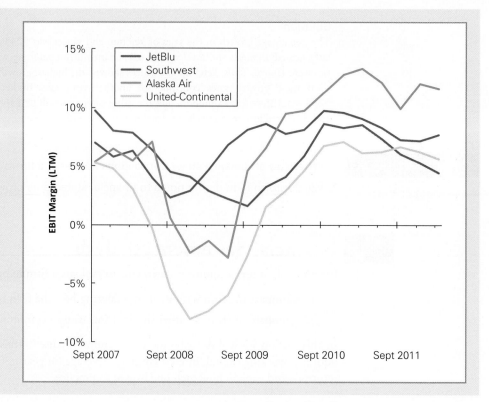

FIGURE 2.1

EBIT Margins for Four U.S. Airlines

Annual (last twelve month) EBIT margins for four U.S. airlines: Alaska Airlines (ALK), JetBlue (JBLU), Southwest (LUV), and United-Continental (UAL). Note the decline in profitability for all airlines in the wake of the 2008 financial crisis, followed by a recovery by mid-2010. Note also the consistently lower profitability of the legacy carrier, United-Continental, relative to its younger peers.

Source: Capital IQ

In addition to the efficiency of operations, differences in operating margins can result from corporate strategy. For example, in December 2011, high-end retailer Nordstrom (JWN) had an operating margin of 11.5% over the past year; Wal-Mart Stores (WMT) had an operating margin of only 5.9%. In this case, Wal-Mart's lower operating margin was not a result of its inefficiency. Rather, the low operating margin is part of Wal-Mart's strategy of offering low prices to sell common products in high volume. Indeed, Wal-Mart's sales were over 41 times higher than those of Nordstrom.

Finally, a firm's **net profit margin** is the ratio of net income to revenues:

$$\text{Net Profit Margin} = \frac{\text{Net Income}}{\text{Sales}} \tag{2.10}$$

The net profit margin shows the fraction of each dollar in revenues that is available to equity holders after the firm pays interest and taxes. In 2012, Vodafone's net profit margin was $7,003/46,417 = 15.09\%$. One must be cautious when comparing net profit margins: While differences in net profit margins can be due to differences in efficiency, they can also result from differences in leverage (or gearing), which determines the amount of interest expense, as well as differences in accounting assumptions.

Liquidity Ratios

Financial analysts often use the information in the firm's balance sheet or statement of financial position to assess its financial solvency or liquidity. Specifically, creditors often compare a firm's current assets and current liabilities to assess whether the firm has sufficient working capital to meet its short-term needs. This comparison can be summarized in the firm's **current ratio**, the ratio of current assets to current liabilities:

$$\text{Current Ratio} = \frac{\text{Current Assets}}{\text{Current Liabilities}}$$

Notice that Vodafone's current ratio increased from $17,003/27,075 = 0.63$ in 2011 to $20,025/24,025 = 0.83$ in 2012.

A more stringent test of the firm's liquidity is the **quick ratio**, which compares only cash and "near cash" assets, such as short-term investments and accounts receivable, to current liabilities. In 2012, Vodafone's quick ratio was $(7,138 + 10,744)/24,025 = 0.74$. A higher current or quick ratio implies less risk of the firm experiencing a cash shortfall in the near future. A reason to exclude inventory is that it may not be that liquid; indeed an increase in the current ratio that results from an unusual increase in inventory could be an indicator that the firm is having difficulty selling its products.

Ultimately, firms need cash to pay employees and meet other obligations. Running out of cash can be very costly for a firm, so firms often gauge their cash position by calculating the **cash ratio**, which is the most stringent liquidity ratio:

$$\text{Cash Ratio} = \frac{\text{Cash}}{\text{Current Liabilities}}$$

Of course, all of these liquidity ratios are limited in that they only consider the firm's current assets. If the firm is able to generate significant cash quickly from its ongoing activities, it might be highly liquid even if these ratios are poor.

EXAMPLE 2.4   **Computing Liquidity Ratios**

Problem
Calculate Vodafone's quick ratio and cash ratio. Based on these measures, how has its liquidity changed between 2011 and 2012?

Solution
In 2011, Vodafone's quick ratio was $(9,259 + 6,262)/27,075 = 0.57$ and its cash ratio was $6,252/27,075 = 0.23$. In 2012, these ratios were 0.74 and $7,138/24,025 = 0.30$, respectively. Thus, Vodafone's cash position, and its quick ratio improved over the period.

Working Capital Ratios

We can use the combined information in the firm's income statement and balance sheet to gauge how efficiently the firm is utilizing its net working capital. To evaluate the speed at which a company turns sales into cash, firms often compute the number of

accounts receivable days—that is, the number of days' worth of sales accounts receivable represents:[7]

$$\text{Accounts Receivable Days} = \frac{\text{Accounts Receivable}}{\text{Average Daily Sales}} \qquad (2.11)$$

Given average daily sales of £46,417 million/365 = £127.17 million in 2012, Vodafone's receivables of £10,744 million represent 10,744/127.17 = 85 days' worth of sales. In other words, on average, Vodafone takes almost three months to collect payment from its customers. In 2011, Vodafone's accounts receivable represented only 74 days' worth of sales. Although the number of receivable days can fluctuate seasonally, a significant unexplained increase could be a cause for concern (perhaps indicating the firm is doing a poor job of collecting from its customers or is trying to boost sales by offering generous credit terms).

There are similar ratios for accounts payable and inventory. For these items, it is natural to compare them to the firm's cost of sales, which should reflect the total amount paid to suppliers and inventory sold. Therefore, **accounts payable days** is defined as:

$$\text{Accounts Payable Days} = \frac{\text{Accounts Payable}}{\text{Average Daily Cost of Sales}} \qquad (2.12)$$

Similarly, **inventory days** = (inventory/average daily cost of sales).[8]

Turnover ratios are an alternative way to measure working capital. We compute turnover ratios by expressing annual revenues or costs as a multiple of the corresponding working capital account. For example,

$$\text{Inventory Turnover} = \frac{\text{Annual Cost of Sales}}{\text{Inventory}} \qquad (2.13)$$

Vodafone's **inventory turnover** in 2012 is 31,546/486 = 64.9, indicating that Vodafone sold roughly 65 times its current stock of inventory during the year. Similarly, **accounts receivable turnover** = (annual sales/accounts receivable) and **accounts payable turnover** = (annual cost of sales/accounts payable). Note that higher turnover corresponds to shorter days, and thus a more efficient use of working capital.

While working capital ratios can be meaningfully compared over time or within an industry, there are wide differences across industries. While the average large U.S. firm had about 45 days' worth of receivables and 65 days' worth of inventory in 2012, airlines tend to have minimal accounts receivable or inventory, as their customers pay in advance and they sell a transportation service as opposed to a physical commodity. On the other hand, distillers and wine producers tend to have very large inventory (over 300 days on average), as their products are often aged prior to sale.

Interest Coverage Ratios

Lenders often assess a firm's ability to meet its interest obligations by comparing its earnings with its interest expenses using an **interest coverage ratio**. One common ratio to consider is the firm's EBIT as a multiple of its interest expenses. A high ratio indicates that the firm is earning much more than is necessary to meet its required interest payments.

---

[7]Accounts receivable days can also be calculated based on the *average* accounts receivable at the end of the current and prior year.

[8]As with accounts receivable days, these ratios can also be calculated using the average accounts payable or inventory balance from the current and prior year.

As a benchmark, creditors often look for an EBIT/Interest coverage ratio in excess of 5× for high-quality borrowers. When EBIT/Interest falls below 1.5, lenders may begin to question a company's ability to repay its debts.

   Depreciation and amortization expenses are deducted when computing EBIT, but they are not actually cash expenses for the firm. Consequently, financial analysts often compute a firm's earnings before interest, taxes, depreciation, and amortization, or **EBITDA**, as a measure of the cash a firm generates from its operations and has available to make interest payments:[9]

$$\text{EBITDA} = \text{EBIT} + \text{Depreciation and Amortization} \qquad (2.14)$$

We can similarly compute the firm's EBITDA/Interest coverage ratio.

EXAMPLE 2.5 **Computing Interest Coverage Ratios**

Problem
Assess Vodafone's ability to meet its interest obligations by calculating interest coverage ratios using both EBIT and EBITDA.

Solution
In 2011 and 2012, Vodafone had the following interest coverage ratios:

$$2011: \quad \frac{\text{EBIT}}{\text{Interest}} = \frac{9,927}{429} = 23.14 \quad \text{and} \quad \frac{\text{EBITDA}}{\text{Interest}} = \frac{9,927 + 6,150}{429} = 37.48$$

$$2012: \quad \frac{\text{EBIT}}{\text{Interest}} = \frac{11,481}{1,932} = 5.94 \quad \text{and} \quad \frac{\text{EBITDA}}{\text{Interest}} = \frac{11,481 + 4,050}{1,932} = 8.04$$

In this case Vodafone's declining interest coverage may be a source of concern for its creditors.

Leverage (Gearing) Ratios

An important piece of information that we can learn from a firm's statement of financial position or balance sheet is the firm's **leverage (gearing)**, or the extent to which it relies on debt as a source of financing. The **debt-equity ratio** is a common ratio used to assess a firm's leverage. We calculate this ratio by dividing the total amount of short- and long-term debt (including current maturities) by the total shareholders' equity:

$$\text{Debt-Equity Ratio} = \frac{\text{Total Debt}}{\text{Total Equity}} \qquad (2.15)$$

We can calculate the debt-equity ratio using either book or market values for equity and debt. From Table 2.1, Vodafone's debt in 2012 includes short-term financial debt (£8,789

---

[9]Because firms often do not separately list depreciation and amortization expenses on the income statement, EBITDA is generally calculated by combining EBIT from the income statement and depreciation and amortization from the statement of cash flows. Note also that because the firm may ultimately need to invest to replace depreciating assets, EBITDA is best viewed as a measure of the firm's *short-run* ability to meet interest payments.

million), and long-term borrowings (£37,349 million), for a total of £46,138 million. Therefore, its *book* debt-equity ratio is 46,438/78,202 = 0.59, using the book value of equity. Note the slight increase from 2011, when the book debt-equity ratio was only (12,377 + 36,584)/87,561 = 0.56.

Because of the difficulty interpreting the book value of equity, the book debt-equity ratio is not especially useful. Indeed, the book value of equity might even be negative, making the ratio meaningless. For example, Domino's Pizza (DPZ) has, based on the strength of its cash flow, consistently borrowed in excess of the book value of its assets. In 2012, it had debt of $1.6 billion, with a total book value of assets of only $600 million and an equity book value of −$1.4 billion!

It is therefore most informative to compare the firm's debt to the market value of its equity. Recall from Example 2.1 that in 2012, the total market value of Vodafone's equity, its market capitalization, is 50,644 million shares × £1.72/share = £87,142 million. Therefore, Vodafone's *market* debt-equity ratio in 2012 is 46,138/87,142 = 0.53, which means Vodafone's debt is a around half of the market value of its equity.[10] As we show later in the text, a firm's market debt-equity ratio has important consequences for the risk and return of its shares.

We can also calculate the fraction of the firm financed by debt in terms of its **debt-to-capital ratio:**

$$\text{Debt-to-Capital Ratio} = \frac{\text{Total Debt}}{\text{Total Equity} + \text{Total Debt}} \quad (2.16)$$

Again, this ratio can be computed using book or market values.

While leverage increases the risk to the firm's equity holders, firms may also hold cash reserves in order to reduce risk. Thus, another useful measure to consider is the firm's **net debt**, or debt in excess of its cash reserves:

$$\text{Net Debt} = \text{Total Debt} - \text{Excess Cash \& Short-term Investments} \quad (2.17)$$

To understand why net debt may be a more relevant measure of leverage, consider a firm with more cash than debt outstanding: Because such a firm could pay off its debts immediately using its available cash, it has not increased its risk and has no effective leverage.

Analogous to the debt-to-capital ratio, we can use the concept of net debt to compute the firm's **debt-to-enterprise value ratio:**

$$\text{Debt-to-Enterprise Value Ratio} = \frac{\text{Net Debt}}{\text{Market Value of Equity} + \text{Net Debt}}$$

$$= \frac{\text{Net Debt}}{\text{Enterprise Value}} \quad (2.18)$$

Given Vodafone's 2012 cash balance of £7,138 million, and total long- and short-term debt of £46,138 million, its net debt is 46,138 − 7,138 = £39,000 million.[11] Given its market value of equity of £87,142 million, Vodafone's enterprise value in 2012 is

---

[10]In this calculation, we have compared the market value of equity to the book value of debt. Strictly speaking, it would be best to use the market value of debt. But because the market value of debt is generally not very different from its book value, this distinction is often ignored in practice.

[11]While net debt should ideally be calculated by deducting cash in excess of the firm's operating needs, absent additional information, it is typical in practice to deduct all cash on the balance sheet.

87,142 + 39000 = £126,142 million, and thus its debt-to-enterprise value ratio is 39,000/126,142 = 30.92%. That is, 30.92% of Vodafone's underlying business activity is financed via debt.

A final measure of leverage is a firm's **equity multiplier**, measured in book value terms as Total Assets/Book Value of Equity. As we will see shortly, this measure captures the amplification of the firm's accounting returns that results from leverage. The market value equity multiplier, which is generally measured as Enterprise Value/Market Value of Equity, indicates the amplification of shareholders' financial risk that results from leverage.

Valuation Ratios

Analysts use a number of ratios to gauge the market value of the firm. The most common is the firm's **price-earnings ratio (P/E)**:

$$P/E \text{ Ratio} = \frac{\text{Market Capitalization}}{\text{Net Income}} = \frac{\text{Share Price}}{\text{Earnings per Share}} \tag{2.19}$$

That is, the P/E ratio is the ratio of the value of equity to the firm's earnings, either on a total basis or on a per-share basis. For example, Vodafone's P/E ratio in 2012 was 87,142/7,003 = 1.72/0.1374 = 12.5. In other words, investors are willing to pay over 12 times Vodafone's earnings to purchase a share.

The P/E ratio is a simple measure that is used to assess whether a share is over- or undervalued based on the idea that the value of a share should be proportional to the level of earnings it can generate for its shareholders. P/E ratios can vary widely across industries and tend to be highest for industries with high expected growth rates. For example, in January 2012, the average large U.S. firm had a P/E ratio of about 17. But software firms, which tend to have above-average growth rates, had an average P/E ratio of 32, while automotive firms, which were still feeling the effects of the recession, had an average P/E ratio of only 9. The risk of the firm will also affect this ratio—all else equal, riskier firms have lower P/E ratios.

Because the P/E ratio considers the value of the firm's equity, it is sensitive to the firm's choice of leverage. The P/E ratio is therefore of limited usefulness when comparing firms with markedly different leverage. We can avoid this limitation by instead assessing the market value of the underlying business using valuation ratios based on the firm's enterprise value. Typical ratios include the ratio of enterprise value to revenue, or enterprise value to operating income, EBIT, or EBITDA. These ratios compare the value of the business to its sales, operating profits, or cash flow. Like the P/E ratio, these ratios are used to make intra-industry comparisons of how firms are priced in the market.

COMMON MISTAKE   **Mismatched Ratios**

When considering valuation (and other) ratios, be sure that the items you are comparing both represent amounts related to the entire firm or that both represent amounts related solely to equity holders. For example, a firm's share price and market capitalization are values associated with the firm's equity. Thus, it makes sense to compare them to the firm's earnings per share or net income, which are amounts to equity holders after interest has been paid to debt holders. We must be careful, however, if we compare a firm's market capitalization to its revenues, operating income, or EBITDA because these amounts are related to the whole firm, and both debt and equity holders have a claim to them. Thus, it is better to compare revenues, operating income, or EBITDA to the enterprise value of the firm, which includes both debt and equity.

EXAMPLE 2.6	**Computing Profitability and Valuation Ratios**

Problem

Consider the following data as of December 2011 for Deutsche Telekom and France Telecom (in € billion):

	Deutsche Telekom	France Telecom
Sales	58.7	45.3
EBIT	5.6	7.9
Depreciation and Amortisation	14.4	6.7
Net Income	0.6	3.8
Market Capitalisation	38.3	22.3
Cash	3.7	8.0
Debt	40.1	32.3

Compare Deutsche Telekom's and France Telecom's EBIT margins, net profit margins, P/E ratios, and the ratio of enterprise value to sales, EBIT, and EBITDA.

Solution

Deutsche Telekom had an EBIT margin of 5.6/58.7 = 9.5%, a net profit margin of 0.6/58.7 = 1.0%, and a P/E ratio of 38.3/0.6 = 63.8. Its enterprise value was 38.3 + 40.1 − 3.7 = €74.7 billion, which has a ratio of 74.7/58.7 = 1.27 to sales, 74.7/5.6 = 13.34 to EBIT and 74.7/(5.6 + 14.4) = 3.74 to EBITDA.

France Telecom had an EBIT margin of 7.9/45.3 = 17.4%, a net profit margin of 3.8/45.3 = 8.4%, and a P/E ratio of 22.3/3.8 = 5.9. Its enterprise value was 22.3+32.3−8.0 = €46.6 billion, which has a ratio of 46.6/45.3 = 1.03 to sales, 46.6/7.9 = 5.90 to EBIT and 46.6/(7.9 + 6.7) = 3.19 to EBITDA.

Note that although France Telecom's profitability margins exceeded those of Deutsche Telekom's, with the exception of EBIT, the other valuation multiples are quite close.

The P/E ratio or ratios to EBIT or EBITDA, are not meaningful if the firm's earnings are negative. In this case, it is common to look at the firm's enterprise value relative to sales. The risk in doing so, however, is that earnings might be negative because the firm's underlying business model is fundamentally flawed, as was the case for many Internet firms in the late 1990s.

Investment Returns

Analysts often evaluate the firm's return on investment by comparing its income to its investment using ratios such as the firm's **return on equity (ROE)**:[12]

$$\text{Return on Equity} = \frac{\text{Net Income}}{\text{Book Value of Equity}} \tag{2.20}$$

Vodafone's ROE in 2012 was 7,003/78,202 = 8.96%. The ROE provides a measure of the return that the firm has earned on its past investments. A high ROE may indicate the firm is able to find investment opportunities that are very profitable.

---

[12]Because net income is measured over the year, the ROE can also be calculated based on the average book value of equity at the end of the current and prior year.

Another common measure is **return on assets (ROA)**, which we calculate as:[13]

$$\text{Return on Assets} = \frac{\text{Net Income} + \text{Interest Expense}}{\text{Book Value of Assets}} \tag{2.21}$$

The ROA calculation includes interest expense in the numerator because the assets in the denominator have been funded by both debt and equity investors.

As a performance measure, ROA has the benefit that it is less sensitive to leverage than ROE. However, it is sensitive to working capital—for example, an equal increase in the firm's receivables and payables will increase total assets and thus lower ROA. To avoid this problem, we can consider the firm's **return on invested capital (ROIC)**:

$$\text{Return on Invested Capital} = \frac{\text{EBIT } (1 - \text{tax rate})}{\text{Book Value of Equity} + \text{Net Debt}} \tag{2.22}$$

The return on invested capital measures the after-tax profit generated by the business itself, excluding any interest expenses (or interest income), and compares it to the capital raised from equity and debt holders that has already been deployed (i.e., is not held as cash). Of the three measures of operating returns, ROIC is the most useful in assessing the performance of the underlying business.

EXAMPLE 2.7

Computing Operating Returns

Problem
Assess how Vodafone's ability to use its assets effectively has changed in the last year by computing the change in its return on assets and return on invested capital.

Solution
In 2012, Vodafone's ROA was $(7,003 + 1,932)/139,576 = 6.4\%$, compared to an ROA in 2011 of $(7,870 + 429)/151,220 = 5.5\%$.

To compute the return on invested capital, we need to calculate after-tax EBIT, which requires an estimate of Vodafone's tax rate. Because Net income = Pretax income $\times$ $(1 - \text{tax rate})$, we can estimate $(1 - \text{tax rate})$ = Net income/Pretax income. Thus, EBIT $\times$ $(1 - \text{tax rate})$ = $11,481 \times (7,003/9,549) = 8,420$ in 2012, and $9,927 \times (7,870/9,498) = 8,226$ in 2011.

To compute invested capital, we add equity and the short- and long-term debt items on the balance sheet, and deduct cash. Thus, ROIC in 2012 was $8,420/(78,202+8,789+37,349-7,138)=7.2\%$, compared with $8,226/(87,561+12,377+36,584-6,252) = 6.3\%$ in 2011.

The improvement in Vodafone's ROA and ROIC from 2011 to 2012 suggests that Vodafone was able to use its assets more effectively and increase its return over this period.

---

[13]ROA is sometimes calculated as Net Income/Assets, inappropriately ignoring the returns generated by the assets that are being used to support the firm's debt obligations (see also the box on Mismatched Ratios on page 41). Also, the interest expense that is added back is sometimes done on an after-tax basis in order to eliminate the benefit of the tax savings provided by debt. Finally, as with ROE, the *average* book value of assets at the beginning and end of the year may be used.

The DuPont Identity

We can gain further insight into a firm's ROE using a tool called the **DuPont Identity** (named for the company that popularized its use), which expresses the ROE in terms of the firm's profitability, asset efficiency, and leverage:

$$\text{ROE} = \underbrace{\left(\frac{\text{Net Income}}{\text{Sales}}\right)}_{\text{Net Profit Margin}} \times \underbrace{\left(\frac{\text{Sales}}{\text{Total Assets}}\right)}_{\text{Asset Turnover}} \times \underbrace{\left(\frac{\text{Total Assets}}{\text{Book Value of Equity}}\right)}_{\text{Equity Multiplier}} \quad (2.23)$$

The first term in the DuPont Identity is the firm's net profit margin, which measures its overall profitability. The second term is the firm's **asset turnover**, which measures how efficiently the firm is utilizing its assets to generate sales. Together, these terms determine the firm's return on assets. We compute ROE by multiplying by a measure of leverage called the equity multiplier, which indicates the value of assets held per pound or dollar of shareholder equity. The greater the firm's reliance on debt financing, the higher the equity multiplier will be. Applying this identity to Vodafone, we see that in 2012 its asset turnover is 46,417/139,576 = 0.33, with an equity multiplier of 139,576/78,202 = 1.79. Given its net profit margin of 15.09%, we can compute its ROE as

$$\text{ROE} = 8.9\% = 15.09\% \times 0.33 \times 1.79$$

EXAMPLE 2.8 | **Determinants of ROE**

Problem

For the year ended December 2011, Deutsche Telekom had sales of €58.7 billion, net income of €0.6 billion, assets of €122.5 billion, and a book value of equity of €39.9 billion. For the same period, France Telecom had sales of €45.3 billion, net income of €3.8 billion, assets of €96.1 billion, and a book value of equity of €29.6 billion. Compare these firms' profitability, asset turnover, equity multipliers, and return on equity during this period. If Deutsche Telekom had been able to match France Telecom's net profit margin during this period, what would its ROE have been?

Solution

Deutsche Telekom's net profit margin (from Example 2.6) was 0.6/58.7 = 1.02%, which was below France Telecom's net profit margin of 3.8/45.3 = 8.39%. However, both Deutsche Telekom and France Telecom have similar asset turnover ratios of 58.7/122.5 = 0.48 and 45.3/96.1 = 0.47 respectively. Finally, France Telecom had greater leverage (in terms of book value), with an equity multiplier of 96.1/29.6 = 3.25, relative to Deutsche Telekom's equity multiplier of 122.5/39.9 = 3.07. Next let's compute the ROE of each firm directly and using the DuPont Identity:

$$\text{Deutsche Telekom} = \frac{0.6}{39.9} = 1.5\% = 1.02\% \times 0.48 \times 3.07$$

$$\text{France Telecom} = \frac{3.8}{29.6} = 12.8\% = 8.39\% \times 0.47 \times 3.25$$

Note that due to its lower net profit margin, Deutsche Telekom has a much lower ROE than France Telecom. If Deutsche Telekom had been able to match France Telecom's net profit margin, its ROE would have been significantly higher: 8.39% × 0.48 × 3.07 = 12.4%.

To conclude our discussion of financial ratios, Table 2.4 presents the various measures of profitability, liquidity, working capital, interest coverage, leverage, valuation, and operating returns.

TABLE 2.4	A Summary of Key Financial Ratios

Profitability Ratios

Gross Margin	$\dfrac{\text{Gross Profit}}{\text{Sales}}$
Operating Margin	$\dfrac{\text{Operating Income}}{\text{Sales}}$
EBIT Margin	$\dfrac{\text{EBIT}}{\text{Sales}}$
Net Profit Margin	$\dfrac{\text{Net Income}}{\text{Sales}}$

Liquidity Ratios

Current Ratio	$\dfrac{\text{Current Assets}}{\text{Current Liabilities}}$
Quick Ratio	$\dfrac{\text{Cash \& Short-term Investments} + \text{Accounts Receivable}}{\text{Current Liabilities}}$
Cash Ratio	$\dfrac{\text{Cash}}{\text{Current Liabilities}}$

Working Capital Ratios

Accounts Receivable Days	$\dfrac{\text{Accounts Receivable}}{\text{Average Daily Sales}}$
Accounts Payable Days	$\dfrac{\text{Accounts Payable}}{\text{Average Daily Cost of Sales}}$
Inventory Days	$\dfrac{\text{Inventory}}{\text{Average Daily Cost of Sales}}$
Accounts Receivable Turnover	$\dfrac{\text{Annual Sales}}{\text{Accounts Receivable}}$
Accounts Payable Turnover	$\dfrac{\text{Annual Cost of Sales}}{\text{Accounts Payable}}$
Inventory Turnover	$\dfrac{\text{Annual Cost of Sales}}{\text{Inventory}}$

Interest Coverage Ratios

EBIT/Interest Coverage	$\dfrac{\text{EBIT}}{\text{Interest Expense}}$
EBITDA/Interest Coverage	$\dfrac{\text{EBITDA}}{\text{Interest Expense}}$

Leverage (Gearing) Ratios

Debt-Equity Ratio	$\dfrac{\text{Total Debt}}{\text{Book (or Market) Value of Equity}}$
Debt-to-Capital Ratio	$\dfrac{\text{Total Debt}}{\text{Total Equity} + \text{Total Debt}}$
Debt-to-Enterprise Value Ratio	$\dfrac{\text{Net Debt}}{\text{Enterprise Value}}$
Equity Multiplier (book)	$\dfrac{\text{Total Assets}}{\text{Book Value of Equity}}$
Equity Multiplier (market)	$\dfrac{\text{Enterprise Value}}{\text{Market Value of Equity}}$

Valuation Ratios

Market-to-Book Ratio	$\dfrac{\text{Market Value of Equity}}{\text{Book Value of Equity}}$
Price-Earnings Ratio	$\dfrac{\text{Share Price}}{\text{Earnings per Share}}$
Enterprise Value Ratios	$\dfrac{\text{Enterprise Value}}{\text{EBIT or EBITDA or Sales}}$

Operating Returns

Asset Turnover	$\dfrac{\text{Sales}}{\text{Total Assets}}$
Return on Equity (ROE)	$\dfrac{\text{Net Income}}{\text{Book Value of Equity}}$
Return on Assets (ROA)	$\dfrac{\text{Net Income} + \text{Interest Expense}}{\text{Book Value of Assets}}$
Return on Invested Capital (ROIC)	$\dfrac{\text{EBIT} (1 - \text{Tax Rate})}{\text{Book Value of Equity} + \text{Net Debt}}$

1. Why is EBITDA used to assess a firm's ability to meet its interest obligations?

2. What is the difference between a firm's book debt-equity ratio and its market debt-equity ratio?

3. To compare the valuations of firms with very different leverage (gearing), which valuation multiples would be most appropriate?

4. What is the DuPont Identity?

2.7 Financial Reporting in Practice

The various financial statements we have examined are of critical importance to investors and financial managers alike. Even with safeguards such as accounting standards and auditors, financial reporting abuses unfortunately do take place. We now review two of the most infamous recent examples.

Enron

Enron was the most well known of the accounting scandals of the early 2000s. Enron started as an operator of natural-gas pipelines but evolved into a global trader dealing in a range of products including gas, oil, electricity, and even broadband Internet capacity. A series of events unfolded that, in December 2001, led Enron to file what was, at the time, the largest bankruptcy filing in U.S. history. By the end of that year, the market value of Enron's shares had fallen by over $60 billion.

Interestingly, throughout the 1990s and up to late 2001, Enron was touted as one of the most successful and profitable companies in America. *Fortune* rated Enron "The Most Innovative Company in America" for six straight years, from 1995 to 2000. But while many aspects of Enron's business were successful, subsequent investigations suggest that Enron executives had been manipulating Enron's financial statements to mislead investors and artificially inflate the price of Enron's stock and maintain its credit rating. In 2000, for example, 96% of Enron's reported earnings were the result of accounting manipulation.[14]

Although the accounting manipulations that Enron used were quite sophisticated, the essence of most of the deceptive transactions was surprisingly simple. Enron sold assets at inflated prices to other firms (or, in many cases, business entities that Enron's CFO Andrew Fastow had created), together with a promise to buy back those assets at an even higher future price. Thus, Enron was effectively borrowing money, receiving cash today in exchange for a promise to pay more cash in the future. But Enron recorded the incoming cash as revenue and then hid the promises to buy them back in a variety of ways.[15] In the end, much of Enron's revenue growth and profits in the late 1990s were the result of this type of manipulation.

WorldCom

Enron's record as the largest bankruptcy of all time lasted only until July 21, 2002, when WorldCom, which at its peak had a market capitalization of $120 billion, filed for bankruptcy. Again, a series of accounting manipulations beginning in 1998 hid the firm's financial problems from investors.

---

[14]John R. Kroger, "Enron, Fraud and Securities Reform: An Enron Prosecutor's Perspective," *University of Colorado Law Review* (December 2009): pp. 57–138.

[15]In some cases, these promises were called "price risk management liabilities" and hidden with other trading activities; in other cases they were off-balance sheet transactions that were not fully disclosed.

In WorldCom's case, the fraud was to reclassify $3.85 billion in operating expenses as long-term capital expenditures. The immediate impact of this change was to boost World-Com's reported earnings: Operating expenses are deducted from earnings immediately, whereas capital expenditures are depreciated slowly over time. Of course, this manipulation would not boost WorldCom's cash flows, because long-term investments must be deducted on the cash flow statement at the time they are made.

Some investors were concerned by WorldCom's excessive investment compared to the rest of the industry. As one investment advisor commented, "Red flags [were] things like big deviations between reported earnings and excess cash flow . . . [and] excessive capital expenditures for a long period of time. That was what got us out of WorldCom in 1999."[16]

Sarbanes-Oxley Act

Enron and WorldCom highlight the importance to investors of accurate and up-to-date financial statements. The problems at Enron, WorldCom, and elsewhere were kept hidden from boards and shareholders until it was too late. In the wake of these scandals, many people felt that the accounting statements of these companies did not present an accurate picture of the financial health of the company. In 2002, the U.S. Congress passed the **Sarbanes-Oxley Act (SOX)**. While SOX contains many provisions, the overall intent of the legislation was to improve the accuracy of information given to both boards and shareholders. SOX attempted to achieve this goal in three ways: (1) by overhauling incentives and the independence in the auditing process, (2) by stiffening penalties for providing false information, and (3) by forcing companies to validate their internal financial control processes.

Auditing firms are supposed to ensure that a company's financial statements accurately reflect the financial state of the firm. In reality, most auditors have a long-standing relationship with their clients and receive lucrative auditing and consulting fees from them. This extended relationship and the desire to continue earning these fees may make the firms less willing to challenge management. SOX addressed this concern by putting strict limits on the amount of non-audit fees (consulting or otherwise) that an accounting firm can earn from a company that it audits. It also required that audit partners rotate every five years to limit the likelihood that auditing relationships become too cosy over long periods of time. Finally, SOX called on the Securities and Exchange Commission (SEC) to force companies to have audit committees that are dominated by outside directors, with at least one outside director having a financial background.

SOX also stiffened the criminal penalties for providing false information to shareholders (fines of up to $5 million and up to 20 years imprisonment), and required both the CEO and CFO to personally attest to the accuracy of the firm's financial statements. Furthermore, CEOs and CFOs must return bonuses or profits from the sale of stock that are later shown to be due to misstated financial reports.

Finally, Section 404 of SOX requires senior management and the boards of public companies to validate and certify the process through which funds are allocated and controlled, and outcomes are monitored. Section 404 has arguably garnered more attention than any other section in SOX because of the large potential compliance costs that it places on firms. These costs can be especially significant (in percentage terms) for small companies, and critics have argued that they are sufficiently onerous to cause some firms to avoid them by remaining privately held.[17]

---

[16]Robert Olstein, as reported in the *Wall Street Journal*, August 23, 2002.

[17]See Chapter 29 for a more detailed discussion of these and other corporate governance issues.

"It's only when the tide goes out that you learn who's been swimming naked." —*Warren Buffett*

On December 11, 2008, federal agents arrested Bernie Madoff, one of the largest and most successful hedge fund managers. It turned out that the $65 billion[18] fund he ran was in fact a fraud. His spectacular performance of the last 17 years, generating consistent annual returns between 10% and 15%, was actually a complete fabrication. Madoff had been running the world's largest Ponzi scheme: That is, he used the capital contributed by new investors to pay off old investors. His strategy was so successful that for more than a decade investors ranging from Steven Spielberg to New York University, as well as a number of large banks and investment advisors, lined up to invest with him. Indeed, Madoff quite likely would have been able to hide the fraud until his deathbed had not the global financial crisis spurred many investors to seek to withdraw funds from their Madoff accounts in order to raise cash and cover losses elsewhere in their portfolios. In addition, the financial crisis meant there were few new investors with both the cash and the willingness to invest. As a result, Madoff did not have enough new capital to pay off the investors who wanted to withdraw their capital, and the scheme finally collapsed.

How was Madoff able to hide perhaps the largest fraud of all time for so long? Rather than simply manipulate his accounting statements, Madoff *made them up* with the assistance of a virtually unknown accounting firm with only one active accountant. Although many investors may have questioned why such a large fund, with $65 billion in assets, would choose an unknown and tiny audit firm, not enough of them recognized this choice as a potential red flag. In addition, because Madoff's firm was private, it was not subject to the strict regulatory requirements for public companies (such as the Sarbanes-Oxley Act) and so had weak reporting requirements. As this case makes clear, when making an investment decision, it is important not only to review the firm's financial statements, but also to consider the reliability and reputation of the auditors who prepared them.

Dodd-Frank Act

To mitigate the compliance burden on small firms in the U.S., the Dodd-Frank Wall Street Reform and Consumer Protection Act passed in 2010 exempts firms with less than $75 million in publicly held shares from the SOX Section 404 requirements. It also requires the SEC to study how it might reduce cost for medium-sized firms with a public float of less than $250 million, and to assess whether such measures would encourage more firms to list on U.S. exchanges.

Dodd-Frank also broadened the whistleblower provisions of SOX, so that an individual who provides "information related to a possible violation of the federal securities laws (including any rules or regulations thereunder)" that results in penalties or recoveries by the SEC or agencies is eligible to receive from 10 to 30% of that penalty or recovery.

CONCEPT CHECK | 1. Describe the transactions Enron used to increase its reported earnings.

2. What is the Sarbanes-Oxley Act, and how was it modified by the Dodd-Frank Act?

---

[18]$65 billion is the total amount Madoff had reported to his investors, including (fictitious) returns; investigators are still trying to determine the exact amount that investors had actually contributed to the fund, but it appears to be in excess of $17 billion (see www.madoff.com).

Here is what you should know after reading this chapter. MyFinanceLab will help you identify what you know and where to go when you need to practice.

2.1 Firms' Disclosure of Financial Information

- Financial statements are accounting reports that a firm issues periodically to describe its past performance.
- Investors, financial analysts, managers, and other interested parties such as creditors rely on financial statements to obtain reliable information about a corporation.
- The main types of financial statements are the balance sheet or statement of financial position, the income statement, the statement of cash flows, and the statement of changes in shareholders' equity.

2.2 The Balance Sheet or Statement of Financial Position

- The balance sheet shows the current financial position (assets, liabilities, and shareholders' equity) of the firm at a single point in time.
- The two sides of the balance sheet must balance:

$$\text{Assets} = \text{Liabilities} + \text{Shareholders' Equity} \tag{2.1}$$

- The firm's net working capital, which is the capital available in the short term to run the business, is the difference between the firm's current assets and current liabilities. Excluding cash and debt, key components of net working capital are accounts receivable, inventory, and accounts payable.
- Many assets (such as property, plant, and equipment) are listed on the firm's balance sheet based on their historical cost rather than their current market value, whereas other assets (such as customer relationships) are not listed at all.
- Shareholders' equity is the book value of the firm's equity. It differs from market value of the firm's equity, its market capitalization, because of the way assets and liabilities are recorded for accounting purposes. A successful firm's market-to-book ratio typically exceeds 1.
- The enterprise value of a firm is the total value of its underlying business operations:

$$\text{Enterprise Value} = \text{Market Value of Equity} + \text{Debt} - \text{Cash} \tag{2.4}$$

2.3 The Income Statement

- The income statement reports the firm's revenues and expenses, and it computes the firm's bottom line of net income (or profit), or earnings, over a given time interval.
- The firm's operating income is equal to its revenues less its cost of goods sold and operating expenses. After adjusting for other, non-operating income or expenses, we have the firm's earnings before interest and taxes, or EBIT.
- Deducting interest and taxes from EBIT gives the firm's net income, which we can divide by the number of shares outstanding to calculate earnings per share (EPS).

2.4 The Statement of Cash Flows

- The statement of cash flows reports the sources and uses of the firm's cash during a given time period, and can be derived from the firm's income statement and the changes in the firm's balance sheet.
- The statement of cash flows shows the cash used (or provided) from operating, investing, and financing activities.

2.5 Other Financial Statement Information

- The change in shareholders' equity can be computed as retained earnings (net income less dividends) plus net sales of stock (new grants or issuances, net of repurchases).
- The management discussion and analysis section of the financial statements contains management's overview of the firm's performance, as well as disclosure of risks the firm faces, including those from off-balance sheet transactions.

- The notes to a firm's financial statements generally contain important details regarding the numbers used in the main statements.

2.6 Financial Statement Analysis

- Financial ratios allow us to (i) compare the firm's performance over time, and (ii) compare the firm to other similar firms.
- Key financial ratios measure the firm's profitability, liquidity, working capital, interest coverage, leverage (gearing), valuation, and operating returns. See Table 2.4 for a summary.
- EBITDA measures the cash a firm generates before capital investments:

$$\text{EBITDA} = \text{EBIT} + \text{Depreciation and Amortization} \tag{2.14}$$

- Net debt measures the firm's debt in excess of its cash reserves:

$$\text{Net Debt} = \text{Total Debt} - \text{Excess Cash \& Short-term Investments} \tag{2.17}$$

- The DuPont Identity expresses a firm's ROE in terms of its profitability, asset efficiency, and leverage:

$$\text{ROE} = \underbrace{\left(\frac{\text{Net Income}}{\text{Sales}}\right)}_{\text{Net Profit Margin}} \times \underbrace{\left(\frac{\text{Sales}}{\text{Total Assets}}\right)}_{\text{Asset Turnover}} \times \underbrace{\left(\frac{\text{Total Assets}}{\text{Book Value of Equity}}\right)}_{\text{Equity Multiplier}} \tag{2.23}$$

2.7 Financial Reporting in Practice

- Recent accounting scandals have drawn attention to the importance of financial statements. New legislation has increased the penalties for fraud and tightened the procedures firms must use to assure that statements are accurate.

Key Terms

accounts payable *p. 26*
accounts payable days *p. 38*
accounts payable turnover *p. 38*
accounts receivable *p. 25*
accounts receivable days *p. 38*
accounts receivable turnover *p. 38*
accrual items *p. 26*
accumulated depreciation *p. 25*
amortization *p. 26*
annual report *p. 22*
asset turnover *p. 44*
assets *p. 24*
auditor *p. 22*
balance sheet *p. 24*
balance sheet equation *p. 25*
book value (or carrying amount) *p. 25*
book value of equity *p. 27*
capital expenditures *p. 32*
capital leases *p. 26*
cash *p. 37*
cash ratio *p. 37*
convertible bonds *p. 30*
current assets *p. 25*
current liabilities *p. 26*
current ratio *p. 37*
debt-equity ratio *p. 39*
debt-to-capital ratio *p. 40*

debt-to-enterprise value ratio *p. 40*
deferred taxes *p. 26*
depreciation expense *p. 25*
diluted EPS *p. 30*
dilution *p. 30*
DuPont Identity *p. 44*
earnings per share (EPS) *p. 30*
EBIT *p. 30*
EBIT margin *p. 35*
EBITDA *p. 39*
enterprise value *p. 28*
equity multiplier *p. 41*
financial statements *p. 22*
Generally Accepted Accounting
    Principles (GAAP) *p. 22*
goodwill (an intangible asset) *p. 25*
gross margin *p. 35*
gross profit *p. 29*
growth stocks *p. 28*
impairment charge *p. 26*
income statement *p. 28*
interest coverage ratio *p. 38*
International Financial Reporting
    Standards *p. 22*
inventories *p. 25*
inventory days *p. 38*
inventory turnover *p. 38*

Further Reading

For a basic primer on financial statements, see T. R. Ittelson, *Financial Statements: A Step-By-Step Guide to Understanding and Creating Financial Reports* (Career Press, 2009).

For additional information on financial accounting, there are many introductory, MBA-level financial accounting textbooks. See T. Dyckman, R. Magee, and G. Pfeiffer, *Financial Accounting* (Cambridge Business Publishers, 2010); and W. Harrison, C. Horngren, and C. W. Thomas, *Financial Accounting* (Prentice Hall, 2013).

For more on financial statement analysis, see J. Whalen, S. Baginski, and M. Bradshaw, *Financial Reporting, Financial Statement Analysis and Valuation: A Strategic Perspective* (South-Western College Pub, 2010); and L. Revsine, D. Collins, B. Johnson, F. Mittelstaedt, *Financial Reporting & Analysis* (McGraw-Hill/Irwin, 2011).

A great deal of public information is available regarding the alleged accounting abuses at Enron Corporation. A useful starting point is a report produced by a committee established by Enron's own board of directors: Report of the Special Investigative Committee of the Board of Directors of Enron (Powers Report), released February 2, 2002 (available online). Information regarding the resolution of Bernard Madoff's Ponzi scheme can be found on the site published by the Securities Investor Protection Act (SIPA) Trustee, www.madoff.com.

Problems

All problems are available in MyFinanceLab. *An asterisk (*) indicates problems with a higher level of difficulty.*

Firms' Disclosure of Financial Information

1. What are the four main financial statements? What checks are there on the accuracy of these statements?

2. Who reads financial statements? List at least three different categories of people. For each category, provide an example of the type of information they might be interested in and discuss why.

3. Find the most recent financial statements for Starbucks Corporation (SBUX) using the following sources:
   a. From the company's Web page www.starbucks.com. (*Hint*: Search for "investor relations.")
   b. From the SEC Web site www.sec.gov. (*Hint*: Search for company filings in the EDGAR database.)
   c. From the Yahoo! Finance Web site http://finance.yahoo.com.
   d. From at least one other source. (*Hint*: Enter "SBUX 10K" at www.google.com.)

The Balance Sheet or Statement of Financial Position

4. Consider the following potential events that might have taken place at Vodafone Group Plc on 31 March, 2012. For each one, indicate which line items in Vodafone's balance sheet would be affected and by how much. Also indicate the change to Vodafone's book value of equity. (In all cases, ignore any tax consequences for simplicity.)
   a. Vodafone used £200 million of its available cash to repay £200 million of its long-term debt.
   b. A warehouse fire destroyed £50 million worth of uninsured inventory.
   c. Vodafone used £50 million in cash and £50 million in new long-term debt to purchase £100 million of buildings worldwide.
   d. A large customer owing £20 million for products it already received declared bankruptcy, leaving no possibility that Vodafone would ever receive payment.
   e. Vodafone's engineers discover a new manufacturing process that will cut the cost of its flagship product by over 50%.
   f. A key competitor announces a radical new pricing policy that will drastically undercut Vodafone's prices.

5. What was the change in Vodafone Group's book value of equity from 2011 to 2012 according to Table 2.1? Does this imply that the market price of Vodafone's shares decreased in 2012? Explain.

6. Use Google finance (www.google.com/finance) to find the balance sheet data for Qualcomm as of the end of 2011. From the balance sheet, answer the following questions:
   a. How much did Qualcomm have in cash, cash equivalents, and marketable securities (short and long-term)?
   b. What were Qualcomm's total accounts receivable?
   c. What were Qualcomm's total assets?
   d. What were Qualcomm's total liabilities? How much of this was long-term debt?
   e. What was the book value of Qualcomm's equity?

7. Find online the annual report for Peet's Coffee and Tea (PEET) for fiscal year 2011 (filed in January 2012). Answer the following questions from their balance sheet:
   a. How much cash did Peet's have at the end of the fiscal year?
   b. What were Peet's' total assets?
   c. What were Peet's' total liabilities? How much debt did Peet's have?
   d. What was the book value of Peet's equity?

8. In early 2009, General Electric (GE) had a book value of equity of $105 billion, 10.5 billion shares outstanding, and a market price of $10.80 per share. GE also had cash of $48 billion, and total debt of $524 billion. Three years later, in early 2012, GE had a book value of equity of $116 billion, 10.6 billion shares outstanding with a market price of $17 per share, cash of $84 billion, and total debt of $410 billion. Over this period, what was the change in GE's
   a. market capitalization?
   b. market-to-book ratio?
   c. enterprise value?

9. In mid-2012, Abercrombie & Fitch (ANF) had a book equity of $1693 million, a price per share of $35.48, and 82.55 million shares outstanding. At the same time, The Gap (GPS) had a book equity of $3017 million, a share price of $27.90, and 489.22 million shares outstanding.
   a. What is the market-to-book ratio of each of these clothing retailers?
   b. What conclusions can you draw by comparing the two ratios?

10. See Table 2.5 showing financial statement data and share price data for Mydeco Corp.
   a. What is Mydeco's market capitalization at the end of each year?
   b. What is Mydeco's market-to-book ratio at the end of each year?
   c. What is Mydeco's enterprise value at the end of each year?

TABLE 2.5	2009–2013 Financial Statement Data and Share Price Data for Mydeco Corp.

Mydeco Corp. 2009–2013   (All data as of fiscal year end; in $ million)

Income Statement	2009	2010	2011	2012	2013
Revenue	404.3	363.8	424.6	510.7	604.1
Cost of Goods Sold	(188.3)	(173.8)	(206.2)	(246.8)	(293.4)
Gross Profit	216.0	190.0	218.4	263.9	310.7
Sales and Marketing	(66.7)	(66.4)	(82.8)	(102.1)	(120.8)
Administration	(60.6)	(59.1)	(59.4)	(66.4)	(78.5)
Depreciation & Amortization	(27.3)	(27.0)	(34.3)	(38.4)	(38.6)
EBIT	61.4	37.5	41.9	57.0	72.8
Interest Income (Expense)	(33.7)	(32.9)	(32.2)	(37.4)	(39.4)
Pretax Income	27.7	4.6	9.7	19.6	33.4
Income Tax	(9.7)	(1.6)	(3.4)	(6.9)	(11.7)
Net Income	18.0	3.0	6.3	12.7	21.7
Shares outstanding (millions)	55.0	55.0	55.0	55.0	55.0
Earnings per share	$0.33	$0.05	$0.11	$0.23	$0.39

Balance Sheet	2009	2010	2011	2012	2013
Assets					
Cash	48.8	68.9	86.3	77.5	85.0
Accounts Receivable	88.6	69.8	69.8	76.9	86.1
Inventory	33.7	30.9	28.4	31.7	35.3
Total Current Assets	171.1	169.6	184.5	186.1	206.4
Net Property, Plant & Equip.	245.3	243.3	309	345.6	347.0
Goodwill & Intangibles	361.7	361.7	361.7	361.7	361.7
Total Assets	778.1	774.6	855.2	893.4	915.1
Liabilities & Shareholders' Equity					
Accounts Payable	18.7	17.9	22.0	26.8	31.7
Accrued Compensation	6.7	6.4	7.0	8.1	9.7
Total Current Liabilities	25.4	24.3	29.0	34.9	41.4
Long-term Debt	500.0	500.0	575.0	600.0	600.0
Total Liabilities	525.4	524.3	604.0	634.9	641.4
Shareholders' Equity	252.7	250.3	251.2	258.5	273.7
Total Liabilities & Shareholders' Equity	778.1	774.6	855.2	893.4	915.1

Statement of Cash Flows	2009	2010	2011	2012	2013
Net Income	18.0	3.0	6.3	12.7	21.7
Depreciation & Amortization	27.3	27.0	34.3	38.4	38.6
Chg. in Accounts Receivable	3.9	18.8	(0.0)	(7.1)	(9.2)
Chg. in Inventory	(2.9)	2.8	2.5	(3.3)	(3.6)
Chg. in Payables & Accrued Comp.	2.2	(1.1)	4.7	5.9	6.5
Cash from Operations	48.5	50.5	47.8	46.6	54.0
Capital Expenditures	(25.0)	(25.0)	(100.0)	(75.0)	(40.0)
Cash from Investing Activities	(25.0)	(25.0)	(100.0)	(75.0)	(40.0)
Dividends Paid	(5.4)	(5.4)	(5.4)	(5.4)	(6.5)
Sale (or purchase) of shares	—	—	—	—	—
Debt Issuance (Pay Down)	—	—	75.0	25.0	—
Cash from Financing Activities	(5.4)	(5.4)	69.6	19.6	(6.5)
Change in Cash	18.1	20.1	17.4	(8.8)	7.5
Mydeco Share Price	$7.92	$3.30	$5.25	$8.71	$10.89

The Income Statement

11. Suppose that in 2013, Vodafone launches an aggressive marketing campaign that boosts sales by 15%. However, their operating margin falls from 24.1% to 19.4%. Suppose that they have no other income, interest expenses are unchanged, and taxes are the same percentage of pretax income as in 2012.
    a. What is Vodafone's EBIT in 2013?
    b. What is Vodafone's net income in 2013?
    c. If Vodafone's P/E ratio and number of shares outstanding remains unchanged, what is Vodafone's share price in 2013?

12. Find online the annual report for Peet's Coffee and Tea (PEET) for fiscal year 2011 (filed in January 2012). Answer the following questions from their income statement:
    a. What were Peet's revenues for fiscal year 2011? By what percentage did revenues grow from the prior year?
    b. What was Peet's operating income for the fiscal year?
    c. What was Peet's average tax rate for the year?
    d. What were Peet's diluted earnings per share in fiscal year 2011? What number of shares is this EPS based on?

13. See Table 2.5 showing financial statement data and share price data for Mydeco Corp.
    a. By what percentage did Mydeco's revenues grow each year from 2010 to 2013?
    b. By what percentage did net income grow each year?
    c. Why might the growth rates of revenues and net income differ?

14. See Table 2.5 showing financial statement data and share price data for Mydeco Corp. Suppose Mydeco repurchases 2 million shares each year from 2010 to 2013. What would its earnings per share be in years 2010–2013? (Assume Mydeco pays for the shares using its available cash and that Mydeco earns no interest on its cash balances.)

15. See Table 2.5 showing financial statement data and share price data for Mydeco Corp. Suppose Mydeco had purchased additional equipment for $12 million at the end of 2010, and this equipment was depreciated by $4 million per year in 2011, 2012, and 2013. Given Mydeco's tax rate of 35%, what impact would this additional purchase have had on Mydeco's net income in years 2010–2013? (Assume the equipment is paid for out of cash and that Mydeco earns no interest on its cash balances.)

16. See Table 2.5 showing financial statement data and share price data for Mydeco Corp. Suppose Mydeco's costs and expenses had been the same fraction of revenues in 2010–2013 as they were in 2009. What would Mydeco's EPS have been each year in this case?

17. Suppose a firm's tax rate is 35%.
    a. What effect would a $10 million operating expense have on this year's earnings? What effect would it have on next year's earnings?
    b. What effect would a $10 million capital expense have on this year's earnings if the capital is depreciated at a rate of $2 million per year for five years? What effect would it have on next year's earnings?

*18. Quisco Systems has 6.5 billion shares outstanding and a share price of $18. Quisco is considering developing a new networking product in house at a cost of $500 million. Alternatively, Quisco can acquire a firm that already has the technology for $900 million worth (at the current price) of Quisco stock. Suppose that without the expense of the new technology, Quisco will have EPS of $0.80.
    a. Suppose Quisco develops the product in house. What impact would the development cost have on Quisco's EPS? Assume all costs are incurred this year and are treated as an R&D expense, Quisco's tax rate is 35%, and the number of shares outstanding is unchanged.
    b. Suppose Quisco does not develop the product in house but instead acquires the technology. What effect would the acquisition have on Quisco's EPS this year? (Note that acquisition expenses do not appear directly on the income statement. Assume the firm was acquired at the start of the year and has no revenues or expenses of its own, so that the only effect on EPS is due to the change in the number of shares outstanding.)

c. Which method of acquiring the technology has a smaller impact on earnings? Is this method cheaper? Explain.

The Statement of Cash Flows

19. Find online the annual report for Peet's Coffee and Tea (PEET) for fiscal year 2011 (filed in January 2012). Answer the following questions from their cash flow statement:

a. How much cash did Peet's generate from operating activities in fiscal year 2011?

b. What was Peet's total depreciation and amortization expense?

c. How much cash was invested in new property and equipment (net of any sales)?

d. How much did Peet's raise from the sale of shares of its stock (net of any purchases)?

20. See Table 2.5 showing financial statement data and share price data for Mydeco Corp.

a. From 2009 to 2013, what was the total cash flow from operations that Mydeco generated?

b. What fraction of the total in (a) was spent on capital expenditures?

c. What fraction of the total in (a) was spent paying dividends to shareholders?

d. What was Mydeco's total retained earnings for this period?

21. See Table 2.5 showing financial statement data and share price data for Mydeco Corp.

a. In what year was Mydeco's net income the lowest?

b. In what year did Mydeco need to reduce its cash reserves?

c. Why did Mydeco need to reduce its cash reserves in a year when net income was reasonably high?

22. See Table 2.5 showing financial statement data and share price data for Mydeco Corp. Use the data from the balance sheet and cash flow statement in 2009 to determine the following:

a. How much cash did Mydeco have at the end of 2008?

b. What were Mydeco's accounts receivable and inventory at the end of 2008?

c. What were Mydeco's total liabilities at the end of 2008?

d. Assuming goodwill and intangibles were equal in 2008 and 2009, what was Mydeco's net property, plant, and equipment at the end of 2008?

23. Can a firm with positive net income run out of cash? Explain.

24. Suppose your firm receives a $5 million order on the last day of the year. You fill the order with $2 million worth of inventory. The customer picks up the entire order the same day and pays $1 million upfront in cash; you also issue a bill for the customer to pay the remaining balance of $4 million in 30 days. Suppose your firm's tax rate is 0% (i.e., ignore taxes). Determine the consequences of this transaction for each of the following:

a. Revenues   b. Earnings   c. Receivables   d. Inventory   e. Cash

25. Nokela Industries purchases a $40 million cyclo-converter. The cyclo-converter will be depreciated by $10 million per year over four years, starting this year. Suppose Nokela's tax rate is 40%.

a. What impact will the cost of the purchase have on earnings for each of the next four years?

b. What impact will the cost of the purchase have on the firm's cash flow for the next four years?

Other Financial Statement Information

26. See Table 2.5 showing financial statement data and share price data for Mydeco Corp.

a. What were Mydeco's retained earnings each year?

b. Using the data from 2009, what was Mydeco's total shareholders' equity in 2008?

27. Find online the annual report for Peet's Coffee and Tea (PEET) for fiscal year 2011 (filed in January 2012). Answer the following questions from the notes to their financial statements:

a. What was Peet's inventory of green coffee at the end of 2011?

b. What property does Peet's lease? What are the minimum lease payments due in 2012?

c. What was the fair value of all share-based compensation Peet's granted to employees in 2011? How many share options did Peet's have outstanding at the end of 2011?

d. What fraction of Peet's 2011 sales came from specialty sales rather than its retail stores? What fraction came from coffee and tea products?

Financial Statement Analysis

28. See Table 2.5 showing financial statement data and share price data for Mydeco Corp.
   a. What were Mydeco's gross margins each year?
   b. Comparing Mydeco's gross margin, EBIT margin, and net profit margin in 2009 and 2013, which margins improved?

29. In fiscal year 2011, Starbucks Corporation (SBUX) had revenue of $11.70 billion, gross profit of $6.75 billion, and net income of $1.25 billion. Peet's Coffee and Tea (PEET) had revenue of $372 million, gross profit of $72.7 million, and net income of $17.8 million.
   a. Compare the gross margins for Starbucks and Peet's.
   b. Compare the net profit margins for Starbucks and Peet's.
   c. Which firm was more profitable in 2011?

30. In mid-2012, Apple had cash and short-term investments of $27.65 billion, accounts receivable of $14.30 billion, current assets of $51.94 billion, and current liabilities of $33.06 billion.
   a. What was Apple's current ratio?
   b. What was Apple's quick ratio?
   c. What was Apple's cash ratio?
   d. In mid-2012, Dell had a cash ratio of 0.67, a quick ratio of 1.11 and a current ratio of 1.35. What can you say about the asset liquidity of Apple relative to Dell?

31. See Table 2.5 showing financial statement data and share price data for Mydeco Corp.
   a. How did Mydeco's accounts receivable days change over this period?
   b. How did Mydeco's inventory days change over this period?
   c. Based on your analysis, has Mydeco improved its management of its working capital during this time period?

32. See Table 2.5 showing financial statement data and share price data for Mydeco Corp.
   a. Compare Mydeco's accounts payable days in 2009 and 2013.
   b. Did this change in accounts payable days improve or worsen Mydeco's cash position in 2013?

33. See Table 2.5 showing financial statement data and share price data for Mydeco Corp.
   a. By how much did Mydeco increase its debt from 2009 to 2013?
   b. What was Mydeco's EBITDA/Interest coverage ratio in 2009 and 2013? Did its coverage ratio ever fall below 2?
   c. Overall, did Mydeco's ability to meet its interest payments improve or decline over this period?

34. See Table 2.5 showing financial statement data and share price data for Mydeco Corp.
   a. How did Mydeco's book debt-equity ratio change from 2009 to 2013?
   b. How did Mydeco's market debt-equity ratio change from 2009 to 2013?
   c. Compute Mydeco's debt-to-enterprise value ratio to assess how the fraction of its business that is debt financed has changed over the period.

35. Use the data in Problem 8 to determine the change, from 2009 to 2012, in GE's
   a. book debt-equity ratio.   b. market debt-equity ratio.

36. You are analyzing the leverage of two firms and you note the following (all values in millions of dollars):

	Debt	Book Equity	Market Equity	EBIT	Interest Expense
Firm A	500	300	400	100	50
Firm B	80	35	40	8	7

   a. What is the market debt-to-equity ratio of each firm?
   b. What is the book debt-to-equity ratio of each firm?
   c. What is the EBIT/interest coverage ratio of each firm?
   d. Which firm may have more difficulty meeting its debt obligations? Explain.

37. See Table 2.5 showing financial statement data and share price data for Mydeco Corp.
    a. Compute Mydeco's PE ratio each year from 2009 to 2013. In which year was it the highest?
    b. What was Mydeco's Enterprise Value to EBITDA ratio each year? In which year was it the highest?
    c. What might explain the differing time pattern of the two valuation ratios?

38. In mid-2012, United Airlines (UAL) had a market capitalization of $6.8 billion, debt of $12.4 billion, and cash of $7.3 billion. United also had annual revenues of $37.4 billion. Southwest Airlines (LUV) had a market capitalization of $6.6 billion, debt of $3.3 billion, cash of $3.3 billion, and annual revenues of $17.0 billion.
    a. Compare the market capitalization-to-revenue ratio (also called the price-to-sales ratio) for United Airlines and Southwest Airlines.
    b. Compare the enterprise value-to-revenue ratio for United Airlines and Southwest Airlines.
    c. Which of these comparisons is more meaningful? Explain.

39. See Table 2.5 showing financial statement data and share price data for Mydeco Corp.
    a. Compute Mydeco's ROE each year from 2009 to 2013.
    b. Compute Mydeco's ROA each year from 2009 to 2013.
    c. Which return is more volatile? Why?

40. See Table 2.5 showing financial statement data and share price data for Mydeco Corp. Was Mydeco able to improve its ROIC in 2013 relative to what it was in 2009?

41. For fiscal year 2011, Peet's Coffee and Tea (PEET) had a net profit margin of 4.78%, asset turnover of 1.73, and a book equity multiplier of 1.21.
    a. Use this data to compute Peet's ROE using the DuPont Identity.
    b. If Peet's managers wanted to increase its ROE by one percentage point, how much higher would their asset turnover need to be?
    c. If Peet's net profit margin fell by one percentage point, by how much would their asset turn-over need to increase to maintain their ROE?

42. For fiscal year 2011, Starbucks Corporation (SBUX) had total revenues of $11.70 billion, net income of $1.25 billion, total assets of $7.36 billion, and total shareholder's equity of $4.38 billion.
    a. Calculate the Starbucks' ROE directly, and using the DuPont Identity.
    b. Comparing with the data for Peet's in Problem 41, use the DuPont Identity to understand the difference between the two firms' ROEs.

43. Consider a retailing firm with a net profit margin of 3.5%, a total asset turnover of 1.8, total assets of $44 million, and a book value of equity of $18 million.
    a. What is the firm's current ROE?
    b. If the firm increased its net profit margin to 4%, what would be its ROE?
    c. If, in addition, the firm increased its revenues by 20% (while maintaining this higher profit margin and without changing its assets or liabilities), what would be its ROE?

Financial Reporting in Practice

44. Find online the annual report for Peet's Coffee and Tea (PEET) for fiscal year 2011 (filed in January 2012).
    a. Which auditing firm certified these financial statements?
    b. Which officers of Peet's certified the financial statements?

45. WorldCom reclassified $3.85 billion of operating expenses as capital expenditures. Explain the effect this reclassification would have on WorldCom's cash flows. (*Hint*: Consider taxes.) WorldCom's actions were illegal and clearly designed to deceive investors. But if a firm could legitimately choose how to classify an expense for tax purposes, which choice is truly better for the firm's investors?

Data Case

This is your second interview with a prestigious brokerage firm for a job as an equity analyst. You survived the morning interviews with the department manager and the Vice President of Equity. Everything has gone so well that they want to test your ability as an analyst. You are seated in a room with a computer and a list with the names of two companies—Ford (F) and Microsoft (MSFT). You have 90 minutes to complete the following tasks:

1. Download the annual income statements, balance sheets, and cash flow statements for the last four fiscal years from MarketWatch (www.marketwatch.com). Enter each company's stock symbol and then go to "financials." Export the statements to Excel by right-clicking while the cursor is inside each statement.

2. Find historical share prices for each firm from Yahoo! Finance (http://finance.yahoo.com). Enter your stock symbol, click "Historical Prices" in the left column, and enter the proper date range to cover the last day of the month corresponding to the date of each financial statement. Use the closing share prices (not the adjusted close). To calculate the firm's market capitalization at each date, multiply the number of shares outstanding (see "Basic Shares Outstanding" on the income statement) by the firm's historic share price.

3. For each of the four years of statements, compute the following ratios for each firm:

   Valuation Ratios
   Price-Earnings Ratio (for EPS use Diluted EPS Total)
   Market-to-Book Ratio
   Enterprise Value-to-EBITDA
   (For debt, include long-term and short-term debt; for cash, include marketable securities.)

   Profitability Ratios
   Operating Margin (Use Operating Income after Depreciation)
   Net Profit Margin
   Return on Equity

   Financial Strength Ratios
   Current Ratio
   Book Debt-Equity Ratio
   Market Debt-Equity Ratio
   Interest Coverage Ratio (EBIT ÷ Interest Expense)

4. Obtain industry averages for each firm from Reuters.com (http://www.reuters.com/finance/stocks). Enter the stock symbol on top of the page in the "Symbol lookup" and then click the "Financials" button.
   a. Compare each firm's ratios to the available industry ratios for the most recent year. (Ignore the "Company" column as your calculations will be different.)
   b. Analyze the performance of each firm versus the industry and comment on any trends in each individual firm's performance. Identify any strengths or weaknesses you find in each firm.

5. Examine the Market-to-Book ratios you calculated for each firm. Which, if any, of the two firms can be considered "growth firms" and which, if any, can be considered "value firms"?

6. Compare the valuation ratios across the two firms. How do you interpret the difference between them?

7. Consider the enterprise value of each firm for each of the four years. How have the values of each firm changed over the time period?

Financial Decision Making and the Law of One Price

I N MID-2007, MICROSOFT DECIDED TO ENTER A BIDDING WAR with competitors Google and Yahoo! for a stake in the fast-growing social networking site, Facebook. How did Microsoft's managers decide that this was a good decision?

Every decision has future consequences that will affect the value of the firm. These consequences will generally include both benefits and costs. For example, after raising its offer, Microsoft ultimately succeeded in buying a 1.6% stake in Facebook, along with the right to place banner ads on the Facebook Web site, for $240 million. In addition to the upfront cost of $240 million, Microsoft also incurred ongoing costs associated with software development for the platform, network infrastructure, and international marketing efforts to attract advertisers. The benefits of the deal to Microsoft included the revenues associated with the advertising sales, together with the appreciation of its 1.6% stake in Facebook. In the end, Microsoft's decision appeared to be a good one—in addition to advertising benefits, by the time of Facebook's IPO in May 2012, the value of Microsoft's 1.6% stake had grown to over $1 billion.

More generally, a decision is good for the firm's investors if it increases the firm's value by providing benefits whose value exceeds the costs. But comparing costs and benefits is often complicated because they occur at different points in time, may be in different currencies, or may have different risks associated with them. To make a valid comparison, we must use the tools of finance to express all costs and benefits in common terms. In this chapter, we introduce a central principle of finance, which we name the *Valuation Principle*, which states that we can use current market prices to determine the value today of the costs and benefits associated with a decision. This principle allows us to apply the concept of *net present value (NPV)* as a way to compare the costs and benefits of a project in terms of a common unit—namely, dollars today. We will then be able to evaluate a decision by answering this question: *Does the cash value today of its benefits exceed the cash value today of its costs?* In addition, we will see that the NPV indicates the net amount by which the decision will increase wealth.

We then turn to financial markets and apply these same tools to determine the prices of securities that trade in the market. We discuss strategies called *arbitrage*, which allow us to exploit situations in which the prices of publicly available investment opportunities do not conform to these values. Because investors trade rapidly to take advantage of arbitrage opportunities, we argue that equivalent investment opportunities trading simultaneously in competitive markets must have the same price. This *Law of One Price* is the unifying theme of valuation that we use throughout this text.

3.1 Valuing Decisions

A financial manager's job is to make decisions on behalf of the firm's investors. For example, when faced with an increase in demand for the firm's products, a manager may need to decide whether to raise prices or increase production. If the decision is to raise production and a new facility is required, is it better to rent or purchase the facility? If the facility will be purchased, should the firm pay cash or borrow the funds needed to pay for it?

In this book, our objective is to explain how to make decisions that increase the value of the firm to its investors. In principle, the idea is simple and intuitive: For good decisions, the benefits exceed the costs. Of course, real-world opportunities are usually complex and so the costs and benefits are often difficult to quantify. The analysis will often involve skills from other management disciplines, as in these examples:

Marketing: to forecast the increase in revenues resulting from an advertising campaign

Accounting: to estimate the tax savings from a restructuring

Economics: to determine the increase in demand from lowering the price of a product

Organizational Behavior: to estimate the productivity gains from a change in management structure

Strategy: to predict a competitor's response to a price increase

Operations: to estimate the cost savings from a plant modernization

For the remainder of this text, we assume that the analysis of these other disciplines has been completed to quantify the costs and benefits associated with a decision. With that task done, the financial manager must compare the costs and benefits and determine the best decision to make for the value of the firm.

Analyzing Costs and Benefits

The first step in decision making is to identify the costs and benefits of a decision. The next step is to quantify these costs and benefits. In order to compare the costs and benefits, we need to evaluate them in the same terms—cash today. Let's make this concrete with a simple example.

Suppose a jewelry manufacturer has the opportunity to trade 400 ounces of silver for 10 ounces of gold today. Because an ounce of gold differs in value from an ounce of silver, it is incorrect to compare 400 ounces to 10 ounces and conclude that the larger quantity is better. Instead, to compare the costs and benefits, we first need to quantify their values in equivalent terms.

Consider the silver. What is its cash value today? Suppose silver can be bought and sold for a current market price of $15 per ounce. Then the 400 ounces of silver we give up has a cash value of[1]

$$(400 \text{ ounces of silver today}) \times (\$15/\text{ounce of silver today}) = \$6000 \text{ today}$$

If the current market price for gold is $900 per ounce, then the 10 ounces of gold we receive has a cash value of

$$(10 \text{ ounces of gold today}) \times (\$900/\text{ounce of gold today}) = \$9000 \text{ today}$$

Now that we have quantified the costs and benefits in terms of a common measure of value, cash today, we can compare them. The jeweler's opportunity has a benefit of $9000 today and a cost of $6000 today, so the net value of the decision is $9000 − $6000 = $3000 today. By accepting the trade, the jewelry firm will be richer by $3000.

Using Market Prices to Determine Cash Values

In evaluating the jeweler's decision, we used the current market price to convert from ounces of silver or gold to dollars. We did not concern ourselves with whether the jeweler thought that the price was fair or whether the jeweler would use the silver or gold. Do such considerations matter? Suppose, for example, that the jeweler does not need the gold, or thinks the current price of gold is too high. Would he value the gold at less than $9000? The answer is no—he can always sell the gold at the current market price and receive $9000 right now. Similarly, he would not value the gold at more than $9000, because even if he really needs the gold or thinks the current price of gold is too low, he can always buy 10 ounces of gold for $9000. Thus, independent of his own views or preferences, the value of the gold to the jeweler is $9000.

This example illustrates an important general principle: Whenever a good trades in a **competitive market**—by which we mean a market in which it can be bought *and* sold at the same price—that price determines the cash value of the good. As long as a competitive market exists, the value of the good will not depend on the views or preferences of the decision maker.

EXAMPLE 3.1   **Competitive Market Prices Determine Value**

Problem
You have just won a radio contest and are disappointed to find out that the prize is four tickets to the Def Leppard reunion tour (face value $40 each). Not being a fan of 1980s power rock, you have no intention of going to the show. However, there is a second choice: two tickets to your favorite band's sold-out show (face value $45 each). You notice that on eBay, tickets to the Def Leppard show are being bought and sold for $30 apiece and tickets to your favorite band's show are being bought and sold at $50 each. Which prize should you choose?

---

[1]You might worry about commissions or other transactions costs that are incurred when buying or selling gold, in addition to the market price. For now, we will ignore transactions costs, and discuss their effect in the appendix to this chapter.

Solution

Competitive market prices, not your personal preferences (nor the face value of the tickets), are relevant here:

Four Def Leppard tickets at $30 apiece = $120 market value

Two of your favorite band's tickets at $50 apiece = $100 market value

Instead of taking the tickets to your favorite band, you should accept the Def Leppard tickets, sell them on eBay, and use the proceeds to buy two tickets to your favorite band's show. You'll even have $20 left over to buy a T-shirt.

Thus, by evaluating cost and benefits using competitive market prices, we can determine whether a decision will make the firm and its investors wealthier. This point is one of the central and most powerful ideas in finance, which we call the **Valuation Principle**:

The value of an asset to the firm or its investors is determined by its competitive market price. The benefits and costs of a decision should be evaluated using these market prices, and when the value of the benefits exceeds the value of the costs, the decision will increase the market value of the firm.

The Valuation Principle provides the basis for decision making throughout this text. In the remainder of this chapter, we first apply it to decisions whose costs and benefits occur at different points in time and develop the main tool of project evaluation, the *Net Present Value Rule*. We then consider its consequences for the prices of assets in the market and develop the concept of the *Law of One Price*.

EXAMPLE 3.2   **Applying the Valuation Principle**

Problem

You are the operations manager at your firm. Due to a pre-existing contract, you have the opportunity to acquire 200 barrels of oil and 3000 pounds of copper for a total of $12,000. The current competitive market price of oil is $50 per barrel and for copper is $2 per pound. You are not sure you need all of the oil and copper, and are concerned that the value of both commodities may fall in the future. Should you take this opportunity?

Solution

To answer this question, you need to convert the costs and benefits to their cash values using market prices:

$$(200 \text{ barrels of oil}) \times (\$50/\text{barrel of oil today}) = \$10,000 \text{ today}$$

$$(3000 \text{ pounds of copper}) \times (\$2/\text{pound of copper today}) = \$6000 \text{ today}$$

The net value of the opportunity is $10,000 + $6000 − $12,000 = $4000 today. Because the net value is positive, you should take it. This value depends only on the *current* market prices for oil and copper. Even if you do not need all the oil or copper, or expect their values to fall, you can sell them at current market prices and obtain their value of $16,000. Thus, the opportunity is a good one for the firm, and will increase its value by $4000.

When Competitive Market Prices Are Not Available

Competitive market prices allow us to calculate the value of a decision without worrying about the tastes or opinions of the decision maker. When competitive prices are not available, we can no longer do this. Prices at retail stores, for example, are one sided: You can buy at the posted price, but you cannot sell the good to the store at that same price. We cannot use these one-sided prices to determine an exact cash value. They determine the maximum value of the good (since it can always be purchased at that price), but an individual may value it for much less depending on his or her preferences for the good.

Let's consider an example. It has long been common for banks to entice new depositors by offering free gifts for opening a new account. In 2012, ThinkForex offered a free

iPad 3 for individuals opening a new account. At the time, the retail price of that model iPad was $539. But because there is no competitive market to trade iPads, the value of the iPad depends on whether you were going to buy one or not.

If you planned to buy the iPad anyway, then the value to you is $539, the price you would otherwise pay for it. But if you did not want or need the iPad, the value of the offer would depend on the price you could get for the iPad. For example, if you could sell the iPad for $450 to your friend, then ThinkForex's offer is worth $450 to you. Thus, depending on your preferences, ThinkForex's offer is worth somewhere between $450 (you don't want an iPad) and $539 (you definitely want one).

CONCEPT CHECK

1. In order to compare the costs and benefits of a decision, what must we determine?

2. If crude oil trades in a competitive market, would an oil refiner that has a use for the oil value it differently than another investor?

3.2 Interest Rates and the Time Value of Money

For most financial decisions, unlike in the examples presented so far, costs and benefits occur at different points in time. For example, typical investment projects incur costs upfront and provide benefits in the future. In this section, we show how to account for this time difference when evaluating a project.

The Time Value of Money

Consider an investment opportunity with the following certain cash flows:

Cost: $100,000 today

Benefit: $105,000 in one year

Because both are expressed in dollar terms, it might appear that the cost and benefit are directly comparable so that the project's net value is $105,000 − $100,000 = $5000. But this calculation ignores the timing of the costs and benefits, and it treats money today as equivalent to money in one year.

In general, a dollar today is worth more than a dollar in one year. If you have $1 today, you can invest it. For example, if you deposit it in a bank account paying 7% interest, you will have $1.07 at the end of one year. We call the difference in value between money today and money in the future the **time value of money**.

The Interest Rate: An Exchange Rate Across Time

By depositing money into a savings account, we can convert money today into money in the future with no risk. Similarly, by borrowing money from the bank, we can exchange money in the future for money today. The rate at which we can exchange money today for money in the future is determined by the current interest rate. In the same way that an exchange rate allows us to convert money from one currency to another, the interest rate allows us to convert money from one point in time to another. In essence, an interest rate is like an exchange rate across time. It tells us the market price today of money in the future.

Suppose the current annual interest rate is 7%. By investing or borrowing at this rate, we can exchange $1.07 in one year for each $1 today. More generally, we define the **risk-free interest rate**, r_f, for a given period as the interest rate at which money can be borrowed or lent without risk over that period. We can exchange $(1 + r_f)$ dollars in the future per dollar today, and vice versa, without risk. We refer to $(1 + r_f)$ as the **interest rate factor** for risk-free cash flows; it defines the exchange rate across time, and has units of "$ in one year/$ today."

As with other market prices, the risk-free interest rate depends on supply and demand. In particular, at the risk-free interest rate the supply of savings equals the demand for borrowing. After we know the risk-free interest rate, we can use it to evaluate other decisions in which costs and benefits are separated in time without knowing the investor's preferences.

Value of Investment in One Year. Let's reevaluate the investment we considered earlier, this time taking into account the time value of money. If the interest rate is 7%, then we can express our costs as

$$\text{Cost} = (\$100{,}000 \text{ today}) \times (1.07 \text{ \$ in one year/\$ today})$$
$$= \$107{,}000 \text{ in one year}$$

Think of this amount as the opportunity cost of spending $100,000 today: We give up the $107,000 we would have had in one year if we had left the money in the bank. Alternatively, if we were to borrow the $100,000, we would owe $107,000 in one year.

Both costs and benefits are now in terms of "dollars in one year," so we can compare them and compute the investment's net value:

$$\$105{,}000 - \$107{,}000 = -\$2000 \text{ in one year}$$

In other words, we could earn $2000 more in one year by putting our $100,000 in the bank rather than making this investment. We should reject the investment: If we took it, we would be $2000 poorer in one year than if we didn't.

Value of Investment Today. The previous calculation expressed the value of the costs and benefits in terms of dollars in one year. Alternatively, we can use the interest rate factor to convert to dollars today. Consider the benefit of $105,000 in one year. What is the equivalent amount in terms of dollars today? That is, how much would we need to have in the bank today so that we would end up with $105,000 in the bank in one year? We find this amount by dividing by the interest rate factor:

$$\text{Benefit} = (\$105{,}000 \text{ in one year}) \div (1.07 \text{ \$ in one year/\$ today})$$
$$= \$105{,}000 \times \frac{1}{1.07} \text{ today}$$
$$= \$98{,}130.84 \text{ today}$$

This is also the amount the bank would lend to us today if we promised to repay $105,000 in one year.[2] Thus, it is the competitive market price at which we can "buy" or "sell" $105,000 in one year.

---

[2]We are assuming the bank will both borrow and lend at the risk-free interest rate. We discuss the case when these rates differ in "Arbitrage with Transactions Costs" in the appendix to this chapter.

Now we are ready to compute the net value of the investment:

$$\$98,130.84 - \$100,000 = -\$1869.16 \text{ today}$$

Once again, the negative result indicates that we should reject the investment. Taking the investment would make us $1869.16 poorer today because we have given up $100,000 for something worth only $98,130.84.

Present Versus Future Value. This calculation demonstrates that our decision is the same whether we express the value of the investment in terms of dollars in one year or dollars today: We should reject the investment. Indeed, if we convert from dollars today to dollars in one year,

$$(-\$1869.16 \text{ today}) \times (1.07 \text{ \$ in one year/\$ today}) = -\$2000 \text{ in one year}$$

we see that the two results are equivalent, but expressed as values at different points in time. When we express the value in terms of dollars today, we call it the **present value (PV)** of the investment. If we express it in terms of dollars in the future, we call it the **future value (FV)** of the investment.

Discount Factors and Rates. When computing a present value as in the preceding calculation, we can interpret the term

$$\frac{1}{1+r} = \frac{1}{1.07} = 0.93458 \text{ \$ today/\$ in one year}$$

as the *price* today of $1 in one year. Note that the value is less than $1—money in the future is worth less today, and so its price reflects a discount. Because it provides the discount at which we can purchase money in the future, the amount $\frac{1}{1+r}$ is called the one-year **discount factor**. The risk-free interest rate is also referred to as the **discount rate** for a risk-free investment.

EXAMPLE 3.3   **Comparing Costs at Different Points in Time**

Problem

The cost of rebuilding the San Francisco Bay Bridge to make it earthquake-safe was approximately $3 billion in 2004. At the time, engineers estimated that if the project were delayed to 2005, the cost would rise by 10%. If the interest rate were 2%, what would be the cost of a delay in terms of dollars in 2004?

Solution

If the project were delayed, it would cost $3 billion × (1.10) = $3.3 billion in 2005. To compare this amount to the cost of $3 billion in 2004, we must convert it using the interest rate of 2%:

$$\$3.3 \text{ billion in 2005} \div (\$1.02 \text{ in 2005/\$ in 2004}) = \$3.235 \text{ billion in 2004}$$

Therefore, the cost of a delay of one year was

$$\$3.235 \text{ billion} - \$3 \text{ billion} = \$235 \text{ million in 2004}$$

That is, delaying the project for one year was equivalent to giving up $235 million in cash.

We can use the risk-free interest rate to determine values in the same way we used competitive market prices. Figure 3.1 illustrates how we use competitive market prices, exchange rates, and interest rates to convert between dollars today and other goods, currencies, or dollars in the future.

FIGURE 3.1

Converting between Dollars Today and Gold, Euros, or Dollars in the Future

We can convert dollars today to different goods, currencies, or points in time by using the competitive market price, exchange rate, or interest rate.

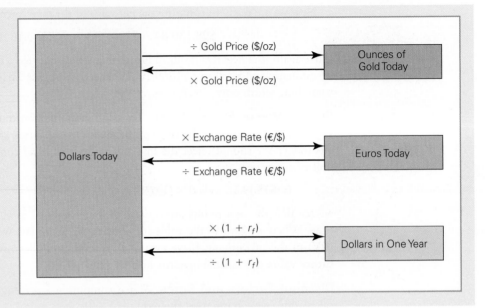

CONCEPT CHECK

1. How do you compare costs at different points in time?

2. If interest rates rise, what happens to the value *today* of a promise of money in one year?

3.3 Present Value and the NPV Decision Rule

In Section 3.2, we converted between cash today and cash in the future using the risk-free interest rate. As long as we convert costs and benefits to the same point in time, we can compare them to make a decision. In practice, however, most corporations prefer to measure values in terms of their present value—that is, in terms of cash today. In this section we apply the Valuation Principle to derive the concept of the *net present value*, or *NPV*, and define the "golden rule" of financial decision making, the *NPV Rule*.

Net Present Value

When we compute the value of a cost or benefit in terms of cash today, we refer to it as the present value (PV). Similarly, we define the **net present value (NPV)** of a project or investment as the difference between the present value of its benefits and the present value of its costs:

Net Present Value

$$NPV = PV(\text{Benefits}) - PV(\text{Costs}) \qquad (3.1)$$

If we use positive cash flows to represent benefits and negative cash flows to represent costs, and calculate the present value of multiple cash flows as the sum of present values for individual cash flows, we can also write this definition as

$$NPV = PV(\text{All project cash flows}) \qquad (3.2)$$

That is, the NPV is the total of the present values of all project cash flows.

Let's consider a simple example. Suppose your firm is offered the following investment opportunity: In exchange for $500 today, you will receive $550 in one year with certainty. If the risk-free interest rate is 8% per year then

$$PV\,(\text{Benefit}) = (\$550 \text{ in one year}) \div (1.08 \text{ \$ in one year/\$ today})$$
$$= \$509.26 \text{ today}$$

This PV is the amount we would need to put in the bank today to generate $550 in one year ($509.26 × 1.08 = $550). In other words, *the present value is the cash cost today of "doing it yourself"—it is the amount you need to invest at the current interest rate to recreate the cash flow.*

Once the costs and benefits are in present value terms, we can compute the investment's NPV:

$$NPV = \$509.26 - \$500 = \$9.26 \text{ today}$$

But what if your firm doesn't have the $500 needed to cover the initial cost of the project? Does the project still have the same value? Because we computed the value using competitive market prices, it should not depend on your tastes or the amount of cash your firm has in the bank. If your firm doesn't have the $500, it could borrow $509.26 from the bank at the 8% interest rate and then take the project. What are your cash flows in this case?

Today: $509.26 (loan) − $500 (invested in the project) = $9.26
In one year: $550 (from project) − $509.26 × 1.08 (loan balance) = $0

This transaction leaves you with exactly $9.26 extra cash today and no future net obligations. So taking the project is like having an extra $9.26 in cash up front. Thus, the NPV expresses the value of an investment decision as an amount of cash received today. *As long as the NPV is positive, the decision increases the value of the firm and is a good decision regardless of your current cash needs or preferences regarding when to spend the money.*

The NPV Decision Rule

Because NPV is expressed in terms of cash today, it simplifies decision making. As long as we have correctly captured all of the costs and benefits of the project, decisions with a positive NPV will increase the wealth of the firm and its investors. We capture this logic in the **NPV Decision Rule**:

When making an investment decision, take the alternative with the highest NPV. Choosing this alternative is equivalent to receiving its NPV in cash today.

Accepting or Rejecting a Project. A common financial decision is whether to accept or reject a project. Because rejecting the project generally has NPV = 0 (there are no new costs or benefits from not doing the project), the NPV decision rule implies that we should

- Accept those projects with positive NPV because accepting them is equivalent to receiving their NPV in cash today, and

- Reject those projects with negative NPV; accepting them would reduce the wealth of investors, whereas not doing them has no cost (NPV = 0).

If the NPV is exactly zero, you will neither gain nor lose by accepting the project rather than rejecting it. It is not a bad project because it does not reduce firm value, but it does not increase value either.

| EXAMPLE 3.4 | The NPV Is Equivalent to Cash Today |

Problem

Your firm needs to buy a new $9500 copier. As part of a promotion, the manufacturer has offered to let you pay $10,000 in one year, rather than pay cash today. Suppose the risk-free interest rate is 7% per year. Is this offer a good deal? Show that its NPV represents cash in your pocket.

Solution

If you take the offer, the benefit is that you won't have to pay $9500 today, which is already in PV terms. The cost, however, is $10,000 in one year. We therefore convert the cost to a present value at the risk-free interest rate:

$$PV(\text{Cost}) = (\$10{,}000 \text{ in one year}) \div (1.07 \text{ \$ in one year/\$ today}) = \$9345.79 \text{ today}$$

The NPV of the promotional offer is the difference between the benefits and the costs:

$$NPV = \$9500 - \$9345.79 = \$154.21 \text{ today}$$

The NPV is positive, so the investment is a good deal. It is equivalent to getting a cash discount today of $154.21, and only paying $9345.79 today for the copier. To confirm our calculation, suppose you take the offer and invest $9345.79 in a bank paying 7% interest. With interest, this amount will grow to $9345.79 \times 1.07 = \$10{,}000$ in one year, which you can use to pay for the copier.

Choosing among Alternatives. We can also use the NPV decision rule to choose among projects. To do so, we must compute the NPV of each alternative, and then select the one with the highest NPV. This alternative is the one that will lead to the largest increase in the value of the firm.

| EXAMPLE 3.5 | Choosing among Alternative Plans |

Problem

Suppose you started a Web site hosting business and then decided to return to school. Now that you are back in school, you are considering selling the business within the next year. An investor has offered to buy the business for $200,000 whenever you are ready. If the interest rate is 10%, which of the following three alternatives is the best choice?

1. Sell the business now.
2. Scale back the business and continue running it while you are in school for one more year, and then sell the business (requiring you to spend $30,000 on expenses now, but generating $50,000 in profit at the end of the year).
3. Hire someone to manage the business while you are in school for one more year, and then sell the business (requiring you to spend $50,000 on expenses now, but generating $100,000 in profit at the end of the year).

Solution

The cash flows and NPVs for each alternative are calculated in Table 3.1. Faced with these three alternatives, the best choice is the one with highest NPV: Hire a manager and sell in one year. Choosing this alternative is equivalent to receiving $222,727 today.

TABLE 3.1	Cash Flows and NPVs for Web Site Business Alternatives		

	Today	In One Year	NPV
Sell Now	$200,000	0	$200,000
Scale Back Operations	−$30,000	$50,000 $200,000	$-30,000 + \dfrac{\$250,000}{1.10} = \$197,273$
Hire a Manager	−$50,000	$100,000 $200,000	$-50,000 + \dfrac{\$300,000}{1.10} = \$222,727$

NPV and Cash Needs

When we compare projects with different patterns of present and future cash flows, we may have preferences regarding when to receive the cash. Some may need cash today; others may prefer to save for the future. In the Web site hosting business example, hiring a manager and selling in one year has the highest NPV. However, this option requires an initial outlay of $50,000, as opposed to selling the business and receiving $200,000 immediately. Suppose you need $60,000 in cash now to pay for school and other expenses. Would selling the business be a better choice in that case?

As was true for the jeweler considering trading silver for gold in Section 3.1, the answer is again no. As long as you can borrow and lend at the 10% interest rate, hiring a manager is the best choice whatever your preferences regarding the timing of the cash flows. To see why, suppose you borrow $110,000 at the rate of 10% and hire the manager. Then you will owe $110,000 \times 1.10 = $121,000$ in one year, for total cash flows shown in Table 3.2. Compare these cash flows with those from selling now, and investing the excess $140,000 (which, at the rate of 10%, will grow to $140,000 \times 1.10 = $154,000$ in one year). Both strategies provide $60,000 in cash today, but the combination of hiring a manager and borrowing generates an additional $179,000 − $154,000 = $25,000 in one year.[3] Thus, even if you need $60,000 now, hiring the manager and selling in one year is still the best option.

TABLE 3.2	Cash Flows of Hiring and Borrowing Versus Selling and Investing	

	Today	In One Year
Hire a Manager	−$50,000	$300,000
Borrow	$110,000	−$121,000
Total Cash Flow	$60,000	$179,000
Versus		
Sell Now	$200,000	$0
Invest	−$140,000	$154,000
Total Cash Flow	$60,000	$154,000

---

[3]Note also that the present value of this additional cash flow, $25,000 ÷ 1.10 = $22,727, is exactly the difference in NPVs between the two alternatives.

This example illustrates the following general principle:

Regardless of our preferences for cash today versus cash in the future, we should always maximize NPV first. We can then borrow or lend to shift cash flows through time and find our most preferred pattern of cash flows.

<table>
<tr><td>CONCEPT CHECK</td><td>1. What is the NPV decision rule?</td></tr>
<tr><td></td><td>2. Why doesn't the NPV decision rule depend on the investor's preferences?</td></tr>
</table>

3.4 Arbitrage and the Law of One Price

So far, we have emphasized the importance of using competitive market prices to compute the NPV. But is there always only one such price? What if the same good trades for different prices in different markets? Consider gold. Gold trades in many different markets, with the largest markets in New York and London. To value an ounce of gold we could look up the competitive price in either of these markets. But suppose gold is trading for $850 per ounce in New York and $900 per ounce in London. Which price should we use?

Fortunately, such situations do not arise, and it is easy to see why. Recall that these are competitive market prices at which you can both buy *and* sell. Thus, you can make money in this situation simply by buying gold for $850 per ounce in New York and then immediately selling it for $900 per ounce in London.[4] You will make $900 − $850 = $50 per ounce for each ounce you buy and sell. Trading 1 million ounces at these prices, you would make $50 million with no risk or investment! This is a case where that old adage, "Buy low, sell high," can be followed perfectly.

Of course, you will not be the only one making these trades. Everyone who sees these prices will want to trade as many ounces as possible. Within seconds, the market in New York would be flooded with buy orders, and the market in London would be flooded with sell orders. Although a few ounces (traded by the lucky individuals who spotted this opportunity first) might be exchanged at these prices, the price of gold in New York would quickly rise in response to all the orders, and the price in London would rapidly fall.[5] Prices would continue to change until they were equalized somewhere in the middle, such as $875 per ounce.

Arbitrage

The practice of buying and selling equivalent goods in different markets to take advantage of a price difference is known as **arbitrage**. More generally, we refer to any situation in which it is possible to make a profit without taking any risk or making any investment as an **arbitrage opportunity**. Because an arbitrage opportunity has a positive NPV, whenever an arbitrage opportunity appears in financial markets, investors will race to take advantage

---

[4]There is no need to transport the gold from New York to London because investors in these markets trade ownership rights to gold that is stored securely elsewhere.

[5]As economists would say, supply would not equal demand in these markets. In New York, demand would be infinite because everyone would want to buy. For equilibrium to be restored so that supply equals demand, the price in New York would have to rise. Similarly, in London there would be infinite supply until the price there fell.

NASDAQ SOES Bandits

The NASDAQ stock market differs from other markets such as the NYSE in that it includes multiple dealers who all trade the same stock. For example, on a given day, as many as ten or more dealers may post prices at which they are willing to trade Apple Computer stock (AAPL). The NASDAQ also has a Small Order Execution System (SOES) that allows individual investors to execute trades directly with a market maker instantly through an electronic system.

When SOES was first launched in the late 1980s, a type of trader referred to as a "SOES bandit" emerged. These traders watched the quotes of different dealers, waiting for arbitrage opportunities to arise. For example, if one dealer was offering to sell AAPL at $580.25 and another was willing to buy at $580.30, the SOES bandit could profit by instantly buying 1000 shares at $580.25 from the first dealer and selling 1000 shares at $580.30 to the second dealer. Such a trade would yield an arbitrage profit of $1000 \times \$0.05 = \$50$.

In the past, by making trades like this one many times per day, these traders could make a reasonable amount of money. Before long, the activity of these traders forced dealers to monitor their own quotes much more actively so as to avoid being "picked off" by these bandits. Today, this sort of arbitrage opportunity rarely appears.*

*See J. Harris and P. Schultz, "The Trading Profits of SOES Bandits," *Journal of Financial Economics* 50(2), (October 1998): 39–62.

of it. Those investors who spot the opportunity first and who can trade quickly will have the ability to exploit it. Once they place their trades, prices will respond, causing the arbitrage opportunity to evaporate.

Arbitrage opportunities are like money lying in the street; once spotted, they will quickly disappear. Thus the normal state of affairs in markets should be that no arbitrage opportunities exist. We call a competitive market in which there are no arbitrage opportunities a **normal market**.[6]

Law of One Price

In a normal market, the price of gold at any point in time will be the same in London and New York. The same logic applies more generally whenever equivalent investment opportunities trade in two different competitive markets. If the prices in the two markets differ, investors will profit immediately by buying in the market where it is cheap and selling in the market where it is expensive. In doing so, they will equalize the prices. As a result, prices will not differ (at least not for long). This important property is the **Law of One Price**:

> *If equivalent investment opportunities trade simultaneously in different competitive markets, then they must trade for the same price in both markets.*

One useful consequence of the Law of One Price is that when evaluating costs and benefits to compute a net present value, we can use any competitive price to determine a cash value, without checking the price in all possible markets.

CONCEPT CHECK

1. If the Law of One Price were violated, how could investors profit?

2. When investors exploit an arbitrage opportunity, how do their actions affect prices?

---

[6]The term *efficient market* is also sometimes used to describe a market that, along with other properties, is without arbitrage opportunities. We avoid the term because it is often vaguely (and inconsistently) defined.

3.5 No-Arbitrage and Security Prices

An investment opportunity that trades in a financial market is known as a **financial security** (or, more simply, a **security**). The notions of arbitrage and the Law of One Price have important implications for security prices. We begin exploring its implications for the prices of individual securities as well as market interest rates. We then broaden our perspective to value a package of securities. Along the way, we will develop some important insights about firm decision making and firm value that will underpin our study throughout this textbook.

Valuing a Security with the Law of One Price

The Law of One Price tells us that the prices of equivalent investment opportunities should be the same. We can use this idea to value a security if we can find another equivalent investment whose price is already known. Consider a simple security that promises a one-time payment to its owner of $1000 in one year's time. Suppose there is no risk that the payment will not be made. One example of this type of security is a **bond**, a security sold by governments and corporations to raise money from investors today in exchange for the promised future payment. If the risk-free interest rate is 5%, what can we conclude about the price of this bond in a normal market?

To answer this question, consider an alternative investment that would generate the same cash flow as this bond. Suppose we invest money at the bank at the risk-free interest rate. How much do we need to invest today to receive $1000 in one year? As we saw in Section 3.3, the cost today of recreating a future cash flow on our own is its present value:

$$PV (\$1000 \text{ in one year}) = (\$1000 \text{ in one year}) \div (1.05 \text{ \$ in one year/\$ today})$$
$$= \$952.38 \text{ today}$$

If we invest $952.38 today at the 5% risk-free interest rate, we will have $1000 in one year's time with no risk.

We now have two ways to receive the same cash flow: (1) buy the bond or (2) invest $952.38 at the 5% risk-free interest rate. Because these transactions produce equivalent cash flows, the Law of One Price implies that, in a normal market, they must have the same price (or cost). Therefore,

$$\text{Price (Bond)} = \$952.38$$

An Old Joke

There is an old joke that many finance professors enjoy telling their students. It goes like this:

A finance professor and a student are walking down a street. The student notices a $100 bill lying on the pavement and leans down to pick it up. The finance professor immediately intervenes and says, "Don't bother; there is no free lunch. If that were a real $100 bill lying there, somebody would already have picked it up!"

This joke invariably generates much laughter because it makes fun of the principle of no arbitrage in competitive markets. But once the laughter dies down, the professor then asks whether anyone has ever *actually* found a real $100 bill lying on the pavement. The ensuing silence is the real lesson behind the joke.

This joke sums up the point of focusing on markets in which no arbitrage opportunities exist. Free $100 bills lying on the pavement, like arbitrage opportunities, are extremely rare for two reasons: (1) Because $100 is a large amount of money, people are especially careful not to lose it, and (2) in the rare event when someone does inadvertently drop $100, the likelihood of your finding it before someone else does is extremely small.

TABLE 3.3	Net Cash Flows from Buying the Bond and Borrowing	
	Today ($)	**In One Year ($)**
Buy the bond	−940.00	+1000.00
Borrow from the bank	+952.38	−1000.00
Net cash flow	+12.38	0.00

Identifying Arbitrage Opportunities with Securities. Recall that the Law of One Price is based on the possibility of arbitrage: If the bond had a different price, there would be an arbitrage opportunity. For example, suppose the bond traded for a price of $940. How could we profit in this situation?

In this case, we can buy the bond for $940 and at the same time borrow $952.38 from the bank. Given the 5% interest rate, we will owe the bank $952.38 × 1.05 = $1000 in one year. Our overall cash flows from this pair of transactions are as shown in Table 3.3. Using this strategy we can earn $12.38 in cash today for each bond that we buy, without taking any risk or paying any of our own money in the future. Of course, as we—and others who see the opportunity—start buying the bond, its price will quickly rise until it reaches $952.38 and the arbitrage opportunity disappears.

A similar arbitrage opportunity arises if the bond price is higher than $952.38. For example, suppose the bond is trading for $960. In that case, we should sell the bond and invest $952.38 at the bank. As shown in Table 3.4, we then earn $7.62 in cash today, yet keep our future cash flows unchanged by replacing the $1000 we would have received from the bond with the $1000 we will receive from the bank. Once again, as people begin selling the bond to exploit this opportunity, the price will fall until it reaches $952.38 and the arbitrage opportunity disappears.

When the bond is overpriced, the arbitrage strategy involves selling the bond and investing some of the proceeds. But if the strategy involves selling the bond, does this mean that only the current owners of the bond can exploit it? The answer is no; in financial markets it is possible to sell a security you do not own by doing a *short sale*. In a **short sale**, the person who intends to sell the security first borrows it from someone who already owns it. Later, that person must either return the security by buying it back or pay the owner the cash flows he or she would have received. For example, we could short sell the bond in the example effectively promising to repay the current owner $1000 in one year. By executing a short sale, it is possible to exploit the arbitrage opportunity when the bond is overpriced even if you do not own it.

TABLE 3.4	Net Cash Flows from Selling the Bond and Investing	
	Today ($)	**In One Year ($)**
Sell the bond	+960.00	−1000.00
Invest at the bank	−952.38	+1000.00
Net cash flow	+7.62	0.00

EXAMPLE 3.6	**Computing the No-Arbitrage Price**

Problem

Consider a security that pays its owner $100 today and $100 in one year, without any risk. Suppose the risk-free interest rate is 10%. What is the no-arbitrage price of the security today (before the first $100 is paid)? If the security is trading for $195, what arbitrage opportunity is available?

Solution

We need to compute the present value of the security's cash flows. In this case there are two cash flows: $100 today, which is already in present value terms, and $100 in one year. The present value of the second cash flow is

$$\$100 \text{ in one year} \div (1.10 \ \$ \text{ in one year}/\$ \text{ today}) = \$90.91 \text{ today}$$

Therefore, the total present value of the cash flows is $100 + $90.91 = $190.91 today, which is the no-arbitrage price of the security.

   If the security is trading for $195, we can exploit its overpricing by selling it for $195. We can then use $100 of the sale proceeds to replace the $100 we would have received from the security today and invest $90.91 of the sale proceeds at 10% to replace the $100 we would have received in one year. The remaining $195 − $100 − $90.91 = $4.09 is an arbitrage profit.

Determining the No-Arbitrage Price. We have shown that at any price other than $952.38, an arbitrage opportunity exists for our bond. Thus, in a normal market, the price of this bond must be $952.38. We call this price the **no-arbitrage price** for the bond.

   By applying the reasoning for pricing the simple bond, we can outline a general process for pricing other securities:

1. Identify the cash flows that will be paid by the security.

2. Determine the "do-it-yourself" cost of replicating those cash flows on our own; that is, the present value of the security's cash flows.

Unless the price of the security equals this present value, there is an arbitrage opportunity. Thus, the general formula is

No-Arbitrage Price of a Security

$$\text{Price(Security)} = PV(\text{All cash flows paid by the security}) \tag{3.3}$$

Determining the Interest Rate from Bond Prices. Given the risk-free interest rate, the no-arbitrage price of a risk-free bond is determined by Eq. 3.3. The reverse is also true: If we know the price of a risk-free bond, we can use Eq. 3.3 to determine what the risk-free interest rate must be if there are no arbitrage opportunities.

   For example, suppose a risk-free bond that pays $1000 in one year is currently trading with a competitive market price of $929.80 today. From Eq. 3.3, we know that the bond's price equals the present value of the $1000 cash flow it will pay:

$$\$929.80 \text{ today} = (\$1000 \text{ in one year}) \div (1 + r_f)$$

We can rearrange this equation to determine the risk-free interest rate:

$$1 + r_f = \frac{\$1000 \text{ in one year}}{\$929.80 \text{ today}} = 1.0755 \ \$ \text{ in one year}/\$ \text{ today}$$

That is, if there are no arbitrage opportunities, the risk-free interest rate must be 7.55%.

Interest rates are calculated by this method in practice. Financial news services report current interest rates by deriving these rates based on the current prices of risk-free government bonds trading in the market.

Note that the risk-free interest rate equals the percentage gain that you earn from investing in the bond, which is called the bond's **return**:

$$\text{Return} = \frac{\text{Gain at End of Year}}{\text{Initial Cost}}$$

$$= \frac{1000 - 929.80}{929.80} = \frac{1000}{929.80} - 1 = 7.55\% \qquad (3.4)$$

Thus, if there is no arbitrage, the risk-free interest rate is equal to the return from investing in a risk-free bond. If the bond offered a higher return than the risk-free interest rate, then investors would earn a profit by borrowing at the risk-free interest rate and investing in the bond. If the bond had a lower return than the risk-free interest rate, investors would sell the bond and invest the proceeds at the risk-free interest rate. No arbitrage is therefore equivalent to the idea that *all risk-free investments should offer investors the same return.*

The NPV of Trading Securities and Firm Decision Making

We have established that positive-NPV decisions increase the wealth of the firm and its investors. Think of buying a security as an investment decision. The cost of the decision is the price we pay for the security, and the benefit is the cash flows that we will receive from owning the security. When securities trade at no-arbitrage prices, what can we conclude about the value of trading them? From Eq. 3.3, the cost and benefit are equal in a normal market and so the NPV of buying a security is zero:

$$NPV \,(\text{Buy security}) = PV \,(\text{All cash flows paid by the security}) - \text{Price (Security)}$$
$$= 0$$

Similarly, if we sell a security, the price we receive is the benefit and the cost is the cash flows we give up. Again the NPV is zero:

$$NPV \,(\text{Sell security}) = \text{Price (Security)} - PV \,(\text{All cash flows paid by the security})$$
$$= 0$$

Thus, the NPV of trading a security in a normal market is zero. This result is not surprising. If the NPV of buying a security were positive, then buying the security would be equivalent to receiving cash today—that is, it would present an arbitrage opportunity. Because arbitrage opportunities do not exist in normal markets, the NPV of all security trades must be zero.

Another way to understand this result is to remember that every trade has both a buyer and a seller. In a competitive market, if a trade offers a positive NPV to one party, it must give a negative NPV to the other party. But then one of the two parties would not agree to the trade. Because all trades are voluntary, they must occur at prices at which neither party is losing value, and therefore for which the trade is zero NPV.

The insight that security trading in a normal market is a zero-NPV transaction is a critical building block in our study of corporate finance. Trading securities in a normal market neither creates nor destroys value: Instead, value is created by the real investment projects in which the firm engages, such as developing new products, opening new stores, or creating more efficient production methods. Financial transactions are not sources of value but instead serve to adjust the timing and risk of the cash flows to best suit the needs of the firm or its investors.

An important consequence of this result is the idea that we can evaluate a decision by focusing on its real components, rather than its financial ones. That is, we can separate the firm's investment decision from its financing choice. We refer to this concept as the **Separation Principle**:

> *Security transactions in a normal market neither create nor destroy value on their own. Therefore, we can evaluate the NPV of an investment decision separately from the decision the firm makes regarding how to finance the investment or any other security transactions the firm is considering.*

EXAMPLE 3.7	Separating Investment and Financing

Problem

Your firm is considering a project that will require an upfront investment of $10 million today and will produce $12 million in cash flow for the firm in one year without risk. Rather than pay for the $10 million investment entirely using its own cash, the firm is considering raising additional funds by issuing a security that will pay investors $5.5 million in one year. Suppose the risk-free interest rate is 10%. Is pursuing this project a good decision without issuing the new security? Is it a good decision with the new security?

Solution

Without the new security, the cost of the project is $10 million today and the benefit is $12 million in one year. Converting the benefit to a present value

$$\$12 \text{ million in one year} \div (1.10 \ \$ \text{ in one year}/\$ \text{ today}) = \$10.91 \text{ million today}$$

we see that the project has an NPV of $10.91 million − $10 million = $0.91 million today.

Now suppose the firm issues the new security. In a normal market, the price of this security will be the present value of its future cash flow:

$$\text{Price(Security)} = \$5.5 \text{ million} \div 1.10 = \$5 \text{ million today}$$

Thus, after it raises $5 million by issuing the new security, the firm will only need to invest an additional $5 million to take the project.

To compute the project's NPV in this case, note that in one year the firm will receive the $12 million payout of the project, but owe $5.5 million to the investors in the new security, leaving $6.5 million for the firm. This amount has a present value of

$$\$6.5 \text{ million in one year} \div (1.10 \ \$ \text{ in one year}/\$ \text{ today}) = \$5.91 \text{ million today}$$

Thus, the project has an NPV of $5.91 million − $5 million = $0.91 million today, as before.

In either case, we get the same result for the NPV. The separation principle indicates that we will get the same result for any choice of financing for the firm that occurs in a normal market. We can therefore evaluate the project without explicitly considering the different financing possibilities the firm might choose.

Valuing a Portfolio

So far, we have discussed the no-arbitrage price for individual securities. The Law of One Price also has implications for packages of securities. Consider two securities, A and B.

Stock Index Arbitrage

Value additivity is the principle behind a type of trading activity known as stock index arbitrage. Common stock indices (such as the Dow Jones Industrial Average and the Standard and Poor's 500) represent portfolios of individual stocks. It is possible to trade the individual stocks in an index on the New York Stock Exchange and NASDAQ. It is also possible to trade the entire index (as a single security) on the futures exchanges in Chicago, or as an exchange-traded fund (ETF) on the NYSE. When the price of the index security is below the total price of the individual stocks, traders buy the index and sell the stocks to capture the price difference. Similarly, when the price of the index security is above the total price of the individual stocks, traders sell the index and buy the individual stocks. The investment banks that engage in stock index arbitrage automate the process by tracking the prices and submitting the orders via computer; as a result, this activity is also referred to as "program trading." It is not uncommon for 20% to 30% of the daily volume of trade on the NYSE to be due to index arbitrage activity via program trading.* The actions of these arbitrageurs ensure that the prices of the index securities and the individual stock prices track each other very closely.

*See http://usequities.nyx.com/markets/program-trading

Suppose a third security, C, has the same cash flows as A and B combined. In this case, security C is equivalent to a combination of the securities A and B. We use the term **portfolio** to describe a collection of securities. What can we conclude about the price of security C as compared to the prices of A and B?

Value Additivity. Because security C is equivalent to the portfolio of A and B, by the Law of One Price, they must have the same price. This idea leads to the relationship known as **value additivity**; that is, the price of C must equal the price of the portfolio, which is the combined price of A and B:

Value Additivity

$$\text{Price(C)} = \text{Price(A + B)} = \text{Price(A)} + \text{Price(B)} \tag{3.5}$$

Because security C has cash flows equal to the sum of A and B, its value or price must be the sum of the values of A and B. Otherwise, an obvious arbitrage opportunity would exist. For example, if the total price of A and B were lower than the price of C, then we could make a profit buying A and B and selling C. This arbitrage activity would quickly push prices until the price of security C equals the total price of A and B.

| EXAMPLE 3.8 | Valuing an Asset in a Portfolio |

Problem

Holbrook Holdings is a publicly traded company with only two assets: It owns 60% of Harry's Hotcakes restaurant chain and an ice hockey team. Suppose the market value of Holbrook Holdings is $160 million, and the market value of the entire Harry's Hotcakes chain (which is also publicly traded) is $120 million. What is the market value of the hockey team?

Solution

We can think of Holbrook as a portfolio consisting of a 60% stake in Harry's Hotcakes and the hockey team. By value additivity, the sum of the value of the stake in Harry's Hotcakes and the hockey team must equal the $160 million market value of Holbrook. Because the 60% stake in Harry's Hotcakes is worth 60% × $120 million = $72 million, the hockey team has a value of $160 million − $72 million = $88 million.

GLOBAL FINANCIAL CRISIS   **Liquidity and the Informational Role of Prices**

In the first half of 2008, as the extent and severity of the decline in the housing market became apparent, investors became increasingly worried about the value of securities that were backed by residential home mortgages. As a result, the volume of trade in the multi-trillion dollar market for mortgage-backed securities plummeted over 80% by August 2008. Over the next two months, trading in many of these securities ceased altogether, making the markets for these securities increasingly illiquid.

Competitive markets depend upon liquidity—there must be sufficient buyers and sellers of a security so that it is possible to trade at any time at the current market price. When markets become illiquid it may not be possible to trade at the posted price. As a consequence, we can no longer rely on market prices as a measure of value.

The collapse of the mortgage-backed securities market created two problems. First was the loss of trading opportunities, making it difficult for holders of these securities to sell them. But a potentially more significant problem was the loss of *information*. Without a liquid, competitive market for these securities, it became impossible to reliably

value these securities. In addition, given that the value of the banks holding these securities was based on the sum of all projects and investments within them, investors could not value the banks either. Investors reacted to this uncertainty by selling both the mortgage-backed securities and securities of banks that held mortgage-backed securities. These actions further compounded the problem by driving down prices to seemingly unrealistically low levels and thereby threatening the solvency of the entire financial system.

The loss of information precipitated by the loss of liquidity played a key role in the breakdown of credit markets. As both investors and government regulators found it increasingly difficult to assess the solvency of the banks, banks found it difficult to raise new funds on their own and also shied away from lending to other banks because of their concerns about the financial viability of their competitors. The result was a breakdown in lending. Ultimately, the government was forced to step in and spend hundreds of billions of dollars in order to (1) provide new capital to support the banks and (2) provide liquidity by creating a market for the now "toxic" mortgage-backed securities.

More generally, value additivity implies that the value of a portfolio is equal to the sum of the values of its parts. That is, the "à la carte" price and the package price must coincide.[7]

Value Additivity and Firm Value. Value additivity has an important consequence for the value of an entire firm. The cash flows of the firm are equal to the total cash flows of all projects and investments within the firm. Therefore, by value additivity, the price or value of the entire firm is equal to the sum of the values of all projects and investments within it. In other words, our NPV decision rule coincides with maximizing the value of the entire firm:

> To maximize the value of the entire firm, managers should make decisions that maximize NPV. The NPV of the decision represents its contribution to the overall value of the firm.

Where Do We Go from Here?

The key concepts we have developed in this chapter—the Valuation Principle, Net Present Value, and the Law of One Price—provide the foundation for financial decision making.

---

[7]This feature of financial markets does not hold in many other *noncompetitive* markets. For example, a round-trip airline ticket often costs much less than two separate one-way tickets. Of course, airline tickets are not sold in a competitive market—you cannot buy *and* sell the tickets at the listed prices. Only airlines can sell tickets, and they have strict rules against reselling tickets. Otherwise, you could make money buying round-trip tickets and selling them to people who need one-way tickets.

The Law of One Price allows us to determine the value of stocks, bonds, and other securities, based on their cash flows, and validates the optimality of the NPV decision rule in identifying projects and investments that create value. In the remainder of the text, we will build on this foundation and explore the details of applying these principles in practice.

For simplicity, we have focused in this chapter on projects that were not risky, and thus had known costs and benefits. The same fundamental tools of the Valuation Principle and the Law of One Price can be applied to analyze risky investments as well, and we will look in detail at methods to assess and value risk in Part IV of the text. Those seeking some early insights and key foundations for this topic, however, are strongly encouraged to read the appendix to this chapter. There we introduce the idea that investors are risk averse, and then use the principle of no-arbitrage developed in this chapter to demonstrate two fundamental insights regarding the impact of risk on valuation:

1. When cash flows are risky, we must discount them at a rate equal to the risk-free interest rate plus an appropriate risk premium; and,

2. The appropriate risk premium will be higher the more the project's returns tend to vary with the overall risk in the economy.

Finally, the chapter appendix also addresses the important practical issue of transactions costs. There we show that when purchase and sale prices, or borrowing and lending rates differ, the Law of One Price will continue to hold, but only up to the level of transactions costs.

CONCEPT CHECK

1. If a firm makes an investment that has a positive NPV, how does the value of the firm change?
2. What is the separation principle?
3. In addition to trading opportunities, what else do liquid markets provide?

MyFinanceLab   Here is what you should know after reading this chapter. MyFinanceLab will help you identify what you know and where to go when you need to practice.

3.1 Valuing Decisions

- To evaluate a decision, we must value the incremental costs and benefits associated with that decision. A good decision is one for which the value of the benefits exceeds the value of the costs.
- To compare costs and benefits that occur at different points in time, in different currencies, or with different risks, we must put all costs and benefits in common terms. Typically, we convert costs and benefits into cash today.
- A competitive market is one in which a good can be bought and sold at the same price. We use prices from competitive markets to determine the cash value of a good.

3.2 Interest Rates and the Time Value of Money

- The time value of money is the difference in value between money today and money in the future. The rate at which we can exchange money today for money in the future by borrowing or investing is the current market interest rate. The risk-free interest rate, r_f, is the rate at which money can be borrowed or lent without risk.

3.3 Present Value and the NPV Decision Rule

- The present value (PV) of a cash flow is its value in terms of cash today.
- The net present value (NPV) of a project is

$$PV(\text{Benefits}) - PV(\text{Costs}) \qquad (3.1)$$

- A good project is one with a positive net present value. The NPV Decision Rule states that when choosing from among a set of alternatives, choose the one with the highest NPV. The NPV of a project is equivalent to the cash value today of the project.
- Regardless of our preferences for cash today versus cash in the future, we should always first maximize NPV. We can then borrow or lend to shift cash flows through time and to find our most preferred pattern of cash flows.

3.4 Arbitrage and the Law of One Price

- Arbitrage is the process of trading to take advantage of equivalent goods that have different prices in different competitive markets.
- A normal market is a competitive market with no arbitrage opportunities.
- The Law of One Price states that if equivalent goods or securities trade simultaneously in different competitive markets, they will trade for the same price in each market. This law is equivalent to saying that no arbitrage opportunities should exist.

3.5 No-Arbitrage and Security Prices

- The No-Arbitrage Price of a Security is

$$PV(\text{All cash flows paid by the security}) \qquad (3.3)$$

- No-arbitrage implies that all risk-free investments should offer the same return.
- The Separation Principle states that security transactions in a normal market neither create nor destroy value on their own. As a consequence, we can evaluate the NPV of an investment decision separately from the security transactions the firm is considering.
- To maximize the value of the entire firm, managers should make decisions that maximize the NPV. The NPV of the decision represents its contribution to the overall value of the firm.
- Value additivity implies that the value of a portfolio is equal to the sum of the values of its parts.

Key Terms

Further Reading

Many of the fundamental principles of this chapter were developed in the classic text by I. Fisher, *The Theory of Interest: As Determined by Impatience to Spend Income and Opportunity to Invest It* (Macmillan, 1930); reprinted (Augustus M. Kelley, 1955).

To learn more about the principle of no arbitrage and its importance as the foundation for modern finance theory, see S. Ross, *Neoclassical Finance* (Princeton University Press, 2004).

For a discussion of arbitrage and rational trading and their role in determining market prices, see M. Rubinstein, "Rational Markets: Yes or No? The Affirmative Case," *Financial Analysts Journal* (May/June 2001): 15–29.

For a discussion of some of the limitations to arbitrage that may arise in practice, see A. Shleifer and R. Vishny, "Limits of Arbitrage," *Journal of Finance*, 52 (1997): 35–55.

Problems   *All problems are available in* MyFinanceLab.

Valuing Decisions

1. Honda Motor Company is considering offering a $2000 rebate on its minivan, lowering the vehicle's price from $30,000 to $28,000. The marketing group estimates that this rebate will increase sales over the next year from 40,000 to 55,000 vehicles. Suppose Honda's profit margin with the rebate is $6000 per vehicle. If the change in sales is the only consequence of this decision, what are its costs and benefits? Is it a good idea?

2. You are an international shrimp trader. A food producer in the Czech Republic offers to pay you 2 million Czech koruna today in exchange for a year's supply of frozen shrimp. Your Thai supplier will provide you with the same supply for 3 million Thai baht today. If the current competitive market exchange rates are 25.50 koruna per dollar and 41.25 baht per dollar, what is the value of this deal?

3. Suppose the current market price of corn is $3.75 per bushel. Your firm has a technology that can convert 1 bushel of corn to 3 gallons of ethanol. If the cost of conversion is $1.60 per bushel, at what market price of ethanol does conversion become attractive?

4. Suppose your employer offers you a choice between a $5000 bonus and 100 shares of the company stock. Whichever one you choose will be awarded today. The stock is currently trading for $63 per share.
   a. Suppose that if you receive the stock bonus, you are free to trade it. Which form of the bonus should you choose? What is its value?
   b. Suppose that if you receive the stock bonus, you are required to hold it for at least one year. What can you say about the value of the stock bonus now? What will your decision depend on?

5. You have decided to take your daughter skiing in Utah. The best price you have been able to find for a roundtrip air ticket is $359. You notice that you have 20,000 frequent flier miles that are about to expire, but you need 25,000 miles to get her a free ticket. The airline offers to sell you 5000 additional miles for $0.03 per mile.
   a. Suppose that if you don't use the miles for your daughter's ticket they will become worthless. What should you do?
   b. What additional information would your decision depend on if the miles were not expiring? Why?

Interest Rates and the Time Value of Money

 6. Suppose the risk-free interest rate is 4%.
   a. Having $200 today is equivalent to having what amount in one year?
   b. Having $200 in one year is equivalent to having what amount today?
   c. Which would you prefer, $200 today or $200 in one year? Does your answer depend on when you need the money? Why or why not?

7. You have an investment opportunity in Japan. It requires an investment of $1 million today and will produce a cash flow of ¥ 114 million in one year with no risk. Suppose the risk-free interest rate in the United States is 4%, the risk-free interest rate in Japan is 2%, and the current competitive exchange rate is ¥ 110 per $1. What is the NPV of this investment? Is it a good opportunity?

8. Your firm has a risk-free investment opportunity where it can invest $160,000 today and receive $170,000 in one year. For what level of interest rates is this project attractive?

Present Value and the NPV Decision Rule

9. You run a construction firm. You have just won a contract to construct a government office building. It will take one year to construct it, requiring an investment of $10 million today and $5 million in one year. The government will pay you $20 million upon the building's completion. Suppose the cash flows and their times of payment are certain, and the risk-free interest rate is 10%.
   a. What is the NPV of this opportunity?
   b. How can your firm turn this NPV into cash today?

10. Your firm has identified three potential investment projects. The projects and their cash flows are shown here:

Project	Cash Flow Today ($)	Cash Flow in One Year ($)
A	−10	20
B	5	5
C	20	−10

Suppose all cash flows are certain and the risk-free interest rate is 10%.
   a. What is the NPV of each project?
   b. If the firm can choose only one of these projects, which should it choose?
   c. If the firm can choose any two of these projects, which should it choose?

11. Your computer manufacturing firm must purchase 10,000 keyboards from a supplier. One supplier demands a payment of $100,000 today plus $10 per keyboard payable in one year. Another supplier will charge $21 per keyboard, also payable in one year. The risk-free interest rate is 6%.
   a. What is the difference in their offers in terms of dollars today? Which offer should your firm take?
   b. Suppose your firm does not want to spend cash today. How can it take the first offer and not spend $100,000 of its own cash today?

Arbitrage and the Law of One Price

12. Suppose Bank One offers a risk-free interest rate of 5.5% on both savings and loans, and Bank Enn offers a risk-free interest rate of 6% on both savings and loans.
   a. What arbitrage opportunity is available?
   b. Which bank would experience a surge in the demand for loans? Which bank would receive a surge in deposits?
   c. What would you expect to happen to the interest rates the two banks are offering?

13. Throughout the 1990s, interest rates in Japan were lower than interest rates in the United States. As a result, many Japanese investors were tempted to borrow in Japan and invest the proceeds in the United States. Explain why this strategy does not represent an arbitrage opportunity.

14. An American Depositary Receipt (ADR) is security issued by a U.S. bank and traded on a U.S. stock exchange that represents a specific number of shares of a foreign stock. For example, Nokia Corporation trades as an ADR with symbol NOK on the NYSE. Each ADR represents one share of Nokia Corporation stock, which trades with symbol NOK1V on the Helsinki stock exchange. If the U.S. ADR for Nokia is trading for $17.96 per share, and Nokia stock is trading on the Helsinki exchange for 14.78 € per share, use the Law of One Price to determine the current $/€ exchange rate.

No-Arbitrage and Security Prices

 15. The promised cash flows of three securities are listed here. If the cash flows are risk-free, and the risk-free interest rate is 5%, determine the no-arbitrage price of each security before the first cash flow is paid.

Security	Cash Flow Today ($)	Cash Flow in One Year ($)
A	500	500
B	0	1000
C	1000	0

16. An Exchange-Traded Fund (ETF) is a security that represents a portfolio of individual stocks. Consider an ETF for which each share represents a portfolio of two shares of Hewlett-Packard (HPQ), one share of Sears (SHLD), and three shares of General Electric (GE). Suppose the current stock prices of each individual stock are as shown here:

Stock	Current Market Price
HPQ	$28
SHLD	$40
GE	$14

a. What is the price per share of the ETF in a normal market?

b. If the ETF currently trades for $120, what arbitrage opportunity is available? What trades would you make?

c. If the ETF currently trades for $150, what arbitrage opportunity is available? What trades would you make?

 17. Consider two securities that pay risk-free cash flows over the next two years and that have the current market prices shown here:

Security	Price Today ($)	Cash Flow in One Year ($)	Cash Flow in Two Years ($)
B1	94	100	0
B2	85	0	100

a. What is the no-arbitrage price of a security that pays cash flows of $100 in one year and $100 in two years?

b. What is the no-arbitrage price of a security that pays cash flows of $100 in one year and $500 in two years?

c. Suppose a security with cash flows of $50 in one year and $100 in two years is trading for a price of $130. What arbitrage opportunity is available?

18. Suppose a security with a risk-free cash flow of $150 in one year trades for $140 today. If there are no arbitrage opportunities, what is the current risk-free interest rate?

 19. Xia Corporation is a company whose sole assets are $100,000 in cash and three projects that it will undertake. The projects are risk-free and have the following cash flows:

Project	Cash Flow Today ($)	Cash Flow in One Year ($)
A	−20,000	30,000
B	−10,000	25,000
C	−60,000	80,000

Xia plans to invest any unused cash today at the risk-free interest rate of 10%. In one year, all cash will be paid to investors and the company will be shut down.

a. What is the NPV of each project? Which projects should Xia undertake and how much cash should it retain?

b. What is the total value of Xia's assets (projects and cash) today?

c. What cash flows will the investors in Xia receive? Based on these cash flows, what is the value of Xia today?

d. Suppose Xia pays any unused cash to investors today, rather than investing it. What are the cash flows to the investors in this case? What is the value of Xia now?

e. Explain the relationship in your answers to parts (b), (c), and (d).

CHAPTER 3
APPENDIX

NOTATION

r_s discount rate
for security s

The Price of Risk

Thus far we have considered only cash flows that have no risk. But in many settings, cash flows are risky. In this section, we examine how to determine the present value of a risky cash flow.

Risky Versus Risk-Free Cash Flows

Suppose the risk-free interest rate is 4% and that over the next year the economy is equally likely to strengthen or weaken. Consider an investment in a risk-free bond, and one in the stock market index (a portfolio of all the stocks in the market). The risk-free bond has no risk and will pay $1100 whatever the state of the economy. The cash flow from an investment in the market index, however, depends on the strength of the economy. Let's assume that the market index will be worth $1400 if the economy is strong but only $800 if the economy is weak. Table 3A.1 summarizes these payoffs.

In Section 3.5, we saw that the no-arbitrage price of a security is equal to the present value of its cash flows. For example, the price of the risk-free bond corresponds to the 4% risk-free interest rate:

$$\text{Price (Risk-free Bond)} = \text{PV (Cash Flows)}$$
$$= (\$1100 \text{ in one year}) \div (1.04 \text{ \$ in one year/\$ today})$$
$$= \$1058 \text{ today}$$

Now consider the market index. An investor who buys it today can sell it in one year for a cash flow of either $800 or $1400, with an average payoff of $\frac{1}{2}(\$800) + \frac{1}{2}(\$1400) = \$1100$. Although this average payoff is the same as the risk-free bond, the market index has a lower price today. It pays $1100 *on average*, but its actual cash flow is risky, so investors are only willing to pay $1000 for it today rather than $1058. What accounts for this lower price?

Risk Aversion and the Risk Premium

Intuitively, investors pay less to receive $1100 on average than to receive $1100 with certainty because they don't like risk. In particular, it seems likely that for most individuals, *the personal cost of losing a dollar in bad times is greater than the benefit of an extra dollar in good times*. Thus, the benefit from receiving an extra $300 ($1400 versus $1100) when the economy is strong is less important than the loss of $300 ($800 versus $1100) when the economy is weak. As a result, investors prefer to receive $1100 with certainty.

The notion that investors prefer to have a safe income rather than a risky one of the same average amount is called **risk aversion**. It is an aspect of an investor's preferences, and different investors may have different degrees of risk aversion. The more risk averse

TABLE 3A.1	Cash Flows and Market Prices (in $) of a Risk-Free Bond and an Investment in the Market Portfolio		
		Cash Flow in One Year	
Security	Market Price Today	Weak Economy	Strong Economy
Risk-free bond	1058	1100	1100
Market index	1000	800	1400

investors are, the lower the current price of the market index will be compared to a risk-free bond with the same average payoff.

Because investors care about risk, we cannot use the risk-free interest rate to compute the present value of a risky future cash flow. When investing in a risky project, investors will expect a return that appropriately compensates them for the risk. For example, investors who buy the market index for its current price of $1000 receive $1100 on average at the end of the year, which is an average gain of $100, or a 10% return on their initial investment. When we compute the return of a security based on the payoff we expect to receive on average, we call it the **expected return**:

$$\text{Expected return of a risky investment} = \frac{\text{Expected gain at end of year}}{\text{Initial cost}} \quad (3A.1)$$

Of course, although the expected return of the market index is 10%, its *actual* return will be higher or lower. If the economy is strong, the market index will rise to 1400, which represents a return of

$$\text{Market return if economy is strong} = (1400 - 1000)/1000 = 40\%$$

If the economy is weak, the index will drop to 800, for a return of

$$\text{Market return if economy is weak} = (800 - 1000)/1000 = -20\%$$

We can also calculate the 10% expected return by computing the average of these actual returns:

$$\tfrac{1}{2}(40\%) + \tfrac{1}{2}(-20\%) = 10\%$$

Thus, investors in the market index earn an expected return of 10% rather than the risk-free interest rate of 4% on their investment. The difference of 6% between these returns is called the market index's **risk premium**. The risk premium of a security represents the additional return that investors expect to earn to compensate them for the security's risk. Because investors are risk averse, the price of a risky security cannot be calculated by simply discounting its expected cash flow at the risk-free interest rate. Rather,

When a cash flow is risky, to compute its present value we must discount the cash flow we expect on average at a rate that equals the risk-free interest rate plus an appropriate risk premium.

The No-Arbitrage Price of a Risky Security

The risk premium of the market index is determined by investors' preferences toward risk. And in the same way we used the risk-free interest rate to determine the no-arbitrage price of other risk-free securities, we can use the risk premium of the market index to value other risky securities. For example, suppose some security "A" will pay investors $600 if the economy is strong and nothing if it is weak. Let's see how we can determine the market price of security A using the Law of One Price.

As shown in Table 3A.2, if we combine security A with a risk-free bond that pays $800 in one year, the cash flows of the portfolio in one year are identical to the cash flows of the market index. By the Law of One Price, the total market value of the bond and security A must equal $1000, the value of the market index. Given a risk-free interest rate of 4%, the market price of the bond is

$$(\$800 \text{ in one year}) \div (1.04 \ \$ \text{ in one year}/\$ \text{ today}) = \$769 \text{ today}$$

| TABLE 3A.2 | Determining the Market Price of Security A (cash flows in $) | | |

		Cash Flow in One Year	
Security	Market Price Today	Weak Economy	Strong Economy
Risk-free bond	769	800	800
Security A	?	0	600
Market index	1000	800	1400

Therefore, the initial market price of security A is $1000 − $769 = $231. If the price of security A were higher or lower than $231, then the value of the portfolio of the bond and security A would differ from the value of the market index, violating the Law of One Price and creating an arbitrage opportunity.

Risk Premiums Depend on Risk

Given an initial price of $231 and an expected payoff of $\frac{1}{2}(0) + \frac{1}{2}(600) = 300$, security A has an expected return of

$$\text{Expected return of security A} = \frac{300 - 231}{231} = 30\%$$

Note that this expected return exceeds the 10% expected return of the market portfolio. Investors in security A earn a risk premium of 30% − 4% = 26% over the risk-free interest rate, compared to a 6% risk premium for the market portfolio. Why are the risk premiums so different?

The reason for the difference becomes clear if we compare the actual returns for the two securities. When the economy is weak, investors in security A lose everything, for a return of −100%, and when the economy is strong, they earn a return of (600 − 231)/231 = 160%. In contrast, the market index loses 20% in a weak economy and gains 40% in a strong economy. Given its much more variable returns, it is not surprising that security A must pay investors a higher risk premium.

Risk Is Relative to the Overall Market

The example of security A suggests that the risk premium of a security will depend on how variable its returns are. But before drawing any conclusions, it is worth considering one further example.

| EXAMPLE 3A.1 | A Negative Risk Premium |

Problem

Suppose security B pays $600 if the economy is weak and $0 if the economy is strong. What are its no-arbitrage price, expected return, and risk premium?

Solution

If we combine the market index and security B together in a portfolio, we earn the same payoff as a risk-free bond that pays $1400, as shown in the following table (cash flows in $).

		Cash Flow in One Year	
Security	Market Price Today	Weak Economy	Strong Economy
Market index	1000	800	1400
Security B	?	600	0
Risk-free bond	1346	1400	1400

Because the market price of the risk-free bond is $1400 ÷ 1.04 = $1346 today, we can conclude from the Law of One Price that security B must have a market price of $1346 − 1000 = $346 today.

If the economy is weak, security B pays a return of (600 − 346)/346 = 73.4%. If the economy is strong, security B pays nothing, for a return of −100%. The expected return of security B is therefore $\frac{1}{2}(73.4\%) + \frac{1}{2}(-100\%) = -13.3\%$. Its risk premium is −13.3% − 4% = −17.3%; that is, security B pays investors 17.3% *less* on average than the risk-free interest rate.

The results for security B are quite striking. Looking at securities A and B in isolation, they seem very similar—both are equally likely to pay $600 or $0. Yet security A has a much lower market price than security B ($231 versus $346). In terms of returns, security A pays investors an expected return of 30%; security B pays −13.3%. Why are their prices and expected returns so different? And why would risk-averse investors be willing to buy a risky security with an expected return below the risk-free interest rate?

To understand this result, note that security A pays $600 when the economy is strong, and B pays $600 when the economy is weak. Recall that our definition of risk aversion is that investors value an extra dollar of income more in bad times than in good times. Thus, because security B pays $600 when the economy is weak and the market index performs poorly, it pays off when investors' wealth is low and they value money the most. In fact, security B is not really "risky" from an investor's point of view; rather, security B is an insurance policy against an economic decline. By holding security B together with the market index, we can eliminate our risk from market fluctuations. Risk-averse investors are willing to pay for this insurance by accepting a return below the risk-free interest rate.

This result illustrates an extremely important principle. The risk of a security cannot be evaluated in isolation. Even when a security's returns are quite variable, if the returns vary in a way that offsets other risks investors are holding, the security will reduce rather than increase investors' risk. As a result, risk can only be assessed relative to the other risks that investors face; that is,

> *The risk of a security must be evaluated in relation to the fluctuations of other investments in the economy. A security's risk premium will be higher the more its returns tend to vary with the overall economy and the market index. If the security's returns vary in the opposite direction of the market index, it offers insurance and will have a negative risk premium.*

Table 3A.3 compares the risk and risk premiums for the different securities we have considered thus far. For each security we compute the difference in its return when the economy is strong versus weak. Note that the risk premium for each security is proportional

TABLE 3A.3	Risk and Risk Premiums for Different Securities			
	Returns			
Security	Weak Economy	Strong Economy	Difference in Returns	Risk Premium
Risk-free bond	4%	4%	0%	0%
Market index	−20%	40%	60%	6%
Security A	−100%	160%	260%	26%
Security B	73%	−100%	−173%	−17.3%

to this difference, and the risk premium is negative when the returns vary in the opposite direction of the market.

Risk, Return, and Market Prices

We have shown that when cash flows are risky, we can use the Law of One Price to compute present values by constructing a portfolio that produces cash flows with identical risk. As shown in Figure 3A.1, computing prices in this way is equivalent to converting between cash flows today and the *expected* cash flows received in the future using a discount rate r_s that includes a risk premium appropriate for the investment's risk:

$$r_s = r_f + (\text{risk premium for investment } s) \qquad (3A.2)$$

For the simple setting considered here with only a single source of risk (the strength of the economy), we have seen that the risk premium of an investment depends on how its returns vary with the overall economy. In Part IV of the text, we show that this result holds for more general settings with many sources of risk and more than two possible states of the economy.

FIGURE 3A.1

Converting between Dollars Today and Dollars in One Year with Risk

When cash flows are risky, Eq. 3A.2 determines the expected return, r_s, that we can use to convert between prices or present values today and the expected cash flow in the future.

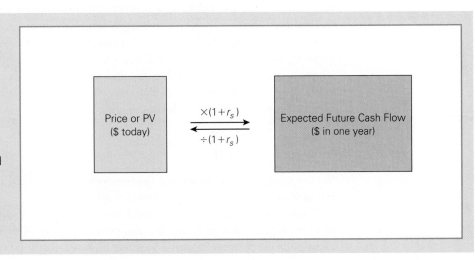

Price or PV ($ today)   ×(1+r_s) →   ← ÷(1+r_s)   Expected Future Cash Flow ($ in one year)

EXAMPLE 3A.2	**Using the Risk Premium to Compute a Price**

Problem

Consider a risky bond with a cash flow of $1100 when the economy is strong and $1000 when the economy is weak. Suppose a 1% risk premium is appropriate for this bond. If the risk-free interest rate is 4%, what is the price of the bond today?

Solution

From Eq. 3A.2, the appropriate discount rate for the bond is

$$r_b = r_f + (\text{Risk Premium for the Bond}) = 4\% + 1\% = 5\%$$

The expected cash flow of the bond is $\frac{1}{2}(\$1100) + \frac{1}{2}(\$1000) = \$1050$ in one year. Thus, the price of the bond today is

$$\text{Bond Price} = (\text{Average cash flow in one year}) \div (1 + r_b \ \$ \text{ in one year}/\$ \text{ today})$$
$$= (\$1050 \text{ in one year}) \div (1.05 \ \$ \text{ in one year}/\$ \text{ today})$$
$$= \$1000 \text{ today}$$

Given this price, the bond's return is 10% when the economy is strong, and 0% when the economy is weak. (Note that the difference in the returns is 10%, which is 1/6 as variable as the market index; see Table 3A.3. Correspondingly, the risk premium of the bond is 1/6 that of the market index as well.)

CONCEPT CHECK	1. Why does the expected return of a risky security generally differ from the risk-free interest rate? What determines the size of its risk premium?
	2. Explain why the risk of a security should not be evaluated in isolation.

Arbitrage with Transactions Costs

In our examples up to this point, we have ignored the costs of buying and selling goods or securities. In most markets, you must pay **transactions costs** to trade securities. As discussed in Chapter 1, when you trade securities in markets such as the NYSE and NASDAQ, you must pay two types of transactions costs. First, you must pay your broker a commission on the trade. Second, because you will generally pay a slightly higher price when you buy a security (the ask price) than you receive when you sell (the bid price), you will also pay the bid-ask spread. For example, a share of Dell Inc. stock (ticker symbol DELL) might be quoted as follows:

Bid: $12.50

Ask: $12.70

We can interpret these quotes as if the competitive price for DELL is $12.60, but there is a transaction cost of $0.10 per share when buying or selling.[8]

What consequence do these transactions costs have for no-arbitrage prices and the Law of One Price? Earlier we stated that the price of gold in New York and London must be identical in competitive markets. Suppose, however, that total transactions costs of $5 per

---

[8]Any price in between the bid price and the ask price could be the competitive price, with differing transaction costs for buying and selling.

ounce are associated with buying gold in one market and selling it in the other. Then if the price of gold is $1450 per ounce in New York and $1452 per ounce in London, the "Buy low, sell high" strategy no longer works:

Cost: $1450 per ounce (buy gold in New York) + $5 (transactions costs)

Benefit: $1452 per ounce (sell gold in London)

NPV: $1452 − $1450 − $5 = −$3 per ounce

Indeed, there is no arbitrage opportunity in this case until the prices diverge by more than $5, the amount of the transactions costs.

In general, we need to modify our previous conclusions about no-arbitrage prices by appending the phrase "up to transactions costs." In this example, there is only one competitive price for gold—up to a discrepancy of the $5 transactions cost. The other conclusions of this chapter have the same qualifier. The package price should equal the à la carte price, up to the transactions costs associated with packaging and unpackaging. The price of a security should equal the present value of its cash flows, up to the transactions costs of trading the security and the cash flows.

Fortunately, for most financial markets, these costs are small. For example, in 2012, typical bid-ask spreads for large NYSE stocks were between 2 and 5 cents per share. As a first approximation we can ignore these spreads in our analysis. Only in situations in which the NPV is small (relative to the transactions costs) will any discrepancy matter. In that case, we will need to carefully account for all transactions costs to decide whether the NPV is positive or negative.

EXAMPLE 3A.3	The No-Arbitrage Price Range

Problem

Consider a bond that pays $1000 at the end of the year. Suppose the market interest rate for deposits is 6%, but the market interest rate for borrowing is 6.5%. What is the no-arbitrage price *range* for the bond? That is, what is the highest and lowest price the bond could trade for without creating an arbitrage opportunity?

Solution

The no-arbitrage price for the bond equals the present value of the cash flows. In this case, however, the interest rate we should use depends on whether we are borrowing or lending. For example, the amount we would need to put in the bank today to receive $1000 in one year is

($1000 in one year) ÷ (1.06 $ in one year/$ today) = $943.40 today

where we have used the 6% interest rate that we will earn on our deposit. The amount that we can borrow today if we plan to repay $1000 in one year is

($1000 in one year) ÷ (1.065 $ in one year/$ today) = $938.97 today

where we have used the higher 6.5% rate that we will have to pay if we borrow.

Suppose the bond price P exceeded $943.40. Then you could profit by selling the bond at its current price and investing $943.40 of the proceeds at the 6% interest rate. You would still receive $1000 at the end of the year, but you would get to keep the difference $($P$ − 943.40) today. This arbitrage opportunity will keep the price of the bond from going higher than $943.40.

Alternatively, suppose the bond price P were less than $938.97. Then you could borrow $938.97 at 6.5% and use P of it to buy the bond. This would leave you with $(938.97 − P)

today, and no obligation in the future because you can use the $1000 bond payoff to repay the loan. This arbitrage opportunity will keep the price of the bond from falling below $938.97.

If the bond price P is between $938.97 and $943.40, then both of the preceding strategies will lose money, and there is no arbitrage opportunity. Thus no arbitrage implies a narrow range of possible prices for the bond ($938.97 to $943.40), rather than an exact price.

To summarize, when there are transactions costs, arbitrage keeps prices of equivalent goods and securities close to each other. Prices can deviate, but not by more than the transactions costs of the arbitrage.

CONCEPT CHECK

1. In the presence of transactions costs, why might different investors disagree about the value of an investment opportunity?

2. By how much could this value differ?

MyFinanceLab

Here is what you should know after reading this chapter. MyFinanceLab will help you identify what you know and where to go when you need to practice.

- When cash flows are risky, we cannot use the risk-free interest rate to compute present values. Instead, we can determine the present value by constructing a portfolio that produces cash flows with identical risk, and then applying the Law of One Price. Alternatively, we can discount the expected cash flows using a discount rate that includes an appropriate risk premium.
- The risk of a security must be evaluated in relation to the fluctuations of other investments in the economy. A security's risk premium will be higher the more its returns tend to vary with the overall economy and the market index. If the security's returns vary in the opposite direction of the market index, it offers insurance and will have a negative risk premium.
- When there are transactions costs, the prices of equivalent securities can deviate from each other, but not by more than the transactions costs of the arbitrage.

Key Terms

expected return *p. 86*
risk aversion *p. 85*
risk premium *p. 86*
transactions costs *p. 90*

Problems

Problems are available in MyFinanceLab. *An asterisk (*) indicates problems with a higher level of difficulty.*

Risky Versus Risk-Free Cash Flows

A.1. The table here shows the no-arbitrage prices of securities A and B that we calculated.

| Security | Market Price Today | Cash Flow in One Year | |
		Weak Economy	Strong Economy
Security A	231	0	600
Security B	346	600	0

a. What are the payoffs of a portfolio of one share of security A and one share of security B?

b. What is the market price of this portfolio? What expected return will you earn from holding this portfolio?

A.2. Suppose security C has a payoff of $600 when the economy is weak and $1800 when the economy is strong. The risk-free interest rate is 4%.
  a. Security C has the same payoffs as which portfolio of the securities A and B in Problem A.1?
  b. What is the no-arbitrage price of security C?
  c. What is the expected return of security C if both states are equally likely? What is its risk premium?
  d. What is the difference between the return of security C when the economy is strong and when it is weak?
  e. If security C had a risk premium of 10%, what arbitrage opportunity would be available?

*A.3.** You work for Innovation Partners and are considering creating a new security. This security would pay out $1000 in one year if the last digit in the closing value of the Dow Jones Industrial index in one year is an even number and zero if it is odd. The one-year risk-free interest rate is 5%. Assume that all investors are averse to risk.
  a. What can you say about the price of this security if it were traded today?
  b. Say the security paid out $1000 if the last digit of the Dow is odd and zero otherwise. Would your answer to part (a) change?
  c. Assume both securities (the one that paid out on even digits and the one that paid out on odd digits) trade in the market today. Would that affect your answers?

*A.4.** Suppose a risky security pays an expected cash flow of $80 in one year. The risk-free rate is 4%, and the expected return on the market index is 10%.
  a. If the returns of this security are high when the economy is strong and low when the economy is weak, but the returns vary by only half as much as the market index, what risk premium is appropriate for this security?
  b. What is the security's market price?

Arbitrage with Transactions Costs

A.5. Suppose Hewlett-Packard (HPQ) stock is currently trading on the NYSE with a bid price of $28.00 and an ask price of $28.10. At the same time, a NASDAQ dealer posts a bid price for HPQ of $27.85 and an ask price of $27.95.
  a. Is there an arbitrage opportunity in this case? If so, how would you exploit it?
  b. Suppose the NASDAQ dealer revises his quotes to a bid price of $27.95 and an ask price of $28.05. Is there an arbitrage opportunity now? If so, how would you exploit it?
  c. What must be true of the highest bid price and the lowest ask price for no arbitrage opportunity to exist?

*A.6.** Consider a portfolio of two securities: one share of Johnson and Johnson (JNJ) stock and a bond that pays $100 in one year. Suppose this portfolio is currently trading with a bid price of $141.65 and an ask price of $142.25, and the bond is trading with a bid price of $91.75 and an ask price of $91.95. In this case, what is the no-arbitrage price range for JNJ stock?

Time, Money, and Interest Rates

THE LAW OF ONE PRICE CONNECTION. For a financial manager, evaluating financial decisions involves computing the value of future cash flows. In Chapter 4, we use the Law of One Price to derive a central concept in financial economics—the *time value of money*. We explain how to value a stream of future cash flows and derive a few useful shortcuts for computing the net present value of various types of cash flow patterns. Chapter 5 considers how to use market interest rates to determine the appropriate discount rate for a set of cash flows. We apply the Law of One Price to demonstrate that the discount rate will depend on the rate of return of investments with maturity and risk similar to the cash flows being valued. This observation leads to the important concept of the *cost of capital* of an investment decision.

Firms raise the capital they need for investment by issuing securities. The simplest security they can issue is a bond. In Chapter 6 use the tools we developed thus far to explain how to value bonds. We will see that the Law of One Price allows us to link bond prices and their yields to the term structure of market interest rates.

The Time Value of Money

NOTATION

r interest rate

C cash flow

FV_n future value on date n

PV present value; annuity spreadsheet notation for the initial amount

C_n cash flow at date n

N date of the last cash flow in a stream of cash flows

NPV net present value

P initial principal or deposit, or equivalent present value

FV future value; annuity spreadsheet notation for an extra final payment

g growth rate

$NPER$ annuity spreadsheet notation for the number of periods or date of the last cash flow

$RATE$ annuity spreadsheet notation for interest rate

PMT annuity spreadsheet notation for cash flow

IRR internal rate of return

PV_n present value on date n

AS DISCUSSED IN CHAPTER 3, TO EVALUATE A PROJECT, A financial manager must compare its costs and benefits. In most cases, these costs and benefits are spread across time. For example, in September 2008, General Motors (GM) unveiled its plans to produce, starting in the 2011 model year, the Chevy Volt, an extended-range electric vehicle. GM's project involved significant upfront research and development costs, with revenues and expenses that will occur many years or even decades into the future. How can financial managers compare cost and benefits that occur over many years?

In order to evaluate a long-term project such as the Chevy Volt, we need tools that allow us to compare cash flows that occur at different points in time. We develop these tools in this chapter. The first tool is a visual method for representing a stream of cash flows: the timeline. After constructing a timeline, we establish three important rules for moving cash flows to different points in time. Using these rules, we show how to compute the present and future values of the costs and benefits of a general stream of cash flows. By converting all cash flows to a common point in time, these tools allow us to compare the costs and benefits of a long-term project, and thus assess its net present value, or NPV. The NPV expresses the net benefit of the project in terms of cash today.

While the general techniques developed in this chapter can be used to value any type of asset, certain types of assets have cash flows that follow a regular pattern. We develop shortcuts for valuing *annuities*, *perpetuities*, and other special cases of assets with cash flows that follow regular patterns.

4.1 The Timeline

We begin our look at valuing cash flows lasting several periods with some basic vocabulary and tools. We refer to a series of cash flows lasting several periods as a **stream of cash flows**. We can represent a stream of cash flows on a **timeline**, a linear representation of the timing of the expected cash flows. Timelines are an important first step in organizing and then solving a financial problem. We use them throughout this text.

To illustrate how to construct a timeline, assume that a friend owes you money. He has agreed to repay the loan by making two payments of $10,000 at the end of each of the next two years. We represent this information on a timeline as follows:

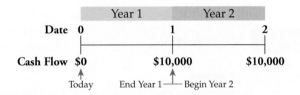

Date 0 represents the present. Date 1 is one year later and represents the end of the first year. The $10,000 cash flow below date 1 is the payment you will receive at the end of the first year. Date 2 is two years from now; it represents the end of the second year. The $10,000 cash flow below date 2 is the payment you will receive at the end of the second year.

To track cash flows on the timeline, interpret each point on the timeline as a specific date. The space between date 0 and date 1 then represents the time period between these dates—in this case, the first year of the loan. Date 0 is the beginning of the first year, and date 1 is the end of the first year. Similarly, date 1 is the beginning of the second year, and date 2 is the end of the second year. By denoting time in this way, date 1 signifies *both* the end of year 1 and the beginning of year 2, which makes sense since those dates are effectively the same point in time.[1]

In this example, both cash flows are inflows. In many cases, however, a financial decision will involve both inflows and outflows. To differentiate between the two types of cash flows, we assign a different sign to each: Inflows are positive cash flows, whereas outflows are negative cash flows.

To illustrate, suppose you're still feeling generous and have agreed to lend your brother $10,000 today. Your brother has agreed to repay this loan in two installments of $6000 at the end of each of the next two years. The timeline is as follows:

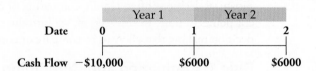

Notice that the first cash flow at date 0 (today) is represented as −$10,000 because it is an outflow. The subsequent cash flows of $6000 are positive because they are inflows.

---

[1]That is, there is no real time difference between a cash flow paid at 11:59 P.M. on December 31 and one paid at 12:01 A.M. on January 1, although there may be some other differences such as taxation that we overlook for now.

So far, we have used timelines to show the cash flows that occur at the end of each year. Actually, timelines can represent cash flows that take place at the end of any time period. For example, if you pay rent each month, you could use a timeline like the one in our first example to represent two rental payments, but you would replace the "year" label with "month."

Many of the timelines included in this chapter are very simple. Consequently, you may feel that it is not worth the time or trouble to construct them. As you progress to more difficult problems, however, you will find that timelines identify events in a transaction or investment that are easy to overlook. If you fail to recognize these cash flows, you will make flawed financial decisions. Therefore, we recommend that you approach *every* problem by drawing the timeline as we do in this chapter.

EXAMPLE 4.1   **Constructing a Timeline**

Problem
Suppose you must pay tuition of $10,000 per year for the next two years. Your tuition payments must be made in equal installments at the start of each semester. What is the timeline of your tuition payments?

Solution
Assuming today is the start of the first semester, your first payment occurs at date 0 (today). The remaining payments occur at semester intervals. Using one semester as the period length, we can construct a timeline as follows:

Date (Semesters)	0	1	2	3	4
Cash Flow	−$5000	−$5000	−$5000	−$5000	$0

CONCEPT CHECK   1. What are the key elements of a timeline?

2. How can you distinguish cash inflows from outflows on a timeline?

4.2 The Three Rules of Time Travel

Financial decisions often require comparing or combining cash flows that occur at different points in time. In this section, we introduce three important rules central to financial decision making that allow us to compare or combine values.

Rule 1: Comparing and Combining Values

Our first rule is that it is only possible to compare or combine values at the same point in time. This rule restates a conclusion introduced in Chapter 3: Only cash flows in the same units can be compared or combined. *A dollar today* and *a dollar in one year* are not equivalent. Having money now is more valuable than having money in the future; if you have the money today you can earn interest on it.

To compare or combine cash flows that occur at different points in time, you first need to convert the cash flows into the same units or *move* them to the same point in time. The next two rules show how to move the cash flows on the timeline.

Rule 2: Moving Cash Flows Forward in Time

Suppose we have $1000 today, and we wish to determine the equivalent amount in one year's time. If the current market interest rate is 10%, we can use that rate as an exchange rate to move the cash flow forward in time. That is,

($1000 today) × (1.10 $ in one year/$ today) = $1100 in one year

In general, if the market interest rate for the year is r, then we multiply by the interest rate factor, $(1 + r)$, to move the cash flow from the beginning to the end of the year. This process of moving a value or cash flow forward in time is known as **compounding**. *Our second rule stipulates that to move a cash flow forward in time, you must compound it.*

We can apply this rule repeatedly. Suppose we want to know how much the $1000 is worth in two years' time. If the interest rate for year 2 is also 10%, then we convert as we just did:

($1100 in one year) × (1.10 $ in two years/$ in one year) = $1210 in two years

Let's represent this calculation on a timeline as follows:

Given a 10% interest rate, all of the cash flows—$1000 at date 0, $1100 at date 1, and $1210 at date 2—are equivalent. They have the same value but are expressed in different units (different points in time). An arrow that points to the right indicates that the value is being moved forward in time—that is, compounded.

The value of a cash flow that is moved forward in time is known as its future value. In the preceding example, $1210 is the future value of $1000 two years from today. Note that the value grows as we move the cash flow further in the future. The difference in value between money today and money in the future represents the **time value of money**, and it reflects the fact that by having money sooner, you can invest it and have more money later as a result. Note also that the equivalent value grows by $100 the first year, but by $110 the second year. In the second year we earn interest on our original $1000, plus we earn interest on the $100 interest we received in the first year. This effect of earning "interest on interest" is known as **compound interest**.

How does the future value change if we move the cash flow three years? Continuing with the same approach, we compound the cash flow a third time. Assuming the competitive market interest rate is fixed at 10%, we get

$1000 × (1.10) × (1.10) × (1.10) = $1000 × (1.10)^3 = $1331

In general, to take a cash flow C forward n periods into the future, we must compound it by the n intervening interest rate factors. If the interest rate r is constant, then

Future Value of a Cash Flow

$$FV_n = C \times \underbrace{(1 + r) \times (1 + r) \times \cdots \times (1 + r)}_{n \text{ times}} = C \times (1 + r)^n \qquad (4.1)$$

FIGURE 4.1

The Composition of Interest over Time

This graph shows the account balance and the composition of interest over time when an investor starts with an initial deposit of $1000, shown in red, in an account earning 10% interest over a 20-year period. Note that the turquoise area representing interest on interest grows, and by year 15 has become larger than the interest on the original deposit, shown in green. In year 20, the interest on interest the investor earned is $3727.50, while the total interest earned on the original $1000 is $2000.

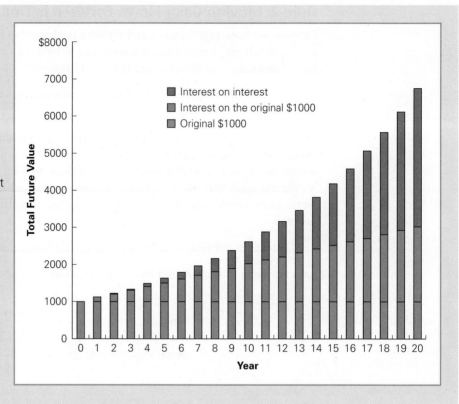

Figure 4.1 shows the importance of earning "interest on interest" in the growth of the account balance over time. The type of growth that results from compounding is called geometric or exponential growth. As Example 4.2 shows, over a long horizon, the effect of compounding can be quite dramatic.

EXAMPLE 4.2

The Power of Compounding

Problem

Suppose you invest $1000 in an account paying 10% interest per year. How much will you have in the account in 7 years? in 20 years? in 75 years?

Solution

You can apply Eq. 4.1 to calculate the future value in each case:

7 years: $\$1000 \times (1.10)^7 = \$1948.72$

20 years: $\$1000 \times (1.10)^{20} = \$6727.50$

75 years: $\$1000 \times (1.10)^{75} = \$1,271,895.37$

Note that at 10% interest, your money will nearly double in 7 years. After 20 years, it will increase almost 7-fold. And if you invest for 75 years, you will be a millionaire!

Rule 3: Moving Cash Flows Back in Time

The third rule describes how to move cash flows backward in time. Suppose you would like to compute the value today of $1000 you anticipate receiving in one year. If the current

Rule of 72

Another way to think about the effect of compounding and discounting is to consider how long it will take your money to double given different interest rates. Suppose we want to know how many years it will take for $1 to grow to a future value of $2. We want the number of years, N, to solve

$$FV = \$1 \times (1 + r)^N = \$2$$

If you solve this formula for different interest rates, you will find the following approximation:

Years to double $\approx 72 \div$ (interest rate in percent)

This simple "Rule of 72" is fairly accurate (i.e., within one year of the exact doubling time) for interest rates higher than 2%. For example, if the interest rate is 9%, the doubling time should be about $72 \div 9 = 8$ years. Indeed, $1.09^8 = 1.99$! So, given a 9% interest rate, your money will approximately double every eight years.[2]

market interest rate is 10%, you can compute this value by converting units as we did in Chapter 3:

($1000 in one year) $\div$ (1.10 $ in one year/$ today) = $909.09 today

That is, to move the cash flow backward in time, we divide it by the interest rate factor, $(1 + r)$, where r is the interest rate. This process of moving a value or cash flow backward in time—finding the equivalent value today of a future cash flow—is known as **discounting**. *Our third rule stipulates that to move a cash flow back in time, we must discount it.*

To illustrate, suppose that you anticipate receiving the $1000 two years from today rather than in one year. If the interest rate for both years is 10%, we can prepare the following timeline:

When the interest rate is 10%, all of the cash flows—$826.45 at date 0, $909.09 at date 1, and $1000 at date 2—are equivalent. They represent the same value in different units (different points in time). The arrow points to the left to indicate that the value is being moved backward in time or discounted. Note that the value decreases as we move the cash flow further back.

The value of a future cash flow at an earlier point on the timeline is its present value at the earlier point in time. That is, $826.45 is the present value at date 0 of $1000 in two years. Recall from Chapter 3 that the present value is the "do-it-yourself" price to produce a future cash flow. Thus, if we invested $826.45 today for two years at 10% interest, we would have a future value of $1000, using the second rule of time travel:

Suppose the $1000 were three years away and you wanted to compute the present value. Again, if the interest rate is 10%, we have

---

[2]See the appendix to this chapter for an explanation of how to calculate the exact doubling time.

That is, the present value today of a cash flow of $1000 in three years is given by

$$\$1000 \div (1.10) \div (1.10) \div (1.10) = \$1000 \div (1.10)^3 = \$751.31$$

In general, to move a cash flow C backward n periods, we must discount it by the n intervening interest rate factors. If the interest rate r is constant, then

Present Value of a Cash Flow

$$PV = C \div (1 + r)^n = \frac{C}{(1 + r)^n} \tag{4.2}$$

EXAMPLE 4.3   **Present Value of a Single Future Cash Flow**

Problem
You are considering investing in a savings bond that will pay $15,000 in 10 years. If the competitive market interest rate is fixed at 6% per year, what is the bond worth today?

Solution
The cash flows for this bond are represented by the following timeline:

Thus, the bond is worth $15,000 in 10 years. To determine the value today, we compute the present value:

$$PV = \frac{15,000}{1.06^{10}} = \$8375.92 \text{ today}$$

The bond is worth much less today than its final payoff because of the time value of money.

Applying the Rules of Time Travel

The rules of time travel allow us to compare and combine cash flows that occur at different points in time. Suppose we plan to save $1000 today, and $1000 at the end of each of the next two years. If we earn a fixed 10% interest rate on our savings, how much will we have three years from today?

Again, we start with a timeline:

The timeline shows the three deposits we plan to make. We need to compute their value at the end of three years.

We can use the rules of time travel in a number of ways to solve this problem. First, we can take the deposit at date 0 and move it forward to date 1. Because it is then in the same time period as the date 1 deposit, we can combine the two amounts to find out the total in the bank on date 1:

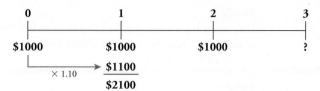

Using the first two rules of time travel, we find that our total savings on date 1 will be $2100. Continuing in this fashion, we can solve the problem as follows:

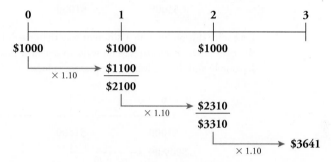

The total amount we will have in the bank at the end of three years is $3641. This amount is the future value of our $1000 savings deposits.

Another approach to the problem is to compute the future value in year 3 of each cash flow separately. Once all three amounts are in year 3 dollars, we can then combine them.

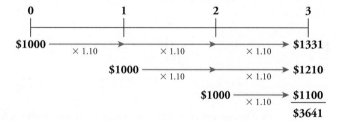

Both calculations give the same future value. As long as we follow the rules, we get the same result. The order in which we apply the rules does not matter. The calculation we choose depends on which is more convenient for the problem at hand. Table 4.1 summarizes the three rules of time travel and their associated formulas.

TABLE 4.1	The Three Rules of Time Travel	
Rule 1	Only values at the same point in time can be compared or combined.	
Rule 2	To move a cash flow forward in time, you must compound it.	Future Value of a Cash Flow $FV_n = C \times (1 + r)^n$
Rule 3	To move a cash flow backward in time, you must discount it.	Present Value of a Cash Flow $PV = C \div (1 + r)^n = \dfrac{C}{(1 + r)^n}$

EXAMPLE 4.4	**Computing the Future Value**

Problem

Let's revisit the savings plan we considered earlier: We plan to save $1000 today and at the end of each of the next two years. At a fixed 10% interest rate, how much will we have in the bank three years from today?

Solution

Let's solve this problem in a different way than we did earlier. First, compute the present value of the cash flows. There are several ways to perform this calculation. Here we treat each cash flow separately and then combine the present values.

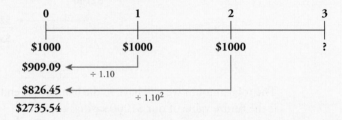

Saving $2735.54 today is equivalent to saving $1000 per year for three years. Now let's compute its future value in year 3:

This answer of $3641 is precisely the same result we found earlier. As long as we apply the three rules of time travel, we will always get the correct answer.

CONCEPT CHECK	1. Can you compare or combine cash flows at different times?
	2. What is compound interest?
	3. How do you move a cash flow backward and forward in time?

4.3 Valuing a Stream of Cash Flows

Most investment opportunities have multiple cash flows that occur at different points in time. In Section 4.2, we applied the rules of time travel to value such cash flows. Now, we formalize this approach by deriving a general formula for valuing a stream of cash flows.

Consider a stream of cash flows: C_0 at date 0, C_1 at date 1, and so on, up to C_N at date N. We represent this cash flow stream on a timeline as follows:

Using the time travel techniques, we compute the present value of this cash flow stream in two steps. First, we compute the present value of each individual cash flow. Then, once the cash flows are in common units of dollars today, we can combine them.

For a given interest rate r, we represent this process on the timeline as follows:

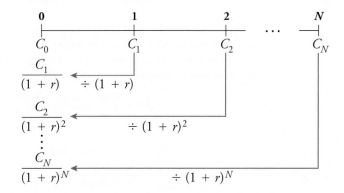

This timeline provides the general formula for the present value of a cash flow stream:

$$PV = C_0 + \frac{C_1}{(1 + r)} + \frac{C_2}{(1 + r)^2} + \cdots + \frac{C_N}{(1 + r)^N} \tag{4.3}$$

We can also write this formula as a summation:

Present Value of a Cash Flow Stream

$$PV = \sum_{n=0}^{N} PV(C_n) = \sum_{n=0}^{N} \frac{C_n}{(1 + r)^n} \tag{4.4}$$

The summation sign, Σ, means "sum the individual elements for each date n from 0 to N." Note that $(1 + r)^0 = 1$, so this shorthand matches precisely Eq. 4.3. That is, the present value of the cash flow stream is the sum of the present values of each cash flow. Recall from Chapter 3 how we defined the present value as the dollar amount you would need to invest today to produce the single cash flow in the future. The same idea holds in this context. The present value is the amount you need to invest today to generate the cash flow stream $C_0, C_1, \ldots, C_N$. That is, receiving those cash flows is equivalent to having their present value in the bank today.

| EXAMPLE 4.5 | **Present Value of a Stream of Cash Flows** |

Problem

You have just graduated and need money to buy a new car. Your rich Uncle Henry will lend you the money so long as you agree to pay him back within four years, and you offer to pay him the rate of interest that he would otherwise get by putting his money in a savings account. Based on your earnings and living expenses, you think you will be able to pay him $5000 in one year, and then $8000 each year for the next three years. If Uncle Henry would otherwise earn 6% per year on his savings, how much can you borrow from him?

Solution
The cash flows you can promise Uncle Henry are as follows:

How much money should Uncle Henry be willing to give you today in return for your promise of these payments? He should be willing to give you an amount that is equivalent to these payments in present value terms. This is the amount of money that it would take him to produce these same cash flows, which we calculate as follows:

$$PV = \frac{5000}{1.06} + \frac{8000}{1.06^2} + \frac{8000}{1.06^3} + \frac{8000}{1.06^4}$$

$$= 4716.98 + 7119.97 + 6716.95 + 6336.75$$

$$= 24{,}890.65$$

Thus, Uncle Henry should be willing to lend you $24,890.65 in exchange for your promised payments. This amount is less than the total you will pay him ($5000 + $8000 + $8000 + $8000 = $29,000) due to the time value of money.

Let's verify our answer. If your uncle kept his $24,890.65 in the bank today earning 6% interest, in four years he would have

$$FV = \$24{,}890.65 \times (1.06)^4 = \$31{,}423.87 \text{ in four years}$$

Now suppose that Uncle Henry gives you the money, and then deposits your payments to him in the bank each year. How much will he have four years from now?

We need to compute the future value of the annual deposits. One way to do so is to compute the bank balance each year:

We get the same answer both ways (within a penny, which is because of rounding).

The last section of Example 4.5 illustrates a general point. If you want to compute the future value of a stream of cash flows, you can do it directly (the second approach used in Example 4.5), or you can first compute the present value and then move it to the future (the first approach). Because we obey the laws of time travel in both cases, we get the same result. This principle can be applied more generally to write the following formula for the future value in year n in terms of the present value of a set of cash flows:

Future Value of a Cash Flow Stream with a Present Value of PV

$$FV_n = PV \times (1 + r)^n \tag{4.5}$$

CONCEPT CHECK
1. How do you calculate the present value of a cash flow stream?
2. How do you calculate the future value of a cash flow stream?

4.4 Calculating the Net Present Value

Now that we have established the rules of time travel and determined how to compute present and future values, we are ready to address our central goal: comparing the costs and benefits of a project to evaluate a long-term investment decision. From our first rule of time travel, to compare cash flows we must value them at a common point in time. A convenient choice is to use present values. In particular, we define the **net present value (NPV)** of an investment decision as follows:

$$NPV = PV(\text{benefits}) - PV(\text{costs}) \tag{4.6}$$

In this context, the benefits are the cash inflows and the costs are the cash outflows. We can represent any investment decision on a timeline as a cash flow stream where the cash outflows (investments) are negative cash flows and the inflows are positive cash flows. Thus, the NPV of an investment opportunity is also the *present value* of the stream of cash flows of the opportunity:

$$NPV = PV(\text{benefits}) - PV(\text{costs}) = PV(\text{benefits} - \text{costs})$$

EXAMPLE 4.6

Net Present Value of an Investment Opportunity

Problem
You have been offered the following investment opportunity: If you invest $1000 today, you will receive $500 at the end of each of the next three years. If you could otherwise earn 10% per year on your money, should you undertake the investment opportunity?

Solution
As always, we start with a timeline. We denote the upfront investment as a negative cash flow (because it is money we need to spend) and the money we receive as a positive cash flow.

To decide whether we should accept this opportunity, we compute the NPV by computing the present value of the stream:

$$NPV = -1000 + \frac{500}{1.10} + \frac{500}{1.10^2} + \frac{500}{1.10^3} = \$243.43$$

Because the NPV is positive, the benefits exceed the costs and we should make the investment. Indeed, the NPV tells us that taking this opportunity is like getting an extra $243.43 that you can spend today. To illustrate, suppose you borrow $1000 to invest in the opportunity and an extra $243.43 to spend today. How much would you owe on the $1243.43 loan in three years? At 10% interest, the amount you would owe would be

$$FV = (\$1000 + \$243.43) \times (1.10)^3 = \$1655 \text{ in three years}$$

At the same time, the investment opportunity generates cash flows. If you put these cash flows into a bank account, how much will you have saved three years from now? The future value of the savings is

$$FV = (\$500 \times 1.10^2) + (\$500 \times 1.10) + \$500 = \$1655 \text{ in three years}$$

As you see, you can use your bank savings to repay the loan. Taking the opportunity therefore allows you to spend $243.43 today at no extra cost.

In principle, we have explained how to answer the question we posed at the beginning of the chapter: How should financial managers evaluate the cash flows from undertaking a multi-year project like the Chevy Volt? We have shown how to compute the NPV of an investment opportunity such as the Chevy Volt that lasts more than one period. In practice, when the number of cash flows exceeds four or five (as it most likely will), the calculations can become tedious. Fortunately, a number of special cases do not require us to treat each cash flow separately. We derive these shortcuts in Section 4.5.

Calculating NPV

While present and future value calculations can be done with a calculator, it is often convenient to evaluate them using a spreadsheet program. For example, the following spreadsheet calculates the NPV in Example 4.6:

	A	B	C	D	E
1	Discount Rate	10.0%			
2	Period	0	1	2	3
3	Cash Flow C_t	(1,000.0)	500.0	500.0	500.0
4	Discount Factor	1.000	0.909	0.826	0.751
5	PV(C_t)	(1,000.0)	454.5	413.2	375.7
6	NPV	243.43			

Rows 1–3 provide the key data of the problem, the discount rate, and the cash flow timeline. Row 4 then calculates the discount factor, $1/(1 + r)^n$, the present value of a dollar received in year n. We multiply each cash flow by the discount factor to convert it to a present value, shown in row 5. Finally, row 6 shows the sum of the present values of all the cash flows, which is the NPV. The formulas in rows 4–6 are shown below:

	A	B	C	D	E
4	Discount Factor	=1/(1+$B$1)^B2	=1/(1+$B$1)^C2	=1/(1+$B$1)^D2	=1/(1+$B$1)^E2
5	PV(C_t)	=B3*B4	=C3*C4	=D3*D4	=E3*E4
6	NPV	=SUM(B5:E5)			

Alternatively, we could have computed the entire NPV in one step, using a single (long) formula. We recommend as a best practice that you avoid that temptation and calculate the NPV step by step. Doing so facilitates error checking and makes clear the contribution of each cash flow to the overall NPV.

Excel's NPV Function

Excel also has a built-in NPV function. This function has the format *NPV*(rate, value1, value2, . . .), where "rate" is the interest rate per period used to discount the cash flows, and "value1", "value2", and so on are the cash flows (or ranges of cash flows). Unfortunately, however, the NPV function computes the present value of the cash flows *assuming the first cash flow occurs at date* 1. Therefore, if a project's first cash flow occurs at date 0, we must add it separately. For example, in the spreadsheet above, we would need the formula

$$= B3 + NPV(B1, C3:E3)$$

to calculate the NPV of the indicated cash flows.

Another pitfall with the NPV function is that cash flows that are left blank are treated differently from cash flows that are equal to zero. If the cash flow is left blank, *both the cash flow and the period are ignored*. For example, consider the example below in which the period 2 cash flow has been deleted:

	A	B	C	D	E
1	Discount Rate	10.0%			
2	Period	0	1	2	3
3	Cash Flow C_t	(1,000.0)	500.0		500.0
4	Discount Factor	1.000	0.909	0.826	0.751
5	PV(C_t)	(1,000.0)	454.5	-	375.7
6	**NPV**	**(169.80)**	=SUM(B5:E5)		
7	NPV function	(132.23)	=B3+NPV(B1,C3:E3)		

Our original method provides the correct solution in row 6, whereas the NPV function used in row 7 treats the cash flow in period 3 as though it occurred at period 2, which is clearly not what is intended and is incorrect.

CONCEPT CHECK

1. How do you calculate the net present value of a cash flow stream?

2. What benefit does a firm receive when it accepts a project with a positive NPV?

4.5 Perpetuities and Annuities

The formulas we have developed so far allow us to compute the present or future value of any cash flow stream. In this section, we consider two special types of cash flow streams, *perpetuities* and *annuities*, and we learn shortcuts for valuing them. These shortcuts are possible because the cash flows follow a regular pattern.

Perpetuities

A **perpetuity** is a stream of equal cash flows that occur at regular intervals and last forever. One example is the British government bond called a **consol** (or perpetual bond). Consol bonds promise the owner a fixed cash flow every year, forever.

Here is the timeline for a perpetuity:

Note from the timeline that the first cash flow does not occur immediately; *it arrives at the end of the first period*. This timing is sometimes referred to as payment *in arrears* and is a standard convention that we adopt throughout this text.

Using the formula for the present value, the present value of a perpetuity with payment C and interest rate r is given by

$$PV = \frac{C}{(1+r)} + \frac{C}{(1+r)^2} + \frac{C}{(1+r)^3} + \cdots = \sum_{n=1}^{\infty} \frac{C}{(1+r)^n}$$

Notice that $C_n = C$ in the present value formula because the cash flow for a perpetuity is constant. Also, because the first cash flow is in one period, $C_0 = 0$.

To find the value of a perpetuity one cash flow at a time would take forever—literally! You might wonder how, even with a shortcut, the sum of an infinite number of positive terms could be finite. The answer is that the cash flows in the future are discounted for an ever-increasing number of periods, so their contribution to the sum eventually becomes negligible.[3]

To derive the shortcut, we calculate the value of a perpetuity by creating our own perpetuity. We can then calculate the present value of the perpetuity because, by the Law of One Price, the value of the perpetuity must be the same as the cost we would incur to create it ourselves. To illustrate, suppose you could invest $100 in a bank account paying 5% interest per year forever. At the end of one year, you will have $105 in the bank—your original $100 plus $5 in interest. Suppose you withdraw the $5 interest and reinvest the $100 for a second year. Again you will have $105 after one year, and you can withdraw $5 and reinvest $100 for another year. By doing this year after year, you can withdraw $5 every year in perpetuity:

Historical Examples of Perpetuities

Companies sometimes issue bonds that they call perpetuities, but in fact are not really perpetuities. For example, in mid-2010, Europe's largest bank, HSBC, sold $3.4 billion of "perpetual" bonds that promise investors a fixed amount each year with no maturity date. But while the bonds have no fixed maturity, they are not exactly true perpetuities as HSBC has the right to pay off the bonds after 5 1/2 years. Thus, the bond's payments might not last forever.

Perpetual bonds were some of the first bonds ever issued. The oldest perpetuities that are still making interest payments were issued in 1624 by the *Hoogheemraadschap Lekdijk Bovendams*, a seventeenth-century Dutch water board responsible for upkeep of the local dikes. To verify that these bonds continue to pay interest, two finance professors at Yale University, William Goetzmann and Geert Rouwenhorst,

purchased one of these bonds in July 2003, and collected 26 years of back interest. On its issue date in 1648, this bond originally paid interest in Carolus guilders. Over the next 355 years, the currency of payment changed to Flemish pounds, Dutch guilders, and most recently euros. Currently, the bond pays interest of €11.34 annually.

Although the Dutch bonds are the oldest perpetuities still in existence, the first perpetuities date from much earlier times. For example, *cencus agreements* and *rentes*, which were forms of perpetuities and annuities, were issued in the twelfth century in Italy, France, and Spain. They were initially designed to circumvent the usury laws of the Catholic Church: Because they did not require the repayment of principal, in the eyes of the church they were not considered loans.

---

[3]In mathematical terms, this is a geometric series, so it converges if $r > 0$.

By investing $100 in the bank today, you can, in effect, create a perpetuity paying $5 per year. The Law of One Price tells us that the same good must have the same price in every market. Because the bank will "sell" us (allow us to create) the perpetuity for $100, the present value of the $5 per year in perpetuity is this "do-it-yourself" cost of $100.

Now let's generalize this argument. Suppose we invest an amount P in the bank. Every year we can withdraw the interest we have earned, $C = r \times P$, leaving the principal, P, in the bank. The present value of receiving C in perpetuity is therefore the upfront cost $P = C/r$. Therefore,

Present Value of a Perpetuity

$$PV(C \text{ in perpetuity}) = \frac{C}{r} \tag{4.7}$$

In other words, by depositing the amount C/r today, we can withdraw interest of $(C/r) \times r = C$ each period in perpetuity. Thus, the present value of the perpetuity is C/r.

Note the logic of our argument. To determine the present value of a cash flow stream, we computed the "do-it-yourself" cost of creating those same cash flows at the bank. This is an extremely useful and powerful approach—and is much simpler and faster than summing those infinite terms![4]

| EXAMPLE 4.7 | **Endowing a Perpetuity** |

Problem

You want to endow an annual MBA graduation party at your alma mater. You want the event to be a memorable one, so you budget $30,000 per year forever for the party. If the university earns 8% per year on its investments, and if the first party is in one year's time, how much will you need to donate to endow the party?

Solution

The timeline of the cash flows you want to provide is

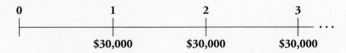

This is a standard perpetuity of $30,000 per year. The funding you would need to give the university in perpetuity is the present value of this cash flow stream. From the formula,

$$PV = C/r = \$30{,}000/0.08 = \$375{,}000 \text{ today}$$

If you donate $375,000 today, and if the university invests it at 8% per year forever, then the MBAs will have $30,000 every year for their graduation party.

---

[4]Another mathematical derivation of this result exists (see the online appendix), but it is less intuitive. This case is a good example of how the Law of One Price can be used to derive useful results.

COMMON MISTAKE　　**Discounting One Too Many Times**

The perpetuity formula assumes that the first payment occurs at the end of the first period (at date 1). Sometimes perpetuities have cash flows that start later in the future. In this case, we can adapt the perpetuity formula to compute the present value, but we need to do so carefully to avoid a common mistake.

To illustrate, consider the MBA graduation party described in Example 4.7. Rather than starting immediately, suppose that the first party will be held two years from today (for the current entering class). How would this delay change the amount of the donation required?

Now the timeline looks like this:

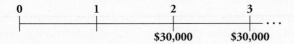

We need to determine the present value of these cash flows, as it tells us the amount of money in the bank needed today to finance the future parties. We cannot apply the perpetuity formula directly, however, because these cash flows are not *exactly* a perpetuity as we defined it. Specifically, the cash flow in the first period is "missing." But consider the situation on date 1—at that point, the first party is one period

away and then the cash flows are periodic. From the perspective of date 1, this *is* a perpetuity, and we can apply the formula. From the preceding calculation, we know we need $375,000 on date 1 to have enough to start the parties on date 2. We rewrite the timeline as follows:

Our goal can now be restated more simply: How much do we need to invest today to have $375,000 in one year? This is a simple present value calculation:

$$PV = \$375,000/1.08 = \$347,222 \text{ today}$$

A common mistake is to discount the $375,000 twice because the first party is in two periods. *Remember—the present value formula for the perpetuity already discounts the cash flows to one period prior to the first cash flow.* Keep in mind that this common mistake may be made with perpetuities, annuities, and all of the other special cases discussed in this section. All of these formulas discount the cash flows to one period prior to the first cash flow.

Annuities

An **annuity** is a stream of N equal cash flows paid at regular intervals. The difference between an annuity and a perpetuity is that an annuity ends after some fixed number of payments. Most car loans, mortgages, and some bonds are annuities. We represent the cash flows of an annuity on a timeline as follows.

Note that just as with the perpetuity, we adopt the convention that the first payment takes place at date 1, one period from today. The present value of an N-period annuity with payment C and interest rate r is

$$PV = \frac{C}{(1+r)} + \frac{C}{(1+r)^2} + \frac{C}{(1+r)^3} + \cdots + \frac{C}{(1+r)^N} = \sum_{n=1}^{N} \frac{C}{(1+r)^n}$$

Present Value of an Annuity. To find a simpler formula, we use the same approach we followed with the perpetuity: find a way to create an annuity. To illustrate, suppose you invest $100 in a bank account paying 5% interest. At the end of one year, you will have $105 in the bank—your original $100 plus $5 in interest. Using the same strategy as for a perpetuity, suppose you withdraw the $5 interest and reinvest the $100 for a second year. Once again you will have $105 after one year, and you can repeat the process, withdrawing $5 and reinvesting $100, every year. For a perpetuity, you left the principal in forever.

Alternatively, you might decide after 20 years to close the account and withdraw the principal. In that case, your cash flows will look like this:

With your initial $100 investment, you have created a 20-year annuity of $5 per year, plus you will receive an extra $100 at the end of 20 years. By the Law of One Price, because it took an initial investment of $100 to create the cash flows on the timeline, the present value of these cash flows is $100, or

$$\$100 = PV(\text{20-year annuity of \$5 per year}) + PV(\$100 \text{ in 20 years})$$

Rearranging terms gives

$$PV(\text{20-year annuity of \$5 per year}) = \$100 - PV(\$100 \text{ in 20 years})$$

$$= 100 - \frac{100}{(1.05)^{20}} = \$62.31$$

So the present value of $5 for 20 years is $62.31. Intuitively, the value of the annuity is the initial investment in the bank account minus the present value of the principal that will be left in the account after 20 years.

We can use the same idea to derive the general formula. First, we invest P in the bank, and withdraw only the interest $C = r \times P$ each period. After N periods, we close the account. Thus, for an initial investment of P, we will receive an N-period annuity of C per period, *plus* we will get back our original P at the end. P is the total present value of the two sets of cash flows, or

$$P = PV(\text{annuity of } C \text{ for } N \text{ periods}) + PV(P \text{ in period } N)$$

By rearranging terms, we compute the present value of the annuity:

$$PV(\text{annuity of } C \text{ for } N \text{ periods}) = P - PV(P \text{ in period } N)$$

$$= P - \frac{P}{(1+r)^N} = P\left(1 - \frac{1}{(1+r)^N}\right) \qquad (4.8)$$

Recall that the periodic payment C is the interest earned every period; that is, $C = r \times P$ or, equivalently, solving for P provides the upfront cost in terms of C,

$$P = C/r$$

Making this substitution for P, in Eq. 4.8, provides the formula for the present value of an annuity of C for N periods.

Present Value of an Annuity[5]

$$PV(\text{annuity of } C \text{ for } N \text{ periods with interest rate } r) = C \times \frac{1}{r}\left(1 - \frac{1}{(1+r)^N}\right) \qquad (4.9)$$

---

[5]An early derivation of this formula is attributed to the astronomer Edmond Halley ("Of Compound Interest," published after Halley's death by Henry Sherwin, Sherwin's Mathematical Tables, London: W. and J. Mount, T. Page and Son, 1761).

EXAMPLE 4.8   **Present Value of a Lottery Prize Annuity**

Problem

You are the lucky winner of the $30 million state lottery. You can take your prize money either as (a) 30 payments of $1 million per year (starting today), or (b) $15 million paid today. If the interest rate is 8%, which option should you take?

Solution

Option (a) provides $30 million in prize money but paid over time. To evaluate it correctly, we must convert it to a present value. Here is the timeline:

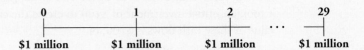

Because the first payment starts today, the last payment will occur in 29 years (for a total of 30 payments).[6] The $1 million at date 0 is already stated in present value terms, but we need to compute the present value of the remaining payments. Fortunately, this case looks like a 29-year annuity of $1 million per year, so we can use the annuity formula:

$$PV(\text{29-year annuity of \$1 million}) = \$1 \text{ million} \times \frac{1}{0.08}\left(1 - \frac{1}{1.08^{29}}\right)$$

$$= \$1 \text{ million} \times 11.16$$

$$= \$11.16 \text{ million today}$$

Thus, the total present value of the cash flows is $1 million + $11.16 million = $12.16 million. In timeline form:

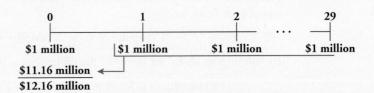

Option (b), $15 million upfront, is more valuable—even though the total amount of money paid is half that of option (a). The reason for the difference is the time value of money. If you have the $15 million today, you can use $1 million immediately and invest the remaining $14 million at an 8% interest rate. This strategy will give you $14 million × 8% = $1.12 million per year in perpetuity! Alternatively, you can spend $15 million − $11.16 million = $3.84 million today, and invest the remaining $11.16 million, which will still allow you to withdraw $1 million each year for the next 29 years before your account is depleted.

Future Value of an Annuity. Now that we have derived a simple formula for the present value of an annuity, it is easy to find a simple formula for the future value. If we want to know the value N years in the future, we move the present value N periods

---

[6]An annuity in which the first payment occurs immediately is sometimes called an *annuity due*. Throughout this text, we always use the term "annuity" to mean one that is paid in arrears.

forward on the timeline; that is, we compound the present value for N periods at interest rate r:

Future Value of an Annuity

$$FV(\text{annuity}) = PV \times (1 + r)^N$$

$$= \frac{C}{r}\left(1 - \frac{1}{(1 + r)^N}\right) \times (1 + r)^N$$

$$= C \times \frac{1}{r}\left((1 + r)^N - 1\right) \tag{4.10}$$

This formula is useful if we want to know how a savings account will grow over time. Let's apply this result to evaluate a retirement savings plan.

EXAMPLE 4.9

Retirement Savings Plan Annuity

Problem

Ellen is 35 years old, and she has decided it is time to plan seriously for her retirement. At the end of each year until she is 65, she will save $10,000 in a retirement account. If the account earns 10% per year, how much will Ellen have saved at age 65?

Solution

As always, we begin with a timeline. In this case, it is helpful to keep track of both the dates and Ellen's age:

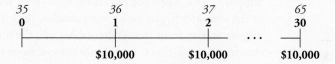

Ellen's savings plan looks like an annuity of $10,000 per year for 30 years. (*Hint:* It is easy to become confused when you just look at age, rather than at both dates and age. A common error is to think there are only $65 - 36 = 29$ payments. Writing down both dates and age avoids this problem.)

To determine the amount Ellen will have in the bank at age 65, we compute the future value of this annuity:

$$FV = \$10,000 \times \frac{1}{0.10}(1.10^{30} - 1)$$

$$= \$10,000 \times 164.49$$

$$= \$1.645 \text{ million at age 65}$$

Growing Cash Flows

So far, we have considered only cash flow streams that have the same cash flow every period. If, instead, the cash flows are expected to grow at a constant rate in each period, we can also derive a simple formula for the present value of the future stream.

Growing Perpetuity. A **growing perpetuity** is a stream of cash flows that occur at regular intervals and grow at a constant rate forever. For example, a growing perpetuity with a first payment of $100 that grows at a rate of 3% has the following timeline:

In general, a growing perpetuity with a first payment C and a growth rate g will have the following series of cash flows:

As with perpetuities with equal cash flows, we adopt the convention that the first payment occurs at date 1. Note a second important convention: *The first payment does not include growth*. That is, the first payment is C, even though it is one period away. Similarly, the cash flow in period n undergoes only $n - 1$ periods of growth. Substituting the cash flows from the preceding timeline into the general formula for the present value of a cash flow stream gives

$$PV = \frac{C}{(1 + r)} + \frac{C(1 + g)}{(1 + r)^2} + \frac{C(1 + g)^2}{(1 + r)^3} + \cdots = \sum_{n=1}^{\infty} \frac{C(1 + g)^{n-1}}{(1 + r)^n}$$

Suppose $g \geq r$. Then the cash flows grow even faster than they are discounted; each term in the sum gets larger, rather than smaller. In this case, the sum is infinite! What does an infinite present value mean? Remember that the present value is the "do-it-yourself" cost of creating the cash flows. An infinite present value means that no matter how much money you start with, it is *impossible* to sustain a growth rate of g *forever* and reproduce those cash flows on your own. Growing perpetuities of this sort cannot exist in practice because no one would be willing to offer one at any finite price. A promise to pay an amount that forever grew faster than the interest rate is also unlikely to be kept (or believed by any savvy buyer).

The only viable growing perpetuities are those where the perpetual growth rate is less than the interest rate, so that each successive term in the sum is less than the previous term and the overall sum is finite. Consequently, we assume that $g < r$ for a growing perpetuity.

To derive the formula for the present value of a growing perpetuity, we follow the same logic used for a regular perpetuity: Compute the amount you would need to deposit today to create the perpetuity yourself. In the case of a regular perpetuity, we created a constant payment forever by withdrawing the interest earned each year and reinvesting the principal. To increase the amount we can withdraw each year, the principal that we reinvest each year must grow. Therefore, we withdraw less than the full amount of interest earned each period, using the remaining interest to increase our principal.

Let's consider a specific case. Suppose you want to create a perpetuity growing at 2%, so you invest $100 in a bank account that pays 5% interest. At the end of one year, you will have $105 in the bank—your original $100 plus $5 in interest. If you withdraw only $3, you will have $102 to reinvest—2% more than the amount you had initially. This amount will then grow to $102 \times 1.05 = $107.10 in the following year, and you can withdraw $3 \times 1.02 = $3.06, which will leave you with principal of

$107.10 − $3.06 = $104.04. Note that $102 × 1.02 = $104.04. That is, both the amount you withdraw and the principal you reinvest grow by 2% each year. On a time-line, these cash flows look like this:

By following this strategy, you have created a growing perpetuity that starts at $3 and grows 2% per year. This growing perpetuity must have a present value equal to the cost of $100.

We can generalize this argument. In the case of an equal-payment perpetuity, we deposited an amount P in the bank and withdrew the interest each year. Because we always left the principal P in the bank, we could maintain this pattern forever. If we want to increase the amount we withdraw from the bank each year by g, then the principal in the bank will have to grow by the same factor g. That is, instead of reinvesting P in the second year, we should reinvest $P(1 + g) = P + gP$. In order to increase our principal by gP, we can only withdraw $C = rP − gP = P(r − g)$. Solving this equation for P, the initial amount deposited in the bank account, gives the present value of a growing perpetuity with initial cash flow C:

Present Value of a Growing Perpetuity

$$PV(\text{growing perpetuity}) = \frac{C}{r - g} \tag{4.11}$$

To understand the formula for a growing perpetuity intuitively, start with the formula for a perpetuity. In the earlier case, you had to put enough money in the bank to ensure that the interest earned matched the cash flows of the regular perpetuity. In the case of a growing perpetuity, you need to put more than that amount in the bank because you have to finance the growth in the cash flows. How much more? If the bank pays interest at a rate of 5%, then all that is left to take out if you want to make sure the principal grows 2% per year is the difference: 5% − 2% = 3%. So instead of the present value of the perpetuity being the first cash flow divided by the interest rate, it is now the first cash flow divided by the *difference* between the interest rate and the growth rate.

EXAMPLE 4.10   **Endowing a Growing Perpetuity**

Problem

In Example 4.7, you planned to donate money to your alma mater to fund an annual $30,000 MBA graduation party. Given an interest rate of 8% per year, the required donation was the present value of

$$PV = \$30,000/0.08 = \$375,000 \text{ today}$$

Before accepting the money, however, the MBA student association has asked that you increase the donation to account for the effect of inflation on the cost of the party in future years. Although $30,000 is adequate for next year's party, the students estimate that the party's cost will rise by 4% per year thereafter. To satisfy their request, how much do you need to donate now?

Solution

The cost of the party next year is $30,000, and the cost then increases 4% per year forever. From the timeline, we recognize the form of a growing perpetuity. To finance the growing cost, you need to provide the present value today of

$$PV = \$30{,}000/(0.08 - 0.04) = \$750{,}000 \text{ today}$$

You need to double the size of your gift!

Growing Annuity. A **growing annuity** is a stream of N growing cash flows, paid at regular intervals. It is a growing perpetuity that eventually comes to an end. The following timeline shows a growing annuity with initial cash flow C, growing at rate g every period until period N:

The conventions used earlier still apply: (1) The first cash flow arrives at the end of the first period, and (2) the first cash flow does not grow. The last cash flow therefore reflects only $N - 1$ periods of growth.

The present value of an N-period growing annuity with initial cash flow C, growth rate g, and interest rate r is given by

Present Value of a Growing Annuity

$$PV = C \times \frac{1}{r - g}\left(1 - \left(\frac{1 + g}{1 + r}\right)^{N}\right) \tag{4.12}$$

Because the annuity has only a finite number of terms, Eq. 4.12 also works when $g > r$.[7] The process of deriving this simple expression for the present value of a growing annuity is the same as for a regular annuity. Interested readers may consult the online appendix for details.

EXAMPLE 4.11	**Retirement Savings with a Growing Annuity**

Problem
In Example 4.9, Ellen considered saving $10,000 per year for her retirement. Although $10,000 is the most she can save in the first year, she expects her salary to increase each year so that she will be able to increase her savings by 5% per year. With this plan, if she earns 10% per year on her savings, how much will Ellen have saved at age 65?

Solution
Her new savings plan is represented by the following timeline:

---

[7]Eq. 4.12 does not work for $g = r$. But in that case, growth and discounting cancel out, and the present value is equivalent to receiving all the cash flows at date 1: $PV = C \times N/(1 + r)$

This example involves a 30-year growing annuity, with a growth rate of 5%, and an initial cash flow of $10,000. The present value of this growing annuity is given by

$$PV = \$10{,}000 \times \frac{1}{0.10 - 0.05}\left(1 - \left(\frac{1.05}{1.10}\right)^{30}\right)$$

$$= \$10{,}000 \times 15.0463$$

$$= \$150{,}463 \text{ today}$$

Ellen's proposed savings plan is equivalent to having $150,463 in the bank *today*. To determine the amount she will have at age 65, we need to move this amount forward 30 years:

$$FV = \$150{,}463 \times 1.10^{30}$$

$$= \$2.625 \text{ million in 30 years}$$

Ellen will have saved $2.625 million at age 65 using the new savings plan. This sum is almost $1 million more than she had without the additional annual increases in savings.

The formula for the growing annuity encompasses all of the other formulas in this section. To see how to derive the other formulas from this one, first consider a growing perpetuity. It is a growing annuity with $N = \infty$. If $g < r$, then

$$\frac{1 + g}{1 + r} < 1,$$

and so

$$\left(\frac{1 + g}{1 + r}\right)^N \to 0 \quad \text{as} \quad N \to \infty.$$

The formula for a growing annuity when $N = \infty$ therefore becomes

$$PV = \frac{C}{r - g}\left(1 - \left(\frac{1 + g}{1 + r}\right)^N\right) = \frac{C}{r - g}(1 - 0) = \frac{C}{r - g},$$

which is the formula for a growing perpetuity. The formulas for a regular annuity and perpetuity also follow from the formula if we let the growth rate $g = 0$. So, if you remember the growing annuity formula, you've got them all!

CONCEPT CHECK

1. How do you calculate the present value of a
   a. Perpetuity?
   b. Annuity?
   c. Growing perpetuity?
   d. Growing annuity?

2. How are the formulas for the present value of a perpetuity, annuity, growing perpetuity, and growing annuity related?

4.6 Using an Annuity Spreadsheet or Calculator

Spreadsheet programs such as Excel, as well as common financial calculators, have a set of functions that perform the calculations that finance professionals do most often. In Excel, the functions are called NPER, RATE, PV, PMT, and FV. The functions are all based on the timeline of an annuity:

The interest rate used to discount these cash flows is denoted by *RATE*. Thus, there are a total of five variables: *NPER*, *RATE*, *PV*, *PMT*, and *FV*. Each function takes four of these variables as inputs and returns the value of the fifth one that ensures that the NPV of the cash flows is zero. That is, the functions all solve the problem

$$NPV = PV + PMT \times \frac{1}{RATE}\left(1 - \frac{1}{(1 + RATE)^{NPER}}\right) + \frac{FV}{(1 + RATE)^{NPER}} = 0 \quad (4.13)$$

In words, the present value of the annuity payments *PMT*, plus the present value of the final payment *FV*, plus the initial amount *PV*, has a net present value of zero. Let's tackle a few examples.

EXAMPLE 4.12

Computing the Future Value in Excel

Problem

Suppose you plan to invest $20,000 in an account paying 8% interest. How much will you have in the account in 15 years?

Solution

We represent this problem with the following timeline:

	0	1	2		*NPER* = 15
	$PV = -\$20{,}000$	$PMT = \$0$	$\$0$	⋯	$FV = ?$

To compute the solution, we enter the four variables we know (*NPER* = 15, *RATE* = 8%, *PV* = −20,000, *PMT* = 0) and solve for the one we want to determine (*FV*) using the Excel function *FV(RATE, NPER, PMT, PV)*. The spreadsheet here calculates a future value of $63,443.

	NPER	RATE	PV	PMT	FV	Excel Formula
Given	15	8.00%	−20,000	0		
Solve for FV					**63,443**	=FV(0.08,15,0,−20000)

Note that we entered *PV* as a negative number (the amount we are putting *into* the bank), and *FV* is shown as a positive number (the amount we can take *out* of the bank). It is important to use signs correctly to indicate the direction in which the money is flowing when using the spreadsheet functions.

To check the result, we can solve this problem directly:

$$FV = \$20{,}000 \times 1.08^{15} = \$63{,}443$$

The Excel spreadsheet in Example 4.12, which is available from MyFinanceLab or from www.pearsonglobaleditions.com/berk, is set up to allow you to compute any one of the five variables. We refer to this spreadsheet as the **annuity spreadsheet**. You simply enter the four input variables on the top line and leave the variable you want to compute blank. The spreadsheet computes the fifth variable and displays the answer on the bottom line. The spreadsheet also displays the Excel function that is used to get the answers. Let's work through a more complicated example that illustrates the convenience of the annuity spreadsheet.

EXAMPLE 4.13

Using the Annuity Spreadsheet

Problem

Suppose that you invest $20,000 in an account paying 8% interest. You plan to withdraw $2000 at the end of each year for 15 years. How much money will be left in the account after 15 years?

Solution

Again, we start with the timeline showing our initial deposit and subsequent withdrawals:

0	1	2	$NPER = 15$
$PV = -\$20,000$	$PMT = \$2000$	$\$2000$	$\$2000 + FV = ?$

Note that PV is negative (money *into* the bank), while PMT is positive (money *out* of the bank). We solve for the final balance in the account, FV, using the annuity spreadsheet:

	NPER	RATE	PV	PMT	FV	Excel Formula
Given	15	8.00%	−20,000	2000		
Solve for FV					9139	=FV(0.08,15,2000,−20000)

We will have $9139 left in the bank after 15 years.

We can also compute this solution directly. One approach is to think of the deposit and the withdrawals as being separate accounts. In the account with the $20,000 deposit, our savings will grow to $63,443 in 15 years, as we computed in Example 4.12. Using the formula for the future value of an annuity, if we borrow $2000 per year for 15 years at 8%, at the end our debt will have grown to

$$\$2000 \times \frac{1}{0.08}(1.08^{15} - 1) = \$54,304$$

After paying off our debt, we will have $63,443 − $54,304 = $9139 remaining after 15 years.

You can also use a handheld financial calculator to do the same calculations. The calculators work in much the same way as the annuity spreadsheet. You enter any four of the five variables, and the calculator calculates the fifth variable.

CONCEPT CHECK

1. What tools can you use to simplify the calculation of present values?

2. What is the process for using the annuity spreadsheet?

4.7 Non-Annual Cash Flows

Until now, we have only considered cash flow streams that occur at annual intervals. Do the same tools apply if the cash flows occur at another interval, say monthly? The answer is yes: Everything we have learned about annual cash flow streams applies to monthly cash flow streams so long as:

1. The interest rate is specified as a monthly rate.

2. The number of periods is expressed in months.

For example, suppose you have a credit card that charges 2% interest per month. If you have a $1000 balance on the card today, and make no payments for six months, your future balance in one year's time will be

$$FV = C \times (1 + r)^n = \$1000 \times (1.02)^6 = \$1126.16$$

We apply the future value formula exactly as before, but with r equal to the *monthly* interest rate and n equal to the number of *months*.

The same logic applies to annuities, as in the following example.

EXAMPLE 4.14   **Evaluating an Annuity with Monthly Cash Flows**

Problem

You are about to purchase a new car and have two options to pay for it. You can pay $20,000 in cash immediately, or you can get a loan that requires you to pay $500 each month for the next 48 months (four years). If the monthly interest rate you earn on your cash is 0.5%, which option should you take?

Solution

Let's start by writing down the timeline of the loan payments:

The timeline shows that the loan is a 48-period annuity. Using the annuity formula the present value is

$$PV(\text{48-period annuity of \$500}) = \$500 \times \frac{1}{0.005}\left(1 - \frac{1}{1.005^{48}}\right)$$

$$= \$21,290$$

Alternatively, we may use the annuity spreadsheet to solve the problem:

	NPER	RATE	PV	PMT	FV	Excel Formula
Given	48	0.50%		500	0	
Solve for PV			(21,290)			=PV(0.005,48,500,0)

Thus, taking the loan is equivalent to paying $21,290 today, which is costlier than paying cash. You should pay cash for the car.

CONCEPT CHECK

1. Do the present and future value formulas depend upon the cash flows occurring at annual intervals?

2. When cash flows occur at a non-annual interval, what interest rate must you use? What number of periods must you use?

4.8 Solving for the Cash Payments

So far, we have calculated the present value or future value of a stream of cash flows. Sometimes, however, we know the present value or future value, but do not know the cash flows. The best example is a loan—you know how much you want to borrow (the present value) and you know the interest rate, but you do not know how much you need to repay each year. Suppose you are opening a business that requires an initial investment of $100,000. Your bank manager has agreed to lend you this money. The terms of the loan state that you will make equal annual payments for the next 10 years and will pay an interest rate of 8% with the first payment due one year from today. What is your annual payment?

From the bank's perspective, the timeline looks like this:

The bank will give you $100,000 today in exchange for 10 equal payments over the next decade. You need to determine the size of the payment C that the bank will require. For the bank to be willing to lend you $100,000, the loan cash flows must have a present value of $100,000 when evaluated at the bank's interest rate of 8%. That is,

$$100,000 = PV(\text{10-year annuity of } C \text{ per year, evaluated at the loan rate})$$

Using the formula for the present value of an annuity,

$$100,000 = C \times \frac{1}{0.08}\left(1 - \frac{1}{1.08^{10}}\right) = C \times 6.71$$

Solving this equation for C gives

$$C = \frac{100,000}{6.71} = \$14,903$$

You will be required to make 10 annual payments of $14,903 in exchange for $100,000 today.

We can also solve this problem with the annuity spreadsheet:

	NPER	RATE	PV	PMT	FV	Excel Formula
Given	10	8.00%	100,000		0	
Solve for PMT				−14,903		=PMT(0.08,10,100000,0)

In general, when solving for a loan payment, think of the amount borrowed (the loan principal) as the present value of the payments when evaluated at the loan rate. If the payments of the loan are an annuity, we can solve for the payment of the loan by inverting the annuity formula. Writing this procedure formally, we begin with the timeline (from the bank's perspective) for a loan with principal P, requiring N periodic payments of C and interest rate r:

Setting the present value of the payments equal to the principal,

$$P = PV(\text{annuity of } C \text{ for } N \text{ periods}) = C \times \frac{1}{r}\left(1 - \frac{1}{(1+r)^N}\right)$$

Solving this equation for C gives the general formula for the loan payment in terms of the outstanding principal (amount borrowed), P; interest rate, r; and number of payments, N:

Loan or Annuity Payment

$$C = \frac{P}{\dfrac{1}{r}\left(1 - \dfrac{1}{(1+r)^N}\right)} \tag{4.14}$$

Note that the cash flow for a perpetuity is simply $C = rP$. Rewriting (4.14) as $C = rP/(1 - 1/(1+r)^N)$, we can see that the payment for an annuity always exceeds the payment of the equivalent value perpetuity, which makes sense because the annuity will eventually end.

| EXAMPLE 4.15 | **Computing a Loan Payment** |

Problem
Your biotech firm plans to buy a new DNA sequencer for $500,000. The seller requires that you pay 20% of the purchase price as a down payment, but is willing to finance the remainder by offering a 48-month loan with equal monthly payments and an interest rate of 0.5% per month. What is the monthly loan payment?

Solution
Given a down payment of 20% × $500,000 = $100,000, your loan amount is $400,000. We start with the timeline (from the seller's perspective), where each period represents one month:

Using Eq. 4.14, we can solve for the loan payment, C, as follows:

$$C = \frac{P}{\dfrac{1}{r}\left(1 - \dfrac{1}{(1+r)^N}\right)} = \frac{400{,}000}{\dfrac{1}{0.005}\left(1 - \dfrac{1}{(1.005)^{48}}\right)}$$

$$= \$9394$$

Using the annuity spreadsheet:

	NPER	RATE	PV	PMT	FV	Excel Formula
Given	48	0.50%	−400,000		0	
Solve for PMT				9,394		=PMT(0.005,48,−400000,0)

Your firm will need to pay $9394 each month to repay the loan.

We can use this same idea to solve for the cash flows when we know the future value rather than the present value. As an example, suppose you have just had a child. You decide to be prudent and start saving this year for her college education. You would like to have $60,000 saved by the time your daughter is 18 years old. If you can earn 7% per year on your savings, how much do you need to save each year to meet your goal?

The timeline for this example is

That is, you plan to save some amount C per year, and then withdraw $60,000 from the bank in 18 years. Therefore, we need to find the annuity payment that has a future value of $60,000 in 18 years. Using the formula for the future value of an annuity from Eq. 4.10,

$$60,000 = FV(\text{annuity}) = C \times \frac{1}{0.07}(1.07^{18} - 1) = C \times 34$$

Therefore, $C = \dfrac{60,000}{34} = \$1765$. So you need to save $1765 per year. If you do, then at a

7% interest rate, your savings will grow to $60,000 by the time your child is 18 years old.

Now let's solve this problem with the annuity spreadsheet:

	NPER	RATE	PV	PMT	FV	Excel Formula
Given	18	7.00%	0		60,000	
Solve for PMT				− 1765		=PMT(0.07,18,0,60000)

Once again, we find that we need to save $1765 for 18 years to accumulate $60,000.

CONCEPT CHECK

1. How can we solve for the required annuity payment for a loan?

2. How can we determine the required amount to save each year to reach a savings goal?

4.9 The Internal Rate of Return

In some situations, you know the present value and cash flows of an investment opportunity but you do not know the interest rate that equates them. This interest rate is called the **internal rate of return (IRR)**, defined as the interest rate that sets the net present value of the cash flows equal to zero.

For example, suppose that you have an investment opportunity that requires a $1000 investment today and will have a $2000 payoff in six years. On a timeline,

One way to analyze this investment is to ask the question: What interest rate, r, would you need so that the NPV of this investment is zero?

$$NPV = -1000 + \frac{2000}{(1 + r)^6} = 0$$

Rearranging gives

$$1000 \times (1 + r)^6 = 2000$$

That is, r is the interest rate you would need to earn on your $1000 to have a future value of $2000 in six years. We can solve for r as follows:

$$1 + r = \left(\frac{2000}{1000} \right)^{1/6} = 1.1225$$

or $r = 12.25\%$. This rate is the IRR of this investment opportunity. Making this investment is like earning 12.25% per year on your money for six years.

When there are just two cash flows, as in the preceding example, it is easy to compute the IRR. Consider the general case in which you invest an amount P today, and receive FV in N years. Then the IRR satisfies the equation $P \times (1 + IRR)^N = FV$, which implies

$$IRR \text{ with two cash flows} = (FV/P)^{1/N} - 1 \qquad (4.15)$$

Note in the formula that we take the total return of the investment over N years, FV/P, and convert it to an equivalent one-year return by raising it to the power $1/N$.

The IRR is also straightforward to calculate for a perpetuity, as we demonstrate in the next example.

EXAMPLE 4.16   **Computing the IRR for a Perpetuity**

Problem

Jessica has just graduated with her MBA. Rather than take the job she was offered at a prestigious investment bank—Baker, Bellingham, and Botts—she has decided to go into business for herself. She believes that her business will require an initial investment of $1 million. After that, it will generate a cash flow of $100,000 at the end of one year, and this amount will grow by 4% per year thereafter. What is the IRR of this investment opportunity?

Solution
The timeline is

The timeline shows that the future cash flows are a growing perpetuity with a growth rate of 4%. Recall from Eq. 4.11 that the PV of a growing perpetuity is $C/(r-g)$. Thus, the NPV of this investment would equal zero if

$$1,000,000 = \frac{100,000}{r - 0.04}$$

We can solve this equation for r

$$r = \frac{100,000}{1,000,000} + 0.04 = 0.14$$

So, the IRR on this investment is 14%.

More generally, if we invest P and receive a perpetuity with initial cash flow C and growth rate g, we can use the growing perpetuity formula to determine

$$IRR \text{ of growing perpetuity} = (C/P) + g \tag{4.16}$$

Now let's consider a more sophisticated example. Suppose your firm needs to purchase a new forklift. The dealer gives you two options: (1) a price for the forklift if you pay cash and (2) the annual payments if you take out a loan from the dealer. To evaluate the loan that the dealer is offering you, you will want to compare the rate on the loan with the rate that your bank is willing to offer you. Given the loan payment that the dealer quotes, how do you compute the interest rate charged by the dealer?

In this case, we need to compute the IRR of the dealer's loan. Suppose the cash price of the forklift is $40,000, and the dealer offers financing with no down payment and four annual payments of $15,000. This loan has the following timeline:

From the timeline it is clear that the loan is a four-year annuity with a payment of $15,000 per year and a present value of $40,000. Setting the NPV of the cash flows equal to zero requires that the present value of the payments equals the purchase price:

$$40,000 = 15,000 \times \frac{1}{r}\left(1 - \frac{1}{(1+r)^4}\right)$$

The value of r that solves this equation, the IRR, is the interest rate charged on the loan. Unfortunately, in this case, there is no simple way to solve for the interest rate r.[8] The only way to solve this equation is to guess values of r until you find the right one.

Start by guessing $r = 10\%$. In this case, the value of the annuity is

$$15{,}000 \times \frac{1}{0.10}\left(1 - \frac{1}{(1.10)^4}\right) = 47{,}548$$

The present value of the payments is too large. To lower it, we need to use a higher interest rate. We guess 20% this time:

$$15{,}000 \times \frac{1}{0.20}\left(1 - \frac{1}{(1.20)^4}\right) = 38{,}831$$

Now the present value of the payments is too low, so we must pick a rate between 10% and 20%. We continue to guess until we find the right rate. Let us try 18.45%:

$$15{,}000 \times \frac{1}{0.1845}\left(1 - \frac{1}{(1.1845)^4}\right) = 40{,}000$$

The interest rate charged by the dealer is 18.45%.

An easier solution than guessing the IRR and manually calculating values is to use a spreadsheet or calculator to automate the guessing process. When the cash flows are an annuity, as in this example, we can use the annuity spreadsheet in Excel to compute the IRR. Recall that the annuity spreadsheet solves Eq. 4.13. It ensures that the NPV of investing in the annuity is zero. When the unknown variable is the interest rate, it will solve for the interest rate that sets the NPV equal to zero—that is, the IRR. For this case,

	NPER	RATE	PV	PMT	FV	Excel Formula
Given	4		40,000	−15,000	0	
Solve for Rate		18.45%				=RATE(4,−15000,40000,0)

The annuity spreadsheet correctly computes an IRR of 18.45%.

EXAMPLE 4.17   **Computing the Internal Rate of Return for an Annuity**

Problem

Baker, Bellingham, and Botts, was so impressed with Jessica that it has decided to fund her business. In return for providing the initial capital of $1 million, Jessica has agreed to pay them $125,000 at the end of each year for the next 30 years. What is the internal rate of return on Baker, Bellingham, and Botts's investment in Jessica's company, assuming she fulfills her commitment?

Solution

Here is the timeline (from Baker, Bellingham, and Botts' perspective):

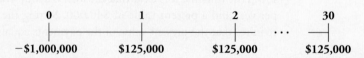

---

[8]With five or more periods and general cash flows, there is *no* general formula to solve for r; trial and error (by hand or computer) is the *only* way to compute the IRR.

The timeline shows that the future cash flows are a 30-year annuity. Setting the NPV equal to zero requires

$$1,000,000 = 125,000 \times \frac{1}{r}\left(1 - \frac{1}{(1 + r)^{30}}\right)$$

Using the annuity spreadsheet to solve for r,

	NPER	RATE	PV	PMT	FV	Excel Formula
Given	30		−1,000,000	125,000	0	
Solve for Rate		**12.09%**				=RATE(30,125000,−1000000,0)

The IRR on this investment is 12.09%. In this case, we can interpret the IRR of 12.09% as the effective interest rate of the loan.

In this chapter, we developed the tools a financial manager needs to apply the NPV rule when cash flows occur at different points in time. As we have seen, the interest rate we use to discount or compound the cash flows is a critical input to any of our present or future value calculations. Throughout the chapter, we have taken the interest rate as given. What determines the interest rate that we should use when discounting cash flows? The Law of One Price implies that we must rely on market information to assess the value of cash flows across time. In Chapter 5, we learn the drivers of market interest rates as well as how they are quoted. Understanding interest rate quoting conventions will also allow us to extend the tools we developed in this chapter to situations where the cash flows are paid, and interest is compounded, more than once per year.

CONCEPT CHECK

1. What is the internal rate of return?

2. In what two cases is the internal rate of return easy to calculate?

USING EXCEL

Excel's IRR Function

Excel also has a built-in function, IRR, that will calculate the IRR of a stream of cash flows. Excel's IRR function has the format, IRR (values, guess), where "values" is the range containing the cash flows, and "guess" is an optional starting guess where Excel begins its search for an IRR. See the example below:

	A	B	C	D	E
1	Period	0	1	2	3
2	Cash Flow C_t	(1,000.0)	300.0	400.0	500.0
3	IRR		8.9% =IRR(B2:E2)		

There are three things to note about the IRR function. First, the values given to the IRR function should include all of the cash flows of the project, including the one at date 0. In this sense, the IRR and NPV functions in Excel are inconsistent. Second, like the NPV function, the IRR ignores the period associated with any blank cells. Finally, as we will discuss in Chapter 7, in some settings the IRR function may fail to find a solution, or may give a different answer, depending on the initial guess.

| MyFinanceLab | Here is what you should know after reading this chapter. MyFinanceLab will help you identify what you know and where to go when you need to practice. |

4.1 The Timeline

- Timelines are a critical first step in organizing the cash flows in a financial problem.

4.2 The Three Rules of Time Travel

- There are three rules of time travel:
  - Only cash flows that occur at the same point in time can be compared or combined.
  - To move a cash flow forward in time, you must compound it.
  - To move a cash flow backward in time, you must discount it.
- The future value in n years of a cash flow C today is

$$C \times (1 + r)^n \tag{4.1}$$

- The number of years it will take for an investment to double in value is approximately equal to 72 divided by the interest rate earned.
- The present value today of a cash flow C received in n years is

$$C \div (1 + r)^n \tag{4.2}$$

4.3 Valuing a Stream of Cash Flows

- The present value of a cash flow stream is

$$PV = \sum_{n=0}^{N} \frac{C_n}{(1 + r)^n} \tag{4.4}$$

- The present value equals the amount you would need in the bank today to recreate the cash flow stream.
- The future value on date n of a cash flow stream with a present value of PV is

$$FV_n = PV \times (1 + r)^n \tag{4.5}$$

4.4 Calculating the Net Present Value

- The net present value (NPV) of an investment opportunity is $PV(\text{benefits} - \text{costs})$. The NPV is the net benefit of the investment in terms of an equivalent amount of cash today.

4.5 Perpetuities and Annuities

- A perpetuity is a constant cash flow C paid every period, forever. The present value of a perpetuity is

$$\frac{C}{r} \tag{4.7}$$

- An annuity is a constant cash flow C paid every period for N periods. The present value of an annuity is

$$C \times \frac{1}{r}\left(1 - \frac{1}{(1 + r)^N}\right) \tag{4.9}$$

The future value of an annuity at the end of the annuity is

$$C \times \frac{1}{r}\left((1 + r)^N - 1\right) \tag{4.10}$$

- In a growing perpetuity or annuity, the cash flows grow at a constant rate g each period. The present value of a growing perpetuity is

$$\frac{C}{r-g} \qquad (4.11)$$

The present value of a growing annuity is

$$C \times \frac{1}{r-g}\left(1 - \left(\frac{1+g}{1+r}\right)^N\right) \qquad (4.12)$$

4.6 Using an Annuity Spreadsheet or Calculator

- Present and future values can be easily calculated using a spreadsheet program. Most programs have built-in formulas for evaluating annuities.

4.7 Non-Annual Cash Flows

- Monthly cash flow streams (or any other period length) can be evaluated in exactly the same way as annual cash flow streams so long as the interest rate and number of periods are expressed in monthly terms.

4.8 Solving for the Cash Payments

- The annuity and perpetuity formulas can be used to solve for the annuity payments when either the present value or the future value is known. The periodic payment on an N-period loan with principal P and interest rate r is

$$C = \frac{P}{\frac{1}{r}\left(1 - \frac{1}{(1+r)^N}\right)} \qquad (4.14)$$

4.9 The Internal Rate of Return

- The internal rate of return (IRR) of an investment opportunity is the interest rate that sets the NPV of the investment opportunity equal to zero.
- When there are only two cash flows, the IRR can be calculated as:

$$IRR \text{ with two cash flows} = (FV/P)^{1/N} - 1 \qquad (4.15)$$

- When the cash flows are a growing perpetuity with a starting cash flow of C with growth rate g, the IRR can be calculated as:

$$IRR \text{ of growing perpetuity} = (C/P) + g \qquad (4.16)$$

Key Terms

Further Reading

The earliest known published work that introduces the ideas in this chapter was in 1202 by the famous Italian mathematician Fibonacci (or Leonardo of Pisa) in Liber Abaci (recently translated into English by Laurence Sigler, *Fibonacci's Liber Abaci, A Translation into Modern English of Leonardo Pisano's Book of Calculation*, Springer-Verlag, 2002). In this book, Fibonacci provides examples demonstrating the rules of time travel for cash flows.

Students who are interested in the early origins of finance and the historical development of the annuity formula will be interested in reading M. Rubinstein, *A History of the Theory of Investments: My Annotated Bibliography* (John Wiley and Sons, 2006) and W. Goetzmann and K. Rouwenhorst, eds., *Origins of Value: Innovations in the History of Finance* (Oxford University Press, 2005).

The material in this chapter should provide the foundation you need to understand the time value of money. For assistance using Excel, other spreadsheet programs, or financial calculators to compute present values, consult available help files and user manuals for additional information and examples.

Students in the lucky position of having to decide how to receive lottery winnings may consult A. Atkins and E. Dyl, "The Lotto Jackpot: The Lump Sum versus the Annuity," *Financial Practice and Education* (Fall/Winter 1995): 107–11.

Problems

All problems are available in MyFinanceLab. *An asterisk (*) indicates problems with a higher level of difficulty.*

The Timeline

1. You have just taken out a five-year loan from a bank to buy an engagement ring. The ring costs $5000. You plan to put down $1000 and borrow $4000. You will need to make annual payments of $1000 at the end of each year. Show the timeline of the loan from your perspective. How would the timeline differ if you created it from the bank's perspective?

2. You currently have a four-year-old mortgage outstanding on your house. You make monthly payments of $1500. You have just made a payment. The mortgage has 26 years to go (i.e., it had an original term of 30 years). Show the timeline from your perspective. How would the timeline differ if you created it from the bank's perspective?

The Three Rules of Time Travel

3. Calculate the future value of $2000 in
   a. Five years at an interest rate of 5% per year.
   b. Ten years at an interest rate of 5% per year.
   c. Five years at an interest rate of 10% per year.
   d. Why is the amount of interest earned in part (a) less than half the amount of interest earned in part (b)?

4. What is the present value of $10,000 received
   a. Twelve years from today when the interest rate is 4% per year?
   b. Twenty years from today when the interest rate is 8% per year?
   c. Six years from today when the interest rate is 2% per year?

5. Your brother has offered to give you either $5000 today or $10,000 in 10 years. If the interest rate is 7% per year, which option is preferable?

6. Consider the following alternatives:
   i. $100 received in one year
   ii. $200 received in five years
   iii. $300 received in ten years

   a. Rank the alternatives from most valuable to least valuable if the interest rate is 10% per year.

   b. What is your ranking if the interest rate is only 5% per year?

   c. What is your ranking if the interest rate is 20% per year?

7. Suppose you invest $1000 in an account paying 8% interest per year.

   a. What is the balance in the account after 3 years? How much of this balance corresponds to "interest on interest"?

   b. What is the balance in the account after 25 years? How much of this balance corresponds to interest on interest?

8. Your daughter is currently eight years old. You anticipate that she will be going to college in 10 years. You would like to have $100,000 in a savings account to fund her education at that time. If the account promises to pay a fixed interest rate of 3% per year, how much money do you need to put into the account today to ensure that you will have $100,000 in 10 years?

9. You are thinking of retiring. Your retirement plan will pay you either $250,000 immediately on retirement or $350,000 five years after the date of your retirement. Which alternative should you choose if the interest rate is

   a. 0% per year?

   b. 8% per year?

   c. 20% per year?

10. Your grandfather put some money in an account for you on the day you were born. You are now 18 years old and are allowed to withdraw the money for the first time. The account currently has $3996 in it and pays an 8% interest rate.

   a. How much money would be in the account if you left the money there until your 25th birthday?

   b. What if you left the money until your 65th birthday?

   c. How much money did your grandfather originally put in the account?

Valuing a Stream of Cash Flows

11. Suppose you receive $100 at the end of each year for the next three years.

   a. If the interest rate is 8%, what is the present value of these cash flows?

   b. What is the future value in three years of the present value you computed in (a)?

   c. Suppose you deposit the cash flows in a bank account that pays 8% interest per year. What is the balance in the account at the end of each of the next three years (after your deposit is made)? How does the final bank balance compare with your answer in (b)?

 12. You have just received a windfall from an investment you made in a friend's business. He will be paying you $10,000 at the end of this year, $20,000 at the end of the following year, and $30,000 at the end of the year after that (three years from today). The interest rate is 3.5% per year.

   a. What is the present value of your windfall?

   b. What is the future value of your windfall in three years (on the date of the last payment)?

 13. You have a loan outstanding. It requires making three annual payments at the end of the next three years of $1000 each. Your bank has offered to allow you to skip making the next two payments in lieu of making one large payment at the end of the loan's term in three years. If the interest rate on the loan is 5%, what final payment will the bank require you to make so that it is indifferent between the two forms of payment?

Calculating the Net Present Value

 14. You have been offered a unique investment opportunity. If you invest $10,000 today, you will receive $500 one year from now, $1500 two years from now, and $10,000 ten years from now.

   a. What is the NPV of the opportunity if the interest rate is 6% per year? Should you take the opportunity?

   b. What is the NPV of the opportunity if the interest rate is 2% per year? Should you take it now?

15. Marian Plunket owns her own business and is considering an investment. If she undertakes the investment, it will pay $4000 at the end of each of the next three years. The opportunity requires an initial investment of $1000 plus an additional investment at the end of the second year of $5000. What is the NPV of this opportunity if the interest rate is 2% per year? Should Marian take it?

Perpetuities and Annuities

16. Your buddy in mechanical engineering has invented a money machine. The main drawback of the machine is that it is slow. It takes one year to manufacture $100. However, once built, the machine will last forever and will require no maintenance. The machine can be built immediately, but it will cost $1000 to build. Your buddy wants to know if he should invest the money to construct it. If the interest rate is 9.5% per year, what should your buddy do?

17. How would your answer to Problem 16 change if the machine takes one year to build?

18. The British government has a consol bond outstanding paying £100 per year forever. Assume the current interest rate is 4% per year.
    a. What is the value of the bond immediately after a payment is made?
    b. What is the value of the bond immediately before a payment is made?

19. What is the present value of $1000 paid at the end of each of the next 100 years if the interest rate is 7% per year?

*20. You are head of the Schwartz Family Endowment for the Arts. You have decided to fund an arts school in the San Francisco Bay area in perpetuity. Every five years, you will give the school $1 million. The first payment will occur five years from today. If the interest rate is 8% per year, what is the present value of your gift?

*21. When you purchased your house, you took out a 30-year annual-payment mortgage with an interest rate of 6% per year. The annual payment on the mortgage is $12,000. You have just made a payment and have now decided to pay the mortgage off by repaying the outstanding balance. What is the payoff amount if
    a. You have lived in the house for 12 years (so there are 18 years left on the mortgage)?
    b. You have lived in the house for 20 years (so there are 10 years left on the mortgage)?
    c. You have lived in the house for 12 years (so there are 18 years left on the mortgage) and you decide to pay off the mortgage immediately *before* the twelfth payment is due?

22. You are 25 years old and decide to start saving for your retirement. You plan to save $5000 at the end of each year (so the first deposit will be one year from now), and will make the last deposit when you retire at age 65. Suppose you earn 8% per year on your retirement savings.
    a. How much will you have saved for retirement?
    b. How much will you have saved if you wait until age 35 to start saving (again, with your first deposit at the end of the year)?

23. Your grandmother has been putting $1000 into a savings account on every birthday since your first (that is, when you turned 1). The account pays an interest rate of 3%. How much money will be in the account on your 18th birthday immediately after your grandmother makes the deposit on that birthday?

24. A rich relative has bequeathed you a growing perpetuity. The first payment will occur in a year and will be $1000. Each year after that, on the anniversary of the last payment you will receive a payment that is 8% larger than the last payment. This pattern of payments will go on forever. If the interest rate is 12% per year,
    a. What is today's value of the bequest?
    b. What is the value of the bequest immediately after the first payment is made?

*25. You are thinking of building a new machine that will save you $1000 in the first year. The machine will then begin to wear out so that the savings *decline* at a rate of 2% per year forever. What is the present value of the savings if the interest rate is 5% per year?

26. You work for a pharmaceutical company that has developed a new drug. The patent on the drug will last 17 years. You expect that the drug's profits will be $2 million in its first year and that this amount will grow at a rate of 5% per year for the next 17 years. Once the patent expires, other pharmaceutical companies will be able to produce the same drug and competition will likely drive profits to zero. What is the present value of the new drug if the interest rate is 10% per year?

27. Your oldest daughter is about to start kindergarten at a private school. Tuition is $10,000 per year, payable at the *beginning* of the school year. You expect to keep your daughter in private school through high school. You expect tuition to increase at a rate of 5% per year over the 13 years of her schooling. What is the present value of the tuition payments if the interest rate is 5% per year? How much would you need to have in the bank now to fund all 13 years of tuition?

28. A rich aunt has promised you $5000 one year from today. In addition, each year after that, she has promised you a payment (on the anniversary of the last payment) that is 5% larger than the last payment. She will continue to show this generosity for 20 years, giving a total of 20 payments. If the interest rate is 5%, what is her promise worth today?

29. You are running a hot Internet company. Analysts predict that its earnings will grow at 30% per year for the next five years. After that, as competition increases, earnings growth is expected to slow to 2% per year and continue at that level forever. Your company has just announced earnings of $1,000,000. What is the present value of all future earnings if the interest rate is 8%? (Assume all cash flows occur at the end of the year.)

*30. Your brother has offered to give you $100, starting next year, and after that growing at 3% for the next 20 years. You would like to calculate the value of this offer by calculating how much money you would need to deposit in the local bank so that the account will generate the same cash flows as he is offering you. Your local bank will guarantee a 6% annual interest rate so long as you have money in the account.
    a. How much money will you need to deposit into the account today?
    b. Using an Excel spreadsheet, show explicitly that you can deposit this amount of money into the account, and every year withdraw what your brother has promised, leaving the account with nothing after the last withdrawal.

Non-Annual Cash Flows

31. Suppose you currently have $5000 in your savings account, and your bank pays interest at a rate of 0.5% per month. If you make no further deposits or withdrawals, how much will you have in the account in five years?

32. Your firm spends $5000 every month on printing and mailing costs, sending statements to customers. If the interest rate is 0.5% per month, what is the present value of eliminating this cost by sending the statements electronically?

33. You have just entered an MBA program and have decided to pay for your living expenses using a credit card that has no minimum monthly payment. You intend to charge $1000 per month on the card for the next 21 months. The card carries a monthly interest rate of 1%. How much money will you owe on the card 22 months from now, when you receive your first statement post-graduation?

*34. Your credit card charges an interest rate of 2% per month. You have a current balance of $1000, and want to pay it off. Suppose you can afford to pay off $100 per month. What will your balance be at the end of one year?

Solving for the Cash Payments

35. You have decided to buy a perpetuity. The bond makes one payment at the end of every year forever and has an interest rate of 5%. If you initially put $1000 into the bond, what is the payment every year?

36. You are thinking of purchasing a house. The house costs $350,000. You have $50,000 in cash that you can use as a down payment on the house, but you need to borrow the rest of the purchase price. The bank is offering a 30-year mortgage that requires annual payments and has an interest rate of 7% per year. What will your annual payment be if you sign up for this mortgage?

 *37. You would like to buy the house and take the mortgage described in Problem 36. You can afford to pay only $23,500 per year. The bank agrees to allow you to pay this amount each year, yet still borrow $300,000. At the end of the mortgage (in 30 years), you must make a *balloon* payment; that is, you must repay the remaining balance on the mortgage. How much will this balloon payment be?

38. You have just made an offer on a new home and are seeking a mortgage. You need to borrow $600,000.
   a. The bank offers a 30-year mortgage with fixed monthly payments and an interest rate of 0.5% per month. What is the amount of your monthly payment if you take this loan?
   b. Alternatively, you can get a 15-year mortgage with fixed monthly payments and an interest rate of 0.4% per month. How much would your monthly payments be if you take this loan instead?

 39. Suppose you take the 30-year mortgage described in Problem 38, part (a). How much will you still owe on the mortgage after 15 years?

 *40. You are thinking about buying a piece of art that costs $50,000. The art dealer is proposing the following deal: He will lend you the money, and you will repay the loan by making the same payment every two years for the next 20 years (i.e., a total of 10 payments). If the interest rate is 4% per year, how much will you have to pay every two years?

 41. You are saving for retirement. To live comfortably, you decide you will need to save $2 million by the time you are 65. Today is your 30th birthday, and you decide, starting today and continuing on every birthday up to and including your 65th birthday, that you will put the same amount into a savings account. If the interest rate is 5%, how much must you set aside each year to make sure that you will have $2 million in the account on your 65th birthday?

 *42. You realize that the plan in Problem 41 has a flaw. Because your income will increase over your lifetime, it would be more realistic to save less now and more later. Instead of putting the same amount aside each year, you decide to let the amount that you set aside grow by 3% per year. Under this plan, how much will you put into the account today? (Recall that you are planning to make the first contribution to the account today.)

*43. You are 35 years old, and decide to save $5000 each year (with the first deposit one year from now), in an account paying 8% interest per year. You will make your last deposit 30 years from now when you retire at age 65. During retirement, you plan to withdraw funds from the account at the end of each year (so your first withdrawal is at age 66). What constant amount will you be able to withdraw each year if you want the funds to last until you are 90?

*44. You have just turned 30 years old, have just received your MBA, and have accepted your first job. Now you must decide how much money to put into your retirement plan. The plan works as follows: Every dollar in the plan earns 7% per year. You cannot make withdrawals until you retire on your sixty-fifth birthday. After that point, you can make withdrawals as you see fit. You decide that you will plan to live to 100 and work until you turn 65. You estimate that to live comfortably in retirement, you will need $100,000 per year starting at the end of the first year of retirement and ending on your 100th birthday. You will contribute the same amount to the plan at the end of every year that you work. How much do you need to contribute each year to fund your retirement?

*45. Problem 44 is not very realistic because most retirement plans do not allow you to specify a fixed amount to contribute every year. Instead, you are required to specify a fixed percentage of your salary that you want to contribute. Assume that your starting salary is $75,000 per year and it will grow 2% per year until you retire. Assuming everything else stays the same as in Problem 44, what percentage of your income do you need to contribute to the plan every year to fund the same retirement income

The Internal Rate of Return

46. You have an investment opportunity that requires an initial investment of $5000 today and will pay $6000 in one year. What is the IRR of this opportunity?

47. Suppose you invest $2000 today and receive $10,000 in five years.
    a. What is the IRR of this opportunity?
    b. Suppose another investment opportunity also requires $2000 upfront, but pays an equal amount at the end of each year for the next five years. If this investment has the same IRR as the first one, what is the amount you will receive each year?

48. You are shopping for a car and read the following advertisement in the newspaper: "Own a new Spitfire! No money down. Four annual payments of just $10,000." You have shopped around and know that you can buy a Spitfire for cash for $32,500. What is the interest rate the dealer is advertising (what is the IRR of the loan in the advertisement)? Assume that you must make the annual payments at the end of each year.

49. A local bank is running the following advertisement in the newspaper: "For just $1000 we will pay you $100 forever!" The fine print in the ad says that for a $1000 deposit, the bank will pay $100 every year in perpetuity, starting one year after the deposit is made. What interest rate is the bank advertising (what is the IRR of this investment)?

50. You are considering purchasing a warehouse. The cost to purchase the warehouse is $500,000. Renting the equivalent space costs $20,000 per year. If the annual interest rate is 6%, at what rate must rental cost increase each year to make the cost of renting comparable to purchasing?

*51. The Tillamook County Creamery Association manufactures Tillamook Cheddar Cheese. It markets this cheese in four varieties: aged 2 months, 9 months, 15 months, and 2 years. At the shop in the dairy, it sells 2 pounds of each variety for the following prices: $7.95, $9.49, $10.95, and $11.95, respectively. Consider the cheese maker's decision whether to continue to age a particular 2-pound block of cheese. At 2 months, he can either sell the cheese immediately or let it age further. If he sells it now, he will receive $7.95 immediately. If he ages the cheese, he must give up the $7.95 today to receive a higher amount in the future. What is the IRR (expressed in percent per month) of the investment of giving up $79.50 today by choosing to store 20 pounds of cheese that is currently 2 months old and instead selling 10 pounds of this cheese when it has aged 9 months, 6 pounds when it has aged 15 months, and the remaining 4 pounds when it has aged 2 years?

Data Case

Assume today is October 31, 2012. Terry Tan is a senior engineer in a large electronic equipment manufacturing company located in Malaysia. He earns US$120,000 per year that he anticipates will grow at 4% per year. Terry has US$800,000 in his savings account. He recently invested this money in a 10-year U.S. Treasury bonds. He is currently 40 years old and he has a bachelor degree in electrical engineering. He hopes to retire at the age of 60.

Due to his extensive work experience and excellent technical skills, Terry recently received two competing job offers from different professional executive search firms. He is considering whether he should accept one of these job offers and is asking your views as a personal financial planning analyst to determine the financial consequences associated with each option.

The first offer is for a Chief Technology Officer position in a large listed firm in Thailand starting January 1, 2013. The base salary for the position is US$80,000 more than what he currently earns and he anticipates that this salary differential will grow at a rate of 6% per year as long as he keeps working. The relocation from Malaysia to Thailand will involve initial start-up costs (to be paid by Terry) and include (i) US$50,000 due at the beginning of the first year in Thailand, (ii) US$40,000 due at the beginning of the second year in Thailand, and (iii) US$30,000 due at the beginning of the third year in Thailand.

The second job offer Terry is considering is for a Deputy President position in a large listed firm in Indonesia also starting January 1, 2013. The base salary for this position is US$100,000 more than what he currently earns and he anticipates that this salary differential will grow at a rate of 5% per year as long as he keeps working. The relocation from Malaysia to Indonesia will involve initial start-up costs (to be paid by Terry) and include (i) US$70,000 due at the beginning of the first year in Indonesia and (ii) US$60,000 due at the beginning of the second year in Indonesia.

1. Determine the interest rate that Terry is currently earning on his savings by going to Yahoo! Finance (http://finance.yahoo.com). Click on the 30-year bond link in the market summary. Next, go to "Historical Prices" and enter the appropriate date (October 31, 2012) to obtain the closing yield or the interest rate that he is earning. Use this interest rate as the discount rate for the remainder of this case.

2. Create a timeline in Excel for his current situation, the position in Thailand, and the position in Indonesia. Use the following assumptions:
   a. Salaries for the year are paid only once, at the end of the year.
   b. The salary increase becomes effective immediately after starting the new job position. That is, because the increases become effective immediately but the salaries are paid at the end of the year, the first salary will be paid exactly one year after starting the new job position.
   c. Ignore the effects of foreign exchange rates, country inflation rates, and personal tax rates.

3. Compute the present value of the salary differential for accepting the job in Thailand. Deduct the present value of the initial start-up costs to derive the net present value of accepting the job in Thailand.

4. Compute the present value of the salary differential for accepting the job in Indonesia. Deduct the present value of the initial start-up costs to derive the net present value of accepting the job in Indonesia.

5. Based on your answers to Questions 3 and 4, what is your advice to Terry?

Solving for the Number of Periods

In addition to solving for cash flows or the interest rate, we can solve for the amount of time it will take a sum of money to grow to a known value. In this case, the interest rate, present value, and future value are all known. We need to compute how long it will take for the present value to grow to the future value.

Suppose we invest $10,000 in an account paying 10% interest, and we want to know how long it will take for the amount to grow to $20,000.

We want to determine N.

In terms of our formulas, we need to find N so that the future value of our investment equals $20,000:

$$FV = \$10,000 \times 1.10^N = \$20,000 \tag{4A.1}$$

One approach is to use trial and error to find N, as with the IRR. For example, with $N = 7$ years, $FV = \$19,487$, so it will take longer than seven years. With $N = 8$ years, $FV = \$21,436$, so it will take between seven and eight years. Alternatively, this problem can be solved on the annuity spreadsheet. In this case, we solve for N:

	NPER	RATE	PV	PMT	FV	Excel Formula
Given		10.00%	−10,000	0	20,000	
Solve for NPER	7.27					=NPER(0.10,0,−10000,20000)

It will take about 7.3 years for our savings to grow to $20,000.

Finally, this problem can be solved mathematically. Dividing both sides of Eq. 4A.1 by $10,000, we have

$$1.10^N = 20,000/10,000 = 2$$

To solve for an exponent, we take the logarithm of both sides, and use the fact that $\ln(x^y) = y \ln(x)$:

$$N \ln(1.10) = \ln(2)$$

$$N = \ln(2)/\ln(1.10) = 0.6931/0.0953 \approx 7.3 \text{ years}$$

EXAMPLE 4A.1   **Solving for the Number of Periods in a Savings Plan**

Problem

You are saving for a down payment on a house. You have $10,050 saved already, and you can afford to save an additional $5000 per year at the end of each year. If you earn 7.25% per year on your savings, how long will it take you to save $60,000?

Solution

The timeline for this problem is

We need to find N so that the future value of our current savings plus the future value of our planned additional savings (which is an annuity) equals our desired amount:

$$10{,}050 \times 1.0725^N + 5000 \times \frac{1}{0.0725}(1.0725^N - 1) = 60{,}000$$

To solve mathematically, rearrange the equation to

$$1.0725^N = \frac{60{,}000 \times 0.0725 + 5000}{10{,}050 \times 0.0725 + 5000} = 1.632$$

We can then solve for N:

$$N = \frac{\ln(1.632)}{\ln(1.0725)} = 7.0 \text{ years}$$

It will take seven years to save the down payment. We can also solve this problem using the annuity spreadsheet:

	NPER	RATE	PV	PMT	FV	Excel Formula
Given		7.25%	−10,050	−5000	60,000	
Solve for N	7.00					=NPER(0.0725,−5000,−10050,60000)

Problems

All problems are available in MyFinanceLab. An asterisk (*) indicates problems with a higher level of difficulty.

*A.1. Your grandmother bought an annuity from Rock Solid Life Insurance Company for $200,000 when she retired. In exchange for the $200,000, Rock Solid will pay her $25,000 per year until she dies. The interest rate is 5%. How long must she live after the day she retired to come out ahead (that is, to get more in *value* than what she paid in)?

*A.2. You are thinking of making an investment in a new plant. The plant will generate revenues of $1 million per year for as long as you maintain it. You expect that the maintenance cost will start at $50,000 per year and will increase 5% per year thereafter. Assume that all revenue and maintenance costs occur at the end of the year. You intend to run the plant as long as it continues to make a positive cash flow (as long as the cash generated by the plant exceeds the maintenance costs). The plant can be built and become operational immediately. If the plant costs $10 million to build, and the interest rate is 6% per year, should you invest in the plant?

Interest Rates

I N CHAPTER 4, WE EXPLORED THE MECHANICS OF COMPUTING present values and future values given a market interest rate. But how do we determine that interest rate? In practice, interest is paid and interest rates are quoted in different ways. For example, in mid-2012, Metropolitan National Bank offered savings accounts with an interest rate of 1.65% paid at the end of each year, while AIG Bank offered an annual interest rate of only 1.60%, but paid on a daily basis. Interest rates can also differ depending on the investment horizon. In July 2012, investors earned less than 0.25% on one-year risk-free U.S. Treasury Bills, but could earn more than 2.3% on twenty-year Treasuries. Interest rates can also vary due to risk or tax consequences: The U.S. government is able to borrow at a lower interest rate than Johnson & Johnson, which in turn can borrow at a lower rate than American Airlines.

In this chapter, we consider the factors that affect interest rates and discuss how to determine the appropriate discount rate for a set of cash flows. We begin by looking at the way interest is paid and interest rates are quoted, and we show how to calculate the effective interest paid in one year given different quoting conventions. We then consider some of the main determinants of interest rates—namely, inflation and government policy. Because interest rates tend to change over time, investors will demand different interest rates for different investment horizons based on their expectations. Finally, we examine the role of risk in determining interest rates and show how to adjust interest rates to determine the effective amount received (or paid) after accounting for taxes.

NOTATION

EAR	effective annual rate
r	interest rate or discount rate
PV	present value
FV	future value
C	cash flow
APR	annual percentage rate
k	number of compounding periods per year
r_r	real interest rate
i	rate of inflation
NPV	net present value
C_n	cash flow that arrives in period n
n	number of periods
r_n	interest rate or discount rate for an n-year term
τ	tax rate

5.1 Interest Rate Quotes and Adjustments

Interest rates are quoted in a variety of ways. While generally stated as an annual rate, the interest payments themselves may occur at different intervals, such as monthly or semiannually. When evaluating cash flows, however, we must use a *discount rate* that matches the time period of our cash flows; this discount rate should reflect the actual return we could earn over that time period. In this section, we explore the mechanics of interpreting and adjusting the interest rate to determine the correct discount rate.

The Effective Annual Rate

Interest rates are often stated as an **effective annual rate (EAR)**, which indicates the actual amount of interest that will be earned at the end of one year.[1] This method of quoting the interest rate is the one we have used thus far in this textbook: in Chapter 4, we used the EAR as the discount rate r in our time value of money calculations. For example, with an EAR of 5%, a $100,000 investment grows to

$$\$100,000 \times (1 + r) = \$100,000 \times (1.05) = \$105,000$$

in one year. After two years it will grow to

$$\$100,000 \times (1 + r)^2 = \$100,000 \times (1.05)^2 = \$110,250$$

Adjusting the Discount Rate to Different Time Periods. The preceding example shows that earning an effective annual rate of 5% for two years is equivalent to earning 10.25% in total interest over the entire period:

$$\$100,000 \times (1.05)^2 = \$100,000 \times 1.1025 = \$110,250$$

In general, by raising the interest rate factor $(1 + r)$ to the appropriate power, we can compute an equivalent interest rate for a longer time period.

We can use the same method to find the equivalent interest rate for periods shorter than one year. In this case, we raise the interest rate factor $(1 + r)$ to the appropriate fractional power. For example, earning 5% interest in one year is equivalent to receiving

$$(1 + r)^{1/2} = (1.05)^{1/2} = \$1.0247$$

for each $1 invested every half year, or equivalently, every six months. That is, a 5% effective annual rate is equivalent to an interest rate of approximately 2.47% earned every six months. We can verify this result by computing the interest we would earn in one year by investing for two six-month periods at this rate:

$$(1 + r_{6mo})^2 = (1.0247)^2 = 1.05 = 1 + r_{1yr}$$

General Equation for Discount Rate Period Conversion. In general, we can convert a discount rate of r for one period to an equivalent discount rate for n periods using the following formula:

$$\text{Equivalent } n\text{-Period Discount Rate} = (1 + r)^n - 1 \qquad (5.1)$$

In this formula, n can be larger than 1 (to compute a rate over more than one period) or smaller than 1 (to compute a rate over a fraction of a period). When computing present

---

[1]The effective annual rate is often referred to as the *effective annual yield* (EAY) or the *annual percentage yield* (APY).

or future values, it is convenient to adjust the discount rate to match the time period of the cash flows. This adjustment is *necessary* to apply the perpetuity or annuity formulas, as shown in Example 5.1.

EXAMPLE 5.1	Valuing Monthly Cash Flows

Problem

Suppose your bank account pays interest monthly with the interest rate quoted as an effective annual rate (EAR) of 6%. What amount of interest will you earn each month? If you have no money in the bank today, how much will you need to save at the end of each month to accumulate $100,000 in 10 years?

Solution

From Eq. 5.1, a 6% EAR is equivalent to earning $(1.06)^{1/12} - 1 = 0.4868\%$ per month. We can write the timeline for our savings plan using *monthly* periods as follows:

That is, we can view the savings plan as a monthly annuity with $10 \times 12 = 120$ monthly payments. We can calculate the total amount saved as the future value of this annuity, using Eq. 4.10:

$$FV(\text{annuity}) = C \times \frac{1}{r}[(1 + r)^n - 1]$$

We can solve for the *monthly* payment C using the equivalent *monthly* interest rate $r = 0.4868\%$, and $n = 120$ months:

$$C = \frac{FV(\text{annuity})}{\frac{1}{r}[(1 + r)^n - 1]} = \frac{\$100{,}000}{\frac{1}{0.004868}[(1.004868)^{120} - 1]} = \$615.47 \text{ per month}$$

We can also compute this result using the annuity spreadsheet:

	NPER	RATE	PV	PMT	FV	Excel Formula
Given	120	0.4868%	0		100,000	
Solve for PMT				−615.47		=PMT(0.004868,120,0,100000)

Thus, if we save $615.47 per month and we earn interest monthly at an effective annual rate of 6%, we will have $100,000 in 10 years.

COMMON MISTAKE	Using the Wrong Discount Rate in the Annuity Formula

The discount rate period must match the periodicity of the cash flows in the annuity formula. In Example 5.1, because the cash flows were monthly, we first must convert the EAR into a monthly discount rate. A common mistake in this case is to treat the annuity as a 10-year annual annuity with a discount rate equal to the EAR of 6%. Doing so, we get

$$C = \frac{\$100{,}000}{\frac{1}{0.06}[(1.06)^{10} - 1]} = \$7586.80$$

which is the amount you would need to invest *per year*, not per month. Note also that if we try to convert this to a monthly amount by dividing by 12, we get 7586.80/12 = 632.23, a higher amount than we need according to Example 5.1. The reason we can save less is that by depositing the cash monthly rather than at the end of each year, we will earn interest on our deposits throughout the year.

Annual Percentage Rates

Banks also quote interest rates in terms of an **annual percentage rate (APR)**, which indicates the amount of **simple interest** earned in one year, that is, the amount of interest earned *without* the effect of compounding. Because it does not include the effect of compounding, the APR quote is typically less than the actual amount of interest that you will earn. To compute the actual amount that you will earn in one year, we must first convert the APR to an effective annual rate.

For example, suppose Granite Bank advertises savings accounts with an interest rate of "6% APR with monthly compounding." In this case, you will earn 6%/12 = 0.5% every month. So an APR with monthly compounding is actually a way of quoting a *monthly* interest rate, rather than an annual interest rate. Because the interest compounds each month, you will earn

$$\$1 \times (1.005)^{12} = \$1.061678$$

at the end of one year, for an effective annual rate of 6.1678%. The 6.1678% that you earn on your deposit is higher than the quoted 6% APR due to compounding: In later months, you earn interest on the interest paid in earlier months.

It is important to remember that because the APR does not reflect the true amount you will earn over one year, *we cannot use the APR itself as a discount rate.* Instead, the APR with k compounding periods is a way of quoting the actual interest earned each compounding period:

$$\text{Interest Rate per Compounding Period} = \frac{APR}{k \text{ periods/year}} \qquad (5.2)$$

Once we have computed the interest earned per compounding period from Eq. 5.2, we can compute the effective annual rate by compounding using Eq. 5.1. Thus the effective annual rate corresponding to an APR with k compounding periods per year is given by the following conversion formula:

Converting an APR to an EAR

$$1 + EAR = \left(1 + \frac{APR}{k}\right)^{k} \qquad (5.3)$$

Table 5.1 shows the effective annual rates that correspond to an APR of 6% with different compounding intervals. The EAR increases with the frequency of compounding because of the ability to earn interest on interest sooner. Investments can compound even more frequently than daily. In principle, the compounding interval could be hourly or every second. In the limit we approach the idea of **continuous compounding**, in which we

TABLE 5.1	Effective Annual Rates for a 6% APR with Different Compounding Periods
Compounding Interval	**Effective Annual Rate**
Annual	$(1 + 0.06/1)^{1} - 1 = 6\%$
Semiannual	$(1 + 0.06/2)^{2} - 1 = 6.09\%$
Monthly	$(1 + 0.06/12)^{12} - 1 = 6.1678\%$
Daily	$(1 + 0.06/365)^{365} - 1 = 6.1831\%$

compound the interest every instant.[2] As a practical matter, compounding more frequently than daily has a negligible impact on the effective annual rate and is rarely observed.

Remember, when working with APRs we must

1. Divide the APR by the number of compounding periods per year to determine the actual interest rate per compounding period (Eq. 5.2).

Then, if the cash flows occur at a different interval than the compounding period,

2. Compute the appropriate discount rate by compounding (Eq. 5.1).

Once you have completed these steps, you can then use the discount rate to evaluate the present or future value of a set of cash flows.

| EXAMPLE 5.2 | **Converting the APR to a Discount Rate** |

Problem

Your firm is purchasing a new telephone system, which will last for four years. You can purchase the system for an upfront cost of $150,000, or you can lease the system from the manufacturer for $4000 paid at the end of each month.[3] Your firm can borrow at an interest rate of 5% APR with semiannual compounding. Should you purchase the system outright or pay $4000 per month?

Solution

The cost of leasing the system is a 48-month annuity of $4000 per month:

Month:	0	1	2	...	48
Payment:		$4000	$4000		$4000

We can compute the present value of the lease cash flows using the annuity formula, but first we need to compute the discount rate that corresponds to a period length of one month. To do so, we convert the borrowing cost of 5% APR with semiannual compounding to a monthly discount rate. Using Eq. 5.2, the APR corresponds to a six-month discount rate of 5%/2 = 2.5%. To convert a six-month discount rate into a one-month discount rate, we compound the six-month rate by 1/6 using Eq. 5.1:

$$(1.025)^{1/6} - 1 = 0.4124\% \text{ per month}$$

(Alternatively, we could first use Eq. 5.3 to convert the APR to an EAR: $1 + EAR = (1 + 0.05/2)^2$ $= 1.050625$. Then we can convert the EAR to a monthly rate using Eq. 5.1: $(1.050625)^{1/12} - 1$ $= 0.4124\%$ per month.)

Given this discount rate, we can use the annuity formula (Eq. 4.9) to compute the present value of the 48 monthly payments:

$$PV = 4000 \times \frac{1}{0.004124}\left(1 - \frac{1}{1.004124^{48}}\right) = \$173,867$$

We can also use the annuity spreadsheet:

	NPER	RATE	PV	PMT	FV	Excel Formula
Given	48	0.4124%		−4,000	0	
Solve for PV			**173,867**			=PV(0.004124,48,−4000,0)

---

[2]A 6% APR with continuous compounding results in an EAR of approximately 6.1837%, which is almost the same as daily compounding. See the appendix for further discussion of continuous compounding.

[3]In addition to these cash flows, there may be tax and accounting considerations when comparing a purchase with a lease. We ignore these complications in this example, but will consider leases in detail in Chapter 25.

Thus, paying $4000 per month for 48 months is equivalent to paying a present value of $173,867 today. This cost is $173,867 − $150,000 = $23,867 higher than the cost of purchasing the system, so it is better to pay $150,000 for the system rather than lease it. We can interpret this result as meaning that at a 5% APR with semiannual compounding, by promising to repay $4000 per month, your firm can borrow $173,867 today. With this loan it could purchase the phone system and have an additional $23,867 to use for other purposes.

1. What is the difference between an EAR and an APR quote?

2. Why can't the APR itself be used as a discount rate?

5.2 Application: Discount Rates and Loans

Now that we have explained how to compute the discount rate from an interest rate quote, let's apply the concept to solve two common financial problems: calculating a loan payment and calculating the remaining balance on a loan.

Computing Loan Payments. To calculate a loan payment, we equate the outstanding loan balance with the present value of the loan payments using the discount rate from the quoted interest rate of the loan, and then solve for the loan payment.

Many loans, such as mortgages and car loans, are **amortizing loans**, which means that each month you pay interest on the loan plus some part of the loan balance. Usually, each monthly payment is the same, and the loan is fully repaid with the final payment. Typical terms for a new car loan might be "6.75% APR for 60 months." When the compounding interval for the APR is not stated explicitly, it is equal to the interval between the payments, or one month in this case. Thus, this quote means that the loan will be repaid with 60 equal monthly payments, computed using a 6.75% APR with monthly compounding. Consider the timeline for a $30,000 car loan with these terms:

The payment, C, is set so that the present value of the cash flows, evaluated using the loan interest rate, equals the original principal amount of $30,000. In this case, the 6.75% APR with monthly compounding corresponds to a one-month discount rate of 6.75%/12 = 0.5625%. So, using the annuity formula to compute the present value of the loan payments, the payment C must satisfy

$$C \times \frac{1}{0.005625}\left(1 - \frac{1}{1.005625^{60}}\right) = 30{,}000$$

and therefore,

$$C = \frac{30{,}000}{\dfrac{1}{0.005625}\left(1 - \dfrac{1}{1.005625^{60}}\right)} = \$590.50$$

Alternatively, we can solve for the payment C using the annuity spreadsheet:

	NPER	RATE	PV	PMT	FV	Excel Formula
Given	60	0.5625%	30,000		0	
Solve for PMT				**−590.50**		=PMT(0.005625,60,30000,0)

Computing the Outstanding Loan Balance. The outstanding balance on a loan, also called the outstanding principal, is equal to the present value of the remaining future loan payments, again evaluated using the loan interest rate.

EXAMPLE 5.3

Computing the Outstanding Loan Balance

Problem

Two years ago your firm took out a 30-year amortizing loan to purchase a small office building. The loan has a 4.80% APR with monthly payments of $2623.33. How much do you owe on the loan today? How much interest did the firm pay on the loan in the past year?

Solution

After 2 years, the loan has 28 years, or 336 months, remaining:

```
0               1               2               336
|───────────────|───────────────|──────  ···  ──|
        −$2623.33       −$2623.33       −$2623.33
```

The remaining balance on the loan is the present value of these remaining payments, using the loan rate of 4.8%/12 = 0.4% per month:

$$\text{Balance after 2 years} = \$2623.33 \times \frac{1}{0.004}\left(1 - \frac{1}{1.004^{336}}\right) = \$484{,}332$$

During the past year, your firm made total payments of $2623.33 × 12 = $31,480 on the loan. To determine the amount that was interest, it is easiest to first determine the amount that was used to repay the principal. Your loan balance one year ago, with 29 years (348 months) remaining, was

$$\text{Balance after 1 year} = \$2623.33 \times \frac{1}{0.004}\left(1 - \frac{1}{1.004^{348}}\right) = \$492{,}354$$

Therefore, the balance declined by $492,354 − $484,332 = $8022 in the past year. Of the total payments made, $8022 was used to repay the principal and the remaining $31,480 − $8022 = $23,458 was used to pay interest.

CONCEPT CHECK

1. How can you compute the outstanding balance on a loan?

2. What is an amortizing loan?

5.3 The Determinants of Interest Rates

How are interest rates determined? Fundamentally, interest rates are determined in the market based on individuals' willingness to borrow and lend. In this section, we look at some of the factors that may influence interest rates, such as inflation, government policy, and expectations of future growth.

GLOBAL FINANCIAL CRISIS   **Teaser Rates and Subprime Loans**

Some loans, such as **adjustable rate mortgages (ARMs)**, have interest rates that are not constant over the life of the loan. When the interest rate on such a loan changes, the loan payments are recalculated based on the loan's current outstanding balance, the new interest rate, and the remaining life of the loan.

Adjustable rate mortgages were the most common type of so-called "subprime" loans made to homebuyers with poor credit histories. These loans often featured low initial rates, aptly named *teaser rates*. After a short period (often 2 to 5 years) the interest rate would jump to a higher rate, implying that the monthly payment would also jump. For example, suppose the rate on the 30-year loan in Example 5.3 was a teaser rate, and that after 2 years the rate increased from 4.8% to 7.2%. Given the remaining balance after two years of $484,332, with the higher interest rate of 7.2%/12 = 0.6% per month, the monthly payment will increase from $2623.33 to

$$\text{New monthly payment} = \frac{\$484{,}332}{\frac{1}{.006}\left(1 - \frac{1}{1.006^{336}}\right)} = \$3355.62$$

While the loan might have been affordable at the initial teaser rate, many subprime borrowers could not afford the higher payments that were required after the loan rate adjusted. Prior to 2007, while interest rates remained low and home prices were high (and increasing), such borrowers were able to avoid default simply by refinancing their loans into new loans that also featured low initial teaser rates. In this way, they were able to keep their payments low. But as mortgage rates increased and housing prices began to decline in 2007, this strategy for keeping their loan payments low was no longer possible. In many cases the outstanding loan balance exceeded the market value of the home, making lenders unwilling to refinance the loans. Stuck with a loan at a now unaffordable interest rate, many homeowners defaulted, and the rate of foreclosure on subprime loans skyrocketed.

To prevent future lenders from using teaser rates to get borrowers into loans they might not ultimately be able to afford, the Dodd-Frank Act requires lenders to verify that borrowers have sufficient income to repay their loans even after the teaser rate expires.

Inflation and Real Versus Nominal Rates

The interest rates that are quoted by banks and other financial institutions, and that we have used for discounting cash flows, are **nominal interest rates**, which indicate the rate at which your money will grow if invested for a certain period. Of course, if prices in the economy are also growing due to inflation, the nominal interest rate does not represent the increase in purchasing power that will result from investing. The rate of growth of your purchasing power, after adjusting for inflation, is determined by the **real interest rate**, which we denote by r_r. If r is the nominal interest rate and i is the rate of inflation, we can calculate the rate of growth of purchasing power as follows:

$$\text{Growth in Purchasing Power} = 1 + r_r = \frac{1+r}{1+i} = \frac{\text{Growth of Money}}{\text{Growth of Prices}} \quad (5.4)$$

We can rearrange Eq. 5.4 to find the following formula for the real interest rate, together with a convenient approximation for the real interest rate when inflation rates are low:

The Real Interest Rate

$$r_r = \frac{r - i}{1 + i} \approx r - i \quad (5.5)$$

That is, the real interest rate is approximately equal to the nominal interest rate less the rate of inflation.[4]

---

[4]The real interest rate should not be used as a discount rate for future cash flows. It can only be used if the cash flows have been adjusted to remove the effect of inflation (in that case, we say the cash flows are in *real terms*). This approach is error prone, however, so throughout this book we will always forecast actual cash flows including any growth due to inflation, and discount using nominal interest rates.

EXAMPLE 5.4	**Calculating the Real Interest Rate**

Problem

At the start of 2008, one-year U.S. government bond rates were about 3.3%, while the rate of inflation that year was 0.1%. At the start of 2011, one-year interest rates were about 0.3%, and inflation that year was about 3.0%. What was the real interest rate in 2008 and 2011?

Solution

Using Eq. 5.5, the real interest rate in 2008 was $(3.3\% - 0.1\%)/(1.001) = 3.20\%$. In 2011, the real interest rate was $(0.3\% - 3.0\%)/(1.03) = -2.62\%$. Note that the real interest rate was negative in 2011, indicating that interest rates were insufficient to keep up with inflation: Investors in U.S. government bonds were able to buy less at the end of the year than they could have purchased at the start of the year. On the other hand, there was hardly any inflation in 2008, and so the real interest rate earned was only slightly below the nominal interest rate.

Figure 5.1 shows the history of U.S. nominal interest rates and inflation rates since 1960. Note that the nominal interest rate tends to move with inflation. Intuitively, individuals' willingness to save will depend on the growth in purchasing power they can expect (given by the real interest rate). Thus, when the inflation rate is high, a higher nominal interest rate is generally needed to induce individuals to save. Note, however, that by historical standards, the last few years have been somewhat exceptional: nominal interest rates have been extremely low, leading to negative real interest rates.

Investment and Interest Rate Policy

Interest rates also affect firms' incentive to raise capital and invest. Consider a risk-free investment opportunity that requires an upfront investment of $10 million and generates

FIGURE 5.1	**U.S. Interest Rates and Inflation Rates, 1962–2012**

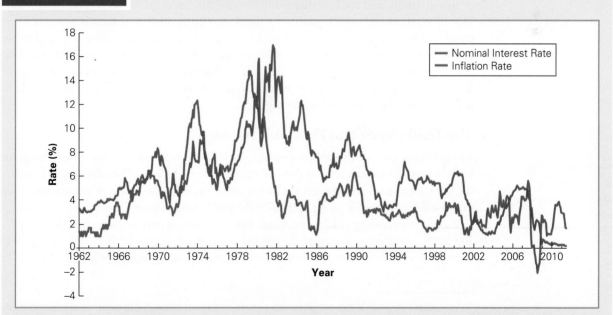

Interest rates are one-year Treasury rates, and inflation rates are the increase in the U.S. Bureau of Labor Statistics' consumer price index over the coming year, with both series computed on a monthly basis The difference between them thus reflects the approximate real interest rate earned by holding Treasuries. Note that interest rates tend to be high when inflation is high.

a cash flow of \$3 million per year for four years. If the risk-free interest rate is 5%, this investment has an NPV of

$$NPV = -10 + \frac{3}{1.05} + \frac{3}{1.05^2} + \frac{3}{1.05^3} + \frac{3}{1.05^4} = \$0.638 \text{ million}$$

If the interest rate is 9%, the NPV falls to

$$NPV = -10 + \frac{3}{1.09} + \frac{3}{1.09^2} + \frac{3}{1.09^3} + \frac{3}{1.09^4} = -\$0.281 \text{ million}$$

and the investment is no longer profitable. The reason, of course, is that we are discounting the positive cash flows at a higher rate, which reduces their present value. The cost of \$10 million occurs today, however, so its present value is independent of the discount rate.

More generally, when the costs of an investment precede the benefits, an increase in the interest rate will decrease the investment's NPV. All else equal, higher interest rates will therefore tend to shrink the set of positive-NPV investments available to firms. The Federal Reserve in the United States and central banks in other countries use this relationship between interest rates and investment to try to guide the economy. They can raise interest rates to reduce investment if the economy is "overheating" and inflation is on the rise, and they can lower interest rates to stimulate investment if the economy is slowing or in recession.

Monetary Policy, Deflation, and the 2008 Financial Crisis. When the 2008 financial crisis struck the economy, the U.S. Federal Reserve responded quickly to mitigate its impact on the broader economy by cutting its short-term interest rate target to 0% by year's end. But while this use of monetary policy is generally quite effective, because consumer prices were falling in late 2008, the inflation rate was negative, and so even with a 0% nominal interest rate the real interest rate remained positive initially. The consequence of this deflation, and the risk that it might continue, meant that the Federal Reserve was "out of ammunition" with regard to its usual weapon against an economic slowdown—it could not lower rates further.[5] This problem was one of the reasons the U.S. and other governments began to consider other measures, such as increased government spending and investment, to stimulate their economies. Former Federal Reserve Governor Kevin Warsh further discusses monetary policy responses to the economic crisis in both the U.S. and Europe in the interview box on page 154.

The Yield Curve and Discount Rates

You may have noticed that the interest rates that banks offer on investments or charge on loans depend on the horizon, or *term*, of the investment or loan. The relationship between the investment term and the interest rate is called the **term structure** of interest rates. We can plot this relationship on a graph called the **yield curve**. Figure 5.2 shows the term structure and corresponding yield curve of risk-free U.S. interest rates in November 2006, 2007, and 2008. In each case, note that the interest rate depends on the horizon, and that the difference between short-term and long-term interest rates was especially pronounced in 2008.

---

[5]Why couldn't the Federal Reserve go further and make nominal interest rates negative? Since individuals can always hold cash (or put their money in a savings account) and earn at least a zero return, the nominal interest rate can never be *significantly* negative. But because storing cash is costly, and because investors viewed many banks as unsafe, short-term U.S. Treasury interest rates were actually slightly negative (down to −0.05%) at several points throughout this period! (See Chapter 6 for further discussion.)

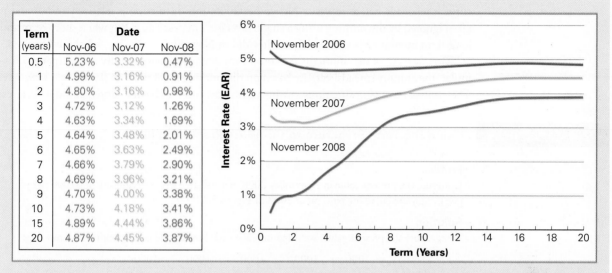

FIGURE 5.2   **Term Structure of Risk-Free U.S. Interest Rates, November 2006, 2007, and 2008**

Term (years)	Date		
	Nov-06	Nov-07	Nov-08
0.5	5.23%	3.32%	0.47%
1	4.99%	3.16%	0.91%
2	4.80%	3.16%	0.98%
3	4.72%	3.12%	1.26%
4	4.63%	3.34%	1.69%
5	4.64%	3.48%	2.01%
6	4.65%	3.63%	2.49%
7	4.66%	3.79%	2.90%
8	4.69%	3.96%	3.21%
9	4.70%	4.00%	3.38%
10	4.73%	4.18%	3.41%
15	4.89%	4.44%	3.86%
20	4.87%	4.45%	3.87%

The figure shows the interest rate available from investing in risk-free U.S. Treasury securities with different investment terms. In each case, the interest rates differ depending on the horizon. (Data from U.S. Treasury STRIPS.)

We can use the term structure to compute the present and future values of a risk-free cash flow over different investment horizons. For example, $100 invested for one year at the one-year interest rate in November 2008 would grow to a future value of

$$\$100 \times 1.0091 = \$100.91$$

at the end of one year, and $100 invested for ten years at the ten-year interest rate in November 2008 would grow to[6]

$$\$100 \times (1.0341)^{10} = \$139.84$$

We can apply the same logic when computing the present value of cash flows with different maturities. A risk-free cash flow received in two years should be discounted at the two-year interest rate, and a cash flow received in ten years should be discounted at the ten-year interest rate. In general, a risk-free cash flow of C_n received in n years has present value

$$PV = \frac{C_n}{(1 + r_n)^n} \tag{5.6}$$

where r_n is the risk-free interest rate (expressed as an EAR) for an n-year term. In other words, when computing a present value we must match the term of the cash flow and term of the discount rate.

Combining Eq. 5.6 for cash flows in different years leads to the general formula for the present value of a cash flow stream:

Present Value of a Cash Flow Stream Using a Term Structure of Discount Rates

$$PV = \frac{C_1}{1 + r_1} + \frac{C_2}{(1 + r_2)^2} + \cdots + \frac{C_N}{(1 + r_N)^N} = \sum_{n=1}^{N} \frac{C_n}{(1 + r_n)^n} \tag{5.7}$$

---

[6]We could also invest for 10 years by investing at the one-year interest rate for 10 years in a row. However, because we do not know what future interest rates will be, our ultimate payoff would not be risk free.

Note the difference between Eq. 5.7 and Eq. 4.4. Here, we use a different discount rate for each cash flow, based on the rate from the yield curve with the same term. When the yield curve is relatively flat, as it was in November 2006, this distinction is relatively minor and is often ignored by discounting using a single "average" interest rate r. But when short-term and long-term interest rates vary widely, as they did in November 2008, Eq. 5.7 should be used.

Warning: All of our shortcuts for computing present values (annuity and perpetuity formulas, the annuity spreadsheet) are based on discounting all of the cash flows *at the same rate*. They *cannot* be used in situations in which cash flows need to be discounted at different rates.

EXAMPLE 5.5   **Using the Term Structure to Compute Present Values**

Problem

Compute the present value in November 2008 of a risk-free five-year annuity of $1000 per year, given the yield curve for November 2008 in Figure 5.2.

Solution

To compute the present value, we discount each cash flow by the corresponding interest rate:

$$PV = \frac{1000}{1.0091} + \frac{1000}{1.0098^2} + \frac{1000}{1.0126^3} + \frac{1000}{1.0169^4} + \frac{1000}{1.0201^5} = \$4775.25$$

Note that we cannot use the annuity formula here because the discount rates differ for each cash flow.

The Yield Curve and the Economy

Figure 5.3 shows the gap between short-term and long-term interest rate historically. Note how sometimes, short-term rates are close to long-term rates, and at other times they may be very different. What accounts for the changing shape of the yield curve?

Interest Rate Determination. The Federal Reserve determines very short-term interest rates through its influence on the **federal funds rate**, which is the rate at which banks can borrow cash reserves on an overnight basis. All other interest rates on the yield curve are set in the market and are adjusted until the supply of lending matches the demand for borrowing at each loan term. As we will see, expectations of future interest rate changes have a major effect on investors' willingness to lend or borrow for longer terms and, therefore, on the shape of the yield curve.

COMMON MISTAKE   **Using the Annuity Formula When Discount Rates Vary by Maturity**

When computing the present value of an annuity, a common mistake is to use the annuity formula with a single interest rate even though interest rates vary with the investment horizon. For example, we *cannot* compute the present value of the five-year annuity in Example 5.5 using the five-year interest rate from November 2008:

$$PV \neq \$1000 \times \frac{1}{0.0201}\left(1 - \frac{1}{1.0201^5}\right) = \$4712.09$$

To find the single interest rate that we could use to value the annuity, we must first compute the present value of the annuity using Eq. 5.7 and then solve for its IRR. For the annuity in Example 5.5, we use the annuity spreadsheet below to find its IRR of 1.55%. The IRR of the annuity is always between the highest and lowest discount rates used to calculate its present value, as is the case in the example below.

	NPER	RATE	PV	PMT	FV	Excel Formula
Given	5		−4,775.25	1000	0	
Solve for Rate		1.55%				=RATE(5,1000,−4775.25,0)

FIGURE 5.3   **Short-Term Versus Long-Term U.S. Interest Rates and Recessions**

One-year and ten-year U.S. Treasury rates are plotted, with the spread between them shaded in blue if the shape of the yield curve is increasing (the one-year rate is below the ten-year rate) and in red if the yield curve is inverted (the one-year rate exceeds the ten-year rate). Gray bars show the dates of U.S. recessions as determined by the National Bureau of Economic Research. Note that inverted yield curves tend to precede recessions by 12–18 months. In recessions, interest rates tend to fall, with short-term rates dropping further. As a result, the yield curve tends to be steep coming out of a recession.

Interest Rate Expectations. Suppose short-term interest rates are equal to long-term interest rates. If investors expect interest rates to rise in the future, they would not want to make long-term investments. Instead, they could do better by investing on a short-term basis and then reinvesting after interest rates rose. Thus, if interest rates are expected to rise, long-term interest rates will tend to be higher than short-term rates to attract investors.

Similarly, if interest rates are expected to fall in the future, then borrowers would not wish to borrow at long-term rates that are equal to short-term rates. They would do better by borrowing on a short-term basis, and then taking out a new loan after rates fall. So, if interest rates are expected to fall, long-term rates will tend to be lower than short-term rates to attract borrowers.

These arguments imply that the shape of the yield curve will be strongly influenced by interest rate expectations. A sharply increasing (*steep*) yield curve, with long-term rates much higher than short-term rates, generally indicates that interest rates are expected to rise in the future (see the yield curve for November 2008 shown in Figure 5.2). A decreasing (*inverted*) yield curve, with long-term rates lower than short-term rates, generally signals an expected decline in future interest rates (see the yield curve for November 2006 shown in Figure 5.2). Because interest rates tend to drop in response to a slowdown in the economy, an inverted yield curve is often interpreted as a negative forecast for economic growth. Indeed, as Figure 5.3 illustrates, each of the last seven recessions in the United States was preceded by a

Kevin M. Warsh, *a lecturer at Stanford's Graduate School of Business and a distinguished visiting fellow at the Hoover Institution,* was a Federal Reserve governor from 2006 to 2011, serving as chief liaison to the financial markets.

QUESTION: *What are the main policy instruments used by central banks to control the economy?*

ANSWER: The Federal Reserve (Fed) deploys several policy tools to achieve its goals of price stability, maximum sustainable employment, and financial stability. Lowering the federal funds short-term interest rate, the primary policy instrument, stimulates the economy. Raising the federal funds rate generally slows the economy. Buying and selling short-term U.S. Treasury securities through *open market operations* is standard practice. Prior to the 2007–2009 financial crisis, the Fed's balance sheet ranged from $700–$900 billion. But when the Fed was unable to lower interest rates further because rates were so close to zero already, it resorted to large-scale, longer-term open market operations to increase liquidity in the financial system in the hopes of stimulating the economy further, thus growing its balance sheet significantly. With *open mouth operations,* the Fed's announcements of its intent to buy or sell assets indicates its desired degree of future policy accommodation, often prompting markets to react by adjusting interest rates immediately. The Fed's Lender-of-Last-Resort authority allows it to lend money against good collateral to troubled institutions under certain conditions.

QUESTION: *What factors limit the effectiveness of Fed policy?*

ANSWER: Monetary policy does not act in isolation. Fiscal (taxing and spending), trade, and regulatory policies have huge consequence on the state of economic and financial conditions. In the short term, monetary policy can help buy time for an economy to improve, but it cannot cure structural failings of an economy in isolation or compensate for the country's growing indebtedness.

QUESTION: *What tools did the Fed create to address the 2007–2009 financial crisis?*

ANSWER: During the darkest days of the crisis, markets did not operate effectively, prices for securities did not clear, and banks and other financial institutions lacked clarity and confidence in the financial wherewithal of each other. One effective, innovative tool, the *Term Auction Facility (TAF),* stimulated the economy by providing cheap and readily available term funding to banks, large and small, on the front lines of the economy, thus encouraging them to extend credit to businesses and consumers. After reducing the policy rate to near zero to help revive the economy, the Fed instituted two *Quantitative Easing (QE)* programs—special purchases of government and agency securities—to increase money supply, promote lending, and according to some proponents, increase prices of riskier assets.

The Fed also addressed the global financial crisis by establishing temporary *central bank liquidity swap lines* with the European Central Bank and other major central banks. Using this facility, a foreign central bank is able to obtain dollar funding for its customers by swapping Euros for dollars or another currency and agreeing to reverse the swap at a later date. The Fed does not take exchange rate risk, but it is subject to the credit risk of its central bank counterparty.

QUESTION: *What tools is the European Central Bank (ECB) using to address the sovereign debt crisis? How does its approach compare to the Fed's approach to the 2007–2009 financial crisis?*

ANSWER: As a novel economic federation, the ECB finds itself in a more difficult position than the Fed. The underlying economies and competitiveness are markedly different across the Eurozone—in Germany versus Greece, for example. From 2007 until mid-2010, many European financiers and policymakers believed that global financial crisis was largely American-made, with some strains exported to the continent. By mid-2010, however, they recognized that it was indeed a global crisis. The ECB is formally charged with a single mandate of ensuring price stability, rather than the broader mandate of the Fed. Still, its actions ultimately mirrored many of those undertaken by the Fed: lowering the effective policy rate to record lows, providing direct liquidity to the Eurozone's financial institutions to avoid a potential run on the banking system, and instituting the Security Market Purchase program (buying sovereign credit of some of its distressed countries).

period in which the yield curve was inverted. Conversely, the yield curve tends to be steep as the economy comes out of a recession and interest rates are expected to rise.[7]

Clearly, the yield curve provides extremely important information for a business manager. In addition to specifying the discount rates for risk-free cash flows that occur at different horizons, it is also a potential leading indicator of future economic growth.

EXAMPLE 5.6	**Comparing Short- and Long-Term Interest Rates**

Problem

Suppose the current one-year interest rate is 1%. If it is known with certainty that the one-year interest rate will be 2% next year and 4% the following year, what will the interest rates r_1, r_2, and r_3 of the yield curve be today? Is the yield curve flat, increasing, or inverted?

Solution

We are told already that the one-year rate $r_1 = 1\%$. To find the two-year rate, note that if we invest $1 for one year at the current one-year rate and then reinvest next year at the new one-year rate, after two years we will earn

$$\$1 \times (1.01) \times (1.02) = \$1.0302$$

We should earn the same payoff if we invest for two years at the current two-year rate r_2:

$$\$1 \times (1 + r_2)^2 = \$1.0302$$

Otherwise, there would be an arbitrage opportunity: If investing at the two-year rate led to a higher payoff, investors could invest for two years and borrow each year at the one-year rate. If investing at the two-year rate led to a lower payoff, investors could invest each year at the one-year rate and borrow at the two-year rate.

Solving for r_2, we find that

$$r_2 = (1.0302)^{1/2} - 1 = 1.499\%$$

Similarly, investing for three years at the one-year rates should have the same payoff as investing at the current three-year rate:

$$(1.01) \times (1.02) \times (1.04) = 1.0714 = (1 + r_3)^3$$

We can solve for $r_3 = (1.0714)^{1/3} - 1 = 2.326\%$. Therefore, the current yield curve has $r_1 = 1\%$, $r_2 = 1.499\%$, and $r_3 = 2.326\%$. The yield curve is increasing as a result of the anticipated higher interest rates in the future.

CONCEPT CHECK	1. What is the difference between a nominal and real interest rate?
	2. How do investors' expectations of future short-term interest rates affect the shape of the current yield curve?

5.4 Risk and Taxes

In this section, we discuss two other factors that are important when evaluating interest rates: risk and taxes.

---

[7]Other factors besides interest rate expectations—most notably risk—can have an impact on the shape of the yield curve. See Chapter 6 for further discussion.

Risk and Interest Rates

We have already seen that interest rates vary with the investment horizon. Interest rates also vary based on the identity of the borrower. For example, Figure 5.4 shows the interest rates required by investors for five-year loans to a number of different borrowers in mid-2012.

Why do these interest rates vary so widely? The lowest interest rate is the rate paid on U.S. Treasury notes. U.S. Treasury securities are widely regarded to be risk free because there is virtually no chance the government will fail to pay the interest and default on these bonds. Thus, when we refer to the "risk-free interest rate," we mean the rate on U.S. Treasuries.

All other borrowers have some risk of default. For these loans, the stated interest rate is the *maximum* amount that investors will receive. Investors may receive less if the company has financial difficulties and is unable to fully repay the loan. To compensate for the risk that they will receive less if the firm defaults, investors demand a higher interest rate than the rate on U.S. Treasuries. The difference between the interest rate of the loan and the Treasury rate will depend on investors' assessment of the likelihood that the firm will default.

Later, we will develop tools to evaluate the risk of different investments and determine the interest rate or discount rate that appropriately compensates investors for the level of risk they are taking. For now, remember that when discounting future cash flows, it is important to use a discount rate that matches both the horizon and the risk of the cash flows. Specifically, *the right discount rate for a cash flow is the rate of return available in the market on other investments of comparable risk and term.*

FIGURE 5.4

Interest Rates on Five-Year Loans for Various Borrowers, July 2012

Interest rates shown based on yields of 5-year bonds for each issuer. Note the variation in interest rates based on the riskiness of the borrower.

Source: FINRA.org.

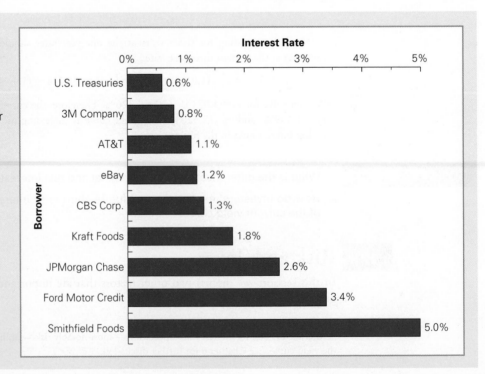

| EXAMPLE 5.7 | **Discounting Risky Cash Flows** |

Problem

Suppose the U.S. government owes your firm $1000, to be paid in five years. Based on the interest rates in Figure 5.4, what is the present value of this cash flow? Suppose instead Smithfield Foods owes your firm $1000. Estimate the present value in this case.

Solution

Assuming we can regard the government's obligation as risk free (there is no chance you won't be paid), then we discount the cash flow using the risk-free Treasury interest rate of 0.6%:

$$PV = \$1000 \div (1.006)^5 = \$970.53$$

The obligation from Smithfield Foods is not risk-free. There is no guarantee that Smithfield Foods will not have financial difficulties and fail to pay the $1000. Because the risk of this obligation is likely to be comparable to the five-year loan quoted in Figure 5.4, the 5% interest rate of the loan is a more appropriate discount rate to use to compute the present value in this case:

$$PV = \$1000 \div (1.05)^5 = \$783.53$$

Note the substantially lower present value of Smithfield's debt compared to the government debt due to Smithfield's higher risk of default.

After-Tax Interest Rates

If the cash flows from an investment are taxed, the investor's actual cash flow will be reduced by the amount of the tax payments. We will discuss the taxation of corporate investments in detail in later chapters. Here, we consider the effect of taxes on the interest earned on savings (or paid on borrowing). Taxes reduce the amount of interest the investor can keep, and we refer to this reduced amount as the **after-tax interest rate**.

Consider an investment that pays 8% interest (EAR) for one year. If you invest $100 at the start of the year, you will earn $8\% \times \$100 = \$8$ in interest at year-end. This interest may be taxable as income.[8] If you are in a 40% tax bracket, you will owe

$$(40\% \text{ income tax rate}) \times (\$8 \text{ interest}) = \$3.20 \text{ tax liability}$$

Thus, you will receive only $\$8 - \$3.20 = \$4.80$ after paying taxes. This amount is equivalent to earning 4.80% interest and not paying any taxes, so the after-tax interest rate is 4.80%.

In general, if the interest rate is r and the tax rate is τ, then for each $1 invested you will earn interest equal to r and owe tax of $\tau \times r$ on the interest. The equivalent after-tax interest rate is therefore

After-Tax Interest Rate

$$r - (\tau \times r) = r(1 - \tau) \tag{5.8}$$

Applying this formula to our previous example of an 8% interest rate and a 40% tax rate, we find the interest rate is $8\% \times (1 - 0.40) = 4.80\%$ after taxes.

---

[8]In the United States, interest income for individuals is taxable as income unless the investment is held in a tax-sheltered retirement account or the investment is from tax-exempt securities (such as municipal bonds). Interest from U.S. Treasury securities is exempt from state and local taxes. Interest income earned by a corporation is also taxed at the corporate tax rate.

We can apply the same calculation to loans. In some cases, the interest on loans is tax deductible.[9] In that case, the cost of paying interest on the loan is offset by the benefit of the tax deduction. The net effect is that when interest on a loan is tax deductible, the effective after-tax interest rate is $r(1 - \tau)$. In other words, the ability to deduct the interest expense lowers the effective after-tax interest rate paid on the loan.

EXAMPLE 5.8

Comparing After-Tax Interest Rates

Problem

Suppose you have a credit card with a 14% APR with monthly compounding, a bank savings account paying 5% EAR, and a home equity loan with a 7% APR with monthly compounding. Your income tax rate is 40%. The interest on the savings account is taxable, and the interest on the home equity loan is tax deductible. What is the effective after-tax interest rate of each instrument, expressed as an EAR? Suppose you are purchasing a new car and are offered a car loan with a 4.8% APR and monthly compounding (which is not tax deductible). Should you take the car loan?

Solution

Because taxes are typically paid annually, we first convert each interest rate to an EAR to determine the actual amount of interest earned or paid during the year. The savings account has a 5% EAR. Using Eq. 5.3, the EAR of the credit card is $(1 + 0.14/12)^{12} - 1 = 14.93\%$, and the EAR of the home equity loan is $(1 + 0.07/12)^{12} - 1 = 7.23\%$.

Next, we compute the after-tax interest rate for each. Because the credit card interest is not tax deductible, its after-tax interest rate is the same as its pre-tax interest rate, 14.93%. The after-tax interest rate on the home equity loan, which is tax deductible, is $7.23\% \times (1 - 0.40) = 4.34\%$. The after-tax interest rate that we will earn on the savings account is $5\% \times (1 - 0.40) = 3\%$.

Now consider the car loan. Its EAR is $(1 + 0.048/12)^{12} - 1 = 4.91\%$. It is not tax deductible, so this rate is also its after-tax interest rate. Therefore, the car loan is not our cheapest source of funds. It would be best to use savings, which has an opportunity cost of foregone after-tax interest of 3%. If we don't have sufficient savings, we should use the home equity loan, which has an after-tax cost of 4.34%. And we should certainly not borrow using the credit card!

CONCEPT CHECK

1. Why do corporations pay higher interest rates on their loans than the U.S. government?

2. How do taxes affect the interest earned on an investment? What about the interest paid on a loan?

5.5 The Opportunity Cost of Capital

As we have seen in this chapter, the interest rates we observe in the market will vary based on quoting conventions, the term of the investment, and risk. The actual return kept by an investor will also depend on how the interest is taxed. In this chapter, we have developed

---

[9]In the United States, interest is tax deductible for individuals only for home mortgages or home equity loans (up to certain limits), some student loans, and loans made to purchase securities. Interest on other forms of consumer debt is not tax deductible. Interest on debt is tax deductible for corporations.

COMMON MISTAKE | **States Dig a $3 Trillion Hole by Discounting at the Wrong Rate**

Almost all states in the United States offer their employees a defined benefit pension plan guaranteeing a retirement income based on the duration of their employment with the state and their final salary. These promised payments are the plan's liabilities—and because the payouts are guaranteed, they are comparable to a risk-free bond. To meet these liabilities, states put aside funds and invest them in risky assets like stocks and corporate bonds.

Unfortunately, states make a critical, but common, mistake when determining their funding requirements: They compute the present value of the liabilities using an arbitrary discount rate (typically 8%) that is unrelated to the riskiness of the plan's liabilities.

Because of their guaranteed nature, the risk-free rate, which is currently well below 8%, is the correct discount rate for plan liabilities.[10] This error has led states to grossly underestimate the value of their liabilities—and underfunded pension plans impose a potential future obligation on taxpayers. How large is this obligation? Professors Robert Novy-Marx and Joshua Rauh[11] found that total state pension underfunding in 2008 amounted to at least $3 *trillion*. They also estimated that there is less than a 5% probability that, over the next 15 years, states will be able to meet their pension obligations without turning to taxpayers. Worse still, states are most likely to need the money in market downturns, precisely when taxpayers are least able to pay.

---

the tools to account for these differences and gained some insights into how interest rates are determined.

In Chapter 3, we argued that the "market interest rate" provides the exchange rate that we need to compute present values and evaluate an investment opportunity. But with so many interest rates to choose from, the term "market interest rate" is inherently ambiguous. Therefore, going forward, we will base the discount rate that we use to evaluate cash flows on the investor's **opportunity cost of capital** (or more simply, the **cost of capital**), which is *the best available expected return offered in the market on an investment of comparable risk and term to the cash flow being discounted.*

The cost of capital is clearly relevant for a firm seeking to raise capital from outside investors. In order to attract funds, the firm must offer an expected return comparable to what investors could earn elsewhere with the same risk and horizon. The same logic applies when a firm considers a project it can fund internally. Because any funds invested in a new project could be returned to shareholders to invest elsewhere, the new project should be taken only if it offers a better return than shareholders' other opportunities.

Thus, the opportunity cost of capital provides the benchmark against which the cash flows of the new investment should be evaluated. For a risk-free project, it will typically correspond to the interest rate on U.S. Treasury securities with a similar term. The cost of capital for risky projects will often exceed this amount, depending on the nature and magnitude of the risk. We will develop tools for estimating the cost of capital for risky projects in Part IV.

CONCEPT CHECK | 1. What is the opportunity cost of capital?

2. Why do different interest rates exist, even in a competitive market?

---

[10]States often justify the 8% rate as the return they expect to earn on their investments. But the risks of their investments and of their liabilities are not comparable (for example, the return on stocks is not guaranteed), so this argument is fundamentally flawed.

[11]R. Novy-Marx and J. Rau, The Liabilities and Risks of State-Sponsored Pension Plans, *Journal of Economic Perspectives—Volume 23, Number 4—Fall 2009.*

MyFinanceLab	Here is what you should know after reading this chapter. MyFinanceLab will help you identify what you know and where to go when you need to practice.

5.1 Interest Rate Quotes and Adjustments

- The effective annual rate (EAR) indicates the actual amount of interest earned in one year. The EAR can be used as a discount rate for annual cash flows.
- Given an EAR, r, the equivalent discount rate for an n-year time interval, where n may be a fraction, is

$$(1 + r)^n - 1 \tag{5.1}$$

- An annual percentage rate (APR) indicates the total amount of interest earned in one year without considering the effect of compounding. APRs cannot be used as discount rates.
- Given an APR with k compounding intervals per year, the interest earned per compounding interval is APR/k.
- Given an APR with k compounding intervals per year, the EAR is given by:

$$1 + EAR = \left(1 + \frac{APR}{k}\right)^k \tag{5.3}$$

- For a given APR, the EAR increases with the compounding frequency.

5.2 Application: Discount Rates and Loans

- Loan rates are typically stated as APRs, with the compounding interval of the APR equal to the payment frequency.
- The outstanding balance of a loan is equal to the present value of the loan payments, when evaluated using the effective interest rate per payment interval based on the loan rate.

5.3 The Determinants of Interest Rates

- Quoted interest rates are nominal interest rates, which indicate the rate of growth of the money invested. The real interest rate indicates the rate of growth of one's purchasing power after adjusting for inflation.
- Given a nominal interest rate r and an inflation rate i, the real interest rate is

$$r_r = \frac{r - i}{1 + i} \approx r - i \tag{5.5}$$

- Nominal interest rates tend to be high when inflation is high and low when inflation is low.
- Higher interest rates tend to reduce the NPV of typical investment projects. The U.S. Federal Reserve raises interest rates to moderate investment and combat inflation and lowers interest rates to stimulate investment and economic growth.
- Interest rates differ with the investment horizon according to the term structure of interest rates. The graph plotting interest rates as a function of the horizon is called the yield curve.
- Cash flows should be discounted using the discount rate that is appropriate for their horizon. Thus the PV of a cash flow stream is

$$PV = \frac{C_1}{1 + r_1} + \frac{C_2}{(1 + r_2)^2} + \cdots + \frac{C_N}{(1 + r_N)^N} = \sum_{n=1}^{N} \frac{C_n}{(1 + r_n)^n} \tag{5.7}$$

- Annuity and perpetuity formulas cannot be applied when discount rates vary with the horizon.
- The shape of the yield curve tends to vary with investors' expectations of future economic growth and interest rates. It tends to be inverted prior to recessions and to be steep coming out of a recession.

5.4 Risk and Taxes

- U.S. government Treasury rates are regarded as risk-free interest rates. Because other borrowers may default, they will pay higher interest rates on their loans.

- The correct discount rate for a cash flow is the expected return available in the market on other investments of comparable risk and term.
- If the interest on an investment is taxed at rate τ, or if the interest on a loan is tax deductible, then the effective after-tax interest rate is

$$r(1 - \tau) \tag{5.8}$$

5.5 The Opportunity Cost of Capital

- The opportunity cost of capital is the best available expected return offered in the market on an investment of comparable risk and term.
- The opportunity cost of capital provides the benchmark against which the cash flows of a new investment should be evaluated.

Key Terms

adjustable rate mortgages (ARMs) *p. 148*
after-tax interest rate *p. 157*
amortizing loan *p. 146*
annual percentage rate (APR) *p. 144*
continuous compounding *p. 144*
(opportunity) cost of capital *p. 159*
effective annual rate (EAR) *p. 142*

federal funds rate *p. 152*
mid-year convention *p. 168*
nominal interest rate *p. 148*
real interest rate *p. 148*
simple interest *p. 144*
term structure *p. 150*
yield curve *p. 150*

Further Reading

For an interesting account of the history of interest rates over the past four millennia, see S. Homer and R. Sylla, *A History of Interest Rates* (John Wiley & Sons, 2005).

For a deeper understanding of interest rates, how they behave with changing market conditions, and how risk can be managed, see J. C. Van Horne, *Financial Market Rates and Flows* (Prentice Hall, 2000).

For further insights into the relationship between interest rates, inflation, and economic growth, see a macroeconomics text such as A. Abel, B. Bernanke, and D. Croushore, *Macroeconomics* (Prentice Hall, 2010).

For further analysis of the yield curve and how it is measured and modeled, see M. Choudhry, *Analyzing and Interpreting the Yield Curve* (John Wiley & Sons, 2004).

Problems

All problems are available in MyFinanceLab. An asterisk (*) indicates problems with a higher level of difficulty.

Interest Rate Quotes and Adjustments

1. Your bank is offering you an account that will pay 20% interest in total for a two-year deposit. Determine the equivalent discount rate for a period length of
   a. Six months.   b. One year.   c. One month.

 2. Which do you prefer: a bank account that pays 5% per year (EAR) for three years or
   a. An account that pays 2½% every six months for three years?
   b. An account that pays 7½% every 18 months for three years?
   c. An account that pays ½% per month for three years?

3. Many academic institutions offer a sabbatical policy. Every seven years a professor is given a year free of teaching and other administrative responsibilities at full pay. For a professor earning $70,000 per year who works for a total of 42 years, what is the present value of the amount she will earn while on sabbatical if the interest rate is 6% (EAR)?

4. You have found three investment choices for a one-year deposit: 10% APR compounded monthly, 10% APR compounded annually, and 9% APR compounded daily. Compute the EAR for each investment choice. (Assume that there are 365 days in the year.)

5. You are considering moving your money to a new bank offering a one-year CD that pays an 8% APR with monthly compounding. Your current bank's manager offers to match the rate you have been offered. The account at your current bank would pay interest every six months. How much interest will you need to earn every six months to match the CD?

6. Your bank account pays interest with an EAR of 5%. What is the APR quote for this account based on semiannual compounding? What is the APR with monthly compounding?

7. Suppose the interest rate is 8% APR with monthly compounding. What is the present value of an annuity that pays $100 every six months for five years?

8. You can earn $50 in interest on a $1000 deposit for eight months. If the EAR is the same regardless of the length of the investment, determine how much interest you will earn on a $1000 deposit for
a. 6 months.   b. 1 year.   c. 1½ years.

9. Suppose you invest $100 in a bank account, and five years later it has grown to $134.39.
a. What APR did you receive, if the interest was compounded semiannually?
b. What APR did you receive if the interest was compounded monthly?

 10. Your son has been accepted into college. This college guarantees that your son's tuition will not increase for the four years he attends college. The first $10,000 tuition payment is due in six months. After that, the same payment is due every six months until you have made a total of eight payments. The college offers a bank account that allows you to withdraw money every six months and has a fixed APR of 4% (semiannual) guaranteed to remain the same over the next four years. How much money must you deposit today if you intend to make no further deposits and would like to make all the tuition payments from this account, leaving the account empty when the last payment is made?

11. You make monthly payments on your mortgage. It has a quoted APR of 5% (monthly compounding). What percentage of the outstanding principal do you pay in interest each month?

Application: Discount Rates and Loans

12. Capital One is advertising a 60-month, 5.99% APR motorcycle loan. If you need to borrow $8000 to purchase your dream Harley Davidson, what will your monthly payment be?

13. Oppenheimer Bank is offering a 30-year mortgage with an EAR of 5⅜% If you plan to borrow $150,000, what will your monthly payment be?

14. You have decided to refinance your mortgage. You plan to borrow whatever is outstanding on your current mortgage. The current monthly payment is $2356 and you have made every payment on time. The original term of the mortgage was 30 years, and the mortgage is exactly four years and eight months old. You have just made your monthly payment. The mortgage interest rate is 6⅜% (APR). How much do you owe on the mortgage today?

15. You have just sold your house for $1,000,000 in cash. Your mortgage was originally a 30-year mortgage with monthly payments and an initial balance of $800,000. The mortgage is currently exactly 18½ years old, and you have just made a payment. If the interest rate on the mortgage is 5.25% (APR), how much cash will you have from the sale once you pay off the mortgage?

16. You have just purchased a home and taken out a $500,000 mortgage. The mortgage has a 30-year term with monthly payments and an APR of 6%.

    a. How much will you pay in interest, and how much will you pay in principal, during the first year?

    b. How much will you pay in interest, and how much will you pay in principal, during the 20th year (i.e., between 19 and 20 years from now)?

17. Your mortgage has 25 years left, and has an APR of 7.625% with monthly payments of $1449.

    a. What is the outstanding balance?

    b. Suppose you cannot make the mortgage payment and you are in danger of losing your house to foreclosure. The bank has offered to renegotiate your loan. The bank expects to get $150,000 for the house if it forecloses. They will lower your payment as long as they will receive at least this amount (in present value terms). If current 25-year mortgage interest rates have dropped to 5% (APR), what is the lowest monthly payment you could make for the remaining life of your loan that would be attractive to the bank?

 *18. You have an outstanding student loan with required payments of $500 per month for the next four years. The interest rate on the loan is 9% APR (monthly). You are considering making an extra payment of $100 today (that is, you will pay an extra $100 that you are not required to pay). If you are required to continue to make payments of $500 per month until the loan is paid off, what is the amount of your final payment? What effective rate of return (expressed as an APR with monthly compounding) have you earned on the $100?

 *19. Consider again the setting of Problem 18. Now that you realize your best investment is to pre-pay your student loan, you decide to prepay as much as you can each month. Looking at your budget, you can afford to pay an extra $250 per month in addition to your required monthly payments of $500, or $750 in total each month. How long will it take you to pay off the loan?

*20. Oppenheimer Bank is offering a 30-year mortgage with an APR of 5.25%. With this mortgage your monthly payments would be $2000 per month. In addition, Oppenheimer Bank offers you the following deal: Instead of making the monthly payment of $2000 every month, you can make half the payment every two weeks (so that you will make 52/2 = 26 payments per year). With this plan, how long will it take to pay off the mortgage of $150,000 if the EAR of the loan is unchanged?

 *21. Your friend tells you he has a very simple trick for shortening the time it takes to repay your mortgage by one-third: Use your holiday bonus to make an extra payment on January 1 of each year (that is, pay your monthly payment due on that day twice). If you take out your mortgage on July 1, so your first monthly payment is due August 1, and you make an extra payment every January 1, how long will it take to pay off the mortgage? Assume that the mortgage has an original term of 30 years and an APR of 12%.

 22. You need a new car and the dealer has offered you a price of $20,000, with the following payment options: (a) pay cash and receive a $2000 rebate, or (b) pay a $5000 down payment and finance the rest with a 0% APR loan over 30 months. But having just quit your job and started an MBA program, you are in debt and you expect to be in debt for at least the next 2½ years. You plan to use credit cards to pay your expenses; luckily you have one with a low (fixed) rate of 15% APR (monthly). Which payment option is best for you?

23. The mortgage on your house is five years old. It required monthly payments of $1402, had an original term of 30 years, and had an interest rate of 10% (APR). In the intervening five years, interest rates have fallen and so you have decided to refinance—that is, you will roll over the outstanding balance into a new mortgage. The new mortgage has a 30-year term, requires monthly payments, and has an interest rate of 6⅝% (APR).

    a. What monthly repayments will be required with the new loan?

    b. If you still want to pay off the mortgage in 25 years, what monthly payment should you make after you refinance?

c. Suppose you are willing to continue making monthly payments of $1402. How long will it take you to pay off the mortgage after refinancing?

d. Suppose you are willing to continue making monthly payments of $1402, and want to pay off the mortgage in 25 years. How much additional cash can you borrow today as part of the refinancing?

24. You have credit card debt of $25,000 that has an APR (monthly compounding) of 15%. Each month you pay the minimum monthly payment only. You are required to pay only the outstanding interest. You have received an offer in the mail for an otherwise identical credit card with an APR of 12%. After considering all your alternatives, you decide to switch cards, roll over the outstanding balance on the old card into the new card, and borrow additional money as well. How much can you borrow today on the new card without changing the minimum monthly payment you will be required to pay?

The Determinants of Interest Rates

25. In 1975, interest rates were 7.85% and the rate of inflation was 12.3% in the United States. What was the real interest rate in 1975? How would the purchasing power of your savings have changed over the year?

26. If the rate of inflation is 5%, what nominal interest rate is necessary for you to earn a 3% real interest rate on your investment?

27. Can the nominal interest rate available to an investor be significantly negative? (*Hint*: Consider the interest rate earned from saving cash "under the mattress.") Can the real interest rate be negative? Explain.

28. Consider a project that requires an initial investment of $100,000 and will produce a single cash flow of $150,000 in five years.
   a. What is the NPV of this project if the five-year interest rate is 5% (EAR)?
   b. What is the NPV of this project if the five-year interest rate is 10% (EAR)?
   c. What is the highest five-year interest rate such that this project is still profitable?

29. Suppose the term structure of risk-free interest rates is as shown below:

Term	1 year	2 years	3 years	5 years	7 years	10 years	20 years
Rate (EAR, %)	1.99	2.41	2.74	3.32	3.76	4.13	4.93

   a. Calculate the present value of an investment that pays $1000 in two years and $2000 in five years for certain.
   b. Calculate the present value of receiving $500 per year, with certainty, at the end of the next five years. To find the rates for the missing years in the table, linearly interpolate between the years for which you do know the rates. (For example, the rate in year 4 would be the average of the rate in year 3 and year 5.)
   *c. Calculate the present value of receiving $2300 per year, with certainty, for the next 20 years. Infer rates for the missing years using linear interpolation. (*Hint*: Use a spreadsheet.)

30. Using the term structure in Problem 29, what is the present value of an investment that pays $100 at the end of each of years 1, 2, and 3? If you wanted to value this investment correctly using the annuity formula, which discount rate should you use?

31. What is the shape of the yield curve given the term structure in Problem 29? What expectations are investors likely to have about future interest rates?

32. Suppose the current one-year interest rate is 6%. One year from now, you believe the economy will start to slow and the one-year interest rate will fall to 5%. In two years, you expect the economy to be in the midst of a recession, causing the Federal Reserve to cut interest rates drastically and the one-year interest rate to fall to 2%. The one-year interest rate will then rise to

3% the following year, and continue to rise by 1% per year until it returns to 6%, where it will remain from then on.

a. If you were certain regarding these future interest rate changes, what two-year interest rate would be consistent with these expectations?

b. What current term structure of interest rates, for terms of 1 to 10 years, would be consistent with these expectations?

c. Plot the yield curve in this case. How does the one-year interest rate compare to the 10-year interest rate?

Risk and Taxes

33. Figure 5.4 shows that CBS's five-year borrowing rate is 1.3% and JPMorgan Chases' is 2.6%. Which would you prefer? $500 from CBS paid today or a promise that the firm will pay you $550 in five years? Which would you choose if JPMorgan Chase offered you the same alternative?

34. Your best taxable investment opportunity has an EAR of 4%. Your best tax-free investment opportunity has an EAR of 3%. If your tax rate is 30%, which opportunity provides the higher after-tax interest rate?

35. Your uncle Fred just purchased a new boat. He brags to you about the low 7% interest rate (APR, monthly compounding) he obtained from the dealer. The rate is even lower than the rate he could have obtained on his home equity loan (8% APR, monthly compounding). If his tax rate is 25% and the interest on the home equity loan is tax deductible, which loan is truly cheaper?

36. You are enrolling in an MBA program. To pay your tuition, you can either take out a standard student loan (so the interest payments are not tax deductible) with an EAR of 5½% or you can use a tax-deductible home equity loan with an APR (monthly) of 6%. You anticipate being in a very low tax bracket, so your tax rate will be only 15%. Which loan should you use?

37. Your best friend consults you for investment advice. You learn that his tax rate is 35%, and he has the following current investments and debts:

- A car loan with an outstanding balance of $5000 and a 4.8% APR (monthly compounding)
- Credit cards with an outstanding balance of $10,000 and a 14.9% APR (monthly compounding)
- A regular savings account with a $30,000 balance, paying a 5.50% EAR
- A money market savings account with a $100,000 balance, paying a 5.25% APR (daily compounding)
- A tax-deductible home equity loan with an outstanding balance of $25,000 and a 5.0% APR (monthly compounding)

a. Which savings account pays a higher after-tax interest rate?

b. Should your friend use his savings to pay off any of his outstanding debts? Explain.

38. Suppose you have outstanding debt with an 8% interest rate that can be repaid any time, and the interest rate on U.S. Treasuries is only 5%. You plan to repay your debt using any cash that you don't invest elsewhere. Until your debt is repaid, what cost of capital should you use when evaluating a new risk-free investment opportunity? Why?

The Opportunity Cost of Capital

39. In the summer of 2008, at Heathrow Airport in London, Bestofthebest (BB), a private company, offered a lottery to win a Ferrari or 90,000 British pounds, equivalent at the time to about $180,000. Both the Ferrari and the money, in 100-pound notes, were on display. If the U.K. interest rate was 5% per year, and the dollar interest rate was 2% per year (EARs), how much did it cost the company in dollars each month to keep the cash on display? That is, what was the opportunity cost of keeping it on display rather than in a bank account? (Ignore taxes.)

40. Your firm is considering the purchase of a new office phone system. You can either pay $32,000 now, or $1000 per month for 36 months.

a. Suppose your firm currently borrows at a rate of 6% per year (APR with monthly compounding). Which payment plan is more attractive?

b. Suppose your firm currently borrows at a rate of 18% per year (APR with monthly compounding). Which payment plan would be more attractive in this case?

41. After reading the Novy-Marx and Rauh article (see the Common Mistake Box on page 159), you decide to compute the total obligation of the state you live in. After some research you determine that your state's promised pension payments amount to $10 billion annually, and you expect this obligation to grow at 2% per year. You determine that the riskiness of this obligation is the same as the riskiness of the state's debt. Based on the pricing of that debt you determine that the correct discount rate for the fund's liabilities is 3% per annum. Currently, based on actuarial calculations using 8% as the discount rate, the plan is neither over- nor underfunded—the value of the liabilities exactly matches the value of the assets. What is the extent of the true unfunded liability?

CHAPTER 5
APPENDIX

NOTATION

e 2.71828...

$\ln$ natural
    logarithm

r_{cc} continuously
    compounded
    discount rate

g_{cc} continuously
    compounded
    growth rate

$\overline{C}_1$ total cash flows
    received in first
    year

Continuous Rates and Cash Flows

In this appendix, we consider how to discount cash flows when interest is paid, or cash flows are received, on a continuous basis.

Discount Rates for a Continuously Compounded APR

Some investments compound more frequently than daily. As we move from daily to hourly ($k = 24 \times 365$) to compounding every second ($k = 60 \times 60 \times 24 \times 365$), we approach the limit of continuous compounding, in which we compound every instant ($k = \infty$). Eq. 5.3 cannot be used to compute the discount rate from an APR quote based on continuous compounding. In this case, the discount rate for a period length of one year—that is, the EAR—is given by Eq. 5A.1:

The EAR for a Continuously Compounded APR

$$(1 + EAR) = e^{APR} \tag{5A.1}$$

where the mathematical constant[12] $e = 2.71828 \ldots$. Once you know the EAR, you can compute the discount rate for any compounding period length using Eq. 5.1.

Alternatively, if we know the EAR and want to find the corresponding continuously compounded APR, we can invert Eq. 5A.1 by taking the natural logarithm (ln) of both sides:[13]

The Continuously Compounded APR for an EAR

$$APR = \ln(1 + EAR) \tag{5A.2}$$

Continuously compounded rates are not often used in practice. Sometimes, banks offer them as a marketing gimmick, but there is little actual difference between daily and continuous compounding. For example, with a 6% APR, daily compounding provides an EAR of $(1 + 0.06/365)^{365} - 1 = 6.18313\%$, whereas with continuous compounding the EAR is $e^{0.06} - 1 = 6.18365\%$.

Continuously Arriving Cash Flows

How can we compute the present value of an investment whose cash flows arrive continuously? For example, consider the cash flows of an online book retailer. Suppose the firm forecasts cash flows of $10 million per year. The $10 million will be received throughout each year, not at year-end; that is, the $10 million is paid *continuously* throughout the year.

We can compute the present value of cash flows that arrive continuously using a version of the growing perpetuity formula. If cash flows arrive, starting immediately, at an initial

---

[12]The constant e raised to a power is also written as the function *exp*. That is, $e^{APR} = exp(APR)$. This function is built into most spreadsheets and calculators.

[13]Recall that $\ln(e^x) = x$

rate of $C per year, and if the cash flows grow at rate g per year, then given a discount rate (expressed as an EAR) of r per year, the present value of the cash flows is

Present Value of a Continuously Growing Perpetuity[14]

$$PV = \frac{C}{r_{cc} - g_{cc}} \tag{5A.3}$$

where $r_{cc} = \ln(1 + r)$ and $g_{cc} = \ln(1 + g)$ are the discount and growth rates expressed as continuously compounded APRs, respectively.

There is another, approximate method for dealing with continuously arriving cash flows. Let $\overline{C}_1$ be the total cash flows that arrive during the first year. Because the cash flows arrive throughout the year, we can think of them arriving "on average" in the middle of the year. In that case, we should discount the cash flows by ½ year less:

$$\frac{C}{r_{cc} - g_{cc}} \approx \frac{\overline{C}_1}{r - g} \times (1 + r)^{1/2} \tag{5A.4}$$

In practice, the approximation in Eq. 5A.4 works quite well. More generally, it implies that when cash flows arrive continuously, we can compute present values reasonably accurately by following a "**mid-year convention**" in which we pretend that all of the cash flows for the year arrive in the middle of the year.

EXAMPLE 5A.1	**Valuing Projects with Continuous Cash Flows**

Problem
Your firm is considering buying an oil rig. The rig will initially produce oil at a rate of 30 million barrels per year. You have a long-term contract that allows you to sell the oil at a profit of $1.25 per barrel. If the rate of oil production from the rig declines by 3% over the year and the discount rate is 10% per year (EAR), how much would you be willing to pay for the rig?

Solution
According to the estimates, the rig will generate profits at an initial rate of (30 million barrels per year) × ($1.25/barrel) = $37.5 million per year. The 10% discount rate is equivalent to a continuously compounded APR of $r_{cc} = \ln(1 + 0.10) = 9.531\%$; similarly, the growth rate has an APR of $g_{cc} = \ln(1 - 0.03) = -3.046\%$. From Eq. 5A.3, the present value of the profits from the rig is

$$PV(\text{profits}) = 37.5/(r_{cc} - g_{cc}) = 37.5/(0.09531 + 0.03046) = \$298.16 \text{ million}$$

Alternatively, we can closely approximate the present value as follows. The initial profit rate of the rig is $37.5 million per year. By the end of the year, the profit rate will have declined by 3% to $37.5 \times (1 - 0.03) = \$36.375$ million per year. Therefore, the average profit rate during the year is approximately $(37.5 + 36.375)/2 = \$36.938$ million. Valuing the cash flows as though they occur at the middle of each year, we have

$$PV(\text{profits}) = [36.938/(r - g)] \times (1 + r)^{1/2}$$
$$= [36.938/(0.10 + 0.03)] \times (1.10)^{1/2} = \$298.01 \text{ million}$$

Note that both methods produce very similar results.

---

[14]Given the perpetuity formula, we can value an annuity as the difference between two perpetuities.

Valuing Bonds

AFTER A FOUR-YEAR HIATUS, THE U.S. GOVERNMENT BEGAN issuing 30-year Treasury bonds again in August 2005. While the move was due in part to the government's need to borrow to fund record budget deficits, the decision to issue 30-year bonds was also a response to investor demand for long-term, risk-free securities backed by the U.S. government. These new 30-year Treasury bonds are part of a much larger market for publicly traded bonds. As of January 2012, the value of traded U.S. Treasury debt was approximately $10 trillion, $2 trillion more than the value of all publicly traded U.S. corporate bonds. If we include bonds issued by municipalities, government agencies, and other issuers, investors had almost $37 trillion invested in U.S. bond markets, compared with just over $15 trillion in U.S. equity markets.[1]

In this chapter, we look at the basic types of bonds and consider their valuation. Understanding bonds and their pricing is useful for several reasons. First, the prices of risk-free government bonds can be used to determine the risk-free interest rates that produce the yield curve discussed in Chapter 5. As we saw there, the yield curve provides important information for valuing risk-free cash flows and assessing expectations of inflation and economic growth. Second, firms often issue bonds to fund their own investments, and the returns investors receive on those bonds is one factor determining a firm's cost of capital. Finally, bonds provide an opportunity to begin our study of how securities are priced in a competitive market. The ideas we develop in this chapter will be helpful when we turn to the topic of valuing stocks in Chapter 9.

We begin the chapter by evaluating the promised cash flows for different types of bonds. Given a bond's cash flows, we can use the Law of One Price to directly relate the bond's return, or yield, and its price. We also

[1] *Source:* Dow Jones Indexes, www.djindexes.com, and Securities Industry and Financial Markets Association, www.sifma.org.

NOTATION

CPN	coupon payment on a bond
n	number of periods
y, YTM	yield to maturity
P	initial price of a bond
FV	face value of a bond
YTM_n	yield to maturity on a zero-coupon bond with n periods to maturity
r_n	interest rate or discount rate for a cash flow that arrives in period n
PV	present value
$NPER$	annuity spreadsheet notation for the number of periods or date of the last cash flow
$RATE$	annuity spreadsheet notation for interest rate
PMT	annuity spreadsheet notation for cash flow
APR	annual percentage rate

describe how bond prices change dynamically over time and examine the relationship between the prices and yields of different bonds. Finally, we consider bonds for which there is a risk of default, so that their cash flows are not known with certainty. As an important application, we look at the behavior of corporate and sovereign bonds during the recent economic crisis.

6.1 Bond Cash Flows, Prices, and Yields

In this section, we look at how bonds are defined and then study the basic relationship between bond prices and their yield to maturity.

Bond Terminology

Recall from Chapter 3 that a bond is a security sold by governments and corporations to raise money from investors today in exchange for promised future payments. The terms of the bond are described as part of the **bond certificate**, which indicates the amounts and dates of all payments to be made. These payments are made until a final repayment date, called the **maturity date** of the bond. The time remaining until the repayment date is known as the **term** of the bond.

Bonds typically make two types of payments to their holders. The promised interest payments of a bond are called **coupons**. The bond certificate typically specifies that the coupons will be paid periodically (e.g., semiannually) until the maturity date of the bond. The principal or **face value** of a bond is the notional amount we use to compute the interest payments. Usually, the face value is repaid at maturity. It is generally denominated in standard increments such as $1000. A bond with a $1000 face value, for example, is often referred to as a "$1000 bond."

The amount of each coupon payment is determined by the **coupon rate** of the bond. This coupon rate is set by the issuer and stated on the bond certificate. By convention, the coupon rate is expressed as an APR, so the amount of each coupon payment, *CPN*, is

Coupon Payment

$$CPN = \frac{\text{Coupon Rate} \times \text{Face Value}}{\text{Number of Coupon Payments per Year}} \tag{6.1}$$

For example, a "$1000 bond with a 10% coupon rate and semiannual payments" will pay coupon payments of $1000 × 10%/2 = $50 every six months.

Zero-Coupon Bonds

The simplest type of bond is a **zero-coupon bond**, which does not make coupon payments. The only cash payment the investor receives is the face value of the bond on the maturity date. **Treasury bills**, which are U.S. government bonds with a maturity of up to one year, are zero-coupon bonds. Recall from Chapter 4 that the present value of a future cash flow is less than the cash flow itself. As a result, prior to its maturity date, the price of a zero-coupon bond is less than its face value. That is, zero-coupon bonds trade at a **discount** (a price lower than the face value), so they are also called **pure discount bonds**.

Suppose that a one-year, risk-free, zero-coupon bond with a $100,000 face value has an initial price of $96,618.36. If you purchased this bond and held it to maturity, you would have the following cash flows:

```
        0                    1
        |————————————————————|
   −$96,618.36          $100,000
```

Although the bond pays no "interest" directly, as an investor you are compensated for the time value of your money by purchasing the bond at a discount to its face value.

Yield to Maturity. Recall that the IRR of an investment opportunity is the discount rate at which the NPV of the cash flows of the investment opportunity is equal to zero. So, the IRR of an investment in a zero-coupon bond is the rate of return that investors will earn on their money if they buy the bond at its current price and hold it to maturity. The IRR of an investment in a bond is given a special name, the **yield to maturity (YTM)** or just the *yield*:

The yield to maturity of a bond is the discount rate that sets the present value of the promised bond payments equal to the current market price of the bond.

Intuitively, the yield to maturity for a zero-coupon bond is the return you will earn as an investor from holding the bond to maturity and receiving the promised face value payment.

Let's determine the yield to maturity of the one-year zero-coupon bond discussed earlier. According to the definition, the yield to maturity of the one-year bond solves the following equation:

$$96{,}618.36 = \frac{100{,}000}{1 + YTM_1}$$

In this case,

$$1 + YTM_1 = \frac{100{,}000}{96{,}618.36} = 1.035$$

That is, the yield to maturity for this bond is 3.5%. Because the bond is risk free, investing in this bond and holding it to maturity is like earning 3.5% interest on your initial investment. Thus, by the Law of One Price, the competitive market risk-free interest rate is 3.5%, meaning all one-year risk-free investments must earn 3.5%.

Similarly, the yield to maturity for a zero-coupon bond with n periods to maturity, current price P, and face value FV solves[2]

$$P = \frac{FV}{(1 + YTM_n)^n} \tag{6.2}$$

Rearranging this expression, we get

Yield to Maturity of an *n*-Year Zero-Coupon Bond

$$YTM_n = \left(\frac{FV}{P}\right)^{1/n} - 1 \tag{6.3}$$

The yield to maturity (YTM_n) in Eq. 6.3 is the per-period rate of return for holding the bond from today until maturity on date n.

Risk-Free Interest Rates. In earlier chapters, we discussed the competitive market interest rate r_n available from today until date n for risk-free cash flows; we used this interest rate as the cost of capital for a risk-free cash flow that occurs on date n. Because a default-free zero-coupon bond that matures on date n provides a risk-free return over the same period, the Law of One Price guarantees that the risk-free interest rate equals the yield to maturity on such a bond.

---

[2]In Chapter 4, we used the notation FV_n for the future value on date n of a cash flow. Conveniently, for a zero-coupon bond, the future value is also its face value, so the abbreviation FV continues to apply.

Risk-Free Interest Rate with Maturity n

$$r_n = YTM_n \tag{6.4}$$

Consequently, we will often refer to the yield to maturity of the appropriate maturity, zero-coupon risk-free bond as *the* risk-free interest rate. Some financial professionals also use the term **spot interest rates** to refer to these default-free, zero-coupon yields.

In Chapter 5, we introduced the yield curve, which plots the risk-free interest rate for different maturities. These risk-free interest rates correspond to the yields of risk-free zero-coupon bonds. Thus, the yield curve we introduced in Chapter 5 is also referred to as the **zero-coupon yield curve**.

EXAMPLE 6.1

Yields for Different Maturities

Problem

Suppose the following zero-coupon bonds are trading at the prices shown below per $100 face value. Determine the corresponding spot interest rates that determine the zero coupon yield curve.

Maturity	1 Year	2 Years	3 Years	4 Years
Price	$96.62	$92.45	$87.63	$83.06

Solution

Using Eq. 6.3, we have

$$r_1 = YTM_1 = (100/96.62) - 1 \quad = 3.50\%$$

$$r_2 = YTM_2 = (100/92.45)^{1/2} - 1 = 4.00\%$$

$$r_3 = YTM_3 = (100/87.63)^{1/3} - 1 = 4.50\%$$

$$r_4 = YTM_4 = (100/83.06)^{1/4} - 1 = 4.75\%$$

GLOBAL FINANCIAL CRISIS   **Pure Discount Bonds Trading at a Premium**

On December 9, 2008, in the midst of one of the worst financial crises in history, the unthinkable happened: For the first time since the Great Depression, U.S. Treasury Bills traded at a negative yield. That is, these risk-free pure discount bonds traded at premium. As Bloomberg.com reported: "If you invested $1 million in three-month bills at today's negative discount rate of 0.01%, for a price of 100.002556, at maturity you would receive the par value for a loss of $25.56."

A negative yield on a Treasury bill implies that investors have an arbitrage opportunity: By *selling* the bill, and holding the proceeds in cash, they would have a risk-free *profit* of $25.56. Why did investors not rush to take advantage of the arbitrage opportunity and thereby eliminate it?

Well, first, the negative yields did not last very long, suggesting that, in fact, investors did rush to take advantage of this opportunity. But second, after closer consideration, the opportunity might not have been a sure risk-free arbitrage. When selling a Treasury security, the investor must choose where to invest, or at least hold, the proceeds. In normal times investors would

be happy to deposit the proceeds with a bank, and consider this deposit to be risk free. But these were not normal times—many investors had great concerns about the financial stability of banks and other financial intermediaries. Perhaps investors shied away from this "arbitrage" opportunity because they were worried that the cash they would receive could not be held safely *anywhere* (even putting it "under the mattress" has a risk of theft!). Thus, we can view the $25.56 as the price investors were willing to pay to have the U.S. Treasury hold their money safely for them at a time when no other investments seemed truly safe.

In July 2012, the same phenomenon repeated itself in Europe when investors purchased newly issued German bonds at a negative yield of −0.06%. The negative yields reflected concern about the safety of European banks. In addition, investors were worried that should the common currency zone break up, countries such as Germany might redenominate their debts into a stronger currency. Investors might therefore be willing to accept a negative yield as a hedge against the Eurozone unraveling.

Coupon Bonds

Like zero-coupon bonds, **coupon bonds** pay investors their face value at maturity. In addition, these bonds make regular coupon interest payments. Two types of U.S. Treasury coupon securities are currently traded in financial markets: **Treasury notes**, which have original maturities from one to 10 years, and **Treasury bonds**, which have original maturities of more than 10 years.

EXAMPLE 6.2

The Cash Flows of a Coupon Bond

Problem

The U.S. Treasury has just issued a five-year, $1000 bond with a 5% coupon rate and semiannual coupons. What cash flows will you receive if you hold this bond until maturity?

Solution

The face value of this bond is $1000. Because this bond pays coupons semiannually, from Eq. 6.1, you will receive a coupon payment every six months of CPN = $1000 × 5%/2 = $25. Here is the timeline, based on a six-month period:

Note that the last payment occurs five years (10 six-month periods) from now and is composed of both a coupon payment of $25 and the face value payment of $1000.

We can also compute the yield to maturity of a coupon bond. Recall that the yield to maturity for a bond is the IRR of investing in the bond and holding it to maturity; it is the *single* discount rate that equates the present value of the bond's remaining cash flows to its current price, shown in the following timeline:

Because the coupon payments represent an annuity, the yield to maturity is the interest rate y that solves the following equation:[3]

Yield to Maturity of a Coupon Bond

$$P = CPN \times \frac{1}{y}\left(1 - \frac{1}{(1+y)^N}\right) + \frac{FV}{(1+y)^N} \tag{6.5}$$

Unfortunately, unlike in the case of zero-coupon bonds, there is no simple formula to solve for the yield to maturity directly. Instead, we need to use either trial-and-error or the annuity spreadsheet we introduced in Chapter 4 (or Excel's IRR function).

---

[3]In Eq. 6.5, we have assumed that the first cash coupon will be paid one period from now. If the first coupon is less than one period away, the cash price of the bond can be found by adjusting the price in Eq. 6.5 by multiplying by $(1 + y)^f$, where f is the fraction of the coupon interval that has already elapsed. (Also, bond prices are often quoted in terms of the *clean price*, which is calculated by deducting from the cash price P an amount, called *accrued interest*, equal to $f \times CPN$. See the box on "Clean and Dirty" bond prices on page 179.)

When we calculate a bond's yield to maturity by solving Eq. 6.5, the yield we compute will be a rate *per coupon interval*. This yield is typically stated as an annual rate by multiplying it by the number of coupons per year, thereby converting it to an APR with the same compounding interval as the coupon rate.

EXAMPLE 6.3

Computing the Yield to Maturity of a Coupon Bond

Problem

Consider the five-year, $1000 bond with a 5% coupon rate and semiannual coupons described in Example 6.2. If this bond is currently trading for a price of $957.35, what is the bond's yield to maturity?

Solution

Because the bond has 10 remaining coupon payments, we compute its yield y by solving:

$$957.35 = 25 \times \frac{1}{y}\left(1 - \frac{1}{(1+y)^{10}}\right) + \frac{1000}{(1+y)^{10}}$$

We can solve it by trial-and-error or by using the annuity spreadsheet:

	NPER	RATE	PV	PMT	FV	Excel Formula
Given	10		−957.35	25	1,000	
Solve for PV		3.00%				=RATE(10,25,−957.35,1000)

Therefore, $y = 3\%$. Because the bond pays coupons semiannually, this yield is for a six-month period. We convert it to an APR by multiplying by the number of coupon payments per year. Thus the bond has a yield to maturity equal to a 6% APR with semiannual compounding.

We can also use Eq. 6.5 to compute a bond's price based on its yield to maturity. We simply discount the cash flows using the yield, as shown in Example 6.4.

EXAMPLE 6.4

Computing a Bond Price from Its Yield to Maturity

Problem

Consider again the five-year, $1000 bond with a 5% coupon rate and semiannual coupons presented in Example 6.3. Suppose you are told that its yield to maturity has increased to 6.30% (expressed as an APR with semiannual compounding). What price is the bond trading for now?

Solution

Given the yield, we can compute the price using Eq. 6.5. First, note that a 6.30% APR is equivalent to a semiannual rate of 3.15%. Therefore, the bond price is

$$P = 25 \times \frac{1}{0.0315}\left(1 - \frac{1}{1.0315^{10}}\right) + \frac{1000}{1.0315^{10}} = \$944.98$$

We can also use the annuity spreadsheet:

	NPER	RATE	PV	PMT	FV	Excel Formula
Given	10	3.15%		25	1,000	
Solve for PV			−944.98			=PV(0.0315,10,25,1000)

Because we can convert any price into a yield, and vice versa, prices and yields are often used interchangeably. For example, the bond in Example 6.4 could be quoted as having a yield of 6.30% or a price of $944.98 per $1000 face value. Indeed, bond traders generally quote bond yields rather than bond prices. One advantage of quoting the yield to maturity rather than the price is that the yield is independent of the face value of the bond. When prices are quoted in the bond market, they are conventionally quoted as a percentage of their face value. Thus, the bond in Example 6.4 would be quoted as having a price of 94.498, which would imply an actual price of $944.98 given the $1000 face value of the bond.

CONCEPT CHECK

1. What is the relationship between a bond's price and its yield to maturity?

2. The risk-free interest rate for a maturity of *n*-years can be determined from the yield of what type of bond?

6.2 Dynamic Behavior of Bond Prices

As we mentioned earlier, zero-coupon bonds trade at a discount—that is, prior to maturity, their price is less than their face value. Coupon bonds may trade at a discount, at a **premium** (a price greater than their face value), or at **par** (a price equal to their face value). In this section, we identify when a bond will trade at a discount or premium as well as how the bond's price will change due to the passage of time and fluctuations in interest rates.

Discounts and Premiums

If the bond trades at a discount, an investor who buys the bond will earn a return both from receiving the coupons *and* from receiving a face value that exceeds the price paid for the bond. As a result, if a bond trades at a discount, its yield to maturity will exceed its coupon rate. Given the relationship between bond prices and yields, the reverse is clearly also true: If a coupon bond's yield to maturity exceeds its coupon rate, the present value of its cash flows at the yield to maturity will be less than its face value, and the bond will trade at a discount.

A bond that pays a coupon can also trade at a premium to its face value. In this case, an investor's return from the coupons is diminished by receiving a face value less than the price paid for the bond. Thus, a bond trades at a premium whenever its yield to maturity is less than its coupon rate.

When a bond trades at a price equal to its face value, it is said to trade at par. A bond trades at par when its coupon rate is equal to its yield to maturity. A bond that trades at a discount is also said to trade below par, and a bond that trades at a premium is said to trade above par.

Table 6.1 summarizes these properties of coupon bond prices.

TABLE 6.1	Bond Prices Immediately After a Coupon Payment	
When the bond price is	We say the bond trades	This occurs when
greater than the face value	"above par" or "at a premium"	Coupon Rate > Yield to Maturity
equal to the face value	"at par"	Coupon Rate = Yield to Maturity
less than the face value	"below par" or "at a discount"	Coupon Rate < Yield to Maturity

| EXAMPLE 6.5 | **Determining the Discount or Premium of a Coupon Bond** |

Problem

Consider three 30-year bonds with annual coupon payments. One bond has a 10% coupon rate, one has a 5% coupon rate, and one has a 3% coupon rate. If the yield to maturity of each bond is 5%, what is the price of each bond per $100 face value? Which bond trades at a premium, which trades at a discount, and which trades at par?

Solution

We can compute the price of each bond using Eq. 6.5. Therefore, the bond prices are

$$P(10\% \text{ coupon}) = 10 \times \frac{1}{0.05}\left(1 - \frac{1}{1.05^{30}}\right) + \frac{100}{1.05^{30}} = \$176.86 \quad \text{(trades at a premium)}$$

$$P(5\% \text{ coupon}) = 5 \times \frac{1}{0.05}\left(1 - \frac{1}{1.05^{30}}\right) + \frac{100}{1.05^{30}} = \$100.00 \quad \text{(trades at par)}$$

$$P(3\% \text{ coupon}) = 3 \times \frac{1}{0.05}\left(1 - \frac{1}{1.05^{30}}\right) + \frac{100}{1.05^{30}} = \$69.26 \quad \text{(trades at a discount)}$$

Most issuers of coupon bonds choose a coupon rate so that the bonds will *initially* trade at, or very close to, par (i.e., at face value). For example, the U.S. Treasury sets the coupon rates on its notes and bonds in this way. After the issue date, the market price of a bond generally changes over time for two reasons. First, as time passes, the bond gets closer to its maturity date. Holding fixed the bond's yield to maturity, the present value of the bond's remaining cash flows changes as the time to maturity decreases. Second, at any point in time, changes in market interest rates affect the bond's yield to maturity and its price (the present value of the remaining cash flows). We explore these two effects in the remainder of this section.

Time and Bond Prices

Let's consider the effect of time on the price of a bond. Suppose you purchase a 30-year, zero-coupon bond with a yield to maturity of 5%. For a face value of $100, the bond will initially trade for

$$P(30 \text{ years to maturity}) = \frac{100}{1.05^{30}} = \$23.14$$

Now let's consider the price of this bond five years later, when it has 25 years remaining until maturity. If the bond's yield to maturity remains at 5%, the bond price in five years will be

$$P(25 \text{ years to maturity}) = \frac{100}{1.05^{25}} = \$29.53$$

Note that the bond price is higher, and hence the discount from its face value is smaller, when there is less time to maturity. The discount shrinks because the yield has not changed, but there is less time until the face value will be received. If you purchased the bond for $23.14 and then sold it after five years for $29.53, the IRR of your investment would be

$$\left(\frac{29.53}{23.14}\right)^{1/5} - 1 = 5.0\%$$

That is, your return is the same as the yield to maturity of the bond. This example illustrates a more general property for bonds: *If a bond's yield to maturity has not changed, then the IRR of an investment in the bond equals its yield to maturity even if you sell the bond early.*

These results also hold for coupon bonds. The pattern of price changes over time is a bit more complicated for coupon bonds, however, because as time passes, most of the cash flows get closer but some of the cash flows disappear as the coupons get paid. Example 6.6 illustrates these effects.

| EXAMPLE 6.6 | The Effect of Time on the Price of a Coupon Bond |

Problem

Consider a 30-year bond with a 10% coupon rate (annual payments) and a $100 face value. What is the initial price of this bond if it has a 5% yield to maturity? If the yield to maturity is unchanged, what will the price be immediately before and after the first coupon is paid?

Solution

We computed the price of this bond with 30 years to maturity in Example 6.5:

$$P = 10 \times \frac{1}{0.05}\left(1 - \frac{1}{1.05^{30}}\right) + \frac{100}{1.05^{30}} = \$176.86$$

Now consider the cash flows of this bond in one year, immediately before the first coupon is paid. The bond now has 29 years until it matures, and the timeline is as follows:

```
   0          1          2              29
   |          |          |    ...        |
  $10        $10        $10         $10 + $100
```

Again, we compute the price by discounting the cash flows by the yield to maturity. Note that there is a cash flow of $10 at date zero, the coupon that is about to be paid. In this case, it is easiest to treat the first coupon separately and value the remaining cash flows as in Eq. 6.5:

$$P(\text{just before first coupon}) = 10 + 10 \times \frac{1}{0.05}\left(1 - \frac{1}{1.05^{29}}\right) + \frac{100}{1.05^{29}} = \$185.71$$

Note that the bond price is higher than it was initially. It will make the same total number of coupon payments, but an investor does not need to wait as long to receive the first one. We could also compute the price by noting that because the yield to maturity remains at 5% for the bond, investors in the bond should earn a return of 5% over the year: $176.86 \times 1.05 = \$185.71$.

What happens to the price of the bond just after the first coupon is paid? The timeline is the same as that given earlier, except the new owner of the bond will not receive the coupon at date zero. Thus, just after the coupon is paid, the price of the bond (given the same yield to maturity) will be

$$P(\text{just after first coupon}) = 10 \times \frac{1}{0.05}\left(1 - \frac{1}{1.05^{29}}\right) + \frac{100}{1.05^{29}} = \$175.71$$

The price of the bond will drop by the amount of the coupon ($10) immediately after the coupon is paid, reflecting the fact that the owner will no longer receive the coupon. In this case, the price is lower than the initial price of the bond. Because there are fewer coupon payments remaining, the premium investors will pay for the bond declines. Still, an investor who buys the bond initially, receives the first coupon, and then sells it earns a 5% return if the bond's yield does not change: $(10 + 175.71)/176.86 = 1.05$.

Figure 6.1 illustrates the effect of time on bond prices, assuming the yield to maturity remains constant. Between coupon payments, the prices of all bonds rise at a rate equal to the yield to maturity as the remaining cash flows of the bond become closer. But as each coupon is paid, the price of a bond drops by the amount of the coupon. When the bond is trading at a premium, the price drop when a coupon is paid will be larger than the price increase between coupons, so the bond's premium will tend to decline as time passes. If the bond is trading at a discount, the price increase between coupons will exceed the drop when a coupon is paid, so the bond's price will rise and its discount will decline as time passes. Ultimately, the prices of all bonds approach the bonds' face value when the bonds mature and their last coupon is paid.

For each of the bonds illustrated in Figure 6.1, if the yield to maturity remains at 5%, investors will earn a 5% return on their investment. For the zero-coupon bond, this return is earned solely due to the price appreciation of the bond. For the 10% coupon bond, this return comes from the combination of coupon payments and price depreciation over time.

Interest Rate Changes and Bond Prices

As interest rates in the economy fluctuate, the yields that investors demand to invest in bonds will also change. Let's evaluate the effect of fluctuations in a bond's yield to maturity on its price.

Consider again a 30-year, zero-coupon bond with a yield to maturity of 5%. For a face value of $100, the bond will initially trade for

$$P(5\% \text{ yield to maturity}) = \frac{100}{1.05^{30}} = \$23.14$$

But suppose interest rates suddenly rise so that investors now demand a 6% yield to maturity before they will invest in this bond. This change in yield implies that the bond price will fall to

$$P(6\% \text{ yield to maturity}) = \frac{100}{1.06^{30}} = \$17.41$$

FIGURE 6.1

The Effect of Time on Bond Prices

The graph illustrates the effects of the passage of time on bond prices when the yield remains constant. The price of a zero-coupon bond rises smoothly. The price of a coupon bond also rises between coupon payments, but tumbles on the coupon date, reflecting the amount of the coupon payment. For each coupon bond, the gray line shows the trend of the bond price just after each coupon is paid.

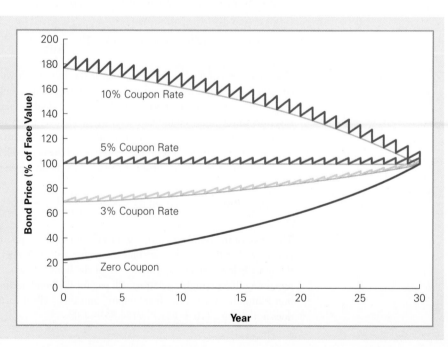

Clean and Dirty Prices for Coupon Bonds

As Figure 6.1 illustrates, coupon bond prices fluctuate around the time of each coupon payment in a sawtooth pattern: The value of the coupon bond rises as the next coupon payment gets closer and then drops after it has been paid. This fluctuation occurs even if there is no change in the bond's yield to maturity.

Because bond traders are more concerned about changes in the bond's price that arise due to changes in the bond's yield, rather than these predictable patterns around coupon payments, they often do not quote the price of a bond in terms of its actual cash price, which is also called the **dirty price** or **invoice price** of the bond. Instead, bonds are often quoted in terms of a **clean price,** which is the bond's cash price less an adjustment for accrued interest, the amount of the next coupon payment that has already accrued:

Clean price = Cash (dirty) price − Accrued interest

Accrued interest = Coupon amount ×

$$\left(\frac{\text{Days since last coupon payment}}{\text{Days in current coupon period}} \right)$$

Note that immediately before a coupon payment is made, the accrued interest will equal the full amount of the coupon, whereas immediately after the coupon payment is made, the accrued interest will be zero. Thus, accrued interest will rise and fall in a sawtooth pattern as each coupon payment passes:

As Figure 6.1 demonstrates, the bonds cash price also has a sawtooth pattern. So if we subtract accrued interest from the bond's cash price and compute the clean price, the sawtooth pattern of the cash price is eliminated. Thus, absent changes in the bond's yield to maturity, its clean price converges smoothly over time to the bond's face value, as shown in the gray lines in Figure 6.1.

Relative to the initial price, the bond price changes by $(17.41 − 23.14)/23.14 = −24.8\%$, a substantial price drop.

This example illustrates a general phenomenon. A higher yield to maturity implies a higher discount rate for a bond's remaining cash flows, reducing their present value and hence the bond's price. Therefore, *as interest rates and bond yields rise, bond prices will fall, and vice versa.*

The sensitivity of a bond's price to changes in interest rates depends on the timing of its cash flows. Because it is discounted over a shorter period, the present value of a cash flow that will be received in the near future is less dramatically affected by interest rates than a cash flow in the distant future. Thus, shorter-maturity zero-coupon bonds are less sensitive to changes in interest rates than are longer-term zero-coupon bonds. Similarly, bonds with higher coupon rates—because they pay higher cash flows upfront—are less sensitive to interest rate changes than otherwise identical bonds with lower coupon rates. The sensitivity of a bond's price to changes in interest rates is measured by the bond's **duration**.[4] Bonds with high durations are highly sensitive to interest rate changes.

| EXAMPLE 6.7 | **The Interest Rate Sensitivity of Bonds** |

Problem
Consider a 15-year zero-coupon bond and a 30-year coupon bond with 10% annual coupons. By what percentage will the price of each bond change if its yield to maturity increases from 5% to 6%?

[4]We define duration formally and discuss this concept more thoroughly in Chapter 30.

Solution

First, we compute the price of each bond for each yield to maturity:

Yield to Maturity	15-Year, Zero-Coupon Bond	30-Year, 10% Annual Coupon Bond
5%	$\dfrac{100}{1.05^{15}} = \$48.10$	$10 \times \dfrac{1}{0.05}\left(1 - \dfrac{1}{1.05^{30}}\right) + \dfrac{100}{1.05^{30}} = \$176.86$
6%	$\dfrac{100}{1.06^{15}} = \$41.73$	$10 \times \dfrac{1}{0.06}\left(1 - \dfrac{1}{1.06^{30}}\right) + \dfrac{100}{1.06^{30}} = \$155.06$

The price of the 15-year zero-coupon bond changes by $(41.73 - 48.10)/48.10 = -13.2\%$ if its yield to maturity increases from 5% to 6%. For the 30-year bond with 10% annual coupons, the price change is $(155.06 - 176.86)/176.86 = -12.3\%$. Even though the 30-year bond has a longer maturity, because of its high coupon rate, its sensitivity to a change in yield is actually less than that of the 15-year zero coupon bond.

In actuality, bond prices are subject to the effects of both the passage of time and changes in interest rates. Bond prices converge to the bond's face value due to the time effect, but simultaneously move up and down due to unpredictable changes in bond yields. Figure 6.2 illustrates

FIGURE 6.2

Yield to Maturity and Bond Price Fluctuations over Time

The graphs illustrate changes in price and yield for a 30-year zero-coupon bond over its life. The top graph illustrates the changes in the bond's yield to maturity over its life. In the bottom graph, the actual bond price is shown in blue. Because the yield to maturity does not remain constant over the bond's life, the bond's price fluctuates as it converges to the face value over time. Also shown is the price if the yield to maturity remained fixed at 4%, 5%, or 6%.

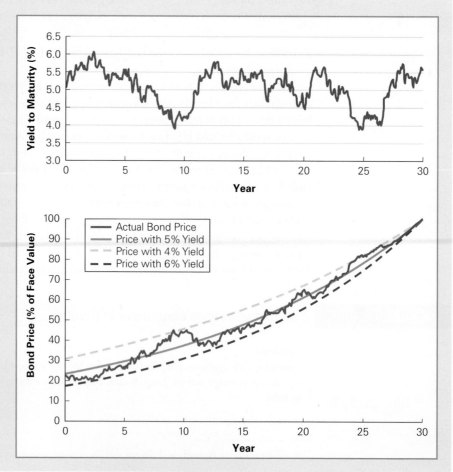

this behavior by demonstrating how the price of the 30-year, zero-coupon bond might change over its life. Note that the bond price tends to converge to the face value as the bond approaches the maturity date, but also moves higher when its yield falls and lower when its yield rises.

As Figure 6.2 demonstrates, prior to maturity the bond is exposed to interest rate risk. If an investor chooses to sell and the bond's yield to maturity has decreased, then the investor will receive a high price and earn a high return. If the yield to maturity has increased, the bond price is low at the time of sale and the investor will earn a low return. In the appendix to this chapter, we discuss one way corporations manage this type of risk.

CONCEPT CHECK

1. If a bond's yield to maturity does not change, how does its cash price change between coupon payments?

2. What risk does an investor in a default-free bond face if he or she plans to sell the bond prior to maturity?

3. How does a bond's coupon rate affect its duration—the bond price's sensitivity to interest rate changes?

6.3 The Yield Curve and Bond Arbitrage

Thus far, we have focused on the relationship between the price of an individual bond and its yield to maturity. In this section, we explore the relationship between the prices and yields of different bonds. Using the Law of One Price, we show that given the spot interest rates, which are the yields of default-free zero-coupon bonds, we can determine the price and yield of any other default-free bond. As a result, the yield curve provides sufficient information to evaluate all such bonds.

Replicating a Coupon Bond

Because it is possible to replicate the cash flows of a coupon bond using zero-coupon bonds, we can use the Law of One Price to compute the price of a coupon bond from the prices of zero-coupon bonds. For example, we can replicate a three-year, $1000 bond that pays 10% annual coupons using three zero-coupon bonds as follows:

We match each coupon payment to a zero-coupon bond with a face value equal to the coupon payment and a term equal to the time remaining to the coupon date. Similarly, we match the final bond payment (final coupon plus return of face value) in three years to a three-year, zero-coupon bond with a corresponding face value of $1100. Because the coupon bond cash flows are identical to the cash flows of the portfolio of zero-coupon bonds, the Law of One Price states that the price of the portfolio of zero-coupon bonds must be the same as the price of the coupon bond.

TABLE 6.2	Yields and Prices (per $100 Face Value) for Zero-Coupon Bonds			
Maturity	1 year	2 years	3 years	4 years
YTM	3.50%	4.00%	4.50%	4.75%
Price	$96.62	$92.45	$87.63	$83.06

To illustrate, assume that current zero-coupon bond yields and prices are as shown in Table 6.2 (they are the same as in Example 6.1). We can calculate the cost of the zero-coupon bond portfolio that replicates the three-year coupon bond as follows:

Zero-Coupon Bond	Face Value Required	Cost
1 year	100	96.62
2 years	100	92.45
3 years	1100	$11 \times 87.63 = 963.93$
	Total Cost:	$1153.00

By the Law of One Price, the three-year coupon bond must trade for a price of $1153. If the price of the coupon bond were higher, you could earn an arbitrage profit by selling the coupon bond and buying the zero-coupon bond portfolio. If the price of the coupon bond were lower, you could earn an arbitrage profit by buying the coupon bond and short selling the zero-coupon bonds.

Valuing a Coupon Bond Using Zero-Coupon Yields

To this point, we have used the zero-coupon bond *prices* to derive the price of the coupon bond. Alternatively, we can use the zero-coupon bond *yields*. Recall that the yield to maturity of a zero-coupon bond is the competitive market interest rate for a risk-free investment with a term equal to the term of the zero-coupon bond. Therefore, the price of a coupon bond must equal the present value of its coupon payments and face value discounted at the competitive market interest rates (see Eq. 5.7 in Chapter 5):

Price of a Coupon Bond

$$P = PV(\text{Bond Cash Flows})$$

$$= \frac{CPN}{1 + YTM_1} + \frac{CPN}{(1 + YTM_2)^2} + \cdots + \frac{CPN + FV}{(1 + YTM_n)^n} \tag{6.6}$$

where CPN is the bond coupon payment, YTM_n is the yield to maturity of a *zero-coupon* bond that matures at the same time as the nth coupon payment, and FV is the face value of the bond. For the three-year, $1000 bond with 10% annual coupons considered earlier, we can use Eq. 6.6 to calculate its price using the zero-coupon yields in Table 6.2:

$$P = \frac{100}{1.035} + \frac{100}{1.04^2} + \frac{100 + 1000}{1.045^3} = \$1153$$

This price is identical to the price we computed earlier by replicating the bond. Thus, we can determine the no-arbitrage price of a coupon bond by discounting its cash flows using the zero-coupon yields. In other words, the information in the zero-coupon yield curve is sufficient to price all other risk-free bonds.

Coupon Bond Yields

Given the yields for zero-coupon bonds, we can use Eq. 6.6 to price a coupon bond. In Section 6.1, we saw how to compute the yield to maturity of a coupon bond from its price. Combining these results, we can determine the relationship between the yields of zero-coupon bonds and coupon-paying bonds.

Consider again the three-year, $1000 bond with 10% annual coupons. Given the zero-coupon yields in Table 6.2, we calculate a price for this bond of $1153. From Eq. 6.5, the yield to maturity of this bond is the rate y that satisfies

$$P = 1153 = \frac{100}{(1+y)} + \frac{100}{(1+y)^2} + \frac{100 + 1000}{(1+y)^3}$$

We can solve for the yield by using the annuity spreadsheet:

	NPER	RATE	PV	PMT	FV	Excel Formula
Given	3		−1,153	100	1,000	
Solve for Rate		4.44%				=RATE(3,100,−1153,1000)

Therefore, the yield to maturity of the bond is 4.44%. We can check this result directly as follows:

$$P = \frac{100}{1.0444} + \frac{100}{1.0444^2} + \frac{100 + 1000}{1.0444^3} = \$1153$$

Because the coupon bond provides cash flows at different points in time, the yield to maturity of a coupon bond is a weighted average of the yields of the zero-coupon bonds of equal and shorter maturities. The weights depend (in a complex way) on the magnitude of the cash flows each period. In this example, the zero-coupon bonds' yields were 3.5%, 4.0%, and 4.5%. For this coupon bond, most of the value in the present value calculation comes from the present value of the third cash flow because it includes the principal, so the yield is closest to the three-year, zero-coupon yield of 4.5%.

EXAMPLE 6.8

Yields on Bonds with the Same Maturity

Problem

Given the following zero-coupon yields, compare the yield to maturity for a three-year, zero-coupon bond; a three-year coupon bond with 4% annual coupons; and a three-year coupon bond with 10% annual coupons. All of these bonds are default free.

Maturity	1 year	2 years	3 years	4 years
Zero-coupon YTM	3.50%	4.00%	4.50%	4.75%

Solution

From the information provided, the yield to maturity of the three-year, zero-coupon bond is 4.50%. Also, because the yields match those in Table 6.2, we already calculated the yield to maturity for the 10% coupon bond as 4.44%. To compute the yield for the 4% coupon bond, we first need to calculate its price. Using Eq. 6.6, we have

$$P = \frac{40}{1.035} + \frac{40}{1.04^2} + \frac{40 + 1000}{1.045^3} = \$986.98$$

The price of the bond with a 4% coupon is $986.98. From Eq. 6.5, its yield to maturity solves the following equation:

$$\$986.98 = \frac{40}{(1+y)} + \frac{40}{(1+y)^2} + \frac{40+1000}{(1+y)^3}$$

We can calculate the yield to maturity using the annuity spreadsheet:

	NPER	RATE	PV	PMT	FV	Excel Formula
Given	3		−986.98	40	1,000	
Solve for Rate		4.47%				=RATE(3,40,−986.98,1000)

To summarize, for the three-year bonds considered

Coupon rate	0%	4%	10%
YTM	4.50%	4.47%	4.44%

Example 6.8 shows that coupon bonds with the same maturity can have different yields depending on their coupon rates. As the coupon increases, earlier cash flows become relatively more important than later cash flows in the calculation of the present value. If the yield curve is upward sloping (as it is for the yields in Example 6.8), the resulting yield to maturity decreases with the coupon rate of the bond. Alternatively, when the zero-coupon yield curve is downward sloping, the yield to maturity will increase with the coupon rate. When the yield curve is flat, all zero-coupon and coupon-paying bonds will have the same yield, independent of their maturities and coupon rates.

Treasury Yield Curves

As we have shown in this section, we can use the zero-coupon yield curve to determine the price and yield to maturity of other risk-free bonds. The plot of the yields of coupon bonds of different maturities is called the **coupon-paying yield curve**. When U.S. bond traders refer to "the yield curve," they are often referring to the coupon-paying Treasury yield curve. As we showed in Example 6.8, two coupon-paying bonds with the same maturity may have different yields. By convention, practitioners always plot the yield of the most recently issued bonds, termed the **on-the-run bonds**. Using similar methods to those employed in this section, we can apply the Law of One Price to determine the zero-coupon bond yields using the coupon-paying yield curve (see Problem 25). Thus, either type of yield curve provides enough information to value all other risk-free bonds.

CONCEPT CHECK

1. How do you calculate the price of a coupon bond from the prices of zero-coupon bonds?

2. How do you calculate the price of a coupon bond from the yields of zero-coupon bonds?

3. Explain why two coupon bonds with the same maturity may each have a different yield to maturity.

6.4 Corporate Bonds

So far in this chapter, we have focused on default-free bonds such as U.S. Treasury securities, for which the cash flows are known with certainty. For other bonds such as **corporate bonds** (bonds issued by corporations), the issuer may default—that is, it might not pay back the full amount promised in the bond prospectus. This risk of default, which is known as the **credit risk** of the bond, means that the bond's cash flows are not known with certainty.

Corporate Bond Yields

How does credit risk affect bond prices and yields? Because the cash flows promised by the bond are the most that bondholders can hope to receive, the cash flows that a purchaser of a bond with credit risk *expects* to receive may be less than that amount. As a result, investors pay less for bonds with credit risk than they would for an otherwise identical default-free bond. Because the yield to maturity for a bond is calculated using the *promised* cash flows, the yield of bonds with credit risk will be higher than that of otherwise identical default-free bonds. Let's illustrate the effect of credit risk on bond yields and investor returns by comparing different cases.

No Default. Suppose that the one-year, zero-coupon Treasury bill has a yield to maturity of 4%. What are the price and yield of a one-year, $1000, zero-coupon bond issued by Avant Corporation? First, suppose that all investors agree that there is *no* possibility that Avant will default within the next year. In that case, investors will receive $1000 in one year for certain, as promised by the bond. Because this bond is risk free, the Law of One Price guarantees that it must have the same yield as the one-year, zero-coupon Treasury bill. The price of the bond will therefore be

$$P = \frac{1000}{1 + YTM_1} = \frac{1000}{1.04} = \$961.54$$

Certain Default. Now suppose that investors believe that Avant will default with certainty at the end of one year and will be able to pay only 90% of its outstanding obligations. Then, even though the bond promises $1000 at year-end, bondholders know they will receive only $900. Investors can predict this shortfall perfectly, so the $900 payment is risk free, and the bond is still a one-year risk-free investment. Therefore, we compute the price of the bond by discounting this cash flow using the risk-free interest rate as the cost of capital:

$$P = \frac{900}{1 + YTM_1} = \frac{900}{1.04} = \$865.38$$

The prospect of default lowers the cash flow investors expect to receive and hence the price they are willing to pay.

Are Treasuries Really Default-Free Securities?

Most investors treat U.S. Treasury securities as risk free, meaning that they believe there is no chance of default (a convention we follow in this book). But are Treasuries really risk free? The answer depends on what you mean by "risk free."

No one can be certain that the U.S. government will never default on its bonds—but most people believe the probability of such an event is very small. More importantly, the default probability is smaller than for any other bond. So saying that the yield on a U.S. Treasury security is risk free really means that the Treasury security is the lowest-risk investment denominated in U.S. dollars in the world.

That said, there have been occasions in the past where Treasury holders did not receive exactly what they were promised: In 1790, Treasury Secretary Alexander Hamilton lowered the interest rate on outstanding debt and in 1933 President Franklin Roosevelt suspended bondholders' right to be paid in gold rather than currency.

A new risk emerged in mid-2011 when a series of large budget deficits brought the United States up against the **debt ceiling**, a constraint imposed by Congress limiting the overall amount of debt the government can incur. An act of Congress was required by August 2011 for the Treasury to meet its obligations and avoid a default. In response to the political uncertainty about whether Congress would raise the ceiling in time, Standard & Poor's downgraded its rating of U.S. Government bonds. Congress ultimately raised the debt ceiling and no default occurred. The incident did, however, serve as a reminder that perhaps no investment is truly "risk free."

Given the bond's price, we can compute the bond's yield to maturity. When computing this yield, we use the *promised* rather than the *actual* cash flows. Thus,

$$YTM = \frac{FV}{P} - 1 = \frac{1000}{865.38} - 1 = 15.56\%$$

The 15.56% yield to maturity of Avant's bond is much higher than the yield to maturity of the default-free Treasury bill. But this result does not mean that investors who buy the bond will earn a 15.56% return. Because Avant will default, the expected return of the bond equals its 4% cost of capital:

$$\frac{900}{865.38} = 1.04$$

Note that *the yield to maturity of a defaultable bond exceeds the expected return of investing in the bond*. Because we calculate the yield to maturity using the promised cash flows rather than the expected cash flows, the yield will always be higher than the expected return of investing in the bond.

Risk of Default.   The two Avant examples were extreme cases, of course. In the first case, we assumed the probability of default was zero; in the second case, we assumed Avant would definitely default. In reality, the chance that Avant will default lies somewhere in between these two extremes (and for most firms, is probably much closer to zero).

To illustrate, again consider the one-year, $1000, zero-coupon bond issued by Avant. This time, assume that the bond payoffs are uncertain. In particular, there is a 50% chance that the bond will repay its face value in full and a 50% chance that the bond will default and you will receive $900. Thus, on average, you will receive $950.

To determine the price of this bond, we must discount this expected cash flow using a cost of capital equal to the expected return of other securities with equivalent risk. If, like most firms, Avant is more likely to default if the economy is weak than if the economy is strong, then—as we demonstrated in Chapter 3—investors will demand a risk premium to invest in this bond. That is, Avant's debt cost of capital, which is the expected return Avant's debt holders will require to compensate them for the risk of the bond's cash flows, will be higher than the 4% risk-free interest rate.

Let's suppose investors demand a risk premium of 1.1% for this bond, so that the appropriate cost of capital is 5.1%.[5] Then the present value of the bond's cash flow is

$$P = \frac{950}{1.051} = \$903.90$$

Consequently, in this case the bond's yield to maturity is 10.63%:

$$YTM = \frac{FV}{P} - 1 = \frac{1000}{903.90} - 1 = 10.63\%$$

Of course, the 10.63% promised yield is the most investors will receive. If Avant defaults, they will receive only $900, for a return of $900/903.90 - 1 = -0.43\%$. The average return is $0.50(10.63\%) + 0.50(-0.43\%) = 5.1\%$, the bond's cost of capital.

Table 6.3 summarizes the prices, expected return, and yield to maturity of the Avant bond under the various default assumptions. Note that the bond's price decreases, and its yield to maturity increases, with a greater likelihood of default. Conversely, *the bond's expected return, which is equal to the firm's debt cost of capital, is less than the yield to maturity*

---

[5]We will develop methods for estimating the appropriate risk premium for risky bonds in Chapter 12.

TABLE 6.3	Bond Price, Yield, and Return with Different Likelihoods of Default		
Avant Bond (1-year, zero-coupon)	Bond Price	Yield to Maturity	Expected Return
Default Free	$961.54	4.00%	4%
50% Chance of Default	$903.90	10.63%	5.1%
Certain Default	$865.38	15.56%	4%

if there is a risk of default. Moreover, a higher yield to maturity does not necessarily imply that a bond's expected return is higher.

Bond Ratings

It would be both difficult and inefficient for every investor to privately investigate the default risk of every bond. Consequently, several companies rate the creditworthiness of bonds and make this information available to investors. By consulting these ratings, investors can assess the creditworthiness of a particular bond issue. The ratings therefore encourage widespread investor participation and relatively liquid markets. The two best-known bond-rating

TABLE 6.4	Bond Ratings

Rating*	Description (Moody's)
Investment Grade Debt	
Aaa/AAA	Judged to be of the best quality. They carry the smallest degree of investment risk and are generally referred to as "gilt edged." Interest payments are protected by a large or an exceptionally stable margin and principal is secure. While the various protective elements are likely to change, such changes as can be visualized are most unlikely to impair the fundamentally strong position of such issues.
Aa/AA	Judged to be of high quality by all standards. Together with the Aaa group, they constitute what are generally known as high-grade bonds. They are rated lower than the best bonds because margins of protection may not be as large as in Aaa securities or fluctuation of protective elements may be of greater amplitude or there may be other elements present that make the long-term risk appear somewhat larger than the Aaa securities.
A/A	Possess many favorable investment attributes and are considered as upper-medium-grade obligations. Factors giving security to principal and interest are considered adequate, but elements may be present that suggest a susceptibility to impairment some time in the future.
Baa/BBB	Are considered as medium-grade obligations (i.e., they are neither highly protected nor poorly secured). Interest payments and principal security appear adequate for the present but certain protective elements may be lacking or may be characteristically unreliable over any great length of time. Such bonds lack outstanding investment characteristics and, in fact, have speculative characteristics as well.
Speculative Bonds	
Ba/BB	Judged to have speculative elements; their future cannot be considered as well assured. Often the protection of interest and principal payments may be very moderate, and thereby not well safeguarded during both good and bad times over the future. Uncertainty of position characterizes bonds in this class.
B/B	Generally lack characteristics of the desirable investment. Assurance of interest and principal payments of maintenance of other terms of the contract over any long period of time may be small.
Caa/CCC	Are of poor standing. Such issues may be in default or there may be present elements of danger with respect to principal or interest.
Ca/CC	Are speculative in a high degree. Such issues are often in default or have other marked shortcomings.
C/C, D	Lowest-rated class of bonds, and issues so rated can be regarded as having extremely poor prospects of ever attaining any real investment standing.

*Ratings: Moody's/Standard & Poor's
Source: www.moodys.com

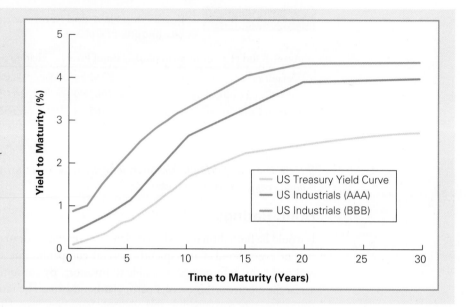

FIGURE 6.3

Corporate Yield Curves for Various Ratings, June 2012

This figure shows the yield curve for U.S. Treasury securities and yield curves for corporate securities with different ratings. Note how the yield to maturity is higher for lower rated bonds, which have a higher probability of default.

Source: Bloomberg

companies are Standard & Poor's and Moody's. Table 6.4 summarizes the rating classes each company uses. Bonds with the highest rating are judged to be least likely to default.

Bonds in the top four categories are often referred to as **investment-grade bonds** because of their low default risk. Bonds in the bottom five categories are often called **speculative bonds**, **junk bonds**, or **high-yield bonds** because their likelihood of default is high. The rating depends on the risk of bankruptcy as well as the bondholders' ability to lay claim to the firm's assets in the event of such a bankruptcy. Thus, debt issues with a low-priority claim in bankruptcy will have a lower rating than issues from the same company that have a high-priority claim in bankruptcy or that are backed by a specific asset such as a building or a plant.

Corporate Yield Curves

Just as we can construct a yield curve from risk-free Treasury securities, we can plot a similar yield curve for corporate bonds. Figure 6.3 shows the average yields of U.S. corporate coupon bonds rated AAA or BBB, as well as the U.S. (coupon-paying) Treasury yield curve. We refer to the difference between the yields of the corporate bonds and the Treasury yields as the **default spread** or **credit spread**. Credit spreads fluctuate as perceptions regarding the probability of default change. Note that the credit spread is high for bonds with low ratings and therefore a greater likelihood of default.

CONCEPT CHECK

1. There are two reasons the yield of a defaultable bond exceeds the yield of an otherwise identical default-free bond. What are they?

2. What is a bond rating?

6.5 Sovereign Bonds

Sovereign bonds are bonds issued by national governments. We have, of course, already encountered an example of a sovereign bond—U.S. Treasury securities. But while U.S. Treasuries are generally considered to be default free, the same cannot be said for bonds issued by many other countries. Until recently, sovereign bond default was considered

GLOBAL FINANCIAL CRISIS   The Credit Crisis and Bond Yields

The financial crisis that engulfed the world's economies in 2008 originated as a credit crisis that first emerged in August 2007. At that time, problems in the mortgage market had led to the bankruptcy of several large mortgage lenders. The default of these firms, and the downgrading of many of the bonds backed by mortgages these firms had originated, caused investors to reassess the risk of other bonds in their portfolios. As perceptions of risk increased and investors attempted to move into safer U.S. Treasury securities, the prices of corporate bonds fell and so their credit spreads rose relative to Treasuries, as shown in Figure 6.4. Panel A of the figure shows the yield spreads for long-term corporate bonds, where we can see that spreads of even the highest-rated Aaa bonds increased dramatically, from a typical level of 0.5% to over 2% by the fall of 2008. Panel B shows a similar pattern for the rate banks had to pay on short-term loans compared to the yields of short-term Treasury bills. This increase in borrowing costs made it more costly for firms to raise the capital needed for new investment, slowing economic growth. The decline in these spreads in early 2009 was viewed by many as an important first step in mitigating the ongoing impact of the financial crisis on the rest of the economy. Note, however, the recent increase in spreads in the wake of the European debt crisis and consequent economic uncertainty.

FIGURE 6.4

Yield Spreads and the Financial Crisis

Panel A shows the yield spread between long-term (30-year) U.S. corporate and Treasury bonds. Panel B shows the yield spread of short-term loans to major international banks (LIBOR) and U.S. Treasury bills (also referred to as the Treasury-Eurodollar or "TED" spread). Note the dramatic increase in these spreads beginning in August 2007 and again in September 2008, before beginning to decline in early 2009. While spreads returned to pre-crisis levels by mid-2011, note the increase in spreads in 2012 in response to the European debt crisis.

Source: Bloomberg.com

an emerging market phenomenon. The recent experience with Greek government bonds served as a wake-up call to investors that governments in the developed world can also default. In 2012, Greece defaulted and wrote off over $100 billion, or about 50%, of its outstanding debt, in the largest sovereign debt restructuring in world history. And Greece is far from unique—as Figure 6.5 shows, there have been periods when more than one-third of all debtor nations were either in default or restructuring their debt.

Because most sovereign debt is risky, the prices and yields of sovereign debt behave much like corporate debt: The bonds issued by countries with high probabilities of default have high yields and low prices. That said, there is a key difference between sovereign default and corporate default.

Unlike a corporation, a country facing difficulty meeting its financial obligations typically has the option to print additional currency to pay its debts. Of course, doing so is likely to lead to high inflation and a sharp devaluation of the currency. Consequently, debt holders carefully consider inflation expectations when determining the yield they are willing to accept because they understand that they may be repaid in money that is worth less than it was when the bonds were issued.

For most countries, the option to "inflate away" the debt is politically preferable to an outright default. That said, defaults do occur, either because the necessary inflation/devaluation would be too extreme, or sometimes because of a change in political regime (for example, Russian Tsarist debt became worthless paper after the 1917 revolution).

European sovereign debt is an interesting special case. Member states of the European Economic and Monetary Union (EMU) all share a common currency, the euro, and so have ceded control of their money supply to the European Central Bank (ECB). As a result, no individual country can simply print money to make debt payments. Furthermore, when the ECB does print money to help pay one country's debt, the subsequent inflation affects all citizens in

| FIGURE 6.5 | **Percent of Debtor Countries in Default or Restructuring Debt, 1800–2006** |

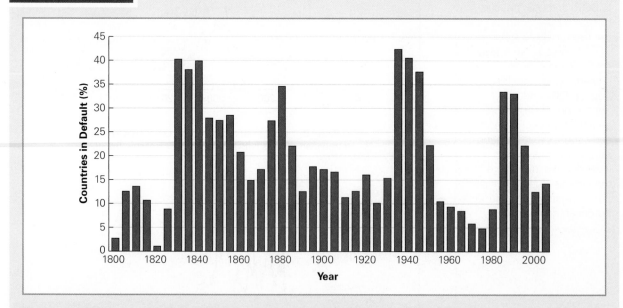

The chart shows, for each 5-year period, the average percentage of debtor countries per year that were either in default or in the process of restructuring their debt. Recent peaks occurred around the time of World War II and the Latin American, Asian, and Russian debt crises in the 1980s and 90s.

Source: Data from *This Time Is Different*, Carmen Reinhart and Kenneth Rogoff, Princeton University Press, 2009.

GLOBAL FINANCIAL CRISIS   **European Sovereign Debt Yields: A Puzzle**

Before the EMU created the euro as a single European currency, the yields of sovereign debt issued by European countries varied widely. These variations primarily reflected differences in inflation expectations and currency risk (see Figure 6.6). However, after the monetary union was put in place at the end of 1998, the yields all essentially converged to the yield on German government bonds. Investors seemed to conclude that there was little distinction between the debt of the European countries in the union—they seemed to feel that all countries in the union were essentially exposed to the same default, inflation and currency risk and thus equally "safe."

Presumably, investors believed that an outright default was unthinkable: They apparently believed that member countries would be fiscally responsible and manage their debt obligations to avoid default at all costs. But as illustrated by Figure 6.6, once the 2008 financial crisis revealed the folly of this assumption, debt yields once again diverged as investors acknowledged the likelihood that some countries (particularly Portugal and Ireland) might be unable to repay their debt and would be forced to default.

In retrospect, rather than bringing fiscal responsibility, the monetary union allowed the weaker member countries to borrow at dramatically lower rates. In response, these countries reacted by increasing their borrowing—and at least in Greece's case, borrowed to the point that default became inevitable.

FIGURE 6.6   **European Government Bond Yields, 1963–2011**

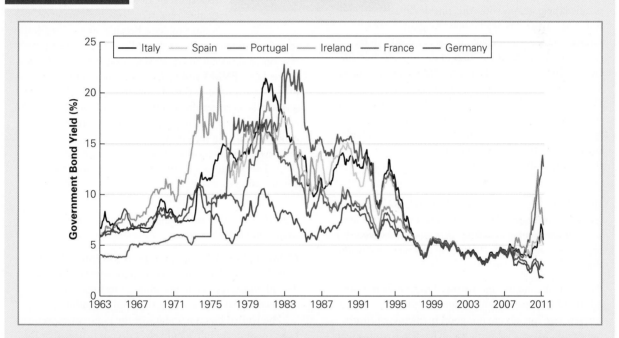

The plot shows the yield on government debt issued by six countries in the European Currency Union. Prior to the euro's introduction in 1999, yields varied in accordance with differing inflation expectations and currency risk. Yields converged once the euro was introduced, but diverged again after the 2008 financial crisis as investors recognized the possibility of default.

Source: Nowakwoski, David, "Government Bonds/Rates: High, Low and Normal," *Roubini Global Economics*, June 8, 2012.

the union, effectively forcing citizens in one country to shoulder the debt burden of another country. Because individual countries do not have discretion to inflate away their debt, default is a real possibility within the EMU. This risk became tangible in 2012 with Greece's default.

CONCEPT CHECK   1. Why do sovereign debt yields differ across countries?

2. What options does a country have if it decides it cannot meet its debt obligations?

Carmen M. Reinhart is the Minos A. Zombanakis Professor of the International Financial System at the John F. Kennedy School of Government, Harvard University. She is co-author of the award-winning book *This Time Is Different: Eight Centuries of Financial Folly*, which documents the striking similarities of the recurring booms and busts characterizing financial history.

INTERVIEW WITH
Carmen M. Reinhart

QUESTION: *Is Europe's sovereign debt crisis an anomaly in the developed world?*

ANSWER: There is a long history of sovereign debt crises in the developed world. Each time prior to the crisis people justified their actions with "this time is different." Two years ago no one thought Greece could default because it was in Europe. In fact, Greece has been in default 48% of the time since 1830. Before World War II, defaults, restructurings, and forced conversions among advanced economies were not rare. Post-World War II, sovereign debt defaults and restructurings have been largely confined to emerging markets such as Chile, Argentina, Peru, Nigeria, and Indonesia, leading people to the false assumption that debt crises were a developing market phenomenon.

QUESTION: *Prior to the 2008/9 financial crisis, the yield spreads on sovereign debt issued by Eurozone countries were very narrow, seeming to indicate that investors believed that the debt was equally safe. Why would investors come to this conclusion?*

ANSWER: Economic and financial indicators in both advanced economies and emerging markets indicate that interest rate spreads are not good predictors of future debt rates. My earlier work with Graciela Kaminsky of early warnings supported this conclusion. Often public and private debt builds up but the spreads do not reflect the added risk. During the boom period, Eurozone countries had very low spreads and very strong credit ratings. Yet the underlying domestic fundamentals did not support these signals of financial health. People convinced themselves that the world was different.

Also, looking exclusively at rising sovereign debt levels can be deceptive. History has shown that private debts before a crisis become public afterwards. In the early 1980s, Chile had a fiscal surplus and still it had a massive debt crisis. In Ireland and Spain in the late 2000s, public debt was under control, but private sector debt, which carried an implicit guarantee, was skyrocketing.

QUESTION: *Since the financial crisis these yields have diverged. What has changed and why?*

ANSWER: People found out that the world was not different; that is, the countries in Europe were not equally risky. Financial crises adversely affect public finances—what starts as a financial crisis morphs into banking and sovereign debt crises. Financial crises related to recessions are deeper and more protracted than normal recessions, creating enormous problems because, even after fiscal stimulus, revenues collapse. In addition, governments take on private debt to circumvent a financial meltdown. In the U.S., FNMA and Freddie Mac moved from the private sector balance sheet before the crisis to the public sector balance sheet afterwards. In Ireland and Spain, public debt became bloated as the governments took on the debts of banks. In the aftermath of the 2007–2008 crisis, the slew of simultaneous crises in advanced economies limited opportunities to grow out of crisis (for example, by increasing exports).

QUESTION: *What's next for Europe? Could the same thing happen in the United States?*

ANSWER: I think Europe's prospects will remain fairly dismal for a while. Europe has been moving very slowly, if at all, to address the implications of its huge debt—deleveraging takes a very long time and is painful.

The United States has many of the same issues. While a U.S. Treasury default is unlikely, I do not believe that the currently low Treasury debt yields imply that the U.S. fundamentals are good. Treasury debt yields are low because of massive official intervention—the Fed and other central banks are buying Treasuries to prevent their currencies from appreciating and to keep their borrowing rates low. This kind of government intervention following a crisis is common. It is why recovery takes so long. Historically, lackluster GDP growth lasts 23 years on average following a financial crisis, and is a dark cloud over U.S. growth prospects.

Here is what you should know after reading this chapter. MyFinanceLab will help you identify what you know and where to go when you need to practice.

6.1 Bond Cash Flows, Prices, and Yields

- Bonds pay both coupon and principal or face value payments to investors. By convention, the coupon rate of a bond is expressed as an APR, so the amount of each coupon payment, *CPN*, is

$$CPN = \frac{\text{Coupon Rate} \times \text{Face Value}}{\text{Number of Coupon Payments per Year}} \tag{6.1}$$

- Zero-coupon bonds make no coupon payments, so investors receive only the bond's face value.
- The internal rate of return of a bond is called its yield to maturity (or yield). The yield to maturity of a bond is the discount rate that sets the present value of the promised bond payments equal to the current market price of the bond.
- The yield to maturity for a zero-coupon bond is given by

$$YTM_n = \left(\frac{FV}{P}\right)^{1/n} - 1 \tag{6.3}$$

- The risk-free interest rate for an investment until date n equals the yield to maturity of a risk-free zero-coupon bond that matures on date n. A plot of these rates against maturity is called the zero-coupon yield curve.
- The yield to maturity for a coupon bond is the discount rate, y, that equates the present value of the bond's future cash flows with its price:

$$P = CPN \times \frac{1}{y}\left(1 - \frac{1}{(1+y)^N}\right) + \frac{FV}{(1+y)^N} \tag{6.5}$$

6.2 Dynamic Behavior of Bond Prices

- A bond will trade at a premium if its coupon rate exceeds its yield to maturity. It will trade at a discount if its coupon rate is less than its yield to maturity. If a bond's coupon rate equals its yield to maturity, it trades at par.
- As a bond approaches maturity, the price of the bond approaches its face value.
- If the bond's yield to maturity has not changed, then the IRR of an investment in a bond equals its yield to maturity even if you sell the bond early.
- Bond prices change as interest rates change. When interest rates rise, bond prices fall, and vice versa.
  - Long-term zero-coupon bonds are more sensitive to changes in interest rates than are short-term zero-coupon bonds.
  - Bonds with low coupon rates are more sensitive to changes in interest rates than similar maturity bonds with high coupon rates.
  - The duration of a bond measures the sensitivity of its price to changes in interest rates.

6.3 The Yield Curve and Bond Arbitrage

- Because we can replicate a coupon-paying bond using a portfolio of zero-coupon bonds, the price of a coupon-paying bond can be determined based on the zero-coupon yield curve using the Law of One Price:

$$P = PV(\text{Bond Cash Flows})$$

$$= \frac{CPN}{1 + YTM_1} + \frac{CPN}{(1 + YTM_2)^2} + \cdots + \frac{CPN + FV}{(1 + YTM_n)^n} \tag{6.6}$$

- When the yield curve is not flat, bonds with the same maturity but different coupon rates will have different yields to maturity.

6.4 Corporate Bonds

- When a bond issuer does not make a bond payment in full, the issuer has defaulted.
  - The risk that default can occur is called default or credit risk.
  - U.S. Treasury securities are generally considered free of default risk.
- The expected return of a corporate bond, which is the firm's debt cost of capital, equals the risk-free rate of interest plus a risk premium. The expected return is less than the bond's yield to maturity because the yield to maturity of a bond is calculated using the promised cash flows, not the expected cash flows.
- Bond ratings summarize the creditworthiness of bonds for investors.
- The difference between yields on Treasury securities and yields on corporate bonds is called the credit spread or default spread. The credit spread compensates investors for the difference between promised and expected cash flows and for the risk of default.

6.5 Sovereign Bonds

- Sovereign bonds are issued by national governments.
- Sovereign bond yields reflect investor expectations of inflation, currency, and default risk.
- Countries may repay their debt by printing additional currency, which generally leads to a rise in inflation and a sharp currency devaluation.
- When "inflating away" the debt is infeasible or politically unattractive, countries may choose to default on their debt.

Key Terms

Further Reading

For readers interested in more details about the bond market, the following texts will prove useful: Z. Bodie, A. Kane, and A. Marcus, *Investments* (McGraw-Hill/Irwin, 2004); F. Fabozzi, *The Handbook of Fixed Income Securities* (McGraw-Hill, 2005); W. Sharpe, G. Alexander, and J. Bailey, *Investments* (Prentice-Hall, 1998); and B. Tuckman, *Fixed Income Securities: Tools for Today's Markets* (John Wiley & Sons, Inc., 2002). C. Reinhart and K. Rogoff, *This Time Is Different* (Princeton University Press, 2010), provides a historical perspective and an excellent discussion of the risk of sovereign debt.

Problems

All problems are available in MyFinanceLab. *An asterisk (*) indicates problems with a higher level of difficulty.*

Bond Cash Flows, Prices, and Yields

1. A 30-year bond with a face value of $1000 has a coupon rate of 5.5%, with semiannual payments.
   a. What is the coupon payment for this bond?
   b. Draw the cash flows for the bond on a timeline.

2. Assume that a bond will make payments every six months as shown on the following timeline (using six-month periods):

0	1	2	3	20
	$20	$20	$20	$20 + $1000

   a. What is the maturity of the bond (in years)?
   b. What is the coupon rate (in percent)?
   c. What is the face value?

3. The following table summarizes prices of various default-free, zero-coupon bonds (expressed as a percentage of face value):

Maturity (years)	1	2	3	4	5
Price (per $100 face value)	$95.51	$91.05	$86.38	$81.65	$76.51

   a. Compute the yield to maturity for each bond.
   b. Plot the zero-coupon yield curve (for the first five years).
   c. Is the yield curve upward sloping, downward sloping, or flat?

4. Suppose the current zero-coupon yield curve for risk-free bonds is as follows:

Maturity (years)	1	2	3	4	5
YTM	5.00%	5.50%	5.75%	5.95%	6.05%

   a. What is the price per $100 face value of a two-year, zero-coupon, risk-free bond?
   b. What is the price per $100 face value of a four-year, zero-coupon, risk-free bond?
   c. What is the risk-free interest rate for a five-year maturity?

5. In the Global Financial Crisis box in Section 6.1, Bloomberg.com reported that the three-month Treasury bill sold for a price of $100.002556 per $100 face value. What is the yield to maturity of this bond, expressed as an EAR?

6. Suppose a 10-year, $1000 bond with an 8% coupon rate and semiannual coupons is trading for a price of $1034.74.
   a. What is the bond's yield to maturity (expressed as an APR with semiannual compounding)?
   b. If the bond's yield to maturity changes to 9% APR, what will the bond's price be?

7. Suppose a five-year, $1000 bond with annual coupons has a price of $900 and a yield to maturity of 6%. What is the bond's coupon rate?

Dynamic Behavior of Bond Prices

8. The prices of several bonds with face values of $1000 are summarized in the following table:

Bond	A	B	C	D
Price	$972.50	$1040.75	$1150.00	$1000.00

For each bond, state whether it trades at a discount, at par, or at a premium.

9. Explain why the yield of a bond that trades at a discount exceeds the bond's coupon rate.

10. Suppose a seven-year, $1000 bond with an 8% coupon rate and semiannual coupons is trading with a yield to maturity of 6.75%.
    a. Is this bond currently trading at a discount, at par, or at a premium? Explain.
    b. If the yield to maturity of the bond rises to 7% (APR with semiannual compounding), what price will the bond trade for?

11. Suppose that General Motors Acceptance Corporation issued a bond with 10 years until maturity, a face value of $1000, and a coupon rate of 7% (annual payments). The yield to maturity on this bond when it was issued was 6%.
    a. What was the price of this bond when it was issued?
    b. Assuming the yield to maturity remains constant, what is the price of the bond immediately before it makes its first coupon payment?
    c. Assuming the yield to maturity remains constant, what is the price of the bond immediately after it makes its first coupon payment?

12. Suppose you purchase a 10-year bond with 6% annual coupons. You hold the bond for four years, and sell it immediately after receiving the fourth coupon. If the bond's yield to maturity was 5% when you purchased and sold the bond,
    a. What cash flows will you pay and receive from your investment in the bond per $100 face value?
    b. What is the internal rate of return of your investment?

13. Consider the following bonds:

Bond	Coupon Rate (annual payments)	Maturity (years)
A	0%	15
B	0%	10
C	4%	15
D	8%	10

    a. What is the percentage change in the price of each bond if its yield to maturity falls from 6% to 5%?
    b. Which of the bonds A–D is most sensitive to a 1% drop in interest rates from 6% to 5% and why? Which bond is least sensitive? Provide an intuitive explanation for your answer.

14. Suppose you purchase a 30-year, zero-coupon bond with a yield to maturity of 6%. You hold the bond for five years before selling it.
    a. If the bond's yield to maturity is 6% when you sell it, what is the internal rate of return of your investment?
    b. If the bond's yield to maturity is 7% when you sell it, what is the internal rate of return of your investment?
    c. If the bond's yield to maturity is 5% when you sell it, what is the internal rate of return of your investment?
    d. Even if a bond has no chance of default, is your investment risk free if you plan to sell it before it matures? Explain.

15. Suppose you purchase a 30-year Treasury bond with a 5% annual coupon, initially trading at par. In 10 years' time, the bond's yield to maturity has risen to 7% (EAR).
    a. If you sell the bond now, what internal rate of return will you have earned on your investment in the bond?
    b. If instead you hold the bond to maturity, what internal rate of return will you earn on your investment in the bond?
    c. Is comparing the IRRs in (a) versus (b) a useful way to evaluate the decision to sell the bond? Explain.

16. Suppose the current yield on a one-year, zero coupon bond is 3%, while the yield on a five-year, zero coupon bond is 5%. Neither bond has any risk of default. Suppose you plan to invest for

one year. You will earn more over the year by investing in the five-year bond as long as its yield does not rise above what level?

The Yield Curve and Bond Arbitrage

For Problems 17–22, assume zero-coupon yields on default-free securities are as summarized in the following table:

Maturity (years)	1	2	3	4	5
Zero-coupon YTM	4.00%	4.30%	4.50%	4.70%	4.80%

17. What is the price today of a two-year, default-free security with a face value of $1000 and an annual coupon rate of 6%? Does this bond trade at a discount, at par, or at a premium?

18. What is the price of a five-year, zero-coupon, default-free security with a face value of $1000?

19. What is the price of a three-year, default-free security with a face value of $1000 and an annual coupon rate of 4%? What is the yield to maturity for this bond?

20. What is the maturity of a default-free security with annual coupon payments and a yield to maturity of 4%? Why?

*21. Consider a four-year, default-free security with annual coupon payments and a face value of $1000 that is issued at par. What is the coupon rate of this bond?

22. Consider a five-year, default-free bond with annual coupons of 5% and a face value of $1000.
   a. Without doing any calculations, determine whether this bond is trading at a premium or at a discount. Explain.
   b. What is the yield to maturity on this bond?
   c. If the yield to maturity on this bond increased to 5.2%, what would the new price be?

*23. Prices of zero-coupon, default-free securities with face values of $1000 are summarized in the following table:

Maturity (years)	1	2	3
Price (per $1000 face value)	$970.87	$938.95	$904.56

Suppose you observe that a three-year, default-free security with an annual coupon rate of 10% and a face value of $1000 has a price today of $1183.50. Is there an arbitrage opportunity? If so, show specifically how you would take advantage of this opportunity? If not, why not?

*24. Assume there are four default-free bonds with the following prices and future cash flows:

Bond	Price Today	Cash Flows		
		Year 1	Year 2	Year 3
A	$934.58	1000	0	0
B	881.66	0	1000	0
C	1,118.21	100	100	1100
D	839.62	0	0	1000

Do these bonds present an arbitrage opportunity? If so, how would you take advantage of this opportunity? If not, why not?

*25. Suppose you are given the following information about the default-free, coupon-paying yield curve:

Maturity (years)	1	2	3	4
Coupon rate (annual payments)	0.00%	10.00%	6.00%	12.00%
YTM	2.000%	3.908%	5.840%	5.783%

a. Use arbitrage to determine the yield to maturity of a two-year, zero-coupon bond.

b. What is the zero-coupon yield curve for years 1 through 4?

Corporate Bonds

26. Explain why the expected return of a corporate bond does not equal its yield to maturity.

27. Grummon Corporation has issued zero-coupon corporate bonds with a five-year maturity. Investors believe there is a 20% chance that Grummon will default on these bonds. If Grummon does default, investors expect to receive only 50 cents per dollar they are owed. If investors require a 6% expected return on their investment in these bonds, what will be the price and yield to maturity on these bonds?

28. The following table summarizes the yields to maturity on several one-year, zero-coupon securities:

Security	Yield (%)
Treasury	3.1
AAA corporate	3.2
BBB corporate	4.2
B corporate	4.9

a. What is the price (expressed as a percentage of the face value) of a one-year, zero-coupon corporate bond with a AAA rating?

b. What is the credit spread on AAA-rated corporate bonds?

c. What is the credit spread on B-rated corporate bonds?

d. How does the credit spread change with the bond rating? Why?

29. Andrew Industries is contemplating issuing a 30-year bond with a coupon rate of 7% (annual coupon payments) and a face value of $1000. Andrew believes it can get a rating of A from Standard and Poor's. However, due to recent financial difficulties at the company, Standard and Poor's is warning that it may downgrade Andrew Industries bonds to BBB. Yields on A-rated, long-term bonds are currently 6.5%, and yields on BBB-rated bonds are 6.9%.

a. What is the price of the bond if Andrew maintains the A rating for the bond issue?

b. What will the price of the bond be if it is downgraded?

 30. HMK Enterprises would like to raise $10 million to invest in capital expenditures. The company plans to issue five-year bonds with a face value of $1000 and a coupon rate of 6.5% (annual payments). The following table summarizes the yield to maturity for five-year (annual-pay) coupon corporate bonds of various ratings:

Rating	AAA	AA	A	BBB	BB
YTM	6.20%	6.30%	6.50%	6.90%	7.50%

a. Assuming the bonds will be rated AA, what will the price of the bonds be?

b. How much total principal amount of these bonds must HMK issue to raise $10 million today, assuming the bonds are AA rated? (Because HMK cannot issue a fraction of a bond, assume that all fractions are rounded to the nearest whole number.)

c. What must the rating of the bonds be for them to sell at par?

d. Suppose that when the bonds are issued, the price of each bond is $959.54. What is the likely rating of the bonds? Are they junk bonds?

31. A BBB-rated corporate bond has a yield to maturity of 8.2%. A U.S. Treasury security has a yield to maturity of 6.5%. These yields are quoted as APRs with semiannual compounding. Both bonds pay semiannual coupons at a rate of 7% and have five years to maturity.

a. What is the price (expressed as a percentage of the face value) of the Treasury bond?

b. What is the price (expressed as a percentage of the face value) of the BBB-rated corporate bond?

c. What is the credit spread on the BBB bonds?

32. The Isabelle Corporation rents prom dresses in its stores across the southern United States. It has just issued a five-year, zero-coupon corporate bond at a price of $74. You have purchased this bond and intend to hold it until maturity.
    a. What is the yield to maturity of the bond?
    b. What is the expected return on your investment (expressed as an EAR) if there is no chance of default?
    c. What is the expected return (expressed as an EAR) if there is a 100% probability of default and you will recover 90% of the face value?
    d. What is the expected return (expressed as an EAR) if the probability of default is 50%, the likelihood of default is higher in bad times than good times, and, in the case of default, you will recover 90% of the face value?
    e. For parts (b–d), what can you say about the five-year, risk-free interest rate in each case?

Sovereign Debt

33. What does it mean for a country to "inflate away" its debt? Why might this be costly for investors even if the country does not default?

34. Suppose the yield on German government bonds is 1%, while the yield on Spanish government bonds is 6%. Both bonds are denominated in euros. Which country do investors believe is more likely to default? Why?

Data Case

You are an intern with Sirius Satellite Radio in their corporate finance division. The firm is planning to issue $50 million of 12% annual coupon bonds with a 10-year maturity. The firm anticipates an increase in its bond rating. Your boss wants you to determine the gain in the proceeds of the new issue if the issue is rated above the firm's current bond rating. To prepare this information, you will have to determine Sirius' current debt rating and the yield curve for their particular rating.

1. Begin by finding the current U.S. Treasury yield curve. At the Treasury Web site (www.treas.gov), search using the term "yield curve" and select "Historic Yield Data." Click on "View Text Version of Treasury Yield Curve." The correct link is likely to be the first link on the page. Download that table into Excel by right clicking with the cursor in the table and selecting "Export to Microsoft Excel."

2. Find the current yield spreads for the various bond ratings. Unfortunately, the current spreads are available only for a fee, so you will use old ones. Go to BondsOnline (www.bondsonline.com) and click "Today's Market." Next, click "Corporate Bond Spreads." Download this table to Excel and copy and paste it to the same file as the Treasury yields.

3. Find the current bond rating for Sirius. Go to Standard & Poor's Web site (www.standardandpoors .com). Select "Find a Rating" from the list at the left of the page, then select "Credit Ratings Search." At this point, you will have to register (it's free) or enter the username and password provided by your instructor. Next, you will be able to search by Organization Name—enter Sirius and select Sirius Satellite Radio. Use the credit rating for the organization, not the specific issue ratings.

4. Return to Excel and create a timeline with the cash flows and discount rates you will need to value the new bond issue.
    a. To create the required spot rates for Sirius' issue, add the appropriate spread to the Treasury yield of the same maturity.
    b. The yield curve and spread rates you have found do not cover every year that you will need for the new bonds. Specifically, you do not have yields or spreads for four-, six-, eight-, and nine-year maturities. Fill these in by linearly interpolating the given yields and spreads. For example, the four-year spot rate and spread will be the average of the three- and five-year rates. The six-year rate and spread will be the average of the five- and seven-year rates. For years 8 and 9 you will have to spread the difference between years 7 and 10 across the two years.

   c. To compute the spot rates for Sirius' current debt rating, add the yield spread to the Treasury rate for each maturity. However, note that the spread is in basis points, which are 1/100th of a percentage point.

   d. Compute the cash flows that would be paid to bondholders each year and add them to the timeline.

5. Use the spot rates to calculate the present value of each cash flow paid to the bondholders.

6. Compute the issue price of the bond and its initial yield to maturity.

7. Repeat Steps 4–6 based on the assumption that Sirius is able to raise its bond rating by one level. Compute the new yield based on the higher rating and the new bond price that would result.

8. Compute the additional cash proceeds that could be raised from the issue if the rating were improved.

CHAPTER 6
APPENDIX

Forward Interest Rates

NOTATION

f_n one-year
forward rate
for year n

Given the risk associated with interest rate changes, corporate managers require tools to help manage this risk. One of the most important is the interest rate forward contract, which is a type of swap contract. An **interest rate forward contract** (also called a **forward rate agreement**) is a contract today that fixes the interest rate for a loan or investment in the future. In this appendix, we explain how to derive forward interest rates from zero-coupon yields.

Computing Forward Rates

A **forward interest rate** (or **forward rate**) is an interest rate that we can guarantee today for a loan or investment that will occur in the future. Throughout this section, we will consider interest rate forward contracts for one-year investments; thus, when we refer to the forward rate for year 5, we mean the rate available *today* on a one-year investment that begins four years from today and is repaid five years from today.

We can use the Law of One Price to calculate the forward rate from the zero-coupon yield curve. The forward rate for year 1 is the rate on an investment that starts today and is repaid in one year; it is equivalent to an investment in a one-year, zero-coupon bond. Therefore, by the Law of One Price, these rates must coincide:

$$f_1 = YTM_1 \tag{6A.1}$$

Now consider the two-year forward rate. Suppose the one-year, zero-coupon yield is 5.5% and the two-year, zero-coupon yield is 7%. There are two ways to invest money risk free for two years. First, we can invest in the two-year, zero-coupon bond at rate of 7% and earn $\$(1.07)^2$ after two years per dollar invested. Second, we can invest in the one-year bond at a rate of 5.5%, which will pay $1.055 at the end of one year, and simultaneously guarantee the interest rate we will earn by reinvesting the $1.055 for the second year by entering into an interest rate forward contract for year 2 at rate f_2. In that case, we will earn $\$(1.055)(1 + f_2)$ at the end of two years. Because both strategies are risk free, by the Law of One Price, they must have the same return:

$$(1.07)^2 = (1.055)(1 + f_2)$$

Rearranging, we have

$$(1 + f_2) = \frac{1.07^2}{1.055} = 1.0852$$

Therefore, in this case the forward rate for year 2 is $f_2 = 8.52\%$.

In general, we can compute the forward rate for year n by comparing an investment in an n-year, zero-coupon bond to an investment in an $(n-1)$ year, zero-coupon bond, with the interest rate earned in the nth year being guaranteed through an interest rate forward contract. Because both strategies are risk free, they must have the same payoff or else an arbitrage opportunity would be available. Comparing the payoffs of these strategies, we have

$$(1 + YTM_n)^n = (1 + YTM_{n-1})^{n-1}(1 + f_n)$$

We can rearrange this equation to find the general formula for the forward interest rate:

$$f_n = \frac{(1 + YTM_n)^n}{(1 + YTM_{n-1})^{n-1}} - 1 \tag{6A.2}$$

EXAMPLE 6A.1

Computing Forward Rates

Problem

Calculate the forward rates for years 1 through 5 from the following zero-coupon yields:

Maturity	1	2	3	4
YTM	5.00%	6.00%	6.00%	5.75%

Solution

Using Eqs. 6A.1 and 6A.2:

$$f_1 = YTM_1 = 5.00\%$$

$$f_2 = \frac{(1 + YTM_2)^2}{(1 + YTM_1)} - 1 = \frac{1.06^2}{1.05} - 1 = 7.01\%$$

$$f_3 = \frac{(1 + YTM_3)^3}{(1 + YTM_2)^2} - 1 = \frac{1.06^3}{1.06^2} - 1 = 6.00\%$$

$$f_4 = \frac{(1 + YTM_4)^4}{(1 + YTM_3)^3} - 1 = \frac{1.0575^4}{1.06^3} - 1 = 5.00\%$$

Note that when the yield curve is increasing in year n (that is, when $YTM_n > YTM_{n-1}$), the forward rate is higher than the zero-coupon yield, $f_n > YTM_n$. Similarly, when the yield curve is decreasing, the forward rate is less than the zero-coupon yield. When the yield curve is flat, the forward rate equals the zero-coupon yield.

Computing Bond Yields from Forward Rates

Eq. 6A.2 computes the forward interest rate using the zero-coupon yields. It is also possible to compute the zero-coupon yields from the forward interest rates. To see this, note that if we use interest rate forward contracts to lock in an interest rate for an investment in year 1, year 2, and so on through year n, we can create an n-year, risk-free investment. The return from this strategy must match the return from an n-year, zero-coupon bond. Therefore,

$$(1 + f_1) \times (1 + f_2) \times \cdots \times (1 + f_n) = (1 + YTM_n)^n \tag{6A.3}$$

For example, using the forward rates from Example 6A.1, we can compute the four-year zero-coupon yield:

$$1 + YTM_4 = [(1 + f_1)(1 + f_2)(1 + f_3)(1 + f_4)]^{1/4}$$

$$= [(1.05)(1.0701)(1.06)(1.05)]^{1/4}$$

$$= 1.0575$$

Forward Rates and Future Interest Rates

A forward rate is the rate that you contract for today for an investment in the future. How does this rate compare to the interest rate that will actually prevail in the future? It is tempting to believe that the forward interest rate should be a good predictor of future interest rates. In reality, this will generally not be the case. Instead, it is a good predictor only when investors do not care about risk.

EXAMPLE 6A.2   **Forward Rates and Future Spot Rates**

Problem
JoAnne Wilford is corporate treasurer for Wafer Thin Semiconductor. She must invest some of the cash on hand for two years in risk-free bonds. The current one-year, zero-coupon yield is 5%. The one-year forward rate is 6%. She is trying to decide between three possible strategies: (1) buy a two-year bond, (2) buy a one-year bond and enter into an interest rate forward contract to guarantee the rate in the second year, or (3) buy a one-year bond and forgo the forward contract, reinvesting at whatever rate prevails next year. Under what scenarios would she be better off following the risky strategy?

Solution
From Eq. 6A.3, both strategies (1) and (2) lead to the same risk-free return of $(1 + YTM_2)^2 = (1 + YTM_1)(1 + f_2) = (1.05)(1.06)$. The third strategy returns $(1.05)(1 + r)$, where r is the one-year interest rate next year. If the future interest rate turns out to be 6%, then the two strategies will offer the same return. Otherwise Wafer Thin Semiconductor is better off with strategy (3) if the interest rate next year is greater than the forward rate—6%—and worse off if the interest rate is lower than 6%.

As Example 6A.2 makes clear, we can think of the forward rate as a break-even rate. If this rate actually prevails in the future, investors will be indifferent between investing in a two-year bond and investing in a one-year bond and rolling over the money in one year. If investors did not care about risk, then they would be indifferent between the two strategies whenever the expected one-year spot rate equals the current forward rate. However, investors *do* generally care about risk. If the expected returns of both strategies were the same, investors would prefer one strategy or the other depending on whether they want to be exposed to future interest rate risk fluctuations. In general, the expected future spot interest rate will reflect investors' preferences toward the risk of future interest rate fluctuations. Thus,

Expected Future Spot Interest Rate = Forward Interest Rate + Risk Premium   (6A.4)

This risk premium can be either positive or negative depending on investors' preferences.[6] As a result, forward rates tend not to be ideal predictors of future spot rates.

---

[6]Empirical research suggests that the risk premium tends to be negative when the yield curve is upward sloping, and positive when it is downward sloping. See E. Fama and R. Bliss, "The Information in Long-Maturity Forward Rates," *American Economic Review* 77(4) (1987): 680–692; and J. Campbell and R. Shiller, "Yield Spreads and Interest Rate Movements: A Bird's Eye View," *Review of Economic Studies* 58(3) (1991): 495–514.

Key Terms

forward interest rate (forward rate) *p. 201*

forward rate agreement *p. 201*

interest rate forward contract *p. 201*

Problems

All problems are available in MyFinanceLab. *An asterisk (*) indicates problems with a higher level of difficulty.*

Problems A.1–A.4 refer to the following table:

Maturity (years)	1	2	3	4	5
Zero-coupon YTM	4.0%	5.5%	5.5%	5.0%	4.5%

A.1. What is the forward rate for year 2 (the forward rate quoted today for an investment that begins in one year and matures in two years)?

A.2. What is the forward rate for year 3 (the forward rate quoted today for an investment that begins in two years and matures in three years)? What can you conclude about forward rates when the yield curve is flat?

A.3. What is the forward rate for year 5 (the forward rate quoted today for an investment that begins in four years and matures in five years)?

*****A.4.** Suppose you wanted to lock in an interest rate for an investment that begins in one year and matures in five years. What rate would you obtain if there are no arbitrage opportunities?

*****A.5.** Suppose the yield on a one-year, zero-coupon bond is 5%. The forward rate for year 2 is 4%, and the forward rate for year 3 is 3%. What is the yield to maturity of a zero-coupon bond that matures in three years?

Valuing Projects and Firms

THE LAW OF ONE PRICE CONNECTION. Now that the basic tools for financial decision making are in place, we can begin to apply them. One of the most important decisions facing a financial manager is the choice of which investments the corporation should make. In Chapter 7, we compare the net present value rule to other investment rules that firms sometimes use and explain why the net present value rule is superior. The process of allocating the firm's capital for investment is known as capital budgeting, and in Chapter 8, we outline the discounted cash flow method for making such decisions. Both chapters provide a practical demonstration of the power of the tools that were introduced in Part II.

Many firms raise the capital they need to make investments by issuing stock to investors. How do investors determine the price they are willing to pay for this stock? And how do managers' investment decisions affect this value? In Chapter 9, Valuing Stocks, we show how the Law of One Price leads to several alternative methods for valuing a firm's equity by considering its future dividends, its free cash flows, or how it compares to similar, publicly traded companies.

Investment Decision Rules

IN 2000, TOSHIBA AND SONY BEGAN EXPERIMENTING WITH new DVD technology, leading to Sony's development of Blu-ray High Definition DVD players and Toshiba's introduction of the HD-DVD player. So began an eight-year format war that ended in February 2008 when Toshiba decided to stop producing HD-DVD players and abandon the format. How did Toshiba and Sony managers arrive at the decision to invest in new DVD formats? And how did Toshiba managers conclude that the best decision was to stop producing HD-DVD? In both cases, the managers made decisions they believed would maximize the value of their firms.

As we will see in this chapter, the NPV investment rule is the decision rule that managers should use to maximize firm value. Nevertheless, some firms use other techniques to evaluate investments and decide which projects to pursue. In this chapter, we explain several commonly used techniques—namely, the *payback rule* and the *internal rate of return rule*. We then compare decisions based on these rules to decisions based on the NPV rule and illustrate the circumstances in which the alternative rules are likely to lead to bad investment decisions. After establishing these rules in the context of a single, stand-alone project, we broaden our perspective to include deciding among alternative investment opportunities. We conclude with a look at project selection when the firm faces capital or other resource constraints.

7.1 NPV and Stand-Alone Projects

We begin our discussion of investment decision rules by considering a take-it-or-leave-it decision involving a single, stand-alone project. By undertaking this project, the firm does not constrain its ability to take other projects. To analyze such a decision, recall the NPV rule:

NPV Investment Rule: *When making an investment decision, take the alternative with the highest NPV. Choosing this alternative is equivalent to receiving its NPV in cash today.*

In the case of a stand-alone project, we must choose between accepting or rejecting the project. The NPV rule then says we should compare the project's NPV to zero (the NPV of doing nothing) and accept the project if its NPV is positive.

Applying the NPV Rule

Researchers at Fredrick's Feed and Farm have made a breakthrough. They believe that they can produce a new, environmentally friendly fertilizer at a substantial cost savings over the company's existing line of fertilizer. The fertilizer will require a new plant that can be built immediately at a cost of $250 million. Financial managers estimate that the benefits of the new fertilizer will be $35 million per year, starting at the end of the first year and lasting forever, as shown by the following timeline:

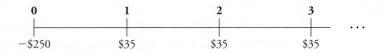

As we explained in Chapter 4, the NPV of this perpetual cash flow stream, given a discount rate r, is

$$NPV = -250 + \frac{35}{r} \tag{7.1}$$

The financial managers responsible for this project estimate a cost of capital of 10% per year. Using this cost of capital in Eq. 7.1, the NPV is $100 million, which is positive. The NPV investment rule indicates that by making the investment, the value of the firm will increase by $100 million today, so Fredrick's should undertake this project.

The NPV Profile and IRR

The NPV of the project depends on the appropriate cost of capital. Often, there may be some uncertainty regarding the project's cost of capital. In that case, it is helpful to compute an **NPV profile**: a graph of the project's NPV over a range of discount rates. Figure 7.1 plots the NPV of the fertilizer project as a function of the discount rate, r.

Notice that the NPV is positive only for discount rates that are less than 14%. When $r = 14\%$, the NPV is zero. Recall from Chapter 4 that the internal rate of return (IRR) of an investment is the discount rate that sets the NPV of the project's cash flows equal to zero. Thus, the fertilizer project has an IRR of 14%.

The IRR of a project provides useful information regarding the sensitivity of the project's NPV to errors in the estimate of its cost of capital. For the fertilizer project, if the cost of capital estimate is more than the 14% IRR, the NPV will be negative, as shown in

NPV of Fredrick's Fertilizer Project

The graph shows the NPV as a function of the discount rate. The NPV is positive only for discount rates that are less than 14%, the internal rate of return (IRR). Given the cost of capital of 10%, the project has a positive NPV of $100 million.

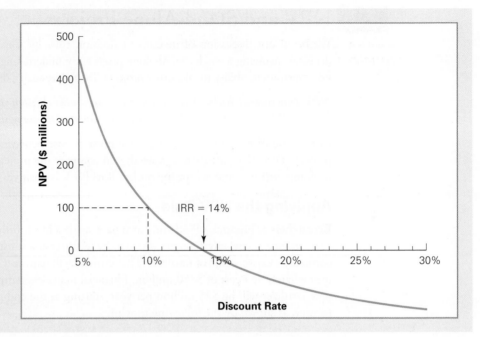

Figure 7.1. Therefore, the decision to accept the project is correct as long as our estimate of 10% is within 4% of the true cost of capital. In general, *the difference between the cost of capital and the IRR is the maximum estimation error in the cost of capital that can exist without altering the original decision.*

Alternative Rules Versus the NPV Rule

Although the NPV rule is the most accurate and reliable decision rule, in practice a wide variety of tools are applied, often in tandem with the NPV rule. In a 2001 study, 75% of the firms John Graham and Campbell Harvey[1] surveyed used the NPV rule for making investment decisions. This result is substantially different from that found in a similar study in 1977 by L. J. Gitman and J. R. Forrester,[2] who found that only 10% of firms used the NPV rule. MBA students in recent years must have been listening to their finance professors! Even so, Graham and Harvey's study indicates that one-fourth of U.S. corporations do not use the NPV rule. Exactly why other capital budgeting techniques are used in practice is not always clear. However, because you may encounter these techniques in the business world, you should know what they are, how they are used, and how they compare to NPV.

As we evaluate alternative rules for project selection in subsequent sections, keep in mind that sometimes other investment rules may give the same answer as the NPV rule, but at other times they may disagree. When the rules conflict, following the alternative rule means that we are either taking a negative NPV investment or turning down a positive NPV investment. In these cases, the alternative rules lead to bad decisions that reduce wealth.

[1]"The Theory and Practice of Corporate Finance: Evidence from the Field," *Journal of Financial Economics* 60 (2001): 187–243.

[2]"A Survey of Capital Budgeting Techniques Used by Major U.S. Firms," *Financial Management* 6 (1977): 66–71.

CONCEPT CHECK 1. Explain the NPV rule for stand-alone projects.

2. What does the difference between the cost of capital and the IRR indicate?

INTERVIEW WITH
Dick Grannis

Dick Grannis is Senior Vice President and Treasurer of QUALCOMM Incorporated, a world leader in digital wireless communications technology and semiconductors, headquartered in San Diego. He joined the company in 1991 and oversees the company's $10 billion cash investment portfolio. He works primarily on investment banking, capital structure, and international finance.

QUESTION: *QUALCOMM has a wide variety of products in different business lines. How does your capital budgeting process for new products work?*

ANSWER: QUALCOMM evaluates new projects (such as new products, equipment, technologies, research and development, acquisitions, and strategic investments) by using traditional financial measurements including discounted cash flow/NPV models, IRR levels, peak funding requirements, the time needed to reach cumulative positive cash flows, and the short-term impact of the investment on our reported net earnings. For strategic investments, we consider the possible value of financial, competitive, technology and/or market value enhancements to our core businesses—even if those benefits cannot be quantified. Overall, we make capital budgeting decisions based on a combination of objective analyses and our own business judgment.

We do not engage in capital budgeting and analysis if the project represents an immediate and necessary requirement for our business operations. One example is new software or production equipment to start a project that has already received approval.

We are also mindful of the opportunity costs of allocating our internal engineering resources on one project vs. another project. We view this as a constantly challenging but worthwhile exercise, because we have many attractive opportunities but limited resources to pursue them.

QUESTION: *How often does QUALCOMM evaluate its hurdle rates and what factors does it consider in setting them? How do you allocate capital across areas and regions and assess the risk of non-U.S. investments?*

ANSWER: QUALCOMM encourages its financial planners to utilize hurdle (or discount) rates that vary according to the risk of the particular project. We expect a rate of return commensurate with the project's risk. Our finance staff considers a wide range of discount rates and chooses one that fits the project's expected risk profile and time horizon. The range can be from 6% to 8% for relatively safe investments in the domestic market to 50% or more for equity investments in foreign markets that may be illiquid and difficult to predict. We re-evaluate our hurdle rates at least every year.

We analyze key factors including: (1) market adoption risk (whether or not customers will buy the new product or service at the price and volume we expect), (2) technology development risk (whether or not we can develop and patent the new product or service as expected), (3) execution risk (whether we can launch the new product or service cost effectively and on time), and (4) dedicated asset risk (the amount of resources that must be consumed to complete the work).

QUESTION: *How are projects categorized and how are the hurdle rates for new projects determined? What would happen if QUALCOMM simply evaluated all new projects against the same hurdle rate?*

ANSWER: We primarily categorize projects by risk level, but we also categorize projects by the expected time horizon. We consider short-term and long-term projects to balance our needs and achieve our objectives. For example, immediate projects and opportunities may demand a great amount of attention, but we also stay focused on long-term projects because they often create greater long-term value for stockholders.

If we were to evaluate all new projects against the same hurdle rate, then our business planners would, by default, consistently choose to invest in the highest risk projects because those projects would appear to have the greatest expected returns in DCF models or IRR analyses. That approach would probably not work well for very long.

7.2 The Internal Rate of Return Rule

One interpretation of the internal rate of return is the average return earned by taking on the investment opportunity. The **internal rate of return (IRR) investment rule** is based on this idea: If the average return on the investment opportunity (i.e., the IRR) is greater than the return on other alternatives in the market with equivalent risk and maturity (i.e., the project's cost of capital), you should undertake the investment opportunity. We state the rule formally as follows:

IRR Investment Rule: *Take any investment opportunity where the IRR exceeds the opportunity cost of capital. Turn down any opportunity whose IRR is less than the opportunity cost of capital.*

Applying the IRR Rule

Like the NPV rule, the internal rate of return investment rule is applied to single, stand-alone projects within the firm. The IRR investment rule will give the correct answer (that is, the same answer as the NPV rule) in many—but not all—situations. For instance, it gives the correct answer for Fredrick's fertilizer opportunity. Looking again at Figure 7.1, whenever the cost of capital is below the IRR (14%), the project has a positive NPV and you should undertake the investment.

In the Fredrick fertilizer example, the NPV rule and the IRR rule coincide, so the IRR rule gives the correct answer. This need not always be the case, however. In fact, *the IRR rule is only guaranteed to work for a stand-alone project if all of the project's negative cash flows precede its positive cash flows.* If this is not the case, the IRR rule can lead to incorrect decisions. Let's examine several situations in which the IRR fails.

Pitfall #1: Delayed Investments

John Star, the founder of SuperTech, the most successful company in the last 20 years, has just retired as CEO. A major publisher has offered to pay Star $1 million upfront if he agrees to write a book about his experiences. He estimates that it will take him three years to write the book. The time that he spends writing will cause him to forgo alternative sources of income amounting to $500,000 per year. Considering the risk of his alternative income sources and available investment opportunities, Star estimates his opportunity cost of capital to be 10%. The timeline of Star's investment opportunity is

0	1	2	3
$1,000,000	−$500,000	−$500,000	−$500,000

The NPV of Star's investment opportunity is

$$NPV = 1,000,000 - \frac{500,000}{1 + r} - \frac{500,000}{(1 + r)^2} - \frac{500,000}{(1 + r)^3}$$

By setting the NPV equal to zero and solving for r, we find the IRR. Using the annuity spreadsheet:

	NPER	RATE	PV	PMT	FV	Excel Formula
Given	3		1,000,000	−500,000	0	
Solve for I		23.38%				=RATE(3,−500000,1000000, 0)

The 23.38% IRR is larger than the 10% opportunity cost of capital. According to the IRR rule, Star should sign the deal. But what does the NPV rule say?

$$NPV = 1{,}000{,}000 - \frac{500{,}000}{1.1} - \frac{500{,}000}{1.1^2} - \frac{500{,}000}{1.1^3} = -\$243{,}426$$

At a 10% discount rate, the NPV is negative, so signing the deal would reduce Star's wealth. He should not sign the book deal.

To understand why the IRR rule fails, Figure 7.2 shows the NPV profile of the book deal. No matter what the cost of capital is, the IRR rule and the NPV rule will give exactly opposite recommendations. That is, the NPV is positive only when the opportunity cost of capital is *above* 23.38% (the IRR). In fact, Star should accept the investment only when the opportunity cost of capital is greater than the IRR, the opposite of what the IRR rule recommends.

Figure 7.2 also illustrates the problem with using the IRR rule in this case. For most investment opportunities, expenses occur initially and cash is received later. In this case, Star gets cash *upfront* and incurs the costs of producing the book *later*. It is as if Star borrowed money—receiving cash today in exchange for a future liability—and when you borrow money you prefer as *low* a rate as possible. In this case the IRR is best interpreted as the rate Star is paying rather than earning, and so Star's optimal rule is to borrow money so long as this rate is *less* than his cost of capital.

Even though the IRR rule fails to give the correct answer in this case, the IRR itself still provides useful information *in conjunction* with the NPV rule. As mentioned earlier, IRR indicates how sensitive the investment decision is to uncertainty in the cost of capital estimate. In this case, the difference between the cost of capital and the IRR is large—13.38%. Star would have to have underestimated the cost of capital by 13.38% to make the NPV positive.

Pitfall #2: Multiple IRRs

Star has informed the publisher that it needs to sweeten the deal before he will accept it. In response, the publisher offers to give him a royalty payment when the book is published in exchange for taking a smaller upfront payment. Specifically, Star will receive $1 million when the book is published and sold four years from now, together with an upfront payment of $550,000. Should he accept or reject the new offer?

FIGURE 7.2

NPV of Star's $1 Million Book Deal

When the benefits of an investment occur before the costs, the NPV is an *increasing* function of the discount rate, and the IRR rule fails.

We begin with the new timeline:

0	1	2	3	4
$550,000	−$500,000	−$500,000	−$500,000	$1,000,000

The NPV of Star's new offer is

$$NPV = 550,000 - \frac{500,000}{1 + r} - \frac{500,000}{(1 + r)^2} - \frac{500,000}{(1 + r)^3} + \frac{1,000,000}{(1 + r)^4}$$

By setting the NPV equal to zero and solving for r, we find the IRR. In this case, there are *two* IRRs—that is, there are two values of r that set the NPV equal to zero. You can verify this fact by substituting IRRs of 7.164% and 33.673% into the equation. Because there is more than one IRR, we cannot apply the IRR rule.

For guidance, let's turn to the NPV rule. Figure 7.3 shows the NPV profile of the new offer. If the cost of capital is *either* below 7.164% or above 33.673%, Star should undertake the opportunity. Otherwise, he should turn it down. Notice that even though the IRR rule fails in this case, the two IRRs are still useful as bounds on the cost of capital. If the cost of capital estimate is wrong, and it is actually smaller than 7.164% or larger than 33.673%, the decision not to pursue the project will change. Even if Star is uncertain whether his actual cost of capital is 10%, as long as he believes it is within these bounds, he can have a high degree of confidence in his decision to reject the deal.

There is no easy fix for the IRR rule when there are multiple IRRs. Although the NPV is negative between the IRRs in this example, the reverse is also possible. Furthermore, there are situations in which more than two IRRs exist.[3] When multiple IRRs exist, our only choice is to rely on the NPV rule.

FIGURE 7.3

NPV of Star's Book Deal with Royalties

In this case, there is more than one IRR, invalidating the IRR rule. In this case, Star should only take the offer if the opportunity cost of capital is *either* below 7.164% or above 33.673%.

---

[3]In general, there can be as many IRRs as the number of times the project's cash flows change sign over time.

The examples in this section illustrate the potential short-comings of the IRR rule when choosing to accept or reject a stand-alone project. As we said at the outset, we can only avoid these problems if all of the negative cash flows of the project precede the positive cash flows. Otherwise, we cannot rely on the IRR rule. However, even in that case, the IRR itself remains a very useful tool. The IRR measures the average return over the life of an investment and indicates the sensitivity of the NPV to estimation error in the cost of capital. Thus, knowing the IRR can be very useful, but relying on it to make investment decisions can be hazardous.

Pitfall #3: Nonexistent IRR

After protracted negotiations, Star is able to get the publisher to increase his initial payment to $750,000, in addition to his $1 million royalty payment when the book is published in four years. With these cash flows, no IRR exists; that is, there is no discount rate that makes the NPV equal to zero. Thus, the IRR rule provides no guidance whatsoever. To evaluate this final offer, let's again look at the NPV profile, shown in Figure 7.4. There we can see that the NPV is positive for any discount rate, and so the offer is attractive. But don't be fooled into thinking the NPV is always positive when the IRR does not exist—it can just as well be negative.

FIGURE 7.4

NPV of Star's Final Offer

In this case, the NPV is positive for every discount rate, and so there is no IRR. Thus, we cannot use the IRR rule.

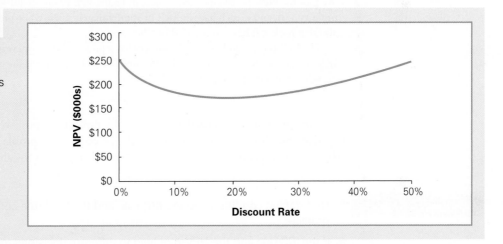

EXAMPLE 7.1   **Problems with the IRR Rule**

Problem
Consider projects with the following cash flows:

Project	0	1	2
A	−375	−300	900
B	−22,222	50,000	−28,000
C	400	400	−1,056
D	−4,300	10,000	−6,000

Which of these projects have an IRR close to 20%? For which of these projects is the IRR rule valid?

FIGURE 7.5

NPV Profiles for Example 7.1

While the IRR Rule works for project A, it fails for each of the other projects.

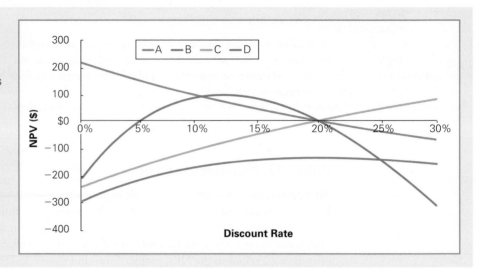

Solution

We plot the NPV profile for each project in Figure 7.5. From the NPV profiles, we can see that projects A, B, and C each have an IRR of approximately 20%, while project D has no IRR. Note also that project B has another IRR of 5%.

The IRR rule is valid only if the project has a positive NPV for every discount rate below the IRR. Thus, the IRR rule is only valid for project A. This project is the only one for which all the negative cash flows precede the positive ones.

As the previous examples demonstrate, if a project has positive cash flows that precede negative ones, it is important to look at the project's NPV profile in order to interpret the IRR. See the appendix to this chapter for a simple approach to calculating the NPV profile in Excel.

CONCEPT CHECK

1. Under what conditions do the IRR rule and the NPV rule coincide for a stand-alone project?

2. If the IRR rule and the NPV rule lead to different decisions for a stand-alone project, which should you follow? Why?

7.3 The Payback Rule

In this section, we examine the *payback rule as an* alternative decision rule for single, stand-alone projects within the firm. The **payback investment rule** states that you should only accept a project if its cash flows pay back its initial investment within a prespecified period. To apply the payback rule, you first calculate the amount of time it takes to pay back the initial investment, called the **payback period**. Then you accept the project if the payback period is less than a prespecified length of time—usually a few years. Otherwise, you reject the project. For example, a firm might adopt any project with a payback period of less than two years.

Applying the Payback Rule

To illustrate the payback rule, we return to the Fredrick's Feed and Farm example.

EXAMPLE 7.2	**The Payback Rule**

Problem

Assume Fredrick's requires all projects to have a payback period of five years or less. Would the firm undertake the fertilizer project under this rule?

Solution

Recall that the project requires an initial investment of $250 million, and will generate $35 million per year. The sum of the cash flows from year 1 to year 5 is $35 \times 5 = $175 million, which will not cover the initial investment of $250 million. In fact, it will not be until year 8 that the initial investment will be paid back ($35 \times 8 = $280 million). Because the payback period for this project exceeds five years, Fredrick's will reject the project.

Relying on the payback rule analysis in Example 7.2, Fredrick's will reject the project. However, as we saw earlier, with a cost of capital of 10%, the NPV is $100 million. Following the payback rule would be a mistake because Fredrick's would pass up a project worth $100 million.

Payback Rule Pitfalls in Practice

The payback rule is not as reliable as the NPV rule because it (1) ignores the project's cost of capital and the time value of money, (2) ignores cash flows after the payback period, and (3) relies on an ad hoc decision criterion (what is the right number of years to require for the payback period?).[4] Despite these failings, about 57% of the firms Graham and Harvey surveyed reported using the payback rule as part of the decision-making process.

Why do some companies consider the payback rule? The answer probably relates to its simplicity. This rule is typically used for small investment decisions—for example, whether to purchase a new copy machine or to service the old one. In such cases, the cost of making an incorrect decision might not be large enough to justify the time required to calculate the NPV. The payback rule also provides budgeting information regarding the length of time capital will be committed to a project. Some firms are unwilling to commit capital to long-term investments without greater scrutiny. Also, if the required payback period is short (one or two years), then most projects that satisfy the payback rule will have a positive NPV. So firms might save effort by first applying the payback rule, and only if it fails take the time to compute NPV.

CONCEPT CHECK	1. Can the payback rule reject projects that have positive NPV? Can it accept projects that have negative NPV?
	2. If the payback rule does not give the same answer as the NPV rule, which rule should you follow? Why?

---

[4]Some companies address the first failing by computing the payback period using discounted cash flows (called discounted payback).

Why Do Rules Other Than the NPV Rule Persist?

Professors Graham and Harvey found that a sizable minority of firms (25%) in their study do not use the NPV rule at all. In addition, more than half of firms surveyed used the payback rule. Furthermore, it appears that most firms use *both* the NPV rule and the IRR rule. Why do firms use rules other than NPV if they can lead to erroneous decisions?

One possible explanation for this phenomenon is that Graham and Harvey's survey results might be misleading. Managers may use the payback rule for budgeting purposes or as a shortcut to get a quick sense of the project before calculating NPV. Similarly, CFOs who were using the IRR as a sensitivity measure in conjunction with the NPV rule might have checked both the IRR box and the NPV box on the survey. Nevertheless, a significant minority of managers surveyed replied that they used only the IRR rule, so this explanation cannot be the whole story.

Managers may use the IRR rule exclusively because you do not need to know the opportunity cost of capital to calculate the IRR. But this benefit is superficial: While you may not need to know the cost of capital to *calculate* the IRR, you certainly need to know the cost of capital when you *apply* the IRR rule. Consequently, the opportunity cost of capital is as important to the IRR rule as it is to the NPV rule.

In our opinion, some firms use the IRR rule exclusively because the IRR sums up the attractiveness of investment opportunity without requiring an assumption about the cost of capital. However, a more useful summary would be a plot of the NPV as a function of the discount rate; that is, the project's NPV profile. The NPV profile also does not require the cost of capital, but it has the distinct advantage of being much more informative and reliable.

7.4 Choosing Between Projects

Thus far, we have considered only decisions where the choice is either to accept or to reject a single, stand-alone project. Sometimes, however, a firm must choose just one project from among several possible projects, that is, the choices are mutually exclusive. For example, a manager may be evaluating alternative package designs for a new product. When choosing any one project excludes us from taking the others, we are facing mutually exclusive investments.

NPV Rule and Mutually Exclusive Investments

When projects are mutually exclusive, we need to determine which projects have a positive NPV and then rank the projects to identify the best one. In this situation, the NPV rule provides a straightforward answer: *Pick the project with the highest NPV*. Because the NPV expresses the value of the project in terms of cash today, picking the project with the highest NPV leads to the greatest increase in wealth.

EXAMPLE 7.3   **NPV and Mutually Exclusive Projects**

Problem

A small commercial property is for sale near your university. Given its location, you believe a student-oriented business would be very successful there. You have researched several possibilities and come up with the following cash flow estimates (including the cost of purchasing the property). Which investment should you choose?

Project	Initial Investment	First-Year Cash Flow	Growth Rate	Cost of Capital
Book Store	$300,000	$63,000	3.0%	8%
Coffee Shop	$400,000	$80,000	3.0%	8%
Music Store	$400,000	$104,000	0.0%	8%
Electronics Store	$400,000	$100,000	3.0%	11%

Solution

Assuming each business lasts indefinitely, we can compute the present value of the cash flows from each as a constant growth perpetuity. The NPV of each project is

$$NPV(\text{Book Store}) = -300{,}000 + \frac{63{,}000}{8\% - 3\%} = \$960{,}000$$

$$NPV(\text{Coffee Shop}) = -400{,}000 + \frac{80{,}000}{8\% - 3\%} = \$1{,}200{,}000$$

$$NPV(\text{Music Store}) = -400{,}000 + \frac{104{,}000}{8\%} = \$900{,}000$$

$$NPV(\text{Electronics Store}) = -400{,}000 + \frac{100{,}000}{11\% - 3\%} = \$850{,}000$$

Thus, all of the alternatives have a positive NPV. But, because we can only choose one, the coffee shop is the best alternative.

IRR Rule and Mutually Exclusive Investments

Because the IRR is a measure of the expected return of investing in the project, you might be tempted to extend the IRR investment rule to the case of mutually exclusive projects by picking the project with the highest IRR. Unfortunately, picking one project over another simply because it has a larger IRR can lead to mistakes. In particular, *when projects differ in their scale of investment, the timing of their cash flows, or their riskiness, then their IRRs cannot be meaningfully compared.*

Differences in Scale. Would you prefer a 500% return on $1, or a 20% return on $1 million? While a 500% return certainly sounds impressive, at the end of the day you will only make $5. The latter return sounds much more mundane, but you will make $200,000. This comparison illustrates an important shortcoming of IRR: Because it is a return, you cannot tell how much value will actually be created without knowing the scale of the investment.

If a project has a positive NPV, then if we can double its size, its NPV will double: By the Law of One Price, doubling the cash flows of an investment opportunity must make it worth twice as much. However, the IRR rule does not have this property—it is unaffected by the scale of the investment opportunity because the IRR measures the average return of the investment. Hence, we cannot use the IRR rule to compare projects of different scales.

As an illustration of this situation, consider the investment in the book store versus the coffee shop in Example 7.3. We can compute the IRR of each as follows:

$$\text{Book Store:} \quad -300{,}000 + \frac{63{,}000}{IRR - 3\%} = 0 \Rightarrow IRR = 24\%$$

$$\text{Coffee Shop:} \quad -400{,}000 + \frac{80{,}000}{IRR - 3\%} = 0 \Rightarrow IRR = 23\%$$

Both projects have IRRs that exceed their cost of capital of 8%. But although the coffee shop has a lower IRR, because it is on a larger scale of investment ($400,000 versus $300,000), it generates a higher NPV ($1.2 million versus $960,000) and thus is more valuable.

Differences in Timing. Even when projects have the same scale, the IRR may lead you to rank them incorrectly due to differences in the timing of the cash flows. The IRR is expressed as a return, but the dollar value of earning a given return—and therefore its NPV—depends on how long the return is earned. Earning a very high annual return is much more valuable if you earn it for several years than if you earn it for only a few days.

As an example, consider the following short-term and long-term projects:

Both projects have an IRR of 50%, but one lasts for one year, while the other has a five-year horizon. If the cost of capital for both projects is 10%, the short-term project has an NPV of $-100 + 150/1.10 = \$36.36$, whereas the long-term project has an NPV of $-100 + 759.375/1.10^5 = \$371.51$. Notice that despite having the same IRR, the long-term project is more than 10 times as valuable as the short-term project.

Even when projects have the same horizon, the pattern of cash flows over time will often differ. Consider again the coffee shop and music store investment alternatives in Example 7.3. Both of these investments have the same initial scale, and the same horizon (infinite). The IRR of the music store investment is

$$\text{Music Store:}\quad -400{,}000 + \frac{104{,}000}{IRR} = 0 \Rightarrow IRR = 26\%$$

But although the music store has a higher IRR than the coffee shop (26% versus 23%), it has a lower NPV ($900,000 versus $1.2 million). The reason the coffee shop has a higher NPV despite having a lower IRR is its higher growth rate. The coffee shop has lower initial cash flows but higher long-run cash flows than the music store. The fact that its cash flows are relatively delayed makes the coffee shop effectively a longer-term investment.

Differences in Risk. To know whether the IRR of a project is attractive, we must compare it to the project's cost of capital, which is determined by the project's risk. Thus, an IRR that is attractive for a safe project need not be attractive for a risky project. As a simple example, while you might be quite pleased to earn a 10% return on a risk-free investment opportunity, you might be much less satisfied to earn a 10% expected return on an investment in a risky start-up company. Ranking projects by their IRRs ignores risk differences.

Looking again at Example 7.3, consider the investment in the electronics store. The IRR of the electronics store is

$$\text{Electronics Store:}\quad -400{,}000 + \frac{100{,}000}{IRR - 3\%} = 0 \Rightarrow IRR = 28\%$$

This IRR is higher than those of all the other investment opportunities. Yet the electronics store has the lowest NPV. In this case, the investment in the electronics store is riskier, as evidenced by its higher cost of capital. Despite having a higher IRR, it is not sufficiently profitable to be as attractive as the safer alternatives.

The Incremental IRR

When choosing between two projects, an alternative to comparing their IRRs is to compute the **incremental IRR**, which is the IRR of the incremental cash flows that would result from replacing one project with the other. The incremental IRR tells us the discount rate

When Can Returns Be Compared?

In this chapter, we have highlighted the many pitfalls that arise when attempting to compare the IRRs of different projects. But there are many situations in which it is quite reasonable to compare returns. For example, if we were thinking of saving money in a savings account for the next year, we would likely compare the effective annual rates associated with different accounts and choose the highest option.

When is it reasonable to compare returns in this way? Remember, *we can only compare returns if the investments (1) have the same scale, (2) have the same timing, and (3) have the*

same risk. While one or more of these conditions are typically violated when we compare two investment projects, they are much more likely to be met when one of the investments is an investment in publicly traded securities or with a bank. When we invest with a bank or in traded securities, we can usually choose the scale of our investment, as well as our investment horizon, so that the opportunities match. In this case, as long as we are comparing opportunities with the same risk, comparing returns is meaningful. (Indeed, this condition was the basis for our definition of the cost of capital in Chapter 5.)

at which it becomes profitable to switch from one project to the other. Then, rather than compare the projects directly, we can evaluate the decision to switch from one to the other using the IRR rule, as in the following example.

EXAMPLE 7.4

Using the Incremental IRR to Compare Alternatives

Problem

Your firm is considering overhauling its production plant. The engineering team has come up with two proposals, one for a minor overhaul and one for a major overhaul. The two options have the following cash flows (in millions of dollars):

Proposal	0	1	2	3
Minor Overhaul	−10	6	6	6
Major Overhaul	−50	25	25	25

What is the IRR of each proposal? What is the incremental IRR? If the cost of capital for both of these projects is 12%, what should your firm do?

Solution

We can compute the IRR of each proposal using the annuity calculator. For the minor overhaul, the IRR is 36.3%:

	NPER	RATE	PV	PMT	FV	Excel Formula
Given	3		−10	6	0	
Solve for Rate		36.3%				=RATE(3,6,−10,0)

For the major overhaul, the IRR is 23.4%:

	NPER	RATE	PV	PMT	FV	Excel Formula
Given	3		−50	25	0	
Solve for Rate		23.4%				=RATE(3,25,−50,0)

Which project is best? Because the projects have different scales, we cannot compare their IRRs directly. To compute the incremental IRR of switching from the minor overhaul to the major overhaul, we first compute the incremental cash flows:

Proposal	0	1	2	3
Major Overhaul	−50	25	25	25
Less: Minor Overhaul	−(−10)	−6	−6	−6
Incremental Cash Flow	−40	19	19	19

These cash flows have an IRR of 20.0%:

	NPER	RATE	PV	PMT	FV	Excel Formula
Given	3		−40	19	0	
Solve for Rate		20.0%				=RATE(3,19,−40,0)

Because the incremental IRR exceeds the 12% cost of capital, switching to the major overhaul looks attractive (i.e., its larger scale is sufficient to make up for its lower IRR). We can check this result using Figure 7.6, which shows the NPV profiles for each project. At the 12% cost of capital, the NPV of the major overhaul does indeed exceed that of the minor overhaul, despite its lower IRR. Note also that the incremental IRR determines the crossover point of the NPV profiles, the discount rate for which the best project choice switches from the major overhaul to the minor one.

FIGURE 7.6

Comparison of Minor and Major Overhauls

Comparing the NPV profiles of the minor and major overhauls in Example 7.4, we can see that despite its lower IRR, the major overhaul has a higher NPV at the cost of capital of 12%. Note also that the incremental IRR of 20% determines the crossover point or discount rate at which the optimal decision changes.

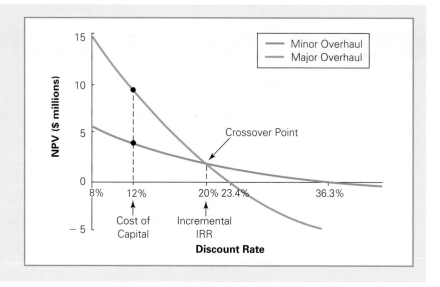

As we saw in Example 7.4, the incremental IRR identifies the discount rate at which the optimal decision changes. However, when using the incremental IRR to choose between projects, we encounter all of the same problems that arose with the IRR rule:

- Even if the negative cash flows precede the positive ones for the individual projects, it need not be true for the incremental cash flows. If not, the incremental IRR is difficult to interpret, and may not exist or may not be unique.

- The incremental IRR can indicate whether it is profitable to switch from one project to another, but it does not indicate whether either project has a positive NPV on its own.

- When the individual projects have different costs of capital, it is not obvious what cost of capital the incremental IRR should be compared to. In this case only the NPV rule, which allows each project to be discounted at its own cost of capital, will give a reliable answer.

COMMON MISTAKE   IRR and Project Financing

Because the IRR is not itself a measure of value, it is easy to manipulate by restructuring the project's cash flows. In particular, it is easy to increase the IRR of a project by financing a portion of the initial investment. A common mistake in practice is to regard this higher IRR as an indication that the financing is attractive. For example, consider an investment in new equipment that will have the following cash flows:

This investment has an IRR of 30%. Now suppose that seller of the equipment offers to lend us $80, so that we only need to pay $20 initially. In exchange, we must pay $100 in one year. By financing the project in this way, the cash flows become

The project's IRR is now $(30/20) - 1 = 50\%$. Does this higher IRR mean that the project is now more attractive? In other words, is the financing a good deal?

The answer is no. Remember, we cannot compare IRRs, so a 50% IRR is not necessarily better than a 30% IRR. In this case, the project with financing is a much smaller scale investment than without financing. In addition, borrowing money is likely to increase the risk of the project. (We'll see explicitly the effect of leverage on risk in Parts IV and V.)

In this particular example, note that we borrowed $80 initially in exchange for paying $100 in one year. The IRR of this loan is $(100/80) - 1 = 25\%$ (this is also the incremental IRR of rejecting the financing). This rate is probably much higher than our firm's borrowing cost if it borrowed through other means. If so, including this financing with the project would be a mistake, despite the higher IRR.

In summary, although the incremental IRR provides useful information by telling us the discount rate at which our optimal project choice would change, using it as a decision rule is difficult and error prone. It is much simpler to use the NPV rule.

CONCEPT CHECK

1. For mutually exclusive projects, explain why picking one project over another because it has a larger IRR can lead to mistakes.

2. What is the incremental IRR and what are its shortcomings as a decision rule?

7.5 Project Selection with Resource Constraints

In principle, the firm should take on all positive-NPV investments it can identify. In practice, there are often limitations on the number of projects the firm can undertake. For example, when projects are mutually exclusive, the firm can only take on one of the projects even if many of them are attractive. Often this limitation is due to resource constraints—for example, there is only one property available in which to open either a coffee shop, or book store, and so on. Thus far, we have assumed that the different projects the firm is considering have the same resource requirements (in Example 7.3, each project would use 100% of the property). In this section, we develop an approach for situations where the choices have differing resource needs.

Evaluating Projects with Different Resource Requirements

In some situations, different projects will demand different amounts of a particular scarce resource. For example, different products may consume different proportions of a firm's production capacity, or might demand different amounts of managerial time and attention.

If there is a fixed supply of the resource so that you cannot undertake all possible opportunities, then the firm must choose the best *set* of investments it can make given the resources it has available.

Often, individual managers work within a budget constraint that limits the amount of capital they may invest in a given period. In this case, the manager's goal is to choose the projects that maximize the total NPV while staying within her budget. Suppose you are considering the three projects shown in Table 7.1. Absent any budget constraint, you would invest in all of these positive-NPV projects. Suppose, however, that you have a budget of at most $100 million to invest. While Project I has the highest NPV, it uses up the entire budget. Projects II and III can both be undertaken (together they also take up the entire budget), and their combined NPV exceeds the NPV of Project I. Thus, with a budget of $100 million, the best choice is to take Projects II and III for a combined NPV of $130 million, compared to just $110 million for Project I alone.

Profitability Index

Note that in the last column of Table 7.1 we included the ratio of the project's NPV to its initial investment. This ratio tells us that for every dollar invested in Project I, we will generate $1.10 in value (over and above the dollar invested).[5] Both Projects II and III generate higher NPVs per dollar invested than Project I, which indicates that they will use the available budget more efficiently.

In this simple example, identifying the optimal combination of projects to undertake is straightforward. In actual situations replete with many projects and resources, finding the optimal combination can be difficult. Practitioners often use the **profitability index** to identify the optimal combination of projects to undertake in such situations:

Profitability Index

$$\text{Profitability Index} = \frac{\text{Value Created}}{\text{Resource Consumed}} = \frac{NPV}{\text{Resource Consumed}} \tag{7.2}$$

The profitability index measures the "bang for your buck"—that is, the value created in terms of NPV per unit of resource consumed. After computing the profitability index, we can rank projects based on it. Starting with the project with the highest index, we move down the ranking, taking all projects until the resource is consumed. In Table 7.1, the ratio we computed in the last column is the profitability index when investment dollars

TABLE 7.1	Possible Projects for a $100 Million Budget		
Project	NPV ($ millions)	Initial Investment ($ millions)	Profitability Index NPV/Investment
I	110	100	1.1
II	70	50	1.4
III	60	50	1.2

---

[5]Practitioners sometimes add 1 to this ratio to include the dollar invested (i.e., Project I generates a total of $2.10 per dollar invested, generating $1.10 in new value). Leaving out the 1 and just considering the *net* present value allows the ratio to be applied to other resources besides cash budgets, as shown in Example 7.5.

are the scarce resource. Note how the "profitability index rule" would correctly select Projects II and III. We can also apply this rule when other resources are scarce, as shown in Example 7.5.

| EXAMPLE 7.5 | **Profitability Index with a Human Resource Constraint** |

Problem

Your division at NetIt, a large networking company, has put together a project proposal to develop a new home networking router. The expected NPV of the project is $17.7 million, and the project will require 50 software engineers. NetIt has a total of 190 engineers available, and the router project must compete with the following other projects for these engineers:

Project	NPV ($ millions)	Engineering Headcount
Router	17.7	50
Project A	22.7	47
Project B	8.1	44
Project C	14.0	40
Project D	11.5	61
Project E	20.6	58
Project F	12.9	32
Total	107.5	332

How should NetIt prioritize these projects?

Solution

The goal is to maximize the total NPV we can create with 190 engineers (at most). We compute the profitability index for each project, using Engineering Headcount in the denominator, and then sort projects based on the index:

Project	NPV ($ millions)	Engineering Headcount (EHC)	Profitability Index (NPV per EHC)	Cumulative EHC Required
Project A	22.7	47	0.483	47
Project F	12.9	32	0.403	79
Project E	20.6	58	0.355	137
Router	17.7	50	0.354	187
Project C	14.0	40	0.350	
Project D	11.5	61	0.189	
Project B	8.1	44	0.184	

We now assign the resource to the projects in descending order according to the profitability index. The final column shows the cumulative use of the resource as each project is taken on until the resource is used up. To maximize NPV within the constraint of 190 engineers, NetIt should choose the first four projects on the list. There is no other combination of projects that will create more value without using more engineers than we have. Note, however, that the resource constraint forces NetIt to forgo three otherwise valuable projects (C, D, and B) with a total NPV of $33.6 million.

Note that in the above examples, the firm's resource constraints cause it to pass up positive-NPV projects. The highest profitability index available from these remaining projects provides useful information regarding the value of that resource to the firm. In Example 7.5, for example, Project C would generate $350,000 in NPV per engineer. If the firm could recruit and train new engineers at a cost of less than $350,000 per engineer, it would be worthwhile to do so in order to undertake Project C. Alternatively, if engineering headcount has been allocated to another division of the firm for projects with a profitability index of less than $350,000 per engineer, it would be worthwhile to reallocate that headcount to this division to undertake Project C.

Shortcomings of the Profitability Index

Although the profitability index is simple to compute and use, for it to be completely reliable, two conditions must be satisfied:

1. The set of projects taken following the profitability index ranking completely exhausts the available resource.

2. There is only a single relevant resource constraint.

To see why the first condition is needed, suppose in Example 7.5 that NetIt has an additional small project with an NPV of only $120,000 that requires three engineers. The profitability index in this case is $0.12/3 = 0.04$, so this project would appear at the bottom of the ranking. However, notice that three of the 190 employees are not being used after the first four projects are selected. As a result, it would make sense to take on this project even though it would be ranked last. This shortcoming can also affect highly ranked projects. For example, in Table 7.1, suppose Project III had an NPV of only $25 million, making it significantly worse than the other projects. Then the best choice would be Project I even though Project II has a higher profitability index.

In many cases, the firm may face multiple resource constraints. For instance, there may be a budget limit as well as a headcount constraint. If more than one resource constraint is binding, then there is no simple index that can be used to rank projects. Instead, linear and integer programming techniques have been developed specifically to tackle this kind of problem. Even if the set of alternatives is large, by using these techniques on a computer we can readily calculate the set of projects that will maximize the total NPV while satisfying multiple constraints (see Further Reading for references).

CONCEPT CHECK

1. Explain why ranking projects according to their NPV might not be optimal when you evaluate projects with different resource requirements.

2. How can the profitability index be used to identify attractive projects when there are resource constraints?

MyFinanceLab

Here is what you should know after reading this chapter. MyFinanceLab will help you identify what you know and where to go when you need to practice.

7.1 NPV and Stand-Alone Projects

- If your objective is to maximize wealth, the NPV rule always gives the correct answer.
- The difference between the cost of capital and the IRR is the maximum amount of estimation error that can exist in the cost of capital estimate without altering the original decision.

7.2 The Internal Rate of Return Rule

- IRR investment rule: Take any investment opportunity whose IRR exceeds the opportunity cost of capital. Turn down any opportunity whose IRR is less than the opportunity cost of capital.
- Unless all of the negative cash flows of the project precede the positive ones, the IRR rule may give the wrong answer and should not be used. Furthermore, there may be multiple IRRs or the IRR may not exist.

7.3 The Payback Rule

- Payback investment rule: Calculate the amount of time it takes to pay back the initial investment (the payback period). If the payback period is less than a prespecified length of time, accept the project. Otherwise, turn it down.
- The payback rule is simple, and favors short-term investments. But it is often incorrect.

7.4 Choosing Between Projects

- When choosing among mutually exclusive investment opportunities, pick the opportunity with the highest NPV.
- We cannot use the IRR to compare investment opportunities unless the investments have the same scale, timing, and risk.
- Incremental IRR: When comparing two mutually exclusive opportunities, the incremental IRR is the IRR of the difference between the cash flows of the two alternatives. The incremental IRR indicates the discount rate at which the optimal project choice changes.

7.5 Project Selection with Resource Constraints

- When choosing among projects competing for the same resource, rank the projects by their profitability indices and pick the set of projects with the highest profitability indices that can still be undertaken given the limited resource.

$$\text{Profitability Index} = \frac{\text{Value Created}}{\text{Resource Consumed}} = \frac{NPV}{\text{Resource Consumed}} \qquad (7.2)$$

- The profitability index is only completely reliable if the set of projects taken following the profitability index ranking completely exhausts the available resource and there is only a single relevant resource constraint.

Key Terms

Further Reading

Readers who would like to know more about what managers actually do should consult J. Graham and C. Harvey, "How CFOs Make Capital Budgeting and Capital Structure Decisions," *Journal of Applied Corporate Finance* 15(1) (2002): 8–23; S. H. Kim, T. Crick, and S. H. Kim, "Do Executives Practice What Academics Preach?" *Management Accounting* 68 (November 1986): 49–52; and P. Ryan and G. Ryan, "Capital Budgeting Practices of the Fortune 1000: How Have Things Changed?" *Journal of Business and Management* 8(4) (2002): 355–364.

For readers interested in how to select among projects competing for the same set of resources, the following references will be helpful: M. Vanhoucke, E. Demeulemeester, and W. Herroelen, "On Maximizing the Net Present Value of a Project Under Renewable Resource Constraints," *Management Science* 47(8) (2001): 1113–1121; and H. M. Weingartner, *Mathematical Programming and the Analysis of Capital Budgeting Problems* (Englewood Cliffs, NJ: Prentice-Hall, 1963).

Problems

All problems are available in MyFinanceLab. *An asterisk (*) indicates problems with a higher level of difficulty.*

NPV and Stand-Alone Projects

1. Your brother wants to borrow $10,000 from you. He has offered to pay you back $12,000 in a year. If the cost of capital of this investment opportunity is 10%, what is its NPV? Should you undertake the investment opportunity? Calculate the IRR and use it to determine the maximum deviation allowable in the cost of capital estimate to leave the decision unchanged.

2. You are considering investing in a start-up company. The founder asked you for $200,000 today and you expect to get $1,000,000 in nine years. Given the riskiness of the investment opportunity, your cost of capital is 20%. What is the NPV of the investment opportunity? Should you undertake the investment opportunity? Calculate the IRR and use it to determine the maximum deviation allowable in the cost of capital estimate to leave the decision unchanged.

3. You are considering opening a new plant. The plant will cost $100 million upfront. After that, it is expected to produce profits of $30 million at the end of every year. The cash flows are expected to last forever. Calculate the NPV of this investment opportunity if your cost of capital is 8%. Should you make the investment? Calculate the IRR and use it to determine the maximum deviation allowable in the cost of capital estimate to leave the decision unchanged.

4. Your firm is considering the launch of a new product, the XJ5. The upfront development cost is $10 million, and you expect to earn a cash flow of $3 million per year for the next five years. Plot the NPV profile for this project for discount rates ranging from 0% to 30%. For what range of discount rates is the project attractive?

5. Bill Clinton reportedly was paid $10 million to write his book *My Way*. The book took three years to write. In the time he spent writing, Clinton could have been paid to make speeches. Given his popularity, assume that he could earn $8 million per year (paid at the end of the year) speaking instead of writing. Assume his cost of capital is 10% per year.
   a. What is the NPV of agreeing to write the book (ignoring any royalty payments)?
   b. Assume that, once the book is finished, it is expected to generate royalties of $5 million in the first year (paid at the end of the year) and these royalties are expected to decrease at a rate of 30% per year in perpetuity. What is the NPV of the book with the royalty payments?

*6. FastTrack Bikes, Inc. is thinking of developing a new composite road bike. Development will take six years and the cost is $200,000 per year. Once in production, the bike is expected to make $300,000 per year for 10 years. Assume the cost of capital is 10%.
   a. Calculate the NPV of this investment opportunity, assuming all cash flows occur at the end of each year. Should the company make the investment?
   b. By how much must the cost of capital estimate deviate to change the decision? (*Hint*: Use Excel to calculate the IRR.)
   c. What is the NPV of the investment if the cost of capital is 14%?

7. OpenSeas, Inc. is evaluating the purchase of a new cruise ship. The ship would cost $500 million, and would operate for 20 years. OpenSeas expects annual cash flows from operating the ship to be $70 million (at the end of each year) and its cost of capital is 12%.
   a. Prepare an NPV profile of the purchase.
   b. Estimate the IRR (to the nearest 1%) from the graph.
   c. Is the purchase attractive based on these estimates?
   d. How far off could OpenSeas' cost of capital be (to the nearest 1%) before your purchase decision would change?

The Internal Rate of Return Rule

(Note: In most cases you will find it helpful to use Excel to compute the IRR.)

8. You are considering an investment in a clothes distributor. The company needs $100,000 today and expects to repay you $120,000 in a year from now. What is the IRR of this investment opportunity? Given the riskiness of the investment opportunity, your cost of capital is 20%. What does the IRR rule say about whether you should invest?

9. You have been offered a very long term investment opportunity to increase your money one hundredfold. You can invest $1000 today and expect to receive $100,000 in 40 years. Your cost of capital for this (very risky) opportunity is 25%. What does the IRR rule say about whether the investment should be undertaken? What about the NPV rule? Do they agree?

10. Does the IRR rule agree with the NPV rule in Problem 3? Explain.

11. How many IRRs are there in part (a) of Problem 5? Does the IRR rule give the right answer in this case? How many IRRs are there in part (b) of Problem 5? Does the IRR rule work in this case?

12. Professor Wendy Smith has been offered the following deal: A law firm would like to retain her for an upfront payment of $50,000. In return, for the next year the firm would have access to 8 hours of her time every month. Smith's rate is $550 per hour and her opportunity cost of capital is 15% (EAR). What does the IRR rule advise regarding this opportunity? What about the NPV rule?

13. Innovation Company is thinking about marketing a new software product. Upfront costs to market and develop the product are $5 million. The product is expected to generate profits of $1 million per year for 10 years. The company will have to provide product support expected to cost $100,000 per year in perpetuity. Assume all profits and expenses occur at the end of the year.
   a. What is the NPV of this investment if the cost of capital is 6%? Should the firm undertake the project? Repeat the analysis for discount rates of 2% and 12%.
   b. How many IRRs does this investment opportunity have?
   c. Can the IRR rule be used to evaluate this investment? Explain.

*14. You own a coal mining company and are considering opening a new mine. The mine itself will cost $120 million to open. If this money is spent immediately, the mine will generate $20 million for the next 10 years. After that, the coal will run out and the site must be cleaned and maintained at environmental standards. The cleaning and maintenance are expected to cost $2 million per year in perpetuity. What does the IRR rule say about whether you should accept this opportunity? If the cost of capital is 8%, what does the NPV rule say?

15. Your firm spends $500,000 per year in regular maintenance of its equipment. Due to the economic downturn, the firm considers forgoing these maintenance expenses for the next three years. If it does so, it expects it will need to spend $2 million in year 4 replacing failed equipment.
   a. What is the IRR of the decision to forgo maintenance of the equipment?
   b. Does the IRR rule work for this decision?
   c. For what costs of capital is forgoing maintenance a good decision?

*16. You are considering investing in a new gold mine in South Africa. Gold in South Africa is buried very deep, so the mine will require an initial investment of $250 million. Once this investment is made, the mine is expected to produce revenues of $30 million per year for the next 20 years. It will cost $10 million per year to operate the mine. After 20 years, the gold will be depleted. The mine must then be stabilized on an ongoing basis, which will cost $5 million per year in perpetuity. Calculate the IRR of this investment. (*Hint*: Plot the NPV as a function of the discount rate.)

17. Your firm has been hired to develop new software for the university's class registration system. Under the contract, you will receive $500,000 as an upfront payment. You expect the development costs to be $450,000 per year for the next three years. Once the new system is in place, you will receive a final payment of $900,000 from the university four years from now.
   a. What are the IRRs of this opportunity?
   b. If your cost of capital is 10%, is the opportunity attractive?
      Suppose you are able to renegotiate the terms of the contract so that your final payment in year 4 will be $1 million.
   c. What is the IRR of the opportunity now?
   d. Is it attractive at these terms?

18. You are considering constructing a new plant in a remote wilderness area to process the ore from a planned mining operation. You anticipate that the plant will take a year to build and cost $100 million upfront. Once built, it will generate cash flows of $15 million at the end of every year over the life of the plant. The plant will be useless 20 years after its completion once the mine runs out of ore. At that point you expect to pay $200 million to shut the plant down and restore the area to its pristine state. Using a cost of capital of 12%,

a. What is the NPV of the project?

b. Is using the IRR rule reliable for this project? Explain.

c. What are the IRRs of this project?

The Payback Rule

19. You are a real estate agent thinking of placing a sign advertising your services at a local bus stop. The sign will cost $5000 and will be posted for one year. You expect that it will generate additional revenue of $500 per month. What is the payback period?

20. You are considering making a movie. The movie is expected to cost $10 million upfront and take a year to make. After that, it is expected to make $5 million when it is released in one year and $2 million per year for the following four years. What is the payback period of this investment? If you require a payback period of two years, will you make the movie? Does the movie have positive NPV if the cost of capital is 10%?

Choosing Between Projects

21. You are deciding between two mutually exclusive investment opportunities. Both require the same initial investment of $10 million. Investment A will generate $2 million per year (starting at the end of the first year) in perpetuity. Investment B will generate $1.5 million at the end of the first year and its revenues will grow at 2% per year for every year after that.

a. Which investment has the higher IRR?

b. Which investment has the higher NPV when the cost of capital is 7%?

c. In this case, for what values of the cost of capital does picking the higher IRR give the correct answer as to which investment is the best opportunity?

22. You have just started your summer internship, and your boss asks you to review a recent analysis that was done to compare three alternative proposals to enhance the firm's manufacturing facility. You find that the prior analysis ranked the proposals according to their IRR, and recommended the highest IRR option, Proposal A. You are concerned and decide to redo the analysis using NPV to determine whether this recommendation was appropriate. But while you are confident the IRRs were computed correctly, it seems that some of the underlying data regarding the cash flows that were estimated for each proposal was not included in the report. For Proposal B, you cannot find information regarding the total initial investment that was required in year 0. And for Proposal C, you cannot find the data regarding additional salvage value that will be recovered in year 3. Here is the information you have:

Proposal	IRR	Year 0	Year 1	Year 2	Year 3
A	60.0%	−100	30	153	88
B	55.0%	?	0	206	95
C	50.0%	−100	37	0	204 +?

Suppose the appropriate cost of capital for each alternative is 10%. Using this information, determine the NPV of each project. Which project should the firm choose?

Why is ranking the projects by their IRR not valid in this situation?

23. Use the incremental IRR rule to correctly choose between the investments in Problem 21 when the cost of capital is 7%. At what cost of capital would your decision change?

24. You work for an outdoor play structure manufacturing company and are trying to decide between two projects:

Year-End Cash Flows ($ thousands)

Project	0	1	2	IRR
Playhouse	−30	15	20	10.4%
Fort	−80	39	52	8.6%

You can undertake only one project. If your cost of capital is 8%, use the incremental IRR rule to make the correct decision.

*25. You are evaluating the following two projects:

Year-End Cash Flows ($ thousands)

Project	0	1	2
X	−30	20	20
Y	−80	40	60

Use the incremental IRR to determine the range of discount rates for which each project is optimal to undertake. Note that you should also include the range in which it does not make sense to take either project.

26. Consider two investment projects, both of which require an upfront investment of $10 million and pay a constant positive amount each year for the next 10 years. Under what conditions can you rank these projects by comparing their IRRs?

27. You are considering a safe investment opportunity that requires a $1000 investment today, and will pay $500 two years from now and another $750 five years from now.
   a. What is the IRR of this investment?
   b. If you are choosing between this investment and putting your money in a safe bank account that pays an EAR of 5% per year for any horizon, can you make the decision by simply comparing this EAR with the IRR of the investment? Explain.

28. AOL is considering two proposals to overhaul its network infrastructure. They have received two bids. The first bid, from Huawei, will require a $20 million upfront investment and will generate $20 million in savings for AOL each year for the next three years. The second bid, from Cisco, requires a $100 million upfront investment and will generate $60 million in savings each year for the next three years.
   a. What is the IRR for AOL associated with each bid?
   b. If the cost of capital for this investment is 12%, what is the NPV for AOL of each bid?
      Suppose Cisco modifies its bid by offering a lease contract instead. Under the terms of the lease, AOL will pay $20 million upfront, and $35 million per year for the next three years. AOL's savings will be the same as with Cisco's original bid.
   c. Including its savings, what are AOL's net cash flows under the lease contract? What is the IRR of the Cisco bid now?
   d. Is this new bid a better deal for AOL than Cisco's original bid? Explain.

Project Selection with Resource Constraints

29. Natasha's Flowers, a local florist, purchases fresh flowers each day at the local flower market. The buyer has a budget of $1000 per day to spend. Different flowers have different profit margins, and also a maximum amount the shop can sell. Based on past experience, the shop has estimated the following NPV of purchasing each type:

	NPV per Bunch	Cost per Bunch	Max. Bunches
Roses	$ 3	$20	25
Lilies	8	30	10
Pansies	4	30	10
Orchids	20	80	5

What combination of flowers should the shop purchase each day?

30. You own a car dealership and are trying to decide how to configure the showroom floor. The floor has 2000 square feet of usable space. You have hired an analyst and asked her to

estimate the NPV of putting a particular model on the floor and how much space each model requires:

Model	NPV	Space Requirement (sq. ft.)
MB345	$3000	200
MC237	5000	250
MY456	4000	240
MG231	1000	150
MT347	6000	450
MF302	4000	200
MG201	1500	150

In addition, the showroom also requires office space. The analyst has estimated that office space generates an NPV of $14 per square foot. What models should be displayed on the floor and how many square feet should be devoted to office space?

31. Kaimalino Properties (KP) is evaluating six real estate investments. Management plans to buy the properties today and sell them five years from today. The following table summarizes the initial cost and the expected sale price for each property, as well as the appropriate discount rate based on the risk of each venture.

Project	Cost Today	Discount Rate	Expected Sale Price in Year 5
Mountain Ridge	$ 3,000,000	15%	$18,000,000
Ocean Park Estates	15,000,000	15%	75,500,000
Lakeview	9,000,000	15%	50,000,000
Seabreeze	6,000,000	8%	35,500,000
Green Hills	3,000,000	8%	10,000,000
West Ranch	9,000,000	8%	46,500,000

KP has a total capital budget of $18,000,000 to invest in properties.
a. What is the IRR of each investment?
b. What is the NPV of each investment?
c. Given its budget of $18,000,000, which properties should KP choose?
d. Explain why the profitably index method could not be used if KP's budget were $12,000,000 instead. Which properties should KP choose in this case?

*32. Orchid Biotech Company is evaluating several development projects for experimental drugs. Although the cash flows are difficult to forecast, the company has come up with the following estimates of the initial capital requirements and NPVs for the projects. Given a wide variety of staffing needs, the company has also estimated the number of research scientists required for each development project (all cost values are given in millions of dollars).

Project Number	Initial Capital	Number of Research Scientists	NPV
I	$10	2	$10.1
II	15	3	19.0
III	15	4	22.0
IV	20	3	25.0
V	30	12	60.2

a. Suppose that Orchid has a total capital budget of $60 million. How should it prioritize these projects?

b. Suppose in addition that Orchid currently has only 12 research scientists and does not anticipate being able to hire any more in the near future. How should Orchid prioritize these projects?

c. If instead, Orchid had 15 research scientists available, explain why the profitability index ranking cannot be used to prioritize projects. Which projects should it choose now?

Data Case

On October 6, 2004, Sirius Satellite Radio announced that it had reached an agreement with Howard Stern to broadcast his radio show exclusively on their system. As a result of this announcement, the Sirius stock price increased dramatically. You are currently working as a stock analyst for a large investment firm and XM Radio, also a satellite radio firm, is one of the firms you track. Your boss wants to be prepared if XM follows Sirius in trying to sign a major personality. Therefore, she wants you to estimate the net cash flows the market had anticipated from the signing of Stern. She advises that you treat the value anticipated by the market as the NPV of the signing, then work backward from the NPV to determine the annual cash flows necessary to generate that value. The potential deal had been rumored for some time prior to the announcement. As a result, the stock price for Sirius increased for several days before the announcement. Thus, your boss advises that the best way to capture all of the value is to take the change in stock price from September 28, 2004, through October 7, 2004. You nod your head in agreement, trying to look like you understand how to proceed. You are relatively new to the job and the term NPV is somewhat familiar to you.

1. To determine the change in stock price over this period, go to Yahoo! Finance (http://finance.yahoo.com) and enter the stock symbol for Sirius (SIRI). Then click "Historical Prices" and enter the appropriate dates. Use the adjusted closing prices for the two dates.

2. To determine the change in value, multiply the change in stock price by the number of shares outstanding. The number of shares outstanding around those dates can be found by going to Sirius' Investor Web site: http://investor.siriusxm.com. Click on "Reports and Filings" on the right, then on "SEC Filings." Select "Annual" in the Document toggle, then select the Excel icon to the right of the Annual Report dated March, 16, 2005. Look on the "Income Statement" sheet of the Excel file to find "Diluted Weighted Average Shares."

3. Because the change in value represents the "expected" NPV of the project, you will have to find the annual net cash flows that would provide this NPV. For this analysis, you will need to estimate the cost of capital for the project. We show how to calculate the cost of capital in subsequent chapters; for now, use the New York University (NYU) cost of capital Web site (http://pages.stern.nyu.edu/~adamodar/New_Home_Page/datafile/wacc.htm). Locate the cost of capital in the far-right column for the "Entertainment Tech" industry.

4. Use the cost of capital from the NYU Web site and the NPV you computed to calculate the constant annual cash flow that provides this NPV. Compute cash flows for 5-, 10-, and 15-year horizons.

5. Your boss mentioned that she believes that the Howard Stern signing by Sirius was actually good for XM because it signaled that the industry has valuable growth potential. To see if she appears to be correct, find the percentage stock price reaction to XM (XMSR) over this same period.

Computing the NPV Profile Using Excel's Data Table Function

As the examples in this chapter demonstrate, interpreting the IRR can be difficult without seeing an investment's full NPV profile. Calculating the NPV for each discount rate can be tedious, however. Here we show an easy method to do so using Excel's **Data Table** functionality.

Consider the NPV and IRR calculations associated with Figure 7.3. As shown in cell B6, the investment has a positive NPV of 11.08 at a 5% discount rate. The project also has two IRRs, shown in cells B8:B9, which we can find by using Excel's IRR function with different initial guesses.

The NPV profile of the project—which shows the NPV for a range of discount rates from 0% to 50%—is shown in cells H2:I13, and corresponds to the data plotted in Figure 7.3. We could construct the NPV profile by plugging each discount rate into cell B1 and recording the resultant NPV from cell B6. Fortunately, Excel automates this "what-if" analysis using a data table. To build the data table, we first enter a column (or row) of data with the discount rates we would like to try, as shown in cells H3:H13. The top of the next column, in cell I2, is a formula whose output we would like to record. In this case the formula in I2 is simply "=B6", the NPV we calculated. To build the data table, we then select cells H2:I13 as shown below, and bring up the Data Table window (from the Data > What-If Analysis menu, or keyboard shortcut Alt-D-T). There we enter B1 as the "column input cell" to indicate that each entry in the column of discount rates should be substituted into cell B1. Upon clicking "ok," Excel will try each discount rate and record the resulting NPV in the table, generating the NPV profile. Moreover, the data table will automatically update should we change any of the project cash flows.

Fundamentals of Capital Budgeting

IN EARLY 2008, MCDONALD'S CORP., THE WORLD'S LEADING fast food restaurant, announced that it would add cappuccinos, lattes, and mochas to its menu of nearly 14,000 U.S. locations over the next two years. John Betts, vice president of national beverage strategy, described the introduction as "the biggest endeavor for McDonald's since our introduction of breakfast 35 years ago." Betts added that McDonald's menu enhancements could add up to $1 billion in sales. The decision by McDonald's to introduce "high-end" coffee options to its menu represents a classic capital budgeting decision. To make such decisions, McDonald's relies primarily on the NPV rule. But how can managers quantify the cost and benefits of a project like this one to compute its NPV?

An important responsibility of corporate financial managers is determining which projects or investments a firm should undertake. *Capital budgeting*, the focus of this chapter, is the process of analyzing investment opportunities and deciding which ones to accept. As we learned in Chapter 7, the NPV rule is the most accurate and reliable method for allocating the firm's resources so as to maximize its value. To implement the NPV rule, we must compute the NPV of our projects and only accept those for which the NPV is positive. The first step in this process is to forecast the project's revenues and costs, and from them estimate the project's expected future cash flows. In this chapter, we will consider in detail the process of estimating a project's expected cash flows, which are crucial inputs in the investment decision process. Using these cash flows, we can then compute the project's NPV—its contribution to shareholder value. Finally, because the cash flow forecasts almost always contain uncertainty, we demonstrate how to compute the sensitivity of the NPV to the uncertainty in the forecasts.

NOTATION

IRR	internal rate of return
$EBIT$	earnings before interest and taxes
τ_c	marginal corporate tax rate
NPV	net present value
NWC_t	net working capital in year t
ΔNWC_t	increase in net working capital between year t and year $t-1$
$CapEx$	capital expenditures
FCF_t	free cash flow in year t
PV	present value
r	projected cost of capital

8.1 Forecasting Earnings

A **capital budget** lists the projects and investments that a company plans to undertake during the coming year. To determine this list, firms analyze alternative projects and decide which ones to accept through a process called **capital budgeting**. This process begins with forecasts of the project's future consequences for the firm. Some of these consequences will affect the firm's revenues; others will affect its costs. Our ultimate goal is to determine the effect of the decision on the firm's cash flows, and evaluate the NPV of these cash flows to assess the consequences of the decision for the firm's value.

As we emphasized in Chapter 2, *earnings are not actual cash flows*. However, as a practical matter, to derive the forecasted cash flows of a project, financial managers often begin by forecasting earnings. Thus, we *begin* by determining the **incremental earnings** of a project—that is, the amount by which the firm's earnings are expected to change as a result of the investment decision. Then, in Section 8.2, we demonstrate how to use the incremental earnings to forecast the *cash flows* of the project.

Let's consider a hypothetical capital budgeting decision faced by managers of the Linksys division of Cisco Systems, a maker of consumer networking hardware. Linksys is considering the development of a wireless home networking appliance, called HomeNet, that will provide both the hardware and the software necessary to run an entire home from any Internet connection. In addition to connecting PCs and printers, HomeNet will control new Internet-capable stereos, digital video recorders, heating and air-conditioning units, major appliances, telephone and security systems, office equipment, and so on. Linksys has already conducted an intensive, $300,000 feasibility study to assess the attractiveness of the new product.

Revenue and Cost Estimates

We begin by reviewing the revenue and cost estimates for HomeNet. HomeNet's target market is upscale residential "smart" homes and home offices. Based on extensive marketing surveys, the sales forecast for HomeNet is 100,000 units per year. Given the pace of technological change, Linksys expects the product will have a four-year life. It will be sold through high-end electronics stores for a retail price of $375, with an expected wholesale price of $260.

Developing the new hardware will be relatively inexpensive, as existing technologies can be simply repackaged in a newly designed, home-friendly box. Industrial design teams will make the box and its packaging aesthetically pleasing to the residential market. Linksys expects total engineering and design costs to amount to $5 million. Once the design is finalized, actual production will be outsourced at a cost (including packaging) of $110 per unit.

In addition to the hardware requirements, Linksys must build a new software application to allow virtual control of the home from the Web. This software development project requires coordination with each of the Web appliance manufacturers and is expected to take a dedicated team of 50 software engineers a full year to complete. The cost of a software engineer (including benefits and related costs) is $200,000 per year. To verify the compatibility of new consumer Internet-ready appliances with the HomeNet system as they become available, Linksys must also install new equipment that will require an upfront investment of $7.5 million.

The software and hardware design will be completed, and the new equipment will be operational, at the end of one year. At that time, HomeNet will be ready to ship. Linksys expects to spend $2.8 million per year on marketing and support for this product.

Incremental Earnings Forecast

Given the revenue and cost estimates, we can forecast HomeNet's incremental earnings, as shown in the spreadsheet in Table 8.1. After the product is developed in year 0, it will generate sales of 100,000 units × $260/unit = $26 million each year for the next four years. The cost of producing these units is 100,000 units × $110/unit = $11 million per year. Thus, HomeNet will produce a gross profit of $26 million − $11 million = $15 million per year, as shown in line 3 of Table 8.1. Note that while revenues and costs occur throughout the year, we adopt the standard convention of listing revenues and costs at the end of the year in which they occur.[1]

The project's operating expenses include $2.8 million per year in marketing and support costs, which are listed as selling, general, and administrative expenses. In year 0, Linksys will spend $5 million on design and engineering, together with 50 × $200,000 = $10 million on software, for a total of $15 million in research and development expenditures.

Capital Expenditures and Depreciation. HomeNet also requires $7.5 million in equipment that will be required to allow third-party manufacturers to upload the specifications and verify the compatibility of any new Internet-ready appliances that they might produce. To encourage the development of compatible products and provide service for existing customers, Linksys expects to continue to operate this equipment even after they phase out the current version of the product. Recall from Chapter 2 that while investments in plant, property, and equipment are a cash expense, they are not directly listed as expenses when calculating *earnings*. Instead, the firm deducts a fraction of the cost of these items each year as depreciation. Several different methods are used to compute depreciation. The simplest method is **straight-line depreciation**, in which the asset's cost (less any expected salvage value) is divided equally over its estimated useful life (we discuss other methods in Section 8.4). If we assume the equipment is purchased at the end of year 0, and then use straight-line depreciation over a five-year life for the new equipment, HomeNet's depreciation expense is $1.5 million per year in years 1 through 5.[2] Deducting

| TABLE 8.1 SPREADSHEET | HomeNet's Incremental Earnings Forecast |

	Year	0	1	2	3	4	5
Incremental Earnings Forecast ($000s)							
1 Sales		—	26,000	26,000	26,000	26,000	—
2 Cost of Goods Sold		—	(11,000)	(11,000)	(11,000)	(11,000)	—
3 **Gross Profit**		—	15,000	15,000	15,000	15,000	—
4 Selling, General, and Administrative		—	(2,800)	(2,800)	(2,800)	(2,800)	—
5 Research and Development		(15,000)	—	—	—	—	
6 Depreciation		—	(1,500)	(1,500)	(1,500)	(1,500)	(1,500)
7 **EBIT**		(15,000)	10,700	10,700	10,700	10,700	(1,500)
8 Income Tax at 40%		6,000	(4,280)	(4,280)	(4,280)	(4,280)	600
9 **Unlevered Net Income**		(9,000)	6,420	6,420	6,420	6,420	(900)

[1]As a result, cash flows that occur at the end of one year will be listed in a different column than those that occur at the start of the next year, even though they may occur only weeks apart. When additional precision is required, cash flows are often estimated on a quarterly or monthly basis. (See also the Appendix to Chapter 5 for a method of converting continuously arriving cash flows to annual ones.)

[2]Recall that although new product sales have ceased, the equipment will remain in use in year 5. Note also that as in Chapter 2, we list depreciation expenses separately rather than include them with other expenses (i.e., COGS, SG&A, and R&D are "clean" and do not include non-cash expenses. Using clean expenses is preferred in financial models.)

these depreciation expenses leads to the forecast for HomeNet's earnings before interest and taxes (EBIT) shown in line 7 of Table 8.1. This treatment of capital expenditures is one of the key reasons why earnings are not an accurate representation of cash flows.

Interest Expenses. In Chapter 2, we saw that to compute a firm's net income, we must first deduct interest expenses from EBIT. When evaluating a capital budgeting decision like the HomeNet project, however, we generally *do not include interest expenses.* Any incremental interest expenses will be related to the firm's decision regarding how to finance the project. Here we wish to evaluate the project on its own, separate from the financing decision.[3] Thus, we evaluate the HomeNet project *as if* Cisco will not use any debt to finance it (whether or not that is actually the case), and we postpone the consideration of alternative financing choices until Part 5 of the book. For this reason, we refer to the net income we compute in the spreadsheet in Table 8.1 as the **unlevered net income** of the project, to indicate that it does not include any interest expenses associated with debt.

Taxes. The final expense we must account for is corporate taxes. The correct tax rate to use is the firm's **marginal corporate tax rate**, which is the tax rate it will pay on an *incremental* dollar of pre-tax income. In Table 8.1, we assume the marginal corporate tax rate for the HomeNet project is 40% each year. The incremental income tax expense is calculated in line 8 as

$$\text{Income Tax} = EBIT \times \tau_c \tag{8.1}$$

where τ_c is the firm's marginal corporate tax rate.

In year 1, HomeNet will contribute an additional $10.7 million to Cisco's EBIT, which will result in an additional $10.7 million $\times$ 40% = $4.28 million in corporate tax that Cisco will owe. We deduct this amount to determine HomeNet's after-tax contribution to net income.

In year 0, however, HomeNet's EBIT is negative. Are taxes relevant in this case? Yes. HomeNet will reduce Cisco's taxable income in year 0 by $15 million. As long as Cisco earns taxable income elsewhere in year 0 against which it can offset HomeNet's losses, Cisco will owe $15 million $\times$ 40% = $6 million *less* in taxes in year 0. The firm should credit this tax savings to the HomeNet project. A similar credit applies in year 5, when the firm claims its final depreciation expense for the equipment.

EXAMPLE 8.1   **Taxing Losses for Projects in Profitable Companies**

Problem

Kellogg Company plans to launch a new line of high-fiber, zero trans fat breakfast pastries. The heavy advertising expenses associated with the new product launch will generate operating losses of $15 million next year for the product. Kellogg expects to earn pretax income of $460 million from operations other than the new pastries next year. If Kellogg pays a 40% tax rate on its pretax income, what will it owe in taxes next year without the new pastry product? What will it owe with the new pastries?

---

[3]This approach is motivated by the Separation Principle (see Chapter 3): When securities are fairly priced, the net present value of a fixed set of cash flows is independent of how those cash flows are financed. Later in the text, we will consider cases in which financing may influence the project's value, and we will extend our capital budgeting techniques accordingly in Chapter 18.

Solution

Without the new pastries, Kellogg will owe $460 million × 40% = $184 million in corporate taxes next year. With the new pastries, Kellogg's pretax income next year will be only $460 million −$15 million = $445 million, and it will owe $445 million × 40% = $178 million in tax. Thus, launching the new product reduces Kellogg's taxes next year by $184 million − $178 million = $6 million.

Unlevered Net Income Calculation. We can express the calculation in the Table 8.1 spreadsheet as the following shorthand formula for unlevered net income:

$$\text{Unlevered Net Income} = EBIT \times (1 - \tau_c)$$
$$= (\text{Revenues} - \text{Costs} - \text{Depreciation}) \times (1 - \tau_c) \quad (8.2)$$

That is, a project's unlevered net income is equal to its incremental revenues less costs and depreciation, evaluated on an after-tax basis.[4]

Indirect Effects on Incremental Earnings

When computing the incremental earnings of an investment decision, we should include *all* changes between the firm's earnings with the project versus without the project. Thus far, we have analyzed only the direct effects of the HomeNet project. But HomeNet may have indirect consequences for other operations within Cisco. Because these indirect effects will also affect Cisco's earnings, we must include them in our analysis.

Opportunity Costs. Many projects use a resource that the company already owns. Because the firm does not need to pay cash to acquire this resource for a new project, it is tempting to assume that the resource is available for free. However, in many cases the resource could provide value for the firm in another opportunity or project. The **opportunity cost** of using a resource is the value it could have provided in its best alternative use.[5] Because this value is lost when the resource is used by another project, we should include the opportunity cost as an incremental cost of the project. In the case of the HomeNet project, suppose the project will require space for a new lab. Even though the lab will be housed in an existing facility, we must include the opportunity cost of not using the space in an alternative way.

EXAMPLE 8.2

The Opportunity Cost of HomeNet's Lab Space

Problem

Suppose HomeNet's new lab will be housed in warehouse space that the company would have otherwise rented out for $200,000 per year during years 1–4. How does this opportunity cost affect HomeNet's incremental earnings?

Solution

In this case, the opportunity cost of the warehouse space is the forgone rent. This cost would reduce HomeNet's incremental earnings during years 1–4 by $200,000 × (1 − 40%) = $120,000, the after-tax benefit of renting out the warehouse space.

---

[4]Unlevered net income is sometimes also referred to as net operating profit after tax (NOPAT).

[5]In Chapter 5, we defined the opportunity cost of capital as the rate you could earn on an alternative investment with equivalent risk. We similarly define the opportunity cost of using an existing asset in a project as the cash flow generated by the next-best alternative use for the asset.

Project Externalities. **Project externalities** are indirect effects of the project that may increase or decrease the profits of other business activities of the firm. For instance, in the McDonald's example in the chapter introduction, some cappuccino purchasers would otherwise have bought an alternative beverage, like a soft drink. When sales of a new product displace sales of an existing product, the situation is often referred to as **cannibalization**. Suppose that approximately 25% of HomeNet's sales come from customers who would have purchased an existing Linksys wireless router if HomeNet were not available. If this reduction in sales of the existing wireless router is a consequence of the decision to develop HomeNet, then we must include it when calculating HomeNet's incremental earnings.

The spreadsheet in Table 8.2 recalculates HomeNet's incremental earnings forecast including the opportunity cost of the lab space and the expected cannibalization of the existing product. The opportunity cost of the lab space in Example 8.2 increases selling, general, and administrative expenses from $2.8 million to $3.0 million. For the cannibalization, suppose that the existing router wholesales for $100 so the expected loss in sales is

$$25\% \times 100,000 \text{ units} \times \$100/\text{unit} = \$2.5 \text{ million}$$

Compared to Table 8.1, the sales forecast falls from $26 million to $23.5 million. In addition, suppose the cost of the existing router is $60 per unit. Then, because Cisco will no longer need to produce as many of its existing wireless routers, the incremental cost of goods sold for the HomeNet project is reduced by

$$25\% \times 100,000 \text{ units} \times (\$60 \text{ cost per unit}) = \$1.5 \text{ million}$$

from $11 million to $9.5 million. HomeNet's incremental gross profit therefore declines by $2.5 million − $1.5 million = $1 million once we account for this externality.

TABLE 8.2 SPREADSHEET   **HomeNet's Incremental Earnings Forecast (Including Cannibalization and Lost Rent)**

	Year	0	1	2	3	4	5
Incremental Earnings Forecast ($000s)							
1 Sales		—	23,500	23,500	23,500	23,500	—
2 Cost of Goods Sold		—	(9,500)	(9,500)	(9,500)	(9,500)	—
3 **Gross Profit**		—	14,000	14,000	14,000	14,000	—
4 Selling, General, and Administrative		—	(3,000)	(3,000)	(3,000)	(3,000)	—
5 Research and Development		(15,000)	—	—	—	—	—
6 Depreciation		—	(1,500)	(1,500)	(1,500)	(1,500)	(1,500)
7 **EBIT**		(15,000)	9,500	9,500	9,500	9,500	(1,500)
8 Income Tax at 40%		6,000	(3,800)	(3,800)	(3,800)	(3,800)	600
9 **Unlevered Net Income**		(9,000)	5,700	5,700	5,700	5,700	(900)

Thus, comparing the spreadsheets in Table 8.1 and Table 8.2, our forecast for HomeNet's unlevered net income in years 1–4 declines from $6.42 million to $5.7 million due to the lost rent of the lab space and the lost sales of the existing router.

Sunk Costs and Incremental Earnings

A **sunk cost** is any unrecoverable cost for which the firm is already liable. Sunk costs have been or will be paid regardless of the decision about whether or not to proceed with the project. Therefore, they are not incremental with respect to the current decision and should not be included in its analysis. For this reason, we did not include in our analysis the $300,000 already expended on the marketing and feasibility studies for HomeNet. Because this $300,000 has already been spent, it is a sunk cost. A good rule to remember is that *if our decision does not affect the cash flow, then the cash flow should not affect our decision*. Below are some common examples of sunk costs you may encounter.

Fixed Overhead Expenses. **Overhead expenses** are associated with activities that are not directly attributable to a single business activity but instead affect many different areas of the corporation. These expenses are often allocated to the different business activities for accounting purposes. To the extent that these overhead costs are fixed and will be incurred in any case, they are not incremental to the project and should not be included. Only include as incremental expenses the *additional* overhead expenses that arise because of the decision to take on the project.

Past Research and Development Expenditures. When a firm has already devoted significant resources to develop a new product, there may be a tendency to continue investing in the product even if market conditions have changed and the product is unlikely to be viable. The rationale sometimes given is that if the product is abandoned, the money that has already been invested will be "wasted." In other cases, a decision is made to abandon a project because it cannot possibly be successful enough to recoup the investment that has already been made. In fact, neither argument is correct: Any money that has already been spent is a sunk cost and therefore irrelevant. The decision to continue or abandon should be based only on the incremental costs and benefits of the product going forward.

Unavoidable Competitive Effects. When developing a new product, firms often worry about the cannibalization of their existing products. But if sales are likely to decline in any case as a result of new products introduced by competitors, then these lost sales are a sunk cost and we should not include them in our projections.

The Sunk Cost Fallacy

Sunk cost fallacy is a term used to describe the tendency of people to be influenced by sunk costs and to "throw good money after bad." That is, people sometimes continue to invest in a project that has a negative NPV because they have already invested a large amount in the project and feel that by not continuing it, the prior investment will be wasted. The sunk cost fallacy is also sometimes called the "Concorde effect," a term that refers to the British and French governments' decision to continue funding the joint development of the Concorde aircraft even after it was clear that sales of the plane would fall far short of what was necessary to justify the cost of continuing its development. Although the project was viewed by the British government as a commercial and financial disaster, the political implications of halting the project—and thereby publicly admitting that all past expenses on the project would result in nothing—ultimately prevented either government from abandoning the project.

Real-World Complexities

We have simplified the HomeNet example in an effort to focus on the types of effects that financial managers consider when estimating a project's incremental earnings. For a real project, however, the estimates of these revenues and costs are likely to be much more complicated. For instance, our assumption that the same number of HomeNet units will be sold each year is probably unrealistic. A new product typically has lower sales initially, as customers gradually become aware of the product. Sales will then accelerate, plateau, and ultimately decline as the product nears obsolescence or faces increased competition.

Similarly, the average selling price of a product and its cost of production will generally change over time. Prices and costs tend to rise with the general level of inflation in the economy. The prices of technology products, however, often fall over time as newer, superior technologies emerge and production costs decline. For most industries, competition tends to reduce profit margins over time. These factors should be considered when estimating a project's revenues and costs.

EXAMPLE 8.3

Product Adoption and Price Changes

Problem

Suppose sales of HomeNet were expected to be 100,000 units in year 1, 125,000 units in years 2 and 3, and 50,000 units in year 4. Suppose also that HomeNet's sale price and manufacturing cost are expected to decline by 10% per year, as with other networking products. By contrast, selling, general, and administrative expenses are expected to rise with inflation by 4% per year. Update the incremental earnings forecast in the spreadsheet in Table 8.2 to account for these effects.

Solution

HomeNet's incremental earnings with these new assumptions are shown in the spreadsheet below:

	Year	0	1	2	3	4	5
Incremental Earnings Forecast ($000s)							
1	Sales	—	23,500	26,438	23,794	8,566	—
2	Cost of Goods Sold	—	(9,500)	(10,688)	(9,619)	(3,463)	—
3	**Gross Profit**	—	14,000	15,750	14,175	5,103	—
4	Selling, General, and Administrative	—	(3,000)	(3,120)	(3,245)	(3,375)	—
5	Research and Development	(15,000)	—	—	—	—	—
6	Depreciation	—	(1,500)	(1,500)	(1,500)	(1,500)	(1,500)
7	**EBIT**	(15,000)	9,500	11,130	9,430	228	(1,500)
8	Income Tax at 40%	6,000	(3,800)	(4,452)	(3,772)	(91)	600
9	**Unlevered Net Income**	**(9,000)**	**5,700**	**6,678**	**5,658**	**137**	**(900)**

For example, sale prices in year 2 will be $260 \times 0.90 = \$234$ per unit for HomeNet, and $\$100 \times 0.90 = \$90$ per unit for the cannibalized product. Thus, incremental sales in year 2 are equal to 125,000 units $\times$ ($234 per unit) $- 31,250$ cannibalized units $\times$ ($90 per unit) $= \$26.438$ million.

CONCEPT CHECK

1. How do we forecast unlevered net income?

2. Should we include sunk costs in the cash flow forecasts of a project? Why or why not?

3. Explain why you must include the opportunity cost of using a resource as an incremental cost of a project.

8.2 Determining Free Cash Flow and NPV

As discussed in Chapter 2, earnings are an accounting measure of the firm's performance. They do not represent real profits: The firm cannot use its earnings to buy goods, pay employees, fund new investments, or pay dividends to shareholders. To do those things, a firm needs cash. Thus, to evaluate a capital budgeting decision, we must determine its consequences for the firm's available cash. The incremental effect of a project on the firm's available cash is the project's **free cash flow**.

In this section, we forecast the free cash flow of the HomeNet project using the earnings forecasts we developed in Section 8.1. We then use this forecast to calculate the NPV of the project.

Calculating Free Cash Flow from Earnings

As discussed in Chapter 2, there are important differences between earnings and cash flow. Earnings include non-cash charges, such as depreciation, but do not include the cost of capital investment. To determine HomeNet's free cash flow from its incremental earnings, we must adjust for these differences.

Capital Expenditures and Depreciation. Depreciation is not a cash expense that is paid by the firm. Rather, it is a method used for accounting and tax purposes to allocate the original purchase cost of the asset over its life. Because depreciation is not a cash flow, we do not include it in the cash flow forecast. Instead, we include the actual cash cost of the asset when it is purchased.

To compute HomeNet's free cash flow, we must add back to earnings the depreciation expense for the new equipment (a non-cash charge) and subtract the actual capital expenditure of $7.5 million that will be paid for the equipment in year 0. We show these adjustments in lines 10 and 11 of the spreadsheet in Table 8.3 (which is based on the incremental earnings forecast of Table 8.2).

TABLE 8.3 SPREADSHEET	Calculation of HomeNet's Free Cash Flow (Including Cannibalization and Lost Rent)

	Year	0	1	2	3	4	5
Incremental Earnings Forecast ($000s)							
1	Sales	—	23,500	23,500	23,500	23,500	—
2	Cost of Goods Sold	—	(9,500)	(9,500)	(9,500)	(9,500)	—
3	**Gross Profit**	—	14,000	14,000	14,000	14,000	—
4	Selling, General, and Administrative	—	(3,000)	(3,000)	(3,000)	(3,000)	—
5	Research and Development	(15,000)	—	—	—	—	—
6	Depreciation	—	(1,500)	(1,500)	(1,500)	(1,500)	(1,500)
7	**EBIT**	(15,000)	9,500	9,500	9,500	9,500	(1,500)
8	Income Tax at 40%	6,000	(3,800)	(3,800)	(3,800)	(3,800)	600
9	**Unlevered Net Income**	**(9,000)**	**5,700**	**5,700**	**5,700**	**5,700**	**(900)**
Free Cash Flow ($000s)							
10	Plus: Depreciation	—	1,500	1,500	1,500	1,500	1,500
11	Less: Capital Expenditures	(7,500)	—	—	—	—	—
12	Less: Increases in NWC	—	(2,100)	—	—	—	2,100
13	**Free Cash Flow**	**(16,500)**	**5,100**	**7,200**	**7,200**	**7,200**	**2,700**

Net Working Capital (NWC). In Chapter 2, we defined net working capital as the difference between current assets and current liabilities. The main components of net working capital are cash, inventory, receivables, and payables:

$$\text{Net Working Capital} = \text{Current Assets} - \text{Current Liabilities}$$
$$= \text{Cash} + \text{Inventory} + \text{Receivables} - \text{Payables} \qquad (8.3)$$

Most projects will require the firm to invest in net working capital. Firms may need to maintain a minimum cash balance[6] to meet unexpected expenditures, and inventories of raw materials and finished product to accommodate production uncertainties and demand fluctuations. Also, customers may not pay for the goods they purchase immediately. While sales are immediately counted as part of earnings, the firm does not receive any cash until the customers actually pay. In the interim, the firm includes the amount that customers owe in its receivables. Thus, the firm's receivables measure the total credit that the firm has extended to its customers. In the same way, payables measure the credit the firm has received from its suppliers. The difference between receivables and payables is the net amount of the firm's capital that is consumed as a result of these credit transactions, known as **trade credit**.

Suppose that HomeNet will have no incremental cash or inventory requirements (products will be shipped directly from the contract manufacturer to customers). However, receivables related to HomeNet are expected to account for 15% of annual sales, and payables are expected to be 15% of the annual cost of goods sold (COGS).[7] HomeNet's net working capital requirements are shown in the spreadsheet in Table 8.4.

Table 8.4 shows that the HomeNet project will require no net working capital in year 0, $2.1 million in net working capital in years 1–4, and no net working capital in year 5. How does this requirement affect the project's free cash flow? Any increases in net working capital represent an investment that reduces the cash available to the firm and so reduces free cash flow. We define the increase in net working capital in year t as

$$\Delta NWC_t = NWC_t - NWC_{t-1} \qquad (8.4)$$

TABLE 8.4 SPREADSHEET	HomeNet's Net Working Capital Requirements

Year	0	1	2	3	4	5
Net Working Capital Forecast ($000s)						
1 Cash Requirements	—	—	—	—	—	—
2 Inventory	—	—	—	—	—	—
3 Receivables (15% of Sales)	—	3,525	3,525	3,525	3,525	—
4 Payables (15% of COGS)	—	(1,425)	(1,425)	(1,425)	(1,425)	—
5 **Net Working Capital**	—	**2,100**	**2,100**	**2,100**	**2,100**	—

[6]The cash included in net working capital is cash that is *not* invested to earn a market rate of return. It includes non-invested cash held in the firm's checking account, in a company safe or cash box, in cash registers (for retail stores), and other sites, which is needed to run the business.

[7]If customers take N days to pay, then accounts receivable will consist of those sales that occurred in the last N days. If sales are evenly distributed throughout the year, receivables will equal $(N/365)$ times annual sales. Thus, receivables equal to 15% of sales corresponds to an average payment period of $N = 15\% \times 365 = 55$ accounts receivable days. The same is true for payables. (See also Eq. 2.11 in Chapter 2.)

We can use our forecast of HomeNet's net working capital requirements to complete our estimate of HomeNet's free cash flow in Table 8.3. In year 1, net working capital increases by $2.1 million. This increase represents a cost to the firm as shown in line 12 of Table 8.3. This reduction of free cash flow corresponds to the fact that $3.525 million of the firm's sales in year 1 and $1.425 million of its costs have not yet been paid.

In years 2–4, net working capital does not change, so no further contributions are needed. In year 5, after the project is shut down, net working capital falls by $2.1 million as the payments of the last customers are received and the final bills are paid. We add this $2.1 million to free cash flow in year 5, as shown in line 12 of Table 8.3.

Now that we have adjusted HomeNet's unlevered net income for depreciation, capital expenditures, and increases to net working capital, we compute HomeNet's free cash flow as shown in line 13 of the spreadsheet in Table 8.3. Note that in the first two years, free cash flow is lower than unlevered net income, reflecting the upfront investment in equipment and net working capital required by the project. In later years, free cash flow exceeds unlevered net income because depreciation is not a cash expense. In the last year, the firm ultimately recovers the investment in net working capital, further boosting the free cash flow.

EXAMPLE 8.4

Net Working Capital with Changing Sales

Problem

Forecast the required investment in net working capital for HomeNet under the scenario in Example 8.3.

Solution

Required investments in net working capital are shown below:

	Year	0	1	2	3	4	5
	Net Working Capital Forecast ($000s)						
1	Receivables (15% of Sales)	—	3,525	3,966	3,569	1,285	—
2	Payables (15% of COGS)	—	(1,425)	(1,603)	(1,443)	(519)	—
3	**Net Working Capital**	—	2,100	2,363	2,126	765	—
4	**Increases in NWC**	—	2,100	263	(237)	(1,361)	(765)

In this case, working capital changes each year. A large initial investment in working capital is required in year 1, followed by a small investment in year 2 as sales continue to grow. Working capital is recovered in years 3–5 as sales decline.

Calculating Free Cash Flow Directly

As we noted at the outset of this chapter, because practitioners usually begin the capital budgeting process by first forecasting earnings, we have chosen to do the same. However, we could have calculated the HomeNet's free cash flow directly by using the following shorthand formula:

Free Cash Flow

$$\text{Free Cash Flow} = \overbrace{(\text{Revenues} - \text{Costs} - \text{Depreciation}) \times (1 - \tau_c)}^{\text{Unlevered Net Income}}$$
$$+ \text{Depreciation} - \text{CapEx} - \Delta NWC \tag{8.5}$$

Note that we first deduct depreciation when computing the project's incremental earnings, and then add it back (because it is a non-cash expense) when computing free cash flow.

Thus, the only effect of depreciation is to reduce the firm's taxable income. Indeed, we can rewrite Eq. 8.5 as

$$\text{Free Cash Flow} = (\text{Revenues} - \text{Costs}) \times (1 - \tau_c) - \text{CapEx} - \Delta NWC$$
$$+ \tau_c \times \text{Depreciation} \tag{8.6}$$

The last term in Eq. 8.6, $\tau_c \times$ Depreciation, is called the **depreciation tax shield**. It is the tax savings that results from the ability to deduct depreciation. As a consequence, depreciation expenses have a *positive* impact on free cash flow. Firms often report a different depreciation expense for accounting and for tax purposes. Because only the tax consequences of depreciation are relevant for free cash flow, we should use the depreciation expense that the firm will use for tax purposes in our forecast.

Calculating the NPV

To compute HomeNet's NPV, we must discount its free cash flow at the appropriate cost of capital.[8] As discussed in Chapter 5, the cost of capital for a project is the expected return that investors could earn on their best alternative investment with similar risk and maturity. We will develop the techniques needed to estimate the cost of capital in Part 4. For now, we assume that Cisco's managers believe that the HomeNet project will have similar risk to other projects within Cisco's Linksys division, and that the appropriate cost of capital for these projects is 12%.

Given this cost of capital, we compute the present value of each free cash flow in the future. As explained in Chapter 4, if the cost of capital $r = 12\%$, the present value of the free cash flow in year t (or FCF_t) is

$$PV(FCF_t) = \frac{FCF_t}{(1 + r)^t} = FCF_t \times \underbrace{\frac{1}{(1 + r)^t}}_{t\text{-year discount factor}} \tag{8.7}$$

We compute the NPV of the HomeNet project in the spreadsheet in Table 8.5. Line 3 calculates the discount factor, and line 4 multiplies the free cash flow by the discount factor to get the present value. The NPV of the project is the sum of the present values of each free cash flow, reported on line 5:[9]

$$NPV = -16{,}500 + 4554 + 5740 + 5125 + 4576 + 1532 = 5027$$

TABLE 8.5 SPREADSHEET	Computing HomeNet's NPV						
Year	**0**	**1**	**2**	**3**	**4**	**5**

Net Present Value ($000s)							
1 **Free Cash Flow**		(16,500)	5,100	7,200	7,200	7,200	2,700
2 Project Cost of Capital	12%						
3 Discount Factor		1.000	0.893	0.797	0.712	0.636	0.567
4 **PV of Free Cash Flow**		(16,500)	4,554	5,740	5,125	4,576	1,532
5 **NPV**		**5,027**					

---

[8]Rather than draw a separate timeline for these cash flows, we can interpret the final line of the spreadsheet in Table 8.3 as the timeline.

[9]We can also compute the NPV using the Excel NPV function to calculate the present value of the cash flows in year 1 through 5, and then add the cash flow in year 0 (i.e., "$=NPV(r, FCF_1:FCF_5)+FCF_0$").

USING EXCEL

Capital Budgeting Using a Spreadsheet Program

Capital budgeting forecasts and analysis are most easily performed in a spreadsheet program. Here we highlight a few best practices when developing your own capital budgets.

Create a Project Dashboard

All capital budgeting analyses begin with a set of assumptions regarding future revenues and costs associated with the investment. Centralize these assumptions within your spreadsheet in a project dashboard so they are easy to locate, review, and potentially modify. Here we show an example for the HomeNet project.

	A / B	C	D	E	F	G	H	I
1	**HomeNet Capital Budget**							
2	**Key Assumptions**		**Year 0**	**Year 1**	**Year 2**	**Year 3**	**Year 4**	**Year 5**
3	*Revenues & Costs*							
4	HomeNet Units Sold		-	100	100	100	100	-
8	HomeNet Ave. Price/Unit		-	$260.00	$260.00	$260.00	$260.00	-
9	HomeNet Cost/Unit		-	$110.00	$110.00	$110.00	$110.00	-
10	Cannibalization Rate		-	25%	25%	25%	25%	-
11	Old Product Ave. Price/Unit		-	$100.00	$100.00	$100.00	$100.00	-
12	Old Product Cost/Unit		-	$60.00	$60.00	$60.00	$60.00	-
13	*Operating Expenses*							
14	Marketing & Support		-	(2,800)	(2,800)	(2,800)	(2,800)	-
15	Lost Rent		-	(200)	(200)	(200)	(200)	-
16	Hardware R&D		(5,000)	-	-	-	-	-
17	Software R&D		(10,000)	-	-	-	-	-
18	Lab Equipment		(7,500)	-	-	-	-	-
19	*Other Assumptions*							
20	*depreciation schedule*		0.0%	20.0%	20.0%	20.0%	20.0%	20.0%
21	*corporate tax rate*		40.0%	40.0%	40.0%	40.0%	40.0%	40.0%
22	*receivables (% sales)*		15.0%	15.0%	15.0%	15.0%	15.0%	15.0%
23	*payables (% cogs)*		15.0%	15.0%	15.0%	15.0%	15.0%	15.0%

Color Code for Clarity

In spreadsheet models, use a blue font color to distinguish numerical assumptions from formulas. For example, HomeNet's revenue and cost estimates are set to a numerical value in year 1, whereas estimates in later years are set to equal to the year 1 estimates. It is therefore clear which cells contain the main assumptions, should we wish to change them at a later date.

Maintain Flexibility

In the HomeNet dashboard, note that we state all assumptions on an annual basis even if we expect them to remain constant. For example, we specify HomeNet's unit volume and average sale price for each year. We can then calculate HomeNet revenues each year based on the corresponding annual assumptions. Doing so provides flexibility if we later determine that HomeNet's adoption rate might vary over time or if we expect prices to follow a trend, as in Example 8.3.

Never Hardcode

So that your assumptions are clear and easy to modify, reference any numerical values you need to develop your projections in the project dashboard. Never "hardcode," or enter numerical values directly into formulas. For example, in the computation of taxes in cell E34 below, we use the formula "$=-E21*E33$" rather than "$=-0.40*E33$". While the latter formula would compute the same answer, because the tax rate is hardcoded it would be difficult to update the model if the forecast for the tax rate were to change.

	A	B	C	D	E	F	G	H	I
26	*Incremental Earnings Forecast*			**Year 0**	**Year 1**	**Year 2**	**Year 3**	**Year 4**	**Year 5**
33		**EBIT**		(15,000)	9,500	9,500	9,500	9,500	(1,500)
34		Taxes		6,000	=-E21*E33	(3,800)	(3,800)	(3,800)	600
35		**Unlevered Net Income**		(9,000)	5,700	5,700	5,700	5,700	(900)

Based on our estimates, HomeNet's NPV is $5.027 million. While HomeNet's upfront cost is $16.5 million, the present value of the additional free cash flow that Cisco will receive from the project is $21.5 million. Thus, taking the HomeNet project is equivalent to Cisco having an extra $5 million in the bank today.

1. What adjustments must you make to a project's unlevered net income to determine its free cash flows?

2. What is the depreciation tax shield?

8.3 Choosing Among Alternatives

Thus far, we have considered the capital budgeting decision to launch the HomeNet product line. To analyze the decision, we computed the project's free cash flow and calculated the NPV. Because *not* launching HomeNet produces an additional NPV of zero for the firm, launching HomeNet is the best decision for the firm if its NPV is positive. In many situations, however, we must compare mutually exclusive alternatives, each of which has consequences for the firm's cash flows. As we explained in Chapter 7, in such cases we can make the best decision by first computing the free cash flow associated with each alternative and then choosing the alternative with the highest NPV.

Evaluating Manufacturing Alternatives

Suppose Cisco is considering an alternative manufacturing plan for the HomeNet product. The current plan is to fully outsource production at a cost of $110 per unit. Alternatively, Cisco could assemble the product in-house at a cost of $95 per unit. However, the latter option will require $5 million in upfront operating expenses to reorganize the assembly facility, and starting in year 1 Cisco will need to maintain inventory equal to one month's production.

To choose between these two alternatives, we compute the free cash flow associated with each choice and compare their NPVs to see which is most advantageous for the firm. When comparing alternatives, we need to compare only those cash flows that differ between them. We can ignore any cash flows that are the same under either scenario (e.g., HomeNet's revenues).

The spreadsheet in Table 8.6 compares the two assembly options, computing the NPV of the cash costs for each. The difference in EBIT results from the upfront cost of setting up the in-house facility in year 0, and the differing assembly costs: $110/unit × 100,000 units/yr = $11 million/yr outsourced, versus $95/unit × 100,000 units/yr = $9.5 million/yr in-house. Adjusting for taxes, we see the consequences for unlevered net income on lines 3 and 9.

Because the options do not differ in terms of capital expenditures (there are none associated with assembly), to compare the free cash flow for each, we only need to adjust for their different net working capital requirements. If assembly is outsourced, payables account for 15% of the cost of goods, or 15% × $11 million = $1.65 million. This amount is the credit Cisco will receive from its supplier in year 1 and will maintain until year 5. Because Cisco will borrow this amount from its supplier, net working capital *falls* by $1.65 million in year 1, adding to Cisco's free cash flow. In year 5, Cisco's net working capital will increase as Cisco pays its suppliers, and free cash flow will fall by an equal amount.

TABLE 8.6 SPREADSHEET	NPV Cost of Outsourced Versus In-House Assembly of HomeNet

	Year	0	1	2	3	4	5
Outsourced Assembly ($000s)							
1 **EBIT**		—	(11,000)	(11,000)	(11,000)	(11,000)	—
2 Income Tax at 40%		—	4,400	4,400	4,400	4,400	—
3 **Unlevered Net Income**		—	(6,600)	(6,600)	(6,600)	(6,600)	—
4 Less: Increases in NWC		—	1,650	—	—	—	(1,650)
5 **Free Cash Flow**		—	**(4,950)**	**(6,600)**	**(6,600)**	**(6,600)**	**(1,650)**
6 NPV at 12%		(19,510)					

	Year	0	1	2	3	4	5
In-House Assembly ($000s)							
7 **EBIT**		(5,000)	(9,500)	(9,500)	(9,500)	(9,500)	—
8 Income Tax at 40%		2,000	3,800	3,800	3,800	3,800	—
9 **Unlevered Net Income**		(3,000)	(5,700)	(5,700)	(5,700)	(5,700)	—
10 Less: Increases in NWC		—	633	—	—	—	(633)
11 **Free Cash Flow**		**(3,000)**	**(5,067)**	**(5,700)**	**(5,700)**	**(5,700)**	**(633)**
12 NPV at 12%		(20,107)					

If assembly is done in-house, payables are $15\% \times \$9.5$ million $= \$1.425$ million. However, Cisco will need to maintain inventory equal to one month's production, which has cost of $\$9.5$ million $\div 12 = \$0.792$ million. Thus, Linksys' net working capital will decrease by $\$1.425$ million $- \$0.792$ million $= \$0.633$ million in year 1 and will increase by the same amount in year 5.

Comparing Free Cash Flows for Cisco's Alternatives

Adjusting for increases to net working capital, we compare the free cash flow of each alternative on lines 5 and 11 and compute their NPVs using the project's 12% cost of capital.[10] In each case, the NPV is negative, as we are evaluating only the costs of production. Outsourcing, however, is somewhat cheaper, with a present value cost of $19.5 million versus $20.1 million if the units are produced in-house.[11]

CONCEPT CHECK
1. How do you choose between mutually exclusive capital budgeting decisions?

2. When choosing between alternatives, what cash flows can be ignored?

---

[10]While we assume it is not the case here, in some settings the risks of these options might differ from the risk of the project overall or from each other, requiring a different cost of capital for each case.

[11]It is also possible to compare these two cases in a single spreadsheet in which we compute the difference in the free cash flows directly, rather than compute the free cash flows separately for each option. We prefer to do them separately, as it is clearer and generalizes to the case when there are more than two options.

8.4 Further Adjustments to Free Cash Flow

In this section, we consider a number of complications that can arise when estimating a project's free cash flow, such as non-cash charges, alternative depreciation methods, liquidation or continuation values, and tax loss carryforwards.

Other Non-Cash Items. In general, other non-cash items that appear as part of incremental earnings should not be included in the project's free cash flow. The firm should include only actual cash revenues or expenses. For example, the firm adds back any amortization of intangible assets (such as patents) to unlevered net income when calculating free cash flow.

Timing of Cash Flows. For simplicity, we have treated the cash flows for HomeNet as if they occur at the end of each year. In reality, cash flows will be spread throughout the year. We can forecast free cash flow on a quarterly, monthly, or even continuous basis when greater accuracy is required.

Accelerated Depreciation. Because depreciation contributes positively to the firm's cash flow through the depreciation tax shield, it is in the firm's best interest to use the most accelerated method of depreciation that is allowable for tax purposes. By doing so, the firm will accelerate its tax savings and increase their present value. In the United States, the most accelerated depreciation method allowed by the IRS is MACRS (Modified Accelerated Cost Recovery System) depreciation. With **MACRS depreciation**, the firm first categorizes assets according to their recovery period. Based on the recovery period, MACRS depreciation tables assign a fraction of the purchase price that the firm can recover each year. We provide MACRS tables and recovery periods for common assets in the appendix.

EXAMPLE 8.5	Computing Accelerated Depreciation

Problem

What depreciation deduction would be allowed for HomeNet's equipment using the MACRS method, assuming the equipment is put into use in year 0 and designated to have a five-year recovery period?

Solution

Table 8A.1 in the appendix provides the percentage of the cost that can be depreciated each year. Based on the table, the allowable depreciation expense for the lab equipment is shown below (in thousands of dollars):

	Year	0	1	2	3	4	5
MACRS Depreciation							
1	Lab Equipment Cost	(7,500)					
2	MACRS Depreciation Rate	20.00%	32.00%	19.20%	11.52%	11.52%	5.76%
3	Depreciation Expense	(1,500)	(2,400)	(1,440)	(864)	(864)	(432)

Note that as long as the equipment is put into use by the end of year 0, the tax code allows us to take our first depreciation expense in year 0. Compared with straight-line depreciation, the MACRS method allows for larger depreciation deductions earlier in the asset's life, which increases the present value of the depreciation tax shield and so will raise the project's NPV. In the case of HomeNet, computing the NPV using MACRS depreciation leads to an NPV of $5.34 million.

Liquidation or Salvage Value. Assets that are no longer needed often have a resale value, or some salvage value if the parts are sold for scrap. Some assets may have a negative liquidation value. For example, it may cost money to remove and dispose of the used equipment.

In the calculation of free cash flow, we include the liquidation value of any assets that are no longer needed and may be disposed of. When an asset is liquidated, any gain on sale is taxed. We calculate the gain on sale as the difference between the sale price and the book value of the asset:

$$\text{Gain on Sale} = \text{Sale Price} - \text{Book Value} \qquad (8.8)$$

The book value is equal to the asset's original cost less the amount it has already been depreciated for tax purposes:

$$\text{Book Value} = \text{Purchase Price} - \text{Accumulated Depreciation} \qquad (8.9)$$

We must adjust the project's free cash flow to account for the after-tax cash flow that would result from an asset sale:[12]

$$\text{After-Tax Cash Flow from Asset Sale} = \text{Sale Price} - (\tau_c \times \text{Gain on Sale}) \qquad (8.10)$$

EXAMPLE 8.6

Adding Salvage Value to Free Cash Flow

Problem

Suppose that in addition to the $7.5 million in new equipment required for HomeNet, some equipment will be transferred to the lab from another Linksys facility. This equipment has a resale value of $2 million and a book value of $1 million. If the equipment is kept rather than sold, its remaining book value can be depreciated next year. When the lab is shut down in year 5, the equipment will have a salvage value of $800,000. What adjustments must we make to HomeNet's free cash flow in this case?

Solution

The existing equipment could have been sold for $2 million. The after-tax proceeds from this sale are an opportunity cost of using the equipment in the HomeNet lab. Thus, we must reduce HomeNet's free cash flow in year 0 by the sale price less any taxes that would have been owed had the sale occurred: $2 million − 40% × ($2 million − $1 million) = $1.6 million.

In year 1, the remaining $1 million book value of the equipment can be depreciated, creating a depreciation tax shield of 40% × $1 million = $400,000. In year 5, the firm will sell the equipment for a salvage value of $800,000. Because the equipment will be fully depreciated at that time, the entire amount will be taxable as a capital gain, so the after-tax cash flow from the sale is $800,000 × (1 − 40%) = $480,000.

The spreadsheet below shows these adjustments to the free cash flow from the spreadsheet in Table 8.3 and recalculates HomeNet's free cash flow and NPV in this case.

	Year	0	1	2	3	4	5
	Free Cash Flow and NPV ($000s)						
1	Free Cash Flow w/o equipment	(16,500)	5,100	7,200	7,200	7,200	2,700
	Adjustments for use of existing equipment						
2	After-Tax Salvage Value	(1,600)	—	—	—	—	480
3	Depreciation Tax Shield	—	400	—	—	—	—
4	**Free Cash Flow with equipment**	**(18,100)**	**5,500**	**7,200**	**7,200**	**7,200**	**3,180**
5	NPV at 12%	4,055					

---

[12]When the sale price is less than the original purchase price of the asset, the gain on sale is treated as a recapture of depreciation and taxed as ordinary income. If the sale price exceeds the original purchase price, then this portion of the gain on sale is considered a capital gain, and in some cases may be taxed at a lower capital gains tax rate.

Terminal or Continuation Value. Sometimes the firm explicitly forecasts free cash flow over a shorter horizon than the full horizon of the project or investment. This is necessarily true for investments with an indefinite life, such as an expansion of the firm. In this case, we estimate the value of the remaining free cash flow beyond the forecast horizon by including an additional, one-time cash flow at the end of the forecast horizon called the **terminal** or **continuation value** of the project. This amount represents the market value (as of the last forecast period) of the free cash flow from the project at all future dates.

Depending on the setting, we use different methods for estimating the continuation value of an investment. For example, when analyzing investments with long lives, it is common to explicitly calculate free cash flow over a short horizon, and then assume that cash flows grow at some constant rate beyond the forecast horizon.

EXAMPLE 8.7

Continuation Value with Perpetual Growth

Problem

Base Hardware is considering opening a set of new retail stores. The free cash flow projections for the new stores are shown below (in millions of dollars):

0	1	2	3	4	5	6
−$10.5	−$5.5	$0.8	$1.2	$1.3	$1.3 × 1.05	$1.3 × (1.05)²

After year 4, Base Hardware expects free cash flow from the stores to increase at a rate of 5% per year. If the appropriate cost of capital for this investment is 10%, what continuation value in year 4 captures the value of future free cash flows in year 5 and beyond? What is the NPV of the new stores?

Solution

Because the future free cash flow beyond year 4 is expected to grow at 5% per year, the continuation value in year 4 of the free cash flow in year 5 and beyond can be calculated as a constant growth perpetuity:

$$\text{Continuation Value in Year } 4 = PV(\text{FCF in Year 5 and Beyond})$$

$$= \frac{FCF_4 \times (1 + g)}{r - g} = \$1.30 \text{ million} \times \frac{1.05}{0.10 - 0.05}$$

$$= \$1.30 \text{ million} \times 21 = \$27.3 \text{ million}$$

Notice that under the assumption of constant growth, we can compute the continuation value as a multiple of the project's final free cash flow.

We can restate the free cash flows of the investment as follows (in thousands of dollars):

Year	0	1	2	3	4
Free Cash Flow (Years 0–4)	(10,500)	(5,500)	800	1,200	1,300
Continuation Value					27,300
Free Cash Flow	(10,500)	(5,500)	800	1,200	28,600

The NPV of the investment in the new stores is

$$NPV = -10,500 - \frac{5500}{1.10} + \frac{800}{1.10^2} + \frac{1200}{1.10^3} + \frac{28,600}{1.10^4} = \$5597$$

or $5.597 million.

Tax Carryforwards. A firm generally identifies its marginal tax rate by determining the tax bracket that it falls into based on its overall level of pretax income. Two additional features of the tax code, called **tax loss carryforwards and carrybacks**, allow corporations to take losses during a current year and offset them against gains in nearby years. Since 1997, companies can "carry back" losses for two years and "carry forward" losses for 20 years. This tax rule means that the firm can offset losses during one year against income for the last two years, or save the losses to be offset against income during the next 20 years. When a firm can carry back losses, it receives a refund for back taxes in the current year. Otherwise, the firm must carry forward the loss and use it to offset future taxable income. When a firm has tax loss carryforwards well in excess of its current pretax income, then additional income it earns today will not increase the taxes it owes until after it exhausts its carryforwards. This delay reduces the present value of the tax liability.

| EXAMPLE 8.8 | **Tax Loss Carryforwards** |

Problem

Verian Industries has outstanding tax loss carryforwards of $100 million from losses over the past six years. If Verian earns $30 million per year in pretax income from now on, when will it first pay taxes? If Verian earns an extra $5 million this coming year, in which year will its taxes increase?

Solution

With pretax income of $30 million per year, Verian will be able to use its tax loss carryforwards to avoid paying taxes until year 4 (in millions of dollars):

Year	1	2	3	4	5
Pretax Income	30	30	30	30	30
Tax Loss Carryforward	−30	−30	−30	−10	
Taxable Income	0	0	0	20	30

If Verian earns an additional $5 million the first year, it will owe taxes on an extra $5 million in year 4:

Year	1	2	3	4	5
Pretax Income	35	30	30	30	30
Tax Loss Carryforward	−35	−30	−30	−5	
Taxable Income	0	0	0	25	30

Thus, when a firm has tax loss carryforwards, the tax impact of current earnings will be delayed until the carryforwards are exhausted. This delay reduces the present value of the tax impact, and firms sometimes approximate the effect of tax loss carryforwards by using a lower marginal tax rate.

| CONCEPT CHECK | 1. Explain why it is advantageous for a firm to use the most accelerated depreciation schedule possible for tax purposes. |

2. What is the continuation or terminal value of a project?

The American Recovery and Reinvestment Act of 2009

On February 17, 2009, President Obama signed into law the American Recovery and Reinvestment Act. The Act, like the earlier Economic Stimulus Act of 2008, included a number of tax changes designed to help businesses and stimulate investment:

Bonus Depreciation. The Act extended a temporary rule (first passed as part of the Economic Stimulus Act of 2008) allowing additional first-year depreciation of 50% of the cost of the asset. By further accelerating the depreciation allowance, this measure increases the present value of the depreciation tax shields associated with new capital expenditures, raising the NPV of such investment.

Increased Section 179 Expensing of Capital Expenditures. Section 179 of the tax code allows small- and medium-sized

businesses to immediately deduct the full purchase price of capital equipment rather than depreciate it over time. Congress doubled the limit for this deduction to a maximum of $250,000 in 2008, and this higher limit was extended by the Act through 2009. Again, being able to receive the tax deductions for such expenses immediately increases their present value and makes investment more attractive.

Extended Loss Carrybacks for Small Businesses. Under the Act, small businesses could carry back losses incurred in 2008 for up to five years, rather than two years. While this extension did not directly affect the NPV of new investments, it meant struggling businesses were more likely to receive refunds of taxes already paid, providing much-needed cash in the midst of the financial crisis.

8.5 Analyzing the Project

When evaluating a capital budgeting project, financial managers should make the decision that maximizes NPV. As we have discussed, to compute the NPV for a project, you need to estimate the incremental cash flows and choose a discount rate. Given these inputs, the NPV calculation is relatively straightforward. The most difficult part of capital budgeting is deciding how to estimate the cash flows and cost of capital. These estimates are often subject to significant uncertainty. In this section, we look at methods that assess the importance of this uncertainty and identify the drivers of value in the project.

Break-Even Analysis

When we are uncertain regarding the input to a capital budgeting decision, it is often useful to determine the **break-even** level of that input, which is the level for which the investment has an NPV of zero. One example of a break-even level that we have already considered is the calculation of the internal rate of return (IRR). Recall from Chapter 7 that the IRR of a project tells you the maximal error in the cost of capital before the optimal investment decision would change. Using the Excel function IRR, the spreadsheet in Table 8.7 calculates an IRR of 24.1% for the free cash flow of the HomeNet project.[13] Hence, the true cost of capital can be as high as 24.1% and the project will still have a positive NPV.

TABLE 8.7 SPREADSHEET	**HomeNet IRR Calculation**						
	Year	**0**	**1**	**2**	**3**	**4**	**5**
NPV ($000s) and IRR							
1 **Free Cash Flow**		(16,500)	5,100	7,200	7,200	7,200	2,700
2 **NPV at 12%**		5,027					
3 **IRR**		24.1%					

---

[13]The format in Excel is = IRR(FCF0:FCF5).

TABLE 8.8	Break-Even Levels for HomeNet

Parameter	Break-Even Level
Units sold	79,759 units per year
Wholesale price	$232 per unit
Cost of goods	$138 per unit
Cost of capital	24.1%

There is no reason to limit our attention to the uncertainty in the cost of capital estimate. In a **break-even analysis**, for each parameter, we calculate the value at which the NPV of the project is zero.[14] Table 8.8 shows the break-even level for several key parameters. For example, based on the initial assumptions, the HomeNet project will break even with a sales level of just under 80,000 units per year. Alternatively, at a sales level of 100,000 units per year, the project will break even with a sales price of $232 per unit.

We have examined the break-even levels in terms of the project's NPV, which is the most useful perspective for decision making. Other accounting notions of break-even are sometimes considered, however. For example, we could compute the **EBIT break-even** for sales, which is the level of sales for which the project's EBIT is zero. While HomeNet's EBIT break-even level of sales is only about 32,000 units per year, given the large upfront investment required in HomeNet, its NPV is −$11.8 million at that sales level.

Sensitivity Analysis

Another important capital budgeting tool is sensitivity analysis. **Sensitivity analysis** breaks the NPV calculation into its component assumptions and shows how the NPV varies as the underlying assumptions change. In this way, sensitivity analysis allows us to explore the effects of errors in our NPV estimates for the project. By conducting a sensitivity analysis, we learn which assumptions are the most important; we can then invest further resources and effort to refine these assumptions. Such an analysis also reveals which aspects of the project are most critical when we are actually managing the project.

To illustrate, consider the assumptions underlying the calculation of HomeNet's NPV. There is likely to be significant uncertainty surrounding each revenue and cost assumption. Table 8.9 shows the base-case assumptions, together with the best and worst cases, for several key aspects of the project.

TABLE 8.9	Best- and Worst-Case Parameter Assumptions for HomeNet

Parameter	Initial Assumption	Worst Case	Best Case
Units sold (thousands)	100	70	130
Sale price ($/unit)	260	240	280
Cost of goods ($/unit)	110	120	100
NWC ($ thousands)	2100	3000	1600
Cannibalization	25%	40%	10%
Cost of capital	12%	15%	10%

[14]These break-even levels can be calculated by simple trial and error within Excel, or using the Excel goal seek or solver tools.

To determine the importance of this uncertainty, we recalculate the NPV of the HomeNet project under the best- and worst-case assumptions for each parameter. For example, if the number of units sold is only 70,000 per year, the NPV of the project falls to −$2.4 million. We repeat this calculation for each parameter. The result is shown in Figure 8.1, which reveals that the most important parameter assumptions are the number of units sold and the sale price per unit. These assumptions deserve the greatest scrutiny during the estimation process. In addition, as the most important drivers of the project's value, these factors deserve close attention when managing the project.

EXAMPLE 8.9

Sensitivity to Marketing and Support Costs

Problem

The current forecast for HomeNet's marketing and support costs is $3 million per year during years 1–4. Suppose the marketing and support costs may be as high as $4 million per year. What is HomeNet's NPV in this case?

Solution

We can answer this question by changing the selling, general, and administrative expense to $4 million in the spreadsheet in Table 8.3 and computing the NPV of the resulting free cash flow. We can also calculate the impact of this change as follows: A $1 million increase in marketing and support costs will reduce EBIT by $1 million and will, therefore, decrease HomeNet's free cash flow by an after-tax amount of $1 million $\times$ (1 − 40%) = $0.6 million per year. The present value of this decrease is

$$PV = \frac{-0.6}{1.12} + \frac{-0.6}{1.12^2} + \frac{-0.6}{1.12^3} + \frac{-0.6}{1.12^4} = -\$1.8 \text{ million}$$

HomeNet's NPV would fall to $5.0 million − $1.8 million = $3.2 million.

FIGURE 8.1

HomeNet's NPV Under Best-and Worst-Case Parameter Assumptions

Green bars show the change in NPV under the best-case assumption for each parameter; red bars show the change under the worst-case assumption. Also shown are the break-even levels for each parameter. Under the initial assumptions, HomeNet's NPV is $5.0 million.

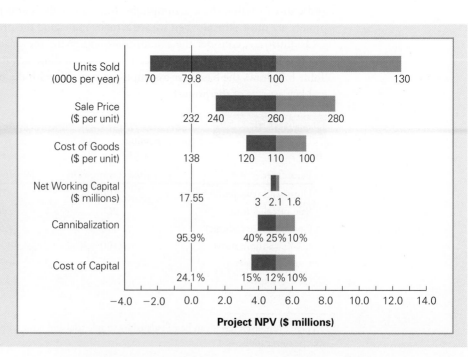

David Holland, Senior Vice President and Treasurer of Cisco, is responsible for managing all funding, risk, and capital market activities related to the firm's $50 billion balance sheet.

INTERVIEW WITH
David Holland

QUESTION: *What is the importance of considering free cash flow, as opposed to just the earnings implications of a financial decision?*

ANSWER: There is an adage saying, "Cash flow is a fact and earnings are an opinion." Earnings use an accounting framework and are governed by many rules, making it hard to know what earnings tell the investor. The economics of cash flow are clear: We can't dispute whether cash has come in or gone out. Cisco's investment decisions are based primarily on cash flow models because they take project risk into account and show the impact on value creation for owners of the business.

QUESTION: *What key financial metrics does Cisco use to make investment decisions?*

ANSWER: Cisco focuses primarily on net present value (NPV) for investment decisions. Robust NPV analysis goes beyond simply accepting projects with positive NPVs and rejecting those with negative NPVs. It identifies the key drivers that affect project success and demonstrates the interplay between factors that affect cash flow. For example, running a model using a lower margin approach shows us the impact on revenue growth and on operating cost structures. We can compare that to a higher margin (premium pricing) approach. The business unit manager learns how to control aspects of the business model to alleviate risk or accelerate the upside potential.

We prefer NPV to internal rate of return (IRR), which may return multiple answers or give false signals as to an investment's profitability, depending on the organization of cash flows. An attraction of IRR analysis is the ease of comparing percentage returns. However, this method hides the scope of a project. A project with a 25% return may generate $1 million in shareholder value, while another with a 13% IRR might produce $1 billion. NPV captures the size of the return in dollar terms and shows a project's impact on share price. NPV also creates an ownership framework for employees whose compensation package includes some form of stock ownership, directly tying the decision-making criteria to stock price.

QUESTION: *When developing a model to analyze a new investment, how do you deal with the uncertainty surrounding estimates, especially for new technologies?*

ANSWER: Cisco relies on strong financial modeling for the thousands of investment decisions we make every year. Our 2500 finance people worldwide work with the internal client—the business lead—to understand the assumptions in the model and to check the model's result against alternative assumptions. Evaluating the cash flows for technology projects, especially new technology, is difficult. When you buy an oil refinery, you can see the throughput and the cash flows. Identifying the relevant savings from a component technology for a larger router or switch product or a strategic move into a new area is more complex and intangible. Scenario and sensitivity analyses and game theory help us control risk by adjusting our strategy. We also look at the qualitative aspects, such as how the strategy fits into the customer sector and the directions customers are moving with their tech platforms.

QUESTION: *How does Cisco adjust for risk?*

ANSWER: To stay competitive in the technology space, we must be prepared to take some level of risk, even in down markets. We apply the same discount rate to all projects in a category, based on their market risk (i.e., sensitivity to market conditions). We do not adjust the discount rate to account for project-specific risks, because our required return has not changed and that would distort the true value of the company. To assess a project's unique risks, we model the upside or downside of cash flows with scenario and sensitivity analysis. We might analyze the sensitivity of a project's NPV to a 1% change in both revenue growth and operating costs. Then we run the model with other assumptions, developing base, optimistic, and bearish cases. We discuss these models with the business lead and rerun the models based on their input. This process improves our potential outcome and project profitability.

Scenario Analysis

In the analysis thus far, we have considered the consequences of varying only one parameter at a time. In reality, certain factors may affect more than one parameter. **Scenario analysis** considers the effect on the NPV of changing multiple project parameters. For example, lowering HomeNet's price may increase the number of units sold. We can use scenario analysis to evaluate alternative pricing strategies for the HomeNet product in Table 8.10. In this case, the current strategy is optimal. Figure 8.2 shows the combinations of price and volume that lead to the same NPV of $5 million for HomeNet as the current strategy. Only strategies with price and volume combinations above the line will lead to a higher NPV.

TABLE 8.10	Scenario Analysis of Alternative Pricing Strategies		
Strategy	Sale Price ($/unit)	Expected Units Sold (thousands)	NPV ($ thousands)
Current strategy	260	100	5027
Price reduction	245	110	4582
Price Increase	275	90	4937

FIGURE 8.2

Price and Volume Combinations for HomeNet with Equivalent NPV

The graph shows alternative price per unit and annual volume combinations that lead to an NPV of $5.0 million. Pricing strategies with combinations above this line will lead to a higher NPV and are superior.

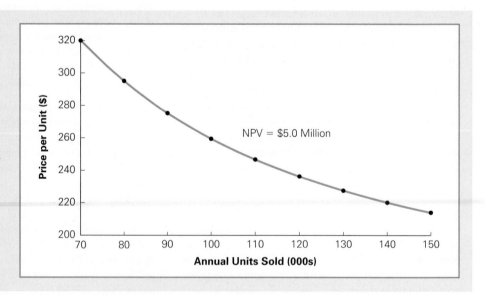

CONCEPT CHECK   1. What is sensitivity analysis?

2. How does scenario analysis differ from sensitivity analysis?

USING EXCEL

Project Analysis Using Excel

Here we describe several useful Excel tools that assist with project analysis.

Goal Seek for Break-Even Analysis

Excel's goal seek function determines the break-even point for key assumptions in our model. For example, to determine the break-even level of units for annual sales, use the Goal Seek window (see the Data > What-If Analysis menu, or keyboard shortcut Alt-A-W-G). The set cell is the cell in which we calculated NPV (cell D51). To set its value to 0 (break-even), we change the average sale price (cell E8). Excel will then use trial and error to find the sale price at which the project's NPV is zero—in this case $231.66.

	A	B	C	D	E	F	G	H	I
1	**HomeNet Capital Budget**								
2	*Key Assumptions*			Year 0	Year 1	Year 2	Year 3	Year 4	Year 5
8	HomeNet Ave. Price/Unit			-	$260.00	$260.00	$260.00	$260.00	-
51	**NPV**			5,026					

Data Tables for Sensitivity Analysis

Data tables, which we introduced in the appendix of Chapter 7 to construct the NPV profile, allow us to compute the sensitivity of NPV to any other input variable in our financial model. Excel can also compute a two-dimensional data table showing the sensitivity of NPV to two inputs simultaneously. For example, the data table below shows NPVs for different combinations of the Hardware R&D budget and HomeNet's manufacturing costs.

	C	D	E	F	G	H
55	NPV			HomeNet Cost / Unit		
56		5,026	$110	$105	$100	$95
57		(5,000)	5,026	5,913	6,800	7,686
58		(5,500)	4,726	5,613	6,500	7,386
59		(6,000)	4,426	5,313	6,200	7,086
60		(6,500)	4,126	5,013	5,900	6,786
61		(7,000)	3,826	4,713	5,600	6,486
62		(7,500)	3,526	4,413	5,300	6,186
63		(8,000)	3,226	4,113	5,000	5,886
64		(8,500)	2,926	3,813	4,700	5,586
65		(9,000)	2,626	3,513	4,400	5,286
66		(9,500)	2,326	3,213	4,100	4,986
67		(10,000)	2,026	2,913	3,800	4,686

(The rows 57–67 in column D are labeled "Hardware R&D Expense")

To construct this data table, put the values of each input along the sides of the table (shown in blue), and a formula for the value we want to compute in the upper left corner (cell D56, which in this case is just a link to the cell in which we computed the NPV). Select the entire table (D56:H67), bring up the Data Table window (see the Data > What-If Analysis menu or keyboard shortcut Alt-D-T), and input the locations in our project dashboard (see page 245) of the cost assumption (row input cell E9) and hardware budget (column input cell D16). The data table shows, for example, that NPV increases if we lower our manufacturing cost to $100 per unit by increasing the hardware budget to $7.5 million.

Scenarios in the Project Dashboard

The project dashboard on page 245 only shows our base-case assumptions. We can build multiple scenarios into our project dashboard by adding additional rows with alternative assumptions, and then using Excel's index function to select the scenario we would like to use in our analysis. For example, rows 5–7 on the next page show alternative annual sales assumptions for HomeNet. We then select the scenario to analyze by entering the appropriate number (in this case 1, 2 or 3) in the highlighted cell (C4), and use the index function to pull the appropriate data into row 4.

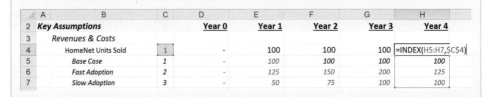

	A	B	C	D	E	F	G	H
2	**Key Assumptions**			**Year 0**	**Year 1**	**Year 2**	**Year 3**	**Year 4**
3		Revenues & Costs						
4		HomeNet Units Sold	1	-	100	100	100	=INDEX(H5:H7,$C$4)
5		Base Case	1	-	100	100	100	100
6		Fast Adoption	2	-	125	150	200	125
7		Slow Adoption	3	-	50	75	100	100

We can then analyze the consequences for each scenario using the one-dimensional data table in C70:D73 below, with column input cell C4.

	A	B	C	D	E
69				NPV	
70		HomeNet Units Sold		5,026	
71		Base Case	1	5,026	
72		Fast Adoption	2	17,227	
73		Slow Adoption	3	(253)	

MyFinanceLab

Here is what you should know after reading this chapter. MyFinanceLab will help you identify what you know and where to go when you need to practice.

8.1 Forecasting Earnings

- Capital budgeting is the process of analyzing investment opportunities and deciding which ones to accept. A capital budget is a list of all projects that a company plans to undertake during the next period.
- We use the NPV rule to evaluate capital budgeting decisions, making decisions that maximize NPV. When deciding to accept or reject a project, we accept projects with a positive NPV.
- The incremental earnings of a project comprise the amount by which the project is expected to change the firm's earnings.
- Incremental earnings should include all incremental revenues and costs associated with the project, including project externalities and opportunity costs, but excluding sunk costs and interest expenses.
  - Project externalities are cash flows that occur when a project affects other areas of the company's business.
  - An opportunity cost is the cost of using an existing asset, measured by the value the asset would have provided in its best alternative use.
  - A sunk cost is an unrecoverable cost that has already been incurred.
  - Interest and other financing-related expenses are excluded to determine the project's unlevered net income.
- We estimate taxes using the marginal tax rate, based on the net income generated by the rest of the firm's operations, as well as any tax loss carrybacks or carryforwards.

■ When evaluating a capital budgeting decision, we first consider the project on its own, separate from the decision regarding how to finance the project. Thus, we ignore interest expenses and compute the unlevered net income contribution of the project:

$$\text{Unlevered Net Income } = EBIT \times (1 - \tau_c)$$

$$= (\text{Revenues} - \text{Costs} - \text{Depreciation}) \times (1 - \tau_c) \qquad (8.2)$$

8.2 Determining Free Cash Flow and NPV

■ We compute free cash flow from incremental earnings by eliminating all non-cash expenses and including all capital investment.
  ▫ Depreciation is not a cash expense, so it is added back.
  ▫ Actual capital expenditures are deducted.
  ▫ Increases in net working capital are deducted. Net working capital is defined as

$$\text{Cash} + \text{Inventory} + \text{Receivables} - \text{Payables} \qquad (8.3)$$

■ The basic calculation for free cash flow is

$$\text{Free Cash Flow} = \overbrace{(\text{Revenues} - \text{Costs} - \text{Depreciation}) \times (1 - \tau_c)}^{\text{Unlevered Net Income}}$$

$$+ \text{Depreciation} - \text{CapEx} - \Delta NWC \qquad (8.5)$$

■ The discount rate for a project is its cost of capital: The expected return of securities with comparable risk and horizon.

8.3 Choosing Among Alternatives

■ When choosing between mutual exclusive investment opportunities, pick the opportunity with the highest NPV.
■ When choosing between alternatives, we only need to include those components of free cash flow that differ among the alternatives.

8.4 Further Adjustments to Free Cash Flow

■ Depreciation expenses affect free cash flow only through the depreciation tax shield. The firm should generally use the most accelerated depreciation schedule that is allowable for tax purposes.
■ Free cash flow should also include the (after-tax) liquidation or salvage value of any assets that are disposed of. It may also include a terminal (continuation) value if the project continues beyond the forecast horizon.
■ When an asset is sold, tax is due on the difference between the sale price and the asset's book value net of depreciation.
■ Terminal or continuation values should reflect the present value of the project's future cash flows beyond the forecast horizon.

8.5 Analyzing the Project

■ Break-even analysis computes the level of a parameter that makes the project's NPV equal zero.
■ Sensitivity analysis breaks the NPV calculation down into its component assumptions, showing how the NPV varies as the values of the underlying assumptions change.
■ Scenario analysis considers the effect of changing multiple parameters simultaneously.

Key Terms

Further Reading

For an excellent overview of the history of the concept of present value and its use in capital budgeting, see M. Rubinstein, "Great Moments in Financial Economics: I. Present Value," *Journal of Investment Management* (First Quarter 2003).

Irving Fisher was one of the first to apply the Law of One Price to propose that any capital project should be evaluated in terms of its present value; see I. Fisher, *The Rate of Interest: Its Nature, Determination and Relation to Economic Phenomena* (Macmillan, 1907). I. Fisher, *The Theory of Interest: As Determined by Impatience to Spend Income and Opportunity to Invest It* (Macmillan, 1930); reprinted (Augustus M. Kelley, 1955).

The use of this approach for capital budgeting was later popularized in the following book: J. Dean, *Capital Budgeting* (Columbia University Press, 1951).

We will revisit the topics of this chapter in Part 6. Additional readings for more advanced topics will be provided there.

Problems

All problems are available in MyFinanceLab. *An asterisk (*) indicates problems with higher level of difficulty.*

Forecasting Earnings

1. Pisa Pizza, a seller of frozen pizza, is considering introducing a healthier version of its pizza that will be low in cholesterol and contain no trans fats. The firm expects that sales of the new pizza will be $20 million per year. While many of these sales will be to new customers, Pisa Pizza estimates that 40% will come from customers who switch to the new, healthier pizza instead of buying the original version.

   a. Assume customers will spend the same amount on either version. What level of incremental sales is associated with introducing the new pizza?

   b. Suppose that 50% of the customers who will switch from Pisa Pizza's original pizza to its healthier pizza will switch to another brand if Pisa Pizza does not introduce a healthier pizza. What level of incremental sales is associated with introducing the new pizza in this case?

2. Kokomochi is considering the launch of an advertising campaign for its latest dessert product, the Mini Mochi Munch. Kokomochi plans to spend $5 million on TV, radio, and print advertising this year for the campaign. The ads are expected to boost sales of the Mini Mochi Munch by $9 million this year and by $7 million next year. In addition, the company expects that new consumers who try the Mini Mochi Munch will be more likely to try Kokomochi's other products. As a result, sales of other products are expected to rise by $2 million each year.

   Kokomochi's gross profit margin for the Mini Mochi Munch is 35%, and its gross profit margin averages 25% for all other products. The company's marginal corporate tax rate is 35% both this year and next year. What are the incremental earnings associated with the advertising campaign?

3. Home Builder Supply, a retailer in the home improvement industry, currently operates seven retail outlets in Georgia and South Carolina. Management is contemplating building an eighth retail store across town from its most successful retail outlet. The company already owns the land for this store, which currently has an abandoned warehouse located on it. Last month, the marketing department spent $10,000 on market research to determine the extent of customer demand for the new store. Now Home Builder Supply must decide whether to build and open the new store.

Which of the following should be included as part of the incremental earnings for the proposed new retail store?
a. The cost of the land where the store will be located.
b. The cost of demolishing the abandoned warehouse and clearing the lot.
c. The loss of sales in the existing retail outlet, if customers who previously drove across town to shop at the existing outlet become customers of the new store instead.
d. The $10,000 in market research spent to evaluate customer demand.
e. Construction costs for the new store.
f. The value of the land if sold.
g. Interest expense on the debt borrowed to pay the construction costs.

4. Hyperion, Inc. currently sells its latest high-speed color printer, the Hyper 500, for $350. It plans to lower the price to $300 next year. Its cost of goods sold for the Hyper 500 is $200 per unit, and this year's sales are expected to be 20,000 units.
a. Suppose that if Hyperion drops the price to $300 immediately, it can increase this year's sales by 25% to 25,000 units. What would be the incremental impact on this year's EBIT of such a price drop?
b. Suppose that for each printer sold, Hyperion expects additional sales of $75 per year on ink cartridges for the next three years, and Hyperion has a gross profit margin of 70% on ink cartridges. What is the incremental impact on EBIT for the next three years of a price drop this year?

 5. After looking at the projections of the HomeNet project, you decide that they are not realistic. It is unlikely that sales will be constant over the four-year life of the project. Furthermore, other companies are likely to offer competing products, so the assumption that the sales price will remain constant is also likely to be optimistic. Finally, as production ramps up, you anticipate lower per unit production costs resulting from economies of scale. Therefore, you decide to redo the projections under the following assumptions: Sales of 50,000 units in year 1 increasing by 50,000 units per year over the life of the project, a year 1 sales price of $260/unit, decreasing by 10% annually and a year 1 cost of $120/unit decreasing by 20% annually. In addition, new tax laws allow you to depreciate the equipment over three rather than five years using straight-line depreciation.
a. Keeping the other assumptions that underlie Table 8.1 the same, recalculate unlevered net income (that is, reproduce Table 8.1 under the new assumptions, and note that we are ignoring cannibalization and lost rent).
b. Recalculate unlevered net income assuming, in addition, that each year 20% of sales comes from customers who would have purchased an existing Linksys router for $100/unit and that this router costs $60/unit to manufacture.

Determining Free Cash Flow and NPV

6. Cellular Access, Inc. is a cellular telephone service provider that reported net income of $250 million for the most recent fiscal year. The firm had depreciation expenses of $100 million, capital expenditures of $200 million, and no interest expenses. Working capital increased by $10 million. Calculate the free cash flow for Cellular Access for the most recent fiscal year.

 7. Castle View Games would like to invest in a division to develop software for video games. To evaluate this decision, the firm first attempts to project the working capital needs for this

operation. Its chief financial officer has developed the following estimates (in millions of dollars):

	Year 1	Year 2	Year 3	Year 4	Year 5
Cash	6	12	15	15	15
Accounts Receivable	21	22	24	24	24
Inventory	5	7	10	12	13
Accounts Payable	18	22	24	25	30

Assuming that Castle View currently does not have any working capital invested in this division, calculate the cash flows associated with changes in working capital for the first five years of this investment.

8. Mersey Chemicals manufactures polypropylene that it ships to its customers via tank car. Currently, it plans to add two additional tank cars to its fleet four years from now. However, a proposed plant expansion will require Mersey's transport division to add these two additional tank cars in two years' time rather than in four years. The current cost of a tank car is $2 million, and this cost is expected to remain constant. Also, while tank cars will last indefinitely, they will be depreciated straight-line over a five-year life for tax purposes. Suppose Mersey's tax rate is 40%. When evaluating the proposed expansion, what incremental free cash flows should be included to account for the need to accelerate the purchase of the tank cars?

9. Elmdale Enterprises is deciding whether to expand its production facilities. Although long-term cash flows are difficult to estimate, management has projected the following cash flows for the first two years (in millions of dollars):

	Year 1	Year 2
Revenues	125	160
Costs of goods sold and operating expenses other than depreciation	40	60
Depreciation	25	36
Increase in net working capital	5	8
Capital expenditures	30	40
Marginal corporate tax rate	35%	35%

a. What are the incremental earnings for this project for years 1 and 2?
b. What are the free cash flows for this project for the first two years?

 10. You are a manager at Percolated Fiber, which is considering expanding its operations in synthetic fiber manufacturing. Your boss comes into your office, drops a consultant's report on your desk, and complains, "We owe these consultants $1 million for this report, and I am not sure their analysis makes sense. Before we spend the $25 million on new equipment needed for this project, look it over and give me your opinion." You open the report and find the following estimates (in thousands of dollars):

	Project Year				
	1	2	...	9	10
Sales revenue	30,000	30,000		30,000	30,000
− Cost of goods sold	18,000	18,000		18,000	18,000
= Gross profit	12,000	12,000		12,000	12,000
− General, sales, and administrative expenses	2,000	2,000		2,000	2,000
− Depreciation	2,500	2,500		2,500	2,500
= Net operating income	7,500	7,500		7,500	7,500
− Income tax	2,625	2,625		2,625	2,625
Net Income	4,875	4,875		4,875	4,875

All of the estimates in the report seem correct. You note that the consultants used straight-line depreciation for the new equipment that will be purchased today (year 0), which is what the accounting department recommended. The report concludes that because the project will increase earnings by $4.875 million per year for 10 years, the project is worth $48.75 million. You think back to your halcyon days in finance class and realize there is more work to be done!

First, you note that the consultants have not factored in that the project will require $10 million in working capital upfront (year 0), which will be fully recovered in year 10. Next, you see they have attributed $2 million of selling, general and administrative expenses to the project, but you know that $1 million of this amount is overhead that will be incurred even if the project is not accepted. Finally, you know that accounting earnings are not the right thing to focus on!

    a. Given the available information, what are the free cash flows in years 0 through 10 that should be used to evaluate the proposed project?

    b. If the cost of capital for this project is 14%, what is your estimate of the value of the new project?

 11. Using the assumptions in part (a) of Problem 5 (assuming there is no cannibalization),

    a. Calculate HomeNet's net working capital requirements (that is, reproduce Table 8.4 under the assumptions in Problem 5(a)).

    b. Calculate HomeNet's FCF (that is, reproduce Table 8.3 under the same assumptions as in (a)).

Choosing Among Alternatives

12. A bicycle manufacturer currently produces 300,000 units a year and expects output levels to remain steady in the future. It buys chains from an outside supplier at a price of $2 a chain. The plant manager believes that it would be cheaper to make these chains rather than buy them. Direct in-house production costs are estimated to be only $1.50 per chain. The necessary machinery would cost $250,000 and would be obsolete after 10 years. This investment could be depreciated to zero for tax purposes using a 10-year straight-line depreciation schedule. The plant manager estimates that the operation would require $50,000 of inventory and other working capital upfront (year 0), but argues that this sum can be ignored since it is recoverable at the end of the 10 years. Expected proceeds from scrapping the machinery after 10 years are $20,000.

If the company pays tax at a rate of 35% and the opportunity cost of capital is 15%, what is the net present value of the decision to produce the chains in-house instead of purchasing them from the supplier?

 13. One year ago, your company purchased a machine used in manufacturing for $110,000. You have learned that a new machine is available that offers many advantages; you can purchase it for $150,000 today. It will be depreciated on a straight-line basis over 10 years, after which it has no salvage value. You expect that the new machine will produce EBITDA (earning before interest, taxes, depreciation, and amortization) of $40,000 per year for the next 10 years. The current machine is expected to produce EBITDA of $20,000 per year. The current machine is being depreciated on a straight-line basis over a useful life of 11 years, after which it will have no salvage value, so depreciation expense for the current machine is $10,000 per year. All other expenses of the two machines are identical. The market value today of the current machine is $50,000. Your company's tax rate is 45%, and the opportunity cost of capital for this type of equipment is 10%. Is it profitable to replace the year-old machine?

 14. Beryl's Iced Tea currently rents a bottling machine for $50,000 per year, including all maintenance expenses. It is considering purchasing a machine instead, and is comparing two options:

    a. Purchase the machine it is currently renting for $150,000. This machine will require $20,000 per year in ongoing maintenance expenses.

b. Purchase a new, more advanced machine for $250,000. This machine will require $15,000 per year in ongoing maintenance expenses and will lower bottling costs by $10,000 per year. Also, $35,000 will be spent upfront in training the new operators of the machine.

Suppose the appropriate discount rate is 8% per year and the machine is purchased today. Maintenance and bottling costs are paid at the end of each year, as is the rental of the machine. Assume also that the machines will be depreciated via the straight-line method over seven years and that they have a 10-year life with a negligible salvage value. The marginal corporate tax rate is 35%. Should Beryl's Iced Tea continue to rent, purchase its current machine, or purchase the advanced machine?

Further Adjustments to Free Cash Flow

15. Markov Manufacturing recently spent $15 million to purchase some equipment used in the manufacture of disk drives. The firm expects that this equipment will have a useful life of five years, and its marginal corporate tax rate is 35%. The company plans to use straight-line depreciation.
    a. What is the annual depreciation expense associated with this equipment?
    b. What is the annual depreciation tax shield?
    c. Rather than straight-line depreciation, suppose Markov will use the MACRS depreciation method for five-year property. Calculate the depreciation tax shield each year for this equipment under this accelerated depreciation schedule.
    d. If Markov has a choice between straight-line and MACRS depreciation schedules, and its marginal corporate tax rate is expected to remain constant, which should it choose? Why?
    e. How might your answer to part (d) change if Markov anticipates that its marginal corporate tax rate will increase substantially over the next five years?

16. Your firm is considering a project that would require purchasing $7.5 million worth of new equipment. Determine the present value of the depreciation tax shield associated with this equipment if the firm's tax rate is 40%, the appropriate cost of capital is 8%, and the equipment can be depreciated
    a. Straight-line over a 10-year period, with the first deduction starting in one year.
    b. Straight-line over a five-year period, with the first deduction starting in one year.
    c. Using MACRS depreciation with a five-year recovery period and starting immediately.
    d. Fully as an immediate deduction.

17. Arnold Inc. is considering a proposal to manufacture high-end protein bars used as food supplements by body builders. The project requires use of an existing warehouse, which the firm acquired three years ago for $1 million and which it currently rents out for $120,000. Rental rates are not expected to change going forward. In addition to using the warehouse, the project requires an up-front investment into machines and other equipment of $1.4 million. This investment can be fully depreciated straight-line over the next 10 years for tax purposes. However, Arnold Inc. expects to terminate the project at the end of eight years and to sell the machines and equipment for $500,000. Finally, the project requires an initial investment into net working capital equal to 10% of predicted first-year sales. Subsequently, net working capital is 10% of the predicted sales over the following year. Sales of protein bars are expected to be $4.8 million in the first year and to stay constant for eight years. Total manufacturing costs and operating expenses (excluding depreciation) are 80% of sales, and profits are taxed at 30%.
    a. What are the free cash flows of the project?
    b. If the cost of capital is 15%, what is the NPV of the project?

18. Bay Properties is considering starting a commercial real estate division. It has prepared the following four-year forecast of free cash flows for this division:

	Year 1	Year 2	Year 3	Year 4
Free Cash Flow	−$185,000	$12,000	$99,000	$240,000

Assume cash flows after year 4 will grow at 3% per year, forever. If the cost of capital for this division is 14%, what is the continuation value in year 4 for cash flows after year 4? What is the value today of this division?

19. Your firm would like to evaluate a proposed new operating division. You have forecasted cash flows for this division for the next five years, and have estimated that the cost of capital is 12%. You would like to estimate a continuation value. You have made the following forecasts for the last year of your five-year forecasting horizon (in millions of dollars):

	Year 5
Revenues	1200
Operating income	100
Net income	50
Free cash flows	110
Book value of equity	400

a. You forecast that future free cash flows after year 5 will grow at 2% per year, forever. Estimate the continuation value in year 5, using the perpetuity with growth formula.

b. You have identified several firms in the same industry as your operating division. The average P/E ratio for these firms is 30. Estimate the continuation value assuming the P/E ratio for your division in year 5 will be the same as the average P/E ratio for the comparable firms today.

c. The average market/book ratio for the comparable firms is 4.0. Estimate the continuation value using the market/book ratio.

20. In September 2008, the IRS changed tax laws to allow banks to utilize the tax loss carryforwards of banks they acquire to shield their future income from taxes (prior law restricted the ability of acquirers to use these credits). Suppose Fargo Bank acquires Covia Bank and with it acquires $74 billion in tax loss carryforwards. If Fargo Bank is expected to generate taxable income of 10 billion per year in the future, and its tax rate is 30%, what is the present value of these acquired tax loss carryforwards given a cost of capital of 8%?

Analyzing the Project

 21. Using the FCF projections in part (b) of Problem 11, calculate the NPV of the HomeNet project assuming a cost of capital of
   a. 10%.
   b. 12%.
   c. 14%.

What is the IRR of the project in this case?

22. For the assumptions in part (a) of Problem 5, assuming a cost of capital of 12%, calculate the following:
   a. The break-even annual sales price decline.
   b. The break-even annual unit sales increase.

 23. Bauer Industries is an automobile manufacturer. Management is currently evaluating a proposal to build a plant that will manufacture lightweight trucks. Bauer plans to use a cost of capital of 12% to evaluate this project. Based on extensive research, it has prepared the following incremental free cash flow projections (in millions of dollars):

	Year 0	Years 1–9	Year 10
Revenues		100.0	100.0
− Manufacturing expenses (other than depreciation)		−35.0	−35.0
− Marketing expenses		−10.0	−10.0
− Depreciation		−15.0	−15.0
= EBIT		40.0	40.0
− Taxes (35%)		−14.0	−14.0
= Unlevered net income		26.0	26.0
+ Depreciation		+15.0	+15.0
− Increases in net working capital		−5.0	−5.0
− Capital expenditures	−150.0		
+ Continuation value			+12.0
= Free cash flow	−150.0	36.0	48.0

   a. For this base-case scenario, what is the NPV of the plant to manufacture lightweight trucks?
   b. Based on input from the marketing department, Bauer is uncertain about its revenue forecast. In particular, management would like to examine the sensitivity of the NPV to the revenue assumptions. What is the NPV of this project if revenues are 10% higher than forecast? What is the NPV if revenues are 10% lower than forecast?
   c. Rather than assuming that cash flows for this project are constant, management would like to explore the sensitivity of its analysis to possible growth in revenues and operating expenses. Specifically, management would like to assume that revenues, manufacturing expenses, and marketing expenses are as given in the table for year 1 and grow by 2% per year every year starting in year 2. Management also plans to assume that the initial capital expenditures (and therefore depreciation), additions to working capital, and continuation value remain as initially specified in the table. What is the NPV of this project under these alternative assumptions? How does the NPV change if the revenues and operating expenses grow by 5% per year rather than by 2%?
   d. To examine the sensitivity of this project to the discount rate, management would like to compute the NPV for different discount rates. Create a graph, with the discount rate on the x-axis and the NPV on the y-axis, for discount rates ranging from 5% to 30%. For what ranges of discount rates does the project have a positive NPV?

 *24.** Billingham Packaging is considering expanding its production capacity by purchasing a new machine, the XC-750. The cost of the XC-750 is $2.75 million. Unfortunately, installing this machine will take several months and will partially disrupt production. The firm has just completed a $50,000 feasibility study to analyze the decision to buy the XC-750, resulting in the following estimates:
   ■ *Marketing*: Once the XC-750 is operating next year, the extra capacity is expected to generate $10 million per year in additional sales, which will continue for the 10-year life of the machine.

■ *Operations*: The disruption caused by the installation will decrease sales by $5 million this year. Once the machine is operating next year, the cost of goods for the products produced by the XC-750 is expected to be 70% of their sale price. The increased production will require additional inventory on hand of $1 million to be added in year 0 and depleted in year 10.

■ *Human Resources*: The expansion will require additional sales and administrative personnel at a cost of $2 million per year.

■ *Accounting*: The XC-750 will be depreciated via the straight-line method over the 10-year life of the machine. The firm expects receivables from the new sales to be 15% of revenues and payables to be 10% of the cost of goods sold. Billingham's marginal corporate tax rate is 35%.

a. Determine the incremental earnings from the purchase of the XC-750.

b. Determine the free cash flow from the purchase of the XC-750.

c. If the appropriate cost of capital for the expansion is 10%, compute the NPV of the purchase.

d. While the expected new sales will be $10 million per year from the expansion, estimates range from $8 million to $12 million. What is the NPV in the worst case? In the best case?

e. What is the break-even level of new sales from the expansion? What is the break-even level for the cost of goods sold?

f. Billingham could instead purchase the XC-900, which offers even greater capacity. The cost of the XC-900 is $4 million. The extra capacity would not be useful in the first two years of operation, but would allow for additional sales in years 3–10. What level of additional sales (above the $10 million expected for the XC-750) per year in those years would justify purchasing the larger machine?

Data Case

Novo Nordisk A/S is a health care company engaging in the discovery, development, and manufacture of pharmaceutical products. Its specialty is diabetes care and its headquarters are in Bagsvaerd, Denmark. The company sells its products all over the world, including in the United States, Japan, China, Russia, India, and Europe.

As a new member of the capital budgeting division of Novo Nordisk A/S, you have been asked to determine the net cash flows and NPV of a proposed new diabetes drug. The drug is expected to be on the market for three years only, because Novo Nordisk A/S expects to launch a new and better version of the drug in the near future. If the project is initiated, it will require an expenditure on research and development of 4% of the total amount that Novo Nordisk A/S spent on research and development in the last financial year. Also, an investment in a new production facility, which is estimated to cost $24 million, will be necessary.

The product revenues for years 1, 2, and 3 are expected to be 0.8%, 0.6%, and 0.4%, respectively, of the total revenue of Novo Nordisk A/S for the last financial year. The cost of goods sold is projected to be $8 million in years 1 and 2, but only $5 million in year 3. Finally, the selling, general, and administrative costs are assumed to be $3 million in years 1 and 2, but only $2 million in year 3.

1. In order to obtain the latest financial statement of Novo Nordisk A/S, go to Yahoo! Finance (http://finance.yahoo.com/) and search for Novo Nordisk A/S by entering the company's ticker symbol, NVO. Go to "Financials" and download the income statement and the balance sheet. Export them to Excel by right clicking while the cursor is inside each statement. When estimating the project details, use data for the most recent year for which the financial statements are available.

2. Novo Nordisk A/S has decided that the investment in the production facility should be depreciated with the straight-line method over the life of the project. Determine the amount of depreciation each year.

3. Calculate the corporate tax rate that Novo Nordisk A/S paid for the last financial year.

4. Use the result of Questions 2 and 3 to calculate the unlevered net income of the project for years 0 to 3.

5. In years 1 to 3, the inventory of the project is 1.5 million, receivables are 15% of the project revenues, and payables are 20% of the project's cost of goods sold. Assume that the project requires no cash. Find the net working capital for the project for each year 1 to 3. Also, find the change in net working capital for each year when assuming the project is terminated in year 3 and the net working capital has to be settled the year after the project ends—that is, find the change in net working capital for years 1 to 4.

6. Calculate the free cash flow for years 0 to 4 using Eq. 8.5 on page 243. Note that you can use the unlevered net income from Question 4.

7. Find the net present value of the project from the calculated free cash flows when assuming that the cost of capital (CoC) for Novo Nordisk A/S is 12%. You may use the NPV function in Excel. Include cash flows 1 through 4 in the NPV function and then subtract the initial cost (i.e., add the initial cash flow CF_0, which is a negative number).

$$NPV(CoC\,;\, CF_1: CF_4) + CF_0$$

8. For a presentation of the new project to your colleagues in the company's capital budgeting division, make a plot of the NPV as a function of the cost of capital. First, calculate the NPV of the project for a range of different assumptions of cost of capital (e.g., 5%, 10%, 15%, . . ., 40%). Then, plot the calculated NPVs as a function of the corresponding cost of capital. From the figure, note the internal rate of return of the project. Verify your result using Excel's IRR function.

| CHAPTER 8 |
| APPENDIX |

MACRS Depreciation

The U.S. tax code allows for accelerated depreciation of most assets. The depreciation method that you use for any particular asset is determined by the tax rules in effect at the time you place the asset into service. (Congress has changed the depreciation rules many times over the years, so many firms that have held property for a long time may have to use several depreciation methods simultaneously.)

For most business property placed in service after 1986, the IRS allows firms to depreciate the asset using the MACRS (Modified Accelerated Cost Recovery System) method. Under this method, you categorize each business asset into a recovery class that determines the time period over which you can write off the cost of the asset. The most commonly used items are classified as shown below:

- *3-year property*: Tractor units, racehorses over 2 years old, and horses over 12 years old.

- *5-year property*: Automobiles, buses, trucks, computers and peripheral equipment, office machinery, and any property used in research and experimentation. Also includes breeding and dairy cattle.

- *7-year property*: Office furniture and fixtures, and any property that has not been designated as belonging to another class.

- *10-year property*: Water transportation equipment, single-purpose agricultural or horticultural structures, and trees or vines bearing fruit or nuts.

- *15-year property*: Depreciable improvements to land such as fences, roads, and bridges.

- *20-year property*: Farm buildings that are not agricultural or horticultural structures.

- *27.5-year property*: Residential rental property.

- *39-year property*: Nonresidential real estate, including home offices. (Note that the value of land may not be depreciated.)

Generally speaking, residential and nonresidential real estate is depreciated via the straight-line method, but other classes can be depreciated more rapidly in early years. Table 8A.1 shows the standard depreciation rates for assets in the other recovery classes; refinements of this table can be applied depending on the month that the asset was placed into service (consult IRS guidelines). The table indicates the percentage of the asset's cost that may be depreciated each year, with year 1 indicating the year the asset was first put into use.

The lower amount in year 1 reflects a "half-year convention" in which the asset is presumed to be in use (and this depreciated) for half of the first year, no matter when it was actually put into use. After year 1, it is assumed that the asset depreciates more rapidly in earlier years.

TABLE 8A.1	MACRS Depreciation Table Showing the Percentage of the Asset's Cost That May Be Depreciated Each Year Based on Its Recovery Period

	Depreciation Rate for Recovery Period					
Year	3 Years	5 Years	7 Years	10 Years	15 Years	20 Years
1	33.33	20.00	14.29	10.00	5.00	3.750
2	44.45	32.00	24.49	18.00	9.50	7.219
3	14.81	19.20	17.49	14.40	8.55	6.677
4	7.41	11.52	12.49	11.52	7.70	6.177
5		11.52	8.93	9.22	6.93	5.713
6		5.76	8.92	7.37	6.23	5.285
7			8.93	6.55	5.90	4.888
8			4.46	6.55	5.90	4.522
9				6.56	5.91	4.462
10				6.55	5.90	4.461
11				3.28	5.91	4.462
12					5.90	4.461
13					5.91	4.462
14					5.90	4.461
15					5.91	4.462
16					2.95	4.461
17						4.462
18						4.461
19						4.462
20						4.461
21						2.231

Valuing Stocks

ON JANUARY 16, 2006, FOOTWEAR AND APPAREL MAKER Kenneth Cole Productions, Inc., announced that its president, Paul Blum, had resigned to pursue "other opportunities." The price of the company's stock had already dropped more than 16% over the prior two years, and the firm was in the midst of a major undertaking to restructure its brand. News that its president, who had been with the company for more than 15 years, was now resigning was taken as a bad sign by many investors. The next day, Kenneth Cole's stock price dropped by more than 6% on the New York Stock Exchange to $26.75, with over 300,000 shares traded, more than twice its average daily volume. How might an investor decide whether to buy or sell a stock such as Kenneth Cole at this price? Why would the stock suddenly be worth 6% less on the announcement of this news? What actions can Kenneth Cole's managers take to increase the stock price?

To answer these questions, we turn to the Law of One Price, which implies that the price of a security should equal the present value of the expected cash flows an investor will receive from owning it. In this chapter, we apply this idea to stocks. Thus, to value a stock, we need to know the expected cash flows an investor will receive and the appropriate cost of capital with which to discount those cash flows. Both of these quantities can be challenging to estimate, and many of the details needed to do so will be developed throughout the remainder of the text. In this chapter, we will begin our study of stock valuation by identifying the relevant cash flows and developing the main tools that practitioners use to evaluate them.

Our analysis begins with a consideration of the dividends and capital gains received by investors who hold the stock for different periods, from which we develop the *dividend-discount model* of stock valuation. Next, we apply Chapter 8's tools to value stocks based on the free cash flows generated by the firm. Having developed these stock valuation methods based on discounted cash flows, we then relate them to the practice of using

NOTATION

P_t stock price at the end of year t

r_E equity cost of capital

N terminal date or forecast horizon

g expected dividend growth rate

Div_t dividends paid in year t

EPS_t earnings per share on date t

PV present value

$EBIT$ earnings before interest and taxes

FCF_t free cash flow on date t

V_t enterprise value on date t

τ_c corporate tax rate

r_{wacc} weighted average cost of capital

g_{FCF} expected free cash flow growth rate

$EBITDA$ earnings before interest, taxes, depreciation, and amortization valuation multiples based on comparable firms. We conclude the chapter by discussing the role of competition in determining the information contained in stock prices, as well as its implications for investors and corporate managers.

9.1 The Dividend-Discount Model

The Law of One Price implies that to value any security, we must determine the expected cash flows an investor will receive from owning it. Thus, we begin our analysis of stock valuation by considering the cash flows for an investor with a one-year investment horizon. We then consider the perspective of investors with longer investment horizons. We show that if investors have the same beliefs, their valuation of the stock will not depend on their investment horizon. Using this result, we then derive the first method to value a stock: the *dividend-discount model*.

A One-Year Investor

There are two potential sources of cash flows from owning a stock. First, the firm might pay out cash to its shareholders in the form of a dividend. Second, the investor might generate cash by choosing to sell the shares at some future date. The total amount received in dividends and from selling the stock will depend on the investor's investment horizon. Let's begin by considering the perspective of a one-year investor.

When an investor buys a stock, she will pay the current market price for a share, P_0. While she continues to hold the stock, she will be entitled to any dividends the stock pays. Let Div_1 be the total dividends paid per share of the stock during the year. At the end of the year, the investor will sell her share at the new market price, P_1. Assuming for simplicity that all dividends are paid at the end of the year, we have the following timeline for this investment:

Of course, the future dividend payment and stock price in the timeline above are not known with certainty; rather, these values are based on the investor's expectations at the time the stock is purchased. Given these expectations, the investor will be willing to buy the stock at today's price as long as the NPV of the transaction is not negative—that is, as long as the current price does not exceed the present value of the expected future dividend and sale price. Because these cash flows are risky, we cannot compute their present value using the risk-free interest rate. Instead, we must discount them based on the **equity cost of capital**, r_E, for the stock, which is the expected return of other investments available in the market with equivalent risk to the firm's shares. Doing so leads to the following condition under which an investor would be willing to buy the stock:

$$P_0 \leq \frac{Div_1 + P_1}{1 + r_E}$$

Similarly, for an investor to be willing to sell the stock, she must receive at least as much today as the present value she would receive if she waited to sell next year:

$$P_0 \geq \frac{Div_1 + P_1}{1 + r_E}$$

But because for every buyer of the stock there must be a seller, *both* equations must hold, and therefore the stock price should satisfy

$$P_0 = \frac{Div_1 + P_1}{1 + r_E} \qquad (9.1)$$

In other words, as we discovered in Chapter 3, in a competitive market, buying or selling a share of stock must be a zero-NPV investment opportunity.

Dividend Yields, Capital Gains, and Total Returns

We can reinterpret Eq. 9.1 if we multiply by $(1 + r_E)$, divide by P_0, and subtract 1 from both sides:

Total Return

$$r_E = \frac{Div_1 + P_1}{P_0} - 1 = \underbrace{\frac{Div_1}{P_0}}_{\text{Dividend Yield}} + \underbrace{\frac{P_1 - P_0}{P_0}}_{\text{Capital Gain Rate}} \qquad (9.2)$$

The first term on the right side of Eq. 9.2 is the stock's **dividend yield**, which is the expected annual dividend of the stock divided by its current price. The dividend yield is the percentage return the investor expects to earn from the dividend paid by the stock. The second term on the right side of Eq. 9.2 reflects the **capital gain** the investor will earn on the stock, which is the difference between the expected sale price and purchase price for the stock, $P_1 - P_0$. We divide the capital gain by the current stock price to express the capital gain as a percentage return, called the **capital gain rate**.

The sum of the dividend yield and the capital gain rate is called the **total return** of the stock. The total return is the expected return that the investor will earn for a one-year investment in the stock. Thus, Eq. 9.2 states that the stock's total return should equal the equity cost of capital. In other words, *the expected total return of the stock should equal the expected return of other investments available in the market with equivalent risk.*

EXAMPLE 9.1

Stock Prices and Returns

Problem

Suppose you expect Walgreen Company (a drugstore chain) to pay dividends of $0.44 per share and trade for $33 per share at the end of the year. If investments with equivalent risk to Walgreen's stock have an expected return of 8.5%, what is the most you would pay today for Walgreen's stock? What dividend yield and capital gain rate would you expect at this price?

Solution

Using Eq. 9.1, we have

$$P_0 = \frac{Div_1 + P_1}{1 + r_E} = \frac{0.44 + 33.00}{1.085} = \$30.82$$

At this price, Walgreen's dividend yield is $Div_1/P_0 = 0.44/30.82 = 1.43\%$. The expected capital gain is $33.00 - \$30.82 = \$2.18$ per share, for a capital gain rate of $2.18/30.82 = 7.07\%$. Therefore, at this price, Walgreen's expected total return is $1.43\% + 7.07\% = 8.5\%$, which is equal to its equity cost of capital.

The Mechanics of a Short Sale

If a stock's expected total return is below that of other investments with comparable risk, investors who own the stock will choose to sell it and invest elsewhere. But what if you don't own the stock—can you profit in this situation?

The answer is yes, by short selling the stock. To short sell a stock, you must contact your broker, who will try to borrow the stock from someone who currently owns it.* Suppose John Doe holds the stock in a brokerage account. Your broker can lend you shares from his account so that you can sell them in the market at the current stock price. Of course, at some point you must close the short sale by buying the shares in the market and returning them to Doe's account. In the meantime, so that John Doe is not made worse off by lending his shares to you, you must pay him any dividends the stock pays.**

The following table compares the cash flows from buying with those from short-selling a stock:

	Date 0	Date t	Date 1
Cash flows from buying a stock	$-P_0$	$+Div_t$	$+P_1$
Cash flows from short-selling a stock	$+P_0$	$-Div_t$	$-P_1$

When you short sell a stock, first you receive the current share price. Then, while your short position remains open, you must pay any dividends made. Finally, you must pay the future stock price to close your position. These cash flows are exactly the reverse of those from buying a stock.

Because the cash flows are reversed, if you short sell a stock, rather than receiving its return, you must *pay* its return to the person you borrowed the stock from. But if this return is less than you expect to earn by investing your money in an alternative investment with equivalent risk, the strategy has a positive NPV and is attractive[†] (We will discuss such strategies further in Chapter 11.)

In practice, short sales typically reflect a desire of some investors to bet against the stock. For example, in July 2008, Washington Mutual stood on the verge of bankruptcy as a result of its exposure to subprime mortgages. Even though its stock price had fallen by more than 90% in the prior year, many investors apparently felt the stock was still not attractive—the **short interest** (number of shares sold short) in Washington Mutual exceeded 500 million, representing more than 50% of Washington Mutual's outstanding shares.

The Cash Flows Associated with a Short Sale

P_0 is the initial price of the stock, P_1 is the price of the stock when the short sale is closed, and Div_t are dividends paid by the stock at any date t between 0 and 1.

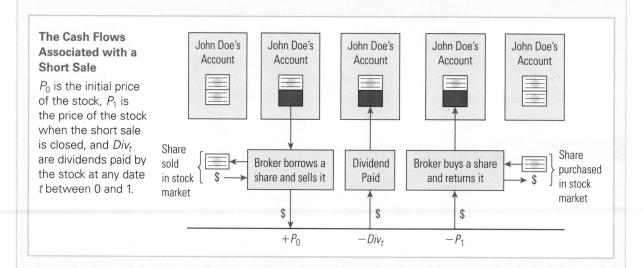

*Selling a stock without first locating a share to borrow is known as a *naked short sale*, and is prohibited by the SEC.

**In practice, John Doe need not know you borrowed his shares. He continues to receive dividends, and if he needs the shares, the broker will replace them either by (1) borrowing shares from someone else or (2) forcing the short-seller to close his position and buy the shares in the market.

†Typically, the broker will charge a fee for finding the shares to borrow, and require the short-seller to deposit collateral guaranteeing the short-seller's ability to buy the stock later. These costs of shorting tend to be small except in unusual circumstances.

The result in Eq. 9.2 is what we should expect: The firm must pay its shareholders a return commensurate with the return they can earn elsewhere while taking the same risk. If the stock offered a higher return than other securities with the same risk, investors would sell those other investments and buy the stock instead. This activity would drive up the stock's current price, lowering its dividend yield and capital gain rate until Eq. 9.2 holds true. If the stock offered a lower expected return, investors would sell the stock and drive down its current price until Eq. 9.2 was again satisfied.

A Multiyear Investor

Eq. 9.1 depends upon the expected stock price in one year, P_1. But suppose we planned to hold the stock for two years. Then we would receive dividends in both year 1 and year 2 before selling the stock, as shown in the following timeline:

$$
\begin{array}{ccccc}
0 & & 1 & & 2 \\
\vdash & & \vdash & & \dashv \\
-P_0 & & Div_1 & & Div_2 + P_2
\end{array}
$$

Setting the stock price equal to the present value of the future cash flows in this case implies[1]

$$P_0 = \frac{Div_1}{1 + r_E} + \frac{Div_2 + P_2}{(1 + r_E)^2} \tag{9.3}$$

Eqs. 9.1 and 9.3 are different: As a two-year investor we care about the dividend and stock price in year 2, but these terms do not appear in Eq. 9.1. Does this difference imply that a two-year investor will value the stock differently than a one-year investor?

The answer to this question is no. While a one-year investor does not care about the dividend and stock price in year 2 directly, she will care about them indirectly because they will affect the price for which she can sell the stock at the end of year 1. For example, suppose the investor sells the stock to another one-year investor with the same beliefs. The new investor will expect to receive the dividend and stock price at the end of year 2, so he will be willing to pay

$$P_1 = \frac{Div_2 + P_2}{1 + r_E}$$

for the stock. Substituting this expression for P_1 into Eq. 9.1, we get the same result as shown in Eq. 9.3:

$$P_0 = \frac{Div_1 + P_1}{1 + r_E} = \frac{Div_1}{1 + r_E} + \frac{1}{1 + r_E} \overbrace{\left(\frac{Div_2 + P_2}{1 + r_E} \right)}^{P_1}$$

$$= \frac{Div_1}{1 + r_E} + \frac{Div_2 + P_2}{(1 + r_E)^2}$$

---

[1]By using the same equity cost of capital for both periods, we are assuming that the equity cost of capital does not depend on the term of the cash flows. Otherwise, we would need to adjust for the term structure of the equity cost of capital (as we did with the yield curve for risk-free cash flows in Chapter 5). This step would complicate the analysis but would not change the results.

Thus, the formula for the stock price for a two-year investor is the same as the one for a sequence of two one-year investors.

The Dividend-Discount Model Equation

We can continue this process for any number of years by replacing the final stock price with the value that the next holder of the stock would be willing to pay. Doing so leads to the general **dividend-discount model** for the stock price, where the horizon N is arbitrary:

Dividend-Discount Model

$$P_0 = \frac{Div_1}{1 + r_E} + \frac{Div_2}{(1 + r_E)^2} + \cdots + \frac{Div_N}{(1 + r_E)^N} + \frac{P_N}{(1 + r_E)^N} \tag{9.4}$$

Eq. 9.4 applies to a single N-year investor, who will collect dividends for N years and then sell the stock, or to a series of investors who hold the stock for shorter periods and then resell it. Note that Eq. 9.4 holds for *any* horizon N. Thus, all investors (with the same beliefs) will attach the same value to the stock, independent of their investment horizons. How long they intend to hold the stock and whether they collect their return in the form of dividends or capital gains is irrelevant. For the special case in which the firm eventually pays dividends and is never acquired, it is possible to hold the shares forever. Consequently, we can let N go to infinity in Eq. 9.4 and write it as follows:

$$P_0 = \frac{Div_1}{1 + r_E} + \frac{Div_2}{(1 + r_E)^2} + \frac{Div_3}{(1 + r_E)^3} + \cdots = \sum_{n=1}^{\infty} \frac{Div_n}{(1 + r_E)^n} \tag{9.5}$$

That is, *the price of the stock is equal to the present value of the expected future dividends it will pay.*

CONCEPT CHECK

1. How do you calculate the total return of a stock?
2. What discount rate do you use to discount the future cash flows of a stock?
3. Why will a short-term and long-term investor with the same beliefs be willing to pay the same price for a stock?

9.2 Applying the Dividend-Discount Model

Eq. 9.5 expresses the value of the stock in terms of the expected future dividends the firm will pay. Of course, estimating these dividends—especially for the distant future—is difficult. A common approximation is to assume that in the long run, dividends will grow at a constant rate. In this section, we will consider the implications of this assumption for stock prices and explore the trade-off between dividends and growth.

Constant Dividend Growth

The simplest forecast for the firm's future dividends states that they will grow at a constant rate, g, forever. That case yields the following timeline for the cash flows for an investor who buys the stock today and holds it:

Because the expected dividends are a constant growth perpetuity, we can use Eq. 4.11 to calculate their present value. We then obtain the following simple formula for the stock price:[2]

Constant Dividend Growth Model

$$P_0 = \frac{Div_1}{r_E - g} \tag{9.6}$$

According to the **constant dividend growth model**, the value of the firm depends on the dividend level for the coming year, divided by the equity cost of capital adjusted by the expected growth rate of dividends.

EXAMPLE 9.2 **Valuing a Firm with Constant Dividend Growth**

Problem

Consolidated Edison, Inc. (Con Edison), is a regulated utility company that services the New York City area. Suppose Con Edison plans to pay $2.36 per share in dividends in the coming year. If its equity cost of capital is 7.5% and dividends are expected to grow by 1.5% per year in the future, estimate the value of Con Edison's stock.

Solution

If dividends are expected to grow perpetually at a rate of 1.5% per year, we can use Eq. 9.6 to calculate the price of a share of Con Edison stock:

$$P_0 = \frac{Div_1}{r_E - g} = \frac{\$2.36}{0.075 - 0.015} = \$39.33$$

For another interpretation of Eq. 9.6, note that we can rearrange it as follows:

$$r_E = \frac{Div_1}{P_0} + g \tag{9.7}$$

Comparing Eq. 9.7 with Eq. 9.2, we see that g equals the expected capital gain rate. In other words, with constant expected dividend growth, the expected growth rate of the share price matches the growth rate of dividends.

Dividends Versus Investment and Growth

In Eq. 9.6, the firm's share price increases with the current dividend level, Div_1, and the expected growth rate, g. To maximize its share price, a firm would like to increase both these quantities. Often, however, the firm faces a trade-off: Increasing growth may require investment, and money spent on investment cannot be used to pay dividends. We can use the constant dividend growth model to gain insight into this trade-off.

---

[2]As we discussed in Chapter 4, this formula requires that $g < r_E$. Otherwise, the present value of the growing perpetuity is infinite. The implication here is that it is impossible for a stock's dividends to grow at a rate $g > r_E$ *forever*. If the growth rate exceeds r_E, it must be temporary, and the constant growth model does not apply.

John Burr Williams' *Theory of Investment Value*

The first formal derivation of the dividend-discount model appeared in the *Theory of Investment Value*, written by John Burr Williams in 1938. The book was an important landmark in the history of corporate finance, because Williams demonstrated for the first time that corporate finance relied on certain principles that could be derived using formal analytical methods. As Williams wrote in the preface:

The truth is that the mathematical method is a new tool of great power whose use promises to lead to notable advances in Investment Analysis. Always it has been the rule in the history of science that the invention of new tools is the key to new discoveries, and we may expect the same rule to hold true in this branch of Economics as well.

Williams' book was not widely appreciated in its day—indeed, legend has it there was a lively debate at Harvard over whether it was acceptable as his Ph.D. dissertation. But Williams went on to become a very successful investor, and by the time he died in 1989, the importance of the mathematical method in corporate finance was indisputable, and the discoveries that resulted from this "new" tool had fundamentally changed its practice. Today, Williams is regarded as the founder of fundamental analysis, and his book pioneered the use of *pro forma* modeling of financial statements and cash flows for valuation purposes, as well as many other ideas now central to modern finance (see Chapter 14 for further contributions).

A Simple Model of Growth. What determines the rate of growth of a firm's dividends? If we define a firm's **dividend payout rate** as the fraction of its earnings that the firm pays as dividends each year, then we can write the firm's dividend per share at date t as follows:

$$Div_t = \underbrace{\frac{\text{Earnings}_t}{\text{Shares Outstanding}_t}}_{EPS_t} \times \text{Dividend Payout Rate}_t \tag{9.8}$$

That is, the dividend each year is the firm's earnings per share (EPS) multiplied by its dividend payout rate. Thus the firm can increase its dividend in three ways:

1. It can increase its earnings (net income).
2. It can increase its dividend payout rate.
3. It can decrease its shares outstanding.

Let's suppose for now that the firm does not issue new shares (or buy back its existing shares), so that the number of shares outstanding is fixed, and explore the trade-off between options 1 and 2.

A firm can do one of two things with its earnings: It can pay them out to investors, or it can retain and reinvest them. By investing cash today, a firm can increase its future dividends. For simplicity, let's assume that if no investment is made, the firm does not grow, so the current level of earnings generated by the firm remains constant. If all increases in future earnings result exclusively from new investment made with retained earnings, then

$$\text{Change in Earnings} = \text{New Investment} \times \text{Return on New Investment} \tag{9.9}$$

New investment equals earnings multiplied by the firm's **retention rate**, the fraction of current earnings that the firm retains:

$$\text{New Investment} = \text{Earnings} \times \text{Retention Rate} \tag{9.10}$$

Substituting Eq. 9.10 into Eq. 9.9 and dividing by earnings gives an expression for the growth rate of earnings:

$$\text{Earnings Growth Rate} = \frac{\text{Change in Earnings}}{\text{Earnings}}$$

$$= \text{Retention Rate} \times \text{Return on New Investment} \qquad (9.11)$$

If the firm chooses to keep its dividend payout rate constant, then the growth in dividends will equal growth of earnings:

$$g = \text{Retention Rate} \times \text{Return on New Investment} \qquad (9.12)$$

Profitable Growth. Eq. 9.12 shows that a firm can increase its growth rate by retaining more of its earnings. However, if the firm retains more earnings, it will be able to pay out less of those earnings and, according to Eq. 9.8, will have to reduce its dividend. If a firm wants to increase its share price, should it cut its dividend and invest more, or should it cut investment and increase its dividend? Not surprisingly, the answer will depend on the profitability of the firm's investments. Let's consider an example.

EXAMPLE 9.3	**Cutting Dividends for Profitable Growth**

Problem

Crane Sporting Goods expects to have earnings per share of $6 in the coming year. Rather than reinvest these earnings and grow, the firm plans to pay out all of its earnings as a dividend. With these expectations of no growth, Crane's current share price is $60.

Suppose Crane could cut its dividend payout rate to 75% for the foreseeable future and use the retained earnings to open new stores. The return on its investment in these stores is expected to be 12%. Assuming its equity cost of capital is unchanged, what effect would this new policy have on Crane's stock price?

Solution

First, let's estimate Crane's equity cost of capital. Currently, Crane plans to pay a dividend equal to its earnings of $6 per share. Given a share price of $60, Crane's dividend yield is $6/$60 = 10%. With no expected growth ($g = 0$), we can use Eq. 9.7 to estimate r_E:

$$r_E = \frac{Div_1}{P_0} + g = 10\% + 0\% = 10\%$$

In other words, to justify Crane's stock price under its current policy, the expected return of other stocks in the market with equivalent risk must be 10%.

Next, we consider the consequences of the new policy. If Crane reduces its dividend payout rate to 75%, then from Eq. 9.8 its dividend this coming year will fall to $Div_1 = EPS_1 \times 75\% = \$6 \times 75\% = \$4.50$. At the same time, because the firm will now retain 25% of its earnings to invest in new stores, from Eq. 9.12 its growth rate will increase to

$$g = \text{Retention Rate} \times \text{Return on New Investment} = 25\% \times 12\% = 3\%$$

Assuming Crane can continue to grow at this rate, we can compute its share price under the new policy using the constant dividend growth model of Eq. 9.6:

$$P_0 = \frac{Div_1}{r_E - g} = \frac{\$4.50}{0.10 - 0.03} = \$64.29$$

Thus, Crane's share price should rise from $60 to $64.29 if it cuts its dividend to increase investment and growth, implying the investment has positive NPV. By using its earnings to invest in projects that offer a rate of return (12%) greater than its equity cost of capital (10%), Crane has created value for its shareholders.

In Example 9.3, cutting the firm's dividend in favor of growth raised the firm's stock price. But this is not always the case, as the next example demonstrates.

EXAMPLE 9.4

Unprofitable Growth

Problem

Suppose Crane Sporting Goods decides to cut its dividend payout rate to 75% to invest in new stores, as in Example 9.3. But now suppose that the return on these new investments is 8%, rather than 12%. Given its expected earnings per share this year of $6 and its equity cost of capital of 10%, what will happen to Crane's current share price in this case?

Solution

Just as in Example 9.3, Crane's dividend will fall to $6 \times 75\% = \$4.50$. Its growth rate under the new policy, given the lower return on new investment, will now be $g = 25\% \times 8\% = 2\%$. The new share price is therefore

$$P_0 = \frac{Div_1}{r_E - g} = \frac{\$4.50}{0.10 - 0.02} = \$56.25$$

Thus, even though Crane will grow under the new policy, the new investments have negative NPV. Crane's share price will fall if it cuts its dividend to make new investments with a return of only 8% when its investors can earn 10% on other investments with comparable risk.

Comparing Example 9.3 with Example 9.4, we see that the effect of cutting the firm's dividend to grow crucially depends on the return on new investment. In Example 9.3, the return on new investment of 12% exceeds the firm's equity cost of capital of 10%, so the investment has a positive NPV. In Example 9.4, the return on new investment is only 8%, so the new investment has a negative NPV (even though it will lead to earnings growth). Thus, *cutting the firm's dividend to increase investment will raise the stock price if, and only if, the new investments have a positive NPV.*

Changing Growth Rates

Successful young firms often have very high initial earnings growth rates. During this period of high growth, firms often retain 100% of their earnings to exploit profitable investment opportunities. As they mature, their growth slows to rates more typical of established companies. At that point, their earnings exceed their investment needs and they begin to pay dividends.

We cannot use the constant dividend growth model to value the stock of such a firm, for several reasons. First, these firms often pay *no* dividends when they are young. Second, their growth rate continues to change over time until they mature. However, we can use the general form of the dividend-discount model to value such a firm by applying the constant growth model to calculate the future share price of the stock P_N once the firm matures and its expected growth rate stabilizes:

Specifically, if the firm is expected to grow at a long-term rate g after year $N + 1$, then from the constant dividend growth model:

$$P_N = \frac{Div_{N+1}}{r_E - g} \qquad (9.13)$$

We can then use this estimate of P_N as a terminal (continuation) value in the dividend-discount model. Combining Eq. 9.4 with Eq. 9.13, we have

Dividend-Discount Model with Constant Long-Term Growth

$$P_0 = \frac{Div_1}{1 + r_E} + \frac{Div_2}{(1 + r_E)^2} + \cdots + \frac{Div_N}{(1 + r_E)^N} + \frac{1}{(1 + r_E)^N}\left(\frac{Div_{N+1}}{r_E - g}\right) \qquad (9.14)$$

EXAMPLE 9.5

Valuing a Firm with Two Different Growth Rates

Problem

Small Fry, Inc., has just invented a potato chip that looks and tastes like a french fry. Given the phenomenal market response to this product, Small Fry is reinvesting all of its earnings to expand its operations. Earnings were $2 per share this past year and are expected to grow at a rate of 20% per year until the end of year 4. At that point, other companies are likely to bring out competing products. Analysts project that at the end of year 4, Small Fry will cut investment and begin paying 60% of its earnings as dividends and its growth will slow to a long-run rate of 4%. If Small Fry's equity cost of capital is 8%, what is the value of a share today?

Solution

We can use Small Fry's projected earnings growth rate and payout rate to forecast its future earnings and dividends as shown in the following spreadsheet:

Year	0	1	2	3	4	5	6
Earnings							
1 EPS Growth Rate (versus prior year)		20%	20%	20%	20%	4%	4%
2 EPS	$2.00	$2.40	$2.88	$3.46	$4.15	$4.31	$4.49
Dividends							
3 Dividend Payout Rate		0%	0%	0%	60%	60%	60%
4 Dividend		$ —	$ —	$ —	$2.49	$2.59	$2.69

Starting from $2.00 in year 0, EPS grows by 20% per year until year 4, after which growth slows to 4%. Small Fry's dividend payout rate is zero until year 4, when competition reduces its investment opportunities and its payout rate rises to 60%. Multiplying EPS by the dividend payout ratio, we project Small Fry's future dividends in line 4.

From year 4 onward, Small Fry's dividends will grow at the expected long-run rate of 4% per year. Thus, we can use the constant dividend growth model to project Small Fry's share price at the end of year 3. Given its equity cost of capital of 8%,

$$P_3 = \frac{Div_4}{r_E - g} = \frac{\$2.49}{0.08 - 0.04} = \$62.25$$

We then apply the dividend-discount model (Eq. 9.4) with this terminal value:

$$P_0 = \frac{Div_1}{1 + r_E} + \frac{Div_2}{(1 + r_E)^2} + \frac{Div_3}{(1 + r_E)^3} + \frac{P_3}{(1 + r_E)^3} = \frac{\$62.25}{(1.08)^3} = \$49.42$$

As this example illustrates, the dividend-discount model is flexible enough to handle any forecasted pattern of dividends.

Limitations of the Dividend-Discount Model

The dividend-discount model values the stock based on a forecast of the future dividends paid to shareholders. But unlike a Treasury bond, whose cash flows are known with virtual certainty, a tremendous amount of uncertainty is associated with any forecast of a firm's future dividends.

Let's consider the example of Kenneth Cole Productions (KCP), mentioned in the introduction to this chapter. In early 2006, KCP paid annual dividends of $0.72. With an equity cost of capital of 11% and expected dividend growth of 8%, the constant dividend growth model implies a share price for KCP of

$$P_0 = \frac{Div_1}{r_E - g} = \frac{\$0.72}{0.11 - 0.08} = \$24$$

which is reasonably close to the $26.75 share price the stock had at the time. With a 10% dividend growth rate, however, this estimate would rise to $72 per share; with a 5% dividend growth rate, the estimate falls to $12 per share. As we see, even small changes in the assumed dividend growth rate can lead to large changes in the estimated stock price.

Furthermore, it is difficult to know which estimate of the dividend growth rate is more reasonable. KCP more than doubled its dividend between 2003 and 2005, but earnings remained relatively flat during that time. Consequently, this rapid rate of dividend growth was not likely to be sustained. Forecasting dividends requires forecasting the firm's earnings, dividend payout rate, and future share count. But future earnings depend on interest expenses (which in turn depend on how much the firm borrows), and the firm's share count and dividend payout rate depend on whether the firm uses a portion of its earnings to repurchase shares. Because borrowing and repurchase decisions are at management's discretion, they can be difficult to forecast reliably.[3] We look at two alternative methods that avoid some of these difficulties in the next section.

CONCEPT CHECK

1. In what three ways can a firm increase its future dividend per share?

2. Under what circumstances can a firm increase its share price by cutting its dividend and investing more?

9.3 Total Payout and Free Cash Flow Valuation Models

In this section, we outline two alternative approaches to valuing the firm's shares that avoid some of the difficulties of the dividend-discount model. First, we consider the *total payout model*, which allows us to ignore the firm's choice between dividends and share repurchases. Then, we consider the *discounted free cash flow model*, which focuses on the cash flows to all of the firm's investors, both debt and equity holders, allowing us to avoid estimating the impact of the firm's borrowing decisions on earnings.

Share Repurchases and the Total Payout Model

In our discussion of the dividend-discount model, we implicitly assumed that any cash paid out by the firm to shareholders takes the form of a dividend. However, in recent years, an increasing number of firms have replaced dividend payouts with *share repurchases*. In a

---

[3]We discuss management's decision to borrow funds or repurchase shares in Part 5.

share repurchase, the firm uses excess cash to buy back its own stock. Share repurchases have two consequences for the dividend-discount model. First, the more cash the firm uses to repurchase shares, the less it has available to pay dividends. Second, by repurchasing shares, the firm decreases its share count, which increases its earnings and dividends on a per-share basis.

In the dividend-discount model, we valued a share from the perspective of a single shareholder, discounting the dividends the shareholder will receive:

$$P_0 = PV(\text{Future Dividends per Share}) \tag{9.15}$$

An alternative method that may be more reliable when a firm repurchases shares is the **total payout model**, which values *all* of the firm's equity, rather than a single share. To do so, we discount the total payouts that the firm makes to shareholders, which is the total amount spent on both dividends *and* share repurchases.[4] Then, we divide by the current number of shares outstanding to determine the share price.

Total Payout Model

$$P_0 = \frac{PV(\text{Future Total Dividends and Repurchases})}{\text{Shares Outstanding}_0} \tag{9.16}$$

We can apply the same simplifications that we obtained by assuming constant growth in Section 9.2 to the total payout method. The only change is that *we discount total dividends and share repurchases and use the growth rate of total earnings (rather than earnings per share) when forecasting the growth of the firm's total payouts*. This method can be more reliable and easier to apply when the firm uses share repurchases.

EXAMPLE 9.6   **Valuation with Share Repurchases**

Problem

Titan Industries has 217 million shares outstanding and expects earnings at the end of this year of $860 million. Titan plans to pay out 50% of its earnings in total, paying 30% as a dividend and using 20% to repurchase shares. If Titan's earnings are expected to grow by 7.5% per year and these payout rates remain constant, determine Titan's share price assuming an equity cost of capital of 10%.

Solution

Titan will have total payouts this year of 50% × $860 million = $430 million. Based on the equity cost of capital of 10% and an expected earnings growth rate of 7.5%, the present value of Titan's future payouts can be computed as a constant growth perpetuity:

$$PV(\text{Future Total Dividends and Repurchases}) = \frac{\$430 \text{ million}}{0.10 - 0.075} = \$17.2 \text{ billion}$$

This present value represents the total value of Titan's equity (i.e., its market capitalization). To compute the share price, we divide by the current number of shares outstanding:

$$P_0 = \frac{\$17.2 \text{ billion}}{217 \text{ million shares}} = \$79.26 \text{ per share}$$

---

[4]Think of the total payouts as the amount you would receive if you owned 100% of the firm's shares: You would receive all of the dividends, plus the proceeds from selling shares back to the firm in the share repurchase.

Using the total payout method, we did not need to know the firm's split between dividends and share repurchases. To compare this method with the dividend-discount model, note that Titan will pay a dividend of $30\% \times \$860$ million/(217 million shares) = $1.19 per share, for a dividend yield of $1.19/79.26 = 1.50\%$. From Eq. 9.7, Titan's expected EPS, dividend, and share price growth rate is $g = r_E - Div_1/P_0 = 8.50\%$. These "per share" growth rates exceed the 7.5% growth rate of total earnings because Titan's share count will decline over time due to share repurchases.[5]

The Discounted Free Cash Flow Model

In the total payout model, we first value the firm's equity, rather than just a single share. The **discounted free cash flow model** goes one step further and begins by determining the total value of the firm to all investors—both equity *and* debt holders. That is, we begin by estimating the firm's enterprise value, which we defined in Chapter 2 as[6]

$$\text{Enterprise Value} = \text{Market Value of Equity} + \text{Debt} - \text{Cash} \quad (9.17)$$

The enterprise value is the value of the firm's underlying business, unencumbered by debt and separate from any cash or marketable securities. We can interpret the enterprise value as the net cost of acquiring the firm's equity, taking its cash, paying off all debt, and thus owning the unlevered business. The advantage of the discounted free cash flow model is that it allows us to value a firm without explicitly forecasting its dividends, share repurchases, or its use of debt.

Valuing the Enterprise. How can we estimate a firm's enterprise value? To estimate the value of the firm's equity, we computed the present value of the firm's total payouts to equity holders. Likewise, to estimate a firm's enterprise value, we compute the present value of the *free cash flow* (FCF) that the firm has available to pay all investors, both debt and equity holders. We saw how to compute the free cash flow for a project in Chapter 8; we now perform the same calculation for the entire firm:

$$\text{Free Cash Flow} = \overbrace{EBIT \times (1 - \tau_c)}^{\text{Unlevered Net Income}} + \text{Depreciation}$$

$$- \text{Capital Expenditures} - \text{Increases in Net Working Capital} \quad (9.18)$$

When we are looking at the entire firm, it is natural to define the firm's **net investment** as its capital expenditures in excess of depreciation:

$$\text{Net Investment} = \text{Capital Expenditures} - \text{Depreciation} \quad (9.19)$$

We can loosely interpret net investment as investment intended to support the firm's growth, above and beyond the level needed to maintain the firm's existing capital. With that definition, we can also write the free cash flow formula as

---

[5]The difference in the per share and total earnings growth rate results from Titan's "repurchase yield" of $(20\% \times \$860$ million/217 million shares)/($79.26/share) = 1%. Indeed, given an expected share price of $79.26 \times 1.085 = \$86.00$ next year, Titan will repurchase $20\% \times \$860$ million ÷ ($86 per share) = 2 million shares next year. With the decline in the number of shares from 217 million to 215 million, EPS grows by a factor of $1.075 \times (217/215) = 1.085$ or 8.5%.

[6]To be precise, by cash we are referring to the firm's cash in excess of its working capital needs, which is the amount of cash it has invested at a competitive market interest rate.

$$\text{Free Cash Flow} = EBIT \times (1 - \tau_c) - \text{Net Investment}$$
$$- \text{Increases in Net Working Capital} \qquad (9.20)$$

Free cash flow measures the cash generated by the firm before any payments to debt or equity holders are considered.

Thus, just as we determine the value of a project by calculating the NPV of the project's free cash flow, we estimate a firm's current enterprise value V_0 by computing the present value of the firm's free cash flow:

Discounted Free Cash Flow Model

$$V_0 = PV(\text{Future Free Cash Flow of Firm}) \qquad (9.21)$$

Given the enterprise value, we can estimate the share price by using Eq. 9.17 to solve for the value of equity and then divide by the total number of shares outstanding:

$$P_0 = \frac{V_0 + \text{Cash}_0 - \text{Debt}_0}{\text{Shares Outstanding}_0} \qquad (9.22)$$

Intuitively, the difference between the discounted free cash flow model and the dividend-discount model is that in the dividend-discount model, the firm's cash and debt are included indirectly through the effect of interest income and expenses on earnings. In the discounted free cash flow model, we ignore interest income and expenses (free cash flow is based on EBIT), but then adjust for cash and debt directly in Eq. 9.22.

Implementing the Model. A key difference between the discounted free cash flow model and the earlier models we have considered is the discount rate. In previous calculations we used the firm's equity cost of capital, r_E, because we were discounting the cash flows to equity holders. Here we are discounting the free cash flow that will be paid to both debt and equity holders. Thus, we should use the firm's **weighted average cost of capital (WACC)**, denoted by r_{wacc}, which is the average cost of capital the firm must pay to all of its investors, both debt and equity holders. If the firm has no debt, then $r_{wacc} = r_E$. But when a firm has debt, r_{wacc} is an average of the firm's debt and equity cost of capital. In that case, because debt is generally less risky than equity, r_{wacc} is generally less than r_E. We can also interpret the WACC as reflecting the average risk of all of the firm's investments. We'll develop methods to calculate the WACC explicitly in Parts 4 and 5.

Given the firm's weighted average cost of capital, we implement the discounted free cash flow model in much the same way as we did the dividend-discount model. That is, we forecast the firm's free cash flow up to some horizon, together with a terminal (continuation) value of the enterprise:

$$V_0 = \frac{FCF_1}{1 + r_{wacc}} + \frac{FCF_2}{(1 + r_{wacc})^2} + \cdots + \frac{FCF_N + V_N}{(1 + r_{wacc})^N} \qquad (9.23)$$

Often, the terminal value is estimated by assuming a constant long-run growth rate g_{FCF} for free cash flows beyond year N, so that

$$V_N = \frac{FCF_{N+1}}{r_{wacc} - g_{FCF}} = \left(\frac{1 + g_{FCF}}{r_{wacc} - g_{FCF}} \right) \times FCF_N \qquad (9.24)$$

The long-run growth rate g_{FCF} is typically based on the expected long-run growth rate of the firm's revenues.

EXAMPLE 9.7	**Valuing Kenneth Cole Using Free Cash Flow**

Problem

Kenneth Cole (KCP) had sales of $518 million in 2005. Suppose you expect its sales to grow at a 9% rate in 2006, but that this growth rate will slow by 1% per year to a long-run growth rate for the apparel industry of 4% by 2011. Based on KCP's past profitability and investment needs, you expect EBIT to be 9% of sales, increases in net working capital requirements to be 10% of any increase in sales, and net investment (capital expenditures in excess of depreciation) to be 8% of any increase in sales. If KCP has $100 million in cash, $3 million in debt, 21 million shares outstanding, a tax rate of 37%, and a weighted average cost of capital of 11%, what is your estimate of the value of KCP's stock in early 2006?

Solution

Using Eq. 9.20, we can estimate KCP's future free cash flow based on the estimates above as follows:

Year	2005	2006	2007	2008	2009	2010	2011
FCF Forecast ($ millions)							
1 Sales	518.0	564.6	609.8	652.5	691.6	726.2	755.3
2 *Growth versus Prior Year*		*9.0%*	*8.0%*	*7.0%*	*6.0%*	*5.0%*	*4.0%*
3 **EBIT** (9% of sales)		50.8	54.9	58.7	62.2	65.4	68.0
4 Less: Income Tax (37% EBIT)		(18.8)	(20.3)	(21.7)	(23.0)	(24.2)	(25.1)
5 Less: Net Investment (8% ΔSales)		(3.7)	(3.6)	(3.4)	(3.1)	(2.8)	(2.3)
6 Less: Inc. in NWC (10% ΔSales)		(4.7)	(4.5)	(4.3)	(3.9)	(3.5)	(2.9)
7 **Free Cash Flow**		23.6	26.4	29.3	32.2	35.0	37.6

Because we expect KCP's free cash flow to grow at a constant rate after 2011, we can use Eq. 9.24 to compute a terminal enterprise value:

$$V_{2011} = \left(\frac{1 + g_{FCF}}{r_{wacc} - g_{FCF}}\right) \times FCF_{2011} = \left(\frac{1.04}{0.11 - 0.04}\right) \times 37.6 = \$558.6 \text{ million}$$

From Eq. 9.23, KCP's current enterprise value is the present value of its free cash flows plus the terminal enterprise value:

$$V_0 = \frac{23.6}{1.11} + \frac{26.4}{1.11^2} + \frac{29.3}{1.11^3} + \frac{32.2}{1.11^4} + \frac{35.0}{1.11^5} + \frac{37.6 + 558.6}{1.11^6} = \$424.8 \text{ million}$$

We can now estimate the value of a share of KCP's stock using Eq. 9.22:

$$P_0 = \frac{424.8 + 100 - 3}{21} = \$24.85$$

Connection to Capital Budgeting. There is an important connection between the discounted free cash flow model and the NPV rule for capital budgeting that we developed in Chapter 8. Because the firm's free cash flow is equal to the sum of the free cash flows from the firm's current and future investments, we can interpret the firm's enterprise value as the total NPV that the firm will earn from continuing its existing projects and initiating new ones. Hence, the NPV of any individual project represents its contribution to the firm's enterprise value. To maximize the firm's share price, we should accept projects that have a positive NPV.

Recall also from Chapter 8 that many forecasts and estimates were necessary to estimate the free cash flows of a project. The same is true for the firm: We must forecast future sales, operating expenses, taxes, capital requirements, and other factors. On the one hand, estimating free cash flow in this way gives us flexibility to incorporate many specific details about the future prospects of the firm. On the other hand, some uncertainty inevitably surrounds each assumption. It is therefore important to conduct a sensitivity analysis, as we described in Chapter 8, to translate this uncertainty into a range of potential values for the stock.

EXAMPLE 9.8	Sensitivity Analysis for Stock Valuation

Problem

In Example 9.7, KCP's revenue growth rate was assumed to be 9% in 2006, slowing to a long-term growth rate of 4%. How would your estimate of the stock's value change if you expected revenue growth of 4% from 2006 on? How would it change if in addition you expected EBIT to be 7% of sales, rather than 9%?

Solution

With 4% revenue growth and a 9% EBIT margin, KCP will have 2006 revenues of 518×1.04 = \$538.7 million, and EBIT of 9%(538.7) = \$48.5 million. Given the increase in sales of $538.7 - 518.0 = \$20.7$ million, we expect net investment of 8%(20.7) = \$1.7 million and additional net working capital of 10%(20.7) = \$2.1 million. Thus, KCP's expected FCF in 2006 is

$$FCF_{06} = 48.5 \ (1 - .37) - 1.7 - 2.1 = \$26.8 \text{ million}$$

Because growth is expected to remain constant at 4%, we can estimate KCP's enterprise value as a growing perpetuity:

$$V_0 = \$26.8/(0.11 - 0.04) = \$383 \text{ million}$$

for an initial share value of $P_0 = (383 + 100 - 3)/21 = \$22.86$. Thus, comparing this result with that of Example 9.7, we see that a higher initial revenue growth of 9% versus 4% contributes about \$2 to the value of KCP's stock.

If, in addition, we expect KCP's EBIT margin to be only 7%, our FCF estimate would decline to

$$FCF_{06} = (.07 \times 538.7)(1 - .37) - 1.7 - 2.1 = \$20.0 \text{ million}$$

for an enterprise value of $V_0 = \$20/(0.11 - 0.04) = \$286$ million and a share value of $P_0 = (286 + 100 - 3)/21 = \$18.24$. Thus, we can see that maintaining an EBIT margin of 9% versus 7% contributes more than \$4.50 to KCP's stock value in this scenario.

Figure 9.1 summarizes the different valuation methods we have discussed thus far. The value of the stock is determined by the present value of its future dividends. We can estimate the total market capitalization of the firm's equity from the present value of the firm's total payouts, which includes dividends and share repurchases. Finally, the present value

FIGURE 9.1	A Comparison of Discounted Cash Flow Models of Stock Valuation

By computing the present value of the firm's dividends, total payouts or free cash flows, we can estimate the value of the stock, the total value of the firm's equity, or the firm's enterprise value.

Present Value of ...	Determines the ...
Dividend Payments	Stock Price
Total Payouts (All Dividends and Repurchases)	Equity Value
Free Cash Flow (Cash available to pay all security holders)	Enterprise Value

of the firm's free cash flow, which is the cash the firm has available to make payments to equity or debt holders, determines the firm's enterprise value.

1. How does the growth rate used in the total payout model differ from the growth rate used in the dividend-discount model?

2. What is the enterprise value of the firm?

3. How can you estimate a firm's stock price based on its projected free cash flows?

9.4 Valuation Based on Comparable Firms

Thus far, we have valued a firm or its stock by considering the expected future cash flows it will provide to its owner. The Law of One Price then tells us that its value is the present value of its future cash flows, because the present value is the amount we would need to invest elsewhere in the market to replicate the cash flows with the same risk.

Another application of the Law of One Price is the method of comparables. In the **method of comparables** (or "comps"), rather than value the firm's cash flows directly, we estimate the value of the firm based on the value of other, comparable firms or investments that we expect will generate very similar cash flows in the future. For example, consider the case of a new firm that is *identical* to an existing publicly traded company. If these firms will generate identical cash flows, the Law of One Price implies that we can use the value of the existing company to determine the value of the new firm.

Of course, identical companies do not exist. Although they may be similar in many respects, even two firms in the same industry selling the same types of products are likely to be of a different size or scale. In this section, we consider ways to adjust for scale differences to use comparables to value firms with similar business, and then discuss the strengths and weaknesses of this approach.

Valuation Multiples

We can adjust for differences in scale between firms by expressing their value in terms of a **valuation multiple**, which is a ratio of the value to some measure of the firm's scale. As an analogy, consider valuing an office building. A natural measure to consider would be the price per square foot for other buildings recently sold in the area. Multiplying the size of the office building under consideration by the average price per square foot would typically provide a reasonable estimate of the building's value. We can apply this same idea to stocks, replacing square footage with some more appropriate measure of the firm's scale.

The Price-Earnings Ratio. The most common valuation multiple is the price-earnings (P/E) ratio, which we introduced in Chapter 2. A firm's P/E ratio is equal to the share price divided by its earnings per share. The intuition behind its use is that when you buy a stock, you are in a sense buying the rights to the firm's future earnings. Because differences in the scale of firms' earnings are likely to persist, you should be willing to pay proportionally more for a stock with higher current earnings. Thus, we can estimate the value of a firm's share by multiplying its current earnings per share by the average P/E ratio of comparable firms.

To interpret the P/E multiple, consider the stock price formula we derived in Eq. 9.6 for the case of constant dividend growth: $P_0 = Div_1/(r_E - g)$. If we divide both sides of this equation by EPS_1, we have the following formula:

$$\text{Forward P/E} = \frac{P_0}{EPS_1} = \frac{Div_1/EPS_1}{r_E - g} = \frac{\text{Dividend Payout Rate}}{r_E - g} \tag{9.25}$$

Eq. 9.25 provides a formula for the firm's **forward P/E**, which is the P/E multiple computed based on its **forward earnings** (expected earnings over the next twelve months). We can also compute a firm's **trailing P/E** ratio using **trailing earnings** (earnings over the prior 12 months).[7] For valuation purposes, the forward P/E is generally preferred, as we are most concerned about future earnings.[8]

Eq. 9.25 implies that if two stocks have the same payout and EPS growth rates, as well as equivalent risk (and therefore the same equity cost of capital), then they should have the same P/E. It also shows that firms and industries with high growth rates, and that generate cash well in excess of their investment needs so that they can maintain high payout rates, should have high P/E multiples.

EXAMPLE 9.9	Valuation Using the Price-Earnings Ratio

Problem

Suppose furniture manufacturer Herman Miller, Inc., has earnings per share of $1.38. If the average P/E of comparable furniture stocks is 21.3, estimate a value for Herman Miller using the P/E as a valuation multiple. What are the assumptions underlying this estimate?

Solution

We estimate a share price for Herman Miller by multiplying its EPS by the P/E of comparable firms. Thus, $P_0 = \$1.38 \times 21.3 = \$29.39$. This estimate assumes that Herman Miller will have similar future risk, payout rates, and growth rates to comparable firms in the industry.

Enterprise Value Multiples. It is also common practice to use valuation multiples based on the firm's enterprise value. As we discussed in Section 9.3, because it represents the total value of the firm's underlying business rather than just the value of equity, using the enterprise value is advantageous if we want to compare firms with different amounts of leverage.

Because the enterprise value represents the entire value of the firm before the firm pays its debt, to form an appropriate multiple, we divide it by a measure of earnings or cash flows before interest payments are made. Common multiples to consider are enterprise value to EBIT, EBITDA (earnings before interest, taxes, depreciation, and amortization), and free cash flow. However, because capital expenditures can vary substantially from period to period (e.g., a firm may need to add capacity and build a new plant one year, but then not need to expand further for many years), most practitioners rely on enterprise value to EBITDA multiples. From Eq. 9.24, if expected free cash flow growth is constant, then

$$\frac{V_0}{EBITDA_1} = \frac{FCF_1/EBITDA_1}{r_{wacc} - g_{FCF}} \tag{9.26}$$

As with the P/E multiple, this multiple is higher for firms with high growth rates and low capital requirements (so that free cash flow is high in proportion to EBITDA).

---

[7]Assuming EPS grows at rate g_0 between date 0 and 1,

$$\text{Trailing P/E} = P_0/EPS_0 = (1 + g_0)\, P_0/EPS_1 = (1 + g_0)\, (\text{Forward P/E})$$

so trailing multiples tend to be higher for growing firms. Thus, when comparing multiples, be sure to be consistent in the use of either trailing or forward multiples across firms.

[8]Because we are interested in the persistent components of the firm's earnings, it is also common practice to exclude extraordinary items that will not be repeated when calculating a P/E ratio for valuation purposes.

EXAMPLE 9.10	**Valuation Using an Enterprise Value Multiple**

Problem

Suppose Rocky Shoes and Boots (RCKY) has earnings per share of $2.30 and EBITDA of $30.7 million. RCKY also has 5.4 million shares outstanding and debt of $125 million (net of cash). You believe Deckers Outdoor Corporation is comparable to RCKY in terms of its underlying business, but Deckers has no debt. If Deckers has a P/E of 13.3 and an enterprise value to EBITDA multiple of 7.4, estimate the value of RCKY's shares using both multiples. Which estimate is likely to be more accurate?

Solution

Using Decker's P/E, we would estimate a share price for RCKY of $P_0 = \$2.30 \times 13.3 = \$30.59$. Using the enterprise value to EBITDA multiple, we would estimate RCKY's enterprise value to be $V_0 = \$30.7$ million $\times 7.4 = \$227.2$ million. We then subtract debt and divide by the number of shares to estimate RCKY's share price: $P_0 = (227.2 - 125)/5.4 = \$18.93$. Because of the large difference in leverage between the firms, we would expect the second estimate, which is based on enterprise value, to be more reliable.

Other Multiples. Many other valuation multiples are possible. Looking at enterprise value as a multiple of sales can be useful if it is reasonable to assume that the firms will maintain similar margins in the future. For firms with substantial tangible assets, the ratio of price to book value of equity per share is sometimes used. Some multiples are specific to an industry. In the cable TV industry, for example, it is natural to consider enterprise value per subscriber.

Limitations of Multiples

If comparable firms were identical, their multiples would match precisely. Of course, firms are not identical. Thus, the usefulness of a valuation multiple will depend on the nature of the differences between firms and the sensitivity of the multiples to these differences.

Table 9.1 lists several valuation multiples for Kenneth Cole as well as for other firms in the footwear industry as of January 2006. Also shown is the average for each multiple, together with the range around the average (in percentage terms). Comparing Kenneth Cole with the industry averages, KCP looks somewhat overvalued according to its P/E (i.e., it trades at a higher P/E multiple), and somewhat undervalued according to the other multiples shown. For all of the multiples, however, a significant amount of dispersion across the industry is apparent. While the enterprise value to EBITDA multiple shows the smallest variation, even with it we cannot expect to obtain a precise estimate of value.

The differences in these multiples are most likely due to differences in their expected future growth rates, profitability, risk (and therefore costs of capital), and, in the case of Puma, differences in accounting conventions between the United States and Germany. Investors in the market understand that these differences exist, so the stocks are priced accordingly. But when valuing a firm using multiples, there is no clear guidance about how to adjust for these differences other than by narrowing the set of comparables used.

Thus, a key shortcoming of the comparables approach is that it does not take into account the important differences among firms. One firm might have an exceptional management team, another might have developed an efficient manufacturing process, or secured a patent on a new technology. Such differences are ignored when we apply a valuation multiple.

| TABLE 9.1 | Stock Prices and Multiples for the Footwear Industry, January 2006 |

Ticker	Name	Stock Price ($)	Market Capitalization ($ millions)	Enterprise Value ($ millions)	P/E	Price/ Book	Enterprise Value/ Sales	Enterprise Value/ EBITDA
KCP	Kenneth Cole Productions	26.75	562	465	16.21	2.22	0.90	8.36
NKE	NIKE, Inc.	84.20	21,830	20,518	16.64	3.59	1.43	8.75
PMMAY	Puma AG	312.05	5,088	4,593	14.99	5.02	2.19	9.02
RBK	Reebok International	58.72	3,514	3,451	14.91	2.41	0.90	8.58
WWW	Wolverine World Wide	22.10	1,257	1,253	17.42	2.71	1.20	9.53
BWS	Brown Shoe Company	43.36	800	1,019	22.62	1.91	0.47	9.09
SKX	Skechers U.S.A.	17.09	683	614	17.63	2.02	0.62	6.88
SRR	Stride Rite Corp.	13.70	497	524	20.72	1.87	0.89	9.28
DECK	Deckers Outdoor Corp.	30.05	373	367	13.32	2.29	1.48	7.44
WEYS	Weyco Group	19.90	230	226	11.97	1.75	1.06	6.66
RCKY	Rocky Shoes & Boots	19.96	106	232	8.66	1.12	0.92	7.55
DFZ	R.G. Barry Corp.	6.83	68	92	9.20	8.11	0.87	10.75
BOOT	LaCrosse Footwear	10.40	62	75	12.09	1.28	0.76	8.30
			Average (excl. KCP)		15.01	2.84	1.06	8.49
			Max (relative to Ave.)		+51%	+186%	+106%	+27%
			Min (relative to Ave.)		−42%	−61%	−56%	−22%

Another limitation of comparables is that they only provide information regarding the value of the firm *relative to* the other firms in the comparison set. Using multiples will not help us determine if an entire industry is overvalued, for example. This issue became especially important during the Internet boom of the late 1990s. Because many of these firms did not have positive cash flows or earnings, new multiples were created to value them (e.g., price to "page views"). While these multiples could justify the value of these firms in relation to one another, it was much more difficult to justify the stock prices of many of these firms using a realistic estimate of cash flows and the discounted free cash flow approach.

Comparison with Discounted Cash Flow Methods

Using a valuation multiple based on comparables is best viewed as a "shortcut" to the discounted cash flow methods of valuation. Rather than separately estimate the firm's cost of capital and future earnings or free cash flows, we rely on the market's assessment of the value of other firms with similar future prospects. In addition to its simplicity, the multiples approach has the advantage of being based on actual prices of real firms, rather than what may be unrealistic forecasts of future cash flows.

On the other hand, discounted cash flows methods have the advantage that they allow us to incorporate specific information about the firm's profitability, cost of capital, or future growth potential, as well as perform sensitivity analysis. Because the true driver of value for any firm is its ability to generate cash flows for its investors, the discounted cash flow methods have the potential to be more accurate and insightful than the use of a valuation multiple.

Stock Valuation Techniques: The Final Word

In the end, no single technique provides a final answer regarding a stock's true value. All approaches require assumptions or forecasts that are too uncertain to provide a definitive assessment of the firm's value. Most real-world practitioners use a combination of these approaches and gain confidence if the results are consistent across a variety of methods.

Figure 9.2 compares the ranges of values for Kenneth Cole Productions using the different valuation methods that we have discussed in this chapter.[9] Kenneth Cole's stock price of $26.75 in January 2006 is within the range estimated by all of these methods. Hence, based on this evidence alone we would not conclude that the stock is obviously under- or overpriced.

| FIGURE 9.2 | **Range of Valuations for KCP Stock Using Alternative Valuation Methods** |

Valuations from multiples are based on the low, high, and average values of the comparable firms from Table 9.1 (see Problems 25 and 26 at the end of the chapter). The constant dividend growth model is based on an 11% equity cost of capital and 4%, 8%, and 10% dividend growth rates, as discussed at the end of Section 9.2. The discounted free cash flow model is based on Example 9.7 with the range of parameters in Problem 22. (Midpoints are based on average multiples or base case assumptions. Red and blue regions show the variation between the lowest-multiple/worst-case scenario and the highest-multiple/best-case scenario. KCP's actual share price of $26.75 is indicated by the gray line.)

CONCEPT CHECK   1. What are some common valuation multiples?

2. What implicit assumptions are made when valuing a firm using multiples based on comparable firms?

---

[9]A chart such as this one, showing the range of values produced by each valuation method, is often referred to as a valuation "football field chart" by practitioners.

Since 2005, Douglas Kehring has been Senior Vice President of Oracle Corporation's Corporate Development and Strategic Planning group, providing planning, advisory, execution, and integration management services to Oracle on mergers and acquisitions and related transactions.

INTERVIEW WITH

Douglas Kehring

QUESTION: *How does Oracle target companies to acquire?*

ANSWER: Oracle uses an ongoing strategic planning process to identify potential acquisition targets. Top-down, the corporate development group works with the CEO's office looking for large, game-changing acquisitions. We also work bottom-up with engineering executives who sponsor potential acquisitions to fill customer needs and product gaps. Together we identify prospects, engage with targets, perform due diligence, develop business plans, and proceed with feasible transactions. Our group also provides the CEO's office with objective opinions of sponsor proposals, based on Oracle's overall needs and priorities. The CEO's office approves all transactions.

We see about 300 to 400 opportunities a year and show all to the appropriate product group executives, including those from venture capital firms and investment bankers. Typically, they express an interest in about 20 to 40, and we sign confidentiality agreements to proceed with a thorough analysis. About 12 of those reach the letter of intent stage, where we issue a term sheet and an exclusivity period to complete the transaction.

QUESTION: *Once you decide to try to acquire a company, how do you determine how much to pay for it?*

ANSWER: The pricing occurs after due diligence but before the letter of intent. From a practical standpoint, we negotiate the price point with the seller—that's where the art comes into play. Our DCF analysis is the most important part in justifying the value. We take into account what we believe we can do with the business from an income statement perspective, to determine the breakeven valuation at the chosen hurdle rate. If we pay less, we'll earn a higher rate of return, and vice versa.

QUESTION: *Discuss the role of both discounted cash flow and comparables analysis in determining the price to pay.*

ANSWER: We use 5-year DCFs, because it takes that long to get to a steady state and predicting beyond that is difficult. The hardest part is determining the income statement inputs. The fifth-year numbers dominate value. Getting to that point depends on how fast you grow the business and how profitable it is. Assumptions are the key. We take a conservative approach, leveraging available information. Overly aggressive sponsor assumptions lead to extreme valuations, creating an acquirer's biggest problems.

The hurdle rate for a project varies. We might use cost of equity or the WACC. Then we ask, "What is right risk/return profile for this transaction?" and adjust the rate accordingly—for example, possibly requiring a higher return for a smaller, more volatile company.

Oracle's 80 completed transactions give us actual experience on which to base more realistic assumptions. We look at variables and attributes—was it a product line, a specific feature, a stand-alone acquisition?—and assess how well we did based on our models, to improve our cash flow analysis for future acquisitions. Then we benchmark using common valuation multiples based on comparable publicly traded companies and similar M&A transactions.

QUESTION: *How does your analysis differ for private versus public companies?*

ANSWER: The basic DCF analysis is no different: We perform the same due diligence for private and public companies and receive the same types of information. Typically, the larger the public company's revenues, the more stable it is and the more professional its orientation and systems. We feel more confident in our risk attributes and the information we receive. In acquiring a public company, we prepare a pro forma statement for the combined entity to determine whether it will increase or decrease our earnings per share.

Of greater concern to us is the target's size. A $2 billion company, whether public or private, has multiple product lines and larger installed bases, reducing its risk profile. A $100 million company may have only one product line and thus, higher risk and volatility. On the other hand, the small company may grow faster than a large one.

9.5 Information, Competition, and Stock Prices

As shown in Figure 9.3, the models described in this chapter link the firm's expected future cash flows, its cost of capital (determined by its risk), and the value of its shares. But what conclusions should we draw if the actual market price of a stock doesn't appear to be consistent with our estimate of its value? Is it more likely that the stock is mispriced or that we made a mistake in our risk and future cash flow estimates? We close this chapter with a consideration of this question and the implications for corporate managers.

Information in Stock Prices

Consider the following situation. You are a new junior analyst assigned to research Kenneth Cole Productions' stock and assess its value. You scrutinize the company's recent financial statements, look at the trends in the industry, and forecast the firm's future earnings, dividends, and free cash flows. You carefully run the numbers and estimate the stock's value at $30 per share. On your way to present your analysis to your boss, you run into a slightly more experienced colleague in the elevator. It turns out your colleague has been researching the same stock and has different beliefs. According to her analysis, the value of the stock is only $20 per share. What would you do?

Most of us in this situation would reconsider our own analysis. The fact that someone else who has carefully studied the stock has come to a very different conclusion is powerful evidence that we might have missed something. In the face of this information from our colleague, we would probably reconsider our analysis and adjust our assessment of the stock's value downward. Of course, our colleague might also revise her opinion based on our assessment. After sharing our analyses, we would likely end up with a consensus estimate somewhere between $20 and $30 per share. That is, at the end of this process our beliefs would be similar.

This type of encounter happens millions of times every day in the stock market. When a buyer seeks to buy a stock, the willingness of other parties to sell the same stock suggests that they value the stock differently, as the NPV of buying and selling the stock cannot *both* be positive. Thus, the information that others are willing to trade should lead buyers and sellers to revise their valuations. Ultimately, investors trade until they reach a consensus regarding the value of the stock. In this way, stock markets aggregate the information and views of many different investors.

| FIGURE 9.3 | The Valuation Triad |

Valuation models determine the relationship among the firm's future cash flows, its cost of capital, and the value of its shares. The stock's expected cash flows and cost of capital can be used to assess its market price. Conversely, the market price can be used to assess the firm's future cash flows or cost of capital.

Thus, if your valuation model suggests a stock is worth $30 per share when it is trading for $20 per share in the market, the discrepancy is equivalent to knowing that thousands of investors—many of them professionals who have access to the best information—disagree with your assessment. This knowledge should make you reconsider your original analysis. You would need a very compelling reason to trust your own estimate in the face of such contrary opinions.

What conclusion can we draw from this discussion? Recall Figure 9.3, in which a valuation model links the firm's future cash flows, its cost of capital, and its share price. In other words, given accurate information about any two of these variables, a valuation model allows us to make inferences about the third variable. Thus, the way we use a valuation model will depend on the quality of our information: The model will tell us the most about the variable for which our prior information is the least reliable.

For a publicly traded firm, its market price should already provide very accurate information, aggregated from a multitude of investors, regarding the true value of its shares. Therefore, in most situations, a valuation model is best applied to tell us something about the firm's future cash flows or cost of capital, based on its current stock price. Only in the relatively rare case in which we have some superior information that other investors lack regarding the firm's cash flows and cost of capital would it make sense to second-guess the stock price.

EXAMPLE 9.11

Using the Information in Market Prices

Problem

Suppose Tecnor Industries will pay a dividend this year of $5 per share. Its equity cost of capital is 10%, and you expect its dividends to grow at a rate of about 4% per year, though you are somewhat unsure of the precise growth rate. If Tecnor's stock is currently trading for $76.92 per share, how would you update your beliefs about its dividend growth rate?

Solution

If we apply the constant dividend growth model based on a 4% growth rate, we would estimate a stock price of $P_0 = 5/(0.10 - 0.04) = \$83.33$ per share. The market price of $76.92, however, implies that most investors expect dividends to grow at a somewhat slower rate. If we continue to assume a constant growth rate, we can solve for the growth rate consistent with the current market price using Eq. 9.7:

$$g = r_E - Div_1/P_0 = 10\% - 5/76.92 = 3.5\%$$

Thus, given this market price for the stock, we should lower our expectations for the dividend growth rate unless we have very strong reasons to trust our own estimate.

Competition and Efficient Markets

The idea that markets aggregate the information of many investors, and that this information is reflected in security prices, is a natural consequence of investor competition. If information were available that indicated that buying a stock had a positive NPV, investors with that information would choose to buy the stock; their attempts to purchase it would then drive up the stock's price. By a similar logic, investors with information that selling a stock had a positive NPV would sell it and the stock's price would fall.

The idea that competition among investors works to eliminate *all* positive-NPV trading opportunities is referred to as the **efficient markets hypothesis**. It implies that securities will be fairly priced, based on their future cash flows, given all information that is available to investors.

The underlying rationale for the efficient markets hypothesis is the presence of competition. What if new information becomes available that affects the firm's value? The degree of competition, and therefore the accuracy of the efficient markets hypothesis, will depend on the number of investors who possess this information. Let's consider two important cases.

Public, Easily Interpretable Information. Information that is available to all investors includes information in news reports, financial statements, corporate press releases, or in other public data sources. If the impact of this information on the firm's future cash flows can be readily ascertained, then all investors can determine the effect of this information on the firm's value.

In this situation, we expect competition between investors to be fierce and the stock price to react nearly instantaneously to such news. A few lucky investors might be able to trade a small quantity of shares before the price fully adjusts. But most investors would find that the stock price already reflected the new information before they were able to trade on it. In other words, we expect the efficient markets hypothesis to hold very well with respect to this type of information.

EXAMPLE 9.12	**Stock Price Reactions to Public Information**

Problem

Myox Labs announces that due to potential side effects, it is pulling one of its leading drugs from the market. As a result, its future expected free cash flow will decline by $85 million per year for the next 10 years. Myox has 50 million shares outstanding, no debt, and an equity cost of capital of 8%. If this news came as a complete surprise to investors, what should happen to Myox's stock price upon the announcement?

Solution

In this case, we can use the discounted free cash flow method. With no debt, $r_{wacc} = r_E = 8\%$. Using the annuity formula, the decline in expected free cash flow will reduce Myox's enterprise value by

$$\$85 \text{ million} \times \frac{1}{0.08}\left(1 - \frac{1}{1.08^{10}}\right) = \$570 \text{ million}$$

Thus, the share price should fall by $570/50 = $11.40 per share. Because this news is public and its effect on the firm's expected free cash flow is clear, we would expect the stock price to drop by this amount nearly instantaneously.

Private or Difficult-to-Interpret Information. Some information is not publicly available. For example, an analyst might spend time and effort gathering information from a firm's employees, competitors, suppliers, or customers that is relevant to the firm's future cash flows. This information is not available to other investors who have not devoted a similar effort to gathering it.

Even when information is publicly available, it may be difficult to interpret. Non-experts in the field may find it difficult to evaluate research reports on new technologies, for example. It may take a great deal of legal and accounting expertise and effort to understand the full consequences of a highly complicated business transaction. Certain consulting experts may have greater insight into consumer tastes and the likelihood of a product's acceptance. In these cases, while the fundamental information may be public, the interpretation of how that information will affect the firm's future cash flows is itself private information.

When private information is relegated to the hands of a relatively small number of investors, these investors may be able to profit by trading on their information.[10] In this case, the efficient markets hypothesis will not hold in the strict sense. However, as these informed traders begin to trade, they will tend to move prices, so over time prices will begin to reflect their information as well.

If the profit opportunities from having this type of information are large, other individuals will attempt to gain the expertise and devote the resources needed to acquire it. As more individuals become better informed, competition to exploit this information will increase. Thus, in the long run, we should expect that the degree of "inefficiency" in the market will be limited by the costs of obtaining the information.

| EXAMPLE 9.13 | **Stock Price Reactions to Private Information** |

Problem

Phenyx Pharmaceuticals has just announced the development of a new drug for which the company is seeking approval from the Food and Drug Administration (FDA). If approved, the future profits from the new drug will increase Phenyx's market value by $750 million, or $15 per share given its 50 million shares outstanding. If the development of this drug was a surprise to investors, and if the average likelihood of FDA approval is 10%, what do you expect will happen to Phenyx's stock price when this news is announced? What may happen to the stock price over time?

Solution

Because many investors are likely to know that the chance of FDA approval is 10%, competition should lead to an immediate jump in the stock price of $10\% \times \$15 = \$1.50$ per share. Over time, however, analysts and experts in the field are likely to do their own assessments of the probable efficacy of the drug. If they conclude that the drug looks more promising than average, they will begin to trade on their private information and buy the stock, and the price will tend to drift higher over time. If the experts conclude that the drug looks less promising than average, they will tend to sell the stock, and its price will drift lower over time. Examples of possible price paths are shown in Figure 9.4. While these experts may be able to trade on their superior information and earn a profit, for uninformed investors who do not know which outcome will occur, the stock may rise or fall and so appears fairly priced at the announcement.

Lessons for Investors and Corporate Managers

The effect of competition based on information about stock prices has important consequences for both investors and corporate managers.

Consequences for Investors. As in other markets, investors should be able to identify positive-NPV trading opportunities in securities markets only if some barrier or restriction to free competition exists. An investor's competitive advantage may take several forms.

---

[10]Even with private information, informed investors may find it difficult to profit from that information, because they must find others who are willing to trade with them; that is, the market for the stock must be sufficiently *liquid*. A liquid market requires that other investors in the market have alternative motives to trade (e.g., selling shares of a stock to purchase a house) and so be willing to trade even when facing the risk that other traders may be better informed. See Chapter 13 for more details.

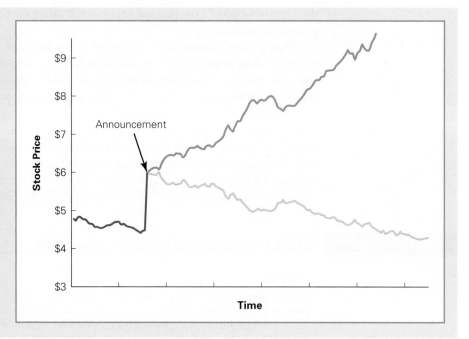

FIGURE 9.4

Possible Stock Price Paths for Example 9.13

Phenyx's stock price jumps on the announcement based on the average likelihood of approval. The stock price then drifts up (green path) or down (gold path) as informed traders trade on their more accurate assessment of the drug's likelihood of approval. Because an uninformed investor does not know which outcome will occur, the stock is fairly priced at the announcement, even though it will appear under- or overpriced ex post.

The investor may have expertise or access to information that is known to only a few people. Alternatively, the investor may have lower trading costs than other market participants and so can exploit opportunities that others would find unprofitable. In all cases, however, the source of the positive-NPV trading opportunity must be something that is hard to replicate; otherwise, any gains would be competed away.

While the fact that positive-NPV trading opportunities are hard to come by may be disappointing, there is some good news as well. If stocks are fairly priced according to our valuation models, then investors who buy stocks can expect to receive future cash flows that fairly compensate them for the risk of their investment. Thus, in such cases the average investor can invest with confidence, even if he is not fully informed.

Implications for Corporate Managers. If stocks are fairly valued according to the models we have described, then the value of the firm is determined by the cash flows that it can pay to its investors. This result has several key implications for corporate managers:

- *Focus on NPV and free cash flow.* A manager seeking to boost the price of her firm's stock should make investments that increase the present value of the firm's free cash flow. Thus, the capital budgeting methods outlined in Chapter 8 are fully consistent with the objective of maximizing the firm's share price.

- *Avoid accounting illusions.* Many managers make the mistake of focusing on accounting earnings as opposed to free cash flows. With efficient markets, the accounting consequences of a decision do not directly affect the value of the firm and should not drive decision making.

- *Use financial transactions to support investment.* With efficient markets, the firm can sell its shares at a fair price to new investors. Thus, the firm should not be constrained from raising capital to fund positive NPV investment opportunities.

Kenneth Cole Productions—What Happened?

The biggest challenge in valuing a stock is forecasting the future. Events will often arise that cause the company's performance to exceed or fall short of analysts' expectations. Often these events are specific to the company itself. But other times the events are beyond the company's control. For example, no one could have predicted the severity of the economic collapse that would ensue in 2008–2009, and the impact it would have on retailers worldwide. Consider what actually happened to Kenneth Cole Productions.

Unanticipated problems within the company meant that the remainder of 2006 was challenging for KCP. Despite strong revenue growth in its wholesale division, its retail stores suffered an unexpected large same-store sales decline of 13%. Overall, KCP revenues grew only 3.6% in 2006, well below analysts' forecasts. Losses in the retail division caused KCP's EBIT margin to drop below 7%.

After the departure of its president, KCP also struggled to find new leadership. As both Chairman and CEO, founder Kenneth Cole was able to spend less time on the creative aspects of the brand, and its image suffered. Sales declined 4.8% in 2007, and its EBIT margin fell to 1%. However there was some cause for optimism—in Spring 2008, KCP hired Jill Granoff, a former Liz Claiborne executive, as its new CEO.

The optimism was short-lived. Like many other retailers, in Fall 2008, KCP was hit hard by the effects of the financial crisis. It found itself saddled with large inventories, and had to aggressively cut prices. By year end, sales had fallen by 3.6%. Worse, KCP reported operating losses, with an EBIT margin of −2%. Analysts forecast that 2009 would be KCP's most difficult year yet, with sales declines exceeding 8% and EBIT margins falling below −4%.

Reflecting its poor performance, KCP cut its dividend in half at the start of 2008 and suspended dividend payments altogether at the start of 2009. The chart below shows KCP's stock price performance—clearly, investors in KCP did not do well over this period, with the stock losing more than 70% of its value by early 2009, with more than half of that loss occurring in the wake of the financial crisis.

As the economy recovered in 2010, KCP returned to profitability, and sales experienced double digit growth. In early 2012, the company's founder, Kenneth Cole, offered to buy the firm from its shareholders. The deal closed on September 25, 2012 for a price $15.25/share, still well under its early 2006 value.

It is important to recognize, however, that while we know *now* that KCP was overpriced in 2006, that does not mean that the market for KCP stock was "inefficient" at that time. Indeed, as we saw earlier, KCP may have been appropriately priced based on reasonable expectations for its future growth that investors had at the time. Unfortunately, due to problems both within KCP and with the broader economy, those expectations were not realized.

The Efficient Markets Hypothesis Versus No Arbitrage

We can draw an important distinction between the efficient markets hypothesis and the notion of a normal market that we introduced in Chapter 3, which is based on the idea of arbitrage. An arbitrage opportunity is a situation in which two securities (or portfolios) with *identical* cash flows have different prices. Because anyone can earn a sure profit in this situation by buying the low-priced security and selling the high-priced one, we expect that investors will immediately exploit and eliminate these opportunities. Thus, in a normal market, arbitrage opportunities will not be found.

The efficient markets hypothesis, that the NPV of investing is zero, is best expressed in terms of returns, as in Eq. 9.2. When the NPV of investing is zero, the price of every security equals the present value of its expected cash flows when discounted at a cost of capital that reflects its risk. So the efficient markets hypothesis implies that securities with *equivalent risk* should have the same *expected return*. The efficient markets hypothesis is therefore incomplete without a definition of "equivalent risk." Furthermore, because investors must *forecast* the riskiness of securities, and may do so differently, there is no reason to expect the efficient markets hypothesis to hold perfectly; it is best viewed as an idealized approximation for highly competitive markets.

To test the validity of the efficient markets hypothesis and, more importantly, to implement the discounted cash flow methods of stock valuation introduced in this chapter, we need a theory of how investors can estimate the risk of investing in a security and how this risk determines the security's expected return. Developing such a theory is the topic of Part 4, which we turn to next.

CONCEPT CHECK

1. State the efficient market hypothesis.

2. What are the implications of the efficient market hypothesis for corporate managers?

MyFinanceLab   Here is what you should know after reading this chapter. MyFinanceLab will help you identify what you know and where to go when you need to practice.

9.1 The Dividend-Discount Model

- The Law of One Price states that the value of a stock is equal to the present value of the dividends and future sale price the investor will receive. Because these cash flows are risky, they must be discounted at the equity cost of capital, which is the expected return of other securities available in the market with equivalent risk to the firm's equity.
- The total return of a stock is equal to the dividend yield plus the capital gain rate. The expected total return of a stock should equal its equity cost of capital:

$$r_E = \frac{Div_1 + P_1}{P_0} - 1 = \underbrace{\frac{Div_1}{P_0}}_{\text{Dividend yield}} + \underbrace{\frac{P_1 - P_0}{P_0}}_{\text{Capital Gain Rate}} \tag{9.2}$$

- When investors have the same beliefs, the dividend-discount model states that, for any horizon N, the stock price satisfies the following equation:

$$P_0 = \frac{Div_1}{1 + r_E} + \frac{Div_2}{(1 + r_E)^2} + \cdots + \frac{Div_N}{(1 + r_E)^N} + \frac{P_N}{(1 + r_E)^N} \tag{9.4}$$

- If the stock eventually pays dividends and is never acquired, the dividend-discount model implies that the stock price equals the present value of all future dividends.

9.2 Applying the Dividend-Discount Model

- The constant dividend growth model assumes that dividends grow at a constant expected rate g. In that case, g is also the expected capital gain rate, and

$$P_0 = \frac{Div_1}{r_E - g} \tag{9.6}$$

- Future dividends depend on earnings, shares outstanding, and the dividend payout rate:

$$Div_t = \underbrace{\frac{\text{Earnings}_t}{\text{Shares Outstanding}_t}}_{EPS_t} \times \text{Dividend Payout Rate}_t \tag{9.8}$$

- If the dividend payout rate and the number of shares outstanding is constant, and if earnings change only as a result of new investment from retained earnings, then the growth rate of the firm's earnings, dividends, and share price is calculated as follows:

$$g = \text{Retention Rate} \times \text{Return on New Investment} \tag{9.12}$$

- Cutting the firm's dividend to increase investment will raise the stock price if, and only if, the new investments have a positive NPV.
- If the firm has a long-term growth rate of g after the period $N + 1$, then we can apply the dividend-discount model and use the constant dividend growth formula to estimate the terminal stock value P_N.
- The dividend-discount model is sensitive to the dividend growth rate, which is difficult to estimate accurately.

9.3 Total Payout and Free Cash Flow Valuation Models

- If the firm undertakes share repurchases, it is more reliable to use the total payout model to value the firm. In this model, the value of equity equals the present value of future total dividends and repurchases. To determine the stock price, we divide the equity value by the initial number of shares outstanding of the firm:

$$P_0 = \frac{PV\,(\text{Future Total Dividends and Repurchases})}{\text{Shares Outstanding}_0} \tag{9.16}$$

- The growth rate of the firm's total payout is governed by the growth rate of earnings, not earnings per share.
- When a firm has leverage, it is more reliable to use the discounted free cash flow model. In this model,
  - We can estimate the firm's future free cash flow as

$$\text{Free Cash Flow} = EBIT \times (1 - \tau_c) - \text{Net Investment}$$
$$- \text{Increases in Net Working Capital} \tag{9.20}$$

  where Net Investment equals the firm's capital expenditures in excess of depreciation.
  - The firm's enterprise value (the market value of equity plus debt, less excess cash) equals the present value of the firm's future free cash flow:

$$V_0 = PV\,(\text{Future Free Cash Flow of Firm}) \tag{9.21}$$

  - We discount cash flows using the weighted average cost of capital, which is the expected return the firm must pay to investors to compensate them for the risk of holding the firm's debt and equity together.
  - We can estimate a terminal enterprise value by assuming free cash flow grows at a constant rate (typically equal to the rate of long-run revenue growth).

■ We determine the stock price by subtracting debt and adding cash to the enterprise value, and then dividing by the initial number of shares outstanding of the firm:

$$P_0 = \frac{V_0 + \text{Cash}_0 - \text{Debt}_0}{\text{Shares Outstanding}_0} \tag{9.22}$$

9.4 Valuation Based on Comparable Firms

■ We can also value stocks by using valuation multiples based on comparable firms. Multiples commonly used for this purpose include the P/E ratio and the ratio of enterprise value to EBITDA. Using multiples assumes that comparable firms have the same risk and future growth as the firm being valued.

■ No valuation model provides a definitive value for the stock. It is best to use several methods to identify a reasonable range for the value.

9.5 Information, Competition, and Stock Prices

■ Stock prices aggregate the information of many investors. Therefore, if our valuation disagrees with the stock's market price, it is most likely an indication that our assumptions about the firm's cash flows are wrong.

■ Competition between investors tends to eliminate positive-NPV trading opportunities. Competition will be strongest when information is public and easy to interpret. Privately informed traders may be able to profit from their information, which is reflected in prices only gradually.

■ The efficient markets hypothesis states that competition eliminates all positive-NPV trades, which is equivalent to stating that securities with equivalent risk have the same expected returns.

■ In an efficient market, investors will not find positive-NPV trading opportunities without some source of competitive advantage. By contrast, the average investor will earn a fair return on his or her investment.

■ In an efficient market, to raise the stock price corporate managers should focus on maximizing the present value of the free cash flow from the firm's investments, rather than accounting consequences or financial policy.

Key Terms

capital gain *p. 273*
capital gain rate *p. 273*
constant dividend growth model *p. 277*
discounted free cash flow model *p. 284*
dividend-discount model *p. 276*
dividend payout rate *p. 278*
dividend yield *p. 273*
efficient markets hypothesis *p. 295*
equity cost of capital *p. 272*
forward earnings *p. 289*
forward P/E *p. 289*

method of comparables *p. 288*
net investment *p. 284*
retention rate *p. 278*
share repurchase *p. 283*
short interest *p. 274*
total payout model *p. 283*
total return *p. 273*
trailing earnings *p. 289*
trailing P/E *p. 289*
valuation multiple *p. 288*
weighted average cost of capital (WACC) *p. 285*

Further Reading

For a more thorough discussion of different stock valuation methods, see T. Copeland, T. Koller, and J. Murrin, *Valuation: Measuring and Managing the Value of Companies* (John Wiley & Sons, 2001).

For a comparison of the discounted free cash flow model and the method of comparables for a sample of 51 highly leveraged transactions, see S. Kaplan and R. Ruback "The Valuation of Cash Flow Forecasts: An Empirical Analysis," *Journal of Finance* 50 (1995): 1059–1093.

An entertaining introduction to efficient markets can be found in B. Malkiel's popular book, *A Random Walk Down Wall Street: Completely Revised and Updated Eighth Edition* (W. W. Norton, 2003).

For a classic discussion of market efficiency, the arguments that support it, and important empirical tests, see E. F. Fama, "Efficient Capital Markets: A Review of Theory and Empirical Work," *Journal of Finance* 25 (1970): 383–417, and "Efficient Capital Markets: II," *The Journal of Finance* 46(5) (1991): 1575–1617. Another review of the literature and apparent anomalies can be found in R. Ball, "The Development, Accomplishments and Limitations of the Theory of Stock Market Efficiency," *Managerial Finance* 20(2,3) (1994): 3–48.

For two sides of the debate of whether the price of Internet companies in the late 1990s could be justified by a valuation model, see: L. Pástor and P. Veronesi, "Was There a Nasdaq Bubble in the Late 1990s?" *Journal of Financial Economics* 81(2006): 61–100; M. Richardson and E. Ofek, "DotCom Mania: The Rise and Fall of Internet Stock Prices," *Journal of Finance* 58 (2003): 1113–1138.

Problems

All problems are available in MyFinanceLab. An asterisk (*) indicates problems with a higher level of difficulty.

The Dividend Discount Model

1. Assume Evco, Inc., has a current price of $50 and will pay a $2 dividend in one year, and its equity cost of capital is 15%. What price must you expect it to sell for right after paying the dividend in one year in order to justify its current price?

2. Anle Corporation has a current price of $20, is expected to pay a dividend of $1 in one year, and its expected price right after paying that dividend is $22.
   a. What is Anle's expected dividend yield?
   b. What is Anle's expected capital gain rate?
   c. What is Anle's equity cost of capital?

3. Suppose Acap Corporation will pay a dividend of $2.80 per share at the end of this year and $3 per share next year. You expect Acap's stock price to be $52 in two years. If Acap's equity cost of capital is 10%:
   a. What price would you be willing to pay for a share of Acap stock today, if you planned to hold the stock for two years?
   b. Suppose instead you plan to hold the stock for one year. What price would you expect to be able to sell a share of Acap stock for in one year?
   c. Given your answer in part (b), what price would you be willing to pay for a share of Acap stock today, if you planned to hold the stock for one year? How does this compare to your answer in part (a)?

4. Krell Industries has a share price of $22 today. If Krell is expected to pay a dividend of $0.88 this year, and its stock price is expected to grow to $23.54 at the end of the year, what is Krell's dividend yield and equity cost of capital?

Applying the Dividend-Discount Model

5. NoGrowth Corporation currently pays a dividend of $2 per year, and it will continue to pay this dividend forever. What is the price per share if its equity cost of capital is 15% per year?

6. Summit Systems will pay a dividend of $1.50 this year. If you expect Summit's dividend to grow by 6% per year, what is its price per share if its equity cost of capital is 11%?

7. Dorpac Corporation has a dividend yield of 1.5%. Dorpac's equity cost of capital is 8%, and its dividends are expected to grow at a constant rate.
   a. What is the expected growth rate of Dorpac's dividends?
   b. What is the expected growth rate of Dorpac's share price?

8. Kenneth Cole Productions (KCP) suspended its dividend at the start of 2009 and as of the middle of 2012, has not reinstated its dividend. Suppose you do not expect KCP to resume paying dividends until July 2014. You expect KCP's dividend in July 2014 to be $1.00 (paid annually), and you expect it to grow by 5% per year thereafter. If KCP's equity cost of capital is 11%, what is the value of a share of KCP in July 2012?

9. In 2006 and 2007, Kenneth Cole Productions (KCP) paid annual dividends of $0.72. In 2008, KCP paid an annual dividend of $0.36, and then paid no further dividends through 2012. Suppose KCP was acquired at the end of 2012 for $15.25 per share.
   a. What would an investor with perfect foresight of the above been willing to pay for KCP at the start of 2006? (*Note*: Because an investor with perfect foresight bears no risk, use a risk-free equity cost of capital of 5%.)
   b. Does your answer to (a) imply that the market for KCP stock was inefficient in 2006?

10. DFB, Inc., expects earnings this year of $5 per share, and it plans to pay a $3 dividend to shareholders. DFB will retain $2 per share of its earnings to reinvest in new projects with an expected return of 15% per year. Suppose DFB will maintain the same dividend payout rate, retention rate, and return on new investments in the future and will not change its number of outstanding shares.
    a. What growth rate of earnings would you forecast for DFB?
    b. If DFB's equity cost of capital is 12%, what price would you estimate for DFB stock?
    c. Suppose DFB instead paid a dividend of $4 per share this year and retained only $1 per share in earnings. If DFB maintains this higher payout rate in the future, what stock price would you estimate now? Should DFB raise its dividend?

11. Cooperton Mining just announced it will cut its dividend from $4 to $2.50 per share and use the extra funds to expand. Prior to the announcement, Cooperton's dividends were expected to grow at a 3% rate, and its share price was $50. With the new expansion, Cooperton's dividends are expected to grow at a 5% rate. What share price would you expect after the announcement? (Assume Cooperton's risk is unchanged by the new expansion.) Is the expansion a positive NPV investment?

12. Procter & Gamble will pay an annual dividend of $0.65 one year from now. Analysts expect this dividend to grow at 12% per year thereafter until the fifth year. After then, growth will level off at 2% per year. According to the dividend-discount model, what is the value of a share of Procter & Gamble stock if the firm's equity cost of capital is 8%?

13. Colgate-Palmolive Company has just paid an annual dividend of $0.96. Analysts are predicting an 11% per year growth rate in earnings over the next five years. After then, Colgate's earnings are expected to grow at the current industry average of 5.2% per year. If Colgate's equity cost of capital is 8.5% per year and its dividend payout ratio remains constant, what price does the dividend-discount model predict Colgate stock should sell for?

14. What is the value of a firm with initial dividend Div, growing for n years (i.e., until year $n + 1$) at rate g_1 and after that at rate g_2 forever, when the equity cost of capital is r?

15. Halliford Corporation expects to have earnings this coming year of $3 per share. Halliford plans to retain all of its earnings for the next two years. For the subsequent two years, the firm will retain 50% of its earnings. It will then retain 20% of its earnings from that point onward. Each year, retained earnings will be invested in new projects with an expected return of 25% per year. Any earnings that are not retained will be paid out as dividends. Assume Halliford's share count remains constant and all earnings growth comes from the investment of retained earnings. If Halliford's equity cost of capital is 10%, what price would you estimate for Halliford stock?

Total Payout and Free Cash Flow Valuation Models

16. Suppose Amazon.com Inc. pays no dividends but spent $2 billion on share repurchases last year. If Amazon's equity cost of capital is 8%, and if the amount spent on repurchases is expected to grow by 6% per year, estimate Amazon's market capitalization. If Amazon has 450 million shares outstanding, what stock price does this correspond to?

17. Maynard Steel plans to pay a dividend of $3 this year. The company has an expected earnings growth rate of 4% per year and an equity cost of capital of 10%.
    a. Assuming Maynard's dividend payout rate and expected growth rate remains constant, and Maynard does not issue or repurchase shares, estimate Maynard's share price.
    b. Suppose Maynard decides to pay a dividend of $1 this year and use the remaining $2 per share to repurchase shares. If Maynard's total payout rate remains constant, estimate Maynard's share price.
    c. If Maynard maintains the dividend and total payout rate given in part (b), at what rate are Maynard's dividends and earnings per share expected to grow?

18. Benchmark Metrics, Inc. (BMI), an all-equity financed firm, just reported EPS of $5.00 per share for 2008. Despite the economic downturn, BMI is confident regarding its current investment opportunities. But due to the financial crisis, BMI does not wish to fund these investments externally. The Board has therefore decided to suspend its stock repurchase plan and cut its dividend to $1 per share (vs. almost $2 per share in 2007), and retain these funds instead. The firm has just paid the 2008 dividend, and BMI plans to keep its dividend at $1 per share in 2009 as well. In subsequent years, it expects its growth opportunities to slow, and it will still be able to fund its growth internally with a target 40% dividend payout ratio, and reinitiating its stock repurchase plan for a total payout rate of 60%. (All dividends and repurchases occur at the end of each year.)

    Suppose BMI's existing operations will continue to generate the current level of earnings per share in the future. Assume further that the return on new investment is 15%, and that reinvestments will account for all future earnings growth (if any). Finally, assume BMI's equity cost of capital is 10%.
    a. Estimate BMI's EPS in 2009 and 2010 (before any share repurchases).
    b. What is the value of a share of BMI at the start of 2009?

19. Heavy Metal Corporation is expected to generate the following free cash flows over the next five years:

Year	1	2	3	4	5
FCF ($ millions)	53	68	78	75	82

After then, the free cash flows are expected to grow at the industry average of 4% per year. Using the discounted free cash flow model and a weighted average cost of capital of 14%:
    a. Estimate the enterprise value of Heavy Metal.
    b. If Heavy Metal has no excess cash, debt of $300 million, and 40 million shares outstanding, estimate its share price.

20. IDX Technologies is a privately held developer of advanced security systems based in Chicago. As part of your business development strategy, in late 2008 you initiate discussions with IDX's founder about the possibility of acquiring the business at the end of 2008. Estimate the value of IDX per share using a discounted FCF approach and the following data:
    ■ Debt: $30 million
    ■ Excess cash: $110 million
    ■ Shares outstanding: 50 million
    ■ Expected FCF in 2009: $45 million
    ■ Expected FCF in 2010: $50 million
    ■ Future FCF growth rate beyond 2010: 5%
    ■ Weighted-average cost of capital: 9.4%

21. Sora Industries has 60 million outstanding shares, $120 million in debt, $40 million in cash, and the following projected free cash flow for the next four years::

	Year	0	1	2	3	4
	Earnings and FCF Forecast ($ millions)					
1	Sales	433.0	468.0	516.0	547.0	574.3
2	*Growth versus Prior Year*		*8.1%*	*10.3%*	*6.0%*	*5.0%*
3	Cost of Goods Sold		(313.6)	(345.7)	(366.5)	(384.8)
4	**Gross Profit**		154.4	170.3	180.5	189.5
5	Selling, General, and Administrative		(93.6)	(103.2)	(109.4)	(114.9)
6	Depreciation		(7.0)	(7.5)	(9.0)	(9.5)
7	**EBIT**		53.8	59.6	62.1	65.2
8	Less: Income Tax at 40%		(21.5)	(23.8)	(24.8)	(26.1)
9	Plus: Depreciation		7.0	7.5	9.0	9.5
10	Less: Capital Expenditures		(7.7)	(10.0)	(9.9)	(10.4)
11	Less: Increase in NWC		(6.3)	(8.6)	(5.6)	(4.9)
12	**Free Cash Flow**		25.3	24.6	30.8	33.3

a. Suppose Sora's revenue and free cash flow are expected to grow at a 5% rate beyond year 4. If Sora's weighted average cost of capital is 10%, what is the value of Sora's stock based on this information?

b. Sora's cost of goods sold was assumed to be 67% of sales. If its cost of goods sold is actually 70% of sales, how would the estimate of the stock's value change?

c. Let's return to the assumptions of part (a) and suppose Sora can maintain its cost of goods sold at 67% of sales. However, now suppose Sora reduces its selling, general, and administrative expenses from 20% of sales to 16% of sales. What stock price would you estimate now? (Assume no other expenses, except taxes, are affected.)

*d. Sora's net working capital needs were estimated to be 18% of sales (which is their current level in year 0). If Sora can reduce this requirement to 12% of sales starting in year 1, but all other assumptions remain as in part (a), what stock price do you estimate for Sora? (*Hint:* This change will have the largest impact on Sora's free cash flow in year 1.)

 22. Consider the valuation of Kenneth Cole Productions in Example 9.7.

a. Suppose you believe KCP's initial revenue growth rate will be between 4% and 11% (with growth slowing in equal steps to 4% by year 2011). What range of share prices for KCP is consistent with these forecasts?

b. Suppose you believe KCP's EBIT margin will be between 7% and 10% of sales. What range of share prices for KCP is consistent with these forecasts (keeping KCP's initial revenue growth at 9%)?

c. Suppose you believe KCP's weighted average cost of capital is between 10% and 12%. What range of share prices for KCP is consistent with these forecasts (keeping KCP's initial revenue growth and EBIT margin at 9%)?

d. What range of share prices is consistent if you vary the estimates as in parts (a), (b), and (c) simultaneously?

23. Kenneth Cole Productions (KCP) was acquired in 2012 for a purchase price of $15.25 per share. KCP has 18.5 million shares outstanding, $45 million in cash, and no debt at the time of the acquisition.

a. Given a weighted average cost of capital of 11%, and assuming no future growth, what level of annual free cash flow would justify this acquisition price?

b. If KCP's current annual sales are $480 million, assuming no net capital expenditures or increases in net working capital, and a tax rate of 35%, what EBIT margin does your answer in part (a) require?

Valuation Based on Comparable Firms

24. You notice that PepsiCo (PEP) has a stock price of $72.62 and EPS of $3.80. Its competitor, the Coca-Cola Company (KO), has EPS of $1.89. Estimate the value of a share of Coca-Cola stock using only this data.

 25. Suppose that in January 2006, Kenneth Cole Productions had EPS of $1.65 and a book value of equity of $12.05 per share.
   a. Using the average P/E multiple in Table 9.1, estimate KCP's share price.
   b. What range of share prices do you estimate based on the highest and lowest P/E multiples in Table 9.1?
   c. Using the average price to book value multiple in Table 9.1, estimate KCP's share price.
   d. What range of share prices do you estimate based on the highest and lowest price to book value multiples in Table 9.1?

 26. Suppose that in January 2006, Kenneth Cole Productions had sales of $518 million, EBITDA of $55.6 million, excess cash of $100 million, $3 million of debt, and 21 million shares outstanding.
   a. Using the average enterprise value to sales multiple in Table 9.1, estimate KCP's share price.
   b. What range of share prices do you estimate based on the highest and lowest enterprise value to sales multiples in Table 9.1?
   c. Using the average enterprise value to EBITDA multiple in Table 9.1, estimate KCP's share price.
   d. What range of share prices do you estimate based on the highest and lowest enterprise value to EBITDA multiples in Table 9.1?

 27. In addition to footwear, Kenneth Cole Productions designs and sells handbags, apparel, and other accessories. You decide, therefore, to consider comparables for KCP outside the footwear industry.
   a. Suppose that Fossil, Inc., has an enterprise value to EBITDA multiple of 9.73 and a P/E multiple of 18.4. What share price would you estimate for KCP using each of these multiples, based on the data for KCP in Problems 25 and 26?
   b. Suppose that Tommy Hilfiger Corporation has an enterprise value to EBITDA multiple of 7.19 and a P/E multiple of 17.2. What share price would you estimate for KCP using each of these multiples, based on the data for KCP in Problems 25 and 26?

 28. Consider the following data for the airline industry for August 1, 2012 (EV = enterprise value, Book = tangible book value, NM = not meaningful because divisor is negative). Discuss the challenges of using multiples to value an airline.

Company Name	Market Cap	EV	EV/Sales	EV/EBITDA	EV/EBIT	P/E	P/Book
Delta Air Lines (DAL)	7,972.7	17,557.7	0.48x	4.1x	6.3x	8.7x	NM
United Continental (UAL)	6,038.9	10,781.9	0.29x	3.2x	5.3x	15.5x	NM
Southwest Airlines (LUV)	6,821.4	6,841.4	0.40x	4.0x	7.3x	21.1x	1.2x
US Airways (LCC)	1,758.1	3,726.1	0.27x	3.6x	4.8x	4.3x	NM
JetBlue Airways (JBLU)	1,441.2	3,122.2	0.65x	4.9x	8.0x	11.9x	0.8x
Alaska Air (ALK)	2,402.5	2,174.2	0.48x	2.7x	4.0x	9.9x	1.9x
SkyWest (SKYW)	333.7	1,551.5	0.42x	5.1x	31.4x	NM	0.3x
Hawaiian (HA)	317.1	480.8	0.27x	2.4x	3.9x	5.5x	3.7x

Source: Capital IQ

Information, Competition, and Stock Prices

29. You read in the paper that Summit Systems from Problem 6 has revised its growth prospects and now expects its dividends to grow at 3% per year forever.
    a. What is the new value of a share of Summit Systems stock based on this information?
    b. If you tried to sell your Summit Systems stock after reading this news, what price would you be likely to get and why?

30. In mid-2012, Coca-Cola Company (KO) had a share price of $39. Its dividend was $1.00 per year, and you expect Coca-Cola to raise this dividend by approximately 7% per year in perpetuity.
    a. If Coca-Cola's equity cost of capital is 8%, what share price would you expect based on your estimate of the dividend growth rate?
    b. Given Coca-Cola's share price, what would you conclude about your assessment of Coca-Cola's future dividend growth?

31. Roybus, Inc., a manufacturer of flash memory, just reported that its main production facility in Taiwan was destroyed in a fire. While the plant was fully insured, the loss of production will decrease Roybus' free cash flow by $180 million at the end of this year and by $60 million at the end of next year.
    a. If Roybus has 35 million shares outstanding and a weighted average cost of capital of 13%, what change in Roybus' stock price would you expect upon this announcement? (Assume the value of Roybus' debt is not affected by the event.)
    b. Would you expect to be able to sell Roybus' stock on hearing this announcement and make a profit? Explain.

32. Apnex, Inc., is a biotechnology firm that is about to announce the results of its clinical trials of a potential new cancer drug. If the trials were successful, Apnex stock will be worth $70 per share. If the trials were unsuccessful, Apnex stock will be worth $18 per share. Suppose that the morning before the announcement is scheduled, Apnex shares are trading for $55 per share.
    a. Based on the current share price, what sort of expectations do investors seem to have about the success of the trials?
    b. Suppose hedge fund manager Paul Kliner has hired several prominent research scientists to examine the public data on the drug and make their own assessment of the drug's promise. Would Kliner's fund be likely to profit by trading the stock in the hours prior to the announcement?
    c. What would limit the fund's ability to profit on its information?

Data Case

As a new analyst for a large brokerage firm, you are anxious to demonstrate the skills you learned in your MBA program and prove that you are worth your attractive salary. Your first assignment is to analyze the stock of the General Electric Corporation. Your boss recommends determining prices based on both the dividend-discount model and discounted free cash flow valuation methods. GE uses a cost of equity of 10.5% and an after-tax weighted average cost of capital of 7.5%. The expected return on new investments is 12%. However, you are a little concerned because your finance professor has told you that these two methods can result in widely differing estimates when applied to real data. You are really hoping that the two methods will reach similar prices. Good luck with that!

1. Go to Yahoo! Finance (http://finance.yahoo.com) and enter the symbol for General Electric (GE). From the main page for GE, gather the following information and enter it onto a spreadsheet:
    a. The current stock price (last trade) at the top of the page.
    b. The current dividend amount, which is in the bottom-right cell in the same box as the stock price.

2. Next, click "Key Statistics" from the left side of the page. From the Key Statistics page, gather the following information and enter it on the same spreadsheet:
   a. The number of shares of stock outstanding.
   b. The Payout ratio.

3. Next, click "Analyst Estimates" from the left side of the page. From the Analyst Estimates page, find the expected growth rate for the next five years and enter it onto your spreadsheet. It will be near the very bottom of the page.

4. Next, click "Income Statement" near the bottom of the menu on the left. Copy and paste the entire three years of income statements into a new worksheet in your existing Excel file. (*Note*: if you are using IE as your browser, you can place the cursor in the middle of the statement, right-click, and select "Export to Microsoft Excel" to download an Excel version.) Repeat this process for both the balance sheet and cash flow statement for General Electric. Keep all the different statements in the same Excel worksheet.

5. To determine the stock value based on the dividend-discount model:
   a. Create a timeline in Excel for five years.
   b. Use the dividend obtained from Yahoo! Finance as the current dividend to forecast the next five annual dividends based on the five-year growth rate.
   c. Determine the long-term growth rate based on GE's payout ratio (which is one minus the retention ratio) using Eq. 9.12.
   d. Use the long-term growth rate to determine the stock price for year five using Eq. 9.13.
   e. Determine the current stock price using Eq. 9.14.

6. To determine the stock value based on the discounted free cash flow method:
   a. Forecast the free cash flows using the historic data from the financial statements downloaded from Yahoo! to compute the three-year average of the following ratios:
      i. EBIT/Sales
      ii. Tax Rate (Income Tax Expense/Income Before Tax)
      iii. Property Plant and Equipment/Sales
      iv. Depreciation/Property Plant and Equipment
      v. Net Working Capital/Sales
   b. Create a timeline for the next seven years.
   c. Forecast future sales based on the most recent year's total revenue growing at the five-year growth rate from Yahoo! for the first five years and the long-term growth rate for years 6 and 7.
   d. Use the average ratios computed in part (a) to forecast EBIT, property, plant and equipment, depreciation, and net working capital for the next seven years.
   e. Forecast the free cash flow for the next seven years using Eq. 9.18.
   f. Determine the horizon enterprise value for year 5 using Eq. 9.24.
   g. Determine the enterprise value of the firm as the present value of the free cash flows.
   h. Determine the stock price using Eq. 9.22.

7. Compare the stock prices from the two methods to the actual stock price. What recommendations can you make as to whether clients should buy or sell GE stock based on your price estimates?

8. Explain to your boss why the estimates from the two valuation methods differ. Specifically, address the assumptions implicit in the models themselves as well as those you made in preparing your analysis. Why do these estimates differ from the actual stock price of GE?

PART

Risk and Return

4

THE LAW OF ONE PRICE CONNECTION. To apply the Law of One Price correctly requires comparing investment opportunities of equivalent risk. In this part of the book, we explain how to measure and compare risks across investment opportunities. Chapter 10 introduces the key insight that investors only demand a risk premium for risk they cannot eliminate without cost by diversifying their portfolios. Hence, only non-diversifiable market risk will matter when comparing investment opportunities. Intuitively, this insight suggests that an investment's risk premium will depend on its sensitivity to market risk. In Chapter 11, we quantify these ideas and derive investors' optimal investment portfolio choices. We then consider the implications of assuming all investors choose their portfolio of investments optimally. This assumption leads to the *Capital Asset Pricing Model* (CAPM), the central model in financial economics that quantifies the notion of "equivalent risk" and thereby provides the relation between risk and return. In Chapter 12, we apply these ideas and consider the practicalities of estimating the cost of capital for a firm and for an individual investment project. Chapter 13 takes a closer look at the behavior of individual, as well as professional, investors. Doing so reveals some strengths and weaknesses of the CAPM, as well as ways we can combine the CAPM with the principle of no arbitrage for a more general model of risk and return.

Capital Markets and the Pricing of Risk

OVER THE FIVE-YEAR PERIOD 2003 THROUGH 2007, investors in General Mills, Inc., earned an average return of 7% per year. Within this period, there was some variation, with the annual return ranging from −1.2% in 2003 to almost 20% in 2006. Over the same period, investors in eBay, Inc., earned an average return of 25%. These investors, however, gained over 90% in 2003 and lost 30% in 2006. Finally, investors in three-month U.S. Treasury bills earned an average return of 2.9% during the period, with a low return of 1.3% in 2004 and a high return of 5% in 2007. Clearly, these three investments offered returns that were very different in terms of their average level and their variability. What accounts for these differences?

In this chapter, we will consider why these differences exist. Our goal is to develop a theory that explains the relationship between average returns and the variability of returns and thereby derive the risk premium that investors require to hold different securities and investments. We then use this theory to explain how to determine the cost of capital for an investment opportunity.

We begin our investigation of the relationship between risk and return by examining historical data for publicly traded securities. We will see, for example, that while stocks are riskier investments than bonds, they have also earned higher average returns. We can interpret the higher average return on stocks as compensation to investors for the greater risk they are taking.

But we will also find that not all risk needs to be compensated. By holding a portfolio containing many different investments, investors can eliminate risks that are specific to individual securities. Only those risks that cannot be eliminated by holding a large portfolio determine the risk premium required by investors. These observations will allow us to refine our definition of what risk is, how we can measure it, and thus, how to determine the cost of capital.

10.1 Risk and Return: Insights from 86 Years of Investor History

We begin our look at risk and return by illustrating how risk affects investor decisions and returns. Suppose your great-grandparents invested $100 on your behalf at the end of 1925. They instructed their broker to reinvest any dividends or interest earned in the account until the beginning of 2012. How would that $100 have grown if it were placed in one of the following investments?

1. Standard & Poor's 500 (S&P 500): A portfolio, constructed by Standard and Poor's, comprising 90 U.S. stocks up to 1957 and 500 U.S. stocks after that. The firms represented are leaders in their respective industries and are among the largest firms, in terms of market value, traded on U.S. markets.

2. Small Stocks: A portfolio, updated quarterly, of U.S. stocks traded on the NYSE with market capitalizations in the bottom 20%.

3. World Portfolio: A portfolio of international stocks from all of the world's major stock markets in North America, Europe, and Asia.[1]

4. Corporate Bonds: A portfolio of long-term, AAA-rated U.S. corporate bonds with maturities of approximately 20 years.[2]

5. Treasury Bills: An investment in one-month U.S. Treasury bills.

Figure 10.1 shows the result, through the start of 2012, of investing $100 at the end of 1925 in each of these five investment portfolios, ignoring transactions costs. During this 86-year period in the United States, small stocks experienced the highest long-term return, followed by the large stocks in the S&P 500, the international stocks in the world portfolio, corporate bonds, and finally Treasury bills. All of the investments grew faster than inflation, as measured by the consumer price index (CPI).

At first glance the graph is striking—had your great-grandparents invested $100 in the small stock portfolio, the investment would be worth more than $2.6 million at the beginning of 2012! By contrast, if they had invested in Treasury bills, the investment would be worth only about $2,000. Given this wide difference, why invest in anything other than small stocks?

But first impressions can be misleading. While over the full horizon stocks (especially small stocks) did outperform the other investments, they also endured periods of significant losses. Had your great-grandparents put the $100 in a small stock portfolio during the Depression era of the 1930s, it would have grown to $181 in 1928, but then fallen to only $15 by 1932. Indeed, it would take until World War II for stock investments to outperform corporate bonds.

Even more importantly, your great-grandparents would have sustained losses at a time when they likely needed their savings the most—in the depths of the Great Depression. A similar story held during the 2008 financial crisis: All of the stock portfolios declined by more than 50%, with the small stock portfolio declining by almost 70% (over $1.5 million!) from its peak in 2007 to its lowest point in 2009. Again, many investors faced a double whammy: an increased risk of being unemployed (as firms started laying off employees)

---

[1]Based on the Morgan Stanley Capital International World Index from 1970. Prior to 1970, the index is constructed by Global Financial Data, with approximate initial weights of 44% North America, 44% Europe, and 12% Asia, Africa, and Australia.

[2]Based on Moody's AAA Corporate Bond Index.

| FIGURE 10.1 | **Value of $100 Invested in 1925 in Stocks, Bonds, or Bills** |

The chart shows the growth in value of $100 invested in 1925 if it were invested in U.S. large stocks, small stocks, world stocks, corporate bonds, or Treasury bills, with the level of the consumer price index (CPI) shown as a reference. Returns were calculated at year-end assuming all dividends and interest are reinvested and excluding transactions costs. Note that while stocks have generally outperformed bonds and bills, they have also endured periods of significant losses (numbers shown represent peak to trough decline, with the decline in small stocks in red and the S&P 500 in blue).

Source: Chicago Center for Research in Security Prices, Standard and Poor's, MSCI, and Global Financial Data.

precisely when the value of their savings eroded. Thus, while the stock portfolios had the best performance over this 86-year period, that performance came at a cost—the risk of large losses in a downturn. On the other hand, Treasury bills enjoyed steady—albeit modest—gains each year.

Few people ever make an investment for 86 years, as depicted in Figure 10.1. To gain additional perspective on the risk and return of these investments, Figure 10.2 shows the results for more realistic investment horizons and different initial investment dates. Panel (a), for example, shows the value of each investment after one year and illustrates that if we rank the investments by the volatility of their annual increases and decreases in value, we obtain the same ranking we observed with regard to performance: Small stocks had the most variable returns, followed by the S&P 500, the world portfolio, corporate bonds, and finally Treasury bills.

Panels (b), (c), and (d) of Figure 10.2 show the results for 5-, 10-, and 20-year investment horizons, respectively. Note that as the horizon lengthens, the relative performance of the stock portfolios improves. That said, even with a 10-year horizon there were periods during which stocks underperformed Treasuries. And while investors in small stocks most often came out ahead, this was not assured even with a 20-year horizon: For investors in

Value of $100 Invested in Alternative Assets for Differing Horizons

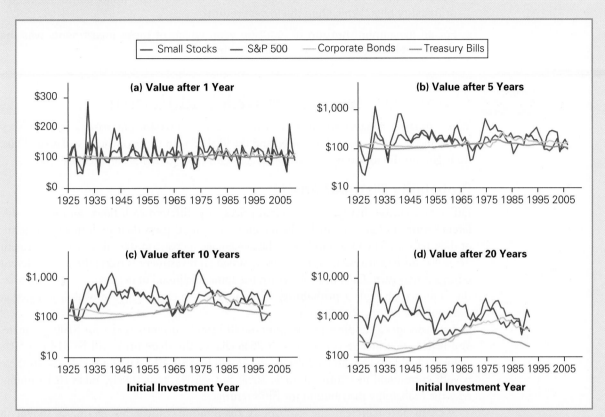

Each panel shows the result of investing $100 at the end of the initial investment year, in each investment opportunity, for horizons of 1, 5, 10, or 20 years. That is, each point on the plot is the result of an investment over the specified horizon, plotted as a function of the initial investment date. Dividends and interest are reinvested and transaction costs are excluded. Note that small stocks show the greatest variation in performance at the one-year horizon, followed by large stocks and then corporate bonds. For longer horizons, the relative performance of stocks improved, but they remained riskier.

Source Data: Chicago Center for Research in Security Prices, Standard and Poor's, MSCI, and Global Financial Data.

the early 1980s, small stocks did worse than both the S&P 500 *and* corporate bonds over the subsequent 20 years. Finally, stock investors with long potential horizons might find themselves in need of cash in intervening years, and be forced to liquidate at a loss relative to safer alternatives.

In Chapter 3, we explained why investors are averse to fluctuations in the value of their investments, and that investments that are more likely to suffer losses in downturns must compensate investors for this risk with higher expected returns. Figures 10.1 and 10.2 provide compelling historical evidence of this relationship between risk and return, just as we should expect in an efficient market. But while it is clear that investors do not like risk and thus demand a risk premium to bear it, our goal in this chapter is to quantify this relationship. We want to explain *how much* investors demand (in terms of a higher expected return) to bear a given level of risk. To do so, we must first develop tools that will allow us to measure risk and return—the objective of the next section.

1. For an investment horizon from 1926 to 2012, which of the following investments had the highest return: the S&P 500, small stocks, world portfolio, corporate bonds, or Treasury bills? Which had the lowest return?

2. For an investment horizon of just one year, which of these investments was the most variable? Which was the least variable?

10.2 Common Measures of Risk and Return

When a manager makes an investment decision or an investor purchases a security, they have some view as to the risk involved and the likely return the investment will earn. Thus, we begin our discussion by reviewing the standard ways to define and measure risks.

Probability Distributions

Different securities have different initial prices, pay different cash flows, and sell for different future amounts. To make them comparable, we express their performance in terms of their returns. The return indicates the percentage increase in the value of an investment per dollar initially invested in the security. When an investment is risky, there are different returns it may earn. Each possible return has some likelihood of occurring. We summarize this information with a **probability distribution**, which assigns a probability, P_R, that each possible return, R, will occur.

Let's consider a simple example. Suppose BFI stock currently trades for $100 per share. You believe that in one year there is a 25% chance the share price will be $140, a 50% chance it will be $110, and a 25% chance it will be $80. BFI pays no dividends, so these payoffs correspond to returns of 40%, 10%, and −20%, respectively. Table 10.1 summarizes the probability distribution for BFI's returns.

We can also represent the probability distribution with a histogram, as shown in Figure 10.3.

Expected Return

Given the probability distribution of returns, we can compute the expected return. We calculate the **expected** (or **mean**) **return** as a weighted average of the possible returns, where the weights correspond to the probabilities.[3]

Expected (Mean) Return

$$\text{Expected Return} = E[R] = \sum_R p_R \times R \qquad (10.1)$$

TABLE 10.1	Probability Distribution of Returns for BFI			
			Probability Distribution	
Current Stock Price ($)	**Stock Price in One Year ($)**		**Return, R**	**Probability, P_R**
	140		0.40	25%
100	110		0.10	50%
	80		−0.20	25%

[3]The notation $\sum_R$ means that we calculate the sum of the expression (in this case, $p_R \times R$) over all possible returns R.

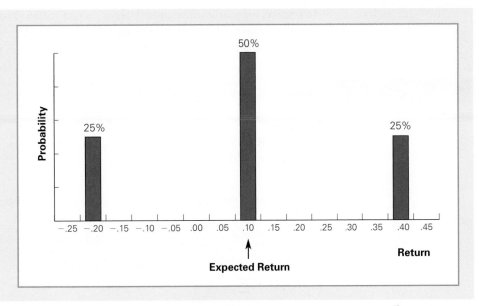

FIGURE 10.3

Probability Distribution of Returns for BFI

The height of a bar in the histogram indicates the likelihood of the associated outcome.

The expected return is the return we would earn on average if we could repeat the investment many times, drawing the return from the same distribution each time. In terms of the histogram, the expected return is the "balancing point" of the distribution, if we think of the probabilities as weights. The expected return for BFI is

$$E[R_{BFI}] = 25\%(-0.20) + 50\%(0.10) + 25\%(0.40) = 10\%$$

This expected return corresponds to the balancing point in Figure 10.3.

Variance and Standard Deviation

Two common measures of the risk of a probability distribution are its *variance* and *standard deviation*. The **variance** is the expected squared deviation from the mean, and the **standard deviation** is the square root of the variance.

Variance and Standard Deviation of the Return Distribution

$$Var(R) = E[(R - E[R])^2] = \sum_R p_R \times (R - E[R])^2$$

$$SD(R) = \sqrt{Var(R)} \tag{10.2}$$

If the return is risk-free and never deviates from its mean, the variance is zero. Otherwise, the variance increases with the magnitude of the deviations from the mean. Therefore, the variance is a measure of how "spread out" the distribution of the return is. The variance of BFI's return is

$$Var(R_{BFI}) = 25\% \times (-0.20-0.10)^2 + 50\% \times (0.10-0.10)^2 + 25\% \times (0.40-0.10)^2$$

$$= 0.045$$

The standard deviation of the return is the square root of the variance, so for BFI,

$$SD(R) = \sqrt{Var(R)} = \sqrt{0.045} = 21.2\% \tag{10.3}$$

In finance, we refer to the standard deviation of a return as its **volatility**. While the variance and the standard deviation both measure the variability of the returns, the standard deviation is easier to interpret because it is in the same units as the returns themselves.[4]

EXAMPLE 10.1   **Calculating the Expected Return and Volatility**

Problem
Suppose AMC stock is equally likely to have a 45% return or a −25% return. What are its expected return and volatility?

Solution
First, we calculate the expected return by taking the probability-weighted average of the possible returns:

$$E[R] = \sum_R p_R \times R = 50\% \times 0.45 + 50\% \times (-0.25) = 10.0\%$$

To compute the volatility, we first determine the variance:

$$Var(R) = \sum_R p_R \times (R - E[R])^2 = 50\% \times (0.45 - 0.10)^2 + 50\% \times (-0.25 - 0.10)^2$$
$$= 0.1225$$

Then, the volatility or standard deviation is the square root of the variance:

$$SD(R) = \sqrt{Var(R)} = \sqrt{0.1225} = 35\%$$

Note that both AMC and BFI have the same expected return, 10%. However, the returns for AMC are more spread out than those for BFI—the high returns are higher and the low returns are lower, as shown by the histogram in Figure 10.4. As a result, AMC has a higher variance and volatility than BFI.

FIGURE 10.4

Probability Distribution for BFI and AMC Returns

While both stocks have the same expected return, AMC's return has a higher variance and standard deviation.

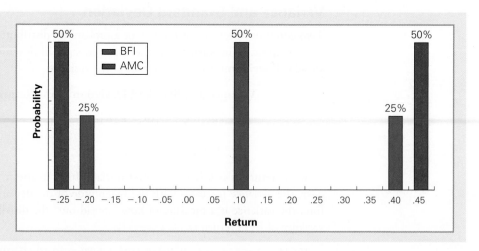

---

[4]While variance and standard deviation are the most common measures of risk, they do not differentiate upside and downside risk. Alternative measures that focus on downside risk include the semivariance (variance of the losses only) and the expected tail loss (the expected loss in the worst x% of outcomes). Because they often produce the same ranking (as in Example 10.1, or if returns are normally distributed) but are more complicated to apply, these alternative measures tend to be used only in special applications.

If we could observe the probability distributions that investors anticipate for different securities, we could compute their expected returns and volatilities and explore the relationship between them. Of course, in most situations we do not know the explicit probability distribution, as we did for BFI. Without that information, how can we estimate and compare risk and return? A popular approach is to extrapolate from historical data, which is a sensible strategy if we are in a stable environment and believe that the distribution of future returns should mirror that of past returns. Let's look at the historical returns of stocks and bonds, to see what they reveal about the relationship between risk and return.

CONCEPT CHECK

1. How do we calculate the expected return of a stock?

2. What are the two most common measures of risk, and how are they related to each other?

10.3 Historical Returns of Stocks and Bonds

In this section, we explain how to compute average returns and volatilities using historical stock market data. The distribution of past returns can be helpful when we seek to estimate the distribution of returns investors may expect in the future. We begin by first explaining how to compute historical returns.

Computing Historical Returns

Of all the possible returns, the **realized return** is the return that actually occurs over a particular time period. How do we measure the realized return for a stock? Suppose you invest in a stock on date t for price P_t. If the stock pays a dividend, Div_{t+1}, on date $t + 1$, and you sell the stock at that time for price P_{t+1}, then the realized return from your investment in the stock from t to $t + 1$ is

$$R_{t+1} = \frac{Div_{t+1} + P_{t+1}}{P_t} - 1 = \frac{Div_{i+1}}{P_t} + \frac{P_{t+1} - P_t}{P_t}$$

$$= \text{Dividend Yield} + \text{Capital Gain Rate} \qquad (10.4)$$

That is, as we discussed in Chapter 9, the realized return, R_{t+1}, is the total return we earn from dividends and capital gains, expressed as a percentage of the initial stock price.[5]

Calculating Realized Annual Returns. If you hold the stock beyond the date of the first dividend, then to compute your return you must specify how you invest any dividends you receive in the interim. To focus on the returns of a single security, let's assume that *you reinvest all dividends immediately and use them to purchase additional shares of the same stock or security.* In this case, we can use Eq. 10.4 to compute the stock's return between dividend payments, and then compound the returns from each dividend interval to compute the return over a longer horizon. For example, if a stock pays dividends at the end of each quarter, with realized returns $R_{Q1}, \ldots, R_{Q4}$ each quarter, then its annual realized return, R_{annual}, is

$$1 + R_{annual} = (1 + R_{Q1})(1 + R_{Q2})(1 + R_{Q3})(1 + R_{Q4}) \qquad (10.5)$$

---

[5]We can compute the realized return for any security in the same way, by replacing the dividend payments with any cash flows paid by the security (e.g., with a bond, coupon payments would replace dividends).

| EXAMPLE 10.2 | **Realized Returns for Microsoft Stock** |

Problem

What were the realized annual returns for Microsoft stock in 2004 and 2008?

Solution

When we compute Microsoft's annual return, we assume that the proceeds from the dividend payment were immediately reinvested in Microsoft stock. That way, the return corresponds to remaining fully invested in Microsoft over the entire period. To do that we look up Microsoft stock price data at the start and end of the year, as well as at any dividend dates (Yahoo!Finance is a good source for such data; see also MyFinanceLab or www.pearsonglobaleditions.com/berk for additional sources). From these data, we can construct the following table (prices and dividends in $/share):

Date	Price	Dividend	Return	Date	Price	Dividend	Return
12/31/03	27.37			12/31/07	35.60		
8/23/04	27.24	0.08	−0.18%	2/19/08	28.17	0.11	−20.56%
11/15/04[6]	27.39	3.08	11.86%	5/13/08	29.78	0.11	6.11%
12/31/04	26.72		−2.45%	8/19/08	27.32	0.11	−7.89%
				11/18/08	19.62	0.13	−27.71%
				12/31/08	19.44		−0.92%

The return from December 31, 2003, until August 23, 2004, is equal to

$$\frac{0.08 + 27.24}{27.37} - 1 = -0.18\%$$

The rest of the returns in the table are computed similarly. We then calculate the annual returns using Eq. 10.5:

$$R_{2004} = (0.9982)(1.1186)(0.9755) - 1 = 8.92\%$$

$$R_{2008} = (0.7944)(1.0611)(0.9211)(0.7229)(0.9908) - 1 = -44.39\%$$

Example 10.2 illustrates two features of the returns from holding a stock like Microsoft. First, both dividends and capital gains contribute to the total realized return—ignoring either one would give a very misleading impression of Microsoft's performance. Second, the returns are risky. In years like 2004 the returns are positive, but in other years like 2008 they are negative, meaning Microsoft's shareholders lost money over the year.

We can compute realized returns in this same way for any investment. We can also compute the realized returns for an entire portfolio, by keeping track of the interest and dividend payments paid by the portfolio during the year, as well as the change in the market value of the portfolio. For example, the realized returns for the S&P 500 index are shown in Table 10.2, which for comparison purposes also lists the returns for Microsoft and for three-month Treasury bills.

---

[6]The large dividend in November 2004 included a $3 special dividend which Microsoft used to reduce its accumulating cash balance and disburse $32 billion in cash to its investors, in the largest aggregate dividend payment in history.

TABLE 10.2	Realized Return for the S&P 500, Microsoft, and Treasury Bills, 2002–2011				
Year End	S&P 500 Index	Dividends Paid*	S&P 500 Realized Return	Microsoft Realized Return	1-Month T-Bill Return
2001	1148.08				
2002	879.82	14.53	−22.1%	−22.0%	1.6%
2003	1111.92	20.80	28.7%	6.8%	1.0%
2004	1211.92	20.98	10.9%	8.9%	1.2%
2005	1248.29	23.15	4.9%	−0.9%	3.0%
2006	1418.30	27.16	15.8%	15.8%	4.8%
2007	1468.36	27.86	5.5%	20.8%	4.7%
2008	903.25	21.85	−37.0%	−44.4%	1.5%
2009	1115.10	27.19	26.5%	60.5%	0.1%
2010	1257.64	25.44	15.1%	−6.5%	0.1%
2011	1257.60	26.59	2.1%	−4.5%	0.0%

*Total dividends paid by the 500 stocks in the portfolio, based on the number of shares of each stock in the index, adjusted until the end of the year, assuming they were reinvested when paid.

Source: Standard & Poor's, Microsoft and U.S. Treasury Data

Comparing Realized Annual Returns. Once we have calculated the realized annual returns, we can compare them to see which investments performed better in a given year. From Table 10.2, we can see that Microsoft stock outperformed the S&P 500 and Treasuries in 2007 and 2009. On the other hand, in 2002 and 2008, Treasury bills performed better than both Microsoft stock and the S&P 500. Note also the overall tendency for Microsoft's return to move in the same direction as the S&P 500, which it did in seven out of the ten years.

Over any particular period we observe only one draw from the probability distribution of returns. However, if the probability distribution remains the same, we can observe multiple draws by observing the realized return over multiple periods. By counting the number of times the realized return falls within a particular range, we can estimate the underlying probability distribution. Let's illustrate this process with the data in Figure 10.1.

Figure 10.5 plots the annual returns for each U.S. investment in Figure 10.1 in a histogram. The height of each bar represents the number of years that the annual returns were in each range indicated on the *x*-axis. When we plot the probability distribution in this way using historical data, we refer to it as the **empirical distribution** of the returns.

Average Annual Returns

The **average annual return** of an investment during some historical period is simply the average of the realized returns for each year. That is, if R_t is the realized return of a security in year t, then the average annual return for years 1 through T is

Average Annual Return of a Security

$$\bar{R} = \frac{1}{T}(R_1 + R_2 + \cdots + R_T) = \frac{1}{T}\sum_{t=1}^{T} R_t \qquad (10.6)$$

Notice that the average annual return is the balancing point of the empirical distribution—in this case, the probability of a return occurring in a particular range is measured by the number of times the realized return falls in that range. Therefore, if the probability

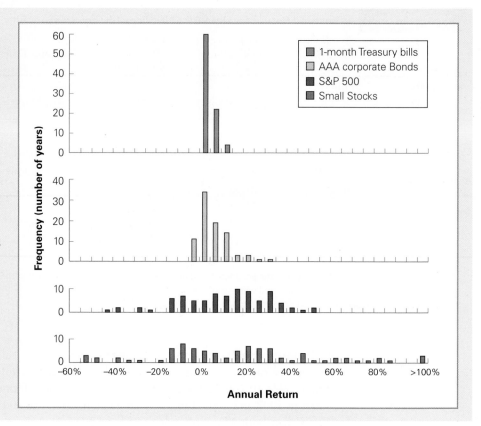

FIGURE 10.5

The Empirical Distribution of Annual Returns for U.S. Large Stocks (S&P 500), Small Stocks, Corporate Bonds, and Treasury Bills, 1926–2011.

The height of each bar represents the number of years that the annual returns were in each 5% range. Note the greater variability of stock returns (especially small stocks) compared to the returns of corporate bonds or Treasury bills.

distribution of the returns is the same over time, the average return provides an estimate of the expected return.

Using the data from Table 10.2, the average return for the S&P 500 for the years 2002–2011 is

$$\bar{R} = \frac{1}{10}(-0.221 + 0.287 + 0.109 + 0.049 + 0.158$$
$$+ 0.055 - 0.37 + 0.265 + 0.151 + 0.021) = 5.0\%$$

The average Treasury bill return from 2002–2011 was 1.8%. Therefore, investors earned 3.2% more on average holding the S&P 500 rather than investing in Treasury bills over this period. Table 10.3 provides the average returns for different U.S. Investments from 1926–2011.

TABLE 10.3	Average Annual Returns for U.S. Small Stocks, Large Stocks (S&P 500), Corporate Bonds, and Treasury Bills, 1926–2011

Investment	Average Annual Return
Small stocks	18.7%
S&P 500	11.7%
Corporate bonds	6.6%
Treasury bills	3.6%

The Variance and Volatility of Returns

Looking at Figure 10.5, we can see that the variability of the returns is very different for each investment. The distribution of small stocks' returns shows the widest spread. The large stocks of the S&P 500 have returns that vary less than those of small stocks, but much more than the returns of corporate bonds or Treasury bills.

To quantify this difference in variability, we can estimate the standard deviation of the probability distribution. As before, we will use the empirical distribution to derive this estimate. Using the same logic as we did with the mean, we estimate the variance by computing the average squared deviation from the mean. We do not actually know the mean, so instead we use the best estimate of the mean—the average realized return.[7]

Variance Estimate Using Realized Returns

$$Var(R) = \frac{1}{T-1} \sum_{t=1}^{T} (R_t - \overline{R})^2 \tag{10.7}$$

We estimate the standard deviation or volatility as the square root of the variance.[8]

EXAMPLE 10.3

Computing a Historical Volatility

Problem
Using the data from Table 10.2, what are the variance and volatility of the S&P 500's returns for the years 2002–2011?

Solution
Earlier, we calculated the average annual return of the S&P 500 during this period to be 5.0%. Therefore,

$$Var(R) = \frac{1}{T-1} \sum_t (R_t - \overline{R})^2$$

$$= \frac{1}{10-1} [(-0.221 - 0.05)^2 + (0.287 - 0.05)^2 + \cdots + (0.021 - 0.05)^2]$$

$$= 0.042$$

The volatility or standard deviation is therefore $SD(R) = \sqrt{Var(R)} = \sqrt{0.042} = 20.5\%$

We can compute the standard deviation of the returns to quantify the differences in the variability of the distributions that we observed in Figure 10.5. These results are shown in Table 10.4.

Comparing the volatilities in Table 10.4 we see that, as expected, small stocks have had the most variable historical returns, followed by large stocks. The returns of corporate bonds and Treasury bills are much less variable than stocks, with Treasury bills being the least volatile investment category.

---

[7]Why do we divide by $T-1$ rather than by T here? It is because we do not know the true expected return, and so must compute deviations from the estimated average return $\overline{R}$. But in calculating the average return from the data, we lose a degree of freedom (in essence, we "use up" one of the data points), so that effectively we only have $T-1$ remaining data points to estimate the variance.

[8]If the returns used in Eq. 10.7 are not annual returns, the variance is typically converted to annual terms by multiplying the number of periods per year. For example, when using monthly returns, we multiply the variance by 12 and, equivalently, the standard deviation by $\sqrt{12}$.

TABLE 10.4	Volatility of U.S. Small Stocks, Large Stocks (S&P 500), Corporate Bonds, and Treasury Bills, 1926–2011

Investment	Return Volatility (Standard Deviation)
Small stocks	39.2%
S&P 500	20.3%
Corporate bonds	7.0%
Treasury bills	3.1%

Estimation Error: Using Past Returns to Predict the Future

To estimate the cost of capital for an investment, we need to determine the expected return that investors will require to compensate them for that investment's risk. If the distribution of past returns and the distribution of future returns are the same, we could look at the return investors expected to earn in the past on the same or similar investments, and assume they will require the same return in the future. However, there are two difficulties with this approach. First,

We do not know what investors expected in the past; we can only observe the actual returns that were realized.

In 2008, for example, investors lost 37% investing in the S&P 500, which is surely not what they expected at the beginning of the year (or they would have invested in Treasury Bills instead!).

If we believe that investors are neither overly optimistic nor pessimistic on average, then over time, the average realized return should match investors' expected return. Armed with this assumption, we can use a security's historical average return to infer its expected return. But now we encounter the second difficulty:

The average return is just an estimate of the true expected return, and is subject to estimation error.

Given the volatility of stock returns, this estimation error can be large even with many years of data, as we will see next.

Standard Error. We measure the estimation error of a statistical estimate by its *standard error*. The **standard error** is the standard deviation of the estimated value of the mean of the actual distribution around its true value; that is, it is the standard deviation of the average return. The standard error provides an indication of how far the sample average might deviate from the expected return. If the distribution of a stock's return is identical each year, and each year's return is independent of prior years' returns,[9] then we calculate the standard error of the estimate of the expected return as follows:

Standard Error of the Estimate of the Expected Return

$$SD \text{ (Average of Independent, Identical Risks)} = \frac{SD \text{ (Individual Risk)}}{\sqrt{\text{Number of Observations}}} \qquad (10.8)$$

---

[9]Saying that returns are independent and identically distributed (IID) means that the likelihood that the return has a given outcome is the same each year and does not depend on past returns (in the same way that the odds of a coin coming up heads do not depend on past flips). It turns out to be a reasonable first approximation for stock returns.

Because the average return will be within two standard errors of the true expected return approximately 95% of the time,[10] we can use the standard error to determine a reasonable range for the true expected value. The **95% confidence interval** for the expected return is

$$\text{Historical Average Return} \pm (2 \times \text{Standard Error}) \tag{10.9}$$

For example, from 1926 to 2011 the average return of the S&P 500 was 11.7% with a volatility of 20.3%. Assuming its returns are drawn from an independent and identical distribution (IID) each year, the 95% confidence interval for the expected return of the S&P 500 during this period is

$$11.7\% \pm 2\left(\frac{20.3\%}{\sqrt{86}}\right) = 11.7\% \pm 4.4\%$$

or a range from 7.3% to 16.1%. Thus, even with 86 years of data, we cannot estimate the expected return of the S&P 500 very accurately. If we believe the distribution may have changed over time and we can use only more recent data to estimate the expected return, then the estimate will be even less accurate.

Limitations of Expected Return Estimates. Individual stocks tend to be even more volatile than large portfolios, and many have been in existence for only a few years, providing little data with which to estimate returns. Because of the relatively large estimation error in such cases, the average return investors earned in the past is not a reliable estimate of a security's expected return. Instead, we need to derive a different method to estimate the expected return that relies on more reliable statistical estimates. In the remainder of this chapter, we will pursue the following alternative strategy: First we will consider how to measure a security's risk, and then we will use the relationship between risk and return— which we must still determine—to estimate its expected return.

EXAMPLE 10.4

The Accuracy of Expected Return Estimates

Problem
Using the returns for the S&P 500 from 2002–2011 only (see Table 10.2), what is the 95% confidence interval you would estimate for the S&P 500's expected return?

Solution
Earlier, we calculated the average return for the S&P 500 during this period to be 5.0%, with a volatility of 20.5% (see Example 10.3). The standard error of our estimate of the expected return is $20.5\% \div \sqrt{10} = 6.5\%$, and the 95% confidence interval is $5.0\% \pm (2 \times 6.5\%)$, or from -8% to 18%. As this example shows, with only a few years of data, we cannot reliably estimate expected returns for stocks.

CONCEPT CHECK

1. How do we estimate the average annual return of an investment?

2. We have 86 years of data on the S&P 500 returns, yet we cannot estimate the expected return of the S&P 500 very accurately. Why?

---

[10]If returns are independent and from a normal distribution, then the estimated mean will be within two standard errors of the true mean 95.44% of the time. Even if returns are not normally distributed, this formula is approximately correct with a sufficient number of independent observations.

Arithmetic Average Returns Versus Compound Annual Returns

We compute average annual returns by calculating an *arithmetic* average. An alternative is the compound annual return (also called the compound annual growth rate, or CAGR), which is computed as the *geometric* average of the annual returns $R_1, \ldots, R_T$:

Compound Annual Return =
$$[(1 + R_1) \times (1 + R_2) \times \ldots \times (1 + R_T)]^{1/T} - 1$$

It is equivalent to the IRR of the investment over the period:

$$(\text{Final Value/Initial Investment})^{1/T} - 1$$

For example, using the data in Figure 10.1, the compound annual return of the S&P 500 from 1926–2011 was

$$(275{,}240/100)^{1/86} - 1 = 9.65\%$$

That is, investing in the S&P 500 from 1926 to 2011 was equivalent to earning 9.65% per year over that time period. Similarly, the compound annual return for small stocks was 12.6%, for corporate bonds was 6.4%, and for Treasury bills was 3.6%.

In each case, the compound annual return is below the average annual return shown in Table 10.3. This difference reflects the fact that returns are volatile. To see the effect of volatility, suppose an investment has annual returns of +20% one year and −20% the next year. The average annual return is $\frac{1}{2}(20\% - 20\%) = 0\%$, but the value of $1 invested after two years is

$$\$1 \times (1.20) \times (0.80) = \$0.96$$

That is, an investor would have lost money. Why? Because the 20% gain happens on a $1 investment, whereas the 20% loss happens on a larger investment of $1.20. In this case, the compound annual return is

$$(0.96)^{1/2} - 1 = -2.02\%$$

This logic implies that the compound annual return will always be below the average return, and the difference grows with the volatility of the annual returns. (Typically, the difference is about half of the variance of the returns.)

Which is a better description of an investment's return? The compound annual return is a better description of the long-run *historical* performance of an investment. It describes the equivalent risk-free return that would be required to duplicate the investment's performance over the same time period. The ranking of the long-run performance of different investments coincides with the ranking of their compound annual returns. Thus, the compound annual return is the return that is most often used for comparison purposes. For example, mutual funds generally report their compound annual returns over the last five or ten years.

Conversely, we should use the arithmetic average return when we are trying to estimate an investment's *expected* return over a *future* horizon based on its past performance. If we view past returns as independent draws from the same distribution, then the arithmetic average return provides an unbiased estimate of the true expected return.[*]

For example, if the investment mentioned above is equally likely to have annual returns of +20% and −20% in the future, then if we observe many two-year periods, a $1 investment will be equally likely to grow to

$$(1.20)(1.20) = \$1.44,$$
$$(1.20)(0.80) = \$0.96,$$
$$(0.80)(1.20) = \$0.96,$$
$$\text{or} \quad (0.80)(0.80) = \$0.64.$$

Thus, the average value in two years will be $(1.44 + 0.96 + 0.96 + 0.64)/4 = \$1$, so that the expected annual and two-year returns will both be 0%.

[*]For this result to hold we must compute the historical returns using the same time interval as the expected return we are estimating; that is, we use the average of past monthly returns to estimate the future monthly return, or the average of past annual returns to estimate the future annual return. Because of estimation error the estimate for different time intervals will generally differ from the result one would get by simply compounding the average annual return. With enough data, however, the results will converge.

10.4 The Historical Trade-Off Between Risk and Return

In Chapter 3, we discussed the idea that investors are risk averse: The benefit they receive from an increase in income is smaller than the personal cost of an equivalent decrease in income. This idea suggests that investors would not choose to hold a portfolio that is more volatile unless they expected to earn a higher return. In this section, we quantify the historical relationship between volatility and average returns.

The Returns of Large Portfolios

In Tables 10.3 and 10.4, we computed the historical average returns and volatilities for several different types of investments. We combine those data in Table 10.5, which lists the volatility and *excess return* for each investment. The **excess return** is the difference between the average return for the investment and the average return for Treasury bills, a risk-free investment, and measures the average risk premium investors earned for bearing the risk of the investment.

In Figure 10.6, we plot the average return versus the volatility of different investments. In addition to the ones we have already considered, we also include data for a large portfolio of mid-cap stocks, or stocks of median size in the U.S. market. Note the positive relationship: The investments with higher volatility have rewarded investors with higher average returns. Both Table 10.5 and Figure 10.6 are consistent with our view that investors are risk averse. Riskier investments must offer investors higher average returns to compensate them for the extra risk they are taking on.

TABLE 10.5	Volatility Versus Excess Return of U.S. Small Stocks, Large Stocks (S&P 500), Corporate Bonds, and Treasury Bills, 1926–2011	
Investment	**Return Volatility (Standard Deviation)**	**Excess Return (Average Return in Excess of Treasury Bills)**
Small stocks	39.2%	15.1%
S&P 500	20.3%	8.1%
Corporate bonds	7.0%	3.0%
Treasury bills	3.1%	0.0%

FIGURE 10.6

The Historical Trade-Off Between Risk and Return in Large Portfolios

Note the general increasing relationship between historical volatility and average return for these large portfolios. In addition to the portfolios in Figure 10.1, also included is a mid-cap portfolio composed of the 10% of U.S. stocks whose size is just above the median of all U.S. stocks. (Data from 1926–2011.)

Source: CRSP, Morgan Stanley Capital International

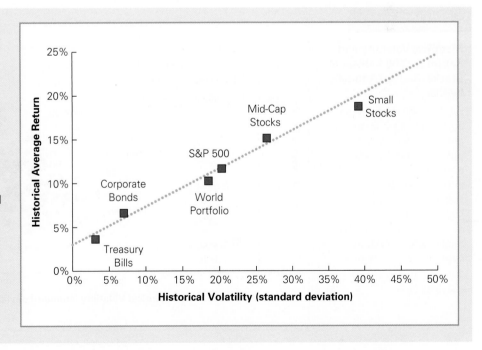

The Returns of Individual Stocks

Figure 10.6 suggests the following simple model of the risk premium: Investments with higher volatility should have a higher risk premium and therefore higher returns. Indeed, looking at Figure 10.6 it is tempting to draw a line through the portfolios and conclude that all investments should lie on or near this line—that is, expected return should rise proportionately with volatility. This conclusion appears to be approximately true for the large portfolios we have looked at so far. Is it correct? Does it apply to individual stocks?

Unfortunately, the answer to both questions is no. Figure 10.7 shows that, if we look at the volatility and return of individual stocks, we do not see any clear relationship between them. Each point represents the volatility and average return from investing in the Nth largest stock traded in the United States (updated quarterly) for $N = 1$ to 500.

We can make several important observations from these data. First, there is a relationship between size and risk: Larger stocks have lower volatility overall. Second, even the largest stocks are typically more volatile than a portfolio of large stocks, the S&P 500. Finally, there is no clear relationship between volatility and return. While the smallest stocks have a slightly higher average return, many stocks have higher volatility and lower average returns than other stocks. And all stocks seem to have higher risk and lower returns than we would have predicted from a simple extrapolation of our data from large portfolios.

Thus, while volatility is perhaps a reasonable measure of risk when evaluating a large portfolio, it is not adequate to explain the returns of individual securities. Why wouldn't investors demand a higher return from stocks with a higher volatility? And how is it that the S&P 500—a portfolio of the 500 largest stocks—is so much less risky than all of the 500 stocks individually? To answer these questions, we need to think more carefully about how to measure risk for an investor.

FIGURE 10.7

Historical Volatility and Return for 500 Individual Stocks, Ranked Annually by Size

Unlike the case for large portfolios, there is no precise relationship between volatility and average return for individual stocks. Individual stocks have higher volatility and lower average returns than the relationship shown for large portfolios. (Annual data from 1926–2011.)

Source: CRSP

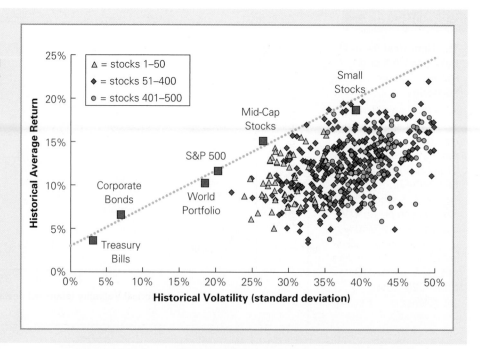

1. What is the excess return?

2. Do expected returns of well-diversified large portfolios of stocks appear to increase with volatility?

3. Do expected returns for individual stocks appear to increase with volatility?

10.5 Common Versus Independent Risk

In this section, we explain why the risk of an individual security differs from the risk of a portfolio composed of similar securities. We begin with an example from the insurance industry.

Theft Versus Earthquake Insurance: An Example

Consider two types of home insurance: theft insurance and earthquake insurance. Let us assume, for the purpose of illustration, that the risk of each of these two hazards is similar for a given home in the San Francisco area. Each year there is about a 1% chance that the home will be robbed and a 1% chance that the home will be damaged by an earthquake. So, the chance the insurance company will pay a claim for a single home is the same for both types of insurance policies. Suppose an insurance company writes 100,000 policies of each type for homeowners in San Francisco. We know that the risks of the individual policies are similar, but are the risks of the portfolios of policies similar?

First, consider theft insurance. Because the chance of a theft in any given home is 1%, we would expect about 1% of the 100,000 homes to experience a robbery. Thus, the number of theft claims will be about 1000 per year. The actual number of claims may be a bit higher or lower each year, but not by much. We can estimate the likelihood that the insurance company will receive different numbers of claims, assuming that instances of theft are independent of one another (that is, the fact that one house is robbed does not change the odds of other houses being robbed). The number of claims will almost always be between 875 and 1125 (0.875% and 1.125% of the number of policies written). In this case, if the insurance company holds reserves sufficient to cover 1200 claims, it will almost certainly have enough to meet its obligations on its theft insurance policies.

Now consider earthquake insurance. Most years, an earthquake will not occur. But because the homes are in the same city, if an earthquake does occur, all homes are likely to be affected and the insurance company can expect as many as 100,000 claims. As a result, the insurance company will have to hold reserves sufficient to cover claims on all 100,000 policies it wrote to meet its obligations if an earthquake occurs.

Thus, although the expected numbers of claims may be the same, earthquake and theft insurance lead to portfolios with very different risk characteristics. For earthquake insurance, the number of claims is very risky. It will most likely be zero, but there is a 1% chance that the insurance company will have to pay claims on *all* the policies it wrote. In this case, the risk of the portfolio of insurance policies is no different from the risk of any single policy—it is still all or nothing. Conversely, for theft insurance, the number of claims in a given year is quite predictable. Year in and year out, it will be very close to 1% of the total number of policies, or 1000 claims. The portfolio of theft insurance policies has almost no risk![11]

---

[11]In the case of insurance, this difference in risk—and therefore in required reserves—can lead to a significant difference in the cost of the insurance. Indeed, earthquake insurance is generally thought to be much more expensive to purchase, even though the risk to an individual household may be similar to other risks, such as theft or fire.

Types of Risk. Why are the portfolios of insurance policies so different when the individual policies themselves are quite similar? Intuitively, the key difference between them is that an earthquake affects all houses simultaneously, so the risk is perfectly correlated across homes. We call risk that is perfectly correlated **common risk**. In contrast, because thefts in different houses are not related to each other, the risk of theft is uncorrelated and independent across homes. We call risks that share no correlation **independent risks**. When risks are independent, some individual homeowners are unlucky and others are lucky, but overall the number of claims is quite predictable. The averaging out of independent risks in a large portfolio is called **diversification**.

The Role of Diversification

We can quantify this difference in terms of the standard deviation of the percentage of claims. First, consider the standard deviation for an individual homeowner. At the beginning of the year, the homeowner expects a 1% chance of placing a claim for either type of insurance. But at the end of the year, the homeowner will have filed a claim (100%) or not (0%). Using Eq. 10.2, the standard deviation is

$$SD\,(\text{Claim}) = \sqrt{Var\,(\text{Claim})}$$
$$= \sqrt{0.99 \times (0 - 0.01)^2 + 0.01 \times (1 - 0.01)^2} = 9.95\%$$

For the homeowner, this standard deviation is the same for a loss from earthquake or theft.

Now consider the standard deviation of the percentage of claims for the insurance company. In the case of earthquake insurance, because the risk is common, the percentage of claims is either 100% or 0%, just as it was for the homeowner. Thus, the percentage of claims received by the earthquake insurer is also 1% on average, with a 9.95% standard deviation.

While the theft insurer also receives 1% of claims on average, because the risk of theft is independent across households, the portfolio is much less risky. To quantify this difference, let's calculate the standard deviation of the average claim using Eq. 10.8. Recall that when risks are independent and identical, the standard deviation of the average is known as the standard error, which declines with the square root of the number of observations. Therefore,

$$SD\,(\text{Percentage Theft Claims}) = \frac{SD\,(\text{Individual Claim})}{\sqrt{\text{Number of Observations}}}$$
$$= \frac{9.95\%}{\sqrt{100,000}} = 0.03\%$$

Thus, there is almost *no* risk for the theft insurer.

The principle of diversification is used routinely in the insurance industry. In addition to theft insurance, many other forms of insurance (e.g., life, health, auto) rely on the fact that the number of claims is relatively predictable in a large portfolio. Even in the case of earthquake insurance, insurers can achieve some diversification by selling policies in different geographical regions or by combining different types of policies. Diversification reduces risk in many other settings. For example, farmers often diversify the types of crops they plant to reduce the risk from the failure of any individual crop. Similarly, firms may diversify their supply chains or product lines to reduce the risk from supply disruptions or demand shocks.

| EXAMPLE 10.5 | Diversification and Gambling |

Problem

Roulette wheels are typically marked with the numbers 1 through 36 plus 0 and 00. Each of these outcomes is equally likely every time the wheel is spun. If you place a bet on any one number and are correct, the payoff is 35:1; that is, if you bet $1, you will receive $36 if you win ($35 plus your original $1) and nothing if you lose. Suppose you place a $1 bet on your favorite number. What is the casino's expected profit? What is the standard deviation of this profit for a single bet? Suppose 9 million similar bets are placed throughout the casino in a typical month. What is the standard deviation of the casino's average revenues per dollar bet each month?

Solution

Because there are 38 numbers on the wheel, the odds of winning are 1/38. The casino loses $35 if you win, and makes $1 if you lose. Therefore, using Eq. 10.1, the casino's expected profit is

$$E\,[\text{Payoff}] = (1/38) \times (-\$35) + (37/38) \times (\$1) = \$0.0526$$

That is, for each dollar bet, the casino earns 5.26 cents on average. For a single bet, we calculate the standard deviation of this profit using Eq. 10.2 as

$$SD\,(\text{Payoff}) = \sqrt{(1/38) \times (-35 - 0.0526)^2 + (37/38) \times (1 - 0.0526)^2} = \$5.76$$

This standard deviation is quite large relative to the magnitude of the profits. But if many such bets are placed, the risk will be diversified. Using Eq. 10.8, the standard deviation of the casino's average revenues per dollar bet (i.e., the standard error of their payoff) is only

$$SD\,(\text{Average Payoff}) = \frac{\$5.76}{\sqrt{9,000,000}} = \$0.0019$$

In other words, by the same logic as Eq. 10.9, there is roughly 95% chance the casino's profit per dollar bet will be in the interval $0.0526 \pm (2 \times 0.0019) = \$0.0488$ to $0.0564. Given $9 million in bets placed, the casino's monthly profits will almost always be between $439,000 and $508,000, which is very little risk. The key assumption, of course, is that each bet is separate so that their outcomes are independent of each other. If the $9 million were placed in a single bet, the casino's risk would be large—losing $35 \times \$9$ million = $315 million if the bet wins. For this reason, casinos often impose limits on the amount of any individual bet.

| CONCEPT CHECK | 1. What is the difference between common risk and independent risk? |
| | 2. Under what circumstances will risk be diversified in a large portfolio of insurance contracts? |

10.6 Diversification in Stock Portfolios

As the insurance example indicates, the risk of a portfolio of insurance contracts depends on whether the individual risks within it are common or independent. Independent risks are diversified in a large portfolio, whereas common risks are not. Let's consider the implication of this distinction for the risk of stock portfolios.[12]

---

[12]Harry Markowitz was the first to formalize the role of diversification in forming an optimal stock market portfolio. See H. Markowitz, "Portfolio Selection," *Journal of Finance* 7 (1952): 77–91.

Firm-Specific Versus Systematic Risk

Over any given time period, the risk of holding a stock is that the dividends plus the final stock price will be higher or lower than expected, which makes the realized return risky. What causes dividends or stock prices, and therefore returns, to be higher or lower than we expect? Usually, stock prices and dividends fluctuate due to two types of news:

1. *Firm-specific news* is good or bad news about the company itself. For example, a firm might announce that it has been successful in gaining market share within its industry.

2. *Market-wide news* is news about the economy as a whole and therefore affects all stocks. For instance, the Federal Reserve might announce that it will lower interest rates to boost the economy.

Fluctuations of a stock's return that are due to firm-specific news are independent risks. Like theft across homes, these risks are unrelated across stocks. This type of risk is also referred to as **firm-specific**, **idiosyncratic**, **unique**, or **diversifiable risk**.

Fluctuations of a stock's return that are due to market-wide news represent common risk. As with earthquakes, all stocks are affected simultaneously by the news. This type of risk is also called **systematic**, **undiversifiable**, or **market risk**.

When we combine many stocks in a large portfolio, the firm-specific risks for each stock will average out and be diversified. Good news will affect some stocks, and bad news will affect others, but the amount of good or bad news overall will be relatively constant. The systematic risk, however, will affect all firms—and therefore the entire portfolio—and will not be diversified.

Let's consider an example. Suppose type S firms are affected *only* by the strength of the economy, which has a 50–50 chance of being either strong or weak. If the economy is strong, type S stocks will earn a return of 40%; if the economy is weak, their return will be −20%. Because these firms face systematic risk (the strength of the economy), holding a large portfolio of type S firms will not diversify the risk. When the economy is strong, the portfolio will have the same return of 40% as each type S firm; when the economy is weak, the portfolio will also have a return of −20%.

Now consider type I firms, which are affected only by idiosyncratic, firm-specific risks. Their returns are equally likely to be 35% or −25%, based on factors specific to each firm's local market. Because these risks are firm specific, if we hold a portfolio of the stocks of many type I firms, the risk is diversified. About half of the firms will have returns of 35%, and half will have returns of −25%, so that the return of the portfolio will be close to the average return of 0.5 (35%) + 0.5 (−25%) = 5%.

Figure 10.8 illustrates how volatility declines with the size of the portfolio for type S and I firms. Type S firms have only systematic risk. As with earthquake insurance, the volatility of the portfolio does not change as the number of firms increases. Type I firms have only idiosyncratic risk. As with theft insurance, the risk is diversified as the number of firms increases, and volatility declines. As is evident from Figure 10.8, with a large number of firms, the risk is essentially eliminated.

Of course, actual firms are not like type S or I firms. Firms are affected by both systematic, market-wide risks and firm-specific risks. Figure 10.8 also shows how the volatility changes with the size of a portfolio containing the stocks of typical firms. When firms carry both types of risk, only the firm-specific risk will be diversified when we combine many firms' stocks into a portfolio. The volatility will therefore decline until only the systematic risk, which affects all firms, remains.

Volatility of Portfolios of Type S and I Stocks

Because type S firms have only systematic risk, the volatility of the portfolio does not change. Type I firms have only idiosyncratic risk, which is diversified and eliminated as the number of firms in the portfolio increases. Typical stocks carry a mix of both types of risk, so that the risk of the portfolio declines as idiosyncratic risk is diversified away, but systematic risk still remains.

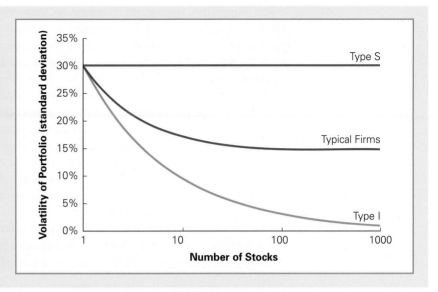

This example explains one of the puzzles shown in Figure 10.7. There we saw that the S&P 500 had much lower volatility than any of the individual stocks. Now we can see why: The individual stocks each contain firm-specific risk, which is eliminated when we combine them into a large portfolio. Thus, the portfolio as a whole can have lower volatility than each of the stocks within it.

EXAMPLE 10.6   **Portfolio Volatility**

Problem
What is the volatility of the average return of ten type S firms? What is the volatility of the average return of ten type I firms?

Solution
Type S firms have equally likely returns of 40% or −20%. Their expected return is $\frac{1}{2}(40\%) + \frac{1}{2}(-20\%) = 10\%$, so

$$SD\,(R_S) = \sqrt{\tfrac{1}{2}(0.40 - 0.10)^2 + \tfrac{1}{2}(-0.20 - 0.10)^2} = 30\%$$

Because all type S firms have high or low returns at the same time, the average return of ten type S firms is also 40% or −20%. Thus, it has the same volatility of 30%, as shown in Figure 10.8.

Type I firms have equally likely returns of 35% or −25%. Their expected return is $\frac{1}{2}(35\%) + \frac{1}{2}(-25\%) = 5\%$, so

$$SD\,(R_I) = \sqrt{\tfrac{1}{2}(0.35 - 0.05)^2 + \tfrac{1}{2}(-0.25 - 0.05)^2} = 30\%$$

Because the returns of type I firms are independent, using Eq. 10.8, the average return of 10 type I firms has volatility of $30\% \div \sqrt{10} = 9.5\%$, as shown in Figure 10.8.

No Arbitrage and the Risk Premium

Consider again type I firms, which are affected only by firm-specific risk. Because each individual type I firm is risky, should investors expect to earn a risk premium when investing in type I firms?

In a competitive market, the answer is no. To see why, suppose the expected return of type I firms exceeds the risk-free interest rate. Then, by holding a large portfolio of many type I firms, investors could diversify the firm-specific risk of these firms and earn a return above the risk-free interest rate without taking on any significant risk.

The situation just described is very close to an arbitrage opportunity, which investors would find very attractive. They would borrow money at the risk-free interest rate and invest it in a large portfolio of type I firms, which offers a higher return with only a tiny amount of risk.[13] As more investors take advantage of this situation and purchase shares of type I firms, the current share prices for type I firms would rise, lowering their expected return—recall that the current share price P_t is the denominator when computing the stock's return as in Eq. 10.4. This trading would stop only after the return of type I firms equaled the risk-free interest rate. Competition between investors drives the return of type I firms down to the risk-free return.

The preceding argument is essentially an application of the Law of One Price: Because a large portfolio of type I firms has no risk, it must earn the risk-free interest rate. This no-arbitrage argument suggests the following more general principle:

The risk premium for diversifiable risk is zero, so investors are not compensated for holding firm-specific risk.

We can apply this principle to all stocks and securities. It implies that the risk premium of a stock is not affected by its diversifiable, firm-specific risk. If the diversifiable risk of stocks were compensated with an additional risk premium, then investors could buy the stocks, earn the additional premium, and simultaneously diversify and eliminate the risk. By doing so, investors could earn an additional premium without taking on additional risk. This opportunity to earn something for nothing would quickly be exploited and eliminated.[14]

Because investors can eliminate firm-specific risk "for free" by diversifying their portfolios, they will not require a reward or risk premium for holding it. However, diversification does not reduce systematic risk: Even holding a large portfolio, an investor will be exposed to risks that affect the entire economy and therefore affect all securities. Because investors are risk averse, they will demand a risk premium to hold systematic risk; otherwise they would be better off selling their stocks and investing in risk-free bonds. Because investors can eliminate firm-specific risk for free by diversifying, whereas systematic risk can be eliminated only by sacrificing expected returns, it is a security's systematic risk that determines the risk premium investors require to hold it. This fact leads to a second key principle:

The risk premium of a security is determined by its systematic risk and does not depend on its diversifiable risk.

This principle implies that a stock's volatility, which is a measure of total risk (that is, systematic risk plus diversifiable risk), is not especially useful in determining the risk premium that investors will earn. For example, consider again type S and I firms. As calculated in Example 10.6, the volatility of a single type S or I firm is 30%. Although both types of firms have the same volatility, type S firms have an expected return of 10% and type I firms have an expected return of 5%. The difference in expected returns derives from the difference in the kind of risk each firm bears. Type I firms have only firm-specific risk, which does not require a risk premium, so the expected return of 5% for type I firms equals the

---

[13]If investors could actually hold a large enough portfolio and completely diversify all the risk, then this would be a true arbitrage opportunity.

[14]The main thrust of this argument can be found in S. Ross, "The Arbitrage Theory of Capital Asset Pricing," *Journal of Economic Theory* 13 (December 1976): 341–360.

GLOBAL FINANCIAL CRISIS   Diversification Benefits During Market Crashes

The figure below illustrates the benefits of diversification over the last 40 years. The blue graph shows the historical volatility of the S&P 500 portfolio (annualized based on daily returns each quarter). The pink graph is the average volatility of the individual stocks in the portfolio (weighted according to the size of each stock). Thus, the pink shaded area is idiosyncratic risk—risk that has been diversified away by holding the portfolio. The blue area is market risk which cannot be diversified.

Market volatility clearly varies, increasing dramatically during times of crisis. But notice also that the fraction of risk that can be diversified away also varies, and seems to decline during times of crisis. For example, since 1970, on average about 50% of the volatility of individual stocks is diversifiable

(i.e., the pink area is about 50% of the total). But as the figure demonstrates, during the 1987 stock market crash, the 2008 financial crisis, and the recent Eurozone debt crisis, this fraction fell dramatically, so that only about 20% of the volatility of individual stocks could be diversified. The combined effect of increased volatility and reduced diversification during the 2008 financial crisis was so severe that the risk that investors care about—market risk—increased *seven*-fold, from 10% to 70%, between 2006 and the last quarter of 2008.

Although you are always better off diversifying, it is important to keep in mind that the benefits of diversification depend on economic conditions. In times of extreme crisis, the benefits may go down, making downturns in the market particularly painful for investors.

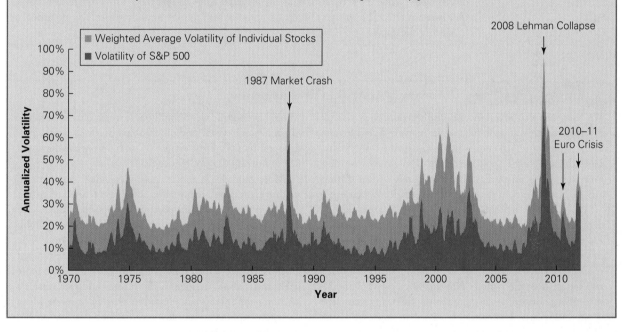

risk-free interest rate. Type S firms have only systematic risk. Because investors will require compensation for taking on this risk, the expected return of 10% for type S firms provides investors with a 5% risk premium above the risk-free interest rate.

We now have an explanation for the second puzzle of Figure 10.7. While volatility might be a reasonable measure of risk for a well-diversified portfolio, it is not an appropriate metric for an individual security. Thus, there should be no clear relationship between volatility and average returns for individual securities. Consequently, to estimate a security's expected return, we need to find a measure of a security's systematic risk.

In Chapter 3, we argued that an investment's risk premium depends on how its returns move in relation to the overall economy. In particular, risk-averse investors will demand a premium to invest in securities that will do poorly in bad times (recall, for example, the performance of small stocks in Figure 10.1 during the Great Depression). This idea coincides with the notion of systematic risk we have defined in this chapter. Economy-wide risk—that is, the risk of recessions and booms—is systematic risk that cannot be diversified. Therefore an asset that moves with the economy contains systematic risk and so requires a risk premium.

EXAMPLE 10.7   **Diversifiable Versus Systematic Risk**

Problem

Which of the following risks of a stock are likely to be firm-specific, diversifiable risks, and which are likely to be systematic risks? Which risks will affect the risk premium that investors will demand?

a. The risk that the founder and CEO retires
b. The risk that oil prices rise, increasing production costs
c. The risk that a product design is faulty and the product must be recalled
d. The risk that the economy slows, reducing demand for the firm's products

Solution

Because oil prices and the health of the economy affect all stocks, risks (b) and (d) are systematic risks. These risks are not diversified in a large portfolio, and so will affect the risk premium that investors require to invest in a stock. Risks (a) and (c) are firm-specific risks, and so are diversifiable. While these risks should be considered when estimating a firm's future cash flows, they will not affect the risk premium that investors will require and, therefore, will not affect a firm's cost of capital.

COMMON MISTAKE   **A Fallacy of Long-Run Diversification**

We have seen that investors can greatly reduce their risk by dividing their investment dollars over many different investments, eliminating the diversifiable risk in their portfolios. Does the same logic apply over time? That is, by investing for many years, can we also diversify the risk we face during any particular year? In the long run, does risk still matter?

Eq. 10.8 tells us that if returns each year are independent, the volatility of the average annual return declines with the number of years that we invest. Of course, as long-term investors, we don't care about the volatility of our *average* return; instead, we care about the volatility of our *cumulative* return over the period. This volatility grows with the investment horizon, as illustrated in the following example.

In 1925, large U.S. stocks increased in value by about 30%. In fact, a $77 investment at the start of 1925 would have grown to $77 × 1.30 = $100 by the end of the year. Notice from Figure 10.1 that a $100 investment in the S&P 500 from 1926 onward would have grown to about $275,000 by the start of 2012. But suppose instead stocks had dropped by 35% in 1925. Then, the initial $77 invested would be worth only $77 × (1 − 35%) = $50 at the beginning of 1926. If returns from then on were unchanged, the investment would be worth half as much in 2012, or $137,500. Thus, despite the long horizon, the difference in the first year's return still has a significant effect on the final payoff.

The financial crisis in 2008 brought home the reality of this fallacy to many investors. Consider for example, a long-term investor who invested $100 in small stocks in 1925. If her investment horizon was 81 years (end of 2006), she would have a little over $2 million. If instead her investment horizon was 83 years (end of 2008) her portfolio would have dropped by over 50% to just $1 million. Again, having a longer horizon did not reduce risk!

More generally, if returns are independent over time so that future returns are not affected by past returns, then any change in the value of our portfolio today will translate into the same percentage change in the value of our portfolio in the future, and there is no diversification over time. The only way the length of the time horizon can reduce risk is if a below-average return today implies that returns are more likely to be above average in the future (and vice versa), a phenomenon sometimes referred to as *mean reversion*. Mean reversion implies that past low returns can be used to predict future high returns in the stock market.

For short horizons of a few years, there is no evidence of mean reversion in the stock market. For longer horizons, there is some evidence of mean reversion historically, but it is not clear how reliable this evidence is (there are not enough decades of accurate stock market data available) or whether the pattern will continue. Even if there is long-run mean reversion in stock returns, a buy-and-hold diversification strategy is still not optimal: Because mean reversion implies that past returns can be used to predict future returns, you should invest more in stocks when returns are predicted to be high, and invest less when they are predicted to be low. This strategy is very different from the diversification we achieve by holding many stocks, where we cannot predict which stocks will have good or bad firm-specific shocks.

1. Explain why the risk premium of diversifiable risk is zero.

2. Why is the risk premium of a security determined only by its systematic risk?

10.7 Measuring Systematic Risk

As we have discussed, investors can eliminate the firm-specific risk in their investments by diversifying their portfolio. Thus, when evaluating the risk of an investment, an investor will care about its systematic risk, which cannot be eliminated through diversification. In exchange for bearing systematic risk, investors want to be compensated by earning a higher return. So, to determine the additional return, or risk premium, investors will require to undertake an investment, we first need to measure the investment's systematic risk.

Identifying Systematic Risk: The Market Portfolio

To measure the systematic risk of a stock, we must determine how much of the variability of its return is due to systematic, market-wide risks versus diversifiable, firm-specific risks. That is, we would like to know how sensitive the stock is to systematic shocks that affect the economy as a whole.

To determine how sensitive a stock's return is to interest rate changes, for example, we would look at how much the return tends to change on average for each 1% change in interest rates. Similarly, to determine how sensitive a stock's return is to oil prices, we would examine the average change in the return for each 1% change in oil prices. In the same way, to determine how sensitive a stock is to systematic risk, we can look at the average change in its return for each 1% change in the return of *a portfolio that fluctuates solely due to systematic risk*.

Thus, the first step to measuring systematic risk is finding a portfolio that contains *only* systematic risk. Changes in the price of this portfolio will correspond to systematic shocks to the economy. We call such a portfolio an **efficient portfolio**. An efficient portfolio cannot be diversified further—that is, there is no way to reduce the risk of the portfolio without lowering its expected return. How can we identify such a portfolio?

As we will see over the next few chapters, the best way to identify an efficient portfolio is one of the key questions in modern finance. Because diversification improves with the number of stocks held in a portfolio, an efficient portfolio should be a large portfolio containing many different stocks. Thus, a natural candidate for an efficient portfolio is the **market portfolio**, which is a portfolio of all stocks and securities traded in the capital markets. Because it is difficult to find data for the returns of many bonds and small stocks, it is common in practice to use the S&P 500 portfolio as an approximation for the market portfolio, under the assumption that the S&P 500 is large enough to be essentially fully diversified.

Sensitivity to Systematic Risk: Beta

If we assume that the market portfolio (or the S&P 500) is efficient, then changes in the value of the market portfolio represent systematic shocks to the economy. We can then measure the systematic risk of a security by calculating the sensitivity of the security's return to the return of the market portfolio, known as the **beta** (β) of the security. More precisely,

The beta of a security is the expected % change in its return given a 1% change in the return of the market portfolio.

| EXAMPLE 10.8 | **Estimating Beta** |

Problem

Suppose the market portfolio tends to increase by 47% when the economy is strong and decline by 25% when the economy is weak. What is the beta of a type S firm whose return is 40% on average when the economy is strong and −20% when the economy is weak? What is the beta of a type I firm that bears only idiosyncratic, firm-specific risk?

Solution

The systematic risk of the strength of the economy produces a 47% − (−25%) = 72% change in the return of the market portfolio. The type S firm's return changes by 40% − (−20%) = 60% on average. Thus the firm's beta is $\beta_S = 60\%/72\% = 0.833$. That is, each 1% change in the return of the market portfolio leads to a 0.833% change in the type S firm's return on average.

The return of a type I firm has only firm-specific risk, however, and so is not affected by the strength of the economy. Its return is affected only by factors specific to the firm. Because it will have the same expected return, whether the economy is strong or weak, $\beta_I = 0\%/72\% = 0$.

Real-Firm Betas. We will look at statistical techniques for estimating beta from historical stock returns in Chapter 12. There we will see that we can estimate beta reasonably accurately using just a few years of data (which was not the case for expected returns, as we saw in Example 10.4). Using the S&P 500 to represent the market's return, Table 10.6 shows the betas of several stocks during 2007–2012. As shown in the table, each 1% change in the return of the market during this period led, on average, to a 1.48% change in the return for eBay, but only a 0.54% change in the return for Coca-Cola.

Interpreting Betas. Beta measures the sensitivity of a security to market-wide risk factors. For a stock, this value is related to how sensitive its underlying revenues and cash flows are to general economic conditions. The average beta of a stock in the market is about 1; that is, the average stock price tends to move about 1% for each 1% move in the overall market. Stocks in cyclical industries, in which revenues and profits vary greatly over the business cycle, are likely to be more sensitive to systematic risk and have betas that exceed 1, whereas stocks of non-cyclical firms tend to have betas that are less than 1.

For example, notice the relatively low betas of Consolidated Edison (a utility company), Abbott Labs (pharmaceuticals), and General Mills and Hershey (food processing). Utilities tend to be stable and highly regulated, and thus are insensitive to fluctuations in the overall market. Drug and food companies are also very insensitive—the demand for their products appears to be unrelated to the booms and busts of the economy as a whole.

At the other extreme, technology stocks tend to have higher betas; consider Apple (1.26), Dell (1.41), eBay (1.48), Autodesk (2.14), and Advanced Micro Devices (2.24). Shocks in the economy have an amplified impact on these stocks: When the market as a whole is up, AMD's stock tends to rise more than twice as much; but when the market stumbles, it tends to fall more than twice as far. Note also the high beta of luxury retailers Saks and Tiffany & Co., compared with the much lower beta of Wal-Mart Stores; presumably their sales respond very differently to economic booms and busts. Finally, we see that highly levered firms in cyclical industries, such as Ford Motor and U.S. Steel, tend to have high betas reflecting their sensitivity to economic conditions.

| CONCEPT CHECK | 1. What is the market portfolio? |

2. Define the beta of a security.

TABLE 10.6	Betas with Respect to the S&P 500 for Individual Stocks (based on monthly data for 2007–2012)

Company	Ticker	Industry	Equity Beta
General Mills	GIS	Packaged Foods	0.20
Consolidated Edison	ED	Utilities	0.28
The Hershey Company	HSY	Packaged Foods	0.28
Abbott Laboratories	ABT	Pharmaceuticals	0.31
Newmont Mining	NEM	Gold	0.32
Wal-Mart Stores	WMT	Superstores	0.35
Clorox	CLX	Household Products	0.39
Kroger	KR	Food Retail	0.42
Altria Group	MO	Tobacco	0.43
Amgen	AMGN	Biotechnology	0.44
McDonald's	MCD	Restaurants	0.47
Procter & Gamble	PG	Household Products	0.47
Pepsico	PEP	Soft Drinks	0.51
Coca-Cola	KO	Soft Drinks	0.54
Johnson & Johnson	JNJ	Pharmaceuticals	0.59
PetSmart	PETM	Specialty Stores	0.75
Molson Coors Brewing	TAP	Brewers	0.78
Nike	NKE	Footwear	0.91
Microsoft	MSFT	Systems Software	1.01
Southwest Airlines	LUV	Airlines	1.09
Intel	INTC	Semiconductors	1.09
Whole Foods Market	WFM	Food Retail	1.10
Foot Locker	FL	Apparel Retail	1.11
Oracle	ORCL	Systems Software	1.12
Amazon.com	AMZN	Internet Retail	1.13
Google	GOOG	Internet Software and Services	1.14
Starbucks	SBUX	Restaurants	1.20
Walt Disney	DIS	Movies and Entertainment	1.21
Cisco Systems	CSCO	Communications Equipment	1.23
Apple	AAPL	Computer Hardware	1.26
PulteGroup	PHM	Homebuilding	1.28
Dell	DELL	Computer Hardware	1.41
salesforce.com	CRM	Application Software	1.47
Marriott International	MAR	Hotels and Resorts	1.48
eBay	EBAY	Internet Software and Services	1.48
Coach	COH	Apparel and Luxury Goods	1.60
Macy's	M	Department Stores	1.67
Juniper Networks	JNPR	Communications Equipment	1.71
Williams-Sonoma	WSM	Home Furnishing Retail	1.72
Tiffany & Co.	TIF	Apparel and Luxury Goods	1.80
Caterpillar	CAT	Construction Machinery	1.85
Ethan Allen Interiors	ETH	Home Furnishings	1.95
Autodesk	ADSK	Application Software	2.14
Harley-Davidson	HOG	Motorcycle Manufacturers	2.23
Advanced Micro Devices	AMD	Semiconductors	2.24
Ford Motor	F	Automobile Manufacturers	2.38
Sotheby's	BID	Auction Services	2.39
Wynn Resorts Ltd.	WYNN	Casinos and Gaming	2.41
United States Steel	X	Steel	2.52
Saks	SKS	Department Stores	2.57

Source: CapitalIQ

10.8 Beta and the Cost of Capital

Throughout this text, we have emphasized that financial managers should evaluate an investment opportunity based on its cost of capital, which is the expected return available on alternative investments in the market with comparable risk and term. For risky investments, this cost of capital corresponds to the risk-free interest rate, plus an appropriate risk premium. Now that we can measure the systematic risk of an investment according to its beta, we are in a position to estimate the risk premium investors will require.

Estimating the Risk Premium

Before we can estimate the risk premium of an individual stock, we need a way to assess investors' appetite for risk. The size of the risk premium investors will require to make a risky investment depends upon their risk aversion. Rather than attempt to measure this risk aversion directly, we can measure it indirectly by looking at the risk premium investors' demand for investing in systematic, or market, risk.

The Market Risk Premium. We can calibrate investors' appetite for market risk from the market portfolio. The risk premium investors earn by holding market risk is the difference between the market portfolio's expected return and the risk-free interest rate:

$$\text{Market Risk Premium} = E[R_{Mkt}] - r_f \qquad (10.10)$$

For example, if the risk-free rate is 5% and the expected return of the market portfolio is 11%, the market risk premium is 6%. In the same way that the market interest rate reflects investors' patience and determines the time value of money, the market risk premium reflects investors' risk tolerance and determines the market price of risk in the economy.

Adjusting for Beta. The market risk premium is the reward investors expect to earn for holding a portfolio with a beta of 1—the market portfolio itself. Consider an investment opportunity with a beta of 2. This investment carries twice as much systematic risk as an investment in the market portfolio. That is, for each dollar we invest in the opportunity, we could invest twice that amount in the market portfolio and be exposed to exactly the same amount of systematic risk. So, by the Law of One Price, because it has twice as much systematic risk, investors will require twice the risk premium to invest in an opportunity with a beta of 2.

COMMON MISTAKE **Beta Versus Volatility**

Recall that beta differs from volatility. Volatility measures total risk—that is, both market and firm-specific risks—so that there is no necessary relationship between volatility and beta. For example, in early 2012 the stocks of Amgen and Cisco Systems had similar volatility. Amgen, however, has a much lower beta. While drug companies face a great deal of risk related to the development and approval of new drugs, this risk is unrelated to the rest of the economy. And though health care expenditures do vary a little with the state of the economy, they vary much less than expenditures on technology. Thus, while their volatilities are similar, much more of the risk of Amgen's stock is diversifiable risk, whereas Cisco's stock has a much greater proportion of systematic risk.

To summarize, we can use the beta of the investment to determine the scale of the investment in the market portfolio that has equivalent systematic risk. Thus, to compensate investors for the time value of their money as well as the systematic risk they are bearing, the cost of capital r_I for an investment with beta β_I should satisfy the following formula:

Estimating the Cost of Capital of an Investment from Its Beta

$$r_I = \text{Risk-Free Interest Rate} + \beta_I \times \text{Market Risk Premium}$$

$$= r_f + \beta_I \times (E[R_{Mkt}] - r_f) \tag{10.11}$$

As an example, let's consider eBay and General Mills stocks, using the beta estimates in Table 10.6. According to Eq. 10.11, if the market risk premium is 6% and the risk-free interest rate is 5%, the equity cost of capital for each of these firms is

$$r_{EBAY} = 5\% + 1.48 \times 6\% = 13.9\%$$

$$r_{GIS} = 5\% + 0.20 \times 6\% = 6.2\%$$

Thus, the difference in the average returns of these two stocks that we reported in the introduction of this chapter is not so surprising. Investors in eBay require a much higher return on average to compensate them for eBay's much higher systematic risk.

EXAMPLE 10.9

Expected Returns and Beta

Problem

Suppose the risk-free rate is 5% and the economy is equally likely to be strong or weak. Use Eq. 10.11 to determine the cost of capital for the type S firms considered in Example 10.8. How does this cost of capital compare with the expected return for these firms?

Solution

If the economy is equally likely to be strong or weak, the expected return of the market is $E[R_{Mkt}] = \frac{1}{2}(0.47) + \frac{1}{2}(-0.25) = 11\%$, and the market risk premium is $E[R_{Mkt}] - r_f = 11\% - 5\% = 6\%$. Given the beta of 0.833 for type S firms that we calculated in Example 10.8, the estimate of the cost of capital for type S firms from Eq. 10.11 is

$$r_s = r_f + \beta_s \times (E[R_{Mkt}] - r_f) = 5\% + 0.833 \times (11\% - 5\%) = 10\%$$

This matches their expected return: $\frac{1}{2}(40\%) + \frac{1}{2}(-20\%) = 10\%$. Thus, investors who hold these stocks can expect a return that appropriately compensates them for the systematic risk they are bearing by holding them (as we should expect in a competitive market).

What happens if a stock has a negative beta? According to Eq. 10.11, such a stock would have a negative risk premium—it would have an expected return below the risk-free rate. While this might seem unreasonable at first, note that stock with a negative beta will tend to do well when times are bad, so owning it will provide insurance against the systematic risk of other stocks in the portfolio. (For an example of such a security, see Example 3A.1 in Chapter 3.) Risk-averse investors are willing to pay for this insurance by accepting a return below the risk-free interest rate.

The Capital Asset Pricing Model

Equation 10.11, for estimating the cost of capital, is often referred to as the **Capital Asset Pricing Model (CAPM)**,[15] the most important method for estimating the cost of capital that is used in practice. In this chapter, we have provided an intuitive justification of the CAPM, and its use of the market portfolio as the benchmark for systematic risk. We provide a more complete development of the model and its assumptions in Chapter 11, where we also detail the portfolio optimization process used by professional fund managers. Then, in Chapter 12, we look at the practicalities of implementing the CAPM, and develop statistical tools for estimating the betas of individual stocks, together with methods for estimating the beta and cost of capital of projects within these firms. Finally, in Chapter 13 we look at the empirical evidence for (and against) the CAPM, both as a model of investor behavior and as forecast of expected returns, and introduce some proposed extensions to the CAPM.

CONCEPT CHECK

1. How can you use a security's beta to estimate its cost of capital?

2. If a risky investment has a beta of zero, what should its cost of capital be according to the CAPM? How can you justify this?

MyFinanceLab

Here is what you should know after reading this chapter. MyFinanceLab will help you identify what you know and where to go when you need to practice.

10.1 A First Look at Risk and Return

- Historically, over long horizons, investments in stocks have outperformed investments in bonds.
- Investing in stocks has also been much riskier than investing in bonds historically. Even over a horizon of 5 years, there have been many occasions in the past that stocks have substantially underperformed bonds.

10.2 Common Measures of Risk and Return

- A probability distribution summarizes information about possible different returns and their likelihood of occurring.
  - The expected, or mean, return is the return we expect to earn on average:

  $$\text{Expected Return} = E[R] = \sum_R p_R \times R \qquad (10.1)$$

  - The variance or standard deviation measures the variability of the returns:

  $$Var(R) = E[(R - E[R])^2] = \sum_R p_R \times (R - E[R])^2$$

  $$SD(R) = \sqrt{Var(R)} \qquad (10.2)$$

  - The standard deviation of a return is also called its volatility.

---

[15]The CAPM was first developed independently by Lintner and Sharpe. See J. Lintner "The Valuation of Risk Assets and the Selection of Risky Investments in Stock Portfolios and Capital Budgets," *Review of Economics and Statistics* 47 (1965): 13–37; and W. Sharpe, "Capital Asset Prices: A Theory of Market Equilibrium Under Conditions of Risk," *Journal of Finance* 19 (1964): 425–442.

10.3 Historical Returns of Stocks and Bonds

- The realized or total return for an investment is the total of the dividend yield and the capital gain rate.
  - Using the empirical distribution of realized returns, we can estimate the expected return and variance of the distribution of returns by calculating the average annual return and variance of realized returns:

$$\bar{R} = \frac{1}{T}(R_1 + R_2 + \cdots + R_T) = \frac{1}{T}\sum_{t=1}^{T} R_t \qquad (10.6)$$

$$Var(R) = \frac{1}{T-1}\sum_{t=1}^{T}(R_t - \bar{R})^2 \qquad (10.7)$$

  - The square root of the estimated variance is an estimate of the volatility of returns.
  - Because a security's historical average return is only an estimate of its true expected return, we use the standard error of the estimate to gauge the amount of estimation error:

$$SD\ (\text{Average of Independent, Identical Risks}) = \frac{SD\ (\text{Individual Risk})}{\sqrt{\text{Number of Observations}}} \qquad (10.8)$$

10.4 The Historical Trade-Off Between Risk and Return

- Comparing historical data for large portfolios, small stocks have had higher volatility and higher average returns than large stocks, which have had higher volatility and higher average returns than bonds.
- There is no clear relationship between the volatility and return of individual stocks.
  - Larger stocks tend to have lower overall volatility, but even the largest stocks are typically more risky than a portfolio of large stocks.
  - All stocks seem to have higher risk and lower returns than would be predicted based on extrapolation of data for large portfolios.

10.5 Common Versus Independent Risk

- The total risk of a security represents both idiosyncratic risk and systematic risk.
  - Variation in a stock's return due to firm-specific news is called idiosyncratic risk. This type of risk is also called firm-specific, unique, or diversifiable risk. It is risk that is independent of other shocks in the economy.
  - Systematic risk, also called market or undiversifiable risk, is risk due to market-wide news that affects all stocks simultaneously. It is risk that is common to all stocks.

10.6 Diversification in Stock Portfolios

- Diversification eliminates idiosyncratic risk but does not eliminate systematic risk.
  - Because investors can eliminate idiosyncratic risk, they do not require a risk premium for taking it on.
  - Because investors cannot eliminate systematic risk, they must be compensated for holding it. As a consequence, the risk premium for a stock depends on the amount of its systematic risk rather than its total risk.

10.7 Measuring Systematic Risk

- An efficient portfolio contains only systematic risk and cannot be diversified further—that is, there is no way to reduce the risk of the portfolio without lowering its expected return.
- The market portfolio contains all shares of all stocks and securities in the market. The market portfolio is often assumed to be efficient.
- If the market portfolio is efficient, we can measure the systematic risk of a security by its beta (β). The beta of a security is the sensitivity of the security's return to the return of the overall market.

10.8 Beta and the Cost of Capital

- The market risk premium is the expected excess return of the market portfolio:

$$\text{Market Risk Premium} = E[R_{Mkt}] - r_f \tag{10.10}$$

It reflects investors' overall risk tolerance and represents the market price of risk in the economy.

- The cost of capital for a risky investment equals the risk-free rate plus a risk premium. The Capital Asset Pricing Model (CAPM) states that the risk premium equals the investment's beta times the market risk premium:

$$r_I = r_f + \beta_I \times (E[R_{Mkt}] - r_f) \tag{10.11}$$

Key Terms

95% confidence interval *p. 325*
average annual return *p. 321*
beta (β) *p. 339*
Capital Asset Pricing Model (CAPM) *p. 342*
common risk *p. 330*
diversification *p. 330*
efficient portfolio *p. 337*
empirical distribution *p. 321*
excess return *p. 327*
expected (mean) return *p. 316*
firm-specific, idiosyncratic, unique, or
   diversifiable risk *p. 332*

independent risk *p. 330*
market portfolio *p. 337*
probability distribution *p. 316*
realized return *p. 319*
standard deviation *p. 317*
standard error *p. 324*
systematic, undiversifiable, or
   market risk *p. 332*
variance *p. 317*
volatility *p. 318*

Further Reading

The original work on diversification was developed in the following papers: H. Markowitz, "Portfolio Selection," *Journal of Finance* 7 (1952): 77–91; A. Roy, "Safety First and the Holding of Assets," *Econometrica* 20 (July 1952): 431–449; and, in the context of insurance, B. deFinetti, "Il problema de pieni," *Giornale dell'Instituto Italiano degli Attuari*, 11 (1940): 1–88.

For information on historical returns of different types of assets, see: E. Dimson, P. Marsh, and M. Staunton, *Triumph of the Optimist: 101 Years of Global Equity Returns* (Princeton University Press, 2002); and Ibbotson Associates, Inc., *Stocks, Bonds, Bills, and Inflation* (Ibbotson Associates, 2009).

Many books address the topics of this chapter in more depth: E. Elton, M. Gruber, S. Brown, and W. Goetzmann, *Modern Portfolio Theory and Investment Analysis* (John Wiley & Sons, 2006); J. Francis, *Investments: Analysis and Management* (McGraw-Hill, 1991); R. Radcliffe, *Investment: Concepts, Analysis, and Strategy* (Harper-Collins, 1994); F. Reilly and K. Brown, *Investment Analysis and Portfolio Management* (Dryden Press, 1996); and Z. Bodie, A. Kane, and A. Marcus, *Investments* (McGraw-Hill/Irwin, 2008).

Problems

All problems are available in MyFinanceLab. *An asterisk (*) indicates problems with a higher level of difficulty.*

Common Measures of Risk and Return

1. The figure below shows the one-year return distribution for RCS stock. Calculate
   a. The expected return.
   b. The standard deviation of the return.

2. The following table shows the one-year return distribution of Startup, Inc. Calculate
a. The expected return.
b. The standard deviation of the return.

Probability	40%	20%	20%	10%	10%
Return	−100%	−75%	−50%	−25%	1000%

3. Characterize the difference between the two stocks in Problems 1 and 2. What trade-offs would you face in choosing one to hold?

Historical Returns of Stocks and Bonds

4. You bought a stock one year ago for $50 per share and sold it today for $55 per share. It paid a $1 per share dividend today.
a. What was your realized return?
b. How much of the return came from dividend yield and how much came from capital gain?

5. Repeat Problem 4 assuming that the stock fell $5 to $45 instead.
a. Is your capital gain different? Why or why not?
b. Is your dividend yield different? Why or why not?

6. Using the data in the following table, calculate the return for investing in Boeing stock (BA) from January 2, 2008, to January 2, 2009, and also from January 3, 2011, to January 3, 2012, assuming all dividends are reinvested in the stock immediately.

Historical Stock and Dividend Data for Boeing

Date	Price	Dividend	Date	Price	Dividend
1/2/2008	86.62		1/3/2011	66.40	
2/6/2008	79.91	0.40	2/9/2011	72.63	0.42
5/7/2008	84.55	0.40	5/11/2011	79.08	0.42
8/6/2008	65.40	0.40	8/10/2011	57.41	0.42
11/5/2008	49.55	0.40	11/8/2011	66.65	0.42
1/2/2009	45.25		1/3/2012	74.22	

7. The last four years of returns for a stock are as follows:

Year	1	2	3	4
Return	−4%	+28%	+12%	+4%

a. What is the average annual return?
b. What is the variance of the stock's returns?
c. What is the standard deviation of the stock's returns?

*8. Assume that historical returns and future returns are independently and identically distributed and drawn from the same distribution.

    a. Calculate the 95% confidence intervals for the expected annual return of four different investments included in Tables 10.3 and 10.4 (the dates are inclusive, so the time period spans 86 years).

    b. Assume that the values in Tables 10.3 and 10.4 are the true expected return and volatility (i.e., estimated without error) and that these returns are normally distributed. For each investment, calculate the probability that an investor will not lose more than 5% in the next year. (*Hint*: you can use the function normdist (*x*,mean,volatility,1) in Excel to compute the probability that a normally distributed variable with a given mean and volatility will fall below *x*.)

    c. Do all the probabilities you calculated in part (b) make sense? If so, explain. If not, can you identify the reason?

9. Using the data in Table 10.2,

    a. What was the average annual return of Microsoft stock from 2002–2011?

    b. What was the annual volatility for Microsoft stock from 2002–2011?

10. Using the data in Table 10.2,

    a. What was the average dividend yield for the SP500 from 2002–2011?

    b. What was the volatility of the dividend yield?

    c. What was the average annual return of the SP500 from 2002–2011 excluding dividends (i.e., from capital gains only)?

    d. What was the volatility of the S&P 500 returns from capital gains?

    e. Were dividends or capital gains a more important component of the S&P 500's average returns during this period? Which were the more important source of volatility?

11. Consider an investment with the following returns over four years:

Year	1	2	3	4
Return	10%	20%	−5%	15%

    a. What is the compound annual growth rate (CAGR) for this investment over the four years?

    b. What is the average annual return of the investment over the four years?

    c. Which is a better measure of the investment's past performance?

    d. If the investment's returns are independent and identically distributed, which is a better measure of the investment's expected return next year?

 12. Download the spreadsheet from MyFinanceLab that contains historical monthly prices and dividends (paid at the end of the month) for Ford Motor Company stock (Ticker: F) from August 1994 to August 1998. Calculate the realized return over this period, expressing your answer in percent per month (i.e., what monthly return would have led to the same cumulative performance as an investment in Ford stock over this period).

 13. Using the same data as in Problem 12, compute the

    a. Average monthly return over this period.

    b. Monthly volatility (or standard deviation) over this period.

14. Explain the difference between the average return you calculated in Problem 13(a) and the realized return you calculated in Problem 12. Are both numbers useful? If so, explain why.

 15. Compute the 95% confidence interval of the estimate of the average monthly return you calculated in Problem 13(a).

The Historical Trade-Off Between Risk and Return

16. How does the relationship between the average return and the historical volatility of individual stocks differ from the relationship between the average return and the historical volatility of large, well-diversified portfolios?

17. Download the spreadsheet from MyFinanceLab containing the data for Figure 10.1.
    a. Compute the average return for each of the assets from 1929 to 1940 (The Great Depression).
    b. Compute the variance and standard deviation for each of the assets from 1929 to 1940.
    c. Which asset was riskiest during the Great Depression? How does that fit with your intuition?

18. Using the data from Problem 17, repeat your analysis over the 1990s.
    a. Which asset was riskiest?
    b. Compare the standard deviations of the assets in the 1990s to their standard deviations in the Great Depression. Which had the greatest difference between the two periods?
    c. If you only had information about the 1990s, what would you conclude about the relative risk of investing in small stocks?

19. What if the last two decades had been "normal"? Download the spreadsheet from MyFinanceLab containing the data for Figure 10.1.
    a. Calculate the arithmetic average return on the S&P 500 from 1926 to 1989.
    b. Assuming that the S&P 500 had simply continued to earn the average return from (a), calculate the amount that $100 invested at the end of 1925 would have grown to by the end of 2011.
    c. Do the same for small stocks.

Common Versus Independent Risk

20. Consider two local banks. Bank A has 100 loans outstanding, each for $1 million, that it expects will be repaid today. Each loan has a 5% probability of default, in which case the bank is not repaid anything. The chance of default is independent across all the loans. Bank B has only one loan of $100 million outstanding, which it also expects will be repaid today. It also has a 5% probability of not being repaid. Explain the difference between the type of risk each bank faces. Which bank faces less risk? Why?

*21. Using the data in Problem 20, calculate
    a. The expected overall payoff of each bank.
    b. The standard deviation of the overall payoff of each bank.

Diversification in Stock Portfolios

22. Consider the following two, completely separate, economies. The expected return and volatility of all stocks in both economies is the same. In the first economy, all stocks move together—in good times all prices rise together and in bad times they all fall together. In the second economy, stock returns are independent—one stock increasing in price has no effect on the prices of other stocks. Assuming you are risk-averse and you could choose one of the two economies in which to invest, which one would you choose? Explain.

23. Consider an economy with two types of firms, S and I. S firms all move together. I firms move independently. For both types of firms, there is a 60% probability that the firms will have a 15% return and a 40% probability that the firms will have a −10% return. What is the volatility (standard deviation) of a portfolio that consists of an equal investment in 20 firms of (a) type S, and (b) type I?

*24. Using the data in Problem 23, plot the volatility as a function of the number of firms in the two portfolios.

25. Explain why the risk premium of a stock does not depend on its diversifiable risk.

26. Identify each of the following risks as most likely to be systematic risk or diversifiable risk:
    a. The risk that your main production plant is shut down due to a tornado.
    b. The risk that the economy slows, decreasing demand for your firm's products.
    c. The risk that your best employees will be hired away.
    d. The risk that the new product you expect your R&D division to produce will not materialize.

27. Suppose the risk-free interest rate is 5%, and the stock market will return either 40% or −20% each year, with each outcome equally likely. Compare the following two investment strategies: (1) invest for one year in the risk-free investment, and one year in the market, or (2) invest for both years in the market.
   a. Which strategy has the highest expected final payoff?
   b. Which strategy has the highest standard deviation for the final payoff?
   c. Does holding stocks for a longer period decrease your risk?

 28. Download the spreadsheet from MyFinanceLab containing the realized return of the S&P 500 from 1929–2008. Starting in 1929, divide the sample into four periods of 20 years each. For each 20-year period, calculate the final amount an investor would have earned given a $1000 initial investment. Also express your answer as an annualized return. If risk were eliminated by holding stocks for 20 years, what would you expect to find? What can you conclude about long-run diversification?

Measuring Systematic Risk

29. What is an efficient portfolio?

30. What does the beta of a stock measure?

31. You turn on the news and find out the stock market has gone up 10%. Based on the data in Table 10.6, by how much do you expect each of the following stocks to have gone up or down: (1) Starbucks, (2) Tiffany & Co., (3) Hershey, and (4) McDonald's.

32. Based on the data in Table 10.6, estimate which of the following investments you expect to lose the most in the event of a severe market down turn: (1) A $1000 investment in eBay, (2) a $5000 investment in Abbott Laboratories, or (3) a $2500 investment in Walt Disney.

33. Suppose the market portfolio is equally likely to increase by 30% or decrease by 10%.
   a. Calculate the beta of a firm that goes up on average by 43% when the market goes *up* and goes down by 17% when the market goes *down*.
   b. Calculate the beta of a firm that goes up on average by 18% when the market goes *down* and goes down by 22% when the market goes *up*.
   c. Calculate the beta of a firm that is expected to go up by 4% *independently* of the market.

Beta and the Cost of Capital

34. Suppose the risk-free interest rate is 4%.
   a. i. Use the beta you calculated for the stock in Problem 33(a) to estimate its expected return.
      ii. How does this compare with the stock's actual expected return?
   b. i. Use the beta you calculated for the stock in Problem 33(b) to estimate its expected return.
      ii. How does this compare with the stock's actual expected return?

35. Suppose the market risk premium is 5% and the risk-free interest rate is 4%. Using the data in Table 10.6, calculate the expected return of investing in
   a. Starbucks' stock.
   b. Hershey's stock.
   c. Autodesk's stock.

36. Given the results to Problem 35, why don't all investors hold Autodesk's stock rather than Hershey's stock?

37. Suppose the market risk premium is 6.5% and the risk-free interest rate is 5%. Calculate the cost of capital of investing in a project with a beta of 1.2.

38. State whether each of the following is inconsistent with an efficient capital market, the CAPM, or both:
   a. A security with only diversifiable risk has an expected return that exceeds the risk-free interest rate.

    b. A security with a beta of 1 had a return last year of 15% when the market had a return of 9%.

    c. Small stocks with a beta of 1.5 tend to have higher returns on average than large stocks with a beta of 1.5.

Data Case

Today is April 30, 2012, and you have just started your new job with a financial planning firm. In addition to studying for all your license exams, you have been asked to review a portion of a client's stock portfolio to determine the risk/return profiles of 12 stocks in the portfolio. Unfortunately, your small firm cannot afford the expensive databases that would provide all this information with a few simple keystrokes, but that's why they hired you. Specifically, you have been asked to determine the monthly average returns and standard deviations for the 12 stocks for the past five years. In the following chapters, you will be asked to do more extensive analyses on these same stocks.

    The stocks (with their symbols in parentheses) are:

Archer Daniels Midland (ADM)	International Business Machines
Boeing (BA)	Corporation (IBM)
Caterpillar (CAT)	JPMorgan Chase & Co. (JPM)
Deere & Co. (DE)	Microsoft (MSFT)
General Mills, Inc. (GIS)	Procter and Gamble (PG)
Google Inc. (GOOG)	Wal-Mart (WMT)
Hershey (HSY)	

1. Collect price information for each stock from Yahoo! Finance (finance.yahoo.com) as follows:

    a. Enter the stock symbol. On the page for that stock, click "Historical Prices" on the left side of the page.

    b. Enter the "start date" as April 30, 2007 and the "end date" as April 30, 2012 to cover the five-year period. Make sure you click "monthly" next to the date.

    c. After hitting "Get Prices," scroll to the bottom of the first page and click "Download to Spreadsheet." If you are asked if you want to open or save the file, click open.

    d. Copy the entire spreadsheet, open Excel, and paste the Web data into a spreadsheet. Delete all the columns except the date and the adjusted close (the first and last columns).

    e. Keep the Excel file open and go back to the Yahoo! Finance Web page and hit the back button. If you are asked if you want to save the data, click no.

    f. When you return to the prices page, enter the next stock symbol and hit "Get Prices" again. Do not change the dates or frequency, but make sure you have the same dates for all the stocks you will download. Again, click "Download to Spreadsheet" and then open the file. Copy the last column, "Adj. Close," paste it into the Excel file and change "Adj. Close" to the stock symbol. Make sure that the first and last prices are in the same rows as the first stock.

    g. Repeat these steps for the remaining 10 stocks, pasting each closing price right next to the other stocks, again making sure that the correct prices on the correct dates all appear on the same rows.

2. Convert these prices to monthly returns as the percentage change in the monthly prices. (*Hint*: Create a separate worksheet within the Excel file.) Note that to compute a return for each month, you need a beginning and ending price, so you will not be able to compute the return for the first month.

3. Compute the mean monthly returns and standard deviations for the monthly returns of each of the stocks.[16] Convert the monthly statistics to annual statistics for easier interpretation (multiply the mean monthly return by 12, and multiply the monthly standard deviation by $\sqrt{12}$).

---

[16] In Eq. 10.4, we showed how to compute returns with stock price and dividend data. The "adjusted close" series from Yahoo! Finance is already adjusted for dividends and splits, so we may compute returns based on the percentage change in monthly adjusted prices.

4. Add a column in your Excel worksheet with the average return across stocks for each month. This is the monthly return to an equally weighted portfolio of these 12 stocks. Compute the mean and standard deviation of monthly returns for the equally weighted portfolio. Double check that the average return on this equally weighted portfolio is equal to the average return of all of the individual stocks. Convert these monthly statistics to annual statistics (as described in Step 3) for interpretation.

5. Using the annual statistics, create an Excel plot with standard deviation (volatility) on the x-axis and average return on the y-axis as follows:
   a. Create three columns on your spreadsheet with the statistics you created in Questions 3 and 4 for each of the individual stocks and the equally weighted portfolio. The first column will have the ticker, the second will have annual standard deviation, and the third will have the annual mean return.
   b. Highlight the data in the last two columns (standard deviation and mean), choose Insert>Chart>XY Scatter Plot. Complete the chart wizard to finish the plot.

6. What do you notice about the average of the volatilities of the individual stocks, compared to the volatility of the equally weighted portfolio?

Optimal Portfolio Choice and the Capital Asset Pricing Model

IN THIS CHAPTER, WE BUILD ON THE IDEAS WE INTRODUCED IN Chapter 10 to explain how an investor can choose an efficient portfolio. In particular, we will demonstrate how to find the optimal portfolio for an investor who wants to earn the highest possible return given the level of volatility he or she is willing to accept by developing the statistical techniques of *mean-variance portfolio optimization*. Both elegant and practical, these techniques are used routinely by professional investors, money managers, and financial institutions. We then introduce the assumptions of the Capital Asset Pricing Model (CAPM), the most important model of the relationship between risk and return. Under these assumptions, the efficient portfolio is the market portfolio of all stocks and securities. As a result, the expected return of any security depends upon its beta with the market portfolio.

In Chapter 10, we explained how to calculate the expected return and volatility of a single stock. To find the efficient portfolio, we must understand how to do the same thing for a portfolio of stocks. We begin this chapter by explaining how to calculate the expected return and volatility of a portfolio. With these statistical tools in hand, we then describe how an investor can create an efficient portfolio out of individual stocks, and consider the implications, if all investors attempt to do so, for an investment's expected return and cost of capital.

In our exploration of these concepts, we take the perspective of a stock market investor. These concepts, however, are also important for a corporate financial manager. After all, financial managers are also investors, investing money on behalf of their shareholders. When a company makes a new investment, financial managers must ensure that the investment has a positive NPV. Doing so requires knowing the cost of capital of the investment opportunity and, as we shall see in the next chapter, the CAPM is the main method used by most major corporations to calculate the cost of capital.

NOTATION

R_i return of security (or investment) i

x_i fraction invested in security i

$E[R_i]$ expected return

r_f risk-free interest rate

$\overline{R}_i$ average return of security (or investment)

$Corr(R_i, R_j)$ correlation between returns of i and j

$Cov(R_i, R_j)$ covariance between returns of i and j

$SD(R)$ standard deviation (volatility) of return R

$Var(R)$ variance of return R

n number of securities in a portfolio

R_{xP} return of portfolio with fraction x invested in portfolio P and $(1 - x)$ invested in the risk-free security

β_i^P beta or sensitivity of the investment i to the fluctuations of the portfolio P

β_i beta of security i with respect to the market portfolio

r_i required return or cost of capital of security i

11.1 The Expected Return of a Portfolio

To find an optimal portfolio, we need a method to define a portfolio and analyze its return. We can describe a portfolio by its **portfolio weights**, the fraction of the total investment in the portfolio held in each individual investment in the portfolio:

$$x_i = \frac{\text{Value of investment } i}{\text{Total value of portfolio}} \qquad (11.1)$$

These portfolio weights add up to 1 (that is, $\Sigma_i x_i = 1$), so that they represent the way we have divided our money between the different individual investments in the portfolio.

As an example, consider a portfolio with 200 shares of the Walt Disney Company worth $30 per share and 100 shares of Coca-Cola worth $40 per share. The total value of the portfolio is $200 \times \$30 + 100 \times \$40 = \$10,000$, and the corresponding portfolio weights x_D and x_C are

$$x_D = \frac{200 \times \$30}{\$10,000} = 60\%, \qquad x_C = \frac{100 \times \$40}{\$10,000} = 40\%$$

Given the portfolio weights, we can calculate the return on the portfolio. Suppose $x_1, \ldots, x_n$ are the portfolio weights of the n investments in a portfolio, and these investments have returns $R_1, \ldots, R_n$. Then the return on the portfolio, R_P, is the weighted average of the returns on the investments in the portfolio, where the weights correspond to portfolio weights:

$$R_P = x_1 R_1 + x_2 R_2 + \cdots + x_n R_n = \sum_i x_i R_i \qquad (11.2)$$

The return of a portfolio is straightforward to compute if we know the returns of the individual stocks and the portfolio weights.

EXAMPLE 11.1 **Calculating Portfolio Returns**

Problem

Suppose you buy 200 shares of the Walt Disney Company at $30 per share and 100 shares of Coca-Cola stock at $40 per share. If Disney's share price goes up to $36 and Coca-Cola's falls to $38, what is the new value of the portfolio, and what return did it earn? Show that Eq. 11.2 holds. After the price change, what are the new portfolio weights?

Solution

The new value of the portfolio is $200 \times \$36 + 100 \times \$38 = \$11,000$, for a gain of $1000 or a 10% return on your $10,000 investment. Disney's return was $36/30 - 1 = 20\%$, and Coca-Cola's was $38/40 - 1 = -5\%$. Given the initial portfolio weights of 60% Disney and 40% Coca-Cola, we can also compute the portfolio's return from Eq. 11.2:

$$R_P = x_D R_D + x_C R_C = 0.6 \times (20\%) + 0.4 \times (-5\%) = 10\%$$

After the price change, the new portfolio weights are

$$x_D = \frac{200 \times \$36}{\$11,000} = 65.45\%, \qquad x_C = \frac{100 \times \$38}{\$11,000} = 34.55\%$$

Without trading, the weights increase for those stocks whose returns exceed the portfolio's return.

Equation 11.2 also allows us to compute the expected return of a portfolio. Using the facts that the expectation of a sum is just the sum of the expectations and that the expectation of a known multiple is just the multiple of its expectation, we arrive at the following formula for a portfolio's expected return:

$$E[R_P] = E\left[\sum_i x_i R_i\right] = \sum_i E[x_i R_i] = \sum_i x_i E[R_i] \qquad (11.3)$$

That is, the expected return of a portfolio is simply the weighted average of the expected returns of the investments within it, using the portfolio weights.

EXAMPLE 11.2

Portfolio Expected Return

Problem

Suppose you invest $10,000 in Ford stock, and $30,000 in Tyco International stock. You expect a return of 10% for Ford and 16% for Tyco. What is your portfolio's expected return?

Solution

You invested $40,000 in total, so your portfolio weights are 10,000/40,000 = 0.25 in Ford and 30,000/40,000 = 0.75 in Tyco. Therefore, your portfolio's expected return is

$$E[R_P] = x_F E[R_F] + x_T E[R_T] = 0.25 \times 10\% + 0.75 \times 16\% = 14.5\%$$

CONCEPT CHECK

1. What is a portfolio weight?

2. How do we calculate the return on a portfolio?

11.2 The Volatility of a Two-Stock Portfolio

As we explained in Chapter 10, combining stocks in a portfolio eliminates some of their risk through diversification. The amount of risk that will remain depends on the degree to which the stocks are exposed to common risks. In this section, we describe the statistical tools that we can use to quantify the risk stocks have in common and determine the volatility of a portfolio.

Combining Risks

Let's begin with a simple example of how risk changes when stocks are combined in a portfolio. Table 11.1 shows returns for three hypothetical stocks, along with their average returns and volatilities. While the three stocks have the same volatility and average return,

---

TABLE 11.1   **Returns for Three Stocks, and Portfolios of Pairs of Stocks**

	Stock Returns			Portfolio Returns	
Year	North Air	West Air	Tex Oil	$1/2R_N + 1/2R_W$	$1/2R_W + 1/2R_T$
2007	21%	9%	−2%	15.0%	3.5%
2008	30%	21%	−5%	25.5%	8.0%
2009	7%	7%	9%	7.0%	8.0%
2010	−5%	−2%	21%	−3.5%	9.5%
2011	−2%	−5%	30%	−3.5%	12.5%
2012	9%	30%	7%	19.5%	18.5%
Average Return	10.0%	10.0%	10.0%	10.0%	10.0%
Volatility	13.4%	13.4%	13.4%	12.1%	5.1%

the pattern of their returns differs. When the airline stocks performed well, the oil stock tended to do poorly (see 2007–2008), and when the airlines did poorly, the oil stock tended to do well (2010–2011).

Table 11.1 also shows the returns for two portfolios of the stocks. The first portfolio consists of equal investments in the two airlines, North Air and West Air. The second portfolio includes equal investments in West Air and Tex Oil. The average return of both portfolios is equal to the average return of the stocks, consistent with Eq. 11.3. However, their volatilities—12.1% and 5.1%—are very different from the individual stocks *and* from each other.

This example demonstrates two important phenomena. First, by combining stocks into a portfolio, we reduce risk through diversification. Because the prices of the stocks do not move identically, some of the risk is averaged out in a portfolio. As a result, both portfolios have lower risk than the individual stocks. Second, the amount of risk that is eliminated in a portfolio depends on the degree to which the stocks face common risks and their prices move together. Because the two airline stocks tend to perform well or poorly at the same time, the portfolio of airline stocks has a volatility that is only slightly lower than that of the individual stocks. The airline and oil stocks, by contrast, do not move together; indeed, they tend to move in opposite directions. As a result, additional risk is canceled out, making that portfolio much less risky. This benefit of diversification is obtained costlessly—without any reduction in the average return.

Determining Covariance and Correlation

To find the risk of a portfolio, we need to know more than the risk and return of the component stocks: We need to know the degree to which the stocks face common risks and their returns move together. In this section, we introduce two statistical measures, *covariance* and *correlation*, that allow us to measure the co-movement of returns.

Covariance. **Covariance** is the expected product of the deviations of two returns from their means. The covariance between returns R_i and R_j is:

Covariance between Returns R_i and R_j

$$Cov(R_i, R_j) = E[(R_i - E[R_i])(R_j - E[R_j])] \tag{11.4}$$

When estimating the covariance from historical data, we use the formula[1]

Estimate of the Covariance from Historical Data

$$Cov(R_i, R_j) = \frac{1}{T-1} \sum_t (R_{i,t} - \overline{R}_i)(R_{j,t} - \overline{R}_j) \tag{11.5}$$

Intuitively, if two stocks move together, their returns will tend to be above or below average at the same time, and the covariance will be positive. If the stocks move in opposite directions, one will tend to be above average when the other is below average, and the covariance will be negative.

Correlation. While the sign of the covariance is easy to interpret, its magnitude is not. It will be larger if the stocks are more volatile (and so have larger deviations from their expected returns), and it will be larger the more closely the stocks move in relation to each

---

[1]As with Eq. 10.7 for historical volatility, we divide by $T - 1$ rather than by T to make up for the fact that we have used the data to compute the average returns $\overline{R}$, eliminating a degree of freedom.

| FIGURE 11.1 | **Correlation** |

Correlation measures how returns move in relation to each other. It is between +1 (returns always move together) and −1 (returns always move oppositely). Independent risks have no tendency to move together and have zero correlation.

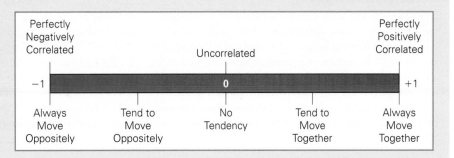

other. In order to control for the volatility of each stock and quantify the strength of the relationship between them, we can calculate the **correlation** between two stock returns, defined as the covariance of the returns divided by the standard deviation of each return:

$$Corr(R_i, R_j) = \frac{Cov(R_i, R_j)}{SD(R_i)\,SD(R_j)} \qquad (11.6)$$

The correlation between two stocks has the same sign as their covariance, so it has a similar interpretation. Dividing by the volatilities ensures that correlation is always between −1 and +1, which allows us to gauge the strength of the relationship between the stocks. As Figure 11.1 shows, correlation is a barometer of the degree to which the returns share common risk and tend to move together. The closer the correlation is to +1, the more the returns tend to move together as a result of common risk. When the correlation (and thus the covariance) equals 0, the returns are *uncorrelated;* that is, they have no tendency to move either together or in opposition to one another. Independent risks are uncorrelated. Finally, the closer the correlation is to −1, the more the returns tend to move in opposite directions.

| EXAMPLE 11.3 | **The Covariance and Correlation of a Stock with Itself** |

Problem
What are the covariance and the correlation of a stock's return with itself?

Solution
Let R_s be the stock's return. From the definition of the covariance,

$$Cov(R_s, R_s) = E[(R_s - E[R_s])(R_s - E[R_s])] = E[(R_s - E[R_s])^2]$$
$$= Var(R_s)$$

where the last equation follows from the definition of the variance. That is, the covariance of a stock with itself is simply its variance. Then,

$$Corr(R_s, R_s) = \frac{Cov(R_s, R_s)}{SD(R_s)\,SD(R_s)} = \frac{Var(R_s)}{SD(R_s)^2} = 1$$

where the last equation follows from the definition of the standard deviation. That is, a stock's return is perfectly positively correlated with itself, as it always moves together with itself in perfect synchrony.

COMMON MISTAKE   Computing Variance, Covariance, and Correlation in Excel

The computer spreadsheet program Excel does not compute the standard deviation, variance, covariance, and correlation consistently. The Excel functions STDEV and VAR correctly use Eq. 10.7 to estimate the standard deviation and variance from historical data. But the Excel function COVAR does *not* use Eq. 11.5; instead, Excel divides by T instead of $T - 1$. Therefore, to estimate the covariance from a sample of historical returns using COVAR, you must correct the inconsistency by multiplying by the number of data points and dividing by the number of data points minus one; i.e., COVAR*$T/(T - 1)$. Alternatively, you can use the function CORREL to compute the correlation, and then estimate the covariance by multiplying the correlation by the standard deviation of each return. Finally, Excel 2010 introduced a new function, COVARIANCE.S, that correctly estimates the covariance from a historical sample.

EXAMPLE 11.4   **Computing the Covariance and Correlation**

Problem

Using the data in Table 11.1, what are the covariance and the correlation between North Air and West Air? Between West Air and Tex Oil?

Solution

Given the returns in Table 11.1, we deduct the mean return (10%) from each and compute the product of these deviations between the pairs of stocks. We then sum them and divide by $T - 1 = 5$ to compute the covariance, as in Table 11.2.

From the table, we see that North Air and West Air have a positive covariance, indicating a tendency to move together, whereas West Air and Tex Oil have a negative covariance, indicating a tendency to move oppositely. We can assess the strength of these tendencies from the correlation, obtained by dividing the covariance by the standard deviation of each stock (13.4%). The correlation for North Air and West Air is 62.4%; the correlation for West Air and Tex Oil is −71.3%.

TABLE 11.2   **Computing the Covariance and Correlation between Pairs of Stocks**

Year	Deviation from Mean			North Air and West Air	West Air and Tex Oil
	$(R_N - \bar{R}_N)$	$(R_W - \bar{R}_W)$	$(R_T - \bar{R}_T)$	$(R_N - \bar{R}_N)(R_W - \bar{R}_W)$	$(R_W - \bar{R}_W)(R_T - \bar{R}_T)$
2007	11%	−1%	−12%	−0.0011	0.0012
2008	20%	11%	−15%	0.0220	−0.0165
2009	−3%	−3%	−1%	0.0009	0.0003
2010	−15%	−12%	11%	0.0180	−0.0132
2011	−12%	−15%	20%	0.0180	−0.0300
2012	−1%	20%	−3%	−0.0020	−0.0060

$$\text{Sum} = \sum_t (R_{i,t} - \bar{R}_i)(R_{j,t} - \bar{R}_j) = \quad 0.0558 \qquad -0.0642$$

Covariance:

$$Cov(R_i, R_j) = \frac{1}{T-1}\text{Sum} = \quad 0.0112 \qquad -0.0128$$

Correlation:

$$Corr(R_i, R_j) = \frac{Cov(R_i, R_j)}{SD(R_i)SD(R_j)} = \quad 0.624 \qquad -0.713$$

TABLE 11.3	Historical Annual Volatilities and Correlations for Selected Stocks (based on monthly returns, 1996–2011)						
	Microsoft	Dell	Alaska Air	Southwest Airlines	Ford Motor	Heinz	General Mills
Volatility (Standard Deviation)	35%	47%	38%	32%	53%	19%	17%
Correlation with							
Microsoft	1.00	0.63	0.24	0.25	0.27	0.17	0.10
Dell	0.63	1.00	0.19	0.24	0.31	0.12	0.09
Alaska Air	0.24	0.19	1.00	0.36	0.15	0.26	0.15
Southwest Airlines	0.25	0.24	0.36	1.00	0.31	0.26	0.22
Ford Motor	0.27	0.31	0.15	0.31	1.00	0.16	0.05
Heinz	0.17	0.12	0.26	0.26	0.16	1.00	0.50
General Mills	0.10	0.09	0.15	0.22	0.05	0.50	1.00

When will stock returns be highly correlated with each other? Stock returns will tend to move together if they are affected similarly by economic events. Thus, stocks in the same industry tend to have more highly correlated returns than stocks in different industries. This tendency is illustrated in Table 11.3, which shows the volatility of individual stock returns and the correlation between them for several common stocks. Consider, for example, Microsoft and Dell. The returns of these two technology stocks have a higher correlation with each other (63%) than with any of the non-technology stocks (31% or lower). The same pattern holds for the airline and food-processing stocks—their returns are most highly correlated with the other firm in their industry, and much less correlated with those outside their industry. General Mills and Heinz have the lowest correlation with each of the other stocks; indeed, General Mills and Ford have a correlation of only 5%, suggesting that these two firms are subject to essentially uncorrelated risks. Note, however, that all of the correlations are positive, illustrating the general tendency of stocks to move together.

EXAMPLE 11.5	Computing the Covariance from the Correlation

Problem

Using the data from Table 11.3, what is the covariance between Microsoft and Dell?

Solution

We can rewrite Eq. 11.6 to solve for the covariance:

$$Cov(R_M, R_D) = Corr(R_M, R_D)SD(R_M)SD(R_D)$$

$$= (0.63)(0.35)(0.47) = 0.1036$$

Computing a Portfolio's Variance and Volatility

We now have the tools to compute the variance of a portfolio. For a two-stock portfolio with $R_P = x_1R_1 + x_2R_2$,

$$Var(R_P) = Cov(R_P, R_P)$$
$$= Cov(x_1R_1 + x_2R_2, x_1R_1 + x_2R_2)$$
$$= x_1x_1Cov(R_1,R_1) + x_1x_2Cov(R_1,R_2) + x_2x_1Cov(R_2,R_1) + x_2x_2Cov(R_2,R_2) \quad (11.7)$$

In the last line of Eq. 11.7, we use the fact that, as with expectations, we can change the order of the covariance with sums and multiples.[2] By combining terms and recognizing, from Example 11.4, that $Cov(R_i, R_i) = Var(R_i)$, we arrive at our main result of this section:

The Variance of a Two-Stock Portfolio

$$Var(R_P) = x_1^2 Var(R_1) + x_2^2 Var(R_2) + 2x_1 x_2 Cov(R_1, R_2) \tag{11.8}$$

As always, the volatility is the square root of the variance, $SD(R_P) = \sqrt{Var(R_P)}$.

Let's check this formula for the airline and oil stocks in Table 11.1. Consider the portfolio containing shares of West Air and Tex Oil. The variance of each stock is equal to the square of its volatility, $0.134^2 = 0.018$. From Example 11.3, the covariance between the stocks is -0.0128. Therefore, the variance of a portfolio with 50% invested in each stock is

$$Var\left(\tfrac{1}{2}R_W + \tfrac{1}{2}R_T\right) = x_W^2 Var(R_W) + x_T^2 Var(R_T) + 2x_W x_T Cov(R_W, R_T)$$
$$= \left(\tfrac{1}{2}\right)^2 (0.018) + \left(\tfrac{1}{2}\right)^2 (0.018) + 2\left(\tfrac{1}{2}\right)\left(\tfrac{1}{2}\right)(-0.0128)$$
$$= 0.0026$$

The volatility of the portfolio is $\sqrt{0.0026} = 5.1\%$, which corresponds to the calculation in Table 11.1. For the North Air and West Air portfolio, the calculation is the same except for the stocks' higher covariance of 0.0112, resulting in a higher volatility of 12.1%.

Equation 11.8 shows that the variance of the portfolio depends on the variance of the individual stocks *and* on the covariance between them. We can also rewrite Eq. 11.8 by calculating the covariance from the correlation (as in Example 11.5):

$$Var(R_P) = x_1^2 SD(R_1)^2 + x_2^2 SD(R_2)^2 + 2x_1 x_2 Corr(R_1, R_2) SD(R_1) SD(R_2) \tag{11.9}$$

Equations 11.8 and 11.9 demonstrate that with a positive amount invested in each stock, the more the stocks move together and the higher their covariance or correlation, the more variable the portfolio will be. The portfolio will have the greatest variance if the stocks have a perfect positive correlation of $+1$.

EXAMPLE 11.6   **Computing the Volatility of a Two-Stock Portfolio**

Problem

Using the data from Table 11.3, what is the volatility of a portfolio with equal amounts invested in Microsoft and Dell stock? What is the volatility of a portfolio with equal amounts invested in Dell and Alaska Air stock?

Solution

With portfolio weights of 50% each in Microsoft and Dell stock, from Eq. 11.9, the portfolio's variance is

$$Var(R_P) = x_M^2 SD(R_M)^2 + x_D^2 SD(R_D)^2 + 2x_M x_D Corr(R_M, R_D) SD(R_M) SD(R_D)$$
$$= (0.50)^2 (0.35)^2 + (0.50)^2 (0.47)^2 + 2(0.50)(0.50)(0.63)(0.35)(0.47)$$
$$= 0.1377$$

---

[2]That is, $Cov(A + B, C) = Cov(A, C) + Cov(B, C)$ and $Cov(mA, B) = m\,Cov(A, B)$.

The volatility is therefore $SD(R) = \sqrt{Var(R)} = \sqrt{0.1377} = 37.1\%$.

For the portfolio of Dell and Alaska Air stock,

$$Var(R_P) = x_M^2 SD(R_M)^2 + x_D^2 SD(R_D)^2 + 2x_M x_D Corr(R_M, R_D)SD(R_M)SD(R_D)$$
$$= (0.50)^2(0.47)^2 + (0.50)^2(0.38)^2 + 2(0.50)(0.50)(0.19)(0.47)(0.38)$$
$$= 0.1083$$

The volatility in this case is $SD(R) = \sqrt{Var(R)} = \sqrt{0.1083} = 32.9\%$.

Note that the portfolio of Dell and Alaska Air stock is less volatile than either of the individual stocks. It is also less volatile than the portfolio of Dell and Microsoft stock. Even though Alaska Air's stock returns are more volatile than Microsoft's, its much lower correlation with Dell's returns leads to greater diversification in the portfolio.

CONCEPT CHECK
1. What does the correlation measure?
2. How does the correlation between the stocks in a portfolio affect the portfolio's volatility?

11.3 The Volatility of a Large Portfolio

We can gain additional benefits of diversification by holding more than two stocks in our portfolio. While these calculations are best done on a computer, by understanding them we can obtain important intuition regarding the amount of diversification that is possible if we hold many stocks.

Large Portfolio Variance

Recall that the return on a portfolio of n stocks is simply the weighted average of the returns of the stocks in the portfolio:

$$R_P = x_1 R_1 + x_2 R_2 + \cdots + x_n R_n = \sum_i x_i R_i$$

Using the properties of the covariance, we can write the variance of a portfolio as follows:

$$Var(R_P) = Cov(R_P, R_P) = Cov(\textstyle\sum_i x_i R_i, R_P) = \sum_i x_i Cov(R_i, R_P) \qquad (11.10)$$

This equation indicates that the *variance of a portfolio is equal to the weighted average covariance of each stock with the portfolio*. This expression reveals that the risk of a portfolio depends on how each stock's return moves in relation to it.

We can reduce the formula even further by replacing the second R_P with a weighted average and simplifying:

$$Var(R_P) = \sum_i x_i Cov(R_i, R_P) = \sum_i x_i Cov(R_i, \textstyle\sum_j x_j R_j)$$
$$= \sum_i \sum_j x_i x_j Cov(R_i, R_j) \qquad (11.11)$$

This formula says that the variance of a portfolio is equal to the sum of the covariances of the returns of all pairs of stocks in the portfolio multiplied by each of their portfolio weights.[3] That is, the overall variability of the portfolio depends on the total co-movement of the stocks within it.

---

[3]Looking back, we can see that Eq. 11.11 generalizes the case of two stocks in Eq. 11.7.

Diversification with an Equally Weighted Portfolio

We can use Eq. 11.11 to calculate the variance of an **equally weighted portfolio**, a portfolio in which the same amount is invested in each stock. An equally weighted portfolio consisting on n stocks has portfolio weights $x_i = 1/n$. In this case, we have the following formula:[4]

Variance of an Equally Weighted Portfolio of n Stocks

$$Var(R_P) = \frac{1}{n}(\text{Average Variance of the Individual Stocks})$$

$$+\left(1 - \frac{1}{n}\right)(\text{Average Covariance between the Stocks}) \qquad (11.12)$$

Equation 11.12 demonstrates that as the number of stocks, n, grows large, the variance of the portfolio is determined primarily by the average covariance among the stocks. As an example, consider a portfolio of stocks selected randomly from the stock market. The historical volatility of the return of a typical large firm in the stock market is about 40%, and the typical correlation between the returns of large firms is about 28%. Using Eq. 11.12, the volatility of an equally weighted portfolio varies with the number of stocks, n, as follows:

$$SD(R_P) = \sqrt{\frac{1}{n}(0.40^2) + \left(1 - \frac{1}{n}\right)(0.28 \times 0.40 \times 0.40)}$$

We graph the volatility for different numbers of stocks in Figure 11.2. Note that the volatility declines as the number of stocks in the portfolio grows. In fact, nearly half of the volatility

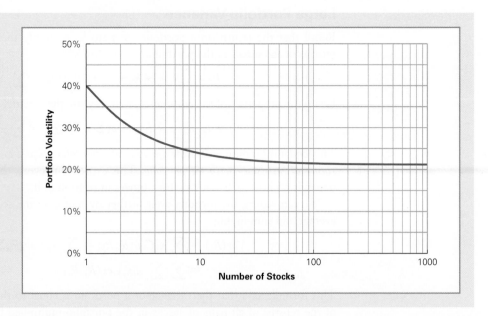

FIGURE 11.2

Volatility of an Equally Weighted Portfolio Versus the Number of Stocks

The volatility declines as the number of stocks in the portfolio increases. Even in a very large portfolio, however, market risk remains.

[4]For an n-stock portfolio, there are n variance terms (any time $i = j$ in Eq. 11.11) with weight $x_i^2 = 1/n^2$ on each, which implies a weight of $n/n^2 = 1/n$ on the average variance. There are $n^2 - n$ covariance terms (all the $n \times n$ pairs minus the n variance terms) with weight $x_i x_j = 1/n^2$ on each, which implies a weight of $(n^2 - n)/n^2 = 1 - 1/n$ on the average covariance.

of the individual stocks is eliminated in a large portfolio as the result of diversification. The benefit of diversification is most dramatic initially: The decrease in volatility when going from one to two stocks is much larger than the decrease when going from 100 to 101 stocks—indeed, almost all of the benefit of diversification can be achieved with about 30 stocks. Even for a very large portfolio, however, we cannot eliminate all of the risk. The variance of the portfolio converges to the average covariance, so the volatility declines to $\sqrt{0.28 \times 0.4 \times 0.4} = 21.17\%$.[5]

EXAMPLE 11.7

Diversification Using Different Types of Stocks

Problem

Stocks within a single industry tend to have a higher correlation than stocks in different industries. Likewise, stocks in different countries have lower correlation on average than stocks within the United States. What is the volatility of a very large portfolio of stocks within an industry in which the stocks have a volatility of 40% and a correlation of 60%? What is the volatility of a very large portfolio of international stocks with a volatility of 40% and a correlation of 10%?

Solution

From Eq. 11.12, the volatility of the industry portfolio as $n \to \infty$ is given by

$$\sqrt{\text{Average Covariance}} = \sqrt{0.60 \times 0.40 \times 0.40} = 31.0\%$$

This volatility is higher than when using stocks from different industries as in Figure 11.2. Combining stocks from the same industry that are more highly correlated therefore provides less diversification. We can achieve superior diversification using international stocks. In this case,

$$\sqrt{\text{Average Covariance}} = \sqrt{0.10 \times 0.40 \times 0.40} = 12.6\%$$

We can also use Eq. 11.12 to derive one of the key results that we discussed in Chapter 10: When risks are independent, we can diversify all of the risk by holding a large portfolio.

EXAMPLE 11.8

Volatility When Risks Are Independent

Problem

What is the volatility of an equally weighted average of n independent, identical risks?

Solution

If risks are independent, they are uncorrelated and their covariance is zero. Using Eq. 11.12, the volatility of an equally weighted portfolio of the risks is

$$SD(R_P) = \sqrt{Var(R_P)} = \sqrt{\frac{1}{n} Var(\text{Individual Risk})} = \frac{SD(\text{Individual Risk})}{\sqrt{n}}$$

This result coincides with Eq. 10.8, which we used earlier to evaluate independent risks. Note that as $n \to \infty$, the volatility goes to 0—that is, a very large portfolio will have *no* risk. In this case, we can eliminate all risk because there is no common risk.

---

[5]You might wonder what happens if the average covariance is negative. It turns out that while the covariance between a pair of stocks can be negative, as the portfolio grows large, the average covariance cannot be negative because the returns of all stocks cannot move in opposite directions simultaneously.

Since 2006 John F. Powers has been president and chief executive officer of the Stanford Management Company, which invests and manages Stanford University's $21.1 billion endowment. Prior to joining Stanford, he served as managing director and the director of research at Offit Hall Capital Management, an investment advisory firm.

QUESTION: *Describe how you manage Stanford's $16.5 billion endowment.*

ANSWER: Our objective is to grow the endowment's value after meeting our 5% annual payout obligation to Stanford University. We begin with the return we think will exceed 5%, account for inflation, and grow modestly, creating a portfolio that combines liquid and private (illiquid) strategies. We run a modified mean-variance optimization model using forward-looking assumptions of return and volatility of our asset classes, to find that place on the efficient frontier that meets our long-term objectives. Once we have our asset allocation strategy, we outsource money to a select group of third-party managers, to capture their expertise, gain access to the higher returns from illiquid assets, and increase diversification. We retain a relatively small portion in market replication instruments, including ETFs, so that we can modify our asset allocation quickly in response to pricing dislocations we perceive in the market.

QUESTION: *You hold assets with very different expected returns. If your goal is to maximize the value of Stanford's endowment, why not just hold those with the highest expected returns?*

ANSWER: Illiquid assets provide us the highest returns. If they dominated our portfolio, we would expose the university to their greater volatility and risk. As an operating business, Stanford requires some predictability of payout now and for future planning. Without diversification and a balanced portfolio, we'd create extreme risks of both spikes and crashes in portfolio value.

We also consider consequences across multiple time periods and in correlation to other assets. Increasing diversification may yield better portfolio performance with lower risk levels. For example, real assets—commodities and real estate—typically have very low correlation with equity markets. However, during the 2008–2009 financial crisis, these assets became highly correlated to credits and equities—they all behaved the same way under pressure, creating a "correlation storm." Ultimately, that led to a reshaping of the portfolio.

QUESTION: *Historically, university endowments have performed extremely well compared to public markets. Why do you think this is?*

ANSWER: Endowment managers recognized early the power of diversification. Their willingness to invest in alternative assets such as private equity funds yielded extraordinary returns. In addition, the declining interest rate environment over the past 25 years rewarded strategies that explicitly or implicitly employ leverage. Our ability to access premier money managers, acquire private assets, and use leveraged strategies like buyouts boosted our returns. From 2001–2011, Stanford's annualized return was 9.3%, compared to 2.7% for the S&P 500 and 5.7% for the U.S. bond market.

QUESTION: *During the financial crisis, did the portfolio achieve the benefits of diversification that you had expected? Has your strategy changed since the financial crisis?*

ANSWER: Because of the above-mentioned "correlation storm," we did not get the expected benefit of diversification. We were nervous about the pricing of investment-grade bonds, which were several standard deviations away from previous levels, and so we substantially reduced our exposure to corporate debt. This created cash and liquidity for us to redeploy funds into attractively priced assets.

Going forward, we expect ongoing episodes of heightened market volatility. Our strategy is to increase the diversification of our portfolio as much as possible. We are working with money managers who buy value-based assets, looking for long-term price appreciation, and increasing exposure to more arbitrage-oriented strategies (less based on fundamentals of equity and corporate credit markets). When markets are under pressure, our goal is to be positioned to be able to acquire stressed assets priced at significant discounts.

Diversification with General Portfolios

The results in the last section depend on the portfolio being equally weighted. For a portfolio with arbitrary weights, we can rewrite Eq. 11.10 in terms of the correlation as follows:

$$Var(R_P) = \sum_i x_i\, Cov(R_i, R_P) = \sum_i x_i\, SD(R_i) SD(R_P) Corr(R_i, R_P)$$

Dividing both sides of this equation by the standard deviation of the portfolio yields the following important decomposition of the volatility of a portfolio:

Volatility of a Portfolio with Arbitrary Weights

$$SD(R_P) = \sum_i \overbrace{x_i \times SD(R_i) \times Corr(R_i, R_P)}^{\text{Security } i\text{'s contribution to the}\atop\text{volatility of the portfolio}} \tag{11.13}$$

Amount   Total   Fraction of i's
of i held   risk of i risk that is
common to P

Equation 11.13 states that each security contributes to the volatility of the portfolio according to its volatility, or total risk, scaled by its correlation with the portfolio, which adjusts for the fraction of the total risk that is common to the portfolio. Therefore, when combining stocks into a portfolio that puts positive weight on each stock, unless all of the stocks have a perfect positive correlation of $+1$ with the portfolio (and thus with one another), the risk of the portfolio will be lower than the weighted average volatility of the individual stocks:

$$SD(R_P) = \sum_i x_i SD(R_i)\, Corr(R_i, R_P) < \sum_i x_i SD(R_i) \tag{11.14}$$

Contrast Eq. 11.14 with Eq. 11.3 for the expected return. The expected return of a portfolio is equal to the weighted average expected return, but the volatility of a portfolio is *less than* the weighted average volatility: We can eliminate some volatility by diversifying.

CONCEPT CHECK

1. How does the volatility of an equally weighted portfolio change as more stocks are added to it?

2. How does the volatility of a portfolio compare with the weighted average volatility of the stocks within it?

11.4 Risk Versus Return: Choosing an Efficient Portfolio

Now that we understand how to calculate the expected return and volatility of a portfolio, we can return to the main goal of the chapter: Determine how an investor can create an efficient portfolio.[6] Let's start with the simplest case—an investor who can choose between only two stocks.

---

[6]The techniques of portfolio optimization were developed in a 1952 paper by Harry Markowitz, as well as in related work by Andrew Roy (1952) and Bruno de Finetti (1940) (see Further Reading).

Efficient Portfolios with Two Stocks

Consider a portfolio of Intel and Coca-Cola stock. Suppose an investor believes these stocks are uncorrelated and will perform as follows:

Stock	Expected Return	Volatility
Intel	26%	50%
Coca-Cola	6%	25%

How should the investor choose a portfolio of these two stocks? Are some portfolios preferable to others?

Let's compute the expected return and volatility for different combinations of the stocks. Consider a portfolio with 40% invested in Intel stock and 60% invested in Coca-Cola stock. We can compute the expected return from Eq. 11.3 as

$$E[R_{40\text{-}60}] = x_I E[R_I] + x_C E[R_C] = 0.40(26\%) + 0.60(6\%) = 14\%$$

We can compute the variance using Eq. 11.9,

$$Var(R_{40\text{-}60}) = x_I^2 SD(R_I)^2 + x_C^2 SD(R_C)^2 + 2x_I x_C Corr(R_I, R_C) SD(R_I) SD(R_C)$$

$$= 0.40^2(0.50)^2 + 0.60^2(0.25)^2 + 2(0.40)(0.60)(0)(0.50)(0.25) = 0.0625$$

so that the volatility is $SD(R_{40\text{-}60}) = \sqrt{0.0625} = 25\%$. Table 11.4 shows the results for different portfolio weights.

Due to diversification, it is possible to find a portfolio with even lower volatility than either stock: Investing 20% in Intel stock and 80% in Coca-Cola stock, for example, has a volatility of only 22.3%. But knowing that investors care about volatility *and* expected return, we must consider both simultaneously. To do so, we plot the volatility and expected return of each portfolio in Figure 11.3. We labeled the portfolios from Table 11.4 with the portfolio weights. The curve (a hyperbola) represents the set of portfolios that we can create using arbitrary weights.

Faced with the choices in Figure 11.3, which ones make sense for an investor who is concerned with both the expected return and the volatility of her portfolio? Suppose the investor considers investing 100% in Coca-Cola stock. As we can see from Figure 11.3, other portfolios—such as the portfolio with 20% in Intel stock and 80% in Coca-Cola stock—make the investor better off in *both* ways: (1) They have a higher expected return, and (2) they have lower volatility. As a result, investing solely in Coca-Cola stock is not a good idea.

TABLE 11.4	Expected Returns and Volatility for Different Portfolios of Two Stocks

Portfolio Weights		Expected Return (%)	Volatility (%)
x_I	x_C	$E[R_P]$	$SD[R_P]$
1.00	0.00	26.0	50.0
0.80	0.20	22.0	40.3
0.60	0.40	18.0	31.6
0.40	0.60	14.0	25.0
0.20	0.80	10.0	22.4
0.00	1.00	6.0	25.0

FIGURE 11.3

Volatility Versus Expected Return for Portfolios of Intel and Coca-Cola Stock

Labels indicate portfolio weights (x_I, x_C) for Intel and Coca-Cola stocks. Portfolios on the red portion of the curve, with at least 20% invested in Intel stock, are efficient. Those on the blue portion of the curve, with less than 20% invested in Intel stock, are inefficient—an investor can earn a higher expected return with lower risk by choosing an alternative portfolio.

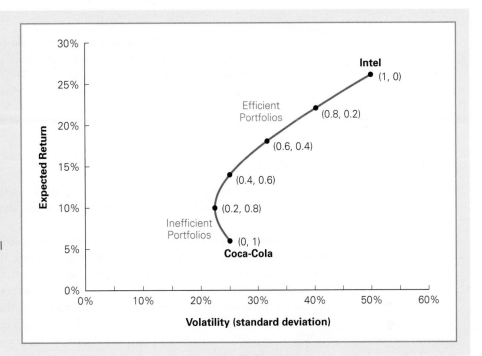

Identifying Inefficient Portfolios. More generally, we say a portfolio is an **inefficient portfolio** whenever it is possible to find another portfolio that is better in terms of both expected return and volatility. Looking at Figure 11.3, a portfolio is inefficient if there are other portfolios above and to the left—that is, to the northwest—of it. Investing solely in Coca-Cola stock is inefficient, and the same is true of all portfolios with more than 80% in Coca-Cola stock (the blue part of the curve). Inefficient portfolios are not optimal for an investor seeking high returns and low volatility.

Identifying Efficient Portfolios. By contrast, portfolios with at least 20% in Intel stock are efficient (the red part of the curve): There is no other portfolio of the two stocks that offers a higher expected return with lower volatility. But while we can rule out inefficient portfolios as inferior investment choices, we cannot easily rank the efficient ones—investors will choose among them based on their own preferences for return versus risk. For example, an extremely conservative investor who cares only about minimizing risk would choose the lowest-volatility portfolio (20% Intel, 80% Coca-Cola). An aggressive investor might choose to invest 100% in Intel stock—even though that approach is riskier, the investor may be willing to take that chance to earn a higher expected return.

EXAMPLE 11.9   **Improving Returns with an Efficient Portfolio**

Problem

Sally Ferson has invested 100% of her money in Coca-Cola stock and is seeking investment advice. She would like to earn the highest expected return possible without increasing her volatility. Which portfolio would you recommend?

Solution

In Figure 11.3, we can see that Sally can invest up to 40% in Intel stock without increasing her volatility. Because Intel stock has a higher expected return than Coca-Cola stock, she will earn higher expected returns by putting more money in Intel stock. Therefore, you should recommend that Sally put 40% of her money in Intel stock, leaving 60% in Coca-Cola stock. This portfolio has the same volatility of 25%, but an expected return of 14% rather than the 6% she has now.

The Effect of Correlation

In Figure 11.3, we assumed that the returns of Intel and Coca-Cola stocks are uncorrelated. Let's consider how the risk and return combinations would change if the correlations were different.

Correlation has no effect on the expected return of a portfolio. For example, a 40–60 portfolio will still have an expected return of 14%. However, the volatility of the portfolio will differ depending on the correlation, as we saw in Section 11.2. In particular, the lower the correlation, the lower the volatility we can obtain. In terms of Figure 11.3, as we lower the correlation and therefore the volatility of the portfolios, the curve showing the portfolios will bend to the left to a greater degree, as illustrated in Figure 11.4.

When the stocks are perfectly positively correlated, we can identify the set of portfolios by the straight line between them. In this extreme case (the red line in Figure 11.4), the volatility of the portfolio is equal to the weighted average volatility of the two stocks—there is no diversification. When the correlation is less than 1, however, the volatility of the portfolios is reduced due to diversification, and the curve bends to the left. The reduction in risk (and the bending of the curve) becomes greater as the correlation decreases. At the other extreme of perfect negative correlation (blue line), the line again becomes straight,

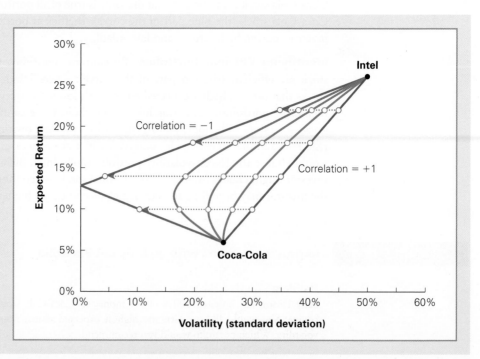

FIGURE 11.4

Effect on Volatility and Expected Return of Changing the Correlation between Intel and Coca-Cola Stock

This figure illustrates correlations of 1, 0.5, 0, −0.5, and −1. The lower the correlation, the lower the risk of the portfolios.

this time reflecting off the vertical axis. In particular, when the two stocks are perfectly negatively correlated, it becomes possible to hold a portfolio that bears absolutely no risk.

Short Sales

Thus far, we have considered only portfolios in which we invest a positive amount in each stock. We refer to a positive investment in a security as a **long position** in the security. But it is also possible to invest a *negative* amount in a stock, called a **short position**, by engaging in a short sale, a transaction in which you sell a stock today that you do not own, with the obligation to buy it back in the future. (For the mechanics of a short sale, see the box on page 274 in Chapter 9). As the next example demonstrates, we can include a short position as part of a portfolio by assigning that stock a negative portfolio weight.

EXAMPLE 11.10	**Expected Return and Volatility with a Short Sale**

Problem
Suppose you have $20,000 in cash to invest. You decide to short sell $10,000 worth of Coca-Cola stock and invest the proceeds from your short sale, plus your $20,000, in Intel. What is the expected return and volatility of your portfolio?

Solution
We can think of our short sale as a negative investment of $-\$10,000$ in Coca-Cola stock. In addition, we invested $+\$30,000$ in Intel stock, for a total net investment of $\$30,000 - \$10,000 = \$20,000$ cash. The corresponding portfolio weights are

$$x_I = \frac{\text{Value of investment in Intel}}{\text{Total value of portfolio}} = \frac{30,000}{20,000} = 150\%$$

$$x_C = \frac{\text{Value of investment in Coca-Cola}}{\text{Total value of portfolio}} = \frac{-10,000}{20,000} = -50\%$$

Note that the portfolio weights still add up to 100%. Using these portfolio weights, we can calculate the expected return and volatility of the portfolio using Eq. 11.3 and Eq. 11.8 as before:

$$E[R_P] = x_I E[R_I] + x_C E[R_C] = 1.50 \times 26\% + (-0.50) \times 6\% = 36\%$$

$$SD(R_P) = \sqrt{Var(R_P)} = \sqrt{x_I^2 Var(R_I) + x_C^2 Var(R_C) + 2x_I x_C Cov(R_I, R_C)}$$

$$= \sqrt{1.5^2 \times 0.50^2 + (-0.5)^2 \times 0.25^2 + 2(1.5)(-0.5)(0)} = 76.0\%$$

Note that in this case, short selling increases the expected return of your portfolio, but also its volatility, above those of the individual stocks.

Short selling is profitable if you expect a stock's price to decline in the future. Recall that when you borrow a stock to short sell it, you are obligated to buy and return it in the future. So when the stock price declines, you receive more upfront for the shares than the cost to replace them in the future. But as the preceding example shows, short selling can be advantageous even if you expect the stock's price to rise, as long as you invest the proceeds in another stock with an even higher expected return. That said, and as the example also shows, short selling can greatly increase the risk of the portfolio.

In Figure 11.5, we show the effect on the investor's choice set when we allow for short sales. Short selling Intel to invest in Coca-Cola is not efficient (blue dashed curve)—other portfolios exist that have a higher expected return *and* a lower volatility. However, because Intel is expected to outperform Coca-Cola, short selling Coca-Cola to invest in Intel is efficient in this case. While such a strategy leads to a higher volatility, it also provides the investor with a higher expected return. This strategy could be attractive to an aggressive investor.

Efficient Portfolios with Many Stocks

Recall from Section 11.3 that adding more stocks to a portfolio reduces risk through diversification. Let's consider the effect of adding to our portfolio a third stock, Bore Industries, which is uncorrelated with Intel and Coca-Cola but is expected to have a very low return of 2%, and the same volatility as Coca-Cola (25%). Figure 11.6 illustrates the portfolios that we can construct using these three stocks.

Because Bore stock is inferior to Coca-Cola stock—it has the same volatility but a lower return—you might guess that no investor would want to hold a long position in Bore. However, that conclusion ignores the diversification opportunities that Bore provides. Figure 11.6 shows the results of combining Bore with Coca-Cola or with Intel (light blue curves), or combining Bore with a 50–50 portfolio of Coca-Cola and Intel (dark blue curve).[7] Notice that some of the portfolios we obtained by combining only Intel and Coca-Cola (black curve) are inferior to these new possibilities.

---

[7]When a portfolio includes another portfolio, we can compute the weight of each stock by multiplying the portfolio weights. For example, a portfolio with 30% in Bore stock and 70% in the *portfolio* of (50% Intel, 50% Coca-Cola) has 30% in Bore stock, 70% × 50% = 35% in Intel stock, and 70% × 50% = 35% in Coca-Cola stock.

FIGURE 11.6

Expected Return and Volatility for Selected Portfolios of Intel, Coca-Cola, and Bore Industries Stocks

By combining Bore (B) with Intel (I), Coca-Cola (C), and portfolios of Intel and Coca-Cola, we introduce new risk and return possibilities. We can also do better than with just Coca-Cola and Intel alone (the black curve). Portfolios of Bore and Coca-Cola (B + C) and Bore and Intel (B + I) are shown in light blue in the figure. The dark blue curve is a combination of Bore with a portfolio of Intel and Coca-Cola.

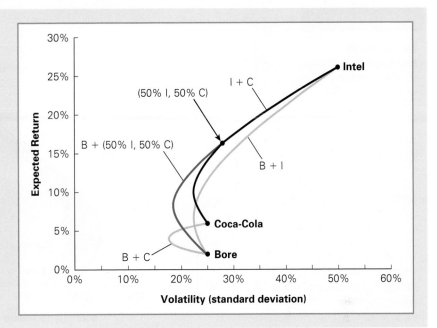

NOBEL PRIZES   Harry Markowitz and James Tobin

The techniques of mean-variance portfolio optimization, which allow an investor to find the portfolio with the highest expected return for any level of variance (or volatility), were developed in an article, "Portfolio Selection," published in the *Journal of Finance* in 1952 by Harry Markowitz. Markowitz's approach has evolved into one of the main methods of portfolio optimization used on Wall Street. In recognition for his contribution to the field, Markowitz was awarded the Nobel Prize for economics in 1990.

Markowitz's work made clear that it is a security's covariance with an investor's portfolio that determines its incremental risk, and thus an investment's risk cannot be evaluated in isolation. He also demonstrated that diversification provided a "free lunch"—the opportunity to reduce risk without sacrificing expected return. In later work Markowitz went on to develop numerical algorithms to compute the efficient frontier for a set of securities.

Many of these same ideas were developed concurrently by Andrew Roy in "Safety First and the Holding of Assets" published in *Econometrica* in the same year. After winning the Nobel Prize, Markowitz graciously wrote "I am often called the father of modern portfolio theory, but Roy can claim an equal share of this honor."* Interestingly, Mark Rubinstein discovered many of these ideas in an earlier 1940 article by Bruno de Finetti in the Italian journal *Giornale*

dell'Instituto Italiano degli Attuari, but the work remained in obscurity until its recent translation in 2004.**

While Markowitz assumed that investors might choose any portfolio on the efficient frontier of risky investments, James Tobin furthered this theory by considering the implications of allowing investors to combine risky securities with a risk-free investment. As we will show in Section 11.5, in that case we can identify a *unique* optimal portfolio of risky securities that does not depend on an investor's tolerance for risk. In his article "Liquidity Preference as Behavior Toward Risk" published in the *Review of Economic Studies* in 1958, Tobin proved a "Separation Theorem," which applied Markowitz's techniques to find this optimal risky portfolio. The Separation Theorem showed that investors could choose their ideal exposure to risk by varying their investments in the optimal portfolio and the risk-free investment. Tobin was awarded the Nobel Prize for economics in 1981 for his contributions to finance and economics.

---

*H. Markowitz, "The Early History of Portfolio Theory: 1600–1960," *Financial Analysts Journal* 55 (1999): 5–16.

**M. Rubinstein, "Bruno de Finetti and Mean-Variance Portfolio Selection," *Journal of Investment Management* 4 (2006) 3–4; the issue also contains a translation of de Finetti's work and comments by Harry Markowitz.

FIGURE 11.7

The Volatility and Expected Return for All Portfolios of Intel, Coca-Cola, and Bore Stock

Portfolios of all three stocks are shown, with the dark blue area showing portfolios without short sales, and the light blue area showing portfolios that include short sales. The best risk–return combinations are on the efficient frontier (red curve). The efficient frontier improves (has a higher return for each level of risk) when we move from two to three stocks.

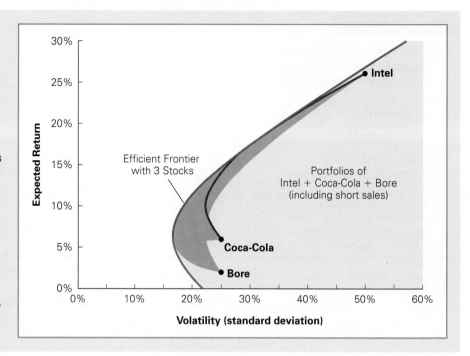

When we combine Bore stock with every portfolio of Intel and Coca-Cola, and allow for short sales as well, we get an entire region of risk and return possibilities rather than just a single curve. This region is shown in the shaded area in Figure 11.7. But note that most of these portfolios are inefficient. The efficient portfolios—those offering the highest possible expected return for a given level of volatility—are those on the northwest edge of the shaded region, which we call the **efficient frontier** for these three stocks. In this case none of the stocks, on its own, is on the efficient frontier, so it would not be efficient to put all our money in a single stock.

When the set of investment opportunities increases from two to three stocks, the efficient frontier improves. Visually, the old frontier with any two stocks is located inside the new frontier. In general, adding new investment opportunities allows for greater diversification and improves the efficient frontier. Figure 11.8 uses historical data to show the effect of increasing the set from three stocks (Exxon Mobil, GE, and IBM) to ten stocks. Even though the added stocks appear to offer inferior risk–return combinations on their own, because they allow for additional diversification, the efficient frontier improves with their inclusion. Thus, to arrive at the best possible set of risk and return opportunities, we should keep adding stocks until all investment opportunities are represented. Ultimately, based on our estimates of returns, volatilities, and correlations, we can construct the efficient frontier for *all* available risky investments showing the best possible risk and return combinations that we can obtain by optimal diversification.

CONCEPT CHECK

1. How does the correlation between two stocks affect the risk and return of portfolios that combine them?

2. What is the efficient frontier?

3. How does the efficient frontier change when we use more stocks to construct portfolios?

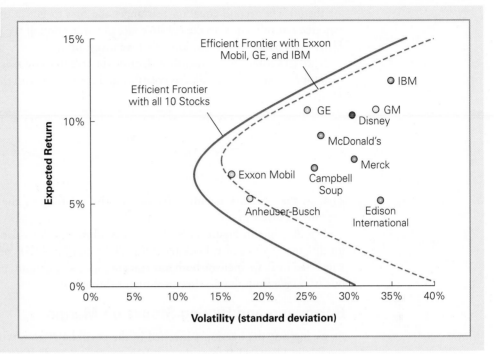

FIGURE 11.8

Efficient Frontier with Three Stocks Versus Ten Stocks

The efficient frontier expands as new investments are added. (Based on monthly returns, 1996–2004.)

11.5 Risk-Free Saving and Borrowing

Thus far, we have considered the risk and return possibilities that result from combining risky investments into portfolios. By including all risky investments in the construction of the efficient frontier, we achieve maximum diversification.

There is another way besides diversification to reduce risk that we have not yet considered: We can keep some of our money in a safe, no-risk investment like Treasury bills. Of course, doing so will reduce our expected return. Conversely, if we are an aggressive investor who is seeking high expected returns, we might decide to borrow money to invest even more in the stock market. In this section we will see that the ability to choose the amount to invest in risky versus risk-free securities allows us to determine the *optimal portfolio* of risky securities for an investor.

Investing in Risk-Free Securities

Consider an arbitrary risky portfolio with returns R_P. Let's look at the effect on risk and return of putting a fraction x of our money in the portfolio, while leaving the remaining fraction $(1 - x)$ in risk-free Treasury bills with a yield of r_f.

Using Eq. 11.3 and Eq. 11.8, we calculate the expected return and variance of this portfolio, whose return we will denote by R_{xP}. First, the expected return is

$$E[R_{xP}] = (1 - x)r_f + xE[R_P]$$
$$= r_f + x(E[R_P] - r_f) \tag{11.15}$$

The first equation simply states that the expected return is the weighted average of the expected returns of Treasury bills and the portfolio. (Because we know up front the current interest rate paid on Treasury bills, we do not need to compute an expected return for them.) The second equation rearranges the first to give a useful interpretation: Our expected return is equal to the risk-free rate plus a fraction of the portfolio's risk premium, $E[R_P] - r_f$, based on the fraction x that we invest in it.

Next, let's compute the volatility. Because the risk-free rate r_f is fixed and does not move with (or against) our portfolio, its volatility and covariance with the portfolio are both zero. Thus,

$$
\begin{aligned}
SD(R_{xP}) &= \sqrt{(1-x)^2 Var(r_f) + x^2 Var(R_P) + 2(1-x)x Cov(r_f, R_P)} \\
&= \sqrt{x^2 Var(R_P)} \\
&= xSD(R_P)
\end{aligned}
\tag{11.16}
$$

That is, the volatility is only a fraction of the volatility of the portfolio, based on the amount we invest in it.

The blue line in Figure 11.9 illustrates combinations of volatility and expected return for different choices of x. Looking at Eq. 11.15 and Eq. 11.16, as we increase the fraction x invested in P, we increase both our risk and our risk premium proportionally. Hence the line is *straight* from the risk-free investment through P.

Borrowing and Buying Stocks on Margin

As we increase the fraction x invested in the portfolio P from 0 to 100%, we move along the line in Figure 11.9 from the risk-free investment to P. If we increase x beyond 100%, we get points beyond P in the graph. In this case, we are short selling the risk-free investment, so we must pay the risk-free return; in other words, we are borrowing money at the risk-free interest rate.

Borrowing money to invest in stocks is referred to as **buying stocks on margin** or using leverage. A portfolio that consists of a short position in the risk-free investment is known

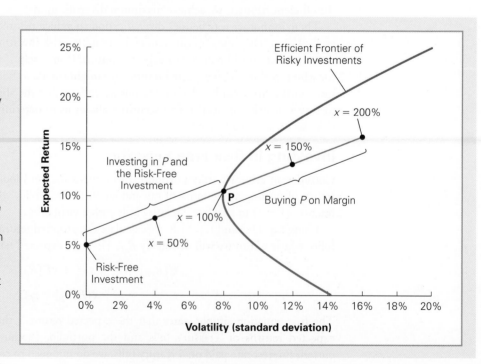

FIGURE 11.9

The Risk–Return Combinations from Combining a Risk-Free Investment and a Risky Portfolio

Given a risk-free rate of 5%, the point with 0% volatility and an expected return of 5% represents the risk-free investment. The blue line shows the portfolios we obtained by investing x in portfolio P and $(1 - x)$ in the risk-free investment. Investments with weight $x > 100\%$ in portfolio P require borrowing at the risk-free interest rate.

as a *levered* portfolio. As you might expect, margin investing is a risky investment strategy. Note that the region of the blue line in Figure 11.9 with $x > 100\%$ has higher risk than the portfolio P itself. At the same time, margin investing can provide higher expected returns than investing in P using only the funds we have available.

| EXAMPLE 11.11 | Margin Investing |

Problem

Suppose you have $10,000 in cash, and you decide to borrow another $10,000 at a 5% interest rate in order to invest $20,000 in portfolio Q, which has a 10% expected return and a 20% volatility. What is the expected return and volatility of your investment? What is your realized return if Q goes up 30% over the year? What if Q falls by 10%?

Solution

You have doubled your investment in Q using margin, so $x = 200\%$. From Eq. 11.15 and Eq. 11.16, we see that you have increased both your expected return and your risk relative to the portfolio Q:

$$E(R_{xQ}) = r_f + x(E[R_Q] - r_f) = 5\% + 2 \times (10\% - 5\%) = 15\%$$

$$SD(R_{xQ}) = xSD(R_Q) = 2 \times (20\%) = 40\%$$

If Q goes up 30%, your investment will be worth $26,000, but you will owe $10,000 \times 1.05 = $10,500 on your loan, for a net payoff of $15,500 or a 55% return on your $10,000 initial investment. If Q drops by 10%, you are left with $18,000 - $10,500 = $7500, and your return is -25%. Thus the use of margin doubled the range of your returns (55% - (-25%) = 80% versus 30% - (-10%) = 40%), corresponding to the doubling of the volatility of the portfolio.

Identifying the Tangent Portfolio

Looking back at Figure 11.9, we can see that portfolio P is not the best portfolio to combine with the risk-free investment. By combining the risk-free asset with a portfolio somewhat higher on the efficient frontier than portfolio P, we will get a line that is steeper than the line through P. If the line is steeper, then for any level of volatility, we will earn a higher expected return.

To earn the highest possible expected return for any level of volatility we must find the portfolio that generates the steepest possible line when combined with the risk-free investment. The slope of the line through a given portfolio P is often referred to as the **Sharpe ratio** of the portfolio:

$$\text{Sharpe Ratio} = \frac{\text{Portfolio Excess Return}}{\text{Portfolio Volatility}} = \frac{E[R_P] - r_f}{SD(R_P)} \tag{11.17}$$

The Sharpe ratio measures the ratio of reward-to-volatility provided by a portfolio.[8] The optimal portfolio to combine with the risk-free asset will be the one with the highest Sharpe ratio, where the line with the risk-free investment just touches, and so is tangent to, the efficient frontier of risky investments, as shown in Figure 11.10. The portfolio that

---

[8]The Sharpe ratio was first introduced by William Sharpe as a measure to compare the performance of mutual funds. See W. Sharpe, "Mutual Fund Performance," *Journal of Business* 39 (1966) 119–138.

generates this tangent line is known as the **tangent portfolio**. All other portfolios of risky assets lie below this line. Because the tangent portfolio has the highest Sharpe ratio of any portfolio in the economy, the tangent portfolio provides the biggest reward per unit of volatility of any portfolio available.[9]

As is evident from Figure 11.10, combinations of the risk-free asset and the tangent portfolio provide the best risk and return trade-off available to an investor. This observation has a striking consequence: The tangent portfolio is efficient and, once we include the risk-free investment, all efficient portfolios are combinations of the risk-free investment and the tangent portfolio. Therefore, the optimal portfolio of *risky* investments no longer depends on how conservative or aggressive the investor is; every investor should invest in the tangent portfolio *independent of his or her taste for risk*. The investor's preferences will determine only how much to invest in the tangent portfolio versus the risk-free investment. Conservative investors will invest a small amount, choosing a portfolio on the line near the risk-free investment. Aggressive investors will invest more, choosing a portfolio that is near the tangent portfolio or even beyond it by buying stocks on margin. But both types of investors will choose to hold the *same* portfolio of risky assets, the tangent portfolio.

We have achieved one of the primary goals of this chapter and explained how to identify *the* efficient portfolio of risky assets. **The efficient portfolio** is the tangent portfolio, the portfolio with the highest Sharpe ratio in the economy. By combining it with the risk-free investment, an investor will earn the highest possible expected return for any level of volatility he or she is willing to bear.

FIGURE 11.10

The Tangent or Efficient Portfolio

The tangent portfolio is the portfolio with the highest Sharpe ratio. Investments on the green line connecting the risk-free investment and the tangent portfolio provide the best risk and return trade-off available to an investor. As a result, we also refer to the tangent portfolio as *the* efficient portfolio.

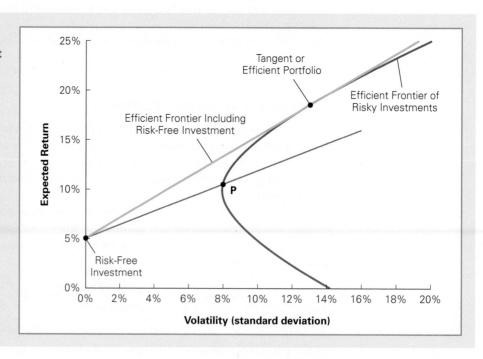

---

[9]The Sharpe ratio can also be interpreted as the number of standard deviations the portfolio's return must fall to underperform the risk-free investment. Thus, if returns are normally distributed, the tangent portfolio is the portfolio with the greatest chance of earning a return above the risk-free rate.

EXAMPLE 11.12	**Optimal Portfolio Choice**

Problem

Your uncle asks for investment advice. Currently, he has $100,000 invested in portfolio P in Figure 11.10, which has an expected return of 10.5% and a volatility of 8%. Suppose the risk-free rate is 5%, and the tangent portfolio has an expected return of 18.5% and a volatility of 13%. To maximize his expected return without increasing his volatility, which portfolio would you recommend? If your uncle prefers to keep his expected return the same but minimize his risk, which portfolio would you recommend?

Solution

In either case the best portfolios are combinations of the risk-free investment and the tangent portfolio. If we invest an amount x in the tangent portfolio T, using Eq. 11.15 and Eq. 11.16, the expected return and volatility are

$$E[R_{xT}] = r_f + x(E[R_T] - r_f) = 5\% + x(18.5\% - 5\%)$$

$$SD(R_{xT}) = x\,SD(R_T) = x(13\%)$$

So, to maintain the volatility at 8%, $x = 8\%/13\% = 61.5\%$. In this case, your uncle should invest $61,500 in the tangent portfolio, and the remaining $38,500 in the risk-free investment. His expected return will then be 5% + (61.5%)(13.5%) = 13.3%, the highest possible given his level of risk.

Alternatively, to keep the expected return equal to the current value of 10.5%, x must satisfy 5% + x(13.5%) = 10.5%, so $x = 40.7\%$. Now your uncle should invest $40,700 in the tangent portfolio and $59,300 in the risk-free investment, lowering his volatility level to (40.7%)(13%) = 5.29%, the lowest possible given his expected return.

CONCEPT CHECK	1. What do we know about the Sharpe ratio of the efficient portfolio?
	2. If investors are holding optimal portfolios, how will the portfolios of a conservative and an aggressive investor differ?

11.6 The Efficient Portfolio and Required Returns

Thus far, we have evaluated the optimal portfolio choice for an investor, and concluded that the tangent or efficient portfolio in Figure 11.10 offers the highest Sharpe ratio and therefore the best risk-return trade-off available. We now turn to the implications of this result for a firm's cost of capital. After all, if a firm wants to raise new capital, investors must find it attractive to increase their investment in it. In this section we derive a condition to determine whether we can improve a portfolio by adding more of a given security, and use it to calculate an investor's required return for holding an investment.

Portfolio Improvement: Beta and the Required Return

Take an arbitrary portfolio P, and let's consider whether we could raise its Sharpe ratio by selling some of our risk-free assets (or borrowing money) and investing the proceeds in an investment i. If we do so, there are two consequences:

1. Expected return: Because we are giving up the risk-free return and replacing it with i's return, our expected return will increase by i's excess return, $E[R_i] - r_f$.

2. Volatility: We will add the risk that i has in common with our portfolio (the rest of i's risk will be diversified). From Eq. 11.13, incremental risk is measured by i's volatility multiplied by its correlation with P: $SD(R_i) \times Corr(R_i, R_P)$.

Is the gain in return from investing in i adequate to make up for the increase in risk? Another way we could have increased our risk would have been to invest more in portfolio P itself. In that case, P's Sharpe ratio,

$$\frac{E[R_P] - r_f}{SD(R_P)},$$

tells us how much the return would increase for a given increase in risk. Because the investment in i increases risk by $SD(R_i) \times Corr(R_i, R_P)$, it offers a larger increase in return than we could have gotten from P alone if[10]

$$\underbrace{E[R_i] - r_f}_{\substack{\text{Additional return} \\ \text{from investment } i}} > \overbrace{\underbrace{SD(R_i) \times Corr(R_i, R_P)}_{\substack{\text{Incremental volatility} \\ \text{from investment } i}} \times \underbrace{\frac{E[R_P] - r_f}{SD(R_P)}}_{\substack{\text{Return per unit of volatility} \\ \text{available from portfolio } P}}}^{\text{Additional return from taking the same risk investing in } P} \qquad (11.18)$$

To provide a further interpretation for this condition, let's combine the volatility and correlation terms in Eq. 11.18 to define the *beta of investment i with portfolio P:*

$$\beta_i^P \equiv \frac{SD(R_i) \times Corr(R_i, R_P)}{SD(R_P)} \qquad (11.19)$$

β_i^P measures the sensitivity of the investment i to the fluctuations of the portfolio P. That is, for each 1% change in the portfolio's return, investment i's return is expected to change by β_i^P% due to risks that i has in common with P. With this definition, we can restate Eq. 11.18 as follows:

$$E[R_i] > r_f + \beta_i^P \times (E[R_P] - r_f)$$

That is, *increasing the amount invested in i will increase the Sharpe ratio of portfolio P if its expected return $E[R_i]$ exceeds its required return given portfolio P, defined as*

$$r_i \equiv r_f + \beta_i^P \times (E[R_P] - r_f) \qquad (11.20)$$

The **required return** is the expected return that is necessary to compensate for the risk investment i will contribute to the portfolio. The required return for an investment i is equal to the risk-free interest rate plus the risk premium of the current portfolio, P, scaled by i's sensitivity to P, β_i^P. If i's expected return exceeds this required return, then adding more of it will improve the performance of the portfolio.

---

[10]We can also write Eq. 11.18 as a comparison of the Sharpe ratio of investment i with the Sharpe ratio of the portfolio scaled by their correlation (the fraction of the risk they have in common):

$$\frac{E[R_i] - r_f}{SD(R_i)} > Corr(R_i, R_p) \times \frac{E[R_p] - r_f}{SD(R_p)}$$

EXAMPLE 11.13	The Required Return of a New Investment

Problem

You are currently invested in the Omega Fund, a broad-based fund with an expected return of 15% and a volatility of 20%, as well as in risk-free Treasuries paying 3%. Your broker suggests that you add a real estate fund to your portfolio. The real estate fund has an expected return of 9%, a volatility of 35%, and a correlation of 0.10 with the Omega Fund. Will adding the real estate fund improve your portfolio?

Solution

Let R_{re} be the return of the real estate fund and R_O be the return of the Omega Fund. From Eq. 11.19, the beta of the real estate fund with the Omega Fund is

$$\beta_{re}^O = \frac{SD(R_{re})\,Corr(R_{re}, R_O)}{SD(R_O)} = \frac{35\% \times 0.10}{20\%} = 0.175$$

We can then use Eq. 11.20 to determine the required return that makes the real estate fund an attractive addition to our portfolio:

$$r_{re} = r_f + \beta_{re}^O(E[R_O] - r_f) = 3\% + 0.175 \times (15\% - 3\%) = 5.1\%$$

Because its expected return of 9% exceeds the required return of 5.1%, investing some amount in the real estate fund will improve our portfolio's Sharpe ratio.

Expected Returns and the Efficient Portfolio

If a security's expected return exceeds its required return, then we can improve the performance of portfolio P by adding more of the security. But how much more should we add? As we buy shares of security i, its correlation (and therefore its beta) with our portfolio will increase, ultimately raising its required return until $E[R_i] = r_i$. At this point, our holdings of security i are optimal. Similarly, if security i's expected return is less than the required return r_i, we should reduce our holdings of i. As we do so the correlation and the required return r_i will fall until $E[R_i] = r_i$.

Thus, if we have no restrictions on our ability to buy or sell securities that are traded in the market, we will continue to trade until the expected return of each security equals its required return—that is, until $E[R_i] = r_i$ holds for all i. At this point, no trade can possibly improve the risk–reward ratio of the portfolio, so our portfolio is the optimal, efficient portfolio. That is, *a portfolio is efficient if and only if the expected return of every available security equals its required return.*

From Eq. 11.20, this result implies the following relationship between the expected return of any security and its beta with the efficient portfolio:

Expected Return of a Security

$$E[R_i] = r_i \equiv r_f + \beta_i^{eff} \times (E[R_{eff}] - r_f) \tag{11.21}$$

where R_{eff} is the return of the efficient portfolio, the portfolio with the highest Sharpe ratio of any portfolio in the economy.

| EXAMPLE 11.14 | **Identifying the Efficient Portfolio** |

Problem

Consider the Omega Fund and real estate fund of Example 11.13. Suppose you have $100 million invested in the Omega Fund. In addition to this position, how much should you invest in the real estate fund to form an efficient portfolio of these two funds?

Solution

Suppose that for each $1 invested in the Omega Fund, we borrow x_{re} dollars (or sell x_{re} worth of Treasury bills) to invest in the real estate fund. Then our portfolio has a return of $R_P = R_O + x_{re}(R_{re} - r_f)$, where R_O is the return of the Omega Fund and R_{re} is the return of the real estate fund. Table 11.5 shows the change to the expected return and volatility of our portfolio as we increase the investment x_{re} in the real estate fund, using the formulas

$$E[R_P] = E[R_O] + x_{re}(E[R_{re}] - r_f)$$

$$Var(R_P) = Var[R_O + x_{re}(R_{re} - r_f)] = Var(R_O) + x_{re}^2 Var(R_{re}) + 2x_{re}Cov(R_{re}, R_O)$$

Adding the real estate fund initially improves the Sharpe ratio of the portfolio, as defined by Eq. 11.17. As we add more of the real estate fund, however, its correlation with our portfolio rises, computed as

$$Corr(R_{re}, R_P) = \frac{Cov(R_{re}, R_P)}{SD(R_{re})SD(R_P)} = \frac{Cov(R_{re}, R_O + x_{re}(R_{re} - r_f))}{SD(R_{re})SD(R_P)}$$

$$= \frac{x_{re}Var(R_{re}) + Cov(R_{re}, R_O)}{SD(R_{re})SD(R_P)}$$

The beta of the real estate fund—computed from Eq. 11.19—also rises, increasing the required return. The required return equals the 9% expected return of the real estate fund at about $x_{re} = 11\%$, which is the same level of investment that maximizes the Sharpe ratio. Thus, the efficient portfolio of these two funds includes $0.11 in the real estate fund per $1 invested in the Omega Fund.

| TABLE 11.5 | **Sharpe Ratio and Required Return for Different Investments in the Real Estate Fund** |

x_{re}	$E[R_P]$	$SD(R_P)$	Sharpe Ratio	$Corr(R_{re}, R_P)$	β_{re}^P	Required Return r_{re}
0%	15.00%	20.00%	0.6000	10.0%	0.18	5.10%
4%	15.24%	20.19%	0.6063	16.8%	0.29	6.57%
8%	15.48%	20.47%	0.6097	23.4%	0.40	8.00%
10%	15.60%	20.65%	0.6103	26.6%	0.45	8.69%
11%	15.66%	20.74%	0.6104	28.2%	0.48	9.03%
12%	15.72%	20.84%	0.6103	29.7%	0.50	9.35%
16%	15.96%	21.30%	0.6084	35.7%	0.59	10.60%

Before we move on, note the significance of Eq. 11.21. This equation establishes the relation between an investment's risk and its expected return. It states that *we can determine the appropriate risk premium for an investment from its beta with the efficient portfolio.* The efficient or tangent portfolio, which has the highest possible Sharpe ratio of any portfolio in the market, provides the benchmark that identifies the systematic risk present in the economy.

In Chapter 10, we argued that the *market portfolio* of all risky securities should be well diversified, and therefore could be used as a benchmark to measure systematic risk. To understand the connection between the market portfolio and the efficient portfolio, we must consider the implications of the collective investment decisions of all investors, which we turn to next.

CONCEPT CHECK
1. When will a new investment improve the Sharpe ratio of a portfolio?
2. An investment's cost of capital is determined by its beta with what portfolio?

11.7 The Capital Asset Pricing Model

As shown in Section 11.6, once we can identify the efficient portfolio, we can compute the expected return of any security based on its beta with the efficient portfolio according to Eq. 11.21. But to implement this approach, we face an important practical problem: To identify the efficient portfolio we must know the expected returns, volatilities, and correlations between investments. These quantities are difficult to forecast. Under these circumstances, how do we put the theory into practice?

To answer this question, we revisit the Capital Asset Pricing Model (CAPM), which we introduced in Chapter 10. This model allows us to identify the efficient portfolio of risky assets without having any knowledge of the expected return of each security. Instead, the CAPM uses the optimal choices investors make to identify the efficient portfolio as the market portfolio, the portfolio of all stocks and securities in the market. To obtain this remarkable result, we make three assumptions regarding the behavior of investors.[11]

The CAPM Assumptions

Three main assumptions underlie the CAPM. The first is a familiar one that we have adopted since Chapter 3:

    1. *Investors can buy and sell all securities at competitive market prices (without incurring taxes or transactions costs) and can borrow and lend at the risk-free interest rate.*

The second assumption is that *all* investors behave as we have described thus far in this chapter, and choose a portfolio of traded securities that offers the highest possible expected return given the level of volatility they are willing to accept:

    2. *Investors hold only efficient portfolios of traded securities—portfolios that yield the maximum expected return for a given level of volatility.*

Of course, there are many investors in the world, and each may have his or her own estimates of the volatilities, correlations, and expected returns of the available securities. But investors don't come up with these estimates arbitrarily; they base them on historical patterns and other information (including market prices) that is widely available to the public. If all investors use publicly available information sources, then their estimates are likely to be similar. Consequently, it is not unreasonable to consider a special case in which all investors have the same estimates concerning future investments and returns, called

---

[11]The CAPM was proposed as a model of risk and return by William Sharpe in a 1964 paper, as well as in related papers by Jack Treynor (1962), John Lintner (1965), and Jan Mossin (1966).

homogeneous expectations. Although investors' expectations are not completely identical in reality, assuming homogeneous expectations should be a reasonable approximation in many markets, and represents the third simplifying assumption of the CAPM:

3. *Investors have homogeneous expectations regarding the volatilities, correlations, and expected returns of securities.*

Supply, Demand, and the Efficiency of the Market Portfolio

If investors have homogeneous expectations, then each investor will identify the same portfolio as having the highest Sharpe ratio in the economy. Thus, all investors will demand the *same* efficient portfolio of risky securities—the tangent portfolio in Figure 11.10—adjusting only their investment in risk-free securities to suit their particular appetite for risk.

But if every investor is holding the tangent portfolio, then the combined portfolio of risky securities of *all* investors must also equal the tangent portfolio. Furthermore, because every security is owned by someone, the sum of all investors' portfolios must equal the portfolio of all risky securities available in the market, which we defined in Chapter 10 as the market portfolio. Therefore, *the efficient, tangent portfolio of risky securities (the portfolio that all investors hold) must equal the market portfolio.*

The insight that the market portfolio is efficient is really just the statement that *demand must equal supply*. All investors demand the efficient portfolio, and the supply of securities is the market portfolio; hence the two must coincide. If a security were not part of the efficient portfolio, then no investor would want to own it, and demand for this security would not equal its supply. This security's price would fall, causing its expected return to rise until it became an attractive investment. In this way, prices in the market will adjust so that the efficient portfolio and the market portfolio coincide, and demand equals supply.

EXAMPLE 11.15   **Portfolio Weights and the Market Portfolio**

Problem
Suppose that after much research, you have identified the efficient portfolio. As part of your holdings, you have decided to invest $10,000 in Microsoft, and $5000 in Pfizer stock. Suppose your friend, who is a wealthier but more conservative investor, has $2000 invested in Pfizer. If your friend's portfolio is also efficient, how much has she invested in Microsoft? If all investors are holding efficient portfolios, what can you conclude about Microsoft's market capitalization, compared to Pfizer's?

Solution
Because all efficient portfolios are combination of the risk-free investment and the tangent portfolio, they share the same proportions of risky stocks. Thus, since you have invested twice as much in Microsoft as in Pfizer, the same must be true for your friend; therefore, she has invested $4000 in Microsoft stock. If all investors hold efficient portfolios, the same must be true of each of their portfolios. Because, collectively, all investors own all shares of Microsoft and Pfizer, Microsoft's market capitalization must therefore be twice that of Pfizer's.

Optimal Investing: The Capital Market Line

When the CAPM assumptions hold, the market portfolio is efficient, so the tangent portfolio in Figure 11.10 is actually the market portfolio. We illustrate this result in Figure 11.11. Recall that the tangent line graphs the highest possible expected return we can achieve for

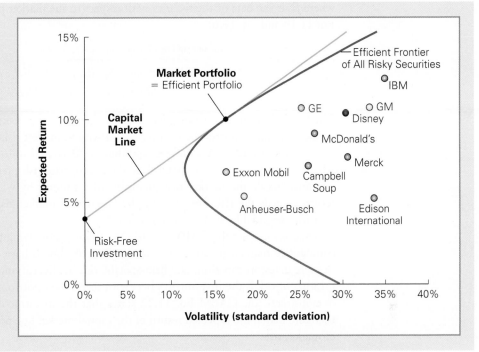

FIGURE 11.11

The Capital Market Line

When investors have homogeneous expectations, the market portfolio and the efficient portfolio coincide. Therefore, the capital market line (CML), which is the line from the risk-free investment through the market portfolio, represents the highest-expected return available for any level of volatility.

any level of volatility. When the tangent line goes through the market portfolio, it is called the **capital market line (CML)**. According to the CAPM, all investors should choose a portfolio on the capital market line, by holding some combination of the risk-free security and the market portfolio.

CONCEPT CHECK

1. Explain why the market portfolio is efficient according to the CAPM.

2. What is the capital market line (CML)?

11.8 Determining the Risk Premium

Under the CAPM assumptions, we can identify the efficient portfolio: It is equal to the market portfolio. Thus, if we don't know the expected return of a security or the cost of capital of an investment, *we can use the CAPM to find it by using the market portfolio as a benchmark.*

Market Risk and Beta

In Eq. 11.21, we showed that the expected return of an investment is given by its beta with the efficient portfolio. But if the market portfolio is efficient, we can rewrite Eq. 11.21 as

The CAPM Equation for the Expected Return

$$E[R_i] = r_i = r_f + \underbrace{\beta_i \times (E[R_{Mkt}] - r_f)}_{\text{Risk premium for security } i}$$

(11.22)

382   **Chapter 11** Optimal Portfolio Choice and the Capital Asset Pricing Model

where β_i is the beta of the security with respect to the market portfolio, defined as (using Eq. 11.19 and Eq. 11.6)

$$\beta_i = \overbrace{\frac{SD(R_i) \times Corr(R_i, R_{Mkt})}{SD(R_{Mkt})}}^{\text{Volatility of } i \text{ that is common with the market}} = \frac{Cov(R_i, R_{Mkt})}{Var(R_{Mkt})} \tag{11.23}$$

The beta of a security measures its volatility due to market risk relative to the market as a whole, and thus captures the security's sensitivity to market risk.

Equation 11.22 is the same result that we derived intuitively at the conclusion of Chapter 10. It states that to determine the appropriate risk premium for any investment, we must rescale the market risk premium (the amount by which the market's expected return exceeds the risk-free rate) by the amount of market risk present in the security's returns, measured by its beta with the market.

We can interpret the CAPM equation as follows. Following the Law of One Price, in a competitive market, investments with similar risk should have the same expected return. Because investors can eliminate firm-specific risk by diversifying their portfolios, the right measure of risk is the investment's beta with the market portfolio, β_i. As the next example demonstrates, the CAPM Eq. 11.22 states that the investment's expected return should therefore match the expected return of the capital market line portfolio with the same level of market risk.

EXAMPLE 11.16   Computing the Expected Return for a Stock

Problem

Suppose the risk-free return is 4% and the market portfolio has an expected return of 10% and a volatility of 16%. Campbell Soup stock has a 26% volatility and a correlation with the market of 0.33. What is Campbell Soup's beta with the market? What capital market line portfolio has equivalent market risk, and what is its expected return?

Solution

We can compute beta using Eq. 11.23:

$$\beta_{CPB} = \frac{SD(R_{CPB})Corr(R_{CPB}, R_{Mkt})}{SD(R_{Mkt})} = \frac{26\% \times 0.33}{16\%} = 0.54$$

That is, for each 1% move of the market portfolio, Campbell Soup stock tends to move 0.54%. We could obtain the same sensitivity to market risk by investing 54% in the market portfolio, and 46% in the risk-free security. Because it has the same market risk, Campbell's soup stock should have the same expected return as this portfolio, which is (using Eq. 11.15 with $x = 0.54$),

$$E[R_{CPB}] = r_f + x(E[R_{Mkt}] - r_f) = 4\% + 0.54(10\% - 4\%)$$

$$= 7.2\%$$

Because $x = \beta_{CPB}$, this calculation is precisely the CAPM Eq. 11.22. Thus, investors will require an expected return of 7.2% to compensate for the risk associated with Campbell Soup stock.

EXAMPLE 11.17   **A Negative-Beta Stock**

Problem

Suppose the stock of Bankruptcy Auction Services, Inc. (BAS), has a negative beta of −0.30. How does its expected return compare to the risk-free rate, according to the CAPM? Does this result make sense?

Solution

Because the expected return of the market is higher than the risk-free rate, Eq. 11.22 implies that the expected return of BAS will be *below* the risk-free rate. For example, if the risk-free rate is 4% and the expected return on the market is 10%,

$$E[R_{BAS}] = 4\% - 0.30(10\% - 4\%) = 2.2\%$$

This result seems odd: Why would investors be willing to accept a 2.2% expected return on this stock when they can invest in a safe investment and earn 4%? A savvy investor will not hold BAS alone; instead, she will hold it in combination with other securities as part of a well-diversified portfolio. Because BAS will tend to rise when the market and most other securities fall, BAS provides "recession insurance" for the portfolio, and investors pay for this insurance by accepting an expected return below the risk-free rate.

NOBEL PRIZE   **William Sharpe on the CAPM**

William Sharpe received the Nobel Prize in 1990 for his development of the Capital Asset Pricing Model. Here are his comments on the CAPM from a 1998 interview with Jonathan Burton:*

Portfolio theory focused on the actions of a single investor with an optimal portfolio. I said, What if everyone was optimizing? They've all got their copies of Markowitz and they're doing what he says. Then some people decide they want to hold more IBM, but there aren't enough shares to satisfy demand. So they put price pressure on IBM and up it goes, at which point they have to change their estimates of risk and return, because now they're paying more for the stock. That process of upward and downward pressure on prices continues until prices reach an equilibrium and everyone collectively wants to hold what's available. At that point, what can you say about the relationship between risk and return? The answer is that expected return is proportionate to beta relative to the market portfolio.

The CAPM was and is a theory of equilibrium. Why should anyone expect to earn more by investing in one security as opposed to another? You need to be compensated for doing badly when times are bad. The security that is going to do badly just when you need money when times are bad is a security you have to hate, and there had better be some

redeeming virtue or else who will hold it? That redeeming virtue has to be that in normal times you expect to do better. The key insight of the Capital Asset Pricing Model is that higher expected returns go with the greater risk of doing badly in bad times. Beta is a measure of that. Securities or asset classes with high betas tend to do worse in bad times than those with low betas.

The CAPM was a very simple, very strong set of assumptions that got a nice, clean, pretty result. And then almost immediately, we all said: Let's bring more complexity into it to try to get closer to the real world. People went on—myself and others—to what I call "extended" Capital Asset Pricing Models, in which expected return is a function of beta, taxes, liquidity, dividend yield, and other things people might care about.

Did the CAPM evolve? Of course. But the fundamental idea remains that there's no reason to expect reward just for bearing risk. Otherwise, you'd make a lot of money in Las Vegas. If there's reward for risk, it's got to be special. There's got to be some economics behind it or else the world is a very crazy place. I don't think differently about those basic ideas at all.

*Jonathan Burton, "Revisiting the Capital Asset Pricing Model," *Dow Jones Asset Manager* (May/June 1998): 20–28.

FIGURE 11.12	The Capital Market Line and the Security Market Line

(a) The CML depicts portfolios combining the risk-free investment and the efficient portfolio, and shows the highest expected return that we can attain for each level of volatility. According to the CAPM, the market portfolio is on the CML and all other stocks and portfolios contain diversifiable risk and lie to the right of the CML, as illustrated for Exxon Mobil (XOM).

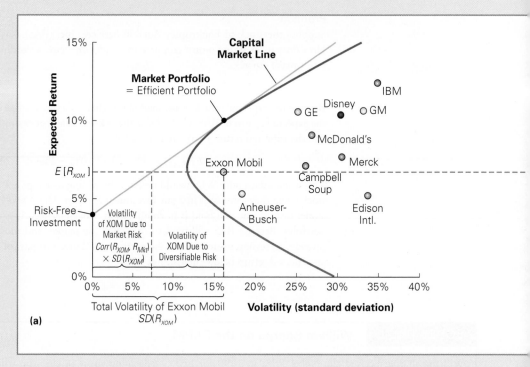

The Security Market Line

Equation 11.22 implies that there is a linear relationship between a stock's beta and its expected return. Panel (b) of Figure 11.12 graphs this line through the risk-free investment (with a beta of 0) and the market (with a beta of 1); it is called the *security market line (SML)*. Under the CAPM assumptions, the **security market line (SML)** is the line along which all individual securities should lie when plotted according to their expected return and beta, as shown in panel (b).

Contrast this result with the capital market line shown in panel (a) of Figure 11.12, where there is no clear relationship between an individual stock's volatility and its expected return. As we illustrate for Exxon Mobil (XOM), a stock's expected return is due only to the fraction of its volatility that is common with the market—$Corr(R_{XOM}, R_{Mkt}) \times SD(R_{XOM})$; the distance of each stock to the right of the capital market line is due to its diversifiable risk. The relationship between risk and return for individual securities becomes evident only when we measure market risk rather than total risk.

Beta of a Portfolio

Because the security market line applies to all tradable investment opportunities, we can apply it to portfolios as well. Consequently, the expected return of a portfolio is given by Eq. 11.22 and therefore depends on the portfolio's beta. Using Eq. 11.23, we calculate the beta of a portfolio $R_p = \sum_i x_i R_i$ as follows:

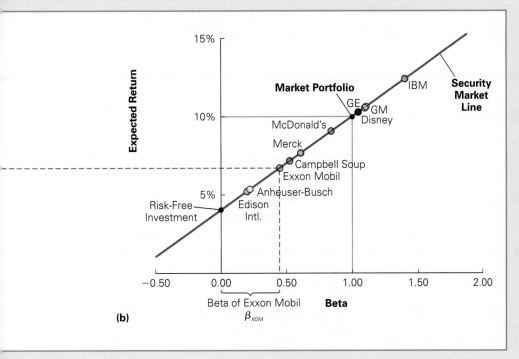

(b) The SML shows the expected return for each security as a function of its beta with the market. According to the CAPM, the market portfolio is efficient, so all stocks and portfolios should lie on the SML.

$$\beta_P = \frac{Cov(R_P, R_{Mkt})}{Var(R_{Mkt})} = \frac{Cov\left(\sum_i x_i R_i, R_{Mkt}\right)}{Var(R_{Mkt})} = \sum_i x_i \frac{Cov(R_i, R_{Mkt})}{Var(R_{Mkt})}$$

$$= \sum_i x_i \beta_i \tag{11.24}$$

In other words, *the beta of a portfolio is the weighted average beta of the securities in the portfolio.*

EXAMPLE 11.18   **The Expected Return of a Portfolio**

Problem

Suppose Kraft Foods' stock has a beta of 0.50, whereas Boeing's beta is 1.25. If the risk-free rate is 4%, and the expected return of the market portfolio is 10%, what is the expected return of an equally weighted portfolio of Kraft Foods and Boeing stocks, according to the CAPM?

Solution

We can compute the expected return of the portfolio in two ways. First, we can use the SML to compute the expected return of Kraft Foods (KFT) and Boeing (BA) separately:

$$E[R_{KFT}] = r_f + \beta_{KFT}(E[R_{Mkt}] - r_f) = 4\% + 0.50(10\% - 4\%) = 7.0\%$$
$$E[R_{BA}] = r_f + \beta_{BA}(E[R_{Mkt}] - r_f) = 4\% + 1.25(10\% - 4\%) = 11.5\%$$

Then, the expected return of the equally weighted portfolio P is

$$E[R_P] = \tfrac{1}{2} E[R_{KFT}] + \tfrac{1}{2} E[R_{BA}] = \tfrac{1}{2}(7.0\%) + \tfrac{1}{2}(11.5\%) = 9.25\%$$

Alternatively, we can compute the beta of the portfolio using Eq. 11.24:

$$\beta_P = \tfrac{1}{2}\beta_{KFT} + \tfrac{1}{2}\beta_{BA} = \tfrac{1}{2}(0.50) + \tfrac{1}{2}(1.25) = 0.875$$

We can then find the portfolio's expected return from the SML:

$$E[R_P] = r_f + \beta_P(E[R_{Mkt}] - r_f) = 4\% + 0.875(10\% - 4\%) = 9.25\%$$

Summary of the Capital Asset Pricing Model

In these last two sections, we have explored the consequences of the CAPM assumptions that markets are competitive, investors choose efficient portfolios, and investors have homogeneous expectations. The CAPM leads to two major conclusions:

- The market portfolio is the efficient portfolio. Therefore, the highest expected return for any given level of volatility is obtained by a portfolio on the capital market line, which combines the market portfolio with risk-free saving or borrowing.

- The risk premium for any investment is proportional to its beta with the market. Therefore, the relationship between risk and the required return is given by the security market line described by Eq. 11.22 and Eq. 11.23.

The CAPM model is based on strong assumptions. Because some of these assumptions do not fully describe investors' behavior, some of the model's conclusions are not completely accurate—it is certainly not the case that every investor holds the market portfolio, for instance. We will examine individual investor behavior in more detail in Chapter 13, where we also consider proposed extensions to the CAPM. Nevertheless, financial economists find the qualitative intuition underlying the CAPM compelling, so it is still the most common and important model of risk and return. While not perfect, it is widely regarded as a very useful approximation and is used by firms and practitioners as a practical means to estimate a security's expected return and an investment's cost of capital. In Chapter 12, we will explain in more detail how to implement the model, looking more closely at the construction of the market portfolio and developing a means to estimate the betas of firms' securities as well as their underlying investments.

CONCEPT CHECK   1. What is the security market line (SML)?

2. According to the CAPM, how can we determine a stock's expected return?

MyFinanceLab

Here is what you should know after reading this chapter. MyFinanceLab will help you identify what you know and where to go when you need to practice.

11.1 The Expected Return of a Portfolio

- The portfolio weight is the initial fraction x_i of an investor's money invested in each asset. Portfolio weights add up to 1.

$$x_i = \frac{\text{Value of investment } i}{\text{Total value of portfolio}} \tag{11.1}$$

- The expected return of a portfolio is the weighted average of the expected returns of the investments within it, using the portfolio weights.

$$E[R_p] = \sum_i x_i E[R_i] \tag{11.3}$$

11.2 The Volatility of a Two-Stock Portfolio

- To find the risk of a portfolio, we need to know the degree to which stock returns move together. Covariance and correlation measure the co-movement of returns.
  - The covariance between returns R_i and R_j is defined by

$$Cov(R_i, R_j) = E[(R_i - E[R_i])(R_j - E[R_j])] \tag{11.4}$$

and is estimated from historical data using

$$Cov(R_i, R_j) = \frac{1}{T-1} \sum_t (R_{i,t} - \overline{R}_i)(R_{j,t} - \overline{R}_j) \tag{11.5}$$

  - The correlation is defined as the covariance of the returns divided by the standard deviation of each return. The correlation is always between -1 and $+1$. It represents the fraction of the volatility due to risk that is common to the securities.

$$Corr(R_i, R_j) = \frac{Cov(R_i, R_j)}{SD(R_i)\, SD(R_j)} \tag{11.6}$$

- The variance of a portfolio depends on the covariance of the stocks within it.
  - For a portfolio with two stocks, the portfolio variance is

$$Var(R_P) = x_1^2 Var(R_1) + x_2^2 Var(R_2) + 2x_1 x_2 Cov(R_1, R_2)$$

$$= x_1^2 SD(R_1)^2 + x_2^2 SD(R_2)^2 + 2x_1 x_2 Corr(R_1, R_2) SD(R_1) SD(R_2) \tag{11.8 and 11.9}$$

  - If the portfolio weights are positive, as we lower the covariance or correlation between the two stocks in a portfolio, we lower the portfolio variance.

11.3 The Volatility of a Large Portfolio

- The variance of an equally weighted portfolio is

$$Var(R_P) = \frac{1}{n}(\text{Average Variance of the Individual Stocks})$$

$$+ \left(1 - \frac{1}{n}\right)(\text{Average Covariance between the Stocks}) \tag{11.12}$$

- Diversification eliminates independent risks. The volatility of a large portfolio results from the common risk between the stocks in the portfolio.
- Each security contributes to the volatility of the portfolio according to its total risk scaled by its correlation with the portfolio, which adjusts for the fraction of the total risk that is common to the portfolio.

$$SD(R_P) = \sum_i x_i \times SD(R_i) \times Corr(R_i, R_P) \tag{11.13}$$

11.4 Risk Versus Return: Choosing an Efficient Portfolio

- Efficient portfolios offer investors the highest possible expected return for a given level of risk. The set of efficient portfolios is called the efficient frontier. As investors add stocks to a portfolio, the efficient portfolio improves.
  - An investor seeking high expected returns and low volatility should invest only in efficient portfolios.
  - Investors will choose from the set of efficient portfolios based on their risk tolerance.

- Investors may use short sales in their portfolios. A portfolio is short those stocks with negative portfolio weights. Short selling extends the set of possible portfolios.

11.5 Risk-Free Saving and Borrowing

- Portfolios can be formed by combining the risk-free asset with a portfolio of risky assets.
  - The expected return and volatility for this type of portfolio is

$$E[R_{xP}] = r_f + x(E[R_p] - r_f) \tag{11.15}$$

$$SD(R_{xP}) = x\,SD(R_P) \tag{11.16}$$

  - The risk–return combinations of the risk-free investment and a risky portfolio lie on a straight line connecting the two investments.
- The goal of an investor who is seeking to earn the highest possible expected return for any level of volatility is to find the portfolio that generates the steepest possible line when combined with the risk-free investment. The slope of this line is called the Sharpe ratio of the portfolio.

$$\text{Sharpe Ratio} = \frac{\text{Portfolio Excess Return}}{\text{Portfolio Volatility}} = \frac{E[R_P] - r_f}{SD(R_P)} \tag{11.17}$$

- The risky portfolio with the highest Sharpe ratio is called the efficient portfolio. The efficient portfolio is the optimal combination of risky investments independent of the investor's appetite for risk. An investor can select a desired degree of risk by choosing the amount to invest in the efficient portfolio relative to the risk-free investment.

11.6 The Efficient Portfolio and Required Returns

- Beta indicates the sensitivity of the investment's return to fluctuations in the portfolio's return. The beta of an investment with a portfolio is

$$\beta_i^P \equiv \frac{SD(R_i) \times Corr(R_i, R_P)}{SD(R_P)} \tag{11.19}$$

- Buying shares of security i improves the Sharpe ratio of a portfolio if its expected return exceeds the required return:

$$r_i \equiv r_f + \beta_i^P \times (E[R_P] - r_f) \tag{11.20}$$

- A portfolio is efficient when $E[R_i] = r_i$ for all securities. The following relationship therefore holds between beta and expected returns for traded securities:

$$E[R_i] = r_i \equiv r_f + \beta_i^{eff} \times (E[R_{eff}] - r_f) \tag{11.21}$$

11.7 The Capital Asset Pricing Model

- Three main assumptions underlie the Capital Asset Pricing Model (CAPM):
  - Investors trade securities at competitive market prices (without incurring taxes or transaction costs) and can borrow and lend at the risk-free rate.
  - Investors choose efficient portfolios.
  - Investors have homogeneous expectations regarding the volatilities, correlations, and expected returns of securities.
- Because the supply of securities must equal the demand for securities, the CAPM implies that the market portfolio of all risky securities is the efficient portfolio.
- Under the CAPM assumptions, the capital market line (CML), which is the set of portfolios obtained by combining the risk-free security and the market portfolio, is the set of portfolios with the highest possible expected return for any level of volatility.

- The CAPM equation states that the risk premium of any security is equal to the market risk premium multiplied by the beta of the security. This relationship is called the security market line (SML), and it determines the required return for an investment:

$$E[R_i] = r_i = r_f + \underbrace{\beta_i \times (E[R_{Mkt}] - r_f)}_{\text{Risk premium for security } i}$$

(11.22)

- The beta of a security measures the amount of the security's risk that is common to the market portfolio or market risk. Beta is defined as follows:

$$\beta_i = \frac{\overbrace{SD(R_i) \times Corr(R_i, R_{Mkt})}^{\text{Volatility of } i \text{ that is common with the market}}}{SD(R_{Mkt})} = \frac{Cov(R_i, R_{Mkt})}{Var(R_{Mkt})}$$

(11.23)

- The beta of a portfolio is the weighted-average beta of the securities in the portfolio.

Key Terms

buying stocks on margin *p. 372*
capital market line (CML) *p. 381*
correlation *p. 355*
covariance *p. 354*
efficient frontier *p. 370*
the efficient portfolio *p. 374*
equally weighted portfolio *p. 360*
homogeneous expectations *p. 380*

inefficient portfolio *p. 365*
long position *p. 367*
portfolio weights *p. 352*
required return *p. 376*
security market line (SML) *p. 384*
Sharpe ratio *p. 373*
short position *p. 367*
tangent portfolio *p. 374*

Further Reading

The following text presents in more depth optimal portfolio choice: W. Sharpe, G. Alexander, and J. Bailey, *Investments* (Prentice Hall, 1999).

Two seminal papers on optimal portfolio choice are: H. Markowitz, "Portfolio Selection," *Journal of Finance* 7 (March 1952): 77–91; and J. Tobin, "Liquidity Preference as Behavior Toward Risk," *Review of Economic Studies* 25 (February 1958): 65–86. While Markowitz's paper had the greatest influence, the application of mean-variance optimization to portfolio theory was developed concurrently by Andrew Roy ("Safety First and the Holding of Assets," *Econometrica* 20 (1952): 431–449). For an analysis of earlier related work by Bruno de Finetti, see M. Rubinstein, "Bruno de Finetti and Mean-Variance Portfolio Selection," *Journal of Investment Management* 4 (2006) 3–4; the issue also contains a translation of de Finetti's work and comments by Harry Markowitz.

For a historical account of how researchers recognized the impact that short-sales constraints may have in the expected returns of assets, see M. Rubinstein, "Great Moments in Financial Economics: III. Short-Sales and Stock Prices," *Journal of Investment Management* 2(1) (First Quarter 2004): 16–31.

The insight that the expected return of a security is given by its beta with an efficient portfolio was first derived in the following paper: R. Roll, "A Critique of the Asset Pricing Theory's Tests," *Journal of Financial Economics* 4 (1977): 129–176.

The following classic papers developed the CAPM: J. Lintner, "The Valuation of Risk Assets and the Selection of Risky Investments in Stock Portfolios and Capital Budgets," *Review of Economics and Statistics* 47 (February 1965): 13–37; J. Mossin, "Equilibrium in a Capital Asset Market," *Econometrica* 34 (1966): 768–783; W. Sharpe, "Capital Asset Prices: A Theory of Market Equilibrium under Conditions of Risk," *Journal of Finance* 19 (September 1964): 425–442; and J. Treynor, "Toward a Theory of the Market Value of Risky Assets," unpublished manuscript (1961).

Problems

All problems are available in MyFinanceLab. An asterisk (*) indicates problems with a higher level of difficulty.

The Expected Return of a Portfolio

1. You are considering how to invest part of your retirement savings. You have decided to put $200,000 into three stocks: 50% of the money in GoldFinger (currently $25/share), 25% of the money in Moosehead (currently $80/share), and the remainder in Venture Associates (currently $2/share). If GoldFinger stock goes up to $30/share, Moosehead stock drops to $60/share, and Venture Associates stock rises to $3 per share,
   a. What is the new value of the portfolio?
   b. What return did the portfolio earn?
   c. If you don't buy or sell shares after the price change, what are your new portfolio weights?

2. You own three stocks: 600 shares of Apple Computer, 10,000 shares of Cisco Systems, and 5000 shares of Colgate-Palmolive. The current share prices and expected returns of Apple, Cisco, and Colgate-Palmolive are, respectively, $500, $20, $100 and 12%, 10%, 8%.
   a. What are the portfolio weights of the three stocks in your portfolio?
   b. What is the expected return of your portfolio?
   c. Suppose the price of Apple stock goes up by $25, Cisco rises by $5, and Colgate-Palmolive falls by $13. What are the new portfolio weights?
   d. Assuming the stocks' expected returns remain the same, what is the expected return of the portfolio at the new prices?

3. Consider a world that only consists of the three stocks shown in the following table:

Stock	Total Number of Shares Outstanding	Current Price per Share	Expected Return
First Bank	100 Million	$100	18%
Fast Mover	50 Million	$120	12%
Funny Bone	200 Million	$30	15%

   a. Calculate the total value of all shares outstanding currently.
   b. What fraction of the total value outstanding does each stock make up?
   c. You hold the market portfolio, that is, you have picked portfolio weights equal to the answer to part b (that is, each stock's weight is equal to its contribution to the fraction of the total value of all stocks). What is the expected return of your portfolio?

4. There are two ways to calculate the expected return of a portfolio: either calculate the expected return using the value and dividend stream of the portfolio as a whole, or calculate the weighted average of the expected returns of the individual stocks that make up the portfolio. Which return is higher?

The Volatility of a Two-Stock Portfolio

 5. Using the data in the following table, estimate (a) the average return and volatility for each stock, (b) the covariance between the stocks, and (c) the correlation between these two stocks.

Year	2007	2008	2009	2010	2011	2012
Stock A	−10%	20%	5%	−5%	2%	9%
Stock B	21%	7%	30%	−3%	−8%	25%

 6. Use the data in Problem 5, consider a portfolio that maintains a 50% weight on stock A and a 50% weight on stock B.
   a. What is the return each year of this portfolio?
   b. Based on your results from part a, compute the average return and volatility of the portfolio.

c. Show that (i) the average return of the portfolio is equal to the average of the average returns of the two stocks, and (ii) the volatility of the portfolio equals the same result as from the calculation in Eq. 11.9.

d. Explain why the portfolio has a lower volatility than the average volatility of the two stocks.

 7. Using your estimates from Problem 5, calculate the volatility (standard deviation) of a portfolio that is 70% invested in stock A and 30% invested in stock B.

 8. Using the data from Table 11.3, what is the covariance between the stocks of Alaska Air and Southwest Airlines?

9. Suppose two stocks have a correlation of 1. If the first stock has an above average return this year, what is the probability that the second stock will have an above average return?

10. Arbor Systems and Gencore stocks both have a volatility of 40%. Compute the volatility of a portfolio with 50% invested in each stock if the correlation between the stocks is (a) +1, (b) 0.50, (c) 0, (d) −0.50, and (e) −1.0. In which cases is the volatility lower than that of the original stocks?

11. Suppose Wesley Publishing's stock has a volatility of 60%, while Addison Printing's stock has a volatility of 30%. If the correlation between these stocks is 25%, what is the volatility of the following portfolios of Addison and Wesley: (a) 100% Addison, (b) 75% Addison and 25% Wesley, and (c) 50% Addison and 50% Wesley.

12. Suppose Avon and Nova stocks have volatilities of 50% and 25%, respectively, and they are perfectly negatively correlated. What portfolio of these two stocks has zero risk?

 13. Suppose Tex stock has a volatility of 40%, and Mex stock has a volatility of 20%. If Tex and Mex are uncorrelated,
a. What portfolio of the two stocks has the same volatility as Mex alone?
b. What portfolio of the two stocks has the smallest possible volatility?

The Volatility of a Large Portfolio

14. Using the data in Table 11.1,
a. Compute the annual returns for a portfolio with 25% invested in North Air, 25% invested in West Air, and 50% invested in Tex Oil.
b. What is the lowest annual return for your portfolio in part a? How does it compare with the lowest annual return of the individual stocks or portfolios in Table 11.1?

15. Using the data from Table 11.3, what is the volatility of an equally weighted portfolio of Microsoft, Alaska Air, and Ford Motor stock?

16. Suppose the average stock has a volatility of 50%, and the correlation between pairs of stocks is 20%. Estimate the volatility of an equally weighted portfolio with (a) 1 stock, (b) 30 stocks, (c) 1000 stocks.

17. What is the volatility (standard deviation) of an equally weighted portfolio of stocks within an industry in which the stocks have a volatility of 50% and a correlation of 40% as the portfolio becomes arbitrarily large?

18. Consider an equally weighted portfolio of stocks in which each stock has a volatility of 40%, and the correlation between each pair of stocks is 20%.
a. What is the volatility of the portfolio as the number of stocks becomes arbitrarily large?
b. What is the average correlation of each stock with this large portfolio?

19. Stock A has a volatility of 65% and a correlation of 10% with your current portfolio. Stock B has a volatility of 30% and a correlation of 25% with your current portfolio. You currently hold both stocks. Which will increase the volatility of your portfolio: (i) selling a small amount of stock B and investing the proceeds in stock A, or (ii) selling a small amount of stock A and investing the proceeds in stock B?

20. You currently hold a portfolio of three stocks, Delta, Gamma, and Omega. Delta has a volatility of 60%, Gamma has a volatility of 30%, and Omega has a volatility of 20%. Suppose you invest 50% of your money in Delta, and 25% each in Gamma and Omega.
    a. What is the highest possible volatility of your portfolio?
    b. If your portfolio has the volatility in (a), what can you conclude about the correlation between Delta and Omega?

Risk Versus Return: Choosing an Efficient Portfolio

21. Suppose Ford Motor stock has an expected return of 20% and a volatility of 40%, and Molson Coors Brewing has an expected return of 10% and a volatility of 30%. If the two stocks are uncorrelated,
    a. What is the expected return and volatility of an equally weighted portfolio of the two stocks?
    b. Given your answer to part a, is investing all of your money in Molson Coors stock an efficient portfolio of these two stocks?
    c. Is investing all of your money in Ford Motor an efficient portfolio of these two stocks?

22. Suppose Intel's stock has an expected return of 26% and a volatility of 50%, while Coca-Cola's has an expected return of 6% and volatility of 25%. If these two stocks were perfectly negatively correlated (i.e., their correlation coefficient is −1),
    a. Calculate the portfolio weights that remove all risk.
    b. If there are no arbitrage opportunities, what is the risk-free rate of interest in this economy?

For Problems 23–26, suppose Johnson & Johnson and the Walgreen Company have expected returns and volatilities shown below, with a correlation of 22%.

	Expected Return	Standard Deviation
Johnson & Johnson	7%	16%
Walgreen Company	10%	20%

23. Calculate (a) the expected return and (b) the volatility (standard deviation) of a portfolio that is equally invested in Johnson & Johnson's and Walgreen's stock.

24. For the portfolio in Problem 23, if the correlation between Johnson & Johnson's and Walgreen's stock were to increase,
    a. Would the expected return of the portfolio rise or fall?
    b. Would the volatility of the portfolio rise or fall?

25. Calculate (a) the expected return and (b) the volatility (standard deviation) of a portfolio that consists of a long position of $10,000 in Johnson & Johnson and a short position of $2000 in Walgreen's.

*26. Using the same data as for Problem 23, calculate the expected return and the volatility (standard deviation) of a portfolio consisting of Johnson & Johnson's and Walgreen's stocks using a wide range of portfolio weights. Plot the expected return as a function of the portfolio volatility. Using your graph, identify the range of Johnson & Johnson's portfolio weights that yield efficient combinations of the two stocks, rounded to the nearest percentage point.

27. A hedge fund has created a portfolio using just two stocks. It has shorted $35,000,000 worth of Oracle stock and has purchased $85,000,000 of Intel stock. The correlation between Oracle's and Intel's returns is 0.65. The expected returns and standard deviations of the two stocks are given in the table below:

	Expected Return	Standard Deviation
Oracle	12.00%	45.00%
Intel	14.50%	40.00%

    a. What is the expected return of the hedge fund's portfolio?
    b. What is the standard deviation of the hedge fund's portfolio?

28. Consider the portfolio in Problem 27. Suppose the correlation between Intel and Oracle's stock increases, but nothing else changes. Would the portfolio be more or less risky with this change?

*29. Fred holds a portfolio with a 30% volatility. He decides to short sell a small amount of stock with a 40% volatility and use the proceeds to invest more in his portfolio. If this transaction reduces the risk of his portfolio, what is the minimum possible correlation between the stock he shorted and his original portfolio?

30. Suppose Target's stock has an expected return of 20% and a volatility of 40%, Hershey's stock has an expected return of 12% and a volatility of 30%, and these two stocks are uncorrelated.
    a. What is the expected return and volatility of an equally weighted portfolio of the two stocks?

    Consider a new stock with an expected return of 16% and a volatility of 30%. Suppose this new stock is uncorrelated with Target's and Hershey's stock.
    b. Is holding this stock alone attractive compared to holding the portfolio in (a)?
    c. Can you improve upon your portfolio in (a) by adding this new stock to your portfolio? Explain.

31. You have $10,000 to invest. You decide to invest $20,000 in Google and short sell $10,000 worth of Yahoo! Google's expected return is 15% with a volatility of 30% and Yahoo!'s expected return is 12% with a volatility of 25%. The stocks have a correlation of 0.9. What is the expected return and volatility of the portfolio?

32. You expect HGH stock to have a 20% return next year and a 30% volatility. You have $25,000 to invest, but plan to invest a total of $50,000 in HGH, raising the additional $25,000 by shorting *either* KBH or LWI stock. Both KBH and LWI have an expected return of 10% and a volatility of 20%. If KBH has a correlation of $+0.5$ with HGH, and LWI has a correlation of -0.50 with HGH, which stock should you short?

Risk-Free Saving and Borrowing

*33. Suppose you have $100,000 in cash, and you decide to borrow another $15,000 at a 4% interest rate to invest in the stock market. You invest the entire $115,000 in a portfolio J with a 15% expected return and a 25% volatility.
    a. What is the expected return and volatility (standard deviation) of your investment?
    b. What is your realized return if J goes up 25% over the year?
    c. What return do you realize if J falls by 20% over the year?

34. You have $100,000 to invest. You choose to put $150,000 into the market by borrowing $50,000.
    a. If the risk-free interest rate is 5% and the market expected return is 10%, what is the expected return of your investment?
    b. If the market volatility is 15%, what is the volatility of your investment?

35. You currently have $100,000 invested in a portfolio that has an expected return of 12% and a volatility of 8%. Suppose the risk-free rate is 5%, and there is another portfolio that has an expected return of 20% and a volatility of 12%.
    a. What portfolio has a higher expected return than your portfolio but with the same volatility?
    b. What portfolio has a lower volatility than your portfolio but with the same expected return?

36. Assume the risk-free rate is 4%. You are a financial advisor, and must choose *one* of the funds below to recommend to each of your clients. Whichever fund you recommend, your clients will then combine it with risk-free borrowing and lending depending on their desired level of risk.

	Expected Return	Volatility
Fund A	10%	10%
Fund B	15%	22%
Fund C	6%	2%

Which fund would you recommend without knowing your client's risk preference?

37. Assume all investors want to hold a portfolio that, for a given level of volatility, has the maximum possible expected return. Explain why, when a risk-free asset exists, all investors will choose to hold the same portfolio of risky stocks.

The Efficient Portfolio and Required Returns

38. In addition to risk-free securities, you are currently invested in the Tanglewood Fund, a broad-based fund of stocks and other securities with an expected return of 12% and a volatility of 25%. Currently, the risk-free rate of interest is 4%. Your broker suggests that you add a venture capital fund to your current portfolio. The venture capital fund has an expected return of 20%, a volatility of 80%, and a correlation of 0.2 with the Tanglewood Fund. Calculate the required return and use it to decide whether you should add the venture capital fund to your portfolio.

39. You have noticed a market investment opportunity that, given your current portfolio, has an expected return that exceeds your required return. What can you conclude about your current portfolio?

40. The Optima Mutual Fund has an expected return of 20%, and a volatility of 20%. Optima claims that no other portfolio offers a higher Sharpe ratio. Suppose this claim is true, and the risk-free interest rate is 5%.
    a. What is Optima's Sharpe Ratio?
    b. If eBay's stock has a volatility of 40% and an expected return of 11%, what must be its correlation with the Optima Fund?
    c. If the SubOptima Fund has a correlation of 80% with the Optima Fund, what is the Sharpe ratio of the SubOptima Fund?

41. You are currently only invested in the Natasha Fund (aside from risk-free securities). It has an expected return of 14% with a volatility of 20%. Currently, the risk-free rate of interest is 3.8%. Your broker suggests that you add Hannah Corporation to your portfolio. Hannah Corporation has an expected return of 20%, a volatility of 60%, and a correlation of 0 with the Natasha Fund.
    a. Is your broker right?
    b. You follow your broker's advice and make a substantial investment in Hannah stock so that, considering only your risky investments, 60% is in the Natasha Fund and 40% is in Hannah stock. When you tell your finance professor about your investment, he says that you made a mistake and should reduce your investment in Hannah. Is your finance professor right?
    c. You decide to follow your finance professor's advice and reduce your exposure to Hannah. Now Hannah represents 15% of your risky portfolio, with the rest in the Natasha fund. Is this the correct amount of Hannah stock to hold?

42. Calculate the Sharpe ratio of each of the three portfolios in Problem 41. What portfolio weight in Hannah stock maximizes the Sharpe ratio?

43. Returning to Problem 38, assume you follow your broker's advice and put 50% of your money in the venture fund.
    a. What is the Sharpe ratio of the Tanglewood Fund?
    b. What is the Sharpe ratio of your new portfolio?
    c. What is the optimal fraction of your wealth to invest in the venture fund? (*Hint*: Use Excel and round your answer to two decimal places.)

The Capital Asset Pricing Model

44. When the CAPM correctly prices risk, the market portfolio is an efficient portfolio. Explain why.

45. A big pharmaceutical company, DRIg, has just announced a potential cure for cancer. The stock price increased from $5 to $100 in one day. A friend calls to tell you that he owns DRIg.

You proudly reply that you do, too. Since you have been friends for some time, you know that he holds the market, as do you, and so you both are invested in this stock. Both of you care only about expected return and volatility. The risk-free rate is 3%, quoted as an APR based on a 365-day year. DRIg made up 0.2% of the market portfolio before the news announcement.

a. On the announcement your overall wealth went up by 1% (assume all other price changes canceled out so that without DRIg, the market return would have been zero). How is your wealth invested?

b. Your friend's wealth went up by 2%. How is he invested?

46. Your investment portfolio consists of $15,000 invested in only one stock—Microsoft. Suppose the risk-free rate is 5%, Microsoft stock has an expected return of 12% and a volatility of 40%, and the market portfolio has an expected return of 10% and a volatility of 18%. Under the CAPM assumptions,

a. What alternative investment has the lowest possible volatility while having the same expected return as Microsoft? What is the volatility of this investment?

b. What investment has the highest possible expected return while having the same volatility as Microsoft? What is the expected return of this investment?

47. Suppose you group all the stocks in the world into two mutually exclusive portfolios (each stock is in only one portfolio): growth stocks and value stocks. Suppose the two portfolios have equal size (in terms of total value), a correlation of 0.5, and the following characteristics:

	Expected Return	Volatility
Value Stocks	13%	12%
Growth Stocks	17%	25%

The risk-free rate is 2%.

a. What is the expected return and volatility of the market portfolio (which is a 50–50 combination of the two portfolios)?

b. Does the CAPM hold in this economy? (*Hint*: Is the market portfolio efficient?)

Determining the Risk Premium

48. Suppose the risk-free return is 4% and the market portfolio has an expected return of 10% and a volatility of 16%. Merck & Co. (Ticker: MRK) stock has a 20% volatility and a correlation with the market of 0.06.

a. What is Merck's beta with respect to the market?

b. Under the CAPM assumptions, what is its expected return?

 49. Consider a portfolio consisting of the following three stocks:

	Portfolio Weight	Volatility	Correlation with the Market Portfolio
HEC Corp	0.25	12%	0.4
Green Midget	0.35	25%	0.6
Alive And Well	0.4	13%	0.5

The volatility of the market portfolio is 10% and it has an expected return of 8%. The risk-free rate is 3%.

a. Compute the beta and expected return of each stock.

b. Using your answer from part a, calculate the expected return of the portfolio.

c. What is the beta of the portfolio?

d. Using your answer from part c, calculate the expected return of the portfolio and verify that it matches your answer to part b.

50. Suppose Autodesk stock has a beta of 2.16, whereas Costco stock has a beta of 0.69. If the risk-free interest rate is 4% and the expected return of the market portfolio is 10%, what is the expected return of a portfolio that consists of 60% Autodesk stock and 40% Costco stock, according to the CAPM?

*51. What is the risk premium of a zero-beta stock? Does this mean you can lower the volatility of a portfolio without changing the expected return by substituting out any zero-beta stock in a portfolio and replacing it with the risk-free asset?

Data Case

Your manager was so impressed with your work analyzing the return and standard deviations of the 12 stocks from Chapter 10 that he would like you to continue your analysis.

Specifically, he wants you to update the stock portfolio by:

- Rebalancing the portfolio with the optimum weights that will provide the best risk and return combinations for the new 12-stock portfolio.

- Determining the improvement in the return and risk that would result from these optimum weights compared to the current method of equally weighting the stocks in the portfolio.

Use the Solver function in Excel to perform this analysis (the time-consuming alternative is to find the optimum weights by trial-and-error).

1. Begin with the equally weighted portfolio analyzed in Chapter 10. Establish the portfolio returns for the stocks in the portfolio using a formula that depends on the portfolio weights. Initially, these weights will all equal 1/12. You would like to allow the portfolio weights to vary, so you will need to list the weights for each stock in separate cells and establish another cell that sums the weights of the stocks. The portfolio returns for each month *must* reference these weights for Excel Solver to be useful.

2. Compute the values for the monthly mean return and standard deviation of the portfolio. Convert these values to annual numbers (as you did in Chapter 10) for easier interpretation.

3. Compute the efficient frontier when short sales are not allowed. Use the Solver tool in Excel (on the Data tab in the analysis section).* To set the Solver parameters:
   a. Set the target cell as the cell of interest, making it the cell that computes the (annual) portfolio standard deviation. Minimize this value.
   b. Establish the "By Changing Cells" by holding the Control key and clicking in each of the 12 cells containing the weights of each stock.
   c. Add constraints by clicking the Add button next to the "Subject to the Constraints" box. One set of constraints will be the weight of each stock that is greater than or equal to zero. Calculate the constraints individually. A second constraint is that the weights will sum to one.
   d. Compute the portfolio with the lowest standard deviation. If the parameters are set correctly, you should get a solution when you click "Solve." If there is an error, you will need to double-check the parameters, especially the constraints.

---

*If the Solver tool is not available, you must load it into Excel as follows:

1. On the File Tab, click Excel Options.

2. Click Add-Ins, and then, in the Manage box, select Excel Add-ins.

3. Click Go.

4. In the Add-Ins available box, select the Solver Add-in check box, and then click OK.
   Tip: If Solver Add-in is not listed in the Add-Ins available box, click Browse to locate the add-in. If you are prompted that the Solver Add-in is not currently installed on your computer, click Yes to install it.

5. After you load the Solver Add-in, the Solver command is available in the Analysis group on the Data tab.

4. Next, compute portfolios that have the lowest standard deviation for a target level of the expected return.

   a. Start by finding the portfolio with an expected return 2% higher than that of the minimum variance portfolio. To do this, add a constraint that the (annual) portfolio return equals this target level. Click "Solve" and record the standard deviation and mean return of the solution (and be sure the mean return equals target—if not, check your constraint).

   b. Repeat step (a) raising the target return in 2% increments, recording the result for each step. Continue to increase the target return and record the result until Solver can no longer find a solution.

   c. At what level does Solver fail to find a solution? Why?

5. Plot the efficient frontier with the constraint of no short sales. To do this, create an XY Scatter Plot (similar to what you did in Chapter 10), with portfolio standard deviation on the x-axis and the return on the y-axis, using the data for the minimum variance portfolio and the portfolios you computed in step 4. How do these portfolios compare to the mean and standard deviation for the equally weighted portfolio analyzed in Chapter 10?

6. Redo your analysis to allow for short sales by removing the constraint that each portfolio weight is greater than or equal to zero. Use Solver to calculate the (annual) portfolio standard deviation for the minimum variance portfolio, and when the annual portfolio returns are set to 0.05, 0.1, 0.2, 0.3, and 0.4. Plot the unconstrained efficient frontier on an XY Scatter Plot. How does allowing short sales affect the frontier?

7. Redo your analysis adding a new risk-free security that has a return of 0.5% (0.005) each month. Include a weight for this security when calculating the monthly portfolio returns. That is, there will now be 13 weights, one for each of the 12 stocks and one for the risk-free security. Again, these weights must sum to 1. Allow for short sales, and use Solver to calculate the (annual) portfolio standard deviation when the annual portfolio returns are set to 0.05, 0.1, 0.2, 0.3, and 0.4. Plot the results on the same XY Scatter Plot, and in addition keep track of the portfolio weights of the optimal portfolio. What do you notice about the relative weights of the different stocks in the portfolio as you change the target return? Can you identify the tangent portfolio?

The CAPM with Differing Interest Rates

In this chapter, we assumed that investors faced the same risk-free interest rate whether they were saving or borrowing. In practice, investors receive a lower rate when they save than they must pay when they borrow. For example, short-term margin loans from a broker are often 1–2% higher than the rates paid on short-term Treasury securities. Banks, pension funds, and other investors with large amounts of collateral can borrow at rates that are generally within 1% of the rate on risk-free securities, but there is still a difference. Do these differences in interest rates affect the conclusions of the CAPM?

The Efficient Frontier with Differing Saving and Borrowing Rates

Figure 11A.1 plots the risk and return possibilities when the saving and borrowing rates differ. In this graph, $r_S = 3\%$ is the rate earned on risk-free savings or lending, and $r_B = 6\%$ is the rate paid on borrowing. Each rate is associated with a different tangent portfolio, labeled T_S and T_B, respectively. A conservative investor who desires a low-risk portfolio can combine the portfolio T_S with saving at rate r_S to achieve risk and return combinations along the lower green line. An aggressive investor who desires high expected returns can invest in the portfolio T_B, using some amount of borrowed funds at rate r_B. By adjusting the amount of borrowing, the investor can achieve risk and return combinations on the upper green line. The combinations on the upper line are not as desirable as the combinations that would result if the investor could borrow at rate r_S, but the investor is unable to borrow at the lower rate. Finally, investors with intermediate preferences may choose portfolios on the portion of the red curve between T_S and T_B, which do not involve borrowing or lending.

Thus, if borrowing and lending rates differ, investors with different preferences will choose different portfolios of risky securities. Any portfolio on the curve from T_S to T_B might be chosen. So, the first conclusion of the CAPM—that the market portfolio is the unique efficient portfolio of risky investments—is no longer valid.

The Security Market Line with Differing Interest Rates

The more important conclusion of the CAPM for corporate finance is the security market line, which relates the risk of an investment to its required return. It turns out that the SML is still valid when interest rates differ. To see why, we make use of the following result:

A combination of portfolios on the efficient frontier of risky investments is also on the efficient frontier of risky investments.[12]

Because all investors hold portfolios on the efficient frontier between T_S and T_B, and because all investors collectively hold the market portfolio, the market portfolio must lie

---

[12] To understand this result intuitively, note that portfolios on the efficient frontier contain no diversifiable risk (otherwise we could reduce risk further without lowering the expected return). But a combination of portfolios that contain no diversifiable risk also contains no diversifiable risk, so it is also efficient.

The CAPM with Different Saving and Borrowing Rates

Investors who save at rate r_S will invest in portfolio T_S, and investors who borrow at rate r_B will invest in portfolio T_B. Some investors may neither save nor borrow and invest in a portfolio on the efficient frontier between T_S and T_B. Because all investors choose portfolios on the efficient frontier from T_S to T_B, the market portfolio is on the efficient frontier between them. The dotted tangent line through the market portfolio determines the interest rate r^* that can be used in the SML.

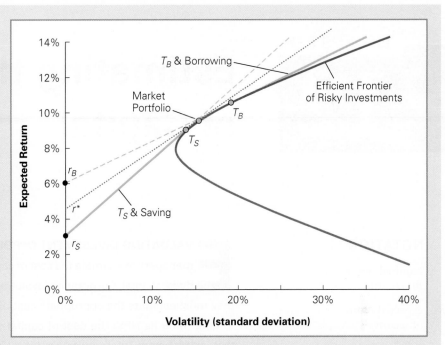

on the frontier between T_S and T_B. As a result, the market portfolio will be tangent for some risk-free interest rate r^* between r_S and r_B, as illustrated by the dotted line in Figure 11A.1. Because our determination of the security market line depends only on the market portfolio being tangent for some interest rate, the SML still holds in the following form:

$$E[R_i] = r^* + \beta_i \times (E[R_{Mkt}] - r^*) \tag{11A.1}$$

That is, the SML holds with some rate r^* between r_S and r_B in place of r_f. The rate r^* depends on the proportion of savers and borrowers in the economy. But even without knowing those proportions, because saving and borrowing rates tend to be close to each other, r^* must be in a narrow range and we can use Eq. 11A.1 to provide reasonable estimates of expected returns.[13]

We can make a similar argument regarding the choice of which risk-free rate to use. As discussed in Chapter 6, the risk-free rate varies with the investment horizon according to the yield curve. When an investor chooses her optimal portfolio, she will do so by finding the tangent line using the risk-free rate that corresponds to her investment horizon. If all investors have the same horizon, then the risk-free rate corresponding to that horizon will determine the SML. If investors have different horizons (but still have homogeneous expectations), then Eq. 11A.1 will hold for some r^* on the current yield curve, with the rate depending on the proportion of investors with each investment horizon.[14]

---

[13]This result was shown by M. Brennan, "Capital Market Equilibrium with Divergent Borrowing and Lending Rates," *Journal of Financial and Quantitative Analysis* 6 (1971): 1197–1205.

[14]We can generalize the arguments in this section further to settings in which there is no risk-free asset; see Fischer Black, "Capital Market Equilibrium with Restricted Borrowing," *Journal of Business* 45 (1972): 444–455, and Mark Rubinstein, "The Fundamental Theorem of Parameter-Preference Security Valuation," *Journal of Financial and Quantitative Analysis* 1 (1973): 61–69.

Estimating the Cost of Capital

EVALUATING INVESTMENT OPPORTUNITIES REQUIRES financial managers to estimate the cost of capital. For example, when executives at Intel Corporation evaluate a capital investment project, they must estimate the appropriate cost of capital for the project in order to determine its NPV. The cost of capital should include a risk premium that compensates Intel's investors for taking on the risk of the new project. How can Intel estimate this risk premium and, therefore, the cost of capital?

In the last two chapters, we have developed a method to answer this question—the Capital Asset Pricing Model. In this chapter, we will apply this knowledge to compute the cost of capital for an investment opportunity. We begin the chapter by focusing on an investment in the firm's stock. We show how to estimate the firm's equity cost of capital, including the practical details of identifying the market portfolio and estimating equity betas. Next, we develop methods to estimate the firm's debt cost of capital, based either on its yield or on its beta. We then consider investing in a new project, and show how to estimate a project's cost of capital based on the unlevered cost of capital of comparable firms. Finally, we introduce the concept of the weighted-average cost of capital as a tool for evaluating levered projects and investments.

12.1 The Equity Cost of Capital

Recall that the cost of capital is the best expected return available in the market on investments with *similar* risk. The Capital Asset Pricing Model (CAPM) provides a practical way to identify an investment with similar risk. Under the CAPM, the market portfolio is a well-diversified, efficient portfolio representing the non-diversifiable risk in the economy. Therefore, investments have similar risk if they have the same sensitivity to market risk, as measured by their beta with the market portfolio.

So, the cost of capital of any investment opportunity equals the expected return of available investments with the same beta. This estimate is provided by the Security Market Line equation of the CAPM, which states that, given the beta, β_i, of the investment opportunity, its cost of capital is:

The CAPM Equation for the Cost of Capital (Security Market Line)

$$r_i = r_f + \underbrace{\beta_i \times (E[R_{Mkt}] - r_f)}_{\text{Risk premium for security } i} \tag{12.1}$$

In other words, investors will require a risk premium comparable to what they would earn taking the same market risk through an investment in the market portfolio.

As our first application of the CAPM, consider an investment in the firm's stock. As we demonstrated in Chapter 9, to value a share of stock, we need to calculate the equity cost of capital. We can do so using Eq. 12.1 if we know the beta of the firm's stock.

EXAMPLE 12.1

Computing the Equity Cost of Capital

Problem

Suppose you estimate that eBay's stock has a volatility of 30% and a beta of 1.45. A similar process for UPS yields a volatility of 35% and a beta of 0.79. Which stock carries more total risk? Which has more market risk? If the risk-free interest rate is 3% and you estimate the market's expected return to be 8%, calculate the equity cost of capital for eBay and UPS. Which company has a higher cost of equity capital?

Solution

Total risk is measured by volatility; therefore, UPS stock has more total risk than eBay. Systematic risk is measured by beta. eBay has a higher beta, so it has more market risk than UPS.

Given eBay's estimated beta of 1.45, we expect the price for eBay's stock to move by 1.45% for every 1% move of the market. Therefore, eBay's risk premium will be 1.45 times the risk premium of the market, and eBay's equity cost of capital (from Eq. 12.1) is

$$r_{EBAY} = 3\% + 1.45 \times (8\% - 3\%) = 3\% + 7.25\% = 10.25\%$$

UPS has a lower beta of 0.79. The equity cost of capital for UPS is

$$r_{UPS} = 3\% + 0.79 \times (8\% - 3\%) = 3\% + 3.95\% = 6.95\%$$

Because market risk cannot be diversified, it is market risk that determines the cost of capital; thus eBay has a higher cost of equity capital than UPS, even though it is less volatile.

While the calculations in Example 12.1 are straightforward, to implement them we need a number of key inputs. In particular, we must do the following:

- Construct the market portfolio, and determine its expected excess return over the risk-free interest rate

- Estimate the stock's beta, or sensitivity to the market portfolio

We explain how to estimate these inputs in more detail in the next two sections.

1. According to the CAPM, we can determine the cost of capital of an investment by comparing it to what portfolio?

2. What inputs do we need to estimate a firm's equity cost of capital using the CAPM?

12.2 The Market Portfolio

To apply the CAPM, we must identify the market portfolio. In this section we examine how the market portfolio is constructed, common proxies that are used to represent the market portfolio, and how we can estimate the market risk premium.

Constructing the Market Portfolio

Because the market portfolio is the total supply of securities, the proportions of each security should correspond to the proportion of the total market that each security represents. Thus, the market portfolio contains more of the largest stocks and less of the smallest stocks. Specifically, the investment in each security i is proportional to its market capitalization, which is the total market value of its outstanding shares:

$$MV_i = (\text{Number of Shares of } i \text{ Outstanding}) \times (\text{Price of } i \text{ per Share}) \qquad (12.2)$$

We then calculate the portfolio weights of each security as follows:

$$x_i = \frac{\text{Market Value of } i}{\text{Total Market Value of All Securities in the Portfolio}} = \frac{MV_i}{\sum_j MV_j} \qquad (12.3)$$

A portfolio like the market portfolio, in which each security is held in proportion to its market capitalization, is called a **value-weighted portfolio**. A value-weighted portfolio is also an **equal-ownership portfolio**: We hold an equal fraction of the total number of shares outstanding of each security in the portfolio. This last observation implies that even when market prices change, to maintain a value-weighted portfolio, we do not need to trade unless the number of shares outstanding of some security changes. Because very little trading is required to maintain it, a value-weighted portfolio is also a **passive portfolio**.

Market Indexes

If we focus our attention on U.S. stocks, then rather than construct the market portfolio ourselves, we can make use of several popular market indexes that try to represent the performance of the U.S. stock market.

Examples of Market Indexes. A **market index** reports the value of a particular portfolio of securities. The S&P 500 is an index that represents a value-weighted portfolio of 500 of the largest U.S. stocks.[1] The S&P 500 was the first widely publicized value-weighted index and is the standard portfolio used to represent "the market portfolio" when using the

---

[1]Standard and Poor's periodically replaces stocks in the index (on average about 20–25 per year). While size is one criterion, S&P tries to maintain appropriate representation of different sectors of the economy and chooses firms that are leaders in their industries. Also, starting in 2005, the value weights in the index are based on the number of shares actually available for public trading, referred to as its **free float**.

Value-Weighted Portfolios and Rebalancing

Because they are passive, value-weighted portfolios are very efficient from a transaction cost perspective because there is no need to rebalance the portfolio weights in the face of price changes. To see why, consider the following example. Suppose we invest $50,000 in a value-weighted portfolio of Microsoft, Google, and Oracle, as shown below:

	Market Data				Our Portfolio	
Stock	Stock Price ($)	Shares Outstanding (billions)	Market Cap ($ billion)	Percent of Total	Initial Investment	Shares Purchased
Microsoft	25.00	10.00	250	50%	$25,000	1000
Google	500.00	0.30	150	30%	$15,000	30
Oracle	20.00	5.00	100	20%	$10,000	500
		Total	500	100%	$50,000	

Note that our investment in each stock is proportional to each stock's market capitalization. In addition, the number of shares purchased is proportional to each stock's outstanding shares.

Now suppose that the price of Microsoft stock increases to $30 per share and Google's stock price drops to $400 per share. Let's compute the new value weights as well as the effect on our portfolio:

Stock	Stock Price ($)	Shares Outstanding (billions)	Market Cap ($ billion)	Percent of Total	Shares Held	New Investment Value
Microsoft	30.00	10.00	300	57.7%	1000	$30,000
Google	400.00	0.30	120	23.1%	30	$12,000
Oracle	20.00	5.00	100	19.2%	500	$10,000
		Total	520	100%		$52,000

Note that although the value weights have changed, the value of our investment in each stock has also changed and remains proportional to each stock's market cap. For example, our weight in Microsoft stock is $30,000/$52,000 = 57.7%, matching its market weight. Thus, there is no need to trade in response to price changes to maintain a value-weighted portfolio. Rebalancing is only required if firms issue or retire shares, or if the set of firms represented by the portfolio changes.

CAPM in practice. Even though the S&P 500 includes only 500 of the more than 7000 individual U.S. stocks in existence, because the S&P 500 includes the largest stocks, it represents more than 70% of the U.S. stock market in terms of market capitalization.

More recently created indexes, such as the Wilshire 5000, provide a value-weighted index of *all* U.S. stocks listed on the major stock exchanges.[2] While more complete than the S&P 500, and therefore more representative of the overall market, its returns are very similar; between 1990 and 2009, the correlation between their weekly returns was nearly 99%. Given this similarity, many investors view the S&P 500 as an adequate measure of overall U.S. stock market performance.

The most widely quoted U.S. stock index is the Dow Jones Industrial Average (DJIA), which consists of a portfolio of 30 large industrial stocks. While somewhat representative, the DJIA clearly does not represent the entire market. Also, the DJIA is a *price-weighted*

---

[2]The Wilshire 5000 began with approximately 5000 stocks when it was first published in 1974 but since then the number of stocks in the index has grown with U.S. equity markets. Similar indices are the Dow Jones U.S. Total Market Index and the S&P Total Market Index.

(rather than value-weighted) *portfolio*. A **price-weighted portfolio** holds an equal number of shares of each stock, independent of their size. Despite being nonrepresentative of the entire market, the DJIA remains widely cited because it is one of the oldest stock market indexes (first published in 1884).

Investing in a Market Index. In addition to capturing the performance of the U.S. market, the S&P 500 and the Wilshire 5000 are both easy to invest in. Many mutual fund companies offer funds, called **index funds**, that invest in these portfolios. In addition, *exchange-traded funds* represent these portfolios. An **exchange-traded fund (ETF)** is a security that trades directly on an exchange, like a stock, but represents ownership in a portfolio of stocks. For example, Standard and Poor's Depository Receipts (SPDR, nick-named "spiders") trade on the American Stock Exchange (symbol SPY) and represent own-ership in the S&P 500. Vanguard's Total Stock Market ETF (symbol VTI, nicknamed "viper") is based on the Wilshire 5000 index. By investing in an index or an exchange-traded fund, an individual investor with only a small amount to invest can easily achieve the benefits of broad diversification.

Although practitioners commonly use the S&P 500 as the market portfolio in the CAPM, no one does so because of a belief that this index is *actually* the market portfolio. Instead they view the index as a **market proxy**—a portfolio whose return they believe closely tracks the true market portfolio. Of course, how well the model works will depend on how closely the market proxy actually tracks the true market portfolio. We will return to this issue in Chapter 13.

The Market Risk Premium

Recall that a key ingredient to the CAPM is the market risk premium, which is the expected excess return of the market portfolio: $E[R_{Mkt}] - r_f$. The market risk premium provides the benchmark by which we assess investors' willingness to hold market risk. Before we can estimate it, we must first discuss the choice of the risk-free interest rate to use in the CAPM.

Determining the Risk-Free Rate. The risk-free interest rate in the CAPM model cor-responds to the risk-free rate at which investors can both borrow and save. We generally determine the risk-free saving rate using the yields on U.S. Treasury securities. Most inves-tors, however, must pay a substantially higher rate to borrow funds. In mid-2012, for example, even the highest credit quality borrowers had to pay almost 0.30% over U.S. Treasury rates on short-term loans. Even if a loan is essentially risk-free, this premium compensates lenders for the difference in liquidity compared with an investment in Trea-suries. As a result, practitioners sometimes use rates from the highest quality corporate bonds in place of Treasury rates in Eq. 12.1.

While U.S. Treasuries are free from default risk, they are subject to interest rate risk unless we select a maturity equal to our investment horizon. Which horizon should we choose when selecting an interest rate from the yield curve? Again, we can extend the CAPM to allow for different investment horizons, and the risk-free rate we choose should correspond to the yield for an "average" horizon.[3] When surveyed, the vast majority of

---

[3]As explained in the Chapter 11 appendix, the precise rate to use depends on investors' horizons and their propensity to borrow or save. As there is no easy way to know these characteristics, judgment is required. Throughout this chapter, we'll try to make clear these gray areas and highlight common practices.

Michael A. Latham is currently chairman of iShares, a unit of BlackRock. iShares is a global exchange-traded funds business that has more than $645 billion in assets under management in over 500 funds. Prior to assuming his current role in 2011, he held a variety of senior executive positions within the iShares business.

INTERVIEW WITH

Michael A. Latham

QUESTION: *Forty years ago, the only way for an individual to hold a well-diversified portfolio like the market portfolio was to buy all the stocks himself. How have investor options changed since then?*

ANSWER: Two major innovations—the passive mutual fund and the exchange-traded fund—have given investors easier access to a well-diversified portfolio. In a traditional (active) mutual fund, the fund has discretion to select investments. In contrast, the primary objective of the passive mutual fund, also known as an index fund, is to replicate holdings in an index that is generally intended to represent "the market"—for example, the S&P 500. Like actively managed mutual funds, investors transact exclusively with the passive mutual fund manager only once a day at a calculated Net Asset Value (NAV).

The next evolution in index investing, the exchange-traded fund (ETF), was introduced approximately 20 years ago and has shown rapid adoption in the past decade. Like index mutual funds, ETFs are a fully diversified basket of securities that typically track a market index. ETFs trade on stock exchanges, experiencing price changes throughout the day, so there is no reliance on a single fund provider for both trading and investment management.

QUESTION: *How does an ETF differ from a mutual fund?*

ANSWER: The ETF structure provides more liquidity because it trades at market prices that change throughout the day. Mutual fund NAVs are set once a day and may require fair value estimations that are subject to pricing inaccuracies. ETFs offer daily disclosure of holdings, versus mutual funds' typical quarterly or semi-annual disclosure. Another major difference is ETFs' greater tax efficiency: Investors typically only realize capital gains when selling their own shares or if the ETF changes the holdings in its underlying index. Mutual funds distribute realized capital gains and losses pro rata to shareholders more frequently than ETFs. Investors buy and sell ETF shares through any broker for a standard brokerage commission. Mutual fund fees vary based on the fund and often include sales and redemption fees that are a percentage of the transaction.

QUESTION: *When creating iShares, you bet that ETFs were going to be very popular. In retrospect you were right. Why have ETFs grown so fast?*

ANSWER: ETFs appeal to a wide variety of client types, from the most sophisticated institutional investors to the broad retail market. Investors recognize the immense benefits of ETFs: easy access, transparency, and flexibility. ETFs give anyone who can buy stocks instant access to well-diversified portfolios that meet a variety of investment needs—whether plain and simple like the S&P 500 or hard-to-access asset classes such as commodities, bonds, emerging markets, or stocks in specific countries, size categories, or industries. Ultimately it's a better, more cost-effective structure than the alternatives; annual ETF fees are typically much lower than comparable mutual funds.

QUESTION: *In the long run, do you expect ETFs and Index Funds to coexist? If so, what kinds of investors might be better served with each vehicle?*

ANSWER: While traditional index mutual funds are currently entrenched in certain markets like pension funds and 401(k)s, I believe that ETFs will continue their phenomenal growth and continue to take share from index mutual funds. ETFs provide virtually all the benefits of index mutual funds, with greater trading and tax efficiency. Many investors still do not understand ETFs, so education remains a primary focus and will fuel growth going forward. In addition, as 401(k) technology platforms evolve to account seamlessly for traded securities, more investors will have access to ETFs. Index mutual funds will continue to fill a need with small investors who employ dollar cost averaging (small dollar repetitive investments), where frequent trading commissions could be cost prohibitive.

large firms and financial analysts report using the yields of long-term (10- to 30-year) bonds to determine the risk-free interest rate.[4]

The Historical Risk Premium. One approach to estimating the market risk premium, $E[R_{Mkt}] - r_f$, is to use the historical average excess return of the market over the risk-free interest rate.[5] With this approach, it is important to measure historical stock returns over the same time horizon as that used for the risk-free interest rate.

Because we are interested in the *future* market risk premium, we face a trade-off in selecting the amount of data we use. As we noted in Chapter 10, it takes many years of data to produce even moderately accurate estimates of expected returns. Yet very old data may have little relevance for investors' expectations of the market risk premium today.

Table 12.1 reports excess returns of the S&P 500 versus one-year and ten-year Treasury rates, based on data since 1926, as well as just the last 50 years. For each time period, note the lower risk premium when we compare the S&P 500 to longer-term Treasuries. This difference primarily arises because, historically, the yield curve has tended to be upward sloping, with long-term interest rates higher than short-term rates.

Table 12.1 also suggests that the market risk premium has declined over time, with the S&P 500 showing a significantly lower excess return over the past 50 years than over the full sample. There are several potential explanations for this decline. First, more investors participate in the stock market today, so that the risk can be shared more broadly. Second, financial innovations such as mutual funds and exchange-traded funds have greatly reduced the costs of diversifying. Third, prior to the recent increase in the wake of the 2008 financial crisis, overall volatility of the market has declined over time. All of these reasons may have reduced the risk of holding stocks, and so diminished the premium investors require. Most researchers and analysts believe that future expected returns for the market are likely to be closer to these more recent historical numbers, in a range of about 4–6% over Treasury bills (and 3–5% over longer term bonds).[6]

TABLE 12.1	Historical Excess Returns of the S&P 500 Compared to One-Year and Ten-Year U.S. Treasury Securities		

	Period	
S&P 500 Excess Return Versus	1926–2012	1962–2012
One-year Treasury	7.7%	5.5%
Ten-year Treasury*	5.9%	3.8%

*Based on a comparison of compounded returns over a ten-year holding period.

---

[4]See Robert Bruner, et al., "Best Practices in Estimating the Cost of Capital: Survey and Synthesis," *Financial Practice and Education* 8 (1998): 13–28.

[5]Because we are interested in the expected return, the correct average to use is the arithmetic average. See Chapter 10.

[6]I. Welch, "Views of Financial Economists On The Equity Premium And Other Issues," *Journal of Business* 73 (2000): 501–537 (with 2009 update), J. Graham and C. Harvey, "The Equity Risk Premium in 2008: Evidence from the Global CFO Outlook Survey," SSRN 2008, and Ivo Welch and Amit Goyal, "A Comprehensive Look at The Empirical Performance of Equity Premium Prediction," *Review of Financial Studies* 21 (2008): 1455–1508.

A Fundamental Approach. Using historical data to estimate the market risk premium suffers from two drawbacks. First, despite using 50 years (or more) of data, the standard errors of the estimates are large (e.g., even using data from 1926, the 95% confidence interval for the excess return is $\pm$ 4.5%). Second, because they are backward looking, we cannot be sure they are representative of current expectations.

As an alternative, we can take a fundamental approach toward estimating the market risk premium. Given an assessment of firms' future cash flows, we can estimate the expected return of the market by solving for the discount rate that is consistent with the current level of the index. For example, if we use the constant expected growth model presented in Chapter 9, the expected market return is equal to

$$r_{Mkt} = \frac{Div_1}{P_0} + g = \text{Dividend Yield} + \text{Expected Dividend Growth Rate} \quad (12.4)$$

While this model is highly inaccurate for an individual firm, the assumption of constant expected growth is more reasonable when considering the overall market. If, for instance, the S&P 500 has a current dividend yield of 2%, and we assume that both earnings and dividends are expected to grow 6% per year, this model would estimate the expected return of the S&P 500 as 8%. Following such methods, researchers generally report estimates in the 3–5% range for the future equity risk premium.[7]

CONCEPT CHECK

1. How do you determine the weight of a stock in the market portfolio?

2. What is a market proxy?

3. How can you estimate the market risk premium?

12.3 Beta Estimation

Having identified a market proxy, the next step in implementing the CAPM is to determine the security's beta, which measures the sensitivity of the security's returns to those of the market. Because beta captures the market risk of a security, as opposed to its diversifiable risk, it is the appropriate measure of risk for a well-diversified investor.

Using Historical Returns

Ideally, we would like to know a stock's beta *in the future;* that is, how sensitive will its future returns be to market risk. In practice, we estimate beta based on the stock's historical sensitivity. This approach makes sense if a stock's beta remains relatively stable over time, which appears to be the case for most firms.

Many data sources provide estimates of beta based on historical data. Typically, these data sources estimate correlations and volatilities from two to five years of weekly or monthly returns and use the S&P 500 as the market portfolio. Table 10.6 on page 339 shows estimated betas for a number of large firms in different industries.

---

[7]See e.g., E. Fama and K. French, "The Equity Premium," *Journal of Finance* 57 (2002): 637–659; and J. Siegel, "The Long-Run Equity Risk Premium," CFA Institute Conference proceedings *Points of Inflection: New Directions for Portfolio Management* (2004). Similarly, L. Pastor, M. Sinha, and B. Swaminathan report a 2–4% implied risk premium over 10-year Treasuries ["Estimating the Intertemporal Risk-Return Tradeoff Using the Implied Cost of Capital," *Journal of Finance* 63 (2008): 2859–2897].

As we discussed in Chapter 10, the differences in betas reflect the sensitivity of each firm's profits to the general health of the economy. For example, Apple, Autodesk, and other technology stocks have high betas (well over 1) because demand for their products usually varies with the business cycle: Companies and consumers tend to invest in technology when times are good, but they cut back on these expenditures when the economy slows. In contrast, the demand for personal and household products has very little relation to the state of the economy. Firms producing these goods, such as Procter & Gamble, tend to have very low betas (near 0.5).

Let's look at Cisco Systems stock as an example. Figure 12.1 shows the monthly returns for Cisco and the monthly returns for the S&P 500 from the beginning of 2000 to 2012. Note the overall tendency for Cisco to have a high return when the market is up and a low return when the market is down. Indeed, Cisco tends to move in the same direction as the market, but with greater amplitude. The pattern suggests that Cisco's beta is larger than 1.

Rather than plot the returns over time, we can see Cisco's sensitivity to the market even more clearly by plotting Cisco's excess return as a function of the S&P 500 excess return, as shown in Figure 12.2. Each point in this figure represents the excess return of Cisco and the S&P 500 from one of the months in Figure 12.1. For example, in November 2002, Cisco was up 33.5% and the S&P 500 was up 5.7% (while risk-free Treasuries returned only 0.12%). Once we have plotted each month in this way, we can then plot the best-fitting line drawn through these points.[8]

FIGURE 12.1   **Monthly Returns for Cisco Stock and for the S&P 500, 2000–2012**

Cisco's returns tend to move in the same direction, but with greater amplitude, than those of the S&P 500.

---

[8]By "best fitting," we mean the line that minimizes the sum of the squared deviations from the line. In Excel, it can be found by adding a linear trendline to the chart.

Identifying the Best-Fitting Line

As the scatterplot makes clear, Cisco's returns have a positive covariance with the market: Cisco tends to be up when the market is up, and vice versa. Moreover, from the best-fitting line, we can see visually that a 10% change in the market's return corresponds to a bit more than a 15% change in Cisco's return. That is, Cisco's return moves more than one and a half times that of the overall market, and Cisco's estimated beta is about 1.6. More generally,

Beta corresponds to the slope of the best-fitting line in the plot of the security's excess returns versus the market excess return.[9]

To understand this result fully, recall that beta measures the market risk of a security—the percentage change in the return of a security for a 1% change in the return of the market portfolio. The best-fitting line in Figure 12.2 captures the components of a security's return that we can explain based on market risk, so its slope is the security's beta. Note though, that in any individual month, the security's returns will be higher or lower than the best-fitting line. Such deviations from the best-fitting line result from risk that is not related to the market as a whole. These deviations are zero on average in the graph, as the points above the line balance out the points below the line. They represent firm-specific risk that is diversifiable and that averages out in a large portfolio.

FIGURE 12.2

Scatterplot of Monthly Excess Returns for Cisco Versus the S&P 500, 2000–2012

Beta corresponds to the slope of the best-fitting line. Beta measures the expected change in Cisco's excess return per 1% change in the market's excess return. Deviations from the best-fitting line correspond to diversifiable, non-market-related risk. In this case, Cisco's estimated beta is approximately 1.60.

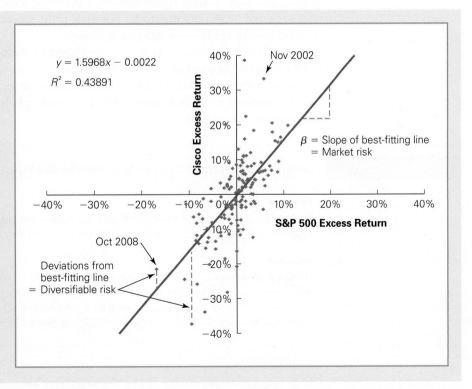

[9]The precise slope can be calculated using Excel's SLOPE() function, or by displaying the equation for the trendline on the chart. (The R^2 in the displayed equation is the square of the correlation between the returns.)

Using Linear Regression

The statistical technique that identifies the best-fitting line through a set of points is called **linear regression**. In Figure 12.2, linear regression corresponds to writing the excess return of a security as the sum of three components:[10]

$$(R_i - r_f) = \alpha_i + \beta_i (R_{Mkt} - r_f) + \varepsilon_i \tag{12.5}$$

The first term, α_i, is the constant or intercept term of the regression. The second term, $\beta_i(R_{Mkt} - r_f)$, represents the sensitivity of the stock to market risk. For example, if the market's return is 1% higher, there is a $\beta_i\%$ increase in the security's return. We refer to the last term, ε_i, as the **error (or residual) term**: It represents the deviation from the best-fitting line and is zero on average (or else we could improve the fit). This error term corresponds to the diversifiable risk of the stock, which is the risk that is unrelated to the market.

If we take expectations of both sides of Eq. 12.5 and rearrange the result, because the average error is zero (that is, $E[\varepsilon_i] = 0$), we get

$$E[R_i] = \underbrace{r_f + \beta_i(E[R_{Mkt}] - r_f)}_{\text{Expected return for } i \text{ from the SML}} + \underbrace{\alpha_i}_{\text{Distance above/below the SML}} \tag{12.6}$$

The constant α_i, referred to as the stock's **alpha**, measures the historical performance of the security relative to the expected return predicted by the security market line—it is the distance the stock's average return is above or below the SML. Thus, we can interpret α_i as a risk-adjusted measure of the stock's historical performance.[11] According to the CAPM, α_i should not be significantly different from zero.

Using Excel's regression data analysis tool for the monthly returns from 2000–2012, Cisco's estimated beta is 1.60, with a 95% confidence interval from 1.3 to 1.9. Assuming Cisco's sensitivity to market risk will remain stable over time, we would expect Cisco's beta to be in this range in the near future. With this estimate in hand, we are ready to estimate Cisco's equity cost of capital.

EXAMPLE 12.2   **Using Regression Estimates to Estimate the Equity Cost of Capital**

Problem

Suppose the risk-free interest rate is 3%, and the market risk premium is 5%. What range for Cisco's equity cost of capital is consistent with the 95% confidence interval for its beta?

Solution

Using the data from 2000 to 2012, and applying the CAPM equation, the estimated beta of 1.6 implies an equity cost of capital of 3% + 1.6(5%) = 11% for Cisco. But our estimate is uncertain, and the 95% confidence interval for Cisco's beta of 1.3 to 1.9 gives a range for Cisco's equity cost of capital from 3% + 1.3(5%) = 9.5% to 3% + 1.9(5%) = 12.5%.

---

[10]In the language of regression, the stock's excess return is the *dependent (or y) variable*, and the market's excess return is the *independent (or x) variable*.

[11]When used in this way, α_i is often referred to as Jensen's alpha. It can be calculated using the INTERCEPT() function in Excel. Using this regression as a test of the CAPM was introduced by F. Black, M. Jensen, and M. Scholes in "The Capital Asset Pricing Model: Some Empirical Tests." In M. Jensen, ed., *Studies in the Theory of Capital Markets.* (Praeger, 1972).

Why Not Estimate Expected Returns Directly?

If the CAPM requires us to use historical data to estimate beta and determine a security's expected return (or an investment's cost of capital), why not just use the security's historical average return as an estimate for its expected return instead? This method would certainly be simpler and more direct.

As we saw in Chapter 10, however, it is extremely difficult to infer the average return of individual stocks from historical data. For example, consider Cisco's stock, which had an average annual return of -1.3% from 2000–2012, and a volatility of 42%. Given 12 years of data, the standard error of our estimate of the expected return is $42\%/\sqrt{12} = 12.1\%$,

leading to a 95% confidence interval of $-1.3\% \pm 24.2\%$! Even with 100 years of data, the confidence bounds would be $\pm 8.4\%$. Of course, Cisco has not existed for 100 years, and even if it had, the firm today would bear little resemblance today to what it was like 100 years ago.

At the same time, using the methods described in this section, we can infer beta from historical data reasonably accurately even with as little as two years of data. In theory at least, the CAPM can provide much more accurate estimates of expected returns for stocks than we could obtain from their historical average return.

The estimate of Cisco's alpha from the regression is -0.22%. In other words, given its beta, Cisco's average monthly return was 0.22% lower than required by the security market line. The standard error of the alpha estimate is about 0.7%, however, so that statistically the estimate is not significantly different from zero. Alphas, like expected returns, are difficult to estimate with much accuracy without a very long data series. Moreover, the alphas for individual stocks have very little persistence.[12] Thus, although Cisco's return underperformed its required return over this time period, it may not necessarily continue to do so.

In this section we have provided an overview of the main methodology for estimating a security's market risk. In the appendix to this chapter, we discuss some additional practical considerations and common techniques for forecasting beta.

CONCEPT CHECK
1. How can you estimate a stock's beta from historical returns?
2. How do we define a stock's alpha, and what is its interpretation?

12.4 The Debt Cost of Capital

In the preceding sections, we have shown how to use the CAPM to estimate the cost of capital of a firm's equity. What about a firm's debt—what expected return is required by a firm's creditors? In this section, we'll consider some of the main methods for estimating a firm's **debt cost of capital**, the cost of capital that a firm must pay on its debt. In addition to being useful information for the firm and its investors, we will see in the next section that knowing the debt cost of capital will be helpful when estimating the cost of capital of a project.

Debt Yields Versus Returns

Recall from Chapter 6 that the yield to maturity of a bond is the IRR an investor will earn from holding the bond to maturity and receiving its promised payments. Therefore, if there is little risk the firm will default, we can use the bond's yield to maturity as an estimate of investors' expected return. If there is a significant risk that the firm will default on its obligation, however, the yield to maturity of the firm's debt, which is its promised return, will overstate investors' expected return.

---

[12]Indeed, over the period 1996–2000, Cisco's return had an alpha of 3.1% per month, significantly outperforming its required return, but as we have seen this positive alpha did not forecast superior future returns.

COMMON MISTAKE   **Using the Debt Yield as Its Cost of Capital**

As we emphasize in this section, the yield to maturity of a firm's debt reflects the *promised* return of the bond, absent default. Investor's expected return from holding the debt will generally be lower, once default risk is taken into account. Nonetheless, it is not uncommon for firms to use the yield on their debt as an approximation of their debt cost of capital. This approximation may be reasonable if the debt is very safe, so that the risk of default is low. When the firm's debt is risky, however, the debt yield will overestimate the debt cost of capital, with the magnitude of the error increasing with the riskiness of the debt.

Consider, for example, that in mid-2009 long-term bonds issued by AMR Corp. (parent company of American Airlines) had a yield to maturity exceeding 20%. These bonds had a CCC rating, and their yield to maturity greatly overstates their expected return given AMR's significant default risk. Indeed, with risk-free rates of 3% and a market risk premium of 5%, an expected return of 20% would imply a debt beta greater than 3 for AMR, which is unreasonably high, and higher even than the equity betas of many firms in the industry.

In fact, AMR filed for bankruptcy on November 29, 2011, with bondholders losing close to 80% of what they were owed. The methods described in this section can provide a much better estimate of a firm's debt cost of capital in cases like AMR's when the likelihood of default is significant.

To understand the relationship between a debt's yield and its expected return, consider a one-year bond with a yield to maturity of y. Thus, for each \$1 invested in the bond today, the bond promises to pay \$$(1 + y)$ in one year. Suppose, however, the bond will default with probability p, in which case bond holders will receive only \$$(1 + y - L)$, where L represents the expected loss per \$1 of debt in the event of default. Then the expected return of the bond is[13]

$$r_d = (1 - p)y + p(y - L) = y - pL$$

$$= \text{Yield to Maturity} - \text{Prob(default)} \times \text{Expected Loss Rate} \qquad (12.7)$$

The importance of these adjustments will naturally depend on the riskiness of the bond, with lower-rated (and higher-yielding) bonds having a greater risk of default. Table 12.2 shows average annual default rates by debt rating, as well as the peak default rates experienced during recessionary periods. To get a sense of the impact on the expected return to debt holders, note that the average loss rate for unsecured debt is about 60%. Thus, for a B-rated bond, during average times the expected return to debt holders would be approximately $0.055 \times 0.60 = 3.3\%$ below the bond's quoted yield. On the other hand, outside of recessionary periods, given its negligible default rate the yield on an AA-rated bond provides a reasonable estimate of its expected return.

TABLE 12.2	Annual Default Rates by Debt Rating (1983–2011)[14]							
Rating:	AAA	AA	A	BBB	BB	B	CCC	CC-C
Default Rate:								
Average	0.0%	0.1%	0.2%	0.5%	2.2%	5.5%	12.2%	14.1%
In Recessions	0.0%	1.0%	3.0%	3.0%	8.0%	16.0%	48.0%	79.0%

Source: "Corporate Defaults and Recovery Rates, 1920–2011," *Moody's Global Credit Policy*, February 2012.

---

[13]While we derived this equation for a one-year bond, the same formula holds for a multi-year bond assuming a constant yield to maturity, default rate, and loss rate.

[14]Average rates are annualized based on a 10-year holding period; recession estimates are based on peak annual rates.

Debt Betas

Alternatively, we can estimate the debt cost of capital using the CAPM. In principle it would be possible to estimate debt betas using their historical returns in the same way that we estimated equity betas. However, because bank loans and many corporate bonds are traded infrequently if at all, as a practical matter we can rarely obtain reliable data for the returns of individual debt securities. Thus, we need another means of estimating debt betas. We will develop a method for estimating debt betas for an individual firm using stock price data in Chapter 21. We can also approximate beta using estimates of betas of bond indices by rating category, as shown in Table 12.3. As the table indicates, debt betas tend to be low, though they can be significantly higher for risky debt with a low credit rating and a long maturity.

EXAMPLE 12.3	Estimating the Debt Cost of Capital

Problem

In mid-2012, homebuilder KB Home had outstanding 6-year bonds with a yield to maturity of 6% and a B rating. If corresponding risk-free rates were 1%, and the market risk premium is 5%, estimate the expected return of KB Home's debt.

Solution

Given the low rating of debt, we know the yield to maturity of KB Home's debt is likely to significantly overstate its expected return. Using the average estimates in Table 12.2 and an expected loss rate of 60%, from Eq. 12.7 we have

$$r_d = 6\% - 5.5\%(0.60) = 2.7\%$$

Alternatively, we can estimate the bond's expected return using the CAPM and an estimated beta of 0.26 from Table 12.3. In that case,

$$r_d = 1\% + 0.26(5\%) = 2.3\%$$

While both estimates are rough approximations, they both confirm that the expected return of KB Home's debt is well below its promised yield.

TABLE 12.3	Average Debt Betas by Rating and Maturity[15]				
By Rating	*A and above*	*BBB*	*BB*	*B*	*CCC*
Avg. Beta	< 0.05	0.10	0.17	0.26	0.31
By Maturity	(BBB and above)	*1–5 Year*	*5–10 Year*	*10–15 Year*	*> 15 Year*
Avg. Beta		0.01	0.06	0.07	0.14

Source: S. Schaefer and I. Strebulaev, "Risk in Capital Structure Arbitrage," Stanford GSB working paper, 2009.

[15]Note that these are average debt betas across industries. We would expect debt betas to be lower (higher) for industries that are less (more) exposed to market risk. One simple way to approximate this difference is to scale the debt betas in Table 12.3 by the relative asset beta for the industry (see Figure 12.4 on page 419).

Note that both of the methods discussed in this section are approximations; more specific information about the firm and its default risk could obviously improve them. Also, we have focused on the debt cost of capital from the perspective of an outside investor. The effective cost of debt to the firm can be lower once the tax deductibility of interest payments is considered. We will return to this issue in Section 12.6.

1. Why does the yield to maturity of a firm's debt generally overestimate its debt cost of capital?

2. Describe two methods that can be used to estimate a firm's debt cost of capital.

12.5 A Project's Cost of Capital

In Chapter 8, we explained how to decide whether or not to undertake a project. Although the project's cost of capital is required to make this decision, we indicated then that we would explain later how to estimate it. We are now ready to fulfill this promise. As we did in Chapter 8, we will assume the project will be evaluated on its own, separate from any financing decisions. Thus, we will assume that the project will be purely equity financed (there will be no debt used to finance it) and consider project financing in Section 12.6.

In the case of a firm's equity or debt, we estimate the cost of capital based on the historical risks of these securities. Because a new project is not itself a publicly traded security, this approach is not possible. Instead, the most common method for estimating a project's beta is to identify comparable firms in the same line of business as the project we are considering undertaking. Indeed, the firm undertaking the project will often be one such comparable firm (and sometimes the only one). Then, if we can estimate the cost of capital of the assets of comparable firms, we can use that estimate as a proxy for the project's cost of capital.

All-Equity Comparables

The simplest setting is one in which we can find an all-equity financed firm (i.e., a firm with no debt) in a single line of business that is comparable to the project. Because the firm is all equity, holding the firm's stock is equivalent to owning the portfolio of its underlying assets. Thus, if the firm's average investment has similar market risk to our project, then we can use the comparable firm's equity beta and cost of capital as estimates for beta and the cost of capital of the project.

Estimating the Beta of a Project from a Single-Product Firm

Problem
You have just graduated with an MBA and have always been a coffee aficionado. During your two years you spent many a night in Peet's Coffee and Tea (PEET), and are wondering whether you might replicate their success in locations where they have not yet expanded. To develop your financial plan, estimate the cost of capital of this opportunity assuming a risk-free rate of 3% and a market risk premium of 5%.

Solution
Checking Google: Finance, we find that Peet's has no debt, and an estimated beta of 0.83. Using Peet's beta as the estimate of the project beta, we can apply Eq. 12.1 to estimate the cost of capital of this investment opportunity as

$$r_{project} = r_f + \beta_{PEET}(E[R_{Mkt}] - r) = 3\% + 0.83 \times 5\% = 7.15\%$$

Thus, assuming our coffee shop has a similar sensitivity to market risk as Peet's, we can estimate the appropriate cost of capital for our investment as 7.15%. In other words, rather than investing in the new coffee shop, you could invest in Peet's coffee shops simply by buying Peet's stock. Given this alternative, to be attractive, the new investment must have an expected return at least equal to that of Peet's stock, which from the CAPM is 7.15%.

Levered Firms as Comparables

The situation is a bit more complicated if the comparable firm has debt. In that case, the cash flows generated by the firm's assets are used to pay both debt and equity holders. As a result, the returns of the firm's equity alone are not representative of the underlying assets; in fact, because of the firm's leverage, the equity will often be much riskier. Thus, the beta of a levered firm's equity will not be a good estimate of the beta of its assets and of our project.

How can we estimate the beta of the comparable firm's assets in this case? As shown in Figure 12.3 we can recreate a claim on the firm's assets by holding *both* its debt and equity simultaneously. Because the firm's cash flows will either be used to pay debt or equity holders, by holding both securities we are entitled to all of the cash flows generated by the firm's assets. The return of the firm's assets is therefore the same as the return of a portfolio of the firm's debt and equity combined. For the same reason, the beta of the firm's assets will match the beta of this portfolio.

The Unlevered Cost of Capital

As we saw in Chapter 11, the expected return of a portfolio is equal to the weighted average of the expected returns of the securities in the portfolio, where the weights correspond to the relative market values of the different securities held. Thus, a firm's **asset cost of capital** or **unlevered cost of capital**, which is the expected return required by the firm's investors to hold the firm's underlying assets, is the weighted average of the firm's equity and debt costs of capital:

$$\begin{pmatrix} \text{Asset or Unlevered} \\ \text{Cost of Capital} \end{pmatrix} = \begin{pmatrix} \text{Fraction of Firm Value} \\ \text{Financed by Equity} \end{pmatrix} \begin{pmatrix} \text{Equity Cost} \\ \text{of Capital} \end{pmatrix} + \begin{pmatrix} \text{Fraction of Firm Value} \\ \text{Financed by Debt} \end{pmatrix} \begin{pmatrix} \text{Debt Cost} \\ \text{of Capital} \end{pmatrix}$$

FIGURE 12.3   Using a Levered Firm as a Comparable for a Project's Risk

If we identify a levered firm whose assets have comparable market risk to our project, then we can estimate the project's cost of capital based on a portfolio of the firm's debt and equity.

Writing this out, if we let E and D be the total market value of equity and debt of the comparable firm, with equity and debt costs of capital r_E and r_D, then we can estimate a firm's asset or unlevered cost of capital r_U as follows:[16]

Asset or Unlevered Cost of Capital

$$r_U = \frac{E}{E+D} r_E + \frac{D}{E+D} r_D \tag{12.8}$$

Unlevered Beta. Because the beta of a portfolio is the weighted-average of the betas of the securities in the portfolio, we have a similar expression for the firm's **asset or unlevered beta**, which we can use to estimate the beta of our project:

Asset or Unlevered Beta

$$\beta_U = \frac{E}{E+D} \beta_E + \frac{D}{E+D} \beta_D \tag{12.9}$$

Let's apply these formulas in an example.

EXAMPLE 12.5   **Unlevering the Cost of Capital**

Problem

Your firm is considering expanding its household products division. You identify Procter & Gamble (PG) as a firm with comparable investments. Suppose PG's equity has a market capitalization of $144 billion and a beta of 0.57. PG also has $37 billion of AA-rated debt outstanding, with an average yield of 3.1%. Estimate the cost of capital of your firm's investment given a risk-free rate of 3% and a market risk-premium of 5%.

Solution

Because investing in this division is like investing in PG's assets by holding its debt and equity, we can estimate our cost of capital based on PG's unlevered cost of capital. First, we estimate PG's equity cost of capital using the CAPM as $r_E = 3\% + 0.57(5\%) = 5.85\%$. Because PG's debt is highly rated, we approximate its debt cost of capital using the debt yield of 3.1%. Thus, PG's unlevered cost of capital is

$$r_U = \frac{144}{144 + 37} 5.85\% + \frac{37}{144 + 37} 3.1\% = 5.29\%$$

Alternatively, we can estimate PG's unlevered beta. Given its high rating, if we assume PG's debt beta is zero we have

$$\beta_U = \frac{144}{144 + 37} 0.57 + \frac{37}{144 + 37} 0 = 0.453$$

Taking this result as an estimate of the beta of our project, we can compute our project's cost of capital from the CAPM as $r_U = 3\% + 0.453(5\%) = 5.27\%$.

The slight difference in r_U using the two methods arises because in the first case, we assumed the expected return of PG's debt is equal to its promised yield of 3.1%, while in the second case, we assumed the debt has a beta of zero, which implies an expected return equal to the risk-free rate of 3% according to the CAPM. The truth is somewhere between the two results, as PG's debt is not completely risk-free.

---

[16]For simplicity, we assume here that the firm in question maintains a constant debt-equity ratio, so that the weights $E/(E + D)$ and $D/(E + D)$ are fixed. As a result, Eq. 12.8 and Eq. 12.9 hold *even in the presence of taxes*. See Chapter 18 for details and an analysis of settings with a changing leverage ratio.

Cash and Net Debt. Sometimes firms maintain large cash balances in excess of their operating needs. This cash represents a risk-free asset on the firm's balance sheet, and reduces the average risk of the firm's assets. Often, we are interested in the risk of the firm's underlying business operations, separate from its cash holdings. That is, we are interested in the risk of the firm's *enterprise value*, which we defined in Chapter 2 as the combined market value of the firm's equity and debt, less any excess cash. In that case, we can measure the leverage of the firm in terms of its **net debt**:

$$\text{Net Debt} = \text{Debt} - \text{Excess Cash and Short-Term Investments} \qquad (12.10)$$

The intuition for using net debt is that if the firm holds $1 in cash and $1 in risk-free debt, then the interest earned on the cash will equal the interest paid on the debt. The cash flows from each source cancel each other, just as if the firm held no cash and no debt.[17]

Note that if the firm has more cash than debt, its net debt will be negative. In this case, its unlevered beta and cost of capital will exceed its equity beta and cost of capital, as the risk of the firm's equity is mitigated by its cash holdings.

EXAMPLE 12.6

Cash and Beta

Problem

In mid-2012, Dell Inc. had a market capitalization of $21 billion, $8 billion in debt, and $13 billion in cash. If its estimated equity beta was 1.41, estimate the beta of Dell's underlying business enterprise.

Solution

Dell has net debt $= (8 - 13) = -\$5$ billion. Therefore, Dell's enterprise value is $(21 - 5) = \$16$ billion, which is the total value of its underlying business on a debt-free basis and excluding cash. Assuming Dell's debt and cash investments are both risk-free, we can estimate the beta of this enterprise value as

$$\beta_U = \frac{E}{E+D}\beta_E + \frac{D}{E+D}\beta_D = \frac{21}{21-5}1.41 + \frac{-5}{21-5}0 = 1.85$$

Note that in this case, Dell's equity is *less* risky than its underlying business activities due to its cash holdings.

Industry Asset Betas

Now that we can adjust for the leverage of different firms to determine their asset betas, it is possible to combine estimates of asset betas for multiple firms in the same industry or line of business. Doing so is extremely useful, as it will enable us to reduce our estimation error and improve the accuracy of the estimated beta for our project.

---

[17]We can also think of the firm's enterprise value V in terms of a portfolio of equity and debt less cash: $V = E + D - C$, where C is excess cash. In that case, the natural extension of Eq. 12.9 is

$$\beta_U = \frac{E}{E+D-C}\beta_E + \frac{D}{E+D-C}\beta_D - \frac{C}{E+D-C}\beta_C$$

(and similarly for Eq. 12.8). The shortcut of using net debt is equivalent if the firm's cash investments and debt have similar market risk, or if the debt beta reflects the combined risk of the firm's debt and cash positions.

| EXAMPLE 12.7 | **Estimating an Industry Asset Beta** |

Problem

Consider the following data for U.S. department stores in mid-2009, showing the equity beta, ratio of net debt to enterprise value (D/V), and debt rating for each firm. Estimate the average and median asset beta for the industry.

Company	Ticker	Equity Beta	D/V	Debt Rating
Dillard's	DDS	2.38	0.59	B
J. C. Penney Company	JCP	1.60	0.17	BB
Kohl's	KSS	1.37	0.08	BBB
Macy's	M	2.16	0.62	BB
Nordstrom	JWN	1.94	0.35	BBB
Saks	SKS	1.85	0.50	CCC
Sears Holdings	SHLD	1.36	0.23	BB

Solution

Note that D/V provides the fraction of debt financing, and $(1 - D/V)$ the fraction of equity financing, for each firm. Using the data for debt betas from Table 12.3, we can apply Eq. 12.9 for each firm. For example, for Dillard's:

$$\beta_U = \frac{E}{E + D}\beta_E + \frac{D}{E + D}\beta_D = (1 - 0.59)2.38 + (0.59)0.26 = 1.13$$

Doing this calculation for each firm, we obtain the following estimates:

Ticker	Equity Beta	D/V	Debt Rating	Debt Beta	Asset Beta
DDS	2.38	0.59	B	0.26	1.13
JCP	1.60	0.17	BB	0.17	1.36
KSS	1.37	0.08	BBB	0.10	1.27
M	2.16	0.62	BB	0.17	0.93
JWN	1.94	0.35	BBB	0.10	1.30
SKS	1.85	0.50	CCC	0.31	1.08
SHLD	1.36	0.23	BB	0.17	1.09
				Average	1.16
				Median	1.13

The large differences in the firms' equity betas are mainly due to differences in leverage. The firms' asset betas are much more similar, suggesting that the underlying businesses in this industry have similar market risk. By combining estimates from several closely related firms in this way, we can get a more accurate estimate of the beta for investments in this industry.

Figure 12.4 shows estimates of industry asset betas for U.S. firms. Note that businesses that are less sensitive to market and economic conditions, such as utilities and household product firms, tend to have lower asset betas than more cyclical industries, such as luxury goods and high technology.

| CONCEPT CHECK | 1. What data can we use to estimate the beta of a project? |
| | 2. Why does the equity beta of a levered firm differ from the beta of its assets? |

FIGURE 12.4   Industry Asset Betas (2012)

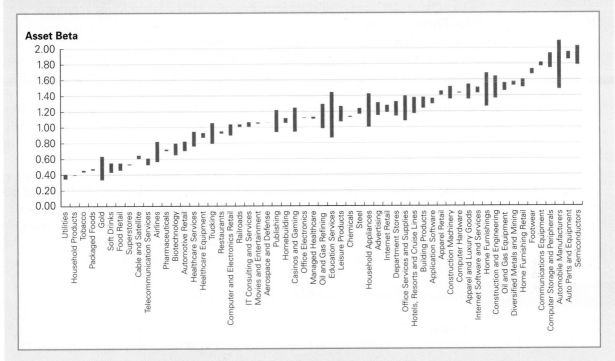

The plot shows median 2-year and 5-year asset betas for firms drawn from the S&P 1500 in selected industries. Note the low asset betas for less cyclical industries such as utilities and household products, versus the much higher asset betas of technology firms, luxury retailers, and capital-intensive cyclical industries (like autos).

Source: Author calculations based on data from CapitalIQ.

12.6 Project Risk Characteristics and Financing

Thus far, we have evaluated a project's cost of capital by comparing it with the unlevered assets of firms in the same line of business. We have also assumed the project itself is unlevered—specifically, it is to be financed solely with equity. In this section we consider why and how we may need to adjust our analysis to account for differences between projects, both in terms of their risk and their mode of financing.

Differences in Project Risk

Firm asset betas reflect the market risk of the *average* project in a firm. But individual projects may be more or less sensitive to market risk. A financial manager evaluating a new investment should try to assess how this project might compare with the average project.

As an example, conglomerate 3M has both a health care division and a computer display and graphics division. These divisions are likely to have very different market risks (note the difference in asset betas between healthcare supplies and computer peripherals in Figure 12.4). 3M's own asset beta will represent an average of the risk of these and 3M's other divisions, and would not be an appropriate measure of risk for projects in either division. Instead, financial managers should evaluate projects based on asset betas of firms that concentrate in a similar line of business. Thus, for multi-divisional firms, identifying a set of "pure play" comparables for each division is helpful in estimating appropriate divisional costs of capital.

Even within a firm with a single line of business, some projects obviously have different market risk characteristics from the firm's other activities. For example, if Cisco Systems were considering whether to buy or lease an office building to expand its headquarters, the cash flows associated with this decision have very different market risk from the cash flows associated with its typical project of developing networking software and hardware, and it should use a different cost of capital. (Indeed, we will discuss the risk and appropriate cost of capital associated with leasing in more detail in Chapter 25.)

Another factor that can affect the market risk of a project is its degree of **operating leverage**, which is the relative proportion of fixed versus variable costs. Holding fixed the cyclicality of the project's revenues, a higher proportion of fixed costs will increase the sensitivity of the project's cash flows to market risk and raise the project's beta. To account for this effect, we should assign projects with an above-average proportion of fixed costs, and thus greater-than-average operating leverage, a higher cost of capital.

EXAMPLE 12.8   **Operating Leverage and Beta**

Problem

Consider a project with expected annual revenues of $120 and costs of $50 in perpetuity. The costs are completely variable, so that the profit margin of the project will remain constant. Suppose the project has a beta of 1.0, the risk-free rate is 5%, and the expected return of the market is 10%. What is the value of this project? What would its value and beta be if the revenues continued to vary with a beta of 1.0, but the costs were instead completely fixed at $50 per year?

Solution

The expected cash flow of the project is $120 − $50 = $70 per year. Given a beta of 1.0, the appropriate cost of capital is $r = 5\% + 1.0(10\% − 5\%) = 10\%$. Thus, the value of the project if the costs are completely variable is $70/10% = $700.

If instead the costs are fixed, then we can compute the value of the project by discounting the revenues and costs separately. The revenues still have a beta of 1.0, and thus a cost of capital of 10%, for a present value of $120/10% = $1200. Because the costs are fixed, we should discount them at the risk-free rate of 5%, so their present value is $50/5% = $1000. Thus, with fixed costs the project has a value of only $1200 − $1000 = $200.

What is the beta of the project now? We can think of the project as a portfolio that is long the revenues and short the costs. The project's beta is the weighted average of the revenue and cost betas, or

$$\beta_P = \frac{R}{R-C}\beta_R - \frac{C}{R-C}\beta_C = \frac{1200}{1200-1000}1.0 - \frac{1000}{1200-1000}0 = 6.0$$

Given a beta of 6.0, the project's cost of capital with fixed costs is $r = 5\% + 6.0(10\% − 5\%) = 35\%$. To verify this result, note that the present value of the expected profits is then $70/35% = 200. As this example shows, increasing the proportion of fixed versus variable costs can significantly increase a project's beta (and reduce its value).

COMMON MISTAKE   **Adjusting for Execution Risk**

When a company launches a new product or makes some other type of new investment, it is often subject to a greater degree of **execution risk**, which is the risk that—due to missteps in the firm's execution—the project may fail to generate the forecasted cash flows. For example, there may be a greater chance of manufacturing delays or marketing mistakes.

Firms sometimes try to adjust for this risk by assigning a higher cost of capital to new projects. Such adjustments are generally incorrect, as this execution risk is typically firm-specific risk, which is diversifiable. (Intuitively, as a shareholder investing in many firms, you can diversify the risk that some firms may suffer execution failures while others do not.) The cost of capital for the project should only depend on its sensitivity to market-wide risks.

Of course, this does not mean that we should ignore execution risk. We should capture this risk in the expected cash flows generated by the project. For example, if a project is expected to generate a free cash flow of $100 next year, but there is a 20% chance it might fail and generate nothing, then our expected free cash flow is only $80. Thus, while the cost of capital remains the same, the expected free cash flow that we discount will be lower the greater the degree of execution risk.

Financing and the Weighted Average Cost of Capital

In Section 12.5, we presumed the project we are evaluating is all-equity financed; that is, the firm does not plan any additional borrowing as a result of the project. What is the importance of this financing assumption, and how might the project's cost of capital change if the firm does use leverage to finance the project?

The complete answer to this question will be the topic of Part 5, where we consider the many implications of the firm's choice of financing policy. We provide a quick preview here of some key results.

Perfect Capital Markets. Let's begin by recalling our discussion in Chapter 3 where we argued that with perfect capital markets—by which we mean no taxes, transactions costs, or other frictions—the choice of financing does not affect the cost of capital or NPV of a project. Rather, a project's cost of capital and NPV are solely determined by its free cash flows. In this setting then, our assumption regarding the project's financing is innocuous. Its cost of capital would be the same whether, and to what extent, it is financed in part with debt. The intuition for this result, which we gave in Chapter 3, is that in a competitive and perfect market, all financing transactions are zero-NPV transactions that do not affect value.

Taxes—A Big Imperfection. When market frictions do exist, the firm's decision regarding how to finance the project may have consequences that affect the project's value. Perhaps the most important example comes from the corporate tax code, which allows the firm to deduct interest payments on debt from its taxable income. As we saw in Chapter 5, if the firm pays interest rate r on its debt, then once the tax deduction is accounted for, the net cost to the firm is given by

$$\text{Effective after-tax interest rate} = r(1 - \tau_C) \tag{12.11}$$

where τ_C is the firm's corporate tax rate.

The Weighted Average Cost of Capital. As we will see in Chapter 15, when the firm finances its own project using debt, it will benefit from the interest tax deduction. One way of including this benefit when calculating the NPV is by using the firm's effective after-tax cost of capital, which we call the **weighted-average cost of capital** or **WACC**:[18]

Weighted Average Cost of Capital (WACC)

$$r_{wacc} = \frac{E}{E + D}r_E + \frac{D}{E + D}r_D(1 - \tau_C) \tag{12.12}$$

Comparing the weighted average cost of capital, r_{wacc}, with the unlevered cost of capital, r_U, defined in Eq. 12.8, note that the WACC is based on the effective after-tax cost of debt, whereas the unlevered cost of capital is based on the firm's pretax cost of debt. The unlevered cost of capital is therefore also referred to as the **pretax WACC**. Let's review the key distinctions between them:

1. The unlevered cost of capital (or pretax WACC) is the expected return investors will earn holding the firm's assets. In a world with taxes, it can be used to evaluate an *all-equity financed project* with the same risk as the firm.

2. The weighted average cost of capital (or WACC) is the effective after-tax cost of capital to the firm. Because interest expense is tax deductible, the WACC is less than the expected return of the firm's assets. In a world with taxes, the WACC can be used to evaluate a project with the same risk and *the same financing as the firm itself.*

Comparing Eq. 12.8 with Eq. 12.12, given a target leverage ratio we can also calculate the WACC as follows:

$$r_{wacc} = r_U - \frac{D}{E + D}\tau_C r_D \tag{12.13}$$

That is, the WACC is equal to the unlevered cost of capital less the tax savings associated with debt. This version of the WACC formula allows us to take advantage of the industry asset betas we estimated in Section 12.5 when determining the WACC.[19] We'll return to consider the WACC in additional detail, as well other implications of the firm's financing decisions, in Part 5.

EXAMPLE 12.9   **Estimating the WACC**

Problem

Dunlap Corp. has a market capitalization of $100 million, and $25 million in outstanding debt. Dunlap's equity cost of capital is 10%, and its debt cost of capital is 6%. What is Dunlap's unlevered cost of capital? If its corporate tax rate is 40%, what is Dunlap's weighted average cost of capital?

Solution

Dunlap's unlevered cost of capital, or pretax WACC, is given by

$$r_U = \frac{E}{E + D}r_E + \frac{D}{E + D}r_D = \frac{100}{125}10\% + \frac{25}{125}6\% = 9.2\%$$

---

[18]The Chapter 18 appendix contains a formal derivation of this formula. Eq. 12.12 assumes the interest on debt equals its expected return r_D, a reasonable approximation if the debt has low risk and trades near par. If not, we can estimate the after-tax debt cost of capital more precisely as $(r_D - \tau_c \bar{r}_D)$, where $\bar{r}_D =$ (current interest expense)/(market value of debt), the *current yield* of the debt.

[19]Eq. 12.13 has an additional advantage: Because we are just using it to estimate the tax shield, we can use the current yield of the debt ($\bar{r}_D$) in place of r_D when debt is risky (see footnote 17).

Thus, we would use a cost of capital of 9.2% to evaluate all-equity financed projects with the same risk as Dunlap's assets.

Dunlap's weighted average cost of capital, or WACC, can be calculated using either Eq. 12.12 or 12.13:

$$r_{wacc} = \frac{E}{E+D}r_E + \frac{D}{E+D}r_D(1-\tau_C) = \frac{100}{125}10\% + \frac{25}{125}6\%(1-40\%) = 8.72\%$$

$$= r_U - \frac{D}{E+D}\tau_C r_D = 9.2\% - \frac{25}{125}(40\%)6\% = 8.72\%$$

We can use the WACC of 8.72% to evaluate projects with the same risk and the same mix of debt and equity financing as Dunlap's assets. It is a lower rate than the unlevered cost of capital to reflect the tax deductibility of interest expenses.

CONCEPT CHECK

1. Why might projects within the same firm have different costs of capital?

2. Under what conditions can we evaluate a project using the firm's weighted average cost of capital?

12.7 Final Thoughts on Using the CAPM

In this chapter, we have developed an approach to estimating a firm's or project's cost of capital using the CAPM. Along the way, we have had to make a number of practical choices, approximations, and estimations. And these decisions were on top of the assumptions of the CAPM itself, which are not completely realistic. At this point, you might be wondering: How reliable, and thus worthwhile, are the results that we obtain following this approach?

While there is no definitive answer to this question, we offer several thoughts. First, the types of approximations that we used to estimate the cost of capital are no different from our other approximations throughout the capital budgeting process. In particular, the revenue and other cash flow projections we must make when valuing a stock or an investment in a new product are likely to be far more speculative than any we have made in estimating the cost of capital. Thus, the imperfections of the CAPM may not be critical in the context of capital budgeting and corporate finance, where errors in estimating project cash flows are likely to have a far greater impact than small discrepancies in the cost of capital.

Second, in addition to being very practical and straightforward to implement, the CAPM-based approach is very robust. While perhaps not perfectly accurate, when the CAPM does generate errors, they tend to be small. Other methods, such as relying on average historical returns, can lead to much larger errors.

Third, the CAPM imposes a disciplined process on managers to identify the cost of capital. There are few parameters available to manipulate in order to achieve a desired result, and the assumptions made are straightforward to document. As a result, the CAPM may make the capital budgeting process less subject to managerial manipulation than if managers could set project costs of capital without clear justification.

Finally, and perhaps most importantly, even if the CAPM model is not perfectly accurate, *it gets managers to think about risk in the correct way*. Managers of widely held corporations should not worry about diversifiable risk, which shareholders can easily eliminate in their own portfolios. They should focus on, and be prepared to compensate investors for, the market risk in the decisions that they make.

Shelagh Glaser

Shelagh Glaser is the Finance Director for Intel's Mobility Group, which provides solutions for the mobile computing market. Prior to that she was Group Controller for Sales & Marketing and co-Group controller for Digital Enterprise Group.

QUESTION: *Does Intel set the discount rate at the corporate or project level?*

ANSWER: We typically set the discount rate at the corporate level. As a company, Intel makes a broad set of products that sell into similar markets so one hurdle rate makes sense for our core business. To justify an investment, every project has to earn or exceed that level of return for our shareholders.

We may use a different discount rate for mergers and acquisitions. For example, recently we've done more software acquisitions. That industry is very different from semi-conductors and has different risk factors, so we take those considerations into account to set the hurdle rate.

QUESTION: *How does Intel compute the cost of capital for new investment opportunities?*

ANSWER: We reexamine our weighted average cost of capital (WACC) each year to see that we have the right inputs and if any have changed: What is the current market risk premium? Are we using the right risk-free rate? How should we weight historical data? We use the CAPM to determine beta but consider whether to continue using the 5-year weekly beta or to change to a daily or monthly beta in the calculation. We also look at the latest studies from academia on what the inputs should be.

Once we have estimated the WACC, we think about the appropriate hurdle rate for our circumstances. We have not changed the hurdle rate in recent years—even though the WACC may have changed—and continue to use a hurdle rate that is above the WACC. This higher hurdle rate reflects our ability to time our investments and helps us choose projects that maximize our expected returns. Intel has more projects with returns above our hurdle than we can invest in, so assessing opportunity cost is a significant aspect of decision making. We may invest in some projects with NPVs below the hurdle rate if they are of strategic importance.

QUESTION: *How do project-specific considerations affect Intel's cost of capital calculation?*

ANSWER: When deciding whether to invest billions in wafer fabrication plants, Intel considers both the physical plant and the product line. We calculate the margin we would need from the product and develop a comprehensive set of metrics to justify the large capital investment. Typically we use our standard hurdle rate and also look at risk factors and the timing of the product launch. Intel's business is driven by the economics of Moore's Law, allowing us to double transistors every 2 years. Each generation of new technology creates cost reductions that enable new fabrication plants to clear the hurdle rate. These plants produce our leading-edge product, which earn our highest margins. To get a premium price, our customers require a product that takes advantage of the performance and power efficiency of the latest technology.

QUESTION: *Has the 2008 financial crisis affected how you evaluate investment opportunities?*

ANSWER: In 2008, the market was very depressed. We continued making R&D investments and reduced spending in other areas, such as marketing and short-term promotion. Cutting R&D would have left us with a gap in our product line in several years, because product development cycles typically run 4 years. In this industry, not keeping the R&D machine flowing, to boost short-term earnings, will harm the company's long-term viability. R&D is critical to our fundamental business model, which may require long-term decisions that negatively impact short-term results.

Intel has a long history of investing to maintain performance leadership during downturns. Intel carries almost no debt. Our capital policy is to maintain sufficient cash for fabrication plants and multiple years of R&D expenses, to avoid depending on capital markets to finance ongoing operations. A painful experience in the 1980s, when Intel's access to capital markets was curtailed, highlighted how this conservative capital policy pays off. Going into this crisis with no debt and an extremely strong cash position has served us well.

Thus, despite its potential flaws, there are very good reasons to use the CAPM as a basis for calculating the cost of capital. In our view, the CAPM is viable, especially when measured relative to the effort required to implement a more sophisticated model (such as the one we will develop in Chapter 13). Consequently, it is no surprise that the CAPM remains the predominant model used in practice to determine the cost of capital.

While the CAPM is likely to be an adequate and practical approach for capital budgeting, you may still wonder how reliable its conclusions are for investors. For example, is holding the market index really the best strategy for investors, or can they do better by trading on news, or hiring a professional fund manager? We consider these questions in Chapter 13.

CONCEPT CHECK

1. Which errors in the capital budgeting process are likely to be more important than discrepancies in the cost of capital estimate?

2. Even if the CAPM is not perfect, why might we continue to use it in corporate finance?

MyFinanceLab

Here is what you should know after reading this chapter. MyFinanceLab will help you identify what you know and where to go when you need to practice.

12.1 The Equity Cost of Capital

- Given a security's beta, we can estimate its cost of capital using the CAPM equation for the security market line:

$$r_i = r_f + \underbrace{\beta_i \times (E[R_{Mkt}] - r_f)}_{\text{Risk premium for security } i} \tag{12.1}$$

12.2 The Market Portfolio

- To implement the CAPM, we must (a) construct the market portfolio, and determine its expected excess return over the risk-free interest rate, and (b) estimate the stock's beta, or sensitivity to the market portfolio.
- The market portfolio is a value-weighted portfolio of all securities traded in the market. According to the CAPM, the market portfolio is efficient.
- In a value-weighted portfolio, the amount invested in each security is proportional to its market capitalization.
- A value-weighted portfolio is also an equal-ownership portfolio. Thus, it is a passive portfolio, meaning no rebalancing is necessary due to daily price changes.
- Because the true market portfolio is difficult if not impossible to construct, in practice we use a proxy for the market portfolio, such as the S&P 500 or Wilshire 5000 indices.
- The risk-free rate in the security market line should reflect an average of the risk-free borrowing and lending rates. Practitioners generally choose the risk-free rate from the yield curve based on the investment horizon.
- While the historical return of the S&P 500 has been about 7.7% more than one-year Treasuries since 1926, research suggests that future excess returns are likely to be lower. Since 1962, the average excess return of the S&P 500 has been 5.5% over one-year Treasuries, and 3.8% over ten-year Treasuries.

12.3 Beta Estimation

- Beta measures a security's sensitivity to market risk. Specifically, beta is the expected change (in %) in the return of a security given a 1% change in the return of the market portfolio.

- To estimate beta, we often use historical returns. Beta corresponds to the slope of the best-fitting line in the plot of a security's excess returns versus the market's excess returns.
- If we regress a stock's excess returns against the market's excess returns, the intercept is the stock's alpha. It measures how the stock has performed historically relative to the security market line.
- Unlike estimating an average return, reliable beta estimates can be obtained with just a few years of data.
- Betas tend to remain stable over time, whereas alphas do not seem to be persistent.

12.4 The Debt Cost of Capital

- Because of default risk, the debt cost of capital, which is its expected return to investors, is less than its yield to maturity, which is its promised return.
- Given annual default and expected loss rates, the debt cost of capital can be estimated as

$$r_d = \text{Yield to Maturity} - \text{Prob (default)} \times \text{Expected Loss Rate} \qquad (12.7)$$

- We can also estimate the expected return for debt based on its beta using the CAPM. However, beta estimates for individual debt securities are hard to obtain. In practice, estimates based on the debt's rating may be used.

12.5 A Project's Cost of Capital

- We can estimate a project's cost of capital based on the asset or unlevered cost of capital of comparable firms in the same line of business. Given a target leverage ratio based on the *market* value of the firm's equity and debt, the firm's unlevered cost of capital is:

$$r_U = \frac{E}{E + D} r_E + \frac{D}{E + D} r_D \qquad (12.8)$$

- We can also estimate the beta of a project as the unlevered beta of a comparable firm:

$$\beta_U = \frac{E}{E + D} \beta_E + \frac{D}{E + D} \beta_D \qquad (12.9)$$

- Because cash holdings will reduce a firm's equity beta, when unlevering betas we can use the firm's net debt, which is debt less excess cash.
- We can reduce estimation error by averaging unlevered betas for several firms in the same industry to determine an industry asset beta.

12.6 Project Risk Characteristics and Financing

- Firm or industry asset betas reflect the market risk of the average project in that firm or industry. Individual projects may be more or less sensitive to the overall market. Operating leverage is one factor that can increase a project's market risk.
- We should not adjust the cost of capital for project-specific risks (such as execution risk). These risks should be reflected in the project's cash flow estimates.
- An unlevered cost of capital can be used to evaluate an equity-financed project. If the project will be financed in part with debt, the firm's effective after-tax cost of debt is less than its expected return to investors. In that case, the weighted average cost of capital can be used:

$$r_{wacc} = \frac{E}{E + D} r_E + \frac{D}{E + D} r_D (1 - \tau_C) \qquad (12.12)$$

- The WACC can also be estimated using industry asset betas as follows:

$$r_{wacc} = r_U - \frac{D}{E + D} \tau_C r_D \qquad (12.13)$$

12.7 Final Thoughts on Using the CAPM

- While the CAPM is not perfect, it is straightforward to use, relatively robust, hard to manipulate, and correctly emphasizes the importance of market risk. As a result, it is the most popular and best available method to use for capital budgeting.

Key Terms

alpha *p. 410*
asset beta *p. 418*
asset cost of capital *p. 415*
debt cost of capital *p. 411*
equal-ownership portfolio *p. 402*
error (or residual) term *p. 410*
exchange-traded fund (ETF) *p. 404*
execution risk *p. 421*
free float *p. 402*
index funds *p. 404*
linear regression *p. 410*

market index *p. 402*
market proxy *p. 404*
net debt *p. 417*
operating leverage *p. 420*
passive portfolio *p. 402*
pretax WACC *p. 422*
price-weighted portfolio *p. 404*
unlevered beta *p. 416*
unlevered cost of capital *p. 415*
value-weighted portfolio *p. 402*
weighted average cost of capital (WACC) *p. 422*

Further Reading

The following articles provide some additional insights on the CAPM: F. Black, "Beta and Return," *Journal of Portfolio Management* 20 (Fall 1993): 8–18; and B. Rosenberg and J. Guy, "Beta and Investment Fundamentals," *Financial Analysts Journal* (May–June 1976): 60–72.

Although not a focus of this chapter, there is an extensive body of literature on testing the CAPM. Besides the articles mentioned in the text, here are a few others that an interested reader might want to consult: W. Ferson and C. Harvey, "The Variation of Economic Risk Premiums," *Journal of Political Economy* 99 (1991): 385–415; M. Gibbons, S. Ross, and J. Shanken, "A Test of the Efficiency of a Given Portfolio," *Econometrica* 57 (1989): 1121–1152; S. Kothari, J. Shanken, and R. Sloan, "Another Look at the Cross-Section of Expected Stock Returns," *Journal of Finance* 50 (March 1995): 185–224; and R. Levy, "On the Short-Term Stationarity of Beta Coefficients," *Financial Analysts Journal* (November–December 1971): 55–62.

Problems

All problems are available in MyFinanceLab. *An asterisk (*) indicates problems with a higher level of difficulty.*

The Equity Cost of Capital

1. Suppose Pepsico's stock has a beta of 0.57. If the risk-free rate is 3% and the expected return of the market portfolio is 8%, what is Pepsico's equity cost of capital?

2. Suppose the market portfolio has an expected return of 10% and a volatility of 20%, while Microsoft's stock has a volatility of 30%.
   a. Given its higher volatility, should we expect Microsoft to have an equity cost of capital that is higher than 10%?
   b. What would have to be true for Microsoft's equity cost of capital to be equal to 10%?

3. Aluminum maker Alcoa has a beta of about 2.0, whereas Hormel Foods has a beta of 0.45. If the expected excess return of the marker portfolio is 5%, which of these firms has a higher equity cost of capital, and how much higher is it?

The Market Portfolio

 4. Suppose all possible investment opportunities in the world are limited to the five stocks listed in the table below. What does the market portfolio consist of (what are the portfolio weights)?

Stock	Price/Share ($)	Number of Shares Outstanding (millions)
A	10	10
B	20	12
C	8	3
D	50	1
E	45	20

5. Using the data in Problem 4, suppose you are holding a market portfolio, and have invested $12,000 in Stock C.

a. How much have you invested in Stock A?

b. How many shares of Stock B do you hold?

c. If the price of Stock C suddenly drops to $4 per share, what trades would you need to make to maintain a market portfolio?

6. Suppose Best Buy stock is trading for $20 per share for a total market cap of $6 billion, and Walt Disney has 1.8 billion shares outstanding. If you hold the market portfolio, and as part of it hold 100 shares of Best Buy, how many shares of Walt Disney do you hold?

7. Standard and Poor's also publishes the S&P Equal Weight Index, which is an equally weighted version of the S&P 500.

a. To maintain a portfolio that tracks this index, what trades would need to be made in response to daily price changes?

b. Is this index suitable as a market proxy?

8. Suppose that in place of the S&P 500, you wanted to use a broader market portfolio of all U.S. stocks and bonds as the market proxy. Could you use the same estimate for the market risk premium when applying the CAPM? If not, how would you estimate the correct risk premium to use?

9. From the start of 1999 to the start of 2009, the S&P 500 had a negative return. Does this mean the market risk premium we should haved used in the CAPM was negative?

Beta Estimation

10. You need to estimate the equity cost of capital for XYZ Corp. You have the following data available regarding past returns:

Year	Risk-free Return	Market Return	XYZ Return
2007	3%	6%	10%
2008	1%	−37%	−45%

a. What was XYZ's average historical return?

b. Compute the market's and XYZ's excess returns for each year. Estimate XYZ's beta.

c. Estimate XYZ's historical alpha.

d. Suppose the current risk-free rate is 3%, and you expect the market's return to be 8%. Use the CAPM to estimate an expected return for XYZ Corp.'s stock.

e. Would you base your estimate of XYZ's equity cost of capital on your answer in part (a) or in part (d)? How does your answer to part (c) affect your estimate? Explain.

*11. Go to Chapter Resources on MyFinanceLab and use the data in the spreadsheet provided to estimate the beta of Nike and Dell stock based on their monthly returns from 2007–2011. (*Hint*: You can use the slope() function in Excel.)

*12. Using the same data as in Problem 11, estimate the alpha of Nike and Dell stock, expressed as % per month. (*Hint*: You can use the intercept() function in Excel.)

*13. Using the same data as in Problem 11, estimate the 95% confidence interval for the alpha and beta of Nike and Dell stock using Excel's regression tool (from the data analysis menu) or the linest() function.

The Debt Cost of Capital

14. In mid-2012, Ralston Purina had AA-rated, 10-year bonds outstanding with a yield to maturity of 2.05%.
   a. What is the highest expected return these bonds could have?
   b. At the time, similar maturity Treasuries have a yield of 1.5%. Could these bonds actually have an expected return equal to your answer in part (a)?
   c. If you believe Ralston Purina's bonds have 0.5% chance of default per year, and that expected loss rate in the event of default is 60%, what is your estimate of the expected return for these bonds?

15. In mid-2009, Rite Aid had CCC-rated, 6-year bonds outstanding with a yield to maturity of 17.3%. At the time, similar maturity Treasuries had a yield of 3%. Suppose the market risk premium is 5% and you believe Rite Aid's bonds have a beta of 0.31. The expected loss rate of these bonds in the event of default is 60%.
   a. What annual probability of default would be consistent with the yield to maturity of these bonds in mid-2009?
   b. In mid-2012, Rite-Aid's bonds had a yield of 8.3%, while similar maturity Treasuries had a yield of 1%. What probability of default would you estimate now?

16. During the recession in mid-2009, homebuilder KB Home had outstanding 6-year bonds with a yield to maturity of 8.5% and a BB rating. If corresponding risk-free rates were 3%, and the market risk premium was 5%, estimate the expected return of KB Home's debt using two different methods. How do your results compare?

17. The Dunley Corp. plans to issue 5-year bonds. It believes the bonds will have a BBB rating. Suppose AAA bonds with the same maturity have a 4% yield. Assume the market risk premium is 5% and use the data in Table 12.2 and Table 12.3.
   a. Estimate the yield Dunley will have to pay, assuming an expected 60% loss rate in the event of default during average economic times. What spread over AAA bonds will it have to pay?
   b. Estimate the yield Dunley would have to pay if it were a recession, assuming the expected loss rate is 80% at that time, but the beta of debt and market risk premium are the same as in average economic times. What is Dunley's spread over AAA now?
   c. In fact, one might expect risk premia and betas to increase in recessions. Redo part (b) assuming that the market risk premium and the beta of debt both increase by 20%; that is, they equal 1.2 times their value in recessions.

A Project's Cost of Capital

18. Your firm is planning to invest in an automated packaging plant. Harburtin Industries is an all-equity firm that specializes in this business. Suppose Harburtin's equity beta is 0.85, the risk-free rate is 4%, and the market risk premium is 5%. If your firm's project is all equity financed, estimate its cost of capital.

19. Consider the setting of Problem 18. You decided to look for other comparables to reduce estimation error in your cost of capital estimate. You find a second firm, Thurbinar Design, which is also engaged in a similar line of business. Thurbinar has a stock price of $20 per share, with 15 million shares outstanding. It also has $100 million in outstanding debt, with a yield on the debt of 4.5%. Thurbinar's equity beta is 1.00.
   a. Assume Thurbinar's debt has a beta of zero. Estimate Thurbinar's unlevered beta. Use the unlevered beta and the CAPM to estimate Thurbinar's unlevered cost of capital.

b. Estimate Thurbinar's equity cost of capital using the CAPM. Then assume its debt cost of capital equals its yield, and using these results, estimate Thurbinar's unlevered cost of capital.

c. Explain the difference between your estimates in part (a) and part (b).

d. You decide to average your results in part (a) and part (b), and then average this result with your estimate from Problem 17. What is your estimate for the cost of capital of your firm's project?

20. IDX Tech is looking to expand its investment in advanced security systems. The project will be financed with equity. You are trying to assess the value of the investment, and must estimate its cost of capital. You find the following data for a publicly traded firm in the same line of business:

Debt Outstanding (book value, AA-rated)	$400 million
Number of shares of common stock	80 million
Stock price per share	$15.00
Book value of equity per share	$6.00
Beta of equity	1.20

What is your estimate of the project's beta? What assumptions do you need to make?

21. In mid-2012, Cisco Systems had a market capitalization of $101 billion. It had A-rated debt of $16 billion as well as cash and short-term investments of $48 billion, and its estimated equity beta at the time was 1.23.

a. What is Cisco's enterprise value?

b. Assuming Cisco's debt has a beta of zero, estimate the beta of Cisco's underlying business enterprise.

22. Consider the following airline industry data from mid-2009:

Company Name	Market Capitalization ($mm)	Total Enterprise Value ($mm)	Equity Beta	Debt Ratings
Delta Air Lines (DAL)	4,938.5	17,026.5	2.04	BB
Southwest Airlines (LUV)	4,896.8	6,372.8	0.966	A/BBB
JetBlue Airways (JBLU)	1,245.5	3,833.5	1.91	B/CCC
Continental Airlines (CAL)	1,124.0	4,414.0	1.99	B

a. Use the estimates in Table 12.3 to estimate the debt beta for each firm (use an average if multiple ratings are listed).

b. Estimate the asset beta for each firm.

c. What is the average asset beta for the industry, based on these firms?

Project Risk Characteristics and Financing

23. Weston Enterprises is an all-equity firm with two divisions. The soft drink division has an asset beta of 0.60, expects to generate free cash flow of $50 million this year, and anticipates a 3% perpetual growth rate. The industrial chemicals division has an asset beta of 1.20, expects to generate free cash flow of $70 million this year, and anticipates a 2% perpetual growth rate. Suppose the risk-free rate is 4% and the market risk premium is 5%.

a. Estimate the value of each division.

b. Estimate Weston's current equity beta and cost of capital. Is this cost of capital useful for valuing Weston's projects? How is Weston's equity beta likely to change over time?

*24. Harrison Holdings, Inc. (HHI) is publicly traded, with a current share price of $32 per share. HHI has 20 million shares outstanding, as well as $64 million in debt. The founder of HHI, Harry Harrison, made his fortune in the fast food business. He sold off part of his fast food empire, and purchased a professional hockey team. HHI's only assets are the hockey team, together with 50% of the outstanding shares of Harry's Hotdogs restaurant chain. Harry's Hotdogs (HDG) has a market capitalization of $850 million, and an enterprise value of $1.05 billion. After a little research, you find that the average asset beta of other fast food restaurant chains is 0.75. You also find that the debt of HHI and HDG is highly rated, and so you decide to estimate the beta of both firms' debt as zero. Finally, you do a regression analysis on HHI's historical stock returns in comparison to the S&P 500, and estimate an equity beta of 1.33. Given this information, estimate the beta of HHI's investment in the hockey team.

25. Your company operates a steel plant. On average, revenues from the plant are $30 million per year. All of the plants costs are variable costs and are consistently 80% of revenues, including energy costs associated with powering the plant, which represent one quarter of the plant's costs, or an average of $6 million per year. Suppose the plant has an asset beta of 1.25, the risk-free rate is 4%, and the market risk premium is 5%. The tax rate is 40%, and there are no other costs.
   a. Estimate the value of the plant today assuming no growth.
   b. Suppose you enter a long-term contract which will supply all of the plant's energy needs for a fixed cost of $3 million per year (before tax). What is the value of the plant if you take this contract?
   c. How would taking the contract in (b) change the plant's cost of capital? Explain.

26. Unida Systems has 40 million shares outstanding trading for $10 per share. In addition, Unida has $100 million in outstanding debt. Suppose Unida's equity cost of capital is 15%, its debt cost of capital is 8%, and the corporate tax rate is 40%.
   a. What is Unida's unlevered cost of capital?
   b. What is Unida's after-tax debt cost of capital?
   c. What is Unida's weighted average cost of capital?

27. You would like to estimate the weighted average cost of capital for a new airline business. Based on its industry asset beta, you have already estimated an unlevered cost of capital for the firm of 9%. However, the new business will be 25% debt financed, and you anticipate its debt cost of capital will be 6%. If its corporate tax rate is 40%, what is your estimate of its WACC?

Data Case

You work in Walt Disney Company's corporate finance and treasury department and have just been assigned to the team estimating Disney's WACC. You must estimate this WACC in preparation for a team meeting later today. You quickly realize that the information you need is readily available online.

1. Go to http://finance.yahoo.com. Under the "Investing Tab" and then "Market Overview," you will find the yield to maturity for ten-year Treasury bonds listed as "10 Yr Bond(%)." Collect this number as your risk-free rate.

2. In the box next to the "Get Quotes" button, type Walt Disney's ticker symbol (DIS) and press enter. Once you see the basic information for Disney, find and click "Key Statistics" on the left side of the screen. From the key statistics, collect Disney's market capitalization (its market value of equity), enterprise value (market-value equity + net debt), cash, and beta.

3. To get Disney's cost of debt and the market value of its long-term debt, you will need the price and yield to maturity on the firm's existing long-term bonds. Go to http://cxa.marketwatch.com/finra/BondCenter/Default.aspx. Under "Quick Bond Search," click "Corporate" and type Disney's ticker symbol. A list of Disney's outstanding bond issues will appear. Assume that

Disney's policy is to use the expected return on noncallable ten-year obligations as its cost of debt. Find the noncallable bond issue that is at least 10 years from maturity. (*Hint*: You will see a column titled "Callable"; make sure the issue you choose has "No" in this column. Bonds may appear on multiple pages.) Find the credit rating and yield to maturity for your chosen bond issue (it is in the column titled "Yield"). Hold the mouse over the table of Disney's bonds and right-click. Select "Export to Microsoft Excel." (Note that this option is available in IE, but may not be in other browsers.) An Excel spreadsheet with all of the data in the table will appear.

4. You now have the price for each bond issue, but you need to know the size of the issue. Returning to the Web page, click "Walt Disney Company" in the first row. This brings up a Web page with all of the information about the bond issue. Scroll down until you find "Amount Outstanding" on the right side. Noting that this amount is quoted in thousands of dollars (e.g., $60,000 means $60 million = $60,000,000), record the issue amount in the appropriate row of your spreadsheet. Repeat this step for all of the bond issues.

5. The price for each bond issue in your spreadsheet is reported as a percentage of the bond's par value. For example, 104.50 means that the bond issue is trading at 104.5% of its par value. You can calculate the market value of each bond issue by multiplying the amount outstanding by (Price ÷ 100). Do so for each issue and then calculate the total of all the bond issues. This is the market value of Disney's debt.

6. Compute the weights for Disney's equity and debt based on the market value of equity and Disney's market value of debt, computed in Step 5.

7. Calculate Disney's cost of equity capital using the CAPM, the risk-free rate you collected in Step 1, and a market risk premium of 5%.

8. Assuming that Disney has a tax rate of 35%, calculate its after-tax debt cost of capital.

9. Calculate Disney's WACC.

10. Calculate Disney's net debt by subtracting its cash (collected in Step 2) from its debt. Recalculate the weights for the WACC using the market value of equity, net debt, and enterprise value. Recalculate Disney's WACC using the weights based on the net debt. How much does it change?

11. How confident are you of your estimate? Which implicit assumptions did you make during your data collection efforts?

Practical Considerations When Forecasting Beta

As discussed in Section 12.3, we can estimate stock betas in practice by regressing past stock returns on returns of the market portfolio. Several practical considerations arise when doing so. Important choices in estimating beta include (1) the time horizon used, (2) the index used as the market portfolio, (3) the method used to extrapolate from past betas to future betas, and (4) the treatment of outliers in the data.

Time Horizon

When estimating beta by using past returns, there is a trade-off regarding which time horizon to use to measure returns. If we use too short a time horizon, our estimate of beta will be unreliable. If we use very old data, they may be unrepresentative of the current market risk of the security. For stocks, common practice is to use at least two years of weekly return data or five years of monthly return data.[20]

The Market Proxy

The CAPM predicts that a security's expected return depends on its beta with regard to the market portfolio of *all* risky investments available to investors. As mentioned earlier, in practice the S&P 500 is used as the market proxy. Other proxies, such as the NYSE Composite Index (a value-weighted index of all NYSE stocks), the Wilshire 5000 index of all U.S. stocks, or an even broader market index that includes both equities and fixed-income securities, are sometimes used as well. When evaluating international stocks, it is common practice to use a country or international market index. It is important to remember, however, that the market risk premium used in Eq. 12.1 must reflect the choice of the market proxy. For example, a lower risk premium should be used if the market proxy includes fixed-income securities.

Beta Variation and Extrapolation

The estimated beta for a firm will tend to vary over time. For example, Figure 12A.1 shows variation in an estimate of Cisco's beta from 1999–2012. Much of this variation is likely due to estimation error. Thus, we should be suspicious of estimates that are extreme relative to historical or industry norms; in fact, many practitioners prefer to use average industry asset betas rather than individual stock betas (see Figure 12.4) in order to reduce estimation error. In addition, evidence suggests that betas tend to regress toward the average beta of 1.0 over time.[21] For both of these reasons, many practitioners use **adjusted betas**, which

---

[20]While daily returns would provide even more sample points, we often do not use them due to the concern—especially for smaller, less liquid stocks—that short-term factors might influence daily returns that are not representative of the longer-term risks affecting the security. Ideally, we should use a return interval equal to our investment horizon. The need for sufficient data, however, makes monthly returns the longest practical choice.

[21]See M. Blume, "Betas and Their Regression Tendencies," *Journal of Finance* 30 (1975): 785–795.

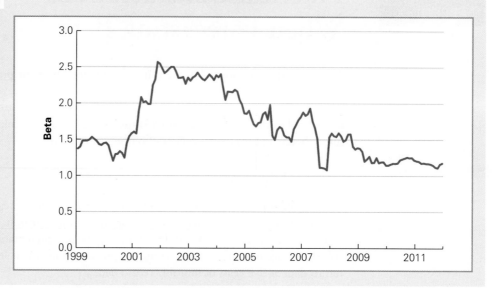

FIGURE 12A.1

Estimated Betas for Cisco Systems, 1999–2012

Estimated betas will vary over time. The estimate for Cisco's beta, based on three years of monthly data, varies from a high of approximately 2.5 in 2002 to a low of 1.1 in 2007. While some of this variation may represent actual changes in the firm's market sensitivity, much of it is likely due to estimation error.

are calculated by averaging the estimated beta with 1.0. For example, Bloomberg computes adjusted betas using the following formula:

$$\text{Adjusted Beta of Security } i = \tfrac{2}{3}\beta_i + \tfrac{1}{3}(1.0) \qquad (12A.1)$$

The estimation methodologies of five data providers appear in Table 12A.1. Each employs a unique methodology, which leads to differences in the reported betas.

Outliers

The beta estimates we obtain from linear regression can be very sensitive to outliers, which are returns of unusually large magnitude.[22] As an example, Figure 12A.2 shows a scatterplot of Genentech's monthly returns versus the S&P 500 for 2002–2004. Based on these returns, we estimate a beta of 1.21 for Genentech. Looking closely at the monthly returns, however, we find two data points with unusually large returns: In April 2002, Genentech's stock price fell by almost 30%, and in May 2003, Genentech's stock price rose by almost 65%. In each case the extreme moves were a reaction to Genentech's announcement of news related to

TABLE 12A.1   Estimation Methodologies Used by Selected Data Providers

	Value Line	Reuters	Bloomberg	Yahoo!	Capital IQ
Returns	Weekly	Monthly	Weekly	Monthly	Weekly, Monthly (5yr)
Horizon	5 years	5 years	2 years	3 years	1, 2, 5 years
Market Index	NYSE Composite	S&P 500	S&P 500	S&P 500	S&P 500 (U.S. Stocks) MSCI (International Stocks)
Adjusted	Adjusted	Unadjusted	Both	Unadjusted	Unadjusted

[22]See, for example, Peter Knez and Mark Ready, "On the Robustness of Size and Book-to-Market in Cross-Sectional Regressions," *Journal of Finance* 52 (1997): 1355–1382.

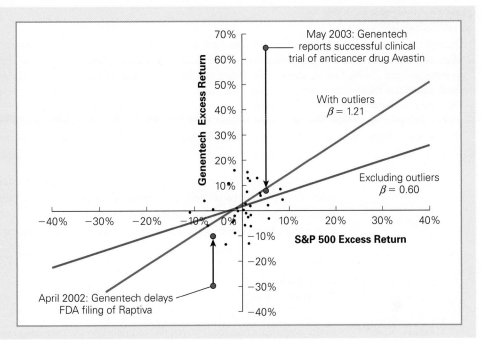

FIGURE 12A.2

Beta Estimation with and without Outliers for Genentech Using Monthly Returns for 2002–2004

Genentech's returns in April 2002 and May 2003 are largely due to firm-specific news. By replacing those returns (blue points) with industry average returns (red points), we obtain a more accurate assessment of Genentech's market risk during this period.

new drug development. In April 2002, Genentech reported a setback in the development of psoriasis drug Raptiva. In May 2003, the company reported the successful clinical trial of its anticancer drug Avastin. These two returns more likely represent firm-specific rather than market-wide risk. But because these large returns happened to occur during months when the market also moved in the same direction, they bias the estimate of beta that results from a standard regression. If we redo the regression replacing Genentech's returns during these two months with the average return of similar biotechnology firms during the same months, we obtain a much lower estimate of 0.60 for Genentech's beta, as shown in Figure 12A.2. This latter estimate is probably a much more accurate assessment of Genentech's true market risk during this period.

There may be other reasons to exclude certain historical data as anomalous when estimating beta. For example, some practitioners advocate ignoring data from 1998–2001 to avoid distortions related to the technology, media, and telecommunications speculative bubble.[23] A similar concern could be raised with regard to the performance of financial stocks during the financial crisis in 2008–2009. On the other hand, including data from recessionary periods may be helpful in evaluating the stock's likely sensitivity to future downturns.

Other Considerations

When using historical returns to forecast future betas, we must be mindful of changes in the environment that might cause the future to differ from the past. For example, if a firm were to change industries, using its historical beta would be inferior to using the beta of other firms in the new industry. Also bear in mind that many practitioners analyze other

---

[23]For example, see A. Annema and M. H. Goedhart, "Better Betas," *McKinsey on Finance* (Winter 2003): 10–13.

| COMMON MISTAKE | Changing the Index to Improve the Fit |

Because we can use regression analysis to estimate beta, it is often incorrectly assumed that a higher goodness of fit will lead to more accurate results. This goodness of fit is measured by the **R-squared** of the regression, which is equal to the square of the correlation between the stock's and market's excess returns.

For example, our regression of Cisco's returns would show a much higher R-squared if we used the NASDAQ 100 index, which has a much heavier concentration of technology stocks, in place of the S&P 500. But remember, the goal of the regression analysis is to determine Cisco's sensitivity to *market* risk. Because the NASDAQ 100 index itself is not well-diversified, it does not capture market risk. Thus, Cisco's beta with respect to the NASDAQ 100 is not a meaningful assessment of its market risk.

information in addition to past returns, such as industry characteristics, firm size, and other financial characteristics of a firm, when they forecast betas. In the end, forecasting betas, like most types of forecasting, is as much art as science, and the best estimates require a thorough knowledge of the particulars of a firm and its industry.

Key Terms

adjusted betas *p. 433*
R-squared *p. 436*

Data Case

In the earlier data case for this chapter, you relied on the beta estimate for Walt Disney provided by Yahoo! Finance. You decide to dig deeper and estimate Disney's equity beta on your own.

1. Get the monthly adjusted prices for Disney and the S&P 500 from Yahoo! Finance (http:// finance.yahoo.com) using the same time period and procedure as in the Chapter 10 Data Case. (The symbol for the S&P 500 in Yahoo! Finance is ^GSPC.)

2. Get the one-month Eurodollar rate from the Federal Reserve Web site (http://www .federalreserve.gov/releases/h15/data.htm).[24] Click on Data Download Program ("DDP" on the top right of the screen). Click the Build Package button and make the following selections:

    1. Series Type—Selected Interest Rates
    2. Instrument—ED Eurodollar deposits (London)
    3. Maturity—1-month
    4. Frequency—Monthly

    Click Go to Package and then Format Package. Select Dates—From 2007 January to 2011 December, and select File Type—Excel. Click Go to download and Download file. Then open and save these rates to an Excel file.

3. To convert the Eurodollar rate to a monthly rate, take the yield and divide it by 100 to convert it to a decimal. Then divide the decimal by 12. The resulting rate will be the monthly risk-free return in the CAPM (you may need to re-sort the dates to match the Yahoo! data).

4. Create separate return columns that compute the excess returns for Walt Disney and the S&P 500. Recall that the excess return is the actual monthly return minus the risk-free rate.

5. Compute the beta of Disney stock based on Eq. 12.5 from this chapter, using the SLOPE function in Excel. How does it compare with the beta currently reported by Yahoo! Finance? Why might the results differ?

6. Compute Disney's alpha over this period using the INTERCEPT function in Excel. How might you interpret this alpha?

---

[24]The Eurodollar deposit rate is the average rate paid on dollar deposits in the London interbank market. It is widely regarded as a close proxy for the risk-free rate because it is a measure of the average borrowing/ lending rate between financial institutions (see the Chapter 11 Appendix).

Investor Behavior and Capital Market Efficiency

AS FUND MANAGER OF LEGG MASON VALUE TRUST, William H. Miller had built a reputation as one of the world's savviest investors. Miller's fund outperformed the overall market every year from 1991–2005, a winning streak no other fund manager came close to matching. But in 2007–2008, Legg Mason Value Trust fell by nearly 65%, almost twice as much as the broader market. While Legg Mason Value Trust outperformed the market in 2009, it lagged again from 2010 until Miller ultimately stepped down as manager and chief investment officer in 2012. As a result of this performance, investors in the fund since 1991 effectively gave back all of the gains they had earned relative to the market in the intervening years and Miller's reputation lay in tatters.[1] Was Miller's performance prior to 2007 merely luck or was his performance in post-2007 the aberration?

According to the CAPM, the market portfolio is efficient, so it should be impossible to consistently do better than the market without taking on additional risk. In this chapter, we will take a close look at this prediction of the CAPM, and assess to what extent the market portfolio is or is not efficient. We will begin by looking at the role of competition in driving the CAPM results, noting that for some investors to beat the market, other investors must be willing to hold portfolios that underperform the market. We then look at the behavior of individual investors, who tend to make a number of mistakes that reduce their returns. But while a few professional fund managers are able to exploit these mistakes and profit from them, it does not appear that much, if any, of these profits make it into the hands of the investors who hold their funds.

On the other hand, we will also consider evidence that certain investment "styles," namely holding small stocks, value stocks, and stocks with high recent returns, perform better than predicted by the CAPM, indicating that the market portfolio may not be efficient. We explore this evidence, and then consider how to calculate the cost of capital if indeed the market portfolio is not efficient by deriving an alternative model of risk—the multifactor asset pricing model.

NOTATION

x_i portfolio weight of investment in i

R_s return of stock or portfolio s

r_f risk-free rate of interest

α_s alpha of stock s

β_s^i beta of stock s with portfolio i

ε_s residual risk of stock s

---

[1]T. Lauricella, "The Stock Picker's Defeat," *Wall Street Journal*, December 10, 2008.

13.1 Competition and Capital Markets

To understand the role of competition in the market, it is useful to consider how the CAPM equilibrium we derived in Chapter 11 might arise based on the behavior of individual investors. In this section, we explain how investors who care only about expected return and variance react to new information and how their actions lead to the CAPM equilibrium.

Identifying a Stock's Alpha

Consider the equilibrium, as we depicted in Figure 11.12 on page 384, where the CAPM holds and the market portfolio is efficient. Now suppose new information arrives such that, *if market prices remain unchanged,* this news would raise the expected return of GM and Exxon Mobil stocks by 2% and lower the expected return of IBM and Anheuser-Busch stocks by 2%, leaving the expected return of the market unchanged.[2] Figure 13.1 illustrates the effect of this change on the efficient frontier. With the new information, the market portfolio is no longer efficient. Alternative portfolios offer a higher expected return and a lower volatility than we can obtain by holding the market portfolio. Investors who are aware of this fact will alter their investments in order to make their portfolios efficient.

To improve the performance of their portfolios, investors who are holding the market portfolio will compare the expected return of each security s with its required return from the CAPM (Eq. 12.1):

$$r_s = r_f + \beta_s \times (E[R_{Mkt}] - r_f) \tag{13.1}$$

FIGURE 13.1

An Inefficient Market Portfolio

If the market portfolio is not equal to the efficient portfolio, then the market is not in the CAPM equilibrium. The figure illustrates this possibility if news is announced that raises the expected return of GM and Exxon Mobil stocks and lowers the expected return of IBM and Anheuser-Busch stocks compared to the situation depicted in Figure 11.12.

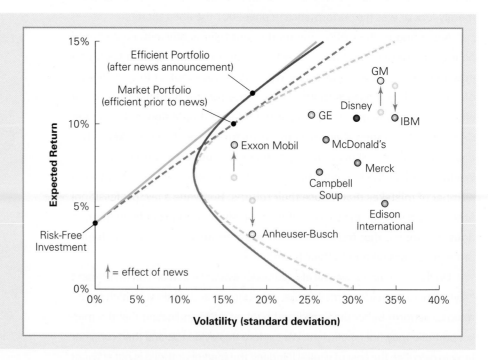

---

[2]In general, news about individual stocks will affect the market's expected return because these stocks are part of the market portfolio. To keep things simple, we assume the individual stock effects cancel out so that the market's expected return remains unchanged.

FIGURE 13.2

Deviations from the Security Market Line

If the market portfolio is not efficient, then stocks will not all lie on the security market line. The distance of a stock above or below the security market line is the stock's alpha. We can improve upon the market portfolio by buying stocks with positive alphas and selling stocks with negative alphas, but as we do so, prices will change and their alphas will shrink toward zero.

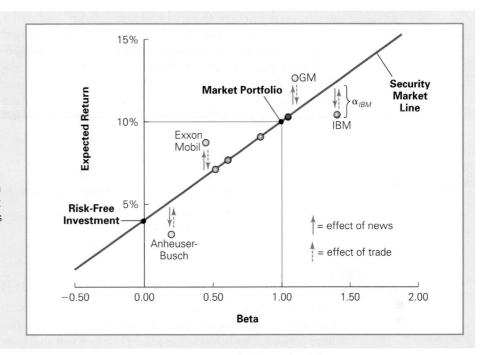

Figure 13.2 shows this comparison. Note that the stocks whose returns have changed are no longer on the security market line. The difference between a stock's expected return and its required return according to the security market line is the stock's alpha:

$$\alpha_s = E[R_s] - r_s \qquad (13.2)$$

When the market portfolio is efficient, all stocks are on the security market line and have an alpha of zero. When a stock's alpha is not zero, investors can improve upon the performance of the market portfolio. As we saw in Chapter 11, the Sharpe ratio of a portfolio will increase if we buy stocks whose expected return exceeds their required return—that is, if we buy stocks with positive alphas. Similarly, we can improve the performance of our portfolio by selling stocks with negative alphas.

Profiting from Non-Zero Alpha Stocks

Faced with the situation in Figure 13.2, savvy investors who are holding the market portfolio will want to buy stock in Exxon Mobil and GM, and sell stock in Anheuser-Busch and IBM. The surge of buy orders for Exxon Mobil and GM will cause their stock prices to rise, and the surge of sell orders for Anheuser-Busch and IBM will cause their stock prices to fall. As stock prices change, so do expected returns. Recall that a stock's total return is equal to its dividend yield plus the capital gain rate. All else equal, an increase in the current stock price will lower the stock's dividend yield and future capital gain rate, thereby lowering its expected return. Thus, as savvy investors attempt to trade to improve their portfolios, they raise the price and lower the expected return of the positive-alpha stocks, and they depress the price and raise the expected return of the negative-alpha stocks, until the stocks are once again on the security market line and the market portfolio is efficient.

Notice that the actions of investors have two important consequences. First, while the CAPM conclusion that the market is always efficient may not literally be true, competition among savvy investors who try to "beat the market" and earn a positive alpha should keep the market portfolio close to efficient much of the time. In that sense, we can view the CAPM as an approximate description of a competitive market.

Second, there may exist trading strategies that take advantage of non-zero alpha stocks, and by doing so actually can beat the market. In the remainder of this chapter we will explore both of these consequences, looking at evidence of the approximate efficiency of the market, as well as identifying trading strategies that may actually do better than the market.

CONCEPT CHECK

1. If investors attempt to buy a stock with a positive alpha, what is likely to happen to its price and expected return? How will this affect its alpha?

2. What is the consequence of investors exploiting non-zero alpha stocks for the efficiency of the market portfolio?

13.2 Information and Rational Expectations

Under what circumstances could an investor profit from trading a non-zero alpha stock? Consider the situation in Figure 13.2 after the news announcement. Because Exxon Mobil has a positive alpha before prices adjust, investors will anticipate that the price will rise and will likely put in buy orders at the current prices. If the information that altered Exxon Mobil's expected return is publically announced, there are likely to be a large number of investors who receive this news and act on it. Similarly, anybody who hears the news will not want to sell at the old prices. That is, there will be a large order imbalance. The only way to remove this imbalance is for the price to rise so that the alpha is zero. Note that in this case it is quite possible for the new prices to come about *without trade*. That is, the competition between investors may be so intense that prices move before any investor can actually trade at the old prices, so no investor can profit from the news.[3]

Informed Versus Uninformed Investors

As the above discussion makes clear, *in order to profit by buying a positive-alpha stock, there must be someone willing to sell it*. Under the CAPM assumption of homogeneous expectations, which states that all investors have the same information, it would seem that all investors would be aware that the stock had a positive alpha and none would be willing to sell.

Of course, the assumption of homogeneous expectations is not necessarily a good description of the real world. In reality, investors have different information and spend varying amounts of effort researching stocks. Consequently, we might expect that sophisticated investors would learn that Exxon Mobil has a positive alpha, and that they would be able to purchase shares from more naïve investors.

However, even differences in the quality of investors' information will not necessarily be enough to generate trade in this situation. An important conclusion of the CAPM is that investors should hold the market portfolio (combined with risk-free investments), and this investment advice *does not depend on the quality of an investor's information or trading skill*. Even naïve investors with no information can follow this investment advice, and as

---

[3]The idea that prices will adjust to information without trade is sometimes referred to as the *no-trade theorem*. (P. Milgrom and N. Stokey, "Information, Trade and Common Knowledge," *Journal of Economic Theory* 26 (1982): 17–27.)

the following example shows, by doing so they can avoid being taken advantage of by more sophisticated investors.

EXAMPLE 13.1   **How to Avoid Being Outsmarted in Financial Markets**

Problem

Suppose you are an investor without access to any information regarding stocks. You know that other investors in the market possess a great deal of information and are actively using that information to select an efficient portfolio. You are concerned that because you are less informed than the average investor, your portfolio will underperform the portfolio of the average investor. How can you prevent that outcome and guarantee that your portfolio will do as well as that of the average investor?

Solution

Even though you are not as well informed, you can guarantee yourself the same return as the average investor simply by holding the market portfolio. Because the aggregate of all investors' portfolios must equal the market portfolio (i.e., demand must equal supply), if you hold the market portfolio then you must make the same return as the average investor.

On the other hand, suppose you don't hold the market portfolio, but instead hold less of some stock, such as Google, than its market weight. This must mean that in aggregate all other investors have over-weighted Google relative to the market. But because other investors are more informed than you are, they must realize Google is a good deal, and so are happy to profit at your expense.

Rational Expectations

Example 13.1 is very powerful. It implies that every investor, regardless of how little information he has access to, can guarantee himself the average return and earn an alpha of zero simply by holding the market portfolio. Thus, no investor should choose a portfolio with a negative alpha. However, because the average portfolio of all investors is the market portfolio, the average alpha of all investors is zero. If no investor earns a negative alpha, then no investor can earn a positive alpha, implying that the market portfolio must be efficient. As a result, the CAPM does not depend on the assumption of homogeneous expectations. Rather it requires only that investors have **rational expectations**, which means that all investors correctly interpret and use their own information, as well as information that can be inferred from market prices or the trades of others.[4]

For an investor to earn a positive alpha and beat the market, some investors must hold portfolios with negative alphas. Because these investors could have earned a zero alpha by holding the market portfolio, we reach the following important conclusion:

The market portfolio can be inefficient (so it is possible to beat the market) only if a significant number of investors either

1. *Do not have rational expectations so that they misinterpret information and believe they are earning a positive alpha when they are actually earning a negative alpha, or*

2. *Care about aspects of their portfolios other than expected return and volatility, and so are willing to hold inefficient portfolios of securities.*

---

[4]See P. DeMarzo and C. Skiadas, "Aggregation, Determinacy, and Informational Efficiency for a Class of Economies with Asymmetric Information," *Journal of Economic Theory* 80 (1998): 123–152.

How do investors actually behave? Do uninformed investors follow the CAPM advice and hold the market portfolio? To shed light on these questions, in the next section we review the evidence on individual investor behavior.

1. How can an uninformed or unskilled investor guarantee herself a non-negative alpha?

2. Under what conditions will it be possible to earn a positive alpha and beat the market?

13.3 The Behavior of Individual Investors

In this section, we examine whether small, individual investors heed the advice of the CAPM and hold the market portfolio. As we will see, many investors do not appear to hold an efficient portfolio, but instead fail to diversify and trade too much. We then consider whether these departures from the market create an opportunity for more sophisticated investors to profit at individual investors' expense.

Underdiversification and Portfolio Biases

One of the most important implications of our discussion of risk and return is the benefit of diversification. By appropriately diversifying their portfolios, investors can reduce risk without reducing their expected return. In that sense, diversification is a "free lunch" that all investors should take advantage of.

Despite this benefit, there is much evidence that individual investors fail to diversify their portfolios adequately. Evidence from the U.S. Survey of Consumer Finances shows that, for households that held stocks, the median number of stocks held by investors in 2001 was four, and 90% of investors held fewer than ten different stocks.[5] Moreover, these investments are often concentrated in stocks of companies that are in the same industry or are geographically close, further limiting the degree of diversification attained. A related finding comes from studying how individuals allocate their retirement savings accounts (401K plans). A study of large plans found that employees invested close to a third of their assets in their employer's own stock.[6] These underdiversification results are not unique to U.S. investors: A comprehensive study of Swedish investors documents that approximately one-half of the volatility in investors' portfolios is due to firm-specific risk.[7]

There are a number of potential explanations for this behavior. One is that investors suffer from a **familiarity bias**, so that they favor investments in companies they are familiar with.[8] Another is that investors have **relative wealth concerns** and care most about the performance of their portfolio relative to that of their peers. This desire to "keep up with the Joneses" can lead investors to choose undiversified portfolios that match those of their colleagues or neighbors.[9] In any case, this underdiversification is one important piece of evidence that individual investors may choose sub-optimal portfolios.

---

[5]V. Polkovnichenko, "Household Portfolio Diversification: A Case for Rank Dependent Preferences," *Review of Financial Studies* 18 (2005): 1467–1502.

[6]S. Benartzi, "Excessive Extrapolation and the Allocation of 401(k) Accounts to Company Stock," *Journal of Finance* 56 (2001): 1747–1764.

[7]J. Campbell, "Household Finance," *Journal of Finance* 61 (2006): 1553–1604.

[8]G. Huberman, "Familiarity Breeds Investment," *Review of Financial Studies* 14 (2001): 659–680.

[9]P. DeMarzo, R. Kaniel, and I. Kremer, "Diversification as a Public Good: Community Effects in Portfolio Choice," *Journal of Finance* 59 (2004): 1677–1715.

Excessive Trading and Overconfidence

According to the CAPM, investors should hold risk-free assets in combination with the market portfolio of all risky securities. In Chapter 12, we demonstrated that because the market portfolio is a value-weighted portfolio, it is also a passive portfolio in the sense that an investor does not need to trade in response to daily price changes in order to maintain it. Thus, if all investors held the market, we would see relatively little trading volume in financial markets.

In reality, a tremendous amount of trading occurs each day. At its peak in 2008, for example, annual turnover on the NYSE was nearly 140%, implying that each share of each stock was traded 1.4 times on average. While average turnover has declined dramatically in the wake of the financial crisis, as shown in Figure 13.3, it is still at levels far in excess of that predicted by the CAPM. Moreover, in a study of trading in individual accounts at a discount brokerage, researchers Brad Barber and Terrance Odean found that individual investors tend to trade very actively, with average turnover almost one and a half times the overall rates reported in Figure 13.3 during the time period of their study.[10]

What might explain this trading behavior? Psychologists have known since the 1960s that uninformed individuals tend to overestimate the precision of their knowledge. For example, many sports fans sitting in the stands confidently second guess the coaching decisions on the field, truly believing that they can do a better job. In finance we call this presumptuousness the **overconfidence bias**. Barber and Odean hypothesized that this kind of behavior also characterizes individual investment decision making: Like sports fans, individual investors believe they can pick winners and losers when, in fact, they cannot; this overconfidence leads them to trade too much.

An implication of this overconfidence bias is that, assuming they have no true ability, investors who trade more will not earn higher returns. Instead, their performance will be

---

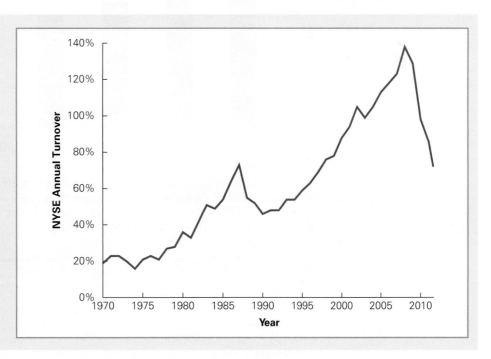

FIGURE 13.3

NYSE Annual Share Turnover, 1970–2011

The plot shows the annual share turnover (number of shares traded in the year/total number of shares). Such high turnover is difficult to reconcile with the CAPM, which implies that investors should hold passive market portfolios. Note also the rapid increase in turnover up through 2008, followed by a dramatic decline post-crisis.

Source: www.nyxdata.com

---

worse once we take into account the costs of trading (due to both commissions and bid-ask spreads). Figure 13.4 documents precisely this result, showing that much investor trading appears not to be based on rational assessments of performance.

As additional evidence, Barber and Odean contrasted the behavior and performance of men versus women.[11] Psychological studies have shown that, in areas such as finance, men tend to be more overconfident than women. Consistent with the overconfidence hypothesis, they documented that men tend to trade more than women, and that their portfolios have lower returns as a result. These differences are even more pronounced for single men and women.

Researchers have obtained similar results in an international context. Using an extraordinarily detailed database on Finnish investors, researchers Mark Grinblatt and Matti Keloharju found that trading activity increases with psychological measures of overconfidence. Interestingly, they also find that trading activity increases with the number of speeding tickets an individual receives, which they interpret as a measure of **sensation seeking**, or the individual's desire for novel and intense risk-taking experiences. In both cases, the increased trading does not appear to be profitable for investors.[12]

FIGURE 13.4   **Individual Investor Returns Versus Portfolio Turnover**

The plot shows average annual return (net of commissions and trading costs) for individual investors at a large discount brokerage from 1991–1997. Investors are grouped into quintiles based on their average annual turnover. While the least-active investors had slightly (but not significantly) better performance than the S&P 500, performance declined with the rate of turnover.

Source: B. Barber and T. Odean, "Trading Is Hazardous to Your Wealth: The Common Stock Investment Performance of Individual Investors," *Journal of Finance* 55 (2000): 773–806.

[11]B. Barber and T. Odean, "Boys Will Be Boys: Gender, Overconfidence, and Common Stock Investment," *Quarterly Journal of Economics* 116 (2001): 261–292.

[12]M. Grinblatt and M. Keloharju, "Sensation Seeking, Overconfidence, and Trading Activity," *Journal of Finance* 64 (2009): 549–578.

Individual Behavior and Market Prices

Thus, in reality, individual investors are underdiversified and trade too much, violating a key prediction of the CAPM. But does this observation imply that the remaining conclusions of the CAPM are invalid?

The answer is not necessarily. If individuals depart from the CAPM in random, idiosyncratic ways, then despite the fact that each individual doesn't hold the market, when we combine their portfolios together these departures will tend to cancel out just like any other idiosyncratic risk. In that case, individuals will hold the market portfolio *in aggregate*, and there will be no effect on market prices or returns. These uninformed investors may simply be trading with themselves—generating trading commissions for their brokers, but without impacting the efficiency of the market.

So, in order for the behavior of uninformed investors to have an impact on the market, there must be patterns to their behavior that lead them to depart from the CAPM in systematic ways, thus imparting systematic uncertainty into prices. For investors' trades to be correlated in this way, they must share a common motivation. Consequently, in Section 13.4, we investigate what might motivate investors to depart from the market portfolio, and show that investors appear to suffer from some common, and predictable, biases.

CONCEPT CHECK

1. Do investors hold well-diversified portfolios?

2. Why is the high trading volume observed in markets inconsistent with the CAPM equilibrium?

3. What must be true about the behavior of small, uninformed investors for them to have an impact on market prices?

13.4 Systematic Trading Biases

For the behavior of individual investors to impact market prices, and thus create a profitable opportunity for more sophisticated investors, there must be predictable, systematic patterns in the types of errors individual investors make. In this section we review some of the evidence researchers have found of such systematic trading biases.

Hanging on to Losers and the Disposition Effect

Investors tend to hold on to stocks that have lost value and sell stocks that have risen in value since the time of purchase. We call this tendency to hang on to losers and sell winners the **disposition effect**. Researchers Hersh Shefrin and Meir Statman, building on the work of psychologists Daniel Kahneman and Amos Tversky, posited that this effect arises due to investors' increased willingness to take on risk in the face of possible losses.[13] It may also reflect a reluctance to "admit a mistake" by taking the loss.

Researchers have verified the disposition effect in many studies. For example, in a study of all trades in the Taiwanese stock market from 1995–1999, investors in aggregate were twice as likely to realize gains as they were to realize losses. Also, nearly 85% of individual investors were subject to this bias.[14] On the other hand, mutual funds and foreign investors

---

[13]H. Shefrin and M. Statman, "The Disposition to Sell Winners Too Early and Ride Losers Too Long: Theory and Evidence," *Journal of Finance* 40 (1985): 777–790, and D. Kahneman and A. Tversky, "Prospect Theory: An Analysis of Decision under Risk," *Econometrica* 47 (1979): 263–291.

[14]B. Barber, Y. T. Lee, Y. J. Liu, and T. Odean, "Is the Aggregate Investor Reluctant to Realize Losses? Evidence from Taiwan," *European Financial Management* 13 (2007): 423–447.

NOBEL PRIZE	**Kahneman and Tversky's Prospect Theory**

In 2002, the Nobel Prize for Economics was awarded to Daniel Kahneman for his development of Prospect Theory with fellow psychologist Amos Tversky (who would have surely shared the prize if not for his death in 1996). Prospect Theory provides a descriptive model of the way individuals make decisions under uncertainty, predicting the choices people *do* make rather than the ones they *should* make. It posits that people evaluate outcomes relative to the status quo or similar reference point (the *framing effect*), will take on risk to avoid realizing losses, and put too much weight on unlikely events. The disposition effect follows from Prospect Theory by assuming investors frame their decisions by comparing the sale price with the purchase price for each stock. In a similar way, Prospect Theory provides an important foundation for much research in behavioral economics and finance.

did not exhibit the same tendency, and other studies have shown that more sophisticated investors appear to be less susceptible to the disposition effect.[15]

This behavioral tendency to sell winners and hang on to losers is costly from a tax perspective. Because capital gains are taxed only when the asset is sold, it is optimal for tax purposes to postpone taxable gains by continuing to hold profitable investments, delaying the tax payment and reducing its present value. On the other hand, investors should capture tax losses by selling their losing investments, especially near the year's end, in order to accelerate the tax write-off.

Of course, hanging on to losers and selling winners might make sense if investors forecast that the losing stocks would ultimately "bounce back" and outperform the winners going forward. While investors may in fact have this belief, it does not appear to be justified—if anything, the losing stocks that small investors continue to hold tend to *underperform* the winners that they sell. According to one study, losers underperformed winners by 3.4% over the year after the winners were sold.[16]

Investor Attention, Mood, and Experience

Individual investors generally are not full-time traders. As a result, they have limited time and attention to spend on their investment decisions, and so may be influenced by attention-grabbing news stories or other events. Studies show that individuals are more likely to buy stocks that have recently been in the news, engaged in advertising, experienced exceptionally high trading volume, or have had extreme (positive or negative) returns.[17]

Investment behavior also seems to be affected by investors' moods. For example, sunshine generally has a positive effect on mood, and studies have found that stock returns tend to be higher when it is a sunny day at the location of the stock exchange. In New York City, the annualized market return on perfectly sunny days is approximately 24.8% per

---

[15]R. Dhar and N. Zhu, "Up Close and Personal: Investor Sophistication and the Disposition Effect," *Management Science* 52 (2006): 726–740.

[16]T. Odean, "Are Investors Reluctant to Realize Their Losses?" *Journal of Finance* 53 (1998): 1775–1798.

[17]See G. Grullon, G. Kanatas, and J. Weston, "Advertising, Breadth of Ownership, and Liquidity," *Review of Financial Studies* 17 (2004): 439–461; M. Seasholes and G. Wu, "Predictable Behavior, Profits, and Attention," *Journal of Empirical Finance* 14 (2007): 590–610; Barber and T. Odean, "All That Glitters: The Effect of Attention and News on the Buying Behavior of Individual and Institutional Investors," *Review of Financial Studies* 21 (2008): 785–818.

year versus 8.7% per year on perfectly cloudy days.[18] Further evidence of the link between investor mood and stock returns comes from the effect of major sports events on returns. One study estimates that a loss in the World Cup elimination stage lowers the next day's stock returns in the losing country by about 0.50%, presumably due to investors' poor mood.[19]

Finally, investors appear to put too much weight on their own experience rather than considering all the historical evidence. As a result, people who grew up and lived during a time of high stock returns are more likely to invest in stocks than people who experienced times when stocks performed poorly.[20]

Herd Behavior

Thus far, we have considered common factors that might lead to correlated trading behavior by investors. An alternative reason why investors make similar trading errors is that they are actively *trying* to follow each other's behavior. This phenomenon, in which individuals imitate each other's actions, is referred to as **herd behavior**.

There are several reasons why traders might herd in their portfolio choices. First, they might believe others have superior information that they can take advantage of by copying their trades. This behavior can lead to an **informational cascade effect** in which traders ignore their own information hoping to profit from the information of others.[21] A second possibility is that, due to relative wealth concerns, individuals choose to herd in order to avoid the risk of underperforming their peers.[22] Third, professional fund managers may face reputational risk if they stray too far from the actions of their peers.[23]

Implications of Behavioral Biases

The insight that investors make mistakes is not news. What is surprising, however, is that these mistakes persist even though they may be economically costly and there is a relatively easy way to avoid them—buying and holding the market portfolio.

Regardless of why individual investors choose not to protect themselves by holding the market portfolio, the fact that they don't has potential implications for the CAPM. If individual investors are engaging in strategies that earn negative alphas, it may be possible for more sophisticated investors to take advantage of this behavior and earn positive alphas. Is there evidence that such savvy investors exist? In Section 13.5, we examine evidence regarding this possibility.

---

[18]Based on data from 1982–1997; see D. Hirshleifer and T. Shumway, "Good Day Sunshine: Stock Returns and the Weather," *Journal of Finance* 58 (2003): 1009–1032.

[19]A. Edmans, D. Garcia, and O. Norli, "Sports Sentiment and Stock Returns," *Journal of Finance* 62 (2007): 1967–1998.

[20]U. Malmendier and S. Nagel, "Depression Babies: Do Macroeconomic Experiences Affect Risk-Taking?", *Quarterly Journal of Economics* 126 (2011): 373–416.

[21]For example, see S. Bikhchandani, D. Hirshleifer, and I. Welch, "A Theory of Fads, Fashion, Custom and Cultural Change as Informational Cascades," *Journal of Political Economy* 100 (1992): 992–1026; and C. Avery and P. Zemsky, "Multidimensional Uncertainty and Herd Behavior in Financial Markets," *American Economic Review* 88 (1998): 724–748.

[22]P. DeMarzo, R. Kaniel, and I. Kremer, "Relative Wealth Concerns and Financial Bubbles," *Review of Financial Studies* 21 (2008): 19–50.

[23]D. Scharfstein and J. Stein, "Herd Behavior and Investment," *American Economic Review* 80 (1990): 465–479.

1. What are several systematic behavioral biases that individual investors fall prey to?

2. What implication might these behavioral biases have for the CAPM?

13.5 The Efficiency of the Market Portfolio

When individual investors make mistakes, can sophisticated investors easily profit at their expense? In order for sophisticated investors to profit from investor mistakes, two conditions must hold. First, the mistakes must be sufficiently pervasive and persistent to affect stock prices. That is, investor behavior must push prices so that non-zero alpha trading opportunities become apparent, as in Figure 13.2. Second, there must be limited competition to exploit these non-zero alpha opportunities. If competition is too intense, these opportunities will be quickly eliminated before any trader can take advantage of them in a significant way. In this section, we examine whether there is any evidence that individual or professional investors can outperform the market without taking on additional risk.

Trading on News or Recommendations

A natural place to look for profitable trading opportunities is in reaction to big news announcements or analysts' recommendations. If enough other investors are not paying attention, perhaps one can profit from these public sources of information.

Takeover Offers. One of the biggest news announcements for a firm, in terms of stock price impact, is when it is the target of a takeover offer. Typically, the offer is for a significant premium to the target's current stock price, and while the target's stock price typically jumps on the announcement, it often does not jump completely to the offer price. While it might seem that this difference creates a profitable trading opportunity, in most cases there is usually remaining uncertainty regarding whether the deal will occur at the initially offered price, at a higher price, or fail to occur at all. Figure 13.5 shows the average response to many such takeover announcements, showing the target stock's **cumulative abnormal return**, which measures the stock's return relative to that predicted based on its beta, at the time of the event. Figure 13.5 reveals that the initial jump in the stock price is high enough so that the stock's future returns do not outperform the market, on average. However, if we *could* predict whether the firm would ultimately be acquired, we could earn profits trading on that information.

Stock Recommendations. We could also consider stock recommendations. For example, popular commentator Jim Cramer makes numerous stock recommendations on his evening television show, *Mad Money*. Do investors profit from following these recommendations? Figure 13.6 shows the results of a recent study that analyzed the average stock price reaction to these recommendations, based on whether the recommendation coincided with a news story about the company. In the case where there is news, it appears that the stock price correctly reflects this information the next day, and stays flat (relative to the market) subsequently. On the other hand, for the stocks without news, there appears to be a significant jump in the stock price the next day, but the stock price then tends to fall relative to the market, generating a negative alpha, over the next several weeks. The authors of the study found that the stocks without news tended to be smaller, less liquid stocks; it appears that the individual investors who buy these stocks based on the recommendation push the price too high. They appear to be subject to an overconfidence bias, trusting too much in Cramer's recommendation and not adequately taking into account the behavior

FIGURE 13.5

Returns to Holding Target Stocks Subsequent to Takeover Announcements

After the initial jump in the stock price at the time of the announcement, target stocks do not appear to earn abnormal subsequent returns on average. However, stocks that are ultimately acquired tend to appreciate and have positive alphas, while those that are not acquired have negative alphas. Thus, an investor could profit from correctly predicting the outcome.

Source: Adapted from M. Bradley, A. Desai, and E. H. Kim, "The Rationale Behind Interfirm Tender Offers: Information or Synergy?" *Journal of Financial Economics* 11 (1983): 183–206.

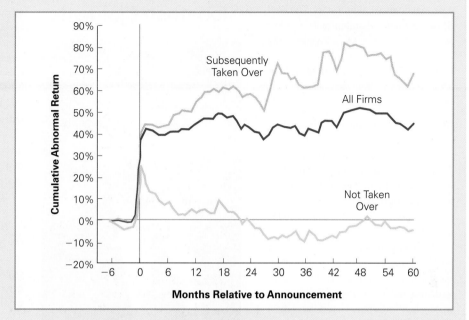

of their fellow investors. The more interesting question is why don't smart investors short these stocks and prevent the overreaction? In fact they do (the amount of short interest rises for these stocks), but because these small stocks are difficult to locate and borrow and therefore costly to short, the price does not correct immediately.

FIGURE 13.6

Stock Price Reactions to Recommendations on *Mad Money*

When recommendations coincide with news, the initial stock price reaction appears correct and future alphas are not significantly different from zero. Without news, the stock price appears to overreact. While sophisticated investors gain by shorting these stocks, costs of shorting limit their ability to do so.

Source: Adapted from J. Engelberg, C. Sasseville, J. Williams, "Market Madness? The Case of Mad Money," *Management Science*, 2011.

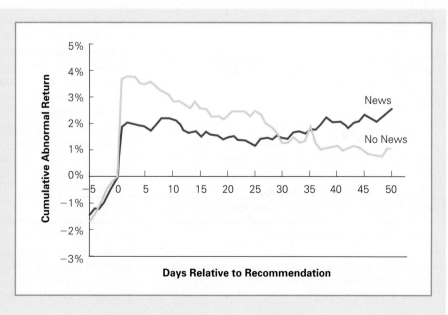

INTERVIEW WITH
Jonathan Clements

Jonathan Clements is the former personal finance columnist for *The Wall Street Journal* and author of *The Little Book of Main Street Money* (Wiley 2009).

QUESTION: *You have written for years on personal finance. How has academic theory influenced investor behavior?*

ANSWER: When I started writing about mutual funds in the 1980s, investors would ask, "What are the best funds?" Today, they are more likely to say, "I'm looking to add a foreign-stock fund to my portfolio. Which funds in that category do you like? Or should I index instead?"

We have gotten away from the blind pursuit of market-beating returns, and there is more focus on portfolio construction and a growing willingness to consider indexing. That reflects the impact of academic research.

What has really influenced investors has been the academic "grunt work" of the past four decades, which has given us a decent grasp of what historical market returns look like. Thanks to that research, many ordinary investors have a better understanding of how stocks have performed relative to bonds. They realize that most actively managed stock mutual funds don't beat the market, and thus, there is a case for indexing. They appreciate that different market sectors perform well at different times, so there is a real value in diversifying.

QUESTION: *Some have critiqued the idea of holding a well-diversified portfolio, arguing that diversification hasn't worked in the 2008–2009 financial crisis. Is diversification still the best strategy?*

ANSWER: Yes, when markets collapse, pretty much every sector gets bludgeoned. But just because investments rise and fall in sync with one another doesn't mean they rise and fall by the same amount. You might have a portfolio where one sector falls 40 percent and another loses 20 percent. Sure, losing 20 percent stings. Still, holding that sector is reducing your portfolio's overall loss, so you are indeed benefiting from diversification.

QUESTION: *Academics talk about efficient frontiers and optimal portfolios. How does that translate into advice for someone looking to build a portfolio?*

ANSWER: While academic research has influenced ordinary investors, we shouldn't overstate the case. To some extent, the research has merely codified what investors already knew intuitively. For instance, investors have always thought about risk as well as return, and they have always been inclined to diversify. The academic research may have made investors a little more rigorous in their thinking, but it didn't radically change their behavior.

Moreover, to the extent that the research doesn't fit with investors' intuition, they have clearly rejected it. Investors still behave in ways that academics would consider sub-optimal. They don't build well-diversified portfolios and then focus on the risk and return of the overall portfolio. Instead, they build moderately diversified portfolios—and then pay a lot of attention to the risk and reward of each investment they own.

QUESTION: *How does risk tolerance affect the type of portfolio a person should build?*

ANSWER: In theory, investors should hold the globally diversified all-asset "market portfolio" and then, depending on their risk tolerance, either add risk-free assets to reduce volatility or use leverage to boost returns. But almost nobody invests that way. In fact, I once tried to find out what the market portfolio looks like—and discovered nobody knows for sure.

Among the vast majority of ordinary investors, the idea of using leverage to buy investments is an anathema. In practice, many are doing just that. They hold a portfolio of assets, including stocks, bonds, and real estate, and they have a heap of debt, including their mortgage, auto loans, and credit-card balances. But the implication—that they effectively have a leveraged stock-market bet—would horrify most investors.

While nobody seems to know what the market portfolio looks like, investors have become willing to consider a broader array of assets, including foreign stocks, real-estate investment trusts, and commodities. I think the trend will continue, as people come to realize that they can lower a portfolio's risk level by adding apparently risky investments.

The Performance of Fund Managers

The previous results suggest that though it may not be easy to profit simply by trading on news, sophisticated investors might be able to do so (for example, by being better able to predict takeover outcomes, or short small stocks). Presumably, professional fund managers, such as those who manage mutual funds, should be in the best position to take advantage of such opportunities. Are they able to find profit-making opportunities in financial markets?

Fund Manager Value-Added. The answer is yes. Calculating a fund's gross alpha (before fees) and scaling it by the fund's assets under management (AUM) indicates that the average mutual fund manager is able to identify profitable trading opportunities worth approximately $2 million per year.[24]

Of course, the fact that the average mutual fund manager is able to find profitable trading opportunities does not imply that all managers do so. In fact, most cannot. The median mutual fund actually destroys value; that is, most fund managers appear to behave much like individual investors by trading so much that their trading costs exceed the profits from any trading opportunities they may find.

Returns to Investors. Do investors benefit by identifying the profit-making funds and investing in them? This time the answer is no—on average investors do not benefit from investing in actively managed mutual funds. As reported in Figure 13.7, typical studies find that the returns to investors of the average domestic U.S. equity fund has a negative alpha. While including funds that hold international stocks leads to an average alpha that is not significantly different from zero, all the studies consistently agree on one thing: on

FIGURE 13.7

Estimated Alphas for U.S. Mutual Funds (1975–2002)

The figure shows average annual alphas for mutual funds by fund type. For each category, the average fund has a negative estimated alpha.

Source: Adapted from R. Kosowski, A. Timmermann, R. Wermers, H. White, "Can Mutual Fund 'Stars' Really Pick Stocks? New Evidence from a Bootstrap Analysis," *Journal of Finance* 61 (2006): 2551–2596.

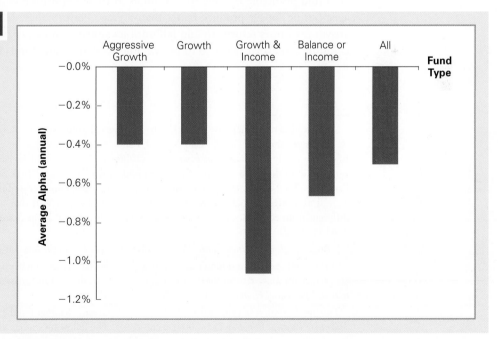

average actively managed mutual funds don't appear to provide superior returns for their investors compared to investing in passive index funds.[25]

Again, the fact that the average mutual fund has a negative alpha does not imply that all mutual funds do. Can investors identify funds that consistently deliver positive alphas to their investors? Morningstar ranks fund managers each year based on their historical performance. For example, Morningstar named Legg Mason's William Miller, whose performance we highlighted in the introduction to this chapter, as manager of the year in 1998 and manager of the decade the following year. As we have already noted, investors who were motivated to invest based on these awards saw poor performance over the next 10 years. Miller's experience is not exceptional. At the end of each year Forbes publishes an Honor Roll of top mutual funds based on an analysis of the past performance and riskiness of the fund. In a famous 1994 study, Vanguard CEO John Bogle compared the returns from investing in the market index with the returns from investing each year in the newly announced Honor Roll funds. Over a 19-year period, the Honor Roll portfolio had an annual return of 11.2%, whereas the market index fund had an annual return of 13.1%.[26] Thus, the superior past performance of these funds was not a good predictor of their future ability to outperform the market. Other studies have confirmed this result, and found little predictability in fund performance.[27]

While these results regarding mutual fund performance might seem surprising, they are consistent with a competitive capital market. If investors could predict that a skilled manager would generate a positive alpha in the future, they would rush to invest with this manager, who would then be flooded with capital. During Legg Mason manager William Miller's meteoric rise, his capital under management grew from about $700 million in 1992 to $28 billion in 2007. But the more capital the manager has to invest, the harder it is to find profitable trading opportunities. If these opportunities are exhausted, the manager can no longer produce better-than-average performance. Ultimately, as new capital arrives the fund's returns should fall until its alpha is no longer positive.[28] Indeed, alphas could be somewhat negative to reflect other benefits these funds provide, or could result

---

[25]Many studies report negative average alphas for mutual funds; see e.g., R. Kosowski, A. Timmermann, R. Wermers, and H. White, "Can Mutual Fund 'Stars' Really Pick Stocks? New Evidence from a Bootstrap Analysis," *Journal of Finance* 61 (2006): 2551–2596 and E. Fama, and K. French, "Luck versus Skill in the Cross Section of Mutual Fund Alpha Estimates," Tuck School of Business Working Paper No. 2009–2056. Using an expanded time period, and considering funds that hold international as well as domestic stocks, J. B. Berk and J. van Binsbergen, find that alphas are not significantly different from zero (*Measuring Managerial Skill in the Mutual Fund Industry*, NBER working paper #18184, 2012).

[26]J. Bogle, *Bogle on Mutual Funds: New Perspectives for the Intelligent Investor*, McGraw-Hill, 1994.

[27]One possible exception is fund fees—ironically, funds that charge a higher percentage fee seem to generate predictably *lower* returns for their investors. See M. Carhart, "On Persistence in Mutual Fund Performance," *Journal of Finance* 52 (1997): 57–82.

[28]This mechanism was proposed by J. Berk and R. Green, "Mutual Fund Flows in Rational Markets," *Journal of Political Economy* 112 (2004): 1269–1295. The following studies all find that new capital flows into funds that do well and out of funds that do poorly: M. Gruber, "Another Puzzle: The Growth in Actively Managed Mutual Funds," *Journal of Finance* 51 (1996): 783–810; E. Sirri and P. Tufano, "Costly Search and Mutual Fund Flows," *Journal of Finance* 53 (1998): 1589–1622; J. Chevalier and G. Ellison, "Risk Taking by Mutual Funds as a Response to Incentives," *Journal of Political Economy* 105 (1997): 1167–1200.

from overconfidence. Investors put too much confidence in their ability to select fund managers and thus commit too much capital to them.[29]

The argument above suggests that when investors identify skilled managers, they should flock to them, so that these managers will manage the largest funds. Consequently, fund size is a strong predictor of the future value added by fund managers.[30] So while investors appear to be good at picking managers, in the end they derive little benefit, because this superior performance is captured by the manager in the form of fees—mutual funds charge approximately the same percentage fee, so the larger funds collect higher aggregate fees. This result is exactly as we should expect: In a competitive labor market, the fund manager should capture the economic rents associated with his or her unique skill.

In summary, while the profits of mutual fund managers imply it is possible to find profitable trading opportunities in markets, being able to do so consistently is a rare talent possessed by only the most skilled fund managers.

Researchers have obtained similar results when evaluating institutional fund managers responsible for managing retirement plans, pension funds, and endowment assets. A study investigating the hiring decisions of plan sponsors found that sponsors picked managers that had significantly outperformed their benchmarks historically (see Figure 13.8). Once

FIGURE 13.8   **Before and After Hiring Returns of Investment Managers**

While plan sponsors tend to hire managers that have significantly outperformed their benchmarks historically, after-hiring performance is similar to the excess return of the average fund (0.64% on a value-weighted basis). Data based on 8755 hiring decisions of 3400 plan sponsors from 1994–2003, and returns are gross of management fees (which tend to range from 0.5%–0.7%/year).

Sources: A. Goyal and S. Wahal, "The Selection and Termination of Investment Management Firms by Plan Sponsors," *Journal of Finance* 63 (2008): 1805–1847 and with J. Busse, "Performance and Persistence in Institutional Investment Management," *Journal of Finance* 63 (2008): 1805–1847.

---

[29]In Miller's case most investors paid dearly for their confidence in him—although his losses post-2007 equaled his gains from 1992, most investors were not invested in 1992, and so they experienced overall performance that lagged the S&P 500. Not surprisingly, after 2007 he experienced large capital outflows, so by the end of 2008 he had only about $1.2 billion under management.

[30]J. B. Berk and J. van Binsbergen, *Measuring Managerial Skill in the Mutual Fund Industry*, NBER working paper #18184 (2012).

hired, however, the performance of these new managers looked very similar to the average fund, with returns exceeding their benchmarks by an amount roughly equal to their management fees.

The Winners and Losers

The evidence in this section suggests that while it may be possible to improve on the market portfolio, it isn't easy. This result is perhaps not so surprising, for as we noted in Section 13.2, the average investor (on a value-weighted basis) earns an alpha of zero, *before* including trading costs. So beating the market should require special skills, such as better analysis of information, or lower trading costs.

Because individual investors are likely to be at a disadvantage on both counts, as well as subject to behavioral biases, the CAPM wisdom that investors should "hold the market" is probably the best advice for most people. Indeed, a comprehensive study of the Taiwan stock market found that individual investors there lose an average of 3.8% per year by trading, with roughly 1/3 of the losses due to poor trades and the remaining 2/3 due to transactions costs.[31]

The same study reported that institutions earn 1.5% per year on average from their trades. But while professional fund managers may profit due to their talent, information, and superior trading infrastructure, the results in this section suggest that little of those profits go to the investors who invest with them.

CONCEPT CHECK

1. Should uninformed investors expect to make money by trading based on news announcements?

2. If fund managers are talented, why do the returns of their funds to investors not have positive alphas?

13.6 Style-Based Techniques and the Market Efficiency Debate

In Section 13.5, we looked for evidence that professional investors could profit at small investors' expense and outperform the market. In this section, we will take a different tack. Rather than looking at managers' profits, we will look at possible *trading strategies*. In particular, many fund managers distinguish their trading strategies based on the types of stocks they tend to hold; specifically, small versus large stocks, and value versus growth stocks. In this section, we will consider these alternative investment styles, and see whether some strategies have generated higher returns historically than the CAPM predicts.

Size Effects

As we reported in Chapter 10, small stocks (those with smaller market capitalizations) have historically earned higher average returns than the market portfolio. Moreover, while small stocks do tend to have high market risk, their returns appear high even accounting for their higher beta, an empirical result we call the **size effect**.

---

[31]Taiwan provides a unique opportunity to study how profits are distributed, because unlike the U.S., the identity of buyers and sellers is tracked for all trades. See B. Barber, Y. Lee, Y. Liu, and T. Odean, "Just How Much Do Individual Investors Lose by Trading?" *Review of Financial Studies* 22 (2009): 609–632.

Excess Return and Market Capitalizations. To compare the performance of portfolios formed based on size, researchers Eugene Fama and Kenneth French[32] divided stocks each year into ten portfolios by ranking them based on their market capitalizations, and collecting the smallest 10% of stocks into the first portfolio, the next 10% into the second portfolio, up to the biggest 10% into the tenth portfolio. They then recorded the monthly excess returns of each decile portfolio over the following year. After repeating this process for each year, they calculated the average excess return of each portfolio and the beta of the portfolio; Figure 13.9 shows the result. As you can see, although the portfolios with higher betas yield higher returns, most portfolios plot above the security market line (SML)—all except one portfolio had a positive alpha. The smallest deciles exhibit the most extreme effect.

Of course, this result could be due to estimation error; as the figure shows, the standard errors are large and none of the alpha estimates is significantly different from zero. However, nine of the ten portfolios plot above the SML. If the positive alphas were due purely to statistical error, we would expect as many portfolios to appear above the line as below it.

| FIGURE 13.9 | **Excess Return of Size Portfolios, 1926–2011** |

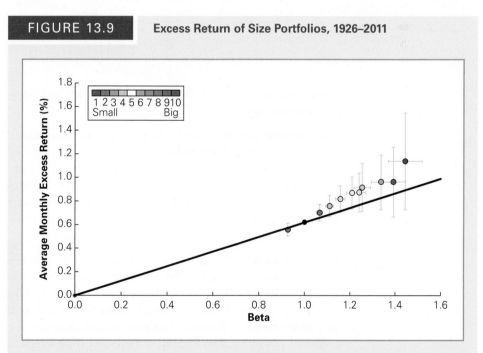

The plot shows the average monthly excess return (the return minus the one-month risk-free rate) for ten portfolios formed in each year based on firms' market capitalizations, plotted as a function of the portfolio's estimated beta. The black line is the security market line. If the market portfolio is efficient and there is no measurement error, all portfolios would plot along this line. The error bars mark the 95% confidence bands of the beta and expected excess return estimates. Note the tendency of small stocks to be above the security market line.

Source: Data courtesy of Kenneth French.

---

[32]See E. Fama and K. French, "The Cross-Section of Stock Returns," *Journal of Finance* 47 (1992): 427–465.

FIGURE 13.10

Excess Return of Book-to-Market Portfolios, 1926–2011

The plot shows the same data as Figure 13.9, with portfolios formed based on stocks' book-to-market ratios rather than size. Note the tendency of value stocks (high book-to-market) to be above the security market line, and growth stocks (low book-to-market) to be near or below the line.

Source: Data courtesy of Kenneth French.

Consequently, a test of whether the alphas of all ten portfolios are jointly all equal to zero can be statistically rejected.

Excess Return and Book-to-Market Ratio. Researchers have found similar results using the **book-to-market ratio**, the ratio of the book value of equity to the market value of equity, to form stocks into portfolios. Recall from Chapter 2 that practitioners refer to stocks with high book-to-market ratios as value stocks, and those with low book-to-market ratios as growth stocks. Figure 13.10 demonstrates that value stocks tend to have positive alphas, and growth stocks tend to have low or negative alphas. Once again, a joint test of whether all 10 portfolios have an alpha of zero is rejected.

Size Effects and Empirical Evidence. The size effect—the observation that small stocks (or stocks with a high book-to-market ratio) have positive alphas—was first discovered in 1981 by Rolf Banz.[33] At the time, researchers did not find the evidence to be convincing because financial economists had been *searching* the data, looking for stocks with positive alphas. Because of estimation error, it is always possible to find stocks with estimated positive alphas; indeed, if we look hard enough, it is also always possible to find something these stocks have in common. As a consequence, many researchers were inclined to attribute Banz's findings to a **data snooping bias**, which is the idea that given enough characteristics, it will always be possible to find some characteristic that by pure chance happens to be correlated with the estimation error of average returns.[34]

---

[33]See R. Banz, "The Relationship between Return and Market Values of Common Stock," *Journal of Financial Economics* 9 (1981): 3–18. A similar relation between stock price (rather than size) and future returns was found by M. Blume and F. Husic, "Price, Beta and Exchange Listing," *Journal of Finance* 28 (1973): 283–299.

[34]David Leinweber, in his book *Nerds on Wall Street* (Wiley Financial, 2008), illustrates this point by searching the data for a patently absurd characteristic that is correlated with returns. He found that over a 13-year period annual butter production in Bangladesh can "explain" annual variation in S&P 500 returns!

After the publication of Banz's study, however, a theoretical reason emerged that explained the relationship between market capitalization and expected returns. Financial economists realized that as long as beta is not a *perfect* measure of risk—either due to estimation error, or because the market portfolio is not efficient—we should *expect* to observe the size effect.[35] To understand why, consider a stock with a positive alpha. All else equal, a positive alpha implies that the stock also has a relatively high expected return. A higher expected return implies a lower price—the only way to offer a higher expected return is for investors to buy the stock's dividend stream at a lower price. A lower price means a lower market capitalization (and similarly a higher book-to-market ratio—market capitalization is in the *denominator* of the book-to-market ratio). Thus, when a financial economist forms a portfolio of stocks with low market capitalizations (or high book-to-market ratios), that collection contains stocks that will likely have higher expected returns and, if the market portfolio is not efficient, positive alphas. Similarly, a stock that plots below the security market line will have a lower expected return and, all else equal, a higher price, implying that it has a higher market capitalization and lower book-to-market ratio. Hence a portfolio of stocks with high market capitalizations or low book-to-market ratios will have negative alphas if the market portfolio is not efficient. Let's illustrate with a simple example.

EXAMPLE 13.2   **Risk and the Market Value of Equity**

Problem

Consider two firms, SM Industries and BiG Corporation, which are expected to pay dividends of $1 million per year in perpetuity. SM's dividend stream is riskier than BiG's, so its cost of capital is 14% per year. BiG's cost of capital is 10%. Which firm has the higher market value? Which firm has the higher expected return? Now assume both stocks have the same estimated beta, either because of estimation error, or because the market portfolio is not efficient. Based on this beta, the CAPM would assign an expected return of 12% to both stocks. How do the market values of the firms relate to their alphas?

Solution

The timeline of dividends is the same for both firms:

To calculate the market value of SM, we calculate the present value of its future expected dividends using the perpetuity formula and a cost of capital of 14%:

$$\text{Market Value of SM} = \frac{1}{0.14} = \$7.143 \text{ million}$$

Similarly, the market value of BiG is

$$\text{Market Value of BiG} = \frac{1}{0.10} = \$10 \text{ million}$$

---

[35]See J. Berk, "A Critique of Size-Related Anomalies," *Review of Financial Studies* 8 (1995): 275–286.

SM has the lower market value, and a higher expected return (14% vs. 10%). It also has the higher alpha:

$$\alpha_{SM} = 0.14 - 0.12 = 2\%$$

$$\alpha_{BiG} = 0.10 - 0.12 = -2\%$$

Consequently, the firm with the lower market value has the higher alpha.

When the market portfolio is not efficient, theory predicts that stocks with low market capitalizations or high book-to-market ratios will have positive alphas. In light of this observation, the size effect is, indeed, potential evidence against the efficiency of the market portfolio.

Momentum

Researchers have also used past stock returns to form portfolios with positive alphas. For example, for the years 1965 to 1989, Narishiman Jegadeesh and Sheridan Titman[36] ranked stocks each month by their realized returns over the prior 6–12 months. They found that the best-performing stocks had positive alphas over the next 3–12 months. This evidence goes against the CAPM: When the market portfolio is efficient, past returns should not predict alphas.

Investors can exploit this result by buying stocks that have had past high returns and (short) selling stocks that have had past low returns, which is called a **momentum strategy**. Jegadeesh and Titman showed that over the period 1965–1989, this strategy would have produced an alpha of over 12% per year.

Implications of Positive-Alpha Trading Strategies

Over the years since the discovery of the CAPM, it has become increasingly clear to researchers and practitioners alike that by forming portfolios based on market capitalization, book-to-market ratios, and past returns, investors can construct trading strategies that have a positive alpha. Given these results, we are left to draw one of two conclusions:

1. Investors are systematically ignoring positive-NPV investment opportunities. That is, the CAPM correctly computes required risk premiums, but investors are ignoring opportunities to earn extra returns without bearing any extra risk, either because they are unaware of them or because the costs to implement the strategies are larger than the NPV of undertaking them.

2. The positive-alpha trading strategies contain risk that investors are unwilling to bear but the CAPM does not capture. That is, a stock's beta with the market portfolio does not adequately measure a stock's systematic risk, and so the CAPM does not correctly compute the risk premium.

The only way a positive-NPV opportunity can persist in a market is if some barrier to entry restricts competition. In this case, it is very difficult to identify what these barriers might be. The existence of these trading strategies has been widely known for more than 15 years. Not only is the information required to form the portfolios readily available, but

---

[36]See N. Jegadeesh and S. Titman, "Returns to Buying Winners and Selling Losers: Implications for Market Efficiency," *Journal of Finance* 48 (1993): 65–91.

Market Efficiency and the Efficiency of the Market Portfolio

In Chapter 9 we introduced the *efficient markets hypothesis*, which states that competition should eliminate positive-NPV trading opportunities or, equivalently, that securities with equivalent risk should have the same expected return. But because "equivalent risk" is not well defined, we cannot test the efficient markets hypothesis directly. The risk measure is well defined under the CAPM assumptions, however, and thus we can test the idea that no positive-NPV trading opportunities exist in the CAPM by testing whether the market portfolio is efficient and all trading strategies have zero alpha.

Some researchers further categorize such tests as tests of *weak form*, *semi-strong form*, and *strong form efficiency*. **Weak form efficiency** states that it should not be possible to profit by trading on information in past prices by, for example, selling winners and hanging on to losers or, conversely, by trading on momentum. **Semi-strong form efficiency** states that it should not be possible to consistently profit by trading on any public information, such as news announcements or analysts' recommendations. Finally **strong form efficiency** states that it should not be possible to consistently profit even by trading on private information.

Note that the efficient markets hypothesis does *not* state that market prices are always correct given *future* information. For example, the 2008 financial crisis made clear that the share prices of many banks and other firms were overvalued in 2007. Given this information, selling bank stocks in 2007 would have been a positive-NPV trading opportunity. But this fact on its own does not contradict market efficiency. We would need to demonstrate that the financial crisis was easily predictable in 2007, and that many investors profited by trading on that knowledge. The scarcity of "winners" in the wake of the financial crisis makes clear that this prediction was by no means obvious at the time. Indeed, the trader most famous for anticipating the banking crisis by shorting mortgage-backed securities, John Paulson, has had mediocre performance since then, with his Advantage Plus fund recording a *52% loss* in 2011, suggesting, perhaps, that his earlier bet might have had to do more with luck, and a healthy appetite for risk, rather than skill.

As the evidence in this chapter makes clear, when we use the CAPM to measure risk, the evidence for market efficiency is mixed: individual investors don't seem to "beat the market" on average, yet at the same time certain trading strategies do appear to be profitable. The key question facing finance researchers is how to correctly measure risk. Do these "profitable" strategies entail systematic risks not identified by the CAPM—making them fairly priced according to some more general model of risk than the CAPM? Or do they represent a true opportunity to earn higher returns without increasing risk?

---

many mutual funds follow momentum-based and market capitalization/book-to-market–based strategies. Hence, the first conclusion does not seem likely.

That leaves the second possibility: The market portfolio is not efficient, and therefore a stock's beta with the market is not an adequate measure of its systematic risk. Stated another way, the profits (positive alphas) from the trading strategy are really returns for bearing risk that investors are averse to and the CAPM does not capture. There are several reasons why the market portfolio might not be efficient. Let's examine each possibility in turn.

Proxy Error. The true market portfolio may be efficient, but the proxy we have used for it may be inaccurate. The true market portfolio consists of all traded investment wealth in the economy, including bonds, real estate, art, precious metals, and so on. We cannot include most of these investments in the market proxy because competitive price data is not available. Consequently, standard proxies like the S&P 500 may be inefficient compared with the true market, and stocks will have nonzero alphas.[37] In this case, the

---

[37]When the true market portfolio is efficient, even a small difference between the proxy and true market portfolio can lead to an insignificant relation between beta and returns. See R. Roll and S. Ross, "On the Cross-Sectional Relation between Expected Returns and Beta," *Journal of Finance* 49 (1) (1994): 101–121.

alphas merely indicate that the wrong proxy is being used; they do not indicate forgone positive-NPV investment opportunities.[38]

Behavioral Biases. As we discussed in Section 13.4, some investors may be subject to systematic behavioral biases. For example, they may be attracted to large growth stocks that receive greater news coverage. Or they may sell winners and hang on to losers, following a contrarian strategy. By falling prey to these biases, these investors are holding inefficient portfolios. More sophisticated investors hold an efficient portfolio, but because supply must equal demand, this efficient portfolio must include more small, value, and momentum stocks to offset the trades of biased investors. While alphas are zero with respect to this efficient portfolio, they are positive when compared with the market portfolio (which is the combined holdings of the biased and sophisticated investors).

Alternative Risk Preferences and Non-Tradable Wealth. Investors may also choose inefficient portfolios because they care about risk characteristics other than the volatility of their traded portfolio. For example, they may be attracted to investments with skewed distributions that have a small probability of an extremely high payoff. As a result, they might be willing to hold some diversifiable risk in order to obtain such a payoff. In addition, investors are exposed to other significant risks outside their portfolio that are not tradable, the most important of which is due to their human capital.[39] For example, a banker at Goldman Sachs is exposed to financial sector risk, while a software engineer is exposed to risk in the high-tech sector. When choosing a portfolio, investors may deviate from the market portfolio to offset these inherent exposures.[40]

It is important to appreciate that just because the market portfolio is not efficient, this does not rule out the possibility of *another* portfolio being efficient. In fact, as we pointed out in Chapter 11, the CAPM pricing relationship holds with *any* efficient portfolio. Consequently, in light of the evidence against the efficiency of the market portfolio, researchers have developed alternative models of risk and return that do not rely on the efficiency of the market portfolio in particular. We develop such a model in Section 13.7.

CONCEPT CHECK

1. What does the existence of a positive-alpha trading strategy imply?

2. If investors have a significant amount of non-tradable (but risky) wealth, why might the market portfolio not be efficient?

---

[38]Because we cannot actually construct the *true* market portfolio of *all* risky investments, the CAPM theory is in some sense untestable (see R. Roll, "A Critique of the Asset Pricing Theory's Tests," *Journal of Financial Economics* 4 (1977): 129–176). Of course, from a corporate manager's perspective, whether the CAPM is testable is irrelevant—as long as an efficient portfolio can be identified, he or she can use it to compute the cost of capital.

[39]Although rare, there are innovative new markets that allow people to trade their human capital to finance their education; see M. Palacios, *Investing in Human Capital: A Capital Markets Approach to Student Funding*, Cambridge University Press, 2004.

[40]Indeed, human capital risk can explain some of the inefficiency of common market proxies. See R. Jagannathan and Z. Wang, "The Conditional CAPM and the Cross-Sections of Expected Returns," *Journal of Finance* 51 (1996): 3–53; and I. Palacios-Huerta, "The Robustness of the Conditional CAPM with Human Capital," *Journal of Financial Econometrics* 1 (2003): 272–289.

13.7 Multifactor Models of Risk

In Chapter 11, we presented the expected return of any marketable security as a function of the expected return of the efficient portfolio:

$$E[R_s] = r_f + \beta_s^{eff} \times (E[R_{eff}] - r_f) \tag{13.3}$$

When the market portfolio is not efficient, to use Eq.13.3 we need to find an alternative method to identify an efficient portfolio.

As a practical matter, it is extremely difficult to identify portfolios that are efficient because we cannot measure the expected return and the standard deviation of a portfolio with great accuracy. Yet, although we might not be able to identify the efficient portfolio itself, we do know some characteristics of the efficient portfolio. First, any efficient portfolio will be well diversified. Second, we can construct an efficient portfolio from other well-diversified portfolios. This latter observation may seem trivial, but it is actually quite useful: It implies that *it is not actually necessary to identify the efficient portfolio itself.* As long as we can identify a *collection* of well-diversified portfolios from which an efficient portfolio can be constructed, we can use the collection itself to measure risk.

Using Factor Portfolios

Assume that we have identified portfolios that we can combine to form an efficient portfolio; we call these portfolios **factor portfolios**. Then, as we show in the appendix, if we use N factor portfolios with returns $R_{F1}, \ldots, R_{FN}$, the expected return of asset s is given by

Multifactor Model of Risk

$$E[R_s] = r_f + \beta_s^{F1}(E[R_{F1}] - r_f) + \beta_s^{F2}(E[R_{F2}] - r_f) + \cdots + \beta_s^{FN}(E[R_{FN}] - r_f)$$

$$= r_f + \sum_{n=1}^{N} \beta_s^{Fn}(E[R_{Fn}] - r_f) \tag{13.4}$$

Here $\beta_s^{F1}, \ldots, \beta_s^{FN}$ are the **factor betas**, one for each risk factor, and have the same interpretation as the beta in the CAPM. Each factor beta is the expected % change in the excess return of a security for a 1% change in the excess return of the factor portfolio (holding the other factors constant).

Equation 13.4 says that we can write the risk premium of any marketable security as the sum of the risk premium of each factor multiplied by the sensitivity of the stock with that factor—the *factor betas*. There is nothing inconsistent between Eq.13.4, which gives the expected return in terms of multiple factors, and Eq.13.3, which gives the expected return in terms of just the efficient portfolio. *Both* equations hold; the difference between them is simply the portfolios that we use. When we use an efficient portfolio, it alone will capture all systematic risk. Consequently, we often refer to this model as a **single-factor model**. If we use multiple portfolios as factors, then together these factors will capture all systematic risk, but note that each factor in Eq.13.4 captures different components of the systematic risk. When we use more than one portfolio to capture risk, the model is known as a **multifactor model**. Each portfolio can be interpreted as either a risk factor itself or a portfolio of stocks correlated with an unobservable risk factor.[41] The model is also referred to as the **Arbitrage Pricing Theory (APT)**.

We can simplify Eq.13.4 a bit further. Think of the expected excess return of each factor, $E[R_{Fn}] - r_f$, as the expected return of a portfolio in which we borrow the funds at rate r_f to invest in the factor portfolio. Because this portfolio costs nothing to construct (we are borrowing the funds to invest), it is called a **self-financing portfolio**. We can also construct a self-financing portfolio by going long some stocks, and going short other stocks with equal market value. In general, a self-financing portfolio is any portfolio with portfolio weights that sum to zero rather than one. If we require that all factor portfolios are self-financing (either by borrowing funds or shorting stocks), then we can rewrite Eq.13.4 as

Multifactor Model of Risk with Self-Financing Portfolios

$$E[R_s] = r_f + \beta_s^{F1}E[R_{F1}] + \beta_s^{F2}E[R_{F2}] + \cdots + \beta_s^{FN}E[R_{FN}]$$

$$= r_f + \sum_{n=1}^{N}\beta_s^{Fn}E[R_{Fn}] \tag{13.5}$$

To recap, it is possible to calculate the cost of capital without actually identifying the efficient portfolio using a multifactor risk model. Rather than relying on the efficiency of a single portfolio (such as the market), multifactor models rely on the weaker condition that we can construct an efficient portfolio from a collection of well-diversified portfolios or factors. We next explain how to select the factors.

Selecting the Portfolios

The most obvious portfolio to use when identifying a collection of portfolios that contain the efficient portfolio is the market portfolio itself. Historically, the market portfolio has commanded a large premium over short-term risk-free investments, such as Treasury bills. Even if the market portfolio is not efficient, it still captures many components of systematic risk. As Figures 13.9 and 13.10 demonstrate, even when the model fails, portfolios with higher average returns *do* tend to have higher betas. Thus, the first portfolio in the collection is a self-financing portfolio that consists of a long position in the market portfolio that is financed by a short position in the risk-free security.

How do we go about picking the other portfolios? As we pointed out earlier, trading strategies based on market capitalization, book-to-market ratios, and momentum appear to have positive alphas, meaning that the portfolios that implement the trading strategy capture risk that is not captured by the market portfolio. Hence, these portfolios are good candidates for the other portfolios in a multifactor model. We will construct three additional portfolios out of these trading strategies: The first trading strategy selects stocks based on their market capitalization, the second uses the book-to-market ratio, and the third uses past returns.

Market Capitalization Strategy. Each year, we place firms into one of two portfolios based on their market value of equity: Firms with market values below the median of NYSE firms form an equally weighted portfolio, S, and firms above the median market value form an equally weighted portfolio, B. A trading strategy that each year buys portfolio S

[41]This form of the multifactor model was originally developed by Stephen Ross, although Robert Merton had developed an alternative multifactor model earlier. See S. Ross, "The Arbitrage Theory of Capital Asset Pricing," *Journal of Economic Theory* 13 (1976): 341–360; and R. Merton, "An Intertemporal Capital Asset Pricing Model," *Econometrica* 41 (1973): 867–887.

(small stocks) and finances this position by short selling portfolio B (big stocks) has produced positive risk-adjusted returns historically. This self-financing portfolio is widely known as the **small-minus-big (SMB) portfolio**.

Book-to-Market Ratio Strategy. A second trading strategy that has produced positive risk-adjusted returns historically uses the book-to-market ratio to select stocks. Each year firms with book-to-market ratios less than the 30th percentile of NYSE firms form an equally weighted portfolio called the low portfolio, L. Firms with book-to-market ratios greater than the 70th percentile of NYSE firms form an equally weighted portfolio called the high portfolio, H. A trading strategy that each year takes a long position in portfolio H, which it finances with a short position in portfolio L, has produced positive risk-adjusted returns. We add this self-financing portfolio (high minus low book-to-market stocks) to our collection and call it the **high-minus-low (HML) portfolio** (we can also think of this portfolio as long value stocks, and short growth stocks).

Past Returns Strategy. The third trading strategy is a momentum strategy. Each year we rank stocks by their return over the last one year,[42] and construct a portfolio that goes long the top 30% of stocks and short the bottom 30%. This trading strategy requires holding this portfolio for a year; we then form a new self-financing portfolio and hold it for another year. We repeat this process annually. The resulting self-financing portfolio is known as the **prior one-year momentum (PR1YR) portfolio**.

Fama-French-Carhart Factor Specification. The collection of these four portfolios—the excess return of the market ($Mkt - r_f$), SMB, HML, and PR1YR—is currently the most popular choice for the multifactor model. Using this collection, the expected return of security s is given by:

Fama-French-Carhart Factor Specification

$$E[R_s] = r_f + \beta_s^{Mkt}(E[R_{Mkt}] - r_f) + \beta_s^{SMB}E[R_{SMB}]$$

$$+ \beta_s^{HML}E[R_{HML}] + \beta_s^{PR1YR}E[R_{PR1YR}] \qquad (13.6)$$

where β_s^{Mkt}, β_s^{SMB}, β_s^{HML}, and β_s^{PR1YR} are the factor betas of stock s and measure the sensitivity of the stock to each portfolio. Because the four portfolios in Eq. 13.6 were identified by Eugene Fama, Kenneth French, and Mark Carhart, we will refer to this collection of portfolios as the **Fama-French-Carhart (FFC) factor specification**.

The Cost of Capital with Fama-French-Carhart Factor Specification

Multifactor models have a distinct advantage over single-factor models in that it is much easier to identify a collection of portfolios that captures systematic risk than just a single portfolio. They also have an important disadvantage, however: We must estimate the expected return of *each* portfolio. Because expected returns are not easy to estimate, each portfolio we add to the collection increases the difficulty of implementing the model. This task is especially complex because it is unclear *which* economic risk the portfolios capture, so we cannot hope to come up with a reasonable estimate of what the return should be

---

[42]Because of short-term trading effects, the most recent month's return is often dropped, so we actually use an 11-month return.

(as we did with the CAPM) based on an economic argument. To implement the model, we have little choice other than to use historical average returns on the portfolios.[43]

Because the returns on the FFC portfolios are so volatile, we use over 80 years of data to estimate the expected return. Table 13.1 shows the monthly average return as well as the 95% confidence bands of the FFC portfolios (we use a value-weighted portfolio of all NYSE, AMEX, and NASDAQ stocks as the proxy for the market portfolio). Even with 80 years of data, however, all of the estimates of the expected returns are imprecise.

TABLE 13.1	FFC Portfolio Average Monthly Returns, 1927–2012	
Factor Portfolio	Average Monthly Return (%)	95% Confidence Band (%)
Mkt $-r_f$	0.61	±0.34
SMB	0.25	±0.20
HML	0.38	±0.22
PR1YR	0.70	±0.29

Source: Kenneth French http://mba.tuck.dartmouth.edu/pages/faculty/ken.french/data_library.html

---

EXAMPLE 13.3   **Using the FFC Factor Specification to Calculate the Cost of Capital**

Problem

You are considering making an investment in a project in the fast food industry. You determine that the project has the same level of non-diversifiable risk as investing in McDonald's stock. Determine the cost of capital by using the FFC factor specification.

Solution

You decide to use data over the past nine years to estimate the factor betas of McDonald's stock (ticker: MCD). Therefore, you regress the monthly excess return (the realized return in each month minus the risk-free rate) of McDonald's stock on the return of each portfolio. The coefficient estimates are the factor betas. Here are the estimates of the four factor betas and their 95% confidence interval based on data from years 2003 through 2011:

Factor	Beta Estimate	Lower 95%	Upper 95%
Mkt	0.687	0.449	0.926
SMB	−0.299	−0.725	0.127
HML	−0.156	−0.561	0.249
PR1YR	0.123	−0.068	0.314

Using these estimates and a risk-free monthly rate of 1.5%/12 = 0.125%, you can calculate the monthly expected return for investing in McDonald's stock:

---

[43]There is a second, more subtle disadvantage to most factor models. Because factor models are designed to price traded securities, there is no guarantee that they will accurately price risks that are not currently traded (e.g., the risk associated with a new technology). In practice, it is assumed that any non-traded risk is idiosyncratic, and therefore does not command a risk premium.

$$E[R_{MCD}] = r_f + \beta_{MCD}^{Mkt}(E[R_{Mkt}] - r_f) + \beta_{MCD}^{SMB}E[R_{SMB}] + \beta_{MCD}^{HML}E[R_{HML}] + \beta_{MCD}^{PR1YR}E[R_{PR1YR}]$$

$$= 0.125\% + 0.687 \times 0.61\% - 0.299 \times 0.25\% - 0.156 \times 0.38\% + 0.123 \times 0.70\%$$

$$= 0.496\%$$

Expressed as an APR, the expected return is $0.496\% \times 12 = 5.95\%$. Thus, the annual cost of capital of the investment opportunity is about 6%. (Note, however the substantial uncertainty both in the factor betas and their expected returns.)

As a comparison, a standard CAPM regression over the same time period leads to an estimated market beta of 0.54 for McDonald's—the market beta differs from the estimate of 0.687 above because we are using only a single factor in the CAPM regression. Using the historical excess return on the market implies an expected return of $0.125\% + 0.54 \times 0.61\% = 0.454\%$ per month, or about 5.5% per year.

The FFC factor specification was identified a little more than 20 years ago. Although it is widely used in academic literature to measure risk, much debate persists about whether it really is a significant improvement over the CAPM.[44] The one area where researchers have found that the FFC factor specification does appear to do better than the CAPM is measuring the risk of actively managed mutual funds. Researchers have found that funds with high returns in the past have positive alphas under the CAPM.[45] When Mark Carhart repeated the same test using the FFC factor specification to compute alphas, he found no evidence that mutual funds with high past returns had future positive alphas.[46]

CONCEPT CHECK

1. What is the advantage of a multifactor model over a single factor model?

2. How can you use the Fama-French-Carhart factor specification to estimate the cost of capital?

13.8 Methods Used in Practice

Given the evidence for and against the efficiency of the market portfolio, what method do managers actually use to calculate the cost of capital? A survey of 392 CFOs conducted by John Graham and Campbell Harvey found that 73.5% of the firms that they questioned use the CAPM to calculate the cost of capital, as indicated in Figure 13.11. They also found that larger firms were more likely to use the CAPM than were smaller firms.

What about the other methods? Among the firms Graham and Harvey surveyed, only about one-third reported using a multifactor model to calculate the cost of capital. Two other methods that some firms in the survey reported using are historical average returns (40%) and the dividend discount model (16%). By dividend discount model, practitioners mean Eq. 9.7 in Chapter 9: They estimate the firm's expected future growth rate and add the current dividend yield to determine the stock's expected total return.

---

[44]See M. Cooper, R. Gutierrez, Jr., and B. Marcum, "On the Predictability of Stock Returns in Real Time," *Journal of Business* 78 (2005): 469–500.

[45]See M. Grinblatt and S. Titman, "The Persistence of Mutual Fund Performance," *Journal of Finance* 47 (1992): 1977–1984; and D. Hendricks, J. Patel, and R. Zeckhauser, "Hot Hands in Mutual Funds: Short-Run Persistence of Performance 1974–1988," *Journal of Finance* 4 (1993): 93–130.

[46]See M. Carhart, "On Persistence in Mutual Fund Performance," *Journal of Finance* 52 (1997): 57–82.

| FIGURE 13.11 | **How Firms Calculate the Cost of Capital** |

The figure shows the percentage of firms that use the CAPM, multifactor models, the historical average return, and the dividend discount model. The dividend discount model was presented in Chapter 9.

Source: J. R. Graham and C. R. Harvey, "The Theory and Practice of Corporate Finance: Evidence from the Field," *Journal of Financial Economics* 60 (2001): 187–243.

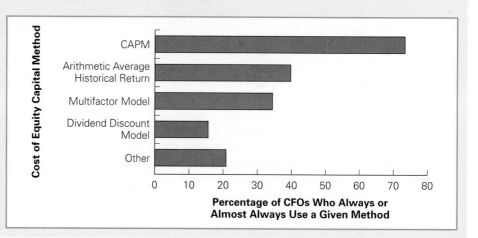

In short, there is no clear answer to the question of which technique is used to measure risk in practice—it very much depends on the organization and the sector. It is not difficult to see why there is so little consensus in practice about which technique to use. *All the techniques we covered are imprecise.* Financial economics has not yet reached the point where we can provide a theory of expected returns that gives a precise estimate of the cost of capital. Consider, too, that all techniques are not equally simple to implement. Because the trade-off between simplicity and precision varies across sectors, practitioners apply the techniques that best suit their particular circumstances.

When making a capital budgeting decision, the cost of capital is just one of several imprecise estimates that go into the NPV calculation. Indeed, in many cases, the imprecision in the cost of capital estimate is less important than the imprecision in the estimate of future cash flows. Often the least complicated models to implement are used most often. In this regard, the CAPM has the dual virtues of being both simple to implement and reasonably reliable.

CONCEPT CHECK

1. Which is the most popular method used by corporations to calculate the cost of capital?

2. What other techniques do corporations use to calculate the cost of capital?

MyFinanceLab

Here is what you should know after reading this chapter. MyFinanceLab will help you identify what you know and where to go when you need to practice.

13.1 Competition and Capital Markets

- The difference between a stock's expected return and its required return according to the security market line is the stock's alpha:

$$\alpha_s = E[R_s] - r_s \tag{13.2}$$

- While the CAPM conclusion that the market is always efficient may not literally be true, competition among savvy investors who try to "beat the market" and earn a positive alpha should keep the market portfolio close to efficient much of the time.

13.2 Information and Rational Expectations

- If all investors have homogeneous expectations, which states that all investors have the same information, all investors would be aware that the stock had a positive alpha and none would be willing to sell. The only way to restore the equilibrium in this case is for the price to rise immediately so that the alpha is zero.

- An important conclusion of the CAPM is that investors should hold the market portfolio (combined with risk-free investments), and this investment advice *does not depend on the quality of an investor's information or trading skill.* By doing so they can avoid being taken advantage of by more sophisticated investors.

- The CAPM requires only that investors have rational expectations, which means that all investors correctly interpret and use their own information, as well as information that can be inferred from market prices or the trades of others.

- The market portfolio can be inefficient only if a significant number of investors either do not have rational expectations or care about aspects of their portfolios other than expected return and volatility.

13.3 The Behavior of Individual Investors

- There is evidence that individual investors fail to diversify their portfolios adequately (underdiversification bias) and favor investments in companies they are familiar with (familiarity bias).

- Investors appear to trade too much. This behavior stems, at least in part, from investor overconfidence: the tendency of uninformed individuals to overestimate the precision of their knowledge.

13.4 Systematic Trading Biases

- In order for the behavior of uninformed investors to have an impact on the market, there must be patterns to their behavior that lead them to depart from the CAPM in systematic ways, thus imparting systematic uncertainty into prices.

- Examples of behavior that could be systematic across investors include the disposition effect (the tendency to hang on to losers and sell winners), investor mood swings that result from common events like weather, and putting too much weight on their own experience. Investors could also herd—actively trying to follow each other's behavior.

13.5 The Efficiency of the Market Portfolio

- It is not easy to profit simply by trading on news, but professional investors might be able to do so by, for example, being better able to predict takeover outcomes. However, in equilibrium, individual investors should not expect to share any of the benefit of this skill by investing with such professional investors. The empirical evidence supports this—on average, investors earn zero alphas when they invest in managed mutual funds.

- Because beating the market requires enough trading skill to overcome transaction costs as well as behavioral biases, CAPM wisdom that investors should "hold the market" is probably the best advice for most people.

13.6 Style-Based Techniques and the Market Efficiency Debate

- The size effect refers to the observation that historically stocks with low market capitalizations have had positive alphas compared to the predictions of the CAPM. The size effect is evidence that the market portfolio is not efficient, which suggests that the CAPM does not accurately model expected returns. Researchers find similar results using the book-to-market ratio instead of firm size.

- A momentum trading strategy that goes long stocks with high past risk-adjusted returns and short stocks with low past returns also generates positive CAPM alphas, providing further evidence that the market portfolio is not efficient and that the CAPM does not accurately model expected returns.

■ Securities may have non-zero alphas if the market portfolio that is used is not a good proxy for the true market portfolio.

■ The market portfolio will be inefficient if some investors' portfolio holdings are subject to systematic behavioral biases.

■ The market portfolio will be inefficient if either investors care about risk characteristics other than the volatility of their traded portfolio or if investors are exposed to other significant risks outside their portfolio that are not tradable, the most important of which is due to their human capital.

13.7 Multifactor Models of Risk

■ When more than one portfolio is used to capture risk, the model is known as a multifactor model. This model is also sometimes called the Arbitrage Pricing Theory (APT). Using a collection of N well-diversified portfolios, the expected return of stock s is

$$E[R_s] = r_f + \beta_s^{F1}(E[R_{F1}] - r_f) + \beta_s^{F2}(E[R_{F2}] - r_f) + \cdots + \beta_s^{FN}(E[R_{FN}] - r_f)$$

$$= r_f + \sum_{n=1}^{N} \beta_s^{Fn}(E[R_{Fn}] - r_f) \tag{13.4}$$

■ A simpler way to write multifactor models is to express risk premiums as the expected return on a self-financing portfolio. A self-financing portfolio is a portfolio that costs nothing to construct. By using the expected returns of self-financing portfolios, the expected return of a stock can be expressed as

$$E[R_s] = r_f + \beta_s^{F1}E[R_{F1}] + \beta_s^{F2}E[R_{F2}] + \cdots + \beta_s^{FN}E[R_{FN}]$$

$$= r_f + \sum_{n=1}^{N} \beta_s^{Fn}E[R_{Fn}] \tag{13.5}$$

■ The portfolios that are most commonly used in a multifactor model are the market portfolio (Mkt), small-minus-big (SMB) portfolio, high-minus-low (HML) portfolio, and prior one-year momentum (PR1YR) portfolio. This model is known as the Fama-French-Carhart factor specification:

$$E[R_s] = r_f + \beta_s^{Mkt}(E[R_{Mkt}] - r_f) + \beta_s^{SMB}E[R_{SMB}]$$

$$+ \beta_s^{HML}E[R_{HML}] + \beta_s^{PR1YR}E[R_{PR1YR}] \tag{13.6}$$

13.8 Methods Used in Practice

■ The CAPM is the most commonly used method in practice to estimate the cost of capital, likely because of its combined simplicity and relative reliability.

Key Terms

Arbitrage Pricing Theory (APT) *p. 462*
book-to-market ratio *p. 456*
cumulative abnormal return *p. 448*
data snooping bias *p. 456*
disposition effect *p. 445*
factor betas *p. 461*
factor portfolios *p. 461*
Fama-French-Carhart (FFC) factor
   specification *p. 463*

familiarity bias *p. 442*
herd behavior *p. 447*
high-minus-low (HML) portfolio *p. 463*
informational cascade effect *p. 447*
momentum strategy *p. 458*
multifactor model *p. 461*
overconfidence bias *p. 443*
prior one-year momentum (PR1YR)
   portfolio *p. 463*

Further Reading

For a simple insightful discussion of why some investors must lose if others win and what this means for mutual fund managers, see W. Sharpe, "The Arithmetic of Active Management," *Financial Analysts Journal*, 47(1) (January–February, 1991): 7–9. The ideas on how information affects markets were developed in a series of influential articles: P. Milgrom and N. Stokey, "Information, Trade and Common Knowledge," *Journal of Economic Theory* 26(11) (1982): 17–27; S. Grossman and J. Stiglitz, "On the Impossibility of Informationally Efficient Markets," *The American Economic Review* 70(3) (June 1980): 393–408; M. Hellwig, "On the Aggregation of Information in Competitive Markets," *Journal of Economic Theory* 22 (1980): 477–498; D. Diamond and R. Verrecchia, "Information Aggregation in a Noisy Rational Expectations Economy," *Journal of Financial Economics* 9 (September 1981): 221–235.

For an overview of the Barber and Odean results on individual investor behavior, see B. Barber and T. Odean, "The Courage of Misguided Convictions: The Trading Behavior of Individual Investors," *Financial Analyst Journal* (November/December 1999): 41–55. For a broad introduction to the topic of behavioral finance, see N. Barberis and R. Thaler, "A Survey of Behavioral Finance," in G. Constantinides, M. Harris, and R. Stulz (ed.), *Handbook of the Economics of Finance Vol. 1*, Elsevier, 2003. For a review of the impact of behavioral theories on corporate finance, see M. Baker, Malcolm, R. Ruback, and J. Wurgler, "Behavioral Corporate Finance: A Survey," in E. Eckbo (ed.), *The Handbook of Corporate Finance: Empirical Corporate Finance*, Elsevier/North Holland, 2007.

For a review of rational explanations for herd behavior in financial markets, see S. Sharma and S. Bikhchandani, "Herd Behavior in Financial Markets—A Review," IMF Working Papers 00/48, 2000. For its role in mispricing and crashes, see M. Brunnermeier, *Asset Pricing under Asymmetric Information: Bubbles, Crashes, Technical Analysis, and Herding*, Oxford University Press, 2001.

Readers interested in a more in-depth exposition of the performance of active managers can consult: J. B. Berk, "Five Myths of Active Portfolio Management," *Journal of Portfolio Management* 31(3): 27.

More detail on the theoretical relation between firm size and returns can be found in J. B. Berk, "Does Size Really Matter?" *Financial Analysts Journal* (September/October 1997): 12–18.

A summary of the empirical evidence on the relationship between risk-adjusted return and market value can be found in the following article: E. Fama and K. French, "The Cross-Section of Expected Stock Returns," *Journal of Finance* 47 (June 1992): 427–465.

The evidence that momentum strategies produce positive risk-adjusted returns was first published in the following article: N. Jegadeesh and S. Titman, "Returns to Buying Winners and Selling Losers: Implications for Stock Market Efficiency," *Journal of Finance* 48 (March 1993): 65–91.

The following two articles provide details on the FFC factor specification: E. Fama and K. French, "Common Risk Factors in the Returns on Stocks and Bonds," *Journal of Financial Economics* 33 (1993): 3–56; and M. Carhart, "On Persistence in Mutual Fund Performance," *Journal of Finance* 52 (March 1997): 57–82.

Finally, because the value of a firm also includes the value of future growth options, Z. Da, R. Guo, and R. Jagannathan, "CAPM for Estimating the Cost of Equity Capital: Interpreting the Empirical Evidence," *Journal of Financial Economics* 103 (2012): 204–220 argue that when it comes to evaluating projects (rather than securities), the CAPM may be *more* reliable than multifactor models.

Problems

All problems are available in MyFinanceLab. *An asterisk (*) indicates problems with a higher level of difficulty.*

Competition and Capital Markets

1. Assume that all investors have the same information and care only about expected return and volatility. If new information arrives about one stock, can this information affect the price and return of other stocks? If so, explain why?

 2. Assume that the CAPM is a good description of stock price returns. The market expected return is 7% with 10% volatility and the risk-free rate is 3%. New news arrives that does not change any of these numbers but it does change the expected return of the following stocks:

	Expected Return	Volatility	Beta
Green Leaf	12%	20%	1.5
NatSam	10%	40%	1.8
HanBel	9%	30%	0.75
Rebecca Automobile	6%	35%	1.2

   a. At current market prices, which stocks represent buying opportunities?
   b. On which stocks should you put a sell order in?

3. Suppose the CAPM equilibrium holds perfectly. Then the risk-free interest rate increases, *and nothing else changes.*
   a. Is the market portfolio still efficient?
   b. If your answer to part a is yes, explain why. If not, describe which stocks would be buying opportunities and which stocks would be selling opportunities.

Information and Rational Expectations

4. You know that there are informed traders in the stock market, but you are uninformed. Describe an investment strategy that guarantees you will not lose money to the informed traders and explain why it works.

5. What are the only conditions under which the market portfolio might not be an efficient portfolio?

6. Explain what the following sentence means: The market portfolio is a fence that protects the sheep from the wolves, but nothing can protect the sheep from themselves.

7. You are trading in a market in which you know there are a few highly skilled traders who are better informed than you are. There are no transaction costs. Each day you randomly choose five stocks to buy and five stocks to sell (by, perhaps, throwing darts at a dartboard).
   a. Over the long run will your strategy outperform, underperform, or have the same return as a buy and hold strategy of investing in the market portfolio?
   b. Would your answer to part a change if all traders in the market were equally well informed and were equally skilled?

The Behavior of Individual Investors

8. Why does the CAPM imply that investors should trade very rarely?

9. Your brother Joe is a surgeon who suffers badly from the overconfidence bias. He loves to trade stocks and believes his predictions with 100% confidence. In fact, he is uninformed like most investors. Rumors are that Vital Signs (a startup that makes warning labels in the medical industry) will receive a takeover offer at $20 per share. Absent the takeover offer, the stock will trade at $15 per share. The uncertainty will be resolved in the next few hours. Your brother believes that the takeover

will occur with certainty and has instructed his broker to buy the stock at any price less than $20. In fact, the true probability of a takeover is 50%, but a few people are informed and know whether the takeover will actually occur. They also have submitted orders. Nobody else is trading in the stock.

a. Describe what will happen to the market price once these orders are submitted if in fact the take-over will occur in a few hours. What will your brother's profits be: positive, negative, or zero?

b. What range of possible prices could result once these orders are submitted if the takeover does not occur? What will your brother's profits be: positive, negative, or zero?

c. What are your brother's expected profits?

10. To put the turnover of Figure 13.3 into perspective, let's do a back of the envelope calculation of what an investor's average turnover per stock would be were he to follow a policy of investing in the S&P 500 portfolio. Because the portfolio is value weighted, the trading would be required when Standard and Poor's changes the constituent stocks. (Let's ignore additional, but less important reasons like new share issuances and repurchases.) Assuming they change 23 stocks a year (the historical average since 1962) what would you estimate the investor's per stock share turnover to be? Assume that the average total number of shares outstanding for the stocks that are added or deleted from the index is the same as the average number of shares outstanding for S&P 500 stocks.

Systematic Trading Biases

11. How does the disposition effect impact investors' tax obligations?

12. Consider the price paths of the following two stocks over six time periods:

	1	2	3	4	5	6
Stock 1	10	12	14	12	13	16
Stock 2	15	11	8	16	15	18

Neither stock pays dividends. Assume you are an investor with the disposition effect and you bought at time 1 and right now it is time 3. Assume throughout this question that you do no trading (other than what is specified) in these stocks.

a. Which stock(s) would you be inclined to sell? Which would you be inclined to hold on to?

b. How would your answer change if right now is time 6?

c. What if you bought at time 3 instead of 1 and today is time 6?

d. What if you bought at time 3 instead of 1 and today is time 5?

13. Suppose that all investors have the disposition effect. A new stock has just been issued at a price of $50, so all investors in this stock purchased the stock today. A year from now the stock will be taken over, for a price of $60 or $40 depending on the news that comes out over the year. The stock will pay no dividends. Investors will sell the stock whenever the price goes up by more than 10%.

a. Suppose good news comes out in 6 months (implying the takeover offer will be $60). What equilibrium price will the stock trade for after the news comes out, that is, the price that equates supply and demand?

b. Assume that you are the only investor who does not suffer from the disposition effect and your trades are small enough to not affect prices. Without knowing what will actually transpire, what trading strategy would you instruct your broker to follow?

The Efficiency of the Market Portfolio

14. Davita Spencer is a manager at Half Dome Asset Management. She can generate an alpha of 2% a year up to $100 million. After that her skills are spread too thin, so cannot add value and her alpha is zero. Half Dome charges a fee of 1% per year on the total amount of money under management (at the beginning of each year). Assume that there are always investors looking for positive alpha and no investor would invest in a fund with a negative alpha. In equilibrium, that is, when no investor either takes out money or wishes to invest new money,

    a. What alpha do investors in Davita's fund expect to receive?

    b. How much money will Davita have under management?

    c. How much money will Half Dome generate in fee income?

15. Assume the economy consisted of three types of people. 50% are fad followers, 45% are passive investors (they have read this book and so hold the market portfolio), and 5% are informed traders. The portfolio consisting all the informed traders has a beta of 1.5 and an expected return of 15%. The market expected return is 11%. The risk-free rate is 5%.

    a. What alpha do the informed traders make?

    b. What is the alpha of the passive investors?

    c. What is the expected return of the fad followers?

    d. What alpha do the fad followers make?

Style-Based Techniques and the Market Efficiency Debate

16. Explain what the size effect is.

*17. Assume all firms have the same expected dividends. If they have different expected returns, how will their market values and expected returns be related? What about the relation between their dividend yields and expected returns?

18. Each of the six firms in the table below is expected to pay the listed dividend payment every year in perpetuity.

Firm	Dividend ($ million)	Cost of Capital (%/Year)
S1	10	8
S2	10	12
S3	10	14
B1	100	8
B2	100	12
B3	100	14

    a. Using the cost of capital in the table, calculate the market value of each firm.

    b. Rank the three S firms by their market values and look at how their cost of capital is ordered. What would be the expected return for a self-financing portfolio that went long on the firm with the largest market value and shorted the firm with the lowest market value? (The expected return of a self-financing portfolio is the weighted average return of the constituent securities.) Repeat using the B firms.

    c. Rank all six firms by their market values. How does this ranking order the cost of capital? What would be the expected return for a self-financing portfolio that went long on the firm with the largest market value and shorted the firm with the lowest market value?

    d. Repeat part c but rank the firms by the dividend yield instead of the market value. What can you conclude about the dividend yield ranking compared to the market value ranking?

19. Consider the following stocks, all of which will pay a liquidating dividend in a year and nothing in the interim:

	Market Capitalization ($ million)	Expected Liquidating Dividend ($ million)	Beta
Stock A	800	1000	0.77
Stock B	750	1000	1.46
Stock C	950	1000	1.25
Stock D	900	1000	1.07

a. Calculate the expected return of each stock.

b. What is the sign of correlation between the expected return and market capitalization of the stocks?

 20. In Problem 19, assume the risk-free rate is 3% and the market risk premium is 7%.

a. What does the CAPM predict the expected return for each stock should be?

b. Clearly, the CAPM predictions are not equal to the actual expected returns, so the CAPM does not hold. You decide to investigate this further. To see what kind of mistakes the CAPM is making, you decide to regress the actual expected return onto the expected return predicted by the CAPM.[47] What is the intercept and slope coefficient of this regression?

c. What are the residuals of the regression in (b)? That is, for each stock compute the difference between the actual expected return and the best fitting line given by the intercept and slope coefficient in (b).

d. What is the sign of the correlation between the residuals you calculated in (b) and market capitalization?

e. What can you conclude from your answers to part b of the previous problem and part d of this problem about the relation between firm size (market capitalization) and returns? (The results do not depend on the particular numbers in this problem. You are welcome to verify this for yourself by redoing the problems with another value for the market risk premium, and by picking the stock betas and market capitalizations randomly.[48])

21. Explain how to construct a positive-alpha trading strategy if stocks that have had relatively high returns in the past tend to have positive alphas and stocks that have had relatively low returns in the past tend to have negative alphas.

*22. If you can use past returns to construct a trading strategy that makes money (has a positive alpha), it is evidence that market portfolio is not efficient. Explain why.

23. Explain why you might expect stocks to have nonzero alphas if the market proxy portfolio is not highly correlated with the true market portfolio, even if the true market portfolio is efficient.

24. Explain why if some investors are subject to systematic behavioral biases, while others pick efficient portfolios, the market portfolio will not be efficient.

25. Explain why an employee who cares only about expected return and volatility will likely underweight the amount of money he invests in his own company's stock relative to an investor who does not work for his company.

Multifactor Models of Risk

For Problems 26–28, refer to the following table of estimated factor betas based on data from 2003–2011.

Factor	MSFT	XOM	GE
MKT	0.965	0.808	1.183
SMB	−0.295	−0.812	−0.475
HML	−0.099	0.196	0.965
PR1YR	0.089	0.376	−0.200

[47]The Excel function SLOPE will produce the desired answers.

[48]The Excel command RAND will produce a random number between 0 and 1.

26. Using the factor beta estimates in the table shown here and the monthly expected return estimates in Table 13.1, calculate the risk premium of General Electric stock (ticker: GE) using the FFC factor specification. (Annualize your result by multiplying by 12.) GE's CAPM beta over the same time period was 1.33. How does the risk premium you would estimate from the CAPM compare?

27. You are currently considering an investment in a project in the energy sector. The investment has the same riskiness as Exxon Mobil stock (ticker: XOM). Using the data in Table 13.1 and the table above, calculate the cost of capital using the FFC factor specification if the current risk-free rate is 3% per year.

28. You work for Microsoft Corporation (ticker: MSFT), and you are considering whether to develop a new software product. The risk of the investment is the same as the risk of the company.
    a. Using the data in Table 13.1 and in the table above, calculate the cost of capital using the FFC factor specification if the current risk-free rate is 3% per year.
    b. Microsoft's CAPM beta over the same time period was 0.84. What cost of capital would you estimate using the CAPM?

14.1 # Equity Versus Debt Financing

The relative proportions of debt, equity, and other securities that a firm has outstanding constitute its **capital structure**. When corporations raise funds from outside investors, they must choose which type of security to issue. The most common choices are financing through equity alone and financing through a combination of debt and equity. We begin our discussion by considering both of these options.

Financing a Firm with Equity

Consider an entrepreneur with the following investment opportunity. For an initial investment of $800 this year, a project will generate cash flows of either $1400 or $900 next year. The cash flows depend on whether the economy is strong or weak, respectively. Both scenarios are equally likely, and are shown in Table 14.1.

TABLE 14.1	The Project Cash Flows	
Date 0	**Date 1**	
	Strong Economy	**Weak Economy**
−$800	$1400	$900

Because the project cash flows depend on the overall economy, they contain market risk. As a result, investors demand a risk premium. The current risk-free interest rate is 5%, and suppose that given the market risk of the investment the appropriate risk premium is 10%.

What is the NPV of this investment opportunity? Given a risk-free interest rate of 5% and a risk premium of 10%, the cost of capital for this project is 15%. Because the expected cash flow in one year is $\frac{1}{2}(\$1400) + \frac{1}{2}(\$900) = \$1150$, we get

$$NPV = -\$800 + \frac{\$1150}{1.15} = -\$800 + \$1000$$
$$= \$200$$

Thus, the investment has a positive NPV.

If this project is financed using equity alone, how much would investors be willing to pay for the firm's shares? Recall from Chapter 3 that, in the absence of arbitrage, the price of a security equals the present value of its cash flows. Because the firm has no other liabilities, equity holders will receive all of the cash flows generated by the project on date 1. Hence, the market value of the firm's equity today will be

$$PV(\text{equity cash flows}) = \frac{\$1150}{1.15} = \$1000$$

So, the entrepreneur can raise $1000 by selling the equity in the firm. After paying the investment cost of $800, the entrepreneur can keep the remaining $200—the project's NPV—as a profit. In other words, the project's NPV represents the value to the initial owners of the firm (in this case, the entrepreneur) created by the project.

TABLE 14.2	Cash Flows and Returns for Unlevered Equity				
	Date 0	Date 1: Cash Flows		Date 1: Returns	
	Initial Value	Strong Economy	Weak Economy	Strong Economy	Weak Economy
Unlevered equity	$1000	$1400	$900	40%	−10%

Equity in a firm with no debt is called **unlevered equity**. Because there is no debt, the date 1 cash flows of the unlevered equity are equal to those of the project. Given equity's initial value of $1000, shareholders' returns are either 40% or −10%, as shown in Table 14.2.

The strong and weak economy outcomes are equally likely, so the expected return on the unlevered equity is $\frac{1}{2}(40\%) + \frac{1}{2}(-10\%) = 15\%$. Because the risk of unlevered equity equals the risk of the project, shareholders are earning an appropriate return for the risk they are taking.

Financing a Firm with Debt and Equity

Financing the firm exclusively with equity is not the entrepreneur's only option. She can also raise part of the initial capital using debt. Suppose she decides to borrow $500 initially, in addition to selling equity. Because the project's cash flow will always be enough to repay the debt, the debt is risk free. Thus, the firm can borrow at the risk-free interest rate of 5%, and it will owe the debt holders $500 \times 1.05 = \$525$ in one year.

Equity in a firm that also has debt outstanding is called **levered equity**. Promised payments to debt holders must be made *before* any payments to equity holders are distributed. Given the firm's $525 debt obligation, the shareholders will receive only $1400 − $525 = $875 if the economy is strong and $900 − $525 = $375 if the economy is weak. Table 14.3 shows the cash flows of the debt, the levered equity, and the total cash flows of the firm.

What price E should the levered equity sell for, and which is the best capital structure choice for the entrepreneur? In an important paper, researchers Franco Modigliani and Merton Miller proposed an answer to this question that surprised researchers and practitioners at the time.[1] They argued that with perfect capital markets, the total value of a firm should not depend on its capital structure. Their reasoning: The firm's total cash flows

TABLE 14.3	Values and Cash Flows for Debt and Equity of the Levered Firm		
	Date 0	Date 1: Cash Flows	
	Initial Value	Strong Economy	Weak Economy
Debt	$500	$525	$525
Levered equity	$E = ?$	$875	$375
Firm	$1000	$1400	$900

---

[1] F. Modigliani and M. Miller, "The Cost of Capital, Corporation Finance and the Theory of Investment," *American Economic Review* 48(3) (1958): 261–297.

still equal the cash flows of the project, and therefore have the same present value of $1000 calculated earlier (see the last line in Table 14.3). Because the cash flows of the debt and equity sum to the cash flows of the project, by the Law of One Price the combined values of debt and equity must be $1000. Therefore, if the value of the debt is $500, the value of the levered equity must be $E = \$1000 - \$500 = \$500$.

Because the cash flows of levered equity are smaller than those of unlevered equity, levered equity will sell for a lower price ($500 versus $1000). However, the fact that the equity is less valuable with leverage does not mean that the entrepreneur is worse off. She will still raise a total of $1000 by issuing both debt and levered equity, just as she did with unlevered equity alone. As a consequence, she will be indifferent between these two choices for the firm's capital structure.

The Effect of Leverage on Risk and Return

Modigliani and Miller's conclusion went against the common view, which stated that even with perfect capital markets, leverage would affect a firm's value. In particular, it was thought that the value of the levered equity would exceed $500, because the present value of its expected cash flow at 15% is

$$\frac{\frac{1}{2}(\$875) + \frac{1}{2}(\$375)}{1.15} = \$543$$

The reason this logic is *not* correct is that leverage increases the risk of the equity of a firm. Therefore, it is inappropriate to discount the cash flows of levered equity at the same discount rate of 15% that we used for unlevered equity. Investors in levered equity require a higher expected return to compensate for its increased risk.

Table 14.4 compares the equity returns if the entrepreneur chooses unlevered equity financing with the case in which she borrows $500 and raises an additional $500 using levered equity. Note that the returns to equity holders are very different with and without leverage. Unlevered equity has a return of either 40% or −10%, for an expected return of 15%. But levered equity has higher risk, with a return of either 75% or −25%. To compensate for this risk, levered equity holders receive a higher expected return of 25%.

We can evaluate the relationship between risk and return more formally by computing the sensitivity of each security's return to the systematic risk of the economy. (In our simple two-state example, this sensitivity determines the security's beta; see also the discussion of

TABLE 14.4	Returns to Equity with and without Leverage					
	Date 0	Date 1: Cash Flows		Date 1: Returns		
	Initial Value	Strong Economy	Weak Economy	Strong Economy	Weak Economy	Expected Return
Debt	$500	$525	$525	5%	5%	5%
Levered equity	$500	$875	$375	75%	−25%	25%
Unlevered equity	$1000	$1400	$900	40%	−10%	15%

TABLE 14.5	Systematic Risk and Risk Premiums for Debt, Unlevered Equity, and Levered Equity	
	Return Sensitivity (Systematic Risk)	**Risk Premium**
	$\Delta R = R(\text{strong}) - R(\text{weak})$	$E[R] - r_f$
Debt	5% − 5% = 0%	5% − 5% = 0%
Unlevered equity	40% − (−10%) = 50%	15% − 5% = 10%
Levered equity	75% − (−25%) = 100%	25% − 5% = 20%

risk in the appendix to Chapter 3.) Table 14.5 shows the return sensitivity and the risk premium for each security. Because the debt's return bears no systematic risk, its risk premium is zero. In this particular case, however, levered equity has twice the systematic risk of unlevered equity. As a result, levered equity holders receive twice the risk premium.

To summarize, in the case of perfect capital markets, if the firm is 100% equity financed, the equity holders will require a 15% expected return. If the firm is financed 50% with debt and 50% with equity, the debt holders will receive a lower return of 5%, while the levered equity holders will require a higher expected return of 25% because of their increased risk. As this example shows, *leverage increases the risk of equity even when there is no risk that the firm will default.* Thus, while debt may be cheaper when considered on its own, it raises the cost of capital for equity. Considering both sources of capital together, the firm's average cost of capital with leverage is $\frac{1}{2}(5\%) + \frac{1}{2}(25\%) = 15\%$, the same as for the unlevered firm.

EXAMPLE 14.1

Leverage and the Equity Cost of Capital

Problem

Suppose the entrepreneur borrows only $200 when financing the project. According to Modigliani and Miller, what should the value of the equity be? What is the expected return?

Solution

Because the value of the firm's total cash flows is still $1000, if the firm borrows $200, its equity will be worth $800. The firm will owe $200 × 1.05 = $210 in one year. Thus, if the economy is strong, equity holders will receive $1400 − $210 = $1190, for a return of $1190/$800 − 1 = 48.75%. If the economy is weak, equity holders will receive $900 − $210 = $690, for a return of $690/$800 − 1 = −13.75%. The equity has an expected return of

$$\tfrac{1}{2}(48.75\%) + \tfrac{1}{2}(-13.75\%) = 17.5\%.$$

Note that the equity has a return sensitivity of 48.75% − (−13.75%) = 62.5%, which is 62.5%/50% = 125% of the sensitivity of unlevered equity. Its risk premium is 17.5% − 5% = 12.5%, which is also 125% of the risk premium of the unlevered equity, so it is appropriate compensation for the risk.

CONCEPT CHECK

1. Why are the value and cash flows of levered equity less than if the firm had issued unlevered equity?

2. How does the risk and cost of capital of levered equity compare to that of unlevered equity? Which is the superior capital structure choice in a perfect capital market?

14.2 Modigliani-Miller I: Leverage, Arbitrage, and Firm Value

In the previous section, we used the Law of One Price to argue that leverage would not affect the total value of the firm (the amount of money the entrepreneur can raise). Instead, it merely changes the allocation of cash flows between debt and equity, without altering the total cash flows of the firm. Modigliani and Miller (or simply MM) showed that this result holds more generally under a set of conditions referred to as **perfect capital markets:**

1. Investors and firms can trade the same set of securities at competitive market prices equal to the present value of their future cash flows.

2. There are no taxes, transaction costs, or issuance costs associated with security trading.

3. A firm's financing decisions do not change the cash flows generated by its investments, nor do they reveal new information about them.

Under these conditions, MM demonstrated the following result regarding the role of capital structure in determining firm value:[2]

MM Proposition I: *In a perfect capital market, the total value of a firm is equal to the market value of the total cash flows generated by its assets and is not affected by its choice of capital structure.*

MM and the Law of One Price

MM established their result with the following simple argument. In the absence of taxes or other transaction costs, the total cash flow paid out to all of a firm's security holders is equal to the total cash flow generated by the firm's assets. Therefore, by the Law of One Price, the firm's securities and its assets must have the same total market value. Thus, as long as the firm's choice of securities does not change the cash flows generated by its assets, this decision will not change the total value of the firm or the amount of capital it can raise.

We can also view MM's result in terms of the Separation Principle introduced in Chapter 3: If securities are fairly priced, then buying or selling securities has an NPV of zero and, therefore, should not change the value of a firm. The future repayments that the firm must make on its debt are equal in value to the amount of the loan it receives upfront. Thus, there is no net gain or loss from using leverage, and the value of the firm is determined by the present value of the cash flows from its current and future investments.

Homemade Leverage

MM showed that the firm's value is not affected by its choice of capital structure. But suppose investors would prefer an alternative capital structure to the one the firm has chosen. MM demonstrated that in this case, investors can borrow or lend on their own and achieve the same result. For example, an investor who would like more leverage than the firm has chosen can borrow and add leverage to his or her own portfolio. When investors use

---

[2]Although it was not widely appreciated at the time, the idea that a firm's value does not depend on its capital structure was argued even earlier by John Burr Williams in his pathbreaking book, *The Theory of Investment Value* (North Holland Publishing, 1938; reprinted by Fraser Publishing, 1997).

MM and the Real World

Students often question why Modigliani and Miller's results are important if, after all, capital markets are not perfect in the real world. While it is true that capital markets are not perfect, all scientific theories begin with a set of idealized assumptions from which conclusions can be drawn. When we apply the theory, we must then evaluate how closely the assumptions hold, and consider the consequences of any important deviations.

As a useful analogy, consider Galileo's law of falling bodies. Galileo overturned the conventional wisdom by showing that, without friction, free-falling bodies will fall at the same rate independent of their mass. If you test this law, you will likely find it does not hold exactly. The reason, of course, is that unless we are in a vacuum, air friction tends to slow some objects more than others.

MM's results are similar. In practice, we will find that capital structure can have an effect on firm value. But just as Galileo's law of falling bodies reveals that we must look to air friction, rather than any underlying property of gravity, to explain differences in the speeds of falling objects, MM's proposition reveals that any effects of capital structure must similarly be due to frictions that exist in capital markets. After exploring the full meaning of MM's results in this chapter, we look at the important sources of these frictions, and their consequences, in subsequent chapters.

leverage in their own portfolios to adjust the leverage choice made by the firm, we say that they are using **homemade leverage**. As long as investors can borrow or lend at the same interest rate as the firm,[3] homemade leverage is a perfect substitute for the use of leverage by the firm.

To illustrate, suppose the entrepreneur uses no leverage and creates an all-equity firm. An investor who would prefer to hold levered equity can do so by using leverage in his own portfolio—that is, he can buy the stock on margin, as illustrated in Table 14.6.

TABLE 14.6	Replicating Levered Equity Using Homemade Leverage		
	Date 0	Date 1: Cash Flows	
	Initial Cost	Strong Economy	Weak Economy
Unlevered equity	$1000	$1400	$900
Margin loan	−$500	−$525	−$525
Levered equity	$500	$875	$375

If the cash flows of the unlevered equity serve as collateral for the margin loan, then the loan is risk-free and the investor should be able to borrow at the 5% rate. Although the firm is unlevered, by using homemade leverage, the investor has replicated the payoffs to the levered equity illustrated in Table 14.3, for a cost of $500. Again, by the Law of One Price, the value of levered equity must also be $500.

Now suppose the entrepreneur uses debt, but the investor would prefer to hold unlevered equity. The investor can replicate the payoffs of unlevered equity by buying both the debt *and* the equity of the firm. Combining the cash flows of the two securities produces cash flows identical to unlevered equity, for a total cost of $1000, as we see in Table 14.7.

In each case, the entrepreneur's choice of capital structure does not affect the opportunities available to investors. Investors can alter the leverage choice of the firm to suit their

---

[3]This assumption is implied by perfect capital markets because the interest rate on a loan should depend only on its risk.

TABLE 14.7	Replicating Unlevered Equity by Holding Debt and Equity		
	Date 0	Date 1: Cash Flows	
	Initial Cost	Strong Economy	Weak Economy
Debt	$500	$525	$525
Levered equity	$500	$875	$375
Unlevered Equity	$1000	$1400	$900

personal tastes either by borrowing and adding more leverage or by holding bonds and reducing leverage. With perfect capital markets, because different choices of capital structure offer no benefit to investors, they do not affect the value of the firm.

EXAMPLE 14.2 — Homemade Leverage and Arbitrage

Problem

Suppose there are two firms, each with date 1 cash flows of $1400 or $900 (as shown in Table 14.1). The firms are identical except for their capital structure. One firm is unlevered, and its equity has a market value of $990. The other firm has borrowed $500, and its equity has a market value of $510. Does MM Proposition I hold? What arbitrage opportunity is available using homemade leverage?

Solution

MM Proposition I states that the total value of each firm should equal the value of its assets. Because these firms hold identical assets, their total values should be the same. However, the problem assumes the unlevered firm has a total market value of $990, whereas the levered firm has a total market value of $510 (equity) + $500 (debt) = $1010. Therefore, these prices violate MM Proposition I.

Because these two identical firms are trading for different total prices, the Law of One Price is violated and an arbitrage opportunity exists. To exploit it, we can borrow $500 and buy the equity of the unlevered firm for $990, re-creating the equity of the levered firm by using homemade leverage for a cost of only $990 − 500 = $490. We can then sell the equity of the levered firm for $510 and enjoy an arbitrage profit of $20.

	Date 0	Date 1: Cash Flows	
	Cash Flow	Strong Economy	Weak Economy
Borrow	$500	−$525	−$525
Buy unlevered equity	−$990	$1400	$900
Sell levered equity	$510	−$875	−$375
Total cash flow	$20	$0	$0

Note that the actions of arbitrageurs buying the unlevered firm and selling the levered firm will cause the price of the unlevered firm's stock to rise and the price of the levered firm's stock to fall until the firms' values are equal and MM Proposition I holds.

The Market Value Balance Sheet

In Section 14.1, we considered just two choices for a firm's capital structure. MM Proposition I, however, applies much more broadly to any choice of debt and equity. In fact, it applies even if the firm issues other types of securities, such as convertible debt or warrants, a type of stock option that we discuss later in the text. The logic is the same: Because investors can buy or sell securities on their own, no value is created when the firm buys or sells securities for them.

One application of MM Proposition I is the useful device known as the market value balance sheet of the firm. A **market value balance sheet** is similar to an accounting balance sheet, with two important distinctions. First, *all* assets and liabilities of the firm are included—even intangible assets such as reputation, brand name, or human capital that are missing from a standard accounting balance sheet. Second, all values are current market values rather than historical costs. On the market value balance sheet, shown in Table 14.8, the total value of all securities issued by the firm must equal the total value of the firm's assets.

The market value balance sheet captures the idea that value is created by a firm's choice of assets and investments. By choosing positive-NPV projects that are worth more than their initial investment, the firm can enhance its value. Holding fixed the cash flows generated by the firm's assets, however, the choice of capital structure does not change the value of the firm. Instead, it merely divides the value of the firm into different securities. Using the market value balance sheet, we can compute the value of equity as follows:

$$\text{Market Value of Equity} = \text{Market Value of Assets} - \text{Market Value of Debt and Other Liabilities} \quad (14.1)$$

EXAMPLE 14.3   **Valuing Equity When There Are Multiple Securities**

Problem
Suppose our entrepreneur decides to sell the firm by splitting it into three securities: equity, $500 of debt, and a third security called a warrant that pays $210 when the firm's cash flows are high and nothing when the cash flows are low. Suppose that this third security is fairly priced at $60. What will the value of the equity be in a perfect capital market?

Solution
According to MM Proposition I, the total value of all securities issued should equal the value of the assets of the firm, which is $1000. Because the debt is worth $500 and the new security is worth $60, the value of the equity must be $440. (You can check this result by verifying that at this price, equity has a risk premium commensurate with its risk in comparison with the securities in Table 14.5.)

Application: A Leveraged Recapitalization

So far, we have looked at capital structure from the perspective of an entrepreneur who is considering financing an investment opportunity. In fact, MM Proposition I applies to capital structure decisions made at any time during the life of the firm.

Let's consider an example. Harrison Industries is currently an all-equity firm operating in a perfect capital market, with 50 million shares outstanding that are trading for $4 per share. Harrison plans to increase its leverage by borrowing $80 million and using the funds to repurchase 20 million of its outstanding shares. When a firm repurchases a significant percentage of its outstanding shares in this way, the transaction is called a **leveraged recapitalization**.

We can view this transaction in two stages. First, Harrison sells debt to raise $80 million in cash. Second, Harrison uses the cash to repurchase shares. Table 14.9 shows the market value balance sheet after each of these stages.

TABLE 14.8	The Market Value Balance Sheet of the Firm

Assets	Liabilities
Collection of Assets and Investments Undertaken by the Firm:	Collection of Securities Issued by the Firm:

Tangible Assets
  Cash
  Plant, property, and equipment
  Inventory and other working capital
  (and so on)
	Debt
	  Short-term debt
	  Long-term debt
	  Convertible debt

Intangible Assets
  Intellectual property
  Reputation
  Human capital
  (and so on)
	Equity
	  Common stock
	  Preferred stock
	  Warrants (options)

Total Market Value of Firm Assets	**Total Market Value of Firm Securities**

Initially, Harrison is an all-equity firm. That is, the market value of Harrison's equity, which is 50 million shares × $4 per share = $200 million, equals the market value of its existing assets. After borrowing, Harrison's liabilities grow by $80 million, which is also equal to the amount of cash the firm has raised. Because both assets and liabilities increase by the same amount, the market value of the equity remains unchanged.

To conduct the share repurchase, Harrison spends the $80 million in borrowed cash to repurchase $80 million ÷ $4 per share = 20 million shares. Because the firm's assets decrease by $80 million and its debt remains unchanged, the market value of the equity must also fall by $80 million, from $200 million to $120 million, for assets and liabilities to remain balanced. The share price, however, is unchanged—with 30 million shares remaining, the shares are worth $120 million ÷ 30 million shares = $4 per share, just as before.

The fact that the share price did not change should not come as a surprise. Because the firm has sold $80 million worth of new debt and purchased $80 million worth of

TABLE 14.9	Market Value Balance Sheet after Each Stage of Harrison's Leveraged Recapitalization (in $ million)

Initial		After Borrowing		After Share Repurchase	
Assets	Liabilities	Assets	Liabilities	Assets	Liabilities
		Cash 80	Debt 80	Cash 0	Debt 80
Existing assets 200	Equity 200	Existing assets 200	Equity 200	Existing assets 200	Equity 120
200	200	280	280	200	200
Shares outstanding (million)	50	Shares outstanding (million)	50	Shares outstanding (million)	30
Value per share	$4.00	Value per share	$4.00	Value per share	$4.00

existing equity, this zero-NPV transaction (benefits = costs) does not change the value for shareholders.

1. Why are investors indifferent to the firm's capital structure choice?

2. What is a market value balance sheet?

3. In a perfect capital market, how will a firm's market capitalization change if it borrows in order to repurchase shares? How will its share price change?

14.3 Modigliani-Miller II: Leverage, Risk, and the Cost of Capital

Modigliani and Miller showed that a firm's financing choice does not affect its value. But how can we reconcile this conclusion with the fact that the cost of capital differs for different securities? Consider again our entrepreneur from Section 14.1. When the project is financed solely through equity, the equity holders require a 15% expected return. As an alternative, the firm can borrow at the risk-free rate of 5%. In this situation, isn't debt a cheaper and better source of capital than equity?

Although debt does have a lower cost of capital than equity, we cannot consider this cost in isolation. As we saw in Section 14.1, while debt itself may be cheap, it increases the risk and therefore the cost of capital of the firm's equity. In this section, we calculate the impact of leverage on the expected return of a firm's stock, or the equity cost of capital. We then consider how to estimate the cost of capital of the firm's assets, and show that it is unaffected by leverage. In the end, the savings from the low expected return on debt, the debt cost of capital, are exactly offset by a higher equity cost of capital, and there are no net savings for the firm.

Leverage and the Equity Cost of Capital

We can use Modigliani and Miller's first proposition to derive an explicit relationship between leverage and the equity cost of capital. Let E and D denote the market value of equity and debt if the firm is levered, respectively; let U be the market value of equity if the firm is unlevered; and let A be the market value of the firm's assets. Then MM Proposition I states that

$$E + D = U = A \tag{14.2}$$

That is, the total market value of the firm's securities is equal to the market value of its assets, whether the firm is unlevered or levered.

We can interpret the first equality in Eq. 14.2 in terms of homemade leverage: By holding a portfolio of the firm's equity and debt, we can replicate the cash flows from holding unlevered equity. Because the return of a portfolio is equal to the weighted average of the returns of the securities in it, this equality implies the following relationship between the returns of levered equity (R_E), debt (R_D), and unlevered equity (R_U):

$$\frac{E}{E + D} R_E + \frac{D}{E + D} R_D = R_U \tag{14.3}$$

If we solve Eq. 14.3 for R_E, we obtain the following expression for the return of levered equity:

$$R_E = R_U + \frac{D}{E}(R_U - R_D) \qquad (14.4)$$

Risk without leverage   Additional risk due to leverage

This equation reveals the effect of leverage on the return of the levered equity. The levered equity return equals the unlevered return, plus an extra "kick" due to leverage. This extra effect pushes the returns of levered equity even higher when the firm performs well ($R_U > R_D$), but makes them drop even lower when the firm does poorly ($R_U < R_D$). The amount of additional risk depends on the amount of leverage, measured by the firm's market value debt-equity ratio, D/E. Because Eq. 14.4 holds for the realized returns, it holds for the *expected* returns as well (denoted by r in place of R). This observation leads to Modigliani and Miller's second proposition:

MM Proposition II: *The cost of capital of levered equity increases with the firm's market value debt-equity ratio,*

Cost of Capital of Levered Equity

$$r_E = r_U + \frac{D}{E}(r_U - r_D) \qquad (14.5)$$

We can illustrate MM Proposition II for the entrepreneur's project in Section 14.1. Recall that if the firm is all-equity financed, the expected return on unlevered equity is 15% (see Table 14.4). If the firm is financed with $500 of debt, the expected return of the debt is the risk-free interest rate of 5%. Therefore, according to MM Proposition II, the expected return on equity for the levered firm is

$$r_E = 15\% + \frac{500}{500}(15\% - 5\%) = 25\%$$

This result matches the expected return calculated in Table 14.4.

EXAMPLE 14.4

Computing the Equity Cost of Capital

Problem
Suppose the entrepreneur of Section 14.1 borrows only $200 when financing the project. According to MM Proposition II, what will be the firm's equity cost of capital?

Solution
Because the firm's assets have a market value of $1000, by MM Proposition I the equity will have a market value of $800. Then, using Eq. 14.5,

$$r_E = 15\% + \frac{200}{800}(15\% - 5\%) = 17.5\%$$

This result matches the expected return calculated in Example 14.1.

Capital Budgeting and the Weighted Average Cost of Capital

We can use the insight of Modigliani and Miller to understand the effect of leverage on the firm's cost of capital for new investments. If a firm is financed with both equity and debt, then the risk of its underlying assets will match the risk of a portfolio of its equity and debt. Thus, the appropriate cost of capital for the firm's assets is the cost of capital of this portfolio, which is simply the weighted average of the firm's equity and debt cost of capital:

Unlevered Cost of Capital (Pretax WACC)

$$r_U \equiv \left(\begin{array}{c} \text{Fraction of Firm Value} \\ \text{Financed by Equity} \end{array} \right) \left(\begin{array}{c} \text{Equity} \\ \text{Cost of Capital} \end{array} \right) + \left(\begin{array}{c} \text{Fraction of Firm Value} \\ \text{Financed by Debt} \end{array} \right) \left(\begin{array}{c} \text{Debt} \\ \text{Cost of Capital} \end{array} \right)$$

$$= \frac{E}{E+D} r_E + \frac{D}{E+D} r_D \tag{14.6}$$

In Chapter 12 we called this cost of capital the firm's unlevered cost of capital, or pretax WACC. There we also introduced the firm's effective after-tax weighted average cost of capital, or WACC, which we compute using the firm's after-tax cost of debt. Because we are in a setting of perfect capital markets, there are no taxes, so the firm's WACC and unlevered cost of capital coincide:

$$r_{wacc} = r_U = r_A \tag{14.7}$$

That is, *with perfect capital markets, a firm's WACC is independent of its capital structure and is equal to its equity cost of capital if it is unlevered, which matches the cost of capital of its assets.*

Figure 14.1 illustrates the effect of increasing the amount of leverage in a firm's capital structure on its equity cost of capital, its debt cost of capital, and its WACC. In the figure,

FIGURE 14.1

WACC and Leverage with Perfect Capital Markets

As the fraction of the firm financed with debt increases, both the equity and the debt become riskier and their cost of capital rises. Yet, because more weight is put on the lower-cost debt, the weighted average cost of capital remains constant.
(a) Equity, debt, and weighted average costs of capital for different amounts of leverage. The rate of increase of r_D and r_E, and thus the shape of the curves, depends on the characteristics of the firm's cash flows.
(b) Calculating the WACC for alternative capital structures. Data in this table correspond to the example in Section 14.1.

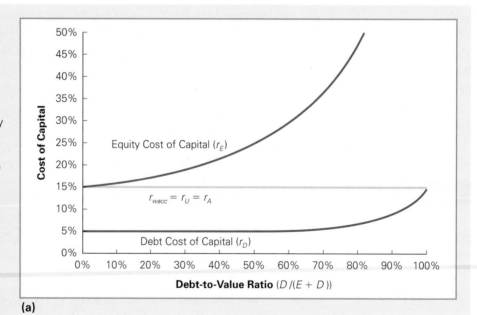

(a)

(b)

E	D	r_E	r_D	$\frac{E}{E+D} r_E + \frac{D}{E+D} r_D$	$= r_{wacc}$
1000	0	15.0%	5.0%	$1.0 \times 15.0\% + 0.0 \times 5.0\%$	$= 15\%$
800	200	17.5%	5.0%	$0.8 \times 17.5\% + 0.2 \times 5.0\%$	$= 15\%$
500	500	25.0%	5.0%	$0.5 \times 25.0\% + 0.5 \times 5.0\%$	$= 15\%$
100	900	75.0%	8.3%[4]	$0.1 \times 75.0\% + 0.9 \times 8.3\%$	$= 15\%$

---

[4]With this level of leverage, the debt is risky with a face value of 1050 and thus a promised yield of 16.67%. Because the firm defaults with 50% probability, the expected return of the debt, r_D, is only 8.33%. The debt, therefore, has a risk premium of 3.33%, which is justified given its return sensitivity of 16.67%.

we measure the firm's leverage in terms of its **debt-to-value ratio**, $D/(E + D)$, which is the fraction of the firm's total value that corresponds to debt. With no debt, the WACC is equal to the unlevered equity cost of capital. As the firm borrows at the low cost of capital for debt, its equity cost of capital rises according to Eq. 14.5. The net effect is that the firm's WACC is unchanged. Of course, as the amount of debt increases, the debt becomes more risky because there is a chance the firm will default; as a result, the debt cost of capital r_D also rises. With 100% debt, the debt would be as risky as the assets themselves (similar to unlevered equity). But even though the debt and equity costs of capital both rise when leverage is high, because more weight is put on the lower-cost debt, the WACC remains constant.

Recall from Chapter 9 that we can calculate the enterprise value of the firm by discounting its future free cash flow using the WACC. Thus, Eq. 14.7 provides the following intuitive interpretation of MM Proposition I: Although debt has a lower cost of capital than equity, leverage does not lower a firm's WACC. As a result, the value of the firm's free cash flow evaluated using the WACC does not change, and so the enterprise value of the firm does not depend on its financing choices. This observation allows us to answer the questions posed for the CFO of EBS at the beginning of this chapter: With perfect capital markets, the firm's weighted average cost of capital, and therefore the NPV of the expansion, is unaffected by how EBS chooses to finance the new investment.

EXAMPLE 14.5   Reducing Leverage and the Cost of Capital

Problem

NRG Energy, Inc. (NRG) is an energy company with a market debt-equity ratio of 2. Suppose its current debt cost of capital is 6%, and its equity cost of capital is 12%. Suppose also that if NRG issues equity and uses the proceeds to repay its debt and reduce its debt-equity ratio to 1, it will lower its debt cost of capital to 5.5%. With perfect capital markets, what effect will this transaction have on NRG's equity cost of capital and WACC? What would happen if NRG issues even more equity and pays off its debt completely? How would these alternative capital structures affect NRG's enterprise value?

Solution

We can calculate NRG's initial WACC and unlevered cost of capital using Eqs. 14.6 and 14.7:

$$r_{wacc} = r_U = \frac{E}{E + D} r_E + \frac{D}{E + D} r_D = \frac{1}{1 + 2}(12\%) + \frac{2}{1 + 2}(6\%) = 8\%$$

Given NRG's unlevered cost of capital of 8%, we can use Eq. 14.5 to calculate NRG's equity cost of capital after the reduction in leverage:

$$r_E = r_U + \frac{D}{E}(r_U - r_D) = 8\% + \frac{1}{1}(8\% - 5.5\%) = 10.5\%$$

The reduction in leverage will cause NRG's equity cost of capital to fall to 10.5%. Note, though, that with perfect capital markets, NRG's WACC remains unchanged at $8\% = \frac{1}{2}(10.5\%) + \frac{1}{2}(5.5\%)$, and there is no net gain from this transaction.

If NRG pays off its debt completely, it will be unlevered. Thus, its equity cost of capital will equal its WACC and unlevered cost of capital of 8%.

In either scenario, NRG's WACC and free cash flows remain unchanged. Thus, with perfect capital markets, its enterprise value will not be affected by these different capital structure choices.

| COMMON MISTAKE | Is Debt Better Than Equity? |

Because debt has a lower cost of capital than equity, a common mistake is to assume that a firm can reduce its overall WACC by increasing the amount of debt financing. If this strategy works, shouldn't a firm take on as much debt as possible, at least as long as the debt is not risky?

This argument ignores the fact that even if the debt is risk free and the firm will not default, adding leverage increases the risk of the equity. Given the increase in risk, equity holders will demand a higher risk premium and, therefore, a higher expected return. The increase in the cost of equity exactly offsets the benefit of a greater reliance on the cheaper debt capital, so that the firm's overall cost of capital remains unchanged.

Computing the WACC with Multiple Securities

We calculated the firm's unlevered cost of capital and WACC in Eqs. 14.6 and 14.7 assuming that the firm has issued only two types of securities (equity and debt). If the firm's capital structure is more complex, however, then r_U and r_{wacc} are calculated by computing the weighted average cost of capital of *all* of the firm's securities.

| EXAMPLE 14.6 | WACC with Multiple Securities |

Problem

Compute the WACC for the entrepreneur's project with the capital structure described in Example 14.3.

Solution

Because the firm has three securities in its capital structure (debt, equity, and the warrant), its weighted average cost of capital is the average return it must pay these three groups of investors:

$$r_{wacc} = r_U = \frac{E}{E+D+W}r_E + \frac{D}{E+D+W}r_D + \frac{W}{E+D+W}r_W$$

From Example 14.3, we know $E = 440$, $D = 500$, and $W = 60$. What are the expected returns for each security? Given the cash flows of the firm, the debt is risk free and has an expected return of $r_D = 5\%$. The warrant has an expected payoff of $\frac{1}{2}(\$210) + \frac{1}{2}(\$0) = \$105$, so its expected return is $r_w = \$105/\$60 - 1 = 75\%$. Equity has a payoff of $(\$1400 - \$525 - \$210) = \$665$ when cash flows are high and $(\$900 - \$525) = \$375$ when cash flows are low; thus, its expected payoff is $\frac{1}{2}(\$665) + \frac{1}{2}(\$375) = \$520$. The expected return for equity is then $r_E = \$520/\$440 - 1 = 18.18\%$. We can now compute the WACC:

$$r_{wacc} = \frac{\$440}{\$1000}(18.18\%) + \frac{\$500}{\$1000}(5\%) + \frac{\$60}{\$1000}(75\%) = 15\%$$

Once again, the firm's WACC and unlevered cost of capital is 15%, the same as if it were all-equity financed.

Levered and Unlevered Betas

Note that Eqs. 14.6 and 14.7 for the weighted-average cost of capital match our calculation in Chapter 12 of a firm's unlevered cost of capital. There, we showed that a firm's unlevered or asset beta is the weighted average of its equity and debt beta:

$$\beta_U = \frac{E}{E+D}\beta_E + \frac{D}{E+D}\beta_D \tag{14.8}$$

Recall that the unlevered beta measures the market risk of the firm's underlying assets, and thus can be used to assess the cost of capital for comparable investments. When a firm changes its capital structure without changing its investments, its unlevered beta will remain unaltered. However, its equity beta will change to reflect the effect of the capital structure change on its risk.[5] Let's rearrange Eq. 14.8 to solve for β_E:

$$\beta_E = \beta_U + \frac{D}{E}(\beta_U - \beta_D) \qquad (14.9)$$

Eq. 14.9 is analogous to Eq. 14.5, with beta replacing the expected returns. It shows that the firm's equity beta also increases with leverage.

EXAMPLE 14.7   **Betas and Leverage**

Problem

Suppose drug retailer CVS has an equity beta of 0.80 and a debt-equity ratio of 0.10. Estimate its asset beta assuming its debt beta is zero. Suppose CVS were to increase its leverage so that its debt-equity ratio was 0.50. Assuming its debt beta were still zero, what would you expect its equity beta to be after the increase in leverage?

Solution

We can estimate the unlevered or asset beta for CVS using Eq. 14.8:

$$\beta_U = \frac{E}{E+D}\beta_E + \frac{D}{E+D}\beta_D = \frac{1}{1+D/E}\beta_E = \frac{1}{1+0.1} \times 0.8 = 0.73$$

With the increase in leverage, CVS's equity beta will increase according to Eq. 14.9:

$$\beta_E = \beta_U + \frac{D}{E}(\beta_U - \beta_D) = 0.73 + 0.5(0.73 - 0) = 1.09$$

Thus, CVS's equity beta (and equity cost of capital) will increase with leverage. Note that if CVS's debt beta also increased, the impact of leverage on its equity beta would be somewhat lower—if debt holders share some of the firm's market risk, the equity holders will need to bear less of it.

The assets on a firm's balance sheet include any holdings of cash or risk-free securities. Because these holdings are risk-free, they reduce the risk—and therefore the required risk premium—of the firm's assets. For this reason, holding excess cash has the opposite effect of leverage on risk and return. From this standpoint, we can view cash as negative debt. Thus, as we stated in Chapter 12, when we are trying to assess a firm's enterprise value— its business assets separate from any cash holdings—it is natural to measure leverage in terms of the firm's net debt, which is its debt less its holdings of excess cash or short-term investments.

---

[5]The relationship between leverage and equity betas was developed by R. Hamada in "The Effect of the Firm's Capital Structure on the Systematic Risk of Common Stocks," *Journal of Finance* 27(2) (1972): 435–452, and by M. Rubinstein in "A Mean-Variance Synthesis of Corporate Financial Theory," *Journal of Finance* 28(1) (1973): 167–181.

EXAMPLE 14.8   **Cash and the Cost of Capital**

Problem

In July 2012, Cisco Systems had a market capitalization of $102.4 billion. It had debt of $16.2 billion as well as cash and short-term investments of $48.6 billion. Its equity beta was 1.23 and its debt beta was approximately zero. What was Cisco's enterprise value at the time? Given a risk-free rate of 2% and a market risk premium of 5%, estimate the unlevered cost of capital of Cisco's business.

Solution

Because Cisco had $16.2 billion in debt and $48.6 billion in cash, Cisco's net debt = $16.2 billion − $48.6 billion = −$32.4 billion. Its enterprise value was therefore $102.4 billion − $32.4 billion = $70 billion.

Given a zero beta for its net debt, Cisco's unlevered beta was

$$\beta_U = \frac{E}{E+D}\beta_E + \frac{D}{E+D}\beta_D = \frac{\$102.4}{\$70}(1.23) + \frac{-\$32.4}{\$70}(0) = 1.80$$

and we can estimate its unlevered cost of capital as $r_U = 2\% + 1.80 \times 5\% = 11\%$. Note that because of its cash holdings, Cisco's equity is less risky than its underlying business.

CONCEPT CHECK   1. How do we compute the weighted average cost of capital of a firm?

2. With perfect capital markets, as a firm increases its leverage, how does its debt cost of capital change? Its equity cost of capital? Its weighted average cost of capital?

NOBEL PRIZE   **Franco Modigliani and Merton Miller**

Franco Modigliani and Merton Miller, the authors of the Modigliani-Miller Propositions, have each won the Nobel Prize in economics for their work in financial economics, including their capital structure propositions. Modigliani won the Nobel Prize in 1985 for his work on personal savings and for his capital structure theorems with Miller. Miller earned his prize in 1990 for his analysis of portfolio theory and capital structure.

Miller once described the MM propositions in an interview this way:

People often ask: Can you summarize your theory quickly? Well, I say, you understand the M&M theorem if you know why this is a joke: The pizza delivery man comes to Yogi Berra after the game and says, "Yogi, how do you want this pizza cut, into quarters or eighths?" And Yogi says, "Cut it in eight pieces. I'm feeling hungry tonight."

Everyone recognizes that's a joke because obviously the number and shape of the pieces don't affect the size of

the pizza. And similarly, the stocks, bonds, warrants, et cetera, issued don't affect the aggregate value of the firm. They just slice up the underlying earnings in different ways. [*]

Modigliani and Miller each won the Nobel Prize in large part for their observation that the value of a firm should be unaffected by its capital structure in perfect capital markets. While the intuition underlying the MM propositions may be as simple as slicing pizza, their implications for corporate finance are far-reaching. The propositions imply that the true role of a firm's financial policy is to deal with (and potentially exploit) financial market imperfections such as taxes and transactions costs. Modigliani and Miller's work began a long line of research into these market imperfections, which we look at over the next several chapters.

_____

[*]Peter J. Tanous, *Investment Gurus* (Prentice Hall Press, 1997).

14.4 Capital Structure Fallacies

MM Propositions I and II state that with perfect capital markets, leverage has no effect on firm value or the firm's overall cost of capital. Here we take a critical look at two incorrect arguments that are sometimes cited in favor of leverage.

Leverage and Earnings per Share

Leverage can increase a firm's expected earnings per share. An argument sometimes made is that by doing so, leverage should also increase the firm's stock price.

Consider the following example. Levitron Industries (LVI) is currently an all-equity firm. It expects to generate earnings before interest and taxes (EBIT) of $10 million over the next year. Currently, LVI has 10 million shares outstanding, and its stock is trading for a price of $7.50 per share. LVI is considering changing its capital structure by borrowing $15 million at an interest rate of 8% and using the proceeds to repurchase 2 million shares at $7.50 per share.

Let's consider the consequences of this transaction in a setting of perfect capital markets. Suppose LVI has no debt. Because LVI pays no interest, and because in perfect capital markets there are no taxes, LVI's earnings would equal its EBIT. Therefore, without debt, LVI would expect earnings per share of

$$EPS = \frac{\text{Earnings}}{\text{Number of Shares}} = \frac{\$10 \text{ million}}{10 \text{ million}} = \$1$$

The new debt will obligate LVI to make interest payments each year of

$$\$15 \text{ million} \times 8\% \text{ interest/year} = \$1.2 \text{ million/year}$$

As a result, LVI will have expected earnings after interest of

$$\text{Earnings} = \text{EBIT} - \text{Interest} = \$10 \text{ million} - \$1.2 \text{ million} = \$8.8 \text{ million}$$

The interest payments on the debt will cause LVI's total earnings to fall. But because the number of outstanding shares will also have fallen to 10 million − 2 million = 8 million shares after the share repurchase, LVI's expected earnings per share is

$$EPS = \frac{\$8.8 \text{ million}}{8 \text{ million}} = \$1.10$$

As we can see, LVI's expected earnings per share increases with leverage.[6] This increase might appear to make shareholders better off and could potentially lead to an increase in the stock price. Yet we know from MM Proposition I that as long as the securities are fairly priced, these financial transactions have an NPV of zero and offer no benefit to shareholders. How can we reconcile these seemingly contradictory results?

The answer is that the risk of earnings has changed. Thus far, we have considered only *expected* earnings per share. We have not considered the consequences of this transaction on the risk of the earnings. To do so, we must determine the effect of the increase in leverage on earnings per share in a variety of scenarios.

Suppose earnings before interest payments are only $4 million. Without the increase in leverage, EPS would be $4 million ÷ 10 million shares = $0.40. With the new debt, however, earnings after interest payments would be $4 million − $1.2 million = $2.8 million, leading to earnings per share of $2.8 million ÷ 8 million shares = $0.35. So, when

---

[6]More generally, leverage will increase expected EPS whenever the firm's after-tax borrowing cost is less than the ratio of expected earnings to the share price (i.e., the reciprocal of its forward P/E multiple, also called the *earnings yield*). For LVI, with no taxes, $8\% < EPS/P = 1/7.50 = 13.33\%$.

FIGURE 14.2

LVI Earnings per Share with and without Leverage

The sensitivity of EPS to EBIT is higher for a levered firm than for an unlevered firm. Thus, given assets with the same risk, the EPS of a levered firm is more volatile.

earnings are low, leverage will cause EPS to fall even further than it otherwise would have. Figure 14.2 presents a range of scenarios.

As Figure 14.2 shows, if earnings before interest exceed $6 million, then EPS is higher with leverage. When earnings fall below $6 million, however, EPS is lower with leverage than without it. In fact, if earnings before interest fall below $1.2 million (the level of the interest expense), then after interest LVI will have negative EPS. So, although LVI's expected EPS rises with leverage, the risk of its EPS also increases. The increased risk can be seen because the line showing EPS with leverage in Figure 14.2 is steeper than the line without leverage, implying that the same fluctuation in EBIT will lead to greater fluctuations in EPS once leverage is introduced. Taken together, these observations are consistent with MM Proposition I. While EPS increases on average, this increase is necessary to compensate shareholders for the additional risk they are taking, so LVI's share price does not increase as a result of the transaction. Let's check this result in an example.

EXAMPLE 14.9   **The MM Propositions and Earnings per Share**

Problem

Assume that LVI's EBIT is not expected to grow in the future and that all earnings are paid as dividends. Use MM Propositions I and II to show that the increase in expected EPS for LVI will not lead to an increase in the share price.

Solution

Without leverage, expected earnings per share and therefore dividends are $1 each year, and the share price is $7.50. Let r_U be LVI's cost of capital without leverage. Then we can value LVI as a perpetuity:

$$P = 7.50 = \frac{Div}{r_U} = \frac{EPS}{r_U} = \frac{1.00}{r_U}$$

Therefore, LVI's current share price implies $r_U = 1/7.50 = 13.33\%$.

The market value of LVI stock without leverage is $7.50 per share $\times$ 10 million shares = $75 million. If LVI uses debt to repurchase $15 million worth of the firm's equity (that is, 2 million shares), then the remaining equity will be worth $75 million − $15 million = $60 million

GLOBAL FINANCIAL CRISIS | Bank Capital Regulation and the ROE Fallacy

In banking jargon, a "capital requirement" obligates a bank to finance itself with a certain minimum amount of equity to ensure that its debt-to-equity ratio will stay below a set level. The permitted level of leverage is very high—international standards allow common equity to represent as little as 2% of a bank's total funding.[7] To put this number in perspective, the equity of a typical non-financial firm exceeds 50% of firm value. Such extreme leverage makes bank equity very risky.

These extreme levels of bank leverage were an important contributing factor to the financial meltdown in 2008 and the subsequent recession: With such a small equity cushion, even a minor drop in asset values can lead to insolvency. Post-crisis, banks have come under increased pressure to reduce leverage with new international rules more than doubling the required proportion of equity financing. Many policymakers believe capital requirements should be increased much more to reduce the risk of the financial sector and the consequent spillovers to the broader economy.

Bankers counter that decreased leverage will lower their return on equity, limiting their ability to compete effectively. According to Josef Ackermann, then CEO of Deutsche Bank, new capital requirements would "depress ROE to levels that make investment into the banking sector unattractive relative to other business sectors."[8] The return on equity is indeed a function of the firm's leverage. As with EPS, lower leverage will tend to decrease the firm's ROE on average, though it will raise the ROE in bad times. But this decrease in average ROE is compensated for by a reduction in the riskiness of equity and therefore the required risk premium. Thus, from an investor's perspective, the reduction in ROE that results solely from a decrease in leverage does *not* make investing in the firm any less attractive. Franco Modigliani and Merton Miller were awarded the Nobel Prize for pointing out that in a perfect market the bank's capital structure cannot affect its competitiveness.

The only way a change in leverage can affect the "attractiveness" of equity (and the competiveness of banks) is if there is a market imperfection. In the next two chapters we will discuss these imperfections and explain why they do give banks a strong incentive to maximize their leverage. Unfortunately, the most important imperfections derive from government subsidies, so the banks' gains from leverage come largely at taxpayer expense.

---

according to MM Proposition I. After the transaction, LVI's debt-equity ratio is $15 million ÷ $60 million $= \frac{1}{4}$. Using MM Proposition II, LVI's equity cost of capital with leverage will be

$$r_E = r_U + \frac{D}{E}(r_U - r_D) = 13.33\% + \frac{1}{4}(13.33\% - 8\%) = 14.66\%$$

Given that expected EPS is now $1.10 per share, the new value of the shares equals

$$P = \frac{\$1.10}{r_E} = \frac{\$1.10}{14.66\%} = \$7.50 \text{ per share}$$

Thus, even though EPS is higher, due to the additional risk, shareholders will demand a higher return. These effects cancel out, so the price per share is unchanged.

Because the firm's earnings per share and price-earnings ratio are affected by leverage, we cannot reliably compare these measures across firms with different capital structures. The same is true for accounting-based performance measures such as return on equity (ROE). Therefore, most analysts prefer to use performance measures and valuation multiples that are based on the firm's earnings before interest has been deducted. For example, the ratio of enterprise value to EBIT (or EBITDA) is more useful when analyzing firms with very different capital structures than is comparing their P/E ratios.

---

[7]Two percent is the Tier 1 Common Equity Requirement of the Basel II Accord, the global regulatory standard for bank capital. Starting in 2013, the new Basel III Accord will raise this requirement gradually to 4.5% by 2015.

[8]J. Ackermann, "The new architecture of financial regulation: Will it prevent another crisis?" Special Paper 194, FMG Deutsche Bank Conference, London School of Economics, October 2010.

Equity Issuances and Dilution

Another often-heard fallacy is that issuing equity will dilute existing shareholders' owner-ship, so debt financing should be used instead. By **dilution**, the proponents of this fallacy mean that if the firm issues new shares, the cash flows generated by the firm must be divided among a larger number of shares, thereby reducing the value of each individual share. The problem with this line of reasoning is that it ignores the fact that the cash raised by issuing new shares will increase the firm's assets. Let's consider an example.

Suppose Jet Sky Airlines (JSA) is a highly successful discount airline serving the south-eastern United States. It currently has no debt and 500 million shares of stock outstanding. These shares are currently trading at $16. Last month the firm announced that it would expand its operations to the Northeast. The expansion will require the purchase of $1 bil-lion of new planes, which will be financed by issuing new equity. How will the share price change when the new equity is issued today?

Based on the current share price of the firm (prior to the issue), the equity and therefore the assets of the firm have a market value of 500 million shares × $16 per share = $8 billion. Because the expansion decision has already been made and announced, in perfect capital markets this value incorporates the NPV associated with the expansion.

Suppose JSA sells 62.5 million new shares at the current price of $16 per share to raise the additional $1 billion needed to purchase the planes.

Assets (in $ million)	Before Equity Issue	After Equity Issue
Cash		1000
Existing assets	8000	8000
Total Value	8000	9000
Shares outstanding (million)	500	562.5
Value per share	$16.00	$16.00

Two things happen when JSA issues equity. First, the market value of its assets grows because of the additional $1 billion in cash the firm has raised. Second, the number of shares increases. Although the number of shares has grown to 562.5 million, the value per share is unchanged: $9 billion ÷ 562.5 million shares = $16 per share.

In general, as long as the firm sells the new shares of equity *at a fair price*, there will be no gain or loss to shareholders associated with the equity issue itself. The money taken in by the firm as a result of the share issue exactly offsets the dilution of the shares. *Any gain or loss associated with the transaction will result from the NPV of the investments the firm makes with the funds raised.*

CONCEPT CHECK

1. If a change in leverage raises a firm's earnings per share, should this cause its share price to rise in a perfect market?

2. True or False: When a firm issues equity, it increases the supply of its shares in the market, which should cause its share price to fall.

14.5 MM: Beyond the Propositions

Since the publication of their original paper, Modigliani and Miller's ideas have greatly influenced finance research and practice. Perhaps more important than the specific propositions themselves is the approach that MM took to derive them. Proposition I was one of the first arguments to show that the Law of One Price could have strong implications for security prices and firm values in a competitive market; it marks the beginning of the modern theory of corporate finance.

Modigliani and Miller's work formalized a new way of thinking about financial markets that was first put forth by John Burr Williams in his 1938 book, *The Theory of Investment Value*. In it Williams argues:

> If the investment value of an enterprise as a whole is by definition the present worth of all its future distributions to security holders, whether on interest or dividend account, then this value in no wise depends on what the company's capitalization is. Clearly, if a single individual or a single institutional investor owned all of the bonds, stocks and warrants issued by the corporation, it would not matter to this investor what the company's capitalization was (except for details concerning the income tax). Any earnings collected as interest could not be collected as dividends. To such an individual it would be perfectly obvious that total interest- and dividend-paying power was in no wise dependent on the kind of securities issued to the company's owner. Furthermore no change in the investment value of the enterprise as a whole would result from a change in its capitalization. Bonds could be retired with stock issues, or two classes of junior securities could be combined into one, without changing the investment value of the company as a whole. Such constancy of investment value is analogous to the indestructibility of matter or energy: it leads us to speak of the Law of the Conservation of Investment Value, just as physicists speak of the Law of the Conservation of Matter, or the Law of the Conservation of Energy.

Thus, the results in this chapter can be interpreted more broadly as the **conservation of value principle** for financial markets: *With perfect capital markets, financial transactions neither add nor destroy value, but instead represent a repackaging of risk (and therefore return).*

The conservation of value principle extends far beyond questions of debt versus equity or even capital structure. It implies that any financial transaction that appears to be a good deal in terms of adding value either is too good to be true or is exploiting some type of market imperfection. To make sure the value is not illusory, it is important to identify the market imperfection that is the source of value. In the next several chapters we will examine different types of market imperfections and the potential sources of value that they introduce for the firm's capital structure choice and other financial transactions.

CONCEPT CHECK

1. Consider the questions facing Dan Harris, CFO of EBS, at the beginning of this chapter. What answers would you give based on the Modigliani-Miller Propositions? What considerations should the capital structure decision be based on?

2. State the conservation of value principle for financial markets.

MyFinanceLab   Here is what you should know after reading this chapter. MyFinanceLab will help you identify what you know and where to go when you need to practice.

14.1 Equity Versus Debt Financing

- The collection of securities a firm issues to raise capital from investors is called the firm's capital structure. Equity and debt are the securities most commonly used by firms. When equity is used without debt, the firm is said to be unlevered. Otherwise, the amount of debt determines the firm's leverage.
- The owner of a firm should choose the capital structure that maximizes the total value of the securities issued.

14.2 Modigliani-Miller I: Leverage, Arbitrage, and Firm Value

- Capital markets are said to be perfect if they satisfy three conditions:
  - Investors and firms can trade the same set of securities at competitive market prices equal to the present value of their future cash flows.
  - There are no taxes, transaction costs, or issuance costs associated with security trading.
  - A firm's financing decisions do not change the cash flows generated by its investments, nor do they reveal new information about them.
- According to MM Proposition I, with perfect capital markets the value of a firm is independent of its capital structure.
  - With perfect capital markets, homemade leverage is a perfect substitute for firm leverage.
  - If otherwise identical firms with different capital structures have different values, the Law of One Price would be violated and an arbitrage opportunity would exist.
- The market value balance sheet shows that the total market value of a firm's assets equals the total market value of the firm's liabilities, including all securities issued to investors. Changing the capital structure therefore alters how the value of the assets is divided across securities, but not the firm's total value.
- A firm can change its capital structure at any time by issuing new securities and using the funds to pay its existing investors. An example is a leveraged recapitalization in which the firm borrows money (issues debt) and repurchases shares (or pays a dividend). MM Proposition I implies that such transactions will not change the share price.

14.3 Modigliani-Miller II: Leverage, Risk, and the Cost of Capital

- According to MM Proposition II, the cost of capital for levered equity is

$$r_E = r_U + \frac{D}{E}(r_U - r_D) \tag{14.5}$$

- Debt is less risky than equity, so it has a lower cost of capital. Leverage increases the risk of equity, however, raising the equity cost of capital. The benefit of debt's lower cost of capital is offset by the higher equity cost of capital, leaving a firm's weighted average cost of capital (WACC) unchanged with perfect capital markets:

$$r_{wacc} = r_A = r_U = \frac{E}{E+D}r_E + \frac{D}{E+D}r_D \tag{14.6, 14.7}$$

- The market risk of a firm's assets can be estimated by its unlevered beta:

$$\beta_U = \frac{E}{E+D}\beta_E + \frac{D}{E+D}\beta_D \tag{14.8}$$

■ Leverage increases the beta of a firm's equity:

$$\beta_E = \beta_U + \frac{D}{E}(\beta_U - \beta_D) \tag{14.9}$$

■ A firm's net debt is equal to its debt less its holdings of cash and other risk-free securities. We can compute the cost of capital and the beta of the firm's business assets, excluding cash, by using its net debt when calculating its WACC or unlevered beta.

14.4 Capital Structure Fallacies

■ Leverage can raise a firm's expected earnings per share and its return on equity, but it also increases the volatility of earnings per share and the riskiness of its equity. As a result, in a perfect market shareholders are not better off and the value of equity is unchanged.

■ As long as shares are sold to investors at a fair price, there is no cost of dilution associated with issuing equity. While the number of shares increases when equity is issued, the firm's assets also increase because of the cash raised, and the per-share value of equity remains unchanged.

14.5 MM: Beyond the Propositions

■ With perfect capital markets, financial transactions are a zero-NPV activity that neither add nor destroy value on their own, but rather repackage the firm's risk and return. Capital structure—and financial transactions more generally—affect a firm's value only because of its impact on some type of market imperfection.

Key Terms

capital structure *p. 479*
conservation of value principle *p. 499*
debt-to-value ratio *p. 491*
dilution *p. 498*
homemade leverage *p. 484*

leveraged recapitalization *p. 486*
levered equity *p. 480*
market value balance sheet *p. 486*
perfect capital markets *p. 483*
unlevered equity *p. 480*

Further Reading

For further details on MM's argument, especially their use of the Law of One Price to derive their results, see MM's original paper: F. Modigliani and M. Miller, "The Cost of Capital, Corporation Finance and the Theory of Investment," *American Economic Review* 48(3) (1958): 261–297.

For a retrospective look at the work of Modigliani and Miller and its importance in corporate finance, see the collection of articles in Volume 2, Issue 4 of the *Journal of Economic Perspectives* (1988), which includes: "The Modigliani-Miller Propositions After Thirty Years," by M. Miller (pp. 99–120), "Comment on the Modigliani-Miller Propositions," by S. Ross (pp. 127–133), "Corporate Finance and the Legacy of Modigliani and Miller," by S. Bhattacharya (pp. 135–147), and "MM—Past, Present, Future," by F. Modigliani (pp. 149–158).

For an interesting interview with Merton Miller about his work, see: P. Tanous, *Investment Gurus* (Prentice Hall Press, 1997).

For a more recent discussion of MM's contribution to the development of capital structure theory, see: R. Cookson, "A Survey of Corporate Finance ('The Party's Over' and 'Debt Is Good for You')," *The Economist* (January 27, 2001): 5–8.

A historical account of Miller-Modigliani's result is provided in these sources: P. Bernstein, *Capital Ideas: The Improbable Origins of Modern Wall Street* (Free Press, 1993); and M. Rubinstein, "Great Moments in Financial Economics: II. Modigliani-Miller Theorem," *Journal of Investment Management* 1(2) (2003).

For more insight into the debate regarding bank capital requirements, and many of the fallacies that have arisen in that debate, see A. Admati, P. DeMarzo, M. Hellwig, and P. Pfleiderer,

"Fallacies, Irrelevant Facts, and Myths in the Discussion of Capital Regulation: Why Bank Equity Is Not Expensive," Rock Center for Corporate Governance Research Paper No. 86, August 2010.

Problems

All problems are available in MyFinanceLab. An asterisk (*) indicates problems with a higher level of difficulty.

Equity Versus Debt Financing

1. Consider a project with free cash flows in one year of $130,000 or $180,000, with each outcome being equally likely. The initial investment required for the project is $100,000, and the project's cost of capital is 20%. The risk-free interest rate is 10%.
   a. What is the NPV of this project?
   b. Suppose that to raise the funds for the initial investment, the project is sold to investors as an all-equity firm. The equity holders will receive the cash flows of the project in one year. How much money can be raised in this way—that is, what is the initial market value of the unlevered equity?
   c. Suppose the initial $100,000 is instead raised by borrowing at the risk-free interest rate. What are the cash flows of the levered equity, and what is its initial value according to MM?

2. You are an entrepreneur starting a biotechnology firm. If your research is successful, the technology can be sold for $30 million. If your research is unsuccessful, it will be worth nothing. To fund your research, you need to raise $2 million. Investors are willing to provide you with $2 million in initial capital in exchange for 50% of the unlevered equity in the firm.
   a. What is the total market value of the firm without leverage?
   b. Suppose you borrow $1 million. According to MM, what fraction of the firm's equity will you need to sell to raise the additional $1 million you need?
   c. What is the value of your share of the firm's equity in cases (a) and (b)?

3. Acort Industries owns assets that will have an 80% probability of having a market value of $50 million in one year. There is a 20% chance that the assets will be worth only $20 million. The current risk-free rate is 5%, and Acort's assets have a cost of capital of 10%.
   a. If Acort is unlevered, what is the current market value of its equity?
   b. Suppose instead that Acort has debt with a face value of $20 million due in one year. According to MM, what is the value of Acort's equity in this case?
   c. What is the expected return of Acort's equity without leverage? What is the expected return of Acort's equity with leverage?
   d. What is the lowest possible realized return of Acort's equity with and without leverage?

4. Wolfrum Technology (WT) has no debt. Its assets will be worth $450 million in one year if the economy is strong, but only $200 million in one year if the economy is weak. Both events are equally likely. The market value today of its assets is $250 million.
   a. What is the expected return of WT stock without leverage?
   b. Suppose the risk-free interest rate is 5%. If WT borrows $100 million today at this rate and uses the proceeds to pay an immediate cash dividend, what will be the market value of its equity just after the dividend is paid, according to MM?
   c. What is the expected return of WT stock after the dividend is paid in part (b)?

Modigliani-Miller I: Leverage, Arbitrage, and Firm Value

5. Suppose there are no taxes. Firm ABC has no debt, and firm XYZ has debt of $5000 on which it pays interest of 10% each year. Both companies have identical projects that generate free cash

flows of $800 or $1000 each year. After paying any interest on debt, both companies use all remaining free cash flows to pay dividends each year.

a. Fill in the table below showing the payments debt and equity holders of each firm will receive given each of the two possible levels of free cash flows.

	ABC		XYZ	
FCF	Debt Payments	Equity Dividends	Debt Payments	Equity Dividends
$ 800				
$1000				

b. Suppose you hold 10% of the equity of ABC. What is another portfolio you could hold that would provide the same cash flows?

c. Suppose you hold 10% of the equity of XYZ. If you can borrow at 10%, what is an alternative strategy that would provide the same cash flows?

6. Suppose Alpha Industries and Omega Technology have identical assets that generate identical cash flows. Alpha Industries is an all-equity firm, with 10 million shares outstanding that trade for a price of $22 per share. Omega Technology has 20 million shares outstanding as well as debt of $60 million.

a. According to MM Proposition I, what is the stock price for Omega Technology?

b. Suppose Omega Technology stock currently trades for $11 per share. What arbitrage opportunity is available? What assumptions are necessary to exploit this opportunity?

7. Cisoft is a highly profitable technology firm that currently has $5 billion in cash. The firm has decided to use this cash to repurchase shares from investors, and it has already announced these plans to investors. Currently, Cisoft is an all-equity firm with 5 billion shares outstanding. These shares currently trade for $12 per share. Cisoft has issued no other securities except for stock options given to its employees. The current market value of these options is $8 billion.

a. What is the market value of Cisoft's non-cash assets?

b. With perfect capital markets, what is the market value of Cisoft's equity after the share repurchase? What is the value per share?

8. Schwartz Industry is an industrial company with 100 million shares outstanding and a market capitalization (equity value) of $4 billion. It has $2 billion of debt outstanding. Management have decided to delever the firm by issuing new equity to repay all outstanding debt.

a. How many new shares must the firm issue?

b. Suppose you are a shareholder holding 100 shares, and you disagree with this decision. Assuming a perfect capital market, describe what you can do to undo the effect of this decision.

9. Zetatron is an all-equity firm with 100 million shares outstanding, which are currently trading for $7.50 per share. A month ago, Zetatron announced it will change its capital structure by borrowing $100 million in short-term debt, borrowing $100 million in long-term debt, and issuing $100 million of preferred stock. The $300 million raised by these issues, plus another $50 million in cash that Zetatron already has, will be used to repurchase existing shares of stock. The transaction is scheduled to occur today. Assume perfect capital markets.

a. What is the market value balance sheet for Zetatron

   i. Before this transaction?

   ii. After the new securities are issued but before the share repurchase?

   iii. After the share repurchase?

b. At the conclusion of this transaction, how many shares outstanding will Zetatron have, and what will the value of those shares be?

Modigliani-Miller II: Leverage, Risk, and the Cost of Capital

10. Explain what is wrong with the following argument: "If a firm issues debt that is risk free, because there is no possibility of default, the risk of the firm's equity does not change. Therefore, risk-free debt allows the firm to get the benefit of a low cost of capital of debt without raising its cost of capital of equity."

11. Consider the entrepreneur described in Section 14.1 (and referenced in Tables 14.1–14.3). Suppose she funds the project by borrowing $750 rather than $500.
    a. According to MM Proposition I, what is the value of the equity? What are its cash flows if the economy is strong? What are its cash flows if the economy is weak?
    b. What is the return of the equity in each case? What is its expected return?
    c. What is the risk premium of equity in each case? What is the sensitivity of the levered equity return to systematic risk? How does its sensitivity compare to that of unlevered equity? How does its risk premium compare to that of unlevered equity?
    d. What is the debt-equity ratio of the firm in this case?
    e. What is the firm's WACC in this case?

12. Hardmon Enterprises is currently an all-equity firm with an expected return of 12%. It is considering a leveraged recapitalization in which it would borrow and repurchase existing shares.
    a. Suppose Hardmon borrows to the point that its debt-equity ratio is 0.50. With this amount of debt, the debt cost of capital is 6%. What will the expected return of equity be after this transaction?
    b. Suppose instead Hardmon borrows to the point that its debt-equity ratio is 1.50. With this amount of debt, Hardmon's debt will be much riskier. As a result, the debt cost of capital will be 8%. What will the expected return of equity be in this case?
    c. A senior manager argues that it is in the best interest of the shareholders to choose the capital structure that leads to the highest expected return for the stock. How would you respond to this argument?

13. Suppose The Washington Post Company (WPO) has no debt and an equity cost of capital of 9.2%. The average debt-to-value ratio for the publishing industry is 13%. What would its cost of equity be if it took on the average amount of debt for its industry at a cost of debt of 6%?

14. Global Pistons (GP) has common stock with a market value of $200 million and debt with a value of $100 million. Investors expect a 15% return on the stock and a 6% return on the debt. Assume perfect capital markets.
    a. Suppose GP issues $100 million of new stock to buy back the debt. What is the expected return of the stock after this transaction?
    b. Suppose instead GP issues $50 million of new debt to repurchase stock.
        i. If the risk of the debt does not change, what is the expected return of the stock after this transaction?
        ii. If the risk of the debt increases, would the expected return of the stock be higher or lower than in part (i)?

15. Hubbard Industries is an all-equity firm whose shares have an expected return of 10%. Hubbard does a leveraged recapitalization, issuing debt and repurchasing stock, until its debt-equity ratio is 0.60. Due to the increased risk, shareholders now expect a return of 13%. Assuming there are no taxes and Hubbard's debt is risk free, what is the interest rate on the debt?

16. Hartford Mining has 50 million shares that are currently trading for $4 per share and $200 million worth of debt. The debt is risk free and has an interest rate of 5%, and the expected return of Hartford stock is 11%. Suppose a mining strike causes the price of Hartford stock to fall 25% to $3 per share. The value of the risk-free debt is unchanged. Assuming there are no taxes and the risk (unlevered beta) of Hartford's assets is unchanged, what happens to Hartford's equity cost of capital?

17. Mercer Corp. is an all-equity firm with 10 million shares outstanding and $100 million worth of debt outstanding. Its current share price is $75. Mercer's equity cost of capital is 8.5%. Mercer has just announced that it will issue $350 million worth of debt. It will use the proceeds from this debt to pay off its existing debt, and use the remaining $250 million to pay an immediate dividend. Assume perfect capital markets.
    a. Estimate Mercer's share price just after the recapitalization is announced, but before the transaction occurs.
    b. Estimate Mercer's share price at the conclusion of the transaction. (*Hint*: Use the market value balance sheet.)
    c. Suppose Mercer's existing debt was risk-free with a 4.25% expected return, and its new debt is risky with a 5% expected return. Estimate Mercer's equity cost of capital after the transaction.

18. In mid-2012, AOL Inc. had $100 million in debt, total equity capitalization of $3.1 billion, and an equity beta of 0.90 (as reported on Yahoo! Finance). Included in AOL's assets was $1.5 billion in cash and risk-free securities. Assume that the risk-free rate of interest is 3% and the market risk premium is 4%.
    a. What is AOL's enterprise value?
    b. What is the beta of AOL's business assets?
    c. What is AOL's WACC?

*19. Indell stock has a current market value of $120 million and a beta of 1.50. Indell currently has risk-free debt as well. The firm decides to change its capital structure by issuing $30 million in additional risk-free debt, and then using this $30 million plus another $10 million in cash to repurchase stock. With perfect capital markets, what will be the beta of Indell stock after this transaction?

Capital Structure Fallacies

20. Yerba Industries is an all-equity firm whose stock has a beta of 1.2 and an expected return of 12.5%. Suppose it issues new risk-free debt with a 5% yield and repurchases 40% of its stock. Assume perfect capital markets.
    a. What is the beta of Yerba stock after this transaction?
    b. What is the expected return of Yerba stock after this transaction?
    Suppose that prior to this transaction, Yerba expected earnings per share this coming year of $1.50, with a forward P/E ratio (that is, the share price divided by the expected earnings for the coming year) of 14.
    c. What is Yerba's expected earnings per share after this transaction? Does this change benefit shareholders? Explain.
    d. What is Yerba's forward P/E ratio after this transaction? Is this change in the P/E ratio reasonable? Explain.

21. You are CEO of a high-growth technology firm. You plan to raise $180 million to fund an expansion by issuing either new shares or new debt. With the expansion, you expect earnings next year of $24 million. The firm currently has 10 million shares outstanding, with a price of $90 per share. Assume perfect capital markets.
    a. If you raise the $180 million by selling new shares, what will the forecast for next year's earnings per share be?
    b. If you raise the $180 million by issuing new debt with an interest rate of 5%, what will the forecast for next year's earnings per share be?
    c. What is the firm's forward P/E ratio (that is, the share price divided by the expected earnings for the coming year) if it issues equity? What is the firm's forward P/E ratio if it issues debt? How can you explain the difference?

22. Zelnor, Inc., is an all-equity firm with 100 million shares outstanding currently trading for $8.50 per share. Suppose Zelnor decides to grant a total of 10 million new shares to employees

as part of a new compensation plan. The firm argues that this new compensation plan will motivate employees and is a better strategy than giving salary bonuses because it will not cost the firm anything.

a. If the new compensation plan has no effect on the value of Zelnor's assets, what will be the share price of the stock once this plan is implemented?

b. What is the cost of this plan for Zelnor's investors? Why is issuing equity costly in this case?

*23. Suppose Levered Bank is funded with 2% equity and 98% debt. Its current market capitalization is $10 billion, and its market to book ratio is 1. Levered Bank earns a 4.22% expected return on its assets (the loans it makes), and pays 4% on its debt.

New capital requirements will necessitate that Levered Bank increase its equity to 4% of its capital structure. It will issue new equity and use the funds to retire existing debt. The interest rate on its debt is expected to remain at 4%.

a. What is Levered Bank's expected ROE with 2% equity?

b. Assuming perfect capital markets, what will Levered Bank's expected ROE be after it increases its equity to 4%?

c. Consider the difference between Levered Bank's ROE and its cost of debt. How does this "premium" compare before and after the Bank's increase in leverage?

d. Suppose the return on Levered Bank's assets has a volatility of 0.25%. What is the volatility of Levered Bank's ROE before and after the increase in equity?

e. Does the reduction in Levered Bank's ROE after the increase equity reduce its attractiveness to shareholders? Explain.

Data Case

You work in the corporate finance division of Nokia at the head office in Finland. Nokia manufactures cell phones and provides Internet services and digital map information worldwide.

The firm has been on low leverage levels in recent years, and your boss is wondering whether there could be positive effects for firm value by having a higher debt level. From his MBA program, he remembers something about capital structure being irrelevant. However, as he graduated quite a while ago, he is not completely sure about it.

So your task is to show him the effects in real numbers. You make the assumption of capital markets being perfect, a point that you will have to explain in the conclusion of your analysis. To be sure, you consider both an increase in debt to repurchase stock (the alternative your boss has in mind) and also a new stock issue to repurchase debt.

1. Obtain the financial information you need for Nokia.

   a. Go to http://finance.yahoo.com and search for Nokia using their ticker symbol "NOK."

      i. Get the current stock price from "Summary" (found to the right of the page).

      ii. Get the number of shares outstanding from "Key Statistics."

      iii. Get the Income Statement and the Balance Sheet. Place your cursor in the Income Statement or the Balance Sheet and right-click. Select "Export to Microsoft Excel." The income statement is only needed for the Data Case in Chapter 15, but you might want to download it now. Save the Income Statement and the Balance Sheet in the same worksheet.

   b. To get the cost of debt for Nokia, go to NASD BondInfo (http://cxa.marketwatch.com/finra/bondcenter/default.aspx). Select "Corporate" and search for Nokia using their ticker symbol "NOK."

      i. The next page contains information for all Nokia's outstanding and recently matured bonds.

      ii. Select the latest yield on the outstanding bond with the shortest remaining maturity.

2. Market debt-to-equity ratio:
   a. Calculate the market value of equity (market capitalization) using the share price and the number of shares outstanding.
   b. Approximate the market value of debt by the book value of net debt. Use "Short/Current Long Term Debt," "Long Term Debt," and "Cash and Cash Equivalents." Use the data given for the most recent year.
   c. Calculate the market debt-to-equity ratio using Eq. 2.15.

3. Cost of capital:
   a. Calculate the cost of capital of levered equity (r_E) using Eq. 14.5 and assuming that the return of unlevered equity is 15%.
   b. Calculate the WACC using Eq. 14.7.

4. Your boss has reviewed your results and has made the following statement: "Since the cost of equity is higher than the cost of debt, why don't we just issue some more debt and buy back some shares? That will bring down our overall cost of capital." Your answer should be based on an analysis of two scenarios: (1) Nokia issues new debt worth 10% of the sum of the existing "Short/Current Long Term Debt" and "Long Term Debt," and immediately buys back shares for the same amount and (2) Nokia issues new equity worth 10% of the sum of the existing "Short/Current Long Term Debt" and "Long Term Debt," and immediately buys back debt for the same amount.

5. Write a short report for your boss that briefly relates the results from Question 4 to the assumption of perfect capital markets. Comment on the implicit assumptions made along the way. How do these assumptions correspond to the "real" world?

Debt and Taxes

N A PERFECT CAPITAL MARKET, THE LAW OF ONE PRICE IMPLIES that all financial transactions have an NPV of zero and neither create nor destroy value. Consequently, in Chapter 14, we found that the choice of debt versus equity financing does not affect the value of a firm: The funds raised from issuing debt equal the present value of the future interest and principal payments the firm will make. While leverage increases the risk and cost of capital of the firm's equity, the firm's weighted average cost of capital (WACC), total value, and share price are unaltered by a change in leverage. That is, *in a perfect capital market, a firm's choice of capital structure is unimportant*.

This statement is at odds, however, with the observation that firms invest significant resources, both in terms of managerial time and effort and investment banking fees, in managing their capital structures. In many instances, the choice of leverage is of critical importance to a firm's value and future success. As we will show, there are large and systematic variations in the typical capital structures for different industries. For example, in July 2012, Amgen, a biotechnology and drug company, had debt of $24 billion, cash of $22 billion, and equity worth more than $64 billion, giving the firm a market debt-equity ratio of 0.38, with very little net debt. In contrast, Navistar International, an auto and truck manufacturer, had a debt-equity ratio of 2.6. Truck manufacturers in general have higher debt ratios than biotechnology and drug companies. If capital structure is unimportant, why do we see such consistent differences in capital structures across firms and industries? Why do managers dedicate so much time, effort, and expense to the capital structure choice?

As Modigliani and Miller made clear in their original work, capital structure does not matter in *perfect* capital markets. Recall from Chapter 14 that a perfect capital market exists under the following assumptions:

1. Investors and firms can trade the same set of securities at competitive market prices equal to the present value of their future cash flows.

2. There are no taxes, transaction costs, or issuance costs associated with security trading.

3. A firm's financing decisions do not change the cash flows generated by its investments, nor do they reveal new information about them.

Thus, if capital structure *does* matter, then it must stem from a market *imperfection*. In this chapter, we focus on one such imperfection—taxes. Corporations and investors must pay taxes on the income they earn from their investments. As we will see, a firm can enhance its value by using leverage to minimize the taxes it, and its investors, pay.

15.1 The Interest Tax Deduction

Corporations must pay taxes on the income that they earn. Because they pay taxes on their profits after interest payments are deducted, interest expenses reduce the amount of corporate tax firms must pay. This feature of the tax code creates an incentive to use debt.

Let's consider the impact of interest expenses on the taxes paid by Macy's, Inc., a retail department store. Macy's had earnings before interest and taxes of approximately $2.5 billion in 2012, and interest expenses of about $430 million. Given Macy's marginal corporate tax rate of 35%,[1] the effect of leverage on Macy's earnings is shown in Table 15.1.

TABLE 15.1	Macy's Income with and without Leverage, Fiscal Year 2012 ($ million)	
	With Leverage	**Without Leverage**
EBIT	$2500	$2500
Interest expense	−430	0
Income before tax	2070	2500
Taxes (35%)	−725	−875
Net income	$1345	$1625

As we can see from Table 15.1, Macy's net income in 2012 was lower with leverage than it would have been without leverage. Thus, Macy's debt obligations reduced the income available to equity holders. But more importantly, the *total* amount available to *all* investors was higher with leverage:

	With Leverage	Without Leverage
Interest paid to debt holders	430	0
Income available to equity holders	1345	1625
Total available to all investors	$1775	$1625

With leverage, Macy's was able to pay out $1775 million in total to its investors, versus only $1625 million without leverage, representing an increase of $150 million.

---

[1]Macy's paid an average tax rate of approximately 35.6 % in 2012, after accounting for other credits and deferrals. Because we are interested in the impact of a change in leverage, Macy's marginal tax rate—the tax rate that would apply to additional taxable income—is relevant to our discussion.

It might seem odd that a firm can be better off with leverage even though its earnings are lower. But recall from Chapter 14 that the value of a firm is the total amount it can raise from all investors, not just equity holders. Because leverage allows the firm to pay out more in total to its investors—including interest payments to debt holders—it will be able to raise more total capital initially.

Where does the additional $150 million come from? Looking at Table 15.1, we can see that this gain is equal to the reduction in taxes with leverage: $875 million − $725 million = $150 million. Because Macy's does not owe taxes on the $430 million of earnings it used to make interest payments, this $430 million is *shielded* from the corporate tax, providing the tax savings of 35% × $430 million = $150 million.

In general, the gain to investors from the tax deductibility of interest payments is referred to as the **interest tax shield**. The interest tax shield is the additional amount that a firm would have paid in taxes if it did not have leverage. We can calculate the amount of the interest tax shield each year as follows:

$$\text{Interest Tax Shield} = \text{Corporate Tax Rate} \times \text{Interest Payments} \qquad (15.1)$$

EXAMPLE 15.1   **Computing the Interest Tax Shield**

Problem

Shown below is the income statement for D.F. Builders (DFB). Given its marginal corporate tax rate of 35%, what is the amount of the interest tax shield for DFB in years 2009 through 2012?

DFB Income Statement ($ million)	2009	2010	2011	2012
Total sales	$3369	$3706	$4077	$4432
Cost of sales	−2359	−2584	−2867	−3116
Selling, general, and administrative expense	−226	−248	−276	−299
Depreciation	−22	−25	−27	−29
Operating income	762	849	907	988
Other income	7	8	10	12
EBIT	769	857	917	1000
Interest expense	−50	−80	−100	−100
Income before tax	719	777	817	900
Taxes (35%)	−252	−272	−286	−315
Net income	$467	$505	$531	$585

Solution

From Eq. 15.1, the interest tax shield is the tax rate of 35% multiplied by the interest payments in each year:

($ million)	2009	2010	2011	2012
Interest expense	−50	−80	−100	−100
Interest tax shield (35% × **interest expense**)	17.5	28	35	35

Thus, the interest tax shield enabled DFB to pay an additional $115.5 million to its investors over this period.

CONCEPT CHECK

1. With corporate income taxes, explain why a firm's value can be higher with leverage even though its earnings are lower.

2. What is the interest tax shield?

15.2 Valuing the Interest Tax Shield

When a firm uses debt, the interest tax shield provides a corporate tax benefit each year. To determine the benefit of leverage for the value of the firm, we must compute the present value of the stream of future interest tax shields the firm will receive.

The Interest Tax Shield and Firm Value

Each year a firm makes interest payments, the cash flows it pays to investors will be higher than they would be without leverage by the amount of the interest tax shield:

$$\begin{pmatrix} \text{Cash Flows to Investors} \\ \text{with Leverage} \end{pmatrix} = \begin{pmatrix} \text{Cash Flows to Investors} \\ \text{without Leverage} \end{pmatrix} + (\text{Interest Tax Shield})$$

Figure 15.1 illustrates this relationship. Here you can see how each dollar of pretax cash flows is divided. The firm uses some fraction to pay taxes, and it pays the rest to investors. By increasing the amount paid to debt holders through interest payments, the amount of the pretax cash flows that must be paid as taxes decreases. The gain in total cash flows to investors is the interest tax shield.

Because the cash flows of the levered firm are equal to the sum of the cash flows from the unlevered firm plus the interest tax shield, by the Law of One Price the same must be true for the present values of these cash flows. Thus, letting V^L and V^U represent the value of the firm with and without leverage, respectively, we have the following change to MM Proposition I in the presence of taxes:

The total value of the levered firm exceeds the value of the firm without leverage due to the present value of the tax savings from debt:

$$V^L = V^U + PV(\text{Interest Tax Shield}) \tag{15.2}$$

FIGURE 15.1   **The Cash Flows of the Unlevered and Levered Firm**

By increasing the cash flows paid to debt holders through interest payments, a firm reduces the amount paid in taxes. The increase in total cash flows paid to investors is the interest tax shield. (The figure assumes a 40% marginal corporate tax rate.)

Clearly, there is an important tax advantage to the use of debt financing. But how large is this tax benefit? To compute the increase in the firm's total value associated with the interest tax shield, we need to forecast how a firm's debt—and therefore its interest payments—will vary over time. Given a forecast of future interest payments, we can determine the interest tax shield and compute its present value by discounting it at a rate that corresponds to its risk.

EXAMPLE 15.2	**Valuing the Interest Tax Shield without Risk**

Problem

Suppose DFB plans to pay $100 million in interest each year for the next 10 years, and then to repay the principal of $2 billion in year 10. These payments are risk free, and DFB's marginal tax rate will remain 35% throughout this period. If the risk-free interest rate is 5%, by how much does the interest tax shield increase the value of DFB?

Solution

In this case, the interest tax shield is 35% × $100 million = $35 million each year for the next 10 years. Therefore, we can value it as a 10-year annuity. Because the tax savings are known and not risky, we can discount them at the 5% risk-free rate:

$$PV(\text{Interest Tax Shield}) = \$35 \text{ million} \times \frac{1}{0.05}\left(1 - \frac{1}{1.05^{10}}\right)$$
$$= \$270 \text{ million}$$

The final repayment of principal in year 10 is not deductible, so it does not contribute to the tax shield.

The Interest Tax Shield with Permanent Debt

In Example 15.2, we know with certainty the firm's future interest payments and associated tax savings. In practice, this case is rare. Typically, the level of future interest payments varies due to changes the firm makes in the amount of debt outstanding, changes in the interest rate on that debt, and the risk that the firm may default and fail to make an interest payment. In addition, the firm's marginal tax rate may fluctuate due to changes in the tax code and changes in the firm's income bracket.

Rather than attempting to account for all possibilities here, let's consider the special case in which the firm issues debt and plans to keep the dollar amount of debt constant forever.[2] For example, the firm might issue a perpetual consol bond, making only interest payments but never repaying the principal. More realistically, suppose the firm issues short-term debt, such as a five-year coupon bond. When the principal is due, the firm raises the money needed to pay it by issuing new debt. In this way, the firm never pays off the principal but simply refinances it whenever it comes due. In this situation, the debt is effectively permanent.

Many large firms have a policy of maintaining a certain amount of debt on their balance sheets. As old bonds and loans mature, new borrowing takes place. The key assumption here is that the firm maintains a *fixed* dollar amount of outstanding debt, rather than an amount that changes with the size of the firm.

---

[2]We discuss how to value the interest tax shield with more complicated leverage policies in Chapter 18.

Pizza and Taxes

In Chapter 14, we mentioned the pizza analogy that Merton Miller once used to describe the MM Propositions with perfect capital markets: No matter how you slice it, you still have the same amount of pizza.

We can extend this analogy to the setting with taxes, but the story is a bit different. In this case, every time equity holders get a slice of pizza, Uncle Sam gets a slice as a tax payment.

But when debt holders get a slice, there is no tax. Thus, by allocating more slices to debt holders rather than to equity holders, more pizza will be available to investors. While the total amount of pizza does not change, there is more pizza left over for investors to consume because less pizza is consumed by Uncle Sam in taxes.

Suppose a firm borrows debt D and keeps the debt permanently. If the firm's marginal tax rate is τ_c, and if the debt is riskless with a risk-free interest rate r_f, then the interest tax shield each year is $\tau_c \times r_f \times D$, and we can value the tax shield as a perpetuity:

$$PV(\text{Interest Tax Shield}) = \frac{\tau_c \times \text{Interest}}{r_f} = \frac{\tau_c \times (r_f \times D)}{r_f}$$

$$= \tau_c \times D$$

The above calculation assumes the debt is risk free and the risk-free interest rate is constant. These assumptions are not necessary, however. As long as the debt is fairly priced, no arbitrage implies that its market value must equal the present value of the future interest payments:[3]

$$\text{Market Value of Debt} = D = PV(\text{Future Interest Payments}) \tag{15.3}$$

If the firm's marginal tax rate is constant,[4] then we have the following general formula:

Value of the Interest Tax Shield of Permanent Debt

$$PV(\text{Interest Tax Shield}) = PV(\tau_c \times \text{Future Interest Payments})$$

$$= \tau_c \times PV(\text{Future Interest Payments})$$

$$= \tau_c \times D \tag{15.4}$$

This formula shows the magnitude of the interest tax shield. Given a 35% corporate tax rate, it implies that for every $1 in new permanent debt that the firm issues, the value of the firm increases by $0.35.

The Weighted Average Cost of Capital with Taxes

The tax benefit of leverage can also be expressed in terms of the weighted average cost of capital. When a firm uses debt financing, the cost of the interest it must pay is offset to some extent by the tax savings from the interest tax shield. For example, suppose a firm

---

[3]Equation 15.3 holds even if interest rates fluctuate and the debt is risky, as long as any new debt is also fairly priced. It requires only that the firm never repay the principal on the debt (it either refinances or defaults on the principal). The result follows by the same argument used in Chapter 9 to show that the price of equity should equal the present value of all future dividends.

[4]The tax rate may not be constant if the firm's taxable income fluctuates sufficiently to change the firm's tax bracket (we discuss this possibility further in Section 15.5).

with a 35% tax rate borrows $100,000 at 10% interest per year. Then its net cost at the end of the year is

		Year-End
Interest expense	$r \times \$100,000 =$	$10,000
Tax savings	$-\tau_c \times r \times \$100,000 =$	−3,500
Effective after-tax cost of debt	$r \times (1 - \tau_c) \times \$100,000 =$	$6,500

The effective cost of the debt is only $6,500/$100,000 = 6.50% of the loan amount, rather than the full 10% interest. Thus, the tax deductibility of interest lowers the effective cost of debt financing for the firm. More generally,[5]

With tax-deductible interest, the effective after-tax borrowing rate is $r(1 - \tau_c)$.

In Chapter 14, we showed that without taxes, the firm's WACC was equal to its unlevered cost of capital, which is the average return that the firm must pay to its investors (equity holders and debt holders). The tax-deductibility of interest payments, however, lowers the effective after-tax cost of debt *to the firm*. As we discussed in Chapter 12, we can account for the benefit of the interest tax shield by calculating the WACC using the effective after-tax cost of debt:

Weighted Average Cost of Capital (After Tax)[6]

$$r_{wacc} = \frac{E}{E + D} r_E + \frac{D}{E + D} r_D (1 - \tau_c) \tag{15.5}$$

The WACC represents the effective cost of capital to the firm, after including the benefits of the interest tax shield. It is therefore lower than the pretax WACC, which is the average return paid to the firm's investors. From Eq. 15.5, we have the following relationship between the WACC and the firm's pretax WACC:

$$r_{wacc} = \underbrace{\frac{E}{E + D} r_E + \frac{D}{E + D} r_D}_{\text{Pretax WACC}} - \underbrace{\frac{D}{E + D} r_D \tau_c}_{\substack{\text{Reduction Due} \\ \text{to Interest Tax Shield}}} \tag{15.6}$$

As we will show in Chapter 18, even in the presence of taxes, a firm's target leverage ratio does not affect the firm's pretax WACC, which equals its unlevered cost of capital and depends only on the risk of the firm's assets.[7] Thus, the higher the firm's leverage, the more the firm exploits the tax advantage of debt, and the lower its WACC is. Figure 15.2 illustrates this decline in the WACC with the firm's leverage ratio.

The Interest Tax Shield with a Target Debt-Equity Ratio

Earlier we calculated the value of the tax shield assuming the firm maintains a constant level of debt. In many cases this assumption is unrealistic—rather than maintain a constant

---

[5]We derived this same result in Chapter 5 when considering the implications of tax-deductible interest for individuals (e.g., with a home mortgage).

[6]We will derive this formula in Chapter 18. See Chapter 12 for methods of estimating the cost of debt (and Eq. 12.12 and footnote 18 on page 422 in the context of the WACC.)

[7]Specifically, if the firm adjusts its leverage to maintain a target debt-equity ratio or interest coverage ratio, then its pretax WACC remains constant and equal to its unlevered cost of capital. See Chapter 18 for a full discussion of the relationship between the firm's levered and unlevered costs of capital.

FIGURE 15.2	The WACC with and without Corporate Taxes

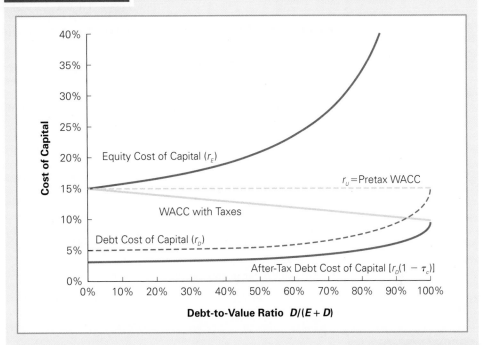

We compute the WACC as a function of the firm's target debt-to-value ratio using Eq. 15.5. As shown in Figure 14.1, the firm's unlevered cost of capital or pretax WACC is constant, reflecting the required return of the firm's investors based on the risk of the firm's assets. However, the (effective after-tax) WACC, which represents the after-tax cost to the firm, declines with leverage as the interest tax shield grows. The figure assumes a marginal corporate income tax rate of $\tau_c = 35\%$.

level of debt, many firms target a specific debt-equity ratio instead. When a firm does so, the level of its debt will grow (or shrink) with the size of the firm.

As we will show formally in Chapter 18, when a firm adjusts its debt over time so that its debt-equity ratio is expected to remain constant, we can compute its value with leverage, V^L, by discounting its free cash flow using the WACC. The value of the interest tax shield can be found by comparing V^L to the unlevered value, V^U, of the free cash flow discounted at the firm's unlevered cost of capital, the pretax WACC.

EXAMPLE 15.3	Valuing the Interest Tax Shield with a Target Debt-Equity Ratio

Problem

Western Lumber Company expects to have free cash flow in the coming year of $4.25 million, and its free cash flow is expected to grow at a rate of 4% per year thereafter. Western Lumber has an equity cost of capital of 10% and a debt cost of capital of 6%, and it pays a corporate tax rate of 35%. If Western Lumber maintains a debt-equity ratio of 0.50, what is the value of its interest tax shield?

Solution

We can estimate the value of Western Lumber's interest tax shield by comparing its value with and without leverage. We compute its unlevered value by discounting its free cash flow at its pretax WACC:

$$\text{Pretax WACC} = \frac{E}{E + D}r_E + \frac{D}{E + D}r_D = \frac{1}{1 + 0.5}10\% + \frac{0.5}{1 + 0.5}6\% = 8.67\%$$

Because Western Lumber's free cash flow is expected to grow at a constant rate, we can value it as a constant growth perpetuity:

$$V^U = \frac{4.25}{8.67\% - 4\%} = \$91 \text{ million}$$

To compute Western Lumber's levered value, we calculate its WACC:

$$\text{WACC} = \frac{E}{E + D}r_E + \frac{D}{E + D}r_D(1 - \tau_c)$$

$$= \frac{1}{1 + 0.5}10\% + \frac{0.5}{1 + 0.5}6\%(1 - 0.35) = 7.97\%$$

Thus, Western Lumber's value including the interest tax shield is

$$V^L = \frac{4.25}{7.97\% - 4\%} = \$107 \text{ million}$$

The value of the interest tax shield is therefore

$$PV(\text{Interest Tax Shield}) = V^L - V^U = 107 - 91 = \$16 \text{ million}$$

CONCEPT CHECK

1. With corporate taxes as the only market imperfection, how does the value of the firm with leverage differ from its value without leverage?

2. How does leverage affect a firm's weighted average cost of capital?

15.3 Recapitalizing to Capture the Tax Shield

When a firm makes a significant change to its capital structure, the transaction is called a recapitalization (or simply a "recap"). In Chapter 14, we introduced a leveraged recapitalization in which a firm issues a large amount of debt and uses the proceeds to pay a special dividend or to repurchase shares. Leveraged recaps were especially popular in the mid- to late-1980s, when many firms found that these transactions could reduce their tax payments.

Let's see how such a transaction might benefit current shareholders. Midco Industries has 20 million shares outstanding with a market price of $15 per share and no debt. Midco has had consistently stable earnings, and pays a 35% tax rate. Management plans to borrow $100 million on a permanent basis through a leveraged recap in which they would use the borrowed funds to repurchase outstanding shares. Their expectation is that the tax savings from this transaction will boost Midco's stock price and benefit shareholders. Let's see if this expectation is realistic.

The Tax Benefit

First, we examine the tax consequences of Midco's leveraged recap. Without leverage, Midco's total market value is the value of its unlevered equity. Assuming the current stock price is the fair price for the shares without leverage:

$$V^U = (20 \text{ million shares}) \times (\$15/\text{share}) = \$300 \text{ million}$$

With leverage, Midco will reduce its annual tax payments. If Midco borrows $100 million using permanent debt, the present value of the firm's future tax savings is

$$PV(\text{Interest Tax Shield}) = \tau_c D = 35\% \times \$100 \text{ million} = \$35 \text{ million}$$

Thus, the total value of the levered firm will be

$$V^L = V^U + \tau_c D = \$300 \text{ million} + \$35 \text{ million} = \$335 \text{ million}$$

This total value represents the combined value of the debt and the equity after the recapitalization. Because the value of the debt is $100 million, the value of the equity is

$$E = V^L - D = \$335 \text{ million} - \$100 \text{ million} = \$235 \text{ million}$$

While total firm value has increased, the value of equity dropped after the recap. How do shareholders benefit from this transaction?

Even though the value of the shares outstanding drops to $235 million, don't forget that shareholders will also receive the $100 million that Midco will pay out through the share repurchase. In total, they will receive the full $335 million, a gain of $35 million over the value of their shares without leverage. Let's trace the details of the share repurchase and see how it leads to an increase in the stock price.

The Share Repurchase

Suppose Midco repurchases its shares at their current price of $15 per share. The firm will repurchase $100 million ÷ $15 per share = 6.667 million shares, and it will then have 20 − 6.667 = 13.333 million shares outstanding. Because the total value of equity is $235 million, the new share price is

$$\frac{\$235 \text{ million}}{13.333 \text{ million shares}} = \$17.625$$

The shareholders who keep their shares earn a capital gain of $17.625 − $15 = $2.625 per share, for a total gain of

$$\$2.625/\text{share} \times 13.333 \text{ million shares} = \$35 \text{ million}$$

In this case, the shareholders who remain after the recap receive the benefit of the tax shield. However, you may have noticed something odd in the previous calculations. We assumed that Midco was able to repurchase the shares at the initial price of $15 per share, and then demonstrated that the shares would be worth $17.625 after the transaction. Why would a shareholder agree to sell the shares for $15 when they are worth $17.625?

No Arbitrage Pricing

The previous scenario represents an arbitrage opportunity. Investors could *buy* shares for $15 immediately before the repurchase, and they could sell these shares immediately afterward at a higher price. But this activity would raise the share price above $15 even before the repurchase: Once investors know the recap will occur, the share price will rise immediately to a level that reflects the $35 million value of the interest tax shield that the firm will receive. That is, the value of the Midco's equity will rise *immediately* from $300 million to $335 million. With 20 million shares outstanding, the share price will rise to

$$\$335 \text{ million} \div 20 \text{ million shares} = \$16.75 \text{ per share}$$

Midco must offer at least this price to repurchase the shares.

With a repurchase price of $16.75, the shareholders who tender their shares and the shareholders who hold their shares both gain $16.75 − $15 = $1.75 per share as a result of the transaction. The benefit of the interest tax shield goes to all 20 million of the original shares outstanding for a total benefit of $1.75/share × 20 million shares = $35 million. In other words,

When securities are fairly priced, the original shareholders of a firm capture the full benefit of the interest tax shield from an increase in leverage.

EXAMPLE 15.4	**Alternative Repurchase Prices**

Problem

Suppose Midco announces a price at which it will repurchase $100 million worth of its shares. Show that $16.75 is the lowest price it could offer and expect shareholders to tender their shares. How will the benefits be divided if Midco offers more than $16.75 per share?

Solution

For each repurchase price, we can compute the number of shares Midco will repurchase, as well as the number of shares that will remain after the share repurchase. Dividing the $235 million total value of equity by the number of remaining shares gives Midco's new share price after the transaction. No shareholders will be willing to sell their shares unless the repurchase price is at least as high as the share price after the transaction; otherwise, they would be better off waiting to sell their shares. As the table shows, the repurchase price must be at least $16.75 for shareholders to be willing to sell rather than waiting to receive a higher price.

Repurchase Price ($/share)	Shares Repurchased (million)	Shares Remaining (million)	New Share Price ($/share)
P_R	$R = 100/P_R$	$N = 20 - R$	$P_N = 235/N$
15.00	6.67	13.33	$17.63
16.25	6.15	13.85	16.97
16.75	5.97	14.03	16.75
17.25	5.80	14.20	16.55
17.50	5.71	14.29	16.45

If Midco offers a price above $16.75, then all existing shareholders will be eager to sell their shares, because the shares will have a lower value after the transaction is completed. In this case, Midco's offer to repurchase shares will be oversubscribed and Midco will need to use a lottery or some other rationing mechanism to choose from whom it will repurchase shares. In that case, more of the benefits of the recap will go to the shareholders who are lucky enough to be selected for the repurchase.

Analyzing the Recap: The Market Value Balance Sheet

We can analyze the recapitalization using the market value balance sheet, a tool we developed in Chapter 14. It states that the total market value of a firm's securities must equal the total market value of the firm's assets. In the presence of corporate taxes, *we must include the interest tax shield as one of the firm's assets.*

We analyze the leveraged recap by breaking this transaction into steps, as shown in Table 15.2. First, the recap is announced. At this point, investors anticipate the future interest tax shield, raising the value of Midco's assets by $35 million. Next, Midco issues $100 million in new debt, increasing both Midco's cash and liabilities by that amount. Finally, Midco uses the cash to repurchase shares at their market price of $16.75. In this step, Midco's cash declines, as does the number of shares outstanding.

TABLE 15.2	Market Value Balance Sheet for the Steps in Midco's Leveraged Recapitalization			
Market Value Balance Sheet ($ million)	Initial	Step 1: Recap Announced	Step 2: Debt Issuance	Step 3: Share Repurchase
Assets				
Cash	0	0	100	0
Original assets (V^U)	300	300	300	300
Interest tax shield	0	35	35	35
Total assets	300	335	435	335
Liabilities				
Debt	0	0	100	100
Equity = Assets − Liabilities	300	335	335	235
Shares outstanding (million)	20	20	20	14.03
Price per share	$15.00	$16.75	$16.75	$16.75

Note that the share price rises at the announcement of the recap. This increase in the share price is due solely to the present value of the (anticipated) interest tax shield. Thus, even though leverage reduces the total value of equity, shareholders capture the benefits of the interest tax shield upfront.[8]

CONCEPT CHECK

1. How can shareholders benefit from a leveraged recap when it reduces the total value of equity?

2. How does the interest tax shield enter into the market value balance sheet?

15.4 Personal Taxes

So far, we have looked at the benefits of leverage with regard to the taxes a corporation must pay. By reducing a firm's corporate tax liability, debt allows the firm to pay more of its cash flows to investors.

Unfortunately for investors, after they receive the cash flows, they are generally taxed again. For individuals, interest payments received from debt are taxed as income. Equity investors also must pay taxes on dividends and capital gains. What are the consequences to firm value of these additional taxes?

Including Personal Taxes in the Interest Tax Shield

The value of a firm is equal to the amount of money the firm can raise by issuing securities. The amount of money an investor will pay for a security ultimately depends on the benefits the investor will receive—namely, the cash flows the investor will receive *after all taxes have been paid*. Thus, just like corporate taxes, personal taxes reduce the cash flows to investors and diminish firm value. As a result, the actual interest tax shield depends on the reduction in the total taxes (both corporate and personal) that are paid.[9]

---

[8] We are ignoring other potential side effects of leverage, such as costs of future financial distress. We discuss such costs in Chapter 16.

[9] This point was made most forcefully in yet another pathbreaking article by Merton Miller, "Debt and Taxes," *Journal of Finance* 32 (1977): 261–275. See also M. Miller and M. Scholes, "Dividends and Taxes," *Journal of Financial Economics* 6 (1978): 333–364.

Personal taxes have the potential to offset some of the corporate tax benefits of leverage that we have described. In particular, in the United States and many other countries, interest income has historically been taxed more heavily than capital gains from equity. Table 15.3 shows recent top federal tax rates in the United States. The average rate on equity income listed in the table is an average of the top capital gains and dividend tax rates.

To determine the true tax benefit of leverage, we need to evaluate the combined effect of both corporate and personal taxes. Consider a firm with $1 of earnings before interest and taxes. The firm can either pay this $1 to debt holders as interest, or it can use the $1 to pay equity holders directly, with a dividend, or indirectly, by retaining earnings so that shareholders receive a capital gain. Figure 15.3 shows the tax consequences of each option.

Using 2012 tax rates, debt offers a clear tax advantage with respect to corporate taxes: For every $1 in pretax cash flows that debt holders receive, equity holders receive $\tau_c = 35\%$ less under current tax rates. But at the personal level, the income tax rate on interest income is $\tau_i = 35\%$, whereas the tax rate on equity income is only $\tau_e = 15\%$. Combining corporate and personal rates leads to the following comparison:

	After-Tax Cash Flows	Using Current Tax Rates
To debt holders	$(1 - \tau_i)$	$(1 - 0.35) = 0.65$
To equity holders	$(1 - \tau_c)(1 - \tau_e)$	$(1 - 0.35)(1 - 0.15) = 0.5525$

While a tax advantage to debt remains, it is not as large as we calculated based on corporate taxes alone. To express the comparison in relative terms, note that equity holders receive

$$\tau^* = \frac{0.65 - 0.5525}{0.65} = 15\%$$

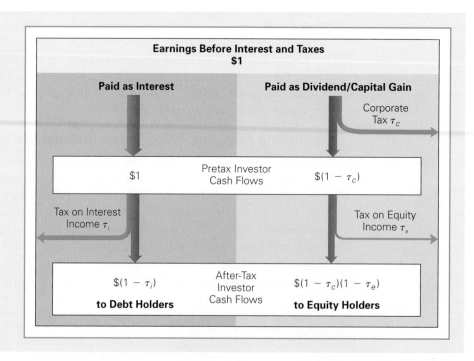

TABLE 15.3	Top Federal Tax Rates in the United States, 1971–2012

		Personal Tax Rates*			
Year	Corporate Tax Rate[†]	Interest Income	Average Rate on Equity Income	Dividends	Capital Gains
1971–1978	48%	70%	53%	70%	35%
1979–1981	46%	70%	49%	70%	28%
1982–1986	46%	50%	35%	50%	20%
1987	40%	39%	33%	39%	28%
1988–1990	34%	28%	28%	28%	28%
1991–1992	34%	31%	30%	31%	28%
1993–1996	35%	40%	34%	40%	28%
1997–2000	35%	40%	30%	40%	20%
2001–2002	35%	39%	30%	39%	20%
2003–2012	35%	35%	15%	15%	15%

*Interest income is taxed as ordinary income. Until 2003, dividends were also taxed as ordinary income. The average tax rate on equity income is an average of dividend and capital gain tax rates (consistent with a 50% dividend payout ratio and annual realization of capital gains), where the capital gain tax rate is the long-term rate applicable to assets held more than one year.

[†]The corporate rate shown is for C corporations with the highest level of income. Marginal rates can be higher for lower brackets. (For example, since 2000, the 35% tax rate applies to income levels above $18.3 million, while the tax rate for income levels between $100,000 and $335,000 is 39%.)

less after taxes than debt holders. In this case, personal taxes reduce the tax advantage of debt from 35% to 15%.

In general, every $1 received after taxes by debt holders from interest payments costs equity holders $(1 - \tau^*)$ on an after-tax basis, where

Effective Tax Advantage of Debt

$$\tau^* = \frac{(1 - \tau_i) - (1 - \tau_c)(1 - \tau_e)}{(1 - \tau_i)} = 1 - \frac{(1 - \tau_c)(1 - \tau_e)}{(1 - \tau_i)} \qquad (15.7)$$

When there are no personal taxes, or when the personal tax rates on debt and equity income are the same ($\tau_i = \tau_e$), this formula reduces to $\tau^* = \tau_c$. But when equity income is taxed less heavily ($\tau_i > \tau_e$), then τ^* is less than τ_c.

EXAMPLE 15.5	Calculating the Effective Tax Advantage of Debt

Problem
What was the effective tax advantage of debt in 1980? In 1990?

Solution
Using Eq. 15.7 and the tax rates in Table 15.3, we can calculate

$$\tau^*_{1980} = 1 - \frac{(1 - 0.46)(1 - 0.49)}{(1 - 0.70)} = 8.2\%$$

$$\tau^*_{1990} = 1 - \frac{(1 - 0.34)(1 - 0.28)}{(1 - 0.28)} = 34\%$$

Given the tax rates at the time, the effective tax advantage of debt was much lower in 1980 than in 1990.

FIGURE 15.4

The Effective Tax Advantage of Debt with and without Personal Taxes, 1971–2012

After adjusting for personal taxes, the tax advantage of debt τ^* is generally below τ_c, but still positive. It has also varied widely with changes to the tax code.

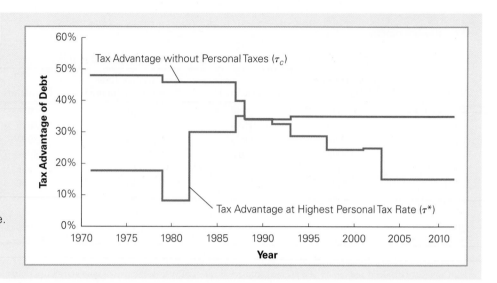

Figure 15.4 shows the effective tax advantage of debt since 1971 in the United States. It has varied widely over time with changes in the tax code.

Valuing the Interest Tax Shield with Personal Taxes

How does the forgoing analysis of personal taxes affect our valuation of the debt tax shield? We postpone a detailed answer to this question until Chapter 18, and limit our discussion here to a few important observations. First, as long as $\tau^* > 0$, then despite any tax disadvantage of debt at the personal level, a net tax advantage for leverage remains. In the case of permanent debt, the value of the firm with leverage becomes

$$V^L = V^U + \tau^* D \tag{15.8}$$

Because the personal tax disadvantage of debt generally implies $\tau^* < \tau_c$, comparing Eq. 15.8 with Eq. 15.4 we see that the benefit of leverage is reduced.

Personal taxes have a similar, but indirect, effect on the firm's weighted average cost of capital. While we still compute the WACC using the corporate tax rate τ_c as in Eq. 15.5, with personal taxes the firm's equity and debt costs of capital will adjust to compensate investors for their respective tax burdens. The net result is that a personal tax disadvantage for debt causes the WACC to decline more slowly with leverage than it otherwise would.

EXAMPLE 15.6

Estimating the Interest Tax Shield with Personal Taxes

Problem
Estimate the value of Midco after its $100 million leveraged recap, accounting for personal taxes in 2012.

Solution
Given $\tau^* = 15\%$ in 2012, and given Midco's current value $V^U = \$300$ million, we estimate $V^L = V^U + \tau^* D = \$300$ million $+ 15\%(\$100$ million$) = \$315$ million. With 20 million original shares outstanding, the stock price would increase by $15 million $\div$ 20 million shares $= \$0.75$ share.

Determining the Actual Tax Advantage of Debt

In estimating the effective tax advantage of debt after taking personal taxes into account, we made several assumptions that may need adjustment when determining the actual tax benefit for a particular firm or investor.

First, with regard to the capital gains tax rate, we assumed that investors paid capital gains taxes every year. But unlike taxes on interest income or dividends, which are paid annually, capital gains taxes are paid only at the time the investor sells the stock and realizes the gain. Deferring the payment of capital gains taxes lowers the present value of the taxes, which can be interpreted as a lower *effective* capital gains tax rate. For example, given a capital gains tax rate of 15% and an interest rate of 6%, holding the asset for 10 more years lowers the effective tax rate this year to $(15\%)/1.06^{10} = 8.4\%$. Also, investors with accrued losses that they can use to offset gains face a zero effective capital gains tax rate. As a consequence, investors with longer holding periods or with accrued losses face a lower tax rate on equity income, decreasing the effective tax advantage of debt.

A second key assumption in our analysis is the computation of the tax rate on equity income τ_e. Using the average dividend and capital gains tax rate is reasonable for a firm that pays out 50% of its earnings as dividends, so that shareholder gains from additional earnings were evenly split between dividends and capital gains. For firms with much higher or much lower payout ratios, however, this average would not be accurate. For example, for firms that do not pay dividends, the capital gains tax rate should be used as the tax rate on equity income.

Finally, we assumed the top marginal federal income tax rates for the investor. In reality, rates vary for individual investors, and many investors face lower rates. (We have also ignored state taxes, which vary widely by state and have an additional impact.) At lower rates, the effects of personal taxes are less substantial. Moreover, *many investors face no personal taxes.* Consider investments held in retirement savings accounts or pension funds that

---

Cutting the Dividend Tax Rate

In January 2003, President George W. Bush unveiled a proposal to boost the U.S. economy with a $674 billion tax cut plan, half of which would come from eliminating taxes on dividends. From the moment it was announced, this tax cut generated tremendous controversy.

Proponents argued that easing the tax bite on investors' dividend income would boost the stock market and stimulate the sluggish economy. Critics quickly denounced it as a tax cut for the rich. But one of the underlying motives of the plan, authored in large part by economist R. Glenn Hubbard, was to end the current distortion in tax laws that encourage companies to accumulate debt because interest is deductible but dividend payments are not.

Levying taxes both on corporate earnings and on the dividends or capital gains paid to investors is known as *double taxation.* The lower rates on capital gains have provided some relief from double taxation. In 2002, however, dividends were still taxed at the same rate as ordinary income, leading to a combined tax rate in excess of 60% on dividends—one of the highest tax rates on dividends of any industrialized nation. As we have seen, this double taxation results in a tax advantage to debt financing.

Ultimately, policymakers agreed to a compromise that reduced the tax rate for individuals on both dividends (for stocks held for more than 60 days) and capital gains (for assets held for more than one year) to 15%. This compromise still gives a tax advantage to debt, but at a decreased level from prior years (see Figure 15.4).

The "Bush tax cuts" (which also lowered income and capital gains tax rates) were originally set to expire at the end of 2010. Fearing their expiration would slow the nascent economic recovery, in December 2010 Congress extended the tax cuts through 2012. As of mid-2012 there is renewed debate regarding a further extension of the tax cuts, which may stimulate growth but would widen the federal deficit.

are not subject to taxes.[10] For these investors, the effective tax advantage of debt is $\tau^* = \tau_c$, the full corporate tax rate. This full tax advantage would also apply to securities dealers for whom interest, dividends, and capital gains are all taxed equivalently as income.

What is the bottom line? Calculating the effective tax advantage of debt accurately is extremely difficult, and this advantage will vary across firms (and from investor to investor). A firm must consider the tax bracket of its typical debt holders to estimate τ_i, and the tax bracket and holding period of its typical equity holders to determine τ_e. If, for instance, a firm's investors hold shares primarily through their retirement accounts, $\tau^* \approx \tau_c$. While τ^* is likely to be somewhat below τ_c for the typical firm, exactly how much lower is open to debate. Our calculation of τ^* in Figure 15.4 should be interpreted as a very rough guide at best.[11]

CONCEPT CHECK

1. Under current law (in 2012), why is there a personal tax disadvantage of debt?

2. How does this personal tax disadvantage of debt change the value of leverage for the firm?

15.5 Optimal Capital Structure with Taxes

In Modigliani and Miller's setting of perfect capital markets, firms could use any combination of debt and equity to finance their investments without changing the value of the firm. In effect, any capital structure was optimal. In this chapter we have seen that taxes change that conclusion because interest payments create a valuable tax shield. Even after adjusting for personal taxes, the value of a firm with leverage exceeds the value of an unlevered firm, and there is a tax advantage to using debt financing.

Do Firms Prefer Debt?

Do firms show a preference for debt in practice? Figure 15.5 illustrates the net new issues of equity and debt by U.S. corporations. For equity, the figure shows the total amount of new equity issued, less the amount retired through share repurchases and acquisitions. For debt, it shows the total amount of new borrowing less the amount of loans repaid.

Figure 15.5 makes clear that when firms raise new capital from investors, they do so primarily by issuing debt. In fact, in most years, aggregate equity issues are negative, meaning that firms are reducing the amount of equity outstanding by buying shares. (This observation does not mean that *all* firms raised funds using debt. Many firms may have sold equity to raise funds. However, at the same time, other firms were buying or repurchasing an equal or greater amount.) The data show a clear preference for debt as a source of external financing for the total population of U.S. firms. Indeed, in aggregate, firms appear to be borrowing in excess of the funds they need for internal use in order to repurchase equity.

While firms seem to prefer debt when raising external funds, not all investment is externally funded. As Figure 15.5 also shows, capital expenditures greatly exceed firms' external financing, implying that most investment and growth is supported by internally generated funds, such as retained earnings. Thus, even though firms have not *issued* new equity, the market value of equity has risen over time as firms have grown. In fact, as shown in

---

[10]Evidence from the mid-1990s suggests that the growth in pension funds has lowered the average marginal tax rate for investors to about half the rates shown in Table 15.3. See J. Poterba, "The Rate of Return to Corporate Capital and Factor Shares: New Estimates Using Revised National Income Accounts and Capital Stock Data," NBER working paper no. 6263 (1997).

[11]For a discussion of methods of estimating τ^* and the need to include personal taxes, see J. Graham, "Do Personal Taxes Affect Corporate Financing Decisions?" *Journal of Public Economics* 73 (1999): 147–185.

FIGURE 15.5

Net External Financing and Capital Expenditures by U.S. Corporations, 1975–2011

In aggregate, firms have raised external capital primarily by issuing debt. These funds have been used to retire equity and fund investment, but the vast majority of capital expenditures are internally funded. (Amounts adjusted for inflation to reflect 2011 dollars.)

Source: Federal Reserve, *Flow of Funds Accounts of the United States*, 2012.

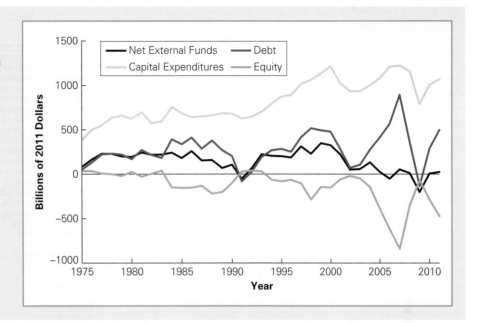

Figure 15.6, debt as a fraction of firm value has varied in a range from 30–50% for the average firm. The average debt-to-value ratio fell during the 1990s bull market, with the trend reversing post-2000 due to declines in the stock market as well as a dramatic increase in debt issuance in response to falling interest rates.

The aggregate data in Figure 15.6 masks two important tendencies. First, the use of leverage varies greatly by industry. Second, many firms retain large cash balances to reduce their effective leverage. These patterns are revealed in Figure 15.7, which shows *net* debt as a fraction of firm enterprise value for a number of industries and the overall market. Note that net debt is negative if a firm's cash holdings exceed its outstanding debt. Clearly, there are large differences in net leverage across industries. Firms in growth industries like biotechnology or high technology carry very little debt and maintain large cash reserves,

FIGURE 15.6

Debt-to-Value Ratio [$D/(E+D)$] of U.S. Firms, 1975–2011

Although firms have primarily issued debt rather than equity, the average proportion of debt in their capital structures has not increased due to the growth in value of existing equity.

Source: Compustat and Federal Reserve, *Flow of Funds Accounts of the United States*, 2012.

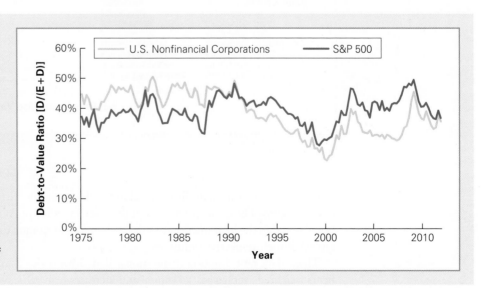

FIGURE 15.7

Net Debt-to-Enterprise Value Ratio for Select Industries

Figure shows industry median levels of net debt (total book value of debt less cash and short-term investments) as a percentage of firm enterprise value (equity market capitalization plus net debt). While the median level of net debt for all U.S. stocks was about 17.5% of firm value, note the large differences by industry.

Source: Capital IQ, 2012.

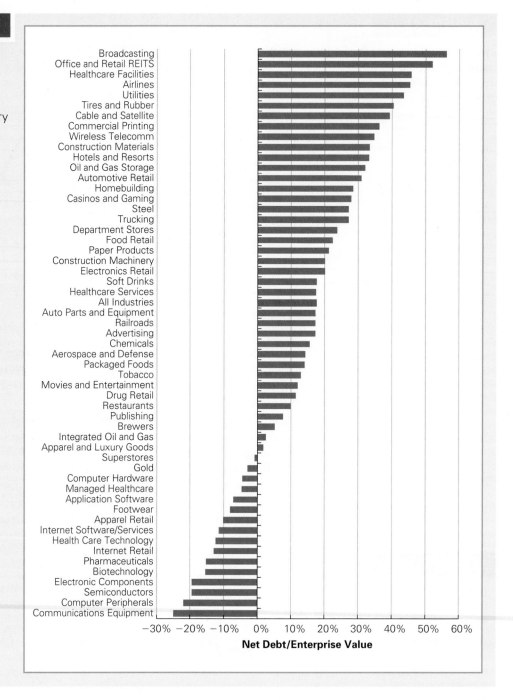

whereas airlines, real estate firms, trucking and automotive firms, and utilities have high leverage ratios. Thus, the differences in the leverage ratios of Amgen and Navistar International noted in the introduction to this chapter are not unique to these firms, but rather are typical of their respective industries.

These data raise important questions. If debt provides a tax advantage that lowers a firm's weighted average cost of capital and increases firm value, why does debt make up less than half of the capital structure of most firms? And why does the leverage choice vary so much across industries, with some firms having no net leverage? To begin to answer these questions, let's consider a bit more carefully what the optimal capital structure is from a tax perspective.

Limits to the Tax Benefit of Debt

To receive the full tax benefits of leverage, a firm need not use 100% debt financing. A firm receives a tax benefit only if it is paying taxes in the first place. That is, the firm must have taxable earnings. This constraint may limit the amount of debt needed as a tax shield.

To determine the optimal level of leverage, compare the three leverage choices shown in Table 15.4 for a firm with earnings before interest and taxes (EBIT) equal to $1000 and a corporate tax rate of $\tau_c = 35\%$. With no leverage, the firm owes tax of $350 on the full $1000 of EBIT. If the firm has high leverage with interest payments equal to $1000, then it can shield its earnings from taxes, thereby saving the $350 in taxes. Now consider a third case, in which the firm has excess leverage so that interest payments exceed EBIT. In this case, the firm has a net operating loss, but there is no increase in the tax savings. Because the firm is paying no taxes already, there is no immediate tax shield from the excess leverage.[12]

Thus, no corporate tax benefit arises from incurring interest payments that regularly exceed EBIT. And, because interest payments constitute a tax disadvantage at the investor level as discussed in Section 15.4, investors will pay higher personal taxes with excess leverage, making them worse off.[13] We can quantify the tax disadvantage for excess interest payments by setting $\tau_c = 0$ (assuming there is no reduction in the corporate tax for excess interest payments) in Eq. 15.7 for τ^*:

$$\tau_{ex}^* = 1 - \frac{(1 - \tau_e)}{(1 - \tau_i)} = \frac{\tau_e - \tau_i}{(1 - \tau_i)} < 0 \tag{15.9}$$

TABLE 15.4	Tax Savings with Different Amounts of Leverage		
	No Leverage	High Leverage	Excess Leverage
EBIT	$1000	$1000	$1000
Interest expense	0	−1000	−1100
Income before tax	1000	0	0
Taxes (35%)	−350	0	0
Net income	650	0	−100
Tax savings from leverage	$0	$350	$350

---

[12]If the firm paid taxes during the prior two years, it could "carry back" the current year's net operating loss to apply for a refund of some of those taxes. Alternatively, the firm could "carry forward" the net operating loss up to 20 years to shield future income from taxes (although waiting to receive the credit reduces its present value). Thus, there can be a tax benefit from interest in excess of EBIT if it does not occur on a regular basis. For simplicity, we ignore carrybacks and carryforwards in this discussion.

[13]Of course, another problem can arise from having excess leverage: The firm may not be able to afford the excess interest and could be forced to default on the loan. We discuss financial distress (and its potential costs) in Chapter 16.

Andrew Balson is a Managing Director of Bain Capital, a leading private investment firm with nearly $57 billion in assets under management. Bain Capital specializes in private equity (PE) and leveraged buyout (LBO) transactions, in which a firm is purchased and recapitalized with debt-to-value ratios often exceeding 70%. Bain Capital has invested in many well-known companies including Burger King, Domino's Pizza, Dunkin' Brands, HCA, Michael's Stores, Sealy Mattress Company, and Toys 'R Us.

INTERVIEW WITH
Andrew Balson

QUESTION: *What is the role of private investment firms such as Bain Capital, and what types of firms make the best LBO candidates?*

ANSWER: Our business serves as an alternate capital market for companies that don't really belong as public companies, either during a transition period or permanently, and don't have a logical fit within another larger corporation. In that context, we've done buyouts for companies across many different industries and types. There really isn't one particular type that is best. We look for companies that are well positioned in their industries, have advantages relative to their competitors, and provide real value to their customers. Some may be underperforming but change can enable them to turn around. Others may be performing well but could do even better. Perhaps the management team has not been given appropriate incentives, or the company has not been optimized or managed aggressively enough. Occasionally, we find a company we can buy at a low price compared to its inherent value. That was a big part of our business 10 years ago but is less so today. We pay relatively full valuations compared to the company's current earnings. This approach works because of our ability to improve current earnings or cash flow.

QUESTION: *How does leverage affect risk and return for investors?*

ANSWER: Based on my experience, if we've found interesting companies where we can change the profit trajectory, leverage will ultimately serve to magnify both the impact of the investments we make and the returns for our investors. Over the past 20 years, the Bain Capital portfolio has far outperformed any equity benchmarks. That performance comes from improved operating profits that are magnified by leverage. Growth is an important driver of our success, so we strive to create efficient capital structures that complement our strategy and enable us to invest in business opportunities. The line between too much and not enough is not distinct, however. We try to use as much debt as we can without changing how our management teams run our businesses.

QUESTION: *How will the 2008 financial crisis affect capital structure and financing policies in the future?*

ANSWER: From 2006 to 2008, debt became more available, and the amount of leverage per $1 of earnings went up dramatically. Companies that typically borrowed four to six times earnings before interest, taxes, depreciation, and amortization (EBITDA) were now borrowing seven to eight times EBITDA. The cost of borrowing went down, spreads tightened, and borrowing terms became more lenient, resulting in "covenant-lite" loans. The market opened its wallet and threw money at PE firms, ultimately driving returns down.

The PE markets began to crack in late spring 2008. Banks had to shore up their balance sheets, leaving no money for buyouts. The PE markets are now reverting to pre-2006 leverage—five times EBITDA—rates, and terms.

QUESTION: *What challenges and opportunities does the financial crisis present for PE firms?*

ANSWER: The fundamental benefits of PE for many companies will persist. PE remains an attractive asset class—at the right leverage and price. The economic uncertainty creates less incentive for sellers of companies, who are more likely to wait out these difficult capital markets. It's a great time to be a PE investor with capital, however. We were able to take substantial minority stakes in companies that interest us, at attractive terms. PE financing is now more expensive, and I think it will remain that way for some time. Companies that need financing now, to grow or make a strategic move, will tap higher-cost capital sources such as PE.

It's also a challenging time for our portfolio companies. Sales in most companies have declined precipitously. We are working with our companies to cut costs and generate liquidity to get them "across the icy river"; and we expect the vast majority to make it.

Note that τ_{ex}^* is negative because equity is taxed less heavily than interest for investors $(\tau_e > \tau_i)$. At 2012 tax rates, this disadvantage is

$$\tau_{ex}^* = \frac{15\% - 35\%}{(1 - 35\%)} = -30.8\%$$

Therefore, the optimal level of leverage from a tax saving perspective is the level such that interest equals EBIT. The firm shields all of its taxable income, and it does not have any tax-disadvantaged excess interest. Figure 15.8 shows the tax savings at different levels of interest payments when EBIT equals $1000 with certainty. In this case, an interest payment of $1000 maximizes the tax savings.

Of course, it is unlikely that a firm can predict its future EBIT precisely. If there is uncertainty regarding EBIT, then with a higher interest expense there is a greater risk that interest will exceed EBIT. As a result, the tax savings for high levels of interest falls, possibly reducing the optimal level of the interest payment, as shown in Figure 15.8.[14] In general, as a firm's interest expense approaches its expected taxable earnings, the marginal tax advantage of debt declines, limiting the amount of debt the firm should use.

Growth and Debt

In a tax-optimal capital structure, the level of interest payments depends on the level of EBIT. What does this conclusion tell us about the optimal fraction of debt in a firm's capital structure?

If we examine young technology or biotechnology firms, we often find that these firms do not have any taxable income. Their value comes mainly from the prospect that they will produce high future profits. A biotech firm might be developing drugs with tremendous potential, but it has yet to receive any revenue from these drugs. Such a firm will not have taxable earnings. In that case, a tax-optimal capital structure does not include debt.

FIGURE 15.8

Tax Savings for Different Levels of Interest

When EBIT is known with certainty, the tax savings is maximized if the interest expense is equal to EBIT. When EBIT is uncertain, the tax savings declines for high levels of interest because of the risk that the interest payment will be in excess of EBIT.

[14]Details of how to compute the optimal level of debt when earnings are risky can be found in a paper by J. Graham, "How Big Are the Tax Benefits of Debt?" *Journal of Finance* 55(5) (2000): 1901–1941.

We would expect such a firm to finance its investments with equity alone. Only later, when the firm matures and becomes profitable, will it have taxable cash flows. At that time it should add debt to its capital structure.

Even for a firm with positive earnings, growth will affect the optimal leverage ratio. To avoid excess interest, this type of firm should have debt with interest payments that are below its expected taxable earnings:

$$\text{Interest} = r_D \times \text{Debt} \le EBIT \quad \text{or} \quad \text{Debt} \le EBIT/r_D$$

That is, from a tax perspective, the firm's optimal level of debt is proportional to its current earnings. However, the value of the firm's equity will depend on the growth rate of earnings: The higher the growth rate, the higher the value of equity is (and equivalently, the higher the firm's price-earnings multiple is). As a result, *the optimal proportion of debt in the firm's capital structure* $[D/(E + D)]$ *will be lower, the higher the firm's growth rate.*[15]

Other Tax Shields

Up to this point, we have assumed that interest is the only means by which firms can shield earnings from corporate taxes. But there are numerous other provisions in the tax laws for deductions and tax credits, such as depreciation, investment tax credits, carryforwards of past operating losses, and the like. For example, many high-tech firms paid little or no taxes in the late 1990s because of tax deductions related to employee stock options (see the box on page 532 for further discussion). To the extent that a firm has other tax shields, its taxable earnings will be reduced and it will rely less heavily on the interest tax shield.[16]

The Low Leverage Puzzle

Do firms choose capital structures that fully exploit the tax advantages of debt? The results of this section imply that to evaluate this question, we should compare the level of firms' interest payments to their taxable income, rather than simply consider the fraction of debt in their capital structures. Figure 15.9 compares interest expenses and EBIT for firms in the S&P 500. It reveals two important patterns. First, firms have used debt to shield less than one third of their income from taxes on average, and only about 50% in downturns (when earnings tend to fall). Second, only about 10% of the time do firms have negative taxable income, and thus would not benefit from an increased interest tax shield. Overall, firms have far less leverage than our analysis of the interest tax shield would predict.[17]

This low level of leverage is not unique to U.S. firms. Table 15.5 shows international leverage levels from a 1995 study by Raghuram Rajan and Luigi Zingales using 1990 data. Note that firms worldwide have similar low proportions of debt financing, with firms in the United Kingdom exhibiting especially low leverage. Also, with the exception of Italy and Canada, firms shield less than half of their taxable income using interest payments. The corporate tax

---

[15]This explanation for the low leverage of high growth firms is developed in a paper by J. Berens and C. Cuny, "The Capital Structure Puzzle Revisited," *Review of Financial Studies* 8 (1995): 1185–1208.

[16]See H. DeAngelo and R. Masulis, "Optimal Capital Structure Under Corporate and Personal Taxation," *Journal of Financial Economics* 8 (1980): 3–27. For a discussion of methods to estimate a firm's marginal tax rate to account for these effects, see J. Graham, "Proxies for the Corporate Marginal Tax Rate," *Journal of Financial Economics* 42 (1996): 187–221.

[17]Additional evidence is provided by J. Graham in "How Big Are the Tax Benefits of Debt?" *Journal of Finance* 55 (2000): 1901–1941, where he estimates that the typical firm exploits less than half of the potential tax benefits of debt.

FIGURE 15.9	

Interest Payments as a Percentage of EBIT and Percentage of Firms with Negative Pretax Income, S&P 500 1975–2011

On average, firms shield less than one third of their income via interest expenses, and these expenses exceed taxable income only about 10% of the time.

Source: Compustat.

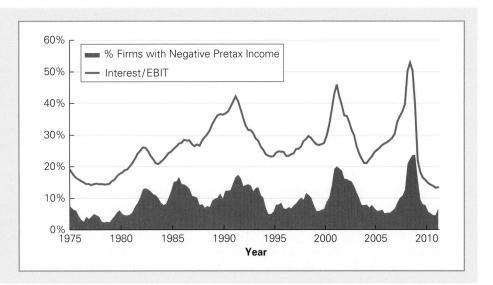

codes are similar across all countries in terms of the tax advantage of debt. Personal tax rates vary more significantly, however, leading to greater variation in τ^*.[18]

Why are firms under-leveraged? Either firms are content to pay more taxes than necessary rather than maximize shareholder value, or there is more to the capital structure story than we have uncovered so far. While some firms may deliberately choose a suboptimal capital structure, it is hard to accept that most firms are acting suboptimally. The consensus of so many managers in choosing low levels of leverage suggests that debt financing has other costs that prevent firms from using the interest tax shield fully.

Talk to financial managers and they will quickly point out a key cost of debt missing from our analysis: Increasing the level of debt increases the probability of bankruptcy. Aside from taxes, another important difference between debt and equity financing is that

TABLE 15.5	International Leverage and Tax Rates (1990)				

Country	$D/(E + D)$	Net of Cash $D/(E + D)$	Interest/EBIT	τ_c	τ^*
United States	28%	23%	41%	34.0%	34.0%
Japan	29%	17%	41%	37.5%	31.5%
Germany	23%	15%	31%	50.0%	3.3%
France	41%	28%	38%	37.0%	7.8%
Italy	46%	36%	55%	36.0%	18.6%
United Kingdom	19%	11%	21%	35.0%	24.2%
Canada	35%	32%	65%	38.0%	28.9%

Source: R. Rajan and L. Zingales, "What Do We Know About Capital Structure? Some Evidence from International Data," *Journal of Finance* 50 (1995): 1421–1460. Data is for median firms and top marginal tax rates.

---

[18]Similar low leverage results continue to hold using more recent data from 2006; see J. Fan, S. Titman, and G. Twite, "An International Comparison of Capital Structure and Debt Maturity Choices," SSRN working paper, 2008.

Employee Stock Options

Employee stock options can serve as an important tax shield for some firms. The typical employee stock option allows employees of a firm to buy the firm's stock at a discounted price (often, the price of the stock when they started employment). When an employee exercises a stock option, the firm is essentially selling shares to the employee at a discount. If the discount is large, the employee can exercise the option and earn a large profit.

The amount of the discount is a cost for the firm's equity holders because selling shares at a price below their market value dilutes the value of the firm's shares. To reflect this cost, the IRS allows firms to deduct the amount of the discount from their earnings for tax purposes. (The IRS taxes employees on the gain, so the tax burden does not go away, but moves from the firm to the employees.) Unlike the interest tax shield, the tax deduction from employee stock options does not add to the value of the firm. If the same amounts were paid to employees through salary rather than options, the firm would be able to deduct the extra salary from its taxable income as well. Until recently, however, employee stock options did not affect EBIT, so that EBIT overstated the taxable income of firms with option expenses.

During the stock market boom of the late 1990s, many technology firms and other firms that issued a large number of employee stock options were able to claim these deductions and lower their taxes relative to what one would naively have imputed from EBIT. In 2000, some of the most profitable companies in the United States (based on net income), such as Microsoft, Cisco Systems, Dell, and Qualcomm, had *no* taxable income—using the stock option deduction, they were able to report a loss for tax purposes.[*] A study by J. Graham, M. Lang, and D. Shackelford reported that in 2000, stock option deductions for the entire NASDAQ 100 exceeded aggregate pretax earnings.[†] For these firms, there would have been no tax advantage associated with debt—which may help explain why they used little to no debt financing.

Since 2006, firms have been required to expense employee stock options. However, the rules for expensing the options are not the same as the tax deduction. As a consequence, even after this rule change, stock options may continue to result in a significant difference between firms' accounting income and their income for tax purposes. For example, Mark Zuckerberg's founding options in Facebook led to an accounting expense of under $10 million, yet provided Facebook with a tax deduction exceeding $2 billion.

[*]See M. Sullivan, "Stock Options Take $50 Billion Bite Out of Corporate Taxes," *Tax Notes* (March 18, 2002): 1396–1401.
[†]"Employee Stock Options, Corporate Taxes and Debt Policy," *Journal of Finance* 59 (2004): 1585–1618.

debt payments *must* be made to avoid bankruptcy, whereas firms have no similar obligation to pay dividends or realize capital gains. If bankruptcy is costly, these costs might offset the tax advantages of debt financing. We explore the role of financial bankruptcy costs and other market imperfections in Chapter 16.

CONCEPT CHECK

1. How does the growth rate of a firm affect the optimal fraction of debt in the capital structure?
2. Do firms choose capital structures that fully exploit the tax advantages of debt?

MyFinanceLab Here is what you should know after reading this chapter. MyFinanceLab will help you identify what you know and where to go when you need to practice.

15.1 The Interest Tax Deduction

- Because interest expense is tax deductible, leverage increases the total amount of income available to all investors.
- The gain to investors from the tax deductibility of interest payments is called the interest tax shield.

$$\text{Interest Tax Shield} = \text{Corporate Tax Rate} \times \text{Interest Payments} \tag{15.1}$$

15.2 Valuing the Interest Tax Shield

■ When we consider corporate taxes, the total value of a levered firm equals the value of an unlevered firm plus the present value of the interest tax shield.

$$V^L = V^U + PV(\text{Interest Tax Shield}) \qquad (15.2)$$

■ When a firm's marginal tax rate is constant, and there are no personal taxes, the present value of the interest tax shield from permanent debt equals the tax rate times the value of the debt, $\tau_c D$.

■ The firm's pretax WACC measures the required return to the firm's investors. Its effective after-tax WACC, or simply the WACC, measures the cost to the firm after including the benefit of the interest tax shield. The two notions are related as follows:

$$r_{wacc} = \frac{E}{E+D}r_E + \frac{D}{E+D}r_D(1-\tau_c) \qquad (15.5)$$

$$= \underbrace{\frac{E}{E+D}r_E + \frac{D}{E+D}r_D}_{\text{Pretax WACC}} - \underbrace{\frac{D}{E+D}r_D\tau_c}_{\substack{\text{Reduction Due} \\ \text{to Interest Tax Shield}}} \qquad (15.6)$$

Absent other market imperfections, the WACC declines with a firm's leverage.

■ When the firm maintains a target leverage ratio, we compute its levered value V^L as the present value of its free cash flows using the WACC, whereas its unlevered value V^U is the present value of its free cash flows using its unlevered cost of capital or pretax WACC.

15.3 Recapitalizing to Capture the Tax Shield

■ When securities are fairly priced, the original shareholders of a firm capture the full benefit of the interest tax shield from an increase in leverage.

15.4 Personal Taxes

■ Personal taxes offset some of the corporate tax benefits of leverage. Every $1 received after taxes by debt holders from interest payments costs equity holders $(1 − τ*)$ on an after-tax basis, where

$$\tau^* = 1 - \frac{(1-\tau_c)(1-\tau_e)}{(1-\tau_i)} \qquad (15.7)$$

15.5 Optimal Capital Structure with Taxes

■ The optimal level of leverage from a tax-saving perspective is the level such that interest equals EBIT. In this case, the firm takes full advantage of the corporate tax deduction of interest, but avoids the tax disadvantage of excess leverage at the personal level.

■ The optimal fraction of debt, as a proportion of a firm's capital structure, declines with the growth rate of the firm.

■ The interest expense of the average firm is well below its taxable income, implying that firms do not fully exploit the tax advantages of debt.

Key Term interest tax shield *p. 510*

Further Reading

In their 1963 paper, "Corporate Income Taxes and the Cost of Capital: A Correction," *American Economic Review* 53 (June 1963): 433–443, Modigliani and Miller adjusted their analysis to incorporate the tax benefits of leverage. Other classic works in how taxation affects the cost of capital and optimal capital structure include: M. King, "Taxation and the Cost of Capital," *Review of Economic Studies* 41 (1974): 21–35; M. Miller, "Debt and Taxes," *Journal of Finance* 32 (1977): 261–275; M. Miller and M. Scholes, "Dividends and Taxes," *Journal of Financial Economics* 6 (1978): 333–364; and J. Stiglitz, "Taxation, Corporate Financial Policy, and the Cost of Capital," *Journal of Public Economics* 2 (1973): 1–34.

For an analysis of how firms respond to tax incentives, see J. MacKie-Mason, "Do Taxes Affect Corporate Financing Decisions?" *Journal of Finance* 45 (1990): 1471–1493. For a recent review of the literature of taxes and corporate finance, see J. Graham, "Taxes and Corporate Finance: A Review," *Review of Financial Studies* 16 (2003): 1075–1129.

These articles analyze in depth several issues regarding taxation and optimal capital structure: M. Bradley, G. Jarrell, and E. Kim, "On the Existence of an Optimal Capital Structure: Theory and Evidence," *The Journal of Finance* 39 (1984): 857–878; M. Brennan and E. Schwartz, "Corporate Income Taxes, Valuation, and the Problem of Optimal Capital Structure," *Journal of Business* 51 (1978): 103–114; H. DeAngelo and R. Masulis, "Optimal Capital Structure Under Corporate and Personal Taxation," *Journal of Financial Economics* 8 (1980): 3–29; and S. Titman and R. Wessels, "The Determinants of Capital Structure Choice," *Journal of Finance* 43 (1988): 1–19.

The following articles contain information on what managers say about their capital structure decisions: J. Graham and C. Harvey, "How Do CFOs Make Capital Budgeting and Capital Structure Decisions?" *Journal of Applied Corporate Finance* 15 (2002): 8–23; R. Kamath, "Long-Term Financing Decisions: Views and Practices of Financial Managers of NYSE Firms," *Financial Review* 32 (1997): 331–356; E. Norton, "Factors Affecting Capital Structure Decisions," *Financial Review* 26 (1991): 431–446; and J. Pinegar and L. Wilbricht, "What Managers Think of Capital Structure Theory: A Survey," *Financial Management* 18 (1989): 82–91.

For additional insight into capital structure decisions internationally, see also F. Bancel and U. Mittoo, "Cross-Country Determinants of Capital Structure Choice: A Survey of European Firms," *Financial Management* 33 (2004): 103–132; R. La Porta, F. Lopez-de-Silanes, A. Shleifer, and R. Vishny, "Legal Determinants of External Finance," *Journal of Finance* 52 (1997): 1131–1152; and L. Booth, V. Aivazian, A. Demirguq-Kunt, and V. Maksimovic, "Capital Structures in Developing Countries," *Journal of Finance* 56 (2001): 87–130.

Problems

All problems are available in MyFinanceLab. *An asterisk (*) indicates problems with a higher level of difficulty.*

The Interest Tax Deduction

1. Pelamed Pharmaceuticals has EBIT of $325 million in 2006. In addition, Pelamed has interest expenses of $125 million and a corporate tax rate of 40%.
   a. What is Pelamed's 2006 net income?
   b. What is the total of Pelamed's 2006 net income and interest payments?
   c. If Pelamed had no interest expenses, what would its 2006 net income be? How does it compare to your answer in part b?
   d. What is the amount of Pelamed's interest tax shield in 2006?

2. Grommit Engineering expects to have net income next year of $20.75 million and free cash flow of $22.15 million. Grommit's marginal corporate tax rate is 35%.
   a. If Grommit increases leverage so that its interest expense rises by $1 million, how will its net income change?
   b. For the same increase in interest expense, how will free cash flow change?

3. Suppose the corporate tax rate is 40%. Consider a firm that earns $1000 before interest and taxes each year with no risk. The firm's capital expenditures equal its depreciation expenses each year, and it will have no changes to its net working capital. The risk-free interest rate is 5%.
   a. Suppose the firm has no debt and pays out its net income as a dividend each year. What is the value of the firm's equity?
   b. Suppose instead the firm makes interest payments of $500 per year. What is the value of equity? What is the value of debt?
   c. What is the difference between the total value of the firm with leverage and without leverage?
   d. The difference in part c is equal to what percentage of the value of the debt?

 4. Braxton Enterprises currently has debt outstanding of $35 million and an interest rate of 8%. Braxton plans to reduce its debt by repaying $7 million in principal at the end of each year for the next five years. If Braxton's marginal corporate tax rate is 40%, what is the interest tax shield from Braxton's debt in each of the next five years?

Valuing the Interest Tax Shield

 5. Your firm currently has $100 million in debt outstanding with a 10% interest rate. The terms of the loan require the firm to repay $25 million of the balance each year. Suppose that the marginal corporate tax rate is 40%, and that the interest tax shields have the same risk as the loan. What is the present value of the interest tax shields from this debt?

6. Arnell Industries has just issued $10 million in debt (at par). The firm will pay interest only on this debt. Arnell's marginal tax rate is expected to be 35% for the foreseeable future.
   a. Suppose Arnell pays interest of 6% per year on its debt. What is its annual interest tax shield?
   b. What is the present value of the interest tax shield, assuming its risk is the same as the loan?
   c. Suppose instead that the interest rate on the debt is 5%. What is the present value of the interest tax shield in this case?

 7. Ten years have passed since Arnell issued $10 million in perpetual interest only debt with a 6% annual coupon, as in Problem 6. Tax rates have remained the same at 35% but interest rates have dropped, so Arnell's current cost of debt capital is 4%.
   a. What is Arnell's annual interest tax shield?
   b. What is the present value of the interest tax shield today?

8. Bay Transport Systems (BTS) currently has $30 million in debt outstanding. In addition to 6.5% interest, it plans to repay 5% of the remaining balance each year. If BTS has a marginal corporate tax rate of 40%, and if the interest tax shields have the same risk as the loan, what is the present value of the interest tax shield from the debt?

9. Safeco Inc. has no debt, and maintains a policy of holding $10 million in excess cash reserves, invested in risk-free Treasury securities. If Safeco pays a corporate tax rate of 35%, what is the cost of permanently maintaining this $10 million reserve? (*Hint*: What is the present value of the additional taxes that Safeco will pay?)

10. Rogot Instruments makes fine violins and cellos. It has $1 million in debt outstanding, equity valued at $2 million, and pays corporate income tax at rate of 35%. Its cost of equity is 12% and its cost of debt is 7%.
    a. What is Rogot's pretax WACC?
    b. What is Rogot's (effective after-tax) WACC?

11. Rumolt Motors has 30 million shares outstanding with a price of $15 per share. In addition, Rumolt has issued bonds with a total current market value of $150 million. Suppose Rumolt's equity cost of capital is 10%, and its debt cost of capital is 5%.
    a. What is Rumolt's pretax weighted average cost of capital?
    b. If Rumolt's corporate tax rate is 35%, what is its after-tax weighted average cost of capital?

12. Summit Builders has a market debt-equity ratio of 0.65 and a corporate tax rate of 40%, and it pays 7% interest on its debt. The interest tax shield from its debt lowers Summit's WACC by what amount?

13. NatNah, a builder of acoustic accessories, has no debt and an equity cost of capital of 15%. Suppose NatNah decides to increase its leverage and maintain a market debt-to-value ratio of 0.5. Suppose its debt cost of capital is 9% and its corporate tax rate is 35%. If NatNah's pretax WACC remains constant, what will its (effective after-tax) WACC be with the increase in leverage?

14. Restex maintains a debt-equity ratio of 0.85, and has an equity cost of capital of 12% and a debt cost of capital of 7%. Restex's corporate tax rate is 40%, and its market capitalization is $220 million.
    a. If Restex's free cash flow is expected to be $10 million in one year, what constant expected future growth rate is consistent with the firm's current market value?
    b. Estimate the value of Restex's interest tax shield.

15. Acme Storage has a market capitalization of $100 million and debt outstanding of $40 million. Acme plans to maintain this same debt-equity ratio in the future. The firm pays an interest rate of 7.5% on its debt and has a corporate tax rate of 35%.
    a. If Acme's free cash flow is expected to be $7 million next year and is expected to grow at a rate of 3% per year, what is Acme's WACC?
    b. What is the value of Acme's interest tax shield?

16. Milton Industries expects free cash flow of $5 million each year. Milton's corporate tax rate is 35%, and its unlevered cost of capital is 15%. The firm also has outstanding debt of $19.05 million, and it expects to maintain this level of debt permanently.
    a. What is the value of Milton Industries without leverage?
    b. What is the value of Milton Industries with leverage?

17. Suppose Microsoft has 8.75 billion shares outstanding and pays a marginal corporate tax rate of 35%. If Microsoft announces that it will pay out $50 billion in cash to investors through a combination of a special dividend and a share repurchase, and if investors had previously assumed Microsoft would retain this excess cash permanently, by how much will Microsoft's share price change upon the announcement?

18. Kurz Manufacturing is currently an all-equity firm with 20 million shares outstanding and a stock price of $7.50 per share. Although investors currently expect Kurz to remain an all-equity firm, Kurz plans to announce that it will borrow $50 million and use the funds to repurchase shares. Kurz will pay interest only on this debt, and it has no further plans to increase or decrease the amount of debt. Kurz is subject to a 40% corporate tax rate.
    a. What is the market value of Kurz's existing assets before the announcement?
    b. What is the market value of Kurz's assets (including any tax shields) just after the debt is issued, but before the shares are repurchased?
    c. What is Kurz's share price just before the share repurchase? How many shares will Kurz repurchase?
    d. What are Kurz's market value balance sheet and share price after the share repurchase?

19. Rally, Inc., is an all-equity firm with assets worth $25 billion and 10 billion shares outstanding. Rally plans to borrow $10 billion and use these funds to repurchase shares. The firm's corporate tax rate is 35%, and Rally plans to keep its outstanding debt equal to $10 billion permanently.
    a. Without the increase in leverage, what would Rally's share price be?
    b. Suppose Rally offers $2.75 per share to repurchase its shares. Would shareholders sell for this price?
    c. Suppose Rally offers $3.00 per share, and shareholders tender their shares at this price. What will Rally's share price be after the repurchase?
    d. What is the lowest price Rally can offer and have shareholders tender their shares? What will its stock price be after the share repurchase in that case?

Personal Taxes

20. Suppose the corporate tax rate is 40%, and investors pay a tax rate of 15% on income from dividends or capital gains and a tax rate of 33.3% on interest income. Your firm decides to add debt so it will pay an additional $15 million in interest each year. It will pay this interest expense by cutting its dividend.

a. How much will debt holders receive after paying taxes on the interest they earn?

b. By how much will the firm need to cut its dividend each year to pay this interest expense?

c. By how much will this cut in the dividend reduce equity holders' annual after-tax income?

d. How much less will the government receive in total tax revenues each year?

e. What is the effective tax advantage of debt τ^*?

21. Apple Corporation had no debt on its balance sheet in 2011, but paid $8 billion in taxes. Suppose Apple were to issue sufficient debt to reduce its taxes by $1 billion per year permanently. Assume Apple's marginal corporate tax rate is 35% and its borrowing cost is 4.5%.

a. If Apple's investors do not pay personal taxes (because they hold their Apple stock in tax-free retirement accounts), how much value would be created (what is the value of the tax shield)?

b. How does your answer change if instead you assume that Apple's investors pay a 15% tax rate on income from equity and a 35% tax rate on interest income?

22. Markum Enterprises is considering permanently adding $100 million of debt to its capital structure. Markum's corporate tax rate is 35%.

a. Absent personal taxes, what is the value of the interest tax shield from the new debt?

b. If investors pay a tax rate of 40% on interest income, and a tax rate of 20% on income from dividends and capital gains, what is the value of the interest tax shield from the new debt?

*23. Garnet Corporation is considering issuing risk-free debt or risk-free preferred stock. The tax rate on interest income is 35%, and the tax rate on dividends or capital gains from preferred stock is 15%. However, the dividends on preferred stock are not deductible for corporate tax purposes, and the corporate tax rate is 40%.

a. If the risk-free interest rate for debt is 6%, what is the cost of capital for risk-free preferred stock?

b. What is the after-tax debt cost of capital for the firm? Which security is cheaper for the firm?

c. Show that the after-tax debt cost of capital is equal to the preferred stock cost of capital multiplied by $(1 - \tau^*)$.

*24. Suppose the tax rate on interest income is 35%, and the average tax rate on capital gains and dividend income is 10%. How high must the marginal corporate tax rate be for debt to offer a tax advantage?

Optimal Capital Structure with Taxes

25. With its current leverage, Impi Corporation will have net income next year of $4.5 million. If Impi's corporate tax rate is 35% and it pays 8% interest on its debt, how much additional debt can Impi issue this year and still receive the benefit of the interest tax shield next year?

*26. Colt Systems will have EBIT this coming year of $15 million. It will also spend $6 million on total capital expenditures and increases in net working capital, and have $3 million in depreciation expenses. Colt is currently an all-equity firm with a corporate tax rate of 35% and a cost of capital of 10%.

a. If Colt's free cash flows are expected to grow by 8.5% per year, what is the market value of its equity today?

b. If the interest rate on its debt is 8%, how much can Colt borrow now and still have non-negative net income this coming year?

c. Is there a tax incentive today for Colt to choose a debt-to-value ratio that exceeds 50%? Explain.

27. PMF, Inc., is equally likely to have EBIT this coming year of $10 million, $15 million, or $20 million. Its corporate tax rate is 35%, and investors pay a 15% tax rate on income from equity and a 35% tax rate on interest income.

   a. What is the effective tax advantage of debt if PMF has interest expenses of $8 million this coming year?

   b. What is the effective tax advantage of debt for interest expenses in excess of $20 million? (Ignore carryforwards.)

   c. What is the expected effective tax advantage of debt for interest expenses between $10 million and $15 million? (Ignore carryforwards.)

   d. What level of interest expense provides PMF with the greatest tax benefit?

Data Case

Your boss was impressed by your analysis about the irrelevance of capital structure from the Data Case in Chapter 14. Still, both of you are aware that taxes are an important imperfection that you would like to take into account. Your boss remembers that there is a tax advantage of debt financing, and he asks you to incorporate that into the analysis, so that he can convince the CEO to increase Nokia's debt level. You remind him that there are also some more subtle considerations about the personal taxes at the investor level that have to be taken into account. To show the effect in numbers, you will compare the effect of a new debt issue for Nokia's share price, given that there are either no taxes, or corporate taxes only, or taxes paid on all levels. Use the financial data for Nokia that you collected in Question 1 for the Data Case in Chapter 14. Assume that the marginal personal tax rate on income from debt is 35% and that the marginal personal tax rate on income from equity is 28%.

1. Calculate the average corporate tax rate for Nokia over the last three years by dividing "Income Tax Expense" by "Income Before Tax." Use the average corporate tax rate as the corporate tax rate when answering the following questions.

2. Calculate the effective tax advantage of debt using Eq. 15.7.

   Nokia is planning to issue new debt worth 10% of the sum of the existing "Short/Current Long Term Debt" and "Long Term Debt," in order to repurchase shares for the same amount. The debt issue will take the form of a 10-year corporate bond (bullet loan) with a yearly coupon equal to the cost of debt (current yield on the corporate bond) found in Question 1 in the Data Case in Chapter 14.

   The management is considering three different tax settings:

     ■ A world with no taxes

     ■ A world with corporate taxes only

     ■ A world with taxes paid on all levels

3. Determine the present value of the interest tax shield for each of the three tax settings.

   a. Draw a timeline with the years from 1 to 10.

   b. Calculate the interest payment on the bonds for each year.

   c. Calculate the interest tax shield in each of the three tax settings.

   d. Calculate the present value of the interest tax shield in each of the three tax settings.

4. Determine the new share price and number of shares outstanding in each of the three tax settings.

   a. Use the current market value of Nokia's equity that you calculated in the Data Case in Chapter 14.

   b. Determine the new market value of the equity if the repurchase occurs.

   c. Determine the share price at which shareholders are willing to sell their shares given the information about the new debt. *Note*: Format the share price with three or four decimals, as the differences in share price might be less than one cent.

   d. Determine the number of shares outstanding after the repurchase.

5. Your boss is considering suggesting even a doubling (i.e., 100% instead of 10% increase) of debt, as Nokia's management wants to maximize the share price. Make him aware of critical assumptions that you made, and discuss the limits of generating tax benefits.

Financial Distress, Managerial Incentives, and Information

MODIGLIANI AND MILLER DEMONSTRATED THAT CAPITAL structure does not matter in a perfect capital market. In Chapter 15, we found a tax benefit of leverage, at least up to the point that a firm's EBIT exceeds the interest payments on the debt. Yet we saw that the average U.S. firm shields less than half of its earnings in this way. Why don't firms use more debt?

We can gain some insight by looking at United Airlines (UAL Corporation). For the five-year period 1996 through 2000, UAL paid interest expenses of $1.7 billion, relative to EBIT of more than $6 billion. During this period, it reported a total provision for taxes on its income statement exceeding $2.2 billion. The company appeared to have a level of debt that did not fully exploit its tax shield. Even so, as a result of high fuel and labor costs, a decline in travel following the terrorist attacks of September 11, 2001, and increased competition from discount carriers, UAL filed for bankruptcy court protection in December 2002. United ultimately emerged from bankruptcy in 2006; after a profitable 2007, it suffered losses and renewed creditor concerns in the wake of the financial crisis in 2008. The airline returned to profitability in 2010 when it announced plans to acquire Continental Airlines. The merger was completed by the end of 2011, although the company attributed a 37% drop in profits in the second quarter of 2012 to ongoing costs associated with the merger. As this case demonstrates, firms such as airlines whose future cash flows are unstable and highly sensitive to shocks in the economy run the risk of bankruptcy if they use too much leverage.

When a firm has trouble meeting its debt obligations we say the firm is in **financial distress**. In this chapter, we consider how a firm's choice of capital structure can, due to market imperfections, affect its costs of financial distress, alter managers' incentives, and signal information to investors. Each of these consequences of the capital structure decision

NOTATION

E market value of equity

D market value of debt

PV present value

β_E equity beta

β_D debt beta

I investment

NPV net present value

V^U value of the unlevered firm

V^L value of the firm with leverage

τ^* effective tax advantage of debt

can be significant, and each may offset the tax benefits of leverage when leverage is high. Thus, these imperfections may help to explain the levels of debt that we generally observe. In addition, because their effects are likely to vary widely across different types of firms, they may help to explain the large discrepancies in leverage choices that exist across industries, as documented in Figure 15.7 in the previous chapter.

16.1 Default and Bankruptcy in a Perfect Market

Debt financing puts an obligation on a firm. A firm that fails to make the required interest or principal payments on the debt is in **default**. After the firm defaults, debt holders are given certain rights to the assets of the firm. In the extreme case, the debt holders take legal ownership of the firm's assets through a process called bankruptcy. Recall that equity financing does not carry this risk. While equity holders hope to receive dividends, the firm is not legally obligated to pay them.

Thus, it seems that an important consequence of leverage is the risk of bankruptcy. Does this risk represent a disadvantage to using debt? Not necessarily. As we pointed out in Chapter 14, Modigliani and Miller's results continue to hold in a perfect market even when debt is risky and the firm may default. Let's review that result by considering a hypothetical example.

Armin Industries: Leverage and the Risk of Default

Armin Industries faces an uncertain future in a challenging business environment. Due to increased competition from foreign imports, its revenues have fallen dramatically in the past year. Armin's managers hope that a new product in the company's pipeline will restore its fortunes. While the new product represents a significant advance over Armin's competitors' products, whether that product will be a hit with consumers remains uncertain. If it is a hit, revenues and profits will grow, and Armin will be worth $150 million at the end of the year. If it fails, Armin will be worth only $80 million.

Armin Industries may employ one of two alternative capital structures: (1) It can use all-equity financing or (2) it can use debt that matures at the end of the year with a total of $100 million due. Let's look at the consequences of these capital structure choices when the new product succeeds, and when it fails, in a setting of perfect capital markets.

Scenario 1: New Product Succeeds. If the new product is successful, Armin is worth $150 million. Without leverage, equity holders own the full amount. With leverage, Armin must make the $100 million debt payment, and Armin's equity holders will own the remaining $50 million.

But what if Armin does not have $100 million in cash available at the end of the year? Although its assets will be worth $150 million, much of that value may come from anticipated *future* profits from the new product, rather than cash in the bank. In that case, if Armin has debt, will it be forced to default?

With perfect capital markets, the answer is no. As long as the value of the firm's assets exceeds its liabilities, Armin will be able to repay the loan. Even if it does not have the cash immediately available, it can raise the cash by obtaining a new loan or by issuing new shares.

For example, suppose Armin currently has 10 million shares outstanding. Because the value of its equity is $50 million, these shares are worth $5 per share. At this price, Armin can raise $100 million by issuing 20 million new shares and use the proceeds to pay off the debt. After the debt is repaid, the firm's equity is worth $150 million. Because there is now a total of 30 million shares, the share price remains $5 per share.

This scenario shows that if a firm has access to capital markets and can issue new securities at a fair price, *then it need not default as long as the market value of its assets exceeds its liabilities*. That is, whether default occurs depends on the relative values of the firm's assets and liabilities, not on its cash flows. Many firms experience years of negative cash flows yet remain solvent.

Scenario 2: New Product Fails. If the new product fails, Armin is worth only $80 million. If the company has all-equity financing, equity holders will be unhappy but there is no immediate legal consequence for the firm. In contrast, if Armin has $100 million in debt due, it will experience financial distress. The firm will be unable to make its $100 million debt payment and will have no choice except to default. In bankruptcy, debt holders will receive legal ownership of the firm's assets, leaving Armin's shareholders with nothing. Because the assets the debt holders receive have a value of $80 million, they will suffer a loss of $20 million relative to the $100 million they were owed. Equity holders in a corporation have limited liability, so the debt holders cannot sue Armin's shareholders for this $20 million—they must accept the loss.

Comparing the Two Scenarios. Table 16.1 compares the outcome of each scenario without leverage and with leverage. Both debt and equity holders are worse off if the product fails rather than succeeds. Without leverage, if the product fails equity holders lose $150 million − $80 million = $70 million. With leverage, equity holders lose $50 million, and debt holders lose $20 million, *but the total loss is the same—$70 million*. Overall, *if the new product fails, Armin's investors are equally unhappy whether the firm is levered and declares bankruptcy or whether it is unlevered and the share price declines.*[1]

TABLE 16.1	Value of Debt and Equity with and without Leverage (in $ million)			
	Without Leverage		With Leverage	
	Success	Failure	Success	Failure
Debt value	—	—	100	80
Equity value	150	80	50	0
Total to all investors	150	80	150	80

This point is important. When a firm declares bankruptcy, the news often makes headlines. Much attention is paid to the firm's poor results and the loss to investors. But the decline in value is not *caused* by bankruptcy: The decline is the same whether or not the firm has leverage. That is, if the new product fails, Armin will experience **economic distress**, which is a significant decline in the value of a firm's assets, whether or not it experiences financial distress due to leverage.

Bankruptcy and Capital Structure

With perfect capital markets, Modigliani-Miller (MM) Proposition I applies: The total value to all investors does not depend on the firm's capital structure. Investors as a group are *not* worse off because a firm has leverage. While it is true that bankruptcy results from

---

[1]There is a temptation to look only at shareholders and to say they are worse off when Armin has leverage because their shares are worthless. In fact, shareholders lose $50 million relative to success when the firm is levered, versus $70 million without leverage. What really matters is the total value to all investors, which will determine the total amount of capital the firm can raise initially.

a firm having leverage, bankruptcy alone does not lead to a greater reduction in the total value to investors. Thus, there is no disadvantage to debt financing, and a firm will have the same total value and will be able to raise the same amount initially from investors with either choice of capital structure.

EXAMPLE 16.1

Bankruptcy Risk and Firm Value

Problem
Suppose the risk-free rate is 5%, and Armin's new product is equally likely to succeed or to fail. For simplicity, suppose that Armin's cash flows are unrelated to the state of the economy (i.e., the risk is diversifiable), so that the project has a beta of 0 and the cost of capital is the risk-free rate. Compute the value of Armin's securities at the beginning of the year with and without leverage, and show that MM Proposition I holds.

Solution
Without leverage, the equity is worth either $150 million or $80 million at year-end. Because the risk is diversifiable, no risk premium is necessary and we can discount the expected value of the firm at the risk-free rate to determine its value without leverage at the start of the year:[2]

$$\text{Equity (unlevered)} = V^U = \frac{\frac{1}{2}(150) + \frac{1}{2}(80)}{1.05} = \$109.52 \text{ million}$$

With leverage, equity holders receive $50 million or nothing, and debt holders receive $100 million or $80 million. Thus,

$$\text{Equity (levered)} = \frac{\frac{1}{2}(50) + \frac{1}{2}(0)}{1.05} = \$23.81 \text{ million}$$

$$\text{Debt} = \frac{\frac{1}{2}(100) + \frac{1}{2}(80)}{1.05} = \$85.71 \text{ million}$$

Therefore, the value of the levered firm is $V^L = E + D = 23.81 + 85.71 = \$109.52$ million. With or without leverage, the total value of the securities is the same, verifying MM Proposition I. The firm is able to raise the same amount from investors using either capital structure.

CONCEPT CHECK

1. With perfect capital markets, does the possibility of bankruptcy put debt financing at a disadvantage?

2. Does the risk of default reduce the value of the firm?

16.2 The Costs of Bankruptcy and Financial Distress

With perfect capital markets, the *risk* of bankruptcy is not a disadvantage of debt—bankruptcy simply shifts the ownership of the firm from equity holders to debt holders without changing the total value available to all investors.

Is this description of bankruptcy realistic? No. Bankruptcy is rarely simple and straightforward—equity holders don't just "hand the keys" to debt holders the moment the firm defaults on a debt payment. Rather, bankruptcy is a long and complicated process that imposes both direct and indirect costs on the firm and its investors, costs that the assumption of perfect capital markets ignores.

---

[2]If the risk were not diversifiable and a risk premium were needed, the calculations here would become more complicated but the conclusion would not change.

The Bankruptcy Code

When a firm fails to make a required payment to debt holders, it is in default. Debt holders can then take legal action against the firm to collect payment by seizing the firm's assets. Because most firms have multiple creditors, without coordination it is difficult to guarantee that each creditor will be treated fairly. Moreover, because the assets of the firm might be more valuable if kept together, creditors seizing assets in a piecemeal fashion might destroy much of the remaining value of the firm.

The U.S. bankruptcy code was created to organize this process so that creditors are treated fairly and the value of the assets is not needlessly destroyed. According to the provisions of the 1978 Bankruptcy Reform Act, U.S. firms can file for two forms of bankruptcy protection: Chapter 7 or Chapter 11.

In **Chapter 7 liquidation**, a trustee is appointed to oversee the liquidation of the firm's assets through an auction. The proceeds from the liquidation are used to pay the firm's creditors, and the firm ceases to exist.

In the more common form of bankruptcy for large corporations, **Chapter 11 reorganization**, all pending collection attempts are automatically suspended, and the firm's existing management is given the opportunity to propose a reorganization plan. While developing the plan, management continues to operate the business. The reorganization plan specifies the treatment of each creditor of the firm. In addition to cash payment, creditors may receive new debt or equity securities of the firm. The value of cash and securities is generally less than the amount each creditor is owed, but more than the creditors would receive if the firm were shut down immediately and liquidated. The creditors must vote to accept the plan, and it must be approved by the bankruptcy court.[3] If an acceptable plan is not put forth, the court may ultimately force a Chapter 7 liquidation of the firm.

Direct Costs of Bankruptcy

The bankruptcy code is designed to provide an orderly process for settling a firm's debts. However, the process is still complex, time-consuming, and costly. When a corporation becomes financially distressed, outside professionals, such as legal and accounting experts, consultants, appraisers, auctioneers, and others with experience selling distressed assets, are generally hired. Investment bankers may also assist with a potential financial restructuring.

These outside experts are costly. Between 2003 and 2005, United Airlines paid a team of over 30 advisory firms an average of $8.6 million per month for legal and professional services related to its Chapter 11 reorganization. Enron spent a then-record $30 million per month on legal and accounting fees in bankruptcy, with the total cost exceeding $750 million. WorldCom paid its advisors $620 million as part of its reorganization to become MCI, and the Lehman Brothers bankruptcy, the largest in history, has reportedly entailed fees of $1.6 billion.[4]

---

[3]Specifically, management holds the exclusive right to propose a reorganization plan for the first 120 days, and this period may be extended indefinitely by the bankruptcy court. Thereafter, any interested party may propose a plan. Creditors who will receive full payment or have their claims fully reinstated under the plan are deemed unimpaired, and do not vote on the reorganization plan. All impaired creditors are grouped according to the nature of their claims. If the plan is approved by creditors holding two-thirds of the claim amount in each group and a majority in the number of the claims in each group, the court will confirm the plan. Even if all groups do not approve the plan, the court may still impose the plan (in a process commonly known as a "cram down") if it deems the plan fair and equitable with respect to each group that objected.

[4]M. Farrell, "Lehman bankruptcy bill: $1.6 billion," CNNMoney, March 6, 2012.

In addition to the money spent by the firm, the creditors may incur costs during the bankruptcy process. In the case of Chapter 11 reorganization, creditors must often wait several years for a reorganization plan to be approved and to receive payment. To ensure that their rights and interests are respected, and to assist in valuing their claims in a proposed reorganization, creditors may seek separate legal representation and professional advice.

Whether paid by the firm or its creditors, these direct costs of bankruptcy reduce the value of the assets that the firm's investors will ultimately receive. In some cases, such as Enron, reorganization costs may approach 10% of the value of the assets. Studies typically report that the average direct costs of bankruptcy are approximately 3% to 4% of the pre-bankruptcy market value of total assets.[5] The costs are likely to be higher for firms with more complicated business operations and for firms with larger numbers of creditors, because it may be more difficult to reach agreement among many creditors regarding the final disposition of the firm's assets. Because many aspects of the bankruptcy process are independent of the size of the firm, the costs are typically higher, in percentage terms, for smaller firms. A study of Chapter 7 liquidations of small businesses found that the average direct costs of bankruptcy were 12% of the value of the firm's assets.[6]

Given the substantial legal and other direct costs of bankruptcy, firms in financial distress can avoid filing for bankruptcy by first negotiating directly with creditors. When a financially distressed firm is successful at reorganizing outside of bankruptcy, it is called a **workout**. Consequently, the direct costs of bankruptcy should not substantially exceed the cost of a workout. Another approach is a **prepackaged bankruptcy** (or "prepack"), in which a firm will *first* develop a reorganization plan with the agreement of its main creditors, and *then* file Chapter 11 to implement the plan (and pressure any creditors who attempt to hold out for better terms). With a prepack, the firm emerges from bankruptcy quickly and with minimal direct costs.[7]

Indirect Costs of Financial Distress

Aside from the direct legal and administrative costs of bankruptcy, many other *indirect* costs are associated with financial distress (whether or not the firm has formally filed for bankruptcy). While these costs are difficult to measure accurately, they are often much larger than the direct costs of bankruptcy.

Loss of Customers. Because bankruptcy may enable or encourage firms to walk away from commitments to their customers, customers may be unwilling to purchase

---

[5]See J. Warner, "Bankruptcy Costs: Some Evidence," *Journal of Finance* 32 (1977): 337–347; L. Weiss, "Bankruptcy Resolution: Direct Costs and Violation of Priority of Claims," *Journal of Financial Economics* 27 (1990): 285–314; E. Altman, "A Further Empirical Investigation of the Bankruptcy Cost Question," *Journal of Finance* 39 (1984): 1067–1089; and B. Betker, "The Administrative Costs of Debt Restructurings: Some Recent Evidence," *Financial Management* 26 (1997): 56–68. L. LoPucki and J. Doherty estimate that due to speedier resolution, the direct costs of bankruptcy fell by more than 50% during the 1990s to approximately 1.5% of firm value ("The Determinants of Professional Fees in Large Bankruptcy Reorganization Cases," *Journal of Empirical Legal Studies* 1 (2004): 111–141).

[6]R. Lawless and S. Ferris, "Professional Fees and Other Direct Costs in Chapter 7 Business Liquidations," *Washington University Law Quarterly* (1997): 1207–1236. For comparative international data, see K. Thorburn, "Bankruptcy Auctions: Costs, Debt Recovery and Firm Survival," *Journal of Financial Economics* 58 (2000): 337–368, and A. Raviv and S. Sundgren, "The Comparative Efficiency of Small-firm Bankruptcies: A Study of the U.S. and the Finnish Bankruptcy Codes," *Financial Management* 27 (1998): 28–40.

[7]See E. Tashjian, R. Lease, and J. McConnell, "An Empirical Analysis of Prepackaged Bankruptcies," *Journal of Financial Economics* 40 (1996): 135–162.

products whose value depends on future support or service from the firm. For example, customers will be reluctant to buy plane tickets in advance from a distressed airline that may cease operations, or to purchase autos from a distressed manufacturer that may fail to honor its warranties or provide replacement parts. Similarly, many technology firms' customers may hesitate to commit to a hardware or software platform that may not be supported or upgraded in the future. In contrast, the loss of customers is likely to be small for producers of raw materials (such as sugar or aluminum), as the value of these goods, once delivered, does not depend on the seller's continued success.[8]

Loss of Suppliers. Customers are not the only ones who retreat from a firm in financial distress. Suppliers may also be unwilling to provide a firm with inventory if they fear they will not be paid. For example, Kmart Corporation filed for bankruptcy protection in January 2002 in part because the decline in its stock price scared suppliers, which then refused to ship goods. Similarly, Swiss Air was forced to shut down because its suppliers refused to fuel its planes. This type of disruption is an important financial distress cost for firms that rely heavily on trade credit. In many cases, the bankruptcy filing itself can alleviate these problems through **debtor-in-possession (DIP) financing**. DIP financing is new debt issued by a bankrupt firm. Because this kind of debt is senior to all existing creditors, it allows a firm that has filed for bankruptcy renewed access to financing to keep operating.

Loss of Employees. Because firms in distress cannot offer job security with long-term employment contracts, they may have difficulty hiring new employees, and existing employees may quit or be hired away. Retaining key employees may be costly: Pacific Gas and Electric Corporation implemented a retention program costing over $80 million to retain 17 key employees while in bankruptcy.[9] This type of financial distress cost is likely to be high for firms whose value is derived largely from their human resources.

Loss of Receivables. Firms in financial distress tend to have difficulty collecting money that is owed to them. According to one of Enron's bankruptcy lawyers, "Many customers who owe smaller amounts are trying to hide from us. They must believe that Enron will never bother with them because the amounts are not particularly large in any individual case."[10] Knowing that the firm might go out of business or at least experience significant management turnover reduces the incentive of customers to maintain a reputation for timely payment.

Fire Sales of Assets. In an effort to avoid bankruptcy and its associated costs, companies in distress may attempt to sell assets quickly to raise cash. To do so, the firm may accept a lower price than would be optimal if it were financially healthy. Indeed, a study of airlines by Todd Pulvino shows that companies in bankruptcy or financial distress sell their aircraft at prices that are 15% to 40% below the prices received by healthier rivals.[11]

---

[8]See S. Titman, "The Effect of Capital Structure on a Firm's Liquidation Decision," *Journal of Financial Economics* 13 (1984): 137–151. T. Opler and S. Titman report 17.7% lower sales growth for highly leveraged firms compared to their less leveraged competitors in R&D-intensive industries during downturns ("Financial Distress and Corporate Performance," *Journal of Finance* 49 (1994): 1015–1040).

[9]R. Jurgens, "PG&E to Review Bonus Program," *Contra Costa Times*, December 13, 2003.

[10]K. Hays, "Enron Asks Judge to Get Tough on Deadbeat Customers," *Associated Press*, August 19, 2003.

[11]"Do Asset Fire-Sales Exist? An Empirical Investigation of Commercial Aircraft Transactions," *Journal of Finance* 53 (1998): 939–978, and "Effects of Bankruptcy Court Protection on Asset Sales," *Journal of Financial Economics* 52 (1999): 151–186. For examples from other industries, see T. Kruse, "Asset Liquidity and the Determinants of Asset Sales by Poorly Performing Firms," *Financial Management* 31 (2002): 107–129.

Discounts are also observed when distressed firms attempt to sell subsidiaries. The costs of selling assets below their value are greatest for firms with assets that lack competitive, liquid markets.

Inefficient Liquidation. Bankruptcy protection can be used by management to delay the liquidation of a firm that should be shut down. A study by Lawrence Weiss and Karen Wruck estimates that Eastern Airlines lost more than 50% of its value while in bankruptcy because management was allowed to continue making negative-NPV investments.[12] On the other hand, companies in bankruptcy may be forced to liquidate assets that would be more valuable if held. For example, as a result of its default, Lehman Brothers was forced to terminate 80% of its derivatives contracts with counterparties, in many cases at purportedly unattractive terms.[13]

Costs to Creditors. Aside from the direct legal costs that creditors may incur when a firm defaults, there may be other indirect costs to creditors. If the loan to the firm was a significant asset for the creditor, default of the firm may lead to costly financial distress *for the creditor*.[14] For example, in the 2008 financial crisis, the Lehman Brothers' bankruptcy in turn helped push many of Lehman's creditors into financial distress as well.

Because bankruptcy is a *choice* the firm's investors and creditors make, there is a limit to the direct and indirect costs on them that result from the firm's decision to go through the bankruptcy process. If these costs were too large, they could be largely avoided by negotiating a workout or doing a prepackaged bankruptcy. Thus, these costs should not exceed the cost of renegotiating with the firm's creditors.[15]

On the other hand, there is no such limit on the indirect costs of financial distress that arise from the firm's customers, suppliers, or employees. Many of these costs are incurred even *prior* to bankruptcy, in anticipation of the fact that the firm may use bankruptcy as an opportunity to renegotiate its contracts and commitments. For example, the firm may use bankruptcy as a way to renege on promises of future employment or retirement benefits for employees, to stop honoring warranties on its products, or to back out of unfavorable delivery contracts with its suppliers. Because of this fear that the firm will not honor its long-term commitments in bankruptcy, highly levered firms may need to pay higher wages to their employees, charge less for their products, and pay more to their suppliers than similar firms with less leverage. Because these costs are not limited by the cost of renegotiating to avoid bankruptcy, they may be substantially greater than other kinds of bankruptcy costs.[16]

---

[12]"Information Problems, Conflicts of Interest, and Asset Stripping: Ch. 11's Failure in the Case of Eastern Airlines," *Journal of Financial Economics* 48, 55–97.

[13]See C. Loomis, "Derivatives: The risk that still won't go away," *Fortune*, June 24, 2009.

[14]While these costs are borne by the creditor and not by the firm, the creditor will consider these potential costs when setting the rate of the loan.

[15]For an insightful discussion of this point, see R. Haugen and L. Senbet, "Bankruptcy and Agency Costs: Their Significance to the Theory of Optimal Capital Structure," *Journal of Financial and Quantitative Analysis* 23 (1988): 27–38.

[16]There is evidence that firms can use bankruptcy to improve efficiency (A. Kalay, R. Singhal, and E. Tashjian, "Is Chapter 11 really costly?" *Journal of Financial Economics*, 84 (2007) 772–796) but that these gains may come at the expense of workers (L. Jacobson, R. LaLonde, and D. Sullivan, "Earnings losses of displaced workers," *American Economic Review* 83 (1993) 685–709). J. Berk, R. Stanton, and J. Zechner, "Human Capital, Bankruptcy and Capital Structure," *Journal of Finance*, 65 (2009) 891–925, argue that firms may choose not to issue debt in order to increase their ability to commit to long-term labor contracts.

GLOBAL FINANCIAL CRISIS   **The Chrysler Prepack**

In November 2008, Chrysler CEO Robert Nardelli flew by private jet to Washington with a simple message: Without a government bailout, a Chrysler bankruptcy was inevitable. Congress was not convinced—it felt that bankruptcy was inevitable with or without a bailout and that the automaker needed to provide a more convincing plan to justify government funding. A return trip in December (this time by automobile) yielded a similar result. Bypassing Congress, outgoing President Bush decided to bail out Chrysler with funds from the Troubled Asset Relief Program (TARP). In the end the government provided Chrysler with $8 billion in debt financing.

As a durable goods manufacturer, a lengthy bankruptcy would have entailed significant bankruptcy costs. Indeed, sales were already suffering in part due to customer concerns about Chrysler's future. In response, President Obama took the unprecedented step of guaranteeing warranties on all new Chrysler cars in March 2009.

Despite all this assistance, on April 30, 2009, Chrysler declared bankruptcy as part of a government-orchestrated prepack. Just 41 days later, Chrysler emerged from bankruptcy as a Fiat-run, employee-owned,[17] and government-financed corporation.

Many potential bankruptcy costs were avoided because of the speed with which Chrysler transited the bankruptcy process following the prepack agreement. Yet, getting the debt holders to agree required additional government capital commitments and unprecedented political pressure. In many cases, the senior debt holders were banks that were already receiving TARP aid. Perhaps as a cost of receiving this aid, they accepted a deal that put the claims of unsecured creditors such as the United Auto Workers ahead of their more senior claims.[18] So, while some creditors may have been harmed, there is no doubt that the unprecedented cooperation among investors, and more importantly, government intervention, avoided a long and costly bankruptcy.

Overall Impact of Indirect Costs. In total, the indirect costs of financial distress can be substantial. When estimating them, however, we must remember two important points. First, we need to identify losses to total firm value (and not solely losses to equity holders or debt holders, or transfers between them). Second, we need to identify the incremental losses that are associated with financial distress, above and beyond any losses that would occur due to the firm's economic distress. A study of highly levered firms by Gregor Andrade and Steven Kaplan estimated a potential loss due to financial distress of 10% to 20% of firm value.[19] Next, we consider the consequences of these potential costs of leverage for firm value.

CONCEPT CHECK

1. If a firm files for bankruptcy under Chapter 11 of the bankruptcy code, which party gets the first opportunity to propose a plan for the firm's reorganization?

2. Why are the losses of debt holders whose claims are not fully repaid not a cost of financial distress, whereas the loss of customers who fear the firm will stop honoring warranties is?

---

[17]The Chrysler employee pension plan owned 55% of Chrysler, Fiat 20%, the U.S. Treasury 8%, and the Canadian government 2%. The rest of the equity was split amongst the remaining debt claimants.

[18]Not all creditors bowed willingly to the government pressure. A group of pension funds opposed the prepack. In the end the Supreme Court sided with the company and refused to hear their appeal. Perhaps not surprisingly, as a result of this intervention, other unionized firms with large underfunded pensions saw their borrowing costs increase as creditors anticipated the possibility of similar resolutions. (See B. Blaylock, A. Edwards, and J. Stanfield, "Creditor Rights and Government Intervention," 2012, http://ssrn.com/abstract=1685618).

[19]"How Costly Is Financial (Not Economic) Distress? Evidence from Highly Leveraged Transactions That Became Distressed," *Journal of Finance* 53 (1998): 1443–1493.

16.3 Financial Distress Costs and Firm Value

The costs of financial distress described in the previous section represent an important departure from Modigliani and Miller's assumption of perfect capital markets. MM assumed that the cash flows of a firm's assets do not depend on its choice of capital structure. As we have discussed, however, levered firms risk incurring financial distress costs that reduce the cash flows available to investors.

Armin Industries: The Impact of Financial Distress Costs

To illustrate how these financial distress costs affect firm value, consider again the example of Armin Industries. With all-equity financing, Armin's assets will be worth $150 million if its new product succeeds and $80 million if the new product fails. In contrast, with debt of $100 million, Armin will be forced into bankruptcy if the new product fails. In this case, some of the value of Armin's assets will be lost to bankruptcy and financial distress costs. As a result, debt holders will receive less than $80 million. We show the impact of these costs in Table 16.2, where we assume debt holders receive only $60 million after accounting for the costs of financial distress.

As Table 16.2 shows, the total value to all investors is now less with leverage than it is without leverage when the new product fails. The difference of $80 million − $60 million = $20 million is due to financial distress costs. These costs will lower the total value of the firm with leverage, and MM's Proposition I will no longer hold, as illustrated in Example 16.2.

EXAMPLE 16.2   **Firm Value When Financial Distress Is Costly**

Problem
Compare the current value of Armin Industries with and without leverage, given the data in Table 16.2. Assume that the risk-free rate is 5%, the new product is equally likely to succeed or fail, and the risk is diversifiable.

Solution
With and without leverage, the payments to equity holders are the same as in Example 16.1. There we computed the value of unlevered equity as $109.52 million and the value of levered equity as $23.81 million. But due to bankruptcy costs, the value of the debt is now

$$\text{Debt} = \frac{\frac{1}{2}(100) + \frac{1}{2}(60)}{1.05} = \$76.19 \text{ million}$$

The value of the levered firm is $V^L = E + D = 23.81 + 76.19 = \$100$ million, which is less than the value of the unlevered firm, $V^U = \$109.52$ million. Thus, due to bankruptcy costs, the value of the levered firm is $9.52 million less than its value without leverage. This loss equals the present value of the $20 million in financial distress costs the firm will pay if the product fails:

$$PV(\text{Financial Distress Costs}) = \frac{\frac{1}{2}(0) + \frac{1}{2}(20)}{1.05} = \$9.52 \text{ million}$$

Who Pays for Financial Distress Costs?

The financial distress costs in Table 16.2 reduce the payments to the debt holders when the new product has failed. In that case, the equity holders have already lost their investment and have no further interest in the firm. It might seem as though these costs are irrelevant

TABLE 16.2	Value of Debt and Equity with and without Leverage (in $ million)			
	Without Leverage		With Leverage	
	Success	Failure	Success	Failure
Debt value	—	—	100	60
Equity value	150	80	50	0
Total to all investors	150	80	150	60

from the shareholders' perspective. Why should equity holders care about costs borne by debt holders?

It is true that after a firm is in bankruptcy, equity holders care little about bankruptcy costs. But debt holders are not foolish—they recognize that when the firm defaults, they will not be able to get the full value of the assets. As a result, they will pay less for the debt initially. How much less? Precisely the amount they will ultimately give up—the present value of the bankruptcy costs.

But if the debt holders pay less for the debt, there is less money available for the firm to pay dividends, repurchase shares, and make investments. That is, this difference is money out of the equity holders' pockets. This logic leads to the following general result:

When securities are fairly priced, the original shareholders of a firm pay the present value of the costs associated with bankruptcy and financial distress.

EXAMPLE 16.3 — Financial Distress Costs and the Stock Price

Problem
Suppose that at the beginning of the year, Armin Industries has 10 million shares outstanding and no debt. Armin then announces plans to issue one-year debt with a face value of $100 million and to use the proceeds to repurchase shares. Given the data in Table 16.2, what will the new share price be? As in the previous examples, assume the risk-free rate is 5%, the new product is equally likely to succeed or fail, and this risk is diversifiable.

Solution
From Example 16.1, the value of the firm without leverage is $109.52 million. With 10 million shares outstanding, this value corresponds to an initial share price of $10.952 per share. In Example 16.2, we saw that with leverage, the total value of the firm is only $100 million. In anticipation of this decline in value, the price of the stock should fall to $100 million ÷ 10 million shares = $10.00 per share on announcement of the recapitalization.

Let's check this result. From Example 16.2, due to bankruptcy costs, the new debt is worth $76.19 million. Thus, at a price of $10 per share, Armin will repurchase 7.619 million shares, leaving 2.381 million shares outstanding. In Example 16.1, we computed the value of levered equity as $23.81 million. Dividing by the number of shares gives a share price after the transaction of

$$\$23.81 \text{ million} \div 2.381 \text{ million shares} = \$10.00 \text{ per share}$$

Thus, the recapitalization will cost shareholders $0.952 per share or $9.52 million in total. This cost matches the present value of financial distress costs computed in Example 16.2. Thus, although debt holders bear these costs in the end, shareholders pay the present value of the costs of financial distress upfront.

1. Armin incurred financial distress costs only in the event that the new product failed. Why might Armin incur financial distress costs even *before* the success or failure of the new product is known?

2. True or False: If bankruptcy costs are only incurred once the firm is in bankruptcy and its equity is worthless, then these costs will not affect the initial value of the firm.

16.4 Optimal Capital Structure: The Trade-Off Theory

We can now combine our knowledge of the benefits of leverage from the interest tax shield (discussed in Chapter 15) with the costs of financial distress to determine the amount of debt that a firm should issue to maximize its value. The analysis presented in this section is called the **trade-off theory** because it weighs the benefits of debt that result from shielding cash flows from taxes against the costs of financial distress associated with leverage.

According to this theory, *the total value of a levered firm equals the value of the firm without leverage plus the present value of the tax savings from debt, less the present value of financial distress costs:*

$$V^L = V^U + PV(\text{Interest Tax Shield}) - PV(\text{Financial Distress Costs}) \qquad (16.1)$$

Equation 16.1 shows that leverage has costs as well as benefits. Firms have an incentive to increase leverage to exploit the tax benefits of debt. But with too much debt, they are more likely to risk default and incur financial distress costs.

The Present Value of Financial Distress Costs

Aside from simple examples, calculating the precise present value of financial distress costs is quite complicated. Three key factors determine the present value of financial distress costs: (1) the probability of financial distress, (2) the magnitude of the costs if the firm is in distress, and (3) the appropriate discount rate for the distress costs. In Example 16.2, when Armin is levered, the present value of its financial distress costs depends on the probability that the new product will fail (50%), the magnitude of the costs if it does fail ($20 million), and the discount rate (5%).

What determines each of these factors? The probability of financial distress depends on the likelihood that a firm will be unable to meet its debt commitments and therefore default. This probability increases with the amount of a firm's liabilities (relative to its assets). It also increases with the volatility of a firm's cash flows and asset values. Thus, firms with steady, reliable cash flows, such as utility companies, are able to use high levels of debt and still have a very low probability of default. Firms whose value and cash flows are very volatile (for example, semiconductor firms) must have much lower levels of debt to avoid a significant risk of default.

The magnitude of the financial distress costs will depend on the relative importance of the costs discussed in Section 16.2, and is also likely to vary by industry. For example, firms, such as technology firms, whose value comes largely from human capital, are likely to incur high costs when they risk financial distress, due to the potential for loss of customers and the need to hire and retain key personnel, as well as a lack of tangible assets that can be easily liquidated. In contrast, firms whose main assets are physical capital, such as real estate firms, are likely to have lower costs of financial distress, because a greater portion of their value derives from assets that can be sold relatively easily.

Finally, the discount rate for the distress costs will depend on the firm's market risk. Note that because distress costs are high when the firm does poorly, the beta of distress costs will have an opposite sign to that of the firm.[20] Also, the higher the firm's beta, the more likely it will be in distress in an economic downturn, and thus the more negative the beta of its distress costs will be. Because a more negative beta leads to a lower cost of capital (below the risk-free rate), other things equal *the present value of distress costs will be higher for high beta firms.*

Optimal Leverage

Figure 16.1 shows how the value of a levered firm, V^L, varies with the level of permanent debt, D, according to Eq. 16.1. With no debt, the value of the firm is V^U. For low levels of debt, the risk of default remains low and the main effect of an increase in leverage is an increase in the interest tax shield, which has present value τ^*D, where τ^* is the effective tax advantage of debt calculated in Chapter 15. If there were no costs of financial distress, the value would continue to increase at this rate until the interest on the debt exceeds the firm's earnings before interest and taxes and the tax shield is exhausted.

The costs of financial distress reduce the value of the levered firm, V^L. The amount of the reduction increases with the probability of default, which in turn increases with the level of the debt D. The trade-off theory states that firms should increase their leverage until it reaches the level D^* for which V^L is maximized. At this point, the tax savings that result from increasing leverage are just offset by the increased probability of incurring the costs of financial distress.

FIGURE 16.1

Optimal Leverage with Taxes and Financial Distress Costs

As the level of debt, D, increases, the tax benefits of debt increase by τ^*D until the interest expense exceeds the firm's EBIT (see Figure 15.8). The probability of default, and hence the present value of financial distress costs, also increase with D. The optimal level of debt, D^*, occurs when these effects balance out and V^L is maximized. D^* will be lower for firms with higher costs of financial distress.

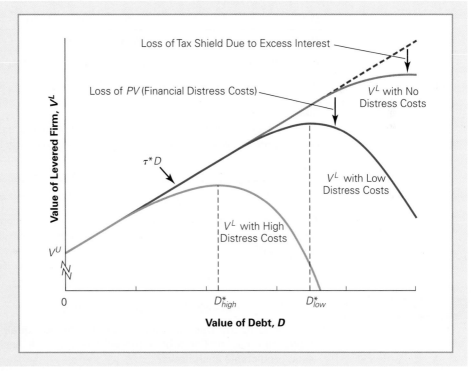

---

[20]For intuition, consider a law firm specializing in bankruptcy. Because profits will be higher in downturns, the law firm will have negative beta. Formally, the beta of distress costs is similar to the beta of a put option on the firm, which we calculate in Chapter 21 (see Figure 21.8). See also H. Almeida and T. Philippon, "The risk-adjusted cost of financial distress," *Journal of Finance* 62 (2007) 2557–2586.

Figure 16.1 also illustrates the optimal debt choices for two types of firms. The optimal debt choice for a firm with low costs of financial distress is indicated by D^*_{low}, and the optimal debt choice for a firm with high costs of financial distress is indicated by D^*_{high}. Not surprisingly, with higher costs of financial distress, it is optimal for the firm to choose lower leverage.

The trade-off theory helps to resolve two puzzles regarding leverage that arose in Chapter 15. First, the presence of financial distress costs can explain why firms choose debt levels that are too low to fully exploit the interest tax shield. Second, differences in the magnitude of financial distress costs and the volatility of cash flows can explain the differences in the use of leverage across industries. That said, bankruptcy costs alone may not be sufficient to explain all of the variation observed. Fortunately, the trade-off theory can be easily extended to include other effects of leverage—which may be even more important than financial distress costs—that we discuss next.

EXAMPLE 16.4   **Choosing an Optimal Debt Level**

Problem

Greenleaf Industries is considering adding leverage to its capital structure. Greenleaf's managers believe they can add as much as $35 million in debt and exploit the benefits of the tax shield (for which they estimate $\tau^* = 15\%$). However, they also recognize that higher debt increases the risk of financial distress. Based on simulations of the firm's future cash flows, the CFO has made the following estimates (in millions of dollars):[21]

Debt	0	10	20	25	30	35
PV(Interest tax shield)	0.00	1.50	3.00	3.75	4.50	5.25
PV(Financial distress costs)	0.00	0.00	0.38	1.62	4.00	6.38

What is the optimal debt choice for Greenleaf?

Solution

From Eq. 16.1, the net benefit of debt is determined by subtracting *PV*(Financial distress costs) from *PV*(Interest tax shield). The net benefit for each level of debt is

Debt	0	10	20	25	30	35
Net benefit	0.00	1.50	2.62	2.13	0.50	−1.13

The level of debt that leads to the highest net benefit is $20 million. Greenleaf will gain $3 million due to tax shields, and lose $0.38 million due to the present value of distress costs, for a net gain of $2.62 million.

CONCEPT CHECK

1. What is the "trade-off" in the trade-off theory?

2. According to the trade-off theory, all else being equal, which type of firm has a higher optimal level of debt: a firm with very volatile cash flows or a firm with very safe, predictable cash flows?

---

[21]The PV of the interest tax shield is computed as τ^*D. The PV of financial distress costs is generally difficult to estimate and requires option valuation techniques we introduce in Part 7.

Exploiting Debt Holders: The Agency Costs of Leverage

In this section, we consider another way that capital structure can affect a firm's cash flows: It can alter managers' incentives and change their investment decisions. If these changes have a negative NPV, they will be costly for the firm.

The type of costs we describe in this section are examples of **agency costs**—costs that arise when there are conflicts of interest between stakeholders. Because top managers often hold shares in the firm and are hired and retained with the approval of the board of directors, which itself is elected by shareholders, managers will generally make decisions that increase the value of the firm's equity. When a firm has leverage, a conflict of interest exists if investment decisions have different consequences for the value of equity and the value of debt. Such a conflict is most likely to occur when the risk of financial distress is high. In some circumstances, managers may take actions that benefit shareholders but harm the firm's creditors and lower the total value of the firm.

We illustrate this possibility by considering Baxter Inc., a firm that is facing financial distress. Baxter has a loan of $1 million due at the end of the year. Without a change in its strategy, the market value of its assets will be only $900,000 at that time, and Baxter will default on its debt. In this situation, let's consider several types of agency costs that might arise.

Excessive Risk-Taking and Asset Substitution

Baxter executives are considering a new strategy that seemed promising initially but appears risky after closer analysis. The new strategy requires no upfront investment, but it has only a 50% chance of success. If it succeeds, it will increase the value of the firm's assets to $1.3 million. If it fails, the value of the firm's assets will fall to $300,000. Therefore, the expected value of the firm's assets under the new strategy is 50% × $1.3 million + 50% × $300,000 = $800,000, a decline of $100,000 from their value of $900,000 under the old strategy. Despite the negative expected payoff, some within the firm have suggested that Baxter should go ahead with the new strategy, in the interest of better serving its shareholders. How can shareholders benefit from this decision?

As Table 16.3 shows, if Baxter does nothing, it will ultimately default and equity holders will get nothing with certainty. Thus, equity holders have nothing to lose if Baxter tries the risky strategy. If the strategy succeeds, equity holders will receive $300,000 after paying off the debt. Given a 50% chance of success, the equity holders' expected payoff is $150,000.

Clearly, equity holders gain from this strategy, even though it has a negative expected payoff. Who loses? The debt holders: If the strategy fails, they bear the loss. As shown in Table 16.3, if the project succeeds, debt holders are fully repaid and receive $1 million. If the project fails, they receive only $300,000. Overall, the debt holders' expected payoff is

TABLE 16.3	Outcomes for Baxter's Debt and Equity under Each Strategy (in $ thousand)			
			New Risky Strategy	
	Old Strategy	Success	Failure	Expected
Value of assets	900	1300	300	800
Debt	900	1000	300	650
Equity	0	300	0	150

$650,000, a loss of $250,000 relative to the $900,000 they would have received under the old strategy. This loss corresponds to the $100,000 expected loss of the risky strategy and the $150,000 gain of the equity holders. Effectively, the equity holders are gambling with the debt holders' money.

This example illustrates a general point: *When a firm faces financial distress, shareholders can gain from decisions that increase the risk of the firm sufficiently, even if they have a negative NPV.* Because leverage gives shareholders an incentive to replace low-risk assets with riskier ones, this result is often referred to as the **asset substitution problem**.[22] It can also lead to over-investment, as shareholders may gain if the firm undertakes negative-NPV, but sufficiently risky, projects.

In either case, if the firm increases risk through a negative-NPV decision or investment, the total value of the firm will be reduced. Anticipating this bad behavior, security holders will pay less for the firm initially. This cost is likely to be highest for firms that can easily increase the risk of their investments.

Debt Overhang and Under-Investment

Suppose Baxter does not pursue the risky strategy. Instead, the firm's managers consider an attractive investment opportunity that requires an initial investment of $100,000 and will generate a risk-free return of 50%. That is, it has the following cash flows (in thousands of dollars):

If the current risk-free rate is 5%, this investment clearly has a positive NPV. The only problem is that Baxter does not have the cash on hand to make the investment.

Could Baxter raise the $100,000 by issuing new equity? Unfortunately, it cannot. Suppose equity holders were to contribute the $100,000 in new capital required. Their payoff at the end of the year is shown in Table 16.4.

Thus, if equity holders contribute $100,000 to fund the project, they get back only $50,000. The other $100,000 from the project goes to the debt holders, whose payoff increases from $900,000 to $1 million. Because the debt holders receive most of the benefit, this project is a negative-NPV investment opportunity for equity holders, even though it offers a positive NPV for the firm.

This example illustrates another general point: *When a firm faces financial distress, it may choose not to finance new, positive-NPV projects.* In this case, when shareholders prefer not to

TABLE 16.4	Outcomes for Baxter's Debt and Equity with and without the New Project (in $ thousand)	
	Without New Project	With New Project
Existing assets	900	900
New project		150
Total firm value	900	1050
Debt	900	1000
Equity	0	50

[22]See M. Jensen and W. Meckling, "Theory of the Firm: Managerial Behavior, Agency Costs and Ownership Structure," *Journal of Financial Economics* 3 (1976): 305–360.

Firms and financial institutions in or near financial distress in the midst of the 2008 financial crisis experienced many of the costs associated with financial distress that we have described, creating further negative consequences for the real economy.

Of particular concern was the seeming unwillingness of banks to make loans to borrowers at reasonable terms. One possible explanation was that the borrowers were not creditworthy and so lending to them was a negative NPV investment. But many, including the banks themselves, pointed to another culprit: banks were subject to debt overhang that made it extremely difficult to raise the capital needed to make positive-NPV loans. Thus, a primary rationale for governmental bailouts during the crisis was to provide banks with capital directly, alleviating their debt overhang and increasing the availability of credit to the rest of the economy.

invest in a positive-NPV project, we say there is a **debt overhang** or **under-investment problem**.[23] This failure to invest is costly for debt holders and for the overall value of the firm, because it is giving up the NPV of the missed opportunities. The cost is highest for firms that are likely to have profitable future growth opportunities requiring large investments.

Cashing Out. When a firm faces financial distress, shareholders have an incentive to withdraw cash from the firm if possible. As an example, suppose Baxter has equipment it can sell for $25,000 at the beginning of the year. It will need this equipment to continue normal operations during the year; without it, Baxter will have to shut down some operations and the firm will be worth only $800,000 at year-end. Although selling the equipment reduces the value of the firm by $100,000, if it is likely that Baxter will default at year-end, this cost would be borne by the debt holders. So, equity holders gain if Baxter sells the equipment and uses the $25,000 to pay an immediate cash dividend. This incentive to liquidate assets at prices below their actual value to the firm is an extreme form of under-investment resulting from the debt overhang.

Estimating the Debt Overhang. How much leverage must a firm have for there to be a significant debt overhang problem? While difficult to estimate precisely, we can use a useful approximation. Suppose equity holders invest an amount I in a new investment project with similar risk to the rest of the firm. Let D and E be the market value of the firm's debt and equity, and let β_D and β_E be their respective betas. Then the following approximate rule applies: equity holders will benefit from the new investment only if[24]

$$\frac{NPV}{I} > \frac{\beta_D D}{\beta_E E} \tag{16.2}$$

---

[23]This agency cost of debt was formalized by S. Myers, "Determinants of Corporate Borrowing," *Journal of Financial Economics* 5 (1977): 147–175.

[24]To understand this result, let dE and dD be the change in the value of equity and debt resulting from an investment with total value $dE + dD = I + NPV$. Equity holders benefit if they gain more than they invest, $I < dE$, which is equivalent to debt holders capturing less than the investment's NPV, $NPV > dD$. Dividing the second inequality by the first, we have $NPV/I > dD/dE$. Eq. 16.2 follows from the approximation $dD/dE \approx \beta_D D/\beta_E E$; that is, the relative sensitivity of debt and equity to changes in asset values are similar whether those changes arise from investment decisions or market conditions. We derive this approximation in Chapter 21.

That is, the project's profitability index (*NPV/I*) must exceed a cutoff equal to the relative riskiness of the firm's debt (β_D/β_E) times its debt-equity ratio (*D/E*). Note that if the firm has no debt (*D* = 0) or its debt is risk free (β_D = 0), then Eq. 16.2 is equivalent to *NPV* > 0. But if the firm's debt is risky, the required cutoff is positive and increases with the firm's leverage. Equity holders will reject positive-NPV projects with profitability indices below the cutoff, leading to under-investment and reduction in firm value.

EXAMPLE 16.5

Estimating the Debt Overhang

Problem

In Example 12.7, we estimated that Sears had an equity beta of 1.36, a debt beta of 0.17, and a debt-equity ratio of 0.30, while Saks had an equity beta of 1.85, a debt beta of 0.31, and a debt-equity ratio of 1.0. For both firms, estimate the minimum NPV such that a new $100,000 investment (which does not change the volatility of the firm) will benefit shareholders. Which firm has the more severe debt overhang?

Solution

We can use Eq. 16.2 to estimate the cutoff level of the profitability index for Sears as $(0.17/1.36) \times 0.30 = 0.0375$. Thus, the NPV would need to equal at least $3750 for the investment to benefit shareholders. For Saks, the cutoff is $(0.31/1.85) \times 1.0 = 0.1675$. Thus, the minimum NPV for Saks is $16,750. Saks has the more severe debt overhang, as its shareholders will reject projects with positive NPVs up to this higher cutoff. Similarly, Saks shareholders would benefit if the firm "cashed out" by liquidating up to $116,750 worth of assets to pay out an additional $100,000 in dividends.

Agency Costs and the Value of Leverage

These examples illustrate how leverage can encourage managers and shareholders to act in ways that reduce firm value. In each case, the equity holders benefit at the expense of the debt holders. But, as with financial distress costs, it is the shareholders of the firm who ultimately bear these agency costs. Although equity holders may benefit at debt holders' expense from these negative-NPV decisions in times of distress, debt holders recognize this possibility and pay less for the debt when it is first issued, reducing the amount the firm can distribute to shareholders. The net effect is a reduction in the initial share price of the firm corresponding to the negative NPV of the decisions.

These agency costs of debt can arise only if there is some chance the firm will default and impose losses on its debt holders. The magnitude of the agency costs increases with the risk, and therefore the amount, of the firm's debt. Agency costs, therefore, represent another cost of increasing the firm's leverage that will affect the firm's optimal capital structure choice.

EXAMPLE 16.6

Agency Costs and the Amount of Leverage

Problem

Would the agency costs described previously arise if Baxter had less leverage and owed $400,000 rather than $1 million?

Solution

If Baxter makes no new investments or changes to its strategy, the firm will be worth $900,000. Thus, the firm will remain solvent and its equity will be worth $900,000 − $400,000 = $500,000.

Consider first the decision to increase risk. If Baxter takes the risky strategy, its assets will be worth either $1.3 million or $300,000, so equity holders will receive $900,000 or $0. In this case, the equity holders' expected payoff with the risky project is only $900,000 × 0.5 = $450,000. Thus equity holders will reject the risky strategy.

What about under-investment? If Baxter raises $100,000 from equity holders to fund a new investment that increases the value of assets by $150,000, the equity will be worth

$$\$900,000 + \$150,000 - \$400,000 = \$650,000$$

This is a gain of $150,000 over the $500,000 equity holders would receive without the investment. Because their payoff has gone up by $150,000 for a $100,000 investment, they will be willing to invest in the new project.

Similarly, Baxter has no incentive to cash out and sell equipment to pay a dividend. If the firm pays the dividend, equity holders receive $25,000 today. But their future payoff declines to $800,000 − $400,000 = $400,000. Thus, they give up $100,000 in one year for a $25,000 gain today. For any reasonable discount rate, this is a bad deal and stockholders will reject the dividend.

The Leverage Ratchet Effect

As we have seen, when an unlevered firm issues new debt, equity holders will bear any anticipated agency or bankruptcy costs via a discount in the price they receive for that new debt. This discount deters the firm from taking on high leverage initially if doing so would reduce the value of the firm.

However, once a firm has debt already in place, some of the agency or bankruptcy costs that result from taking on additional leverage will fall on *existing* debt holders. Because that debt has already been sold, the negative consequences for these debt holders will not be borne by shareholders. As a result, shareholders may benefit from taking on higher leverage even though it might reduce the total value of the firm. (This result is another manifestation of the "cashing out" effect of debt overhang—levered firms may have an incentive to borrow further and disburse the proceeds to shareholders.)

Finally, debt overhang will inhibit firms from reducing leverage once it is in place. In this case, if the firm tries to buy back debt, existing debt holders will gain (and debt holders who sell will demand a premium) due to the reduction in risk, agency costs, and bankruptcy costs associated with lower leverage.

The **leverage ratchet effect** captures the observations that, once existing debt is in place, (1) shareholders may have an incentive to increase leverage even if it decreases the value of the firm,[25] and (2) shareholders will not have an incentive to decrease leverage by buying back debt, even if it will increase the value of the firm.[26]

EXAMPLE 16.7   **Debt Overhang and the Leverage Ratchet Effect**

Problem

Show that Baxter's shareholders would not gain by reducing leverage from $1 million to $400,000, even though firm value would increase by eliminating the cost of underinvestment.

---

[25]For an analysis of this effect and its consequence on loan markets, see D. Bizer and P. DeMarzo, "Sequential Banking," *Journal of Political Economy*, 100 (1992): 41–61.

[26]This result holds quite generally as long as the debt must be repurchased at its ex-post fair value; see A. Admati, P. DeMarzo, M. Hellwig, and P. Pfleiderer, "Debt Overhang and Capital Regulation," http://papers.ssrn.com/sol3/papers.cfm?abstract_id=2031204.

Solution

Recall that with $1 million in debt, Baxter would choose to forgo an investment in a positive NPV risk-free project (see Table 16.4). Thus, its equity would be worth zero, and its debt would be worth $900,000. Also, as shown in Example 16.6, if the debt level were $400,000 instead of $1 million, the problem would not exist–equity holders would choose to take the positive NPV investment and firm value would increase by the NPV of the project.

Even so, equity holders will not choose to reduce debt. Because the debt will be default-free after the buyback, and given the risk-free rate of 5%, each debt holder must be repaid at least $1/1.05 = $0.952 per dollar of principal, or would otherwise prefer to hold onto their debt while others sell. Therefore, to reduce its debt to $400,000, Baxter would need to raise $600,000/1.05 = $571,429 from equity holders. Baxter could then raise another $100,000 from equity holders to invest in the new project. In the end, the value of the firm would be $1.05 million, and after paying $400,000 in debt, equity holders would receive $650,000. But this amount is less than the total of $671,429 equity holders would need to invest upfront.

The reason equity holders do not gain by reducing debt in Example 16.7 is that in order to buy back the debt, the company must pay its post-transaction market value, which includes the value of the anticipated investment. A similar outcome would apply to the case of excessive risk-taking. By reducing debt, equity holders lose their incentive to take on a risky negative NPV investment. While this effect increases the value of the firm, equity holders would not gain as they would be forced to pay a price for the debt that reflects the value of eliminating the incentives for excessive risk-taking.

Debt Maturity and Covenants

Firms can do several things to mitigate the agency costs of debt. First, note that the magnitude of agency costs likely depends on the maturity of debt. With long-term debt, equity holders have more opportunities to profit at the debt holders' expense before the debt matures. Thus, agency costs are smallest for short-term debt.[27] For example, if Baxter's debt were due today, the firm would be forced to default or renegotiate with debt holders before it could increase risk, fail to invest, or cash out. However, by relying on short-term debt the firm will be obligated to repay or refinance its debt more frequently. Short-term debt may also increase the firm's risk of financial distress and its associated costs.

Second, as a condition of making a loan, creditors often place restrictions on the actions that the firm can take. Such restrictions are referred to as **debt covenants**. Covenants may limit the firm's ability to pay large dividends or restrict the types of investments that the firm can make. They also typically limit the amount of new debt the firm can take on. By preventing management from exploiting debt holders, these covenants may help to reduce agency costs. Conversely, because covenants hinder management flexibility, they have the potential to get in the way of positive NPV opportunities and so can have costs of their own.[28]

CONCEPT CHECK

1. Why do firms have an incentive to both take excessive risk and under-invest when they are in financial distress?

2. Why would debt holders desire covenants that restrict the firm's ability to pay dividends, and why might shareholders also benefit from this restriction?

---

[27] See S. Johnson, "Debt Maturity and the Effects of Growth Opportunities and Liquidity on Leverage," *Review of Financial Studies* 16 (March 2003): 209–236.

[28] For an analysis of the costs and benefits of bond covenants, see C. Smith and J. Warner, "On Financial Contracting: An Analysis of Bond Covenants," *Journal of Financial Economics* 7 (1979): 117–161.

16.6 Motivating Managers: The Agency Benefits of Leverage

In Section 16.5, we took the view that managers act in the interests of the firm's equity holders, and we considered the potential conflicts of interest between debt holders and equity holders when a firm has leverage. Of course, managers also have their own personal interests, which may differ from those of both equity holders and debt holders. Although managers often do own shares of the firm, in most large corporations they own only a very small fraction of the outstanding shares. And while the shareholders, through the board of directors, have the power to fire managers, they rarely do so unless the firm's performance is exceptionally poor.[29]

This separation of ownership and control creates the possibility of **management entrenchment**: facing little threat of being fired and replaced, managers are free to run the firm in their own best interests. As a result, managers may make decisions that benefit themselves at investors' expense. In this section, we consider how leverage can provide incentives for managers to run the firm more efficiently and effectively. The benefits we describe in this section, in addition to the tax benefits of leverage, give the firm an incentive to use debt rather than equity financing.

Concentration of Ownership

One advantage of using leverage is that it allows the original owners of the firm to maintain their equity stake. As major shareholders, they will have a strong interest in doing what is best for the firm. Consider the following simple example:

Ross Jackson is the owner of a successful furniture store. He plans to expand by opening several new stores. Ross can either borrow the funds needed for expansion or raise the money by selling shares in the firm. If he issues equity, he will need to sell 40% of the firm to raise the necessary funds.

If Ross uses debt, he retains ownership of 100% of the firm's equity. As long as the firm does not default, any decision Ross makes that increases the value of the firm by $1 increases the value of his own stake by $1. But if Ross issues equity, he retains only 60% of the equity. Thus, Ross gains only $0.60 for every $1 increase in firm value.

The difference in Ross's ownership stake changes his incentives in running the firm. Suppose the value of the firm depends largely on Ross's personal effort. Ross is then likely to work harder, and the firm will be worth more, if he receives 100% of the gains rather than only 60%.

Another effect of issuing equity is Ross's temptation to enjoy corporate perks, such as a large office with fancy artwork, a corporate limo and driver, a corporate jet, or a large expense account. With leverage, Ross is the sole owner and will bear the full cost of these perks. But with equity, Ross bears only 60% of the cost; the other 40% will be paid for by the new equity holders. Thus, with equity financing, it is more likely that Ross will overspend on these luxuries.

The costs of reduced effort and excessive spending on perks are another form of agency cost. These agency costs arise in this case due to the dilution of ownership that occurs when equity financing is used. Who pays these agency costs? As always, if securities are fairly

---

[29]See, for example, J. Warner, R. Watts, and K. Wruck, "Stock Prices and Top Management Changes," *Journal of Financial Economics* 20 (1988): 461–492, though more recent evidence suggests that management turnover may be more sensitive to poor performance than previously measured (see D. Jenter and K. Lewellen, "Performance-induced CEO turnover," working paper, 2012).

priced, the original owners of the firm pay the cost. In our example, Ross will find that if he chooses to issue equity, the new investors will discount the price they will pay to reflect Ross's lower effort and increased spending on perks. In this case, using leverage can benefit the firm by preserving ownership concentration and avoiding these agency costs.[30]

Reduction of Wasteful Investment

While ownership is often concentrated for small, young firms, ownership typically becomes diluted over time as a firm grows. First, the original owners of the firm may retire, and the new managers likely will not hold a large ownership stake. Second, firms often need to raise more capital for investment than can be sustained using debt alone (recall the discussion of growth and leverage in Chapter 15). Third, owners will often choose to sell off their stakes and invest in a well-diversified portfolio to reduce risk.[31] As a result, for large U.S. firms, most CEOs own less than 1% of their firms' shares.

With such low ownership stakes, the potential for conflict of interest between managers and equity holders is high. Appropriate monitoring and standards of accountability are required to prevent abuse. While most successful firms have implemented appropriate mechanisms to protect shareholders, each year scandals are revealed in which managers have acted against shareholders' interests.

While overspending on personal perks may be a problem for large firms, these costs are likely to be small relative to the overall value of the firm. A more serious concern for large corporations is that managers may make large, unprofitable investments: Bad investment decisions have destroyed many otherwise successful firms. But what would motivate managers to make negative-NPV investments?

Some financial economists explain a manager's willingness to engage in negative-NPV investments as *empire building*. According to this view, managers prefer to run large firms rather than small ones, so they will take on investments that increase the size—rather than the profitability—of the firm. One potential reason for this preference is that managers of large firms tend to earn higher salaries, and they may also have more prestige and garner greater publicity than managers of small firms. As a result, managers may expand (or fail to shut down) unprofitable divisions, pay too much for acquisitions, make unnecessary capital expenditures, or hire unnecessary employees.

Another reason that managers may over-invest is that they are overconfident. Even when managers attempt to act in shareholders' interests, they may make mistakes. Managers tend to be bullish on the firm's prospects and so may believe that new opportunities are better than they actually are. They may also become committed to investments the firm has already made and continue to invest in projects that should be canceled.[32]

---

[30]This potential benefit of leverage is discussed by M. Jensen and W. Meckling, "Theory of the Firm: Managerial Behavior, Agency Costs and Ownership Structure," *Journal of Financial Economics* 3 (1976): 305–360. However, because managers who own a large block of shares are more difficult to replace, increasing ownership concentration at lower levels (e.g., in the 5%–25% range) may increase entrenchment and *reduce* incentives; see R. Morck, A. Shleifer, and R. Vishny, "Management Ownership and Market Valuation," *Journal of Financial Economics* 20 (1988): 293–315.

[31]According to one study, original owners tend to reduce their stake by more than 50% within nine years after the firm becomes a public company (B. Urošević, "Essays in Optimal Dynamic Risk Sharing in Equity and Debt Markets," 2002, University of California, Berkeley).

[32]For evidence of the relationship between CEO overconfidence and investment distortions, see U. Malmendier and G. Tate, "CEO Overconfidence and Corporate Investment," *Journal of Finance* 60 (2005): 2661–2700; J. Heaton "Managerial Optimism and Corporate Finance," *Financial Management* 31 (2002): 33–45; and R. Roll, "The Hubris Hypothesis of Corporate Takeovers," *Journal of Business* 59 (1986): 197–216.

Excessive Perks and Corporate Scandals

While most CEOs and managers exercise proper restraint when spending shareholders' money, there have been some highly publicized exceptions that have come to light as corporate scandals.

Former Enron CFO Andrew Fastow reportedly used complicated financial transactions to enrich himself with at least $30 million of shareholder money. Tyco Corporation's ex-CEO Dennis Kozlowski will be remembered for his $6000 shower curtain, $6300 sewing basket, and $17 million Fifth Avenue condo, all paid for with Tyco funds. In total, he and former CFO Mark Swartz were convicted of pilfering $600 million from company coffers.* Former WorldCom CEO Bernie Ebbers, who was convicted for his role in the firm's $11 billion accounting scandal, borrowed more than $400 million from the company at favorable

terms from late 2000 to early 2002. Among other things, he used the money from these loans to give gifts to friends and family, as well as build a house.† John Rigas and his son Timothy, former CEO and CFO of Adelphia Communications, were convicted of stealing $100 million from the firm as well as hiding $2 billion in corporate debt.

But these are exceptional cases. And they were not, in and of themselves, the cause of the firms' downfalls, but rather a symptom of a broader problem of a lack of oversight and accountability within these firms, together with an opportunistic attitude of the managers involved.

---

*M. Warner, "Exorcism at Tyco," *Fortune*, April 28, 2003.
†A. Backover, "Report Slams Culture at WorldCom," *USA Today*, November 5, 2002.

For managers to engage in wasteful investment, they must have the cash to invest. This observation is the basis of the **free cash flow hypothesis**, the view that wasteful spending is more likely to occur when firms have high levels of cash flow in excess of what is needed to make all positive-NPV investments and payments to debt holders.[33] Only when cash is tight will managers be motivated to run the firm as efficiently as possible. According to this hypothesis, leverage increases firm value because it commits the firm to making future interest payments, thereby reducing excess cash flows and wasteful investment by managers.[34]

A related idea is that leverage can reduce the degree of managerial entrenchment because managers are more likely to be fired when a firm faces financial distress. Managers who are less entrenched may be more concerned about their performance and less likely to engage in wasteful investment. In addition, when the firm is highly levered, creditors themselves will closely monitor the actions of managers, providing an additional layer of management oversight.[35]

Leverage and Commitment

Leverage may also tie managers' hands and commit them to pursue strategies with greater vigor than they would without the threat of financial distress. For example, when American Airlines was in labor negotiations with its unions in April 2003, the firm was able to win wage concessions by explaining that higher costs would push it into bankruptcy. (A similar situation enabled Delta Airlines to persuade its pilots to accept a 33% wage cut in November 2004.) Without the threat of financial distress,

---

[33]The hypothesis that excess cash flow induces empire building was put forth by M. Jensen, "Agency Costs of Free Cash Flow, Corporate Finance, and Takeovers," *American Economic Review* 76 (1986): 323–329.

[34]Of course, managers could also raise new capital for wasteful investment. But investors would be reluctant to contribute to such an endeavor and would offer unfavorable terms. In addition, raising external funds would attract greater scrutiny and public criticism regarding the investment.

[35]See, for example, M. Harris and A. Raviv, "Capital Structure and the Informational Role of Debt," *Journal of Finance* 45 2 (1990): 321–349.

GLOBAL FINANCIAL CRISIS   Moral Hazard, Government Bailouts, and the Appeal of Leverage

The term **moral hazard** refers to the idea that individuals will change their behavior if they are not fully exposed to its consequences. Discussion of moral hazard's role in the 2008 financial crisis has centered on mortgage brokers, investment bankers, and corporate managers who earned large bonuses when their businesses did well, but did not need to repay these bonuses later when things turned sour. The agency costs described in this chapter represent another form of moral hazard, as equity holders may take excessive risk or pay excessive dividends if the negative consequences will be borne by bondholders.

How are such abuses by equity holders normally held in check? Bondholders will either charge equity holders for the risk of this abuse by increasing the cost of debt, or, more likely, equity holders will credibly commit not to take on excessive risk by, for example, agreeing to very strong bond covenants and other monitoring.

Ironically, despite the potential immediate benefits of the federal bailouts in response to the 2008 financial crisis, by protecting the bondholders of many large corporations, the government may have simultaneously weakened this disciplining mechanism and thereby increased the likelihood of future crises. With this precedent in place, all lenders to corporations deemed "too big to fail" may presume they have an implicit government guarantee, thus lowering their incentives to insist on strong covenants and to monitor whether those covenants are being satisfied.[36] Without this monitoring the likelihood of future abuses by equity holders and managers has likely been increased, as has the government's liability.

Moral hazard might also help to explain why bankers are opposed to higher capital requirements. As we pointed out in Chapter 14, in a perfect market, capital requirements cannot affect the competitiveness of banks. However, because both deposit insurance and government bailouts subsidize bank debt, banks' borrowing costs do not reflect either their risk or the costs associated with default. Thus, higher leverage *both* reduces banks' tax obligations and increases the benefit they receive in bankruptcy from these subsidies, greatly favoring debt in the trade-off between tax subsidies and bankruptcy costs. Because taxpayers ultimately pay for these subsidies, the benefits of leverage to bank shareholders come largely at taxpayer expense.[37]

American's managers might not have reached agreement with the union as quickly or achieved the same wage concessions.[38]

A firm with greater leverage may also become a fiercer competitor and act more aggressively in protecting its markets because it cannot risk the possibility of bankruptcy. This commitment to aggressive behavior can scare off potential rivals. (This argument could work in reverse: A firm weakened by too much leverage might become so financially fragile that it crumbles in the face of competition, allowing other firms to erode its markets.)[39]

---

[36]As an example, a number of large banks continued to pay dividends during the crisis even after receiving bailout funds. Had the funds been raised from outside investors without any government guarantee, it is very likely the new investors would have restricted such payouts.

[37]See A. Admati, P. DeMarzo, M. Hellwig, and P. Pfleiderer, "Fallacies, Irrelevant Facts, and Myths in the Discussion of Capital Regulation: Why Bank Equity Is Not Expensive," Rock Center for Corporate Governance Research Paper No. 86, August 2010.

[38]See E. Perotti and K. Spier, "Capital Structure as a Bargaining Tool: The Role of Leverage in Contract Renegotiation," *American Economic Review* 83 (1993): 1131–1141. Debt can also affect a firm's bargaining power with its suppliers; see S. Dasgupta and K. Sengupta, "Sunk Investment, Bargaining and Choice of Capital Structure," *International Economic Review* 34 (1993): 203–220; O. Sarig, "The Effect of Leverage on Bargaining with a Corporation," *Financial Review* 33 (1998): 1–16; and C. Hennessy and D. Livdan, "Debt, Bargaining, and Credibility in Firm-Supplier Relationships," *Journal of Financial Economics* 93 (2009): 382–399. Debt may also enhance a target's bargaining power in a control contest; see M. Harris and A. Raviv, "Corporate Control Contests and Capital Structure," *Journal of Financial Economics* 20 (1988): 55–86; and R. Israel, "Capital Structure and the Market for Corporate Control: The Defensive Role of Debt Financing," *Journal of Finance* 46 (1991): 1391–1409.

[39]See J. Brander and T. Lewis, "Oligopoly and Financial Structure: The Limited Liability Effect," *American Economic Review* 76 (1986): 956–970. In an empirical study, J. Chevalier finds that leverage reduces the competitiveness of supermarket firms ("Capital Structure and Product-Market Competition: Empirical Evidence from the Supermarket Industry," *American Economic Review* 85 (1995): 415–435). P. Bolton and D. Scharfstein discuss the effects of not having deep pockets in "A Theory of Predation Based on Agency Problems in Financial Contracting," *American Economic Review* 80 (1990): 93–106.

CONCEPT CHECK
1. In what ways might managers benefit by overspending on acquisitions?

2. How might shareholders use the firm's capital structure to prevent this problem?

16.7 Agency Costs and the Trade-Off Theory

We can now adjust Eq. 16.1 for the value of the firm to include the costs and benefits of the incentives that arise when the firm has leverage. This more complete equation follows:

$$V^L = V^U + PV(\text{Interest Tax Shield}) - PV(\text{Financial Distress Costs})$$
$$- PV(\text{Agency Costs of Debt}) + PV(\text{Agency Benefits of Debt}) \qquad (16.3)$$

The net effect of the costs and benefits of leverage on the value of a firm is illustrated in Figure 16.2. With no debt, the value of the firm is V^U. As the debt level increases, the firm benefits from the interest tax shield (which has present value τ^*D). The firm also benefits from improved incentives for management, which reduce wasteful investment and perks. If the debt level is too large, however, firm value is reduced due to the loss of tax benefits (when interest exceeds EBIT), financial distress costs, and the agency costs of leverage. The optimal level of debt, D^*, balances the costs and benefits of leverage.

The Optimal Debt Level

It is important to note that the relative magnitudes of the different costs and benefits of debt vary with the characteristics of the firm. Likewise, the optimal level of debt varies. As an example, let's contrast the optimal capital structure choice for two types of firms.[40]

FIGURE 16.2

Optimal Leverage with Taxes, Financial Distress, and Agency Costs

As the level of debt, D, increases, the value of the firm increases from the interest tax shield as well as improvements in managerial incentives. If leverage is too high, however, the present value of financial distress costs, as well as the agency costs from debt holder–equity holder conflicts, dominates and reduces firm value. The optimal level of debt, D^*, balances these benefits and costs of leverage.

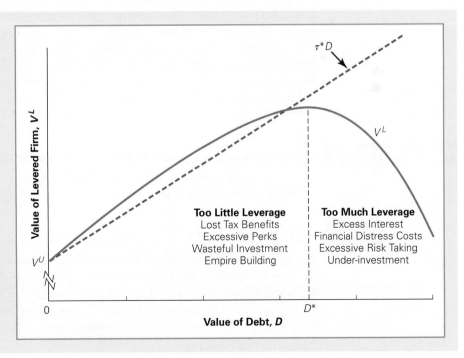

---

[40]For an empirical estimation of the variation in Figure 16.2 across firms and industries, see J. van Binsbergen, J. Graham, and J. Yang, "The Cost of Debt," *Journal of Finance*, 65 (2010): 2089–2136, and A. Korteweg, "The Net Benefits to Leverage," *Journal of Finance*, 65 (2010): 2137–2170.

R&D-Intensive Firms. Firms with high R&D costs and future growth opportunities typically maintain low debt levels. These firms tend to have low current free cash flows, so they need little debt to provide a tax shield or to control managerial spending. In addition, they tend to have high human capital, so there will be large costs as a result of financial distress. Also, these firms may find it easy to increase the risk of their business strategy (by pursuing a riskier technology) and often need to raise additional capital to fund new investment opportunities. Thus, their agency costs of debt are also high. Biotechnology and technology firms often maintain less than 10% leverage.

Low-Growth, Mature Firms. Mature, low-growth firms with stable cash flows and tangible assets often fall into the high-debt category. These firms tend to have high free cash flows with few good investment opportunities. Thus, the tax shield and incentive benefits of leverage are likely to be high. With tangible assets, the financial distress costs of leverage are likely to be low, as the assets can be liquidated for close to their full value. Examples of low-growth industries in which firms typically maintain greater than 20% leverage include real estate, utilities, and supermarket chains.

Debt Levels in Practice

The trade-off theory explains how firms *should* choose their capital structures to maximize value to current shareholders. Evaluating whether they actually do so is not so straightforward, however, as many of the costs of leverage are hard to measure.

Why might firms *not* choose an optimal capital structure? Capital structure decisions, like investment decisions, are made by managers who have their own incentives. Proponents of the **management entrenchment theory** of capital structure believe that managers choose a capital structure primarily to avoid the discipline of debt and maintain their own entrenchment. Thus, managers seek to *minimize* leverage to prevent the job loss that would accompany financial distress. Managers are constrained from using too little debt, however, to keep shareholders happy. If managers sacrifice too much firm value, disgruntled shareholders may try to replace them or sell the firm to an acquirer. Under this hypothesis, firms will have leverage that is less than the optimal level D^* in Figure 16.2, and increase it toward D^* only in response to a takeover threat or the threat of shareholder activism.[41]

CONCEPT CHECK

1. Describe how management entrenchment can affect the value of the firm.

2. Coca-Cola Enterprises is almost 50% debt financed, while Intel, a technology firm, has no net debt. Why might these firms choose such different capital structures?

16.8 Asymmetric Information and Capital Structure

Throughout this chapter, we have assumed that managers, stockholders, and creditors have the same information. We have also assumed that securities are fairly priced: The firm's shares and debt are priced according to their true underlying value. These assumptions may not always be accurate in practice. Managers' information about the firm and its future cash flows is likely to be superior to that of outside investors—there is **asymmetric information**

---

[41]See J. Zwiebel, "Dynamic Capital Structure Under Managerial Entrenchment," *American Economic Review* 86 (1996): 1197–1215; L. Zingales and W. Novaes, "Capital Structure Choice When Managers Are in Control: Entrenchment versus Efficiency," *Journal of Business* 76 (2002): 49–82; and E. Morellec, "Can Managerial Discretion Explain Observed Leverage Ratios?" *Review of Financial Studies* 17 (2004): 257–294.

between managers and investors. In this section, we consider how asymmetric information may motivate managers to alter a firm's capital structure.

Leverage as a Credible Signal

Consider the plight of Kim Smith, CEO of Beltran International, who believes her company's stock is undervalued. Market analysts and investors are concerned that several of Beltran's key patents will expire soon, and that new competition will force Beltran to cut prices or lose customers. Smith believes that new product innovations and soon-to-be-introduced manufacturing improvements will keep Beltran ahead of its competitors and enable it to sustain its current profitability well into the future. She seeks to convince investors of Beltran's promising future and to increase Beltran's current stock price.

One potential strategy is to launch an investor relations campaign. Smith can issue press releases, describing the merits of the new innovations and the manufacturing improvements. But Smith knows that investors may be skeptical of these press releases if their claims cannot be verified. After all, managers, much like politicians, have an incentive to sound optimistic and confident about what they can achieve.

Because investors expect her to be biased, to convince the market Smith must take actions that give credible signals of her knowledge of the firm. That is, she must take actions that the market understands she would be unwilling to do unless her statements were true. This idea is more general than manager–investor communication; it is at the heart of much human interaction. We call it the **credibility principle**:

Claims in one's self-interest are credible only if they are supported by actions that would be too costly to take if the claims were untrue.

This principle is the essence behind the adage, "Actions speak louder than words."

One way a firm can credibly convey its strength to investors is by making statements about its future prospects that investors and analysts can ultimately verify. Because the penalties for intentionally deceiving investors are large,[42] investors will generally believe such statements.

For example, suppose Smith announces that pending long-term contracts from the U.S., British, and Japanese governments will increase revenues for Beltran by 30% next year. Because this statement can be verified after the fact, it would be costly to make it if untrue. For deliberate misrepresentation, the U.S. Securities and Exchange Commission (SEC) would likely fine the firm and file charges against Smith. The firm could also be sued by its investors. These large costs would likely outweigh any potential benefits to Smith and Beltran for temporarily misleading investors and boosting the share price. Thus, investors will likely view the announcement as credible.

But what if Beltran cannot yet reveal specific details regarding its future prospects? Perhaps the contracts for the government orders have not yet been signed or cannot be disclosed for other reasons. How can Smith credibly communicate her positive information regarding the firm?

One strategy is to commit the firm to large future debt payments. If Smith is right, then Beltran will have no trouble making the debt payments. But if Smith is making false claims and the firm does not grow, Beltran will have trouble paying its creditors and will experience financial distress. This distress will be costly for the firm and also for Smith, who will likely lose her job. Thus, Smith can use leverage as a way to convince investors that she does have information that the firm will grow, even if she cannot provide verifiable details about the sources of growth. Investors know that Beltran would be at risk of defaulting without

---

[42]The Sarbanes-Oxley Act of 2002 increased the penalties for securities fraud to include up to 10 years of imprisonment.

growth opportunities, so they will interpret the additional leverage as a credible signal of the CEO's confidence. The use of leverage as a way to signal good information to investors is known as the **signaling theory of debt**.[43]

EXAMPLE 16.7	Debt Signals Strength

Problem

Suppose that Beltran currently uses all-equity financing, and that Beltran's market value in one year's time will be either $100 million or $50 million depending on the success of the new strategy. Currently, investors view the outcomes as equally likely, but Smith has information that success is virtually certain. Will leverage of $25 million make Smith's claims credible? How about leverage of $55 million?

Solution

If leverage is substantially less than $50 million, Beltran will have no risk of financial distress regardless of the outcome. As a result, there is no cost of leverage even if Smith does not have positive information. Thus, leverage of $25 million would not be a credible signal of strength to investors.

However, leverage of $55 million is likely to be a credible signal. If Smith has no positive information, there is a significant chance that Beltran will face bankruptcy under this burden of debt. Thus Smith would be unlikely to agree to this amount of leverage unless she is certain about the firm's prospects.

Issuing Equity and Adverse Selection

Suppose a used-car dealer tells you he is willing to sell you a nice looking sports car for $5000 less than its typical price. Rather than feel lucky, perhaps your first reaction should be one of skepticism: If the dealer is willing to sell it for such a low price, there must be something wrong with the car—it is probably a "lemon."

The idea that buyers will be skeptical of a seller's motivation for selling was formalized by George Akerlof.[44] Akerlof showed that if the seller has private information about the quality of the car, then his *desire to sell* reveals the car is probably of low quality. Buyers are therefore reluctant to buy except at heavily discounted prices. Owners of high-quality cars are reluctant to sell because they know buyers will think they are selling a lemon and offer only a low price. Consequently, the quality and prices of cars sold in the used-car market are both low. This result is referred to as **adverse selection**: The selection of cars sold in the used-car market is worse than average.

Adverse selection extends beyond the used-car market. In fact, it applies in any setting in which the seller has more information than the buyer. Adverse selection leads to the **lemons principle**:

When a seller has private information about the value of a good, buyers will discount the price they are willing to pay due to adverse selection.

We can apply this principle to the market for equity.[45] Suppose the owner of a start-up company tells you that his firm is a wonderful investment opportunity—and then offers to

---

[43]See S. Ross, "The Determination of Financial Structure: The Incentive-Signalling Approach," *Bell Journal of Economics* 8 (1977): 23–40.

[44]"The Market for Lemons: Quality, Uncertainty, and the Market Mechanism," *Quarterly Journal of Economics* 84 (1970): 488–500.

[45]See H. Leland and D. Pyle, "Information Asymmetries, Financial Structure and Financial Intermediation," *Journal of Finance* 32 (1977): 371–387.

The 2001 Nobel Prize in Economics

In 2001, George Akerlof, Michael Spence, and Joseph Stiglitz jointly received the Nobel Prize in economics for their analyses of markets with asymmetric information and adverse selection. In this chapter, we discuss the implications of their theory for firm capital structure. This theory, however, has much broader applications. As described on the Nobel Prize Web site (www.nobelprize.org):

Many markets are characterized by asymmetric information: Actors on one side of the market have much better information than those on the other. Borrowers know more than lenders about their repayment prospects, managers

and boards know more than shareholders about the firm's profitability, and prospective clients know more than insurance companies about their accident risk. During the 1970s, this year's Laureates laid the foundation for a general theory of markets with asymmetric information. Applications have been abundant, ranging from traditional agricultural markets to modern financial markets. The Laureates' contributions form the core of modern information economics.

© The Nobel Foundation.

---

sell you 70% of his stake in the firm. He states that he is selling *only* because he wants to diversify. Although you appreciate this desire, you also suspect the owner may be eager to sell such a large stake because he has negative information about the firm's future prospects. That is, he may be trying to cash out before the bad news becomes known.[46]

As with the used-car dealer, a firm owner's desire to sell equity may lead you to question how good an investment opportunity it really is. Based on the lemons principle, you therefore reduce the price you are willing to pay. This discount of the price due to adverse selection is a potential cost of issuing equity, and it may make owners with good information refrain from issuing equity.

EXAMPLE 16.8   **Adverse Selection in Equity Markets**

Problem

Zycor stock is worth either $100 per share, $80 per share, or $60 per share. Investors believe each case is equally likely, and the current share price is equal to the average value of $80.

Suppose the CEO of Zycor announces he will sell most of his holdings of the stock to diversify. Diversifying is worth 10% of the share price—that is, the CEO would be willing to receive 10% less than the shares are worth to achieve the benefits of diversification. If investors believe the CEO knows the true value, how will the share price change if he tries to sell? Will the CEO sell at the new share price?

Solution

If the true value of the shares were $100, the CEO would not be willing to sell at the market price of $80 per share, which would be 20% below their true value. So, if the CEO tries to sell, shareholders can conclude the shares are worth either $80 or $60. In that case, share price should fall to the average value of $70. But again, if the true value were $80, the CEO would be willing to sell for $72, but not $70 per share. So, if he still tries to sell, investors will know the true value is $60 per share. Thus, the CEO will sell only if the true value is the lowest possible price, $60 per share. If the CEO knows the firm's stock is worth $100 or $80 per share, he will not sell even though he would prefer to diversify.

---

[46]Again, if the owner of the firm (or the car, in the earlier example) has very specific information that can be verified ex-post, there are potential legal consequences for not revealing that information to a buyer. Generally, however, there is a great deal of subtle information the seller might have that would be impossible to verify.

In explaining adverse selection, we considered an owner of a firm selling his or her *own* shares. What if a manager of the firm decides to sell securities on the *firm's* behalf? If the securities are sold at a price below their true value, the buyer's windfall represents a cost for the firm's current shareholders. Acting on behalf of the current shareholders, the manager may be unwilling to sell.[47]

Let's consider a simple example. Gentec is a biotech firm with no debt, and its 20 million shares are currently trading at $10 per share, for a total market value of $200 million. Based on the prospects for one of Gentec's new drugs, management believes the true value of the company is $300 million, or $15 per share. Management believes the share price will reflect this higher value after the clinical trials for the drug are concluded next year.

Gentec has already announced plans to raise $60 million from investors to build a new research lab. It can raise the funds today by issuing 6 million new shares at the current price of $10 per share. In that case, after the good news comes out, the value of the firm's assets will be $300 million (from the existing assets) plus $60 million (new lab), for a total value of $360 million. With 26 million shares outstanding, the new share price will be $360 million ÷ 26 million shares = $13.85 per share.

But suppose Gentec waits for the good news to come out and the share price to rise to $15 *before* issuing the new shares. At that time, the firm will be able to raise the $60 million by selling 4 million shares. The firm's assets will again be worth a total of $360 million, but Gentec will have only 24 million shares outstanding, which is consistent with the share price of $360 million ÷ 24 million shares = $15 per share.

Thus, issuing new shares when management knows they are underpriced is costly for the original shareholders. Their shares will be worth only $13.85 rather than $15. As a result, if Gentec's managers care primarily about the firm's current shareholders, they will be reluctant to sell securities at a price that is below their true value. If they believe the shares are underpriced, managers will prefer to wait until after the share price rises to issue equity.

This preference not to issue equity that is underpriced leads us to the same lemons problem we had before: Managers who know securities have a high value will not sell, and those who know they have a low value will sell. Due to this adverse selection, investors will be willing to pay only a low price for the securities. The lemons problem creates a cost for firms that need to raise capital from investors to fund new investments. If they try to issue equity, investors will discount the price they are willing to pay to reflect the possibility that managers are privy to bad news.

Implications for Equity Issuance

Adverse selection has a number of important implications for equity issuance. First and foremost, the lemons principle directly implies that

1. **The stock price declines on the announcement of an equity issue.** When a firm issues equity, it signals to investors that its equity may be overpriced. As a result, investors are not willing to pay the pre-announcement price for the equity and so the stock price declines. Numerous studies have confirmed this result,

---

[47]S. Myers and N. Majluf demonstrated this result, and a number of its implications for capital structure, in an influential paper, "Corporate Financing and Investment Decisions When Firms Have Information that Investors Do Not Have," *Journal of Financial Economics* 13 (1984): 187–221.

finding that the stock price falls about 3% on average on the announcement of an equity issue by a publicly traded U.S. firm.[48]

As was true for Gentec, managers issuing equity have an incentive to delay the issue until any news that might positively affect the stock price becomes public. In contrast, there is no incentive to delay the issue if managers expect negative news to come out. These incentives lead to the following pattern:

2. **The stock price tends to rise prior to the announcement of an equity issue.** This result is also supported empirically, as illustrated in Figure 16.3 using data from a study by Deborah Lucas and Robert McDonald. They found that stocks with equity issues outperformed the market by almost 50% in the year and a half prior to the announcement of the issue.

Managers may also try to avoid the price decline associated with adverse selection by issuing equity at times when they have the smallest informational advantage over investors. For example, because a great deal of information is released to investors at the time of earnings announcements, equity issues are often timed to occur immediately after these announcements. That is,

3. **Firms tend to issue equity when information asymmetries are minimized, such as immediately after earnings announcements.** Studies have confirmed this timing and reported that the negative stock price reaction is smallest immediately after earnings announcements.[49]

FIGURE 16.3

Stock Returns Before and After an Equity Issue

Stocks tend to rise (relative to the market) before an equity issue is announced. Upon announcement, stock prices fall on average. This figure shows the average return relative to the market before and after announcements using data from D. Lucas and R. McDonald, "Equity Issues and Stock Price Dynamics," *Journal of Finance* 45 (1990): 1019–1043.

[48]See, e.g., P. Asquith and D. Mullins, "Equity Issues and Offering Dilution," *Journal of Financial Economics* 15 (1986): 61–89; R. Masulis and A. Korwar, "Seasoned Equity Offerings: An Empirical Investigation," *Journal of Financial Economics* 15 (1986): 91–118; and W. Mikkelson and M. Partch, "Valuation Effects of Security Offerings and the Issuance Process," *Journal of Financial Economics* 15 (1986): 31–60.

[49]R. Korajczyk, D. Lucas, and R. McDonald, "The Effect of Information Releases on the Pricing and Timing of Equity Issues," *Review of Financial Studies* 4 (1991): 685–708.

Implications for Capital Structure

Because managers find it costly to issue equity that is underpriced, they may seek alternative forms of financing. While debt issues may also suffer from adverse selection, because the value of low-risk debt is not very sensitive to managers' private information about the firm (but is instead determined mainly by interest rates), the degree of underpricing will tend to be smaller for debt than for equity. Of course, a firm can avoid underpricing altogether by financing investment using its cash (retained earnings) when possible. Thus,

> *Managers who perceive the firm's equity is underpriced will have a preference to fund investment using retained earnings, or debt, rather than equity.*

The converse to this statement is also true: Managers who perceive the firm's equity to be overpriced will prefer to issue equity, as opposed to issuing debt or using retained earnings, to fund investment. However, due to the negative stock price reaction when issuing equity, it is less likely that equity will be overpriced. In fact, absent other motives to issue equity, if both managers and investors behave rationally, the price drop upon announcement may be sufficient to deter managers from issuing equity except as a last resort.

The idea that managers will prefer to use retained earnings first, and will issue new equity only as a last resort, is often referred to as the **pecking order hypothesis**, put forth by Stewart Myers.[50] While difficult to test directly, this hypothesis is consistent with the aggregate data on corporate financing in Figure 16.4, which shows that firms tend to be net repurchasers (rather than issuers) of equity, whereas they are issuers of debt. Moreover, the vast majority of investment is funded by retained earnings, with net external financing amounting to less than 25% of capital expenditures in most years, and about 10% on average. These observations can also be consistent with the trade-off theory of capital structure, however, and there is substantial evidence that firms do not follow a *strict* pecking order, as firms often issue equity even when borrowing is possible.[51]

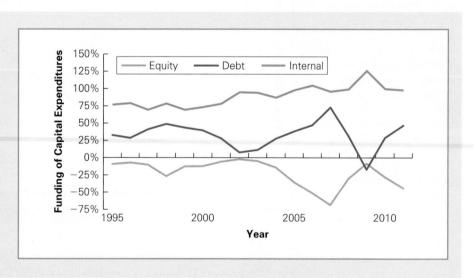

FIGURE 16.4

Aggregate Sources of Funding for Capital Expenditures, U.S. Corporations

The chart shows net equity and debt issues as a percentage of total capital expenditures. In aggregate, firms tend to repurchase equity and issue debt. But more than 75% of capital expenditures are funded from retained earnings.

Source: Federal Reserve Flow of Funds

---

[50]S. Myers, "The Capital Structure Puzzle," *Journal of Finance* 39 (1984): 575–592.

[51]For example, see M. Leary and M. Roberts, "The Pecking Order, Debt Capacity, and Information Asymmetry," *Journal of Financial Economics*, 95 (2010) 332–355.

EXAMPLE 16.9	The Pecking Order of Financing Alternatives

Problem

Axon Industries needs to raise $10 million for a new investment project. If the firm issues one-year debt, it may have to pay an interest rate of 7%, although Axon's managers believe that 6% would be a fair rate given the level of risk. However, if the firm issues equity, they believe the equity may be underpriced by 5%. What is the cost to current shareholders of financing the project out of retained earnings, debt, and equity?

Solution

If the firm spends $10 million out of retained earnings, rather than paying that money out to shareholders as a dividend, the cost to shareholders is $10 million. Using debt costs the firm $10 \times (1.07) = 10.7 million in one year, which has a present value based on management's view of the firm's risk of $10.7 \div (1.06) = 10.094 million. Finally, if equity is underpriced by 5%, then to raise $10 million the firm will need to issue $10.5 million in new equity. Thus, the cost to existing shareholders will be $10.5 million. Comparing the three, retained earnings are the cheapest source of funds, followed by debt, and finally by equity.

Aside from a general preference for using retained earnings or debt as a source of funding rather than equity, adverse selection costs do not lead to a clear prediction regarding a firm's overall capital structure. Instead, these costs imply that the managers' choice of financing will depend, in addition to the other costs and benefits discussed in this chapter, on whether they believe the firm is currently underpriced or overpriced by investors. This dependence is sometimes referred to as the **market timing** view of capital structure: The firm's overall capital structure depends in part on the market conditions that existed when it sought funding in the past. As a result, similar firms in the same industry might end up with very different, but nonetheless optimal, capital structures.[52]

Indeed, even the pecking order hypothesis does not provide a clear prediction regarding capital structure on its own. While it argues that firms should prefer to use retained earnings, then debt, and then equity as funding sources, retained earnings are merely another form of equity financing (they increase the value of equity while the value of debt remains unchanged). Therefore, firms might have low leverage either because they are unable to issue additional debt and are forced to rely on equity financing or because they are sufficiently profitable to finance all investment using retained earnings.

CONCEPT CHECK	1. How does asymmetric information explain the negative stock price reaction to the announcement of an equity issue?
	2. Why might firms prefer to fund investments using retained earnings or debt rather than issuing equity?

---

[52]See J. Wurgler and M. Baker, "Market Timing and Capital Structure," *Journal of Finance* 57 (2002): 1–32.

16.9 Capital Structure: The Bottom Line

Over the past three chapters, we have examined a number of factors that might influence a firm's choice of capital structure. What is the bottom line for a financial manager?

The most important insight regarding capital structure goes back to Modigliani and Miller: With perfect capital markets, a firm's security choice alters the risk of the firm's equity, but it does not change its value or the amount it can raise from outside investors. Thus, the optimal capital structure depends on market imperfections, such as taxes, financial distress costs, agency costs, and asymmetric information.

Of all the different possible imperfections that drive capital structure, the most clear-cut, and possibly the most significant, is taxes. The interest tax shield allows firms to repay investors and avoid the corporate tax. Each dollar of permanent debt financing provides the firm with a tax shield worth τ^* dollars, where τ^* is the effective tax advantage of debt. For firms with consistent taxable income, this benefit of leverage is important to consider.

While firms should use leverage to shield their income from taxes, how much of their income should they shield? If leverage is too high, there is an increased risk that a firm may not be able to meet its debt obligations and will be forced to default. While the risk of default is not itself a problem, financial distress may lead to other consequences that reduce the value of the firm. Firms must, therefore, balance the tax benefits of debt against the costs of financial distress.

Agency costs and benefits of leverage are also important determinants of capital structure. Too much debt can motivate managers and equity holders to take excessive risks or under-invest in a firm. When free cash flows are high, too little leverage may encourage wasteful spending. This effect may be especially important for firms in countries lacking strong protections for investors against self-interested managers.[53] When agency costs are significant, short-term debt may be the most attractive form of external financing.

A firm must also consider the potential signaling and adverse selection consequences of its financing choice. Because bankruptcy is costly for managers, increasing leverage can signal managers' confidence in the firm's ability to meet its debt obligations. When managers have different views regarding the value of securities, managers can benefit current shareholders by issuing the most overpriced securities. However, new investors will respond to this incentive by lowering the price they are willing to pay for securities that the firm issues, leading to negative price reaction when a new issue is announced. This effect is most pronounced for equity issues, because the value of equity is most sensitive to the manager's private information. To avoid this "lemons cost," firms should rely first on retained earnings, then debt, and finally equity. This pecking order of financing alternatives will be most important when managers are likely to have a great deal of private information regarding the value of the firm.

Finally, it is important to recognize that because actively changing a firm's capital structure (for example, by selling or repurchasing shares or bonds) entails transactions costs, firms may be unlikely to change their capital structures unless they depart significantly from the optimal level. As a result, most changes to a firm's debt-equity ratio are likely to occur passively, as the market value of the firm's equity fluctuates with changes in the firm's stock price.[54]

---

[53]See J. Fan, S. Titman, and G. Twite, "An International Comparison of Capital Structure and Debt Maturity Choices," SSRN working paper, 2008.

[54]See I. Strebulaev, "Do Tests of Capital Structure Theory Mean What They Say?," *Journal of Finance* 62 (2007) 1747–1787.

1. Consider the differences in leverage across industries shown in Figure 15.7. To what extent can you account for these differences?

2. What are some reasons firms might depart from their optimal capital structure, at least in the short run?

MyFinanceLab

Here is what you should know after reading this chapter. MyFinanceLab will help you identify what you know and where to go when you need to practice.

16.1 Default and Bankruptcy in a Perfect Market

- In the Modigliani-Miller setting, leverage may result in bankruptcy, but bankruptcy alone does not reduce the value of the firm. With perfect capital markets, bankruptcy shifts ownership from the equity holders to debt holders without changing the total value available to all investors.

16.2 The Costs of Bankruptcy and Financial Distress

- U.S. firms can file for bankruptcy protection under the provisions of the 1978 Bankruptcy Reform Act.
  - In a Chapter 7 liquidation, a trustee oversees the liquidation of the firm's assets.
  - In a Chapter 11 reorganization, management attempts to develop a reorganization plan that will improve operations and maximize value to investors. If the firm cannot successfully reorganize, it may be liquidated under Chapter 7 bankruptcy.
- Bankruptcy is a costly process that imposes both direct and indirect costs on a firm and its investors.
  - Direct costs include the costs of experts and advisors such as lawyers, accountants, appraisers, and investment bankers hired by the firm or its creditors during the bankruptcy process.
  - Indirect costs include the loss of customers, suppliers, employees, or receivables during bankruptcy. Firms also incur indirect costs when they need to sell assets at distressed prices.

16.3 Financial Distress Costs and Firm Value

- When securities are fairly priced, the original shareholders of a firm pay the present value of the costs associated with bankruptcy and financial distress.

16.4 Optimal Capital Structure: The Trade-Off Theory

- According to the trade-off theory, the total value of a levered firm equals the value of the firm without leverage plus the present value of the tax savings from debt minus the present value of financial distress costs:

$$V^L = V^U + PV(\text{Interest Tax Shield}) - PV(\text{Financial Distress Costs}) \quad (16.1)$$

Optimal leverage is the level of debt that maximizes V^L.

16.5 Exploiting Debt Holders: The Agency Costs of Leverage

- Agency costs arise when there are conflicts of interest between stakeholders. A highly levered firm with risky debt faces the following agency costs:
  - Asset substitution: Shareholders can gain by making negative-NPV investments or decisions that sufficiently increase the firm's risk.
  - Debt overhang: Shareholders may be unwilling to finance new, positive-NPV projects.
  - Cashing out: Shareholders have an incentive to liquidate assets at prices below their market values and distribute the proceeds as a dividend.

- With debt overhang, equity holders will benefit from new investment only if

$$\frac{NPV}{I} > \frac{\beta_D D}{\beta_E E} \tag{16.2}$$

- When a firm has existing debt, debt overhang leads to a leverage ratchet effect:
  - Shareholders may have an incentive to increase leverage even if it decreases the value of the firm.
  - Shareholders will not have an incentive to decrease leverage by buying back debt, even if it will increase the value of the firm.

16.6 Motivating Managers: The Agency Benefits of Leverage

- Leverage has agency benefits and can improve incentives for managers to run a firm more efficiently and effectively due to
  - Increased ownership concentration: Managers with higher ownership concentration are more likely to work hard and less likely to consume corporate perks.
  - Reduced free cash flow: Firms with less free cash flow are less likely to pursue wasteful investments.
  - Reduced managerial entrenchment and increased commitment: The threat of financial distress and being fired may commit managers more fully to pursue strategies that improve operations.

16.7 Agency Costs and the Trade-Off Theory

- We can extend the trade-off theory to include agency costs. The value of a firm, including agency costs and benefits, is:

$$V^L = V^U + PV(\text{Interest Tax Shield}) - PV(\text{Financial Distress Costs})$$

$$- PV(\text{Agency Costs of Debt}) + PV(\text{Agency Benefits of Debt}) \tag{16.3}$$

Optimal leverage is the level of debt that maximizes V^L.

16.8 Asymmetric Information and Capital Structure

- When managers have better information than investors, there is asymmetric information. Given asymmetric information, managers may use leverage as a credible signal to investors of the firm's ability to generate future free cash flow.
- According to the lemons principle, when managers have private information about the value of a firm, investors will discount the price they are willing to pay for a new equity issue due to adverse selection.
- Managers are more likely to sell equity when they know a firm is overvalued. As a result,
  - The stock price declines when a firm announces an equity issue.
  - The stock price tends to rise prior to the announcement of an equity issue because managers tend to delay equity issues until after good news becomes public.
  - Firms tend to issue equity when information asymmetries are minimized.
  - Managers who perceive that the firm's equity is underpriced will have a preference to fund investment using retained earnings, or debt, rather than equity. This result is called the pecking order hypothesis.

16.9 Capital Structure: The Bottom Line

- There are numerous frictions that drive the firm's optimal capital structure. However, if there are substantial transactions costs to changing the firm's capital structure, most changes in the firm's leverage are likely to occur passively, based on fluctuations in the firm's stock price.

Key Terms

adverse selection *p. 566*
agency costs *p. 553*
asset substitution problem *p. 554*
asymmetric information *p. 564*
Chapter 7 liquidation *p. 543*
Chapter 11 reorganization *p. 543*
credibility principle *p. 565*
debt covenants *p. 558*
debt overhang *p. 555*
debtor-in-possession (DIP) financing *p. 545*
default *p. 540*
economic distress *p. 541*
financial distress *p. 539*

free cash flow hypothesis *p. 561*
lemons principle *p. 566*
leverage ratchet effect *p. 557*
management entrenchment *p. 559*
management entrenchment theory *p. 564*
market timing *p. 571*
moral hazard *p. 562*
pecking order hypothesis *p. 570*
prepackaged bankruptcy *p. 544*
signaling theory of debt *p. 566*
trade-off theory *p. 550*
under-investment problem *p. 555*
workout *p. 544*

Further Reading

For a survey of alternative theories of capital structure, see M. Harris and A. Raviv, "The Theory of Capital Structure," *Journal of Finance* 46 (1991): 197–355. For a textbook treatment, see J. Tirole, *The Theory of Corporate Finance*, Princeton University Press, 2005.

In this chapter, we did not discuss how firms dynamically manage their capital structures. Although this topic is beyond the scope of this book, interested readers can consult the following papers: R. Goldstein, N. Ju, and H. Leland, "An EBIT-Based Model of Dynamic Capital Structure," *Journal of Business* 74 (2001): 483–512; O. Hart and J. Moore, "Default and Renegotiation: A Dynamic Model of Debt," *Quarterly Journal of Economics* 113(1) (1998): 1–41; C. Hennessy and T. Whited, "Debt Dynamics," *Journal of Finance* 60(3) (2005): 1129–1165; and H. Leland, "Agency Costs, Risk Management, and Capital Structure," *Journal of Finance* 53(4) (1998): 1213–1243.

For an empirical study of how firms' capital structures evolve in response to changes in their stock price, and how these dynamics relate to existing theories, see I. Welch, "Capital Structure and Stock Returns," *Journal of Political Economy* 112 (2004): 106–131. See also I. Strebulaev, "Do Tests of Capital Structure Theory Mean What They Say?" *Journal of Finance* 62 (2007): 1747–1787, for an analysis of the importance of adjustment costs in interpreting firms' capital structure choices.

Explaining much of the within-industry variation in capital structure remains an important puzzle. Interested readers should consult M. Lemmon, M. Roberts, and J. Zender, "Back to the beginning: Persistence and the cross-section of corporate capital structure," *Journal of Finance* 63 (2008): 1575–1608. For an empirical estimation of Figure 16.2 by industry, see A. Korteweg, "The Net Benefits to Leverage," *Journal of Finance*, 65 (2010), 2137–2170.

Results of empirical tests of the pecking order theory can be found in E. Fama and K. French, "Testing Tradeoff and Pecking Order Predictions About Dividends and Debt," *Review of Financial Studies* 15(1): 1–33; M. Frank and V. Goyal, "Testing the Pecking Order Theory of Capital Structure," *Journal of Financial Economics* 67(2) (2003): 217–248; and L. Shyam-Sunder and S. Myers, "Testing Static Tradeoff Against Pecking Order Models of Capital Structure," *Journal of Financial Economics* 51(2) (1999): 219–244.

Problems

All problems in are available in MyFinanceLab. *An asterisk (*) indicates problems with a higher level of difficulty.*

Default and Bankruptcy in a Perfect Market

 1. Gladstone Corporation is about to launch a new product. Depending on the success of the new product, Gladstone may have one of four values next year: $150 million, $135 million, $95 million, or $80 million. These outcomes are all equally likely, and this risk is diversifiable.

Gladstone will not make any payouts to investors during the year. Suppose the risk-free interest rate is 5% and assume perfect capital markets.

a. What is the initial value of Gladstone's equity without leverage?

Now suppose Gladstone has zero-coupon debt with a $100 million face value due next year.

b. What is the initial value of Gladstone's debt?

c. What is the yield-to-maturity of the debt? What is its expected return?

d. What is the initial value of Gladstone's equity? What is Gladstone's total value with leverage?

2. Baruk Industries has no cash and a debt obligation of $36 million that is now due. The market value of Baruk's assets is $81 million, and the firm has no other liabilities. Assume perfect capital markets.

a. Suppose Baruk has 10 million shares outstanding. What is Baruk's current share price?

b. How many new shares must Baruk issue to raise the capital needed to pay its debt obligation?

c. After repaying the debt, what will Baruk's share price be?

The Costs of Bankruptcy and Financial Distress

3. When a firm defaults on its debt, debt holders often receive less than 50% of the amount they are owed. Is the difference between the amount debt holders are owed and the amount they receive a *cost* of bankruptcy?

4. Which type of firm is more likely to experience a loss of customers in the event of financial distress:

a. Campbell Soup Company or Intuit, Inc. (a maker of accounting software)?

b. Allstate Corporation (an insurance company) or Adidas AG (maker of athletic footwear, apparel, and sports equipment)?

5. Which type of asset is more likely to be liquidated for close to its full market value in the event of financial distress:

a. An office building or a brand name?

b. Product inventory or raw materials?

c. Patent rights or engineering "know-how"?

6. Suppose Tefco Corp. has a value of $100 million if it continues to operate, but has outstanding debt of $120 million that is now due. If the firm declares bankruptcy, bankruptcy costs will equal $20 million, and the remaining $80 million will go to creditors. Instead of declaring bankruptcy, management proposes to exchange the firm's debt for a fraction of its equity in a workout. What is the minimum fraction of the firm's equity that management would need to offer to creditors for the workout to be successful?

7. You have received two job offers. Firm A offers to pay you $85,000 per year for two years. Firm B offers to pay you $90,000 for two years. Both jobs are equivalent. Suppose that firm A's contract is certain, but that firm B has a 50% chance of going bankrupt at the end of the year. In that event, it will cancel your contract and pay you the lowest amount possible for you to not quit. If you did quit, you expect you could find a new job paying $85,000 per year, but you would be unemployed for 3 months while you search for it.

a. Say you took the job at firm B. What is the least firm B can pay you next year in order to match what you would earn if you quit?

b. Given your answer to part (a), and assuming your cost of capital is 5%, which offer pays you a higher present value of your expected wage?

c. Based on this example, discuss one reason why firms with a higher risk of bankruptcy may need to offer higher wages to attract employees.

Financial Distress Costs and Firm Value

8. As in Problem 1, Gladstone Corporation is about to launch a new product. Depending on the success of the new product, Gladstone may have one of four values next year: $150 million,

$135 million, $95 million, or $80 million. These outcomes are all equally likely, and this risk is diversifiable. Suppose the risk-free interest rate is 5% and that, in the event of default, 25% of the value of Gladstone's assets will be lost to bankruptcy costs. (Ignore all other market imperfections, such as taxes.)

a. What is the initial value of Gladstone's equity without leverage?

Now suppose Gladstone has zero-coupon debt with a $100 million face value due next year.

b. What is the initial value of Gladstone's debt?

c. What is the yield-to-maturity of the debt? What is its expected return?

d. What is the initial value of Gladstone's equity? What is Gladstone's total value with leverage?

Suppose Gladstone has 10 million shares outstanding and no debt at the start of the year.

e. If Gladstone does not issue debt, what is its share price?

f. If Gladstone issues debt of $100 million due next year and uses the proceeds to repurchase shares, what will its share price be? Why does your answer differ from that in part (e)?

9. Kohwe Corporation plans to issue equity to raise $50 million to finance a new investment. After making the investment, Kohwe expects to earn free cash flows of $10 million each year. Kohwe currently has 5 million shares outstanding, and it has no other assets or opportunities. Suppose the appropriate discount rate for Kohwe's future free cash flows is 8%, and the only capital market imperfections are corporate taxes and financial distress costs.

a. What is the NPV of Kohwe's investment?

b. Given these plans, what is Kohwe's value per share today?

Suppose Kohwe borrows the $50 million instead. The firm will pay interest only on this loan each year, and it will maintain an outstanding balance of $50 million on the loan. Suppose that Kohwe's corporate tax rate is 40%, and expected free cash flows are still $10 million each year.

c. What is Kohwe's share price today if the investment is financed with debt?

Now suppose that with leverage, Kohwe's expected free cash flows will decline to $9 million per year due to reduced sales and other financial distress costs. Assume that the appropriate discount rate for Kohwe's future free cash flows is still 8%.

d. What is Kohwe's share price today given the financial distress costs of leverage?

10. You work for a large car manufacturer that is currently financially healthy. Your manager feels that the firm should take on more debt because it can thereby reduce the expense of car warranties. To quote your manager, "If we go bankrupt, we don't have to service the warranties. We therefore have lower bankruptcy costs than most corporations, so we should use more debt." Is he right?

Optimal Capital Structure: The Trade-Off Theory

11. Apple Computer has no debt. As Problem 21 in Chapter 15 makes clear, by issuing debt Apple can generate a very large tax shield potentially worth over $10 billion. Given Apple's success, one would be hard pressed to argue that Apple's management are naïve and unaware of this huge potential to create value. A more likely explanation is that issuing debt would entail other costs. What might these costs be?

12. Hawar International is a shipping firm with a current share price of $5.50 and 10 million shares outstanding. Suppose Hawar announces plans to lower its corporate taxes by borrowing $20 million and repurchasing shares.

a. With perfect capital markets, what will the share price be after this announcement?

Suppose that Hawar pays a corporate tax rate of 30%, and that shareholders expect the change in debt to be permanent.

b. If the only imperfection is corporate taxes, what will the share price be after this announcement?

c. Suppose the only imperfections are corporate taxes and financial distress costs. If the share price rises to $5.75 after this announcement, what is the PV of financial distress costs Hawar will incur as the result of this new debt?

13. Your firm is considering issuing one-year debt, and has come up with the following estimates of the value of the interest tax shield and the probability of distress for different levels of debt:

	Debt Level (in $ million)						
	0	40	50	60	70	80	90
PV (interest tax shield, in $ million)	0.00	0.76	0.95	1.14	1.33	1.52	1.71
Probability of Financial Distress	0%	0%	1%	2%	7%	16%	31%

Suppose the firm has a beta of zero, so that the appropriate discount rate for financial distress costs is the risk-free rate of 5%. Which level of debt above is optimal if, in the event of distress, the firm will have distress costs equal to
a. $2 million?
b. $5 million?
c. $25 million?

14. Marpor Industries has no debt and expects to generate free cash flows of $16 million each year. Marpor believes that if it permanently increases its level of debt to $40 million, the risk of financial distress may cause it to lose some customers and receive less favorable terms from its suppliers. As a result, Marpor's expected free cash flows with debt will be only $15 million per year. Suppose Marpor's tax rate is 35%, the risk-free rate is 5%, the expected return of the market is 15%, and the beta of Marpor's free cash flows is 1.10 (with or without leverage).
a. Estimate Marpor's value without leverage.
b. Estimate Marpor's value with the new leverage.

15. Real estate purchases are often financed with at least 80% debt. Most corporations, however, have less than 50% debt financing. Provide an explanation for this difference using the trade-off theory.

Exploiting Debt Holders: The Agency Costs of Leverage

16. On May 14, 2008, General Motors paid a dividend of $0.25 per share. During the same quarter GM lost a staggering $15.5 billion or $27.33 *per share*. Seven months later the company asked for billions of dollars of government aid and ultimately declared bankruptcy just over a year later, on June 1, 2009. At that point a share of GM was worth only a little more than a dollar.
a. If you ignore the possibility of a government bailout, the decision to pay a dividend given how close the company was to financial distress is an example of what kind of cost?
*b. What would your answer be if GM executives anticipated that there was a possibility of a government bailout should the firm be forced to declare bankruptcy?

17. Dynron Corporation's primary business is natural gas transportation using its vast gas pipeline network. Dynron's assets currently have a market value of $150 million. The firm is exploring the possibility of raising $50 million by selling part of its pipeline network and investing the $50 million in a fiber-optic network to generate revenues by selling high-speed network bandwidth. While this new investment is expected to increase profits, it will also substantially increase Dynron's risk. If Dynron is levered, would this investment be more or less attractive to equity holders than if Dynron had no debt?

18. Consider a firm whose only asset is a plot of vacant land, and whose only liability is debt of $15 million due in one year. If left vacant, the land will be worth $10 million in one year. Alternatively, the firm can develop the land at an upfront cost of $20 million. The developed land will be worth $35 million in one year. Suppose the risk-free interest rate is 10%, assume all cash flows are risk-free, and assume there are no taxes.
a. If the firm chooses not to develop the land, what is the value of the firm's equity today? What is the value of the debt today?
b. What is the NPV of developing the land?

c. Suppose the firm raises $20 million from equity holders to develop the land. If the firm develops the land, what is the value of the firm's equity today? What is the value of the firm's debt today?

d. Given your answer to part (c), would equity holders be willing to provide the $20 million needed to develop the land?

19. Sarvon Systems has a debt-equity ratio of 1.2, an equity beta of 2.0, and a debt beta of 0.30. It currently is evaluating the following projects, none of which would change the firm's volatility (amounts in $ million):

Project	A	B	C	D	E
Investment	100	50	85	30	75
NPV	20	6	10	15	18

a. Which project will equity holders agree to fund?
b. What is the cost to the firm of the debt overhang?

20. Zymase is a biotechnology start-up firm. Researchers at Zymase must choose one of three different research strategies. The payoffs (after-tax) and their likelihood for each strategy are shown below. The risk of each project is diversifiable.

Strategy	Probability	Payoff (in $ million)
A	100%	75
B	50%	140
	50%	0
C	10%	300
	90%	40

a. Which project has the highest expected payoff?
b. Suppose Zymase has debt of $40 million due at the time of the project's payoff. Which project has the highest expected payoff for equity holders?
c. Suppose Zymase has debt of $110 million due at the time of the project's payoff. Which project has the highest expected payoff for equity holders?
d. If management chooses the strategy that maximizes the payoff to equity holders, what is the expected agency cost to the firm from having $40 million in debt due? What is the expected agency cost to the firm from having $110 million in debt due?

21. Petron Corporation's management team is meeting to decide on a new corporate strategy. There are four options, each with a different probability of success and total firm value in the event of success, as shown below:

	Strategy			
	A	B	C	D
Probability of Success	100%	80%	60%	40%
Firm Value if Successful (in $ million)	50	60	70	80

Assume that for each strategy, firm value is zero in the event of failure.
a. Which strategy has the highest expected payoff?
b. Suppose Petron's management team will choose the strategy that leads to the highest expected value of Petron's equity. Which strategy will management choose if Petron currently has

     i. No debt?

     ii. Debt with a face value of $20 million?

     iii. Debt with a face value of $40 million?

  c. What agency cost of debt is illustrated in your answer to part (b)?

 22. Consider the setting of Problem 21, and suppose Petron Corp. has debt with a face value of $40 million outstanding. For simplicity assume all risk is idiosyncratic, the risk-free interest rate is zero, and there are no taxes.

  a. What is the expected value of equity, assuming Petron will choose the strategy that maximizes the value of its equity? What is the total expected value of the firm?

  b. Suppose Petron issues equity and buys back its debt, reducing the debt's face value to $5 million. If it does so, what strategy will it choose after the transaction? Will the total value of the firm increase?

  c. Suppose you are a debt holder, deciding whether to sell your debt back to the firm. If you expect the firm to reduce its debt to $5 million, what price would you demand to sell your debt?

  d. Based on your answer to (c), how much will Petron need to raise from equity holders in order to buy back the debt?

  e. How much will equity holders gain or lose by recapitalizing to reduce leverage? How much will debt holders gain or lose? Would you expect Petron's management to choose to reduce its leverage?

 *23. Consider the setting of Problems 21 and 22, and suppose Petron Corp. must pay a 25% tax rate on the amount of the final payoff that is paid to equity holders. It pays no tax on payments to, or capital raised from, debt holders.

  a. Which strategy will Petron choose with no debt? Which will it choose with a face value of $10 million, $30 million, or $50 million in debt? (Assume management maximizes the value of equity, and in the case of ties, will choose the safer strategy.)

  b. Given your answer to (a), show that the total combined value of Petron's equity and debt is maximized with a face value of $30 million in debt.

  c. Show that if Petron has $30 million in debt outstanding, shareholders can gain by increasing the face value of debt to $50 million, even though this will reduce the total value of the firm.

  d. Show that if Petron has $50 million in debt outstanding, shareholders will lose by buying back debt to reduce the face value of debt to $30 million, even though that will increase the total value of the firm.

Motivating Managers: The Agency Benefits of Leverage

24. You own your own firm, and you want to raise $30 million to fund an expansion. Currently, you own 100% of the firm's equity, and the firm has no debt. To raise the $30 million solely through equity, you will need to sell two-thirds of the firm. However, you would prefer to maintain at least a 50% equity stake in the firm to retain control.

  a. If you borrow $20 million, what fraction of the equity will you need to sell to raise the remaining $10 million? (Assume perfect capital markets.)

  b. What is the smallest amount you can borrow to raise the $30 million without giving up control? (Assume perfect capital markets.)

 25. Empire Industries forecasts net income this coming year as shown below (in thousands of dollars):

EBIT	$1000
Interest expense	0
Income before tax	1000
Taxes	−350
Net income	**$650**

Approximately $200,000 of Empire's earnings will be needed to make new, positive-NPV investments. Unfortunately, Empire's managers are expected to waste 10% of its net income on needless perks, pet projects, and other expenditures that do not contribute to the firm. All remaining income will be returned to shareholders through dividends and share repurchases.

a. What are the two benefits of debt financing for Empire?

b. By how much would each $1 of interest expense reduce Empire's dividend and share repurchases?

c. What is the increase in the *total* funds Empire will pay to investors for each $1 of interest expense?

26. Ralston Enterprises has assets that will have a market value in one year as follows:

Probability	1%	6%	24%	38%	24%	6%	1%
Value (in $ million)	70	80	90	100	110	120	130

That is, there is a 1% chance the assets will be worth $70 million, a 6% chance the assets will be worth $80 million, and so on. Suppose the CEO is contemplating a decision that will benefit her personally but will reduce the value of the firm's assets by $10 million. The CEO is likely to proceed with this decision unless it substantially increases the firm's risk of bankruptcy.

a. If Ralston has debt due of $75 million in one year, the CEO's decision will increase the probability of bankruptcy by what percentage?

b. What level of debt provides the CEO with the biggest incentive not to proceed with the decision?

Agency Costs and the Trade-Off Theory

27. Although the major benefit of debt financing is easy to observe—the tax shield—many of the indirect costs of debt financing can be quite subtle and difficult to observe. Describe some of these costs.

28. If it is managed efficiently, Remel Inc. will have assets with a market value of $50 million, $100 million, or $150 million next year, with each outcome being equally likely. However, managers may engage in wasteful empire building, which will reduce the firm's market value by $5 million in all cases. Managers may also increase the risk of the firm, changing the probability of each outcome to 50%, 10%, and 40%, respectively.

a. What is the expected value of Remel's assets if it is run efficiently?

Suppose managers will engage in empire building unless that behavior increases the likelihood of bankruptcy. They will choose the risk of the firm to maximize the expected payoff to equity holders.

b. Suppose Remel has debt due in one year as shown below. For each case, indicate whether managers will engage in empire building, and whether they will increase risk. What is the expected value of Remel's assets in each case?

i. $44 million

ii. $49 million

iii. $90 million

iv. $99 million

c. Suppose the tax savings from the debt, after including investor taxes, is equal to 10% of the expected payoff of the debt. The proceeds from the debt, as well as the value of any tax savings, will be paid out to shareholders immediately as a dividend when the debt is issued. Which debt level in part (b) is optimal for Remel?

29. Which of the following industries have low optimal debt levels according to the trade-off theory? Which have high optimal levels of debt?

    a. Tobacco firms

    b. Accounting firms

    c. Mature restaurant chains

    d. Lumber companies

    e. Cell phone manufacturers

30. According to the managerial entrenchment theory, managers choose capital structure so as to preserve their control of the firm. On the one hand, debt is costly for managers because they risk losing control in the event of default. On the other hand, if they do not take advantage of the tax shield provided by debt, they risk losing control through a hostile takeover.

    Suppose a firm expects to generate free cash flows of $90 million per year, and the discount rate for these cash flows is 10%. The firm pays a tax rate of 40%. A raider is poised to take over the firm and finance it with $750 million in permanent debt. The raider will generate the same free cash flows, and the takeover attempt will be successful if the raider can offer a premium of 20% over the current value of the firm. According to the managerial entrenchment hypothesis, what level of permanent debt will the firm choose?

Asymmetric Information and Capital Structure

31. Info Systems Technology (IST) manufactures microprocessor chips for use in appliances and other applications. IST has no debt and 100 million shares outstanding. The correct price for these shares is either $14.50 or $12.50 per share. Investors view both possibilities as equally likely, so the shares currently trade for $13.50.

    IST must raise $500 million to build a new production facility. Because the firm would suffer a large loss of both customers and engineering talent in the event of financial distress, managers believe that if IST borrows the $500 million, the present value of financial distress costs will exceed any tax benefits by $20 million. At the same time, because investors believe that managers know the correct share price, IST faces a lemons problem if it attempts to raise the $500 million by issuing equity.

    a. Suppose that if IST issues equity, the share price will remain $13.50. To maximize the long-term share price of the firm once its true value is known, would managers choose to issue equity or borrow the $500 million if

       i. They know the correct value of the shares is $12.50?

       ii. They know the correct value of the shares is $14.50?

    b. Given your answer to part (a), what should investors conclude if IST issues equity? What will happen to the share price?

    c. Given your answer to part (a), what should investors conclude if IST issues debt? What will happen to the share price in that case?

    d. How would your answers change if there were no distress costs, but only tax benefits of leverage?

32. During the Internet boom of the late 1990s, the stock prices of many Internet firms soared to extreme heights. As CEO of such a firm, if you believed your stock was significantly overvalued, would using your stock to acquire non-Internet stocks be a wise idea, even if you had to pay a small premium over their fair market value to make the acquisition?

*33. "We R Toys" (WRT) is considering expanding into new geographic markets. The expansion will have the same business risk as WRT's existing assets. The expansion will require an initial investment of $50 million and is expected to generate perpetual EBIT of $20 million per year. After the initial investment, future capital expenditures are expected to equal depreciation, and no further additions to net working capital are anticipated.

WRT's existing capital structure is composed of $500 million in equity and $300 million in debt (market values), with 10 million equity shares outstanding. The unlevered cost of capital is 10%, and WRT's debt is risk free with an interest rate of 4%. The corporate tax rate is 35%, and there are no personal taxes.

a. WRT initially proposes to fund the expansion by issuing equity. If investors were not expecting this expansion, and if they share WRT's view of the expansion's profitability, what will the share price be once the firm announces the expansion plan?

b. Suppose investors think that the EBIT from WRT's expansion will be only $4 million. What will the share price be in this case? How many shares will the firm need to issue?

c. Suppose WRT issues equity as in part (b). Shortly after the issue, new information emerges that convinces investors that management was, in fact, correct regarding the cash flows from the expansion. What will the share price be now? Why does it differ from that found in part (a)?

d. Suppose WRT instead finances the expansion with a $50 million issue of permanent risk-free debt. If WRT undertakes the expansion using debt, what is its new share price once the new information comes out? Comparing your answer with that in part (c), what are the two advantages of debt financing in this case?

Payout Policy

FOR MANY YEARS, MICROSOFT CORPORATION CHOSE TO distribute cash to investors primarily by repurchasing its own stock. During the five fiscal years ending June 2004, for example, Microsoft spent an average of $5.4 billion per year on share repurchases. Microsoft began paying dividends to investors in 2003, with what CFO John Connors called "a starter dividend" of $0.08 per share. Then, on July 20, 2004, Microsoft stunned financial markets by announcing plans to pay the largest single cash dividend payment in history, a one-time dividend of $32 billion, or $3 per share, to all shareholders of record on November 17, 2004. Since then Microsoft has repurchased over $100 billion in shares, and raised its quarterly dividend 7 times, so that by late 2012 its dividend was $0.23 per share, representing a 3.5% annual dividend yield.

When a firm's investments generate free cash flow, the firm must decide how to use that cash. If the firm has new positive-NPV investment opportunities, it can reinvest the cash and increase the value of the firm. Many young, rapidly growing firms reinvest 100% of their cash flows in this way. But mature, profitable firms such as Microsoft often find that they generate more cash than they need to fund all of their attractive investment opportunities. When a firm has excess cash, it can hold those funds as part of its cash reserves or pay the cash out to shareholders. If the firm decides to follow the latter approach, it has two choices: It can pay a dividend or it can repurchase shares from current owners. These decisions represent the firm's payout policy.

In this chapter, we show that, as with capital structure, a firm's payout policy is shaped by market imperfections, such as taxes, agency costs, transaction costs, and asymmetric information between managers and investors. We look at why some firms prefer to pay dividends, whereas others rely exclusively on share repurchases. In addition, we explore why some firms build up large cash reserves, while others pay out their excess cash.

17.1 Distributions to Shareholders

Figure 17.1 illustrates the alternative uses of free cash flow.[1] The way a firm chooses between these alternatives is referred to as its **payout policy**. We begin our discussion of a firm's payout policy by considering the choice between paying dividends and repurchasing shares. In this section, we examine the details of these methods of paying cash to shareholders.

Dividends

A public company's board of directors determines the amount of the firm's dividend. The board sets the amount per share that will be paid and decides when the payment will occur. The date on which the board authorizes the dividend is the **declaration date**. After the board declares the dividend, the firm is legally obligated to make the payment.

The firm will pay the dividend to all shareholders of record on a specific date, set by the board, called the **record date**. Because it takes three business days for shares to be registered, only shareholders who purchase the stock at least three days prior to the record date receive the dividend. As a result, the date two business days prior to the record date is known as the **ex-dividend date**; anyone who purchases the stock on or after the ex-dividend date will not receive the dividend. Finally, on the **payable date** (or **distribution date**), which is generally about a month after the record date, the firm mails dividend checks to the registered shareholders. Figure 17.2 shows these dates for Microsoft's $3.00 dividend.

Most companies that pay dividends pay them at regular, quarterly intervals. Companies typically adjust the amount of their dividends gradually, with little variation in the amount of the dividend from quarter to quarter. Occasionally, a firm may pay a one-time, **special dividend** that is usually much larger than a regular dividend, as was Microsoft's $3.00 dividend in 2004. Figure 17.3 shows the dividends paid by GM from 1983 to 2008. In addition to regular dividends, GM paid special dividends in December 1997 and again in May 1999 (associated with spin-offs of subsidiaries, discussed further in Section 17.7).

FIGURE 17.1

Uses of Free Cash Flow

A firm can retain its free cash flow, either investing or accumulating it, or pay out its free cash flow through a dividend or share repurchase. The choice between these options is determined by the firm's payout policy.

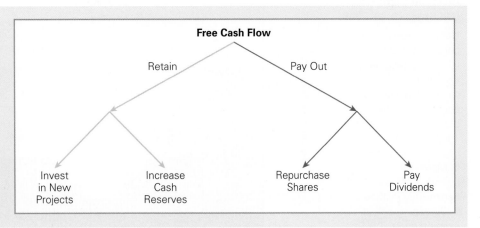

---

[1]Strictly speaking, Figure 17.1 is for an all-equity firm. For a levered firm, free cash flow would also have to be used to support interest and principal payments to debt holders.

FIGURE 17.2   **Important Dates for Microsoft's Special Dividend**

Declaration Date Board declares special dividend of $3.00/share	**Ex-Dividend Date** Buyers of stock on or after this date do not receive dividend	**Record Date** Shareholders recorded by this date receive dividend	**Payable Date** Eligible shareholders receive payments of $3.00/share
July 20, 2004	November 15, 2004	November 17, 2004	December 2, 2004

Microsoft declared the dividend on July 20, 2004, payable on December 2 to all shareholders of record on November 17. The ex-dividend date was two business days earlier, or November 15, 2004.

Notice that GM split its stock in March 1989 so that each owner of one share received a second share. This kind of transaction is called a 2-for-1 stock split. More generally, in a **stock split** or **stock dividend**, the company issues additional shares rather than cash to its shareholders. In the case of GM's stock split, the number of shares doubled, but the dividend per share was cut in half (from $1.50 per share to $0.75 per share), so that the total amount GM paid out as a dividend was the same just before and just after the split. (We discuss stock splits and stock dividends further in Section 17.7.) While GM raised its dividends throughout the 1980s, it cut its dividend during the recession in the early 1990s. GM raised its dividends again in the late 1990s, but was forced to cut its dividend again in early 2006 and suspend them altogether in July 2008 in response to financial difficulties. One year later GM filed for Chapter 11 bankruptcy and its existing shareholders were

FIGURE 17.3

Dividend History for GM Stock, 1983–2008

Until suspending its dividends in July 2008, GM had paid a regular dividend each quarter since 1983. GM paid additional special dividends in December 1997 and May 1999, and had a 2-for-1 stock split in March 1989. GM ultimately filed for bankruptcy in June of 2009 wiping out all existing equity holders. GM has since emerged from bankruptcy and issued new stock, but as of 2012, has yet to pay a dividend.

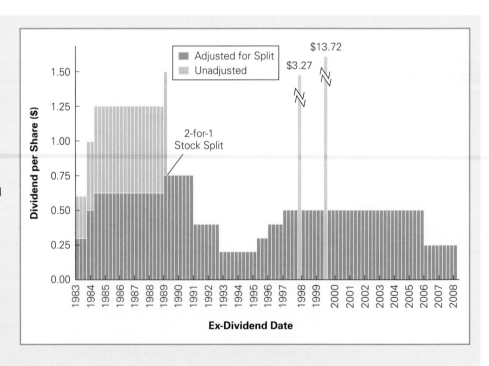

wiped out. GM has since emerged from bankruptcy and issued new shares, but has not (as of 2012) reintroduced a dividend payment.

Dividends are a cash outflow for the firm. From an accounting perspective, dividends generally reduce the firm's current (or accumulated) retained earnings. In some cases, dividends are attributed to other accounting sources, such as paid-in capital or the liquidation of assets. In this case, the dividend is known as a **return of capital** or a **liquidating dividend**. While the source of the funds makes little difference to a firm or to investors directly, there is a difference in tax treatment: A return of capital is taxed as a capital gain rather than as a dividend for the investor.[2]

Share Repurchases

An alternative way to pay cash to investors is through a share repurchase or buyback. In this kind of transaction, the firm uses cash to buy shares of its own outstanding stock. These shares are generally held in the corporate treasury, and they can be resold if the company needs to raise money in the future. We now examine three possible transaction types for a share repurchase.

Open Market Repurchase. An **open market repurchase** is the most common way that firms repurchase shares. A firm announces its intention to buy its own shares in the open market, and then proceeds to do so over time like any other investor. The firm may take a year or more to buy the shares, and it is not obligated to repurchase the full amount it originally stated. Also, the firm must not buy its shares in a way that might appear to manipulate the price. For example, SEC guidelines recommend that the firm not purchase more than 25% of the average daily trading volume in its shares on a single day, nor make purchases at the market open or within 30 minutes of the close of trade.[3]

While open market share repurchases represent about 95% of all repurchase transactions,[4] other methods are available to a firm that wants to buy back its stock. These methods are used when a firm wishes to repurchase a substantial portion of its shares, often as part of a recapitalization.

Tender Offer. A firm can repurchase shares through a **tender offer** in which it offers to buy shares at a prespecified price during a short time period—generally within 20 days. The price is usually set at a substantial premium (10%–20% is typical) to the current market price. The offer often depends on shareholders tendering a sufficient number of shares. If shareholders do not tender enough shares, the firm may cancel the offer and no buyback occurs.

A related method is the **Dutch auction** share repurchase, in which the firm lists different prices at which it is prepared to buy shares, and shareholders in turn indicate how many shares they are willing to sell at each price. The firm then pays the lowest price at which it can buy back its desired number of shares.

Targeted Repurchase. A firm may also purchase shares directly from a major shareholder in a **targeted repurchase**. In this case the purchase price is negotiated directly with the seller. A targeted repurchase may occur if a major shareholder desires to sell a large number of shares but the market for the shares is not sufficiently liquid to sustain such a large

---

[2]There is also a difference in the accounting treatment. A cash dividend reduces the cash and retained earnings shown on the balance sheet, whereas a return of capital reduces paid-in capital. This accounting difference has no direct economic consequence, however.

[3]SEC Rule 10b-18, introduced in 1983, defines guidelines for open market share repurchases.

[4]G. Grullon and D. Ikenberry, "What Do We Know About Stock Repurchases?" *Journal of Applied Corporate Finance* 13(1) (2000): 31–51.

sale without severely affecting the price. Under these circumstances, the shareholder may be willing to sell shares back to the firm at a discount to the current market price. Alternatively, if a major shareholder is threatening to take over the firm and remove its management, the firm may decide to eliminate the threat by buying out the shareholder—often at a large premium over the current market price. This type of transaction is called **greenmail**.

1. How is a stock's ex-dividend date determined, and what is its significance?

2. What is a Dutch auction share repurchase?

17.2 Comparison of Dividends and Share Repurchases

If a corporation decides to pay cash to shareholders, it can do so through either dividend payments or share repurchases. How do firms choose between these alternatives? In this section, we show that in the perfect capital markets setting of Modigliani and Miller, the method of payment does not matter.

Consider the case of Genron Corporation, a hypothetical firm. Genron has $20 million in excess cash and no debt. The firm expects to generate additional free cash flows of $48 million per year in subsequent years. If Genron's unlevered cost of capital is 12%, then the enterprise value of its ongoing operations is

$$\text{Enterprise Value} = PV(\text{Future FCF}) = \frac{\$48 \text{ million}}{12\%} = \$400 \text{ million}$$

Including the cash, Genron's total market value is $420 million.

Genron's board is meeting to decide how to pay out its $20 million in excess cash to shareholders. Some board members have advocated using the $20 million to pay a $2 cash dividend for each of Genron's 10 million outstanding shares. Others have suggested repurchasing shares instead of paying a dividend. Still others have proposed that Genron raise additional cash and pay an even larger dividend today, in anticipation of the high future free cash flows it expects to receive. Will the amount of the current dividend affect Genron's share price? Which policy would shareholders prefer?

Let's analyze the consequences of each of these three alternative policies and compare them in a setting of perfect capital markets.

Alternative Policy 1: Pay Dividend with Excess Cash

Suppose the board opts for the first alternative and uses all excess cash to pay a dividend. With 10 million shares outstanding, Genron will be able to pay a $2 dividend immediately. Because the firm expects to generate future free cash flows of $48 million per year, it anticipates paying a dividend of $4.80 per share each year thereafter. The board declares the dividend and sets the record date as December 14, so that the ex-dividend date is December 12. Let's compute Genron's share price just before and after the stock goes ex-dividend.

The fair price for the shares is the present value of the expected dividends given Genron's equity cost of capital. Because Genron has no debt, its equity cost of capital equals its unlevered cost of capital of 12%. Just before the ex-dividend date, the stock is said to trade **cum-dividend** ("with the dividend") because anyone who buys the stock will be entitled to the dividend. In this case,

$$P_{cum} = \text{Current Dividend} + PV(\text{Future Dividends}) = 2 + \frac{4.80}{0.12} = 2 + 40 = \$42$$

After the stock goes ex-dividend, new buyers will not receive the current dividend. At this point the share price will reflect only the dividends in subsequent years:

$$P_{ex} = PV(\text{Future Dividends}) = \frac{4.80}{0.12} = \$40$$

The share price will drop on the ex-dividend date, December 12. The amount of the price drop is equal to the amount of the current dividend, $2. We can also determine this change in the share price using a simple market value balance sheet (values in millions of dollars):

	December 11 (Cum-Dividend)	December 12 (Ex-Dividend)
Cash	20	0
Other assets	400	400
Total market value	420	400
Shares (millions)	10	10
Share price	$42	$40

As the market value balance sheet shows, the share price falls when a dividend is paid because the reduction in cash decreases the market value of the firm's assets. Although the stock price falls, holders of Genron stock do not incur a loss overall. Before the dividend, their stock was worth $42. After the dividend, their stock is worth $40 and they hold $2 in cash from the dividend, for a total value of $42.[5]

The fact that the stock price falls by the amount of the dividend also follows from the assumption that no opportunity for arbitrage exists. If it fell by less than the dividend, an investor could earn a profit by buying the stock just before it goes ex-dividend and selling it just after, as the dividend would more than cover the capital loss on the stock. Similarly, if the stock price fell by more than the dividend, an investor could profit by selling the stock just before it goes ex-dividend and buying it just after. Therefore, no arbitrage implies

In a perfect capital market, when a dividend is paid, the share price drops by the amount of the dividend when the stock begins to trade ex-dividend.

Alternative Policy 2: Share Repurchase (No Dividend)

Suppose that Genron does not pay a dividend this year, but instead uses the $20 million to repurchase its shares on the open market. How will the repurchase affect the share price?

With an initial share price of $42, Genron will repurchase $20 million ÷ $42 per share = 0.476 million shares, leaving only $10 - 0.476 = 9.524$ million shares outstanding. Once again, we can use Genron's market value balance sheet to analyze this transaction:

	December 11 (Before Repurchase)	December 12 (After Repurchase)
Cash	20	0
Other assets	400	400
Total market value of assets	420	400
Shares (millions)	10	9.524
Share price	$42	$42

---

[5]For simplicity, we have ignored the short delay between the ex-dividend date and the payable date of the dividend. In reality, the shareholders do not receive the dividend immediately, but rather the *promise* to receive it within several weeks. The stock price adjusts by the present value of this promise, which is effectively equal to the amount of the dividend unless interest rates are extremely high.

In this case, the market value of Genron's assets falls when the company pays out cash, but the number of shares outstanding also falls. The two changes offset each other, so the share price remains the same.

Genron's Future Dividends. We can also see why the share price does not fall after the share repurchase by considering the effect on Genron's future dividends. In future years, Genron expects to have $48 million in free cash flow, which can be used to pay a dividend of $48 million ÷ 9.524 million shares = $5.04 per share each year. Thus, with a share repurchase, Genron's share price today is

$$P_{rep} = \frac{5.04}{0.12} = \$42$$

In other words, by not paying a dividend today and repurchasing shares instead, Genron is able to raise its dividends *per share* in the future. The increase in future dividends compensates shareholders for the dividend they give up today. This example illustrates the following general conclusion about share repurchases:

> *In perfect capital markets, an open market share repurchase has no effect on the stock price, and the stock price is the same as the cum-dividend price if a dividend were paid instead.*

Investor Preferences. Would an investor prefer that Genron issue a dividend or repurchase its stock? Both policies lead to the same *initial* share price of $42. But is there a difference in shareholder value *after* the transaction? Consider an investor who currently holds 2000 shares of Genron stock. Assuming the investor does not trade the stock, the investor's holdings after a dividend or share repurchase are as follows:

Dividend	Repurchase
$40 × 2000 = $80,000 stock	$42 × 2000 = $84,000 stock
$ 2 × 2000 = $ 4,000 cash	

In either case, the value of the investor's portfolio is $84,000 immediately after the transaction. The only difference is the distribution between cash and stock holdings. Thus, it might seem the investor would prefer one approach or the other based on whether she needs the cash.

But if Genron repurchases shares and the investor wants cash, she can raise cash by selling shares. For example, she can sell $4000 ÷ $42 per share = 95 shares to raise about $4000 in cash. She will then hold 1905 shares, or 1905 × $42 ≈ $80,000 in stock. Thus, in the case of a share repurchase, by selling shares an investor can create a **homemade dividend**.

Similarly, if Genron pays a dividend and the investor does not want the cash, she can use the $4000 proceeds of the dividend to purchase 100 additional shares at the ex-dividend share price of $40 per share. As a result she will hold 2100 shares, worth 2100 × $40 = $84,000.[6] We summarize these two cases below:

Dividend + Buy 100 shares	Repurchase + Sell 95 shares
$40 × 2100 = $84,000 stock	$42 × 1905 ≈ $80,000 stock
	$42 × 95 ≈ $ 4,000 cash

---

[6]In fact, many firms allow investors to register for a dividend reinvestment program, or *DRIP*, which automatically reinvests any dividends into new shares of the stock.

| COMMON MISTAKE | Repurchases and the Supply of Shares |

There is a misconception that when a firm repurchases its own shares, the price rises due to the decrease in the supply of shares outstanding. This intuition follows naturally from the standard supply and demand analysis taught in micro-economics. Why does that analysis not apply here?

When a firm repurchases its own shares, two things happen. First, the supply of shares is reduced. At the same time, however, the value of the firm's assets declines when it spends its cash to buy the shares. If the firm repurchases its shares at their market price, these two effects offset each other, leaving the share price unchanged.

This result is similar to the dilution fallacy discussed in Chapter 14: When a firm issues shares at their market price, the share price does not fall due to the increase in supply. The increase in supply is offset by the increase in the firm's assets that results from the cash it receives from the issuance.

By selling shares or reinvesting dividends, the investor can create any combination of cash and stock desired. As a result, the investor is indifferent between the various payout methods the firm might employ:

In perfect capital markets, investors are indifferent between the firm distributing funds via dividends or share repurchases. By reinvesting dividends or selling shares, they can replicate either payout method on their own.

Alternative Policy 3: High Dividend (Equity Issue)

Let's look at a third possibility for Genron. Suppose the board wishes to pay an even larger dividend than $2 per share right now. Is that possible and, if so, will the higher dividend make shareholders better off?

Genron plans to pay $48 million in dividends starting next year. Suppose the firm wants to start paying that amount today. Because it has only $20 million in cash today, Genron needs an additional $28 million to pay the larger dividend now. It could raise cash by scaling back its investments. But if the investments have positive NPV, reducing them would lower firm value. An alternative way to raise more cash is to borrow money or sell new shares. Let's consider an equity issue. Given a current share price of $42, Genron could raise $28 million by selling $28 million ÷ $42 per share = 0.67 million shares. Because this equity issue will increase Genron's total number of shares outstanding to 10.67 million, the amount of the dividend per share each year will be

$$\frac{\$48 \text{ million}}{10.67 \text{ million shares}} = \$4.50 \text{ per share}$$

Under this new policy, Genron's cum-dividend share price is

$$P_{cum} = 4.50 + \frac{4.50}{0.12} = 4.50 + 37.50 = \$42$$

As in the previous examples, the initial share value is unchanged by this policy, and increasing the dividend has no benefit to shareholders.

| EXAMPLE 17.1 | Homemade Dividends |

Problem

Suppose Genron does not adopt the third alternative policy, and instead pays a $2 dividend per share today. Show how an investor holding 2000 shares could create a homemade dividend of $4.50 per share × 2000 shares = $9000 per year on her own.

Solution

If Genron pays a $2 dividend, the investor receives $4000 in cash and holds the rest in stock. To receive $9000 in total today, she can raise an additional $5000 by selling 125 shares at $40 per share just after the dividend is paid. In future years, Genron will pay a dividend of $4.80 per share. Because she will own $2000 - 125 = 1875$ shares, the investor will receive dividends of $1875 \times \$4.80 = \$9000$ per year from then on.

Modigliani–Miller and Dividend Policy Irrelevance

In our analysis we considered three possible dividend policies for the firm this year: (1) pay out all cash as a dividend, (2) pay no dividend and use the cash instead to repurchase shares, or (3) issue equity to finance a larger dividend. These policies are illustrated in Table 17.1.

Table 17.1 shows an important trade-off: If Genron pays a higher *current* dividend per share, it will pay lower *future* dividends per share. For example, if the firm raises the current dividend by issuing equity, it will have more shares and therefore smaller free cash flows per share to pay dividends in the future. If the firm lowers the current dividend and repurchases its shares, it will have fewer shares in the future, so it will be able to pay a higher dividend per share. The net effect of this trade-off is to leave the total present value of all future dividends, and hence the current share price, unchanged.

The logic of this section matches that in our discussion of capital structure in Chapter 14. There we explained that in perfect capital markets, buying and selling equity and debt are zero-NPV transactions that do not affect firm value. Moreover, any choice of leverage by a firm could be replicated by investors using homemade leverage. As a result, the firm's choice of capital structure is irrelevant.

Here we have established the same principle for a firm's choice of a dividend. Regardless of the amount of cash the firm has on hand, it can pay a smaller dividend (and use the remaining cash to repurchase shares) or a larger dividend (by selling equity to raise cash). Because buying or selling shares is a zero-NPV transaction, such transactions have no effect on the initial share price. Furthermore, shareholders can create a homemade dividend of any size by buying or selling shares themselves.

Modigliani and Miller developed this idea in another influential paper published in 1961.[7] As with their result on capital structure, it went against the conventional wisdom

| TABLE 17.1 | Genron's Dividends per Share Each Year Under the Three Alternative Policies |

	Initial Share Price	Dividend Paid ($ per share)			
		Year 0	Year 1	Year 2	. . .
Policy 1:	$42.00	2.00	4.80	4.80	. . .
Policy 2:	$42.00	0	5.04	5.04	. . .
Policy 3:	$42.00	4.50	4.50	4.50	. . .

[7]See M. Modigliani and M. Miller, "Dividend Policy, Growth, and the Valuation of Shares," *Journal of Business* 34 (1961): 411–433. See also J. B. Williams, *The Theory of Investment Value* (Harvard University Press, 1938).

COMMON MISTAKE The Bird in the Hand Fallacy

"A bird in the hand is worth two in the bush."

The **bird in the hand hypothesis** states that firms choosing to pay higher current dividends will enjoy higher stock prices because shareholders prefer current dividends to future ones (with the same present value). According to this view, alternative policy 3 would lead to the highest share price for Genron.

Modigliani and Miller's response to this view is that with perfect capital markets, shareholders can generate an equivalent homemade dividend at any time by selling shares. Thus, the dividend choice of the firm should not matter.*

---

*The bird in the hand hypothesis is proposed in early studies of dividend policy. See M. Gordon, "Optimal Investment and Financing Policy," *Journal of Finance* 18 (1963): 264–272, and J. Lintner, "Dividends, Earnings, Leverage, Stock Prices and the Supply of Capital to Corporations," *Review of Economics and Statistics* 44 (1962): 243–269.

---

that dividend policy could change a firm's value and make its shareholders better off even absent market imperfections. We state here their important proposition:

MM Dividend Irrelevance: **In perfect capital markets, holding fixed the investment policy of a firm, the firm's choice of dividend policy is irrelevant and does not affect the initial share price.**

Dividend Policy with Perfect Capital Markets

The examples in this section illustrate the idea that by using share repurchases or equity issues a firm can easily alter its dividend payments. Because these transactions do not alter the value of the firm, neither does dividend policy.

This result may at first seem to contradict the idea that the price of a share should equal the present value of its future dividends. As our examples have shown, however, a firm's choice of dividend today affects the dividends it can afford to pay in the future in an offsetting fashion. Thus, while dividends *do* determine share prices, a firm's choice of dividend policy does not.

As Modigliani and Miller make clear, the value of a firm ultimately derives from its underlying free cash flow. A firm's free cash flow determines the level of payouts that it can make to its investors. In a perfect capital market, whether these payouts are made through dividends or share repurchases does not matter. Of course, in reality capital markets are not perfect. As with capital structure, it is the imperfections in capital markets that should determine the firm's dividend and payout policy.

CONCEPT CHECK

1. True or False: When a firm repurchases its own shares, the price rises due to the decrease in the supply of shares outstanding.

2. In a perfect capital market, how important is the firm's decision to pay dividends versus repurchase shares?

17.3 The Tax Disadvantage of Dividends

As with capital structure, taxes are an important market imperfection that influences a firm's decision to pay dividends or repurchase shares.

| TABLE 17.2 | Long-Term Capital Gains Versus Dividend Tax Rates in the United States, 1971–2012 |

Year	Capital Gains	Dividends
1971–1978	35%	70%
1979–1981	28%	70%
1982–1986	20%	50%
1987	28%	39%
1988–1990	28%	28%
1991–1992	28%	31%
1993–1996	28%	40%
1997–2000	20%	40%
2001–2002	20%	39%
2003–*	15%	15%

*The current tax rates are set to expire in 2013 unless they are extended by Congress. The tax rates shown are for financial assets held for more than one year. For assets held one year or less, capital gains are taxed at the ordinary income tax rate (currently 35% for the highest bracket); the same is true for dividends if the assets are held for less than 61 days. Because the capital gains tax is not paid until the asset is sold, for assets held for longer than one year the *effective* capital gains tax rate is equal to the present value of the rate shown, when discounted by the after-tax risk-free interest rate for the additional number of years the asset is held.

Taxes on Dividends and Capital Gains

Shareholders typically must pay taxes on the dividends they receive. They must also pay capital gains taxes when they sell their shares. Table 17.2 shows the history of U.S. tax rates applied to dividends and long-term capital gains for investors in the highest tax bracket.

Do taxes affect investors' preferences for dividends versus share repurchases? When a firm pays a dividend, shareholders are taxed according to the dividend tax rate. If the firm repurchases shares instead, and shareholders sell shares to create a homemade dividend, the homemade dividend will be taxed according to the capital gains tax rate. If dividends are taxed at a higher rate than capital gains, which has been true until the most recent change to the tax code, shareholders will prefer share repurchases to dividends.[8] And although recent tax code changes equalized the tax rates on dividends and capital gains, because capital gains taxes are deferred until the asset is sold, there is still a tax advantage for share repurchases over dividends for long-term investors.

The higher tax rate on dividends also makes it undesirable for a firm to raise funds to pay a dividend. Absent taxes and issuance costs, if a firm raises money by issuing shares and then gives that money back to shareholders as a dividend, shareholders are no better or worse off—they get back the money they put in. When dividends are taxed at a higher rate than capital gains, however, this transaction hurts shareholders because they will receive less than their initial investment.

---

[8]Some countries tax dividends at a lower rate than capital gains. The same holds currently in the U.S. for stocks held between 61 days and one year.

EXAMPLE 17.2	Issuing Equity to Pay a Dividend

Problem

Suppose a firm raises $10 million from shareholders and uses this cash to pay them $10 million in dividends. If the dividend is taxed at a 40% rate, and if capital gains are taxed at a 15% rate, how much will shareholders receive after taxes?

Solution

Shareholders will owe 40% of $10 million, or $4 million in dividend taxes. Because the value of the firm will fall when the dividend is paid, shareholders' capital gain on the stock will be $10 million less when they sell, lowering their capital gains taxes by 15% of $10 million or $1.5 million. Thus, in total, shareholders will pay $4 million − $1.5 million = $2.5 million in taxes, and they will receive back only $7.5 million of their $10 million investment.

Optimal Dividend Policy with Taxes

When the tax rate on dividends exceeds the tax rate on capital gains, shareholders will pay lower taxes if a firm uses share repurchases for all payouts rather than dividends. This tax savings will increase the value of a firm that uses share repurchases rather than dividends. We can also express the tax savings in terms of a firm's equity cost of capital. Firms that use dividends will have to pay a higher pre-tax return to offer their investors the same after-tax return as firms that use share repurchases.[9] As a result, the optimal dividend policy when the dividend tax rate exceeds the capital gain tax rate is to *pay no dividends at all*.

While firms do still pay dividends, substantial evidence shows that many firms have recognized their tax disadvantage. For example, prior to 1980, a majority of firms used dividends exclusively to distribute cash to shareholders (see Figure 17.4). But the fraction of dividend-paying firms declined dramatically from 1978–2002, falling by more than half.

FIGURE 17.4	Trends in the Use of Dividends and Repurchases

This figure shows the percentage of publicly traded U.S. industrial firms each year that paid dividends or repurchased shares. Note the broad decline in the fraction of firms using dividends from 1975 to 2002, falling from 75% to 35%. This trend has reversed since the 2003 dividend tax cut. The fraction of firms repurchasing shares each year has averaged about 30%.

Source: Compustat.

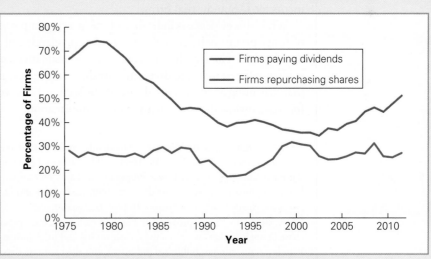

---

[9]For an extension of the CAPM that includes investor taxes, see M. Brennan, "Taxes, Market Valuation and Corporation Financial Policy," *National Tax Journal* 23 (1970): 417–427.

FIGURE 17.5	**The Changing Composition of Shareholder Payouts**

This figure shows the value of share repurchases as a percentage of total payouts to shareholders (dividends and repurchases). By the late 1990s share repurchases surpassed dividends to become the largest form of corporate payouts for U.S. industrial firms. Note, however, the declines in repurchases during economic downturns.

Source: Compustat data for U.S. firms, excluding financial firms and utilities.

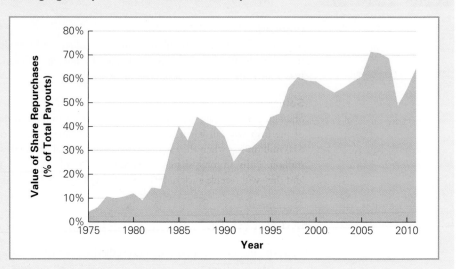

The trend away from dividends has noticeably reversed, however, since the 2003 reduction in the dividend tax rate.[10]

Figure 17.4 does not tell the full story of the shift in corporate payout policy, however. We see a more dramatic trend if we compare the dollar amounts of both forms of corporate payouts. Figure 17.5 shows the relative importance of share repurchases as a proportion of total payouts to shareholders. While dividends accounted for more than 80% of corporate payouts until the early 1980s, the importance of share repurchases grew dramatically in the mid-1980s after the SEC gave guidelines that provided firms a "safe harbor" from accusations of stock-price manipulation.[11] Repurchase activity slowed during the 1990–1991 recession, but by the end of the 1990s repurchases exceeded the value of dividend payments for U.S. industrial firms.[12]

While this evidence is indicative of the growing importance of share repurchases as a part of firms' payout policies, it also shows that dividends still remain a key form of payouts to shareholders. The fact that firms continue to issue dividends despite their tax disadvantage is often referred to as the **dividend puzzle**.[13] In the next section, we consider some factors that may mitigate this tax disadvantage. In Section 17.6, we examine alternative motivations for using dividends based on asymmetric information.

---

[10]See G. Grullon and R. Michaely, "Dividends, Share Repurchase, and the Substitution Hypothesis," *Journal of Finance* 57 (2002): 1649–1684, and E. Fama and K. French, "Disappearing Dividends: Changing Firm Characteristics or Lower Propensity to Pay?" *Journal of Financial Economics* 60 (2001): 3–43. For an examination of recent trends since 2000, see B. Julio and D. Ikenberry, "Reappearing Dividends," *Journal of Applied Corporate Finance* 16 (2004): 89–100.

[11]SEC Rule 10b-18 (adopted in 1982 and amended in 2003) provides guidelines on the manner of purchase (a single broker on a given day), their timing and price (not at the open nor close of trade, no higher than last transaction or published bid price), and their volume (less than 25% of trading volume).

[12]For further evidence that repurchases are replacing dividends, see A. Dittmar and R. Dittmar, "Stock Repurchase Waves: An Examination of the Trends in Aggregate Corporate Payout Policy," 2004 working paper, University of Michigan, and G. Grullon and R. Michaely, "Dividends, Share Repurchases, and the Substitution Hypothesis," *Journal of Finance* 57 (2002): 1649–1684.

[13]See F. Black, "The Dividend Puzzle," *Journal of Portfolio Management* 2 (1976): 5–8.

1. What is the optimal dividend policy when the dividend tax rate exceeds the capital gains tax rate?

2. What is the dividend puzzle?

17.4 Dividend Capture and Tax Clienteles

While many investors have a tax preference for share repurchases rather than dividends, the strength of that preference depends on the difference between the dividend tax rate and the capital gains tax rate that they face. Tax rates vary by income, jurisdiction, investment horizon, and whether the stock is held in a retirement account. Because of these differences, firms may attract different groups of investors depending on their dividend policy. In this section, we look in detail at the tax consequences of dividends as well as investor strategies that may reduce the impact of dividend taxes on firm value.

The Effective Dividend Tax Rate

To compare investor preferences, we must quantify the combined effects of dividend and capital gains taxes to determine an effective dividend tax rate for an investor. For simplicity, consider an investor who buys a stock today just before it goes ex-dividend, and sells the stock just after.[14] By doing so, the investor will qualify for, and capture, the dividend. If the stock pays a dividend of amount Div, and the investor's dividend tax rate is τ_d, then her after-tax cash flow from the dividend is $Div(1 - \tau_d)$.

In addition, because the price just before the stock goes ex-dividend, P_{cum}, exceeds the price just after, P_{ex}, the investor will expect to incur a capital loss on her trade. If her tax rate on capital gains is τ_g, her after-tax loss is $(P_{cum} - P_{ex})(1 - \tau_g)$.

Therefore, the investor earns a profit by trading to capture the dividend if the after-tax dividend exceeds the after-tax capital loss. Conversely, if the after-tax capital loss exceeds the after-tax dividend, the investor benefits by selling the stock just before it goes ex-dividend and buying it afterward, thereby avoiding the dividend. In other words, there is an arbitrage opportunity unless the price drop and dividend are equal after taxes:

$$(P_{cum} - P_{ex})(1 - \tau_g) = Div(1 - \tau_d) \tag{17.1}$$

We can write Eq. 17.1 in terms of the share price drop as

$$P_{cum} - P_{ex} = Div \times \left(\frac{1 - \tau_d}{1 - \tau_g} \right) = Div \times \left(1 - \frac{\tau_d - \tau_g}{1 - \tau_g} \right) = Div \times (1 - \tau_d^*) \tag{17.2}$$

where we define τ_d^* to be the **effective dividend tax rate**:

$$\tau_d^* = \left(\frac{\tau_d - \tau_g}{1 - \tau_g} \right) \tag{17.3}$$

---

[14]We could equally well consider a long-term investor deciding between selling the stock just before or just after the ex-dividend date. The analysis would be identical (although the applicable tax rates will depend on the holding period).

The effective dividend tax rate τ_d^* measures the additional tax paid by the investor per dollar of after-tax capital gains income that is instead received as a dividend.[15]

| EXAMPLE 17.3 | **Changes in the Effective Dividend Tax Rate** |

Problem

Consider an individual investor in the highest U.S. tax bracket who plans to hold a stock for more than one year. What was the effective dividend tax rate for this investor in 2002? How did the effective dividend tax rate change in 2003? (Ignore state taxes.)

Solution

From Table 17.2 , in 2002 we have $\tau_d = 39\%$ and $\tau_g = 20\%$. Thus,

$$\tau_d^* = \frac{0.39 - 0.20}{1 - 0.20} = 23.75\%$$

This indicates a significant tax disadvantage of dividends; each \$1 of dividends is worth only \$0.7625 in capital gains. However, after the 2003 tax cut, $\tau_d = 15\%$, $\tau_g = 15\%$, and

$$\tau_d^* = \frac{0.15 - 0.15}{1 - 0.15} = 0\%$$

Therefore, the 2003 tax cut eliminated the tax disadvantage of dividends for a one-year investor.

Tax Differences Across Investors

The effective dividend tax rate τ_d^* for an investor depends on the tax rates the investor faces on dividends and capital gains. These rates differ across investors for a variety of reasons.

Income Level. Investors with different levels of income fall into different tax brackets and face different tax rates.

Investment Horizon. Capital gains on stocks held one year or less, and dividends on stocks held for less than 61 days, are taxed at higher ordinary income tax rates. Long-term investors can defer the payment of capital gains taxes (lowering their effective capital gains tax rate even further). Investors who plan to bequeath stocks to their heirs may avoid the capital gains tax altogether.

Tax Jurisdiction. U.S. investors are subject to state taxes that differ by state. For example, New Hampshire imposes a 5% tax on income from interest and dividends, but no tax on capital gains. Foreign investors in U.S. stocks are subject to 30% withholding for dividends they receive (unless that rate is reduced by a tax treaty with their home country). There is no similar withholding for capital gains.

Type of Investor or Investment Account. Stocks held by individual investors in a retirement account are not subject to taxes on dividends or capital gains.[16] Similarly,

---

[15]For identification and empirical support for Eq. 17.2 and 17.3, see E. Elton and M. Gruber, "Marginal Stockholder Tax Rates and the Clientele Effect," *Review of Economics and Statistics* 52 (1970): 68–74. For investor reaction to major tax code changes see J. Koski, "A Microstructure Analysis of Ex-Dividend Stock Price Behavior Before and After the 1984 and 1986 Tax Reform Acts," *Journal of Business* 69 (1996): 313–338.

stocks held through pension funds or nonprofit endowment funds are not subject to dividend or capital gains taxes. Corporations that hold stocks are able to exclude 70% of dividends they receive from corporate taxes, but are unable to exclude capital gains.[17]

To illustrate, consider four different investors: (1) a "buy and hold" investor who holds the stock in a taxable account and plans to transfer the stock to her heirs, (2) an investor who holds the stock in a taxable account but plans to sell it after one year, (3) a pension fund, and (4) a corporation. Under the current maximum U.S. federal tax rates, the effective dividend tax rate for each would be as follows:

1. Buy and hold individual investor: $\tau_d = 15\%$, $\tau_g = 0$, and $\tau_d^* = 15\%$

2. One-year individual investor: $\tau_d = 15\%$, $\tau_g = 15\%$, and $\tau_d^* = 0$

3. Pension fund: $\tau_d = 0$, $\tau_g = 0$, and $\tau_d^* = 0$

4. Corporation: Given a corporate tax rate of 35%, $\tau_d = (1 - 70\%) \times 35\% = 10.5\%$, $\tau_g = 35\%$, and $\tau_d^* = -38\%$

As a result of their different tax rates, these investors have varying preferences regarding dividends. Long-term investors are more heavily taxed on dividends, so they would prefer share repurchases to dividend payments. One-year investors, pension funds, and other non-taxed investors have no tax preference for share repurchases over dividends; they would prefer a payout policy that most closely matches their cash needs. For example, a non-taxed investor who desires current income would prefer high dividends so as to avoid the brokerage fees and other transaction costs of selling the stock.

Finally, the negative effective dividend tax rate for corporations implies that corporations enjoy a tax *advantage* associated with dividends. For this reason, a corporation that chooses to invest its cash will prefer to hold stocks with high dividend yields.

Clientele Effects

Table 17.3 summarizes the different preferences across investor groups. These differences in tax preferences create **clientele effects**, in which the dividend policy of a firm is optimized for the tax preference of its investor clientele. Individuals in the highest tax brackets have a preference for stocks that pay no or low dividends, whereas tax-free investors and corporations have a preference for stocks with high dividends. In this case, a firm's dividend policy is optimized for the tax preference of its investor clientele.

Evidence supports the existence of tax clienteles. For example, Franklin Allen and Roni Michaely[18] report that in 1996 individual investors held 54% of all stocks by market value, yet received only 35% of all dividends paid, indicating that individuals tend to hold stocks with low dividend yields. Of course, the fact that high-tax investors receive any dividends at

---

[16]While taxes (or penalties) may be owed when the money is withdrawn from the retirement account, these taxes do not depend on whether the money came from dividends or capital gains.

[17]Corporations can exclude 80% if they own more than 20% of the shares of the firm paying the dividend.

[18]F. Allen and R. Michaely, "Payout Policy," in G. Constantinides, M. Harris, and R. Stulz, eds., *Handbook of the Economics of Finance: Corporate Finance Volume* 1A (Elsevier, 2003).

TABLE 17.3	Differing Dividend Policy Preferences Across Investor Groups	
Investor Group	**Dividend Policy Preference**	**Proportion of Investors**
Individual investors	Tax disadvantage for dividends Generally prefer share repurchase (except for retirement accounts)	~52%
Institutions, pension funds	No tax preference Prefer dividend policy that matches income needs	~47%
Corporations	Tax advantage for dividends	~1%

Source: Proportions based on *Federal Reserve Flow of Funds Accounts.*

all implies that the clienteles are not perfect—dividend taxes are not the only determinants of investors' portfolios.

Another clientele strategy is a dynamic clientele effect, also called the **dividend-capture theory**.[19] This theory states that absent transaction costs, investors can trade shares at the time of the dividend so that non-taxed investors receive the dividend. That is, non-taxed investors need not hold the high-dividend-paying stocks all the time; it is necessary only that they hold them when the dividend is actually paid.

An implication of this theory is that we should see large volumes of trade in a stock around the ex-dividend day, as high-tax investors sell and low-tax investors buy the stock in anticipation of the dividend, and then reverse those trades just after the ex-dividend date. Consider Figure 17.6, which illustrates the price and volume for the stock of Value Line, Inc., during 2004. On April 23, Value Line announced it would use its accumulated cash to pay a special dividend of $17.50 per share, with an ex-dividend date of May 20. Note the substantial increase in the volume of trade around the time of the special dividend. The volume of trade in the month following the special dividend announcement was more than 25 times the volume in the month prior to the announcement. In the three months following the announcement of the special dividend, the cumulative volume exceeded 65% of the total shares available for trade.

While this evidence supports the dividend-capture theory, it is also true that many high-tax investors continue to hold stocks even when dividends are paid. For a small ordinary dividend, the transaction costs and risks of trading the stock probably offset the benefits associated with dividend capture.[20] Only large special dividends, such as in the case of Value Line, tend to generate significant increases in volume. Thus, while clientele

---

[19]This idea is developed by A. Kalay, "The Ex-Dividend Day Behavior of Stock Prices: A Reexamination of the Clientele Effect," *Journal of Finance* 37 (1982): 1059–1070. See also J. Boyd and R. Jagannathan, "Ex-Dividend Price Behavior of Common Stocks," *Review of Financial Studies* 7 (1994): 711–741, who discuss the complications that arise with multiple tax clienteles.

[20]Dividend-capture strategies are risky because the stock price may fluctuate for unrelated reasons before the transaction can be completed. J. Koski and R. Michaely, "Prices, Liquidity, and the Information Content of Trades," *Review of Financial Studies* 13 (2000): 659–696, show that this risk can be eliminated by negotiating a purchase and sale simultaneously, but with settlement dates before and after the ex-dividend date. When such transactions are possible, the amount of dividend-related volume is greatly increased.

| FIGURE 17.6 | **Volume and Share Price Effects of Value Line's Special Dividend** |

On announcement of the special dividend of $17.50 per share, Value Line's share price rose, as did the volume of trade. The share price dropped by $17.91 on the ex-dividend date, and the volume gradually declined over the following weeks. This pattern of volume is consistent with non-taxed investors buying the stock before the ex-dividend date and selling it afterward. (We consider reasons for the jump in the stock price on the announcement of the dividend in Sections 17.5 and 17.6 .)

effects and dividend-capture strategies reduce the relative tax disadvantage of dividends, they do not eliminate it.[21]

CONCEPT CHECK

1. Under what conditions will investors have a tax preference for share repurchases rather than dividends?

2. What does the dividend-capture theory imply about the volume of trade in a stock around the ex-dividend day?

---

[21]Dividend capture strategies are one reason it is difficult to find evidence that dividend yields affect the equity cost of capital. While evidence was found by R. Litzenberger and K. Ramaswamy ["The Effects of Personal Taxes and Dividends on Capital Asset Prices: Theory and Empirical Evidence," *Journal of Financial Economics* 7 (1979): 163–195], this evidence is contradicted by F. Black and M. Scholes ["The Effects of Dividend Yield and Dividend Policy on Common Stock Prices and Returns," *Journal of Financial Economics* 1 (1974): 1–22]. A. Kalay and R. Michaely provide an explanation for these differing results, and do not find a significant impact of dividend yields on expected returns ["Dividends and Taxes: A Reexamination," *Financial Management* 29 (2000): 55–75].

17.5 Payout Versus Retention of Cash

Looking back at Figure 17.1, we have thus far considered only one aspect of a firm's payout policy: the choice between paying dividends and repurchasing shares. But how should a firm decide the amount it should pay out to shareholders and the amount it should retain?

To answer this question, first, we must consider what the firm will do with cash that it retains. It can invest the cash in new projects or in financial instruments. We will demonstrate that in the context of perfect capital markets, once a firm has taken all positive-NPV investments, it is indifferent between saving excess cash and paying it out. But once we consider market imperfections, there is a trade-off: Retaining cash can reduce the costs of raising capital in the future, but it can also increase taxes and agency costs.

Retaining Cash with Perfect Capital Markets

If a firm retains cash, it can use those funds to invest in new projects. If new positive-NPV projects are available, this decision is clearly the correct one. Making positive-NPV investments will create value for the firm's investors, whereas saving the cash or paying it out will not. However, once the firm has already taken all positive-NPV projects, any additional projects it takes on are zero or negative-NPV investments. Taking on negative-NPV investments will reduce shareholder value, as the benefits of such investments do not exceed their costs.

Of course, rather than waste excess cash on negative-NPV projects, a firm can hold the cash in the bank or use it to purchase financial assets. The firm can then pay the money to shareholders at a future time or invest it when positive-NPV investment opportunities become available.

What are the advantages and disadvantages of retaining cash and investing in financial securities? In perfect capital markets, buying and selling securities is a zero-NPV transaction, so it should not affect firm value. Shareholders can make any investment a firm makes on their own if the firm pays out the cash. Thus, it should not be surprising that with perfect capital markets, the retention versus payout decision—just like the dividend versus share repurchase decision—is irrelevant to total firm value.

EXAMPLE 17.4   **Delaying Dividends with Perfect Markets**

Problem

Barston Mining has $100,000 in excess cash. Barston is considering investing the cash in one-year Treasury bills paying 6% interest, and then using the cash to pay a dividend next year. Alternatively, the firm can pay a dividend immediately and shareholders can invest the cash on their own. In a perfect capital market, which option will shareholders prefer?

Solution

If Barston pays an immediate dividend, the shareholders receive $100,000 today. If Barston retains the cash, at the end of one year the company will be able to pay a dividend of

$$\$100,000 \times (1.06) = \$106,000$$

This payoff is the same as if shareholders had invested the $100,000 in Treasury bills themselves. In other words, the present value of this future dividend is exactly $106,000 \div (1.06) = \$100,000$. Thus, shareholders are indifferent about whether the firm pays the dividend immediately or retains the cash.

As Example 17.4 illustrates, there is no difference for shareholders if the firm pays the cash immediately or retains the cash and pays it out at a future date. This example provides yet another illustration of Modigliani and Miller's fundamental insight regarding financial policy irrelevance in perfect capital markets:

MM Payout Irrelevance: *In perfect capital markets, if a firm invests excess cash flows in financial securities, the firm's choice of payout versus retention is irrelevant and does not affect the initial value of the firm.*

Thus, the decision of whether to retain cash depends on market imperfections, which we turn to next.

Taxes and Cash Retention

Example 17.4 assumed perfect capital markets, and so ignored the effect of taxes. How would our result change with taxes?

EXAMPLE 17.5	Retaining Cash with Corporate Taxes

Problem

Suppose Barston must pay corporate taxes at a 35% rate on the interest it will earn from the one-year Treasury bill paying 6% interest. Would pension fund investors (who do not pay taxes on their investment income) prefer that Barston use its excess cash to pay the $100,000 dividend immediately or retain the cash for one year?

Solution

If Barston pays an immediate dividend, shareholders receive $100,000 today. If Barston retains the cash for one year, it will earn an after-tax return on the Treasury bills of

$$6\% \times (1 - 0.35) = 3.90\%$$

Thus, at the end of the year, Barston will pay a dividend of $100,000 \times (1.039) = \$103,900$.

This amount is less than the $106,000 the investors would have earned if they had invested the $100,000 in Treasury bills themselves. Because Barston must pay corporate taxes on the interest it earns, there is a tax disadvantage to retaining cash. Pension fund investors will therefore prefer that Barston pays the dividend now.

As Example 17.5 shows, corporate taxes make it costly for a firm to retain excess cash. This effect is the very same effect we identified in Chapter 15 with regard to leverage: When a firm pays interest, it receives a tax deduction for that interest, whereas when a firm receives interest, it owes taxes on the interest. As we discussed in Chapter 14, cash is equivalent to *negative* leverage, so the tax advantage of leverage implies a tax disadvantage to holding cash.

EXAMPLE 17.6	Microsoft's Special Dividend

Problem

In the introduction to this chapter, we described Microsoft's special dividend of $3 per share, or $32 billion, during late 2004. If Microsoft had instead retained that cash permanently, what would the present value of the additional taxes be?

Solution

If Microsoft retained the cash, the interest earned on it would be subject to a 35% corporate tax rate. Because the interest payments are risk free, we can discount the tax payments at the risk-free interest rate (assuming Microsoft's marginal corporate tax rate will remain constant or that changes to it have a beta of zero). Thus, the present value of the tax payments on Microsoft's additional interest income would be

$$\frac{\$32 \text{ billion} \times r_f \times 35\%}{r_f} = \$32 \text{ billion} \times 35\% = \$11.2 \text{ billion}$$

Equivalently, on a per share basis, Microsoft's tax savings from paying out the cash rather than retaining it is $\$3 \times 35\% = \$1.05$ per share.

Adjusting for Investor Taxes

The decision to pay out versus retain cash may also affect the taxes paid by shareholders. While pension and retirement fund investors are tax exempt, most individual investors must pay taxes on interest, dividends, and capital gains. How do investor taxes affect the tax disadvantage of retaining cash?

We illustrate the tax impact with a simple example. Consider a firm whose only asset is $100 in cash, and suppose all investors face identical tax rates. Let's compare the option of paying out this cash as an immediate dividend of $100 with the option of retaining the $100 permanently and using the interest earned to pay dividends.

Suppose the firm pays out its cash immediately as a dividend and shuts down. Because the ex-dividend price of the firm is zero (it has shut down), using Eq. 17.2 we find that before the dividend is paid the firm has a share price of

$$P_{cum} = P_{ex} + Div_0 \times \left(\frac{1 - \tau_d}{1 - \tau_g}\right) = 0 + 100 \times \left(\frac{1 - \tau_d}{1 - \tau_g}\right) \tag{17.4}$$

This price reflects the fact that the investor will pay tax on the dividend at rate τ_d, but will receive a tax credit (at capital gains tax rate τ_g) for the capital loss when the firm shuts down.

Alternatively, the firm can retain the cash and invest it in Treasury bills, earning interest at rate r_f each year. After paying corporate taxes on this interest at rate τ_c, the firm can pay a perpetual dividend of

$$Div = 100 \times r_f \times (1 - \tau_c)$$

each year and retain the $100 in cash permanently. What price will an investor pay for the firm in this case? The investor's cost of capital is the after-tax return that she could earn by investing in Treasury bills on her own: $r_f \times (1 - \tau_i)$, where τ_i is the investor's tax rate on interest income. Because the investor must pay taxes on the dividends as well, the value of the firm if it retains the $100 is[22]

$$P_{retain} = \frac{Div \times (1 - \tau_d)}{r_f \times (1 - \tau_i)} = \frac{100 \times r_f \times (1 - \tau_c) \times (1 - \tau_d)}{r_f \times (1 - \tau_i)}$$

$$= 100 \times \frac{(1 - \tau_c)(1 - \tau_d)}{(1 - \tau_i)} \tag{17.5}$$

---

[22]There is no capital gains tax consequence in this case because the share price will remain the same each year.

Comparing Eq. 17.4 and Eq. 17.5,

$$P_{retain} = P_{cum} \times \frac{(1 - \tau_c)(1 - \tau_g)}{(1 - \tau_i)} = P_{cum} \times (1 - \tau_{retain}^*) \qquad (17.6)$$

where τ_{retain}^* measures the effective tax disadvantage of retaining cash:

$$\tau_{retain}^* = \left(1 - \frac{(1 - \tau_c)(1 - \tau_g)}{(1 - \tau_i)} \right) \qquad (17.7)$$

Because the dividend tax will be paid whether the firm pays the cash immediately or retains the cash and pays the interest over time, the dividend tax rate does not affect the cost of retaining cash in Eq. 17.7.[23] The intuition for Eq. 17.7 is that when a firm retains cash, it must pay corporate tax on the interest it earns. In addition, the investor will owe capital gains tax on the increased value of the firm. In essence, the interest on retained cash is taxed twice. If the firm paid the cash to its shareholders instead, they could invest it and be taxed only once on the interest that they earn. The cost of retaining cash therefore depends on the combined effect of the corporate and capital gains taxes, compared to the single tax on interest income. Using 2012 tax rates (see Table 15.3), $\tau_c = \tau_i = 35\%$ and $\tau_g = 15\%$, we get an effective tax disadvantage of retained cash of $\tau_{retain}^* = 15\%$. Thus, after adjusting for investor taxes, there remains a substantial tax *disadvantage* for the firm to retaining excess cash.

Issuance and Distress Costs

If there is a tax disadvantage to retaining cash, why do some firms accumulate large cash balances? Generally, they retain cash balances to cover potential future cash shortfalls. For example, if there is a reasonable likelihood that future earnings will be insufficient to fund future positive-NPV investment opportunities, a firm may start accumulating cash to make up the difference. This motivation is especially relevant for firms that may need to fund large-scale research and development projects or large acquisitions.

The advantage of holding cash to cover future potential cash needs is that this strategy allows a firm to avoid the transaction costs of raising new capital (through new debt or equity issues). The direct costs of issuance range from 1% to 3% for debt issues and from 3.5% to 7% for equity issues. There can also be substantial indirect costs of raising capital due to the agency and adverse selection (lemons) costs discussed in Chapter 16. Therefore, a firm must balance the tax costs of holding cash with the potential benefits of not having to raise external funds in the future. Firms with very volatile earnings may also build up

---

[23]Equation 17.7 also holds if the firm uses any (constant) mix of dividends and share repurchases. However, if the firm initially retains cash by cutting back only on share repurchases, and then later uses the cash to pay a mix of dividends and repurchases, then we would replace τ_g in Eq. 17.7 with the average tax rate on dividends and capital gains, $\tau_e = \alpha\tau_d + (1 - \alpha)\tau_g$, where α is the proportion of dividends versus repurchases. In that case, τ_{retain}^* equals the effective tax disadvantage of debt τ^* we derived in Eq. 15.7, where we implicitly assumed that debt was used to fund a share repurchase (or avoid an equity issue), and that the future interest payments displaced a mix of dividends and share repurchases. Using τ_g here is sometimes referred to as the "new view" or "trapped-equity" view of retained earnings; see, for example, A. Auerbach, "Tax Integration and the 'New View' of the Corporate Tax: A 1980s Perspective," *Proceedings of the National Tax Association–Tax Institute of America* (1981): 21–27. Using τ_e corresponds to the "traditional view"; see, for example, J. Poterba and L. Summers, "Dividend Taxes, Corporate Investment, and 'Q'," *Journal of Public Economics* 22 (1983): 135–167.

cash reserves to enable them to weather temporary periods of operating losses. By holding sufficient cash, these firms can avoid financial distress and its associated costs.

Agency Costs of Retaining Cash

There is no benefit to shareholders when a firm holds cash above and beyond its future investment or liquidity needs, however. In fact, in addition to the tax cost, there are likely to be agency costs associated with having too much cash in the firm. As discussed in Chapter 16, when firms have excessive cash, managers may use the funds inefficiently by continuing money-losing pet projects, paying excessive executive perks, or over-paying for acquisitions. In addition, unions, the government, or other entities may take advantage of the firm's "deep pockets."[24] Leverage is one way to reduce a firm's excess cash and avoid these costs; dividends and share repurchases perform a similar role by taking cash out of the firm.

For highly levered firms, equity holders have an additional incentive to pay out cash. Due to the debt overhang problem discussed in Chapter 16, some of the value of the retained cash will benefit debt holders. As a result, equity holders may prefer to "cash out" and increase the firm's payouts. Anticipating this, debt holders will charge a higher cost of debt, or include covenants restricting the firm's payout policy (see the discussion in Section 16.5).

Thus, paying out excess cash through dividends or share repurchases can boost the stock price by reducing waste or the transfer of the firm's resources to other stakeholders. This potential savings, together with tax benefits, likely explains the roughly $10 increase in Value Line's stock price on the announcement of its special dividend, shown in Figure 17.6.

EXAMPLE 17.7   **Cutting Negative-NPV Growth**

Problem

Rexton Oil is an all-equity firm with 100 million shares outstanding. Rexton has $150 million in cash and expects future free cash flows of $65 million per year. Management plans to use the cash to expand the firm's operations, which will in turn increase future free cash flows by 12%. If the cost of capital of Rexton's investments is 10%, how would a decision to use the cash for a share repurchase rather than the expansion change the share price?

Solution

If Rexton uses the cash to expand, its future free cash flows will increase by 12% to $65 million × 1.12 = $72.8 million per year. Using the perpetuity formula, its market value will be $72.8 million ÷ 10% = $728 million, or $7.28 per share.

If Rexton does not expand, the value of its future free cash flows will be $65 million ÷ 10% = $650 million. Adding the cash, Rexton's market value is $800 million, or $8.00 per share. If Rexton repurchases shares, there will be no change to the share price: It will repurchase $150 million ÷ $8.00/share = 18.75 million shares, so it will have assets worth $650 million with 81.25 million shares outstanding, for a share price of $650 million ÷ 81.25 million shares = $8.00/share.

---

[24]For example, while Ford's larger cash balances helped it weather the 2008 financial crisis, it also did not receive the same government subsidies or labor concessions as its more troubled competitors.

In this case, cutting investment and growth to fund a share repurchase increases the share price by $0.72 per share. The reason is the expansion has a negative NPV: It costs $150 million, but increases future free cash flows by only $7.8 million, for an NPV of

$$-\$150 \text{ million} + \$7.8 \text{ million}/10\% = -\$72 \text{ million, or } -\$0.72 \text{ per share}$$

Ultimately, firms should choose to retain cash for the same reasons they would use low leverage[25]—to preserve financial slack for future growth opportunities and to avoid financial distress costs. These needs must be balanced against the tax disadvantage of holding cash and the agency cost of wasteful investment. It is not surprising, then, that high-tech and biotechnology firms, which typically choose to use little debt, also tend to retain and accumulate large amounts of cash. See Table 17.4 for a list of some U.S. firms with large cash balances.

As with capital structure decisions, however, payout policies are generally set by managers whose incentives may differ from those of shareholders. Managers may prefer to retain and maintain control over the firm's cash rather than pay it out. The retained cash can be used to fund investments that are costly for shareholders but have benefits for managers (for instance, pet projects and excessive salaries), or it can simply be held as a means to reduce leverage and the risk of financial distress that could threaten managers' job security. According to the managerial entrenchment theory of payout policy, managers pay out cash only when pressured to do so by the firm's investors.[26]

CONCEPT CHECK

1. Is there an advantage for a firm to retain its cash instead of paying it out to shareholders in perfect capital markets?

2. How do corporate taxes affect the decision of a firm to retain excess cash?

TABLE 17.4	Firms with Large Cash Balances (September 2012)		
Ticker	Company	Cash & ST Investments ($ billion)	Percentage of Market Capitalization
MSFT	Microsoft Corporation	62.0	24%
CSCO	Cisco Systems, Inc.	48.7	47%
GOOG	Google Inc.	43.3	19%
JNJ	Johnson & Johnson	32.3	17%
GM	General Motors Company	31.6	84%
ORCL	Oracle Corporation	30.7	19%

Source: Google Finance.

---

[25]As discussed in Chapter 14, we can interpret excess cash as negative debt. As a consequence, the trade-offs from holding excess cash are very similar to those involved in the capital structure decision.

[26]Recall from Section 16.7 that the managerial entrenchment theory of capital structure argued that managers choose low leverage to avoid the discipline of debt and preserve their job security. Applied to payout policy, the same theory implies that managers will reduce leverage further by choosing to hold too much cash.

17.6 Signaling with Payout Policy

One market imperfection that we have not yet considered is asymmetric information. When managers have better information than investors regarding the future prospects of the firm, their payout decisions may signal this information. In this section, we look at managers' motivations when setting a firm's payout policy, and we evaluate what these decisions may communicate to investors.

Dividend Smoothing

Firms can change dividends at any time, but in practice they vary the sizes of their dividends relatively infrequently. For example, General Motors (GM) changed the amount of its regular dividend only eight times over a 20-year period. Yet during that same period, GM's earnings varied widely, as shown in Figure 17.7.

The pattern seen with GM is typical of most firms that pay dividends. Firms adjust dividends relatively infrequently, and dividends are much less volatile than earnings. This practice of maintaining relatively constant dividends is called **dividend smoothing**. Firms also increase dividends much more frequently than they cut them. For example, from 1971 to 2001, only 5.4% of dividend changes by U.S. firms were decreases.[27] In a classic survey of corporate executives, John Lintner[28] suggested that these observations resulted from (1) management's belief that investors prefer stable dividends with sustained growth, and (2) management's desire to maintain a long-term target level of dividends as a fraction of earnings. Thus firms raise their dividends only when they perceive

FIGURE 17.7

GM's Earnings and Dividends per Share, 1985–2008

Compared to GM's earnings, its dividend payments were relatively stable. (Data adjusted for splits, earnings exclude extraordinary items.)

Source: Compustat and CapitalIQ.

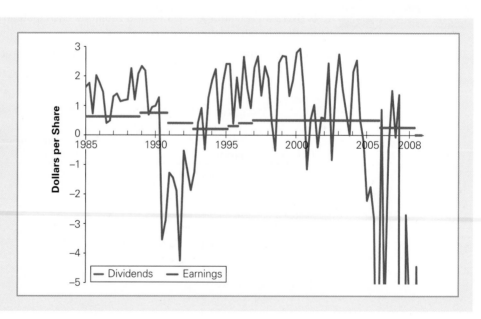

[27]F. Allen and R. Michaely, "Payout Policy," in G. Constantinides, M. Harris, and R. Stulz, eds., *Handbook of the Economics of Finance: Corporate Finance Volume* 1A (Elsevier, 2003).

[28]J. Lintner, "Distribution of Incomes of Corporations Among Dividends, Retained Earnings and Taxes," *American Economic Review* 46 (1956): 97–113.

a long-term sustainable increase in the expected level of future earnings, and cut them only as a last resort.[29]

How can firms keep dividends smooth as earnings vary? As we have already discussed, firms can maintain almost any level of dividend in the short run by adjusting the number of shares they repurchase or issue and the amount of cash they retain. However, due to the tax and transaction costs of funding a dividend with new equity issues, managers do not wish to commit to a dividend that the firm cannot afford to pay out of regular earnings. For this reason, firms generally set dividends at a level they expect to be able to maintain based on the firm's earnings prospects.

Dividend Signaling

If firms smooth dividends, the firm's dividend choice will contain information regarding management's expectations of future earnings. When a firm increases its dividend, it sends a positive signal to investors that management expects to be able to afford the higher dividend for the foreseeable future. Conversely, when managers cut the dividend, it may signal that they have given up hope that earnings will rebound in the near term and so need to reduce the dividend to save cash. The idea that dividend changes reflect managers' views about a firm's future earnings prospects is called the **dividend signaling hypothesis**.

Studies of the market's reaction to dividend changes are consistent with this hypothesis. For example, during the period 1967–1993, firms that raised their dividend by 10% or more saw their stock prices rise by 1.34% after the announcement, while those that cut their dividend by 10% or more experienced a price decline of −3.71%.[30] The average size of the stock price reaction increases with the magnitude of the dividend change, and is larger for dividend cuts.[31]

Dividend signaling is similar to the use of leverage as a signal that we discussed in Chapter 16. Increasing debt signals that management believes the firm can afford the future interest payments, in the same way that raising the dividend signals the firm can afford to maintain the dividends in the future. However, while cutting the dividend is costly for managers in terms of their reputation and the reaction of investors, it is by no means as costly as failing to make debt payments. As a consequence, we would expect dividend changes to be a somewhat weaker signal than leverage changes. Indeed, empirical studies have found average stock price increases of more than 10% when firms replace equity with debt, and decreases of 4% to 10% when firms replace debt with equity.[32]

---

[29]While perhaps a good description of how firms *do* set their dividends, as we have shown in this chapter there is no clear reason why firms *should* smooth their dividends, nor convincing evidence that investors prefer this practice.

[30]See G. Grullon, R. Michaely, and B. Swaminathan, "Are Dividend Changes a Sign of Firm Maturity?" *Journal of Business* 75 (2002): 387–424. The effects are even larger for dividend initiations (+3.4%) and omissions (−7%), according to studies by R. Michaely, R. Thaler, and K. Womack, "Price Reactions to Dividend Initiations and Omissions: Overreaction or Drift?" *Journal of Finance* 50 (1995): 573–608, and similar results by P. Healy and K. Palepu, "Earnings Information Conveyed by Dividend Initiations and Omissions," *Journal of Financial Economics* 21 (1988): 149–176.

[31]Not all of the evidence is consistent with dividend signaling, however. For example, it has been difficult to document a relationship between dividend changes and realized future earnings [S. Benartzi, R. Michaely, and R. Thaler, "Do Changes in Dividends Signal the Future or the Past?" *Journal of Finance* 52 (1997): 1007–1034].

[32]C. Smith, "Raising Capital: Theory and Evidence," in D. Chew, ed., *The New Corporate Finance* (McGraw-Hill, 1993).

Royal & SunAlliance's Dividend Cut

In some quarters, Julian Hance must have seemed like a heretic. On November 8, 2001, the finance director of Royal & SunAlliance, a U.K.-based insurance group with £12.6 billion (€20.2 billion) in annual revenue, did the unthinkable—he announced that he would cut the firm's dividend.

Many observers gasped at the decision. Surely, they argued, cutting the dividend was a sign of weakness. Didn't companies only cut their dividend when profits were falling?

Quite the contrary, countered Hance. With insurance premiums rising around the world, particularly following the World Trade Center tragedy, Royal & SunAlliance believed that its industry offered excellent growth opportunities. "The outlook for business in 2002 and beyond makes a compelling case for reinvesting capital in the business rather than returning it to shareholders," explained Hance.

The stock market agreed with him, sending Royal & SunAlliance's shares up 5% following its dividend news. "Cutting the dividend is a positive move," observes Matthew Wright, an insurance analyst at Credit Lyonnais. "It shows the company expects future profitability to be good."

Source: Justin Wood, CFO Europe.com, December 2001.

While an increase of a firm's dividend may signal management's optimism regarding its future cash flows, it might also signal a lack of investment opportunities. For example, Microsoft's move to initiate dividends in 2003 was largely seen as a result of its declining growth prospects as opposed to a signal about its increased future profitability.[33] Conversely, a firm might cut its dividend to exploit new positive-NPV investment opportunities. In this case, the dividend decrease might lead to a positive—rather than negative—stock price reaction (see the box on Royal and SunAlliance's dividend cut). In general, we must interpret dividends as a signal in the context of the type of new information managers are likely to have.

Signaling and Share Repurchases

Share repurchases, like dividends, may also signal managers' information to the market. However, several important differences distinguish share repurchases and dividends. First, managers are much less committed to share repurchases than to dividend payments. As we noted earlier, when firms announce authorization for an open market share repurchase, they generally announce the maximum amount they plan to spend on repurchases. The actual amount spent, however, may be far less. Also, it may take several years to complete the share repurchase.[34] Second, unlike with dividends, firms do not smooth their repurchase activity from year to year. As a result, announcing a share repurchase today does not necessarily represent a long-term commitment to repurchase shares. In this regard, share repurchases may be less of a signal than dividends about future earnings of a firm.

A third key difference between dividends and share repurchases is that the cost of a share repurchase depends on the market price of the stock. If managers believe the stock is currently overvalued, a share repurchase will be costly to the shareholders who choose to hold on to their shares because buying the stock at its current (overvalued) price is a negative-NPV investment. By contrast, repurchasing shares when managers perceive the stock to

---

[33]See "An End to Growth?" *The Economist* (July 22, 2004): 61.

[34]C. Stephens and M. Weisbach, "Actual Share Reacquisitions in Open-Market Repurchase Programs," *Journal of Finance* 53 (1998): 313–333, consider how firms' actual repurchases compare to their announced plans. For details on share repurchase programs' implementation, see D. Cook, L. Krigman, and J. Leach, "On the Timing and Execution of Open Market Repurchases," *Review of Financial Studies* 17 (2004): 463–498.

be undervalued is a positive-NPV investment for these shareholders. Thus, if managers are acting in the interest of long-term shareholders and attempting to maximize the firm's future share price, they will be more likely to repurchase shares if they believe the stock to be undervalued. (If, on the other hand, managers act in the interest of all shareholders—including those who sell—then there is no such incentive: Any gain to those who remain is a cost to those who sell at the low price.)

In a 2004 survey, 87% of CFOs agreed that firms should repurchase shares when their stock price is a good value relative to its true value,[35] implicitly indicating that most CFOs believe that they should act in the interests of the long-term shareholders. Share repurchases are therefore a credible signal that management believes its shares are underpriced. Thus, if investors believe that managers have better information regarding the firm's prospects than they do, then investors should react favorably to share repurchase announcements. Indeed they do: The average market price reaction to the announcement of an open market share repurchase program is about 3% (with the size of the reaction increasing in the portion of shares outstanding sought).[36] The reaction is much larger for fixed-price tender offers (12%) and Dutch auction share repurchases (8%).[37] Recall that these methods of repurchase are generally used for very large repurchases conducted in a very short timeframe and are often part of an overall recapitalization. Also, the shares are repurchased at a premium to the current market price. Thus, tender offers and Dutch auction repurchases are even stronger signals than open market repurchases that management views the current share price as undervalued.

EXAMPLE 17.8	**Share Repurchases and Market Timing**

Problem

Clark Industries has 200 million shares outstanding, a current share price of $30, and no debt. Clark's management believes that the shares are underpriced, and that the true value is $35 per share. Clark plans to pay $600 million in cash to its shareholders by repurchasing shares at the current market price. Suppose that soon after the transaction is completed, new information comes out that causes investors to revise their opinion of the firm and agree with management's assessment of Clark's value. What is Clark's share price after the new information comes out? How would the share price differ if Clark waited until after the new information came out to repurchase the shares?

Solution

Clark's initial market cap is $30/share × 200 million shares = $6 billion, of which $600 million is cash and $5.4 billion corresponds to other assets. At the current share price, Clark will

---

[35]A. Brav, J. Graham, C. Harvey, and R. Michaely, "Payout Policy in the 21st Century," *Journal of Financial Economics* 77 (2005): 483–527.

[36]See D. Ikenberry, J. Lakonishok, and T. Vermaelen, "Market Underreaction to Open Market Share Repurchases," *Journal of Financial Economics* 39 (1995): 181–208, and G. Grullon and R. Michaely, "Dividends, Share Repurchases, and the Substitution Hypothesis," *Journal of Finance* 57 (2002): 1649–1684. For a signaling explanation of why the stock price will positively react to the announcement even though it is not a commitment to purchase shares, see J. Oded, "Why Do Firms Announce Open-Market Repurchase Programs?" *Review of Financial Studies* 18 (2005): 271–300.

[37]R. Comment and G. Jarrell, "The Relative Signaling Power of Dutch-Auction and Fixed-Price Self-tender Offers and Open-Market Share Repurchases," *Journal of Finance* 46 (1991): 1243–1271.

repurchase $600 million ÷ $30/share = 20 million shares. The market value balance sheet before and after the transaction is shown below (in millions of dollars):

	Before Repurchase	After Repurchase	After New Information
Cash	600	0	0
Other assets	5400	5400	6400
Total market value of assets	6000	5400	6400
Shares (millions)	200	180	180
Share Price	$30	$30	$35.56

According to management, Clark's initial market capitalization should be $35/share × 200 million shares = $7 billion, of which $6.4 billion would correspond to other assets. As the market value balance sheet shows, after the new information comes out, Clark's share price will rise to $35.556.

If Clark waited for the new information to come out before repurchasing the shares, it would buy shares at a market price of $35 per share. Thus, it would repurchase only 17.1 million shares. The share price after the repurchase would be $6.4 billion ÷ 182.9 shares = $35.

By repurchasing shares while the stock is underpriced, the ultimate share price is $0.556 higher, representing a gain of $0.556 × 180 million shares = $100 million for long-term shareholders. This gain equals the loss to the selling shareholders from selling 20 million shares at a price that is $5 below their true value.

As this example shows, the gain from buying shares when the stock is underpriced leads to an increase in the firm's long-run share price. Similarly, buying shares when the stock is overpriced will reduce the long-run share price. The firm may therefore try to time its repurchases appropriately. Anticipating this strategy, shareholders may interpret a share repurchase as a signal that the firm is undervalued.

CONCEPT CHECK

1. What possible signals does a firm give when it cuts its dividend?

2. Would managers acting in the interests of long-term shareholders be more likely to repurchase shares if they believe the stock is undervalued or overvalued?

17.7 Stock Dividends, Splits, and Spin-Offs

In this chapter, we have focused on a firm's decision to pay cash to its shareholders. But a firm can pay another type of dividend that does not involve cash: a stock dividend. In this case, each shareholder who owns the stock before it goes ex-dividend receives additional shares of stock of the firm itself (a stock split) or of a subsidiary (a spin-off). Here we briefly review these two types of transactions.

Stock Dividends and Splits

If a company declares a 10% stock dividend, each shareholder will receive one new share of stock for every 10 shares already owned. Stock dividends of 50% or higher are generally referred to as stock splits. For example, with a 50% stock dividend, each shareholder will receive one new share for every two shares owned. Because a holder of two shares will end up holding three new shares, this transaction is also called a 3:2 ("3-for-2") stock split. Similarly, a 100% stock dividend is equivalent to a 2:1 stock split.

John Connors was Senior Vice President and Chief Financial Officer of Microsoft. He retired in 2005 and is now a partner at Ignition Partners, a Seattle venture capital firm.

QUESTION: *Microsoft declared a dividend for the first time in 2003. What goes into the decision of a company to initiate a dividend?*

ANSWER: Microsoft was in a unique position. The company had never paid a dividend and was facing shareholder pressure to do something with its $60 billion cash buildup. The company considered five key questions in developing its distribution strategy:

1. Can the company sustain payment of a cash dividend in perpetuity and increase the dividend over time? Microsoft was confident it could meet that commitment and raise the dividend in the future.

2. Is a cash dividend a better return to stockholders than a stock buyback program? These are capital structure decisions: Do we want to reduce our shares outstanding? Is our stock attractively priced for a buyback, or do we want to distribute the cash as a dividend? Microsoft had plenty of capacity to issue a dividend *and* continue a buyback program.

3. What is the tax effect of a cash dividend versus a buyback to the corporation and to shareholders? From a tax perspective to shareholders, it was largely a neutral decision in Microsoft's case.

4. What is the psychological impact on investors, and how does it fit the story of the stock for investors? This is a more qualitative factor. A regular ongoing dividend put Microsoft on a path to becoming an attractive investment for income investors.

5. What are the public relations implications of a dividend program? Investors don't look to Microsoft to hold cash but to be a leader in software development and provide equity growth. So they viewed the dividend program favorably.

QUESTION: *How does a company decide whether to increase its dividend, have a special dividend, or repurchase its stock to return capital to investors?*

INTERVIEW WITH
John Connors

ANSWER: The decision to increase the dividend is a function of cash flow projections. Are you confident that you have adequate cash flow to sustain this and future increases? Once you increase the dividend, investors expect future increases as well. Some companies establish explicit criteria for dividend increases. In my experience as a CFO, the analytic framework involves a set of relative comparables. What are the dividend payouts and dividend yields of the market in general and of your peer group, and where are we relative to them? We talk to significant investors and consider what is best for increasing shareholder value long-term.

A special dividend is a very efficient form of cash distribution that generally involves a nonrecurring situation, such as the sale of a business division or a cash award from a legal situation. Also, companies without a comprehensive distribution strategy use special dividends to reduce large cash accumulations. For Microsoft, the 2004 special dividend and announcement of the stock dividend and stock buyback program resolved the issue of what to do with all the cash and clarified our direction going forward.

QUESTION: *What other factors go into dividend decisions?*

ANSWER: Powerful finance and accounting tools help us to make better and broader business decisions. But these decisions involve as much psychology and market thinking as math. You have to consider non-quantifiable factors such as the psychology of investors. Not long ago, everyone wanted growth stocks; no one wanted dividend-paying stocks. Now dividend stocks are in vogue. You must also take into account your industry and what the competition is doing. In many tech companies, employee ownership in the form of options programs represents a fairly significant percentage of fully diluted shares. Dividend distributions reduce the price of the stock and hence the value of options.

At the end of the day, you want to be sure that your cash distribution strategy helps your overall story with investors.

With a stock dividend, a firm does not pay out any cash to shareholders. As a result, the total market value of the firm's assets and liabilities, and therefore of its equity, is unchanged. The only thing that is different is the number of shares outstanding. The stock price will therefore fall because the same total equity value is now divided over a larger number of shares.

Let's illustrate a stock dividend for Genron. Suppose Genron paid a 50% stock dividend (a 3:2 stock split) rather than a cash dividend. Table 17.5 shows the market value balance sheet and the resulting share price before and after the stock dividend.

TABLE 17.5	Cum- and Ex-Dividend Share Price for Genron with a 50% Stock Dividend ($ million)	
	December 11(Cum-Dividend)	December 12(Ex-Dividend)
Cash	20	20
Other assets	400	400
Total market value of assets	420	420
Shares (millions)	10	15
Share price	$42	$28

A shareholder who owns 100 shares before the dividend has a portfolio worth $42 × 100 = $4200. After the dividend, the shareholder owns 150 shares worth $28, giving a portfolio value of $28 × 150 = $4200. (Note the important difference between a stock split and a share issuance: When the company issues shares, the number of shares increases, but the firm also raises cash to add to its existing assets. If the shares are sold at a fair price, the stock price should not change.)

Unlike cash dividends, stock dividends are not taxed. Thus, from both the firm's and shareholders' perspectives, there is no real consequence to a stock dividend. The number of shares is proportionally increased and the price per share is proportionally reduced so that there is no change in value.

Why, then, do companies pay stock dividends or split their stock? The typical motivation for a stock split is to keep the share price in a range thought to be attractive to small investors. Stocks generally trade in lots of 100 shares, and in any case do not trade in units less than one share. As a result, if the share price rises significantly, it might be difficult for small investors to afford one share, let alone 100. Making the stock more attractive to small investors can increase the demand for and the liquidity of the stock, which may in turn boost the stock price. On average, announcements of stock splits are associated with a 2% increase in the stock price.[38]

Most firms use splits to keep their share prices from exceeding $100. From 1990 to 2000, Cisco Systems split its stock nine times, so that one share purchased at the IPO split into 288 shares. Had it not split, Cisco's share price at the time of its last split in March 2000 would have been 288 × $72.19, or $20,790.72.

---

[38]S. Nayak and N. Prabhala, "Disentangling the Dividend Information in Splits: A Decomposition Using Conditional Event-Study Methods," *Review of Financial Studies* 14 (2001): 1083–1116. For evidence that stock splits attract individual investors, see R. Dhar, W. Goetzmann, and N. Zhu, "The Impact of Clientele Changes: Evidence from Stock Splits," *Yale ICF Working Paper* no. 03-14 (2004). While splits seem to increase the number of shareholders, evidence of their impact on liquidity is mixed; see, for example, T. Copeland, "Liquidity Changes Following Stock Splits," *Journal of Finance* 34 (1979): 115–141, and J. Lakonishok and B. Lev, "Stock Splits and Stock Dividends: Why, Who and When," *Journal of Finance* 42 (1987): 913–932.

Firms also do not want their stock prices to fall too low. First, a stock price that is very low raises transaction costs for investors. For example, the spread between the bid and ask price for a stock has a minimum size of one tick ($0.01 for the NYSE and NASDAQ exchanges) independent of the stock price. In percentage terms, the tick size is larger for stocks with a low price than for stocks with a high price. Also, exchanges require stocks to maintain a minimum price to remain listed on an exchange (for example, the NYSE and NASDAQ require listed firms to maintain a price of at least $1 per share).

If the price of the stock falls too low, a company can engage in a **reverse split** and reduce the number of shares outstanding. For example, in a 1:10 reverse split, every 10 shares of stock are replaced with a single share. As a result, the share price increases tenfold. Reverse splits became necessary for many dot-coms after the Internet bust in 2000, and similarly for some financial firms in the wake of the financial crisis. Citigroup, for instance, split its stock 7 times between 1990 and 2000, for a cumulative increase of 12:1. But in May 2011 it implemented a 1:10 reverse split to increase its stock price from $4.50 to $45 per share.

Through a combination of splits and reverse splits, firms can keep their share prices in any range they desire. As Figure 17.8 shows, almost all firms have share prices below $100 per share, with 90% of firms' share prices between $2.50 and $65 per share.

Spin-Offs

Rather than pay a dividend using cash or shares of its own stock, a firm can also distribute shares of a subsidiary in a transaction referred to as a **spin-off**. Non-cash special dividends are commonly used to spin off assets or a subsidiary as a separate company. For example, after selling 15% of Monsanto Corporation in an IPO in October 2000, Pharmacia Corporation announced in July 2002 that it would spin off its remaining 85% holding of Monsanto Corporation. The spin-off was accomplished through a special dividend in which each Pharmacia shareholder received 0.170593 share of Monsanto per share of Pharmacia owned. After receiving the Monsanto shares, Pharmacia shareholders could trade them separately from the shares of the parent firm.

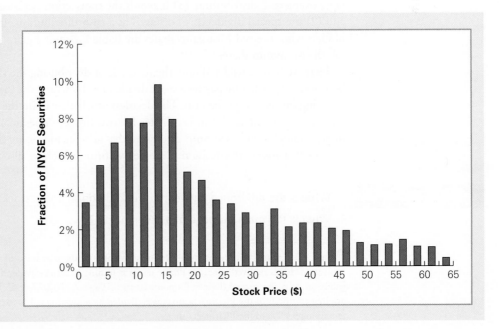

FIGURE 17.8

Distribution of Share Prices on the NYSE (January 2012)

By using splits and reverse splits, most firms keep their share prices between $2.50 and $65 to reduce transaction costs for investors. The median share price is $18.

Berkshire Hathaway's A & B Shares

Many managers split their stock to keep the price affordable for small investors, making it easier for them to buy and sell the stock. Warren Buffett, chairman and chief executive of Berkshire Hathaway, disagrees. As he commented in Berkshire's 1983 annual report: "We are often asked why Berkshire does not split its stock . . . we want [shareholders] who think of themselves as business owners with the intention of staying a long time. And, we want those who keep their eyes focused on business results, not market prices." In its 40-year history, Berkshire Hathaway has never split its stock.

As a result of Berkshire Hathaway's strong performance and the lack of stock splits, the stock price climbed. By 1996, it exceeded $30,000 per share. Because this price was much too expensive for some small investors, several financial intermediaries created unit investment trusts whose only investment was Berkshire shares. (Unit investment trusts are similar to mutual funds, but their investment portfolio is fixed.) Investors could buy smaller interests in these trusts, effectively owning Berkshire stock with a much lower initial investment.

In response, in February 1996, Buffett announced the creation of a second class of Berkshire Hathaway stock, the Class B shares. Each owner of the original shares (now called Class A shares) was offered the opportunity to convert each A share into 30 B shares. "We're giving shareholders a do-it-yourself split, if they care to do it," Buffett said. Through the B shares, investors could own Berkshire stock with a smaller investment, and they would not have to pay the extra transaction costs required to buy stock through the unit trusts.

Meanwhile, the value of the A shares has continued to rise. After reaching a peak of $148,000 in late 2007, the price of one share of Berkshire Hathaway Class A shares was more than $130,000 per share in November 2012.*

---

*Buffet's logic for not splitting the stock is a bit puzzling. If an extremely high stock price were advantageous, Buffet could have obtained it much sooner through a reverse split of the stock.

On the distribution date of August 13, 2002, Monsanto shares traded for an average price of $16.21. Thus, the value of the special dividend was

$$0.170593 \text{ Monsanto shares} \times \$16.21 \text{ per share} = \$2.77 \text{ per share}$$

A shareholder who initially owned 100 shares of Pharmacia stock would receive 17 shares of Monsanto stock, plus cash of $0.0593 \times \$16.21 = \$0.96$ in place of the fractional shares.

Alternatively, Pharmacia could have sold the shares of Monsanto and distributed the cash to shareholders as a cash dividend. The transaction Pharmacia chose offers two advantages over a cash distribution: (1) It avoids the transaction costs associated with such a sale, and (2) the special dividend is not taxed as a cash distribution. Instead, Pharmacia shareholders who received Monsanto shares are liable for capital gains tax only at the time they sell the Monsanto shares.[39]

Here we have considered only the methods of distributing the shares of the firm that has been spun off, either by paying a stock dividend or by selling the shares directly and then distributing (or retaining) the cash. The decision of whether to do the spin-off in the first place raises a new question: When is it better for two firms to operate as separate entities, rather than as a single combined firm? The issues that arise in addressing this question are the same as those that arise in the decision to merge two firms, which we discuss further in Chapter 28.

CONCEPT CHECK

1. What is the difference between a stock dividend and a stock split?

2. What is the main purpose of a reverse split?

---

[39]The capital gain is computed by allocating a fraction of the cost basis of the Pharmacia shares to the Monsanto shares received. Because Pharmacia was trading at an ex-dividend price of $42.54 on the distribution date, the special dividend amounted to $6.1\% = 2.77/(2.77 + 42.54)$ of total value. Thus, the original cost basis of the Pharmacia stock was divided by allocating 6.1% to the Monsanto shares and the remaining 93.9% to the Pharmacia shares.

MyFinanceLab

Here is what you should know after reading this chapter. MyFinanceLab will help you identify what you know and where to go when you need to practice.

17.1 Distributions to Shareholders

- When a firm wants to distribute cash to its shareholders, it can pay a cash dividend or it can repurchase shares.
  - Most companies pay regular, quarterly dividends. Sometimes firms announce one-time, special dividends.
  - Firms repurchase shares using an open market repurchase, a tender offer, a Dutch auction repurchase, or a targeted repurchase.
- On the declaration date, firms announce that they will pay dividends to all shareholders of record on the record date. The ex-dividend date is the first day on which the stock trades without the right to an upcoming dividend; it is usually two trading days prior to the record date. Dividend checks are mailed on the payment date.
- In a stock split or a stock dividend, a company distributes additional shares rather than cash to shareholders.

17.2 Comparison of Dividends and Share Repurchases

- In perfect capital markets, the stock price falls by the amount of the dividend when a dividend is paid. An open market share repurchase has no effect on the stock price, and the stock price is the same as the cum-dividend price if a dividend were paid instead.
- The Modigliani-Miller dividend irrelevance proposition states that in perfect capital markets, holding fixed the investment policy of a firm, the firm's choice of dividend policy is irrelevant and does not affect the initial share price.

17.3 The Tax Disadvantage of Dividends

- In reality, capital markets are not perfect, and market imperfections affect firm dividend policy.
- If taxes are the only important market imperfection, when the tax rate on dividends exceeds the tax rate on capital gains, the optimal dividend policy is for firms to pay no dividends. Firms should use share repurchases for all payouts.

17.4 Dividend Capture and Tax Clienteles

- The effective dividend tax rate, τ_d^*, measures the net tax cost to the investor per dollar of dividend income received:

$$\tau_d^* = \left(\frac{\tau_d - \tau_g}{1 - \tau_g} \right) \tag{17.3}$$

- The effective dividend tax rate varies across investors for several reasons, including income level, investment horizon, tax jurisdiction, and type of investment account.
- Different investor taxes create clientele effects, in which the dividend policy of a firm suits the tax preference of its investor clientele.

17.5 Payout Versus Retention of Cash

- Modigliani-Miller payout policy irrelevance says that, in perfect capital markets, if a firm invests excess cash flows in financial securities, the firm's choice of payout versus retention is irrelevant and does not affect the value of the firm.

- Corporate taxes make it costly for a firm to retain excess cash. Even after adjusting for investor taxes, retaining excess cash brings a substantial tax disadvantage for a firm. The effective tax disadvantage of retaining cash is given by

$$\tau^*_{retain} = \left(1 - \frac{(1 - \tau_c)(1 - \tau_g)}{(1 - \tau_i)} \right) \tag{17.7}$$

- Even though there is a tax disadvantage to retaining cash, some firms accumulate cash balances. Cash balances help firms minimize the transaction costs of raising new capital when they have future potential cash needs. However, there is no benefit to shareholders from firms holding cash in excess of future investment needs.
- In addition to the tax disadvantage of holding cash, agency costs may arise, as managers may be tempted to spend excess cash on inefficient investments and perks. Without pressure from shareholders, managers may choose to horde cash to spend in this way or as a means of reducing a firm's leverage and increasing their job security.
- Dividends and share repurchases help minimize the agency problem of wasteful spending when a firm has excess cash. They also reduce the transfer of value to debt holders or other stakeholders.
- Firms typically maintain relatively constant dividends. This practice is called dividend smoothing.

17.6 Signaling with Payout Policy

- The idea that dividend changes reflect managers' views about firms' future earnings prospects is called the dividend signaling hypothesis.
  - Managers usually increase dividends only when they are confident the firm will be able to afford higher dividends for the foreseeable future.
  - When managers cut the dividend, it may signal that they have lost hope that earnings will improve.
- Share repurchases may be used to signal positive information, as repurchases are more attractive if management believes the stock is undervalued at its current price.

17.7 Stock Dividends, Splits, and Spin-Offs

- With a stock dividend, shareholders receive either additional shares of stock of the firm itself (a stock split) or shares of a subsidiary (a spin-off). The stock price generally falls proportionally with the size of the split.
- A reverse split decreases the number of shares outstanding, and therefore results in a higher share price.

Key Terms

Further Reading

For a comprehensive review of the literature on payout policy, see F. Allen and R. Michaely, "Payout Policy," in G. Constantinides, M. Harris, and R. Stulz, eds., *Handbook of the Economics of Finance: Corporate Finance Volume* 1A (Elsevier, 2003).

The literature on payout policy is extensive. Readers interested in specific issues might find the following articles interesting:

On the information content of payout policy: K. Dewenter and V. Warther, "Dividends, Asymmetric Information, and Agency Conflicts: Evidence from a Comparison of the Dividend Policies of Japanese and U.S. Firms," *Journal of Finance* 53 (1998): 879–904; E. Dyl and R. Weigand, "The Information Content of Dividend Initiations: Additional Evidence," *Financial Management* 27 (1998): 27–35; and G. Grullon and R. Michaely, "The Information Content of Share Repurchase Programs," *Journal of Finance* 59 (2004): 651–680.

On the decision corporations make between dividends and share repurchases: L. Bagwell and J. Shoven, "Cash Distributions to Shareholders," *Journal of Economic Perspectives* 3 (1989): 129–140; M. Barclay and C. Smith, "Corporate Payout Policy: Cash Dividends Versus Open-Market Repurchases," *Journal of Financial Economics* 22 (1988): 61–82; A. Dittmar, "Why Do Firms Repurchase Stock?" *Journal of Business* 73 (2000): 331–355; G. Fenn and N. Liang, "Corporate Payout Policy and Managerial Stock Incentives," *Journal of Financial Economics* 60 (2001): 45–72; W. Guay and J. Harford, "The Cash-Flow Permanence and Information Content of Dividend Increases Versus Repurchases," *Journal of Financial Economics* 57 (2000): 385–415; M. Jagannathan, C. Stephens, and M. Weisbach, "Financial Flexibility and the Choice Between Dividends and Stock Repurchases," *Journal of Financial Economics* 57 (2000): 355–384; K. Kahle, "When a Buyback Isn't a Buyback: Open Market Repurchases and Employee Options," *Journal of Financial Economics* 63 (2002): 235–261; and M. Rozeff, "How Companies Set Their Dividend Payout Ratios," in Joel M. Stern and Donald H. Chew, eds., *The Revolution in Corporate Finance* (Basil Blackwell, 1986).

On tax clienteles: F. Allen, A. Bernardo, and I. Welch, "A Theory of Dividends Based on Tax Clienteles," *Journal of Finance* 55 (2000): 2499–2536.

On the timing of share repurchases: P. Brockman and D. Chung, "Managerial Timing and Corporate Liquidity: Evidence from Actual Share Repurchases," *Journal of Financial Economics* 61 (2001): 417–448; and D. Cook, L. Krigman, and J. Leach, "On the Timing and Execution of Open Market Repurchases," *Review of Financial Studies* 17 (2004): 463–498.

Problems

All problems are available in MyFinanceLab. *An asterisk (*) indicates problems with a higher level of difficulty.*

Distributions to Shareholders

1. What options does a firm have to spend its free cash flow (after it has satisfied all interest obligations)?

2. ABC Corporation announced that it will pay a dividend to all shareholders of record as of Monday, April 2, 2012. It takes three business days of a purchase for the new owners of a share of stock to be registered.
   a. When is the last day an investor can purchase ABC stock and still get the dividend payment?
   b. When is the ex-dividend day?

3. Describe the different mechanisms available to a firm to use to repurchase shares.

Comparison of Dividends and Share Repurchases

4. RFC Corp. has announced a $1 dividend. If RFC's price last price cum-dividend is $50, what should its first ex-dividend price be (assuming perfect capital markets)?

5. EJH Company has a market capitalization of $1 billion and 20 million shares outstanding. It plans to distribute $100 million through an open market repurchase. Assuming perfect capital markets:
   a. What will the price per share of EJH be right before the repurchase?
   b. How many shares will be repurchased?
   c. What will the price per share of EJH be right after the repurchase?

6. KMS Corporation has assets with a market value of $500 million, $50 million of which are cash. It has debt of $200 million, and 10 million shares outstanding. Assume perfect capital markets.
   a. What is its current stock price?
   b. If KMS distributes $50 million as a dividend, what will its share price be after the dividend is paid?
   c. If instead, KMS distributes $50 million as a share repurchase, what will its share price be once the shares are repurchased?
   d. What will its new market debt-equity ratio be after either transaction?

7. Natsam Corporation has $250 million of excess cash. The firm has no debt and 500 million shares outstanding with a current market price of $15 per share. Natsam's board has decided to pay out this cash as a one-time dividend.
   a. What is the ex-dividend price of a share in a perfect capital market?
   b. If the board instead decided to use the cash to do a one-time share repurchase, in a perfect capital market what is the price of the shares once the repurchase is complete?
   c. In a perfect capital market, which policy, in part a or b, makes investors in the firm better off?

8. Suppose the board of Natsam Corporation decided to do the share repurchase in Problem 7 part b, but you, as an investor, would have preferred to receive a dividend payment. How can you leave yourself in the same position as if the board had elected to make the dividend payment instead?

9. Suppose you work for Oracle Corporation, and part of your compensation takes the form of stock options. The value of the stock option is equal to the difference between Oracle's stock price and an exercise price of $10 per share at the time that you exercise the option. As an option holder, would you prefer that Oracle use dividends or share repurchases to pay out cash to shareholders? Explain.

10. Suppose B&E Press paid dividends at the end of each year according to the schedule below. It also reduced its share count by repurchasing 5 million shares at the end of each year at the ex-dividend stock prices shown. (Assume perfect capital markets.)

	2009	2010	2011	2012	2013
Ex-Dividend Stock Price ($/share)	10.00	12.00	8.00	11.00	15.00
Dividend ($/share)		0.50	0.50	0.50	0.50
Shares Outstanding (millions)	100	95	90	85	80

   a. What is total market value of B&E's equity, and what is the total amount paid out to shareholders, at the end of each year?
   b. If B&E had made the same total payouts using dividends only (and so kept is share count constant), what dividend would it have paid and what would its ex-dividend share price have been each year?
   c. If B&E had made the same total payouts using repurchases only (and so paid no dividends), what share count would it have had and what would its share price have been each year?
   d. Consider a shareholder who owns 10 shares of B&E initially, does not sell any shares, and reinvests all dividends at the ex-dividend share price. Would this shareholder have preferred the payout policy in (b), (c), or the original policy?

The Tax Disadvantage of Dividends

11. The HNH Corporation will pay a constant dividend of $2 per share, per year, in perpetuity. Assume all investors pay a 20% tax on dividends and that there is no capital gains tax. Suppose that other investments with equivalent risk to HNH stock offer an after-tax return of 12%.

   a. What is the price of a share of HNH stock?

   b. Assume that management makes a surprise announcement that HNH will no longer pay dividends but will use the cash to repurchase stock instead. What is the price of a share of HNH stock now?

12. Using Table 17.2, for each of the following years, state whether dividends were tax disadvantaged or not for individual investors with a one-year investment horizon:

   a. 1985   b. 1989   c. 1995   d. 1999   e. 2005

Dividend Capture and Tax Clienteles

13. What was the effective dividend tax rate for a U.S. investor in the highest tax bracket who planned to hold a stock for one year in 1981? How did the effective dividend tax rate change in 1982 when the Reagan tax cuts took effect? (Ignore state taxes.)

14. The dividend tax cut passed in 2003 lowered the effective dividend tax rate for a U.S. investor in the highest tax bracket to a historic low. During which other periods in the last 35 years was the effective dividend tax rate as low?

15. Suppose that all capital gains are taxed at a 25% rate, and that the dividend tax rate is 50%. Arbuckle Corp. is currently trading for $30, and is about to pay a $6 special dividend.

   a. Absent any other trading frictions or news, what will its share price be just after the dividend is paid?

   Suppose Arbuckle made a surprise announcement that it would do a share repurchase rather than pay a special dividend.

   b. What net tax savings per share for an investor would result from this decision?

   c. What would happen to Arbuckle's stock price upon the announcement of this change?

16. You purchased CSH stock for $40 one year ago and it is now selling for $50. The company has announced that it plans a $10 special dividend. You are considering whether to sell the stock now, or wait to receive the dividend and then sell.

   a. Assuming 2008 tax rates, what ex-dividend price of CSH will make you indifferent between selling now and waiting?

   b. Suppose the capital gains tax rate is 20% and the dividend tax rate is 40%, what ex-dividend price would make you indifferent now?

17. On Monday, November 15, 2004, TheStreet.com reported: "An experiment in the efficiency of financial markets will play out Monday following the expiration of a $3.08 dividend privilege for holders of Microsoft." The story went on: "The stock is currently trading ex-dividend both the special $3 payout and Microsoft's regular $0.08 quarterly dividend, meaning a buyer doesn't receive the money if he acquires the shares now." Microsoft stock ultimately opened for trade at $27.34 on the ex-dividend date (November 15), down $2.63 from its previous close.

   a. Assuming that this price drop resulted only from the dividend payment (no other information affected the stock price that day), what does this decline in price imply about the effective dividend tax rate for Microsoft?

   b. Based on this information, which of the following investors are most likely to be the marginal investors (the ones who determine the price) in Microsoft stock: i. long-term individual investors, ii. one-year individual investors, iii. pension funds, iv. corporations

18. At current tax rates, which of the following investors are most likely to hold a stock that has a high dividend yield: i. individual investors, ii. pension funds, iii. mutual funds, iv. corporations

19. Que Corporation pays a regular dividend of $1 per share. Typically, the stock price drops by $0.80 per share when the stock goes ex-dividend. Suppose the capital gains tax rate is 20%, but investors pay different tax rates on dividends. Absent transactions costs, what is the highest dividend tax rate of an investor who could gain from trading to capture the dividend?

20. A stock that you know is held by long-term individual investors paid a large one-time dividend. You notice that the price drop on the ex-dividend date is about the size of the dividend payment. You find this relationship puzzling given the tax disadvantage of dividends. Explain how the dividend-capture theory might account for this behavior.

Payout Versus Retention of Cash

21. Clovix Corporation has $50 million in cash, 10 million shares outstanding, and a current share price of $30. Clovix is deciding whether to use the $50 million to pay an immediate special dividend of $5 per share, or to retain and invest it at the risk-free rate of 10% and use the $5 million in interest earned to increase its regular annual dividend of $0.50 per share. Assume perfect capital markets.
   a. Suppose Clovix pays the special dividend. How can a shareholder who would prefer an increase in the regular dividend create it on her own?
   b. Suppose Clovix increases its regular dividend. How can a shareholder who would prefer the special dividend create it on her own?

 22. Assume capital markets are perfect. Kay Industries currently has $100 million invested in short-term Treasury securities paying 7%, and it pays out the interest payments on these securities each year as a dividend. The board is considering selling the Treasury securities and paying out the proceeds as a one-time dividend payment.
   a. If the board went ahead with this plan, what would happen to the value of Kay stock upon the announcement of a change in policy?
   b. What would happen to the value of Kay stock on the ex-dividend date of the one-time dividend?
   c. Given these price reactions, will this decision benefit investors?

 23. Redo Problem 21, but assume that Kay must pay a corporate tax rate of 35%, and investors pay no taxes.

24. Harris Corporation has $250 million in cash, and 100 million shares outstanding. Suppose the corporate tax rate is 35%, and investors pay no taxes on dividends, capital gains, or interest income. Investors had expected Harris to pay out the $250 million through a share repurchase. Suppose instead that Harris announces it will permanently retain the cash, and use the interest on the cash to pay a regular dividend. If there are no other benefits of retaining the cash, how will Harris' stock price change upon this announcement?

 25. Redo Problem 21, but assume the following:
   a. Investors pay a 15% tax on dividends but no capital gains taxes or taxes on interest income, and Kay does not pay corporate taxes.
   b. Investors pay a 15% tax on dividends and capital gains, and a 35% tax on interest income, while Kay pays a 35% corporate tax rate.

26. Raviv Industries has $100 million in cash that it can use for a share repurchase. Suppose instead Raviv invests the funds in an account paying 10% interest for one year.
   a. If the corporate tax rate is 40%, how much additional cash will Raviv have at the end of the year net of corporate taxes?
   b. If investors pay a 20% tax rate on capital gains, by how much will the value of their shares have increased, net of capital gains taxes?
   c. If investors pay a 30% tax rate on interest income, how much would they have had if they invested the $100 million on their own?
   d. Suppose Raviv retained the cash so that it would not need to raise new funds from outside investors for an expansion it has planned for next year. If it did raise new funds, it would have to pay issuance fees. How much does Raviv need to save in issuance fees to make retaining the cash beneficial for its investors? (Assume fees can be expensed for corporate tax purposes.)

27. Use the data in Table 15.3 to calculate the tax disadvantage of retained cash in the following:
    a. 1998
    b. 1976

Signaling with Payout Policy

28. Explain under which conditions an increase in the dividend payment can be interpreted as a signal of the following:
    a. Good news
    b. Bad news

29. Why is an announcement of a share repurchase considered a positive signal?

 *30. AMC Corporation currently has an enterprise value of $400 million and $100 million in excess cash. The firm has 10 million shares outstanding and no debt. Suppose AMC uses its excess cash to repurchase shares. After the share repurchase, news will come out that will change AMC's enterprise value to either $600 million or $200 million.
    a. What is AMC's share price prior to the share repurchase?
    b. What is AMC's share price after the repurchase if its enterprise value goes up? What is AMC's share price after the repurchase if its enterprise value declines?
    c. Suppose AMC waits until after the news comes out to do the share repurchase. What is AMC's share price after the repurchase if its enterprise value goes up? What is AMC's share price after the repurchase if its enterprise value declines?
    d. Suppose AMC management expects good news to come out. Based on your answers to parts (b) and (c), if management desires to maximize AMC's ultimate share price, will they undertake the repurchase before or after the news comes out? When would management undertake the repurchase if they expect bad news to come out?
    e. Given your answer to part d, what effect would you expect an announcement of a share repurchase to have on the stock price? Why?

Stock Dividends, Splits, and Spin-Offs

31. Berkshire Hathaway's A shares are trading at $120,000. What split ratio would it need to bring its stock price down to $50?

 32. Suppose the stock of Host Hotels & Resorts is currently trading for $20 per share.
    a. If Host issued a 20% stock dividend, what will its new share price be?
    b. If Host does a 3:2 stock split, what will its new share price be?
    c. If Host does a 1:3 reverse split, what will its new share price be?

33. Explain why most companies choose to pay stock dividends (split their stock).

34. When might it be advantageous to undertake a reverse stock split?

35. After the market close on May 11, 2001, Adaptec, Inc., distributed a dividend of shares of the stock of its software division, Roxio, Inc. Each Adaptec shareholder received 0.1646 share of Roxio stock per share of Adaptec stock owned. At the time, Adaptec stock was trading at a price of $10.55 per share (cum-dividend), and Roxio's share price was $14.23 per share. In a perfect market, what would Adaptec's ex-dividend share price be after this transaction?

Data Case

In your role as a consultant at a wealth management firm, you have been assigned a very powerful client who holds one million shares of Cisco Systems, Inc. purchased on February 28, 2003. In researching Cisco, you discovered that they are holding a large amount of cash. Additionally, your client is upset that the Cisco stock price has been somewhat stagnant as of late. The client is considering approaching the Board of Directors with a plan for half of the cash the firm has accumulated, but can't decide whether a share repurchase or a special dividend would be best. You have been asked to determine which initiative would generate the greatest amount of money after taxes, assuming that with a share repurchase your client would keep the same proportion of ownership. Because both dividends and capital gains are taxed at the same rate (15%), your client has assumed that there is no difference between the repurchase and the dividend. To confirm, you need to "run the numbers" for each scenario.

1. Go to http://finance.yahoo.com, enter the symbol for Cisco (CSCO), and click "Key Statistics."
   a. Record the current price and the number of shares outstanding.
   b. Click on "Balance Sheet" under "Financials." Copy and paste the balance sheet data into Excel.

2. Using one-half of the most recent cash and cash equivalents reported on the balance sheet (in thousands of dollars), compute the following:
   a. The number of shares that would be repurchased given the current market price.
   b. The dividend per share that could be paid given the total number of shares outstanding.

3. Go to http://finance.yahoo.com to obtain the price at which your client purchased the stock on February 28, 2003.
   a. Enter the symbol for Cisco and click "Get Quotes."
   b. Click "Historical Prices," enter the date your client purchased the stock as the start date and the end date, and hit "Enter." Record the adjusted closing price.

4. Compute the total cash that would be received by your client under the repurchase and the dividend both before taxes and after taxes.

5. The calculation in Step 4 reflects your client's immediate cash flow and tax liability, but it does not consider the final payoff for the client after any shares not sold in a repurchase are liquidated. To incorporate this feature, you first decide to see what happens if the client sells all remaining shares of stock immediately after the dividend or the repurchase. Assume that the stock price will fall by the amount of the dividend if a dividend is paid. What are the client's total after-tax cash flows (considering both the payout and the capital gain) under the repurchase of the dividend in this case?

6. Under which program would your client be better off before taxes? Which program is better after taxes, assuming the remaining shares are sold immediately after the dividend is paid?

7. Because your client is unlikely to sell all 1 million shares today, at the time of dividend/repurchase, you decide to consider two longer holding periods: Assume that under both plans the client sells all remaining shares of stock 5 years later, or the client sells 10 years later. Assume that the stock will return 10% per year going forward. Also assume that Amazon will pay no other dividends over the next 10 years.
   a. What would the stock price be after 5 years or 10 years if a dividend is paid now?
   b. What would the stock price be after 5 years or 10 years if Amazon repurchases shares now?
   c. Calculate the total after-tax cash flows at both points in time (when the dividend payment or the share repurchase takes place, and when the rest of the shares are sold) for your client if the remaining shares are sold in 5 years under both initiatives. Compute the difference between the cash flows under both initiatives at each point in time. Repeat assuming the shares are sold in 10 years.

8. Repeat Question 7 assuming the stock will return 20% per year going forward. What do you notice about the difference in the cash flows under the two initiatives when the return is 20% and 10%?

9. Calculate the NPV of the difference in the cash flows under both holding period assumptions for a range of discount rates. Based on your answer to Question 8, what is the correct discount rate to use?

Advanced Valuation

THE LAW OF ONE PRICE CONNECTION. In this part of the text, we return to the topic of valuation and integrate our understanding of risk, return, and the firm's choice of capital structure. Chapter 18 combines the knowledge of the first five parts of the text and develops the three main methods for capital budgeting with leverage and market imperfections: The weighted average cost of capital (WACC) method, the adjusted present value (APV) method, and the flow-to-equity (FTE) method. While the Law of One Price guarantees that all three methods ultimately lead to the same assessment of value, we will identify conditions that can make one method easiest to apply. Chapter 19 applies Chapter 18's methods of valuation to value a corporation in the context of a leveraged acquisition. Chapter 19 thus serves as a capstone case that illustrates how all the concepts developed thus far in the text are used to make complex real-world financial decisions.

Capital Budgeting and Valuation with Leverage

NOTATION

FCF_t free cash flows at date t

r_{wacc} weighted average cost of capital

r_E, r_D equity and debt costs of capital

r_D^* equity-equivalent debt cost of capital

E market value of equity

D market value of debt (net of cash)

τ_c marginal corporate tax rate

D_t incremental debt of project on date t

V_t^L value of a levered investment on date t

d debt-to-value ratio

r_U unlevered cost of capital

V^U unlevered value of investment

T^s value of predetermined tax shields

k interest coverage ratio

Int_t interest expense on date t

D^s debt net of predetermined tax shields

ϕ permanence of the debt level

τ_e, τ_i tax rate on equity and interest income

τ^* effective tax advantage of debt

IN FALL 2012, GENERAL ELECTRIC COMPANY HAD A MARKET capitalization of approximately $235 billion. With net debt of over $354 billion, GE's total enterprise value was $589 billion, making it the second most valuable business in the world (just behind Apple, and ahead of Exxon Mobil). GE's businesses include power generation and air transportation equipment, health care and medical equipment, consumer appliances, consumer and commercial financing and insurance, as well as entertainment through its affiliate, NBC Universal. With a debt-to-value ratio exceeding 50%, leverage is clearly part of GE's business strategy. How should a firm that uses leverage, like GE, incorporate the costs and benefits associated with leverage into its capital budgeting decisions? And how should a firm adjust for the differences in risk, and debt capacity, associated with its different business activities?

We introduced capital budgeting in Chapter 7. There, we outlined the following basic procedure: First, we estimate the incremental free cash flow generated by the project; then we discount the free cash flow based on the project's cost of capital to determine the NPV. Thus far, we have focused on all-equity financed projects. In this chapter, we integrate the lessons from Parts 4 and 5 into our capital budgeting framework and consider alternative financing arrangements. In particular, we address how the financing decision of the firm can affect both the cost of capital and the set of cash flows that we ultimately discount.

We begin by introducing the three main methods for capital budgeting with leverage and market imperfections: the weighted average cost of capital (WACC) method, the adjusted present value (APV) method, and the flow-to-equity (FTE) method. While their details differ, when appropriately applied each method produces the same estimate of an investment's (or firm's) value. As we shall see, the choice of method is thus guided by which is the simplest to use in a given setting. Ultimately, we will develop recommendations regarding the best method to use depending on the firm's financing policy.

Throughout this chapter, we focus on the intuition and implementation of the main capital budgeting methods. The appendix to this chapter provides additional details about the justification for and assumptions behind some of the results we use in the chapter. It also introduces advanced computational techniques that can be used in Excel to solve for leverage and value simultaneously.

18.1 Overview of Key Concepts

We introduce the three main methods of capital budgeting in Sections 18.2 through 18.4. Before we turn to the specifics, we will revisit some important ideas we encountered earlier in the text that underpin the valuation methods.

Chapter 15 demonstrated that because interest payments are deductible as an expense for the corporation, debt financing creates a valuable interest tax shield for the firm. We can include the value of this tax shield in the capital budgeting decision in several ways. First, we can use the *WACC method*, explained in Section 18.2, in which we discount the unlevered free cash flows using the weighted-average cost of capital, or WACC. Because we calculate the WACC using the effective *after-tax* interest rate as the cost of debt, this method incorporates the tax benefit of debt implicitly through the cost of capital.

Alternatively, we can first value a project's free cash flows without leverage by discounting them using the unlevered cost of capital. We can then separately estimate and add the present value of the interest tax shields from debt. This method, in which we explicitly add the value of the interest tax shields to the project's unlevered value, is called the *adjusted present value (APV) method*, which we explain in Section 18.3.

Our third method makes use of the observation in Chapter 9 that rather than value the firm based on its free cash flows, we can also value its equity based on the total payouts to shareholders. The *flow-to-equity (FTE) method*, introduced in Section 18.4, applies this idea to value the incremental payouts to equity associated with a project.

To illustrate these methods most clearly, we begin the chapter by applying each method to a single example in which we have made a number of simplifying assumptions:

1. *The project has average risk.* We assume initially that the market risk of the project is equivalent to the average market risk of the firm's investments. In that case, the project's cost of capital can be assessed based on the risk of the firm.

2. *The firm's debt-equity ratio is constant.* Initially, we consider a firm that adjusts its leverage to maintain a constant debt-equity ratio in terms of market values. This policy determines the amount of debt the firm will take on when it accepts a new project. It also implies that the risk of the firm's equity and debt, and therefore its weighted average cost of capital, will not fluctuate due to leverage changes.

3. *Corporate taxes are the only imperfection.* We assume initially that the main effect of leverage on valuation is due to the corporate tax shield. We ignore personal taxes and issuance costs, and we assume that other imperfections (such as financial distress or agency costs) are not significant at the level of debt chosen.

While these assumptions are restrictive, they are also a reasonable approximation for many projects and firms. The first assumption is likely to fit typical projects of firms with investments concentrated in a single industry. The second assumption, while unlikely to hold exactly, reflects the fact that firms tend to increase their levels of debt as they grow larger; some may even have an explicit target for their debt-equity ratio. Finally, for firms without very high levels of debt, the interest tax shield is likely to be the most important market imperfection affecting the capital budgeting decision. Hence, the third assumption is a reasonable starting point to begin our analysis.

Of course, while these three assumptions are reasonable in many situations, there are certainly projects and firms for which they do not apply. The remainder of the chapter therefore relaxes these assumptions and shows how to generalize the methods to more complicated settings. In Section 18.5, we adjust these methods for projects whose risk or debt capacity is substantially different from the rest of the firm. These adjustments are especially important for multidivisional firms, such as GE. In Section 18.6, we consider alternative leverage policies for the firm (rather than maintaining a constant debt-equity ratio) and adapt the APV method to handle such cases. We consider the consequence of other market imperfections, such as issuance, distress, and agency costs, on valuation in Section 18.7. Finally, in Section 18.8, we investigate a number of advanced topics, including periodically adjusted leverage policies and the effect of investor taxes.

CONCEPT CHECK

1. What are the three methods we can use to include the value of the tax shield in the capital budgeting decision?

2. In what situation is the risk of a project likely to match that of the overall firm?

18.2 The Weighted Average Cost of Capital Method

The WACC method takes the interest tax shield into account by using the after-tax cost of capital as the discount rate. When the market risk of the project is similar to the average market risk of the firm's investments, then its cost of capital is equal to the firm's weighted average cost of capital (WACC). As we showed in Chapter 15, the WACC incorporates the benefit of the interest tax shield by using the firm's *after-tax* cost of capital for debt:

$$r_{wacc} = \frac{E}{E+D}r_E + \frac{D}{E+D}r_D(1-\tau_c)$$ (18.1)

In this formula,

E = market value of equity r_E = equity cost of capital

D = market value of debt (net of cash) r_D = debt cost of capital

τ_c = marginal corporate tax rate

For now, we assume that the firm maintains a constant debt-equity ratio and that the WACC calculated in Eq. 18.1 remains constant over time.[1] Because the WACC incorporates the tax savings from debt, we can compute the *levered value* of an investment, which is its value including the benefit of interest tax shields given the firm's leverage policy, by discounting its future free cash flow using the WACC. Specifically, if FCF_t is the expected

---

[1]In Section 18.8, we consider the case in which the WACC changes over time due to changes in leverage.

free cash flow of an investment at the end of year t, then the investment's initial levered value, V_0^L, is[2]

$$V_0^L = \frac{FCF_1}{1 + r_{wacc}} + \frac{FCF_2}{(1 + r_{wacc})^2} + \frac{FCF_3}{(1 + r_{wacc})^3} + \cdots \qquad (18.2)$$

Using the WACC to Value a Project

Let's apply the WACC method to value a project. Avco, Inc., is a manufacturer of custom packaging products. Avco is considering introducing a new line of packaging, the RFX series, that will include an embedded radio-frequency identification (RFID) tag, which is a miniature radio antenna and transponder that allows a package to be tracked much more efficiently and with fewer errors than standard bar codes.

Avco engineers expect the technology used in these products to become obsolete after four years. During the next four years, however, the marketing group expects annual sales of $60 million per year for this product line. Manufacturing costs and operating expenses are expected to be $25 million and $9 million, respectively, per year. Developing the product will require upfront R&D and marketing expenses of $6.67 million, together with a $24 million investment in equipment. The equipment will be obsolete in four years and will be depreciated via the straight-line method over that period. Avco bills the majority of its customers in advance, and it expects no net working capital requirements for the project. Avco pays a corporate tax rate of 40%. Given this information, the spreadsheet in Table 18.1 forecasts the project's expected free cash flow.[3]

The market risk of the RFX project is expected to be similar to that for the company's other lines of business. Thus, we can use Avco's equity and debt to determine the weighted average cost of capital for the new project. Table 18.2 shows Avco's current market value balance sheet and equity and debt costs of capital. Avco has built up $20 million in cash for

	TABLE 18.1 SPREADSHEET	Expected Free Cash Flow from Avco's RFX Project				
	Year	0	1	2	3	4
	Incremental Earnings Forecast ($ million)					
1	Sales	—	60.00	60.00	60.00	60.00
2	Cost of Goods Sold	—	(25.00)	(25.00)	(25.00)	(25.00)
3	**Gross Profit**	—	35.00	35.00	35.00	35.00
4	Operating Expenses	(6.67)	(9.00)	(9.00)	(9.00)	(9.00)
5	Depreciation	—	(6.00)	(6.00)	(6.00)	(6.00)
6	**EBIT**	(6.67)	20.00	20.00	20.00	20.00
7	Income Tax at 40%	2.67	(8.00)	(8.00)	(8.00)	(8.00)
8	**Unlevered Net Income**	(4.00)	12.00	12.00	12.00	12.00
	Free Cash Flow					
9	Plus: Depreciation	—	6.00	6.00	6.00	6.00
10	Less: Capital Expenditures	(24.00)	—	—	—	—
11	Less: Increases in NWC	—	—	—	—	—
12	**Free Cash Flow**	**(28.00)**	**18.00**	**18.00**	**18.00**	**18.00**

---

[2]See this chapter's appendix for a formal justification of this result.
[3]The spreadsheets shown in this chapter are available for download from MyFinanceLab.

TABLE 18.2	Avco's Current Market Value Balance Sheet ($ million) and Cost of Capital without the RFX Project

Assets		Liabilities		Cost of Capital	
Cash	20	Debt	320	Debt	6%
Existing Assets	600	Equity	300	Equity	10%
Total Assets	620	Total Liabilities and Equity	620		

investment needs, so that its *net* debt is $D = 320 - 20 = \$300$ million. Avco's enterprise value, which is the market value of its non-cash assets, is $E + D = \$600$ million. Avco intends to maintain a similar (net) debt-equity ratio for the foreseeable future, including any financing related to the RFX project.

With this capital structure, Avco's weighted average cost of capital is

$$r_{wacc} = \frac{E}{E+D}r_E + \frac{D}{E+D}r_D(1-\tau_c) = \frac{300}{600}(10.0\%) + \frac{300}{600}(6.0\%)(1-0.40)$$

$$= 6.8\%$$

We can determine the value of the project, including the tax shield from debt, by calculating the present value of its future free cash flows, V_0^L, using the WACC:

$$V_0^L = \frac{18}{1.068} + \frac{18}{1.068^2} + \frac{18}{1.068^3} + \frac{18}{1.068^4} = \$61.25 \text{ million}$$

Because the upfront cost of launching the product line is only $28 million, this project is a good idea—taking the project results in an NPV of $61.25 - 28 = \$33.25$ million for the firm.

Summary of the WACC Method

To summarize, the key steps in the WACC valuation method are as follows:

1. Determine the free cash flow of the investment.
2. Compute the weighted average cost of capital using Eq. 18.1.
3. Compute the value of the investment, including the tax benefit of leverage, by discounting the free cash flow of the investment using the WACC.

In many firms, the corporate treasurer performs the second step, calculating the firm's WACC. This rate can then be used throughout the firm as the companywide cost of capital for new investments *that are of comparable risk to the rest of the firm and that will not alter the firm's debt-equity ratio.* Employing the WACC method in this way is very simple and straightforward. As a result, it is the method that is most commonly used in practice for capital budgeting purposes.

EXAMPLE 18.1	Valuing an Acquisition Using the WACC Method

Problem

Suppose Avco is considering the acquisition of another firm in its industry that specializes in custom packaging. The acquisition is expected to increase Avco's free cash flow by $3.8 million the first year, and this contribution is expected to grow at a rate of 3% per year from then on. Avco has negotiated a purchase price of $80 million. After the transaction, Avco will adjust its capital structure to maintain its current debt-equity ratio. If the acquisition has similar risk to the rest of Avco, what is the value of this deal?

Solution

The free cash flows of the acquisition can be valued as a growing perpetuity. Because its risk matches the risk for the rest of Avco, and because Avco will maintain the same debt-equity ratio going forward, we can discount these cash flows using the WACC of 6.8%. Thus, the value of the acquisition is

$$V^L = \frac{3.8}{6.8\% - 3\%} = \$100 \text{ million}$$

Given the purchase price of $80 million, the acquisition has an NPV of $20 million.

Implementing a Constant Debt-Equity Ratio

Thus far, we have simply assumed the firm adopted a policy of keeping its debt-equity ratio constant. In fact, an important advantage of the WACC method is that you do not need to know how this leverage policy is implemented in order to make the capital budgeting decision. Nevertheless, keeping the debt-equity ratio constant has implications for how the firm's total debt will change with new investment. For example, Avco currently has a debt-equity ratio of $300/300 = 1$ or, equivalently, a debt-to-value ratio $[D/(E+D)]$ of 50%. To maintain this ratio, the firm's new investments must be financed with debt equal to 50% of their market value.

By undertaking the RFX project, Avco adds new assets to the firm with initial market value $V_0^L = \$61.25$ million. Therefore, to maintain its debt-to-value ratio, Avco must add $50\% \times 61.25 = \$30.625$ million in new net debt.[4] Avco can add this net debt either by reducing cash or by borrowing and increasing debt. Suppose Avco decides to spend its $20 million in cash and borrow an additional $10.625 million. Because only $28 million is required to fund the project, Avco will pay the remaining $30.625 - 28 = \$2.625$ million to shareholders through a dividend (or share repurchase). Table 18.3 shows Avco's market value balance sheet with the RFX project in this case.

TABLE 18.3	Avco's Current Market Value Balance Sheet ($ million) with the RFX Project		
Assets		**Liabilities**	
Cash	—	Debt	330.625
Existing Assets	600.00		
RFX Project	61.25	Equity	330.625
Total Assets	661.25	Total Liabilities and Equity	661.25

---

[4]We can also evaluate the project's debt as follows: Of the $28 million upfront cost of the project, 50% ($14 million) will be financed with debt. In addition, the project generates an NPV of $33.25 million, which will increase the market value of the firm. To maintain a debt-equity ratio of 1, Avco must add debt of $50\% \times 33.25 = \$16.625$ million at the time when the NPV of the project is anticipated (which could occur before the new investment is made). Thus, the total new debt is $14 + 16.625 = \$30.625$ million.

This financing plan maintains Avco's 50% debt-to-value ratio. The market value of Avco's equity increases by $330.625 - 300 = \$30.625$ million. Adding the dividend of $2.625 million, the shareholders' total gain is $30.625 + 2.625 = \$33.25$ million, which is exactly the NPV we calculated for the RFX project.

What happens over the life of the project? First, we define an investment's **debt capacity**, D_t, as the amount of debt at date t that is required to maintain the firm's target debt-to-value ratio, d. If V_t^L, is the project's levered continuation value on date t—that is, the levered value of its free cash flow after date t—then

$$D_t = d \times V_t^L \tag{18.3}$$

We compute the debt capacity for the RFX project in the spreadsheet in Table 18.4. Starting with the project's free cash flow, we compute its levered continuation value at each date (line 2) by discounting the future free cash flow at the WACC as in Eq. 18.2. Because the continuation value at each date includes the value of all subsequent cash flows, it is even simpler to compute the value at each date by working backward from period 4, discounting next period's free cash flow and continuation value:

$$V_t^L = \frac{FCF_{t+1} + \overbrace{V_{t+1}^L}^{\substack{\text{Value of FCF in year} \\ t+2 \text{ and beyond}}}}{1 + r_{wacc}} \tag{18.4}$$

Once we have computed the project's value V_t^L at each date, we apply Eq. 18.3 to compute the project's debt capacity at each date (line 3). As the spreadsheet shows, the project's debt capacity declines each year, and falls to zero by the end of year 4.

TABLE 18.4 SPREADSHEET	Continuation Value and Debt Capacity of the RFX Project over Time					
Year	**0**	**1**	**2**	**3**	**4**
Project Debt Capacity ($ million)						
1 **Free Cash Flow**		(28.00)	18.00	18.00	18.00	18.00
2 Levered Value, V^L (at r_{wacc} = 6.8%)		61.25	47.41	32.63	16.85	—
3 **Debt Capacity, D_t (at d = 50%)**		**30.62**	**23.71**	**16.32**	**8.43**	—

EXAMPLE 18.2   **Debt Capacity for an Acquisition**

Problem
Suppose Avco proceeds with the acquisition described in Example 18.1. How much debt must Avco use to finance the acquisition and still maintain its debt-to-value ratio? How much of the acquisition cost must be financed with equity?

Solution
From the solution to Example 18.2, the market value of the assets acquired in the acquisition, V^L, is $100 million. Thus, to maintain a 50% debt-to-value ratio, Avco must increase its debt by $50 million. The remaining $30 million of the $80 million acquisition cost will be financed with new equity. In addition to the $30 million in new equity, the value of Avco's existing shares will increase by the $20 million NPV of the acquisition, so in total the market value of Avco's equity will rise by $50 million.

1. Describe the key steps in the WACC valuation method.

2. How does the WACC method take into account the tax shield?

18.3 The Adjusted Present Value Method

The **adjusted present value (APV)** method is an alternative valuation method in which we determine the levered value V^L of an investment by first calculating its *unlevered value* V^U, which is its value without any leverage, and then adding the value of the interest tax shield. That is, as we showed in Chapter 15:[5]

The APV Formula

$$V^L = APV = V^U + PV\,(\text{Interest Tax Shield}) \qquad (18.5)$$

As we did with the WACC method, we focus solely on the corporate tax benefits of debt for now and defer the discussion of other consequences of leverage to Section 18.7. As Eq. 18.5 shows, the APV method incorporates the value of the interest tax shield directly, rather than by adjusting the discount rate as in the WACC method. Let's demonstrate the APV method by returning to Avco's RFX project.

The Unlevered Value of the Project

From the free cash flow estimates in Table 18.1, the RFX project has an upfront cost of $28 million, and it generates $18 million per year in free cash flow for the next four years. The first step in the APV method is to calculate the value of these free cash flows using the project's cost of capital if it were financed without leverage.

What is the project's unlevered cost of capital? Because the RFX project has similar risk to Avco's other investments, its unlevered cost of capital is the same as for the firm as a whole. Thus, as we did in Chapter 12, we can calculate the unlevered cost of capital using Avco's pretax WACC, the average return the firm's investors expect to earn:

Unlevered Cost of Capital with a Target Leverage Ratio

$$r_U = \frac{E}{E + D}\,r_E + \frac{D}{E + D}\,r_D = \text{Pretax WACC} \qquad (18.6)$$

To understand why the firm's unlevered cost of capital equals its pretax WACC, note that the pretax WACC represents investors' required return for holding the entire firm (equity and debt). Thus, it will depend only on the firm's overall risk. So long as the firm's leverage choice does not change the overall risk of the firm, the pretax WACC must be the same whether the firm is levered or unlevered—recall Figure 15.2 on page 515.

Of course, this argument relies on the assumption that the overall risk of the firm is independent of the choice of leverage. As we showed in Chapter 14, this assumption always holds in a perfect market. It will also hold in a world with taxes whenever the risk of the tax shield is the same as the risk of the firm (so the size of the tax shield will not change the overall riskiness of the firm). In this chapter's appendix, we show that the tax shield will have the same risk as the firm if the firm maintains a *target leverage ratio*. A **target leverage ratio**

---

[5]Stewart Myers developed the application of APV to capital budgeting, see "Interactions of Corporate Financing and Investment Decisions—Implications for Capital Budgeting," *Journal of Finance* 29 (1974): 1–25.

means that the firm adjusts its debt proportionally to the project's value, or its cash flows, so that a constant debt-equity ratio is a special case.

Applying Eq. 18.6 to Avco, we find its unlevered cost of capital to be

$$r_U = 0.50 \times 10.0\% + 0.50 \times 6.0\% = 8.0\%$$

Avco's unlevered cost of capital is less than its equity cost of capital of 10.0% (which includes the financial risk of leverage), but is more than its WACC of 6.8% (which incorporates the tax benefit of leverage).

Given our estimate of the unlevered cost of capital r_U and the project's free cash flows, we calculate the project's value without leverage:

$$V^U = \frac{18}{1.08} + \frac{18}{1.08^2} + \frac{18}{1.08^3} + \frac{18}{1.08^4} = \$59.62 \text{ million}$$

Valuing the Interest Tax Shield

The value of the unlevered project, V^U, calculated above does not include the value of the tax shield provided by the interest payments on debt—it is the value of the project were it purely equity financed. Given the project's debt capacity from Table 18.4, we can estimate the expected interest payments and the tax shield as shown in the spreadsheet in Table 18.5. The interest paid in year t is estimated based on the amount of debt outstanding at the end of the prior year:

$$\text{Interest paid in year } t = r_D \times D_{t-1} \tag{18.7}$$

The interest tax shield is equal to the interest paid multiplied by the corporate tax rate τ_c.

TABLE 18.5 SPREADSHEET	Expected Debt Capacity, Interest Payments, and Tax Shield for Avco's RFX Project				

Year	0	1	2	3	4
Interest Tax Shield ($ million)					
1 Debt Capacity, D_t (at $d = 50\%$)	30.62	23.71	16.32	8.43	—
2 Interest Paid (at $r_D = 6\%$)		1.84	1.42	0.98	0.51
3 **Interest Tax Shield (at $\tau_c = 40\%$)**		0.73	0.57	0.39	0.20

To compute the present value of the interest tax shield, we need to determine the appropriate cost of capital. The interest tax shields shown in Table 18.5 are expected values, and the true amount of the interest tax shield each year will vary with the cash flows of the project. Because Avco maintains a fixed debt-equity ratio, if the project does well, its value will be higher, it will support more debt, and the interest tax shield will be higher. If the project goes poorly, its value will fall, Avco will reduce its debt level, and the interest tax shield will be lower. Thus, the tax shield will fluctuate with, and therefore share the risk of, the project itself:[6]

> *When the firm maintains a target leverage ratio, its future interest tax shields have similar risk to the project's cash flows, so they should be discounted at the project's unlevered cost of capital.*

[6]In Section 18.6, we consider the case in which the debt levels are fixed in advance, and so do *not* fluctuate with the project cash flows. As we will see, in that case the tax shield has lower risk, and thus a lower cost of capital, than the project.

For Avco's RFX project, we have

$$PV(\text{interest tax shield}) = \frac{0.73}{1.08} + \frac{0.57}{1.08^2} + \frac{0.39}{1.08^3} + \frac{0.20}{1.08^4} = \$1.63 \text{ million}$$

To determine the value of the project with leverage, we add the value of the interest tax shield to the unlevered value of the project:[7]

$$V^L = V^U + PV(\text{interest tax shield}) = 59.62 + 1.63 = \$61.25 \text{ million}$$

Again, given the $28 million initial investment required, the RFX project has an NPV with leverage of $61.25 - 28 = \$33.25$ million, which matches precisely the value we computed in Section 18.2 using the WACC approach.

Summary of the APV Method

To determine the value of a levered investment using the APV method, we proceed as follows:

1. Determine the investment's value without leverage, V^U, by discounting its free cash flows at the unlevered cost of capital, r_U. With a constant debt-equity ratio, r_U may be estimated using Eq. 18.6.

2. Determine the present value of the interest tax shield.
   a. Determine the expected interest tax shield: Given expected debt D_t on date t, the interest tax shield on date $t + 1$ is $\tau_c\, r_D\, D_t$.[8]
   b. Discount the interest tax shield. If a constant debt-equity ratio is maintained, using r_U is appropriate.

3. Add the unlevered value, V^U, to the present value of the interest tax shield to determine the value of the investment with leverage, V^L.

The APV method is more complicated than the WACC method because we must compute two separate valuations: the unlevered project and the interest tax shield. Furthermore, in this example, to determine the project's debt capacity for the interest tax shield calculation, we relied on the calculation in Table 18.4, *which depended on the value of the project*. Thus, we need to know the debt level to compute the APV, but with a constant debt-equity ratio we need to know the project's value to compute the debt level. As a result, implementing the APV approach with a constant debt-equity ratio requires solving for the project's debt and value *simultaneously*. (See this chapter's appendix for an example of this calculation.)

Despite its complexity, the APV method has some advantages. As we shall see in Section 18.6, it can be easier to apply than the WACC method when the firm does not maintain a constant debt-equity ratio. It also provides managers with an explicit valuation of the tax shield itself. In the case of Avco's RFX project, the benefit of the interest tax shield is

---

[7]Because we are using the same discount rate for the free cash flow and the tax shield, the cash flows of the project and the tax shield can be combined first and then discounted at the rate r_U. These combined cash flows are also referred to as the capital cash flows (CCF): CCF = FCF + Interest Tax Shield. This method is known as the CCF or "compressed APV" method [see S. Kaplan and R. Ruback, "The Valuation of Cash Flow Forecasts: An Empirical Analysis," *Journal of Finance* 50 (1995): 1059–1093; and R. Ruback, "Capital Cash Flows: A Simple Approach to Valuing Risky Cash Flows," *Financial Management* 31 (2002): 85–103].

[8]The return on the debt need not come solely from interest payments, so this value is an approximation. The same approximation is implicit in the definition of the WACC (for additional precision, see footnote 28 in this chapter's appendix).

relatively small. Even if tax rates were to change, or if Avco decided for other reasons not to increase its debt, the profitability of the project would not be jeopardized. However, this need not always be the case. Consider again the acquisition in Example 18.1, where the APV method makes clear that the gain from the acquisition crucially depends on the interest tax shield.

EXAMPLE 18.3

Using the APV Method to Value an Acquisition

Problem

Consider again Avco's acquisition from Examples 18.1 and 18.2. The acquisition will contribute $3.8 million in free cash flows the first year, which will grow by 3% per year thereafter. The acquisition cost of $80 million will be financed with $50 million in new debt initially. Compute the value of the acquisition using the APV method, assuming Avco will maintain a constant debt-equity ratio for the acquisition.

Solution

First, we compute the value without leverage. Given Avco's unlevered cost of capital of $r_U = 8\%$, we get

$$V^U = 3.8/(8\% - 3\%) = \$76 \text{ million}$$

Avco will add new debt of $50 million initially to fund the acquisition. At a 6% interest rate, the interest expense the first year is $6\% \times 50 = \$3$ million, which provides an interest tax shield of $40\% \times 3 = \$1.2$ million. Because the value of the acquisition is expected to grow by 3% per year, the amount of debt the acquisition supports—and, therefore, the interest tax shield—is expected to grow at the same rate. The present value of the interest tax shield is

$$PV \text{ (interest tax shield)} = 1.2/(8\% - 3\%) = \$24 \text{ million}$$

The value of the acquisition with leverage is given by the APV:

$$V^L = V^U + PV \text{ (interest tax shield)} = 76 + 24 = \$100 \text{ million}$$

This value is identical to the value computed in Example 18.1 and implies an NPV of $100 - 80 = \$20$ million for the acquisition. Without the benefit of the interest tax shield, the NPV would be $76 - 80 = -\$4$ million.

We can easily extend the APV approach to include other market imperfections such as financial distress, agency, and issuance costs. We discuss these complexities further in Section 18.7.

CONCEPT CHECK

1. Describe the adjusted present value (APV) method.

2. At what rate should we discount the interest tax shield when a firm maintains a target leverage ratio?

18.4 The Flow-to-Equity Method

In the WACC and APV methods, we value a project based on its free cash flow, which is computed ignoring interest and debt payments. Some students find these methods confusing because, if the goal is to determine the benefit of the project to shareholders, it seems to them that we should focus on the cash flows that *shareholders* will receive.

In the **flow-to-equity (FTE)** valuation method, we explicitly calculate the free cash flow available to equity holders *after taking into account all payments to and from debt holders*. The cash flows to equity holders are then discounted using the *equity* cost of capital.[9] Despite this difference in implementation, the FTE method produces the same assessment of the project's value as the WACC or APV methods.

Calculating the Free Cash Flow to Equity

The first step in the FTE method is to determine the project's **free cash flow to equity (FCFE)**. The FCFE is the free cash flow that remains after adjusting for interest payments, debt issuance, and debt repayment. The spreadsheet shown in Table 18.6 calculates the FCFE for Avco's RFX project.

Comparing the FCFE estimates in Table 18.6 with the free cash flow estimates in Table 18.1, we notice two changes. First, we deduct interest expenses (from Table 18.5) on line 7, before taxes. As a consequence, we compute the incremental net income of the project on line 10, rather than its *unlevered* net income as we do when computing free cash flows. The second change is line 14, where we add the proceeds from the firm's net borrowing activity. These proceeds are positive when the firm increases its net debt; they are negative when the firm reduces its net debt by repaying principal (or retaining cash). For the RFX project, Avco issues $30.62 million in debt initially. At date 1, however, the debt capacity of the project falls to $23.71 million (see Table 18.4), so that Avco must repay $30.62 - 23.71 = \$6.91$ million of the debt.[10] In general, given the project's debt capacity D_t,

$$\text{Net Borrowing at Date } t = D_t - D_{t-1} \tag{18.8}$$

TABLE 18.6 SPREADSHEET	Expected Free Cash Flows to Equity from Avco's RFX Project					
Year		**0**	**1**	**2**	**3**	**4**
Incremental Earnings Forecast ($ million)						
1	Sales	—	60.00	60.00	60.00	60.00
2	Cost of Goods Sold	—	(25.00)	(25.00)	(25.00)	(25.00)
3	**Gross Profit**	—	35.00	35.00	35.00	35.00
4	Operating Expenses	(6.67)	(9.00)	(9.00)	(9.00)	(9.00)
5	Depreciation	—	(6.00)	(6.00)	(6.00)	(6.00)
6	**EBIT**	(6.67)	20.00	20.00	20.00	20.00
7	Interest Expense	—	(1.84)	(1.42)	(0.98)	(0.51)
8	**Pretax Income**	(6.67)	18.16	18.58	19.02	19.49
9	Income Tax at 40%	2.67	(7.27)	(7.43)	(7.61)	(7.80)
10	**Net Income**	(4.00)	10.90	11.15	11.41	11.70
Free Cash Flow to Equity						
11	Plus: Depreciation	—	6.00	6.00	6.00	6.00
12	Less: Capital Expenditures	(24.00)	—	—	—	—
13	Less: Increases in NWC	—	—	—	—	—
14	Plus: Net Borrowing	30.62	(6.92)	(7.39)	(7.89)	(8.43)
15	**Free Cash Flow to Equity**	**2.62**	**9.98**	**9.76**	**9.52**	**9.27**

---

[9]The FTE approach is very similar to the total payout method for valuing the firm described in Chapter 9. In that method, we value the total dividends and repurchases that the firm pays to shareholders. It is also equivalent to the residual income valuation method used in accounting.

[10]The $0.01 million difference in the spreadsheet is due to rounding.

As an alternative to Table 18.6, we can compute a project's FCFE directly from its free cash flow. Because interest payments are deducted before taxes in line 7, we adjust the firm's FCF by their after-tax cost. We then add net borrowing to determine FCFE:

Free Cash Flow to Equity

$$FCFE = FCF - \underbrace{(1 - \tau_c) \times (\text{Interest Payments})}_{\text{After-tax interest expense}} + (\text{Net Borrowing}) \qquad (18.9)$$

We illustrate this alternative calculation for Avco's RFX project in Table 18.7. Note that the project's FCFE is lower than its FCF in years 1 through 4 due to the interest and principal payments on the debt. In year 0, however, the proceeds from the loan more than offset the negative free cash flow, so FCFE is positive (and equal to the dividend we calculated in Section 18.2).

Valuing Equity Cash Flows

The project's free cash flow to equity shows the expected amount of additional cash the firm will have available to pay dividends (or conduct share repurchases) each year. Because these cash flows represent payments to equity holders, they should be discounted at the project's equity cost of capital. Given that the risk and leverage of the RFX project are the same as for Avco overall, we can use Avco's equity cost of capital of $r_E = 10.0\%$ to discount the project's FCFE:

$$NPV(FCFE) = 2.62 + \frac{9.98}{1.10} + \frac{9.76}{1.10^2} + \frac{9.52}{1.10^3} + \frac{9.27}{1.10^4} = \$33.25 \text{ million}$$

The value of the project's FCFE represents the gain to shareholders from the project. It is identical to the NPV we computed using the WACC and APV methods.

Why isn't the project's NPV lower now that we have deducted interest and debt payments from the cash flows? Recall that these costs of debt are offset by cash received when the debt is issued. Looking back at Table 18.6, the cash flows from debt in lines 7 and 14 have an NPV of zero assuming the debt is fairly priced.[11] In the end, the only effect on value comes from a reduction in the tax payments, leaving the same result as with the other methods.

Summary of the Flow-to-Equity Method

The key steps in the flow-to-equity method for valuing a levered investment are as follows:

1. Determine the free cash flow to equity of the investment using Eq. 18.9.
2. Determine the equity cost of capital, r_E.
3. Compute the contribution to equity value, E, by discounting the free cash flow to equity using the equity cost of capital.

---

[11]The interest and principal payments for the RFX project are as follows:

	Year	0	1	2	3	4
1	Net Borrowing	30.62	(6.92)	(7.39)	(7.89)	(8.43)
2	Interest Expense	—	(1.84)	(1.42)	(0.98)	(0.51)
3	**Cash Flow from Debt**	**30.62**	**(8.76)**	**(8.81)**	**(8.87)**	**(8.93)**

Because these cash flows have the same risk as the debt, we discount them at the debt cost of capital of 6% to compute their NPV:

$$30.62 + \frac{-8.76}{1.06} + \frac{-8.81}{1.06^2} + \frac{-8.87}{1.06^3} + \frac{-8.93}{1.06^4} = 0.$$

TABLE 18.7 SPREADSHEET	Computing FCFE from FCF for Avco's RFX Project					
	Year	**0**	**1**	**2**	**3**	**4**
Free Cash Flow to Equity ($ million)						
1 **Free Cash Flow**		(28.00)	18.00	18.00	18.00	18.00
2 After-tax Interest Expense		—	(1.10)	(0.85)	(0.59)	(0.30)
3 Net Borrowing		30.62	(6.92)	(7.39)	(7.89)	(8.43)
4 **Free Cash Flow to Equity**		**2.62**	**9.98**	**9.76**	**9.52**	**9.27**

Applying the FTE method was simplified in our example because the project's risk and leverage matched the firm's, and the firm's equity cost of capital was expected to remain constant. Just as with the WACC, however, this assumption is reasonable only if the firm maintains a constant debt-equity ratio. If the debt-equity ratio changes over time, the risk of equity—and, therefore, its cost of capital—will change as well.

In this setting, the FTE approach has the same disadvantage associated with the APV approach: We need to compute the project's debt capacity to determine interest and net borrowing before we can make the capital budgeting decision. For this reason, in most settings the WACC is easier to apply. The FTE method can offer an advantage when calculating the value of equity for the entire firm, if the firm's capital structure is complex and the market values of other securities in the firm's capital structure are not known. In that case, the FTE method allows us to compute the value of equity directly. In contrast, the WACC and APV methods compute the firm's enterprise value, so that a separate valuation of the other components of the firm's capital structure is needed to determine the value of equity. Finally, by emphasizing a project's implication for equity, the FTE method may be viewed as a more transparent method for discussing a project's benefit to shareholders—a managerial concern.

What Counts as "Debt"?

Firms often have many types of debt as well as other liabilities, such as leases. Practitioners use different guidelines to determine which to include as debt when computing the WACC. Some use only long-term debt. Others use both long-term and short-term debt, plus lease obligations. Students are often confused by these different approaches and are left wondering: Which liabilities should be included as debt?

In fact, any choice will work if done correctly. We can view the WACC and FTE methods as special cases of a more general approach in which we *value the after-tax cash flows from a set of the firm's assets and liabilities by discounting them at the after-tax weighted average cost of capital of the firm's remaining assets and liabilities*. In the WACC method, the FCF does not include the interest and principal payments on

debt, so debt is included in the calculation of the weighted average cost of capital. In the FTE method, the FCFE incorporates the after-tax cash flows to and from debt holders, so debt is excluded from the weighted average cost of capital (which is simply the equity cost of capital).

Other combinations are also possible. For example, long-term debt can be included in the weighted average cost of capital, and short-term debt can be included as part of the cash flows. Similarly, other assets (such as cash) or liabilities (such as leases) can be included either in the weighted average cost of capital or as part of the cash flow. All such methods, if applied consistently, will lead to an equivalent valuation. Typically, the most convenient choice is the one for which the assumption of a constant debt-to-value ratio is a reasonable approximation.

| EXAMPLE 18.4 | **Using the FTE Method to Value an Acquisition** |

Problem

Consider again Avco's acquisition from Examples 18.1 through 18.3. The acquisition will contribute $3.8 million in free cash flows the first year, growing by 3% per year thereafter. The acquisition cost of $80 million will be financed with $50 million in new debt initially. What is the value of this acquisition using the FTE method?

Solution

Because the acquisition is being financed with $50 million in new debt, the remaining $30 million of the acquisition cost must come from equity:

$$FCFE_0 = -80 + 50 = -\$30 \text{ million}$$

In one year, the interest on the debt will be $6\% \times 50 = \$3$ million. Because Avco maintains a constant debt-equity ratio, the debt associated with the acquisition is also expected to grow at a 3% rate: $50 \times 1.03 = \$51.5$ million. Therefore, Avco will borrow an additional $51.5 - 50 = \$1.5$ million in one year.

$$FCFE_1 = +3.8 - (1 - 0.40) \times 3 + 1.5 = \$3.5 \text{ million}$$

After year 1, FCFE will also grow at a 3% rate. Using the cost of equity $r_E = 10\%$, we compute the NPV:

$$NPV(FCFE) = -30 + 3.5/(10\% - 3\%) = \$20 \text{ million}$$

This NPV matches the result we obtained with the WACC and APV methods.

| CONCEPT CHECK | 1. Describe the key steps in the flow to equity method for valuing a levered investment. |
| | 2. Why does the assumption that the firm maintains a constant debt-equity ratio simplify the flow-to-equity calculation? |

18.5 Project-Based Costs of Capital

Up to this point, we have assumed that both the risk and the leverage of the project under consideration matched those characteristics for the firm as a whole. This assumption allowed us, in turn, to assume that the cost of capital for a project matched the cost of capital of the firm.

In the real world, specific projects often differ from the average investment made by the firm. Consider General Electric Company, discussed in the introduction to this chapter. Projects in its health care division are likely to have different market risk than projects in air transportation equipment or at NBC Universal. Projects may also vary in the amount of leverage they will support—for example, acquisitions of real estate or capital equipment are often highly levered, whereas investments in intellectual property are not. In this section, we show how to calculate the cost of capital for the project's cash flows when a project's risk and leverage differ from those for the firm overall.

Estimating the Unlevered Cost of Capital

We begin by reviewing the method introduced in Chapter 12 to calculate the unlevered cost of capital of a project with market risk that is very different from the rest of the firm. Suppose Avco launches a new plastics manufacturing division that faces different market risks than its main packaging business. What unlevered cost of capital would be appropriate for this division?

We can estimate r_U for the plastics division by looking at other single-division plastics firms that have similar business risks. For example, suppose two firms are comparable to the plastics division and have the following characteristics:

Firm	Equity Cost of Capital	Debt Cost of Capital	Debt-to-Value Ratio, $D/(E+D)$
Comparable #1	12.0%	6.0%	40%
Comparable #2	10.7%	5.5%	25%

Assuming that both firms maintain a target leverage ratio, we can estimate the unlevered cost of capital for each competitor by using the pretax WACC from Eq. 18.6:

$$\text{Competitor 1:} \quad r_U = 0.60 \times 12.0\% + 0.40 \times 6.0\% = 9.6\%$$

$$\text{Competitor 2:} \quad r_U = 0.75 \times 10.7\% + 0.25 \times 5.5\% = 9.4\%$$

Based on these comparable firms, we estimate an unlevered cost of capital for the plastics division of about 9.5%.[12] With this rate in hand, we can use the APV approach to calculate the value of Avco's investment in plastic manufacturing. To use either the WACC or FTE method, however, we need to estimate the project's equity cost of capital, which will depend on the incremental debt the firm will take on as a result of the project.

Project Leverage and the Equity Cost of Capital

Suppose the firm will fund the project according to a target leverage ratio. This leverage ratio may differ from the firm's overall leverage ratio, as different divisions or types of investments may have different optimal debt capacities. We can rearrange terms in Eq. 18.6 to get the following expression for the equity cost of capital:[13]

$$r_E = r_U + \frac{D}{E}(r_U - r_D) \tag{18.10}$$

Equation 18.10 shows that the project's equity cost of capital depends on its unlevered cost of capital, r_U, and the debt-equity ratio of the incremental financing that will be put in place to support the project. For example, suppose that Avco plans to maintain an equal mix of debt and equity financing as it expands into plastics manufacturing, and it expects its borrowing cost to remain at 6%. Given its 9.5% unlevered cost of capital, the plastics division's equity cost of capital is

$$r_E = 9.5\% + \frac{0.50}{0.50}(9.5\% - 6\%) = 13.0\%$$

Once we have the equity cost of capital, we can use Eq. 18.1 to determine the division's WACC:

$$r_{wacc} = 0.50 \times 13.0\% + 0.50 \times 6.0\% \times (1 - 0.40) = 8.3\%$$

---

[12]If we are using the CAPM to estimate expected returns, this procedure is equivalent to unlevering the betas of comparable firms using Eq. 12.9:

$$\beta_U = [E/(E+D)]\,\beta_E + [D/(D+E)]\,\beta_D.$$

[13]We derived this same expression with perfect capital markets in Eq. 14.5.

Based on these estimates, Avco should use a WACC of 8.3% for the plastics division, compared to the WACC of 6.8% for the packaging division that we calculated in Section 18.2.

In fact, we can combine Eq. 18.1 and Eq. 18.10 to obtain a direct formula for the WACC when the firm maintains a target leverage ratio for the project. If d is the project's debt-to-value ratio, $D/(E + D)$, then[14]

Project-Based WACC Formula

$$r_{wacc} = r_U - d\tau_c r_D \qquad (18.11)$$

For example, in the case of Avco's plastics division:

$$r_{wacc} = 9.5\% - 0.50 \times 0.40 \times 6\% = 8.3\%$$

EXAMPLE 18.5	**Computing Divisional Costs of Capital**

Problem

Hasco Corporation is a multinational provider of lumber and milling equipment. Currently, Hasco's equity cost of capital is 12.7%, and its borrowing cost is 6%. Hasco has traditionally maintained a 40% debt-to-value ratio. Hasco engineers have developed a GPS-based inventory control tracking system, which the company is considering developing commercially as a separate division. Management views the risk of this investment as similar to that of other technology companies' investments, with comparable firms typically having an unlevered cost of capital of 15%. Suppose Hasco plans to finance the new division using 10% debt financing (a constant debt-to-value ratio of 10%) with a borrowing rate of 6%, and its corporate tax rate is 35%. Estimate the unlevered, equity, and weighted average costs of capital for each division.

Solution

For the lumber and milling division, we can use the firm's current equity cost of capital $r_E = 12.7\%$ and debt-to-value ratio of 40%. Then

$$r_{wacc} = 0.60 \times 12.7\% + 0.40 \times 6\% \times (1 - 0.35) = 9.2\%$$

$$r_U = 0.60 \times 12.7\% + 0.40 \times 6\% = 10.0\%$$

For the technology division, we estimate its unlevered cost of capital using comparable firms: $r_U = 15\%$. Because Hasco's technology division will support 10% debt financing,

$$r_E = 15\% + \frac{0.10}{0.90}(15\% - 6\%) = 16\%$$

$$r_{wacc} = 15\% - 0.10 \times 0.35 \times 6\% = 14.8\%$$

Note that the cost of capital is quite different across the two divisions.

Determining the Incremental Leverage of a Project

To determine the equity or weighted average cost of capital for a project, we need to know the amount of debt to associate with the project. For capital budgeting purposes, the project's financing is the *incremental* financing that results if the firm takes on the project. That is, it is the change in the firm's total debt (net of cash) with the project versus without the project.

---

[14]We derive Eq. 18.11 (which is equivalent to Eq. 12.13) by comparing the WACC and pretax WACC in Eq. 18.1 and Eq. 18.6. This formula was proposed by R. Harris and J. Pringle, "Risk Adjusted Discount Rates: Transition from the Average Risk Case," *Journal of Financial Research* 8 (1985): 237–244.

| COMMON MISTAKE | Re-Levering the WACC |

When computing the WACC using its definition in Eq. 18.1, always remember that the equity and debt costs of capital, r_E and r_D, will change for different choices of the firm's leverage ratio. For example, consider a firm with a debt-to-value ratio of 25%, a debt cost of capital of 6.67%, an equity cost of capital of 12%, and a tax rate of 40%. From Eq. 18.1, its current WACC is

$$r_{wacc} = 0.75(12\%) + 0.25(6.67\%)(1 - 0.40)$$
$$= 10\%$$

Suppose the firm increases its debt-to-value ratio to 50%. It is tempting to conclude that its WACC will fall to

$$0.50(12\%) + 0.50(6.67\%)(1 - 0.40) = 8\%$$

In fact, when the firm increases leverage, its equity and debt cost of capital will rise. To compute the new WACC correctly, we must first determine the firm's unlevered cost of capital from Eq. 18.6:

$$r_U = 0.75(12\%) + 0.25(6.67\%) = 10.67\%$$

If the firm's debt cost of capital rises to 7.34% with the increase in leverage, then from Eq. 18.10 its equity cost of capital will rise as well:

$$r_E = 10.67\% + \frac{0.50}{0.50}(10.67\% - 7.34\%) = 14\%$$

Using Eq. 18.1, with the new equity and debt cost of capital, we can correctly compute the new WACC:

$$r_{wacc} = 0.50(14\%) + 0.50(7.34\%)(1 - 0.40)$$
$$= 9.2\%$$

We can also calculate the new WACC using Eq. 18.11:

$$r_{wacc} = 10.67\% - 0.50(0.40)(7.34\%) = 9.2\%$$

Note that if we fail to incorporate the effect of an increase in leverage on the firm's equity and debt costs of capital, we will overestimate the reduction in its WACC.

The incremental financing of a project need not correspond to the financing that is directly tied to the project. As an example, suppose a project involves buying a new warehouse, and the purchase of the warehouse is financed with a mortgage for 90% of its value. However, if the firm has an overall policy to maintain a 40% debt-to-value ratio, it will reduce debt elsewhere in the firm once the warehouse is purchased in an effort to maintain that ratio. In that case, the appropriate debt-to-value ratio to use when evaluating the warehouse project is 40%, not 90%.

Here are some important concepts to remember when determining the project's incremental financing.

Cash Is Negative Debt. A firm's leverage should be evaluated based on its debt net of any cash. Thus, if an investment will reduce the firm's cash holdings, it is equivalent to the firm adding leverage. Similarly, if the positive free cash flow from a project will increase the firm's cash holdings, then this growth in cash is equivalent to a reduction in the firm's leverage.

A Fixed Equity Payout Policy Implies 100% Debt Financing. Consider a firm whose dividend payouts and expenditures on share repurchases are set in advance and will not be affected by a project's free cash flow. In this case, the only source of financing is *debt*—any cash requirement of the project will be funded using the firm's cash or borrowing, and any cash that the project produces will be used to repay debt or increase the firm's cash. As a result, the incremental effect of the project on the firm's financing is to change the level of debt, so this project is 100% debt financed (that is, its debt-to-value ratio $d = 1$). If the firm's payout policy is fixed for the life of a project, the appropriate WACC for the project is $r_U - \tau_c r_D$. This case can be relevant for a highly levered firm that devotes its free cash flow to paying down its debt or for a firm that is hoarding cash.

Optimal Leverage Depends on Project *and* Firm Characteristics. Projects with safer cash flows can support more debt before they increase the risk of financial distress for the firm. But, as we discussed in Part 5, the likelihood of financial distress that a firm can bear depends on the magnitude of the distress, agency, and asymmetric information costs that it may face. These costs are not specific to a project, but rather depend on the characteristics of the entire firm. As a consequence, the optimal leverage for a project will depend on the characteristics of both the project and the firm.

Safe Cash Flows Can Be 100% Debt Financed. When an investment has risk-free cash flows, a firm can offset these cash flows 100% with debt and leave its overall risk unchanged. If it does so, the appropriate discount rate for safe cash flows is $r_D(1 - \tau_c)$.

EXAMPLE 18.6	**Debt Financing at Apple**

Problem

In mid-2012, Apple Inc. held nearly $28 billion in cash and securities and no debt. Consider a project with an unlevered cost of capital of $r_U = 12\%$. Suppose Apple's payout policy is completely fixed during the life of this project, so that the free cash flow from the project will affect only Apple's cash balance. If Apple earns 4% interest on its cash holdings and pays a 35% corporate tax rate, what cost of capital should Apple use to evaluate the project?

Solution

Because the inflows and outflows of the project change Apple's cash balance, the project is financed by 100% debt; that is, $d = 1$. The appropriate cost of capital for the project is

$$r_{wacc} = r_U - \tau_c r_D = 12\% - 0.35 \times 4\% = 10.6\%$$

Note that the project is effectively 100% debt financed, because even though Apple itself had no debt, if the cash had not been used to finance the project, Apple would have had to pay taxes on the interest the cash earned.

CONCEPT CHECK	1. How do we estimate a project's unlevered cost of capital when the project's risk is different from that of a firm?
	2. What is the incremental debt associated with a project?

18.6 APV with Other Leverage Policies

To this point, we have assumed that the incremental debt of a project is set to maintain a constant debt-equity (or, equivalently, debt-to-value) ratio. While a constant debt-equity ratio is a convenient assumption that simplifies the analysis, not all firms adopt this leverage policy. In this section, we consider two alternative leverage policies: constant interest coverage and predetermined debt levels.

When we relax the assumption of a constant debt-equity ratio, the equity cost of capital and WACC for a project will change over time as the debt-equity ratio changes. As a result, the WACC and FTE method are difficult to implement (see Section 18.8 for further details). The APV method, however, is relatively straightforward to use and is therefore the preferred method with alternative leverage policies.

Constant Interest Coverage Ratio

As discussed in Chapter 15, if a firm is using leverage to shield income from corporate taxes, then it will adjust its debt level so that its interest expenses grow with its earnings. In this case, it is natural to specify the firm's incremental interest payments as a target fraction, k, of the project's free cash flow:[15]

$$\text{Interest Paid in Year } t = k \times FCF_t \tag{18.12}$$

When the firm keeps its interest payments to a target fraction of its FCF, we say it has a **constant interest coverage ratio**.

To implement the APV approach, we must compute the present value of the tax shield under this policy. Because the tax shield is proportional to the project's free cash flow, it has the same risk as the project's cash flow and so should be discounted at the same rate—that is, the unlevered cost of capital, r_U. But the present value of the project's free cash flow at rate r_U is the unlevered value of the project. Thus,

$$PV(\text{Interest Tax Shield}) = PV(\tau_c k \times FCF) = \tau_c k \times PV(FCF)$$
$$= \tau_c k \times V^U \tag{18.13}$$

That is, with a constant interest coverage policy, the value of the interest tax shield is proportional to the project's unlevered value. Using the APV method, the value of the project with leverage is given by the following formula:

Levered Value with a Constant Interest Coverage Ratio

$$V^L = V^U + PV(\text{Interest Tax Shield}) = V^U + \tau_c k \times V^U$$
$$= (1 + \tau_c k) V^U \tag{18.14}$$

For example, we calculated the unlevered value of Avco's RFX project as $V^U = \$59.62$ million in Section 18.3. If Avco targets interest to be 20% of its free cash flow, the value with leverage is $V^L = [1 + 0.4\,(20\%)]\,59.62 = \$64.39$ million. (This result differs from the value of $61.25 million for the project that we calculated in Section 18.3, where we assumed a different leverage policy of a 50% debt-to-value ratio.)

Equation 18.14 provides a simple rule to determine an investment's levered value based on a leverage policy that may be appropriate for many firms.[16] Note also that if the investment's free cash flows are expected to grow at a constant rate, then the assumption of constant interest coverage and a constant debt-equity ratio are equivalent, as in the following example.

---

[15]It might be even better to specify interest as a fraction of taxable earnings. Typically, however, taxable earnings and free cash flows are roughly proportional, so the two specifications are very similar. Also, for Eq. 18.12 to hold exactly, the firm must adjust debt continuously throughout the year. We will relax this assumption in Section 18.8 to a setting in which the firm adjusts debt periodically based on its expected level of future free cash flow (see Example 18.10).

[16]J. Graham and C. Harvey report that a majority of firms target a credit rating when issuing debt ["The Theory and Practice of Corporate Finance: Evidence from the Field," *Journal of Financial Economics* 60 (2001)]. The interest coverage ratios are important determinants of credit ratings. Firms and rating agencies also consider the *book* debt-equity ratio, which often fluctuates more closely with a firm's cash flows, rather than with its market value. (For example, book equity increases when the firm invests in physical capital to expand, which generally results in higher cash flows.)

EXAMPLE 18.7	Valuing an Acquisition with Target Interest Coverage

Problem

Consider again Avco's acquisition from Examples 18.1 and 18.2. The acquisition will contribute $3.8 million in free cash flows the first year, growing by 3% per year thereafter. The acquisition cost of $80 million will be financed with $50 million in new debt initially. Compute the value of the acquisition using the APV method assuming Avco will maintain a constant interest coverage ratio for the acquisition.

Solution

Given Avco's unlevered cost of capital of $r_U = 8\%$, the acquisition has an unlevered value of

$$V^U = 3.8/(8\% - 3\%) = \$76 \text{ million}$$

With $50 million in new debt and a 6% interest rate, the interest expense the first year is $6\% \times 50 = \$3$ million, or $k = \text{Interest}/FCF = 3/3.8 = 78.95\%$. Because Avco will maintain this interest coverage, we can use Eq. 18.14 to compute the levered value:

$$V^L = (1 + \tau_c k)V^U = [1 + 0.4 \, (78.95\%)] \, 76 = \$100 \text{ million}$$

This value is identical to the value computed using the WACC method in Example 18.1, where we assumed a constant debt-equity ratio.

Predetermined Debt Levels

Rather than set debt according to a target debt-equity ratio or interest coverage level, a firm may adjust its debt according to a fixed schedule that is known in advance. Suppose, for example, that Avco plans to borrow $30.62 million and then will reduce the debt on a fixed schedule to $20 million after one year, to $10 million after two years, and to zero after three years. The RFX project will have no other consequences for Avco's leverage, regardless of its success. How can we value an investment like this one when its future *debt levels*, rather than the *debt-equity ratio*, are known in advance?

Because the debt levels are known, we can immediately compute the interest payments and the corresponding interest tax shield, as shown in Table 18.8.

At what rate should we discount this tax shield to determine the present value? In Section 18.3, we used the project's unlevered cost of capital because the amount of debt—and, therefore, the tax shield—fluctuated with the value of the project itself and so had similar risk. However, with a fixed debt schedule, the amount of the debt will not fluctuate. In this case, the tax shield is less risky than the project, so it should be discounted at a lower rate.

TABLE 18.8 SPREADSHEET	Interest Payments and Interest Tax Shield Given a Fixed Debt Schedule for Avco's RFX Project

	Year	0	1	2	3	4
Interest Tax Shield ($ million)						
1	**Debt Capacity, D_t (fixed schedule)**	30.62	20.00	10.00	—	—
2	Interest Paid (at $r_D = 6\%$)		1.84	1.20	0.60	—
3	**Interest Tax Shield (at $\tau_c = 40\%$)**		0.73	0.48	0.24	—

Indeed, the risk of the tax shield is similar to the risk of the debt payments. Therefore, we advise the following general rule:[17]

> When debt levels are set according to a fixed schedule, we can discount the predetermined interest tax shields using the debt cost of capital, r_D.

In Avco's case, $r_D = 6\%$:

$$PV \text{ (Interest Tax Shield)} = \frac{0.73}{1.06} + \frac{0.48}{1.06^2} + \frac{0.24}{1.06^3} = \$1.32 \text{ million}$$

We then combine the value of the tax shield with the unlevered value of the project (which we already computed in Section 18.3) to determine the APV:

$$V^L = V^U + PV \text{ (Interest Tax Shield)} = 59.62 + 1.32 = \$60.94 \text{ million}$$

The value of the interest tax shield computed here, \$1.32 million, differs from the value of \$1.63 million we computed in Section 18.3 based on constant debt-equity ratio. Comparing the firm's debt in the two cases, we see that it is paid off more rapidly in Table 18.8 than in Table 18.4. Also, because the debt-equity ratio for the project changes over time in this example, the project's WACC also changes, making it difficult—though not impossible—to apply the WACC method to this case. We show how to do so, and verify that we get the same result, as part of the advanced topics in Section 18.8.

A particularly simple example of a predetermined debt level occurs when the firm has permanent fixed debt, maintaining the same level of debt forever. We discussed this debt policy in Section 15.2 and showed that if the firm maintains a fixed level of debt, D, the value of the tax shield is $\tau_c \times D$.[18] Hence, the value of the levered project in this case is

Levered Value with Permanent Debt

$$V^L = V^U + \tau_c \times D \tag{18.15}$$

A Cautionary Note: When debt levels are predetermined, the firm will not adjust its debt based on fluctuations to its cash flows or value according to a target leverage ratio, and the risk of the interest tax shield differs from the risk of the cash flows. As a result, *the firm's pretax WACC no longer coincides with its unlevered cost of capital, so Eq. 18.6, Eq. 18.10, and Eq. 18.11 do not apply.* (For example, if we compute the WACC using Eq. 18.11 and apply it in the case of permanent debt, the value we estimate will *not* be consistent with Eq. 18.15.) For the correct relationship between the firm's WACC, unlevered, and equity cost of capital, we need to use more general versions of these equations, which we provide in Eq. 18.20 and Eq. 18.21 in Section 18.8.

A Comparison of Methods

We have introduced three methods for valuing levered investments: WACC, APV, and FTE. How do we decide which method to use in which circumstances?

When used consistently, each method produces the same valuation for the investment. Thus, the choice of method is largely a matter of convenience. As a general rule, the

---

[17]The risk of the tax shield is not literally equivalent to that of the debt payments, because it is based on only the interest portion of the payments and is subject to the risk of fluctuations in the firm's marginal tax rate. Nevertheless, this assumption is a reasonable approximation absent much more detailed information.

[18]Because the interest tax shield is $\tau_c r_D D$ in perpetuity, using the discount rate r_D we get $PV \text{(Interest Tax Shield)} = \tau_c r_D D / r_D = \tau_c D$.

WACC method is the easiest to use when the firm will maintain a fixed debt-to-value ratio over the life of the investment. For alternative leverage policies, the APV method is usually the most straightforward approach. The FTE method is typically used only in complicated settings for which the values of other securities in the firm's capital structure or the interest tax shield are themselves difficult to determine.

<table>
<tr><td>CONCEPT CHECK</td><td>1. What condition must the firm meet to have a constant interest coverage policy?

2. What is the appropriate discount rate for tax shields when the debt schedule is fixed in advance?</td></tr>
</table>

18.7 Other Effects of Financing

The WACC, APV, and FTE methods determine the value of an investment incorporating the tax shields associated with leverage. However, as we discussed in Chapter 16, some other potential imperfections are associated with leverage. In this section, we investigate ways to adjust our valuation to account for imperfections such as issuance costs, security mispricing, and financial distress and agency costs.

Issuance and Other Financing Costs

When a firm takes out a loan or raises capital by issuing securities, the banks that provide the loan or underwrite the sale of the securities charge fees. Table 18.9 lists the typical fees for common transactions. The fees associated with the financing of the project are a cost that should be included as part of the project's required investment, reducing the NPV of the project.

For example, suppose a project has a levered value of $20 million and requires an initial investment of $15 million. To finance the project, the firm will borrow $10 million and fund the remaining $5 million by reducing dividends. If the bank providing the loan charges fees (after any tax deductions) totaling $200,000, the project NPV is

$$NPV = V^L - (\text{Investment}) - (\text{After Tax Issuance Costs}) = 20 - 15 - 0.2 = \$4.8 \text{ million}$$

TABLE 18.9	**Typical Issuance Costs for Different Securities, as a Percentage of Proceeds**[19]

Financing Type	Underwriting Fees
Bank loans	< 2%
Corporate bonds	
Investment grade	1–2%
Non-investment grade	2–3%
Equity issues	
Initial public offering	8–9%
Seasoned equity offering	5–6%

---

[19]Fees vary by transaction size; estimates here are based on typical legal, underwriting, and accounting fees for a $50 million transaction. For example, see I. Lee, S. Lochhead, J. Ritter, and Q. Zhao, "The Cost of Raising Capital," *Journal of Financial Research* 19 (1996): 59–74.

Security Mispricing

With perfect capital markets, all securities are fairly priced and issuing securities is a zero-NPV transaction. However, as discussed in Chapter 16, sometimes management may believe that the securities they are issuing are priced at less than (or more than) their true value. If so, the NPV of the transaction, which is the difference between the actual money raised and the true value of the securities sold, should be included when evaluating the decision. For example, if the financing of the project involves an equity issue, and if management believes that the equity will sell at a price that is less than its true value, this mispricing is a cost of the project for the *existing* shareholders.[20] It can be deducted from the project NPV in addition to other issuance costs.

When a firm borrows funds, a mispricing scenario arises if the interest rate charged differs from the rate that is appropriate given the actual risk of the loan. For example, a firm may pay an interest rate that is too high if news that would improve its credit rating has not yet become public. With the WACC method, the cost of the higher interest rate will result in a higher weighted average cost of capital and a lower value for the investment. With the APV method, we must add to the value of the project the NPV of the loan cash flows when evaluated at the "correct" rate that corresponds to their actual risk.[21]

| EXAMPLE 18.8 | Valuing a Loan |

Problem

Gap, Inc., is considering borrowing \$100 million to fund an expansion of its stores. Given investors' uncertainty regarding its prospects, Gap will pay a 6% interest rate on this loan. The firm's management knows, however, that the actual risk of the loan is extremely low and that the appropriate rate on the loan is 5%. Suppose the loan is for five years, with all principal being repaid in the fifth year. If Gap's marginal corporate tax rate is 40%, what is the net effect of the loan on the value of the expansion?

Solution

Shown below are the cash flows (in \$ million) and interest tax shields of a fair loan, at a 5% interest rate, and of the above-market rate loan Gap will receive, with a 6% interest rate. For each loan, we compute both the NPV of the loan cash flows and the present value of the interest tax shields, using the correct rate $r_D = 5\%$.

		Year	0	1	2	3	4	5
1	Fair Loan		100.00	(5.00)	(5.00)	(5.00)	(5.00)	(105.00)
2	Interest Tax Shield			2.00	2.00	2.00	2.00	2.00
3	At $r_D = 5\%$:							
4	NPV(Loan Cash Flows)		0.00					
5	PV(Interest Tax Shield)		8.66					
6	Actual Loan		100.00	(6.00)	(6.00)	(6.00)	(6.00)	(106.00)
7	Interest Tax Shield			2.40	2.40	2.40	2.40	2.40
8	At $r_D = 5\%$:							
9	NPV(Loan Cash Flows)		(4.33)					
10	PV(Interest Tax Shield)		10.39					

For the fair loan, note that the NPV of the loan cash flows is zero. Thus, the benefit of the loan on the project's value is the present value of the interest tax shield of \$8.66 million. For

---

[20] New shareholders, of course, benefit from receiving the shares at a low price.

[21] We must also use the correct rate for r_D when levering or unlevering the cost of capital.

the actual loan, the higher interest rate increases the value of the interest tax shield but implies a negative NPV for the loan cash flows. The combined effect of the loan on the project's value is

$$NPV \text{ (Loan Cash Flows)} + PV \text{ (Interest Tax Shield)} = -4.33 + 10.39 = \$6.06 \text{ million}$$

While leverage is still valuable due to the tax shields, paying the higher interest rate reduces its benefit to the firm by $8.66 - 6.06 = \$2.60$ million.

Financial Distress and Agency Costs

As discussed in Chapter 16, one consequence of debt financing is the possibility of financial distress and agency costs. Because these costs affect the future free cash flows that will be generated by the project, they can be incorporated directly into the estimates of the project's expected free cash flows. When the debt level—and, therefore, the probability of financial distress—is high, the expected free cash flow will be reduced by the expected costs associated with financial distress and agency problems. (Conversely, as we also noted in Chapter 16, in some situations the threat of default can also prompt management to improve efficiency and thereby increase the firm's free cash flow.)

Financial distress and agency costs also have consequences for the cost of capital. For example, financial distress is more likely to occur when economic times are bad. As a result, the costs of distress cause the value of the firm to fall further in a market downturn. Financial distress costs therefore tend to increase the sensitivity of the firm's value to market risk, further raising the cost of capital for highly levered firms.[22]

How do we incorporate financial distress costs into the valuation methods described in this chapter? One approach is to adjust our free cash flow estimates to account for the costs, and increased risk, resulting from financial distress. An alternative method is to first value the project ignoring these costs, and then add the present value of the incremental cash flows associated with financial distress and agency problems separately. Because these costs tend to occur only when a firm is in (or near) default, valuing them is complicated and best done using the option valuation techniques introduced in Part 7. In some special

---

GLOBAL FINANCIAL CRISIS   Government Loan Guarantees

In times of crisis, firms may appeal to the federal government for financial assistance. Often, such aid comes in the form of subsidized loans or loan guarantees. For example, in the wake of the September 11, 2001 tragedy, the U.S. government made available $10 billion in loan guarantees to enable air carriers to obtain credit. U.S. Airways received the largest loan guarantee of $900 million, and America West Airlines received the second largest, for $429 million. Ultimately, these loans were repaid without taxpayer expense.

Loan guarantees were also an important part of the government's response to the 2008 financial crisis. The U.S. government has insured over $1 trillion in debt issued by financial institutions or assets held by the banks. The government also made over $500 billion in direct loans to distressed firms. Moreover, firms and banks viewed as "too big to fail" were thought to have implicit guarantees even if they did not have explicit ones.

These guarantees enabled firms to obtain loans at a lower interest rate than they otherwise would have received without government assistance. If these loans were fairly priced at market rates, then the loans obtained with the help of the federal guarantee had a positive NPV for the borrowers, and were equivalent to a direct cash subsidy. If, on the other hand, market rates for these loans were too high—due perhaps to asymmetric information or a lack of available lenders—then these loans and guarantees may have improved terms for borrowers at a lower cost to taxpayers than a direct cash bailout.

---

[22]In other words, distress costs tend to have a negative beta (they are higher in bad times). Because they are a *cost*, including them in the firm's free cash flows will raise the beta of the firm.

cases, however, we can use the values of the firm's existing securities to estimate the value of distress costs, as in the following example.

EXAMPLE 18.9

Valuing Distress Costs

Problem

Your firm has zero coupon debt with a face value of $100 million due in 5 years time, and no other debt outstanding. The current risk-free rate is 5%, but due to default risk the yield to maturity of the debt is 12%. You believe that in the event of default, 1/3 of the losses are attributable to bankruptcy and distress costs. (For example, if the debt holders lose $60 million and recover $40 million, $20 million of the loss in value would not have occurred if the firm had been unlevered and thus avoided bankruptcy.) Estimate the present value of the distress costs.

Solution

With a 12% yield, the current market value of the firm's debt is $100/1.12^5 = $56.74 million. If the firm's debt were risk-free, its market value would be $100/1.05^5 = $78.35 million. The difference in these values, $78.35 − $56.74 = $21.61 million, is the present value of the debt holders' expected losses in default. If 1/3 of these losses is due to bankruptcy and distress costs, then the present value of these costs is $21.61/3 = $7.2 million.

CONCEPT CHECK

1. How do we deal with issuance costs and security mispricing costs in our assessment of a project's value?

2. How would financial distress and agency costs affect a firm's use of leverage?

18.8 Advanced Topics in Capital Budgeting

In the previous sections, we have highlighted the most important methods for capital budgeting with leverage and demonstrated their application in common settings. In this section, we consider several more complicated scenarios and show how our tools can be extended to these cases. First, we consider leverage policies in which firms keep debt fixed in the short run, but adjust to a target leverage ratio in the long run. Second, we look at the relationship between a firm's equity and unlevered cost of capital for alternative leverage policies. Third, we implement the WACC and FTE methods when the firm's debt-equity ratio changes over time. We then conclude the section by incorporating the effects of personal taxes.

Periodically Adjusted Debt

To this point, we have considered leverage policies in which debt is either adjusted continuously to a target leverage ratio[23] or set according to a fixed plan that will never change. As Figure 18.1 shows, most real-world firms do not, in fact, appear to adjust debt levels continuously to maintain a target leverage ratio at all times. (See Figure 15.6 in Chapter 15 for the behavior of aggregate leverage ratios over time.) Instead, most firms allow the debt-equity ratio of the firm to stray from the target and periodically adjust leverage to bring it back into line with the target. Next, we consider the effect of such a debt policy.

---

[23]While we have simplified our exposition earlier in the chapter by calculating debt and interest payments on an annual basis, the formulas we have used in the case of a target leverage ratio or interest coverage ratio are based on the assumption that the firm maintains the target leverage ratio or interest coverage during the year.

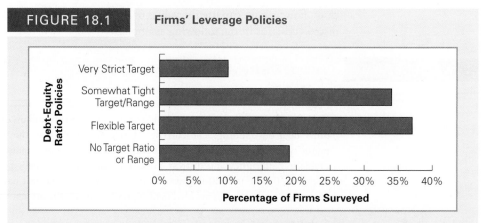

FIGURE 18.1   **Firms' Leverage Policies**

Of 392 CFOs surveyed by Professors J. Graham and C. Harvey, 81% reported having a target debt-equity ratio. However, only 10% of respondents viewed the target as set in stone. Most were willing to let the debt-equity ratio of the firm stray from the target and periodically adjust leverage to bring it back into line.

Source: J. R. Graham and C. Harvey, "The Theory and Practice of Corporate Finance: Evidence from the Field," *Journal of Financial Economics* 60 (2001): 187–243.

Suppose the firm adjusts its leverage every s periods, as shown in Figure 18.2. Then the firm's interest tax shields up to date s are predetermined, so they should be discounted at rate r_D. In contrast, interest tax shields that occur after date s depend on future adjustments the firm will make to its debt, so they are risky. If the firm will adjust the debt according to a target debt-equity ratio or interest coverage level, then the future interest tax shields should be discounted at rate r_D for the periods that they are known, but at rate r_U for all earlier periods when they are still risky.

An important special ase is when the debt is adjusted annually. In that case, the expected interest expense on date t, Int_t, is known as of date $t-1$. Therefore, we discount the interest tax shield at rate r_D for one period, from date t to $t-1$ (because it will be known at that time), and then discount it from date $t-1$ to 0 at rate r_U:

$$PV(\tau_c \times Int_t) = \frac{\tau_c \times Int_t}{(1+r_U)^{t-1}(1+r_D)} = \frac{\tau_c \times Int_t}{(1+r_U)^t} \times \left(\frac{1+r_U}{1+r_D}\right) \qquad (18.16)$$

Equation 18.16 implies that we can value the tax shield by discounting it at rate r_U as before, and then multiply the result by the factor $(1+r_U)/(1+r_D)$ to account for the fact that the tax shield is known one year in advance.

This same adjustment can be applied to other valuation methods as well. For example, when the debt is adjusted annually rather than continuously to a target debt-to-value ratio d, the project-based WACC formula of Eq. 18.11 becomes[24]

$$r_{wacc} = r_U - d\,\tau_c\, r_D \frac{1+r_U}{1+r_D} \qquad (18.17)$$

---

[24]An equivalent WACC formula was proposed by J. Miles and J. Ezzell, "The Weighted Average Cost of Capital, Perfect Capital Markets and Project Life: A Clarification," *Journal of Financial and Quantitative Analysis* 15 (1980): 719–730.

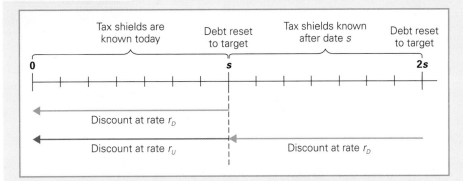

FIGURE 18.2   **Discounting the Tax Shield with Periodic Adjustments**

If the debt is reset to a target leverage ratio every s periods, then interest tax shields within the first s periods are known and should be discounted at rate r_D. Interest tax shields that occur after date s are not yet known, so they should be discounted at rate r_D for the periods when they will be known and at rate r_U for earlier periods.

Similarly, when the firm sets debt annually based on its expected future free cash flow, the constant interest coverage model in Eq. 18.14 becomes

$$V^L = \left(1 + \tau_c k \frac{1 + r_U}{1 + r_D}\right)V^U \tag{18.18}$$

Example 18.10 illustrates these methods in a constant growth setting.

EXAMPLE 18.10   **Annual Debt Ratio Targeting**

Problem
Celmax Corporation expects free cash flows this year of $7.36 million and a future growth rate of 4% per year. The firm currently has $30 million in debt outstanding. This leverage will remain fixed during the year, but at the end of each year Celmax will increase or decrease its debt to maintain a constant debt-equity ratio. Celmax pays 5% interest on its debt, pays a corporate tax rate of 40%, and has an unlevered cost of capital of 12%. Estimate Celmax's value with this leverage policy.

Solution
Using the APV approach, the unlevered value is $V^U = 7.36/(12\% - 4\%) = \$92.0$ million. In the first year, Celmax will have an interest tax shield of $\tau_c\, r_D\, D = 0.40 \times 5\% \times \$30$ million $= \$0.6$ million. Because Celmax will adjust its debt after one year, the tax shields are expected to grow by 4% per year with the firm. The present value of the interest tax shield is therefore

$$PV\,(\text{Interest Tax Shield}) = \underbrace{\frac{0.6}{(12\% - 4\%)}}_{PV \text{ at rate } r_U} \times \underbrace{\left(\frac{1.12}{1.05}\right)}_{\substack{\text{Debt is set 1 year} \\ \text{in advance}}} = \$8.0 \text{ million}$$

Therefore, $V^L = V^U + PV\,(\text{Interest Tax Shield}) = 92.0 + 8.0 = \$100.0$ million.

We can also apply the WACC method. From Eq. 18.17, Celmax's WACC is

$$r_{wacc} = r_U - d\,\tau_c\,r_D\frac{1 + r_U}{1 + r_D} = 12\% - \frac{30}{100}(0.40)(5\%)\frac{1.12}{1.05}$$

$$= 11.36\%$$

Therefore, $V^L = 7.36/(11.36\% - 4\%) = \$100$ million.

Finally, the constant interest coverage model can be applied (in this setting with constant growth, a constant debt-equity ratio implies a constant interest coverage ratio). Given interest of $5\% \times \$30$ million $= \$1.50$ million this year, from Eq. 18.18,

$$V^L = \left(1 + \tau_c\,k\frac{1 + r_U}{1 + r_D}\right)V^U$$

$$= \left(1 + 0.40 \times \frac{1.50}{7.36} \times \frac{1.12}{1.05}\right)92.0 = \$100 \text{ million}$$

Leverage and the Cost of Capital

The relationship between leverage and the project's costs of capital in Eq. 18.6, Eq. 18.10, and Eq. 18.11 relies on the assumption that the firm maintains a target leverage ratio. That relationship holds because in that case the interest tax shields have the same risk as the firm's cash flows. But when debt is set according to a fixed schedule for some period of time, the interest tax shields for the scheduled debt are known, relatively safe cash flows. These safe cash flows will reduce the effect of leverage on the risk of the firm's equity. To account for this effect, we should deduct the value of these "safe" tax shields from the debt—in the same way that we deduct cash—when evaluating a firm's leverage. That is, if T^s is the present value of the interest tax shields from predetermined debt, the risk of a firm's equity will depend on its *debt net of the predetermined tax shields*:

$$D^s = D - T^s \tag{18.19}$$

We show in this chapter's appendix that Eq. 18.6 and Eq. 18.10 continue to apply with D replaced by D^s, so that the more general relationship between the unlevered and equity costs of capital are related as follows:

Leverage and the Cost of Capital with a Fixed Debt Schedule

$$r_U = \frac{E}{E + D^s}r_E + \frac{D^s}{E + D^s}r_D \quad \text{or, equivalently,} \quad r_E = r_U + \frac{D^s}{E}(r_U - r_D) \tag{18.20}$$

We can also combine Eq. 18.20 with the definition of the WACC in Eq. 18.1 and generalize the project-based WACC formula in Eq. 18.11:

Project WACC with a Fixed Debt Schedule

$$r_{wacc} = r_U - d\,\tau_c\,[r_D + \phi(r_U - r_D)] \tag{18.21}$$

where $d = D/(D + E)$ is the debt-to-value ratio, and $\phi = T^s/(\tau_c D)$ is a measure of the permanence of the debt level, D. Here are three cases commonly used in practice, which differ according to the frequency with which the debt is assumed to adjust to the growth of the investment:[25]

1. Continuously adjusted debt: $T^s = 0$, $D^s = D$, and $\phi = 0$

2. Annually adjusted debt: $T^s = \dfrac{\tau_c r_D D}{1 + r_D}$, $D^s = D\left(1 - \tau_c \dfrac{r_D}{1 + r_D}\right)$, and $\phi = \dfrac{r_D}{1 + r_D}$

3. Permanent debt: $T^s = \tau_c D$, $D^s = D(1 - \tau_c)$, and $\phi = 1$

Finally, note that unless d and ϕ remain constant over time, the WACC and equity cost of capital must be computed period by period.

EXAMPLE 18.11

APV and WACC with Permanent Debt

Problem

International Paper Company is considering the acquisition of additional forestland in the southeastern United States. The wood harvested from the land will generate free cash flows of $4.5 million per year, with an unlevered cost of capital of 7%. As a result of this acquisition, International Paper will permanently increase its debt by $30 million. If International Paper's tax rate is 35%, what is the value of this acquisition using the APV method? Verify this result using the WACC method.

Solution

Using the APV method, the unlevered value of the land is $V^U = FCF/r_U = 4.5/0.07 = \$64.29$ million. Because the debt is permanent, the value of the tax shield is $\tau_c D = 0.35(30) = 10.50$. Therefore, $V^L = 64.29 + 10.50 = \$74.79$ million.

To use the WACC method, we apply Eq. 18.21 with $\phi = T^s/(\tau_c D) = 1$ and $d = 30/74.79 = 40.1\%$. Therefore, the WACC for the investment is

$$r_{wacc} = r_U - d\,\tau_c r_U = 7\% - 0.401 \times 0.35 \times 7\% = 6.017\%$$

and $V^L = 4.5/0.06017 = \$74.79$ million.

The WACC or FTE Method with Changing Leverage

When a firm does not maintain a constant debt-equity ratio for a project, the APV method is generally the most straightforward method to apply. The WACC and FTE methods become more difficult to use because when the proportion of debt financing changes, the project's equity cost of capital and WACC will not remain constant over time. With a bit of care, however, these methods can still be used (and, of course, will lead to the same result as the APV method).

As an example, let's see how we would apply the WACC or FTE methods to the RFX project when Avco has the fixed debt schedule we analyzed earlier using the APV method. The spreadsheet in Table 18.10 computes the equity cost of capital and WACC for the

---

[25]Case 1 reduces to the Harris-Pringle formula (see footnote 14), case 2 is the Miles-Ezzell formula (see footnote 24), and case 3 is equivalent to the Modigliani-Miller-Hamada formula with permanent debt. See F. Modigliani and M. Miller, "Corporate Income Taxes and the Cost of Capital: A Correction," *American Economic Review* 53 (1963): 433–443; and R. Hamada, "The Effect of a Firm's Capital Structure on the Systematic Risks of Common Stocks," *Journal of Finance* 27 (1972): 435–452.

TABLE 18.10 SPREADSHEET	Adjusted Present Value and Cost of Capital for Avco's RFX Project with a Fixed Debt Schedule

Year	0	1	2	3	4
Unlevered Value ($ million)					
1 Free Cash Flow	(28.00)	18.00	18.00	18.00	18.00
2 Unlevered Value, V^U (at $r_u = 8.0\%$)	59.62	46.39	32.10	16.67	—
Interest Tax Shield					
3 Debt Schedule, D_t	30.62	20.00	10.00	—	—
4 Interest Paid (at $r_d = 6\%$)	—	1.84	1.20	0.60	—
5 Interest Tax Shield (at $\tau_c = 40\%$)	—	0.73	0.48	0.24	—
6 Tax Shield Value, T^s (at $r_D = 6.0\%$)	1.32	0.67	0.23	—	—
Adjusted Present Value					
7 **Levered Value, $V^L = V^U + T^s$**	**60.94**	**47.05**	**32.33**	**16.67**	**—**
Effective Leverage and Cost of Capital					
8 Equity, $E = V^L - D$	30.32	27.05	22.33	16.67	—
9 Effective Debt, $D^s = D - T^s$	29.30	19.33	9.77	—	—
10 Effective Debt-Equity Ratio, D^s/E	0.966	0.715	0.438	0.000	
11 **Equity Cost of Capital, r_E**	**9.93%**	**9.43%**	**8.88%**	**8.00%**	
12 **WACC, r_{wacc}**	**6.75%**	**6.95%**	**7.24%**	**8.00%**	

RFX project each year given the fixed debt schedule shown in line 3. The project's value is computed using the APV method in line 7 as the total of the unlevered and tax shield values. With the project's equity value and net debt D^s in hand, we can use Eq. 18.20 to calculate the project's equity cost of capital each year (line 11). Note that the equity cost of capital declines over time as the project's leverage ratio D^s/E declines. By year 3, the debt is fully repaid and the equity cost of capital equals the unlevered cost of capital of 8%.

Given the project's equity cost of capital, we compute its WACC using Eq. 18.1 in line 12. For example, at the beginning of the project,

$$r_{wacc} = \frac{E}{E+D}r_E + \frac{D}{E+D}r_D(1 - \tau_c)$$

$$= \frac{30.32}{60.94}9.93\% + \frac{30.62}{60.94}6\%(1 - 0.40) = 6.75\%$$

Note that as the leverage of the project falls, its WACC rises, until it eventually equals the unlevered cost of capital of 8% when the project debt is fully repaid at year 3.

Once we have computed the WACC or the equity cost of capital, we can value the project using the WACC or FTE method. Because the cost of capital changes over time, we must use a different discount rate each year when applying these methods. For example, using the WACC method, the levered value each year is computed as

$$V_t^L = \frac{FCF_{t+1} + V_{t+1}^L}{1 + r_{wacc}(t)} \tag{18.22}$$

where $r_{wacc}(t)$ is the project's WACC in year t. This calculation is shown in Table 18.11. Note that the levered value matches the result from the APV method (line 7 in Table 18.10). The same approach can be used when applying the FTE method.[26]

---

[26]You will notice, however, that we used the APV to compute the debt-equity ratio each period, which we needed to calculate r_E and r_{wacc}. If we had not already solved for the APV, we would need to determine the project's value and WACC simultaneously, using the approach described in this chapter's appendix.

TABLE 18.11 SPREADSHEET	WACC Method for Avco's RFX Project with a Fixed Debt Schedule					
Year	**0**	**1**	**2**	**3**	**4**

	Year	0	1	2	3	4
WACC Method ($ million)						
1 Free Cash Flow		(28.00)	18.00	18.00	18.00	18.00
2 WACC, r_{wacc}			6.75%	6.95%	7.24%	8.00%
3 **Levered Value V^L (at r_{wacc})**		**60.94**	**47.05**	**32.33**	**16.67**	—

Personal Taxes

As we discussed in Chapter 15, leverage has tax consequences for both investors and corporations. For individuals, interest income from debt is generally taxed more heavily than income from equity (capital gains and dividends). So how do personal taxes affect our valuation methods?

If investors are taxed on the income they receive from holding equity or debt, it will raise the return they require to hold those securities. That is, the equity and debt cost of capital in the market *already* reflects the effects of investor taxes. As a result, *the WACC method does not change in the presence of investor taxes*; we can continue to compute the WACC according to Eq. 18.1 and compute the levered value as in Section 18.2.

The APV approach, however, requires modification in the presence of investor taxes because it requires that we compute the unlevered cost of capital. This computation *is* affected by the presence of investor taxes. Let τ_e be the tax rate investors pay on equity income (dividends) and τ_i be the tax rate investors pay on interest income. Then, given an expected return on debt r_D, define r_D^* as the expected return on equity income that would give investors the same after-tax return: $r_D^*(1 - \tau_e) = r_D(1 - \tau_i)$. So

$$r_D^* \equiv r_D \frac{(1 - \tau_i)}{(1 - \tau_e)} \tag{18.23}$$

Because the unlevered cost of capital is for a hypothetical firm that is all equity, investors' tax rates on income for such a firm are the equity rates, so we must use the rate r_D^* when computing the unlevered cost of capital. Therefore, Eq. 18.20 becomes

Unlevered Cost of Capital with Personal Taxes

$$r_U = \frac{E}{E + D^s} r_E + \frac{D^s}{E + D^s} r_D^* \tag{18.24}$$

Next, we must compute the interest tax shield using the effective tax advantage of debt, τ^*, in place of τ_c. The effective tax rate τ^* incorporates the investors' tax rate on equity income, τ_e, and on interest income, τ_i, and was defined in Chapter 15 as follows:

$$\tau^* = 1 - \frac{(1 - \tau_c)(1 - \tau_e)}{(1 - \tau_i)} \tag{18.25}$$

Then, we calculate the interest tax shield using tax rate τ^* and interest rate r_D^*:

$$\text{Interest Tax Shield in Year } t = \tau^* \times r_D^* \times D_{t-1} \tag{18.26}$$

Finally we discount the interest tax shields at rate r_U if the firm maintains a target leverage ratio or at rate r_D^* if the debt is set according to a predetermined schedule.[27]

EXAMPLE 18.12 | **Using the APV Method with Personal Taxes**

Problem

Apex Corporation has an equity cost of capital of 14.4% and a debt cost of capital of 6%, and the firm maintains a debt-equity ratio of 1. Apex is considering an expansion that will contribute $4 million in free cash flows the first year, growing by 4% per year thereafter. The expansion will cost $60 million and will be financed with $40 million in new debt initially with a constant debt-equity ratio maintained thereafter. Apex's corporate tax rate is 40%; the tax rate on interest income is 40%; and the tax rate on equity income is 20%. Compute the value of the expansion using the APV method.

Solution

First, we compute the value without leverage. From Eq. 18.23, the debt cost of capital of 6% is equivalent to an equity rate of

$$r_D^* = r_D \frac{1 - \tau_i}{1 - \tau_e} = 6\% \times \frac{1 - 0.40}{1 - 0.20} = 4.5\%$$

Because Apex maintains a constant debt-equity ratio, $D^s = D$ and Apex's unlevered cost of capital is, using Eq. 18.24,

$$r_U = \frac{E}{E + D^s} r_E + \frac{D^s}{E + D^s} r_D^* = 0.50 \times 14.4\% + 0.50 \times 4.5\% = 9.45\%$$

Therefore, $V^U = 4/(9.45\% - 4\%) = \$73.39$ million.

From Eq. 18.25, the effective tax advantage of debt is

$$\tau^* = 1 - \frac{(1 - \tau_c)(1 - \tau_e)}{(1 - \tau_i)} = 1 - \frac{(1 - 0.40)(1 - 0.20)}{(1 - 0.40)} = 20\%$$

Apex will add new debt of $40 million initially, so from Eq. 18.26 the interest tax shield is $20\% \times 4.5\% \times 40 = \$0.36$ million the first year (note that we use r_D^* here). With a growth rate of 4%, the present value of the interest tax shield is

$$PV \text{ (Interest Tax Shield)} = 0.36/(9.45\% - 4\%) = \$6.61 \text{ million}$$

Therefore, the value of the expansion with leverage is given by the APV:

$$V^L = V^U + PV \text{ (Interest Tax Shield)} = 73.39 + 6.61 = \$80 \text{ million}$$

Given the cost of $60 million, the expansion has an NPV of $20 million.

Let's check this result using the WACC method. Note that the expansion has the same debt-to-value ratio of $40/80 = 50\%$ as the firm overall. Thus, its WACC is equal to the firm's WACC:

$$r_{wacc} = \frac{E}{E + D} r_E + \frac{D}{E + D} r_D (1 - \tau_c)$$

$$= 0.50 \times 14.4\% + 0.50 \times 6\% \times (1 - 0.40) = 9\%$$

Therefore, $V^L = 4/(9\% - 4\%) = \$80$ million, as before.

---

[27]If the debt is permanent, for example, the value of the tax shield is $\tau^* r_D^* D/r_D^* = \tau^* D$. as shown in Chapter 15.

As Example 18.12 illustrates, the WACC method is much simpler to apply than the APV method in the case with investor taxes. More significantly, the WACC approach does not require knowledge of investors' tax rates. This fact is important because in practice, estimating the marginal tax rate of the investor can be very difficult.

However, if the investment's leverage or risk does not match the firm's, then investor tax rates are required even with the WACC method, as we must unlever and/or re-lever the firm's cost of capital using Eq. 18.24. When the investor's tax rate on interest income exceeds that on equity income, an increase in leverage will lead to a smaller reduction in the WACC (see Problem 26).

CONCEPT CHECK

1. When a firm has pre-determined tax shields, how do we measure its net debt when calculating its unlevered cost of capital?

2. If the firm's debt-equity ratio changes over time, can the WACC method still be applied?

MyFinanceLab
Here is what you should know after reading this chapter. MyFinanceLab will help you identify what you know and where to go when you need to practice.

18.1 Overview of Key Concepts
- The three main methods of capital budgeting are weighted average cost of capital (WACC), adjusted present value (APV), and flow-to-equity (FTE).

18.2 The Weighted Average Cost of Capital
- The key steps in the WACC valuation method are as follows:
  - Determine the unlevered free cash flows of the investment.
  - Compute the weighted average cost of capital:

$$r_{wacc} = \frac{E}{E+D}r_E + \frac{D}{E+D}r_D(1-\tau_c) \qquad (18.1)$$

  - Compute the value with leverage, V^L, by discounting the free cash flows of the investment using the WACC.

18.3 The Adjusted Present Value Method
- To determine the value of a levered investment using the APV method, proceed as follows:
  - Determine the investment's value without leverage, V^U, by discounting its free cash flows at the unlevered cost of capital, r_U.
  - Determine the present value of the interest tax shield.
    a. Given debt D_t on date t, the tax shield on date $t+1$ is $\tau_c r_D D_t$.
    b. If the debt level varies with the investment's value or free cash flow, use discount rate r_U. (If the debt is predetermined, discount the tax shield at rate r_D. See Section 18.6.)
  - Add the unlevered value V^U to the present value of the interest tax shield to determine the value of the investment with leverage, V^L.

18.4 The Flow-to-Equity Method
- The key steps in the flow-to-equity method for valuing a levered investment are as follows:
  - Determine the free cash flow to equity of the investment:

$$FCFE = FCF - (1-\tau_c) \times (\text{Interest Payments}) + (\text{Net Borrowing}) \qquad (18.9)$$

  - Compute the contribution to equity value, E, by discounting the free cash flow to equity using the equity cost of capital.

18.5 Project-Based Costs of Capital

■ If a project's risk is different from that of the firm as a whole, we must estimate its cost of capital separately from the firm's cost of capital. We estimate the project's unlevered cost of capital by looking at the unlevered cost of capital for other firms with similar market risk as the project.

■ With a target leverage ratio, the unlevered, equity, and weighted average costs of capital are related as follows:

$$r_U = \frac{E}{E+D}r_E + \frac{D}{E+D}r_D = \text{Pretax WACC} \tag{18.6}$$

$$r_E = r_U + \frac{D}{E}(r_U - r_D) \tag{18.10}$$

$$r_{wacc} = r_U - d\,\tau_c\,r_D, \tag{18.11}$$

where $d = D/(D+E)$ is the project's debt-to-value ratio.

■ When assessing the leverage associated with a project, we must consider its incremental impact on the debt, net of cash balances, of the firm overall and not just the specific financing used for that investment.

18.6 APV with Other Leverage Policies

■ A firm has a constant interest coverage policy if it sets debt to maintain its interest expenses as a fraction, k, of free cash flow. The levered value of a project with such a leverage policy is $V^L = (1 + \tau_c k)V^U$.

■ When debt levels are set according to a fixed schedule:
  ▪ We can discount the predetermined interest tax shields using the debt cost of capital, r_D.
  ▪ The unlevered cost of capital can no longer be computed as the pretax WACC (see Section 18.8).

■ If a firm chooses to keep the level of debt at a constant level, D, permanently, then the levered value of a project with such a leverage policy is $V^L = V^U + \tau_c \times D$.

■ In general, the WACC method is the easiest to use when a firm has a target debt-equity ratio that it plans to maintain over the life of the investment. For other leverage policies, the APV method is usually the most straightforward method.

18.7 Other Effects of Financing

■ Issuance costs and any costs or gains from mispricing of issued securities should be included in the assessment of a project's value.

■ Financial distress costs are likely to (1) lower the expected free cash flow of a project and (2) raise the firm's cost of capital. Taking these effects into account, together with other agency and asymmetric information costs, may limit a firm's use of leverage.

18.8 Advanced Topics in Capital Budgeting

■ If a firm adjusts its debt annually to a target leverage ratio, the value of the interest tax shield is enhanced by the factor $(1 + r_U)/(1 + r_D)$.

■ If the firm does not adjust leverage continuously, so that some of the tax shields are predetermined, the unlevered, equity, and weighted average costs of capital are related as follows:

$$r_U = \frac{E}{E+D^s}r_E + \frac{D^s}{E+D^s}r_D \text{ or, equivalently, } r_E = r_U + \frac{D^s}{E}(r_U - r_D) \tag{18.20}$$

$$r_{wacc} = r_U - d\,\tau_c\,[r_D + \phi(r_U - r_D)] \tag{18.21}$$

where $d = D/(D + E)$ is the debt-to-value ratio of the project, $D^s = D - T^s$, and T^s is the value of predetermined interest tax shields, and $\phi = T^s/(\tau_c D)$ reflects the permanence of the debt level.

■ The WACC method does not need to be modified to account for investor taxes. For the APV method, we use the interest rate

$$r_D^* \equiv r_D \frac{(1 - \tau_i)}{(1 - \tau_e)} \tag{18.23}$$

in place of r_D and we replace τ_c with the effective tax rate:

$$\tau^* = 1 - \frac{(1 - \tau_c)(1 - \tau_e)}{(1 - \tau_i)} \tag{18.25}$$

■ If the investment's leverage or risk does not match the firm's, then investor tax rates are required even with the WACC method, as we must unlever and/or re-lever the firm's cost of capital using

$$r_U = \frac{E}{E + D^s} r_E + \frac{D^s}{E + D^s} r_D^* \tag{18.24}$$

Key Terms

adjusted present value (APV) *p. 633*
constant interest coverage ratio *p. 645*
debt capacity *p. 632*

flow-to-equity (FTE) *p. 637*
free cash flow to equity (FCFE) *p. 637*
target leverage ratio *p. 633*

Further Reading

For a further treatment of the valuation with leverage, see: T. Copeland, T. Koller, and J. Murrin, *Valuation: Measuring and Managing the Value of Companies* (McGraw-Hill, 2000); and S. Pratt, R. Reilly, and R. Schweihs, *Valuing a Business: The Analysis and Appraisal of Closely Held Companies* (McGraw-Hill, 2000).

For a more detailed treatment of the issues discussed in this chapter, see: E. Arzac and L. Glosten, "A Reconsideration of Tax Shield Valuation," *European Financial Management* 11 (2005): 453–461; R. Harris and J. Pringle, "Risk-Adjusted Discount Rates—Extensions from the Average-Risk Case," *Journal of Financial Research* 8 (1985): 237–244; I. Inselbag and H. Kaufold, "Two DCF Approaches in Valuing Companies Under Alternative Financing Strategies (and How to Choose Between Them)," *Journal of Applied Corporate Finance* 10 (1997): 114–122; T. Luehrman, "Using APV: A Better Tool for Valuing Operations," *Harvard Business Review* 75 (1997): 145–154; J. Miles and J. Ezzell, "The Weighted Average Cost of Capital, Perfect Capital Markets, and Project Life: A Clarification," *Journal of Financial and Quantitative Analysis* 15 (1980): 719–730; J. Miles and J. Ezzell, "Reformulation Tax Shield Valuation: A Note," *Journal of Finance* 40 (1985): 1485–1492; R. Ruback, "Capital Cash Flows: A Simple Approach to Valuing Risky Cash Flows," *Financial Management* 31 (2002): 85–104; and R. Taggart, "Consistent Valuation and Cost of Capital Expressions with Corporate and Personal Taxes," *Financial Management* 20 (1991): 8–20.

Problems

All problems are available in MyFinanceLab. *An asterisk (*) indicates problems with a higher level of difficulty.*

Overview of Key Concepts

1. Explain whether each of the following projects is likely to have risk similar to the average risk of the firm.
   a. The Clorox Company considers launching a new version of Armor All designed to clean and protect notebook computers.
   b. Google, Inc., plans to purchase real estate to expand its headquarters.

c. Target Corporation decides to expand the number of stores it has in the southeastern United States.

d. GE decides to open a new Universal Studios theme park in China.

2. Suppose Caterpillar, Inc., has 665 million shares outstanding with a share price of $74.77, and $25 billion in debt. If in three years, Caterpillar has 700 million shares outstanding trading for $83 per share, how much debt will Caterpillar have if it maintains a constant debt-equity ratio?

3. In 2012, Intel Corporation had a market capitalization of $121 billion, debt of $7.2 billion, cash of $14.7 billion, and EBIT of nearly $18 billion. If Intel were to increase its debt by $1 billion and use the cash for a share repurchase, which market imperfections would be most relevant for understanding the consequence for Intel's value? Why?

The Weighted Average Cost of Capital Method

4. Suppose Goodyear Tire and Rubber Company is considering divesting one of its manufacturing plants. The plant is expected to generate free cash flows of $1.5 million per year, growing at a rate of 2.5% per year. Goodyear has an equity cost of capital of 8.5%, a debt cost of capital of 7%, a marginal corporate tax rate of 35%, and a debt-equity ratio of 2.6. If the plant has average risk and Goodyear plans to maintain a constant debt-equity ratio, what after-tax amount must it receive for the plant for the divestiture to be profitable?

5. Suppose Alcatel-Lucent has an equity cost of capital of 10%, market capitalization of $10.8 billion, and an enterprise value of $14.4 billion. Suppose Alcatel-Lucent's debt cost of capital is 6.1% and its marginal tax rate is 35%.
   a. What is Alcatel-Lucent's WACC?
   b. If Alcatel-Lucent maintains a constant debt-equity ratio, what is the value of a project with average risk and the following expected free cash flows?

Year	0	1	2	3
FCF	−100	50	100	70

   c. If Alcatel-Lucent maintains its debt-equity ratio, what is the debt capacity of the project in part b?

6. Acort Industries has 10 million shares outstanding and a current share price of $40 per share. It also has long-term debt outstanding. This debt is risk free, is four years away from maturity, has annual coupons with a coupon rate of 10%, and has a $100 million face value. The first of the remaining coupon payments will be due in exactly one year. The riskless interest rates for all maturities are constant at 6%. Acort has EBIT of $106 million, which is expected to remain constant each year. New capital expenditures are expected to equal depreciation and equal $13 million per year, while no changes to net working capital are expected in the future. The corporate tax rate is 40%, and Acort is expected to keep its debt-equity ratio constant in the future (by either issuing additional new debt or buying back some debt as time goes on).
   a. Based on this information, estimate Acort's WACC.
   b. What is Acort's equity cost of capital?

The Adjusted Present Value Method

7. Suppose Goodyear Tire and Rubber Company has an equity cost of capital of 8.5%, a debt cost of capital of 7%, a marginal corporate tax rate of 35%, and a debt-equity ratio of 2.6. Suppose Goodyear maintains a constant debt-equity ratio.
   a. What is Goodyear's WACC?
   b. What is Goodyear's unlevered cost of capital?
   c. Explain, intuitively, why Goodyear's unlevered cost of capital is less than its equity cost of capital and higher than its WACC.

8. You are a consultant who was hired to evaluate a new product line for Markum Enterprises. The upfront investment required to launch the product line is $10 million. The product will generate free cash flow of $750,000 the first year, and this free cash flow is expected to grow at a rate of 4% per year. Markum has an equity cost of capital of 11.3%, a debt cost of capital of 5%, and a tax rate of 35%. Markum maintains a debt-equity ratio of 0.40.
   a. What is the NPV of the new product line (including any tax shields from leverage)?
   b. How much debt will Markum initially take on as a result of launching this product line?
   c. How much of the product line's value is attributable to the present value of interest tax shields?

9. Consider Alcatel-Lucent's project in Problem 5.
   a. What is Alcatel-Lucent's unlevered cost of capital?
   b. What is the unlevered value of the project?
   c. What are the interest tax shields from the project? What is their present value?
   d. Show that the APV of Alcatel-Lucent's project matches the value computed using the WACC method.

The Flow-to-Equity Method

10. Consider Alcatel-Lucent's project in Problem 5.
    a. What is the free cash flow to equity for this project?
    b. What is its NPV computed using the FTE method? How does it compare with the NPV based on the WACC method?

11. In year 1, AMC will earn $2000 before interest and taxes. The market expects these earnings to grow at a rate of 3% per year. The firm will make no net investments (i.e., capital expenditures will equal depreciation) or changes to net working capital. Assume that the corporate tax rate equals 40%. Right now, the firm has $5000 in risk-free debt. It plans to keep a constant ratio of debt to equity every year, so that on average the debt will also grow by 3% per year. Suppose the risk-free rate equals 5%, and the expected return on the market equals 11%. The asset beta for this industry is 1.11.
    a. If AMC were an all-equity (unlevered) firm, what would its market value be?
    b. Assuming the debt is fairly priced, what is the amount of interest AMC will pay next year? If AMC's debt is expected to grow by 3% per year, at what rate are its interest payments expected to grow?
    c. Even though AMC's debt is *riskless* (the firm will not default), the future growth of AMC's debt is uncertain, so the exact amount of the future interest payments is risky. Assuming the future interest payments have the same beta as AMC's assets, what is the present value of AMC's interest tax shield?
    d. Using the APV method, what is AMC's total market value, V^L? What is the market value of AMC's equity?
    e. What is AMC's WACC? (*Hint*: Work backward from the FCF and V^L.)
    f. Using the WACC method, what is the expected return for AMC equity?
    g. Show that the following holds for AMC: $\beta_A = \dfrac{E}{D+E}\beta_E + \dfrac{D}{D+E}\beta_D$.
    h. Assuming that the proceeds from any increases in debt are paid out to equity holders, what cash flows do the equity holders expect to receive in one year? At what rate are those cash flows expected to grow? Use that information plus your answer to part f to derive the market value of equity using the FTE method. How does that compare to your answer in part d?

Project-Based Costs of Capital

12. Prokter and Gramble (PKGR) has historically maintained a debt-equity ratio of approximately 0.20. Its current stock price is $50 per share, with 2.5 billion shares outstanding. The firm enjoys very stable demand for its products, and consequently it has a low equity beta of 0.50

and can borrow at 4.20%, just 20 basis points over the risk-free rate of 4%. The expected return of the market is 10%, and PKGR's tax rate is 35%.

a. This year, PKGR is expected to have free cash flows of $6.0 billion. What constant expected growth rate of free cash flow is consistent with its current stock price?

b. PKGR believes it can increase debt without any serious risk of distress or other costs. With a higher debt-equity ratio of 0.50, it believes its borrowing costs will rise only slightly to 4.50%. If PKGR announces that it will raise its debt-equity ratio to 0.5 through a leveraged recap, determine the increase in the stock price that would result from the anticipated tax savings.

13. Amarindo, Inc. (AMR), is a newly public firm with 10 million shares outstanding. You are doing a valuation analysis of AMR. You estimate its free cash flow in the coming year to be $15 million, and you expect the firm's free cash flows to grow by 4% per year in subsequent years. Because the firm has only been listed on the stock exchange for a short time, you do not have an accurate assessment of AMR's equity beta. However, you do have beta data for UAL, another firm in the same industry:

	Equity Beta	Debt Beta	Debt-Equity Ratio
UAL	1.5	0.30	1

AMR has a much lower debt-equity ratio of 0.30, which is expected to remain stable, and its debt is risk free. AMR's corporate tax rate is 40%, the risk-free rate is 5%, and the expected return on the market portfolio is 11%.

a. Estimate AMR's equity cost of capital.

b. Estimate AMR's share price.

 14. Remex (RMX) currently has no debt in its capital structure. The beta of its equity is 1.50. For each year into the indefinite future, Remex's free cash flow is expected to equal $25 million. Remex is considering changing its capital structure by issuing debt and using the proceeds to buy back stock. It will do so in such a way that it will have a 30% debt-equity ratio after the change, and it will maintain this debt-equity ratio forever. Assume that Remex's debt cost of capital will be 6.5%. Remex faces a corporate tax rate of 35%. Except for the corporate tax rate of 35%, there are no market imperfections. Assume that the CAPM holds, the risk-free rate of interest is 5%, and the expected return on the market is 11%.

a. Using the information provided, complete the following table:

	Debt-Equity Ratio	Debt Cost of Capital	Equity Cost of Capital	Weighted Average Cost of Capital
Before change in capital structure	0	N/A		
After change in capital structure	0.30	6.5%		

b. Using the information provided and your calculations in part a, determine the value of the tax shield acquired by Remex if it changes its capital structure in the way it is considering.

APV with Other Leverage Policies

15. You are evaluating a project that requires an investment of $90 today and provides a single cash flow of $115 for sure one year from now. You decide to use 100% debt financing, that is, you will borrow $90. The risk-free rate is 5% and the tax rate is 40%. Assume that the investment is fully depreciated at the end of the year, so without leverage you would owe taxes on the difference between the project cash flow and the investment, that is, $25.

a. Calculate the NPV of this investment opportunity using the APV method.

b. Using your answer to part a, calculate the WACC of the project.

c. Verify that you get the same answer using the WACC method to calculate NPV.

d. Finally, show that flow-to-equity also correctly gives the NPV of this investment opportunity.

16. Tybo Corporation adjusts its debt so that its interest expenses are 20% of its free cash flow. Tybo is considering an expansion that will generate free cash flows of $2.5 million this year and is expected to grow at a rate of 4% per year from then on. Suppose Tybo's marginal corporate tax rate is 40%.

a. If the unlevered cost of capital for this expansion is 10%, what is its unlevered value?

b. What is the levered value of the expansion?

c. If Tybo pays 5% interest on its debt, what amount of debt will it take on initially for the expansion?

d. What is the debt-to-value ratio for this expansion? What is its WACC?

e. What is the levered value of the expansion using the WACC method?

17. You are on your way to an important budget meeting. In the elevator, you review the project valuation analysis you had your summer associate prepare for one of the projects to be discussed:

	0	1	2	3	4
EBIT		10.0	10.0	10.0	10.0
Interest (5%)		−4.0	−4.0	−3.0	−2.0
Earnings Before Taxes		6.0	6.0	7.0	8.0
Taxes		−2.4	−2.4	−2.8	−3.2
Depreciation		25.0	25.0	25.0	25.0
Cap Ex	−100.0				
Additions to NWC	−20.0				20.0
Net New Debt	80.0	0.0	−20.0	−20.0	−40.0
FCFE	−40.0	28.6	8.6	9.2	9.8
NPV at 11% Equity Cost of Capital	5.9				

Looking over the spreadsheet, you realize that while all of the cash flow estimates are correct, your associate used the flow-to-equity valuation method and discounted the cash flows using the *company's* equity cost of capital of 11%. However, the project's incremental leverage is very different from the company's historical debt-equity ratio of 0.20: For this project, the company will instead borrow $80 million upfront and repay $20 million in year 2, $20 million in year 3, and $40 million in year 4. Thus, the *project's* equity cost of capital is likely to be higher than the firm's, not constant over time—invalidating your associate's calculation.

Clearly, the FTE approach is not the best way to analyze this project. Fortunately, you have your calculator with you, and with any luck you can use a better method before the meeting starts.

a. What is the present value of the interest tax shield associated with this project?

b. What are the free cash flows of the project?

c. What is the best estimate of the project's value from the information given?

18. Your firm is considering building a $600 million plant to manufacture HDTV circuitry. You expect operating profits (EBITDA) of $145 million per year for the next 10 years. The plant will be depreciated on a straight-line basis over 10 years (assuming no salvage value for tax purposes). After 10 years, the plant will have a salvage value of $300 million (which, since it will

be fully depreciated, is then taxable). The project requires $50 million in working capital at the start, which will be recovered in year 10 when the project shuts down. The corporate tax rate is 35%. All cash flows occur at the end of the year.

a. If the risk-free rate is 5%, the expected return of the market is 11%, and the asset beta for the consumer electronics industry is 1.67, what is the NPV of the project?

b. Suppose that you can finance $400 million of the cost of the plant using 10-year, 9% coupon bonds sold at par. This amount is incremental new debt associated specifically with this project and will not alter other aspects of the firm's capital structure. What is the value of the project, including the tax shield of the debt?

Other Effects of Financing

 19. DFS Corporation is currently an all-equity firm, with assets with a market value of $100 million and 4 million shares outstanding. DFS is considering a leveraged recapitalization to boost its share price. The firm plans to raise a fixed amount of permanent debt (i.e., the outstanding principal will remain constant) and use the proceeds to repurchase shares. DFS pays a 35% corporate tax rate, so one motivation for taking on the debt is to reduce the firm's tax liability. However, the upfront investment banking fees associated with the recapitalization will be 5% of the amount of debt raised. Adding leverage will also create the possibility of future financial distress or agency costs; shown below are DFS's estimates for different levels of debt:

Debt amount ($ million):	0	10	20	30	40	50
Present value of expected distress and agency costs ($ million):	0.0	−0.3	−1.8	−4.3	−7.5	−11.3

a. Based on this information, which level of debt is the best choice for DFS?

b. Estimate the stock price once this transaction is announced.

20. Your firm is considering a $150 million investment to launch a new product line. The project is expected to generate a free cash flow of $20 million per year, and its unlevered cost of capital is 10%. To fund the investment, your firm will take on $100 million in permanent debt.

a. Suppose the marginal corporate tax rate is 35%. Ignoring issuance costs, what is the NPV of the investment?

b. Suppose your firm will pay a 2% underwriting fee when issuing the debt. It will raise the remaining $50 million by issuing equity. In addition to the 5% underwriting fee for the equity issue, you believe that your firm's current share price of $40 is $5 per share less than its true value. What is the NPV of the investment including any tax benefits of leverage? (Assume all fees are on an after-tax basis.)

21. Consider Avco's RFX project from Section 18.3. Suppose that Avco is receiving government loan guarantees that allow it to borrow at the 6% rate. Without these guarantees, Avco would pay 6.5% on its debt.

a. What is Avco's unlevered cost of capital given its true debt cost of capital of 6.5%?

b. What is the unlevered value of the RFX project in this case? What is the present value of the interest tax shield?

c. What is the NPV of the loan guarantees? (*Hint*: Because the actual loan amounts will fluctuate with the value of the project, discount the expected interest savings at the unlevered cost of capital.)

d. What is the levered value of the RFX project, including the interest tax shield and the NPV of the loan guarantees?

Advanced Topics in Capital Budgeting

22. Arden Corporation is considering an investment in a new project with an unlevered cost of capital of 9%. Arden's marginal corporate tax rate is 40%, and its debt cost of capital is 5%.

a. Suppose Arden adjusts its debt continuously to maintain a constant debt-equity ratio of 50%. What is the appropriate WACC for the new project?

b. Suppose Arden adjusts its debt once per year to maintain a constant debt-equity ratio of 50%. What is the appropriate WACC for the new project now?

c. Suppose the project has free cash flows of $10 million per year, which are expected to decline by 2% per year. What is the value of the project in parts a and b now?

23. XL Sports is expected to generate free cash flows of $10.9 million per year. XL has permanent debt of $40 million, a tax rate of 40%, and an unlevered cost of capital of 10%.

a. What is the value of XL's equity using the APV method?

b. What is XL's WACC? What is XL's equity value using the WACC method?

c. If XL's debt cost of capital is 5%, what is XL's equity cost of capital?

d. What is XL's equity value using the FTE method?

 *24. Propel Corporation plans to make a $50 million investment, initially funded completely with debt. The free cash flows of the investment and Propel's incremental debt from the project follow:

Year	0	1	2	3
Free cash flows	−50	40	20	25
Debt	50	30	15	0

Propel's incremental debt for the project will be paid off according to the predetermined schedule shown. Propel's debt cost of capital is 8%, and its tax rate is 40%. Propel also estimates an unlevered cost of capital for the project of 12%.

a. Use the APV method to determine the levered value of the project at each date and its initial NPV.

b. Calculate the WACC for this project at each date. How does the WACC change over time? Why?

c. Compute the project's NPV using the WACC method.

d. Compute the equity cost of capital for this project at each date. How does the equity cost of capital change over time? Why?

e. Compute the project's equity value using the FTE method. How does the initial equity value compare with the NPV calculated in parts a and c?

*25. Gartner Systems has no debt and an equity cost of capital of 10%. Gartner's current market capitalization is $100 million, and its free cash flows are expected to grow at 3% per year. Gartner's corporate tax rate is 35%. Investors pay tax rates of 40% on interest income and 20% on equity income.

a. Suppose Gartner adds $50 million in permanent debt and uses the proceeds to repurchase shares. What will Gartner's levered value be in this case?

b. Suppose instead Gartner decides to maintain a 50% debt-to-value ratio going forward. If Gartner's debt cost of capital is 6.67%, what will Gartner's levered value be in this case?

*26. Revtek, Inc., has an equity cost of capital of 12% and a debt cost of capital of 6%. Revtek maintains a constant debt-equity ratio of 0.5, and its tax rate is 35%.

a. What is Revtek's WACC given its current debt-equity ratio?

b. Assuming no personal taxes, how will Revtek's WACC change if it increases its debt-equity ratio to 2 and its debt cost of capital remains at 6%?

c. Now suppose investors pay tax rates of 40% on interest income and 15% on income from equity. How will Revtek's WACC change if it increases its debt-equity ratio to 2 in this case?

d. Provide an intuitive explanation for the difference in your answers to parts b and c.

Data Case

Toyota Motor Company is expanding the production of their gas-electric hybrid drive systems and plans to shift production in the United States. To enable the expansion, they are contemplating investing $1.5 billion in a new plant with an expected 10-year life. The anticipated free cash flows from the new plant would be $220 million the first year of operation and grow by 10% for each of the next two years and then 5% per year for the remaining seven years. As a newly hired MBA in the capital budgeting division you have been asked to evaluate the new project using the WACC, Adjusted Present Value, and Flow-to-Equity methods. You will compute the appropriate costs of capital and the net present values with each method. Because this is your first major assignment with the firm, they want you to demonstrate that you are capable of handling the different valuation methods. You must seek out the information necessary to value the free cash flows but will be provided some directions to follow. (This is an involved assignment, but at least you don't have to come up with the actual cash flows for the project!)

1. Go to Yahoo! Finance (http://finance.yahoo.com) and get the quote for Toyota (symbol: TM).

   a. Under "Financials," click on the income statement. The income statements for the last three fiscal years will appear. Copy and paste the data into Excel.

   b. Go back to the Web page and select "Balance Sheets" from the top of the page. Repeat the download procedure for the balance sheets, then copy and paste them into the same worksheet as the income statements.

   c. Click "Historical prices" in the left column, and find Toyota's stock price for the last day of the month at the end of each of the past four fiscal years. Record the stock price on each date in your spreadsheet.

2. Create a timeline in Excel with the free cash flows for the 10 years of the project.

3. Determine the WACC using Eq. 18.1.

   a. For the cost of debt, r_D:

      i. Go to NasdBondInfo.com (http://cxa.marketwatch.com/finra/BondCenter/Default.aspx) and click to search by symbol. Enter Toyota's symbol, select the Corporate toggle, and press "Enter."

      ii. Look at the average credit rating for Toyota long-term bonds. If you find that they have a rating of A or above, then you can make the approximation that the cost of debt is the risk-free rate. If Toyota's credit rating has slipped, use Table 12.3 to estimate the beta of debt from the credit rating.

   b. For the cost of equity, r_E:

      i. Get the yield on the 10-year U.S. Treasury Bond from Yahoo! Finance (http://finance.yahoo.com). Scroll down to the Market Summary. Enter that yield as the risk-free rate.

      ii. Find the beta for Toyota from Yahoo! Finance. Enter the symbol for Toyota and click "Key Statistics." The beta for Toyota will be listed there.

      iii. Use a market risk premium of 4.50% to compute r_E using the CAPM. If you need to, repeat the exercise to compute r_D.

   c. Determine the values for E and D for Eq. 18.1 for Toyota and the debt-to-value and equity-to-value ratios.

      i. To compute the net debt for Toyota, add the long-term debt and the short-term debt and subtract cash and cash equivalents for each year on the balance sheet.

      ii. Obtain the historical number of shares outstanding from Google Finance (www.google.com/finance). Enter Toyota's ticker in the search box, click "Financials." Look on the income statement for "Diluted Weighted Average Shares." Multiply the historical stock prices by the number of shares outstanding you collected to compute Toyota's market capitalization at the end of each fiscal year.

iii. Compute Toyota's enterprise value at the end of each fiscal year by combining the values obtained for its equity market capitalization and its net debt.

iv. Compute Toyota's debt-to-value ratio at the end of each year by dividing its net debt by its enterprise value. Use the average ratio from the last four years as an estimate for Toyota's target debt-to-value ratio.

d. Determine Toyota's tax rate by dividing the income tax by earnings before tax for each year. Take the average of the four rates as Toyota's marginal corporate tax rate.

e. Compute the WACC for Toyota using Eq. 18.1.

4. Compute the NPV of the hybrid engine expansion given the free cash flows you calculated using the WACC method of valuation.

5. Determine the NPV using the Adjusted Present Value Method, and also using the Flow-to-Equity method. In both cases, assume Toyota maintains the target leverage ratio you computed in Question 3c.

6. Compare the results under the three methods and explain how the resulting NPVs are achieved under each of the three different methods.

Foundations and Further Details

In this appendix, we look at the foundations for the WACC method, and for the relationship between a firm's levered and unlevered costs of capital. We also address how we can solve for a firm's leverage policy and value simultaneously.

Deriving the WACC Method

The WACC can be used to value a levered investment, as in Eq. 18.2. Consider an investment that is financed by both debt and equity. Because equity holders require an expected return of r_E on their investment and debt holders require a return of r_D, the firm will have to pay investors a total of

$$E(1 + r_E) + D(1 + r_D) \tag{18.A1}$$

next year. What is the value of the investment next year? The project generates free cash flows of FCF_1 at the end of the year. In addition, the interest tax shield of the debt provides a tax savings of $\tau_c \times$ (interest on debt) $\approx \tau_c\, r_D\, D$.[28] Finally, if the investment will continue beyond next year, it will have a continuation value of V_1^L. Thus, to satisfy investors, the project cash flows must be such that

$$E(1 + r_E) + D(1 + r_D) = FCF_1 + \tau_c r_D D + V_1^L \tag{18A.2}$$

Because $V_0^L = E + D$, we can write the WACC definition in Eq. 18.1 as

$$r_{wacc} = \frac{E}{V_0^L} r_E + \frac{D}{V_0^L} r_D (1 - \tau_c) \tag{18.A3}$$

If we move the interest tax shield to the left side of Eq. 18A.2, we can use the definition of the WACC to rewrite Eq. 18A.2 as follows:

$$\underbrace{E(1 + r_E) + D[1 + r_D(1 - \tau_c)]}_{V_0^L(1 + r_{wacc})} = FCF_1 + V_1^L \tag{18.A4}$$

---

[28]The return on the debt r_D need not come solely from interest payments. If C_t is the coupon paid and D_t is the market value of the debt in period t, then in period t, r_D is defined as

$$r_D = \frac{E[\text{Coupon Payment} + \text{Capital Gain}]}{\text{Current Price}} = \frac{E[C_{t+1} + D_{t+1} - D_t]}{D_t}$$

The return that determines the firm's interest expense is

$$\bar{r}_D = \frac{E[C_{t+1} + \overline{D}_{t+1} - \overline{D}_t]}{D_t}$$

where D_t is the value of the debt on date t according to a fixed schedule set by the tax code based on the difference between the bond's initial price and its face value, which is called the bond's *original issue discount* (OID). (If the bond is issued at par and the firm will not default on the next coupon, then $\overline{D}_t = \overline{D}_{t+1}$ and $\bar{r}_D = C_{t+1}/D_t$, which is the bond's *current yield*.) Thus, the true after-tax cost of debt is $(r_D - \tau_c \bar{r}_D)$. In practice, the distinction between r_D and $\bar{r}_D$ is often ignored, and the after-tax cost of debt is computed as $r_D(1 - \tau_c)$. Also, the debt's yield to maturity is often used in place of r_D. Because the yield ignores default risk, it overstates r_D and thus the WACC. See Chapter 12 for alternative methods.

Dividing by $(1 + r_{wacc})$, we can express the value of the investment today as the present value of next period's free cash flows and continuation value:

$$V_0^L = \frac{FCF_1 + V_1^L}{1 + r_{wacc}} \tag{18.A5}$$

In the same way, we can write the value in one year, V_1^L, as the discounted value of the free cash flows and continuation value of the project in year 2. If the WACC is the same next year, then

$$V_0^L = \frac{FCF_1 + V_1^L}{1 + r_{wacc}} = \frac{FCF_1 + \dfrac{FCF_2 + V_2^L}{1 + r_{wacc}}}{1 + r_{wacc}} = \frac{FCF_1}{1 + r_{wacc}} + \frac{FCF_2 + V_2^L}{(1 + r_{wacc})^2} \tag{18.A6}$$

By repeatedly replacing each continuation value, and *assuming the WACC remains constant*, we can derive Eq. 18.2:[29]

$$V_0^L = \frac{FCF_1}{1 + r_{wacc}} + \frac{FCF_2}{(1 + r_{wacc})^2} + \frac{FCF_3}{(1 + r_{wacc})^3} + \cdots \tag{18.A7}$$

That is, *the value of a levered investment is the present value of its future free cash flows using the weighted average cost of capital.*

The Levered and Unlevered Cost of Capital

In this appendix, we derive the relationship between the levered and unlevered cost of capital for the firm. Suppose an investor holds a portfolio of all of the equity and debt of the firm. Then the investor will receive the free cash flows of the firm plus the tax savings from the interest tax shield. These are the same cash flows an investor would receive from a portfolio of the unlevered firm (which generates the free cash flows) and a separate "tax shield" security that paid the investor the amount of the tax shield each period. Because these two portfolios generate the same cash flows, by the Law of One Price they have the same market values:

$$V^L = E + D = V^U + T \tag{18.A8}$$

where T is the present value of the interest tax shield. Equation 18.A8 is the basis of the APV method. Because these portfolios have equal cash flows, they must also have identical expected returns, which implies

$$E\,r_E + D\,r_D = V^U r_U + T r_T \tag{18.A9}$$

where r_T is the expected return associated with the interest tax shields. The relationship between r_E, r_D, and r_U will depend on the expected return r_T, which is determined by the risk of the interest tax shield. Let's consider the two cases discussed in the text.

Target Leverage Ratio

Suppose the firm adjusts its debt continuously to maintain a target debt-to-value ratio, or a target ratio of interest to free cash flow. Because the firm's debt and interest payments will vary with the firm's value and cash flows, it is reasonable to expect the risk of the interest

---

[29]This expansion is the same approach we took in Chapter 9 to derive the discounted dividend formula for the stock price.

tax shield will equal that of the firm's free cash flow, so $r_T = r_U$. Making this assumption, which we return to below, Eq. 18A.9 becomes

$$E\,r_E + D\,r_D = V^U r_U + T r_U = (V^U + T) r_U$$
$$= (E + D) r_U \tag{18.A10}$$

Dividing by $(E + D)$ leads to Eq. 18.6.

Predetermined Debt Schedule

Suppose some of the firm's debt is set according to a predetermined schedule that is independent of the growth of the firm. Suppose the value of the tax shield from the scheduled debt is T^s, and the remaining value of the tax shield $T - T^s$ is from debt that will be adjusted according to a target leverage ratio. Because the risk of the interest tax shield from the scheduled debt is similar to the risk of the debt itself, Eq. 18A.9 becomes

$$E\,r_E + D\,r_D = V^U r_U + T r_T = V^U r_U + (T - T^s) r_U + T^s r_D \tag{18.A11}$$

Subtracting $T^s r_D$ from both sides, and using $D^s = D - T^s$,

$$E\,r_E + D^s r_D = (V^U + T - T^s) r_U = (V^L - T^s) r_U$$
$$= (E + D^s) r_U \tag{18.A12}$$

Dividing by $(E + D^s)$ leads to Eq. 18.20.

Risk of the Tax Shield with a Target Leverage Ratio

Above, we assumed that with a target leverage ratio, it is reasonable to assume that $r_T = r_U$. Under what circumstances should this be the case?

We define a target leverage ratio as a setting in which the firm adjusts its debt at date t to be a proportion $d(t)$ of the investment's value, or a proportion $k(t)$ of its free cash flow. (The target ratio for either policy need not be constant over time, but can vary according to a predetermined schedule.)

With either policy, the value at date t of the incremental tax shield from the project's free cash flow at date s, FCF_s, is proportional to the value of the cash flow $V_t^L(FCF_s)$, so it should be discounted at the same rate as FCF_s. Therefore, the assumption $r_T = r_U$ follows as long as at each date the cost of capital associated with the value of each future free cash flow is the same (a standard assumption in capital budgeting).[30]

Solving for Leverage and Value Simultaneously

When we use the APV method, we need to know the debt level to compute the interest tax shield and determine the project's value. But if a firm maintains a constant debt-to-value ratio, we need to know the project's value to determine the debt level. How can we apply the APV method in this case?

When a firm maintains a constant leverage ratio, to use the APV method we must solve for the debt level and the project value simultaneously. While complicated to do by hand, it is (fortunately) easy to do in Excel. We begin with the spreadsheet shown in Table 18A.1, which illustrates the standard APV calculation outlined in Section 18.3 of the text. For now, we have just inserted arbitrary values for the project's debt capacity in line 3.

---

[30]If the risk of the individual cash flows differs, then r_T will be a weighted average of the unlevered costs of capital of the individual cash flows, with the weights depending on the schedule d or k. See P. DeMarzo, "Discounting Tax Shields and the Unlevered Cost of Capital," 2005, http://ssrn.com/abstract=1488437.

TABLE 18A.1 SPREADSHEET	Adjusted Present Value for Avco's RFX Project with Arbitrary Debt Levels					
Year	**0**	**1**	**2**	**3**	**4**
Unlevered Value ($ million)						
1 Free Cash Flow	(28.00)	18.00	18.00	18.00	18.00
2 Unlevered Value, V^U (at r_u = 8.0%)	59.62	46.39	32.10	16.67	—
Interest Tax Shield						
3 Debt Capacity (arbitrary)	30.00	20.00	10.00	5.00	—
4 Interest Paid (at r_d = 6%)	—	1.80	1.20	0.60	0.30
5 Interest Tax Shield (at τ_c = 40%)	—	0.72	0.48	0.24	0.12
6 Tax Shield Value, T (at r_u = 8.0%)	1.36	0.75	0.33	0.11	—
Adjusted Present Value						
7 **Levered Value, $V^L = V^U + T$**	**60.98**	**47.13**	**32.42**	**16.78**	**—**

Note that the debt capacity specified in line 3 is not consistent with a 50% debt-to-value ratio for the project. For example, given the value of $60.98 million in year 0, the initial debt capacity should be 50% × $60.98 million = $30.49 million in year 0. But if we change each debt capacity in line 3 to a *numerical* value that is 50% of the value in line 7, the interest tax shield and the project's value will change, and we will still not have a 50% debt-to-value ratio.

The solution is to enter in line 3 a *formula* that sets the debt capacity to be 50% of the project's value in line 7 in the same year. Now line 7 depends on line 3, and line 3 depends on line 7, creating a circular reference in the spreadsheet (and you will most likely receive an error message). By changing the calculation option in Excel to calculate the spreadsheet iteratively (File > Options > Formulas and check the Enable iterative calculation box), Excel will keep calculating until the values in line 3 and line 7 of the spreadsheet are consistent, as shown in Table 18A.2.

TABLE 18A.2 SPREADSHEET	Adjusted Present Value for Avco's RFX Project with Debt Levels Solved Iteratively					
Year	**0**	**1**	**2**	**3**	**4**
Unlevered Value ($ million)						
1 Free Cash Flow	(28.00)	18.00	18.00	18.00	18.00
2 Unlevered Value, V^U (at r_u = 8.0%)	59.62	46.39	32.10	16.67	—
Interest Tax Shield						
3 Debt Capacity (at d = 50%)	30.62	23.71	16.32	8.43	—
4 Interest Paid (at r_d = 6%)	—	1.84	1.42	0.98	0.51
5 Interest Tax Shield (at τ_c = 40%)	—	0.73	0.57	0.39	0.20
6 Tax Shield Value, T (at r_u = 8.0%)	1.63	1.02	0.54	0.19	—
Adjusted Present Value						
7 **Levered Value, $V^L = V^U + T$**	**61.25**	**47.41**	**32.63**	**16.85**	**—**

The same method can be applied when using the WACC method with known debt levels. In that case, we need to know the project's value to determine the debt-to-value ratio and compute the WACC, and we need to know the WACC to compute the project's value. Again, we can use iteration within Excel to determine simultaneously the project's value and debt-to-value ratio.

Valuation and Financial Modeling: A Case Study

NOTATION

R_s	return on security s
r_f	risk-free rate
α_s	the alpha of security s
β_s	the beta of security s
R_{mkt}	return of the market portfolio
$E[R_{mkt}]$	expected return of the market portfolio
ε_s	the regression error term
β_U	the beta of an unlevered firm
β_E	the beta of equity
β_D	the beta of debt
r_U	unlevered cost of capital
r_{wacc}	weighted average cost of capital
r_D	debt cost of capital
V_T^L	continuing value of a project at date T
V^U	unlevered value
FCF_t	free cash flow at date t
g	growth rate
T^s	predetermined tax shield value

THE GOAL OF THIS CHAPTER IS TO APPLY THE FINANCIAL tools we have developed thus far to demonstrate how they are used in practice to build a valuation model of a firm. In this chapter, we will value a hypothetical firm, Ideko Corporation. Ideko is a privately held designer and manufacturer of specialty sports eyewear based in Chicago. In mid-2005, its owner and founder, June Wong, has decided to sell the business, after having relinquished management control about four years ago. As a partner in KKP Investments, you are investigating purchasing the company. If a deal can be reached, the acquisition will take place at the end of the current fiscal year. In that event, KKP plans to implement operational and financial improvements at Ideko over the next five years, after which it intends to sell the business.

Ideko has total assets of $87 million and annual sales of $75 million. The firm is also quite profitable, with earnings this year of almost $7 million, for a net profit margin of 9.3%. You believe a deal could be struck to purchase Ideko's equity at the end of this fiscal year for an acquisition price of $150 million, which is almost double Ideko's current book value of equity. Is this price reasonable?

We begin the chapter by estimating Ideko's value using data for comparable firms. We then review KKP's operating strategies for running the business after the acquisition, to identify potential areas for improvements. We build a financial model to project cash flows that reflect these operating improvements. These cash flow forecasts enable us to value Ideko using the APV model introduced in Chapter 18 and estimate the return on KKP's investment. Finally, we explore the sensitivity of the valuation estimates to our main assumptions.

19.1 Valuation Using Comparables

As a result of preliminary conversations with Ideko's founder, you have estimates of Ideko's income and balance sheet information for the current fiscal year shown in Table 19.1. Ideko currently has debt outstanding of $4.5 million, but it also has a substantial cash balance. To obtain your first estimate of Ideko's value, you decide to value Ideko by examining comparable firms.

A quick way to gauge the reasonableness of the proposed price for Ideko is to compare it to that of other publicly traded firms using the method of comparable firms introduced in Chapter 9. For example, at a price of $150 million, Ideko's price-earnings (P/E) ratio is 150,000/6939 = 21.6, roughly equal to the market average P/E ratio in mid-2005.

It is even more informative to compare Ideko to firms in a similar line of business. Although no firm is exactly comparable to Ideko in terms of its overall product line, three firms with which it has similarities are Oakley, Inc.; Luxottica Group; and Nike, Inc. The closest competitor is Oakley, which also designs and manufactures sports eyewear. Luxottica Group is an Italian eyewear maker, but much of its business is prescription eyewear; it also owns and operates a number of retail eyewear chains. Nike is a manufacturer of specialty sportswear products, but its primary focus is footwear. You also decide to compare Ideko to a portfolio of firms in the sporting goods industry.

A comparison of Ideko's proposed valuation to this peer set, as well as to the average firm in the sporting goods industry, appears in Table 19.2. The table not only lists P/E ratios, but also shows each firm's enterprise value (EV) as a multiple of sales and EBITDA (earnings before interest, taxes, depreciation, and amortization). Recall that enterprise value is the total value of equity plus net debt, where net debt is debt less cash and investments in marketable securities that are not required as part of normal operations. Ideko has $4.5 million in debt, and you estimate that it holds $6.5 million of cash in excess of its working capital needs. Thus, Ideko's enterprise value at the proposed acquisition price is 150 + 4.5 − 6.5 = $148 million.

At the proposed price, Ideko's P/E ratio is low relative to those of Oakley and Luxottica, although it is somewhat above the P/E ratios of Nike and the industry overall. The same

TABLE 19.1 SPREADSHEET	Estimated 2005 Income Statement and Balance Sheet Data for Ideko Corporation

Income Statement ($ 000)	Year 2005		Balance Sheet ($ 000)	Year 2005
1 Sales	75,000		**Assets**	
2 Cost of Goods Sold			1 Cash and Equivalents	12,664
3 Raw Materials	(16,000)		2 Accounts Receivable	18,493
4 Direct Labor Costs	(18,000)		3 Inventories	6,165
5 Gross Profit	41,000		**4 Total Current Assets**	37,322
6 Sales and Marketing	(11,250)		5 Property, Plant, and Equipment	49,500
7 Administrative	(13,500)		6 Goodwill	—
8 EBITDA	16,250		**7 Total Assets**	86,822
9 Depreciation	(5,500)		**Liabilities and Stockholders' Equity**	
10 EBIT	10,750		8 Accounts Payable	4,654
11 Interest Expense (net)	(75)		9 Debt	4,500
12 Pretax Income	10,675		**10 Total Liabilities**	9,154
13 Income Tax	(3,736)		**11 Stockholders' Equity**	77,668
14 Net Income	6,939		**12 Total Liabilities and Equity**	86,822

| TABLE 19.2 | Ideko Financial Ratios Comparison, Mid-2005 |

Ratio	Ideko (Proposed)	Oakley, Inc.	Luxottica Group	Nike, Inc.	Sporting Goods Industry
P/E	21.6×	24.8×	28.0×	18.2×	20.3×
EV/Sales	2.0×	2.0×	2.7×	1.5×	1.4×
EV/EBITDA	9.1×	11.6×	14.4×	9.3×	11.4×
EBITDA/Sales	21.7%	17.0%	18.5%	15.9%	12.1%

can be said for Ideko's valuation as a multiple of sales. Thus, based on these two measures, Ideko looks "cheap" relative to Oakley and Luxottica, but is priced at a premium relative to Nike and the average sporting goods firm. The deal stands out, however, when you compare Ideko's enterprise value relative to EBITDA. The acquisition price of just over nine times EBITDA is below that of all of the comparable firms as well as the industry average. Ideko's low EBITDA multiple is a result of its high profit margins: At $16{,}250/75{,}000 = 21.7\%$, its EBITDA margin exceeds that of all of the comparables.

While Table 19.2 provides some reassurance that the acquisition price is reasonable compared to other firms in the industry, it by no means establishes that the acquisition is a good investment opportunity. As with any such comparison, the multiples in Table 19.2 vary substantially. Furthermore, they ignore important differences such as the operating efficiency and growth prospects of the firms, and they do not reflect KKP's plans to improve Ideko's operations. To assess whether this investment is attractive requires a careful analysis both of the operational aspects of the firm and of the ultimate cash flows the deal is expected to generate and the return that should be required.

| EXAMPLE 19.1 | **Valuation by Comparables** |

Problem

What range of acquisition prices for Ideko is implied by the range of multiples for P/E, EV/Sales, and EV/EBITDA in Table 19.2?

Solution

For each multiple, we can find the highest and lowest values across all three firms and the industry portfolio. Applying each multiple to the data for Ideko in Table 19.1 yields the following results:

Multiple	Range		Price (in $ million)	
	Low	High	Low	High
P/E	18.2×	28.0×	126.3	194.3
EV/Sales	1.4×	2.7×	107.0	204.5
EV/EBITDA	9.3×	14.4×	153.1	236.0

For example, Nike has the lowest P/E multiple of 18.2. Multiplying this P/E by Ideko's earnings of $6.94 million gives a value of $18.2 \times 6.94 = \$126.3$ million. The highest multiple of enterprise value to sales is 2.7 (Luxottica); at this multiple, Ideko's enterprise value is $2.7 \times 75 = \$202.5$ million. Adding Ideko's excess cash and subtracting its debt implies a purchase price of $202.5 + 6.5 - 4.5 = \$204.5$ million. The table above demonstrates that while comparables provide a useful benchmark, they cannot be relied upon for a precise estimate of value.

CONCEPT CHECK

1. What is the purpose of the valuation using comparables?

2. If the valuation using comparables indicates the acquisition price is reasonable compared to other firms in the industry, does it establish that the acquisition is a good investment opportunity?

19.2 The Business Plan

While comparables provide a useful starting point, whether this acquisition is a successful investment for KKP depends on Ideko's post-acquisition performance. Thus, it is necessary to look in detail at Ideko's operations, investments, and capital structure, and to assess its potential for improvements and future growth.

Operational Improvements

On the operational side, you are quite optimistic regarding the company's prospects. The market is expected to grow by 5% per year, and Ideko produces a superior product. Ideko's market share has not grown in recent years because current management has devoted insufficient resources to product development, sales, and marketing. Conversely, Ideko has overspent on administrative costs. Indeed, Table 19.1 reveals that Ideko's current administrative expenses are 13,500/75,000 = 18% of sales, a rate that exceeds its expenditures on sales and marketing (15% of sales). This is in stark contrast to its rivals, which spend less on administrative overhead than they do on sales and marketing.

KKP plans to cut administrative costs immediately and redirect resources to new product development, sales, and marketing. By doing so, you believe Ideko can increase its market share from 10% to 15% over the next five years. The increased sales demand can be met in the short run using the existing production lines by increasing overtime and running some weekend shifts. However, once the growth in volume exceeds 50%, Ideko will definitely need to undertake a major expansion to increase its manufacturing capacity.

The spreadsheet in Table 19.3 shows sales and operating cost assumptions for the next five years based on this plan. In the spreadsheet, numbers in blue represent data that has been entered, whereas numbers in black are calculated based on the data provided. For example, given the current market size of 10 million units and an expected growth rate of 5% per year, the spreadsheet calculates the expected market size in years 1 through 5. Also shown is the expected growth in Ideko's market share.

TABLE 19.3 SPREADSHEET   **Ideko Sales and Operating Cost Assumptions**

		Year	2005	2006	2007	2008	2009	2010
Sales Data		**Growth/Year**						
1	Market Size	(000 units)	5.0%	10,000	10,500	11,025	11,576	12,155	12,763
2	Market Share		1.0%	10.0%	11.0%	12.0%	13.0%	14.0%	15.0%
3	Average Sales Price	($/unit)	2.0%	75.00	76.50	78.03	79.59	81.18	82.81
Cost of Goods Data								
4	Raw Materials	($/unit)	1.0%	16.00	16.16	16.32	16.48	16.65	16.82
5	Direct Labor Costs	($/unit)	4.0%	18.00	18.72	19.47	20.25	21.06	21.90
Operating Expense and Tax Data								
6	Sales and Marketing	(% sales)		15.0%	16.5%	18.0%	19.5%	20.0%	20.0%
7	Administrative	(% sales)		18.0%	15.0%	15.0%	14.0%	13.0%	13.0%
8	Tax Rate			35.0%	35.0%	35.0%	35.0%	35.0%	35.0%

Note that Ideko's average selling price is expected to increase because of a 2% inflation rate each year. Likewise, manufacturing costs are expected to rise. Raw materials are forecast to increase at a 1% rate and, although you expect some productivity gains, labor costs will rise at a 4% rate due to additional overtime. The table also shows the reallocation of resources from administration to sales and marketing over the five-year period.

EXAMPLE 19.2

Production Capacity Requirements

Problem

Based on the data in Table 19.3, what production capacity will Ideko require each year? When will an expansion be necessary?

Solution

Production volume each year can be estimated by multiplying the total market size and Ideko's market share in Table 19.3:

	Year	2005	2006	2007	2008	2009	2010
Production Volume (000 units)							
1	Market Size	10,000	10,500	11,025	11,576	12,155	12,763
2	Market Share	10.0%	11.0%	12.0%	13.0%	14.0%	15.0%
3	Production Volume (1 × 2)	1,000	1,155	1,323	1,505	1,702	1,914

Based on this forecast, production volume will exceed its current level by 50% by 2008, necessitating an expansion then.

Capital Expenditures: A Needed Expansion

The spreadsheet in Table 19.4 shows the forecast for Ideko's capital expenditures over the next five years. Based on the estimates for capital expenditures and depreciation, this spreadsheet tracks the book value of Ideko's plant, property, and equipment starting from its level at the beginning of 2005. Note that investment is expected to remain at its current level over the next two years, which is roughly equal to the level of depreciation. Ideko will expand its production during this period by using its existing plant more efficiently. In 2008, however, a major expansion of the plant will be necessary, leading to a large increase in capital expenditures in 2008 and 2009.

The depreciation entries in Table 19.4 are based on the appropriate depreciation schedule for each type of property. Those calculations are quite specific to the nature of the property and are not detailed here. The depreciation shown will be used for tax purposes.[1]

TABLE 19.4 SPREADSHEET

Ideko Capital Expenditure Assumptions

	Year	2005	2006	2007	2008	2009	2010
Fixed Assets and Capital Investment ($ 000)							
1	Opening Book Value	50,000	49,500	49,050	48,645	61,781	69,102
2	Capital Investment	5,000	5,000	5,000	20,000	15,000	8,000
3	Depreciation	(5,500)	(5,450)	(5,405)	(6,865)	(7,678)	(7,710)
4	Closing Book Value	49,500	49,050	48,645	61,781	69,102	69,392

---

[1]Firms often maintain separate books for accounting and tax purposes, and they may use different depreciation assumptions for each. Remember that because depreciation affects cash flows through its tax consequences, tax depreciation is more relevant for valuation.

Working Capital Management

To compensate for its weak sales and marketing efforts, Ideko has sought to retain the loyalty of its retailers in part by maintaining a very lax credit policy. This policy affects Ideko's working capital requirements: For every extra day that customers take to pay, another day's sales revenue is added to accounts receivable (rather than received in cash). From Ideko's current income statement and balance sheet (Table 19.1), we can estimate the number of days of receivables:

$$\text{Accounts Receivable Days} = \frac{\text{Accounts Receivable (\$)}}{\text{Sales Revenue (\$/yr)}} \times 365 \text{ days/yr}$$

$$= \frac{18{,}493}{75{,}000} \times 365 \text{ days} = 90 \text{ days} \qquad (19.1)$$

The standard for the industry is 60 days, and you believe that Ideko can tighten its credit policy to achieve this goal without sacrificing sales.

You also hope to improve Ideko's inventory management. Ideko's balance sheet in Table 19.1 lists inventory of $6.165 million. Of this amount, approximately $2 million corresponds to raw materials, while the rest is finished goods. Given raw material expenditures of $16 million for the year, Ideko currently holds $(2/16) \times 365 = 45.6$ days' worth of raw material inventory. While maintaining a certain amount of inventory is necessary to avoid production stoppages, you believe that, with tighter controls of the production process, 30 days' worth of inventory will be adequate.

Capital Structure Changes: Levering Up

With little debt, excess cash, and substantial earnings, Ideko appears to be significantly underleveraged. You plan to greatly increase the firm's debt, and have obtained bank commitments for loans of $100 million should an agreement be reached. These term loans will have an interest rate of 6.8%, and Ideko will pay interest only during the next five years. The firm will seek additional financing in 2008 and 2009 associated with the expansion of its manufacturing plant, as shown in the spreadsheet in Table 19.5. While Ideko's credit quality should improve over time, the steep slope of the yield curve suggests interest rates may increase; therefore, on balance, you expect Ideko's borrowing rate to remain at 6.8%.

Given Ideko's outstanding debt, its interest expense each year is computed as[2]

$$\text{Interest in Year } t = \text{Interest Rate} \times \text{Ending Balance in Year } (t-1) \qquad (19.2)$$

The interest on the debt will provide a valuable tax shield to offset Ideko's taxable income.

TABLE 19.5 SPREADSHEET	Ideko's Planned Debt and Interest Payments						
Year		**2005**	**2006**	**2007**	**2008**	**2009**	**2010**
Debt and Interest Table ($ 000)							
1 Outstanding Debt		100,000	100,000	100,000	115,000	120,000	120,000
2 Interest on Term Loan	6.80%		(6,800)	(6,800)	(6,800)	(7,820)	(8,160)

---

[2]Equation 19.2 assumes that changes in debt occur at the end of the year. If debt changes throughout the year, it is more accurate to compute interest expenses based on the average level of debt during the year.

TABLE 19.6 SPREADSHEET	Sources and Uses of Funds for the Ideko Acquisition

Acquisition Financing ($ 000)				
Sources			**Uses**	
1 New Term Loan	100,000		Purchase Ideko Equity	150,000
2 Excess Ideko Cash	6,500		Repay Existing Ideko Debt	4,500
3 KKP Equity Investment	53,000		Advisory and Other Fees	5,000
4 Total Sources of Funds	159,500		Total Uses of Funds	159,500

In addition to the tax benefit, the loan will allow KKP to limit its investment in Ideko and preserve its capital for other investments and acquisitions. The sources and uses of funds for the acquisition are shown in Table 19.6. In addition to the $150 million purchase price for Ideko's equity, $4.5 million will be used to repay Ideko's existing debt. With $5 million in advisory and other fees associated with the transaction, the acquisition will require $159.5 million in total funds. KKP's sources of funds include the new loan of $100 million as well as Ideko's own excess cash (which KKP will have access to). Thus, KKP's required equity contribution to the transaction is $159.5 - 100 - 6.5 = \$53$ million.

CONCEPT CHECK

1. What are the different operational improvements KKP plans to make?

2. Why is it necessary to consider these improvements to assess whether the acquisition is attractive?

19.3 Building the Financial Model

The value of any investment opportunity arises from the future cash flows it will generate. To estimate the cash flows resulting from the investment in Ideko, we begin by projecting Ideko's future earnings. We then consider Ideko's working capital and investment needs and estimate its free cash flow. With these data in hand, we can forecast Ideko's balance sheet and statement of cash flows.

Forecasting Earnings

We can forecast Ideko's income statement for the five years following the acquisition based on the operational and capital structure changes proposed. This income statement is often referred to as a **pro forma** income statement, because it is not based on actual data but rather depicts the firm's financials under a given set of hypothetical assumptions. The pro forma income statement translates our expectations regarding the operational improvements KKP can achieve at Ideko into consequences for the firm's earnings.

To build the pro forma income statement, we begin with Ideko's sales. Each year, sales can be calculated from the estimates in Table 19.3 as follows:

$$\text{Sales} = \text{Market Size} \times \text{Market Share} \times \text{Average Sales Price} \qquad (19.3)$$

For example, in 2006, Ideko has projected sales of 10.5 million $\times$ 11% $\times$ 76.5 = \$88.358 million. The spreadsheet in Table 19.7 shows Ideko's current (2005) sales as well as projections for five years after the acquisition (2006–2010).

TABLE 19.7 SPREADSHEET	Pro Forma Income Statement for Ideko, 2005–2010

	Year	2005	2006	2007	2008	2009	2010
Income Statement ($ 000)							
1 **Sales**		75,000	88,358	103,234	119,777	138,149	158,526
2 Cost of Goods Sold							
3 Raw Materials		(16,000)	(18,665)	(21,593)	(24,808)	(28,333)	(32,193)
4 Direct Labor Costs		(18,000)	(21,622)	(25,757)	(30,471)	(35,834)	(41,925)
5 **Gross Profit**		41,000	48,071	55,883	64,498	73,982	84,407
6 Sales and Marketing		(11,250)	(14,579)	(18,582)	(23,356)	(27,630)	(31,705)
7 Administrative		(13,500)	(13,254)	(15,485)	(16,769)	(17,959)	(20,608)
8 **EBITDA**		16,250	20,238	21,816	24,373	28,393	32,094
9 Depreciation		(5,500)	(5,450)	(5,405)	(6,865)	(7,678)	(7,710)
10 **EBIT**		10,750	14,788	16,411	17,508	20,715	24,383
11 Interest Expense (net)		(75)	(6,800)	(6,800)	(6,800)	(7,820)	(8,160)
12 **Pretax Income**		10,675	7,988	9,611	10,708	12,895	16,223
13 Income Tax		(3,736)	(2,796)	(3,364)	(3,748)	(4,513)	(5,678)
14 **Net Income**		**6,939**	**5,193**	**6,247**	**6,960**	**8,382**	**10,545**

The next items in the income statement detail the cost of goods sold. The raw materials cost can be calculated from sales as

$$\text{Raw Materials} = \text{Market Size} \times \text{Market Share} \times \text{Raw Materials per Unit} \quad (19.4)$$

In 2006, the cost of raw materials is 10.5 million $\times$ 11% $\times$ 16.16 = $18.665 million. The same method can be applied to determine the direct labor costs. Sales, marketing, and administrative costs can be computed directly as a percentage of sales. For example:

$$\text{Sales and Marketing} = \text{Sales} \times (\text{Sales and Marketing \% of Sales}) \quad (19.5)$$

Therefore, sales and marketing costs are forecast to be $88.358 million $\times$ 16.5% = $14.579 million in 2006.

Deducting these operating expenses from Ideko's sales, we can project EBITDA over the next five years as shown in line 8 of Table 19.7. Subtracting the depreciation expenses we estimated in Table 19.4, we arrive at Ideko's earnings before interest and taxes. Next, we deduct interest expenses according to the schedule given in Table 19.5.[3] The final expense is the corporate income tax, which we computed using the tax rate in Table 19.3 as

$$\text{Income Tax} = \text{Pretax Income} \times \text{Tax Rate} \quad (19.6)$$

After income taxes, we are left with Ideko's projected pro forma net income as the bottom line in Table 19.7. Based on our projections, net income will rise by 52% from $6.939 million to $10.545 million at the end of five years, although it will drop in the near term due to the large increase in interest expense from the new debt.

---

[3]This interest expense should be offset by any interest earned on investments. As we discuss later in this chapter, we assume that Ideko does not invest its excess cash balances, but instead pays them out to its owner, KKP. Thus, net interest expenses are solely due to Ideko's outstanding debt.

EXAMPLE 19.3	**Forecasting Income**

Problem

By what percentage is Ideko's EBITDA expected to grow over the five-year period? By how much would it grow if Ideko's market share remained at 10%?

Solution

EBITDA will increase from $16.25 million to $32.09 million, or $(32.09/16.25) - 1 = 97\%$, over the five years. With a 10% market share rather than a 15% market share, sales will be only $(10\%/15\%) = 66.7\%$ of the forecast in Table 19.7. Because Ideko's operating expenses are proportional to its unit sales, its expenses and EBITDA will also be 66.7% of the current estimates. Thus, EBITDA will grow to $66.7\% \times 32.09 = \$21.40$ million, which is an increase of only $(21.40/16.25) - 1 = 32\%$.

Working Capital Requirements

The spreadsheet in Table 19.8 lists Ideko's current working capital requirements and forecasts the firm's future working capital needs. (See Chapter 26 for a further discussion of working capital requirements and their determinants.) This forecast includes the plans to tighten Ideko's credit policy, speed up customer payments, and reduce Ideko's inventory of raw materials.

Based on these working capital requirements, the spreadsheet in Table 19.9 forecasts Ideko's net working capital (NWC) over the next five years. Each line item in the spreadsheet is found by computing the appropriate number of days' worth of the corresponding revenue or expense from the income statement (Table 19.7). For example, accounts receivable in 2006 is calculated as[4]

$$\text{Accounts Receivable} = \text{Days Required} \times \frac{\text{Annual Sales}}{365 \text{ days/yr}}$$

$$= 60 \text{ days} \times \frac{\$88.358 \text{ million/yr}}{365 \text{ days/yr}} = \$14.525 \text{ million} \quad (19.7)$$

TABLE 19.8 SPREADSHEET	Ideko's Working Capital Requirements

	Year	2005	>2005
Working Capital Days			
Assets	**Based on:**	**Days**	**Days**
1 Accounts Receivable	Sales Revenue	90	60
2 Raw Materials	Raw Materials Costs	45	30
3 Finished Goods	Raw Materials + Labor Costs	45	45
4 Minimum Cash Balance	Sales Revenue	30	30
Liabilities			
5 Wages Payable	Direct Labor + Admin Costs	15	15
6 Other Accounts Payable	Raw Materials + Sales and Marketing	45	45

[4]If products are highly seasonal, large fluctuations in working capital may occur over the course of the year. When these effects are important, it is best to develop forecasts on a quarterly or monthly basis so that the seasonal effects can be tracked.

TABLE 19.9 SPREADSHEET	Ideko's Net Working Capital Forecast					

Year	2005	2006	2007	2008	2009	2010
Working Capital ($ 000)						
Assets						
1 Accounts Receivable	18,493	14,525	16,970	19,689	22,709	26,059
2 Raw Materials	1,973	1,534	1,775	2,039	2,329	2,646
3 Finished Goods	4,192	4,967	5,838	6,815	7,911	9,138
4 Minimum Cash Balance	6,164	7,262	8,485	9,845	11,355	13,030
5 Total Current Assets	30,822	28,288	33,067	38,388	44,304	50,872
Liabilities						
6 Wages Payable	1,294	1,433	1,695	1,941	2,211	2,570
7 Other Accounts Payable	3,360	4,099	4,953	5,938	6,900	7,878
8 Total Current Liabilities	4,654	5,532	6,648	7,879	9,110	10,448
Net Working Capital						
9 Net Working Capital (5 − 8)	26,168	22,756	26,419	30,509	35,194	40,425
10 Increase in Net Working Capital		(3,412)	3,663	4,089	4,685	5,231

Similarly, Ideko's inventory of finished goods will be $45 \times (18.665 + 21.622)/365 = \$4.967$ million.

Table 19.9 also lists Ideko's minimum cash balance each year. This balance represents the minimum level of cash needed to keep the business running smoothly, allowing for the daily variations in the timing of income and expenses. Firms generally earn little or no interest on these balances, which are held in cash or in a checking or short-term savings accounts. As a consequence, we account for this opportunity cost by including the minimal cash balance as part of the firm's working capital.

We assume that Ideko will earn no interest on this minimal balance. (If it did, this interest would reduce the firm's net interest expense in the income statement.) We also assume that Ideko will pay out as dividends all cash not needed as part of working capital. Therefore, Ideko will hold no excess cash balances or short-term investments above the minimal level reported in Table 19.9. If Ideko were to retain excess funds, these balances would be considered part of its financing strategy (reducing its net debt), and not as part of its working capital.[5]

Ideko's net working capital for each year is computed in Table 19.9 as the difference between the forecasted current assets and current liabilities. Increases in net working capital represent a cost to the firm. Note that as a result of the improvements in accounts receivable and inventory management, Ideko will reduce its net working capital by more than $3.4 million in 2006. After this initial savings, working capital needs will increase in conjunction with the growth of the firm.

Forecasting Free Cash Flow

We now have the data needed to forecast Ideko's free cash flows over the next five years. Ideko's earnings are available from the income statement (Table 19.7), as are its depreciation and interest expenses. Capital expenditures are available from Table 19.4, and changes in net working capital can be found in Table 19.9. We combine these items to estimate the free cash flows in the spreadsheet in Table 19.10.

---

[5]Firms often hold excess cash in anticipation of future investment needs or possible cash shortfalls. Because Ideko can rely on KKP to provide needed capital, excess cash reserves are unnecessary.

TABLE 19.10 SPREADSHEET	Ideko's Free Cash Flow Forecast					
Year	**2005**	**2006**	**2007**	**2008**	**2009**	**2010**
Free Cash Flow ($ 000)						
1 Net Income		5,193	6,247	6,960	8,382	10,545
2 Plus: After-Tax Interest Expense		4,420	4,420	4,420	5,083	5,304
3 **Unlevered Net Income**		9,613	10,667	11,380	13,465	15,849
4 Plus: Depreciation		5,450	5,405	6,865	7,678	7,710
5 Less: Increases in NWC		3,412	(3,663)	(4,089)	(4,685)	(5,231)
6 Less: Capital Expenditures		(5,000)	(5,000)	(20,000)	(15,000)	(8,000)
7 **Free Cash Flow of Firm**		13,475	7,409	(5,845)	1,458	10,328
8 Plus: Net Borrowing		—	—	15,000	5,000	—
9 Less: After-Tax Interest Expense		(4,420)	(4,420)	(4,420)	(5,083)	(5,304)
10 **Free Cash Flow to Equity**		9,055	2,989	4,735	1,375	5,024

To compute Ideko's free cash flow, which excludes cash flows associated with leverage, we first adjust net income by adding back the after-tax interest payments associated with the net debt in its capital structure:[6]

After-Tax Interest Expense =
$$(1 - \text{Tax Rate}) \times (\text{Interest on Debt} - \text{Interest on Excess Cash}) \qquad (19.8)$$

Because Ideko has no excess cash, its after-tax interest expense in 2006 is $(1 - 35\%) \times 6.8$ = $4.42 million, providing unlevered net income of $5.193 + 4.42 = \$9.613$ million. We could also compute the unlevered net income in Table 19.10 by starting with EBIT and deducting taxes. In 2006, for example, EBIT is forecasted as $14.788 million, which amounts to $14.788 \times (1 - 35\%) = \$9.613$ million after taxes.

To compute Ideko's free cash flow from its unlevered net income, we add back depreciation (which is not a cash expense), and deduct Ideko's increases in net working capital and capital expenditures. The free cash flow on line 7 of Table 19.10 shows the cash the firm will generate for its investors, both debt and equity holders. While Ideko will generate substantial free cash flow over the next five years, the level of free cash flow varies substantially from year to year. It is highest in 2006 (due mostly to the large reduction in working capital) and is forecasted to be negative in 2008 (when the plant expansion will begin).

To determine the free cash flow to equity, we first add Ideko's net borrowing (that is, increases to net debt):

Net Borrowing in Year t = Net Debt in Year t − Net Debt in Year $(t - 1)$ \qquad (19.9)

Ideko will borrow in 2008 and 2009 as part of its expansion. We then deduct the after-tax interest payments that were added in line 2.

As shown in the last line of Table 19.10, during the next five years Ideko is expected to generate a positive free cash flow to equity, which will be used to pay dividends to KKP. The free cash flow to equity will be highest in 2006; by 2010, KKP will recoup a significant fraction of its initial investment.

---

[6]If Ideko had some interest income or expenses from working capital, we would *not* include that interest here. We adjust only for interest that is related to the firm's *financing*—that is, interest associated with debt and *excess* cash (cash not included as part of working capital).

INTERVIEW WITH
Joseph L. Rice, III

Joseph L. Rice, III is a founding partner and the former chairman of Clayton, Dubilier & Rice (CD&R). The firm is among the most respected private equity firms in the world. Its investments span a number of industry segments with enterprise values ranging from $1 billion to $15 billion.

QUESTION: *How has private equity business changed since you began in the industry?*

ANSWER: The term "private equity" is very broad and today can cover virtually every kind of investing, short of investing in the stock or bond markets. The buyout business represents a significant component of the private equity market. Since I started in 1966, I've seen many changes as the asset class has matured. In the 1960s and 1970s, the buyout business had relatively little following. Limited capital availability kept transactions small, and we relied on unconventional funding sources. The total purchase price of my first transaction was approximately $3 million, financed through a secured bank line and from individuals contributing amounts ranging from $25,000 to $50,000. In contrast, in 2005, we bought Hertz from Ford for approximately $15 billion.

As the industry has evolved, the attractive returns generated from buyout investments has attracted broader interest from both institutions and high net worth individuals. Buyout firms apply a variety of value creation models, including financial engineering, multiple arbitrage, and industry sector bets, such as technology or healthcare. Today there is more focus on generating returns from improving business performance—which has always been CD&R's underlying investment approach. The character of the businesses that we buy has also changed. Traditionally, this was an asset-heavy business, with much of the financing coming from banks that lent against percentages of inventory and receivables and the liquidation value of hard assets. Now it's become more of a cash flow business.

QUESTION: *What makes a company a good buyout candidate?*

ANSWER: We look to acquire good businesses at fair prices. Acquiring non-core, underperforming divisions of large companies and making them more effective has been a fertile investment area for CD&R. These divestiture buyouts tend to be complex and require experience and patience to execute. For example, we were in discussions with Ford management for three years prior to leading the Hertz division acquisition.

After running a series of projections based on information from management, we develop a capital structure designed to insure the viability of the acquisition candidate. We are relatively unconcerned with EPS but are very return conscious, focusing on cash and creating long-term shareholder value. We must also believe that we can generate a return on equity that meets our standards and justifies our investors' commitments to us.

We also acquire businesses confronting strategic issues where our operating expertise can bring value, such as Kinko's, a great brand franchise that we reorganized and expanded. We prefer service and distribution businesses to large manufacturers because of the wage differential between Asia and the United States and Europe. We also prefer businesses with a diversity of suppliers and customers and where there are multiple levers under our control to improve operating performance.

QUESTION: *Post acquisition, what is the role of the private equity firm?*

ANSWER: CD&R brings both a hands-on ownership style and capital. After closing a transaction, we assess current management's capability to do the job our investment case calls for. If necessary, we build and strengthen the management team. Then we work with them to determine the appropriate strategy to produce outstanding results. Finally, we aggressively pursue productivity, cost reduction, and growth initiatives to enhance operating and financial performance. At Kinko's, we restructured 129 separate S-corporations into one centralized corporation and installed a new management team. Our key strategic decision was transforming Kinko's from a loose confederation of consumer and small business-oriented copy shops into a highly networked company serving major corporations. In the end, that is what made the company an attractive acquisition for FedEx in 2004.

EXAMPLE 19.4	Leverage and Free Cash Flow

Problem

Suppose Ideko does not add leverage in 2008 and 2009, but instead keeps its debt fixed at $100 million until 2010. How would this change in its leverage policy affect its expected free cash flow? How would it affect the free cash flow to equity?

Solution

Because free cash flow is based on unlevered net income, it will not be affected by Ideko's leverage policy. Free cash flow to equity will be affected, however. Net borrowing will be zero each year, and the firm's after-tax interest expense will remain at the 2006 level of $4.42 million:

	Year	2005	2006	2007	2008	2009	2010
Free Cash Flow ($ 000)							
1	**Free Cash Flow of Firm**		13,475	7,409	(5,845)	1,458	10,328
2	Plus: Net Borrowing		—	—	—	—	—
3	Less: After-Tax Interest Expense		(4,420)	(4,420)	(4,420)	(4,420)	(4,420)
4	**Free Cash Flow to Equity**		9,055	2,989	(10,265)	(2,962)	5,908

In this case, Ideko will have a negative free cash flow to equity in 2008 and 2009. That is, without additional borrowing, KKP will have to invest additional capital in the firm to fund the expansion.

The Balance Sheet and Statement of Cash Flows (Optional)

The information we have calculated so far can be used to project Ideko's balance sheet and statement of cash flows through 2010. While these statements are not critical for our valuation, they often prove helpful in providing a more complete picture of how a firm will grow during the forecast period. These statements for Ideko are shown in the spreadsheets in Table 19.11 and Table 19.12.

The statement of cash flows in Table 19.11 starts with net income. Cash from operating activities includes depreciation as well as changes to working capital items (other than cash) from Table 19.9. Note that increases in accounts receivable or inventory are a *use* of cash, whereas an increase in accounts payable is a *source* of cash. Cash from investing activities includes the capital expenditures in Table 19.4. Cash from financing activities includes changes in outstanding debt from Table 19.5, and dividends or stock issuance determined by the free cash flow to equity in Table 19.10. (If free cash flow to equity were negative in any year, it would appear as stock issuance in line 13 in Table 19.11.) As a final check on the calculations, note that the change in cash and cash equivalents on line 15 in Table 19.11 equals the change in the minimum cash balance shown in Table 19.9.

For the balance sheet, we must begin by adjusting Ideko's closing 2005 balance sheet from Table 19.1 to account for the transaction. The transaction will affect the firm's goodwill, stockholders' equity, and its cash and debt balances. We show these changes by constructing a new "pro forma" 2005 balance sheet that represents the firm just after the transaction closes (see Table 19.12). Let's consider how each change is determined.

First, we calculate goodwill as the difference between the acquisition price and the value of the net assets acquired:

$$\text{New Goodwill} = \text{Acquisition Price} - \text{Value of Net Assets Acquired} \quad (19.10)$$

In this case, the acquisition price is the $150 million purchase price for Ideko's existing equity. For the net assets acquired, we use Ideko's existing book value of equity, $77.668

TABLE 19.11 SPREADSHEET	Pro Forma Statement of Cash Flows for Ideko, 2005–2010					
Year	**2005**	**2006**	**2007**	**2008**	**2009**	**2010**
Statement of Cash Flows ($ 000)						
1 **Net Income**		5,193	6,247	6,960	8,382	10,545
2 Depreciation		5,450	5,405	6,865	7,678	7,710
3 Changes in Working Capital						
4 Accounts Receivable		3,968	(2,445)	(2,719)	(3,020)	(3,350)
5 Inventory		(336)	(1,112)	(1,242)	(1,385)	(1,544)
6 Accounts Payable		878	1,116	1,231	1,231	1,338
7 **Cash from Operating Activities**		15,153	9,211	11,095	12,885	14,699
8 Capital Expenditures		(5,000)	(5,000)	(20,000)	(15,000)	(8,000)
9 Other Investment		—	—	—	—	—
10 **Cash from Investing Activities**		(5,000)	(5,000)	(20,000)	(15,000)	(8,000)
11 Debt Issuance (or Repayment)		—	—	15,000	5,000	—
12 Dividends		(9,055)	(2,989)	(4,735)	(1,375)	(5,024)
13 Sale (or Purchase) of Stock		—	—	—	—	—
14 **Cash from Financing Activities**		(9,055)	(2,989)	10,265	3,625	(5,024)
15 **Change in Cash** (7 + 10 + 14)		**1,098**	**1,223**	**1,360**	**1,510**	**1,675**

million, *excluding* any pre-existing goodwill ($0). Thus, new goodwill is $150 - (77.668 - 0) = \$72.332$ million.[7]

TABLE 19.12 SPREADSHEET	Pro Forma Balance Sheet for Ideko, 2005–2010					
Year	**2005PF**	**2006**	**2007**	**2008**	**2009**	**2010**
Balance Sheet ($ 000)						
Assets						
1 Cash and Cash Equivalents	6,164	7,262	8,485	9,845	11,355	13,030
2 Accounts Receivable	18,493	14,525	16,970	19,689	22,709	26,059
3 Inventories	6,165	6,501	7,613	8,854	10,240	11,784
4 **Total Current Assets**	30,822	28,288	33,067	38,388	44,304	50,872
5 Property, Plant, and Equipment	49,500	49,050	48,645	61,781	69,102	69,392
6 Goodwill	72,332	72,332	72,332	72,332	72,332	72,332
7 **Total Assets**	152,654	149,670	154,044	172,501	185,738	192,597
Liabilities						
8 Accounts Payable	4,654	5,532	6,648	7,879	9,110	10,448
9 Debt	100,000	100,000	100,000	115,000	120,000	120,000
10 **Total Liabilities**	104,654	105,532	106,648	122,879	129,110	130,448
Stockholders' Equity						
11 Starting Stockholders' Equity		48,000	44,138	47,396	49,621	56,628
12 Net Income	(5,000)	5,193	6,247	6,960	8,382	10,545
13 Dividends		(9,055)	(2,989)	(4,735)	(1,375)	(5,024)
14 Sale (or Purchase) of Stock	53,000	—	—	—	—	—
15 **Stockholders' Equity**	48,000	44,138	47,396	49,621	56,628	62,149
16 **Total Liabilities and Equity**	152,654	149,670	154,044	172,501	185,738	192,597

---

[7]We have simplified somewhat the balance sheet adjustments in the goodwill calculation. In particular, the book values of Ideko's assets and liabilities may be "stepped up" to reflect current fair values, and a portion of the excess purchase price may be allocated to intangible assets as opposed to goodwill.

Building a three-statement financial model is complex, and even experienced financial modelers make mistakes. Audit your model to check for errors using the following best practices.

Do Not Use Stockholders' Equity as a Plug

Because the balance sheet must balance, it is tempting to calculate stockholders' equity in the spreadsheet as the difference between total assets and total liabilities. Doing so, however, nullifies a key benefit of the balance sheet as an audit tool on the rest of the financial model. As a best practice, always calculate stockholders' equity directly as shown here. Then, in a line below the balance sheet, include a "check" line that tests whether total assets equal total liabilities and equity each year—and if the difference is non-zero, display it in a bold red font so the errror is apparent.

   If the model does have an error, the amount of the difference will provide a clue to its source: If the difference is a constant each year, it is likely to result from one of the adjustments in the initial pro forma balance sheet; if it varies over time, check each line of the balance sheet to be sure the trends make sense (e.g., that inventories grow with sales), and check the sign of each line item in the statement of cash flows to make sure all sources of cash are positive and all uses of cash are negative (especially working capital).

Check the Cash and Payout Policy

Check that the firm's cash and payouts match its intended policy. In this case, we forecast that Ideko would pay out all excess cash going forward. Thus, its cash balances in the balance sheet should match the minimum balances specified in Table 19.9. If not, be sure to audit the free cash flow to equity calculation in Table 19.10. Note also that in this example, free cash flow to equity (i.e., dividends) was an output of the model. We could have alternatively assumed Ideko would retain its excess cash. In that case, free cash flow to equity would be zero (no dividends would be paid), and changes in cash (and thus the firm's net borrowing) would be outputs.

Next, consider stockholders' equity, which we calculate as

$$\text{New Stockholders' Equity} = \text{Equity Contributions} - \text{Expensed Transaction Fees} \quad (19.11)$$

In this case, we deduct the $5 million in advisory fee expenses from KKP's initial equity contribution of $53 million to calculate new shareholders' equity of $48 million.[8]

   Finally, we adjust Ideko's cash and debt balances by deducting the excess cash of $6.5 million used to help fund the transaction, eliminating Ideko's existing debt (which will be repaid), and adding the new debt incurred of $100 million. These steps complete the pro forma 2005 balance sheet as of the completion of the transaction and are shown in Table 19.12.

   To construct the balance sheet going forward, adjust the cash balance to reflect the change in cash from line 15 of the statement of cash flows in Table 19.11. All other current assets and liabilities come from the net working capital spreadsheet (Table 19.9). The inventory entry on the balance sheet includes both raw materials and finished goods. Property, plant, and equipment information comes from the capital expenditure spreadsheet (Table 19.4), and the debt comes from Table 19.5. From Eq. 2.7, stockholders' equity increases each year through retained earnings (net income less dividends) and new capital

---

[8]Under SFAS 141R, as of December 2008, acquisition-related advisory and legal fees should be expensed as incurred. To illustrate this method, we have applied it here. Financing fees related to debt issuance, on the other hand, are not deducted from shareholders' equity, but are instead capitalized as a new asset and amortized over the loan's term. For simplicity, we have ignored these fees and any related tax consequences.

contributions (stock issuances net of repurchases). Dividends after 2005 are equal to positive free cash flows to equity from Table 19.10, whereas negative free cash flows to equity represent a stock issuance. As a check on the calculations, note that the balance sheet does, indeed, balance: Total assets equal total liabilities and equity.[9]

Ideko's book value of equity will decline in 2006, as Ideko reduces its working capital and pays out the savings as part of a large dividend. The firm's book value will then rise as it expands. Ideko's book debt-equity ratio will decline from $100,000/48,000 = 2.1$ to $120,000/62,149 = 1.9$ during the five-year period.

CONCEPT CHECK

1. What is a pro forma income statement?

2. How do we calculate the firm's free cash flow, and the free cash flow to equity?

19.4 Estimating the Cost of Capital

To value KKP's investment in Ideko, we need to assess the risk associated with Ideko and estimate an appropriate cost of capital. Because Ideko is a private firm, we cannot use its own past returns to evaluate its risk, but must instead rely on comparable publicly traded firms. In this section, we use data from the comparable firms identified earlier to estimate a cost of capital for Ideko.

Our approach is as follows. First, we use the techniques developed in Part 4 to estimate the equity cost of capital for Oakley, Luxottica Group, and Nike. Then, we estimate the unlevered cost of capital for each firm based on its capital structure. We use the unlevered cost of capital of the comparable firms to estimate Ideko's unlevered cost of capital. Once we have this estimate, we can use Ideko's capital structure to determine its equity cost of capital or WACC, depending on the valuation method employed.

CAPM-Based Estimation

To determine an appropriate cost of capital, we must first determine the appropriate measure of risk. KKP's investment in Ideko will represent a large fraction of its portfolio. As a consequence, KKP itself is not well diversified. But KKP's investors are primarily pension funds and large institutional investors, which are themselves well diversified and which evaluate their performance relative to the market as a benchmark. Thus, you decide that estimating market risk using the CAPM approach is justified.

Using the CAPM, we can estimate the equity cost of capital for each comparable firm based on the beta of its equity. As outlined in Chapter 12, the standard approach to estimating an equity beta is to determine the historical sensitivity of the stock's returns to the market's returns by using linear regression to estimate the slope coefficient in the equation:

$$\underbrace{R_s - r_f}_{\substack{\text{Excess return} \\ \text{of stock } s}} = \alpha_s + \beta_s \underbrace{(R_{mkt} - r_f)}_{\substack{\text{Excess return} \\ \text{of market portfolio}}} + \varepsilon_s \qquad (19.12)$$

---

[9] In Table 19.12, goodwill is assumed to remain constant. If the transaction were structured as an acquisition of assets (as opposed to stock), the goodwill would be amortizable over 15 years for tax reporting as per section 197 of the Internal Revenue Code. For financial accounting purposes, goodwill is not amortized but is subject to an impairment test at least once a year as specified in FASB 142 (though changes in goodwill due to impairment have no tax accounting consequence).

TABLE 19.13	Equity Betas with Confidence Intervals for Comparable Firms			
	Monthly Returns		**10-Day Returns**	
Firm	Beta	95% C.I.	Beta	95% C.I.
Oakley	1.99	1.2 to 2.8	1.37	0.9 to 1.9
Luxottica	0.56	0.0 to 1.1	0.86	0.5 to 1.2
Nike	0.48	−0.1 to 1.0	0.69	0.4 to 1.0

As a proxy for the market portfolio, we will use a value-weighted portfolio of all NYSE, AMEX, and NASDAQ stocks. With data from 2000 to 2004, we calculate the excess return—the realized return minus the yield on a one-month Treasury security—for each firm and for the market portfolio. We then estimate the equity beta for each firm by regressing its excess return onto the excess return of the market portfolio. We perform the regression for both monthly returns and 10-day returns. The estimated equity betas, together with their 95% confidence intervals, are shown in Table 19.13.

While we would like to assess risk and, therefore, estimate beta based on longer horizon returns (consistent with our investors' investment horizon), the confidence intervals we obtain using monthly data are extremely wide. These confidenc intervals narrow somewhat when we use 10-day returns. In any case, the results make clear that a fair amount of uncertainty persists when we estimate the beta for an individual firm.

Unlevering Beta

Given an estimate of each firm's equity beta, we next "unlever" the beta based on the firm's capital structure. Here we use Eq. 12.9 (which is equivalent, in terms of returns, to calculating the pretax WACC as in Eq. 18.6):

$$\beta_U = \left(\frac{\text{Equity Value}}{\text{Enterprise Value}} \right) \beta_E + \left(\frac{\text{Net Debt Value}}{\text{Enterprise Value}} \right) \beta_D \qquad (19.13)$$

Recall that we must use the *net* debt of the firm—that is, we must subtract any cash from the level of debt—so we use the enterprise value of the firm as the sum of debt and equity in the formula.[10] Table 19.14 shows the capital structure for each comparable firm. Oakley has no debt, while Luxottica has about 17% debt in its capital structure. Nike holds cash that exceeds its debt, leading to a negative net debt in its capital structure.

Table 19.14 also estimates the unlevered beta of each firm. Here, we have used an equity beta for each firm within the range of the results from Table 19.13. Given the low or negative debt levels for each firm, assuming a beta for debt of zero is a reasonable approximation. Then, we compute an unlevered beta for each firm according to Eq. 19.13.

The range of the unlevered betas for these three firms is large. Both Luxottica and Nike have relatively low betas, presumably reflecting the relative noncyclicality of their core businesses (prescription eyewear for Luxottica and athletic shoes for Nike). Oakley has a much

---

[10]Recall from Chapter 18 that Eq. 19.13 assumes that the firm will maintain a target leverage ratio. If the debt is expected to remain fixed for some period, we should also deduct the value of the predetermined tax shields from the firm's net debt.

TABLE 19.14	Capital Structure and Unlevered Beta Estimates for Comparable Firms				
Firm	$\dfrac{E}{E+D}$	$\dfrac{D}{E+D}$	β_E	β_D	β_U
Oakley	1.00	0.00	1.50	—	1.50
Luxottica	0.83	0.17	0.75	0	0.62
Nike	1.05	−0.05	0.60	0	0.63

higher unlevered beta, perhaps because the high-end specialty sports eyewear it produces is a discretionary expense for most consumers.

Ideko's Unlevered Cost of Capital

The data from the comparable firms provides guidance to us for estimating Ideko's unlevered cost of capital. Ideko's products are not as high end as Oakley's eyewear, so their sales are unlikely to vary as much with the business cycle as Oakley's sales do. However, Ideko does not have a prescription eyewear division, as Luxottica does. Ideko's products are also fashion items rather than exercise items, so we expect Ideko's cost of capital to be closer to Oakley's than to Nike's or Luxottica's. Therefore, we use 1.20 as our preliminary estimate for Ideko's unlevered beta, which is somewhat above the average of the comparables in Table 19.14.

We use the security market line of the CAPM to translate this beta into a cost of capital for Ideko. In mid-2005, one-year Treasury rates were approximately 4%; we use this rate for the risk-free interest rate. We also need an estimate of the market risk premium. Since 1960, the average annual return of the value-weighted market portfolio of U.S. stocks has exceeded that of one-year Treasuries by approximately 5%. However, this estimate is a backward-looking number. As we mentioned in Chapter 12, some researchers believe that future stock market excess returns are likely to be lower than this historical average. To be conservative in our valuation of Ideko, we will use 5% as the expected market risk premium.

Based on these choices, our estimate of Ideko's unlevered cost of capital is

$$r_U = r_f + \beta_U (E[R_{mkt}] - r_f) = 4\% + 1.20(5\%)$$
$$= 10\%$$

Of course, as our discussion has made clear, this estimate contains a large amount of uncertainty. Thus, we will include sensitivity analysis with regard to the unlevered cost of capital in our analysis.

EXAMPLE 19.5	Estimating the Unlevered Cost of Capital

Problem

Using the monthly equity beta estimates for each firm in Table 19.13, what range of unlevered cost of capital estimates is possible?

Solution

Oakley has the highest equity beta of 1.99, which is also its unlevered beta (it has no debt). With this beta, the unlevered cost of capital would be $r_U = 4\% + 1.99(5\%) = 13.95\%$. At the other extreme, given its capital structure, Luxottica's equity beta of 0.56 implies an unlevered beta of $(0.56)(0.83) = 0.46$. With this beta, the unlevered cost of capital would be $r_U = 4\% + 0.46(5\%) = 6.3\%$.

As with any analysis based on comparables, experience and judgment are necessary to come up with a reasonable estimate of the unlevered cost of capital. In this case, our choice would be guided by industry norms, an assessment of which comparable is closest in terms of market risk, and possibly knowledge of how cyclical Ideko's revenues have been historically.

1. What is a standard approach to estimate an equity beta?

2. How do we estimate a firm's unlevered cost of capital using data from comparable publicly traded firms?

19.5 Valuing the Investment

Thus far, we have forecasted the first five years of cash flows from KKP's investment in Ideko, and we have estimated the investment's unlevered cost of capital. In this section, we combine these inputs to estimate the value of the opportunity. The first step is to develop an estimate of Ideko's value at the end of our five-year forecast horizon. To do so, we consider both a multiples approach and a discounted cash flow (DCF) valuation using the WACC method. Given Ideko's free cash flow and continuation value, we then estimate its total enterprise value in 2005 using the APV method. Deducting the value of debt and KKP's initial investment from our estimate of Ideko's enterprise value gives the NPV of the investment opportunity. In addition to NPV, we look at some other common metrics, including IRR and cash multiples.

The Multiples Approach to Continuation Value

Practitioners generally estimate a firm's continuation value (also called the terminal value) at the end of the forecast horizon using a valuation multiple. While forecasting cash flows explicitly is useful in capturing those specific aspects of a company that distinguish the firm from its competitors in the short run, in the long run firms in the same industry typically have similar expected growth rates, profitability, and risk. As a consequence, multiples are likely to be relatively homogeneous across firms. Thus, applying a multiple is potentially as reliable as estimating the value based on an explicit forecast of distant cash flows.

Of the different valuation multiples available, the EBITDA multiple is most often used in practice. In most settings, the EBITDA multiple is more reliable than sales or earnings multiples because it accounts for the firm's operating efficiency and is not affected by leverage differences between firms. We estimate the continuation value using an EBITDA multiple as follows:

$$\text{Continuation Enterprise Value at Forecast Horizon} = \\ \text{EBITDA at Horizon} \times \text{EBITDA Multiple at Horizon} \qquad (19.14)$$

From the income statement in Table 19.7, Ideko's EBITDA in 2010 is forecast to be $32.09 million. If we assume its EBITDA multiple in 2010 is unchanged from the value of 9.1 that we calculated at the time of the original purchase, then Ideko's continuation value in 2010 is $32.09 \times 9.1 = \$292.05$ million. This calculation is shown in the spreadsheet in Table 19.15. Given Ideko's outstanding debt of $120 million in 2010, this estimate corresponds to an equity value of $172.05 million.

TABLE 19.15 SPREADSHEET	Continuation Value Estimate for Ideko

Continuation Value: Multiples Approach ($ 000)		Common Multiples	
1 EBITDA in 2010	32,094	**Common Multiples**	
2 EBITDA multiple	9.1×	EV/Sales	1.8×
3 **Continuation Enterprise Value**	**292,052**	P/E (levered)	16.3×
4 Debt	(120,000)	P/E (unlevered)	18.4×
5 **Continuation Equity Value**	**172,052**		

Table 19.15 also shows Ideko's sales and P/E multiples based on this continuation value. The continuation value is 1.8 times Ideko's 2010 sales, and the equity value is 16.3 times Ideko's 2010 earnings. Because the P/E multiple is affected by leverage, we also report Ideko's **unlevered P/E ratio**, which is calculated as its continuing enterprise value divided by its unlevered net income in 2010 (listed in Table 19.10). Ideko would have this P/E ratio if it had no debt in 2010, so this information is useful when comparing Ideko to unlevered firms in the industry.

We can use the various multiples to assess the reasonableness of our estimated continuation value. While the value-to-sales ratio is high compared to the overall sporting goods industry, these multiples are otherwise low relative to the comparables in Table 19.2. If we expect these industry multiples to remain stable, this estimate of Ideko's continuation value seems reasonable (if not relatively conservative).

The Discounted Cash Flow Approach to Continuation Value

One difficulty with relying solely on comparables when forecasting a continuation value is that we are comparing *future* multiples of the firm with *current* multiples of its competitors. In 2010, the multiples of Ideko and the comparables we have chosen may all be very different, especially if the industry is currently experiencing abnormal growth. To guard against such a bias, it is wise to check our estimate of the continuation value based on fundamentals using a discounted cash flow approach.

To estimate a continuation value in year T using discounted cash flows, we assume a constant expected growth rate, g, and a constant debt-equity ratio. As explained in Chapter 18, when the debt-equity ratio is constant, the WACC valuation method is the simplest to apply:

$$\text{Enterprise Value in Year } T = V_T^L = \frac{FCF_{T+1}}{r_{wacc} - g} \tag{19.15}$$

To estimate free cash flow in year $T + 1$, recall that free cash flow is equal to unlevered net income plus depreciation, less capital expenditures and increases in net working capital (see Table 19.10):

$$FCF_{T+1} = \text{Unlevered Net Income}_{T+1} + \text{Depreciation}_{T+1}$$
$$- \text{Increases in NWC}_{T+1} - \text{Capital Expenditures}_{T+1} \tag{19.16}$$

Suppose the firm's sales are expected to grow at a nominal rate g. If the firm's operating expenses remain a fixed percentage of sales, then its unlevered net income will also grow at rate g. Similarly, the firm's receivables, payables, and other elements of net working capital will grow at rate g.

What about capital expenditures? The firm will need new capital to offset depreciation; it will also need to add capacity as its production volume grows. Given a sales growth rate g, we may expect that the firm will need to expand its investment in fixed assets at about the same rate. In that case,[11]

$$\text{Capital Expenditures}_{T+1} = \text{Depreciation}_{T+1} + g \times \text{Fixed Assets}_T$$

Thus, given a growth rate of g for the firm, we can estimate its free cash flow as

$$FCF_{T+1} = (1 + g) \times \text{Unlevered Net Income}_T$$
$$-g \times \text{Net Working Capital}_T - g \times \text{Fixed Assets}_T \quad (19.17)$$

Together, Eq. 19.15 and Eq. 19.17 allow us to estimate a firm's continuation value based on its long-run growth rate.

EXAMPLE 19.6

A DCF Estimate of the Continuation Value

Problem

Estimate Ideko's continuation value in 2010 assuming a future expected growth rate of 5%, a future debt-to-value ratio of 40%, and a debt cost of capital of 6.8%.

Solution

In 2010, Ideko's unlevered net income is forecasted to be $15.849 million (Table 19.10), with working capital of $40.425 million (Table 19.9). It has fixed assets of $69.392 million (Table 19.4). From Eq. 19.17, we can estimate Ideko's free cash flow in 2011:

$$FCF_{2011} = (1.05)(15.849) - (5\%)(40.425) - (5\%)(69.392) = \$11.151 \text{ million}$$

This estimate represents nearly an 8% increase over Ideko's 2010 free cash flow of $10.328 million. It exceeds the 5% growth rate of sales due to the decline in the required additions to Ideko's net working capital as its growth rate slows.

With a debt-to-value ratio of 40%, Ideko's WACC can be calculated from Eq. 18.11 or Eq. 12.13:

$$r_{wacc} = r_U - d\,\tau_c\, r_D = 10\% - 0.40(0.35)\,6.8\% = 9.05\%$$

Given the estimate of Ideko's free cash flow and WACC, we can estimate Ideko's continuation value in 2010:

$$V^L_{2010} = \frac{11.151}{9.05\% - 5\%} = \$275.33 \text{ million}$$

This continuation value represents a terminal EBITDA multiple of $275.33/32.09 = 8.6$.

Both the multiples approach and the discounted cash flow approach are useful in deriving a realistic continuation value estimate. Our recommendation is to combine both approaches, as we do in Table 19.16. As shown in the spreadsheet, our projected EBITDA

---

[11]Here, fixed assets are measured according to their book value net of accumulated depreciation. This level of capital expenditures is required to maintain the firm's ratio of sales to fixed assets (also called its fixed asset turnover ratio). An alternative approach—which is preferable if we anticipate a change in the turnover ratio—is to estimate increases in NWC and net investment (capital expenditures in excess of depreciation) in Eq. 19.16 as a target percentage of the *change* in sales, as we did in Chapter 9 (see Example 9.7), where the target percentage is the expected long-run ratio of NWC and PP&E to sales.

TABLE 19.16 SPREADSHEET	Discounted Cash Flow Estimate of Continuation Value, with Implied EBITDA Multiple

Continuation Value: DCF and EBITDA Multiple ($ 000)

1	Long-Term Growth Rate	5.3%		
2	Target $D/(E + D)$	40.0%		
3	Projected WACC	9.05%		
Free Cash Flow in 2011				
4	Unlevered Net Income	16,695	**Continuation Enterprise Value**	**292,052**
5	Less: Increase in NWC	(2,158)		
6	Less: Net Investment*	(3,705)	**Implied EBITDA Multiple**	**9.1×**
7	Free Cash Flow	10,832		

*Net investment equals the difference between capital expenditures and depreciation, so subtracting this amount is equivalent to adding back depreciation and subtracting capital expenditures (see Eq. 9.20).

multiple of 9.1 can be justified by the discounted cash flow method with a nominal long-term growth rate of about 5.3%.[12] Given an expected future inflation rate of 2.5%, this nominal rate represents a real growth rate of about 2.8%. This implied growth rate is another important reality check for our continuation value estimate. If it is much higher than our expectations of long-run growth for the industry as a whole, we should be more skeptical of the estimate being used.

APV Valuation of Ideko's Equity

Our estimate of Ideko's continuation value summarizes the value of the firm's free cash flow beyond the forecast horizon. We can combine it with our forecast for free cash flow through 2010 (Table 19.10, line 7) to estimate Ideko's value today. Recall from Chapter 18

COMMON MISTAKE	Continuation Values and Long-Run Growth

The continuation value is one of the most important estimates when valuing a firm. A common mistake is to use an overly optimistic continuation value, which will lead to an upward bias in the estimated current value of the firm. Be aware of the following pitfalls:

Using multiples based on current high growth rates. Continuation value estimates are often based on current valuation multiples of existing firms. But if these firms are currently experiencing high growth that will eventually slow down, their multiples can be expected to decline over time. In this scenario, if we estimate a continuation value based on today's multiples without accounting for this decline as growth slows, the estimate will be biased upward.

Ignoring investment necessary for growth. When using the discounted cash flow method, we cannot assume

that $FCF_{T+1} = FCF_T (1 + g)$ if the firm's growth rate has changed between T and $T + 1$. Whenever the growth rate changes, expenditures on working and fixed capital will be affected, and we must take this effect into account as we do in Eq. 19.17.

Using unsustainable long-term growth rates. When using the discounted cash flow method, we must choose a long-term growth rate for the firm. By choosing a high rate, we can make the continuation value estimate extremely high. In the long run, however, firms cannot continue to grow faster than the overall economy. Thus, we should be suspicious of long-term growth rates that exceed the expected rate of GDP growth, which has averaged between 2.5% and 3.5% in *real* terms (that is, not including inflation) in the United States over the past several decades.

---

[12]The exact nominal growth rate needed to match an EBITDA multiple of 9.1 is 5.33897%, which can be found using Solver in Excel.

| TABLE 19.17 SPREADSHEET | APV Estimate of Ideko's Initial Equity Value |

	Year	2005	2006	2007	2008	2009	2010
APV Method ($ 000)							
1 Free Cash Flow			13,475	7,409	(5,845)	1,458	10,328
2 **Unlevered Value** V^U (at 10%)		202,732	209,530	223,075	251,227	274,891	292,052
3 Interest Tax Shield			2,380	2,380	2,380	2,737	2,856
4 **Tax Shield Value** T^S (at 6.8%)		10,428	8,757	6,972	5,067	2,674	—
5 **APV:** $V^L = V^U + T^S$		213,160	218,287	230,047	256,294	277,566	292,052
6 Debt		(100,000)	(100,000)	(100,000)	(115,000)	(120,000)	(120,000)
7 **Equity Value**		**113,160**	**118,287**	**130,047**	**141,294**	**157,566**	**172,052**

that because the debt is paid on a fixed schedule during the forecast period, the APV method is the easiest valuation method to apply.

The steps to estimate Ideko's value using the APV method are shown in the spreadsheet in Table 19.17. First, we compute Ideko's unlevered value V^U, which is the firm's value if we were to operate the company without leverage during the forecast period and sell it for its continuation value at the end of the forecast horizon. Thus, the final value in 2010 would be the continuation value we estimated in Table 19.15. The value in earlier periods includes the free cash flows paid by the firm (from Table 19.10) discounted at the unlevered cost of capital r_U that we estimated in Section 19.4[13]:

$$V_{t-1}^U = \frac{FCF_t + V_t^U}{1 + r_U} \qquad (19.18)$$

Next, we incorporate Ideko's interest tax shield during the forecast horizon. The interest tax shield equals the tax rate of 35% (Table 19.3) multiplied by Ideko's scheduled interest payments (see Table 19.5). Because the debt levels are predetermined, we compute the value T^s of the tax shield by discounting the tax savings at the debt interest rate, $r_D = 6.80\%$:

$$T_{t-1}^s = \frac{\text{Interest Tax Shield}_t + T_t^s}{1 + r_D} \qquad (19.19)$$

Combining the unlevered value and the tax shield value gives the APV, which is Ideko's enterprise value given the planned leverage policy. By deducting debt, we obtain our estimate for the value of Ideko's equity during the forecast period.

Thus, our estimate for Ideko's initial enterprise value is $213 million, with an equity value of $113 million. As KKP's initial cost to acquire Ideko's equity is $53 million (see Table 19.6), based on these estimates the deal looks attractive, with an NPV of $113 million − $53 million = $60 million.

A Reality Check

At this point, it is wise to step back and assess whether our valuation results make sense. Does an initial enterprise value of $213 million for Ideko seem reasonable compared to the values of other firms in the industry?

---

[13]Note that in 2010, we use the continuation value of $292 million as the final "unlevered" value, even though this value might include future tax shields (as in Example 19.6). This approach is correct as we are using the APV calculation only to value the additional tax shields earned during the forecast horizon. Combining discounting methodologies as we have done here is very useful in situations like this one in which the firm is likely to be recapitalized at the exit horizon.

> **COMMON MISTAKE** **Missing Assets or Liabilities**
>
> When computing the enterprise value of a firm from its free cash flows, remember that we are valuing only those assets and liabilities whose cash flow consequences are included in our projections. Any "missing" assets or liabilities must be added to the APV estimate to determine the value of equity. In this case, we deduct the firm's debt and add any excess cash or other marketable securities that have not been included (for Ideko, excess cash has already been paid out and will remain at zero, so
>
> no adjustment is needed). We also adjust for any other assets or liabilities that have not been explicitly considered. For example, if a firm owns vacant land, or if it has patents or other rights whose potential cash flows were not included in the projections, the value of these assets must be accounted for separately. The same is true for liabilities such as stock option grants, potential legal liabilities, leases (if the lease payments were not included in earnings), or underfunded pension liabilities.

Here again, multiples are helpful. Let's compute the initial valuation multiples that would be implied by our estimated enterprise value of $213 million and compare them to Ideko's closest competitors as we did in Table 19.2. Table 19.18 provides our results.

Naturally, the valuation multiples based on the estimated enterprise value of $213 million, which would correspond to a purchase price of $215 million given Ideko's existing debt and excess cash, are higher than those based on a purchase price of $150 million. They are now at the top end or somewhat above the range of the values of the other firms that we used for comparison. While these multiples are not unreasonable given the operational improvements that KKP plans to implement, they indicate that our projections may be somewhat optimistic and depend critically on KKP's ability to achieve the operational improvements it plans.

Our estimated initial EBITDA multiple of 13.1 also exceeds the multiple of 9.1 that we assumed for the continuation value. Thus, our estimate forecasts a decline in the EBITDA multiple, which is appropriate given our expectation that growth will be higher in the short run. If the multiple did not decline, we should question whether our continuation value is too optimistic.

IRR and Cash Multiples

While the NPV method is the most reliable method when evaluating a transaction like KKP's acquisition of Ideko, real-world practitioners often use IRR and the *cash multiple* (or multiple of money) as alternative valuation metrics. We discuss both of these methods in this section.

To compute the IRR, we must compute KKP's cash flows over the life of the transaction. KKP's initial investment in Ideko, from Table 19.6, is $53 million. KKP will then receive cash dividends from Ideko based on the free cash flow to equity reported in Table 19.10. Finally, we assume that KKP will sell its equity share in Ideko at the end of five years,

| | **TABLE 19.18** | Ideko Financial Ratios Comparison, Mid-2005, Based on Discounted Cash Flow Estimate Versus Proposed Purchase Price |

Ratio	Ideko (Estimated Value)	Ideko (Purchase Price)	Oakley, Inc.	Luxottica Group	Nike, Inc.	Sporting Goods
P/E	31.0×	21.6×	24.8×	28.0×	18.2×	20.3×
EV/Sales	2.8×	2.0×	2.0×	2.7×	1.5×	1.4×
EV/EBITDA	13.1×	9.1×	11.6×	14.4×	9.3×	11.4×

TABLE 19.19 SPREADSHEET	IRR and Cash Multiple for KKP's Investment in Ideko

	Year	2005	2006	2007	2008	2009	2010
IRR and Cash Multiple							
1 Initial Investment		(53,000)					
2 Free Cash Flow to Equity			9,055	2,989	4,735	1,375	5,024
3 Continuation Equity Value							172,052
4 KKP Cash Flows		(53,000)	9,055	2,989	4,735	1,375	177,077
5 **IRR**		**33.3%**					
6 **Cash Multiple**		**3.7×**					

receiving the continuation equity value. We combine these data to determine KKP's cash flows in the spreadsheet in Table 19.19. Given the cash flows, we compute the IRR of the transaction, which is 33.3%.

While an IRR of 33.3% might sound attractive, it is not straightforward to evaluate in this context. To do so, we must compare it to the appropriate cost of capital for KKP's investment. Because KKP holds an equity position in Ideko, we should use Ideko's equity cost of capital. Of course, Ideko's leverage ratio changes over the five-year period, which will change the risk of its equity. Thus, there is no single cost of capital to compare to the IRR.[14]

The spreadsheet in Table 19.19 also computes the cash multiple for the transaction. The **cash multiple** (also called the **multiple of money** or **absolute return**) is the ratio of the total cash received to the total cash invested. The cash multiple for KKP's investment in Ideko is

$$\text{Cash Multiple} = \frac{\text{Total Cash Received}}{\text{Total Cash Invested}}$$

$$= \frac{9055 + 2989 + 4735 + 1375 + 177,077}{53,000} = 3.7 \quad (19.20)$$

That is, KKP expects to receive a return that is 3.7 times its investment in Ideko. The cash multiple is a common metric used by investors in transactions such as this one. It has an obvious weakness: The cash multiple does not depend on the amount of time it takes to receive the cash, nor does it account for the risk of the investment. It is therefore useful only for comparing deals with similar time horizons and risk.

CONCEPT CHECK

1. What are the main methods of estimating the continuation value of the firm at the end of the forecast horizon?

2. What are the potential pitfalls of analyzing a transaction like this one based on its IRR or cash multiple?

---

[14]See the appendix to this chapter for a calculation of Ideko's annual equity cost of capital.

19.6 Sensitivity Analysis

Any financial valuation is only as accurate as the estimates on which it is based. Before concluding our analysis, it is important to assess the uncertainty of our estimates and to determine their potential impact on the value of the deal.

Once we have developed the spreadsheet model for KKP's investment in Ideko, it is straightforward to perform a sensitivity analysis to determine the impact of changes in different parameters on the deal's value. For example, the spreadsheet in Table 19.20 shows the sensitivity of our estimates of the value of KKP's investment to changes in our assumptions regarding the exit EBITDA multiple that KKP obtains when Ideko is sold, as well as Ideko's unlevered cost of capital.

In our initial analysis, we assumed an exit EBITDA multiple of 9.1. Table 19.20 shows that each 1.0 increase in the multiple represents about $20 million in initial value.[15] KKP will break even on its $53 million investment in Ideko with an exit multiple of slightly more than 6.0. The table also shows, however, that an exit multiple of 6.0 is consistent with a future growth rate for Ideko of less than 2%, which is even less than the expected rate of inflation and perhaps unrealistically low.

TABLE 19.20 SPREADSHEET	Sensitivity Analysis for KKP's Investment in Ideko					
Exit EBITDA Multiple	6.0	7.0	8.0	9.1	10.0	11.0
Implied Long-Run Growth Rate	1.60%	3.43%	4.53%	**5.34%**	5.81%	6.21%
Ideko Enterprise Value (in $ million)	151.4	171.3	191.2	**213.2**	231.1	251.0
KKP Equity Value (in $ million)	51.4	71.3	91.2	**113.2**	131.1	151.0
KKP IRR	14.8%	22.1%	28.0%	**33.3%**	37.1%	40.8%
Unlevered Cost of Capital	9.0%	10.0%	11.0%	12.0%	13.0%	14.0%
Implied Long-Run Growth Rate	3.86%	**5.34%**	6.81%	8.29%	9.76%	11.24%
Ideko Enterprise Value (in $ million)	222.1	**213.2**	204.7	196.7	189.1	181.9
KKP Equity Value (in $ million)	122.1	**113.2**	104.7	96.7	89.1	81.9

Table 19.20 also illustrates the effect of a change to our assumption about Ideko's unlevered cost of capital. A higher unlevered cost of capital reduces the value of KKP's investment; yet, even with a rate as high as 14%, the equity value exceeds KKP's initial investment. However, if the unlevered cost of capital exceeds 12%, the implied long-term growth rate that justifies the assumed exit EBITDA multiple of 9.1 is probably unrealistically high. Thus, if we believe the unlevered cost of capital falls within this range, we should lower our forecast for the exit EBITDA multiple, which will further reduce the value of KKP's equity. Conversely, if we are confident in our estimate of the exit multiple, this analysis lends further support to our choice for the unlevered cost of capital.

The exercises at the end of this chapter continue the sensitivity analysis by considering different levels of market share growth and changes to working capital management.

CONCEPT CHECK

1. What is the purpose of the sensitivity analysis?

2. Table 19.20 shows the sensitivity analysis for KKP's investment in Ideko. Given this information, do you recommend the acquisition of Ideko?

---

[15]In fact, we can calculate this directly as the present value of Ideko's projected EBITDA in 2010: ($32.094 million)/$(1.10^5)$ = $19.928 million.

Here is what you should know after reading this chapter. MyFinanceLab will help you identify what you know and where to go when you need to practice.

19.1 Valuation Using Comparables

- Valuation using comparables may be used as a preliminary way to estimate the value of a firm. Common multiples include the price-earnings ratio, and the ratio of enterprise value to sales or EBITDA.

19.2 The Business Plan

- When evaluating an acquisition it is necessary to look in detail at the company's operations, investments, and capital structure, and to assess its potential for improvements and future growth.

19.3 Building the Financial Model

- The value of an investment ultimately depends on the firm's future cash flows. To estimate cash flows, one must first develop forecasts for the target firm's operations, investments, and capital structure.
- A financial model may be used to project the future cash flows from an investment.
  - A pro forma income statement projects the firm's earnings under a given set of hypothetical assumptions.
  - The financial model should also consider future working capital needs and capital expenditures to estimate future free cash flows.
  - Based on these estimates, we can forecast the balance sheet and statement of cash flows.
- When forecasting the balance sheet, we must first adjust the firm's initial balance sheet to reflect the transaction, including:

$$\text{New Goodwill} = \text{Acquisition Price} - \text{Value of Net Assets Acquired} \tag{19.10}$$

$$\text{New Stockholders' Equity} = \text{Equity Contributions} - \text{Expensed Transaction Fees} \tag{19.11}$$

- Checking whether the balance sheet balances is an important audit tool for the consistency of the financial model.

19.4 Estimating the Cost of Capital

- To value an investment, we need to assess its risk and estimate an appropriate cost of capital. One method for doing so is to use the CAPM.
  - Use the CAPM to estimate the equity cost of capital for comparable firms, based on their equity betas.
  - Given an estimate of each comparable firm's equity beta, unlever the beta based on the firm's capital structure.
  - Use the CAPM and the estimates of unlevered betas for comparable firms to estimate the unlevered cost of capital for the investment.

19.5 Valuing the Investment

- In addition to forecasting cash flows for a few years, we need to estimate the firm's continuation value at the end of the forecast horizon.
  - One method is to use a valuation multiple based on comparable firms.
  - To estimate a continuation value in year T using discounted cash flows, it is common practice to assume a constant expected growth rate g and a constant debt-equity ratio:

$$\text{Enterprise Value in Year } T = V_T^L = \frac{FCF_{T+1}}{r_{wacc} - g} \tag{19.15}$$

- Given the forecasted cash flows and an estimate of the cost of capital, the final step is to combine these inputs to estimate the value of the opportunity. We may use the valuation methods described in Chapter 18 to calculate firm value.

- While the NPV method is the most reliable approach for evaluating an investment, practitioners often use the IRR and cash multiple as alternative valuation metrics.
  - We use the cash flows over the lifetime of the investment to calculate the IRR.
  - The cash multiple for an investment is the ratio of the total cash received to the total cash invested:

$$\text{Cash Multiple} = \frac{\text{Total Cash Received}}{\text{Total Cash Invested}} \qquad (19.20)$$

19.6 Sensitivity Analysis

- Sensitivity analysis is useful for evaluating the uncertainty of estimates used for valuation, and the impact of this uncertainty on the value of the deal.

Key Terms

cash multiple (multiple of money, absolute return) *p. 698*

pro forma *p. 680*
unlevered P/E ratio *p. 693*

Further Reading

For more detail on the issues involved in the valuation and financial modeling of companies and projects, see: T. Koller, M. Goedhart, and D. Wessels, *Valuation: Measuring and Managing the Value of Companies* (John Wiley & Sons, 2010); S. Benninga and O. Sarig, *Corporate Finance: A Valuation Approach* (McGraw-Hill/Irwin, 1996); E. Arzac, *Valuation for Mergers, Buyouts and Restructuring* (John Wiley & Sons, 2007); S. Pratt, R. Reilly, and R. Schweihs, *Valuing a Business: The Analysis and Appraisal of Closely Held Companies* (McGraw-Hill, 2007); and J. Rosenbaum and J. Pearl, *Investment Banking* (John Wiley & Sons, 2009).

Problems

All problems are available in MyFinanceLab. *An asterisk (*) indicates problems with a higher level of difficulty.*

1. You would like to compare Ideko's profitability to its competitors' profitability using the EBITDA/sales multiple. Given Ideko's current sales of $75 million, use the information in Table 19.2 to compute a range of EBITDA for Ideko assuming it is run as profitably as its competitors.

The Business Plan

2. Assume that Ideko's market share will increase by 0.5% per year rather than the 1% used in the chapter. What production capacity will Ideko require each year? When will an expansion become necessary (when production volume will exceed the current level by 50%)?

3. Under the assumption that Ideko market share will increase by 0.5% per year, you determine that the plant will require an expansion in 2010. The cost of this expansion will be $15 million. Assuming the financing of the expansion will be delayed accordingly, calculate the projected interest payments and the amount of the projected interest tax shields (assuming that the interest rates on the term loans remain the same as in the chapter) through 2010.

Building the Financial Model

 4. Under the assumption that Ideko's market share will increase by 0.5% per year (and the investment and financing will be adjusted as described in Problem 3), you project the following depreciation:

Year	2005	2006	2007	2008	2009	2010
Fixed Assets and Capital Investment ($ 000)						
2 New Investment	5,000	5,000	5,000	5,000	5,000	20,000
3 Depreciation	(5,500)	(5,450)	(5,405)	(5,365)	(5,328)	(6,795)

Using this information, project net income through 2010 (that is, reproduce Table 19.7 under the new assumptions).

 5. Under the assumptions that Ideko's market share will increase by 0.5% per year (implying that the investment, financing, and depreciation will be adjusted as described in Problems 3 and 4) and that the forecasts in Table 19.8 remain the same, calculate Ideko's working capital requirements though 2010 (that is, reproduce Table 19.9 under the new assumptions).

 6. Under the assumptions that Ideko's market share will increase by 0.5% per year (implying that the investment, financing, and depreciation will be adjusted as described in Problems 3 and 4) but that the projected improvements in net working capital do not transpire (so the numbers in Table 19.8 remain at their 2005 levels through 2010), calculate Ideko's working capital requirements though 2010 (that is, reproduce Table 19.9 under these assumptions).

7. Forecast Ideko's free cash flow (reproduce Table 19.10), assuming Ideko's market share will increase by 0.5% per year; investment, financing, and depreciation will be adjusted accordingly; and the projected improvements in working capital occur (that is, under the assumptions in Problem 5).

8. Forecast Ideko's free cash flow (reproduce Table 19.10), assuming Ideko's market share will increase by 0.5% per year; investment, financing, and depreciation will be adjusted accordingly; and the projected improvements in working capital do *not* occur (that is, under the assumptions in Problem 6).

 ***9.** Reproduce Ideko's balance sheet and statement of cash flows, assuming Ideko's market share will increase by 0.5% per year; investment, financing, and depreciation will be adjusted accordingly; and the projected improvements in working capital occur (that is, under the assumptions in Problem 5).

 ***10.** Reproduce Ideko's balance sheet and statement of cash flows, assuming Ideko's market share will increase by 0.5% per year; investment, financing, and depreciation will be adjusted accordingly; and the projected improvements in working capital do *not* occur (that is, under the assumptions in Problem 6).

Estimating the Cost of Capital

11. Calculate Ideko's unlevered cost of capital when Ideko's unlevered beta is 1.1 rather than 1.2, and all other required estimates are the same as in the chapter.

12. Calculate Ideko's unlevered cost of capital when the market risk premium is 6% rather than 5%, the risk-free rate is 5% rather than 4%, and all other required estimates are the same as in the chapter.

Valuing the Investment

13. Using the information produced in the income statement in Problem 4, use EBITDA as a multiple to estimate the continuation value in 2010, assuming the current value remains unchanged (reproduce Table 19.15). Infer the EV/sales and the unlevered and levered P/E ratios implied by the continuation value you calculated.

14. How does the assumption on future improvements in working capital affect your answer to Problem 13?

15. Approximately what expected future long-run growth rate would provide the same EBITDA multiple in 2010 as Ideko has today (i.e., 9.1)? Assume that the future debt-to-value ratio is held constant at 40%; the debt cost of capital is 6.8%; Ideko's market share will increase by 0.5% per year until 2010; investment, financing, and depreciation will be adjusted accordingly; and the projected improvements in working capital occur (i.e., the assumptions in Problem 5).

16. Approximately what expected future long-run growth rate would provide the same EBITDA multiple in 2010 as Ideko has today (i.e., 9.1)? Assume that the future debt-to-value ratio is held constant at 40%; the debt cost of capital is 6.8%; Ideko's market share will increase by 0.5% per year; investment, financing, and depreciation will be adjusted accordingly; and the projected improvements in working capital do *not* occur (i.e., the assumptions in Problem 6).

17. Using the APV method, estimate the value of Ideko and the NPV of the deal using the continuation value you calculated in Problem 13 and the unlevered cost of capital estimate in Section 19.4. Assume that the debt cost of capital is 6.8%; Ideko's market share will increase by 0.5% per year until 2010; investment, financing, and depreciation will be adjusted accordingly; and the projected improvements in working capital occur (i.e., the assumptions in Problem 5).

18. Using the APV method, estimate the value of Ideko and the NPV of the deal using the continuation value you calculated in Problem 13 and the unlevered cost of capital estimate in Section 19.4. Assume that the debt cost of capital is 6.8%; Ideko's market share will increase by 0.5% per year; investment, financing, and depreciation will be adjusted accordingly; and the projected improvements in working capital do *not* occur (i.e., the assumptions in Problem 6).

19. Use your answers from Problems 17 and 18 to infer the value today of the projected improvements in working capital under the assumptions that Ideko's market share will increase by 0.5% per year and that investment, financing, and depreciation will be adjusted accordingly.

CHAPTER 19
APPENDIX

NOTATION

r_E equity
　　cost of
　　capital

Compensating Management

The success of KKP's investment critically depends on its ability to execute the operational improvements laid out in its business plan. KKP has learned from experience that it is much more likely to achieve its goals if the management team responsible for implementing the changes is given a strong incentive to succeed. KKP therefore considers allocating 10% of Ideko's equity to a management incentive plan. This equity stake would be vested over the next five years, and it would provide Ideko's senior executives with a strong financial interest in the success of the venture. What is the cost to KKP of providing this equity stake to the management team? How will this incentive plan affect the NPV of the acquisition?

To determine the value of the acquisition to KKP, we must include the cost of the 10% equity stake granted to management. Because the grant vests after five years, management will not receive any of the dividends paid by Ideko during that time. Instead, management will receive the equity in five years time, at which point we have estimated the value of Ideko's equity to be $172 million (see Table 19.15). Thus, the cost of management's stake in 2010 is equal to 10% × $172 million = $17.2 million according to our estimate. We must determine the present value of this amount today.

Because the payment to the managers is an equity claim, to compute its present value we must use an equity cost of capital. We take an FTE valuation approach to estimate the cost of management's share in Ideko, shown in the spreadsheet in Table 19A.1.

To compute Ideko's equity cost of capital r_E, we use Eq. 18.20, which applies when the debt levels of the firm follow a known schedule:

$$r_E = r_U + \frac{D - T^s}{E}(r_U - r_D)$$

Using the debt, equity, and tax shield values from the spreadsheet in Table 19.17 to compute the effective leverage ratio $(D - T^s)/E$, we compute r_E each year as shown in the spreadsheet. We then compute the cost of management's equity share by discounting at this rate:

$$\text{Cost of Management's Share}_t = \frac{\text{Cost of Management's Share}_{t+1}}{1 + r_E(t)} \qquad (19A.1)$$

Once we have determined the cost of management's equity share, we deduct it from the total value of Ideko's equity (from Table 19.17) to determine the value of KKP's share of Ideko's equity, shown as the last line of the spreadsheet. Given the initial cost of the acquisition to KKP of $53 million, KKP's NPV from the investment, including the cost of management's compensation, is $103.58 million − $53 million = $50.58 million.

TABLE 19A.1 SPREADSHEET	FTE Estimate of the Cost of Management's Share and KKP's Equity Value					

	Year	2005	2006	2007	2008	2009	2010
Management/KKP Share ($ 000)							
1　Management Payoff (10% share)							17,205
2　Effective Leverage $(D - T^s)/E$		0.792	0.771	0.715	0.778	0.745	
3　Equity Cost of Capital r_E		12.53%	12.47%	12.29%	12.49%	12.38%	
4　**Cost of Management's Share**		(9,576)	(10,777)	(12,120)	(13,610)	(15,309)	(17,205)
5　Ideko Equity Value		113,160	118,287	130,047	141,294	157,566	172,052
6　**KKP Equity**		**103,583**	**107,511**	**117,927**	**127,684**	**142,256**	**154,847**

Glossary

10-K The annual form that U.S. companies use to file their financial statements with the U.S. Securities and Exchange Commission (SEC).

10-Q The quarterly reporting form that U.S. companies use to file their financial statements with the U.S. Securities and Exchange Commission (SEC).

95% confidence interval A confidence interval gives a range of values which is likely to include an unknown parameter. If independent samples are taken repeatedly from the same population, then the true parameter will lie outside the 95% confidence interval 5% of the time. For a normal distribution, the interval corresponds to approximately 2 standard deviations on both sides of the mean.

absolute return *See* cash multiple.

accounts payable The amounts owed to creditors for products or services purchased with credit.

accounts payable days An expression of a firm's accounts payable in terms of the number of days' worth of cost of goods sold that the accounts payable represents.

accounts payable turnover The ratio of annual cost of sales to accounts payable. A measure of how quickly the firm is paying its suppliers.

accounts receivable Amounts owed to a firm by customers who have purchased goods or services on credit.

accounts receivable days An expression of a firm's accounts receivable in terms of the number of days' worth of sales that the accounts receivable represents.

accounts receivable turnover The ratio of annual sales to accounts receivable. A measure of how efficiently the firm is managing accounts receivable.

accumulated depreciation The cumulative depreciation of an asset up to a given point in its life; equal to last period's accumulated depreciation plus the current period's depreciation expense.

adjustable rate mortgages (ARMs) Mortgages with interest rates that are not constant over the life of the mortgage. These were the most common type of "subprime" loans.

adjusted betas A beta that has been adjusted toward 1 to account for estimation error.

adjusted present value (APV) A valuation method to determine the levered value of an investment by first calculating its unlevered value (its value without any leverage) and then adding the value of the interest tax shield and deducting any costs that arise from other market imperfections.

adverse selection The idea that when the buyers and sellers have different information, the average quality of assets in the market will differ from the average quality overall.

after-tax interest rate Reflects the amount of interest an investor can keep after taxes have been deducted.

agency costs Costs that arise when there are conflicts of interest between a firm's stakeholders.

agency problem When decision makers, despite being hired as the agents of other stakeholders, put their own self-interest ahead of the interests of the stakeholders.

alpha The difference between a stock's expected return and its required return according to the security market line.

amortization A charge that captures the change in value of acquired assets. Like depreciation, amortization is not an actual cash expense.

amortizing loan A loan on which the borrower makes monthly payments that include interest on the loan plus some part of the loan balance.

annual percentage rate (APR) Indicates the amount of interest earned in one year without the effect of compounding.

annual report The yearly summary of business sent by U.S. public companies to their shareholders that accompanies or includes the financial statement.

annuity A stream of equal periodic cash flows over a specified time period. These cash flows can be inflows of returns earned on investments or outflows of funds invested to earn future returns.

annuity spreadsheet An Excel spreadsheet that can compute any one of the five variables of *NPER, RATE, PV, PMT,* and *FV.* Given any four input variables the spreadsheet computes the fifth.

APR *See* annual percentage rate.

APT *See* Arbitrage Pricing Theory.

APV *See* adjusted present value.

arbitrage The practice of buying and selling equivalent goods or portfolios to take advantage of a price difference.

arbitrage opportunity Any situation in which it is possible to make a profit without taking any risk or making any investment.

Arbitrage Pricing Theory (APT) A model that uses more than one portfolio to capture systematic risk. The portfolios themselves can be thought of as either the risk factor itself or a portfolio of stocks correlated with an unobservable risk factor. Also referred to as a multifactor model.

ARM *See* adjustable rate mortgages.

ask price The price at which a market maker or specialist is willing to sell a security.

asset beta *See* unlevered beta.

asset cost of capital The expected return required by the firm's investors to hold the firm's underlying assets; the weighted average of the firm's equity and debt costs of capital.

asset substitution problem   When a firm faces financial distress, shareholders can gain from decisions that increase the risk of the firm sufficiently, even if they have negative NPV.

asset turnover   The ratio of sales to assets, a measure of how efficiently the firm is utilizing its assets to generate sales.

assets   The cash, inventory, property, plant and equipment, and other investments a company has made.

auditor   A neutral third party that corporations are required to hire that checks the annual financial statements to ensure they are prepared according to GAAP, and to verify that the information is reliable.

average annual return   The arithmetic average of an investment's realized returns for each year.

balance sheet   A list of a firm's assets and liabilities that provides a snapshot of the firm's financial position at a given point in time.

balance sheet identity   Total assets equals total liabilities plus stockholders' equity.

beta   The expected percent change in the excess return of a security for a 1% change in the excess return of the market (or other benchmark) portfolio.

bid price   The price at which a market maker or specialist is willing to buy a security.

bid-ask spread   The amount by which the ask price exceeds the bid price.

bird in the hand hypothesis   The thesis that firms choosing to pay higher current dividends will enjoy higher stock prices because shareholders prefer current dividends to future ones (with the same present value).

bond   A security sold by governments and corporations to raise money from investors today in exchange for the promised future payment.

bond certificate   States the terms of a bond as well as the amounts and dates of all payments to be made.

book value   The acquisition cost of an asset less its accumulated depreciation.

book value of equity   The difference between the book value of a firm's assets and its liabilities; also called stockholders' equity, it represents the net worth of a firm from an accounting perspective.

book-to-market ratio   The ratio of the book value of equity to the market value of equity.

break-even   The level for which an investment has an NPV of zero.

break-even analysis   A calculation of the value of each parameter for which the NPV of the project is zero.

buying stocks on margin (using leverage)   Borrowing money to invest in stocks.

"C" corporations   Corporations that have no restrictions on who owns their shares or the number of shareholders, and therefore cannot qualify for subchapter S treatment and are subject to direct taxation.

CAGR   *See* compound annual growth rate.

cannibalization   When sales of a firm's new product displace sales of one of its existing products.

Capital Asset Pricing Model (CAPM)   An equilibrium model of the relationship between risk and return that characterizes a security's expected return based on its beta with the market portfolio.

capital budget   Lists all of the projects that a company plans to undertake during the next period.

capital budgeting   The process of analyzing investment opportunities and deciding which ones to accept.

capital expenditures   Purchases of new property, plant, and equipment.

capital gain   The amount by which the sale price of an asset exceeds its initial purchase price.

capital gain rate   An expression of a capital gain as a percentage of the initial price of the asset.

capital market line (CML)   When plotting expected returns versus volatility, the line from the risk-free investment through the efficient portfolio of risky stocks (the portfolio that has the highest possible Sharpe ratio). In the context of the CAPM, it is the line from the risk-free investment through the market portfolio. It shows the highest possible expected return that can be obtained for any given volatility.

capital structure   The relative proportions of debt, equity, and other securities that a firm has outstanding.

CAPM   *See* Capital Asset Pricing Model.

carryback or carryforward   *See* tax loss carryforwards and carrybacks.

cash multiple (multiple of money, absolute return)   The ratio of the total cash received to the total cash invested.

cash ratio   The ratio of cash to current liabilities. It is the most stringent liquidity ratio.

Chapter 11 reorganization   A common form of bankruptcy for large corporations in which all pending collection attempts are automatically suspended, and the firm's existing management is given the opportunity to propose a reorganization plan. While developing the plan, management continues to operate the business as usual. The creditors must vote to accept the plan, and it must be approved by the bankruptcy court. If an acceptable plan is not put forth, the court may ultimately force a Chapter 7 liquidation of the firm.

Chapter 7 liquidation   A provision of the U.S. bankruptcy code in which a trustee is appointed to oversee the liquidation of a firm's assets through an auction. The proceeds from the liquidation are used to pay the firm's creditors, and the firm ceases to exist.

chief executive officer (CEO)   The person charged with running the corporation by instituting the rules and policies set by the board of directors.

chief financial officer (CFO)   The most senior financial manager, who often reports directly to the CEO.

clean expenses   Expenses that do not include non-cash charges such as depreciation or amortization. While it differs from some accounting treatment, using clean expenses is preferred in financial models.

clean price   A bond's cash price less an adjustment for accrued interest, the amount of the next coupon payment that has already accrued.

clientele effects   When the dividend policy of a firm reflects the tax preference of its investor clientele.

CML   *See* capital market line.

common risk   Perfectly correlated risk.

competitive market   A market in which goods can be bought and sold at the same price.

compound annual growth rate (CAGR)   Geometric average annual growth rate; year-over-year growth rate which, if applied to the initial value and compounded, will lead to the final value.

compound interest   The effect of earning "interest on interest."

compounding   The process of converting a cash flow to its future value, taking into to account the fact that interest is earned on prior interest payments.

conservation of value principle   With perfect capital markets, financial transactions neither add nor destroy value, but instead represent a repackaging of risk (and therefore return).

consol   A bond that promises its owner a fixed cash flow every year, forever.

constant dividend growth model   A model for valuing a stock by viewing its dividends as a constant growth perpetuity.

constant interest coverage ratio   When a firm keeps its interest payments equal to a target fraction of its free cash flows.

continuation value   The current value of all future free cash flow from continuing a project or investment. *See also* terminal value.

continuous compounding   The compounding of interest every instant (an infinite number of times per year).

convertible bonds   Corporate bonds with a provision that gives the bondholder an option to convert each bond owned into a fixed number of shares of common stock.

corporate bonds   Bonds issued by a corporation.

corporate governance   The system of controls, regulations, and incentives designed to minimize agency costs between managers and investors and prevent corporate fraud.

corporation   A legally defined, artificial being, separate from its owners.

correlation   The covariance of the returns divided by the standard deviation of each return; a measure of the common risk shared by stocks that does not depend on their volatility.

cost of capital   The expected return available on securities with equivalent risk and term to a particular investment.

coupon bonds   Bonds that pay regular coupon interest payments up to maturity, when the face value is also paid.

coupon rate   Determines the amount of each coupon payment of a bond. The coupon rate, expressed as an APR, is set by the issuer and stated on the bond certificate.

coupon-paying yield curve   A plot of the yield of coupon bonds of different maturities.

coupons   The promised interest payments of a bond.

covariance   The expected product of the deviation of each return from its mean.

credibility principle   The principle that claims in one's self-interest are credible only if they are supported by actions that would be too costly to take if the claims were untrue.

credit rating   A rating assigned by a rating agency that assesses the likelihood that a borrower will default.

credit risk   The risk of default by the issuer of any bond that is not default free; it is an indication that the bond's cash flows are not known with certainty.

credit spread   The difference between the risk-free interest rate on U.S. Treasury notes and the interest rates on all other loans. The magnitude of the credit spread will depend on investors' assessment of the likelihood that a particular firm will default.

cum-dividend   When a stock trades before the ex-dividend date, entitling anyone who buys the stock to the dividend.

cumulative abnormal return   Measure of a stock's cumulative return relative to that predicted based on its beta.

current assets   Cash or assets that could be converted into cash within one year. This category includes marketable securities, accounts receivable, inventories, and pre-paid expenses such as rent and insurance.

current liabilities   Liabilities that will be satisfied within one year. They include accounts payable, notes payable, short-term debt, current maturities of long-term debt, salary or taxes owed, and deferred or unearned revenue.

current ratio   The ratio of current assets to current liabilities.

current yield   Coupon amount expressed as a percentage of the current price of a bond.

data snooping bias   The idea that given enough characteristics, it will always be possible to find some characteristic that by pure chance happens to be correlated with the estimation error of a regression.

data table   An Excel function that allows the user to perform sensitivity analysis by computing updated output values (for example, NPV or IRR) by changing one or two assumptions or input variables (such as the discount rate or growth rate).

debt capacity   The amount of debt at a particular date that is required to maintain the firm's target debt-to-value ratio.

debt ceiling   A constraint imposed by the U.S. Congress limiting the overall amount of debt the government can incur.

debt cost of capital   The cost of capital, or expected return, that a firm must pay on its debt.

debt covenants   Conditions of making a loan in which creditors place restrictions on actions that a firm can take.

debt overhang   When shareholders choose not to invest in a positive-NPV project because some of the gains from investment will accrue to debtholders.

debt-equity ratio   The ratio of a firm's total amount of short- and long-term debt (including current maturities) to the value of its equity, which may be calculated based on market or book values.

debt-to-capital ratio   The ratio of a firm's total amount of short- and long-term debt (including current maturities) to the sum of the value of its debt and the value of its equity, which may be calculated based on market or book values.

debt-to-enterprise-value ratio   The fraction of a firm's enterprise value that corresponds to net debt.

debt-to-value ratio   Ratio of debt to debt plus equity, in terms of market values. It is also common to use net debt in place of debt (the debt-to-enterprise value ratio).

debtor-in-possession (DIP) financing   New debt issued by a bankrupt firm; this debt is senior to all existing creditors, providing renewed access to financing to allow a firm that has filed for bankruptcy to keep operating.

declaration date   The date on which a public company's board of directors authorizes the payment of a dividend.

default   When a firm fails to make the required interest or principal payments on its debt, or violates a debt covenant.

default spread   *See* credit spread.

deferred taxes   An asset or liability that results from the difference between a firm's tax expenses as reported for accounting purposes, and the actual amount paid to the taxing authority.

depreciation   A yearly deduction a firm makes from the value of its fixed assets (other than land) over time according to a depreciation schedule that depends on an asset's life span.

depreciation expense   Amount deducted, for accounting purposes, from an asset's value to reflect wear and tear over a given period.

depreciation tax shield   The tax savings that result from the ability to deduct depreciation.

diluted EPS   A firm's disclosure of its potential for dilution from options it has awarded which shows the earnings per share the company would have if the stock options were exercised.

dilution   An increase in the total number of shares that will divide a fixed amount of earnings; often occurs when stock options are exercised or convertible bonds are converted.

dirty price (invoice price)   A bond's actual cash price.

discount   The amount by which a cash flow exceeds its present value. The process of converting a cash flow to its present value.

discount factor   The value today of a dollar received in the future.

discount rate   The rate used to discount a stream of cash flows; the cost of capital of a stream of cash flows.

discounted free cash flow model   A method for estimating a firm's enterprise value by discounting its future free cash flow.

discounting   The process of converting a cash flow to its present value.

disposition effect   The tendency to hold on to stocks that have lost value and sell stocks that have risen in value since the time of purchase.

distribution date   *See* payable date.

diversifiable risk   *See* firm-specific risk.

diversification   The averaging of independent risks in a large portfolio.

dividend payments   Payments made at the discretion of the corporation to its equity holders.

dividend payout rate   The fraction of a firm's earnings that the firm pays as dividends each year.

dividend puzzle   When firms continue to issue dividends despite their tax disadvantage.

dividend signaling hypothesis   The idea that dividend changes reflect managers' views about a firm's future earnings prospects.

dividend smoothing   The practice of maintaining relatively constant dividends.

dividend yield   The expected annual dividend of a stock divided by its current price. The dividend yield is the percentage return an investor expects to earn from the dividend paid by the stock.

dividend-capture theory   The theory that absent transaction costs, investors can trade shares at the time of the dividend so that non-taxed investors receive the dividend.

dividend-discount model   A model that values shares of a firm according to the present value of the future dividends the firm will pay.

Dodd-Frank Act   A 2010 Congressional act that sought to bring about financial stability by bringing about sweeping changes to the financial regulatory system in response to the 2008 financial crisis.

DuPont Identity   Expression of the ROE in terms of the firm's profitability, asset efficiency, and leverage.

duration   The sensitivity of a bond's price to changes in interest rates. The value-weighted average maturity of a bond's cash flows.

Dutch auction   A share repurchase method in which the firm lists different prices at which it is prepared to buy shares, and shareholders in turn indicate how many shares they are willing to sell at each price. The firm then pays the lowest price at which it can buy back its desired number of shares.

EAR   *See* effective annual rate.

earnings per share (EPS)   A firm's net income divided by the total number of shares outstanding.

earnings yield   Ratio of expected earnings to share price; reciprocal of the forward P/E multiple.

EBIT   A firm's earnings before interest and taxes are deducted.

EBIT break-even   The level of sales for which a project's EBIT is zero.

EBIT margin   The ratio of EBIT to sales.

EBITDA   A computation of a firm's earnings before interest, taxes, depreciation, and amortization are deducted.

economic distress   A significant decline in the value of a firm's assets, whether or not the firm experiences financial distress due to leverage.

effective annual rate (EAR)   The total amount of interest that will be earned at the end of one year.

effective dividend tax rate   The effective dividend tax rate measures the additional tax paid by the investor per dollar of after-tax capital gain income that is instead received as a dividend.

efficient frontier   The set of portfolios that can be formed from a given set of investments with the property that each portfolio has the highest possible expected return that can be attained without increasing its volatility.

efficient market   When the cost of capital of an investment depends only on its systematic risk, and not its diversifiable risk.

efficient markets hypothesis   The idea that competition among investors works to eliminate all positive-NPV trading opportunities. It implies that securities will be fairly priced, based on their future cash flows, given all information that is available to investors.

efficient portfolio   A portfolio that contains only systematic risk. An efficient portfolio cannot be diversified further; there is no way to reduce the volatility of the portfolio without lowering its expected return. The efficient portfolio is the tangent portfolio, the portfolio with the highest Sharpe ratio in the economy.

empirical distribution   A plot showing the frequency of outcomes based on historical data.

enterprise value   The total market value of a firm's equity and debt, less the value of its cash and marketable securities. It measures the value of the firm's underlying business.

EPS   *See* earnings per share.

equal-ownership portfolio   A portfolio containing an equal fraction of the total number of shares outstanding of each security in the portfolio. Equivalent to a value-weighted portfolio.

equally weighted portfolio   A portfolio in which the same dollar amount is invested in each stock.

equity   The collection of all the outstanding shares of a corporation.

equity cost of capital   The expected rate of return available in the market on other investments with equivalent risk to the firm's shares.

equity holder (also shareholder or stockholder)   An owner of a share of stock in a corporation.

equity multiplier   Measure of leverage that indicates the value of assets held per dollar of shareholder equity.

error (or residual) term   Represents the deviation from the best-fitting line in a regression. It is zero on average and uncorrelated with any regressors.

ESO   *See* executive/employee stock option.

ETF   *See* exchange traded fund.

European options   Options that allow their holders to exercise the option only on the expiration date; holders cannot exercise before the expiration date.

ex-dividend date   A date, two days prior to a dividend's record date, on or after which anyone buying the stock will not be eligible for the dividend.

excess return   The difference between the average return for an investment and the average return for a risk-free investment.

exchange-traded fund (ETF)   A security that trades directly on an exchange, like a stock, but represents ownership in a portfolio of stocks.

execution risk   The risk that a misstep in the firm's execution may cause a project to fail to generate the forecasted cashflows.

executive stock option (ESO)   A common practice for compensating executives by granting them call options on their company's stock.

expected (mean) return   A computation for the return of a security based on the average payoff expected.

face value   The notional amount of a bond used to compute its interest payments. The face value of the bond is generally due at the bond's maturity. Also called par value or principal amount.

factor betas The sensitivity of the stock's excess return to the excess return of a factor portfolio, as computed in a multifactor regression.

factor portfolios Portfolios that can be combined to form an efficient portfolio.

Fama-French-Carhart (FFC) factor specification A multi-factor model of risk and return in which the factor portfolios are the market, small-minus-big, high-minus-low, and PR1YR portfolios identified by Fama, French, and Carhart.

familiarity bias The tendency of investors to favor investments in companies with which they are familiar.

FCFE *See* free cash flow to equity.

federal funds rate The overnight loan rate charged by banks with excess reserves at a Federal Reserve bank (called federal funds) to banks that need additional funds to meet reserve requirements. The federal funds rate is influenced by the Federal Reserve's monetary policy, and itself influences other interest rates in the market.

FFC factor specification *See* Fama-French-Carhart factor specification.

financial distress When a firm has difficulty meeting its debt obligations.

financial security An investment opportunity that trades in a financial market.

financial statements Firm-issued (usually quarterly and annually) accounting reports with past performance information.

firm-specific, idiosyncratic, unique, or diversifiable risk Fluctuations of a stock's return that are due to firm-specific news and are independent risks unrelated across stocks.

flow to equity (FTE) A valuation method that calculates the free cash flow available to equity holders taking into account all payments to and from debt holders. The cash flows to equity holders are then discounted using the equity cost of capital.

forward interest rate (forward rate) An interest rate guaranteed today for a loan or investment that will occur in the future.

forward P/E A firm's price-earnings (P/E) ratio calculated using forward earnings.

forward rate agreement *See* interest rate forward contract.

free cash flow The incremental effect of a project on a firm's available cash.

free cash flow hypothesis The view that wasteful spending is more likely to occur when firms have high levels of cash flow in excess of what is needed after making all positive-NPV investments and payments to debt holders.

free cash flow to equity (FCFE) The free cash flow that remains after adjusting for interest payments, debt issuance, and debt repayment.

free float The number of shares actually available for public trading. Since 2005, this has been used to compute the value weights of the S&P 500 Index.

FTE *See* flow to equity.

future value The value of a cash flow that is moved forward in time.

futures contract A forward contract that is traded on an exchange.

GAAP *See* Generally Accepted Accounting Principles.

Generally Accepted Accounting Principles (GAAP) A common set of rules and a standard format for public companies to use when they prepare their financial reports.

goodwill The difference between the price paid for a company and the book value assigned to its assets.

greenmail When a firm avoids a threat of takeover and removal of its management by a major shareholder by buying out the shareholder, often at a large premium over the current market price.

gross margin The ratio of gross profit to revenues (sales).

gross profit The third line of an income statement that represents the difference between a firm's sales revenues and its costs.

growing annuity A stream of cash flows paid at regular intervals and growing at a constant rate, up to some final date.

growing perpetuity A stream of cash flows that occurs at regular intervals and grows at a constant rate forever.

growth stocks Firms with high market-to-book ratios.

herd behavior The tendency of investors to make similar trading errors by actively imitating other investors' actions.

high-minus-low (HML) portfolio An annually updated portfolio that is long stocks with high book-to-market ratios and short stocks with low book-to-market ratios.

high-yield bonds Bonds below investment grade which trade with a high yield to maturity to compensate investors for their high risk of default.

HML portfolio *See* high-minus-low portfolio.

homemade dividend When an investor creates a cash payout from their holdings of a stock by simply selling some portion of their shares.

homemade leverage When investors use leverage in their own portfolios to adjust the leverage choice made by a firm.

homogeneous expectations A theoretical situation in which all investors have the same estimates concerning future investment returns.

hostile takeover A situation in which an individual or organization, sometimes referred to as a corporate raider, purchases a large fraction of a target corporation's stock and in doing so gets enough votes to replace the target's board of directors and its CEO.

idiosyncratic risk *See* firm-specific risk.

impairment charge Captures the change in value of the acquired assets; is not an actual cash expense.

income statement A list of a firm's revenues and expenses over a period of time.

incremental earnings The amount by which a firm's earnings are expected to change as a result of an investment decision.

incremental IRR The IRR of the incremental cash flows associated with replacing one project with another, or changing from one decision to another.

incremental IRR investment rule Applies the IRR rule to the difference between the cash flows of two mutually exclusive alternatives (the *increment* to the cash flows of one investment over the other).

independent risk Risks that bear no relation to each other. If risks are independent, then knowing the outcome of one provides no information about the other. Independent risks are always uncorrelated, but the reverse need not be true.

index funds Mutual funds that invest in stocks in proportion to their representation in a published index, such as the S&P 500 or Wilshire 5000.

inefficient portfolio Describes a portfolio for which it is possible to find another portfolio that has higher expected return and lower volatility.

informational cascade effect When traders ignore their own information hoping to profit from the information of others.

intangible assets Non-physical assets, such as intellectual property, brand names, trademarks, and goodwill. Intangible assets appear on the balance sheet as the difference between the price paid for an acquisiton and the book value assigned to its tangible assets.

interest coverage ratio An assessment by lenders of a firm's leverage. Common ratios consider operating income, EBIT, or EBITDA as a multiple of the firm's interest expenses.

interest rate factor   One plus the interest rate, it is the rate of exchange between dollars today and dollars in the future.

interest rate forward contract   A contract today that fixes the interest rate for a loan or investment in the future.

interest tax shield   The reduction in taxes paid due to the tax deductibility of interest payments.

internal rate of return (IRR)   The interest rate that sets the net present value of the cash flows equal to zero.

internal rate of return (IRR) investment rule   A decision rule that accepts any investment opportunity where IRR exceeds the opportunity cost of capital. This rule is only optimal in special circumstances, and often leads to errors if misapplied.

inventories   A firm's raw materials as well as its work-in-progress and finished goods.

inventory turnover   The ratio of the annual cost of sales to inventory. A measure of how efficiently a firm is managing its inventory.

investment-grade bonds   Bonds in the top four categories of creditworthiness with a low risk of default.

invoice price   *See* dirty price.

IRR   *See* internal rate of return.

IRR investment rule   *See* internal rate of return investment rule.

Jensen's alpha   The constant term in a regression of a security's excess returns against those of the market portfolio. It can be interpreted as a risk-adjusted measure of the security's past performance.

junk bonds   Bonds in one of the bottom five categories of creditworthiness (below investment grade) that have a high risk of default.

"just-in-time" (JIT) inventory management   When a firm acquires inventory precisely when needed so that its inventory balance is always zero, or very close to it.

Law of One Price   In competitive markets, securities or portfolios with the same cash flows must have the same price.

LBO   *See* leveraged buyout.

lemons principle   When a seller has private information about the value of a good, buyers will discount the price they are willing to pay due to adverse selection.

leverage   The amount of debt held in a portfolio or issued by a firm. *See also* buying stocks on margin.

leverage ratchet effect   Once existing debt is in place, shareholders may have an incentive to increase leverage even if it decreases the value of the firm, and shareholders may prefer not to decrease leverage by buying back debt even when it will increase the value of the firm.

leverage ratio (of an option)   A measure of leverage obtained by looking at debt as a proportion of value, or interest payments as a proportion of cash flows.

leveraged buyout (LBO)   When a group of private investors purchases all the equity of a public corporation and finances the purchase primarily with debt.

leveraged recapitalization   When a firm uses borrowed funds to pay a large special dividend or repurchase a significant amount of its outstanding shares.

levered equity   Equity in a firm with outstanding debt.

liabilities   A firm's obligations to its creditors.

limited liability   When an investor's liability is limited to her initial investment.

limited liability company (LLC)   A limited partnership without a general partner.

limited partnership   A partnership with two kinds of owners, general partners and limited partners.

linear regression   The statistical technique that identifies the best-fitting line through a set of points.

liquid   Describes an investment that can easily be turned into cash because it can be sold immediately at a competitive market price.

liquidating dividend   A return of capital to shareholders from a business operation that is being terminated.

liquidation   Closing down a business and selling off all its assets; often the result of the business declaring bankruptcy.

LLC   *See* limited liability company.

long position   A positive investment in a security.

long-term assets   Net property, plant, and equipment, as well as property not used in business operations, start-up costs in connection with a new business, investments in long-term securities, and property held for sale.

long-term debt   Any loan or debt obligation with a maturity of more than a year.

long-term liabilities   Liabilities that extend beyond one year.

MACRS depreciation   The most accelerated cost recovery system allowed by the IRS. Based on the recovery period, MACRS depreciation tables assign a fraction of the purchase price that the firm can depreciate each year.

management discussion and analysis (MD&A)   A preface to the financial statements in which a company's management discusses the recent year (or quarter), providing a background on the company and any significant events that may have occurred.

management entrenchment   A situation arising as the result of the separation of ownership and control in which managers may make decisions that benefit themselves at investors' expense.

management entrenchment theory   A theory that suggests managers choose a capital structure to avoid the discipline of debt and maintain their own job security.

margin   Collateral that investors are required to post when buying or selling securities that could generate losses beyond the initial investment.

marginal corporate tax rate   The tax rate a firm will pay on an incremental dollar of pretax income.

market capitalization   The total market value of equity; equals the market price per share times the number of shares.

market index   The market value of a broad-based portfolio of securities.

market makers   Individuals on the trading floor of a stock exchange who match buyers with sellers.

market portfolio   A value-weighted portfolio of all shares of all stocks and securities in the market.

market proxy   A portfolio whose return is believed to closely track the true market portfolio.

market risk   *See* systematic risk.

market timing   The strategy of buy or selling securities (or an asset class) based on a forecast of future price movements.

market timing view of capital structure   The idea that capital structure decisions are made in part to exploit under or over-pricing of the stock in the market.

market value balance sheet   Similar to an accounting balance sheet, with two key distinctions: First, all assets and liabilities of the firm are included, even intangible assets such as reputation, brand name, or human capital that are missing from a standard accounting balance sheet; second, all values are current market values rather than historical costs.

market-to-book ratio (price-to-book [PB] ratio)   The ratio of a firm's market (equity) capitalization to the book value of its stockholders' equity.

marketable securities   Short-term, low-risk investments that can be easily sold and converted to cash (such as money market investments, like government debt, that mature within a year).

maturity date   The final repayment date of a bond.

MD&A   *See* management discussion and analysis.

method of comparables   An estimate of the value of a firm based on the value of other, comparable firms or other investments that are expected to generate very similar cash flows in the future.

mid-year convention   A method of discounting in which cash flows that arrive continuously throughout the year are treated as though they arrive at the middle of the year. This mid-year convention is a reasonable approximation to continuous discounting.

momentum strategy   Buying stocks that have had past high returns, and (short) selling stocks that have had past low returns.

moral hazard   When purchasing insurance reduces a firm's incentive to avoid risk.

multifactor model   A model that uses more than one risk factor to capture risk. *See also* Arbitrage Pricing Theory (APT).

multiple of money   *See* cash multiple.

multiple regression   A regression with more than one independent variable.

naked short sale   Short sale in which the seller fails to locate shares to borrow before executing the sale.

net debt   Total debt outstanding minus any cash balances.

net income or earnings   The last or "bottom line" of a firm's income statement that is a measure of the firm's income over a given period of time.

net investment   The firm's capital expenditures in excess of depreciation.

net operating profit after tax (NOPAT)   *See* unlevered net income.

net present value (NPV)   The difference between the present value of a project's or investment's benefits and the present value of its costs.

Net Present Value (NPV) Decision Rule   When making an investment decision, take the alternative with the highest NPV. Choosing this alternative is equivalent to receiving its NPV in cash today. Also known as NPV Investment Rule.

net profit margin   The ratio of net income to revenues, it shows the fraction of each dollar in revenues that is available to equity holders after the firm pays interest and taxes.

net working capital   The difference between a firm's current assets and current liabilities that represents the capital available in the short-term to run the business.

no-arbitrage price   In a normal market, when the price of a security equals the present value of the cash flows paid by the security.

no-trade theorem   The idea that when investors have rational expectations, prices will adjust to reflect new information before any trades can occur.

nominal interest rates   Interest rates quoted by banks and other financial institutions that indicate the rate at which money will grow if invested for a certain period of time.

NOPAT   Net operating profit after tax; equivalent to unlevered net income.

normal market   A competitive market in which there are no arbitrage opportunities.

NPV   *See* net present value.

NPV Decision Rule   *See* Net Present Value (NPV) Decision Rule.

NPV Investment Rule   *See* Net Present Value (NPV) Decision Rule.

NPV profile   Graph that projects NPV over a range of discount rates.

off-balance sheet transactions   Transactions or arrangements that can have a material impact on a firm's future performance yet do not appear on the balance sheet.

on-the-run bonds   The most recently issued treasury security of a particular original maturity.

open market repurchase   When a firm repurchases shares by buying its shares in the open market.

operating income   A firm's gross profit less its operating expenses.

operating leverage   Relative proportion of fixed versus variable costs.

operating margin   The ratio of operating income to revenues, it reveals how much a company has earned from each dollar of sales before interest and taxes are deducted.

opportunity cost   The value a resource could have provided in its best alternative use.

opportunity cost of capital   The best available expected return offered in the market on an investment of comparable risk and term to the cash flow being discounted; the return the investor forgoes on an alternative investment of equivalent riskiness and term when the investor takes on a new investment.

overconfidence bias   The tendency of individual investors to trade too much based on the mistaken belief that they can pick winners and losers better than investment professionals.

overhead expenses   Those expenses associated with activities that are not directly attributable to a single business activity but instead affect many different areas of a corporation.

paid-in capital   Capital contributed by stockholders through the purchase of stock from the corporation at a price in excess of its par value.

par   A price at which coupon bonds trade that is equal to their face value.

partnership   A sole proprietorship with more than one owner.

passive portfolio   A portfolio that is not rebalanced in response to price changes.

payable date (distribution date)   A date, generally within a month after the record date, on which a firm mails dividend checks to its registered stockholders.

payback investment rule   The simplest investment rule. Only projects that pay back their initial investment within the payback period are undertaken.

payback period   A specified amount of time used in the payback investment rule. Only investments that pay back their initial investment within this amount of time are undertaken.

payout policy   The way a firm chooses between the alternative ways to pay cash out to equity holders.

pecking order hypothesis   The idea that managers will prefer to fund investments by first using retained earnings, then debt and equity only as a last resort.

perfect capital markets   A set of conditions in which investors and firms can trade the same set of securities at competitive market prices with no frictions such as taxes, transaction costs, issuance costs, asymmetric information, or agency costs.

perpetuity   A stream of equal cash flows that occurs at regular intervals and lasts forever.

portfolio   A collection of securities.

portfolio weights   The fraction of the total investment in a portfolio held in each individual investment in the portfolio.

PR1YR portfolio   *See* prior one-year momentum portfolio.

premium   A price at which coupon bonds trade that is greater than their face value. Also, the price a firm pays to purchase insurance, allowing the firm to exchange a random future loss for a certain upfront expense.

prepackaged bankruptcy   A method for avoiding many of the legal and other direct costs of bankruptcy in which a firm first develops a reorganization plan with the agreement of its main creditors, and then files Chapter 11 to implement the plan.

present value (PV)   The value of a cost or benefit computed in terms of cash today.

pretax WACC   The weighted average cost of capital computed using the pretax cost of debt; it can be used to estimate the unlevered cost of capital for a firm that maintains a target leverage ratio.

price-earnings ratio (P/E)   The ratio of the market value of equity to the firm's earnings, or its share price to its earnings per share.

price-to-book (PB) ratio   *See* market-to-book ratio.

price-weighted portfolio   A portfolio that holds an equal number of shares of each stock, independent of their size.

primary market   Market used when a corporation itself issues new shares of stock and sells them to investors.

prior one-year momentum (PR1YR) portfolio   A self-financing portfolio that goes long on the top 30% of stocks with the highest prior year returns, and short on the 30% with the lowest prior year returns, each year.

private company   A company whose shares do not trade on a public market.

private equity firm   A firm organized very similarly to venture capital firms that invests in the equity of existing privately held firms rather than startup companies.

pro forma   Describes a statement that is not based on actual data but rather depicts a firm's financials under a given set of hypothetical assumptions.

probability distribution   A graph that provides the probability of every possible discrete state.

profitability index   Measures the NPV per unit of resource consumed.

profitability index rule   Recommends investment whenever the profitability index exceeds some predetermined number.

project externalities   Indirect effects of a project that may increase or decrease the profits of other business activities of a firm.

public companies   Those corporations whose stock is traded on a stock market or exchange, providing shareholders the ability to quickly and easily convert their investments into cash.

pure discount bonds   *See* zero-coupon bonds.

PV   *See* present value.

quick ratio   The ratio of current assets other than inventory to current liabilities.

R-squared   In the CAPM regression, the square of the correlation between the stock's and market's excess returns. More generally, the fraction of the variance of the independent variable that is explained in a regression.

rational expectations   The idea that investors may have different information regarding expected returns, correlations, and volatilities, but they correctly interpret that information and the information contained in market prices and adjust their estimates of expected returns in a rational way.

real interest rate   The rate of growth of purchasing power after adjusting for inflation.

realized return   The return that actually occurs over a particular time period.

record date   When a firm pays a dividend, only shareholders of record on this date receive the dividend.

regression   A statistical technique that estimates a linear relationship between two variables (the dependent and independent variable) by fitting a line that minimizes the squared distance between the data and the line.

relative wealth concerns   When investors are concerned about the performance of their portfolio relative to that of their peers, rather than its absolute performance.

repurchase yield   Amount spent on repurchases during the year divided by the firm's equity market capitalization at the start of the year. The repurchase yield plus the dividend yield provides a measure of the firm's total payouts.

required return   The expected return of an investment that is necessary to compensate for the risk of undertaking the investment.

residual income valuation method   Valuation method based on discounting earnings net of changes in the book value of equity; equivalent to the flow to equity method.

residual term   *See* error term.

retained earnings   The difference between a firm's net income and the amount it spends on dividends.

retention rate   The fraction of a firm's current earnings that the firm retains.

return   The difference between the selling price and purchasing price of an asset plus any cash distributions expressed as a percentage of the buying price.

return of capital   When a firm, instead of paying dividends out of current earnings (or accumulated retained earnings), pays dividends from other sources, such as paid-in capital or the liquidation of assets.

return on assets (ROA)   The ratio of net income plus interest expense to the total book value of the firm's assets. This measure of ROA includes the benefit of the interest tax shield associated with leverage. As a benchmark, ROA is most comparable to the firm's unlevered cost of capital.

return on equity (ROE)   The ratio of a firm's net income to the book value of its equity. As a benchmark, ROE is most comparable to the firm's required return on equity.

return on invested capital (ROIC)   The ratio of a firm's after-tax profit excluding any interest expense (or income) to the sum of the book value of its equity and net debt. As a benchmark, ROIC is most comparable to the firm's weighted average cost of capital.

reverse split   When the price of a company's stock falls too low and the company reduces the number of outstanding shares.

risk aversion   When investors prefer to have a safe future payment rather than an uncertain one of the same expected amount.

risk premium   Represents the additional return that investors expect to earn to compensate them for a security's risk.

risk-free interest rate   The interest rate at which money can be borrowed or lent without risk over a given period.

ROA   *See* return on assets.

ROE   *See* return on equity.

ROIC   *See* return on invested capital.

"S" corporations   Those corporations that elect subchapter S tax treatment and are allowed, by the U.S. Internal Revenue Tax code, an exemption from double taxation.

Sarbanes-Oxley Act (SOX)   A 2002 Congressional act intended to improve the accuracy of information given to both boards and to shareholders.

scenario analysis   An important capital budgeting tool that determines how the NPV varies as a number of the underlying assumptions are changed simultaneously.

secondary market   Market shares continue to trade on after the initial transaction between the corporation and investors.

security   *See* financial security.

security market line (SML)   The pricing implication of the CAPM, it specifies a linear relation between the risk premium of a security and its beta with the market portfolio.

self-financing portfolio   A portfolio that costs nothing to construct.

semi-strong form efficiency   The theory that consistent profits should not be possible from trading on any public information, such as news announcements or analysts' recommendations.

sensation seeking   The increase in trading activity due to an individual's desire for novel or intense risk-taking experiences.

sensitivity analysis   An important capital budgeting tool that determines how the NPV varies as a single underlying assumption is changed.

Separation Principle   In a perfect market, the NPV of an investment decision can be evaluated separately from any financial transactions a firm is considering.

share repurchase   A situation in which a firm uses cash to buy back its own stock.

shareholder (also stockholder or equity holder)   An owner of a share of stock in a corporation.

Sharpe ratio   The excess return of an asset divided by the volatility of the return of the asset; a measure of the reward per unit risk.

short interest   The number of shares sold short.

short position   A negative amount invested in a stock.

short sale   Selling a security you do not own.

short-term debt   Debt with a maturity of less than one year.

signaling theory of debt   The use of leverage as a way to signal information to investors.

simple interest   Interest earned without the effect of compounding.

single-factor model   A model using an efficient portfolio, capturing all systemic risk alone.

size effect   The observation that small stocks (or stocks with a high book-to-market ratio) have higher returns.

small-minus-big (SMB) portfolio   A portfolio resulting from a trading strategy that each year buys a small market value portfolio and finances that position by selling short a large market value portfolio.

SMB portfolio   *See* small-minus-big portfolio.

SML   *See* security market line.

sole proprietorship   A business owned and run by one person.

sovereign bonds   Bonds issued by national governments.

sovereign debt   Debt issued by a national government.

SOX   *See* Sarbanes-Oxley Act.

special dividend   A one-time dividend payment a firm makes that is usually much larger than a regular dividend.

specialists   Individuals on the trading floor of the NYSE who match buyers with sellers; also called market makers.

speculative bonds   Bonds in one of the bottom five categories of creditworthiness that have a high risk of default.

spin-off   When a firm sells a subsidiary by selling shares in the subsidiary alone.

spot interest rates   Default-free, zero-coupon yields.

standard deviation   A common method used to measure the risk of a probability distribution, it is the square root of the variance, the expected squared deviation from the mean.

standard error   The standard deviation of the estimated value of the mean of the actual distribution around its true value; that is, it is the standard deviation of the average return.

statement of cash flows   An accounting statement that shows how a firm has used the cash it earned during a set period.

statement of financial performance   Statement showing the firm's revenues and expenses over a period of time. *See also* income statement.

statement of financial position   List of the firm's assets and liabilities that provides a snapshot of the firm's financial position at a given point in time. *See also* balance sheet.

statement of stockholders' equity   An accounting statement that breaks down the stockholders' equity computed on the balance sheet into the amount that came from issuing new shares versus retained earnings.

stock   The ownership or equity of a corporation divided into shares.

stock dividend   *See* stock split.

stock exchanges   *See* stock markets.

stock markets (also stock exchanges)   Organized markets on which the shares of many corporations are traded.

stock options   A form of compensation a firm gives to its employees that gives them the right to buy a certain number of shares of stock by a specific date at a specific price.

stock split (stock dividend)   When a company issues a dividend in shares of stock rather than cash to its shareholders.

stockholder (also shareholder or equity holder)   An owner of a share of stock or equity in a corporation.

stockholders' equity   An accounting measure of a firm's net worth that represents the difference between the firm's assets and its liabilities.

straight-line depreciation   A method of depreciation in which an asset's cost is divided equally over its life.

stream of cash flows   A series of cash flows lasting several periods.

strong form efficiency   The theory that it should not be possible to consistently profit even by trading on private information.

subprime mortgages   Mortgages for which borrowers do not meet typical credit standards, and thus have a high default probability.

sunk cost   Any unrecoverable cost for which a firm is already liable.

sunk cost fallacy   The idea that once a manager makes a large investment, he should not abandon a project.

systematic, undiversifiable, or market risk   Fluctuations of a stock's return that are due to market-wide news representing common risk.

takeover   Refers to two mechanisms, either a merger or an acquisition, by which ownership and control of a firm can change.

takeover synergies   Value obtained from an acquisition that could not be obtained if the target remained an independent firm; i.e., value in excess of the firm's standalone value.

tangent portfolio   A portfolio with the highest Sharpe ratio; the point of tangency to the efficient frontier of a line drawn from the risk-free asset; the market portfolio if the CAPM holds.

target leverage ratio   When a firm adjusts its debt proportionally to a project's value or its cash flows (where the proportion need not remain constant). A constant market debt-equity ratio is a special case.

targeted repurchase   When a firm purchases shares directly from a specific shareholder.

tax loss carryforwards and carrybacks   Two features of the U.S. tax code that allow corporations to take losses during a current year and offset them against gains in nearby years. Since 1997, companies can "carry back" losses for two years and "carry forward" losses for 20 years.

TED (Treasury-Eurodollar) spread   Difference in interest rates between the three-month London Inter-Bank Offered Rate (LIBOR) and three-month U.S. Treasury bills.

tender offer   A public announcement of an offer to all existing security holders to buy back a specified amount of outstanding securities at a prespecified price over a prespecified period of time.

term   Time remaining until the final repayment date of a bond.

term structure   The relationship between the investment term and the interest rate.

terminal (continuation) value   The value of a project's remaining free cash flows beyond the forecast horizon. This amount represents the market value (as of the last forecast period) of the free cash flow from the project at all future dates. *See also* continuation value.

TEV (total enterprise value)   *See* enterprise value.

time value of money   The difference in value between money today and money in the future; also, the observation that two cash flows at two different points in time have different values.

timeline   A linear representation of the timing of (potential) cash flows.

total enterprise value (TEV)   *See* enterprise value.

total payout model   A firm's total payouts to equity holders (i.e., all the cash distributed as dividends and stock repurchases) are discounted and then divided by the current number of shares outstanding to determine the share price.

total return   The sum of a stock's dividend yield and its capital gain rate.

trade credit   The difference between receivables and payables that is the net amount of a firm's capital consumed as a result of those credit transactions; the credit that a firm extends to its customers.

trade-off theory   The firm picks its capital structure by trading off the benefits of the tax shield from debt against the costs of financial distress and agency costs.

trailing earnings   A firm's earnings over the prior 12 months.

trailing P/E   The computation of a firm's P/E using its trailing earnings.

transaction cost   In most markets, an expense such as a broker commission and the bid-ask spread investors must pay in order to trade securities.

Treasury bills   Zero-coupon bonds, issued by the U.S. government, with a maturity of up to one year.

Treasury bonds   A type of U.S. Treasury coupon securities, currently traded in financial markets, with original maturities of more than ten years.

Treasury Inflation-Protected Securities (TIPS)   *See* TIPS.

Treasury notes   A type of U.S. Treasury coupon securities, currently traded in financial markets, with original maturities from one to ten years.

treasury stock method   Method of computing a firm's fully diluted share count by including the net new shares potentially created by unexercised in-the-money warrants and options. This method assumes any proceeds the company receives from the exercise are used to repurchase shares. It is equivalent to adding shares with the same market value as the intrinsic value of the options.

turnover ratios   Measures of working capital computed by expressing annual revenues or costs as a multiple of the corresponding working capital account (accounts receivable, accounts payable, and inventory)

under-investment problem   A situation in which equity holders choose not to invest in a positve NPV project because the firm is in financial distress and the value of undertaking the investment opportunity will accrue to bondholders rather than themselves.

undiversifiable risk   *See* systematic risk.

unique risk   *See* firm-specific risk.

unlevered beta   Measures the risk of a firm were it unlevered; beta of the firm's assets; measures the market risk of the firm's business activities, ignoring any additional risk due to leverage.

unlevered cost of capital   The cost of capital of a firm, were it unlevered; for a firm that maintains a target leverage ratio, it can be estimated as the weighted average cost of capital computed without taking into account taxes (pretax WACC).

unlevered equity   Equity in a firm with no debt.

unlevered net income   Net income plus after-tax interest expense; equivalently, after-tax EBIT. *See also* net operating profit after tax (NOPAT).

unlevered P/E ratio   The enterprise value of a firm divided by its unlevered net income in a particular year.

unsystematic risk   *See* firm-specific risk.

valuation multiple   A ratio of a firm's value to some measure of the firm's scale or cash flow.

Valuation Principle   The value of an asset to the firm or its investors is determined by its competitive market price: The benefits and costs of a decision should be evaluated using these market prices, and when the value of the benefits exceeds the value of the costs, the decision will increase the market value of the firm.

value additivity   A relationship determined by the Law of One Price, in which the price of an asset that consists of other assets must equal the sum of the prices of the other assets.

value stocks   Firms with low market-to-book ratios.

value-weighted portfolio   A portfolio in which each security is held in proportion to its market capitalization. Also called an equal-ownership portfolio, because it consists of the same fraction of the outstanding shares of each security.

variance   A method to measure the risk of a probability distribution, it is the expected squared deviation from the mean.

volatility   The standard deviation of a return.

WACC   *See* weighted average cost of capital.

weak form efficiency   The theory that it should not be possible to profit by trading on information in past prices by, for example, selling winners and hanging on to losers or, conversely, by trading on momentum.

weighted average cost of capital (WACC)   The average of a firm's equity and after-tax cost of capital, weighted by the fraction of the firm's enterprise value that corresponds to equity and debt, respectively. Discounting free cash flows using the WACC computes their value including the interest tax shield.

workout   A method for avoiding a declaration of bankruptcy in which a firm in financial distress negotiates directly with its creditors to reorganize.

yield curve   A plot of bond yields as a function of the bonds' maturity date.

yield to maturity (YTM)   The discount rate that sets the present value of the promised bond payments equal to the current market price of the bond. Equivalently, it is the IRR of an investment in a bond that is held to maturity and does not default.

YTM   *See* yield to maturity.

zero-coupon bond   A bond that makes only one payment at maturity.

zero-coupon yield curve   A plot of the yield of risk-free zero-coupon bonds (STRIPS) as a function of the bond's maturity date.

Index

	COMMON MISTAKE boxes alert students to frequently made mistakes stemming from misunderstanding core concepts and calculations—in the classroom and in the field.	GLOBAL FINANCIAL CRISIS boxes reflect the reality of the recent financial crisis and ongoing sovereign debt crisis, noting lessons learned. 15 boxes across the book illustrate and analyze key details.	INTERVIEWS with notable practitioners—15 in total—highlight leaders in the field and address the effect of the financial crisis.
CHAPTER 1 *The Corporation*		The Dodd-Frank Act The Dodd-Frank Act on Corporate Compensation and Governance	David Viniar, Goldman Sachs Jean-François Théodore, NYSE-Euronext
CHAPTER 2 *Introduction to Financial Statement Analysis: IFRS*	Mismatched Ratios	Bernard Madoff's Ponzi Scheme	Sue Frieden, Ernst & Young
CHAPTER 3 *Financial Decision Making and the Law of One Price*		Liquidity and the Informational Role of Prices	
CHAPTER 4 *The Time Value of Money*	Discounting One Too Many Times		
CHAPTER 5 *Interest Rates*	Using the Wrong Discount Rate in the Annuity Formula Using the Annuity Formula When Discount Rates Vary by Maturity States Dig a $3 Trillion Hole by Discounting at the Wrong Rate	Teaser Rates and Subprime Loans	Kevin M. Warsh, Stanford University
CHAPTER 6 *Valuing Bonds*		Pure Discount Bonds Trading at a Premium The Credit Crisis and Bond Yields European Sovereign Debt Yields: A Puzzle	Carmen M. Reinhart, Harvard University
CHAPTER 7 *Investment Decision Rules*	IRR Versus the IRR Rule IRR and Project Financing		Dick Grannis, QUALCOMM
CHAPTER 8 *Fundamentals of Capital Budgeting*	The Opportunity Cost of an Idle Asset	The American Recovery and Reinvestment Act of 2009	David Holland, Cisco
CHAPTER 9 *Valuing Stocks*			Douglas Kehring, Oracle
CHAPTER 10 *Capital Markets and the Pricing of Risk*	A Fallacy of Long-Run Diversification Beta Versus Volatility	Diversification Benefits During Market Crashes	

	COMMON MISTAKE boxes alert students to frequently made mistakes stemming from misunderstanding core concepts and calculations—in the classroom and in the field.	GLOBAL FINANCIAL CRISIS boxes reflect the reality of the recent financial crisis and ongoing sovereign debt crisis, noting lessons learned. 15 boxes across the book illustrate and analyze key details.	INTERVIEWS with notable practitioners—15 in total—highlight leaders in the field and address the effect of the financial crisis.
CHAPTER 11 *Optimal Portfolio Choice and the Capital Asset Pricing Model*	Computing Variance, Covariance, and Correlation in Excel		John Powers, The Stanford Management Company
CHAPTER 12 *Estimating the Cost of Capital*	Using the Debt Yield as Its Cost of Capital Adjusting for Execution Risk Changing the Index to Improve the Fit		Michael A. Latham, iShares Shelagh Glaser, Intel
CHAPTER 13 *Investor Behavior and Capital Market Efficiency*			Jonathan Clements, author; former personal finance columnist for *The Wall Street Journal*
CHAPTER 14 *Capital Structure in a Perfect Market*	Is Debt Better Than Equity?	Bank Capital Regulation and the ROE Fallacy	
CHAPTER 15 *Debt and Taxes*			Andrew Balson, Bain Capital
CHAPTER 16 *Financial Distress, Managerial Incentives, and Information*		The Chrysler Prepack Bailouts, Distress Costs, and Debt Overhang Moral Hazard, Government Bailout, and the Appeal of Leverage	
CHAPTER 17 *Payout Policy*	Repurchases and the Supply of Shares The Bird in the Hand Fallacy		John Connors, Ignition Partners; formerly Microsoft
CHAPTER 18 *Capital Budgeting and Valuation with Leverage*	Re-Levering the WACC	Government Loan Guarantees	
CHAPTER 19 *Valuation and Financial Modeling: A Case Study*	Continuation Values and Long-Run Growth Missing Assets or Liabilities		Joseph L. Rice, III, Clayton, Dubilier & Rice